Introduction to Psychology

Exploration and Application **Fifth Edition**

Introduction to Psychology

Exploration and Application

Fifth Edition

Dennis Coon
Department of Psychology
Santa Barbara City College, California

West Publishing Company
St. Paul • New York • Los Angeles • San Francisco

A study guide has been developed to assist you in mastering the concepts presented in this text. The study guide clarifies concepts by presenting them in concise, condensed form. It reinforces your understanding of terms, concepts, and individuals and also provides a programmed review and self-test questions. The study guide is available from your local bookstore under the title, *Study Guide to Accompany Introduction to Psychology: Exploration and Application*, prepared by Faren Akins.

A *Mastery Study Guide* written by Tom Bond also is available to accompany this book. The *Mastery Study Guide* is specially designed for self-paced, or PSI, courses. It is also highly appropriate for any course in which true mastery of concepts is the goal.

If you cannot locate either of these books in the bookstore, ask your bookstore manager to order them for you.

50 W. Kellogg Boulevard
P.O. Box 64526
St. Paul, MN 55164-1003

Printed in the United States of America

96 95 94 93 92 91 8 7 6

Library of Congress Cataloging-in-Publication Data

Coon, Dennis.
Introduction to psychology.

Bibliography: p.
Includes index.
1. Psychology. I. Title.
BF121.C625 1989 150 88-33859
ISBN 0-314-47349-1

COPY EDITING: Janet Greenblatt
ARTWORK: John & Jean Foster, Barbara Barnett, Marsha Dohrmann
COMPOSITION: Parkwood Composition Service, Inc.
COVER: Stanton Macdonald-Wright, "Subjective Time," Oil on canvas, 53″ × 46″, 1958. Courtesy Joseph Chowning Gallery, San Francisco.

Acknowledgments

The author is indebted to the following for permission to reproduce copyrighted materials.

Fig. 1–2 *(upper right)* © Art Sweezy, Stock Boston; *(upper left)* © Bruce Rosenblum, The Picture Cube; *(lower right)* © 1987 Lynn Johnson, Black Star; *(lower left)* © Susan Van Etten, The Picture Cube.
Fig. 1–4 © Susan Kuklin, Photo Researchers.
Fig. 1–5 Brown Brothers.
Fig. 1–6 Brown Brothers.
Fig. 1–7 Brown Brothers.
Fig. 1–8 United Press International.
Fig. 1–9 The Bettmann Archive.
Fig. 1–10 © Ted Polumbaum.
Fig. 2–1 © Richard Wood, The Picture Cube.
Fig. 2–3 National Geographic Society Magazine. Photo by Baron Hugo van Lawick.
P. 35 Cartoon courtesy of Peter Mueller.
Fig. 2–9 Mike Kagan, Monkmeyer Press.
Fig. 2–11 Photo by Lynn Goldsmith/LGI © 1986.
Fig. 3–10 Courtesy Richard Haier, University of California, Irvine.
Fig. 3–18 © Michael Serino, The Picture Cube.
Fig. 4–10 *(left)* © Harvey Eisner, Taurus; *(right)* © David M. Campione, Taurus.
Fig. 4–13 © Jeffry W. Myers, Stock Boston.
Fig. 4–16 © Jon L. Barken, The Picture Cube.
Fig. 4–27 NASA.
Fig. 5–1 Photo by Kevin McMahon.
Fig. 5–4 © E. R. Degginger, Animals, Animals.
Fig. 5–8 Enrico Ferdrelli/DOT.
Fig. 5–10 B. Julesz. *Foundations of Cyclopean Perception.* Copyright © 1971, University of Chicago Press.
Fig. 5–12 M. C. Escher "Still Life and Street" © 1988 M. C. Escher Heirs/Cordon Art—Baarn, Holland. Collection Haags Gemeentemuseum, The Hague.
Fig. 5–13 From "Pictoral Perception and Culture" by J. B. Deregowski. Copyright © 1972 by *Scientific American,* Inc. All rights reserved.
Fig. 5–16 Baron Wolman.
Fig. 5–17 © Dan Francis, Mardan Photography.
Fig. 5–22 From "Cognitive Determinants of Fixation Location During Picture Viewing" by G. R. Loftus & N. H. Mackworth, *Journal of Experimental Psychology,* 4, 1987, 565–572.
Fig. 5–23 Erdelyi, M. H. and A. G. Applebaum, "Cognitive Masking: The Disruptive Effects of an Emotional Stimulus Upon the Perception of Contiguous Neutral Items." *Bulletin of the Psychonomic Society.* 1973, 1, 59–61.
Fig. 5–24 Al Held, *The Big N.* (1965), Synthetic polymer paint on canvas, 9'3⅜" X 9'. Collection, The Museum of Modern Art, New York. Mrs. Armand P. Bartos Fund.
P. 133 Kapleau, Phillip. *The Three Pillars of Zen,* Harper & Row, 1966.
Fig. 6–3 Yale Joel, LIFE Magazine, © Time Inc.
Fig. 6–4 © 1981 Martin M. Potker, Taurus.
Fig. 6–6 Courtesy of Healthdyne, Inc.
Fig. 6–7 Wide World Photos.
Table 6–2 Stanford Hypnotic Scale, adapted from Weitzenhofler and Hilgard. Stanford University Press, 1959.
Fig. 6–8 Dan Francis, Mardan Photography.
Fig. 6–9 Dan Francis, Mardan Photography.

(Acknowledgments continued following index)

Contents in Brief

Contents

Chapter 5
Perceiving the World 112

Chapter 6
States of Consciousness 139

Part Three

Learning and Cognition 175

Chapter 7
Conditioning and Learning I 176

HAPPY TO PA
JACK-POTS

Chapter 13
Health, Stress, and Coping 335

Part Five

Human Development and Personality 361

Chapter 14
Child Development 362

Chapter 15
From Birth to Death: Life-Span Development 393

Chapter 16
Dimensions of Personality 420

Chapter 17
Theories of Personality 443

Chapter 18
Intelligence 467

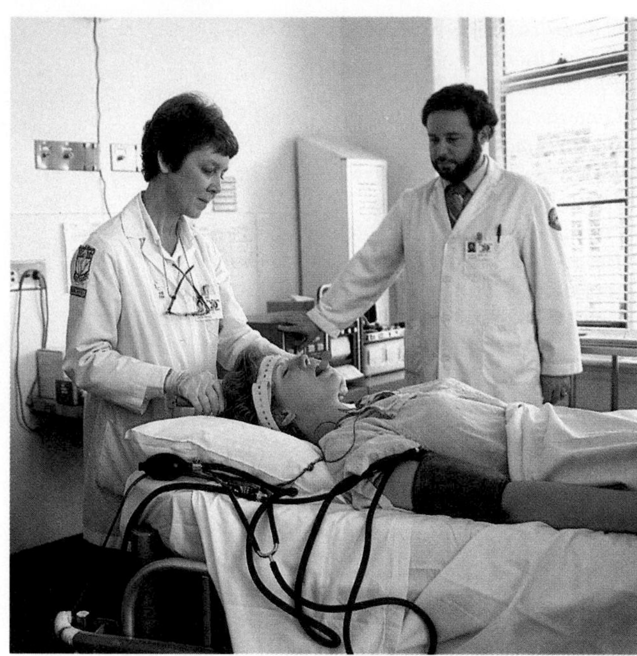

Chapter 21 Insight Therapy 544

Chapter 22 Behavior Therapy 565

Part Seven

Self and Society 583

Chapter 26 Applied Psychology 656

Preface to the Fifth Edition

To the Student

Psychology is a large and rapidly growing field. It is at once familiar, exotic, commonplace, surprising, and challenging. Most of all, psychology is changing. Indeed, this book can be no more than a "snapshot" of a colorful passing scene. And yet, it is rapid change that makes psychology especially fascinating: What, really, could be more intriguing than our evolving understanding of human behavior?

In a very real sense, psychology is about each of us. Psychology asks, "How can we step outside of ourselves for a more objective look at how we live, think, and act?" Psychologists believe the answer is through careful thought, observation, and inquiry. As simple as this may seem, it is the guiding light for everything that follows in this book.

I sincerely hope that you will find psychology as fascinating as I have. In this text, I have done all that I could imagine to make your first encounter with psychology enjoyable and worthwhile. To help you get off to a good start, Chapter 1 includes a discussion of how to study effectively. The ideas covered there will help you get the most out of this text, class lectures, and your psychology course as a whole. In the remaining chapters, I hope that the delight I have found in my own students' curiosity, insights, imagination, and interests will be apparent. Please view this book as a long letter from me to you. It is, in a very real sense, written about you, for you, and to you.

To the Instructor

This book differs from traditional texts in a number of important ways. If you are already familiar with its format, a description of Fifth Edition changes follows shortly. If the text is unfamiliar, a brief account of its design and underlying philosophy is in order.

A Book for Students As an instructor I have learned that selecting a textbook is half the battle in teaching a course. A good text does much of the work of imparting information to students. This frees class time for discussion and it leaves students asking for more. When a book overwhelms students or cools their interest, teaching becomes an uphill battle. For this reason, I have worked hard to make this a clear, readable, and interesting text.

I believe an important question to ask of the introductory course is "What will students remember next year, or in 10 years?" Consequently, I have tried to give students a clear grasp of major concepts, rather than bury them in details. At the same time, I have tried to provide a broad overview that does justice to psychology's diversity. I think students will find this book full of intellectual challenge, and teachers will find traditional topics covered to their satisfaction. In addition, I have made a special effort to relate psychology to common experiences and to practical problems of daily life.

A major feature of this book is the *Applications* section in each chapter. These selections explicitly bridge the gap between psychological theory and practical application. I believe students have every right to ask, "Does this mean anything to me? Can I use it? Why should I learn it if I can't?" No matter how interesting or intellectually stimulating, a text that fails to show the practical value of adopting new ideas is irrelevant in a very basic sense. The Applications sections spell out how students can use the principles of psychology. By doing so, they breathe life into its concepts.

At the end of each chapter you will find a separate *Exploration*. These sections cover current issues, topics from psychology's frontiers, or subjects likely to promote thought and discussion. In essence, they serve as supplemental readings within the text, to provide a taste of changing issues and ideas in psychology. Because Explorations conclude each chapter, they are easy to assign or delete at your discretion.

A Format for Learning

Before this book first appeared, psychology texts made surprisingly little use of learning principles to teach psychology. The extensive use of learning aids herein is based on my belief that students can be guided into more effective study and reading habits while they learn course content. Each chapter is built around the well-known SQ3R study-reading formula. Thus, in addition to helping students learn psychology, the chapter format encourages the development of valuable study skills. Student response to this feature of the text has been very positive, with many students reporting that they transfer the SQ3R technique to other texts as well.

Notice how the time-tested steps of the SQ3R method—*survey, question, read, recite, and review*—underlie the design of each chapter.

Survey A short *Chapter Preview* arouses reader interest, gives an overview of the chapter, and focuses attention on the task at hand. A new boxed outline, titled *In This Chapter,* accompanies the Preview and lists upcoming topics. After that, *Survey Questions* spotlight major issues so that students will read with a purpose.

Question Throughout each chapter, *Guide Questions* act as advance organizers to prime students to look for important ideas as they read. This helps ensure that reading is an active learning experience. Guide Questions also create a dialogue in which student questions and reactions are anticipated. This clarifies difficult points in a lively give-and-take between questions and responses. And, significantly, Guide Questions model critical thinking skills, to encourage reflection and inquiry.

Read The readability of each chapter has been carefully controlled for maximum student involvement and comprehension. I rewrote nearly every line of this edition in an effort to make the text as clear and accessible as possible. To further facilitate comprehension, the text employs a full array of traditional learning aids. These include boldface type and phonetic pronunciations for important terms, bullet summaries, a detailed glossary (also with pronunciations), summary tables, a detailed index, and a robust illustration program.

The *Compare* boxes that appear at selected points in each chapter are new in this edition. Each Compare box contains two or more precise definitions to help students differentiate between terms that are often confused (for example, negative reinforcement and punishment). Making comparisons encourages students to sharpen key distinctions and to think about what they are learning.

Special boxed *Highlights*—which discuss recent research, interesting topics, and original viewpoints—are judiciously placed in each chapter. Highlights serve as stimulating but non-intrusive supplements to the main text.

Chapters throughout the text have been kept short so that each can be read in a single session. This brevity provides excellent flexibility regarding the order in which chapters are assigned. It also gives students a sense of closure or completion at the end of each assignment.

Recite Every few pages, a *Learning Check* allows students to test their understanding and recall of the preceding discussion. Learning Checks are short, non-comprehensive quizzes that require students to stop and actively process information. Students who miss any questions are encouraged to back-track and clarify their understanding before reading more. Completing each Learning Check serves as a form of recitation to enhance learning. It also provides feedback so that students can gauge their progress.

Review As mentioned earlier, an Applications section follows the core of each chapter. Applications show students how psychological concepts relate to practical problems, including problems in their own lives. Through these discussions, students review and extend the ideas they have learned. Applications help reinforce and consolidate learning by illustrating psychology's practicality.

An Exploration follows each Applications section. In most cases, students must be familiar with chapter concepts to fully appreciate an Exploration. This again motivates students to review what they have learned and broaden their understanding.

To complete the review phase of the SQ3R method, a point-by-point *Chapter Summary* provides a concise synopsis of all major topics. Each chapter concludes with a provocative series of *Questions For Discussion* that may be used in class.

Fifth Edition Changes

As in most sciences, there is a stable core of information in psychology that changes little from year to year. Yet, at the same time, psychology continues to produce a wealth of new data and ideas. My challenge in this revision was thus two-fold. First, I wanted to refine and distill the core content of the text. Second, I wanted to introduce students to exciting advances in psychology.

Readers will have to judge for themselves, but I believe that tightening some parts of the text to make room for new information actually strengthened the presentation of core topics. As a result, I was able to include, in almost every chapter, new ideas that I personally found fascinating. I sincerely hope that readers will share my excitement about the new information and insights that psychology has produced in recent years.

Chapter Format With this revision, the chapter format has evolved in several ways. The new "In This Chapter" outlines that accompany Chapter Previews are designed to help students gain an overview of chapter content. Survey Questions are now bulleted for easier reading. The "Compare" boxes are new. Highlights are very carefully repositioned within the chapter design. The Applications are boxed, but they are printed on white paper to make it clear that they are an integral part of each chapter. It is also notable that Chapter Summaries now follow the Explorations. This move was requested by many adopters and reviewers. It allows the summary to cover the entire chapter, and it signals to students that all major sections of the chapter should be read.

New Topics and Updated Coverage Virtually every chapter of the Fifth Edition has been rewritten, reorganized, or improved, with new information evident on every page. I have drawn on hundreds of new references (many as recent as 1988) for this revision. This edition includes one entirely new Chapter Preview and several that are revised. There are 19 new Highlights. Examples include new discussions of subliminal messages in rock music, police detectives' use of cognitive interviewing to improve eyewitness' memories, and seasonal affective disorders. Six new or substantially revised Applications appear in this edition. Eight Explorations are entirely new or extensively updated.

Combined with line-by-line updates, the content changes in this edition are too numerous to describe here. I would, nevertheless, like to give at least a sample of new or revised topics. These include: empiricism, women in psychology, psychology as a profession, major perspectives in psychology (ch. 1); research methods and critical thinking, firewalking (ch. 2); brain-and-behavior links, split-brain research, laterality, PET scans of the brain at work (ch. 3); theories of color vision and the sense of smell, alleged use of subliminal messages in rock music (ch. 4); the moon illusion, attention, top-down and bottom-up processing (ch. 5); sleep, cocaine abuse, nicotine, sensory deprivation, drug abuse (ch. 6); prepared fear theory, human learning (ch. 7); using punishment wisely, the impact of TV as a model, breaking bad habits, buffering television's impact on children (ch. 8); the "feeling of knowing," the permanence of memory, flashbulb memories, ways to improve memory, cognitive interviewing and eyewitness recall (ch. 9); contemporary cognitive research, heuristics, intuitive thought, artificial intelligence, expertise (ch. 10); circadian rhythms, jet lag, and shift work, "yo-yo dieting," intrinsic motivation, behavioral weight-control (ch. 11); theories of emotion, the facial feedback hypothesis, behavioral lie catching, Sternberg's triarchic theory of love (ch. 12); health psychology and behavioral medicine, behavioral risk factors, health promoting behaviors, Type A behavior, the hardy personality, stress and the immune system, meditation (ch. 13); parenting styles, social development, attachment and daycare, Piagetian stages, early childhood education programs, moral development (ch. 14); childhood problems, midlife development, aging, death and bereavement (ch. 15); traits, types, self-concept, theories of personality, situations and dispositions, shyness, genetics and personality (ch. 16); possible selves, self-monitoring (ch. 17); the *Army Alpha,* deviation IQ, retardation, the heredity-environment debate, confluence model, the Larry P. case (ch. 18); DSM-III-R, child molestation, anxiety disorders, personality disorders, depression and suicidal thinking (ch. 19); DSM-III-R, ECT, depression, schizophrenia, seasonal affective disorder, psychiatric commitment and civil rights (ch. 20); short-term dynamic therapy, psychotherapy outcome research, counseling skills and helping behaviors (ch. 21); covert behavior modification (ch. 22); self-handicapping and alcohol abuse, excessive obedience to authority (ch. 23); aggression, superordinate goals and nuclear holocaust (ch. 24); recent survey data, gender differences, homosexuality, AIDS and sexual responsibility, sexual problems, maintaining intimacy in relationships (ch. 25); human factors engineering, business management, environmental psychology, law and psychology, jury behavior (ch. 26).

Supporting Materials

Offering an introductory course in psychology is one of the most challenging of all teaching assignments. To ease your task and enrich your course, an enlarged and improved array of supporting materials has been created.

Study Guides Two excellent study guides will again be available to accompany the text. To structure learning, each chapter of Faren Akins' *Study Guide* provides a list of key terms and concepts, a programmed review, a practice test, and a crossword puzzle based on the text. Tom Bond's *Mastery Study Guide* offers a very thorough review and a chance to practice concepts presented in the text. The MSG includes a list of important terms and individuals, learning objectives (with space for student responses), two tests ("Do You Know the Information,"

"Can You Apply the Information"), and a fill-in-the-blanks Chapter Review.

WESTUDY A microcomputer tutorial program called WESTUDY is available to accompany this edition of the text. WESTUDY poses questions to students in three easy-to-run formats: a multiple-choice review, a race, and a college bowl contest. When used by one or more students, WESTUDY is a motivating and enjoyable study aid.

Transparencies I am very pleased to report that Bill Dwyer, who has enhanced this text in other ways, has created a set of transparencies to enliven classroom presentations. Bill's transparencies are on acetate, in color, and they look so good I am anxious to use them myself. Contact your West representative for more information.

Instructor's Manual The *Instructor's Manual* for this edition has undergone a major revision by Michael Sosulski. The manual includes learning objectives, film suggestions, demonstrations, new supplemental lectures, new classroom exercises, and suggested readings. It also contains general teaching strategies and references, diagnostic reading tests, and other helpful materials. All *Instructor's Manual* materials are now grouped by chapter for easy use.

Testbank William Dwyer and Michael Zeller collaborated to update and improve the *Testbank*. This high-quality collection now consists of 3,000 multiple-choice questions. Over 1,000 of these items are new and many more conceptual questions are included. The *Testbank* also offers essay questions for each chapter. All test items are incorporated into WESTEST, a microcomputer test-generation program that is available by request.

Psychware *Psychware* is a CAI package to enrich the introductory course. Robert S. Slotnick and the New York Institute of Technology have developed a stimulating collection of tutorials, simulations, and experiments for use on microcomputers. Each exercise is highly interactive and features engaging graphics. By using *Psychware*, students can apply the principles of operant conditioning, they can test their short-term memory, they can explore social behavior or gain insight into Piaget's stages of cognitive development, and much more.

Audio Cassettes New with this edition are audio cassettes scripted by Janice Hartgrove-Freile. These cassettes provide a concise review of major ideas from each chapter of the text. They can be used to further reinforce learning, and they make it possible for students to review while on the move. Cassettes are available free to adopters for further copying, or they can be sold directly by your bookstore.

Videotapes Also new is an exciting pair of 60-minute videotapes from PBS's award-winning series, "The Brain." Segments of these videos apply to subjects throughout the text, but they are especially relevant to Chapters 3, 4, 6, 11, 12, 13, and 20. Topics are carefully indexed on the tapes for classroom use and an instructor's manual is included. These tapes are available free to qualified adopters of the text.

Summary I sincerely hope that teachers and students will consider this book and its supporting materials a refreshing change from the ordinary. Writing and revising it has been quite an adventure. In the pages that follow, I think the reader will find an attractive blend of the theoretical and the practical, plus many of the most exciting ideas in psychology.

Acknowledgements

The enterprise of psychology is a cooperative effort requiring the talents and energies of a large community of scholars, teachers, researchers, and students. As with earlier versions of this text, this edition has combined the efforts of a large number of people. I would like to thank first the many students who sent comments, suggestions, and letters of encouragement.

To the professional users/reviewers who gave their time and expertise I extend my sincere thanks. I deeply appreciate the contributions of all those who have, over the years, contributed to this text's evolution. I especially wish to thank those who helped make this edition a reality:

Brian R. Bate,
Cuyahoga Community College

Charles Croll,
Broome Community College, New York

Daniel B. Cruse,
University of Miami, Florida

Lorraine P. Dieudonne,
Foothill College

Paul W. Fenton,
University of Wisconsin, Stout

Linda E. Flickinger,
Saint Clair County Community College, Michigan

Chris Fraser,
Gippsland Institute of Advanced Education, Australia

Christopher Frost, Southwest Texas State University

David A. Gershaw, Arizona Western College

Michael E. Gorman, Michigan Technological University

David A. Griesé, State University of New York, Farmingdale

John Grivas, Monash University, Australia

Janice Hartgrove-Freile, North Harris County College

Barbara Honhart, Lansing Community College

Myles E. Johnson, Normandale Community College

Pat Jones, Brevard Community College

Phil Lau, DeAnza College

Edward R. McCrary III, El Camino College

Andrew Neher, Cabrillo College

Cora F. Patterson, University of Southwestern Louisiana

Steven J. Pollock, Moorpark College, California

James J. Ryan, University of Wisconsin, La Crosse

Francine Smolucha, Moraine Valley Community College, Illinois

Michael C. Sosulski, College of DuPage

I would also like to thank the following individuals who provided advice and guidance during the writing of the Fifth Edition.

Faren Akins
Charles A. Alexander
Scott W. Allen
Stuart Appelle
James W. Armstrong
Alan Auerbach
K. Barsz
Wayne Bartz
Tom Bond
Steven H. Brown
André Cedras
Donna K. Duffy
Fred H. Fahringer
Edna Fiedler
Walter J. Flakus
William F. Ford
David A. Griesé
Janice Hartgrove-Freile
George Hill
Randall E. Jarrell
George W. Johnson
Stuart Karabenick
Peter Kokesnik
Wolanyo Kpo
James H. Nelson
Mike Ostrowski
John A. Paris
Dick Rasor
Sue S. Schmitt
Chuck Titus
Joseph Vielbig

I would also like to thank the psychologists whose work has so obviously enhanced this text and its supporting materials: Faren Akins, Tom Bond, David Cunningham, Bill Dwyer, Janice Hartgrove-Freile, Michael Sosulski, and Michael Zeller. It has been a pleasure working with such talented and supportive colleagues.

Getting a text into print seems almost miraculous at times. With this fact in mind, I would like to thank Janet Greenblatt for her meticulous editing. Likewise, I am indebted to Bob Jucha for his strong editorial support, and to Bill Stryker for his many days, evenings, and weekends of dedicated design and production work. Thanks also to Kristen McCarthy for combining originality with practicality. These individuals and many others at West Publishing Company have made this text a reality.

Finally, I would like to express my continuing gratitude to Clyde H. Perlee, Jr., everyone's favorite Editor in Chief, for his patience, inspiration, and friendship. This is his book as well as mine.

Last of all, I would like to thank my wife Sevren, whose emotional support and countless hours of help made this book possible.

Dennis Coon

Part One

An Introduction to Psychology and Psychologists

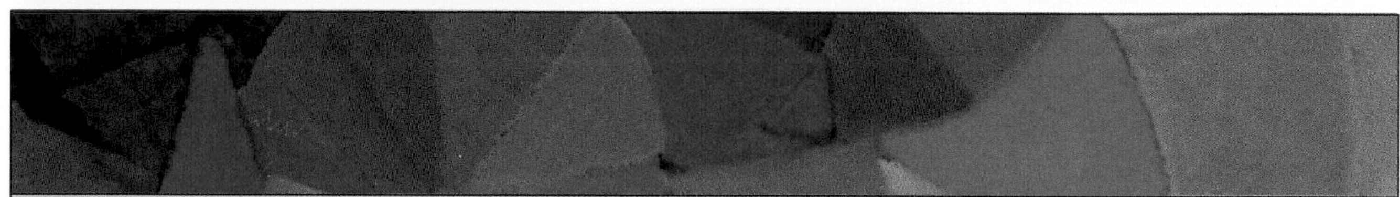

Chapter 1

Psychology and Psychologists

In This Chapter

Defining psychology
Science and empiricism
Psychology's goals
A brief history of psychology
Psychology today
The profession of psychology

Applications

The psychology of studying

Exploration

False psychologies

Chapter Preview

Why Study Psychology?

You are a universe, a collection of worlds within worlds. Your brain is possibly the most complicated and amazing device in existence. Through its action, you are capable of art, music, science, philosophy, and war. Your capacities for love and compassion coexist with your potential for aggression, hatred, and . . . murder? You are the most frustrating riddle ever written, a mystery at times even to yourself. You are a unique event in human history. At the same time, you are like everyone who has ever lived. Your thoughts, emotions, and actions, your behavior and conscious experience are the subject of this book.

Look around you. Newspapers, magazines, radio, and television abound with psychological information. Psychology is discussed in homes, schools, businesses, and bars. Psychology is an explosive, exciting, and ever-changing panorama of people and ideas. You can hardly call yourself "educated" without knowing something about it.

There is another reason for studying psychology. Socrates said, "Know thyself," and although we must envy those who have walked on the moon or cruised the ocean's dreamlike depths, the ultimate frontier still lies close to home. Psychologist D. O. Hebb put it this way: "What is psychology all about? Psychology is about the mind: the central issue, the great mystery, the toughest problem of all" (Hebb, 1974).

Psychology is a journey into inner space. This book is a travel guide. Psychologists can't claim to have "the answers" to all your questions. But they can show you the contours of the landscape already explored. More importantly, you may find skills in psychology that will aid you in your own search for answers. Ultimately, the answers must be your own, but studying psychology is a rich starting point.

Survey Questions

- What is psychology? What are its goals?
- How did psychology emerge as a field of knowledge?
- What are the major trends and specialties in psychology?
- Can psychology be applied to improve study skills and grades?
- How does psychology differ from false systems that also claim to explain behavior?

Psychology: Psyche = Mind; Logos = Knowledge or Study

Question: What is psychology?

Psychology is memory, stress, therapy, love, persuasion, hypnosis, perception, death, conformity, creativity, learning, personality, aging, intelligence, sexuality, emotion, and many, many more topics. Psychology has become such an enormous and colorful beast that no short description can do it justice.

It is important, then, to be open-minded as you begin this course. Consider it an adventure, and judge after you have seen what psychology has to offer. By the time you have read this entire book, you will begin to have an overall picture of what psychology is and what psychologists do. For now, let's just say that **psychology** *is the scientific study of human and animal behavior.*

Compare: Psychology and Related Sciences

Anthropology: The science of human origins, evolution, and cultures.

Biology: The science of life and living organisms: plant, animal, and human.

Psychology: The science of human and animal behavior.

Sociology: The science of the forms and functions of human groups.

Question: What does behavior refer to in the definition of psychology?

Behavior Anything you do—eating, sleeping, talking, thinking, or sneezing—is a behavior. So is dreaming, gambling, taking drugs, watching TV, learning Spanish, basket weaving, or reading this book. The term *behavior* can refer to **covert** (private, internal) activities, such as thinking, as well as **overt** (visible) actions. Psychologists are interested in both visible behavior *and* hidden mental events.

Much of our overt behavior can be studied by direct observation. But how do we study mental activities such as problem solving, daydreaming, or remembering? Often it takes detective work to *deduce* what is happening internally from what can be observed directly. For example, try answering these questions: Is a horse bigger than a mouse? Is a collie bigger than a German shepherd?

If you are like most people, you answered the first question faster than the second. Why? Most people report that they form metal images of the animals to compare their size. A slower answer, therefore, suggests that it is more difficult to compare mental images that are similar in size (Moyer & Bayer, 1976). Although we couldn't actually observe thinking, we were able to learn something interesting about it just the same. When indirect observations consistently point to a conclusion, we can be reasonably certain it is correct.

Empiricism

Question: It seems that psychologists try to be objective in their observations. Is that correct?

Yes. Psychologists are keenly aware that opinions, or claims made by an "authority," may be wrong. They therefore have a special respect for **empirical evidence,** which is information gained by observation and measurement. Whenever possible, psychologists settle differences by collecting **data** (facts or evidence). This allows them to compare what each has observed and draw accurate conclusions. Would you say it's true, for instance, that "you can't teach an old dog new tricks"? Why argue about it? A psychologist would get 10 "new" dogs, 10 "used" dogs, and 10 "old" dogs and then try to teach them all new tricks to find out!

The heart of the empirical attitude is summarized by the phrase, "Let's take a look" (Stanovich, 1986). Here's an example: Have you ever wondered if drivers become more hostile and aggressive when the weather gets hot and uncomfortable? Psychologists Douglas Kenrick and Steven MacFarlane (1986) decided to collect some data to investigate. Kenrick and MacFarlane arranged to have a car parked at a green light in a one-lane intersection. In Phoenix, Arizona. In temperatures ranging from 88° to 116°. Then they recorded the number of times other drivers honked at the stalled car, and how long they honked.

The results are shown in Figure 1–1. As you can see, higher temperatures were clearly linked to an increase in the amount of time spent leaning on the horn (which may be why cars come equipped with horns and not cannons). While these findings are not surprising, they do add to our understanding of links between discomfort and aggression.

An empirical approach seems natural in fields like biology and physics. Yet, in psychology, we are often tempted to accept what seems reasonable, rather than what *is*. For example, see if you can tell, from your own experience or common sense, which of the following statements are true. Then we will compare your answers with answers arrived at empirically.

Fig. 1–1 *Results of an empirical study. The graph shows that horn honking by frustrated motorists becomes more likely as air temperature increases. This suggests that physical discomfort is associated with interpersonal hostility. Riots and assaults also increase during hot weather. Here we see a steady rise in aggression as temperatures go higher. However, hostile actions that require physical exertion, such as a fistfight, may become* less *likely at very high temperatures. (Data from Kenrick & MacFarlane, 1986.)*

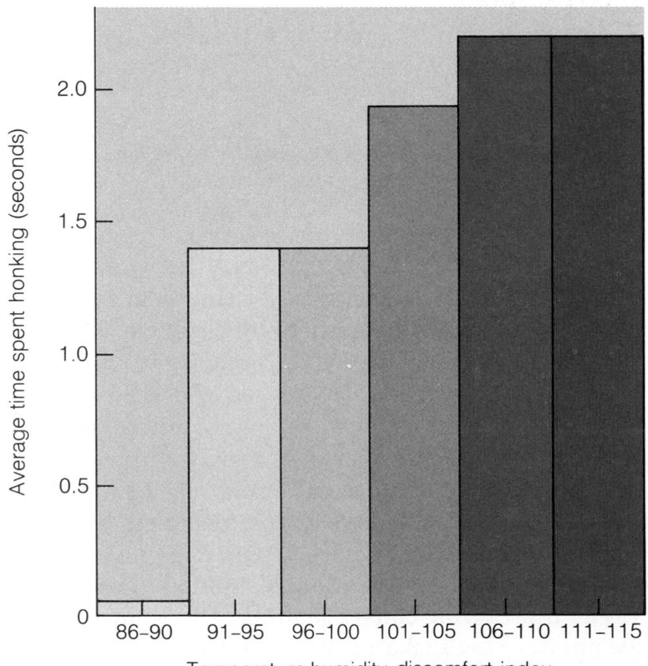

Are These Ideas True or False?

1. If you happened to step on a nail, you would feel it instantly. True or false? (Chapter 3)
2. A one-eyed man could not land an airplane. True or false? (Chapter 5)
3. The apparent size of the moon is greatly magnified by the atmosphere when the moon is low in the sky. True or false? (Chapter 5)
4. When hypnotized, witnesses to crimes can be made to have perfect memory of what they saw. True or false? (Chapter 6)
5. Brain activity almost ceases at various times during sleep. True or false? (Chapter 6)
6. Punishment is the most effective way to reinforce the learning of new habits. True or false? (Chapter 8)
7. All memories are permanent, if only there were some way to retrieve them. True or false? (Chapter 9)
8. People who have high IQs are also usually highly creative. True or false? (Chapter 10)
9. The lie detector (polygraph) is highly accurate at identifying attempts to deceive. True or false? (Chapter 12)
10. Stress is almost always bad for you. True or false? (Chapter 13)
11. Intelligence is completely inherited from one's parents. True or false? (Chapter 18)
12. Those who threaten suicide rarely actually commit suicide. True or false? (Chapter 19)
13. Schizophrenics have two or more distinct personalities. True or false? (Chapter 20)
14. If your car breaks down, you are more likely to get help from a passerby on a busy highway than on a lightly traveled country road. True or false? (Chapter 24)

Scoring this quiz is easy. Empirical research has shown that all of the statements are *false*. (To find out why, you may want to look ahead at the chapters cited in parentheses.) If you missed some questions, don't despair. The point is simply this: Psychology became a science when psychologists began to do experiments, make observations, and seek evidence, and you will become a better observer of human behavior if you do the same.

Science Empiricism alone is not enough to make a science. True **scientific observation** must also be *systematic*. That is, it has to be structured so that observations reveal something about the underlying nature of behavior

(Stanovich, 1986). To return to an earlier example, little would be gained if you drove around a city and made haphazard observations of aggressive horn honking. To be scientific, observations must be carefully planned and recorded. In the next chapter we will look more closely at how this is done.

Question: I've heard that psychology isn't scientific. You have said that it is. Is it?

Psychology is definitely a science. But it is also fair to say that it is a "young" science. For various reasons, the study of certain topics in psychology is still difficult. Sometimes, psychologists are unable to answer questions because of ethical or practical concerns. What would happen, for instance, if a child were placed in a soundproof, lightproof box for the first 5 years of life? This question will probably never be directly answered. (However, many times an indirect answer can be obtained by studying animals.) In other cases, social attitudes may limit what questions can be answered scientifically. Very little was known about human sexual response until William Masters, a gynecologist, and Virginia Johnson, a psycholo-

Fig. 1–2 *The variety and complexity of human behavior make psychological investigation challenging. How would you explain the behaviors shown here?*

gist, directly recorded physical responses to sexual intercourse. Such research would have been impossible to carry out and publish earlier in psychology's history. Likewise, much of what we know about the psychology of death has been learned in recent years, as this once taboo subject has come under study.

More often, questions go unanswered for lack of a suitable **research method**. For years, the reports of people who said they never dream had to be considered accurate. But with an advance in technology, the EEG (electroencephalograph, or brain wave machine) was developed. It then became possible to tell reliably when a person is dreaming. People who "never dream," it turns out, dream frequently. They also vividly remember their dreams when awakened during one. Through use of the EEG, the study of dreaming has become scientific (Fig. 1–3). Many people think of scientific research as dull and painstaking. But as you can see, it takes creativity to find new methods for answering long-standing questions. The fact that psychology is a young science makes it all the more exciting. More importantly, what we *do* know today adds up to a large and highly useful body of knowledge.

Animals

You may have wondered why animals were mentioned in our definition of psychology. It may surprise you to learn that as a group, psychologists are interested in natural laws governing the behavior of *any* living creature—from flatworms to humans. Indeed, specialists known as **comparative psychologists** may spend their entire careers studying rats, cats, dogs, turtles, chimpanzees, or other animals (Fig. 1–4). Comparative psychologists compare the behavior of different species to learn about their similarities and differences. When psychologists study animals, they must be very careful to avoid the **anthropomorphic fallacy** (AN-thro-po-MORE-fik: attributing human thoughts, feelings, or motives to animals).

Question: Why is it risky to attribute motives or emotions to animals?

The temptation to assume that an animal is "angry," "jealous," "bored," or "guilty" can be strong, but it often leads to false conclusions. As an example, let's say I observe gorillas in the wild (where food is plentiful) and conclude that by nature gorillas are not very "greedy." You, on the other hand, place two hungry gorillas in a cage with a banana, stand back to watch the action, and conclude that gorillas are in fact *very* "greedy." Actually, all we have observed is that competition for food is related to the amount of food available. Allowing the human concept of greed into the picture just clouds our understanding of gorilla behavior.

Question: Are comparative psychologists the only ones who study animals?

Fig. 1–3 *The scientific study of dreaming was made possible by use of the EEG, a device that records the tiny electrical potentials generated by the brain of a sleeping subject. The EEG converts these electrical potentials to a written record of brain activity.*

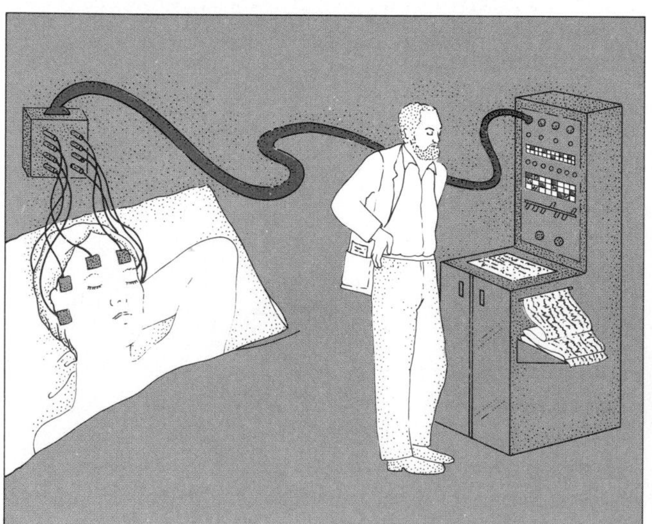

Fig. 1–4 *Some of the most interesting research with animals has focused on attempts to teach primates to communicate using sign language. (See Chapter 10 for more information.) The risk of anthropomorphizing animals in such research is very high.*

No. Other research psychologists also use animals in experiments. Usually this is done to discover principles that help solve human problems. Studies of topics as diverse as obesity, memory, stress, psychosis, therapy, and aging have been enriched by animal research. More importantly, animals sometimes serve as **models,** providing the *only* information available on a subject. For instance, most of what is known about the brain is based on animal research.

Psychological knowledge also benefits animals. For example, behavioral research has provided ways to avoid the killing of animals, such as coyotes, crows, or deer, that destroy crops or livestock. Moreover, the successful care of endangered species in zoos relies on behavioral research. So, too, does the training of guide dogs for the blind (Miller, 1985). For these and other reasons, animals are very much a part of psychology. In fact, a government panel (which included animal welfare advocates) concluded that in psychology there is often no substitute for ethically done animal research (Fisher, 1986).

Psychology's Goals

What do psychologists hope to achieve? In general, the goals of psychology are to **describe, understand, predict,** and **control** behavior. Beyond this, psychology's ultimate goal is to gather knowledge for the benefit of humanity.

What do psychology's goals mean in practice? Assume that we would like to answer the following questions: What happens when a person has an injury on the right side of the brain? Is there more than one type of memory? How does creative problem solving differ from ordinary thought? Do autistic children react differently to their parents than to other adults? The answer to each question requires a careful **description** of behavior, the first goal of psychology.

Question: But a description doesn't explain anything, does it?

Right. Useful knowledge begins with accurate description, or naming and classifying. But descriptions fail to answer the important "why" questions. *Why* do more women attempt suicide, and *why* do more men complete it? *Why* does discomfort encourage aggression? *Why* are bystanders often unwilling to help in an emergency?

Psychology's second goal, **understanding** behavior, is met when we can *explain* why an event occurs. Take the last question as an example. Research on "bystander apathy" has shown that people often fail to help when *other* possible helpers are nearby. Why? Because a "diffusion of responsibility" occurs, so that no one person feels required to pitch in. Generally, the larger the number of potential helpers present, the less likely it is that help will be given (Darley & Latane, 1968). Now we have an explanation of a perplexing problem. (See Chapter 24 for more details.)

Psychology's third goal is **prediction.** Notice that the explanation for bystander apathy makes a prediction about the chances of getting help. Anyone who has been stranded by car trouble on a busy freeway will recognize the accuracy of this prediction.

Prediction in psychology is rarely as precise as it is in "hard sciences" like physics or chemistry. Just the same, behavioral predictions are often quite useful. For example, psychological theory correctly predicted that students high in test-taking anxiety would perform better if given reassurance and advice during testing (Sarason, 1975). Here's another example: Psychological research predicts that you will suffer less jet lag if you fly east early in the day and west late in the day. (See Chapter 11 to learn why.) Prediction is especially important in **psychometrics.** Specialists in this area use various tests to predict such things as success in school, work, or career (see Chapter 26).

Question: Description, explanation, and prediction seem reasonable, but is control a valid goal for psychology?

Control is a frequently misunderstood goal, probably because it sounds like a threat to personal freedom. However, control simply means altering conditions that influence behavior in predictable ways. For example, if a psychologist suggests changes in a classroom that help children learn better, the psychologist has exerted control. If the psychologist uses conditioning principles to help a person overcome a crippling fear of heights, control is involved. Control is also present if behavioral research is used to design an aircraft instrument panel that reduces pilot errors. Clearly, psychology can provide the means for changing behavior. But, as is true of knowledge in other areas, psychological principles must be used wisely and humanely (Kipnis, 1987).

In summary, psychology's goals are a natural outgrowth of our desire to understand behavior. For the many topics studied in psychology, the goals boil down to asking:

What is the nature of this behavior? (description)
Why does it occur? (explanation)
Can we predict when it will occur? (prediction)
What conditions affect it? (control)

Learning Check

To improve your memory of this chapter, see if you can answer these questions. If you miss any, skim over the preceding material before continuing, to make sure you understand what you have just read.

1. Psychology is the ______________ study of the ______________ of humans and animals.

2. Information gained through direct observation and measurement is called ______________ evidence.

3. The ______________ fallacy involves attributing human feelings and motives to animals.

4. Which of the following questions relates most directly to the goal of *understanding* behavior?
a. Do the scores of men and women differ on tests of thinking abilities?
b. Why does a blow to the head cause memory loss?
c. Will productivity in a business office increase if room temperature is raised or lowered?
d What percentage of college students suffer from test anxiety?

5. All sciences are interested in the control of the phenomena they study. T or F?

Answers:

1. scientific, behavior **2.** empirical **3.** anthropomorphic **4.** *b* **5.** F (Astronomy and archeology are examples of sciences that do not share psychology's fourth goal.)

A Brief History of Psychology's Brief History

Psychology has a long past but a short history. Psychology's past is centuries old because it includes **philosophy,** the study of knowledge, reality, and human nature. In contrast, the history of modern psychology began only about 100 years ago. As sciences go, psychology is the new kid on the block: Easily 9 out of 10 persons to ever work in the field are alive today. Of course, to some students this history is still "not short enough!" Yet, the ideas in psychology's past are intimately tied to the present. To understand where psychology is now, let's take a brief look at its short history.

Into the Lab Psychology's history as a science began in 1879 at Leipzig, Germany. There, the "father of psychology," **Wilhelm Wundt** (VILL-helm Voont), created the first psychological laboratory so that he could study *conscious experience.* How, he wondered, are sensations, images, and feelings formed? To find out, Wundt observed and carefully measured **stimuli*** of various kinds (lights, sounds, weights). He then used **introspection,** or "looking inward," to examine his reactions to them. Wundt called this approach **experimental self-observation** (Blumenthal, 1979). Over the years, he used it to study vision, hearing, taste, touch, reaction time, memory, feelings, time perception, and many other subjects.

*Stimulus: singular; stimuli (STIM-you-lie): plural.

Experimental self-observation was a highly developed skill, much like the skill needed to be a professional wine taster. Wundt's subjects had to make at least 10,000 practice observations before they were allowed to take part in a real experiment (Lieberman, 1979). By using such careful observation and measurement, psychology was truly off to a good start.

Structuralism Wundt's ideas were carried to the United States by one of his students, a man named Edward B. Titchener (TICH-in-er). In America, Wundt's ideas became known as **structuralism** because they dealt with the structure of mental life. The structuralists hoped to develop a sort of "mental chemistry" by *analyzing* experience into basic "elements" or "building blocks."

Question: How could they do that? You can't analyze experience like you can a chemical compound, can you?

Perhaps not, but the structuralists tried, mostly by using introspection. In this approach, a subject might heft an apple and then decide that he or she had experienced the elements "hue" (color), "roundness," and "weight." Another example of the kind of question that might have interested a structuralist is, What basic tastes mix together to create complex flavors as different as liver, lime, bacon, or burnt-almond fudge?

It soon became clear that introspection was a poor way to answer many questions. The biggest problem was that structuralists frequently *disagreed.* And when they did, there was no way of settling differences. If two researchers came up with different lists of basic taste sensations, for example, who was to say which was right? Despite such limitations, "looking inward" still has a role in psychology. The study of hypnosis, meditation, drug effects, problem solving, and many other topics would be incomplete if subjects did not describe their private experiences.

Functionalism William James, an American psychologist, broadened psychology to include animal behavior, religious experience, abnormal behavior, and a number of other interesting topics (Fig. 1–6).

The term **functionalism** comes from an interest in how the mind *functions* to adapt us to our environment. To James, consciousness was an ever-changing *stream* or *flow* of images and sensations—not a set of lifeless building blocks, as the structuralists claimed.

The functionalists were strongly influenced by Charles Darwin. According to Darwin, creatures evolve, through **natural selection,** in ways that favor their survival. This means that features that help animals adapt to their environment are retained in evolution. Similarly, the functionalists wanted to find out how thought, perception, habits, and emotions aid human adaptation. In short, they wanted to study the mind *in use*.

Question: What effect did functionalism have on modern psychology?

Functionalism brought the study of animals into psychology by linking human and animal adaptation. It also aided the growth of **educational psychology.** Functionalists stressed that learning makes us more adaptable, and they urged psychologists to help improve education. Today, educational psychologists develop tests and do research on classroom dynamics, teaching styles, and learning. Functionalism also spurred the rise of **industrial psychology,** a specialty involving the study of people at work. (See Chapter 26.)

Behaviorism: Stimulus-Response Psychology Functionalism was soon challenged by a new viewpoint called **behaviorism.** Behaviorist John B. Watson objected to defining psychology as the study of the "mind" or "conscious experience" (Fig. 1–7). He also considered introspection unscientific. Watson found that he could study animal behavior even though he couldn't ask animals questions or know what they were thinking. He simply observed the relationship between **stimuli** (events in the environment) and an animal's **responses.** Why not, he argued, apply the same objectivity to the study of humans?

Watson soon adopted Russian physiologist Ivan Pavlov's (ee-VAHN PAV-lahv) **conditioned response** concept to explain most behavior. (A conditioned response is a learned reaction to a particular stimulus.) Watson's enthusiasm for conditioning obviously had reached extremes when he proclaimed:

> Give me a dozen healthy infants, well-formed, and my own special world to bring them up in and I'll guarantee to take any one at random and train him to become any type of specialist I might select—doctor, lawyer, artist, merchant-chief, and yes, beggarman and thief. (Watson, 1913)

Question: Would most psychologists agree with Watson's claim?

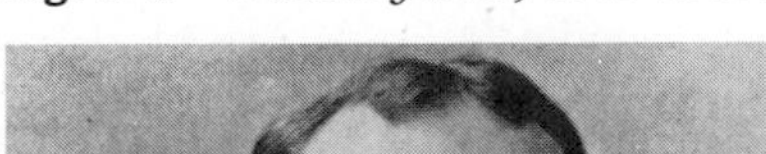

Fig. 1–5 *Wilhelm Wundt, 1832–1920.*

Fig. 1–6 *William James, 1842–1910.*

Fig. 1–7 *John B. Watson, 1878–1958.*

Today, most would probably consider it an overstatement. Just the same, behaviorism has had a profound effect on modern psychology. One of the best-known modern behaviorists, B. F. Skinner, has said:

> The environment is the key causal matrix. . . . In order to understand human behavior we must take into account what the environment does to an organism before and after it responds. Behavior is shaped and maintained by its consequences. (Skinner, 1971)

Skinner, too, has been criticized. Skinner's emphasis on visible behavior tends to ignore thought and subjective experience. This has led some observers to the tongue-in-cheek charge that Skinnerian psychology has "lost consciousness." Despite such criticisms, most psychologists would probably agree that human behavior is greatly influenced by learning.

Behaviorists deserve credit for discovering much of what we know about learning, conditioning, and the proper use of reward and punishment. A system called **behavior modification** is another valuable product of behaviorism. In behavior modification, conditioning principles are used to solve problems such as overeating, phobias, and childhood misbehavior. (See Chapter 22 for more information.)

Question: Were all the early psychologists men? So far, no women have been mentioned.

For the most part, men dominated science and education at the turn of the century. Nevertheless, women were active in psychology from its beginning. Highlight 1–1 gives some details.

● HIGHLIGHT 1–1
Women in Psychology

Histories of psychology abound in "forefathers" but seldom mention women. This situation exists largely because men dominated academic life in the late 1800s. Women, in fact, were actively discouraged from seeking advanced degrees. Even so, by 1906, in America about 1 psychologist in every 10 was a woman. Who were these "foremothers" of psychology? Several who became well known in the field were Mary Calkins, Christine Ladd-Franklin, Lillien Martin, and Margaret Washburn.

Christine Ladd-Franklin was the first American woman to complete requirements for the doctorate in psychology, in 1882. However, her degree was not awarded because of a university policy that denied women the doctorate. The first woman to be awarded a Ph.D. in psychology was Margaret Washburn, in 1894. Over the next 15 years, many more women followed Washburn's pioneering lead.

Today, the number of males and females receiving doctoral degrees in psychology is roughly equal. (New female Ph.D.'s actually exceeded males in 1984.) And in recent years, the number of female psychology graduates at the bachelor's level has far exceeded the number of male psychology graduates. Clearly, psychology has become a profession shared equally by men and women. (Sources: Furumoto & Scarborough, 1986; Howard et al., 1986.)

Gestalt Psychology Imagine for a moment that you have just heard a familiar tune, such as "Yankee Doodle," played on a tuba. Next it is played on a high-pitched violin. Even though none of the original sounds are used, the melody will still be recognizable as long as the *relationship* between the notes is the same. Now, what if the original notes were played in the correct order, but at a rate of one per hour? What would we have? Nothing. The separated notes would no longer be a melody. Perceptually, the melody is somehow more than the sum of its parts. It was observations such as this that launched the **Gestalt** school of thought in psychology.

The German word *Gestalt* (geh-SHTALT) means "form," "pattern," or "whole." The Gestalt viewpoint was first advanced by the German psychologist Max Wertheimer (VERT-hi-mer) (Fig. 1–8). It is a mistake, he said, to analyze psychological events into pieces, or "elements," as the structuralists did. Instead, the Gestaltists tried to study experiences as *wholes*. Their slogan was, "The whole exceeds the sum of its parts."

As with a melody, many other experiences resist analysis into parts, or pieces. For this reason, the Gestalt viewpoint remains influential in the study of perception and personality. It has also given rise to a type of psychotherapy. If you are curious about what Gestalt therapy is like, look ahead to Chapter 21.

Psychoanalytic Psychology As the mainstream of psychology grew more objective, scientific, and experimental, an Austrian physician named Sigmund Freud was developing his own theory of behavior. Freud's point of departure was his belief that mental life is like an iceberg: Only a portion is exposed to view. According to

Freud, our behavior is influenced by vast areas of **unconscious** thoughts, impulses, and desires, which cannot be known directly. This idea added a new dimension not only to psychology, but to art, literature, and history as well.

Freud theorized that many unconscious thoughts are of a threatening, sexual, or aggressive nature. Hence, they are *repressed* (actively held out of awareness). But sometimes, he said, they are revealed by dreams, emotions, or slips of the tongue. ("Freudian slips" are often humorous, as when a student who is tardy for class says, "I'm sorry I couldn't get here any later.") Freud also insisted that all thoughts, emotions, and actions are *determined* (nothing is an accident). He brought new awareness of the importance of childhood for later personality development ("The child is father to the man"). Most of all, perhaps, Freud is best known for creating a method of psychotherapy called **psychoanalysis**.

Freud had not held sway for very long before some of his students, including Carl Jung, began to break away from him. These psychologists developed their own theories and became known as **neo-Freudians** (*neo* means "new" or "recent"). Today, Freud's ideas have been altered, revised, and adapted to the point that few strictly psychoanalytic psychologists are left. However, Freud's legacy is still evident in various **psychodynamic** approaches to psychology. Psychodynamic theories focus on the interplay of internal forces in the personality.

Humanistic Psychology A fairly recent development in psychology is a point of view known as **humanism.** Humanism is sometimes called the "third force" in psychology. (Psychodynamic psychology and behaviorism are the other two.)

Question: How is the humanistic approach different from others?

Psychologists Carl Rogers, Abraham Maslow, and others developed the humanistic viewpoint to counter the negativity they saw in other views. Humanists reject the Freudian idea that personality is ruled by unconscious forces. They are also uncomfortable with the behavioristic idea that we are controlled by the environment. Both views show a strong undercurrent of **determinism,** the idea that behavior is determined by forces beyond our control. In contrast the humanists stress **free will,** the human ability to make choices. Humanists do admit that past experiences affect personality. However, they also believe that people can freely *choose* to live more creative, meaningful, and satisfying lives.

Humanists helped stimulate interest in psychological needs for love, self-esteem, belonging, self-expression, and creativity. Such needs, they point out, are as important as our biological needs for food and water. For example, newborn infants deprived of human love and emotional warmth may die just as surely as they would if deprived of food.

Question: How scientific is the humanistic approach?

Humanists collect data and seek evidence to support their ideas, but for the most part they tend to be less interested in attempts to treat psychology as an objective, behavioral science. Instead, they stress the importance of such *sub-*

Fig. 1–8 *Max Wertheimer, 1880–1941.*

Fig. 1–9 *Sigmund Freud, 1856–1939.*

Fig. 1–10 *Abraham Maslow, 1908–1970.*

jective factors as one's self-image, self-evaluation, and frame of reference.

Self-image refers to your total perception of yourself, including images of your body, personality, and abilities. **Self-evaluation** consists of positive and negative feelings you hold toward yourself. The mental and emotional perspective you use to judge events is your **frame of reference.** As you can see from these terms, humanists seek to understand how people perceive themselves and experience the world.

A unique feature of the humanistic approach is Maslow's description of **self-actualization.** Self-actualization is the need to develop one's potential fully, to lead a rich and meaningful life, and to become the best person one can become. According to the humanists, everyone has this potential. The humanists seek ways to allow it to emerge. (For a summary of psychology's early development, see Table 1–1.)

Psychology Today At one time, schools of thought in psychology were almost like political parties. Loyalty to each view was fierce, and clashes between schools were common. Today, traditional schools of thought have given way to a blending of ideas. Certainly, loyalties and specialties still exist. But many psychologists are **eclectic** (ek-LEK-tik: drawing from many sources) and embrace a variety of theoretical views. Even so, five major perspectives are evident in modern psychology. These are the **behavioristic, humanistic,** and **psychodynamic** views, plus the increasingly important **cognitive** and **psychobiological** perspectives (Table 1–2).

The value of biological approaches for understanding behavior has risen dramatically in recent years. **Psychobiologists** believe that eventually we will be able to explain all behavior in terms of physical mechanisms. This optimism is based on exciting new knowledge about how the brain works and how it relates to thought, feelings, perception, abnormal behavior, and other important topics.

A similar trend is occurring in **cognitive psychology.** *Cognition* means "thinking" or "knowing." Cognitive psychologists study thoughts, expectations, language, perception, problem solving, consciousness, creativity, and other mental processes. Some of these topics were neglected for so many years that psychology can be said to have recently "regained consciousness." Computer models of human thinking have been especially important in spurring recent advances in cognitive psychology.

Whatever their theoretical leanings, modern psychologists prefer facts and principles that have survived rigorous scientific testing. In a moment, we will further explore what psychologists do and identify some of their specialties. First, see if you can correctly match the items in the following Learning Check.

Learning Check

Match:

1. ____ Philosophy
2. ____ Wundt
3. ____ Structuralism
4. ____ Functionalism
5. ____ Behaviorism
6. ____ Gestalt
7. ____ Psychoanalytic
8. ____ Humanistic
9. ____ Cognitive
10. ____ Washburn
11. ____ Psychobiology

A. Against analysis; studied whole experiences
B. "Mental chemistry" and introspection
C. Emphasizes self-actualization and personal growth
D. Interested in unconscious causes of behavior
E. Gave rise to educational and industrial psychology
F. First woman Ph.D. in psychology
G. Studied stimuli and responses, conditioning
H. Part of psychology's "long past"
I. Concerned with thinking, language, problem solving
J. Used "experimental self-observation"
K. Relates behavior to the brain, physiology, and genetics
L. Also known as engineering psychology

Answers:

1. H 2. J 3. B 4. E 5. G 6. A 7. D 8. C 9. I 10. F 11. K

Table 1–1 The Early Development of Psychology

APPROXIMATE ORIGIN	DATE	NOTABLE EVENTS
Experimental psychology	1875	■ First psychology course offered by William James
	1878	■ First American Ph.D. in psychology awarded.
	1879	■ Wilhelm Wundt establishes first psychology laboratory in Germany
	1883	■ First American psychology lab founded at Johns Hopkins University
	1886	■ First American psychology textbook published by John Dewey
Structuralism	1898	■ Edward Titchener advances psychology based on introspection
Functionalism	1890	■ James publishes *Principles of Psychology*
	1892	■ American Psychological Association founded
Psychoanalytic psychology	1895	■ Sigmund Freud publishes first studies
	1900	■ Freud publishes *The Interpretation of Dreams*
Behaviorism	1906	■ Ivan Pavlov reports his research on conditioning
	1913	■ John Watson presents behavioristic view
Gestalt psychology	1912	■ Max Wertheimer and others advance Gestalt viewpoint
Neo-Freudianism	1914	■ Carl Jung breaks with Freud

Table 1–2 Five Ways To Look at Behavior

Psychodynamic view	Emphasizes unconscious impulses, desires, and conflicts; views behavior as the result of clashing forces within personality; negative, pessimistic view of human nature
Behavioristic view	Emphasizes the study of observable behavior and the effects of learning; stresses the influence of external rewards and punishments; neutral, scientific, and somewhat mechanistic view of human nature
Humanistic view	Focuses on subjective experience, human problems, potentials, and ideals; emphasizes self-image and self-actualization to explain behavior; positive, philosophical view of human nature
Psychobiological view	Seeks to explain behavior through activity of the brain and nervous system, physiology, genetics, the endocrine system, biochemistry, and evolution; neutral, reductionistic, mechanistic view of human nature
Cognitive view	Concerned with thinking, knowing, perception, understanding, memory, decision making, and judgment; explains behavior in terms of information processing; neutral, somewhat computer-like view of human nature

Psychologists—Guaranteed Not To Shrink

Question: What is the difference between a psychologist and a psychiatrist?
Answer: About $20 an hour. (And going up.)

There is often confusion about the differences among psychologists, psychiatrists, psychoanalysts, counselors, and other mental health professionals. It is quite inaccurate to think of them all as "shrinks." Each title reflects distinct differences in training and emphasis.

A **psychologist** usually has a master's degree or a doctorate in psychology. These degrees usually require from 3 to 8 years of postgraduate training in psychological theory and research methods. Depending on their interests, psychologists may teach, do research, give psychological tests, or serve as consultants to business, industry, government, or the military. (This statement applies to psychiatrists and psychoanalysts, too.) Psychologists interested in treating emotional problems specialize in **clinical** or **counseling psychology** (see Table 1–3).

The practice of counseling psychology was once limited to problems not involving serious mental disorder, such as adjustment at work or school. In recent years, however, an increasing number of counseling psychologists have shifted to doing psychotherapy primarily. As a result, differences between counseling and clinical psychology are beginning to fade (Fitzgerald & Osipow, 1986; Watkins et al., 1986).

To enter the profession of psychology today, you would probably find it necessary to have a doctorate (Ph.D., Psy.D., or Ed.D) to be licensed or to qualify for employment. (For more information, see Appendix A, Careers in Psychology, at the end of the text.) Most clinical psychologists now have a Ph.D. or a Psy.D. The Psy.D. (Doctor of Psychology) is a new degree that emphasizes practical clinical skills rather than research (McNett, 1982).

Like clinical psychologists, **psychiatrists** are also interested in human problems, but they are trained differently. A psychiatrist is a physician. After learning general medicine, psychiatrists specialize in abnormal behavior and psychotherapy. Psychiatrists often become "talking doctors" who spend much of their time doing psychotherapy. In practice, then, the major difference between clinical psychologists and psychiatrists is that psychiatrists are trained to treat the physical causes of psychological problems. In the vast majority of cases, they do so by prescribing drugs, something a psychologist cannot do.

To be a **psychoanalyst,** you must have a moustache and goatee, spectacles, a German accent, and a well-padded couch—or so the TV and movie stereotype goes. Actually, to become an analyst, you must have an M.D. or Ph.D. degree plus further specialized training in the theory and practice of Freudian psychoanalysis. In other words, either a physician or a psychologist may become an analyst by completing more training. Analysts typically undergo psychoanalysis themselves before applying the method to others.

Question: Is psychoanalysis widely used?

Traditional Freudian analysis is expensive and time-consuming. This fact is gradually making psychoanalysts something of a rare breed. Today, few psychiatrists and almost no psychologists become analysts, and fewer clients seek analysis. In practice, many psychotherapists find that a flexible and eclectic approach is most effective.

In many states, **counselors** (such as marriage and family counselors, child counselors, or school counselors) also do mental health work. To be a licensed counselor typically requires a master's degree plus 1 or 2 years of full-time supervised counseling experience. Almost all of a counselor's postgraduate education is related to practical helping skills, with little emphasis on research.

Question: Do psychologists have to have a license?

The Profession of Psychology Before the American Psychological Association (APA) began a push for licensing and certification, it was possible in many states for virtually anyone to purchase an inexpensive license and "hang out a shingle" as a "psychologist."

Now, to be legally called a psychologist, a person must meet rigorous educational requirements. To work as a clinical or counseling psychologist, he or she must have a license issued by a state examining board. However, the law does not prevent you from calling yourself anything else you choose—therapist, rebirther, primal feeling facilitator, cosmic aura balancer, or Rolfer—or from selling your "services" to anyone willing to pay. Beware of people advertising under such self-proclaimed titles. Even if their intentions are honorable, their training may be limited or nonexistent. A fully trained, certified counselor or psychologist who chooses to use a particular type of therapy is not the same as someone "trained" solely in that technique.

Unfortunately, psychology, like medicine, has attracted a fringe of opportunists, quacks, and charlatans who seek to profit by taking advantage of human needs, fears, and suffering. (See this chapter's Exploration section.) What happens when the escapades of these "not-really psychologists" make the news or when a friend or relative has a bad experience with one? Often, psychologists take the blame. This is truly unfortunate. Most psychologists take pride in following a professional code established by the APA that stresses (1) an accurate statement of professional qualifications, (2) confidential handling of personal information in teaching, practice, or research, and above all, (3) protection of the client's welfare. The APA also encourages psychologists to make their services available to anyone who seeks them, regardless of social considerations. Many psychologists do at least some of their work for free when clients are unable to pay. Many more do volunteer work in their communities.

● How To Be a Psychologist—Let Us Count the Ways

Question: Do all psychologists do therapy and treat abnormal behavior?

No. Even when combined, clinical and counseling psychology account for only about 50 percent of psychologists. The rest are found in a large number of other specialties. At present, there are 45 divisions of the APA, each reflecting a special skill area or interest. Some of the major specialties are listed in Table 1–3 (also see Fig. 1–11). Roughly 1 psychologist out of every 3 is employed full-time at a college or university. In these settings they teach and may also do research, consulting, or therapy. Some do **basic research,** in which they seek knowledge for the sake of knowledge. Others who plan to put their findings to immediate use do **applied research.** Some, of course, do research of both types.

Question: What kinds of topics would a research psychologist at a university study?

Here is a sampling of typical research topics.

Developmental Psychology "I am interested in development from conception until death. I am trying to learn how people grow and change over time. My inter-

Table 1–3 Kinds of Psychologists and What They Do

SPECIALTY		TYPICAL ACTIVITIES
Clinical and counseling psychologists	A*	Does psychotherapy and personal counseling, helps with emotional and behavioral problems, researches clinical problems, is involved in community mental health
Industrial psychologist	A	Selects job applicants, does skills analysis, evaluates on-job training, improves work environments and human relations in work setting
Educational psychologist	A	Conducts research on classroom dynamics, teaching styles, and learning variables; develops educational tests, evaluates educational programs, acts as consultant for schools
Consumer psychologist	A	Researches and tests packaging, advertising, and marketing methods, determines characteristics of product users, conducts public opinion polling
School psychologist	A	Does psychological testing, emotional and vocational counseling of students, detects and treats learning disabilities, improves learning and motivation in the classroom.
Developmental psychologist	A, B	Carries out basic and applied research on child development, adult developmental trends, and aging; does clinical work with disturbed children; acts as consultant to preschools, programs for the aged, and so forth
Engineering psychologist	A	Does applied research on design of machinery, controls, airplanes, automobiles, and so on for business, industry, and the military
Medical psychologist	A	Studies the relationship between stress, personality, and disease (heart attacks, high blood pressure, ulcers); manages emotional problems associated with illness or disability
Environmental psychologist	A, B	Studies the effects of urban noise pollution, crowding, attitudes toward environment, and human use of space, acts as consultant for design of industrial environments, schools, housing for elderly, and urban architecture
Forensic psychologist	A	Studies problems of crime and crime prevention, rehabilitation programs in prisons, courtroom dynamics, psychology and law, selects candidates for police work
Experimental psychologist	B	Applies scientific research methods to study of human and animal behavior; may conduct research in the areas of comparative animal behavior, learning, sensation/perception, personality, physiology, motivation/emotion, social behavior, or cognition

*Research is typically applied (A), basic (B), or both.

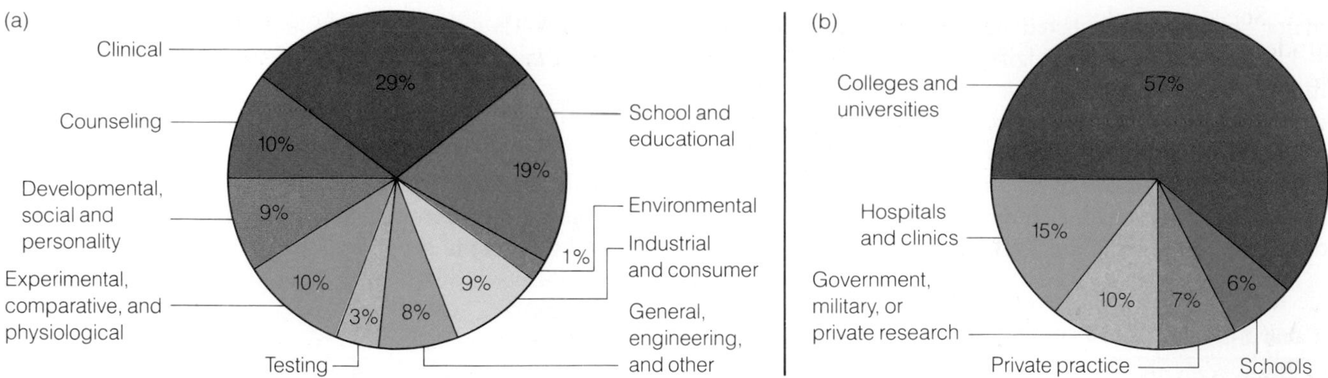

Fig. 1–11 *(a) Specialties in psychology. Percentages are approximate (from Howard et al., 1986). (b) Where psychologists work (from Pion, 1986). Notice that most psychologists specialize in applied areas and work in applied settings.*

ests stretch over the whole life span, but I am especially interested in early childhood. My colleagues and I seek the principles whereby a child develops the ability to think, speak, perceive, and act. Broadly speaking, I am interested in how adult personality and skills emerge from childhood, but my current research is more limited. I am studying the effects of stimulating childhood environments on the development of intelligence."

Learning "I'm also interested in how people get to be the way they are, but in a much more abstract sense. I believe that most human behavior is learned. At any given moment, I would describe your behavior as the result of your personal learning history. By studying various kinds of learning, conditioning, and memory in humans and animals, I am helping to construct theories about how learning occurs and what factors affect it. My doctoral dissertation was on avoidance learning. I had rats learn to press a bar in order to avoid receiving an electric shock that followed the onset of a signal light. Right now, I'm studying the effects of patterns of reinforcement on learning in pigeons."

Personality "In many ways, my area is both the most rewarding and the most frustrating. Personality theorists draw on the findings of all other research areas as well as their own in an effort to create as total a picture and understanding of human personality as possible. I concern myself with the structure and dynamics of personality, motivation, and individual differences. I am studying the personality profiles of college students who score high on tests of creativity."

Sensation and Perception "How do we come to know the world? How does information 'get into' our nervous systems? How is it processed and given pattern and meaning? These are my concerns. I am using an information-processing theory called signal detection to study the visual perception of random shapes."

Comparative Psychology "I've always been interested in basic questions about animal behavior. I am especially fascinated by porpoises. For the last three years, I've been studying the porpoise's echolocation ability. We did a lot of testing underwater in pools to determine the animals' sensory limits. In a typical study, we asked porpoises to select between different shapes and surfaces while they were blindfolded. If they chose the right target, we rewarded them with food. Their ability to discriminate in this way is really superb."

Physiological Psychology "The brain and nervous system are my meat . . . so to speak. I work within the realm of psychobiology. It is my belief that ultimately all other areas in psychology—learning, perception, even personality and abnormal behavior—will be explained by the action of nerve cells and brain chemicals. I have been doing some exciting research on the role of the hypothalamus in hunger. I find that if I remove part of the hypothalamus in the brain of a rat, the rat will eat and gain weight until it looks like a furry water balloon. If I remove an area just a few millimeters away, the rat will starve to death if not force-fed."

Social Psychology "I study people in a group setting, or under any circumstance in which social factors play a part. Social psychologists in general are interested in attitudes, social influence, riots, conformity, leadership, racism, friendship, and a growing list of other topics. My personal interest is interpersonal attraction. I place two strangers together in a room for a short time and investigate factors that affect their degree of attraction toward each other."

This small sample should give you an idea of the diversity of psychological research. It also hints at some of the kinds of information covered later in this book.

A good summary of our discussion so far is provided by psychologists Gary VandenBos and Brenda Bryant:

> Psychologists are explorers and discoverers. They explore the reactions of human beings to small frustrations and great successes, to pleasing colors and the aftermath of disaster, always looking for answers to how and why people think, feel, and behave as they do. . . . The psychologist, regardless of where he or she may work, is always applying what is known in an effort to resolve the unknown. The psychologist, no matter how small the question being asked may appear to be, is looking for the larger answer. (VandenBos & Bryant, 1987)

Giving Psychology Away—An Introduction to Applications

Question: Will learning psychology benefit me personally?

Yes, and more than you might imagine. A special quality of psychology is that its concepts are available to everyone. As former APA president George Miller says:

> The secrets of our trade need not be reserved for highly trained specialists. Psychological facts should be passed out freely to all who need and can use them. (Miller, 1969)

Miller (1980) has urged psychologists to "give psychology away," and that's exactly what this book is meant to do.

To help you get the most out of psychology, each chapter of this text includes an *Applications* section like the one that follows. These sections discuss ideas you can actually use, now or in the future. Our first Applications section tells how psychology can help you study more effectively, a topic that may come in handy very soon.

Learning Check

See if you can answer these questions before continuing.

1. Which of the following can prescribe drugs?
a. a psychologist *b.* a psychiatrist *c.* a psychoanalyst *d.* a counselor

2. A psychologist who specializes in treating human emotional difficulties is called a ______________ psychologist.

3. Roughly 40 percent of psychologists specialize in counseling psychology. T or F?

4. Seeking knowledge for the sake of knowledge is called ______________ research.

Match the following research areas with the topics they cover.

5. ___ Developmental psychology — **A.** Attitudes, groups, leadership
6. ___ Learning — **B.** Conditioning, memory
7. ___ Personality — **C.** The psychology of law
8. ___ Sensation and perception — **D.** Brain and nervous system
9. ___ Physiological psychology — **E.** Child psychology
10. ___ Social psychology — **F.** Individual differences, motivation
11. ___ Comparative psychology — **G.** Animal behavior
H. Processing sensory information

12. Who among the following would most likely be involved in the detection and treatment of learning disabilities?
a. a consumer psychologist *b.* a forensic psychologist *c.* an experimental psychologist *d.* a school psychologist

Answers:
1. *b* **2.** clinical or counseling **3.** F **4.** basic **5.** E **6.** B **7.** F **8.** H **9.** D **10.** A **11.** G **12.** *d*

Applications: The Psychology of Studying

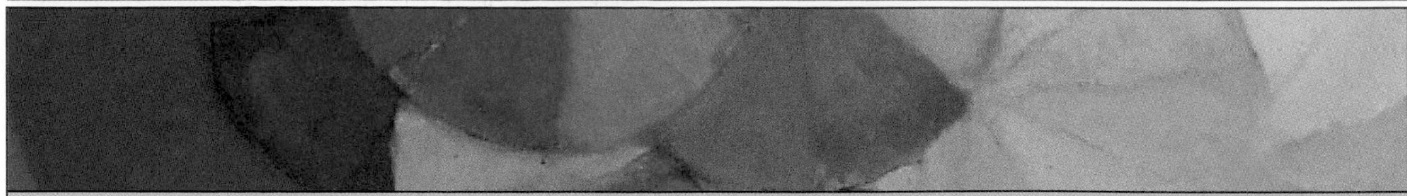

Do you find learning exciting and rewarding? Or painful and intimidating? The second reaction is common even among bright students if they lack basic "tools of the trade." Even if you're not one of those students, you may be able to improve your study skills. Would you like to learn more in less time? There is a good chance you can if you apply the methods described here.

The SQ3R Method—How To Tame a Textbook

Have you ever finished a reading assignment, only to discover later that you remembered little of what you read? This problem plagues students everywhere. But fortunately, an excellent solution exists. Over 40 years ago, educator Francis Robinson developed a superb reading technique called the **SQ3R method.** Robinson's method is simply a way of studying while you read. The symbols S-Q-R-R-R stand for survey, question, read, recite, and review. Following these five steps can help you understand ideas quickly, remember more, and review effectively for tests (Robinson, 1941):

S = *Survey.* Look ahead through a chapter before you begin reading. As you do, read only topic headings, captions for illustrations, and any chapter summary or review. This step should give you an overall picture of what lies ahead.

Q = *Question.* To focus your attention as you read, turn each topic heading into one or more questions. For example, the heading "Stages of Sleep" could raise questions such as: "Is there more than one stage of sleep?" "What are the stages of sleep?" "How do they differ?" Asking questions will increase your interest, and it helps relate new ideas to what you already know, for better comprehension.

R1 = *Read.* The first R in SQ3R refers to *read.* As you read, try to answer the questions you asked. Read in short "bites," from *one topic heading* to the next, then stop. (If the material is very difficult you may even want to read only a paragraph or two at a time.)

R2 = *Recite.* The second R stands for *recite.* After you have read from one topic heading to the next, you should stop and recite. That is, try to silently answer your questions. Or better yet, summarize what you've read in brief notes. If you can't summarize main ideas in your own words, scan back over the section until you can. Until you can remember what you just read, there's little point to reading more.

After you have read a short "bite" of information, turn the next topic heading into questions. Then read to the next heading. Again, you should look for answers as you read, and you should recite before moving on. Repeat the question-read-recite cycle until you've read the entire chapter.

R3 = *Review.* When you've finished reading, skim back over the chapter, or read your notes. Then check your memory by reciting and quizzing yourself again. Or better yet, get someone to ask you questions about each topic to see if you can answer in your own words.

Question: Does this method really work?

Experiments show that using the SQ3R method improves both reading comprehension and grades (Boker, 1974; Driskell & Kelly, 1980). Simply reading straight through a chapter often leads to a case of intellectual "indigestion." That's why it's important that you stop often to think, question, recite, review, and "digest" information.

How to Use this Text With practice, the SQ3R method can be applied to any book. However, as you may have guessed, its steps are built into this text to help you use them.

Each chapter opens with a *Preview,* plus a short outline titled *In This Chapter.* This is followed by *Survey Questions* that identify main points to look for as you read. You can use these features to get an overview of each chapter. Before you begin reading, however, take a minute or two to make your own survey of the chapter. Once you begin reading, additional questions in the text will help clarify ideas and focus your attention. Research shows that this arrangement leads to improved learning and memory (Boker, 1974; Melton, 1978).

Every few pages, *Learning Checks* allow you to recite by testing your memory of important points. (Again, you should also take notes or recite on your own.) If you only have 15 or 20 minutes to study between classes, or if you would like to study chapters in smaller sections, Learning checks make a good stopping place. Near the end of each chapter is an *Applications* section, like this one, filled with practical information. Then, to extend your knowledge, a short *Exploration* covers an interesting topic related to the core of the chapter.

Applications

Finally, a *Chapter Summary* restates key ideas so you can do a final review.

As you read, new terms will be defined where they first appear in the text. Key terms are printed in **boldface type** and occasionally followed by pronunciations. (Capital letters show which syllables are accented.) As a further study aid, a **glossary,** or "mini-dictionary," of terms also appears near the end of this book. Perhaps you should take a moment to find it now.

Together, these features should make learning psychology enjoyable and effective, but there is still more you can do on your own.

Effective Note-Taking—Good Students, Take Note!

Question: The SQ3R method may be good for reading, but what about taking notes in class when it's difficult to know what's important?

Effective note-taking requires active listening. **Active listeners** know how to control their attention to avoid classroom daydreaming. Here's a listening/note-taking plan that works for many students. The important steps are summarized by the letters **LISAN,** pronounced like the word *listen* (Carman & Adams, 1985).

L = *Lead. Don't follow.* Try to anticipate what the instructor is going to say. As in SQ3R, try to set up questions as guides. Questions can come from the instructor's study guides or the reading assignments.

I = *Ideas.* Every lecture is based on a core of important ideas. Usually, an idea is introduced and examples or explanations are given. Ask yourself often, "What is the main idea now? What ideas support it?"

S = *Signal words.* Listen for words that tell you the direction the instructor is taking. For instance, here are some groups of signal words:

There are three reasons why . . .	Here come ideas
Most important is . . .	Main idea
On the contrary . . .	Opposite idea
As an example . . .	Support for main idea
Therefore . . .	Conclusion

A = *Actively listen.* Sit where you can hear and where you can be seen if you need to ask a question. Look at the instructor while he or she talks. Bring questions you want answered from the last lecture or from your reading. Raise your hand at the beginning of class or approach your instructor before the lecture begins. Do anything that helps you to be active.

N = *Note-taking.* As you listen, write down only key points. Listen to everything, but be selective and don't try to write everything down. If you are too busy writing, you may not grasp what is being said. Any gaps in your notes can be filled in immediately after class.

Here is something more you should know: A revealing study (Palkovitz & Lore, 1980) found that most students take reasonably good notes—and then don't use them! Most students wait until just before exams to review their notes. By then the notes have lost much of their meaning. This practice may help explain why students do poorly on test items based on lectures (Thielens, 1987). If you don't want your notes to seem like hieroglyphics or "chicken scratches," it pays to review them *on a regular basis.* And remember, whenever it is important to listen effectively, the letters LISAN are a good guide.

Study Habits—Avoiding the Last-Minute Blues

It is important to realize that virtually every topic is interesting to someone, somewhere. Although I may not be interested in the sex life of the South American tree frog, a biologist might be fascinated. If you wait for your teachers to "make" their courses interesting, you are missing the point. Interest is a matter of *your attitude.* Students and teachers *together* make a class rewarding. It's a big mistake to blame poor performance in college on circumstances "beyond your control." Students who believe that success is due to effort and motivation do better in the long run (Noel, et al., 1987).

With the preceding in mind, let's consider a few things you can do to improve your study habits.

Study in a Specific Place It goes almost without saying that you should study in a quiet, well-lighted area free of distractions. If possible, you should also have at least one place where you only study. Do nothing else at that spot: Keep magazines, radios, friends, pets, posters, games, puzzles, food, lovers, sports cars, elephants, pianos, televisions, hang gliders, kazoos, and other distractions out of the area. In this way, studying will become strongly linked with one specific place (Beneke & Harris, 1972). Then, rather than trying to force yourself to study by "willpower," all you have to do is go to your study area. Once there, you'll find it relatively easy to get started.

Use Spaced Study Sessions It is quite reasonable to review intensely before an exam. However, if you are actually learning information for the first time ("cramming"), you are

Applications

asking for trouble. Research suggests that spaced practice is a more efficient way to study. Spaced practice consists of a large number of relatively short study sessions, rather than one or two long ones (called massed practice). (It might be worth remembering that if you "massed up" your studying, you probably messed it up too.)

Cramming places a tremendous burden on memory. It is far better to learn small amounts on a daily basis and to review frequently. It also makes sense to reward yourself with a treat of some kind after each of your study sessions, to keep yourself motivated between tests.

Try Mnemonics Students sometimes complain about having to memorize for classes. But learning has to start somewhere, and memorizing is often the first step. Psychologists now know a great deal about how to improve memory. Since many of the most important points are summarized in Chapter 9, let's consider just one technique here.

A **mnemonic** (nee-MON-ik) is a memory aid. Most mnemonics link new information to ideas or images that are easy to remember. For example, to remember the early schools of psychology (structuralism, functionalism, behaviorism, Gestalt, psychoanalytic, and humanistic), it might be helpful to make up a sentence like this: "Strutting is fun behavior, guessed the psycho-human." As silly as this may seem, it could provide the extra cues you need to remember when you are under pressure on a test. As another example, imagine you want to remember that the Spanish word for duck is *pato* (pronounced POT-oh). To use a mnemonic, you could picture a duck in a pot or a duck wearing a pot for a hat (Pressley et al., 1980).

Obviously, there are many ways to create mnemonics. If you would like to learn more, look ahead to Chapter 9.

Test Yourself Many students overlook one of the best ways to improve test scores: When studying, you can arrange to take several practice tests before the real one in class. In other words, studying should include self-testing by use of flash cards, Learning Checks, a study guide, or questions you ask yourself. As you study, ask as many questions as you can and be sure you can answer them. Studying without testing yourself is like practicing for a basketball game without shooting any baskets.

Overlearn There is something else to keep in mind: Many students *underprepare* for exams, and most *overestimate* how well they will do on exams (Murray, 1980). A solution to both problems is overlearning. To overlearn, you should continue studying beyond bare mastery of a topic. This means that you need to give yourself time for extra study and review after you think you are prepared for a test. Here's another reason for overlearning:

The Perils of Multiple Choice

College students were given 15 minutes to study a passage on human rights. They also were told to expect an essay, multiple-choice, "memory," or unspecified type of test. In fact, all students took the same test, which included multiple-choice and short-answer questions. Students expecting multiple-choice questions scored *lowest,* even on the multiple-choice questions (Foos & Clark, 1984).

Before tests, students always ask, "Will it be essay or multiple choice?" But as the experiment shows, it is best to approach all tests as if they were essays. By doing so, you will learn information more completely, so that you will really "know your stuff" when you take the test.

Question: All of these study techniques are fine. But what can I do about procrastination?

Procrastination

A tendency to procrastinate is almost universal among college students. (When campus workshops on procrastination are offered, many students never get around to signing up!) Even when procrastination doesn't lead to failure, it can cause much suffering. Procrastinators put off work until the last moment, work only under pressure, skip classes, give false reasons for late work, and feel ashamed of their last-minute efforts (Burka & Yuen, 1983).

Question: Why do so many students procrastinate?

It is fairly natural to put off long-range assignments, at school and elsewhere. However, there are added reasons for student procrastination. Psychologists Jane Burka and Lenora Yuen observe that many students seem to equate performance in school with their *personal worth.* By procrastinating, students can blame poor work on a late start, rather than a lack of ability. After all, it wasn't their best effort, was it?

Perfectionism is a related problem. If you have high expectations for yourself, you may find it hard to start an assignment. Students with high standards expect the impossible from themselves and end up with all-or-nothing work habits (Burka & Yuen, 1983).

Time Management Burka and Yuen supervise a program for procrastinators at the University of California, Berkeley.

Applications

Eventually, they say, most procrastinators must face the self-worth conflict; but progress can be made by learning better study skills and more effective time management. Since we have already discussed study skills, let's consider time management.

A **formal time schedule** can do much to prevent procrastination and maintain motivation in school. To prepare your schedule, make a chart showing all of the hours in each day of the week. Then fill in times that are already committed: sleep, meals, classes, work, team practices, lessons, appointments, and so forth. Next, fill in times when you will study for various classes, and label them. Finally, label the remaining hours as open or free times.

The beauty of keeping a schedule is that you know you are making an honest effort to do well in your classes. In addition to getting more done, you will avoid the trap of yearning to play while you work and feeling guilty about not working when you play. The key to time management is to treat your study times as serious commitments, like class meetings or a job. Be sure to respect your free times, too, so you don't get stale or discouraged.

Many students also find it helpful to set **specific goals** for themselves (Pintrich & McKeachie, 1987). If you have trouble staying motivated, it's a good idea to set goals for the semester, the week, the day, and even for single study sessions. Be realistic when setting your goals, but don't underestimate yourself either.

Taking Tests—Are You "Test Wise"?

Question: If I have read and studied effectively, is there anything else I can do to improve my grades?

Learning is only a first step. You must then be able to show what you know on a test. Here are some guidelines for improving your test-taking skills.

Objective Tests Objective tests (multiple-choice and true-false items) test your ability to recognize a correct statement among wrong answers or a true statement against a false one. If you are taking an objective test, try this:

1. Read the directions carefully; they may give you good advice or clues for the test. If the directions are not clear, ask the instructor to clarify them.
2. Read *all* the choices for each question before you make a decision. If you immediately think that *a* is correct, for instance, and stop reading, you might miss seeing a last choice like "both *a* and *d*" that is a better answer.
3. Read rapidly and skip items you are uncertain about. Later questions may give you "free information" that will help you answer difficult items. Return to skipped items if time allows.
4. Eliminate certain alternatives. With a four-choice-per-item multiple-choice test, the odds are 1 in 4 that you could guess right. If you can eliminate two alternatives, your guessing odds improve to 50-50.
5. Unless there is a penalty for guessing, be sure to answer every question. Even if you are not sure of an answer, you may be right. If you skip a question, it is automatically wrong. When you are forced to guess, don't make the mistake of choosing the longest answer or the letter you've used the least. Both of these strategies produce lower scores than pure random guessing (Shatz, 1986).
6. There is a bit of folk wisdom that says "Don't change your answers on a multiple-choice test. Your first choice is usually right." Careful study of this idea has shown it is *false*. If you change answers, you are more likely to gain points than lose them (Benjamin et al. 1984). This is especially true if you feel *very* uncertain of your first answer. ("When in doubt, scratch it out!") When you have strong doubts, your second answer is more likely to be correct (Johnson, 1975). In fact, even if you are only moderately confident about your new answer, you will probably still come out ahead by making the change (Ramsey et al. 1987).

Essay Tests Essay questions are a weak spot for those students who lack organization, fail to support main ideas, or don't write directly to the question. When you take an essay exam, try the following:

1. Read the question carefully. Make sure that you note key words, such as *compare, contrast, discuss, evaluate, analyze*, and *describe*. These words all demand a certain emphasis in your answer.
2. Think about your answer before putting words on paper. It's a good idea to make a brief list of the points you want to make. Just list them in any order as they come to mind. Then rearrange your ideas in the order you want to write them.
3. Don't beat around the bush or pad your answer. Be direct. Make a point and support it. Get your list of ideas into words.
4. Look over your essay for spelling errors, sentence errors, and grammatical errors. Save this for last. Your *ideas* are of first importance. You can work on spelling and grammar separately if they affect your grades.

A Final Word There is a distinction made in Zen between "live words" and "dead words." Live words come from personal experience; dead words are "about" a subject. This book can only be a collection of dead words without your personal

Applications

involvement. It is designed to help you learn psychology, but it cannot do it for you. You will find many helpful, useful, and exciting ideas in the pages that follow. To make them yours, you must set out to *actively* learn as much as you can. The ideas presented here should get you off to a good start. Good luck!

For more information, consult any of the following books:

Annis, L. F. *Study Techniques*. Dubuque, IA: Brown, 1983.

Burka, J. B., and L. M. Yuen. *Procrastination: Why You Do It; What To Do About It*. Menlo Park; CA; Addison-Wesley, 1983.

Carman, R. A., and W. R. Adams. *Study Skills: A Student's Guide for Survival*. New York: Wiley, 1985.

Deese, J., and E. K. Deese. *How to Study*. New York: McGraw-Hill, 1979.

Ellis, A., and W. J. Knaus. *Overcoming Procrastination*. New York: Rational Living, 1977.

Learning Check

1. The three *R*s in SQ3R stand for "read, recite, and review." T or F?
2. When using the LISAN method, students try to write down as much of a lecture as possible so that their notes are complete. T or F?
3. Spaced study sessions are usually superior to massed practice. T or F?
4. According to recent research, you should almost always stick with your first answer on multiple-choice tests. T or F?
5. To use the technique known as overlearning, you should continue to study after you feel you have begun to master a topic. T or F?
6. Procrastination is related to seeking perfection and equating self-worth with grades. T or F?

Answers:
1. T 2. F 3. T 4. F 5. T 6. T

Exploration: Pseudo-psychologies—Palms, Planets, and Personality

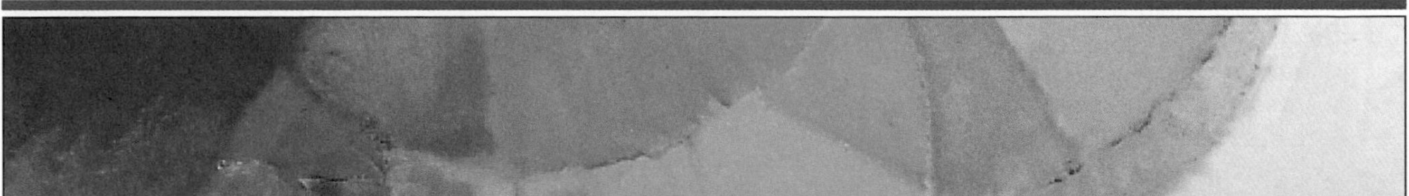

Pseudo-psychologies (SUE-doe-psychologies) are dubious and unfounded systems that resemble psychology. Many pseudo-psychologies offer a highly developed system that gives the appearance of science but is actually false. (*Pseudo* means "false.") Unlike the real thing, pseudo-psychologies are not based on empirical observation or scientific testing. Let's begin by considering some of the less convincing pseudo-psychologies.

Palmistry Palmistry claims that lines in the hand reveal personality and predict a person's future. Lines that are longer or shorter, more bent or less bent, clear or indistinct supposedly predict destiny, fortune, length of life, occupation, and health. The fact that palmistry assumes that the hands tell the story of the whole body is hard enough to swallow, but ignoring the effects of dishwater, manual labor, or hand lotion is inexcusable. Even so, palmists can still be found separating the gullible from their money in many cities.

Phrenology During the nineteenth century, a German anatomy teacher, Franz Gall, popularized the theory that personality is revealed by the shape of the skull. Phrenologists assumed that parts of the brain responsible for various "mental faculties" caused bumps on the head. By feeling these bumps, phrenologists claimed to read a person's abilities.

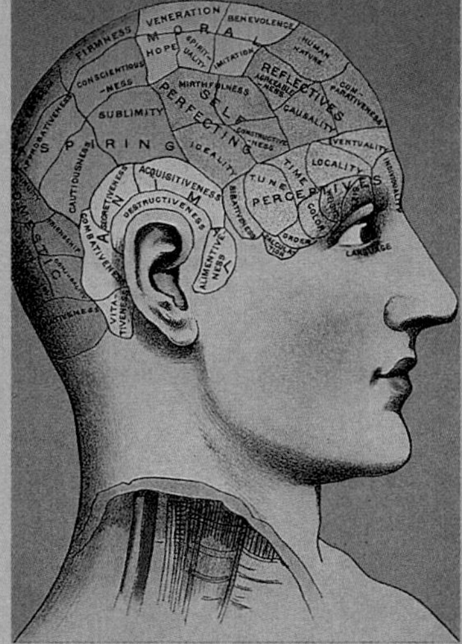

Fig. 1–12 *Phrenology was an attempt to assess personality characteristics by examining various areas of the skull. Phrenologists used charts such as the one shown here as guides. Like other pseudo-psychologists, phrenologists made no attempt to empirically verify their concepts.*

Phrenology faded rapidly when a better understanding of the brain showed that this is impossible. For instance, the area of the brain that controls hearing was listed on phrenology charts as the center for "combativeness" and "destructiveness"!

Graphology Graphologists believe that they can identify personality traits and predict job performance from handwriting. Graphology is only moderately popular in the United States, although at least 3000 companies in this country use handwriting analysis to evaluate job applicants. In European countries, graphology is widely used for job placement and advancement. These uses are troubling to psychologists because studies show that graphologists score close to zero in tests of accuracy in rating personality (Guilford, 1959). In fact, in one study, graphologists did no better than untrained college students in rating personality and sales success, based on the handwriting of a group of salespersons (Rafaeli & Klimoski, 1983). In another recent study, graphologists scored no better than chance at predicting the professions of 40 people (Ben-Shakhar et al., 1986).

Why do graphologists continue to attract devotees? Probably many businesses are glad to give graphologists the responsibility for making important decisions. That way if a poor worker is hired the personnel manager can always blame the graphologist. (By the way, graphology's failure at revealing personality should be distinguished from its proved value for detecting forgeries.)

Question: If the pseudo-psychologies have no scientific basis, how do they survive and why are they popular?

There are several reasons, all of which can be demonstrated by a critique of astrology.

Exploration

Astrology Astrology is probably the most popular pseudo-psychology. Astrologers assume that the position of the stars and planets at the time of a person's birth determines personality traits and affects behavior. Like other pseudo-psychologies, astrology has repeatedly been shown to have no scientific validity (Jerome, 1975). The objections to astrology are numerous and devasting, as shown by the following:

Problems in the Stars

1. The zodiac has shifted by one full constellation since astrology was first set up. However, most astrologers simply ignore this shift. (In other words, if astrology calls you a Scorpio, you are really a Libra, and so forth.)
2. There is no connection between the "compatibility" of the astrological signs of couples and their marriage and divorce rates.
3. Studies have found no connection between astrological signs and leadership, physical characteristics, career choice, or personality traits.
4. The force of gravity exerted by the physician's body at the moment of birth is greater than that exerted by the stars. Also, astrologers have failed to explain why the moment of birth should be more important than the moment of conception.
5. A study of over 3000 predictions by famous astrologers found that only a small percentage were fulfilled. These "successful" predictions tended to be vague ("There will be a tragedy somewhere in the eastern United States in the spring") or easily guessed from current events. (Sources: "Astrology and Astronomy," 1983; Culver & Ianna, 1979; Pasachoff, 1981; Randi, 1980.)

In short, astrology doesn't work.

Question: Then why does it so often seem to work?

Uncritical Acceptance If you have ever had your astrological chart done, you may have been impressed with its seeming accuracy. Careful reading shows many such charts to be made up of mostly flattering traits. Naturally, when your personality is described in *desirable* terms, it is hard to deny that the description has the "ring of truth." How much acceptance would astrology receive if the characteristics of a birth sign read like this:

> **Virgo:** You are the logical type and hate disorder. Your nitpicking is unbearable to your friends. You are cold, unemotional, and usually fall asleep while making love. Virgos make good doorstops.

Positive Instances Even when an astrological description of personality contains a mixture of good and bad traits, it may seem accurate. To find out why, read the following personality description.

Your Personality Profile

> You have a strong need for other people to like you and for them to admire you. You have a tendency to be critical of yourself. You have a great deal of unused energy which you have not turned to your advantage. While you have some personality weaknesses, you are generally able to compensate for them. Your sexual adjustment has presented some problems for you. Disciplined and controlled on the outside, you tend to be worrisome and insecure inside. At times you have serious doubts as to whether you have made the right decision or done the right thing. You prefer a certain amount of change and variety and become dissatisfied when hemmed-in by restrictions and limitations. You pride yourself on being an independent thinker and do not accept other opinions without satisfactory proof. You have found it unwise to be too frank in revealing yourself to others. At times you are extroverted, affable, sociable, while at other times you are introverted, wary, and reserved. Some of your aspirations tend to be pretty unrealistic.*

Does this describe your personality? A psychologist read this summary individually to 79 college students who had taken a personality test. Twenty-nine said it was an "excellent" description of their personality; 30 said it was "good"; 15 said it was "average"; and 5 said it was "poor." Thus, only 5 students out of 79 felt that the description failed to adequately capture their personality.

Reread the description and you will see that it contains both sides of several personality dimensions ("At times you are extroverted . . . while at other times you are introverted. . . ."). Its apparent accuracy is an illusion based on the **fallacy of positive instances,** in which a person remembers or notices things that confirm his or her expectations and forgets the rest. The pseudo-psychologies thrive on this effect. For example, you can always find "Leo characteristics" in a Leo. If you looked, however, you could also find "Gemini characteristics," "Scorpio characteristics," or whatever.

*Reprinted with permission of author and publisher from R. E. Ulrich, T. J. Stachnik, and N. R. Stainton, "Student acceptance of generalized personality interpretations," *Psychological Reports* 13, (1963): 831–834.

Exploration

The Barnum Effect P. T. Barnum, the famed circus showman, had a formula for success: "Always have a little something for everybody." Like the all-purpose personality description, palm readings, fortunes, horoscopes, and other products of pseudo-psychology are stated in such *general* terms that they can hardly miss. There is always "a little something for everybody." If you doubt this, read *all 12* of the daily horoscopes found in newspapers for several days. You will find that predictions for other signs fit events as well as those for your own sign do.

Question: Couldn't that be because commercial horoscopes don't take into account a person's specific time of birth?

If they did, they would not be any more accurate, just more convincing. In one experiment, people were given standardized horoscopes. Some had provided only their sign. Others gave the year, month, and day of their birth. All were then given *the same* personality description. The result? Those who had provided more detailed information considered their horoscope more accurate (Snyder & Schenkel, 1975). Thus, the more hocus pocus a fortune teller, palmist, or astrologer goes through, the more believable the results become.

Compare:

Uncritical acceptance The tendency to believe generally positive or flattering descriptions of oneself.

Fallacy of positive instances The tendency to remember or notice information that fits one's expectations, while forgetting discrepancies.

Barnum Effect The tendency to consider a personal description accurate if it is stated in very general terms.

A Final Note Astrology's popularity shows the difficulty many people have separating valid psychology from systems that seem valid but are not. The goal of this discussion, then, has been to make you a more critical observer of human behavior and to clarify what is, and what is not, psychology. In Chapter 2, you will get a chance to further sharpen your critical skills as we investigate the research methods used in psychology. In the meantime, here is what the "stars" say about your future:

> Emphasis now on education and personal improvement. A learning experience of lasting value awaits you. Take care of scholastic responsibilities before engaging in recreation. Research new possibility. The number 2 figures prominently in your future.

Learning Check

1. ______________________ is the out-dated theory that personality is revealed by the skull. It was popularized by Franz ______________________.
2. The fallacy of positive instances refers to graphology's accepted value for the detection of forgeries. T or F?
3. Personality descriptions provided by pseudo-psychologies are stated in general terms, which provide "a little something for everybody." This fact is the basis of the
   a. palmist's fallacy *b.* uncritical acceptance pattern *c.* fallacy of positive instances *d.* Barnum effect
4. The more accurate the information given an astrologer concerning a person's time and place of birth, the more accurate the astrological descriptions of personality become. T or F?
5. The more accurate the information given an astrologer, the more empirical the resulting horoscope becomes. T or F?

Answers:
1. Phrenology, Gall 2. F 3. *d* 4. F 5. F

Chapter Summary

• **Psychology** is the scientific study of human and animal behavior. Its goals are to **describe, understand, predict,** and **control** behavior.

• Whenever possible, psychologists seek **empirical** (objective and observable) **evidence** based on **scientific observation.**

• Not all psychological questions are answerable, usually because of ethical, practical, technical, or methodological limitations.

• Psychologists study animals as well as people, either out of interest in animals themselves or to use animals as models for human behavior. One danger in studying animals is the **anthropomorphic fallacy,** the tendency to treat animals as if they had human characteristics.

• Accurate description is one goal of psychology, but psychologists also seek understanding and the ability to predict and control behavior. Psychologists engage in control when they alter conditions that affect behavior in predictable ways.

• The history of psychology begins with **philosophy,** an "armchair" approach to understanding human behavior.

• The first psychological laboratory was established in Germany by **Wilhelm Wundt,** who tried to apply scientific methods to the study of conscious experience.

• The first school of thought in psychology was **structuralism,** a kind of "mental chemistry" based on Wundt's ideas and the method of **introspection.**

• Structuralism was followed by **functionalism, behaviorism,** and **Gestalt** psychology. The **psychoanalytic** approach, which emphasizes unconscious determinants of behavior, developed separately. A more recent development is **humanistic** psychology.

• Five main streams of thought that can be seen in modern psychology are **behaviorism, humanism,** the **psychodynamic** approach, **psychobiology,** and **cognitive** psychology. However, there is a strong trend toward blending the best features of many viewpoints.

• **Psychologists, psychiatrists, psychoanalysts,** and **counselors** work in the field of mental health, although their training and methods differ considerably.

• **Clinical** and **counseling** psychologists, who do psychotherapy, represent only one of dozens of specialties in psychology. Other representative areas of specialization are **industrial, educational, consumer, school, developmental, engineering, medical, environmental, forensic, psychometric,** and **experimental** psychology.

• Psychological research may be **basic** or **applied.** Some common research specialties are comparative, learning, sensation, perception, personality, physiology, motivation and emotion, social, cognitive, and developmental psychology.

• The elements of **effective study skills** include the SQ3R method, active listening and note-taking, a positive attitude toward learning, use of a specific study area, spaced practice, mnemonics, self-testing, overlearning, time management, goal setting, and test-taking skills.

• Numerous **pseudo-psychologies** exist. These false systems are frequently confused with valid psychology. Belief in pseudo-psychologies is based in part on **uncritical acceptance,** the **fallacy of positive instances,** and the **Barnum effect.**

Questions For Discussion

1. The goals of psychology are a refinement of things we do every day. Can you relate instances in which you have sought to describe, predict, understand, or control behavior? Do you consider control of behavior an acceptable goal for psychology? Why or why not?

2. Should psychologists study animals? Most people anthropomorphize pets. How could this be a problem in the objective study of animals? In your opinion, can we learn anything about humans by studying animals?

3. In what ways is your behavior controlled by the environment? Do you believe that you have free will? Is there any way to tell if a "free choice" is really determined by your past?

4. How did you picture psychology and psychologists before reading this chapter? Has your image changed? How accurate are television and movie portrayals of psychologists? What psychological specialty do you consider most interesting at this point?

5. Presently, a number of nonphysicians can prescribe certain medications under certain conditions. Examples include optometrists, nurse practitioners, and physician assistants. In your opinion, should psychologists be trained to prescribe mood-altering drugs?

6. Can you name additional systems of thought that you suspect are pseudo-psychologies? What are their claims? Can you use the points made in the Exploration section to explain their attraction for believers?

7. Return to the quiz at the beginning of the chapter. Why are all the statements false? Explain those that you can.

8. Discuss the limitations of the following widely used "psychological" terms and "insights" (dubbed "psychobabble" by one critic): "I really felt like we were *getting into each other's heads*." "She's really *together*, you know, really *laid back*." "You gotta *go with your feelings* and *let it happen* if you don't want to be *uptight*." "We give each other the *space* to be our *true selves*." "I'm really *getting in touch with myself*." "Most problems are due to a lack of *total and honest communication*."

Chapter 2

Research Methods in Psychology

In This Chapter
The scientific method
Naturalistic observation
Correlational method
Experimental method
Clinical method
Survey method
Applications
Reading the popular press
Exploration
The ethics of research

Chapter Preview

From Common Sense to Controlled Observation

Comment overheard on campus: "I don't know why he bothers taking psychology classes. Psychology is just common sense." Is psychology common sense? Is common sense a good source of information?

Consider some ***commonsense statements.*** *Let's say that your grandfather has gone back to college. What do people say? "Ah . . . never too old to learn." And what do they say when he loses interest and quits? "Well, you can't teach an old dog new tricks." Let's examine another commonsense statement. It is frequently said that "absence makes the heart grow fonder." Those of us separated from friends and lovers can take comfort in this knowledge—until we remember "Out of sight, out of mind"! Much of what passes for common sense is equally vague and inconsistent. Notice also that most of these* B.S. *statements work best after the fact. (*B.S.*, of course, stands for* Before Science.*)*

Common sense is not without value; without it, many of us would not be alive. Yet, common sense can often prevent us from seeking better information or seeing the truth. Albert Einstein reportedly said, "Common sense is the layer of prejudice laid down in our minds before we are 18." In the early stages of the scientific revolution, people laughed at the idea that the world is round. (Anyone with eyes could see that it wasn't.) They laughed at Pasteur when he proposed that microorganisms cause disease. (How could creatures too small to be seen kill a healthy human?) Scientific ideas such as these directly contradicted the common sense of their time. Now, few people argue with the findings of sciences such as chemistry, physics, and biology. But many still write off psychology as "just common sense."

Jab a hat pin into your finger. The sensation of pain seems instantaneous. We can go no further with personal observation. However, by using electrical recorders to measure nerve impulses, psychologists have found that such impulses travel at a maximum speed of 120 meters per second. This is one-third the speed of sound. That's fast, but certainly not instantaneous. Pain from the finger takes at least a hundredth of a second to reach the brain.

As you can see, psychologists use careful measurement and specialized research techniques to avoid the pitfalls of "common sense." Their techniques are the topic of this chapter.

Survey Questions

- How do psychologists collect information?
- What are the advantages and disadvantages of each major research method?
- How is an experiment performed?
- How does the scientific method relate to critical thinking?
- How dependable is psychological information found in the popular press?
- What ethical questions does psychological research raise?

Scientific Method—Can a Horse Add?

In the United States today, it is still possible to find people who believe the earth is flat. To the "flat-earther" the earth is disk-shaped, with the North Pole at the center and the South Pole ringing the outer edge.

Question: How could anyone believe such a thing after seeing the astronauts' photographs of the earth?

Flat-earthers point out that the opposite side of large lakes can be seen through binoculars; therefore, the earth must be a flat surface. Also, a person who jumps up in the air for 1 second does not come down 190 miles away. Surely, they say, this proves that the earth cannot be a rotating globe (McCain & Segal, 1969).

Obviously, the flat-earthers have made the wrong observations, in the wrong way, and for the wrong reasons—*if* they are interested in the truth. In many ways, psychologists in search of accurate information must avoid the same trap of faulty observation. To do so, they use the **scientific method,** which is based on the collection of solid observable evidence, accurate description and measurement, precise definition, controlled observation, and repeatable results. In its ideal form the scientific method has five steps:

1. **Observation**
2. **Defining a problem**
3. **Proposing a hypothesis**
4. **Experimentation**
5. **Theory formulation**

Question: What is a hypothesis?

A **hypothesis** (hi-POTH-eh-sis) is a tentative explanation of an event or observation. In common terms, a hypothesis is a clearly stated and *testable* hunch or educated guess

Fig. 2–1 *Applying the scientific method to the study of behavior requires careful observation. Here, a student programs a computer to record a rat's responses in a learning experiment.*

about the causes of behavior. For example, on the basis of your own observations, you might hypothesize that "Frustration encourages aggression." How would you test this hypothesis? First you would have to decide how you were going to frustrate people. (This part might be fun.) Then you would have to find a way of measuring whether or not they became more aggressive. (Not so much fun if you plan to be nearby.) Your plans would serve as **operational definitions** of frustration and aggression. Operational definitions state the exact procedures used to represent a concept.

Operational definitions are important because they allow abstract concepts to be tested in real-world terms. From the realm of ideas, we must somehow get down to observable events (Fig. 2–2). Thus, for the sake of observation, frustration might be defined as "preventing a child from playing with a favorite toy." Aggression might be defined as "the number of times the child strikes a toy punching bag." In another study, frustration could be operationally defined as "interrupting an adult before he or she can finish a puzzle and win a $100 prize." And aggression might be "the number of times a frustrated individual insults the person who prevented work on the puzzle." In general, concepts become more useful when they have been tested with a variety of operational definitions.

Forming a hypothesis and performing other major steps in the scientific method can be illustrated with the story of Clever Hans, a "wonder horse" (Rosenthal, 1965). Clever Hans seemed to solve difficult math problems, which he answered by tapping his foot. If you asked Hans, "What is 12 times 2, minus 18," Hans would tap his foot 6 times. Hans was so astonishing that an inquiring scientist decided to discover how Hans was able to perform. Assume that you are the scientist and that you are just itching to find out how Hans *really* does his trick.

Your investigation of Hans' math skills would probably begin with careful **observation** of both horse and owner while Hans was performing. Assume that these observations fail to reveal any obvious cheating. Then the *problem* becomes more clearly **defined:** What signals Hans to start and stop tapping his foot? Your first **hypothesis** might be that the owner is giving Hans a signal. Your proposed test (an **experiment** of sorts) would be to make the owner leave the room. Then someone else could ask Hans questions. Your test would either confirm or deny the owner's role. This would support or eliminate the cheating hypothesis. By changing the conditions under which you observe Hans, you have **controlled** the situation to gain more information from your observations.

Incidentally, Hans could still answer when his owner was out of the room. But a brilliant series of controlled observations revealed Hans' secret. If Hans couldn't see the questioner, he couldn't answer. It seems that questioners always *lowered their heads* (to look at Hans' foot) after asking a question. This was Hans' cue to start tapping. When Hans had tapped the correct number, a questioner would always *look up* to see if Hans was going to stop. This was Hans' cue to stop tapping!

Question: What about theory formulation?

Since Clever Hans' ability to do math was an isolated problem, no theorizing was involved. However, in actual research, theory building is quite important. A **theory** allows the results of a large number of observations to be summarized. A good theory accounts for existing data,

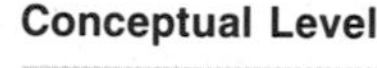

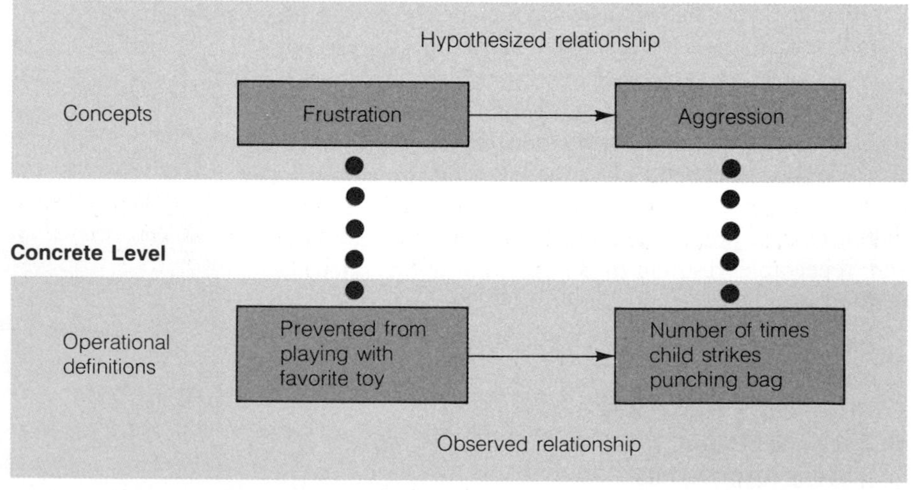

Fig. 2–2 *Operational definitions are used to link concepts with concrete observations. Do you think the examples given are reasonable operational definitions of frustration and aggression? Operational definitions vary in how well they represent concepts. For this reason, many different experiments may be necessary to draw clear conclusions about hypothesized relationships in psychology.*

predicts new observations, and guides further research. Theories of forgetting, personality, mental illness, and the like, are valuable products of psychological research. Without them, psychologists would drown in a sea of disconnected facts.

Research Methods In their search for accurate information and useful theories, psychologists study behavior in many ways: They observe behavior as it unfolds in natural settings (**naturalistic observation**); they make measurements to discover relationships between events (**correlational method**); they use the powerful technique of controlled experimentation (**experimental method**); they study adjustment problems and therapies in the psychological clinic (**clinical method**); and they use questionnaires and surveys to poll large groups of people (**survey method**). Let's see how each of these is used to advance psychological knowledge.

● Naturalistic Observation—Psychology Steps Out!

Instead of waiting to haphazardly encounter a behavior of interest, psychologists may set out to **actively observe** subjects in a **natural setting.** A good example of this style of research is the work of Jane Goodall. She and her staff have been observing chimpanzees in Tanzania since 1960. A quote from her book *In the Shadow of Man* captures the excitement of a scientific discovery:

> Quickly focusing my binoculars, I saw that it was a single chimpanzee, and just then he turned my direction. . . . He was squatting beside the red earth mound of a termite nest, and as I watched I saw him carefully push a long grass stem into a hole in the mound. After a moment he withdrew it and picked something from the end with his mouth. I was too far away to make out what he was eating, but it was obvious that he was actually using a grass stem as a tool (Fig. 2–3). (van Lawick-Goodall, 1971)

Notice that naturalistic observation only provides *descriptions* of behavior. To explain what has been observed often requires more information from other research methods. Just the same, Goodall's discovery forced many scientists to change their definition of humans. Previously, humans had been regarded as the only tool-making animals.

Question: Chimpanzees in zoos use objects as tools. Doesn't that demonstrate the same thing?

Not necessarily. An advantage of naturalistic observation is that the behavior under study has not been tampered with by outside influences. Only by observing chimps in their natural environment can we tell if they use tools without human interference.

Fig. 2–3 *A special moment in Jane Goodall's naturalistic study of chimpanzees. A chimp uses a grass stem to extract a meal from a termite nest. (Photo by Baron Hugo van Lawick.© National Geographic Society.)*

Question: But doesn't the presence of human observers in an animal colony affect the animals' behavior?

Effects of the Observer Yes. A major problem with naturalistic studies is the **effect of the observer** on the observed. Quite often, the presence of an observer may change the behavior of the observed. Naturalists studying animal colonies must be very careful to keep their distance and avoid the temptation to "make friends" with the animals. Likewise, if you were interested in student-teacher interactions, you couldn't simply walk into a classroom and begin taking notes. A stranger in the room might affect both the students and the teacher. When possible, this problem is minimized by **concealing the observer.** For example, Arnold Gesell and his associates (1940) observed preschoolers through one-way vision screens to find the ages at which children first sit up, walk, talk, and so forth.

Observer bias is a closely related problem, in which observers see what they *expect* to see or record only selected details. Teachers in one study were told to watch elementary school children (all normal) who had been labeled as either learning disabled, mentally retarded, emotionally disturbed, or normal. The ratings teachers gave the children differed markedly, depending on the labels used (Foster & Ysseldyke, 1976). Psychologists doing naturalistic studies make a special effort to minimize observer bias by keeping **careful records**.

Despite its problems, naturalistic observation can provide a wealth of information and raise many interesting questions (Sommer, 1977). In most scientific research it is an excellent starting point.

Correlational Studies—In Search of the Perfect Relationship

Let's say that a psychologist notes an association between the IQs of children and their parents, between physical attractiveness and social popularity, between anxiety and test performance, or even between crime and weather conditions. In each instance, two observations or events are **co-related** (linked together in an orderly way). A **correlational study** finds the degree of correlation, or relationship, between two existing traits, behaviors, or events (Myers, 1980).

Unlike naturalistic observation, correlational studies can be done either in the lab or in the natural environment. First, two factors of interest are measured. Then a statistical technique is used to find their degree of correlation. (See Appendix B for more information.) For example, we could find the correlation between the average number of hours slept each night and daytime anxiety levels. If the correlation is large, knowing the number of hours slept would allow us to predict a person's anxiety level. Likewise, knowing anxiety level would allow prediction of sleep needs.

Question: How is the degree of correlation expressed?

Correlations can be expressed as a **coefficient of correlation.** This is simply a number falling somewhere between +1.00 and −1.00 (see Appendix B). If the number is zero or close to zero, it indicates a weak or nonexistent relationship. For example, the correlation between shoe size and intelligence is zero. (Sorry, size-12 readers.) If the correlation is +1.00, a **perfect positive relationship** exists; if it is −1.00, a **perfect negative relationship** has been discovered.

Correlations in psychology are rarely perfect. Most fall somewhere between zero and plus or minus 1. The closer the correlation coefficient is to +1.00 or −1.00, the stronger the relationship. For example, identical twins are likely to have almost identical IQs. In contrast, parents and their children have IQs that are only generally similar. The correlation between IQs of parents and children is .35; that between identical twins is .86.

Question: What do the terms "positive" and "negative" correlation mean?

A positive correlation shows that increases in one measure are matched by increases in the other (or decreases are accompanied by decreases). For example, there is a positive correlation between high school grades and college grades; students who do better in high school tend to do better in college (and the reverse). In a negative correlation, *increases* in the first measure are associated with *decreases* in the second (Fig. 2–4). We might observe, for instance, that the higher the air temperature, the lower the activity level of animals in a zoo. (Also see Highlight 2–1.)

Question: Would that show that air temperature causes changes in activity level?

It might seem so, but we cannot be sure without performing an experiment. Correlational studies help us dis-

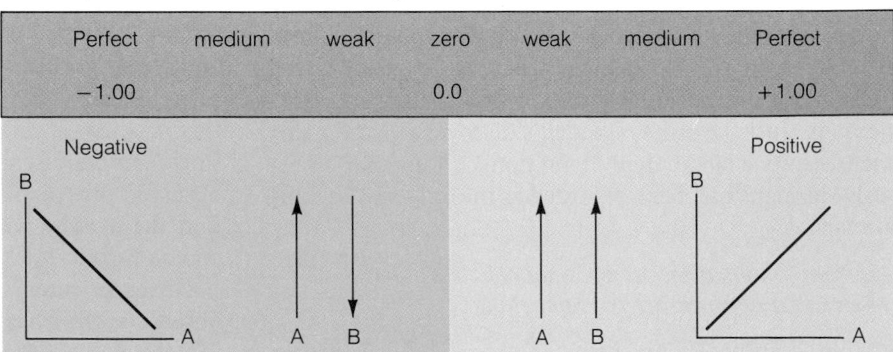

Fig. 2–4 *In a negative correlation, increases in one measure are associated with decreases in the other. In a positive correlation, increases in one measure are associated with increases in the other.*

HIGHLIGHT 2-1
Relationships in Psychology

Do students who study more get better grades? To answer this question, we could record the number of hours different students study each week. Then we could match hours studied with grades earned. Suppose we find that low amounts of study time correspond to low grades and high amounts of studying are linked with high grades. If this were the case, there would be a **positive relationship** between studying and grades. Similarly, we might discover that students who watch many hours of television each day tend to get lower grades than those who watch few hours. (This is the well-known TV zombie effect.) This time, a **negative relationship** would exist. That is, low viewing times go with high grades, and high viewing times go with low grades. Obviously, these examples are only hypothetical. However, when real patterns of this sort can be identified, they have great value. Relationships summarize large amounts of data and allow prediction as well.

Drawing graphs of relationships often helps clarify their nature. For example, Figure 2–5 shows the results of a memory experiment. Before being tested, subjects learned from 1 to 20 word lists. The question was, How well would they remember the last list? The graph shows that when no other lists were memorized, 80 percent of the test list was remembered. When 3 other lists were memorized, scores on the last list dropped to 43 percent (blue arrows). When 10 other lists were memorized, recall fell even further, to 22 percent (red arrows). Overall, there was a negative relationship between the number of lists memorized and recall of the last list. (The meaning of this finding is discussed in Chapter 10. For now, let's just say that you shouldn't memorize the telephone book before studying for a test.)

Some graphs reveal a **linear** (straight-line) **relationship.** Others are **curvilinear** (kur-vih-LIN-ee-er), consisting of a curved line, like Figure 2–5. In either case, relationships need not be perfect to be useful. Suppose, for instance, that we randomly select 10 people. We then compare the number of years of college completed with each person's income at age 25. If we were to obtain results like those shown in Figure 2–6, it would be clear that there is a strong positive relationship between education and earnings. A pattern like this might be of great interest to a high school student thinking about whether to attend college.

The shaded area and the colored line in Figure 2–6 show that the relationship is approximately linear, but not perfect. (If it were perfect, all the dots would lie on the

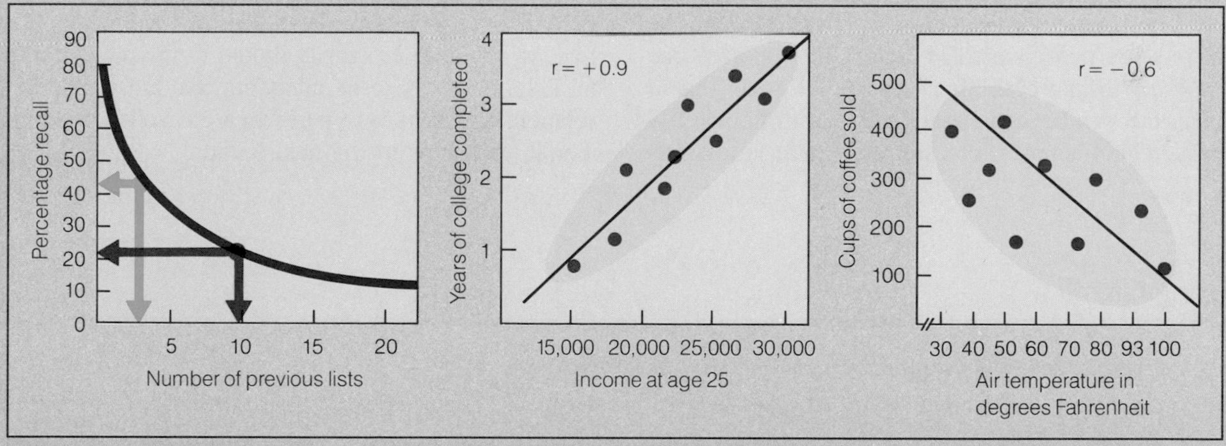

Fig. 2–5 *Effects of interference on memory. A graph of the approximate relationship between percentage recalled and number of different word lists memorized. (Adapted from Underwood, 1957)*

Fig. 2–6 *The relationship between years of college completed and personal income (hypothetical data).*

Fig. 2–7 *The relationship between air temperature and amount of coffee consumed (hypothetical data).*

HIGHLIGHT 2–1
Continued

colored line.) The correlation coefficient (*r*) also shows that the relationship is strong, and positive, but not perfect. (How often do you find a perfect relationship?) If the relationship *were* perfect, the coefficient would be 1.00.

For comparison, Figure 2–7 plots more hypothetical data. Assume that the manager of a college cafeteria has recorded the amount of coffee sold on 10 different days, as well as the air temperature on each day. Notice again that the relationship appears to be linear. However, this time it is negative. Also note how the shaded area and the correlation coefficient both indicate a weaker relationship. Even so, knowing the correlation between temperature and coffee drinking would help anyone planning how much "mud" to brew each morning. On a higher plane, psychologists seek to identify relationships concerning memory, perception, stress, aging, therapy, and a host of similar topics. Much of this book is a summary of such relationships.

cover relationships and make useful predictions. However, correlation *does not demonstrate causation*. (There is an exception, but it involves an advanced technique beyond the scope of this book.) Just because one thing *appears* to be related to another does not mean that a cause-and-effect connection exists. The animals' activity might be affected by seasonal changes in weight, hormone levels, or even the feeding schedule at the zoo.

Here is another example of mistaking correlation for causation: What if a psychologist discovered that the blood of schizophrenic patients contained a certain chemical not found in people functioning normally? Would this show that the chemical *causes* schizophrenia? Again, it may seem so, but schizophrenia could cause the chemical to form. Or, both schizophrenia and the chemical might be caused by some unknown third factor. Just because one thing *appears* to cause another does not *confirm* that it does. This fact can be seen clearly in the case of obviously noncausal relationships. For example, there is a correlation between the number of churches in American cities and the number of bars; the more churches, the more bars. Does this mean that drinking makes you religious? Does it mean that religion makes you thirsty? No one, of course, would leap to such conclusions about cause and effect in this instance. But in less obvious situations, it's tempting.

Exactly 9 months after a major power failure in New York State, doctors and nurses in New York hospitals noticed a sharp rise in the birthrate. News reports of this event implied that when the lights and TVs went off, people had nothing better to do, and the result was a baby boom 9 months later. A closer look at the birthrate would show that it fluctuates up and down all year. The baby boom was but one of dozens of small peaks. Therefore, it was not necessarily linked to the power failure at all. The best way to be confident that a cause-and-effect relationship exists is to perform a controlled experiment. You'll learn how in the next section.

Learning Check

Before reading on, answer the following questions about what you have just read.

1. Most of psychology can rightfully be called common sense because psychologists prefer naturalistic observation to controlled observation. T or F?
2. A hypothesis is any careful observation made in a controlled experiment. T or F?
3. Two problems in naturalistic observation are
   a. getting subjects to cooperate and identifying correlations
   b. defining a problem and proposing a hypothesis
   c. the effects of the observer and observer bias
   d. running the experiment and making careful records
4. Correlation typically does not demonstrate causation. T or F?

5. Which correlation coefficient represents the strongest relationship?
a. −0.86 *b.* +0.66 *c.* +0.10 *d.* +0.09

6. A relationship that does not form a straight line when it is graphed is described as ______________________.

Answers:
1. F 2. F 3. *c* 4. T 5. *a* 6. curvilinear

The Psychology Experiment—Where Cause Meets Effect

One of the most powerful research tools is the **experiment.** Psychologists carefully control conditions in an experiment to identify cause-and-effect relationships. To perform a psychological experiment, you would do the following:

1. Directly vary a condition you think might cause changes in a behavior.
2. Create two or more groups of subjects. These groups should be alike in all ways *except* the condition you are varying.
3. Record whether varying the condition has any effect on behavior.

Assume, for example, that you want to find out if hunger affects memory. First, you would form two groups of people. Then you could give one group a memory test while its members were hungry. The second group would take the same test after eating a meal. By comparing average memory scores for the two groups, you could tell if hunger affects memory.

As you can see, the simplest psychological experiment is based on two groups of **subjects** (animals or people). One group is called the **experimental group;** the other becomes the **control group.** The control group and the experimental group are treated exactly alike except for the one condition you intentionally vary. This condition is called the *independent variable.*

A **variable** is any condition that can change and that might affect the outcome of the experiment. Identifying causes and effects in an experiment involves three types of variables:

1. Independent variables are the conditions altered or varied by the experimenter. Independent variables are suspected *causes* in the experiment.
2. Dependent variables measure the results of the experiment. Dependent variables reveal the *effects* that independent variables have on behavior.
3. Extraneous variables are conditions that a researcher wishes to prevent from affecting the outcome of the experiment.

Let's examine another simple experiment. Suppose you notice that you seem to study better while listening to music. This suggests the hypothesis that music improves learning. We could test this idea experimentally by forming two groups of people. One group studies with music. The other studies without music. Then we could compare their scores on a test. The group exposed to music is the experimental group because the independent variable (music) is present. The group not exposed to music is the control group.

Question: Is a control group really needed? Can't people just study with music on to see if they do better?

Without a control group it would be impossible to tell if music had any effect on learning. The control group provides a *point of reference* for comparison with scores of the experimental group. If the average test score of the experimental group is higher than that of the control group, it can be concluded that music improves learning efficiency. If the average is lower than the control group's average, we will know that music slows learning. If there is no difference, we know that the independent variable has no effect on learning.

In the experiment described, the amount learned (indicated by scores on the test) is the **dependent variable.** We are asking the question, Does the independent variable *affect* the dependent variable? (Does music affect or influence learning?) Another way to think of this is that the results of an experiment are measured by the dependent variable, which *depends* on the independent variable. (The amount learned depends on whether or not music accompanies study.)

Question: How do we know that the people in one group aren't more intelligent than those in the other group?

It's true that personal differences among subjects might influence the outcome of an experiment. However, these can be controlled by *randomly assigning* subjects to the two groups. **Random assignment** means that a subject has an equal chance of being a member of either the experimental group or the control group. Random assignment helps ensure that subject differences are evenly balanced across the two groups. Even in fairly small groups, this results in few differences in the number of people in each group who are geniuses or dunces, hungry, hung over, tall, music lovers, or whatever.

Other **extraneous,** or outside, variables—such as the amount of study time, the sex of subjects, the temperature in the room, the time of day, the amount of light, and so forth—must also be prevented from affecting the outcome of an experiment. But how? Usually this is done by making all conditions except the independent variable *exactly* alike for both groups. When all conditions are the same for both groups—*except* the presence or absence of music—then a difference in the amount learned *must* be caused by the music (Fig. 2–8).

Now let's summarize more formally. In a psychological experiment two or more groups of subjects are treated

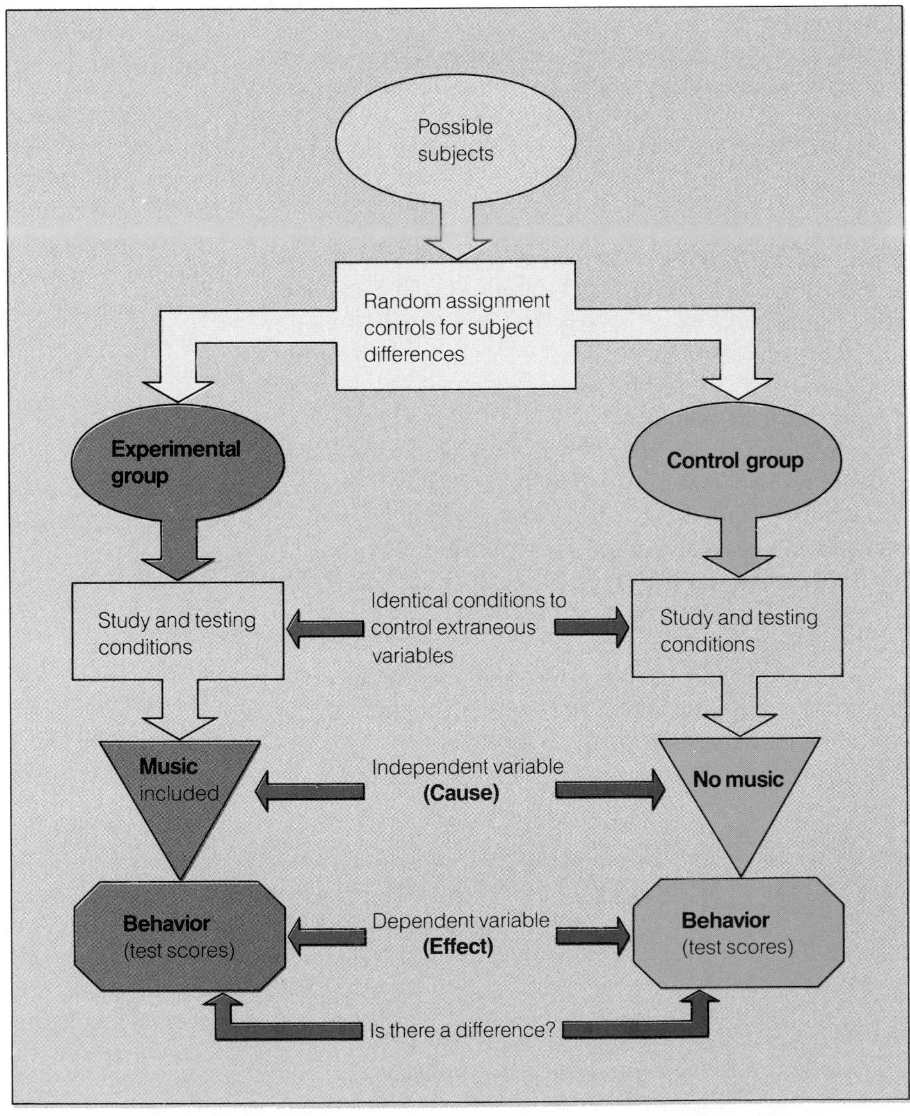

Fig. 2–8 *Elements of a simple psychological experiment to assess the effects of music during study on test scores.*

differently with respect to the independent variable. In all other ways they are treated the same. That is, extraneous variables are equalized for all groups in the experiment. This prevents conditions we are not interested in from affecting the results of the experiment. The effect of the independent variable (or variables) on some behavior (the dependent variable) is then measured. In a carefully controlled experiment, differences in the independent variable can be the only possible **cause** for any **effect** noted in the dependent variable. This allows clear cause-and-effect connections to be identified.

Question: Experiments seem to set up artificial situations. Do experimental findings have anything to do with the real world?

Field Experiments There are many advantages to being able to "custom design" conditions in a laboratory experiment. But there is also a degree of artificiality. An alternative is the **field experiment,** which uses the "real world" as a laboratory. Here is an illustration:

One Good Flat Deserves Another

James Bryan and Mary Test (1971) were interested in whether people are more likely to help someone in distress when they have just seen someone else being helped. To find out, they parked a Ford Mustang with a flat tire on a busy street. An inflated tire leaned against the car, and a young woman stood nearby. Of the 2000 cars that passed, only 35 stopped in this control condition. In the experimental condition, a second car was parked one-quarter mile back from the test car. A woman stood watching a man change a tire on the second car. Of the 2000 vehicles that first passed this staged helping scene, 58 stopped to help the woman in the test car.

Such "real-life" experiments are becoming more popular among psychologists as a way to bridge the gap between laboratory studies and everyday life. You may have even taken part in an experiment without knowing it!

Question: Is the difference between 35 helpers and 58 helpers really enough to draw a conclusion?

Significance The problem of deciding whether or not an independent variable made a difference is handled statistically. Articles in psychology journals almost always include the statement, "Results were **statistically significant.**" What this means is that the obtained results would occur very rarely *by chance alone*. To be statistically significant, a difference must be large enough so that it would occur by chance in less than 5 experiments out of 100. (See Appendix B for more information.) Of course, research findings also become more convincing when they can be duplicated or repeated (see Highlight 2–2).

HIGHLIGHT 2–2
Could You Repeat That, Please?

A key element in any science is the ability to **replicate** (repeat) observations or experiments. In contrast, a failure to replicate observations is a major failing of **parascience** (that which resembles science, but is not truly scientific). A good example is the idea that plants have feelings. This claim, which received wide media coverage, was largely based on "experiments" performed by Cleve Backster, a polygraph expert. (The polygraph is commonly referred to as a lie detector; see Chapter 12.)

Backster claimed that plants wired to a lie detector responded to music, threats (such as a lighted match), and other stimuli. However, when scientists tried to repeat the experiments, using either identical or improved methods, the results were completely negative (Galston & Slayman, 1983).

A long list of other purported wonders—from "pyramid power" to dowsing to moon madness—have likewise disappeared in the light of careful scrutiny. Psychology, too, has admittedly had its share of unrepeatable results. But what separates psychology and other sciences from parascience is that they are self-correcting.

When a finding cannot be repeated, the scientific response is, "We don't believe the result." Maintaining such high standards can be frustrating at times. Among other things, it requires a willingness to change one's beliefs as new or better evidence comes along. Yet, the end result is highly satisfying. High standards of evidence and a demand for repeatability ensure that science moves slowly, but surely, toward the truth.

Placebo Effects—Sugar Pills and Salt Water

Assume that we want to perform an experiment to see if Dexedrine (a powerful central nervous system stimulant) affects learning. An accurate test of the drug will *not* occur if, before studying, members of the experimental group are given a Dexedrine pill and control group members get nothing.

Question: Why not? The experimental group gets the drug and the control group doesn't. If there is a difference in learning scores, it must be due to the action of the drug, right?

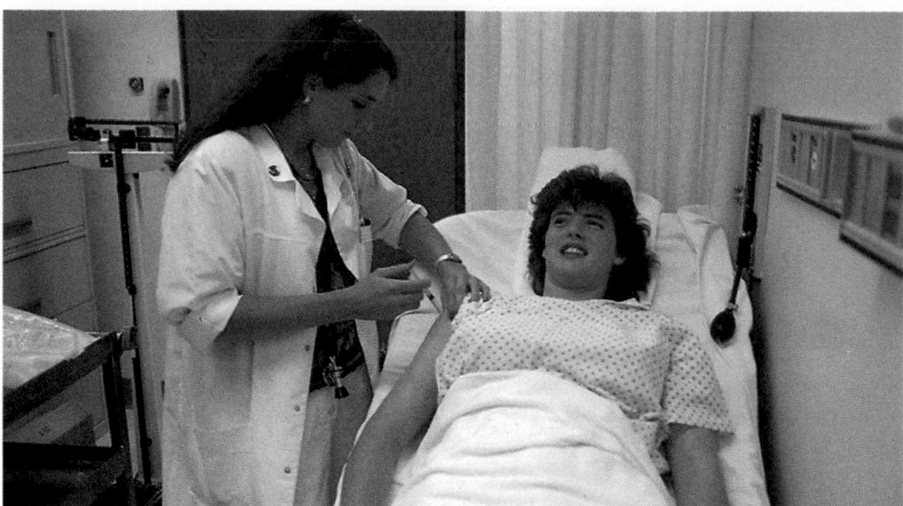

Fig. 2–9 *The placebo effect is a major factor in medical treatments. Would you also expect the placebo effect to occur in psychotherapy?*

No, because an error has been made: The drug is not the only difference between the experimental group and the control group. Members of the experimental group swallow a pill, and control subjects do not. Without using a **placebo** (plah-SEE-bo), it is impossible to tell if the drug affects learning. It might be that those who swallow a pill *expect* to do better. This alone might alter their performance.

Question: What is a placebo? Why would it make a difference?

A placebo is a fake pill or injection. A placebo's beneficial effects come from what it suggests rather than from what it contains. Sugar pills and saline (saltwater) injections are common placebos.

Although they have little or no direct chemical effect, placebos can have a tremendous *psychological* impact. As an example of how powerful the **placebo effect** can be, one study showed that an injection of saline solution was 70 percent as effective as morphine in reducing pain for hospital patients (Beecher, 1959). This fact is well known to physicians. For years they have prescribed placebos for complaints that they feel have no physical basis (Jospe, 1978). Exactly how placebos relieve pain is not fully understood, but experiments suggest that expectations trigger the release of brain chemicals called **endorphins** (Cohen, 1977; Levine et al., 1979). Endorphins are similar to painkilling opiate drugs such as morphine.

To control for placebo effects, a psychologist doing drug research could use a **single-blind** arrangement. In this approach, *all* subjects get a pill or injection. The experimental group gets the real drug and the control group gets a placebo. Thus, subjects are *blind* as to whether they are receiving the drug. But this is not enough. Experimenters must also be blind as to whether they are giving the drug or a placebo to a particular subject. **Double-blind** experiments prevent the researcher from unconsciously influencing subjects' reactions. Typically, someone else prepares the pills or injections, so that the experimenters don't know until after testing who got what.

Question: How could the researcher influence the subject?

The Experimenter Effect Psychologists face an interesting problem not shared by physicists and chemists. Human subjects are very sensitive to hints from an experimenter about what is expected of them. The **experimenter effect,** as this is called, can have a powerful impact on a subject's behavior (Rosenthal, 1976).

The experimenter effect even applies outside the laboratory, where expectations have been shown to influence people in interesting ways. Psychologist Robert Rosenthal (1973) reports a typical example: At the U.S. Air Force Academy Preparatory School, 100 airmen were randomly assigned to one of five math classes. Their teachers were unaware of this random assignment. Instead, the teachers were told that their students were selected for high or low levels of ability. Students in the classes labeled "high-ability" improved much more in math scores than those in "low-ability" classes. Yet, initially, the classes were all of equal ability.

Apparently, the teachers subtly communicated their expectations to the students. This, in turn, created a **self-fulfilling prophecy** that affected the students' performance. That is, students tended to perform as they expected to perform. In short, people sometimes become what we prophesy for them. It is wise to remember that others tend to live *up* or *down* to our expectations of them.

Learning Check

1. Anything that can change (vary) and that might affect the behavior of subjects is called a ________.
2. To understand cause and effect, a simple psychological experiment is based on creating two groups: the ________ group and the ________ group.
3. There are three types of variables to consider in an experiment: independent variables (which are manipulated by the experimenter); ________ variables (which measure the outcome of the experiment); and ________ variables (factors not of interest in a particular experiment).
4. A researcher performs an experiment to learn if room temperature affects the amount of aggression displayed by college students under crowded conditions in a simulated prison environment. In this experiment, the independent variable is
   a. room temperature
   b. the amount of aggression
   c. crowding
   d. the simulated prison environment
5. A procedure used to control both the placebo effect and the experimenter effect in drug experiments is the
   a. correlation method
   b. extraneous prophecy
   c. double blind technique
   d. random assignment of subjects

Answers:
1. variable 2. experimental, control 3. independent, dependent, extraneous 4. *a* 5. *c*

The Clinical Method—Data by the Case

Many experiments that might be revealing are impractical, unethical, or impossible to perform. In instances such as these, information may be gained from **case studies.** A case study is an in-depth focus on all aspects of a single subject. Case studies are used heavily by clinical psychologists.

Case studies may sometimes be thought of as **natural clinical tests** of the effects of unusual variables. Gunshot wounds, brain tumors, accidental poisonings, and similar disasters have provided much information on the functioning of the human brain. One remarkable case from the history of psychology is reported by Dr. J. M. Harlow (1868). Phineas Gage, a young foreman on a work crew, had a 13 pound steel rod blown through the front of his brain by an excavating charge (Fig. 2–10). Amazingly, he survived the accident, but not without undergoing a profound personality change. Dr. Harlow carefully recorded all details of what was perhaps the first in-depth case study of an accidental **frontal lobotomy** (the destruction of front brain matter).

Over 120 years later, a Los Angeles carpenter named Michael Melnick was the victim of a similar freakish accident. Melnick fell from the second story of a house under construction and impaled his head on a steel reinforcing rod. Incredibly, he recovered completely, with no sign of lasting ill effects (*Los Angeles Times*, 1981). Melnick's very different reaction to a similar injury shows why psychologists prefer controlled experiments and often use lab animals for studies of the brain. Case studies lack formal control groups. This, of course, limits the conclusions that can be drawn from clinical observations. Nevertheless, when a purely psychological problem is under study, the clinical method may be the *only* source of information.

Fig. 2–10 *Some of the earliest information on the effects of damage to frontal areas of the brain came from a case study of the accidental injury of Phineas Gage.*

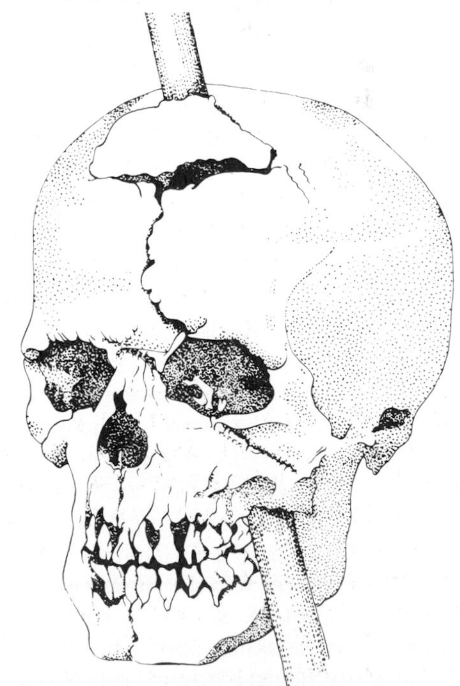

A classic psychological case study is *The Three Faces of Eve* (Thigpen & Cleckley, 1957). Eve White was a mild, restrained suburban housewife who in the course of psychiatric treatment revealed the existence of a second separate personality. This second personality, Eve Black, was the antithesis of Eve White. Eve Black was childish, mischievous, and erotically flirtatious. Eve Black knew about Eve White and openly talked about the times she had disobeyed her parents or gotten drunk and had then "gone into" Eve White. After Eve Black's escapades, Eve White faced her punishment or bore her hangover. But she did so with bewilderment because she did not know of Eve Black's existence. Eventually, this duality was resolved when a third personality—who called herself Jane—emerged. Jane ultimately separated from Eve White's husband and began a relatively stable new life marked by the slow development of a progression of other personalities.

Now in her 50s, the former Eve White has manifested 21 different personalities over the years. The careful recording of all pertinent facts in cases like this is essential to psychology. *Multiple personality* is a rare event, and there are no experimental means for producing it. (Multiple personality is discussed further in Chapter 19.)

Survey Method—Here, Have a Sample

Sometimes, psychologists would like to ask everyone in the world a few well chosen questions: "Have you ever smoked marijuana?" "Have you engaged in premarital sexual intercourse?" "What is your marital status now, and were your parents ever separated or divorced?" "Do you favor abortion?" The answers to questions such as these can reveal much about significant psychological events in the lives of large groups of people. But since it is impractical to question everyone, psychologists use the **survey method**.

In a survey, people in a **representative sample** are asked a series of carefully worded questions. A representative sample includes the same proportion of men, women, professionals, blue collar workers, Republicans, Democrats, whites, blacks, and so on, as found in the population as a whole.

A careful survey can provide an accurate picture of how large segments of the general population feel about current issues. This is true even though only a small percentage of people are polled. However, some psychologists have questioned—tongue in cheek—psychology's claim that its conclusions apply to people in general. The distinguished psychologist Edward Tolman once noted how much of American psychology is based on two sets of subjects: rats and college sophomores. Tolman urged his colleagues to remember that rats certainly are not people and that college sophomores may not be!

Question: How accurate is the survey method?

Modern surveys like the Gallup and Harris polls are quite accurate. The Gallup poll has erred in its election predictions by only 1.5 percent since 1954. This high level of accuracy has not always existed. During the 1936 presidential election, a well-known magazine, the *Literary Digest,* predicted that Alfred Landon would defeat Franklin Roosevelt by a large margin. Roosevelt defeated Landon by a landslide!

Question: How could the poll have been so wrong?

The answer lies in the way the sample was taken. Most people in the poll were contacted by *telephone*. In 1936, during the Great Depression, people who had phones were much more wealthy than average, and the wealthy favored Landon. Thus, the sample was biased rather than representative.

Even when questions are carefully stated and the sample is representative, a survey may be limited by another problem. If a psychologist were to ask you detailed questions about your sexual history and current sexual behavior, how accurate would your replies be? Would you be self-conscious and perhaps not completely frank? Or might you have a tendency to exaggerate? Replies to survey questions are not always *accurate* or *truthful*. Many people show a distinct **courtesy bias,** or tendency to give answers that are agreeable and socially acceptable. For example, pollsters working on an election found that black persons talking to white interviewers were less likely to admit support for a black candidate. Similarly, white persons talking to black interviewers were more likely to claim support for the black candidate (McKean, 1984).

Despite their limitations, surveys frequently produce useful information. For instance, in recent years, working women have complained of sexual harassment at their jobs. How widespread is this problem? A survey of working men and women conducted by psychologist Barbara Gutek provides an answer. Gutek (1981) found that 53 percent of women but only 37 percent of men had experienced some form of sexual harassment at work. Although such information does not solve the problem of sexual harassment, it is a first step toward understanding it and remedying it.

Summary and A Look Ahead

Question: Is so much emphasis on research really necessary in psychology?

Table 2–1 Comparison of Psychological Research Methods

	ADVANTAGES	DISADVANTAGES
Naturalistic observation	Behavior is observed in a natural setting; much information is obtained, and hypotheses and questions for additional research are formed	Little or no control is possible; observed behavior may be altered by the presence of the observer; observations may be biased; causes cannot be conclusively identified
Correlational method	Demonstrates the existence of relationships; allows prediction; can be used in lab, clinic, or natural settings	Little or no control is possible; relationships may be coincidental; cause-and-effect relationships cannot be confirmed
Experimental method	Clear cause-and-effect relationships can be identified; powerful controlled observations can be staged; no need to wait for natural event	May be somewhat artificial; some natural behavior not easily studied in laboratory (field experiments may avoid these objections)
Clinical method	Takes advantage of "natural experiments" and allows investigation of rare or unusual problems or events	Little control is possible; subjective interpretation is often necessary; a single case may be misleading or unrepresentative
Survey method	Allows information about large numbers of people to be gathered; can address questions not answered by other approaches	Obtaining a representative sample is critical and can be difficult to do; answers may be inaccurate; people may not do what they say or say what they do

In a word, yes. As we have seen, science is a powerful way of asking questions about the world and getting trustworthy answers. More importantly, we might ask, What is the alternative to using the scientific method? In most areas of knowledge, including psychology, wiping out scientific advances would mean a return to the Dark Ages. Your awareness of this fact, along with an understanding of current research methods, should help make you a more critical observer of human behavior. Table 2–1 summarizes many of the important ideas we have covered. We should also add that a good scientific theory is always stated in terms that make it **falsifiable**. In other words, its concepts and assertions can be put to a test. True science focuses on solvable problems. It avoids pie-in-the-sky theorizing that cannot be tested (Stanovich, 1986).

To complete our discussion, this chapter's Applications section offers a critical look at information reported in the popular press. Unfortunately, these reports abound with sloppy thinking, misinformation, and pie-in-the-sky theories. The first words that spring to your lips when you read outlandish claims should be, "Prove it." The Applications discussion gives some pointers on what to look for. Following the Applications section is an Exploration on the ethics of psychological research. You should find these topics an interesting way to conclude our look at research in psychology.

Learning Check

1. Case studies can often be thought of as natural tests and are frequently used by clinical psychologists. T or F?

2. For the survey method to be valid, a representative sample of people must be polled. T or F?

3. The phenomenon of multiple personality would most likely be investigated by use of
a. a representative sample *c.* the double-blind procedure
b. field experiments *d.* case studies

4. A problem with the survey method is that answers to questions may not always be ____________ or ____________.

Answers:
1. T 2. T 3. *d* 4. accurate, truthful

Applications: Psychology in the News—Notes on Reading the Popular Press

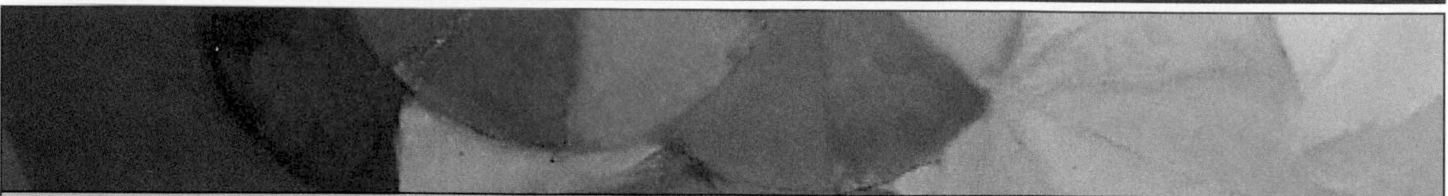

The popularity of psychology has spurred extensive coverage of psychological research and theories in magazines and newspapers. Unfortunately, much of what is covered is based on wishful thinking rather than science. Here are some suggestions for telling the difference.

Suggestion 1 Be skeptical. Psychological reports in the popular press tend to be made uncritically and with a definite bias toward the reporting of sensational findings. Remember, saying "That's incredible" means "That's not believable"—which is quite often true.

Example: Some years ago, stories appeared reporting research on "dermo-optical perception." According to these reports, people had been found who could identify colors and read print (even under glass) while blindfolded. These feats supposedly were performed using the fingertips. Many articles treated them as evidence of a "sixth sense," or "X-ray eyes."

Martin Gardner, a scientist whose hobby is magic, suggests that such "abilities" are based on what stage magicians call a "nose peek." Gardner says that it is impossible to prepare a blindfold (without doing damage to the eyes) that does not leave a tiny space on each side of the nose through which a person can peek. In accordance with this criticism, the phenomenal abilities reported in the first dermo-optical perception experiments disappeared each time the opportunity to peek was controlled (Gardner, 1966).

Here is another indication of the need to be skeptical. Psychologist Philip Zimbardo tells with amusement about mentioning to a reporter that in two mental hospitals in which Zimbardo worked, women patients seemed to use more obscenities than male patients did. Zimbardo emphasizes that this was nothing more than a casual statement. Clearly, it was not based on data of any kind. Yet, when it was reported in *The New York Times,* it became an "observation" that he had "noted" over a long period of time. When *Newsweek* reported the *Times* article, the relationship that was "noted" became one that had been "found." Ultimately, *Playboy's* version stated, "A number of psychologists, *The New York Times* reports, have found that women of every social level have become increasingly uninhibited in their use of obscene language" (*Playboy,* 1969). Zimbardo was the only authority mentioned to confirm this amazing "fact" (Ruch & Zimbardo, 1971)!

Suggestion 2 Consider the source of information. It should come as no surprise that information given to sell a product often reflects a desire for profit rather than the objective truth. Here is a typical advertising claim: "Government tests have proved that no pain reliever is stronger or more effective than Brand X aspirin." A statement like this usually means that there was *no difference* between the product and others tested. No other pain reliever was stronger or more effective, but none was weaker either.

Keep the source in mind when reading the claims of makers of home biofeedback machines, sleep-learning devices, and the like. Remember also that psychological services may be merchandised as well. Be wary of expensive courses that promise instant mental health and happiness, increased efficiency, memory, ESP or psychic ability, control of the unconscious mind, an end to the smoking habit, and so on. Usually they are supported by a few testimonials and many unsupported claims.

Psychic claims should be viewed with special caution. Stage mentalists make their living by deceiving the public. Understandably, they are highly interested in promoting belief in their nonexistent powers. Psychic phenomena, when (and if) they do occur, are quite unpredictable. It would be impossible for a mentalist to do three shows a night, six nights a week without consistently using deception.

Question: I've seen some amazing things on T.V. Could you give an example of how I may have been fooled?

Here is a typical stage mentalist's routine. The mentalist picks an audience member "at random" and begins telling him personal things that the mentalist "could not possibly know." How does the mentalist do it? Easy! One of the mentalist's assistants stood in line outside the theater and eavesdropped on conversations before the show. The assistant then made careful note of where the audience member was seated. The seating location and the overheard information were then passed to the mentalist. The mentalist then announces, "You have an aunt . . . Aunt Bessy . . . she has been very ill . . . you were thinking about her earlier this evening . . . you had a flat tire on the way here this evening."

Suggestion 3 Ask yourself if there was a control group. The importance of a control group in any experiment is frequently overlooked by the unsophisticated—an error to which you are no longer susceptible! The popular press is full of reports of "experiments" performed without control groups: "Talking to Plants Speeds Growth"; "Special Diet

Applications

Controls Hyperactivity in Children"; "Food Shows Less Spoilage in Pyramid Chamber"; "Graduates of Firewalking Seminar Risk their Soles."

Consider the last example for a moment. In recent years, expensive commercial courses have been promoted to teach people to walk barefoot on hot coals. (Why anyone would want to do this is itself an interesting question.) Firewalkers supposedly protect their feet with a technique called "neurolinguistic programming." Many people have paid good money to learn the technique, and most do manage a quick walk on the coals. But is the technique necessary? And is anything remarkable happening? We need a comparison group!

Fortunately, physicist Bernard Leikind has provided one. Leikind showed with volunteers that anyone (with reasonably callused feet) can walk over a bed of coals without being burned. The reason is that the coals, which are light, fluffy carbon, transmit little heat when touched. The principle involved is similar to briefly putting your hand in a hot oven. If you touch a pan, you will be burned because metal transfers heat efficiently. But if your hand stays in the heated air, you'll be fine because air transmits little heat (Mitchell, 1987). Mystery solved.

Fig. 2–11 *Firewalking is based on simple physics, not on any form of supernatural psychological control. The temperature of the coals may be as high as 1200°F. However, coals are like the air in a hot oven: They are very inefficient at transferring heat during brief contact.*

Suggestion 4 Look for errors in distinguishing between correlation and causation. An earlier discussion should make it clear that it is dangerous to presume that one thing has *caused* another on the basis of correlation. In spite of this, you will see many claims based on questionable correlations. Recently, a nutritionist was quoted in the news as saying that drinking excessive amounts of milk may cause juvenile delinquency. (This must have been a real hit with the National Dairy Association.) On what did he base this conclusion? Adolescent males who are often in trouble, he said, drink greater than average amounts of milk.

This correlation is certainly interesting. But in no way does it demonstrate that milk causes delinquency. It could easily be, for instance, that young males who mature early are more likely to be aggressive or get into trouble. Maturing early involves rapid growth. And rapid growth promotes hunger. It is entirely possible that this is the only link between milk and delinquency. Or perhaps some other unknown factor is involved.

Here's another example of mistaking correlation for causation. Jeanne Dixon, a popular astrologer, once answered a group of prominent scientists—who had declared that there is no scientific foundation for astrology—by saying, "They would do well to check the records at their local police stations, where they will learn that the rate of violent crime rises and falls with lunar cycles" (Dixon, 1975). Dixon, of course, believes that the moon affects human behavior.

Question: If it is true that violent crime is more frequent at certain times of the month, doesn't that prove her point?

Far from it. Increased crime could be due to darker nights, the fact that bills fall due at the first of the month, or any number of similar factors. More importantly, direct studies of the alleged "lunar effect" have shown that it doesn't occur (Rotton & Kelly, 1985). Moonstruck criminals, along with "moon madness," are a fiction.

Suggestion 5 Be sure to distinguish between observation and inference. If you see a person *crying*, is it correct to assume that he or she is *sad*? Although it seems reasonable to make this assumption, it is actually quite risky. We can observe objectively that the person is crying, but to *infer* sadness may be in error. It could be that the individual has just peeled 5 pounds of onions. Or maybe he or she just won a million-dollar lottery or is trying contact lenses for the first time.

Psychologists, politicians, physicians, scientists, and other experts often go far beyond the available facts in their claims. This does not mean that their inferences, opinions, and inter-

Applications

pretations have no value; the opinion of an expert on the causes of mental illness, criminal behavior, learning problems, or whatever can be revealing. But be careful to distinguish between fact and opinion. Here is an example that illustrates why this is important.

> A 54-year-old schizophrenic patient was rewarded for holding a broom that was given to her by a ward attendant. If she held the broom, she was given a cigarette by another attendant. The purpose of this experiment was to determine if rewards should be used to alter the patient's listless behavior (she had been hospitalized for 23 years and refused to do anything on the ward). Soon the patient spent much of her time holding the broom. At this point, two psychiatrists were invited to observe the patient through a one-way mirror. One psychiatrist's interpretation of the broom-holding behavior was that it was a symbolic expression of deep-seated unfulfilled desires. According to him, the broom could be a symbol for (1) "a child that gives her love and she gives him in return her devotion," (2) "a phallic symbol," or (3) "the scepter of an omnipotent queen" (Ayllon et al., 1965).

The psychiatrist *observed* that the patient spent much of her time holding a broom. He *inferred* that this behavior had deep psychological meaning. In fact, she held the broom for one reason: She received cigarettes for doing so!

Suggestion 6 Beware of over-simplifications, especially those motivated by monetary gain. Courses or programs that offer a "new personality in three sessions," "six steps to love and fulfillment in marriage," or newly discovered "secrets of unlocking the powers of the mind" should be immediately suspect.

An excellent example of over-simplification is provided by a brochure entitled, "Dr. Joyce Brothers Asks: How Do You Rate as a 'Superwoman'?" Dr. Brothers, a "media" psychologist who has no private practice and is not known for research, wrote the brochure as a consultant for the Aerosol Packaging Council of the Chemical Specialties Manufacturers Association. A typical suggestion in this brochure tells how to enhance a marriage: "Sweep him off to a weekend hideaway. Tip: When he's not looking, spray a touch of your favorite *aerosol* cologne mist on the bedsheets and pillows" (italics added). Sure, Joyce. . . .

Suggestion 7 Remember, "for example" is no proof. After reading this chapter, you should be sensitive to the danger of selecting single examples. If you read, "Law student passes state bar exam using sleep-learning device," don't rush out to buy one. Systematic research has shown that these devices are of little or no value (Koukkou & Lehmann, 1968). A corollary to this suggestion is to ask, Are the reported observations important or widely applicable?

Examples, anecdotes, single cases, and testimonials are all potentially deceptive. Unfortunately, *individual cases* tell nothing about what is true *in general* (Stanovich, 1986). For instance, studies of large groups of people show that smoking increases the likelihood of lung cancer. It doesn't matter if you know a life long heavy smoker who is 94 years old. The general finding is the one to remember.

Summary Journalist Alvin Toffler and others have suggested that we are in the midst of an "information explosion." Indeed, we are all bombarded daily with such a mass of new information that it is difficult to absorb it. The available knowledge, even in a limited area like psychology, biology, medicine, or contemporary rock music, is so vast that no single person can completely know and comprehend it.

With this situation in mind, it becomes increasingly important that you become a critical, selective, and informed consumer of information. And if you think that the value of scientific thought is restricted to the laboratory, remember the words of Oliver Wendell Holmes: "All life is an experiment."

Learning Check

1. Newspaper accounts of dermo-optical perception have generally reported only the results of carefully designed psychological experiments. T or F?
2. Stage mentalists and psychics often use deception in their acts. T or F?
3. Blaming the lunar cycle for variations in the rate of violent crime is an example of mistaking correlation for causation. T or F?
4. Psychiatric interpretations of a patient's broom-holding behavior (described earlier) show the importance of using a control group in experiments. T or F?

Answers:
1. F 2. T 3. T 4. F

● Exploration: Smile, You're on Candid Camera!—The Ethics of Psychological Research

Several years ago, social psychologist Philip Zimbardo and his associates set up a simulated prison at Stanford University. Their goal was to probe the effects of imprisonment on otherwise healthy individuals. Students were recruited to play the roles of prisoners and guards. Much to everyone's surprise, the 2-week experiment had to be called off 6 days after it began. The "guards" had become so sadistic that 4 of the 10 "prisoners" suffered severe emotional reactions, including crying, depression, anxiety, and rage (Zimbardo, et al., 1973). (This experiment is discussed further in Chapter 23.)

The Stanford prison experiment is only one of several to raise serious ethical questions. Were the participants permanently harmed? Did the information gained justify the emotional costs? Are such experiments dehumanizing? Questions like these have drawn attention to three issues to which researchers must be particularly sensitive. These are: *deception, invasion of privacy,* and *lasting harm.* Each issue is illustrated by the following experiments. See if you think they are ethical.

Deception In many experiments the true interests of a researcher are hidden by deception. This approach is often considered necessary to obtain genuine reactions. For example, a researcher interested in guilt once led subjects to believe that they had broken an expensive piece of machinery. During the experiment, the machine suddenly popped loudly, released a plume of smoke, and sputtered to a stop. As embarrassed subjects were about to leave, the experimenter asked them to sign a petition he was supposedly circulating. The petition called for a doubling of tuition fees at the school. Almost all control subjects had refused to sign the same petition. However, because of their guilt, more than 50 percent of the experimental subjects signed (Rubin, 1970). Was deception really necessary to answer the researcher's question?

Invasion of Privacy A second area of debate concerns the extent to which invasion of privacy should be allowed in psychological research. One study that has been both criticized and defended involved secret observation of men in a rest room. Psychologist Eric Knowles was interested in the stress caused by "personal space" invasions. An observer concealed himself in a toilet stall in a public rest room and used a hidden periscope to monitor activity at the urinals. As predicted, urination took longer to begin when an assistant occupied a urinal next to the unsuspecting subject (Middlemist, et al., 1976; Koocher, 1977). This finding is interesting, but does it justify the invasion of privacy used to obtain it?

Lasting Harm Do psychological experiments ever do lasting harm to participants? This is perhaps the most serious ethical question of all. A classic experiment on obedience to authority illustrates the problem. In the study, subjects thought they were giving painful and dangerous electrical shocks to another person (Milgram, 1974). (No shocks were actually given; see Chapter 23.) Belief that they were hurting someone proved extremely stressful for most subjects. Many left the experiment shaken and upset. Some presumably suffered guilt and distress for some time afterward.

This experiment may sound clearly unethical, but the researcher, Stanley Milgram, did follow-up studies on the participants. Most felt positive about their experience and claimed they were glad they had taken part. Many added that they had learned something of value about themselves. But what about the few who felt otherwise? As in medical research, there are no easy answers to the ethical questions raised by psychology.

Most students find the studies just described interesting and informative. How can the search for knowledge be properly balanced with human rights? As a reply to this question, the American Psychological Association has adopted guidelines that state in part: "Psychologists must carry out investigations with respect for the people who participate and with concern for their dignity and welfare." To ensure that this is the case, most college psychology de-

Exploration

partments have ethics committees that oversee proposed research. Nevertheless, no easy answers exist for the ethical questions raised by some research. How do *you* think a psychologist should decide if his or her research is ethical?

Becoming a Subject The ethics of research may turn out to be highly pertinent for many students. As mentioned earlier, college students are frequently asked to serve as subjects in psychology experiments. If you become a subject, what should you expect? First of all, count on having an interesting and educational experience. There is no better way to learn how research is done than to observe it firsthand. Beyond that, you have a right to expect that your reactions will remain confidential; that you will be debriefed about the purpose of the research; that you will receive an interpretation of your responses or test results; and finally, that the results of the research project will be made available to you.

Psychological research can be truly fascinating. If you do participate as a subject, you may end up wanting to try experiments or answer questions of your own. Many careers in psychology were launched in just this way.

Learning Check

1. Deception is regarded as a necessary part of almost all psychology experiments. T or F?
2. Most of the subjects who participated in Milgram's obedience experiment felt that they had not been harmed. T or F?
3. The major ethical question raised by the Stanford prison experiment concerned an invasion of privacy. T or F?
4. In the United States, the American Psychological Association must rule on whether or not an experiment is ethical before it is performed. T or F?

Answers:
1. F 2. T 3. F 4. F

Chapter Summary

• The **scientific method** is used to improve upon common sense and avoid the pitfalls of informal observation. Important steps in scientific investigation usually include **observing, defining a problem,** proposing a **hypothesis, experimenting,** and forming a **theory.**

• Before they can be investigated, psychological concepts must be given **operational definitions.**

• **Naturalistic observation** is a starting place in many investigations. Three problems with this approach are: the effects of the observer on the observed, observer bias, and an inability to explain observed behavior.

• In the **correlational method,** relationships between two traits, responses, or events are measured. Then a **correlation coefficient** is calculated to gauge the strength of the relationship. Correlations allow prediction, but they are usually insufficient to demonstrate cause-and-effect connections.

• **Relationships** in psychology may be **positive** or **negative, linear** or **curvilinear.** Relationships are often clarified by graphing.

• Cause-and-effect relationships are best identified by **controlled experiments.** In an experiment, two or more groups of subjects are formed. These groups differ only with regard to the **independent variable** (condition of interest as a cause in the experiment). Effects on the **dependent variable** are then measured. All other conditions **(extraneous variables)** are held constant. It must be possible to **replicate** (repeat) observations or experiments for them to be meaningful.

• In experiments testing drugs, a **placebo** (fake pill or injection) must be used to control for the effects of expectations. Drug research also frequently employs a **double-blind** procedure so that neither subjects nor experimenters know who is receiving a drug.

• A related problem is the **experimenter effect.** This is the tendency for experimenters to subtly and unconsciously influence the outcome of an experiment. Expectations can create a **self-fulfilling prophecy,** in which a person changes in the direction of the expectation.
• The **clinical method** employs **case studies,** which are in-depth records of a single subject. Case studies provide important information on topics that would not be studied any other way.
• In the **survey method,** people in a **representative sample** are asked a series of carefully worded questions. Responses to these questions provide information on the attitudes and psychological functioning of large groups of people.
• Information in the popular media varies greatly in quality and accuracy. It is wise to approach such information with skepticism and caution. This is especially true with regard to the **source of information, uncontrolled observation, correlation and causation, inferences, oversimplification,** and **single examples.**
• Psychological research raises a number of ethical questions. Three **ethical issues** of particular importance are **deception, invasion of privacy,** and **lasting harm.**

Questions for Discussion

1. Can you think of some "commonsense" statements (other than those already mentioned) that contradict each other? Why do you think such contradictions go unnoticed?
2. Let's say you are interested in investigating the unspoken rules that govern the spacing of people in public places. What research techniques would you use? Can you propose some field experiments that might be performed?
3. What type of correlation would you expect to find between noise levels and productivity in an office? Between income and education? Between physical attractiveness and frequency of dating? Between class attendance and grades? Between use of alcohol by parents and their children? How would you demonstrate a causal link in any of these cases?
4. Regarding self-fulfilling prophecies, how have the expectations of teachers, parents, or friends affected your expectations for yourself? If you have attended a school with slow, normal, and accelerated classes, what advantages and disadvantages do you see in such a system?
5. In your opinion, is it dishonest or unethical for a physician to administer placebos to patients? Why or why not?
6. Have you ever taken part in a survey? On the basis of your participation, how accurate do you think surveys are? What are the flaws of typical "person on the street" surveys often done by local newspapers?
7. Compared to things done regularly by the government, the military, business, and educational institutions, most psychology experiments are pretty tame. With this in mind, what is your position on the ethical questions raised in the Exploration section?
8. Do you consider the experiments described in the Exploration section ethical? Why or why not? What changes would you make if you were repeating the experiments?
9. There is a loophole in the statement, "I've been taking vitamin C tablets, and I haven't had a cold all year." What is it?

Part Two

Foundations of Human Consciousness

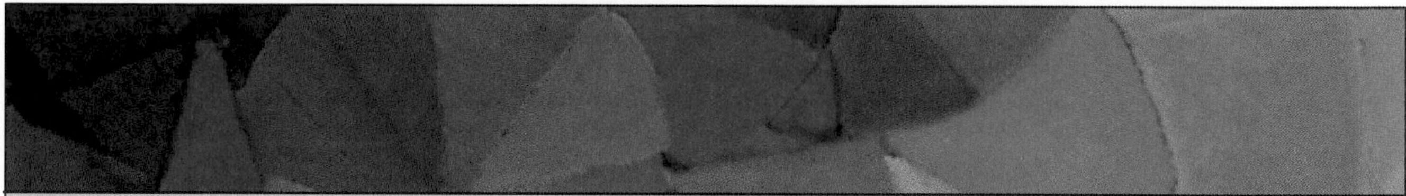

Chapter 3

The Brain, Biology, and Behavior

In This Chapter

Neurons and nerve impulses
The nervous system
The cerebral cortex
The subcortex
The brain in perspective
The endocrine system

Applications

Handedness and brain organization

Exploration

Electrical stimulation of the brain

Chapter Preview

Worlds Within Worlds Within Worlds

Imagine yourself smaller than the period at the end of this sentence. Then join me as we enter a bizarre microscopic world. Surrounding us is a tangle of spidery branches, delicate fibers, and transparent globes. As we watch, pulsing waves of electrical energy flash through the fibers, scattering in thousands of directions. Meanwhile, all is bathed in a swirling sea of exotic chemicals. We are indeed in a strange realm. Yet there is beauty here, and mind-bending complexity—for we have just entered that most amazing of all computers, the human brain.

Crack open the fragile shell of the skull and you find, in the truest sense, "worlds within worlds within worlds." The human brain is about the size of a large grapefruit. Weighing a little over 3 pounds, it consists of some 100 billion nerve cells called ***neurons*** *(NEW-rons).*

Neurons specialize in carrying and processing information. They also activate muscles and glands. Thus, everything you think, do, or feel can be traced back to these tiny cells. The mass of neurons we call the brain allows humans to make music of exquisite beauty, to seek a cure for cancer, or to read a book like this one.

Each neuron in the brain's "enchanted loom" is linked to as many as 10,000 others. This network makes it possible to combine and store an exceedingly large amount of information. In fact, there may be more possible *pathways between neurons in a single human brain than there are atoms in the entire universe!*

Scientists have long known that the brain is the organ of consciousness and action. But only recently have they been able to demonstrate it directly. To prove the point, researcher José Delgado once entered a bullring with a cape and a radio transmitter. The bull charged. Delgado retreated. At the last possible instant the speeding bull stopped short. Why? Because Delgado's radio activated electrodes implanted deep within the bull's brain. These, in turn, stimulated "control centers" that brought the bull to a halt.

Physiological psychology *is the study of how the brain and nervous system relate to behavior. It is clear that answers to many age-old questions of mind, consciousness, and knowledge lie buried within the brain (Thompson, 1985). Let us enter this fascinating realm for a closer look at our biological heritage and human potential.*

Survey Questions

- How do nerve cells operate and communicate?
- What are the functions of major parts of the nervous system?
- What happens when the brain is injured?
- How does the glandular system relate to the nervous system?
- How do right- and left-handed individuals differ?
- Can the brain be controlled artificially?

Neurons—Building a "Biocomputer"

As physiological psychologist Paul MacLean once remarked, the towering question today is whether we can master the brain before we blow ourselves to smithereens through our mastery of physics and chemistry. Unraveling the mysteries of the brain begins with neurons, the basic units of the human "biocomputer." A single neuron is not very smart. Yet, when neurons are joined in vast networks, they produce intelligence and consciousness.

Question: How do neurons carry information?

Parts of a Neuron The nervous system is made up of long "chains" of neurons. No two neurons are exactly alike in size or shape, but most have four basic parts (Fig. 3–1). Notice first the **dendrites** (DEN-drytes), which look like the roots of a tree. The dendrites specialize in receiving messages from other neurons. The cell body, or **soma** (SOH-mah), also accepts incoming information, which it collects and combines. Every so often, these messages cause the soma to send a nerve impulse down a long, thin fiber called an **axon** (AK-sahn).

Most axons branch at their ends to form **axon terminals.** These branches link with the dendrites and somas of other neurons. In this way, information is passed from neuron to neuron. Some axons are only about 0.1 millimeter long. (That's about the width of a pencil line.) Other axons stretch up to a meter through the adult nervous system. Like miniature cables, axons carry messages from the sensory organs to the brain, from the brain to muscles or glands, or simply from one neuron to the next.

The Nerve Impulse Each neuron is like a tiny biological battery ready to be discharged. Electrically charged molecules called **ions** (EYE-ons) are found in differing numbers inside and outside of each nerve cell (Fig. 3–2). As a result, a tiny difference in electrical charge exists across the **cell membrane** (or "skin"). The inside of human neurons registers about minus 70 millivolts compared to outside the cell. (A millivolt is one-thousandth of a volt.) This electrical charge is called the **resting potential.**

Messages arriving from other neurons alter the resting potential until it reaches a **threshold,** or trigger point, for firing. The threshold for human neurons averages about minus 50 millivolts (see Fig. 3–2). When a neuron reaches this point, a nerve impulse, or **action potential,** sweeps down the axon.

The action potential occurs because tiny tunnels, called **ion channels,** pierce the axon membrane. These channels are normally closed by molecular "gates." During an action potential, the gates pop open and allow sodium ions to rush into the axon (Thompson, 1985). This happens first near the soma. Then, as the action potential moves along, the gates open in sequence down the length of the axon.

The threshold for firing makes the action potential an **all-or-nothing** event; an impulse occurs completely or not at all. You might find it helpful to picture the axon as a row of dominoes set on end. Tipping over the dominoes is an all-or-nothing event. Once the first domino drops, a wave of falling dominoes will zip rapidly to the end of the line. Similarly, when a nerve impulse is trig-

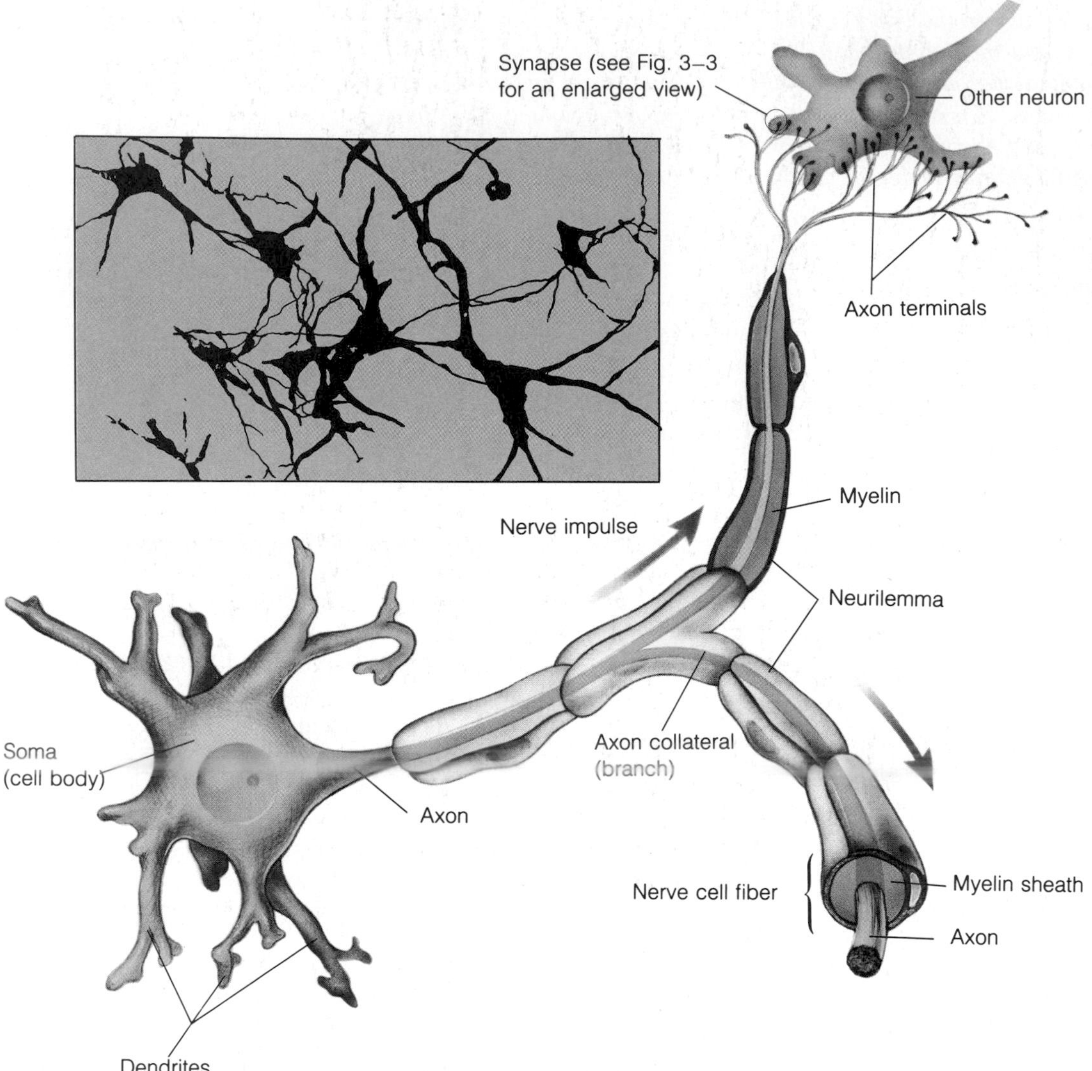

Fig. 3–1 *An example of a neuron, or nerve cell, showing several of its important features. The right foreground shows a nerve cell fiber in cross section, and the upper left inset gives a more realistic picture of the shape of neurons. The nerve impulse usually travels from the dendrites and soma to the branching ends of the axon. The neuron shown here is a motor neuron. Motor neurons originate in the brain or spinal cord and send their axons to the muscles or glands of the body.*

gered near the soma, a wave of activity (the action potential) travels down the axon to the axon terminals.

After each nerve impulse, the cell briefly drops below its resting level. This drop is called a **negative afterpotential.** It is due to an outward flow of potassium ions that occurs while the membrane gates are open. After each nerve impulse, the neuron must recharge. It does this by shifting ions back across the cell membrane until the resting potential is restored.

It takes about one-thousandth of a second for a neuron to fire an impulse and return to its resting level. For this reason, a maximum of about 1000 nerve impulses per second is possible. However, firing rates of 1 per second to 300 or 400 per second are more typical (Steven, 1979).

Question: How fast do nerve impulses travel along the axon?

Impulses travel at about 2.5 meters (roughly, 8 feet) per second in small, thin axons and up to 100 meters per second (about 225 miles per hour) in large axons. The larger the diameter of an axon, the faster it conducts. The speed of nerve impulses is also higher when **myelin** (MY-eh-lin) is present. Myelin is a fatty layer that covers some axons. Where the layer is broken by small gaps, nerve impulses move faster by jumping from gap to gap.

As you can see, nerve impulses are far from instanta-

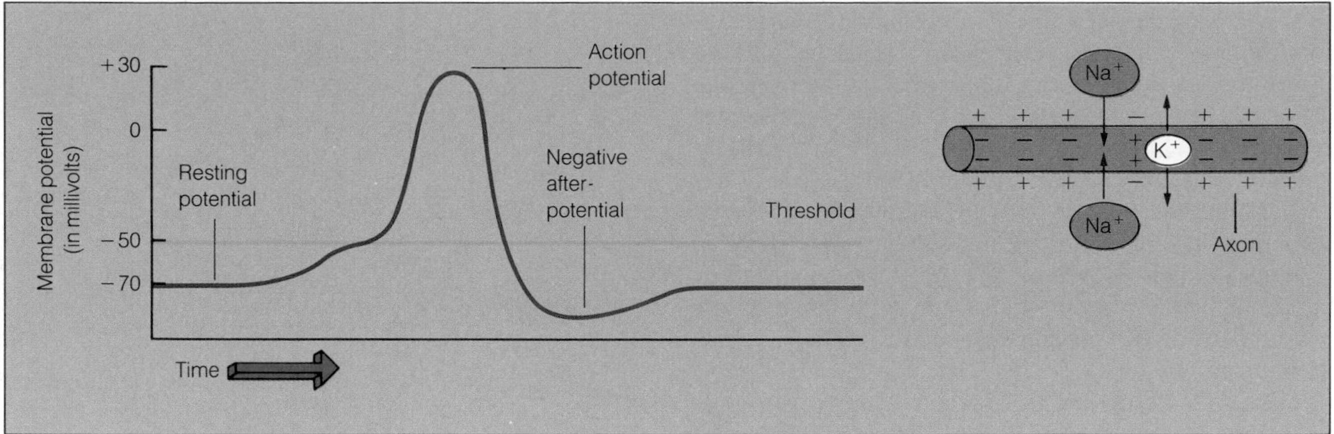

Fig. 3–2 *Electrochemical changes in a nerve cell generate an action potential. When positively charged sodium ions (Na^+) rush into the cell, its potential briefly becomes positive. This is the action potential. After the action potential, an outward flow of positive potassium ions (K^+) restores the negative charge of the resting potential. (See text for further explanation.)*

neous. If someone steps on your toes, it takes one-fiftieth of a second for your brain to get the message!

Question: How is information carried from one neuron to another?

Neurotransmitters We have seen that the nerve impulse is primarily an electrical event. This is why electrically stimulating the brain affects behavior. (A good example is José Delgado's "electronic bullfighting" described in the Chapter Preview.) In contrast, communication between neurons is *molecular*. A nerve impulse that reaches the tips of the axon terminals causes **neurotransmitters** (NEW-row-TRANS-mit-ers) to be released. Small amounts of these potent chemicals cross the tiny gap, or **synapse** (SIN-aps), between neurons. Transmitter molecules then attach to special **receptor sites** on the soma and dendrites of the next neuron (Fig. 3–3). (Transmitters also activate receptor sites on muscles and glands.)

Question: Does the release of a neurotransmitter immediately trigger an action potential in the next neuron?

Not always. Transmitters may *excite* the next neuron (move it closer to firing) or *inhibit* it (make an impulse less likely). At any instant, a neuron receives messages from hundreds of thousands of other neurons. If several "exciting" messages arrive close in time, and they are not canceled by "inhibiting" messages, the neuron reaches its trigger point. This means that chemical messages are *combined* before a neuron "decides" to fire its all-or-nothing action potential. Multiply these events by 100 billion neurons and 100 trillion synapses and you have an amazing computer—one that fits into a space smaller than a shoe box.

There are now some 30 known or suspected neurotransmitters in the brain. Among the more important "chemical messengers" are acetylcholine, adrenaline, noradrenaline, serotonin, dopamine, histamine, and various amino acids (Krieger, 1983).

Fig. 3–3 *A highly magnified view of the synapse shown in Fig. 3–1. Transmitter molecules cross the synaptic gap to affect the next neuron. The size of the gap is exaggerated here; it is actually only about one-millionth of an inch. Transmitter molecules vary in their effect: Some excite the next neuron and some inhibit its activity.*

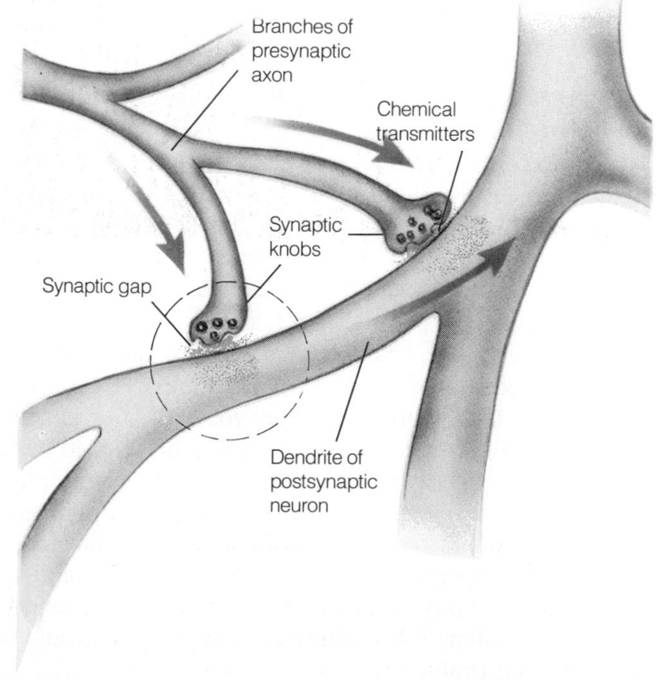

The large variety of transmitter chemicals is one reason why thousands of drugs affect mood and behavior. Many drugs operate by imitating, duplicating, or blocking the actions of neurotransmitters. For example, a transmitter called **acetylcholine** (ah-SEET-ul-KOH-leen) normally activates muscles. However, the drug **curare** (cue-RAH-ree) also attaches to receptor sites on muscles. This prevents acetylcholine from reaching the sites (Evarts, 1979; Thompson, 1985). As a result, a person or animal given curare will be paralyzed—a fact known to South American Indians of the Amazon River Basin, who use curare as an arrow poison.

The mind-altering drug mescaline, which is similar to noradrenaline, is an example of a drug that imitates a brain transmitter (Iversen, 1979). Similarly, the drugs LSD and psilocybin ("magic mushrooms") appear to act directly on receptor sites for the transmitter serotonin (Jacobs, 1987).

Neural Regulators A stunning series of recent discoveries has revealed a new class of brain transmitters. These are called **neuropeptides** (NEW-row-PEP-tides), or simply brain peptides. Neuropeptides do not carry messages directly. Instead, these chemicals seem to *regulate* the activity of other neurons. In doing so, they affect memory, pain, emotion, pleasure, mood, hunger, sexual behavior, and other basic processes (Krieger, 1983). An example of a brain peptide in action is shown in Figure 3–4. As you can see in the drawing, some neurons have specific receptor sites for opiate drugs such as morphine.

Question: Why would the brain have opiate receptors? After all, the human body isn't born with opium in it.

This is exactly the question that started a search for natural opiate-like peptides in the brain. Scientists found that the brain produces opiate-like neural regulators called **enkephalins** (en-KEF-ah-lins) to relieve pain and stress (Iversen, 1979). Related chemicals called **endorphins** (en-DORF-ins) are released by the pituitary gland (Thompson, 1985). It now appears that phenomena as diverse as "runner's high," the placebo effect, and acupuncture may be explained by the action of enkephalins and endorphins. (See Chapter 4 for more information.)

When you touch something hot, you jerk your hand away. The neural messages for this action are carried by neurotransmitters. At the same time, pain may cause the brain to release enkephalins and endorphins. These chemical regulators reduce the pain so that it is not too disabling (Thompson, 1985). Ultimately, an understanding of how peptides regulate brain activities may help explain depression, schizophrenia, drug addiction, and other puzzling problems.

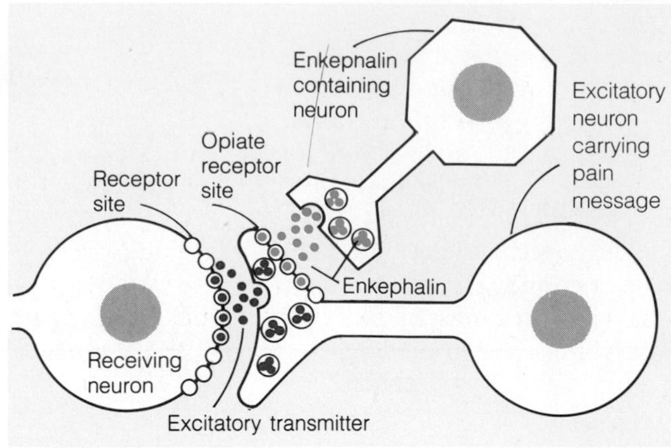

Fig. 3–4 *This simplified diagram shows how natural opiates may operate in the brain to relieve pain. Neurons carrying pain messages appear to have receptor sites for opiate-like transmitters called* enkephalins. *Release of enkephalins by "regulator" neurons suppresses activity in pain-carrying neurons. This suppression blocks or reduces the flow of pain messages. (Adapted from Iversen, 1979.)*

A Brief Tour of the Nervous System—Wired for Action

Picture two people playing catch with a Frisbee. To an outside observer this activity appears interesting, but certainly not amazing. Yet, consider what is going on inside the body: To toss the Frisbee or catch it, a huge amount of information must be sensed, interpreted, and directed to countless muscle fibers. The neural circuits of the body are ablaze with activity. Let's explore the "wiring diagram" that makes this possible.

Neurons and Nerves

Question: Are neurons the same as nerves?

No. Neurons are tiny individual cells. Nerves can be seen with the unaided eye. Rather than being single cells, **nerves** are large bundles of neuron fibers (axons and dendrites). Many nerves have a whitish color because they are made up mainly of axons coated with myelin. A thin layer of cells called the **neurilemma** (NEW-rih-LEM-ah) is also wrapped around most nerve cell fibers outside of the brain and spinal cord. (Return to Fig. 3–1.)

The neurilemma is important because it provides a "tunnel" through which damaged nerve cell fibers can grow when repairing themselves. If you were to accidentally sever a finger, and if it were sewn back on, there is a good chance the nerves would regenerate. In fact, you could expect feeling to creep back at a rate of about 1 millimeter per day.

Neurons in the *brain* and *spinal cord* cannot be replaced by the body, so they must last a lifetime. If the spinal cord is torn, cut, or crushed, a person may permanently lose use of the body below the point of injury. Also, if the cell body of a neuron is destroyed *anywhere* in the nervous system, the cell will die. This is the cause of polio, a crippling disease in which the cell bodies of neurons controlling muscles are destroyed. (For a fascinating exception to the preceding statements, see Highlight 3–1.)

Question: Why wouldn't something as important as brain cells be replaced like other cells in the body?

Very likely, it is because new connections, or "circuits," are created in the brain during learning. If brain cells were frequently replaced, everything you learned would be wiped out day after day (Thompson, 1985).

The Nervous System

Taken as a whole, the nervous system is a single unified structure. Dividing it into smaller parts, however, makes it easier to understand. As seen in Figures 3–5 and 3–6, the **central nervous system** can be distinguished from the **peripheral nervous system.** The central nervous system (CNS) consists of the brain and spinal cord.

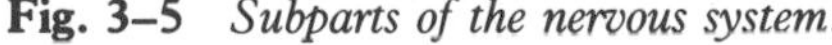

Fig. 3–5 *Subparts of the nervous system.*

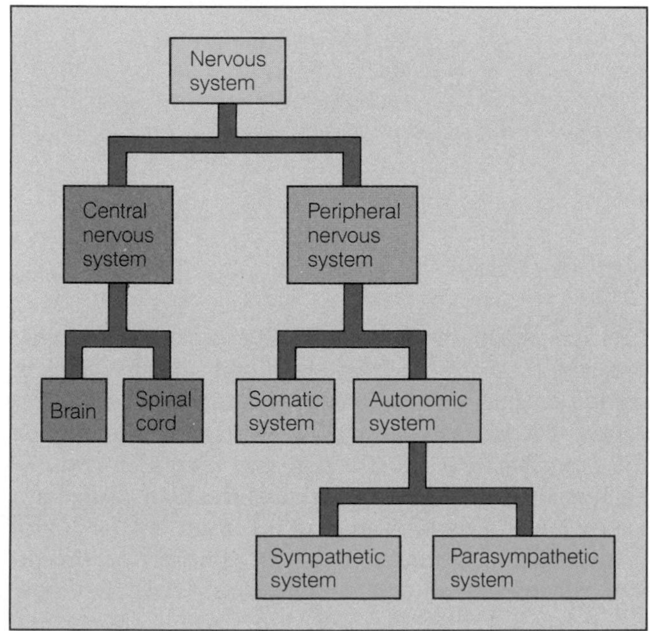

● HIGHLIGHT 3–1
Brain Grafts

Transplanting brain tissue may sound more like science fiction than fact. Nevertheless, it seems likely that brain grafts will someday be used to correct a variety of brain diseases and injuries.

As you know, damaged brain cells are lost forever. The natural question then becomes, Can they be replaced artificially? There is growing evidence that in some cases the answer is yes. Damage can sometimes be repaired with grafts of healthy brain cells. In one experiment, the brains of rats were damaged in an area that affects learning. Some of the rats then received implants of healthy brain tissue in the damaged region. Others remained untreated. Next, a maze-learning test was conducted, with encouraging results: Rats that received implants did significantly better than those left untreated (Labbe et al., 1983). In addition, the grafts appeared to have "taken," or actually linked up with existing brain tissue.

Implants may also provide a cure for some brain-centered diseases. For instance, the crippling effects of Parkinson's disease are caused by a loss of brain cells that release dopamine. (Recall that dopamine is a transmitter substance.) In recent years, a number of human patients with severe Parkinson's disease have had dopamine-producing tissue from their own adrenal glands grafted into their brains. In most cases, the patients have improved noticeably (Kolata, 1983).

Obviously, it's a little early to think about seeking a brain graft to get you through final exams. Transplants are highly experimental at present, and it is not known if foreign tissue can be transplanted in humans, as it has been in animals. Just the same, brain grafting has profound implications. By doing transplants, it may become possible to repair some brain and spinal injuries that are now irreversible. Imagine what that could mean to a person confined to a wheelchair or someone suffering the aftereffects of a stroke. Although it is unwise to raise false hopes, the basic elements of a solution to such problems are beginning to fall into place.

Question: How are the CNS and the peripheral nervous system related?

The Peripheral Nervous System The peripheral system is composed of nerves that carry information to and from the CNS. The peripheral system has two subparts: (1) the **somatic** system, which carries messages to and from the sense organs and skeletal muscles, and (2) the

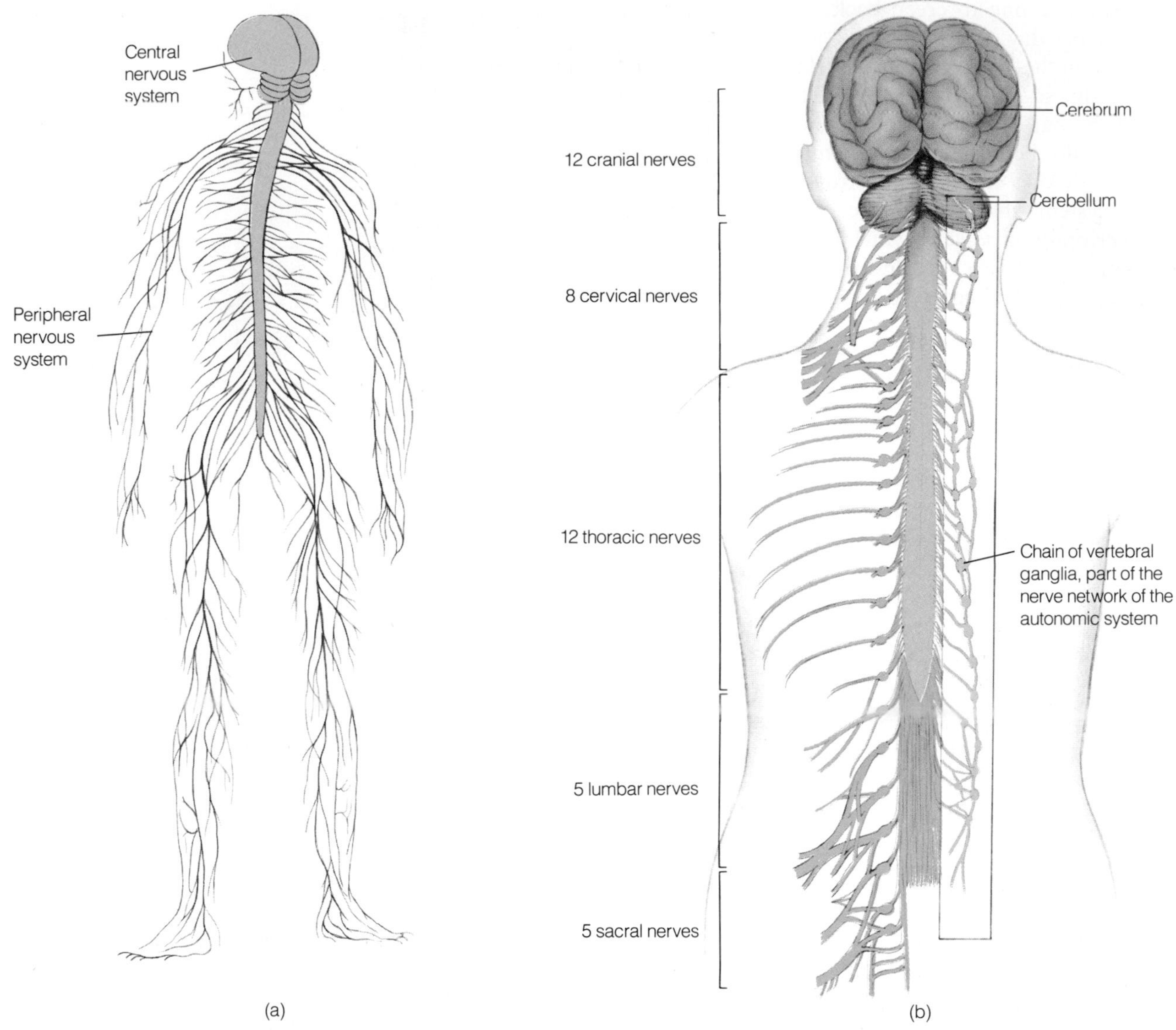

Fig. 3–6 *(a) Central and peripheral nervous systems. (b) Spinal nerves, cranial nerves, and the autonomic nervous system.*

autonomic system, which serves the internal organs and glands of the body. The autonomic nervous system (ANS) can be subdivided into the **sympathetic** and **parasympathetic** branches. Both branches are related to emotional responses, such as crying, sweating, heart rate, and other involuntary behavior (Fig. 3–7).

The ANS, along with the somatic system, coordinates the inner and outer worlds of the body. If a large and angry-looking dog lunges at you, the somatic system helps control the muscles for running. At the same time, the autonomic system raises blood pressure, quickens the heart, and so forth.

Question: How do the branches of the autonomic system differ?

The sympathetic branch is an "emergency" system that prepares the body for "fight or flight" during times of danger or emotion. In essence, it arouses the body for action. The parasympathetic or "sustaining" branch, on the other hand, is most active *soon after* a stressful or emotional event. Its role is to quiet the body and return it to a lower level of arousal (Thompson, 1985). It also helps maintain vital functions such as heart rate, breathing, and digestion at moderate levels. Of course, both

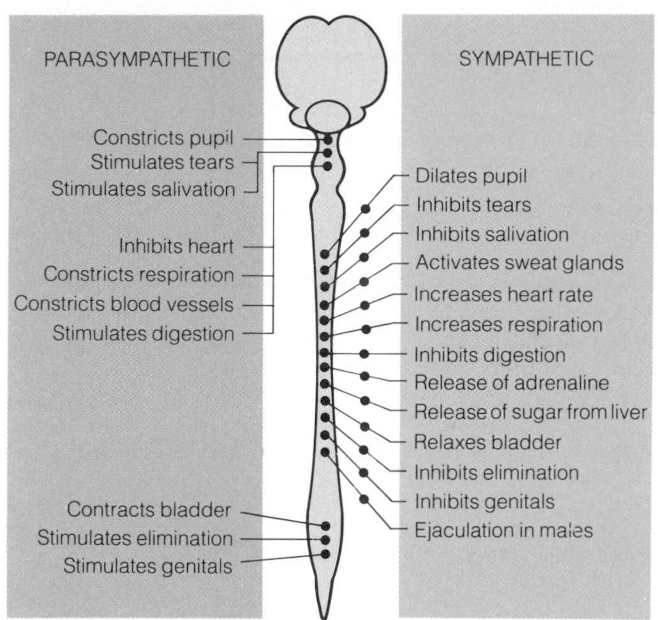

Fig. 3–7 *Sympathetic and parasympathetic branches of the autonomic nervous system. Both branches control involuntary functions. The sympathetic system generally activates the body, whereas the parasympathetic system generally quiets it. The sympathetic branch relays through a chain of ganglia (clusters of cell bodies) outside the spinal cord.*

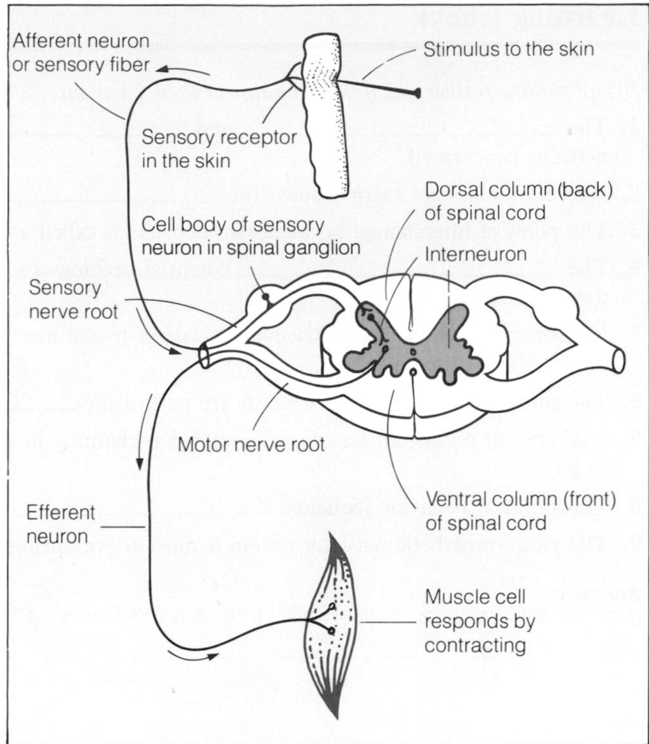

Fig. 3–8 *A simple sensory-motor (reflex) arc. A simple reflex is set in motion by a stimulus to the skin (or other part of the body). The nerve impulse travels to the spinal cord and then back out to a muscle, which contracts. Reflexes provide an "automatic" protective device for the body.*

branches of the ANS are active at all times. Their activity combines to determine if the body is aroused or quieted. (See Chapter 12 for more information on the autonomic system.)

The Spinal Cord The spinal cord is important because it acts like a cable connecting the brain to other parts of the body. If you were to cut through the spinal cord, you would see columns of **white matter.** This nerve tissue is made up of axons that leave the spinal cord to form peripheral nerves. Return to Figure 3–6b and you will see that there are 30 pairs of these **spinal nerves** leaving the spinal cord, plus one pair leaving the bottom tip. The 31 pairs, together with 12 more nerves that leave the brain directly (the **cranial nerves**), place the entire body in sensory and motor communication with the brain.

Question: How is the spinal cord related to behavior?

Within the spinal cord itself, the simplest behavior pattern (a **reflex arc**) can be carried out without any help from the brain (see Fig. 3–8). Imagine that one of our Frisbee players steps on a thorn. This is detected in the foot by a **sensory neuron,** and a message (in the form of an action potential) is fired off to the spinal cord.

The sensory neuron synapses with a **connector neuron** (or **interneuron**) inside the spinal cord. The connector neuron in turn activates another connector cell (in this case a **motor neuron**) that leads back to muscle fibers. The muscle fibers are made up of **effector cells,** which contract and cause the foot to withdraw. Note that brain activity is not required for a reflex arc. The body can react to protect itself without calling on the brain.

In reality, more complex activity usually accompanies even a simple reflex. For example, muscles of the limb on the opposite side of the body must contract to support the shift in weight. Even this can be done by the spinal cord, but it involves many more cells and several levels of the spinal nerves.

Perhaps you have realized how adaptive it is to have a spinal cord capable of responding on its own. Such automatic responses leave the brain of our Frisbee ace free to deal with more important information—such as the location of trees, lampposts, and attractive onlookers—as he or she makes a grandstand catch.

Learning Check

Before reading further, see if you can answer these questions.

1. The ________________ and ________________ are receiving areas where information from other neurons is accepted.
2. Nerve impulses are carried down the ________________.
3. The point of interchange between two neurons is called a myelin. T or F?
4. The ________________ potential becomes an ________________ potential when a neuron passes the threshold for firing.
5. Neuropeptides are a newly discovered class of transmitter substances that includes naturally occurring opiate-like chemicals called enkephalins. T or F?
6. The somatic and autonomic systems are part of the ________________ nervous system.
7. Sodium and potassium ions flow through ion channels in the synapse to trigger a nerve impulse in the receiving neuron. T or F?
8. The simplest behavior sequence is a ________________.
9. The parasympathetic nervous system is most active during times of high emotion. T or F?

Answers:

1. dendrites, soma **2.** axon **3.** F **4.** resting, action **5.** T **6.** peripheral **7.** F **8.** reflex arc **9.** F

● The Cerebral Cortex—My, What a Big Brain You Have!

In many ways, humans are pretty unimpressive creatures. Fragile, weak, born naked and helpless, humans are excelled by animals in almost every category of strength, speed, and sensory sensitivity. The one area in which humans excel is intelligence.

Question: Do humans have the largest brain?

Surprisingly, no. Elephant brains weigh 13 pounds, and whale brains, 19 pounds. At 3 pounds, the human brain seems puny—until we figure the proportion of brain weight to body weight. We then find that an elephant's brain is 1/1000 of its weight; the ratio for sperm whales is 1 to 10,000. The ratio for humans is 1 to 60 (Cohen, 1974). If someone tells you that you have a "whale of a brain" be sure to find out if they mean size or ratio!

Question: What about dolphins?

The only other creatures that compare well to humans in both brain size and *brain-body ratio* are dolphins and porpoises. It is possible, although not established, that these animals may be as intelligent as humans (or more so). Researchers have already shown that dolphins communicate with sounds as complex as our own (Wursig, 1979). However, this does not automatically mean that they use these sounds to generate a language as complex as our own. Also, it may be that dolphins and propoises use larger portions of their brains for swimming, coordination, and "lower" sensory-motor functions.

So, relatively speaking, humans have very highly developed brains. More importantly, as we move from lower to higher animals, an ever-increasing proportion of the brain is devoted to the **cerebral cortex** (seh-REE-brel or ser-EH-brel) (see Fig. 3–9). In humans, the cerebral cortex accounts for no less than 70 percent of the neurons in the central nervous system.

Corticalization The cerebral cortex looks a little like a giant, wrinkled walnut. It covers most of the visible portions of the brain with a mantle of **gray matter** (spongy tissue made up mostly of cell bodies). The cortex in lower animals is small and smooth; in humans it is the largest brain structure. The fact that humans are more intelligent than other animals is related to this **corticalization** (KORE-tih-kal-ih-ZAY-shun), or increase in the size and wrinkling of the cortex. It is a mistake, however, to think that simple differences in brain size produce differences in human intelligence. Highlight 3–2 tells why.

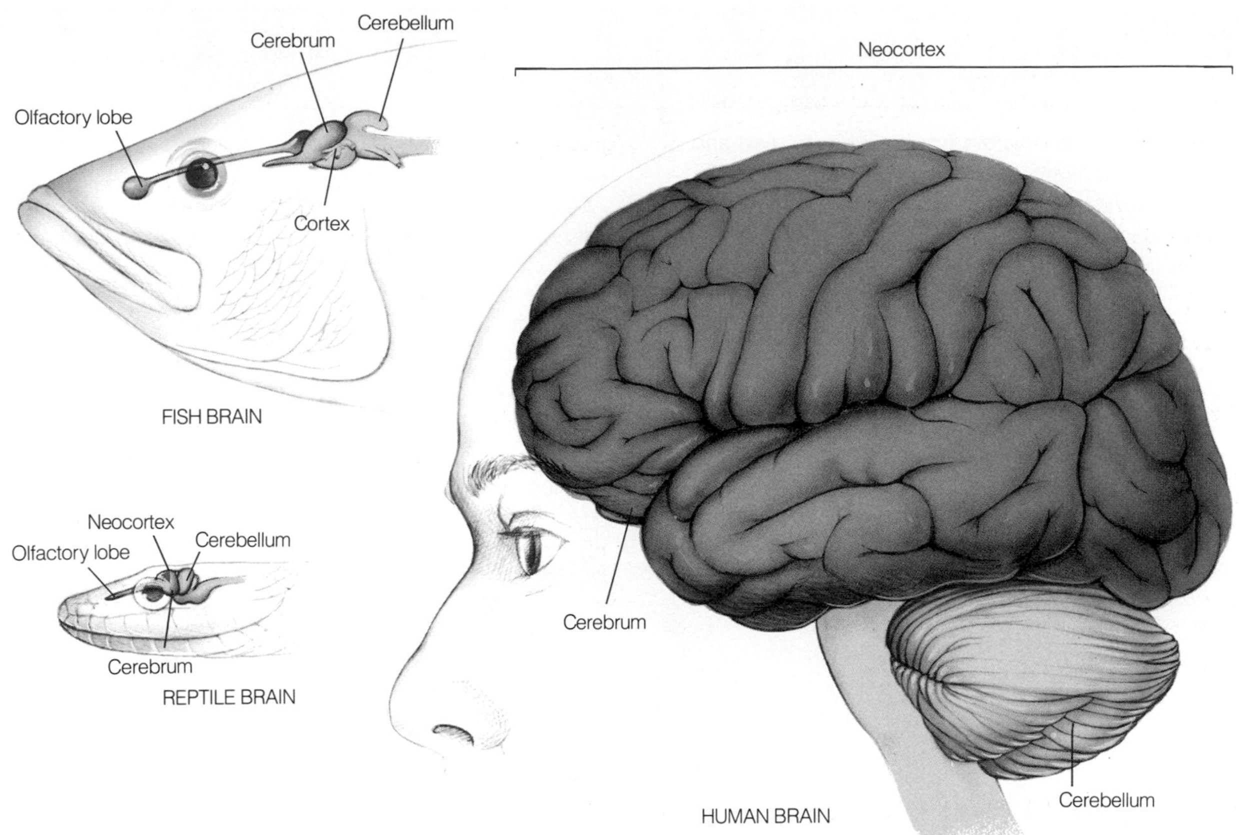

Fig. 3–9 *An illustration showing the increased relative size of the human cerebral cortex, a significant factor in human adaptability and intelligence. Wrinkling of the cerebrum also allows more cortical surface area within the confines of the human skull.*

Cerebral Hemispheres The cortex is composed of two sides, or **hemispheres** (half-globes). The two hemispheres are connected by a thick band of fibers called the **corpus callosum** (KORE-pus-kah-LOH-sum). Surprisingly, the two halves control opposite sides of the body. The left side of the brain mainly controls the right side of the body. The right half of the brain mainly controls left body areas. Thus, if a person has an injury or stroke that damages the right hemisphere, we can expect parts of the left side of the body to be paralyzed or to lose sensation. The reverse occurs for damage to the left hemisphere.

Hemispheric Specialization

We turn now to some very remarkable findings. In 1981, psychobiologist Roger Sperry won a Nobel Prize for his work on the special abilities of the cerebral hemispheres. Sperry and other scientists have shown that the right and left sides of the brain differ on tests of language, perception, music, and other capabilities.

Question: How is it possible to test only one side of the brain?

One way is to work with people who have had a type of surgery in which the corpus callosum is cut to control severe epilepsy. The result of these "split-brain" operations is essentially a person with two brains in one body (Sperry, 1968). After the surgery, it is a simple matter to route information to one hemisphere or the other (see Fig. 3–11).

"Split Brains" In both animals and humans, separating the hemispheres results in a doubling of conscious-

HIGHLIGHT 3–2
The Brain at Work

According to folklore, a person with a large head and a high forehead is likely to be intelligent. But brain efficiency probably has more to do with intelligence than brain size does. Psychologist Richard J. Haier and his colleagues found that the brains of people who perform well on mental tests consume less energy than the brains of poor performers (Haier et al., 1988).

Haier measured brain activity with a technique called **positron emission tomography** (tuh-MOG-ruh-fee), or PET. A PET scan records the amount of glucose (sugar) used by brain cells. The harder neurons work, the more sugar they use. By using harmless, radioactively labeled glucose, it is possible to record an image of how hard the brain is working (Fig. 3–10).

What did PET scans reveal when subjects took a difficult reasoning test? Researchers found that the brains of those who scored *lowest* on the test used the *most* glucose. Although we might assume that smart brains are hardworking brains, the reverse appears to be true. Brighter subjects actually used less energy to get the right answers than poor performers did. Haier believes that this shows that intelligence is related to brain efficiency: Less efficient brains work harder and still accomplish less. We've all had days like that!

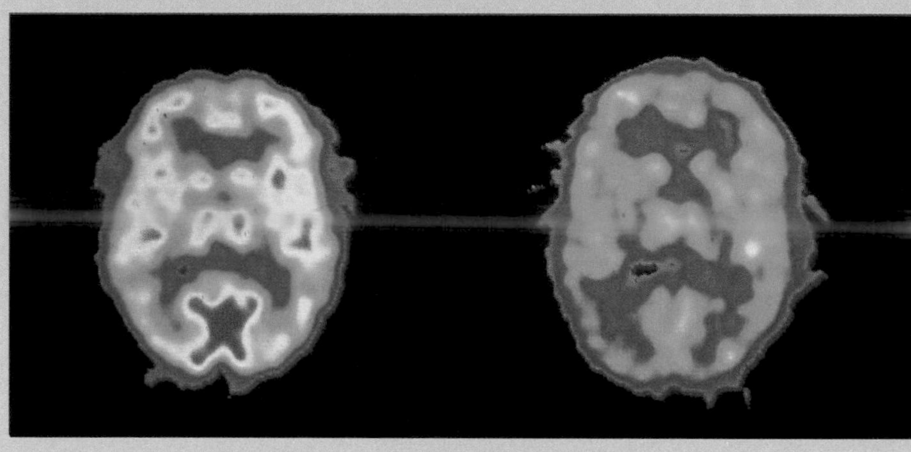

Fig. 3–10 *In the images you see here, red, orange, and yellow indicate high consumption of glucose; green, blue, and pink show areas of low glucose use. The PET scan of the brain on the left shows that a man who solved 11 out of 36 reasoning problems burned more glucose than the man on the right, who solved 33.*

ness. As Sperry (1968) says, "In other words, each hemisphere seems to have its own separate and private sensations; its own perceptions; its own concepts; and its own impulses to act."

Question: How does a split-brain person function after the operation?

Sometimes, having two "brains" in one body creates quite a dilemma. Researcher Michael Gazzaniga (1970) says that while dressing, one of his split-brain patients sometimes found himself pulling his pants down with one hand and pulling them up with the other. Once, the patient grabbed his wife with his left hand and shook her violently. Gallantly, his right hand came to her aid and grabbed the belligerent left hand.

Despite such conflicts, it is far more typical for split-brain patients to act completely normal. The reason is that both halves of the brain have about the same experience at the same time. Also, if a conflict arises, one hemisphere usually overrides the other.

Split-brain effects become most apparent in specialized testing. For example, a dollar sign can be flashed to the right brain and a question mark to the left brain. (Figure 3–11 and 3–12 show how this is possible.) Next, the person is asked to draw what he or she saw, using the left hand, out of sight. The left hand draws a dollar sign. If the person is then asked to point with the right hand to a picture of what the hidden left hand drew, he or she will point to a question mark (Sperry, 1968). In short, for the split-brain person, one hemisphere may not know

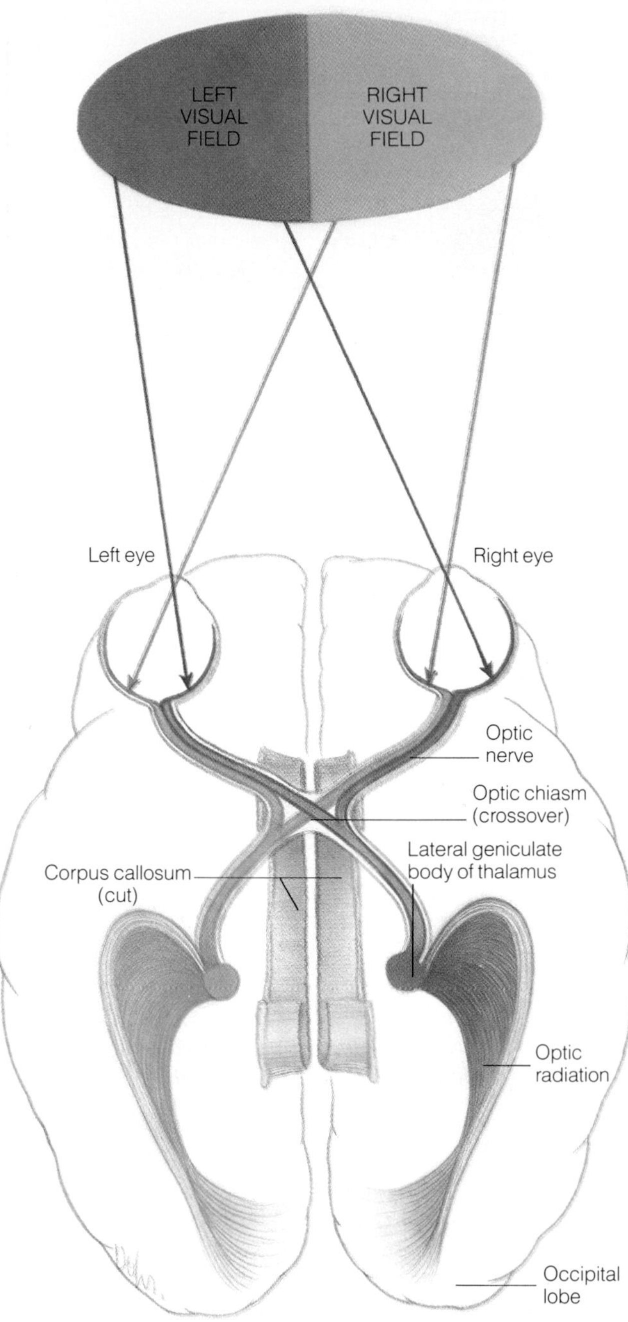

Fig. 3–11 *Basic nerve pathways of vision. Notice that the left portion of each eye connects only to the left half of the brain; likewise, the right portion of each eye connects to the right brain. When the corpus callosum is cut, a "split brain" results. Then visual information can be directed to one hemisphere or the other by flashing it in the right or left visual field as the person stares straight ahead.*

what is happening in the other. This has to be the ultimate case of the "right hand not knowing what the left hand is doing"!

Question: Earlier it was stated that the hemispheres differ in abilities; in what ways do they differ?

Right Brain/Left Brain The brain divides its work in interesting ways. For example, language is a specialty of the left hemisphere. Roughly 95 percent of all adults use the left side of the brain for speaking, writing, and understanding language. In addition, the left hemisphere is superior at math, at judging time and rhythm, and at ordering or coordinating complex movements (especially those needed for speech) (Corballis, 1980).

In contrast, the right hemisphere responds to only the simplest language and numbers. Working with the right hemisphere is a little like talking to a child who only understands a dozen words or so. To answer questions, the right hemisphere must point to objects or make other nonverbal responses (see Fig. 3–12).

At one time, the right brain was regarded as the "minor" hemisphere. But we now know that it has talents of its own. The right hemisphere is superior at perceptual skills such as recognizing patterns, faces, and melodies. It is also involved in detecting and expressing emotion (Geschwind, 1979). The right brain is better at visualization and at "manipulo-spatial" skills, such as arranging blocks to match a pattern, putting together a puzzle, or drawing a picture (Gazzaniga & Le Doux, 1978).

The superiority of the right hemisphere at spatial tasks leads to another intriguing split-brain observation. A common test of spatial ability involves solving a geometric puzzle. On this test the split-brain patient's left hand can typically perform quite well, but the right hand cannot. As Robert Ornstein (1972) reports,

> Professor Sperry often shows an interesting film clip of the right hand attempting to solve the problem and failing, whereupon the patient's left hand cannot restrain itself and "corrects" the right—as when you know the answer to a problem and watch me making mistakes, and cannot refrain from telling me the answer.

Question: Do people normally solve puzzles with just their right hemisphere? Do they do other things with the left?

If you were to solve a puzzle like the one mentioned, your spatially oriented right hemisphere would indeed be more active than the left. But at the same time, your left hemisphere would be more active than it was before you started the puzzle. Thus, while activity may focus on one hemisphere, the skills of both sides of the brain

LEFT BRAIN
- Language
- Speech
- Writing
- Calculation
- Time Sense
- Rhythm
- Ordering of complex movements

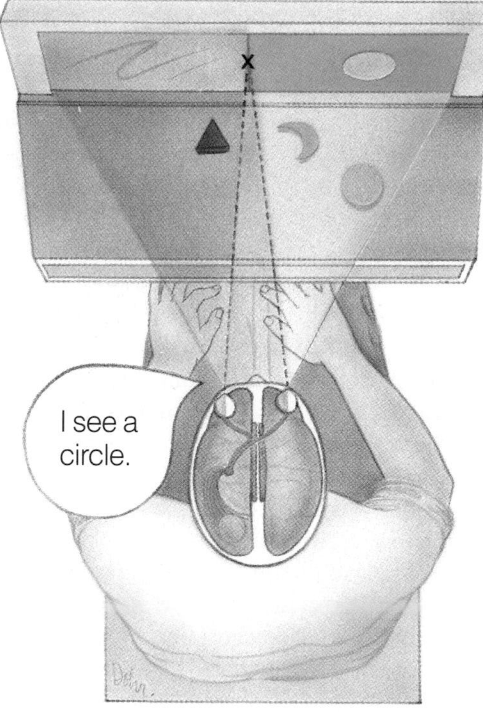

LEFT HEMISPHERE

RIGHT BRAIN
- Nonverbal
- Perceptual skills
- Visualization
- Recognition of patterns, faces, melodies
- Recognition and expression of emotion
- Spatial skills
- Simple language comprehension

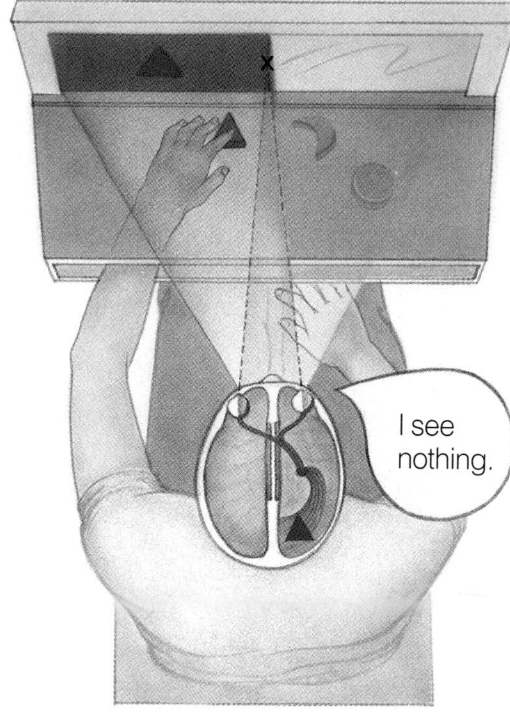

RIGHT HEMISPHERE

Fig. 3–12 *If a circle is flashed to the left brain and a split-brain patient is asked to say what he or she saw, the circle is easily named. The person can also pick out the circle by touching shapes with the right hand, out of sight under a tabletop (shown semitransparent in drawing). However, the left hand will be unable to identify the shape. If a triangle is flashed to the right brain, the person cannot say what was seen (speech is controlled by the left hemisphere). The person will also be unable to identify the correct shape by touch with the right hand. Now, however, the left hand will have no difficulty picking out the hidden triangle. Separate testing of each hemisphere reveals distinct specializations, as listed above. (Figure adapted from an illustration by Edward Kasper in McKean, 1985.)*

are *combined* in most activities. Perhaps this is why lawyers, artists, and psychologists showed no differences in a test of right and left hemisphere activity (Arndt & Berger, 1978; Ornstein & Galin, 1976). Books and courses that claim to teach you to use the "right brain" to be more creative, and the like, ignore the fact that the entire brain is used at all times.

In general, the left hemisphere is mainly involved with analysis (breaking information into parts). It also processes information sequentially (in order, one item after the next). The right hemisphere appears to process information simultaneously and holistically (all at once) (Springer & Deutsch, 1985).

Cerebral Maps of Reality

In addition to the hemispheres, the cerebral cortex can be divided into several smaller areas, or **lobes** (see Fig. 3–13).

Question: What is known about the function of the lobes?

The functions of areas in each of the lobes have been "mapped" by clinical and experimental studies. Experimentally, the surface of the cortex can be activated by touching it with a small electrified needle or wire called an **electrode.** When this is done to a patient undergoing brain surgery (using only local painkillers), the patient can report what effect the stimulation had. The functions

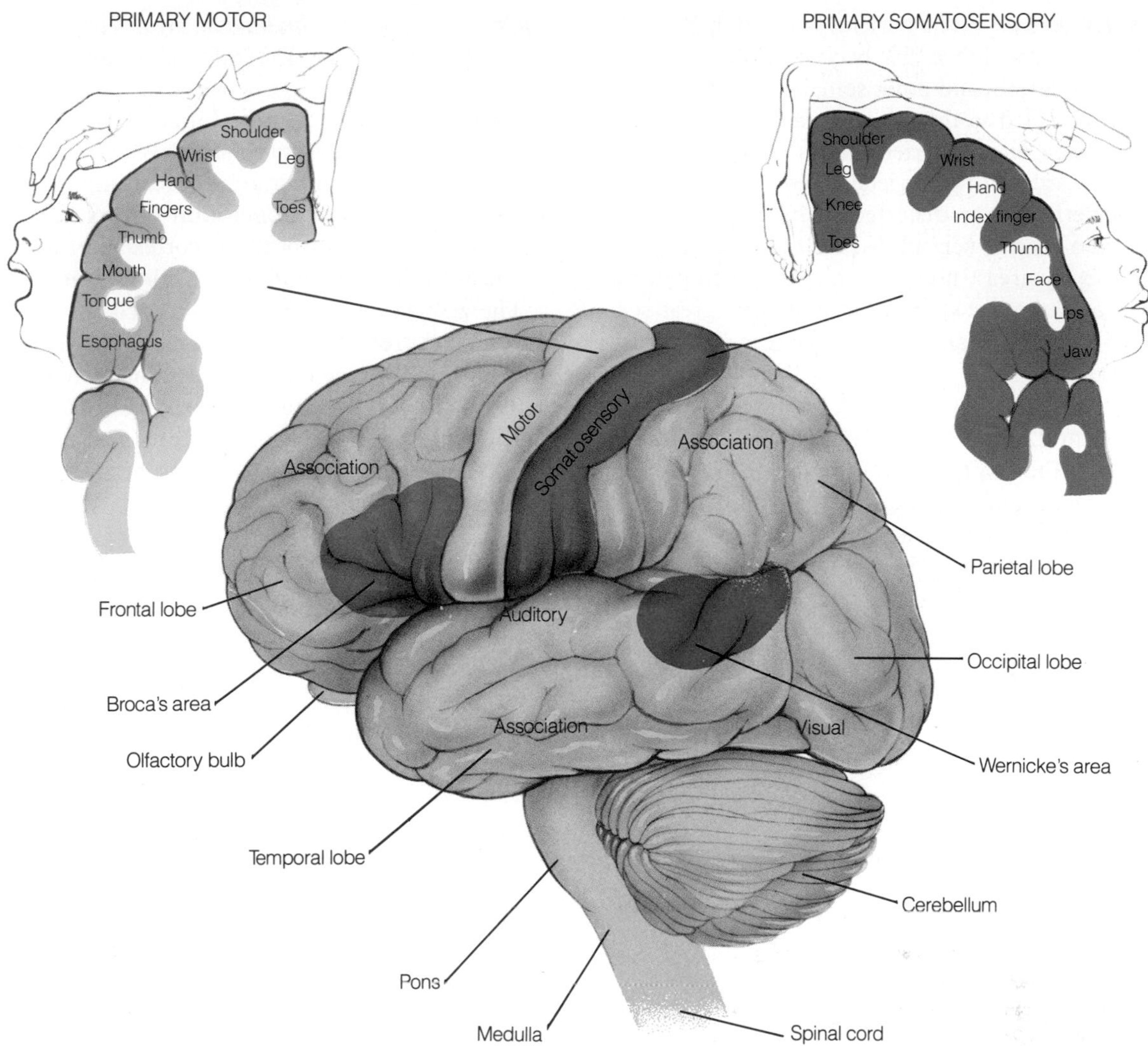

Fig. 3–13 *The lobes of the cerebral cortex and the primary sensory, motor, and association areas on each. The top diagrams show (in cross section) the relative amounts of cortex "assigned" to the sensory and motor control of various parts of the body. (The left cross section, or "slice," is viewed from the back of the brain; the right slice is shown from the front.)*

of the cortex have also been identified by the clinical studies of changes in personality, behavior, or sensory capacity caused by brain diseases or injuries. Let us consider the outcome of such studies.

The Occipital Lobes The occipital lobes (ok-SIP-ih-tal), located at the back of the brain, are the primary **visual area** of the cortex. Patients with *tumors* (cell growths that interfere with brain activity) in the occipital lobes experience blind spots in areas of their vision.

Question: Do the visual areas of the cortex correspond directly to what is seen?

Visual images are mapped onto the cortex, but the map is greatly stretched and distorted (Carlson, 1981). It is important to avoid thinking of the visual area as being like a little TV screen in the brain. Visual information creates complex patterns of activity in nerve cells; it does *not* make a TV-like image. Even if we were tempted to visualize this activity as a "picture," we would still have to ask, "Who's watching the TV?" It is a classic error to think of the brain in terms of some **homunculus** (huh-MUN-cue-lus: little man) that makes decisions or observes incoming information. (See Highlight 4–1 in Chapter 4.)

The Parietal Lobes The parietal lobes (puh-RYE-ih-tal) are located just above the occipital lobes. Touch, temperature, pressure, and other somatic, or bodily, sensations are channeled to the **somatosensory** (so-mat-ŏh-SEN-so-ree) **area** on the parietal lobes. The correspondence between areas of the parietal lobes and parts of the body is not perfect. The distorted body in Figure 3–13 shows that as a map of sensations, the cortex reflects the *sensitivity* of body areas, not their size. For example, the lips are large in the drawing because of their great sensitivity, while the back and trunk, which are less sensitive, are much smaller.

The Temporal Lobes The temporal lobes are located on each side of the brain. Auditory information projects directly to the temporal lobes, making them the site where hearing registers. If we were to stimulate the **primary auditory area** of a temporal lobe, our subject would "hear" a series of sounds. These sounds would increase in pitch as we moved from the top to the bottom. Stimulating in another direction, we would find an orderly change in loudness (Carlson, 1981). This indicates that sound qualities are clearly mapped on the surface of the cortex.

For most people, the left temporal lobe also contains a language "center." (For some, this area is on the right temporal lobe.) Damage to this area can severely limit ability to use language. (More on this later.)

The Frontal Lobes The frontal lobes perform a mixture of functions. For one thing, **olfactory** (smell) information registers on the underside of the frontal lobes. Another important area is the **motor cortex,** an arch of tissue running over the top of the brain. This area directs the body's muscles. If the motor cortex is stimulated with a brief electrical current, muscular twitches will be observed in various parts of the body. Like the somatosensory area, the motor cortex corresponds to the importance of bodily areas, not to their size. The hands, for example, get more area than the feet (see Fig. 3–13).

More complex behaviors are also related to the frontal lobes. When frontal brain areas are removed, animals lose the ability to judge the passage of time, to hold the solution to a problem in mind, or to respond to emotionally unpleasant situations. Damage to the frontal lobes in humans tends to alter personality and decrease emotionality. Doing intellectual tasks based on reasoning or planning also seems to rely on the frontal lobes. Patients with frontal lobe damage often get "stuck" on such tasks and repeat the same wrong answers over and over (Springer & Deutsch, 1985).

Question: The sensory and motor areas leave a lot of the cortex unaccounted for. What do the remaining areas do?

Associative Areas In the human brain, primary sensory and motor areas make up only a small part of the cerebral cortex. All other areas, including parts of all the lobes, are called the **association cortex.** The size and relative amount of association cortex increase strikingly as one ascends the evolutionary scale (Thompson, 1985).

The association cortex seems to process and combine information from the various senses. It is probably also related to higher mental abilities. The frontal lobes' link with thinking skills is a good example of such abilities. Additional clues to the workings of the association cortex come from studies of humans with brain injuries.

Brain Injuries

As mentioned earlier, damage to motor areas on the right brain may paralyze the left side of the body; this is reversed for damage to the left brain. Damage to the right hemisphere may also cause a curious problem called **neglect.** Affected patients pay no attention to the left side of visual space. Often, the patient will not eat food on the left side of a plate and may refuse to acknowledge a paralyzed left arm as his or her own. (See Fig. 3–14.) Surprisingly, left hemisphere damage usually does not produce similar neglect of the right side of space (Springer & Deutsch, 1985).

Brain injuries may also impair the special abilities of the left and right hemispheres. A person with damage in the left brain may lose the ability to speak, read, write, or spell. Yet, the same person may remain able to draw or hum with skill. Persons with right brain damage may get lost while driving, or they may have difficulty understanding diagrams and pictures. Yet, they can speak and read as before (Gardner, 1975; Thompson, 1985).

Regarding emotions, a person with left brain damage may not understand what you say, but he or she will pick up your emotional tone. With right hemisphere damage, the person can understand what is said, but fails to recognize if it is spoken in an angry or humorous way (Geschwind, 1975).

Question: Is it fair to say that damage to the left hemisphere is generally more serious?

Generally it is, because speech and language are so essential. However, if you are an artist, the right brain may be the "major hemisphere" from your point of view. It has been observed, for instance, that painters can still

Fig. 3–14 *Spatial neglect. A patient with right hemisphere damage was asked to copy three model drawings. Notice the obvious neglect of the left side in his drawings. Similar instances of neglect occur in many patients with right hemisphere damage. (From* Left brain, right brain, *Revised Edition by S. P. Springer and G. Deutsch, copyright 1981, 1985. Reprinted with the permission of W. H. Freeman and Company.)*

paint after left brain damage. But an artist with right brain damage may neglect the left side of the canvas, distort outlines, or portray bizarre and repulsive subject matter (Gardner, 1975).

Aphasia Two areas of the cortex are particularly related to language. One, called **Broca's area** (BRO-cahs), lies on the left frontal lobe. The second, known as **Wernicke's area** (VER-nick-ees), is found on the left temporal lobe (see Fig. 3–13). Injury to either area can cause **aphasia** (ah-FAZE-yah), meaning an impaired ability to use language.

Question: What kinds of impairment take place?

Persons with damage in Broca's area can read, and they can understand the speech of others, but they have great difficulty speaking or writing themselves. Typically, their grammar and pronunciation are poor and their speech is slow and labored. For example, the person may say "bife" for bike, "seep" for sleep, or "zokaid" for zodiac. Generally, the person knows what he or she wants to say but can't seem to utter the words (Geschwind, 1979).

In Wernicke's aphasia, the person has problems with the *meaning* of words, not grammar or pronunciation. Whereas someone with Broca's aphasia might say "tssair" when shown a picture of a chair, a Wernicke's patient might say "stool." People with injuries to Wernicke's area often speak in incredibly roundabout ways to avoid using certain nouns. While discussing her son's career, one patient said:

> Well he was two years away, away down for nothing. He didn't do it and got out and said I want to go over there and . . . how to do things, what he's doing now. (Goodglass, 1980.)

It is obvious that both Broca's area and Wernicke's area are crucial for normal language use. It is not surprising to find, then, that they are interconnected in the brain.

"Mindblindness" One of the most fascinating results of brain injury is **agnosia** (ag-KNOW-zyah). This condition is sometimes referred to as "mindblindness" because it involves an inability to identify seen objects. If shown a candle, for instance, someone with an agnosia might describe it as a long narrow object tapering at the top. The person might even draw it accurately and still fail to name it. However, if the person is allowed to feel the candle, he or she will name it immediately (Benton, 1980).

Question: Are agnosias limited to objects?

No. A fascinating form of "mindblindness" is **facial agnosia,** the inability to identify familiar persons. For instance, one patient with facial agnosia was unable to recognize her husband or mother when they visited her in the hospital, and she could not identify pictures of her children. However, when visitors spoke, she knew them immediately from their voices (Benton, 1980).

The study of facial agnosias shows that a brain area devoted to recognizing others is located on the underside of the occipital lobes. These areas appear to have no other function. Why would part of the brain be set aside solely for recognizing faces? From an evolutionary standpoint, it is not really so surprising. After all, we are social animals, for whom facial recognition is very important (Geschwind, 1979). This specialization is one more example of what a marvelous organ of consciousness we possess.

Learning Check

See if you can successfully match the following.

1.	____ Corpus callosum	**A.**	Visual area
2.	____ Occipital lobes	**B.**	Language, speech, writing
3.	____ Parietal lobes	**C.**	Motor cortex and abstract thinking
4.	____ Temporal lobes	**D.**	Spatial skills, visualization, pattern recognition
5.	____ Frontal lobes	**E.**	Speech disturbances
6.	____ Association cortex	**F.**	Causes sleep
7.	____ Aphasias	**G.**	Increased ratio of cortex in brain
8.	____ Corticalization	**H.**	Bodily sensations
9.	____ Left hemisphere	**I.**	Treatment for severe epilepsy
10.	____ Right hemisphere	**J.**	Inability to identify seen objects
11.	____ "Split brain"	**K.**	Fibers connecting the cerebral hemispheres
12.	____ Agnosia	**L.**	Cortex that is not sensory or motor in function
		M.	Hearing

Answers:
1. K **2.** A **3.** H **4.** M **5.** C **6.** L **7.** E **8.** G **9.** B **10.** D **11.** I **12.** J

The Subcortex—At the Core of the (Brain) Matter

Question: What do brain areas below the cortex do?

A person can lose large portions of the cerebrum and still survive. As a matter of fact, if damage is limited to the less crucial areas of the cortex, little visible change may take place. Not so with the brain areas below the cortex. Most of these are so basic to normal functioning that damage may endanger a person's life.

Question: Why are the lower brain areas so important?

Below the cerebral cortex and completely covered by it are structures known as the **subcortex.** The subcortex can be divided into three general areas called the **brainstem** or **hindbrain,** the **midbrain,** and the **forebrain.** (The forebrain also includes the cerebral cortex, which has already been discussed because of its size and importance.) For our purposes, the midbrain can be viewed primarily as a link between the brain structures above and below it. Therefore, let us focus on the forebrain and the hindbrain to appreciate their importance (see Fig. 3–15).

The Hindbrain

As the spinal cord enters the skull to join the brain, it widens into the brainstem, consisting mainly of the **medulla** (meh-DUL-ah) and the **cerebellum** (ser-ah-BEL-uhm). The *medulla* contains centers important for the reflex control of vital life functions, including heart rate, breathing, swallowing, and the like. Various drugs, diseases, or injuries can interrupt the vital functions of the medulla enough to end or endanger life. That's why a karate chop to the back of the neck, like those depicted in movies, can be extremely dangerous.

The *cerebellum,* which looks like a miniature cerebral cortex, lies at the base of the brain. The cerebellum is closely connected to many areas in the brain and spinal cord. It primarily regulates posture, muscle tone, and muscular coordination. The cerebellum may also play a role in some types of memory (see Chapter 9).

Question: What happens if the cerebellum is injured?

Without an intact cerebellum, seemingly simple tasks like walking, running, or playing catch are impossible. The importance of the cerebellum is shown by the effects of a crippling disease called *spinocerebellar degeneration.* The

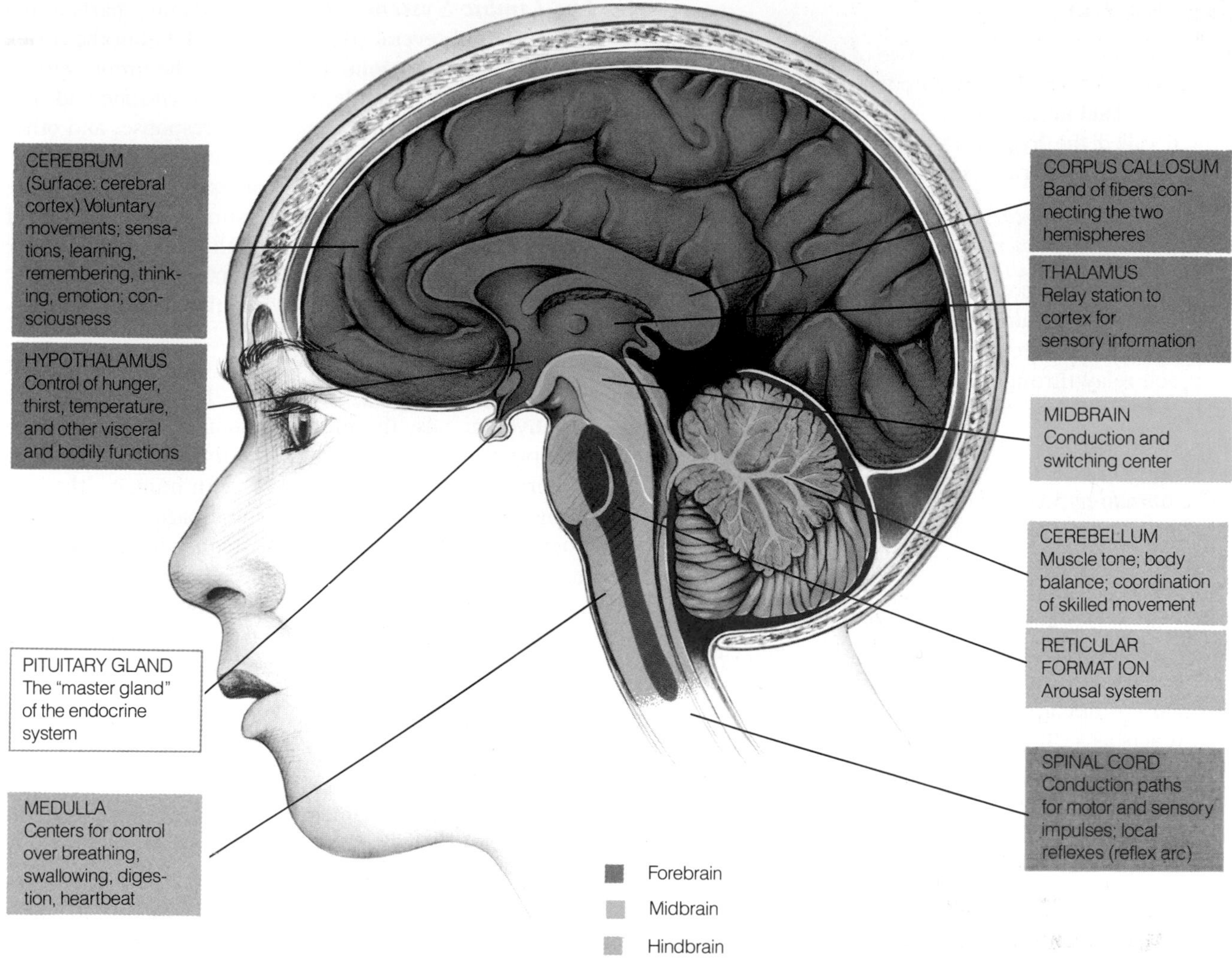

Fig. 3–15 *This simplified drawing shows the main structures of the human brain and describes some of their most important functions.*

first symptoms of this disease are tremor, dizziness, and muscular weakness. Soon, affected persons find that they under-reach or over-reach for objects. Eventually, they have difficulty standing, walking, or even feeding themselves.

Reticular Formation In a space within the medulla and brainstem is a *network* of fibers and cell bodies called the **reticular** (reh-TICK-you-ler) **formation** (RF).

The RF is important for several reasons. First, it acts as a kind of central clearinghouse for most information coming to and from the brain. Second, the reticular formation gives priority to some incoming messages, while excluding others. In this way, the RF affects *attention*. Without the RF, we would be overwhelmed with useless information from the environment. Third, and perhaps most important, the reticular formation is responsible for alertness and wakefulness.

Incoming messages from the sense organs branch into the reticular formation. There, they form a **reticular activating system** (RAS). The RAS bombards the cortex with stimulation, keeping it active and alert (Malmo, 1975). Researchers have found that destroying the RAS causes animals to enter a coma resembling sleep. In contrast, electrical stimulation of the same area instantly awakens sleeping animals (Moruzzi & Magoun, 1949; Lindsley et al., 1949). The sleepy driver who snaps to attention when an animal appears in the middle of the road can thank the RAS for arousing the rest of the brain.

The Forebrain

Like gemstones of nerve tissue, two of the most important parts of the body lie buried deep within the center of the brain. The **thalamus** (THAL-uh-mus) and an area just below it called the **hypothalamus** (HI-po-THAL-uh-mus) are part of the forebrain (see Fig. 3–15).

Question: How could these be any more important than other areas already described?

The thalamus is a football-shaped structure that acts as a final "switching station" for sensory messages on their way to the cortex. Information from vision, hearing, taste, and touch relay through the thalamus. Sensory messages undergo initial analysis there as well. Injury to even small areas of the thalamus can cause deafness, blindness, or loss of any other sense, except smell.

The human hypothalamus is about the size of a thumbnail. Small as it may be, the hypothalamus is a kind of master control center for emotion and many basic motives (Thompson, 1985). The hypothalamus affects behaviors as diverse as sex, rage, temperature control, hormone release, eating and drinking, sleep, waking, and emotion. The hypothalamus is a sort of "crossroads" that connects with many other areas of the cortex and subcortex. As such, it acts as a "final path" for many kinds of behavior leaving the brain. You might think of the hypothalamus as the last area in the brain where many behaviors are organized or "decided on." (See Chapter 11 for a discussion of the role of the hypothalamus in hunger and thirst.)

The Limbic System The hypothalamus, parts of the thalamus, and several structures buried within the cortex form the **limbic system** (Fig. 3–16). The limbic system has an unmistakable role in producing *emotion* and motivated behavior. Rage, fear, sexual response, and other instances of intense arousal can be obtained from various points in the limbic system. For example, cats can be made aggressive by electrically stimulating the limbic system. Typically, they will crouch, hiss, expose their claws, lean forward, and tense their muscles—all characteristic of defense or attack. (See this chapter's Exploration.)

During evolution, the limbic system was the earliest layer of the forebrain to develop. In lower, relatively primitive animals, the limbic system helps organize the appropriate response to stimuli: feeding, fleeing, fighting, or reproduction (Thompson, 1985). In humans, the link to emotion remains. However, some parts of the limbic system have taken on additional, higher-level functions. For example, one part appears to be important for forming lasting memories. This is the **hippocampus** (HIP-oh-CAMP-us), found at the core of the temporal lobes. A link between the hippocampus and memory may explain why stimulating the temporal lobes can produce memory-like or dreamlike experiences. (See Chapter 9 for more information on this point.)

One of the most exciting discoveries in psychobiology was the finding that animals will learn to press a lever to deliver electrical stimulation to the limbic system as a reward (Olds & Milner, 1954). Since the original dis-

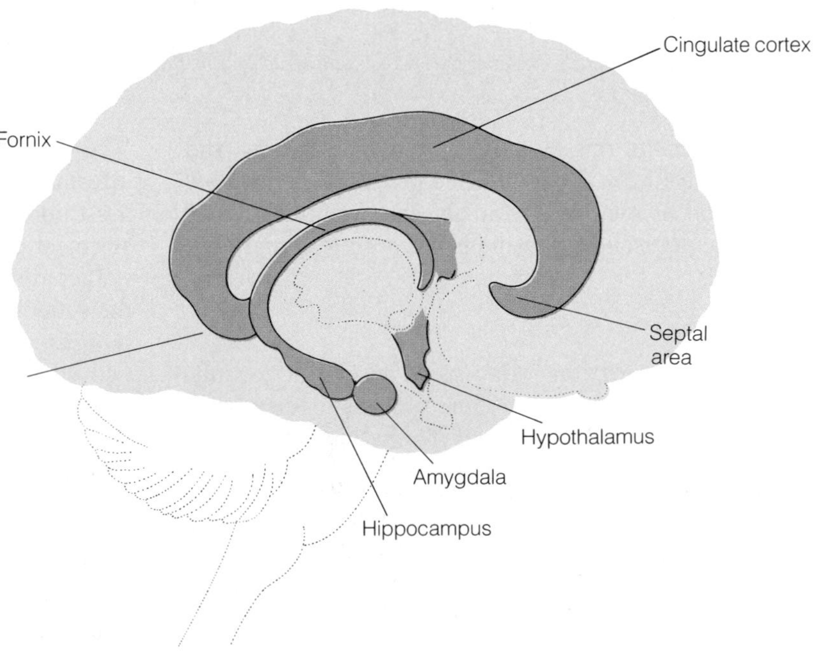

Fig. 3–16 *Parts of the limbic system are shown in this highly simplified drawing. Although it is not apparent in the drawing, the hippocampus and the amygdala extend out into the temporal lobes at each side of the brain. The limbic system is a sort of "primitive core" of the brain strongly associated with emotion.*

covery, many additional areas of the limbic system have been shown to act as reward, or "pleasure," pathways in the brain. Many are found in the hypothalamus, where they overlap with areas associated with drives such as thirst, sex, and hunger (Olds, 1977). (See Chapter 7.)

Punishment, or "aversive," areas have also been found in the limbic system. When these areas are stimulated, animals show discomfort and will work to turn off the stimulation. Since a great deal of human and animal behavior is directed by seeking pleasure and avoiding pain, these discoveries continue to fascinate psychologists.

The Brain in Perspective—Beyond the Biocomputer

We have seen that the human brain is an impressive assembly of billions of sensitive cells and nerve fibers. The brain controls vital bodily functions, keeps track of the external world, issues commands to the muscles and glands, responds to current needs, creates the magic of consciousness, and regulates its own behavior—*all* at the same time. Each of these basic needs is met by the action of one or more of the three main brain divisions: Control of vital bodily functions is carried out by the hindbrain (with some assistance from the hypothalamus in the forebrain); gathering sensory information and issuing motor commands takes place at all three levels of the brain; and response selection, learning, memory, and higher thought processes are controlled by the forebrain, particularly the cortex and association areas.

Redundancy A final note of caution is now in order. For the sake of simplicity, we have assigned functions to each "part" of the brain as if it were a computer. This is only a half-truth. In reality, the brain is a vast information-processing system. Incoming information scatters to structures all over the brain and converges again as it goes out to muscles and glands. The overall system acts in ways that go far beyond any view that considers only "parts" or "brain centers" (Nauta & Fiertag, 1979; Thompson, 1985). To say the least, the brain is much, much more complicated than implied here.

One reason for the brain's great complexity is its tremendous **redundancy,** or duplication, throughout. The brain may use dozens of areas to carry out a function that any one area could manage alone. Because of such redundancy, the brain has an impressive ability to reorganize itself after injury.

Question: Does it make any difference at what age a person experiences a brain injury?

Plasticity Yes. In response to brain damage, children usually show greater **plasticity** (flexibility) of brain reorganization than adults. Like adults, children cannot replace destroyed brain cells. But even when there is severe damage to the left hemisphere, children under the age of 7 can usually shift language processing to the right brain. In fact, people have been located who were born without a corpus callosum, having in effect "natural" split brains. As adults these people can answer questions from both hemispheres, write with both hands, draw with both hands, and solve block-design puzzles with both hands (Sperry, 1974). After age 10, such plasticity becomes rare.

Potential In the final analysis, the brain is both highly vulnerable and amazingly resilient. In one astounding case, a child had the entire left hemisphere of his brain removed at age 5. As an adult he was paralyzed on the right side and blind in his right visual field. But he was able to speak, read, write, and comprehend so well that he maintained a double major in college and has an above-average IQ (Smith & Sugar, 1975).

Cases like the one just described suggest that full use of the brain's potential may still lie ahead. At the same time that such injuries help us understand the brain's limitations, they raise questions about how the undamaged brain might be used more fully. Perhaps the future will see significant breakthroughs in enhancement of memory, intelligence, or recovery from brain damage. For now it is exciting to think that the human brain hasn't yet yielded all its secrets.

The Endocrine System—Slow but Sure Messenger Service

The nervous system is not the only communication network in the body. The **endocrine system** (IN-duh-krin) is the second great communication system. The endocrine system is made up of a number of glands that pour chemicals directly into the bloodstream (see Fig. 3–17). These chemicals, called **hormones,** are carried throughout the body, where they affect internal activities and behavior. Hormones are chemically related to neurotransmitters. Like transmitters, hormones activate cells in the body. To respond, the cells must have receptor sites for the hormone (Thompson, 1985).

Question: How do hormones affect behavior?

Although we are seldom aware of them, hormones affect us in a multitude of ways. Here is a brief sample: Hormone output from the adrenal glands rises during stress-

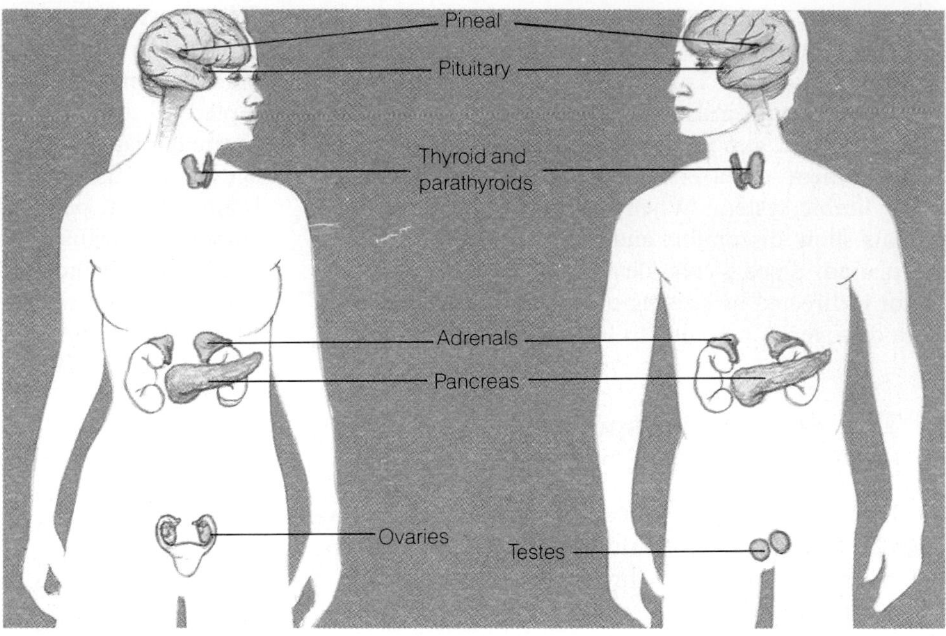

Fig. 3–17 *Locations of the endocrine glands in the male and female.*

ful situations; androgens ("male" hormones) are related to the sex drive in both males and females; hormones secreted during times of high emotion intensify memory formation; at least some of the emotional turmoil of adolescence is due to elevated hormone levels; different hormones predominate when you are angry, rather than fearful (Hoyenga & Hoyenga, 1984). Since this is just a sample, let's consider some additional effects hormones have on the body and behavior.

The **pituitary** is a small, grape-sized structure hanging from the base of the brain (return to Fig. 3–15). One of the pituitary's more important roles is regulation of growth. During childhood, the pituitary secretes a hormone that speeds body development. If too little **growth hormone** is released, a person may remain far smaller than average (see Highlight 3–3). Too much growth hormone produces **giantism.** (See Figure 3–18.) Secretion of too much growth hormone late in the growth period causes the arms, hands, feet, and facial bones to become enlarged. This condition, called **acromegaly** (AK-row-MEG-uh-lee), distorts appearance in a way that some people have turned into successful careers as sideshow entertainers, wrestlers, and the like.

The pituitary also regulates the functioning of other glands (especially the thyroid, adrenal glands, and ovaries or testes). These glands in turn regulate such bodily processes as reproduction, metabolism, and responses to stress. In women, the pituitary also controls the production of milk during pregnancy. Because of its many effects, the pituitary is often called the "master gland." But the master has a master: The pituitary is directed by the hypothalamus, which lies above it in the brain. In this way, the hypothalamus affects glands throughout the body. This, then, is the major link between the brain and the glandular system (Schally et al., 1977).

The **thyroid gland** is found in the neck, on each side of the windpipe. The thyroid regulates **metabolism**—the rate at which energy is produced and expended in the body. As a consequence, it can have a sizable effect on personality. A person with an overactive thyroid (termed **hyperthyroidism**) tends to be thin, tense, excitable, and nervous. An underactive thyroid **(hypothyroidism)** in an adult can cause inactivity, sleepiness, slowness, and overweight. In infancy, hypothyroidism limits development of the nervous system and can cause severe mental retardation (see Chapter 18).

When you are frightened or angry, a number of important actions take place in your body to prepare it for action: Your heart rate and blood pressure are raised; stored sugar is released into the bloodstream for quick energy; the muscles tense and receive more blood; and the blood is prepared to clot more quickly in case of injury. As we discussed earlier, these changes are brought about by the autonomic nervous system. Specifically, the sympathetic branch of the ANS causes the hormones **adrenaline** and **noradrenaline** to be released by the adrenal glands. (As mentioned earlier, the same substances also act as neurotransmitters.)

Fig. 3–18 *Underactivity of the pituitary gland may produce a dwarf; overactivity, a giant.*

● **HIGHLIGHT 3–3**
A Short Topic

Children who lag far behind in growth may suffer lasting emotional scars from rejection by peers or adults. One of the more common causes of limited growth is insufficient growth hormone. If this condition is not treated, a child may fall 6 to 12 inches behind age-mates in height. As adults, some will be **hypopituitary dwarfs** (HI-po-pih-TU-ih-ter-ee). Such individuals are perfectly proportioned, but tiny.

For many years, dwarfism could be treated only with injections of human growth hormone. Supplies were extracted from the pituitary glands of human cadavers—a painstaking and expensive process. Now, a relatively cheap synthetic growth hormone is available. Regular injections of this hormone can raise a hypopituitary child's height by several inches, usually to the short side of average.

Unfortunately, synthetic growth hormone may bring problems as well as good. If not carefully administered, it can cause giantism, acromegaly, diabetes, or other medical problems. There are also ethical concerns. Already, some parents and children have been bitterly disappointed and further upset when the child failed to grow as much as expected. In addition, some children have found it difficult to adjust to becoming more "ordinary." Many go from playing with younger children to being ignored by age-mates. There may even be a risk that some competitive parents will pressure physicians to increase growth of "normal short" children.

With all this in mind, perhaps it is fair to say that the success of growth hormone therapy should be measured by increased emotional well-being—not merely by an increase in stature. (Abstracted from Franklin, 1984.)

The adrenal glands are located just under the back of the rib cage, atop the kidneys. The **adrenal medulla,** or inner core of the adrenal glands, is the source of adrenaline and noradrenaline. The **adrenal cortex,** or outer "bark" of the adrenal glands, produces a second set of hormones called corticoids (KOR-tih-coids). One of their jobs is to regulate salt balance in the body. A deficiency of certain corticoids can evoke a powerful craving for the taste of salt in humans (Beach, 1975). The corticoids also help the body adjust to stress, and they are a secondary source of sex hormones. (For a full discussion of the role of sex glands in development, see Chapter 25.)

Perhaps you have heard about the use of "anabolic steroids" by athletes who want to "bulk up" or promote muscle growth. These drugs are a synthetic version of one of the male corticoids. Like all of the corticoids, they are quite powerful and therefore dangerous. There is no evidence that they improve performance, and they may cause voice deepening or baldness in women and shrinkage of the testicles or breast enlargement in men (*Sexual Medicine,* April 1980). For some users they may cause emotional disturbances and near-psychotic reactions (Harrison & Katz, 1987).

An oversecretion of the adrenal sex hormones can cause **virilism,** in which a woman grows a beard or a man's voice becomes so low it is difficult to understand. Oversecretion in children may cause **premature puberty,** resulting in full sexual development. One of the most remarkable cases on record is that of a 5-year-old Peruvian girl who gave birth to a son (Strange, 1965).

In this brief discussion of the endocrine system, we have considered only a few of the more important glands. Nevertheless, this should give you an appreciation of how completely behavior and personality are tied to the ebb and flow of hormones in the body.

In the upcoming Applications section, we return to the brain to see how hand preference relates to brain organization. In the Exploration that concludes the chapter, we will examine the fascinating effects of stimulating the brain electrically.

Learning Check

Here is a chance to check your memory of the preceding discussions.

1. Three major divisions of the brain are the brainstem or ______________, the ______________, and the ______________.

2. Reflex centers for heartbeat and respiration are found in the
a. cerebellum *b.* thalamus *c.* medulla *d.* RF

3. A portion of the reticular formation, known as the RAS, serves as an ______________ system in the brain.
a. activating *b.* adrenal *c.* adjustment *d.* aversive

4. The ______________ is a final relay, or "switching station," for sensory information on its way to the cortex.

5. "Reward" and "punishment" areas are found throughout the ______________ system, which is also related to emotion.

6. Redundancy and early plasticity underlie the brain's surprising capacity for recovery from some types of brain injuries in early childhood. T or F?

7. Undersecretion from the thyroid can cause
a. dwarfism *b.* giantism *c.* overweight *d.* mental retardation

8. The body's ability to resist stress is related to the action of the adrenal ______________.

Answers:
1. hindbrain, midbrain, forebrain **2.** *c* **3.** *a* **4.** thalamus **5.** limbic **6.** T **7.** *c*, *d* (in infancy) **8.** cortex

Applications: Handedness—If Your Brain Is Right, What's Left?

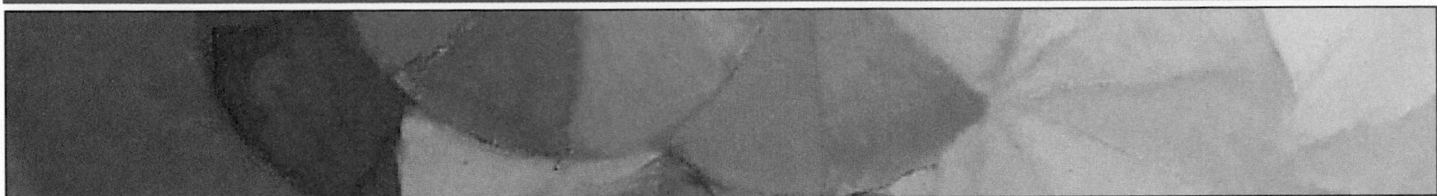

In the English language, "what's right is right," but what's left may be wrong. We have left-handed compliments, left-overs, people with "two left feet," those who are left behind, left out, and . . . left-handed. On the other hand (so to speak), we have the right way, the right whale, the right angle, the "right-hand man" (or woman), righteousness, and . . . the right-handed.

The Sinister Hand Left-handedness has a long and undeserved bad reputation. Southpaws have been accused of being clumsy, stubborn (for refusing to use their right hand), and maladjusted. One 1930s psychologist described the left-handed as "Awkward in the house, and clumsy in their games, they are fumblers and bunglers at whatever they do." But as any lefty will tell you, and modern psychology has confirmed, none of this is true. The supposed clumsiness of lefties is merely a result of living in a right-handed world: If it can be gripped, turned, folded, held, or pulled, it's probably designed for the right hand. Even toilet handles are on the right side.

What causes handedness? Why are there more right-handed than left-handed people? How do left-handed and right-handed people differ? Does being left-handed really create problems? Are there any benefits to being left-handed? The answers to most of these questions lead us back to the brain, where handedness begins. Let's see what research has revealed about handedness, the brain, and you.

Hand Dominance To begin with, you might find it interesting to compare your hands by copying the following design on a piece of paper, once with your right hand and once with your left. You should notice a definite superiority when your dominant hand is used. The interesting thing about this exercise is that there's no real difference in the strength or dexterity of the hands themselves. The agility of the dominant hand is an outward expression of superior motor control on one side of the brain (Herron, 1980).

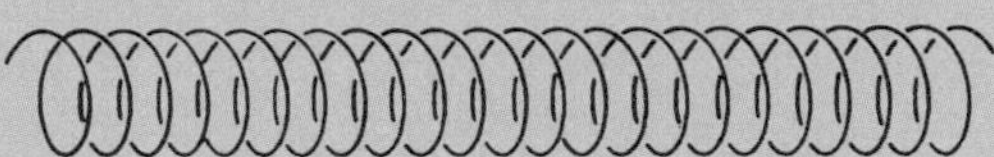

Question: If a person is left-handed, does that mean the right hemisphere is dominant?

Not necessarily. It's true that the right hemisphere controls the left hand, but a left-handed person's language-producing, dominant hemisphere may be on the opposite side of the brain.

Brain Dominance About 97 percent of right-handers process speech in the left hemisphere and are left brain dominant. A good 60 percent of left-handers produce speech from the left hemisphere, just as right-handed people do. About a quarter of all lefties and 3 percent of righties use their right brain for language. Approximately 15 percent of left-handers use both sides of the brain for language processing (Corballis, 1980; Herron, 1980).

Question: Is there any way for a person to tell which of his or her hemispheres is dominant?

One interesting clue is based on the way you write. Right-handed individuals who write with a straight hand, and lefties who write with a hooked hand, are usually left brain dominant for language. Left-handed people who write with their hand below the line, and righties who use a hooked position, are usually right brain dominant (Levy & Reid, 1976; Pines, 1980). Are your friends right brained or left brained? (See Fig. 3–19.)

Before you leap to any conclusions, be aware that writing position is not a foolproof sign of brain organization. The only sure way to determine brain dominance is to do a medical test that involves briefly anesthetizing one cerebral hemisphere at a time (Springer & Deutsch, 1985).

Question: How common is left-handedness, and what causes it?

Handedness Animals such as monkeys show definite hand preferences. However, in most animal groups there is a 50-50 split of right and left "handedness." Among humans, the split is about 90-10, with right-handedness being most common. The prevalence of right-handedness in humans probably reflects the left brain's specialization for language production (Corballis, 1980). Evidence exists that the majority of humans have been right-handed for at least 50 centuries (Coren & Porac, 1977).

It was long believed that children don't express clear-cut handedness until they are 4 or 5. But a study shows that hand preference for many children is stabilized by 18 months of age or earlier (Gottfried & Bathurst, 1983). Such early preferences underscore the fact that handedness cannot be dictated. Parents should never try to force a left-handed child to use the right hand. To do so may invite speech or reading problems because handedness is hereditary (Herron, 1980).

Applications

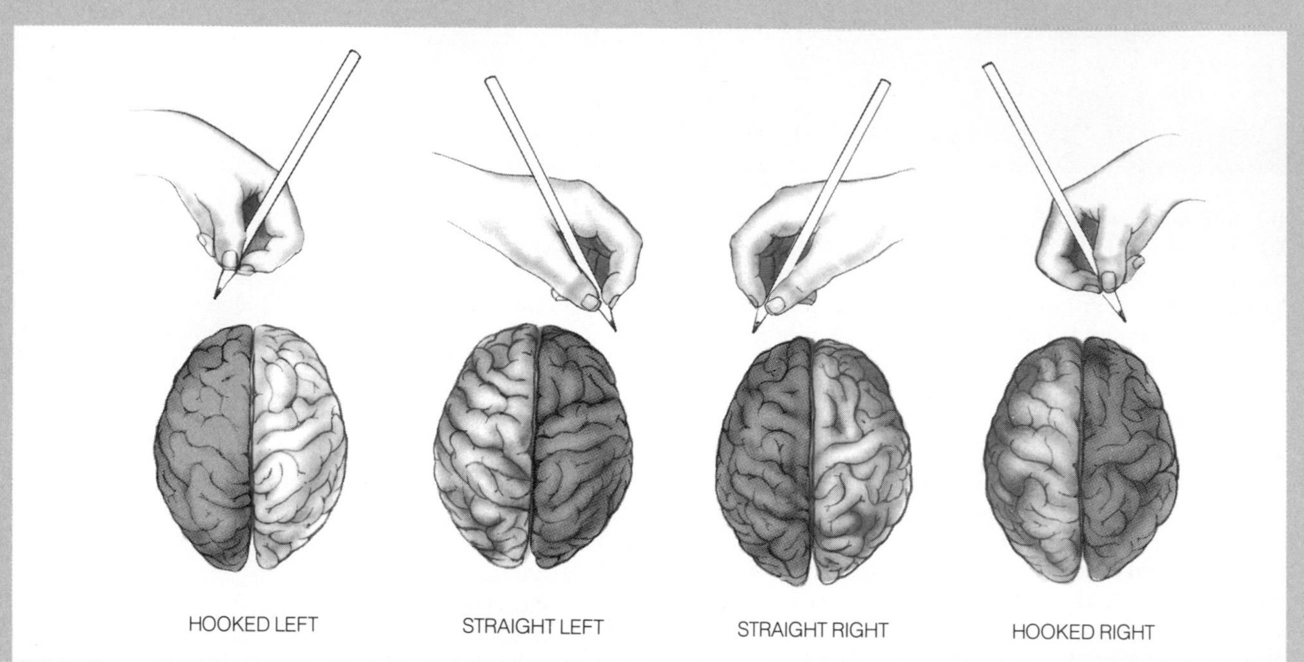

Fig. 3–19 *Research suggests that the hand position used in writing may indicate which brain hemisphere is used for language. (Redrawn from an illustration by M. E. Challinor.)*

Question: Are there any drawbacks to being left-handed?

Other than the fact that lefties must live in a right-handed world, there seem to be none. A large-scale study of high school students in California found no differences in school achievement between left- and right-handers and no physical or mental defects associated with left-handedness (Hardyck et al., 1976). In fact, there may actually be some advantages to being left-handed.

Advantage Left Throughout history a notable number of artists have been lefties, from Leonardo da Vinci and Michelangelo to Pablo Picasso and M. C. Escher. Conceivably, since the right hemisphere is superior at imagery and visual abilities, there is some advantage to using the left hand for drawing or painting (Pines, 1980; Springer & Deutsch, 1985). Whether this is true or not, the left-handed do seem better at putting together verbal and pictorial symbols or ideas—which may be why there are more left-handed architects than would be expected (Herron, 1980).

One striking feature of lefties is that they are generally less **lateralized** than the right-handed. This means that there is less distinct specialization in the two sides of their brains. In fact, even the physical size and shape of their cerebral hemispheres are more alike. If you are a lefty, you can take pride in the fact that your brain is less lopsided than the brains of your right-handed friends (Corballis, 1980)! In general, left-handers are more symmetrical on almost everything, including eye dominance, fingerprints—even foot size (Corballis, 1980).

In some situations less lateralization may be a real advantage. For instance, individuals who are moderately left-handed, or ambidextrous, seem to have better than average pitch memory, which is a basic musical skill (Deutsch, 1978). Correspondingly, more musicians are ambidextrous than would normally be expected. It's not clear, however, if those who are musically gifted were initially less lateralized or if playing music develops both hands or possibly both sides of the brain (Springer & Deutsch, 1985).

Math abilities may also benefit from fuller use of the right hemisphere. Students who are extremely gifted in math are much more likely to be left-handed or ambidextrous than other students are (Benbow, 1986). The clearest advantage of being left-handed shows up when there is a brain injury. Because of their milder lateralization, left-handed individuals typically experience less language loss after damage to either brain hemisphere, and they recover more easily (Geschwind, 1979). Maybe having "two left feet" isn't so bad after all.

Applications

Learning Check

1. About 97 percent of left-handed people process language on the left side of the brain, the same as right-handed people do. T or F?
2. Left-handed individuals who write with their hand below the line are likely to be right-brain dominant. T or F?
3. Most animals, like most humans, show a preference for the right limb. T or F?
4. In general, left-handed individuals show less lateralization in the brain and in fact throughout the body. T or F?
5. A recent study of high school students demonstrated that left-handed individuals are superior in school achievement. T or F?

Answers:
1. F 2. T 3. F 4. T 5. F

● Exploration: Electrical Stimulation of the Brain—The Promise and Peril of Brain Control

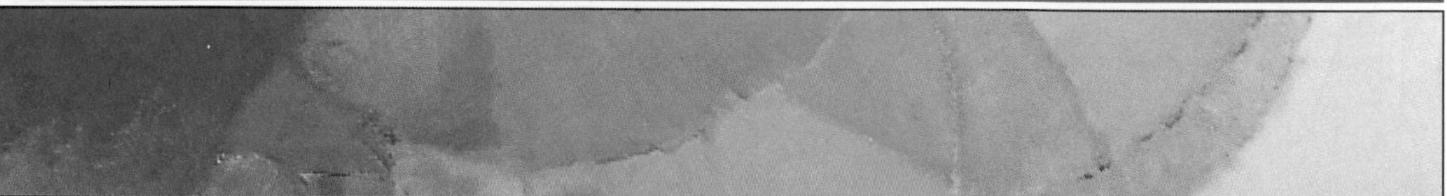

Electrical stimulation of the brain (ESB) has made direct control over the machinery of the brain a reality. In some instances, ESB is capable of calling forth animal and human behavior with almost robotlike precision. ESB begins with **electrode implantation:** the placing of electrical stimulating devices in strategic areas of the brain. Usually, these are fine steel or platinum wires or needles inserted through the skull, run under the scalp, and collected at a single external socket. By this means, as many as two dozen or more separate brain sites can be electrically stimulated on command.

ESB electrodes can be activated at a distance by use of radio transmitters and receivers. Further advances promise increasingly smaller receivers and stimulating devices, eventually the size of a postage stamp or less. In addition to removing any outward signs of ESB implants, miniaturization may eventually allow placement of a microcomputer in the brain, perhaps as a means of controlling epileptic seizures or of artificially increasing intelligence.

Question: How is ESB used now?

ESB is used extensively in animal research as a means of exploring brain-behavior connections. An important advantage of ESB is that it allows an animal (or person) to function normally, with the brain intact, while the experimenter turns various brain areas on and off.

An early experiment by W. R. Hess demonstrated that full-blown rage could be elicited from cats by ESB. Since then, ESB has proved capable of putting animals and humans through the paces of most basic behaviors. Stimulation applied to the proper brain area can instantly bring about terror, anxiety, rage, sexual desire, aggression, alertness, escape, eating, drinking, sleeping, movement of limbs, euphoria, memories, speech, tears, and more.

Question: How do humans respond to ESB?

ESB experiments with humans have understandably been limited to situations involving extraordinary medical need. For example, ESB may be used to identify brain areas that are triggering violent outbursts so that they may be removed surgically.

When tested by ESB, one patient reacted with a sudden outburst of anger upon stimulation of the amygdala (ah-MIG-dah-luh: a part of the limbic system), saying, "I feel like I want to get up from this chair! Please don't let me do it! Don't do this to me. I don't want to be mean!" When asked by the interviewer if she would like to hit him, she said, "Yeah I want to hit something. I want to get something and just tear it up!" The patient was then given a stack of paper, which she tore to shreds (King, 1961). Later, she explained that she had not really been angry at the interviewer. She just had an overwhelming desire to hit or destroy anything and everything.

Electrodes at other locations produce decidedly different reactions. When the temporal lobe was activated, one patient giggled and made funny comments, saying she enjoyed the stimulation very much. Repetition of the stimulation made the patient flirtatious, and she ended by openly expressing her desire to marry the therapist. When stimulation ceased, she again became quiet, reserved, and proper, without excessive friendliness.

Question: Could ESB be used to control a person completely against his or her will?

José Delgado, who has done some of the most advanced work with ESB, believes it could not. As evidence, he cites research on stimulated aggression in animal colonies. Monkeys receiving ESB become aggressive in direct proportion to their rank in the "pecking order" of the colony. When they are at the bottom of the pecking order, stimulation causes few attacks on other monkeys. When they are near the top, aggressive outbursts and attacks are easily triggered. Thus, to the question, "Could a ruthless dictator stand at a master radio transmitter and stimulate the brains of a mass of hopelessly enslaved people?," Delgado replies, "Fortunately it is beyond the theoretical and practical limits of ESB."

So, at this point in its development,

Exploration

ESB cannot really cause a person to behave like a robot. It is true, as we have seen, that a person's emotional reactivity can be influenced, making the person more aggressive or amorous, for instance. But in most cases, the behavioral details of these feelings are modified by the individual's personality and by the situation. If someone were intent on controlling or disrupting the behavior of another person, it would be far easier to do it with drugs. Even minute traces of some drugs, such as LSD, can alter activity throughout the brain. The threat of a terrorist putting LSD in a city water supply would be a far more realistic danger than ESB could ever be.

What, then, does the future hold for ESB? Will it provide a way to block unbearable pain, overcome epileptic seizures, end uncontrollable violence, reverse some forms of mental retardation, or link the brain to a computer? All are possible. What are the ethical implications of present ESB research? Will more precise brain control become possible? What impact does ESB research have on your conceptions of personality, mind, and free will?

(Sources: Delgado, 1969; 1970; London, 1971.)

Learning Check

1. ESB is done primarily by electrically stimulating the spinal cord. T or F?
2. Stimulation of the amygdala causes a person to become hostile and aggressive. T or F?
3. Behaviors induced by ESB are, for the most part, unaffected by external circumstances. T or F?
4. The chances of ESB being used to control the behavior of a large number of people against their will is very low. T or F?

Answers:

1. F 2. T 3. F 4. T

Chapter Summary

- The brain and nervous system are made up of linked nerve cells called **neurons.** Neurons are arranged in long chains and dense networks. They pass information from one to another through **synapses.**
- The basic conducting structure of neurons is the **axon,** but **dendrites** (a receiving area), the **soma** (the cell body and also a receiving area), and **axon terminals** (the branching ends of an axon) are also involved in communication.
- The firing of an **action potential** (nerve impulse) is basically electrical, whereas communication between neurons is chemical. Neurons release chemicals called **neurotransmitters** at the synapse. These cross to **receptor sites** on the receiving cell, causing it to be excited or inhibited. Transmitters called **neuropeptides** appear to regulate activity in the brain.
- **Nerves** are made of axons and associated tissues. Neurons and nerves in the peripheral nervous system can often **regenerate;** damage in the central nervous system is *permanent* unless a repair is attempted by **grafting** or implanting healthy tissue.
- The nervous system can be divided into the **central nervous system** (the brain and spinal cord) and the **peripheral nervous system,** which includes the **somatic** (bodily) and **autonomic** (involuntary) nervous systems. The autonomic system has two divisions: the **sympathetic** (emergency, activating) branch and the **parasympathetic** (sustaining, conserving) branch.
- The human brain is marked by advanced **corticalization,** or enlargement of the **cerebral cortex.** The **left cerbral hemisphere** contains speech or language "centers" in most people. It also specializes in writing, performing calculations, judging time and rhythm, and ordering complex movements. The **right hemisphere** is largely nonverbal. It excels at spatial and perceptual skills, visualization, and recognition of patterns, faces, and melodies.
- **"Split brains"** have been created in animals and humans by cutting the **corpus callosum.** The split-brain individual shows a remarkable degree of independence between the right and left hemispheres. Under some circumstances, the hemispheres function as separate brain units.
- The most basic functions of the **lobes** of the cerebral cortex are as follows: **occipital** lobes—vision; **parietal** lobes—bodily sensation; **temporal** lobes—hearing and language; **frontal** lobes—smell, motor control, speech, and abstract thought.
- There are a number of **association areas** on the cortex that are neither sensory nor motor in function. These are related to more complex skills such as language, memory, recognition, and problem solving. Damage to either **Broca's area** or **Wernicke's area** causes speech and language problems known as **aphasias.** Damage in other areas may cause **agnosia,** the inability to identify objects by sight.
- The brain as a whole can be subdivided into three general areas: the **forebrain, midbrain,** and **hindbrain.**
- The **subcortex** includes several crucial brain structures. The **medulla** contains centers essential for reflex control of heart rate, breathing, and other "vegetative" functions. The **cerebellum** maintains coordination, posture, and muscle tone. The **reticular formation** directs sensory and motor messages, and part of it, known as the **RAS,** acts as an activating system for the brain. The **thalamus** carries sensory information to the cortex. The **hypothalamus** exerts powerful control over eating, drinking, sleep cycles, body temperature, and other basic motives and behaviors. The **limbic system** is strongly related to emotion. It also contains distinct reward and punishment areas and an area known as the **hippocampus** that is important for forming memories.
- The **endocrine system** provides **chemical** communication in the body through the release of **hormones** into the bloodstream. Many of the endocrine glands are influenced by the **pituitary** (the "master gland"), which is in turn influenced by the hypothalamus. The endocrine glands influence moods, behavior, and even personality.
- The vast majority of people are right-handed and therefore left brain dominant for motor skills. Ninety-seven percent of right-handed persons and 60 percent of the left-handed also produce speech from the left hemisphere. In general, the left-handed are less strongly **lateralized** in brain function than are right-handed persons.
- Electrical stimulation of the brain (**ESB**) has been used to study the functions of various areas. ESB holds promise as a medical treatment. It is unlikely that it could ever be used to forcibly control behavior.

Questions for Discussion

1. If you could change the brain or nervous system in any way to improve them, how would you do it, and why?

2. What effect would you expect a drug to have if it raised the firing threshold for neurons? If it blocked passage of neurotransmitters across the synapse? If it mimicked the effect of a neurotransmitter? If it stimulated the RF? If it suppressed activity in the medulla?

3. Have you known someone who has had a stroke or other brain injury? What were the effects? How did the person cope with the injury?

4. A member of your family has been having outbursts of hostile and aggressive behavior. In the past year, they have become virtually uncontrollable. ESB has been recommended as the only remaining possible treatment. Would you condone its use? What limitations (if any) do you think should be imposed on ESB procedures?

5. Do you think a sharp distinction between right and left hemisphere function is valid? For example, are there verbal skills involved in music, dance, or art?

6. Robert Ornstein has urged us to recognize that full use of human potential should take advantage of the specialized skills of both cerebral hemispheres. Roger Sperry has charged that "our educational system tends to neglect the nonverbal form of intellect. What it comes down to is that modern society discriminates against the right hemisphere." Do you agree? What changes would you make in educational systems if you do?

7. What would be some of the possible advantages and disadvantages to having a "split brain"?

8. If a person were kept alive with only the spinal cord intact, what kinds of responses would be possible? What if both the spinal cord and medulla were functioning? The spinal cord, medulla, and cerebellum? The spinal cord, medulla, and subcortex? All brain areas except the association cortex?

9. If your brain were removed, replaced by another, and moved to a new body, which would you consider to be yourself, your old body with the new brain, or your new body with the old brain?

10. Can the brain ever expect to understand itself completely? Or is the brain studying the brain like trying to lift yourself by your bootstraps?

11. If the parents of a normal-sized child wanted to give the child growth hormone to make him or her taller, would you consider it ethical? Why or why not?

12. Brain transplants done on lab animals typically make use of fetal brain tissue. It is possible that cells for transplants will eventually be grown in laboratory dishes. If this does not prove possible, and fetal cells are the only source for transplants, would you consider transplants ethical? If so, under what conditions?

Chapter 4

Sensation and Reality

In This Chapter

General properties of sensory systems

Sensory thresholds and limits

Vision and visual problems

Hearing and deafness

Smell and taste

Somesthetic senses

Adaptation, attention, and gating

Applications

Controlling pain

Exploration

The vestibular system and motion sickness

Chapter Preview

Sensation—A Window on the World

At this very moment, you are bathed in a swirling kaleidoscope of light, heat, pressure, vibrations, molecules, radiation, mechanical forces, and other physical energies. Without the senses, all of this would seem like a void of darkness and silence. The next time you drink in the beauty of a sunset, a flower, or a friend, remember this: ***Sensation*** *makes it all possible.*

It is apparent that the world as we know it is created from sensory impressions. Less obvious is that what passes for "reality" is shaped by the senses. Our sensory organs can detect only a limited range of physical energies. Thus, events go unrecorded when the senses are not attuned to them. We have, for instance, no receptors for atomic radiation, X-rays, or microwaves. For this reason, it is possible to be injured by each of these energies without being aware of it.

Yellow Is Amazing, but Red Is Best *What would the world be like if new senses could be added—if we could "see" gamma rays, "hear" changes in barometric pressure, or "taste" light? We can only guess. It is far easier to imagine losing or regaining a sensory system. Consider the words of Bob Edens, who had his sight restored at age 51 after being blind since birth:*

> I never would have dreamed that yellow is so . . . so yellow. I don't have the words, I'm amazed by yellow. But red is my favorite color. I just can't believe red. I can't wait to get up each day to see what I can see. And at night I look at the stars in the sky and the flashing lights. You could never know how wonderful everything is. I saw some bees the other day, and they were magnificent. I saw a truck drive by in the rain and throw a spray in the air. It was marvelous. And did I mention, I saw a falling leaf just drifting through the air?

If you are ever tempted to take everyday sensory impressions for granted, remember Bob Edens. As his words show, sensation is our window on the world. All our meaningful behavior, our awareness of physical reality, and our ideas about the universe ultimately spring from the senses. It may be no exaggeration, then, to claim that our topic for this chapter is quite . . . "sensational."

Survey Questions

- In general, how do sensory systems function?
- What are the limits of our sensory sensitivity?
- How do each of the major senses work, and what causes common sensory problems, such as deafness or color blindness?
- Why are we more aware of some sensations than others?
- How can pain be reduced or controlled in everyday situations?

General Properties of Sensory Systems—What You See Is What You Get

We begin with a paradox. On one hand we have the magnificent power of the senses. In one instant you can view a star light-years away, and in the next, you can peer into the microscopic universe of a dewdrop. Yet vision, like the other senses, is also narrowly limited in sensitivity so that it acts as a **data reduction system.** That is, our senses routinely "boil down" floods of information into a select stream of useful data.

Sensory selection can be seen in the fact that "light" is only a small slice of a broader range of energies. In addition to visible light, the **electromagnetic spectrum** includes infrared and ultraviolet light, radio waves, television broadcasts, gamma rays, and other energies (see Fig. 4–2). If our eyes were not limited to light sensitivity, "seeing" would be like getting hundreds of different "channels" at once. The confusion would be overwhelming. Obviously, *selection* of information is important.

Question: How are selection and data reduction accomplished?

Some selection occurs simply because sensory receptors are biological *transducers*. A **transducer** is a device that converts one kind of energy into another. For example, a phonograph needle converts vibrations into electrical signals. Scrape the needle with your finger and the speakers will blast out sound. However, if you shine a light on the needle, or put it in cold water, the speakers will remain silent. (The owner of the stereo, however, may get quite loud at this point!) Similarly, each sensory organ is most sensitive to a select range of energy, which it most easily translates into nerve impulses.

As they transduce information, many sensory systems **analyze** the environment into important *features* before sending messages to the brain. **Perceptual features** are basic elements of a stimulus pattern, such as lines, shapes, edges, spots, or colors. The neural circuits of many sensory systems act as **feature detectors.** In other words, they are highly attuned to specific stimulus patterns. Frog eyes, for example, are especially sensitive to small, dark, moving spots. Researcher Jerome Lettvin (1961) calls this sensitivity a "bug detector." It seems that the frog's eyes are "wired" to detect bugs flying nearby. But the insect (spot) must be moving. A frog may starve to death surrounded by dead flies.

In addition to selection and analysis, sensory systems **code** important features of the world into messages understood by the brain (Hubel & Wiesel, 1979). To see coding at work, try this simple demonstration:

> Close your eyes for a moment. Then take your fingertips and press firmly on your eyelids. Apply enough pressure to "squash" your eyes slightly. Do this for about 30 seconds and observe what happens. (Readers with eye problems or contact lenses should not try this.)

If you followed the instructions, you probably saw stars, checkerboards, and flashes of color called **phosphenes** (FOSS-feens). The reason for this is that the receptor cells in the eye, which normally respond to light, are also somewhat sensitive to pressure. Notice, though, that the eye is only prepared to code stimulation—including pressure—into *visual* features. As a result, you experience *light sensations,* not pressure. Also important in producing this effect is **localization of function** in the brain.

Question: What does localization of function mean?

It means that the sensory receptors send messages to specific locations in the brain. Some brain areas receive visual information, others receive auditory information, still others receive taste, and so forth. Thus, the sensation you experience ultimately depends on which area of the brain is activated.

One practical implication of such localization is that it may be possible to artificially stimulate specific brain areas to restore sight, hearing, or other senses. Researchers have already tested a system that uses a miniature television camera to create electrical signals that are applied to the visual cortex of the brain (Dobelle et al., 1974; Dobelle, 1977). (See Fig. 4–1.) Unfortunately, artificial vision of this type still faces major hurdles. However, artificial hearing is proving more workable—as we will see later.

It is fascinating to realize that experiences such as "seeing" and "hearing" ultimately take place in the brain, not in the eye or ear. Each sense organ is merely the first link in a long chain that ends in the cell and fiber forest of the brain. Much as we may be tempted to think so, our sensory systems do not operate like cameras or tape recorders, sending back "pictures" of the world. Rather, they collect, transduce, analyze, code, and transmit an unending flow of data to an active, information-hungry brain. This incoming flow of information is what we refer to as **sensation.** When the brain organizes sensations into meaningful patterns, we speak of *perception,* which is the topic of Chapter 5.) In a moment we will see how each of the senses operates. But first, let's explore a little more the question of how sensitive we are to our "sensational" world.

Fig. 4–1 *Artist's concept of an artificial visual system. Images received by an artificial eye would be transmitted to electrodes placed in the visual area of the brain (shown in cutaway view). The artificial eye, which operates like a television camera, might be placed in the eye socket as shown in the drawing. A major barrier to such systems is the brain's tendency to reject implanted electrodes.*

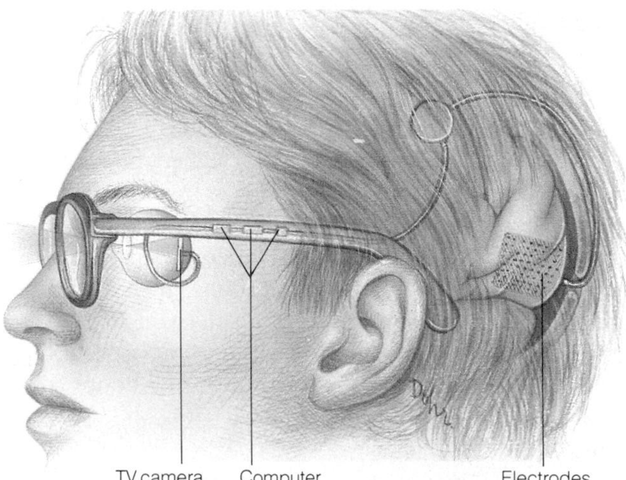

● Psychophysics—Taking It to the Limit

Question: What is the quietest sound that can be heard? The weakest light that can be seen? The lightest touch that can be felt?

The sense organs are our link to reality. What are their limits? An approach called **psychophysics** provides some answers. In psychophysics, changes in *physical* stimuli are measured and related to *psychological* sensations, such as loudness, brightness, or taste. A basic question psychophysics asks is, What is the absolute minimum amount of energy necessary for a sensation to occur? The answer defines the **absolute threshold** for a sensory system.

Testing for absolute thresholds shows just how sensitive we are. For example, it only takes 3 photons of light striking the retina to produce a sensation. A **photon** (FOE-tahn) is the smallest possible "package" of light energy, and responding to 3 photons is the equivalent of seeing a candle flame 30 miles away! Table 4–1 gives the approximate absolute thresholds for the five major senses.

Some sensory systems have upper limits as well as lower ones. For example, when the ears are tested for pitch (higher and lower tones), we find that humans can hear sounds down to 20 **hertz** (vibrations per second) and up to about 20,000 hertz. This is an impressive range—from the lowest rumble of a pipe organ to the highest squeak of a stereo "tweeter." On the lower end, the threshold is as low as practical. If the ears could respond to tones below 20 hertz, you would hear the movements of your own muscles (Oster, 1984). Imagine how disturbing it would be to hear your body creak and groan like an old ship each time you moved.

The 20,000 hertz upper threshold for human hearing, on the other hand, could easily be higher. Dogs, bats, cats, and other animals can hear sounds well above this limit. That's why a "silent" dog whistle (which may make sounds as high as 40,000 or 50,000 hertz) can be heard by dogs, but not by humans. For dogs, the sound exists. For humans, it is beyond awareness. It's easy to see how thresholds define the limits of the sensory world in which we live. (If you want to buy a stereo system for your dog, you will have a hard time finding one that reproduces sounds above 20,000 hertz!)

Table 4–1 Absolute Thresholds

SENSORY MODALITY	ABSOLUTE THRESHOLD
Vision	Candle flame seen at 30 miles on a clear, dark night
Hearing	Tick of a watch under quiet conditions at 20 feet
Taste	1 teaspoon of sugar in 2 gallons of water
Smell	1 drop of perfume diffused into a three-room apartment
Touch	A bee's wing falling on your cheek from 1 centimeter above

(From Galanter, 1962)

Perceptual Defense and Subliminal Perception

Question: Wouldn't the absolute threshold be different for different people?

Not only do absolute thresholds vary from person to person, they also vary from time to time for a single person. The type of stimulus, the state of one's nervous system, and the costs of false "detections" all make a difference. Emotional factors are also important. Unpleasant stimuli, for example, may *raise* the threshold for recognition. This effect is called **perceptual defense.** It was first demonstrated in experiments on the perception of "dirty" and "clean" words (McGinnies, 1949). So-called dirty words such as *whore, rape, bitch,* and *penis* were briefly flashed on a screen. These words took longer to recognize than did "clean" words such as *wharf, rope, batch,* and *pencil.*

Question: Couldn't it be that people wanted to be really sure they had seen a word like penis *before saying it?*

Yes. For many years, psychologists worried about this and other flaws in the original experiment. But later research that avoided these problems suggests that perceptual defense does occur (Erdelyi, 1974). Apparently, it is possible to process information on more than one level and to resist information that causes anxiety, discomfort, or embarrassment (Dember & Warm, 1979).

Question: Is this "subliminal" perception?

Basically, yes. Anytime information is processed below the normal **limen** (LIE-men: threshold or limit) for awareness, it is **subliminal.** Subliminal perception was demonstrated by an experiment in which people saw a series of shapes flashed on a screen for 1/1000 second each. Later, they were allowed to see these shapes and other "new" shapes for as long as they wanted. At that time, they rated how much they liked each shape. Even though they could not tell "old" shapes from "new," they gave "old" shapes higher ratings (Kunst-Wilson & Zajonc, 1980). It seems that the "old" shapes had become familiar and thus more "likable," but at a level below normal awareness.

Question: Could that be applied to advertising?

The urge to manipulate shoppers must be strong, since many businesses have tried subliminal advertising over the years. But do subliminal sales pitches actually work? Let's see.

In one early attempt at subliminal advertising, a New Jersey theater flashed the words *Eat popcorn* and *Drink Coca-Cola* on the screen for 1/3000 second every 5 seconds during movies. Since the words were presented so briefly, they were below the normal threshold for awareness. During the 6 weeks the messages ran, the firm claimed an increase of 57.5 percent in popcorn sales and an 18.1 percent increase in Coca-Cola sales.

In the furor that followed this "experiment," some states rushed to pass laws against the "invisible sell." However, they really had nothing to fear. Subliminal advertising has proved largely ineffective (McBurney & Collings, 1984; Vokey & Read, 1985). Such early "experiments" appeared to succeed only because they didn't take into account weather conditions, the time of year, the films shown, the type of audience, snack bar displays, and so forth.

To summarize, there is evidence that subliminal perception occurs. However, well-controlled experiments have shown that subliminal stimuli are basically *weak* stimuli. Advertisers are better off using the loudest, clearest, most attention-demanding stimuli available—as most do. Despite the evidence, some advertisers still use subliminal messages. Maybe *they* haven't gotten the message. For details on a related controversy, see Highlight 4–1.

Difference Thresholds

Psychophysics also studies **difference thresholds.** Here we are asking, How much must a stimulus *change* (increase or decrease) before it becomes *just noticeably different?* The study of just noticeable differences **(JNDs)** led to one of psychology's first natural "laws." Called *Weber's law* (VAY-bears), it can be roughly stated as fol-

HIGHLIGHT 4–1
Rock Music: Subliminal Messages or Subliminal Myths?

In the latest uproar over subliminal perception, critics heatedly charged that spoken messages recorded backward ("backmasking") in rock music are perceived unconsciously by listeners.

Psychologists John Vokey and Don Read (1985) point out that religious leaders, journalists, and lawmakers merely *assumed* that if subliminal messages exist in records, they must affect listeners. But do they? Vokey and Read decided to find out.

Vokey and Read recorded a variety of sentences backward, including selections from Lewis Carroll's *Jabberwocky* and the twenty-third psalm of the Bible. In a series of tests using the backward sentences, Vokey and Read found no evidence of conscious or unconscious recognition of their meaning. They were also unable to influence subjects' behavior with backward messages.

Undoubtedly, a few misguided musicians have placed backward messages in their recordings—some of which are highly offensive. However, Vokey and Read's research shows that subliminal messages in music offer no threat to listeners. Musicians who have played this game are just fooling themselves.

lows: The amount of change needed to produce a JND is a constant *proportion* of the original stimulus intensity.

Question: What does this mean in practice?

Let's take an example. Pretend that you are sitting in a room in which there are 10 candles burning. Ten candles is the original stimulus intensity. Let's say that we begin lighting candles until the room becomes just noticeably brighter. If this takes 3 more candles, how many more candles will we have to light in a room in which 20 candles are burning in order to cause a just noticeable increase in brightness? Your first guess may be 3, but remember, the JND is a *proportion*. We will have to light 6 candles if we start with 20; 9 if we start with 30; and 12 if we start with 40. The table you see here lists Weber's proportions for some common judgments.

Pitch	1/333 (1/3 of 1 percent)
Weight	1/50
Loudness	1/10
Taste	1/5

Notice the big difference in auditory sensitivity (pitch and loudness) compared to taste. Very small changes in hearing are easy to detect. A voice or a musical instrument that is off pitch 1/3 of 1 percent will be noticeable. For taste, we find that a 20 percent change is necessary to produce a JND. If a cup of coffee has 5 teaspoons of sugar in it, one more (1/5 of 5) will have to be added before there is a noticeable increase in sweetness. It takes a lot of cooks to spoil the broth.

Weber's law is really just an approximation, because it applies mainly to stimuli in the mid-range. For other than pure sensory judgments, it is even more approximate. In spite of this, there is a lesson to be learned from it. Consider judgments of money, for instance. If you discovered that you had been overcharged $5 on the purchase of a shirt, would you return to demand your money? If you discovered that you had been overcharged $5 on the purchase of an automobile, would you return to demand your money? If your answer to the first question is yes, then rationally, your answer to the second should be yes, too. It may not be, however, since the larger base price of a car makes $5 seem a very small difference.

It's now time to examine each of the senses in more detail. In the next section, we will begin with vision, which is perhaps the most magnificent sensory system of all.

Learning Check

Before you read more, it might be a good idea to stop for a quick check on some of the ideas we have covered.

1. Sensory receptors are biological ______________, or devices for converting one type of energy to another.
2. Lettvin found that a frog's eyes are especially sensitive to phosphenes. T or F?
3. Important features of the environment are transmitted to the brain through a process known as
   a. phosphenation *b.* coding *c.* detection *d.* programming

4. The minimum amount of stimulation necessary for a sensation to occur defines the ________________ ________________.

5. A stimulus that causes discomfort or embarrassment may have to be viewed longer before it is perceived because of ________________ ________________.

6. Subliminal stimuli have been shown to have a powerful effect on the behavior of viewers, especially when embedded in movies. T or F?

Answers:

1. transducers 2. F 3. b 4. absolute threshold 5. perceptual defense 6. F

Vision—Catching Some Rays

Question: Which of the senses is most essential?

There really isn't an answer to this question. Nevertheless, for most people loss of vision is the single most devastating sensory disability. Because of its great importance, we will explore vision in more detail than the other senses. Let's begin with the basic dimensions of light and vision.

Dimensions of Vision Recall that the room in which you are sitting is filled with **electromagnetic radiation,** including light and other energies. The **visible spectrum** is made up of light of various wavelengths. The spectrum starts at wavelengths of 400 nanometers (nan-OM-et-ers). A nanometer is one-billionth of a meter. Wavelengths at this end of the spectrum produce sensations of purple or violet. Increasingly longer wavelengths produce blue, green, yellow, and orange, until we reach red, with a wavelength of 700 nanometers (Fig. 4–2).

This physical property of light—its *wavelength*—corresponds to the psychological experience of **hue,** or the specific color of a stimulus. White light is made up of a mixture of frequencies from the entire spectrum. Colors produced by a very *narrow band* of wavelengths are said to be very **saturated,** or "pure." A third dimension of vision, **brightness,** corresponds roughly to the *amplitude* (or "height") of light waves; light of greater amplitude carries more energy and appears brighter.

Structure of the Eye

Question: Is it true that the eye is like a camera?

By pushing the issue a bit, the eye could be used as a camera. When the light-sensitive back surface of the eye is bathed in alum solution, the last image to strike it will appear like a tiny photograph. This fact might make for a great murder mystery, but it's not much of a way to take a photograph. In any case, several of the basic elements of eyes and cameras are similar. Both have a **lens** that focuses images on a light-sensitive layer at the back of a closed space. In a camera, this layer is the film; in the eye, it is a layer of **photoreceptors** (light-sensitive cells) about the size and thickness of a postage stamp, called the **retina** (Fig. 4–3).

Question: How does the eye focus?

Focusing The front of the eye has a clear covering called the **cornea.** The curvature of this transparent "window" bends light rays inward. Next, the lens, which is elastic, is stretched or thickened by a series of muscles, so that more or less additional bending of light occurs. This bending, fattening, and stretching of the lens is called **accommodation.** In cameras, focusing is done more simply—by changing the distance between the lens and the film.

Visual Problems The shape of the eye also affects focusing. If the eye is too short, nearby objects cannot be focused, but distant objects are clear. This is called *farsightedness,* or **hyperopia** (HI-per-OH-pea-ah). If the eyeball is too long, the image falls short of the retina, and distant objects cannot be focused. This condition results in *nearsightedness,* or **myopia** (my-OH-pea-ah). When the cornea or the lens is *misshapen,* part of the visual field will be focused and part will be fuzzy. This problem is called **astigmatism** (ah-STIG-mah-tiz-em). All three visual defects can be corrected by placing glasses or contact lenses in front of the eye. These added lenses change the path of incoming light to restore crisp focusing (Fig. 4–4).

Sometimes, with age, the lens becomes less flexible and less able to accommodate. Since the lens must do its greatest bending to focus nearby objects, the result is **presbyopia** (prez-bee-OH-pea-ah: old vision), or farsightedness due to aging. Perhaps you have seen a grandparent or older friend reading a newspaper at arm's length because of presbyopia. Also, if you now wear glasses for

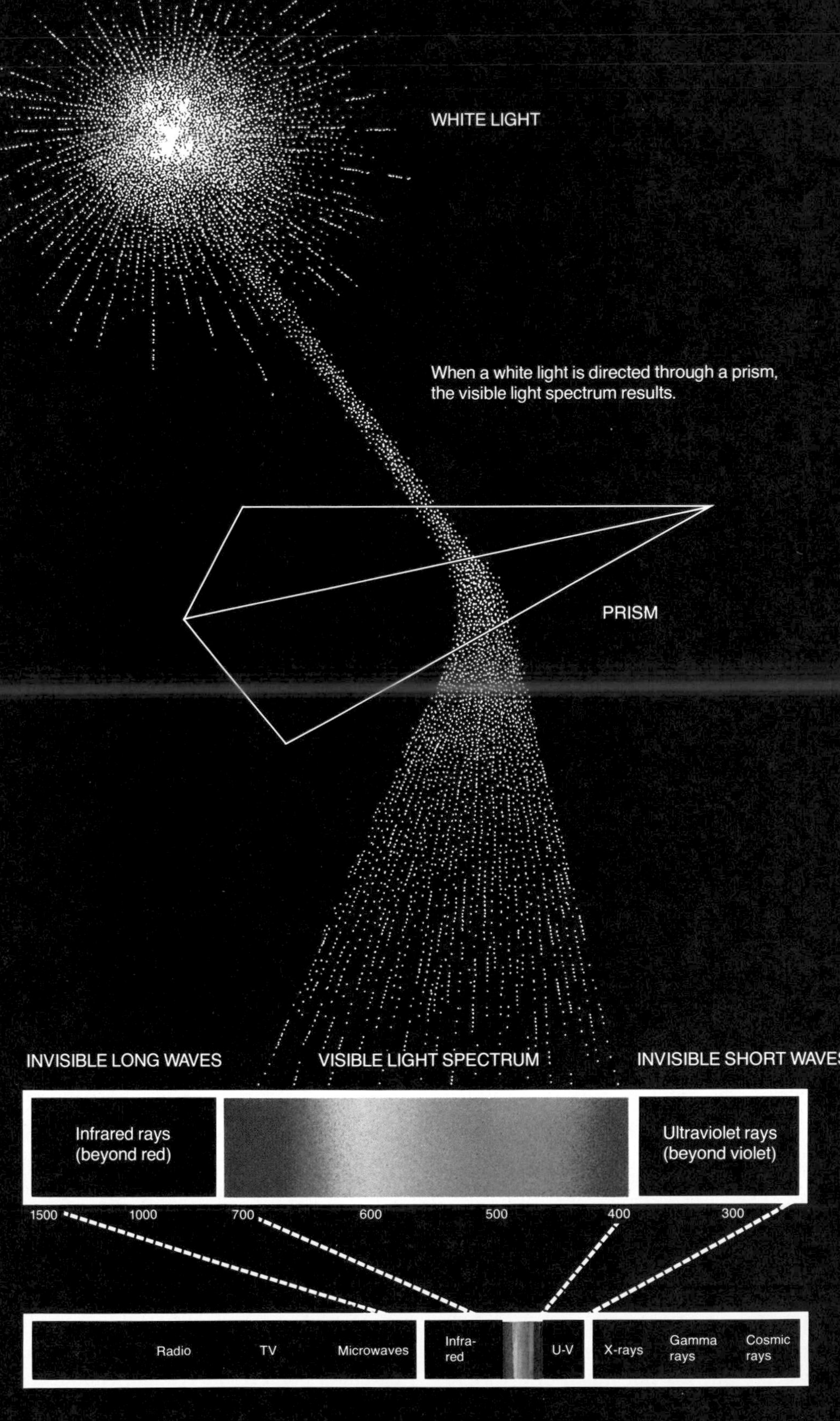

Fig. 4–2 *The visible spectrum.*

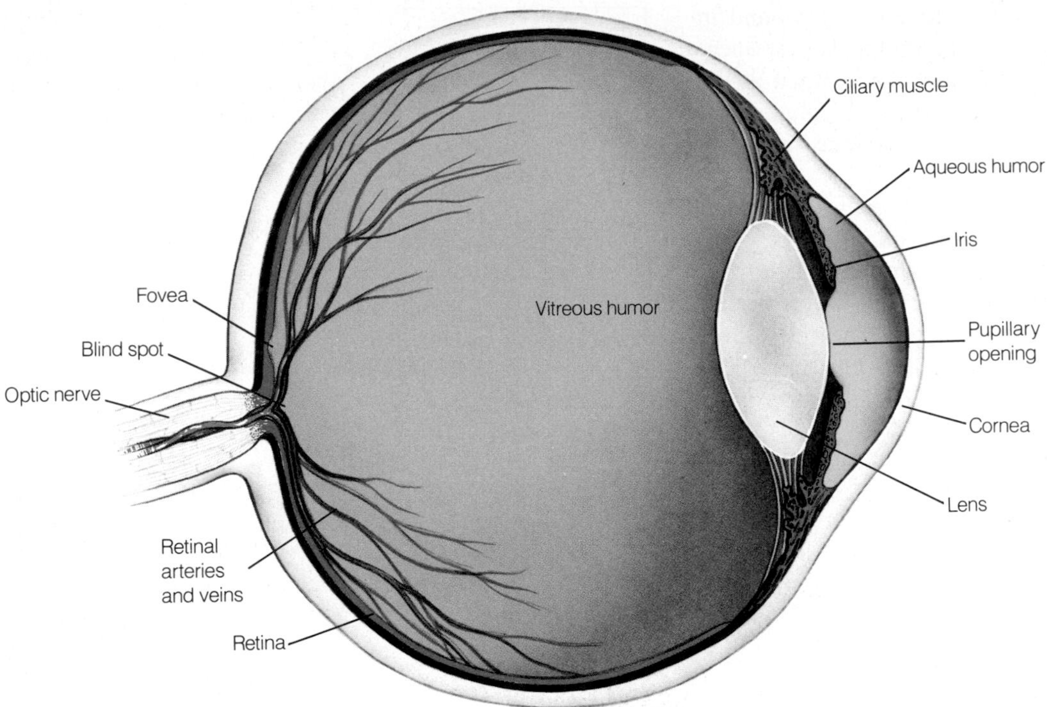

Fig. 4–3 *The human eye, a simplified view.*

nearsightedness, you may need bifocals as you age. Bifocal lenses correct near vision *and* distance vision.

Light Control There is one more major similarity between the eye and a camera. In front of the lens in both is a mechanism to control the amount of light entering. This mechanism in a camera is the diaphragm; in the eye it is the **iris** (Fig. 4–5). The iris is a colored circular muscle that expands and contracts to control the size of the **pupil,** the opening at the center of the eye.

The iris is quite important for normal vision. The retina can adapt to changing light conditions, but only very slowly. By making rapid adjustments, the iris allows us to move quickly from darkness to bright sunlight, or the

Fig. 4–4 *Visual defects and corrective lenses: (a) A myopic (longer than usual) eye. The concave lens spreads light rays just enough to increase the eye's focal length. (b) A hyperopic (shorter than usual) eye. The convex lens increases refraction (bending), returning the point of focus to the retina. (c) An astigmatic (lens or cornea not symmetrical) eye. In astigmatism, parts of vision are sharp and parts are unfocused. Lenses to correct astigmatism are non-symmetrical.*

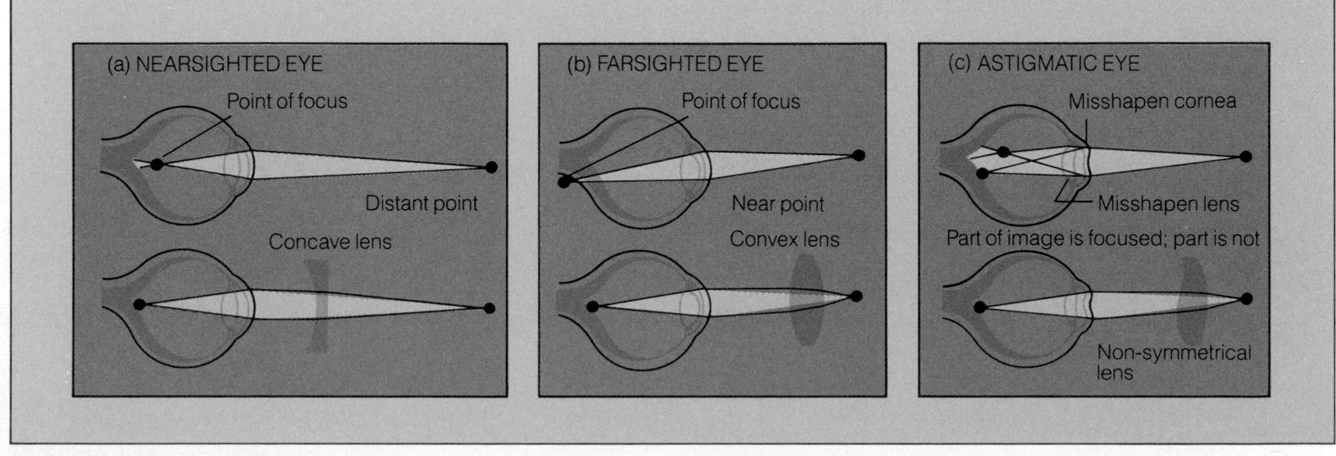

reverse. In dim light the pupils **dilate** (enlarge), and in bright light they **constrict** (narrow). At the largest opening of the iris, the pupil is 17 times larger than at the smallest. Were it not for this, you would be blinded for quite some time upon walking into a darkened room.

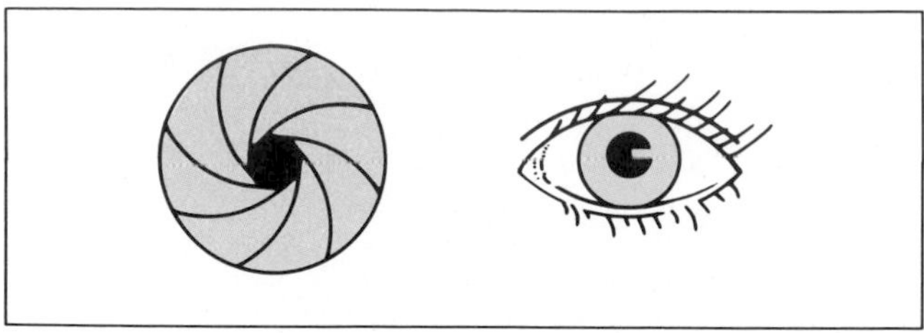

Fig. 4–5 *The diaphragm and iris*

Rods and Cones At this point, our eye-camera comparison breaks down. From the retina on, vision becomes a complex system for analyzing patterns of light (see Highlight 4–2). Besides, the eye would make a very strange camera. First of all, the eye has two types of "film," consisting of receptor cells called **rods** and **cones.** The cones, numbering about 6.5 million in each eye, work

HIGHLIGHT 4–2
How the Brain Sees the World

Early ideas of vision often assumed an almost movielike projection of "pictures" to the brain. But as mentioned in Chapter 3, this mistaken notion immediately raises the question, Who's watching the movie? Thanks to the Nobel Prize–winning work of psychobiologists David Hubel and Torsten Wiesel, we now know that vision acts more like a computer than like a television or movie camera.

Hubel and Wiesel directly recorded the activities of single cells in the visual cortex of the brain. As they did, they noted the area of the retina to which each cell responded. Then they shone lights of various sizes and shapes on the retina and recorded how often the corresponding brain cell fired nerve impulses (Figure 4–6).

The results were fascinating. Many brain cells responded only to lines of a certain width or orientation. These same cells didn't get the least bit "excited" over a dot of light or overall illumination. Other cells responded only to lines at certain angles, or lines of certain lengths, or lines moving in a particular direction (Hubel, 1979; Hubel & Wiesel, 1979).

The upshot of such findings is that cells in the brain, like the frog's retina described earlier, act as feature detectors. The brain seems to first analyze incoming information into lines, angles, shading, movement, and other basic features. Then, other brain areas combine these features into meaningful visual experiences. (This concept is discussed further in Chapter 5.) Reading the letters on this page is a direct result of such feature analysis. Given the size of the task, it's little wonder that as much as 30 percent of the human brain may be involved in vision.

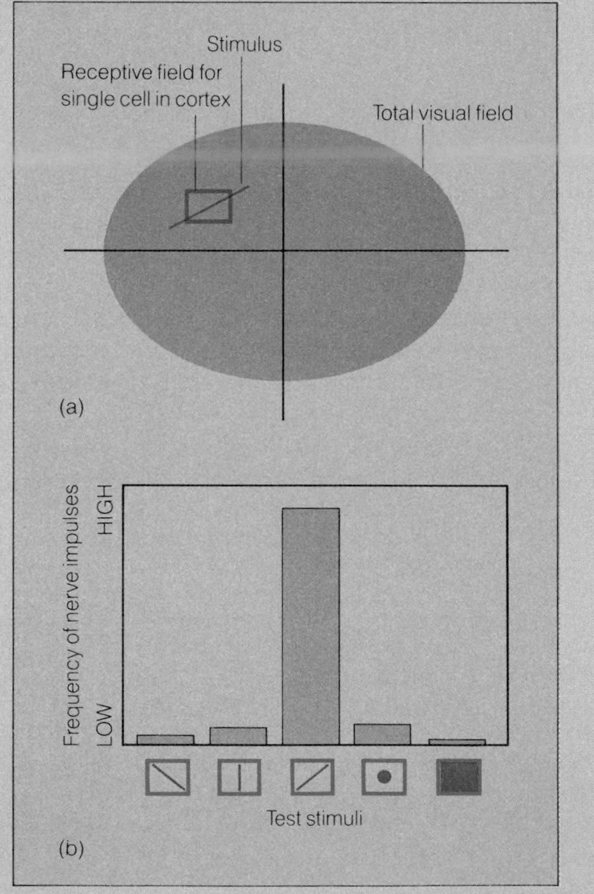

Fig. 4–6 *The top drawing (a) shows how much of the total field of vision a "typical" brain cell responds to. The bar graph below (b) illustrates how a brain cell may act as a feature detector. Notice how the cell primarily responds to just one type of stimulus. (Adapted from Hubel, 1979.)*

best in bright light. They also produce *color* sensations and pick up fine details. In contrast, the rods, numbering about 100 million, are unable to detect colors. Pure rod vision is *black and white*. However, the rods are much more sensitive to light than the cones are. The rods therefore allow us to see in very dim light.

Compared to the film in a camera, the visual receptors are backward. The rods and cones point toward the *back* of the eye, away from incoming light (Fig. 4–7). In addition, the "film" has a hole in it. Each eye has a **blind spot** because there are no receptors where the optic nerve leaves the eye (Fig. 4–8). And last, the eye is constantly in motion. This would be disastrous for a camera, but as we shall see later, it is essential for normal vision.

Question: Are there other differences between the rods and cones?

Visual Acuity The cones lie mainly at the center of the eye. In fact, there is a small cup-shaped area in the middle of the retina called the **fovea** (FOE-vee-ah) that contains *only* cones—about 50,000 of them. If you look at your thumbnail at arm's length, its image just about covers the fovea. Like a newspaper photograph made of many small dots, the tightly packed cones of the fovea produce the greatest visual **acuity,** or sharpness. In other words, vision is sharpest when an image falls on the fovea. Acuity steadily decreases as images are moved to the edge of the retina.

Figure 4–9 describes a widely used rating system for acuity. If vision can be corrected to no better than 20/200 acuity, a person is considered legally blind. With 20/200 vision, the world is seen as nothing but a blur.

Question: What is the purpose of the rest of the retina?

Peripheral Vision Areas outside the fovea also get light, creating a large region of **peripheral** (side) **vision.** The rods are most numerous about 20 degrees from the center of the retina, so much peripheral vision is rod vision. Fortunately, the rods are quite sensitive to *movement*. Thus, while the eye gives its best acuity to the center of vision, it maintains a radarlike scan for movement in side vision. Seeing "out of the corner of the eye" is important for sports, driving, and walking down dark alleys. Those who have lost peripheral vision suffer from **tunnel vision,** a condition much like wearing blinders.

Sailors, pilots, astronomers, and military spotters have long made use of another interesting fact about peripheral vision. Although the rods give poor acuity, they are many

Fig. 4–7 *Anatomy of the retina, light-sensitive element of the eye. Note that light does not fall directly on the rods and cones. It must first pass through the outer layers of the retina. Only about one-half of the light falling on the front of the eye reaches the rods and cones—testimony to the eye's amazing light sensitivity. The rods and cones are much smaller than implied here. The smallest receptors are 1 micron (one-millionth of a meter) wide.*

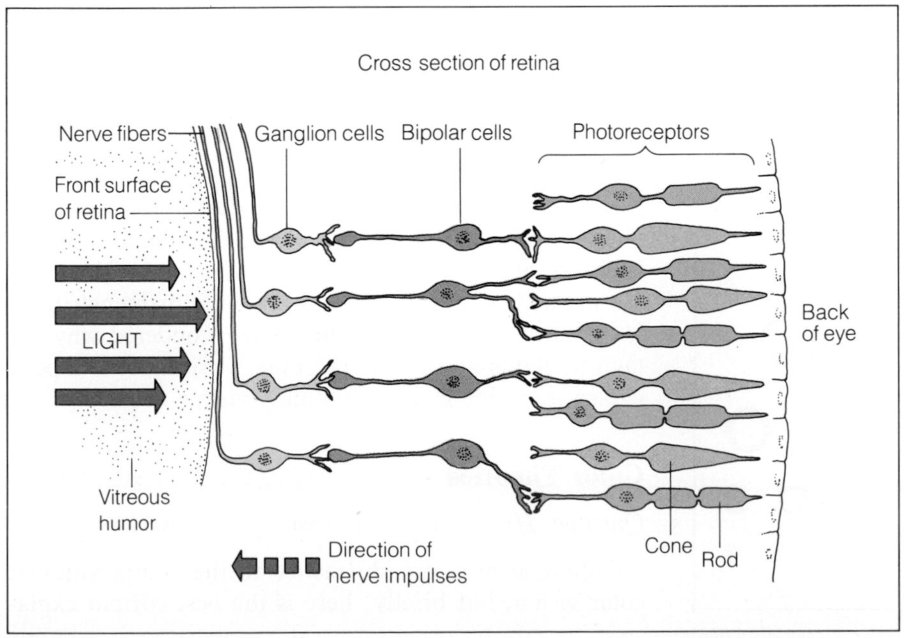

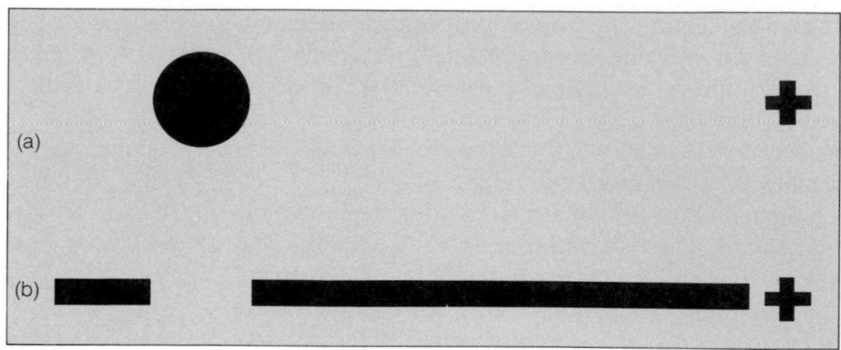

Fig. 4–8 *Experiencing the blind spot. (a) With the right eye closed, stare at the upper right cross. Hold the book about 1 foot from your eye and slowly move it back and forth. You should be able to locate a position that causes the black spot to disappear. When it does, it has fallen on the blind spot. (b) Repeat the procedure described, but stare at the lower cross. When the white space falls on the blind spot, the black line will appear to be continuous. This may help you understand why you do not usually experience a blind spot in your visual field.*

times more responsive to light than the cones are. Since most rods are 20 degrees to each side of the fovea, the best night vision is obtained by looking *next to* an object you wish to see. Test this yourself some night by looking at, and next to, a very dim star.

Fig. 4–9 *Tests of visual acuity. Here are some common tests of visual acuity. In (a), sharpness is indicated by the smallest grating still seen as individual lines. Part (b) requires that you read rows of letters of diminishing size until you can no longer distinguish them. The Landolt rings (c) require no familiarity with letters. All that is required is a report of which side has a break in it. Normal acuity is designated as 20/20 vision: At 20 feet in distance, you can distinguish what the average person can see at 20 feet. If your vision is 20/40, you can only see at 20 feet what the average person can see at 40 feet. If your vision is 20/200, you need glasses! Vision that is 20/12 would mean that you can see at 20 feet what the average person must be 8 feet nearer to see, indicating better than average acuity. American astronaut Gordon Cooper, who claimed to see railroad lines in northern India from 100 miles above, had 20/12 acuity.*

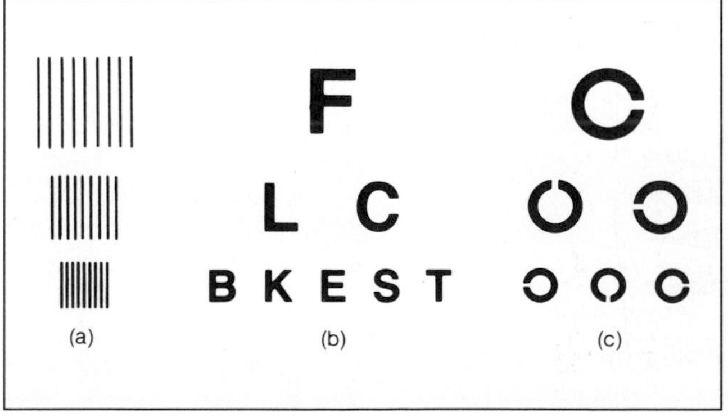

Color Vision—There's More to It Than Meets the Eye

What would you say is the brightest color? Red? Yellow? Blue? Actually, there are two answers to this question, one for the rods and one for the cones. The rods and cones differ in *maximal color sensitivity,* a difference that has practical importance. The cones are most sensitive to the *yellowish green* region of the spectrum. In other words, if all colors are tested in daylight (with each reflecting the same total amount of light) then yellowish green appears *brightest.* The increased use of yellow fire trucks and of Day-Glo yellow vests worn by roadside work crews reflects this fact (Fig. 4–10).

Question: To what color are the rods most sensitive?

Remember that the rods do not produce color sensations. If very dim colored lights are used, no color will be seen. Even so, one light will appear brighter than the others. When tested this way, the rods are most sensitive to *blue-green* lights. Thus, at night or in dim light, when rod vision prevails, the brightest-colored light will be one that is blue or blue-green. For this reason, police and highway patrol cars in many states now have blue emergency lights for night work. Also, you may have wondered why the taxiway lights at airports are blue. It seems like a poor choice, but blue is actually highly visible to pilots.

Color Theories

Question: How do the cones record color sensations?

No short answer can do justice to the complexities of color vision, but briefly, here is the best current expla-

Fig. 4–10 *Yellow-green fire trucks are far more visible in daylight because their color matches the cones' sensitivity peak. However, many cities continue to prefer red trucks because of tradition.*

nation. The **trichromatic theory** (TRY-kro-MAT-ik) of color vision holds that there are three types of cones, each most sensitive to a specific color: red, green, or blue. Other colors are assumed to result from combinations of these three, whereas black and white sensations are produced by the rods.

A basic problem with the trichromatic theory is that four colors seem psychologically primary: red, green, blue, and yellow. A second view, known as the **opponent-process theory,** attempts to explain why you can't have a reddish green or a yellowish blue. According to this theory, the visual system analyzes color into "either-or" messages. It is assumed that the visual system can produce messages for either red or green, yellow or blue, black or white. Coding one color in a pair (red, for instance) seems to block the opposite message (green), so a reddish green is impossible, but a yellowish red (orange) can occur.

According to opponent-process theory, fatigue caused by making one response produces an **afterimage** of the opposite color as the system recovers. To see an afterimage of this type, look at Figure 4–11 and follow the instructions given there.

Question: Which color theory is correct?

Fig. 4–11 *Negative afterimages. Stare at the dot near the middle of the flag for at least 30 seconds. Then look immediately at a plain sheet of white paper or a white wall. You will see the American flag in its normal colors. Reduced sensitivity in yellow, green, and black receptors in the eye, caused by prolonged staring, results in the appearance of complementary colors. Project the afterimage of the flag on other colored surfaces to get additional effects.*

Both! The three-color theory applies to the retina, where three types of light-sensitive **visual pigments** have been found. As predicted, each pigment is most sensitive to a different wavelength of light. The three peaks of sensitivity fall in roughly the red, green, and blue regions. As a result, the three types of cones fire nerve impulses at different rates when various colors are viewed (Fig. 4–12). In further support of the three-color theory, researchers recently confirmed that each cone contains only one pigment and that each pigment is controlled by its own gene (Nathan et al., 1986).

In contrast, the opponent-process theory seems to explain events recorded in the optic pathways *after* information leaves the eye. So both theories appear to be correct at a particular level in the visual system.

Color Blindness and Color Weakness

Do you know anyone who regularly draws hoots or laughter by wearing clothes of wildly clashing colors? Or someone who sheepishly tries to avoid saying what color an object is? If so, you probably know someone who is color-blind.

Fig. 4–12 *Firing rates of blue, green, and red cones in response to different colors. The larger the colored circle, the higher the firing rates. Colors are coded by activity in all three types of cones in the normal eye. (Adapted from Goldstein, 1984.)*

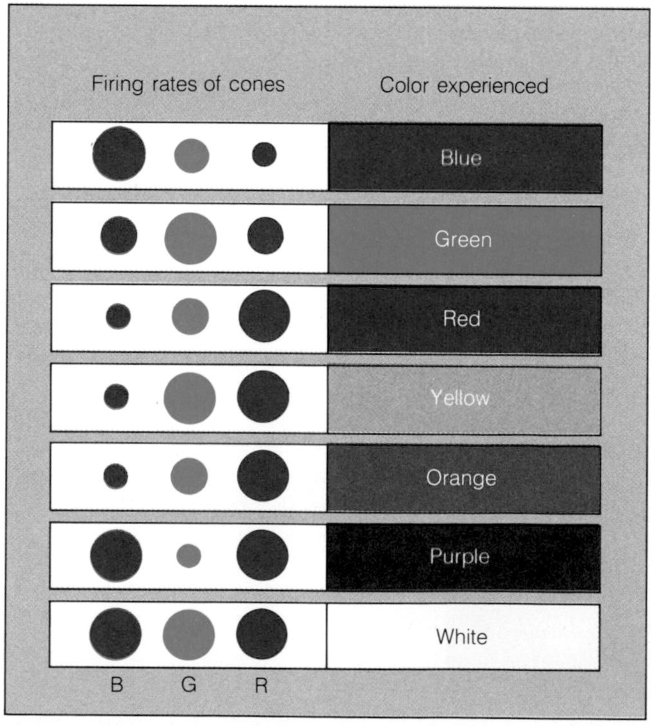

Question: What is it like to be color-blind? What causes color blindness?

A person who is completely **color-blind** sees the world as if it were a black and white movie. How do we know? In a few rare cases, people have been color-blind in only one eye and can compare (Hsia & Graham, 1965). Two colors of equal brightness look exactly alike to the color-blind individual. The color-blind person either lacks cones or has cones that do not function normally (Rushton, 1975).

Total color blindness is rare. **Color weakness,** or partial color blindness, is more common. Approximately 8 percent of the male population (but less than 1 percent of women) are red-green color-blind. (Another form of color weakness, involving yellow and blue, is extremely rare.)

Color blindness is caused by changes in the genes that control red, green, and blue pigments in the cones (Nathans et al., 1986). Red-green color blindness is a recessive, sex-linked trait. This means that it is carried on the *X*, or female, chromosome. Women have two *X* chromosomes, so if they receive only one defective color gene, they still have normal vision. Color-blind men, however, have only one *X* chromosome, so they can inherit the defect from their mothers (who are usually not color-blind themselves). The red-green color-blind individual sees both reds and greens as the same color, usually a yellowish brown (Rushton, 1975) (see Fig. 4–13).

Question: Then how can color-blind individuals drive? Don't they have trouble with traffic lights?

Red-green color-blind individuals have normal vision for yellow and blue, so their main problem is telling red lights from green. In practice, this is not difficult. In the United States, the red light is always on top, and the green light is brighter than the red. Also, to help remedy this problem, most modern traffic signals have a "red" light that has a background of yellow light mixed with it, and a "green" light that is really blue-green.

Question: How can a person tell if he or she is color-blind?

A common test for color blindness and weakness is the **Ishihara** test. In the test, numbers and other designs made of dots are placed on a background also made of dots. The background and the numbers are of different colors (red and green, for example). A person who is color-blind sees only a collection of dots. The person with normal color vision can detect the presence of the numbers or designs. Figure 4–14 is a replica of the Ishihara test. You should not consider Figure 4–14 a true test of color vision, but it may give you some idea of whether or not you are color-blind.

(a) (b) (c)

Fig. 4–13 *Color blindness and color weakness. (a) Photograph illustrates normal color vision. (b) Photograph is printed in blue and yellow and gives an impression of what a red-green color-blind person sees. (c) Photograph simulates total color blindness.*

Dark Adaptation—Let There Be Light!

Question: What happens to the eyes when they adapt to a dark room?

Dark adaptation is the dramatic increase in light sensitivity that occurs after entering the dark. Consider walking into a theater. If you enter from a brightly lighted lobby, you practically need to be led to your seat. After a short time, however, you can see the entire room in detail (including the couple kissing over in the corner). Studies of dark adaptation show that it takes about 30 to 35 minutes of complete darkness to reach maximum visual sensitivity (Fig. 4–15). When dark adaptation is complete, the eye can detect lights 10,000 times weaker than those to which it was originally sensitive.

Question: What causes dark adaptation?

Like the cones, the rods also contain a light-sensitive **visual pigment.** When struck by light, visual pigments bleach, or break down chemically. (The afterimages caused by flashbulbs are a direct result of this bleaching.) To restore light sensitivity, the visual pigments must recombine, which takes time. Night vision is due mainly to an increase of the rod pigment, **rhodopsin** (row-DOP-sin). When completely dark-adapted, the human eye is almost as sensitive to light as the eye of an owl.

Before artificial lighting, gradual adaptation at sunset posed few problems. Now we are often caught in temporary semiblindness. Usually this isn't dangerous, but it can be. Even though dark adaptation takes a long time, it can be wiped out by just a few seconds of viewing bright light. Try this demonstration:

See (and Don't See) for Yourself

Spend 15 or 20 minutes in a darkened room. At the end of this time, you should be able to see clearly. Now, close your left eye and cover it tightly with your hand. Turn on a bright light for 1 or 2 seconds and look at it with your right eye. With the light off again, compare the vision in your two eyes, first opening one and then the other. You will be completely blinded in your right eye.

This experience should convince you of the wisdom of the warning to avoid looking at the headlights of approaching cars during night driving. Under normal conditions, glare recovery takes about 20 seconds, plenty of time for an accident. After a few drinks, it may take 30 to 50 percent longer, because alcohol dilates the pupils, allowing more light to enter.

Question: Is there any way to speed up dark adaptation?

The rods are *insensitive* to extremely red light. To take advantage of this lack of sensitivity, submarines and airplane cockpits are illuminated with red light. So are the ready rooms for fighter pilots and ground crews (Fig. 4–16). In each case, this allows people to move quickly into the dark without having to adapt. Because the red light doesn't stimulate the rods, it is as if they had already spent time in the dark.

Question: Can eating carrots really improve vision?

One of the "ingredients" of rhodopsin is **retinal,** which

ARE YOU COLOR BLIND?

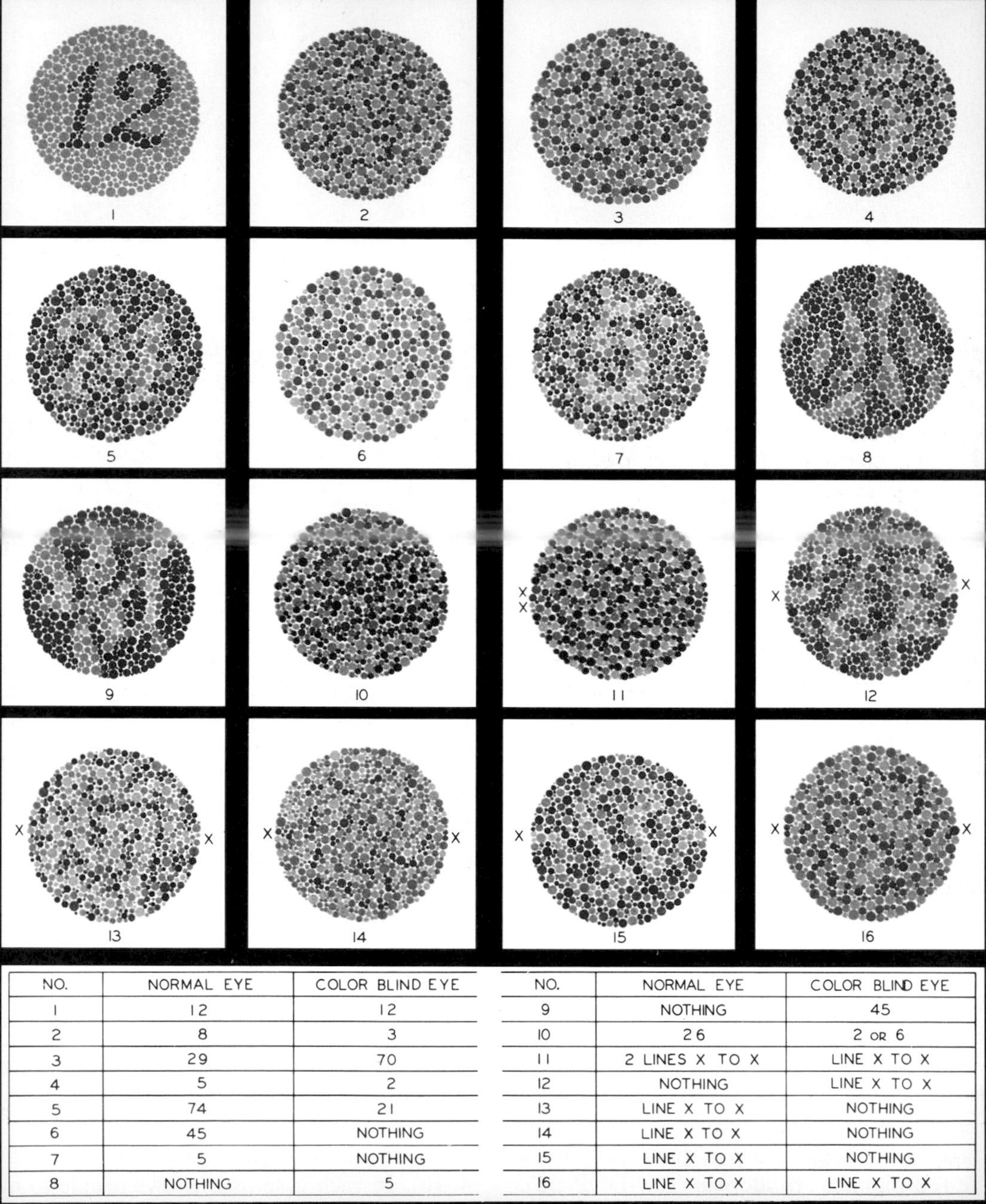

NO.	NORMAL EYE	COLOR BLIND EYE	NO.	NORMAL EYE	COLOR BLIND EYE
1	12	12	9	NOTHING	45
2	8	3	10	26	2 OR 6
3	29	70	11	2 LINES X TO X	LINE X TO X
4	5	2	12	NOTHING	LINE X TO X
5	74	21	13	LINE X TO X	NOTHING
6	45	NOTHING	14	LINE X TO X	NOTHING
7	5	NOTHING	15	LINE X TO X	NOTHING
8	NOTHING	5	16	LINE X TO X	LINE X TO X

Fig. 4–14 *Replica of a test for color blindness.*

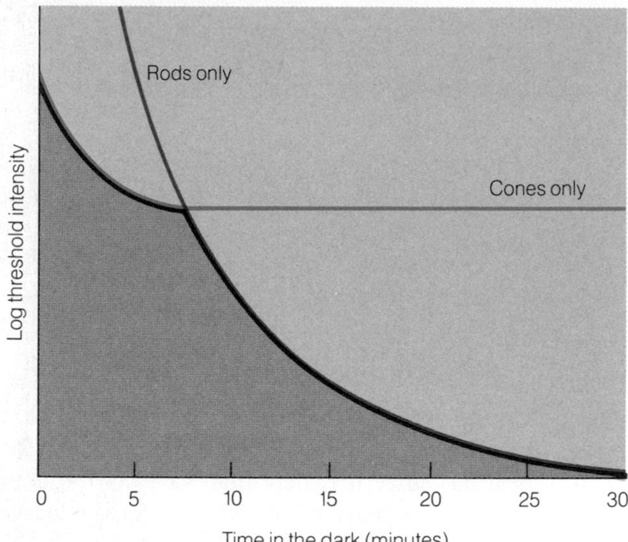

Fig. 4–15 *Typical course of dark adaptation. The black line shows how the threshold for vision lowers as a person spends time in the dark. (A lower threshold means that less light is needed for vision.) The green line shows that the cones adapt first, but they soon cease adding to light sensitivity. Rods, shown by the red line, adapt more slowly. However, they continue to add to improved night vision long after the cones are fully adapted.*

Fig. 4–16 *Red light allows dark adaptation to occur because it provides little or no stimulation to the rods.*

the body makes from vitamin A. When too little vitamin A is available, less rhodopsin is produced. Thus, a person lacking vitamin A may develop **night blindness.** In night blindness, the person sees normally in bright light while using the cones, but becomes totally blind at night when the rods must function. Carrots are an excellent source of vitamin A, so they could improve night vision for someone suffering a deficiency, but not the vision of anyone with an adequate diet (Carlson, 1981).

Learning Check

After such an extended discussion of vision, you may find it helpful to review the following questions.

1. The ____________ ____________ is made up of electromagnetic radiation with wavelengths between 400 and 700 nanometers.

2. *Match:*

____ Myopia	**A.**	Farsightedness
____ Hyperopia	**B.**	Elongated eye
____ Presbyopia	**C.**	Farsightedness due to aging
____ Astigmatism	**D.**	Lack of cones in fovea
	E.	Misshapen cornea or lens

3. In dim light, vision depends mainly on the ____________; color and fine detail are produced by the ____________.

4. The fovea has the greatest visual acuity because of the large concentration of rods found there. T or F?

5. Hubel and Wiesel found that cells in the visual cortex of the brain function as ____________ ____________.

6. The term 20/20 vision means that a person can see at 20 feet what can normally be seen from 20 feet. T or F?

7. When using the cones, the most visible color is
a. reddish orange *b.* blue-green *c.* yellow-orange *d.* yellowish green

8. The eyes become more sensitive to light at night because of a process known as ____________ ____________.

Answers:
1. visible spectrum **2.** B, A, C, E **3.** rods, cones **4.** F **5.** feature detectors **6.** T **7.** *d* **8.** dark adaptation

Hearing—Good Vibrations

Rock, classical, jazz, country, pop—whatever your musical taste, you have probably been moved or soothed by the riches of sound. Hearing also provides the brain with a wealth of information not available through the other senses, such as the approach of an unseen car or the information imparted by spoken language.

Question: What is the stimulus for hearing?

If you throw a stone into a quiet pond, a circle of waves will spread in all directions. In much the same way, sound travels as a series of invisible waves of **compression** (peaks) and **rarefaction** (RARE-eh-fak-shun: valleys) in the air. Any vibrating object—a tuning fork, the string of a musical instrument, or the vocal cords—will produce **sound waves** by setting air molecules in motion. Other materials, such as fluids or solids, will also carry sound. But sound does not travel in a vacuum. Movies that show characters reacting to the "roar" of alien starships or to titanic battles in deep space are in error.

The **frequency** of sound waves (the number of waves per second) corresponds to the perceived **pitch** of a sound. The **amplitude,** or physical "height," of a sound wave tells how much energy it contains. Psychologically, amplitude corresponds to sensed **loudness** (Fig. 4–17).

Question: How are sounds converted to nerve impulses?

What we call the "ear" is only the **pinna** (PIN-ah), or visible, external part of the ear. In addition to being a good place to hang earrings or balance pencils, the pinna acts like a funnel to concentrate sounds. After they are guided into the ear, sound waves collide with the **eardrum (tympanic membrane),** which is like a tight drumhead within the ear canal. The sound waves set the eardrum in motion. This, in turn, causes three small bones called the **auditory ossicles** (OSS-ih-kuls) to vibrate (Fig. 4–18). The third ossicle is attached to a second membrane, or drumhead, called the **oval window.** As the oval window moves back and forth, it makes waves in a fluid within the **cochlea** (KOCK-lee-ah). The cochlea is really the organ of hearing, since it is here that waves in the fluid are detected by tiny **hair cells,** which generate nerve impulses to be sent to the brain.

Question: How are higher and lower sounds detected?

The **frequency theory** of hearing states that as pitch rises, nerve impulses of the same frequency are fed into the auditory nerve. This explains how sounds up to about 4000 hertz reach the brain. But higher tones require a different explanation. The **place theory** of hearing states that high tones register most strongly at the base of the cochlea (near the oval window). Lower tones, on the other hand, mostly move hair cells near the outer tip of the cochlea. Pitch is therefore signaled by the area of the cochlea most strongly activated. Place theory also explains why hunters sometimes lose hearing in a narrow pitch range. "Hunter's notch," as this is called, occurs

Fig. 4–17 *Waves of compression in the air, or vibrations, are the stimulus for hearing. The frequency of sound waves determines their pitch. The amplitude determines loudness.*

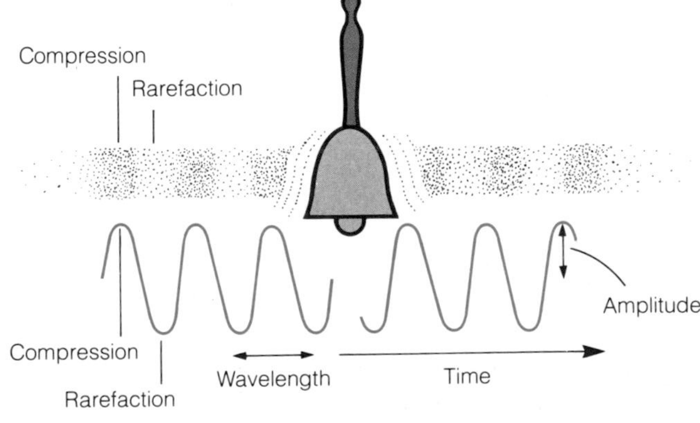

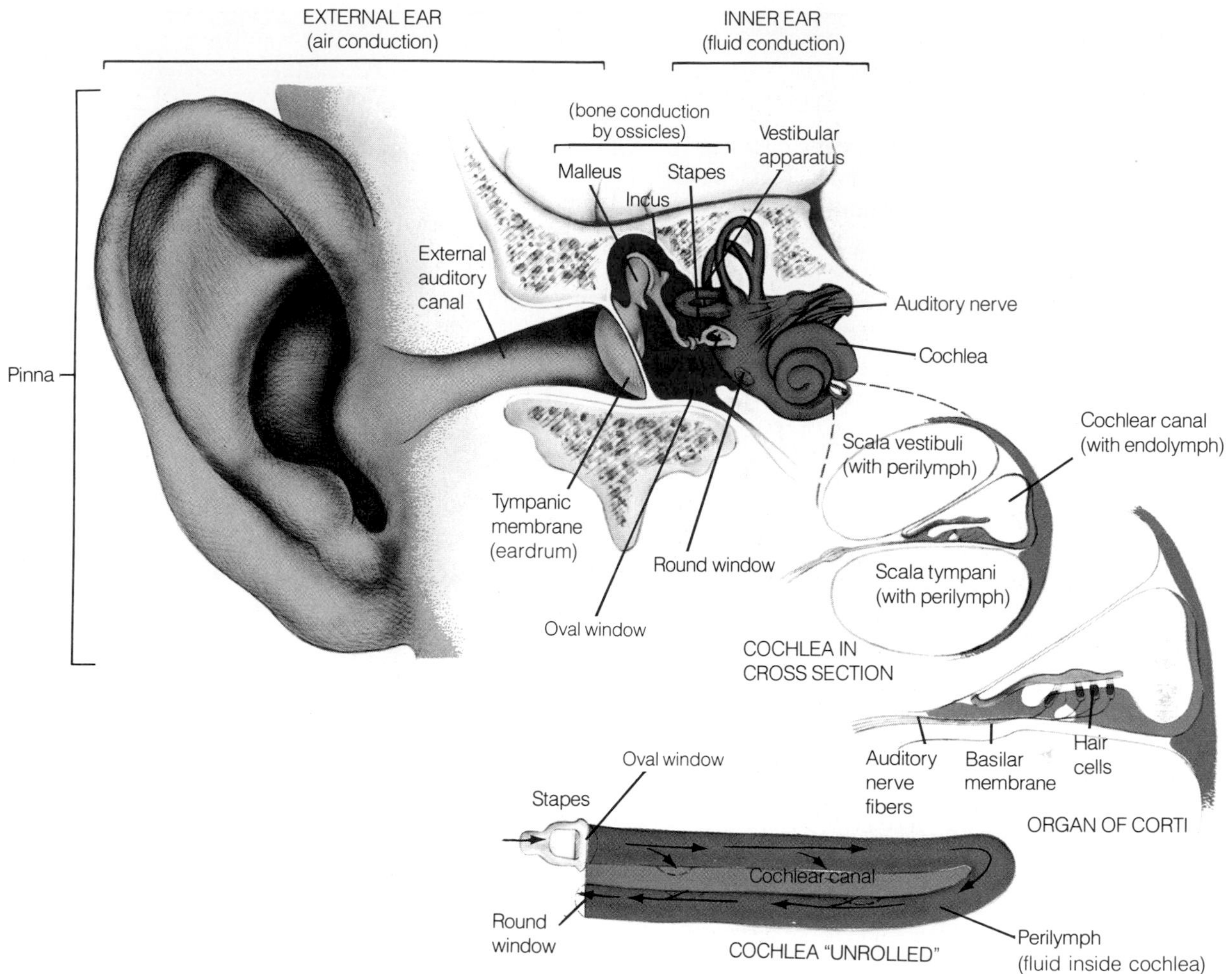

Fig. 4–18 *Anatomy of the ear. The entire ear is a mechanism for changing waves of air pressure into nerve impulses. Inset in foreground shows that as the stapes moves the oval window, the round window bulges outward, allowing waves to ripple through fluid in the cochlea. The waves move membranes near the hair cells, causing the cells to bend. The hair cells then generate nerve impulses carried to the brain. (See enlarged cross sections of cochlea.)*

when hair cells are damaged in the area activated by the pitch of gunfire.

Question: What causes other types of deafness?

Deafness There are three principal types of deafness. **Conduction deafness** occurs when the eardrums or ossicles are damaged or immobilized by disease or injury. Such damage reduces the transfer of sounds to the inner ear. In many cases, conduction deafness can be overcome by a hearing aid, which makes sounds louder and clearer.

Nerve deafness is a hearing loss resulting from damage to the hair cells or auditory nerve. Hearing aids are of no help in this case, because auditory messages are blocked from reaching the brain. However, a new artificial hearing system is making it possible for some persons with nerve deafness to break through the wall of silence (see Highlight 4–3).

A third problem, called **stimulation deafness,** is of special interest, because many jobs, hobbies, and pastimes can cause it. Stimulation deafness occurs when very loud sounds damage hair cells in the cochlea (as in hunter's notch). If you work in a noisy environment or enjoy loud music, motorcycling, snowmobiling, hunting, or similar pursuits, you may be risking stimulation deafness. The hair cells, which are about as thick as a cobweb, are very fragile and easily damaged.

HIGHLIGHT 4–3
Artificial Hearing

Researchers have recently found that in many cases of "nerve" deafness, the nerve is actually intact. This finding has spurred development of **cochlear implants** that bypass hair cells and stimulate the auditory nerves directly (Fig. 4–19).

As you can see, wires from a microphone carry electrical signals to an external coil. A matching coil under the skin picks up the signals and carries them to one or more areas of the cochlea. Early implants allowed patients to hear only low-frequency sounds, such as a dog's bark or the horn of a speeding car. Newer multichannel models make use of place theory to separate higher and lower tones. This has allowed some formerly deaf persons to hear human voices and other higher-frequency sounds (Baker, 1988; Franklin, 1984).

At present, artificial hearing remains crude. Most implant patients describe the sound as "like a radio that isn't quite tuned in." In fact, 30 percent of all adults who have tried implants have given up on them (Dreyfuss, 1985). But the implants are sure to improve. And even now, it is hard to argue with enthusiasts like Kristen Cloud. Shortly after Kristen received an implant, she was able to hear a siren and avoid being struck by a speeding car (Williams, 1984). She says simply, "The implant saved my life."

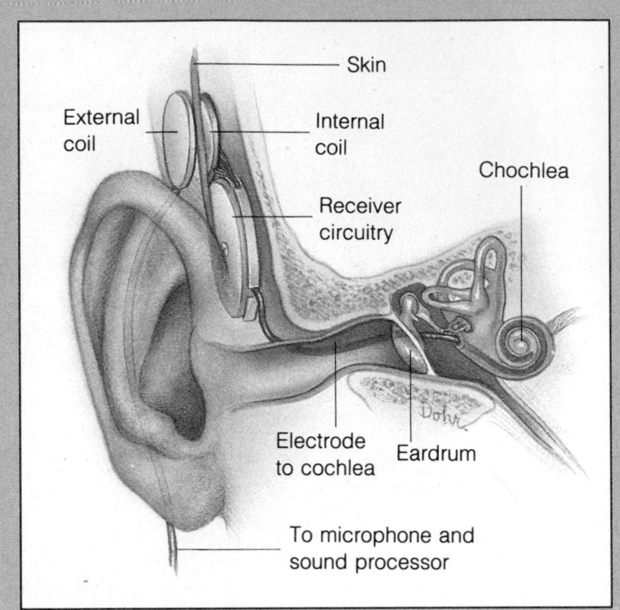

Fig. 4–19. *A cochlear implant, or "artificial ear."*

Question: How loud must a sound be to be hazardous?

The danger of hearing loss depends on both the loudness of sound and how long you are exposed to it. Daily exposure to 85 decibels or more may cause permanent hearing loss. Even short periods of 120 decibels (a rock concert) may cause a **temporary threshold shift,** or temporary loss of hearing. Brief exposure to 150 decibels (jet airplane nearby) can cause permanent deafness (Apfel, 1977; Lipscomb, 1974).

You might find it interesting to check the decibel ratings of some of your activities in Figure 4–20 as a way of estimating hearing risk. Don't be fooled by the numbers, though. Decibels are plotted on a logarithmic scale (like earthquake intensity!). Every 20 decibels increases the amount of energy in a sound by a factor of 10. In other words, a rock concert at 120 decibels is not just twice as powerful as a normal voice at 60 decibels. It is actually 1000 times stronger. This is why music, as well as noise, can do damage. People who sit directly in front of the speaker columns at highly amplified musical concerts run considerable risk of hearing loss. Rock musicians Neil Young and David Lee Roth have been sued by fans who claim their hearing was damaged at concerts. Walkman-style stereo headphones also present a danger. If you can hear the sound from the headset on the person standing next to you, the volume is probably damaging the user's ears.

If a ringing sensation known as **tinnitus** (tin-NYE-tus) follows exposure to loud sounds, chances are that hair cells have been damaged (Dunkle, 1982; McFadden & Wightman, 1983). Almost everyone has tinnitus at times, especially with increasing age. But after repeated sounds that produce this warning, you can expect to become permanently hard-of-hearing (Apfel, 1977). The next time you are exposed to a very loud sound, remember Figure 4–20 and take precautions against damage. (Remember, too, that for temporary ear protection, fingers are always handy.)

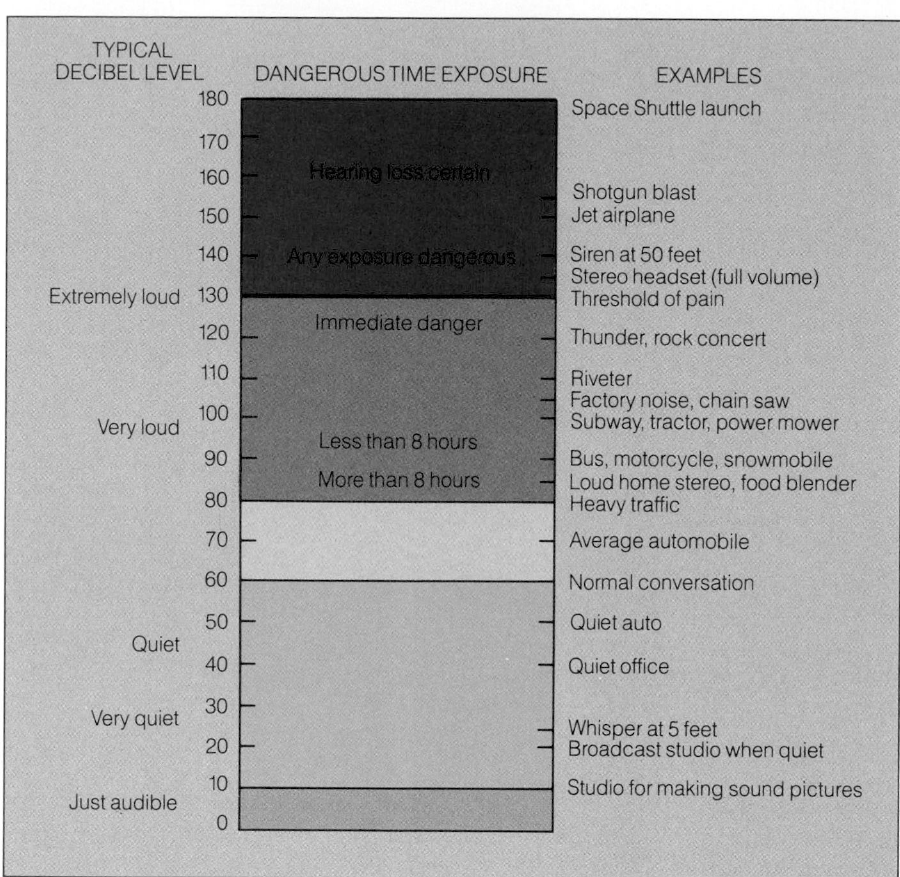

Fig. 4–20 *The loudness of sound is measured in decibels. Zero decibels is the faintest sound most people can hear. Sound in the range of 110 decibels is uncomfortably loud. Prolonged exposure to sounds above 85 decibels may damage the inner ear. Rock music, which may rate 120 decibels, is known to have caused hearing loss in musicians and may affect audiences as well. Sounds of 130 decibels pose an immediate danger to hearing.*

● Smell and Taste—The Nose Knows When the Tongue Can't Tell

Unless you are a wine taster, a perfume blender, a chef, or a gourmet, you may think of **olfaction** (smell) and **gustation** (taste) as least important among the senses. Certainly, a person could survive without these two **chemical senses.** Just the same, the chemical senses occasionally prevent poisonings, and they add pleasure to our lives every day. Let's see how they operate.

The Sense of Smell The receptors for smell respond primarily to gaseous molecules carried in the air. As air enters the nose, it passes over roughly 20 million nerve fibers embedded in the lining of the upper nasal passages. Airborne molecules passing over the exposed fibers trigger nerve signals that are sent to the brain (Fig. 4–21).

Question: How are different odors produced?

This is still something of a mystery. One hint comes from the fact that it is possible to develop a sort of "smell blindness" for a single odor. This loss, called an **anosmia** (an-NOSE-me-ah), suggests that there are specific receptors for different odors. Indeed, scientists have noticed that molecules having a particular odor are quite similar in shape. Specific shapes have been identified for the following odors: *floral* (flower-like), *camphoric* (camphor-like), *musky* (Have you ever smelled a sweaty musk ox?), *minty* (mint-like), and *etherish* (like ether or cleaning fluid). This does not mean, however, that there are different olfactory receptors comparable to the three types of cones in vision (Gesteland, 1986). Each receptor in the nose is probably sensitive to many molecules or combinations of molecules.

It is currently believed that there are different shaped "holes," or depressions, on the odor receptors. Like a piece fit in a puzzle, a molecule produces an odor when it matches up with a hole of the same shape. This is called the **lock and key theory.** Although there are some exceptions, the theory seems to explain many odors.

A recent large-scale test found that 1.2 percent of the population cannot smell at all (Gilbert & Wysocki, 1987). People with total anosmia typically find that olfaction is

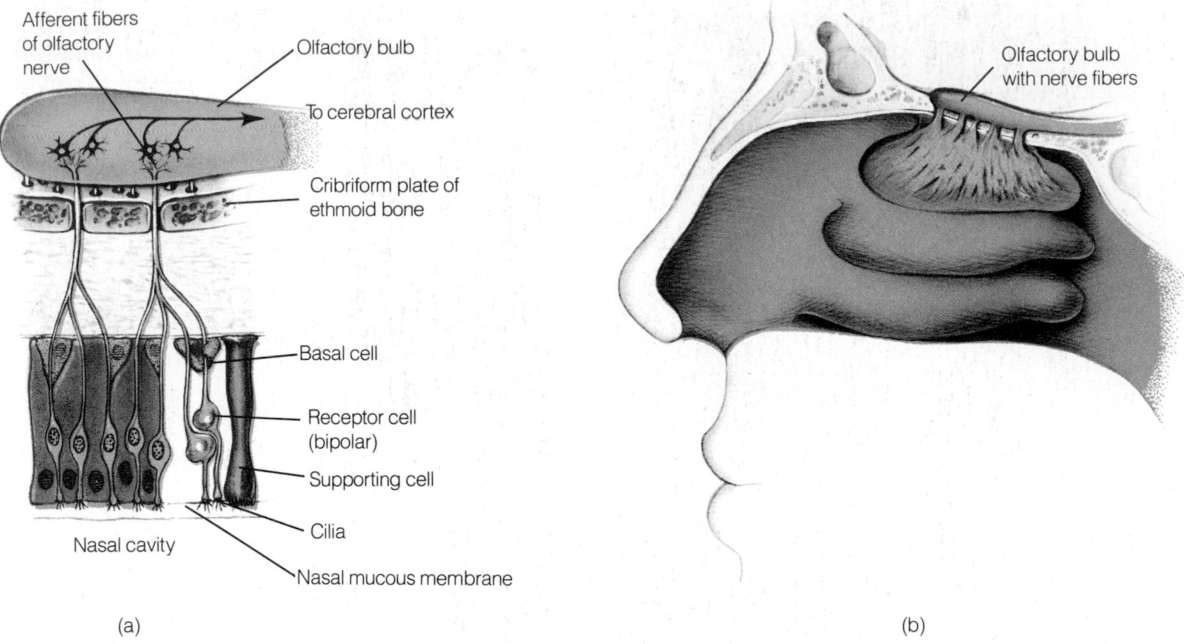

Fig. 4–21 *Receptors for the sense of smell (olfaction). Olfactory nerve fibers respond to gaseous molecules. Receptor cells are shown in cross section at left of part (a).*

not such a minor sense after all. One anosmic individual, for instance, failed to notice that his apartment building was on fire. He was awakened just in time by neighbors, not by the smell of smoke (Monmaney, 1987). Even in everyday terms, anosmia can be a real loss. Many anosmics are unable to cook, and they may be poisoned by spoiled food.

Question: What causes anosmia?

Risks include infections, allergies, and blows to the head (which may tear the olfactory nerves). Exposure to chemicals such as ammonia, photo-developing chemicals, and hair-dressing potions can also cause anosmia. If you value your sense of smell, be careful what you breathe.

Taste There are at least four basic taste sensations: *sweet, salt, sour,* and *bitter.* We are most sensitive to bitter, less sensitive to sour, even less sensitive to salt, and least sensitive to sweet. This order may have helped prevent poisonings when most humans foraged for food, because bitter and sour foods are more likely to be inedible.

Question: If there are only four tastes, how can there be so many different flavors?

Flavors seem more varied than suggested by the four taste qualities because we tend to include sensations of texture, temperature, smell, and even pain ("hot" chili peppers) along with taste. Smell is particularly important in determining flavor. Small bits of apple, potato, and onion "taste" almost exactly alike when the nose is plugged. It is probably no exaggeration to say that subjective flavor is one-half smell. This is why food loses its "taste" when you have a cold.

The four primary tastes are detected by **taste buds** located mainly on the top of the tongue, but also at other points inside the mouth (Fig. 4–22). As food is chewed, it dissolves and enters the taste buds, where it sets off nerve impulses to the brain. Like the skin senses, taste receptors are not equally distributed. Look at Figure 4–22 and you will see that some areas of the tongue are more sensitive to certain tastes than others.

Question: People seem to have very different tastes. Why is that?

Some differences are genetic. The chemical phenylthiocarbamine (FEEN-il-thi-oh-CAR-bah-meen), or PTC, tastes bitter to about 70 percent of those tested and has no taste for the other 30 percent. The sense of taste also varies with age. Taste cells have a life of only several days. With aging, cell replacement slows down, so the sense of taste diminishes (Beidler, 1963). This is why many foods you disliked in childhood have now become acceptable. Children who will not eat vegetables, spinach, liver, and so on, may be having a very different taste

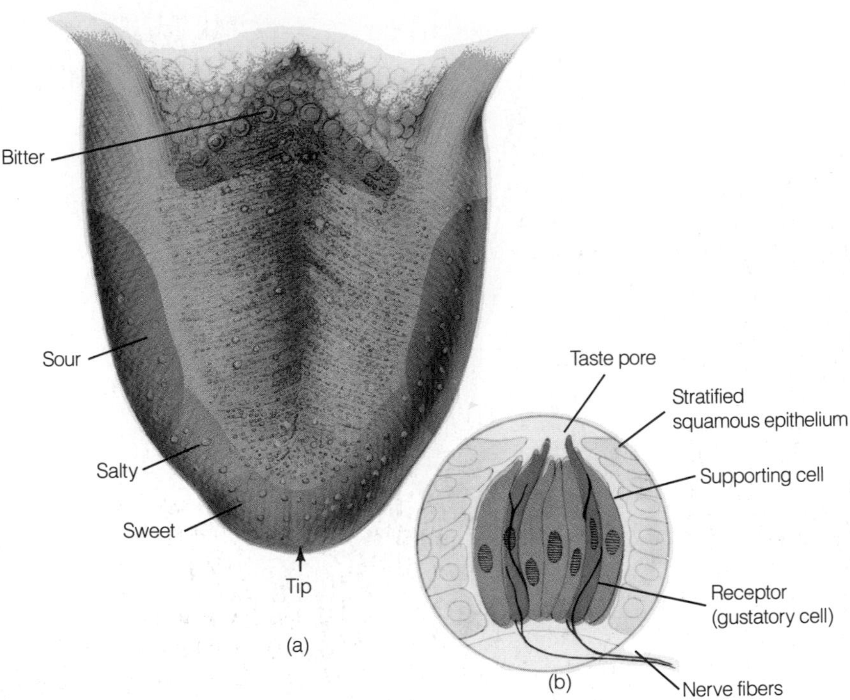

Fig. 4–22 *Receptors for taste: (a) Position of receptors (taste buds) especially sensitive to four taste qualities. (b) Detail of a taste bud within the tongue. The buds also occur in other parts of the digestive system.*

experience than the adult urging the child to eat. Aside from this fact, however, most taste preferences are acquired. Would you eat the coagulated secretion of the modified skin glands of a cow after it had undergone bacterial decomposition? If you would, you are a *cheese* fancier (Matthews & Knight, 1963)!

● The Somesthetic Senses—Flying by the Seat of Your Pants

A gymnast "flying" through a routine on the uneven bars may rely as much on the **somesthetic senses** as on vision. Even the most routine activities, such as walking, running, or passing a sobriety test, would be impossible without somesthetic information from the body.

Question: What are the somesthetic senses?

The somesthetic senses (*soma* means "body," *esthetic* means "feel") include the **skin senses** (touch), the **kinesthetic senses** (receptors in the muscles and joints that detect body position and movement), and the **vestibular senses** (receptors in the inner ear used to maintain balance). (The vestibular senses also contribute to motion sickness, as discussed in this chapter's Exploration.) Because of their importance, let us focus on the skin senses.

Skin receptors produce at least five different sensations: *light touch, pressure, pain, cold,* and *warmth.* Receptors with particular shapes appear to specialize somewhat in various sensations (Fig. 4–23). However, the surface of the eye, which only has free nerve endings, can produce all five sensations (Carlson, 1981). Altogether, the skin has about 200,000 nerve endings for temperature, 500,000 for touch and pressure, and 3 million for pain.

Question: Does the number of receptors in an area of skin relate to its sensitivity?

Yes. Your skin could be "mapped" by applying heat, cold, touch, pressure, or pain to points all over your body. Such testing would show that the skin receptors are found in varying numbers, and that sensitivity generally matches the number of receptors in a given area. As a rough-and-ready illustration, try this two-point touch test:

> The density of touch receptors on various body areas can be checked by having a friend apply two pencil points to the skin with varying distances between them. Without looking, you should respond "one" or "two" each time. Record the distance between the pencils each time you feel two points.

You should find that two points are recognizable when they are 1/10 inch apart on the fingertips, 1/4 inch on the

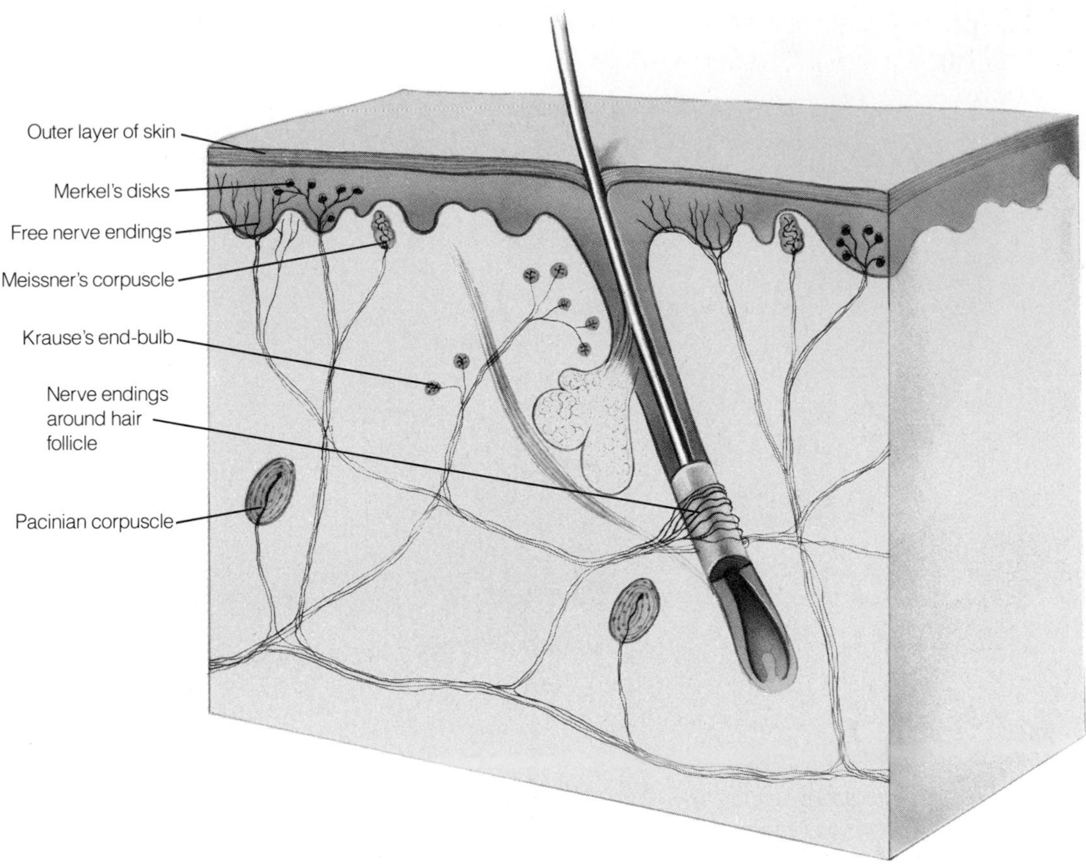

Fig. 4–23 *The skin senses include touch, pressure, pain, cold, and warmth. This drawing shows different forms the skin receptors can take. Other shapes were once recognized, but most turned out to be variations of the shapes shown. The only clearly specialized receptor is the Pacinian corpuscle, which is highly sensitive to pressure. Free nerve endings are receptors for pain and any of the other sensations. For reasons that are not clear, cold is sensed near the surface of the skin, and warmth is sensed deeper. (Carlson, 1981.)*

nose, and 3 inches at the middle of the back. Generally speaking, important areas such as the lips, tongue, face, hands, and genitals, have a higher density of receptors.

Question: There are many more pain receptors than other kinds. Why is pain so heavily represented, and does the concentration of pain receptors also vary?

Like the other skin senses, pain receptors vary in their distribution. There are an average of about 232 pain points per square centimeter behind the knee, 184 per centimeter on the buttocks (an area preferred by many parents for spankings), 60 on the pad of the thumb, and 44 on the tip of the nose (Geldard, 1972). (Is it better, then, to be pinched on the nose than behind the knee? It depends on what you like!)

Actually, there are two kinds of pain. Pain carried by *large* nerve fibers is sharp, bright, fast, and seems to come from specific body areas. This is the body's **warning system.** Give yourself a small jab with a pin and you will feel this type of pain. As you do this, notice that warning pain quickly disappears. Much as we may dislike warning pain, it is usually a signal that the body has been, or is about to be, damaged. Without warning pain, we would be unable to detect or prevent injury (Melzack & Dennis, 1978).

A second type of pain is carried by *small* nerve fibers. This type is slower, nagging, aching, widespread, and very unpleasant. It gets worse if the pain stimulus is repeated. This is the body's **reminding system** (Melzack & Dennis, 1978). A sad thing about the reminding system is that it often causes agony even when the reminder is useless, as in terminal cancer, or when pain continues after an injury has healed. Later in the chapter we will return to pain to learn how it can be controlled. If you got carried away with the pin demonstration, maybe you should read ahead now!

Adaptation, Attention, and Gating—Tuning In and Tuning Out

Each of the senses we have described is continuously active. Even so, many sensory events never reach awareness. One reason for this is *sensory adaptation,* a second is *selective attention,* and a third is *sensory gating.* Let's see how information is filtered by these processes.

Sensory Adaptation Think about walking into a house where fried fish, sauerkraut, and head cheese were prepared for dinner. (Some dinner!) You would probably pass out at the door, yet people who have been in the house for some time will be unaware of the food odors because of **sensory adaptation.** Sensory adaptation refers to a decrease in sensory response to a constant or unchanging stimulus.

Fortunately, the olfactory (smell) receptors are among the most quickly adapting. When exposed to a constant odor, they send fewer and fewer nerve impulses to the brain until the odor is no longer noticed. Adaptation to sensations of pressure from a wristwatch, waistband, ring, or glasses is based on the same principle. Sensory receptors generally respond best to *changes* in stimulation. As David Hubel says, "We need above all to know about changes; no one wants or needs to be reminded 16 hours a day that his shoes are on" (Hubel, 1979).

Question: If change is necessary to prevent sensory adaptation, why doesn't vision undergo adaptation like the sense of smell does? If you stare at something, it certainly doesn't go away.

The rods and cones, like other receptor cells, would respond less to a constant stimulus were it not for the fact that the eye normally makes thousands of tiny movements every minute. These movements are caused by tremors in the eye muscles known as **physiological nystagmus** (nis-TAG-mus). Although they are too small to be seen, these movements shift visual images from one receptor cell to another.

Constant shifting of the eyes ensures that images always fall on fresh, unfatigued receptors. Evidence for this comes from experiments in which subjects are fitted with a special contact lens that has a miniature slide projector attached to it (Fig. 4–24a). Since the projector follows the exact movements of the eye, an image can be stabilized on the retina. When this is done, projected geometric designs fade from view within a few seconds (Pritchard, 1961). You can get the same effect by staring at Figure 4–24b. Since the lighter circle does not form a distinct edge, the retina adapts to the brightness difference and the circle gradually disappears.

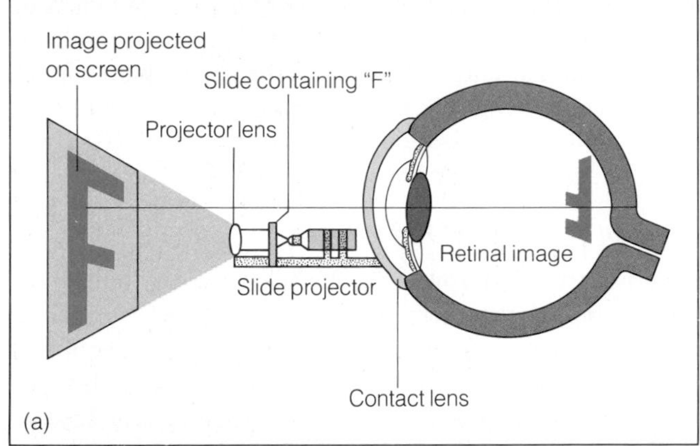

Fig. 4–24 *Stabilized images. (a) Miniature slide projector attached to a contact lens moves each time the eye moves. As a result, the projected image disappears in a few seconds because it does not move on the retina. (b) A similar effect occurs when changes in brightness do not define a distinct edge. In this case, eye movements cannot prevent adaptation. Therefore, if you stare at the dot, the lighter area will disappear. (After Cornsweet, 1970.)*

Selective Attention The so-called "seat-of-your-pants phenomenon" also relates to the functioning of sensory systems. As you sit reading this chapter, receptors for touch and pressure in the seat of your pants are sending nerve impulses to your brain. Even though these sensations have been present all along, you were probably not aware of them until just now. The seat-of-your-pants phenomenon is an example of **selective attention.** We are able to "tune in on" any of the many sensory messages bombarding us while excluding others. Another familiar example of this is the "cocktail party effect." When you are in a group of people, surrounded by voices, you can still select and attend to the voice of the person with whom you are conversing. Or if that person gets dull, you can eavesdrop on conversations all over the room. (Be sure to smile and nod your head occasionally!)

Question: What makes this possible?

Selective attention appears to be based on the ability of various brain structures to select and divert incoming sensory messages (see Chapter 3). But what about messages that haven't reached the brain? Is it possible that some are blocked while others are allowed to pass? Recent evidence suggests there are **sensory gates** that control the flow of incoming nerve impulses in just this way.

Compare:

Sensory adaptation A decline in the number of nerve impulses generated by sensory receptors exposed to an unchanging stimulus.

Selective attention Voluntarily focusing on a selected portion of sensory input, most likely by rerouting messages within the brain.

Sensory gating Alteration of incoming sensory messages in the spinal cord, before they reach the brain.

Sensory Gating of Pain A fascinating example of sensory gating is provided by Ronald Melzack and Patrick Wall, who are studying "pain gates" in the spinal cord (Melzack & Wall, 1983). Melzack and Wall noticed, as you may have, that one type of pain will sometimes cancel another. This suggests that pain messages from different nerve fibers pass through the same neural "gate" in the spinal cord. If the gate is "closed" by one pain message, other messages may not be able to pass through.

Question: How is the gate closed?

Messages carried by large, fast nerve fibers seem to close the spinal pain gate directly. Doing so can prevent slower, "reminding system" pain from reaching the brain. Pain clinics use this effect by applying a mild electrical current to the skin. Such stimulation, felt only as a mild tingling, can greatly reduce more agonizing pain (Melzack & Dennis, 1978).

Messages from small, slow fibers seem to take a different route. After going through the pain gate, they pass on to a "central biasing system" in the brain. Under some circumstances, the brain then sends a message back down the spinal cord, closing the pain gates (Melzack & Dennis, 1978). (See Fig. 4–25.) Melzack and Wall believe that this type of gating explains the painkilling effects of acupuncture (Fig. 4–26). As the acupuncturist's needles are twirled, heated, or electrified, they activate small pain fibers. These relay through the biasing system to close the gates to intense or chronic pain (Melzack & Wall, 1983).

Acupuncture has an interesting side effect not predicted by sensory gating. People given acupuncture often report feelings of light-headedness, relaxation, or euphoria. How are these feelings explained? The answer seems to lie in the body's newly discovered ability to produce opiate-like chemicals. To combat pain, the brain causes the pituitary gland to release a chemical called **beta-endorphin** (BAY-tah-en-DOR-fin: from *endo*, "within," and *orphin*, "opiate") which is similar to morphine (Snyder & Childers, 1979). Endorphins are related to a class of brain chemicals known as enkephalins, discussed in Chapter 3.

Receptor sites for endorphins are found in large numbers in the limbic system and other brain areas associated with pleasure, pain, and emotion (Feldman & Quenzer, 1984). Both acupuncture and electrical stimulation cause a buildup of endorphins in the brain. In other words, the nervous system makes it own "drugs" to block pain. Actually, this ties in nicely with the idea of pain gates.

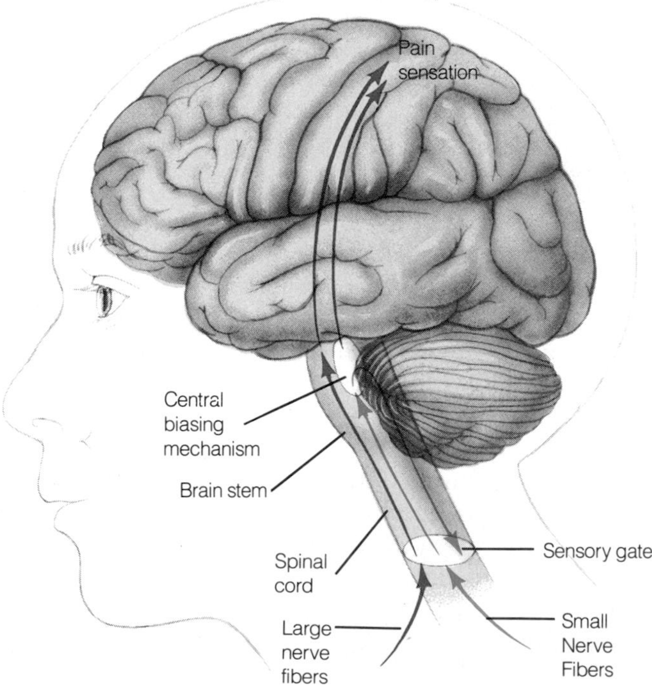

Fig. 4–25 *Diagram of a sensory gate for pain. A series of pain impulses going through the gate may prevent other pain messages from passing through. Or pain messages may relay through a "central biasing mechanism" that exerts control over the gate, closing it to other impulses.*

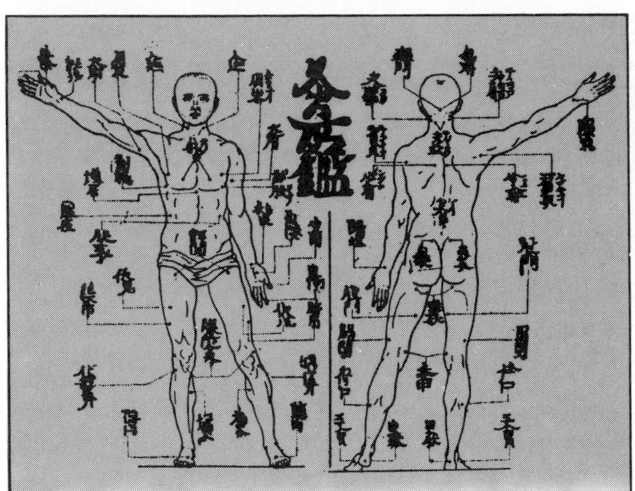

Fig. 4–26 *An acupuncturist's chart. Modern research has begun to explain the painkilling effects of acupuncture. (See text.)*

The central biasing system, which closes pain gates in the spinal cord, is highly sensitive to morphine and other opiate painkillers (Melzack & Wall, 1983).

The discovery of endorphins and their painkilling effect has caused quite a stir in psychology. At long last it appears possible to explain a number of puzzling phenomena, including runner's "high," masochism, acupuncture, and the euphoria sometimes associated with childbirth and painful initiation rites in primitive cultures. In each instance, there is reason to believe that pain and stress cause the release of endorphins (Kruger & Liebskind, 1984). These, in turn, induce feelings of pleasure or euphoria similar to morphine intoxication (Cannon et al., 1978).

The "high" often felt by long-distance runners serves as a good example of the endorphin effect. In one experiment, subjects were tested for pain tolerance. After running 1 mile, each was tested again. In the second test, all could withstand pain about 70 percent longer than before. The runners were then given naloxone, a drug that blocks the effects of endorphins. Following another 1-mile run, the subjects were tested again. This time they had lost their earlier protection from pain (Haier et al., 1981). People who say they are "addicted" to running may be closer to the truth than they realize. And more importantly, we may at last have an explanation for those hardy souls who take hot saunas followed by cold showers!

The severity of pain is also affected by a variety of psychological factors. Since you may not want to try acupuncture or electrical stimulation to control everyday pain, the following Applications describes several practical ways to reduce pain. Before we turn to this useful topic, here's a Learning Check.

Learning Check

1. Which of the following is *not* important for the transduction of sound?
a. the pinna *b.* ossicles *c.* phosphenes *d.* the oval window *e.* hair cells

2. Daily exposure to sounds with a loudness of ______________ decibles may cause permanent hearing loss.

3. Cochlear implants have been used primarily to overcome
a. conduction deafness *b.* stimulation deafness *c.* nerve deafness *d.* tinnitus

4. Olfaction appears to be at least partially explained by the ______________ ______________ ______________ theory of molecule shapes and receptor sites.

5. From the standpoint of survival, we are fortunate that bitter tastes register primarily on the tip of the tongue. T or F?

6. Which of the following is a somesthetic sense?
a. gustation *b.* olfaction *c.* rarefaction *d.* kinesthesis

7. Warning pain is carried by ______________ nerve fibers.

8. Sensory adaptation refers to an increase in sensory response that accompanies a constant or unchanging stimulus. T or F?

9. The brain-centered ability to influence what sensations we will receive is called
a. sensory gating *b.* central adaptation *c.* selective attention *d.* sensory biasing

10. The pain killing effects of acupuncture appear to result from ______________ ______________ and the release of beta-endorphin.

Answers:
1. *c* **2.** 85 **3.** *c* **4.** lock and key **5.** F **6.** *d* **7.** large **8.** F **9.** *c* **10.** sensory gating

Applications: Controlling Pain—This Won't Hurt a Bit

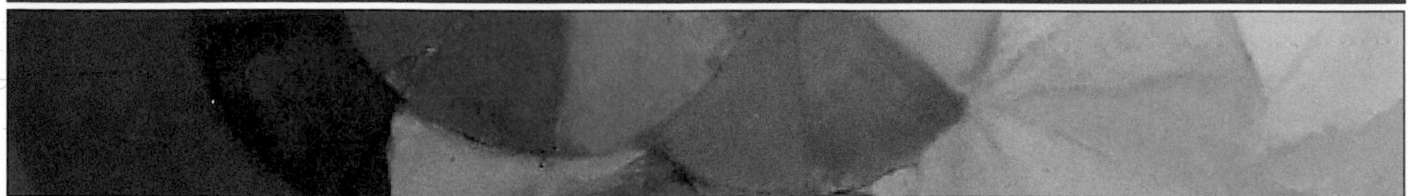

There are many indications that pain may be controlled psychologically. In India, fakirs pierce their cheeks with needles or sit on beds of spikes. In other cultures, people endure tatooing, stretching, cutting, burning, and the like, with little apparent pain. How is such insensitivity achieved? There is no evidence that these people lack normal pain responses. Very likely, the answer lies in four factors that can be used by anyone to alter the amount of pain felt in a particular situation. These are: (1) **anxiety,** (2) **control,** (3) **attention,** and (4) **interpretation.**

Anxiety The basic sensory message of pain can be separated from emotional reactions to it (Melzack, 1978). Fear or high levels of anxiety almost always increase pain (Barber, 1959). A dramatic reversal of this effect is the surprising lack of pain displayed by soldiers wounded in battle. Being excused from further combat apparently produces a flood of relief. This emotional state leaves many soldiers insensitive to wounds that would agonize a civilian (Melzack & Wall, 1983).

Control A moment's reflection should convince you that the most upsetting pain is that over which you have no control. Loss of control seems to increase pain by increasing anxiety and emotional distress. People who are allowed to regulate, avoid, or control a painful stimulus suffer less (Craig, 1978). In general, the more control one *feels* over a painful stimulus, the less pain experienced (Kruger & Liebskind, 1984).

Attention Distraction can also radically reduce pain. Pain, even though it is highly persistent, can be selectively "tuned out" (at least partially), just like any other sensation. Subjects in one experiment who were exposed to intense pain experienced the greatest relief when they were distracted by the task of viewing color slides and describing them aloud (Kanfer & Goldfoot, 1968). In another experiment, pain was lessened when subjects concentrated on trying to name all their high school courses and teachers (Ahles et al., 1983). For the same reason, you may have temporarily forgotten about a toothache or similar pain while absorbed in a movie or book.

Interpretation The meaning or interpretation given a painful stimulus also affects pain (Keefe, 1982). For example, if you give a child a swat on the behind while playing, you'll probably get a burst of laughter. Yet the same swat given as punishment may bring tears (Bresler & Trubo, 1979). The effects of interpretation have also been demonstrated in the lab. In one experiment, it was found that thinking of pain as pleasurable (denying the pain) greatly increased pain tolerance (Neufeld, 1970).

Coping with Pain

Question: How can these facts be applied?

In a sense, they have already been applied to childbirth. **Prepared childbirth training,** which promotes birth with a minimum of drugs or painkillers, uses all four factors. To prepare for natural childbirth, the expectant mother learns in great detail what to anticipate at each stage of labor. This greatly relieves her fears and anxieties. During labor, she attends to sensations that mark her progress and she adjusts her breathing accordingly. Her attention is shifted to sensations other than pain, and her positive attitude is maintained by use of the term *contractions* rather than *labor pains*. Finally, because of her months of preparation and her active participation, she feels *in control* of the situation.

Natural childbirth techniques reduce pain by an average of about 30 percent. Many women find this reduction quite helpful. However, it is important to remember that labor can produce very severe pain. A woman should not feel guilty if she needs painkillers during labor. Many women who have had prepared childbirth training still end up asking for an epidural block (Melzack, 1984).

With more moderate pain, reduced anxiety, redirected attention, and added control can make quite a difference. In any situation where pain can be anticipated (a trip to the doctor, dentist, and so on), lowered anxiety may be achieved by making sure that you are *fully informed*. Be sure that everything that will happen or could happen to you is explained. Also, be sure to fully discuss any fears you have. If you are physically tense, the use of relaxation exercises can help lower your level of arousal. (Relaxation techniques are described in detail in the Applications section in Chapter 22. The desensitization procedure described there may also help reduce anxiety.)

Distraction and Reinterpretation Some dentists are now equipped to help you shift attention away from pain. Patients are actively distracted with video games and headphones carrying music. In other situations, focusing on some external

Applications

object may help you shift attention away from pain. Pick a tree outside a window, a design on the wall, or some other stimulus and examine it in great detail. Prior practice in meditation can be a tremendous aid to such attention shifts. (Meditation techniques are described in Chapter 13.) Research suggests that distraction of this type works best for mild or brief pain. For chronic or strong pain, reinterpretation is more effective (McCaul & Malott, 1984).

Question: Is there any way to increase control over a painful stimulus?

Counterirritation Practically speaking, the choices may be limited. You may be able to arrange a signal with a doctor or dentist that will give you control over whether a painful procedure will continue. A second possibility is more unusual. Ronald Melzack's gate-control theory of pain suggests that sending *mild* pain messages to the spinal cord and brain may effectively close the neurological gates to more severe or unpredictable pain. Medical texts have long recognized this effect. Physicians have found that intense surface stimulation of the skin can control pain from other parts of the body. Likewise, a brief, mildly painful stimulus can relieve more severe pain. Such procedures, known as **counterirritation,** are evident in some of the oldest techniques used to control pain: applying ice packs, hot-water bottles, or mustard packs to other parts of the body (Melzack, 1974).

These facts suggest a way to minimize pain that is based on increased control, counterirritation, and the release of endorphins. If you pinch yourself, you can easily *create and endure* pain equal to that produced by many medical procedures (receiving an injection, having a tooth drilled, and so on). The pain doesn't seem too bad because you have control over it, and it is predictable. This fact might be used to *mask* one pain with a second painful stimulus that is under your control. For instance, if you are having a tooth filled, try pinching yourself or digging a fingernail into a knuckle while the dentist is working. Focus your attention on the pain you are creating, and increase its intensity anytime the dentist's work becomes more painful. This suggestion may not work for you, but casual observation suggests that it can be a useful technique for controlling pain in some circumstances. Generations of children have used it to take the edge off a spanking.

Learning Check

1. Like heightened anxiety, increased control tends to increase subjective pain. T or F?
2. In one experiment, subjects given the task of viewing color slides and describing them aloud experienced less pain than subjects who paid attention to the pain stimulus. T or F?
3. Imagining a pleasant experience can be an effective way of reducing pain in some situations. T or F?
4. The concept of counterirritation holds that relaxation and desensitization are key elements of pain control. T or F?

Answers:

1. F 2. T 3. T 4. F

Exploration: Sensation in Space—Adapting to an Alien Environment

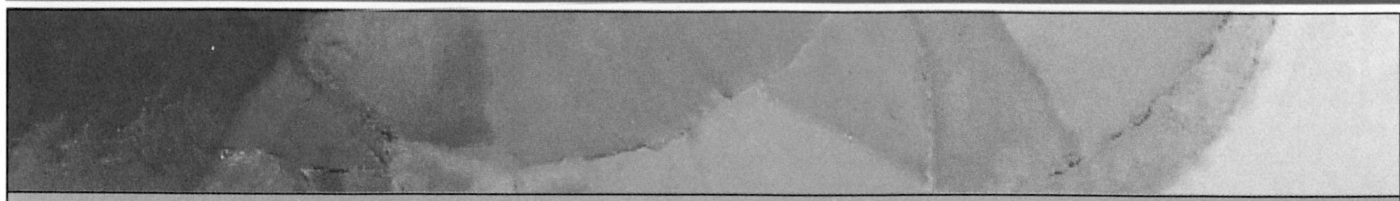

On television, astronauts are often shown playfully enjoying the acrobatics made possible by weightlessness (Fig. 4–27). But adapting to life in space is not as easy or pleasant as such images imply (Johnson, 1984). Indeed, if you were to ride into space, chances are about 50-50 that your first experience in orbit would be throwing up (Joyce, 1984). At least one-half of all astronauts have suffered from **space adaptation syndrome,** or "space sickness."

Question: Is that like seasickness?

Space Sickness Space sickness is a type of motion sickness. Like seasickness, car sickness, and airsickness, its first signs are dizziness and mild disorientation. However, space sickness usually does not produce the pallor, "cold sweating," and nausea so common on earth. In most types of motion sickness, these signs warn that vomiting is about to occur. But in space, vomiting is usually sudden and unexpected. Seeing another astronaut drift by upside down or viewing the earth at an odd angle is often all it takes to trigger repeated vomiting (Connors et al., 1985).

Fig. 4–27 *Weightlessness presents astronauts with a real challenge in sensory adaptation.*

The Vestibular System

Question: What causes motion sickness?

Motion sickness is directly related to the vestibular system (Fig. 4–28). Fluid-filled sacs called **otolith organs** (OH-toe-lith) contain tiny crystals in a soft, gelatin-like mass. The tug of gravity or rapid head movements can cause the mass to shift. This, in turn, stimulates hairlike receptor cells, allowing us to sense gravity and movement.

Three fluid-filled tubes called the **semicircular canals** are also part of the vestibular system. If you could climb inside these tubes, you would find that head movements cause the fluid to swirl about. As the fluid moves, it bends a small "flap," or "float," within a wider part of the canal called the **ampulla** (am-PULL-ah). This bending again stimulates hair cells and signals head rotation.

Motion Sickness The most widely accepted explanation of motion sickness is the **sensory conflict theory.** According to this theory, dizziness and nausea occur when sensations from the vestibular system fail to match information received from the eyes and body.

You can create an example of sensory conflict by turning around repeatedly until you become dizzy. Doing so sets the fluid spinning in the semicircular canals. When you stop, the fluid continues to swirl about, so the brain thinks your head is still moving. This causes the eyes to move involuntarily and makes the world seem like it is still spinning.

On solid ground, information from the vestibular system, vision, and kinesthesis usually matches. However, in a heaving, pitching boat, car, or airplane, a serious mismatch can occur—causing disorientation and finally heaving of another kind.

Question: Why would sensory conflict cause nausea?

According to the most popular theory, you can blame (or thank) evolution. Many poisons disturb the coordination of messages from the vestibular system, vision, and the

Exploration

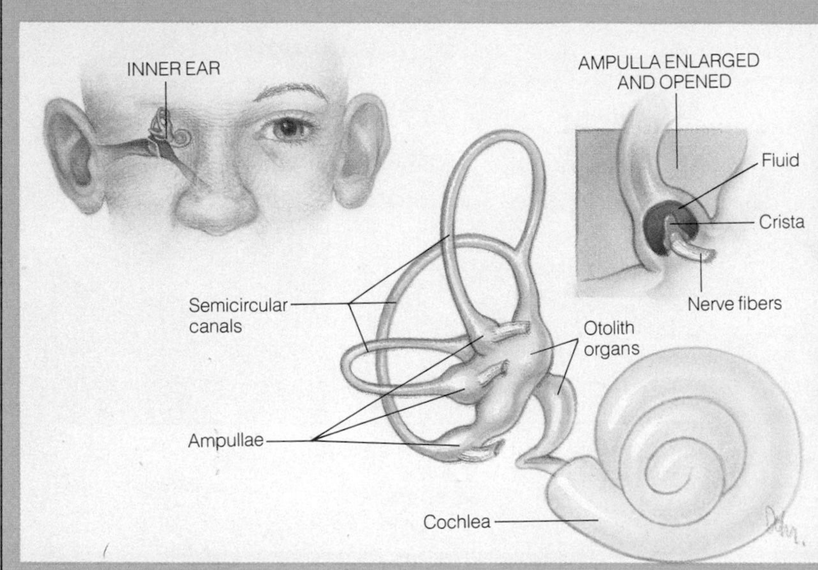

Fig. 4–28 *The vestibular system.*

body. Therefore, we may have evolved so that we react to sensory conflict by vomiting to expel poison. The value of this reaction, however, may be of little comfort to anyone who has ever been "green" and miserable with motion sickness.

In space, sensory conflict can be especially intense. During weightlessness, merely pulling on one's shoes can result in a backward somersault. Under such conditions, the otolith organs send unexpected signals to the brain, and head movements are no longer confirmed by the semicircular canals. Few of the messages the brain receives from the vestibular system and kinesthetic receptors agree with a lifetime of past experience (Engle & Lott, 1980).

Question: How long does it take to adapt to weightlessness?

Space sickness usually disappears in 2 or 3 days. Recent research suggests that this adaptation occurs because astronauts shift to using visual cues instead of vestibular information. Later, this same shift can cause "earth sickness." Immediately after returning to earth (especially after very long missions), some astronauts have experienced dizziness and nausea. All had considerable difficulty in standing with their eyes closed for the first day or two (von Baumgarten et al., 1984).

How to Minimize Motion Sickness

Researchers trying to prevent space sickness have learned a great deal about what helps and what doesn't. The following points may be of some aid to you here on earth.

- Medical treatment for space sickness has concentrated on drugs. The most successful so far is scopolamine, which is available by prescription. Non-prescription "sea sickness" pills also offer some protection. Alcohol and other intoxicating drugs, however, usually make motion sickness worse.
- Soviet cosmonauts have had some success with a system that limits head movements for the first two days in space. In a boat, car, or airplane, it helps to move your head as little as possible. You may even want to place a towel around your neck to restrict head movement. (If it doesn't help, you may soon find another use for it!)
- To minimize sensory conflict, stay out of the cabin on boats. In cars and airplanes, try closing your eyes. Or as an alternative, fixate your eyes on an unmoving point (such as the horizon) or look above the horizon at the unmoving sky.
- If possible, you should lie down. The otoliths are less sensitive to vertical movements when you are horizontal, and your head will move less.
- Anxiety seems to intensify motion sickness. Some of the astronauts have had success at learning to focus their attention on pleasant, distracting thoughts. If you do the same, be sure to also breathe slowly and deeply. (Breathing can, in fact, be a good focus for attention (Nicogossian & Parker, 1982).

Space sickness is only one of the behavioral challenges of space travel. In fact, the long-term effects of space flight are still largely unknown. Although space missions seem relatively routine, astronauts remain true pioneers in a strange and alien sensory environment.

Exploration

Learning Check

1. At least 150 out of every 200 astronauts have suffered from space sickness. T or F?
2. Head movements are detected primarily in the semicircular canals, gravity by the otolith organs. T or F?
3. Sensory conflict theory appears to explain space sickness, but it does not seem to apply to other types of motion sickness. T or F?
4. The drug amphetamine has been used successfully to prevent motion sickness. T or F?

Answers:
1. F 2. T 3. F 4. F

Chapter Summary

- Sensory organs **transduce** physical energies into nerve impulses. Because of **selectivity,** limited **sensitivity, feature detection,** and **coding** patterns, the senses act as **data reduction systems.** Sensory response can be partially understood in terms of **localization of function** in the brain.
- The minimum amount of physical energy necessary to produce a sensation defines the **absolute threshold.** The amount of change necessary to produce a **just noticeable difference** in a stimulus defines a **difference threshold.** The study of thresholds and related topics is called **psychophysics.**
- Threatening or anxiety-provoking stimuli may raise the threshold for recognition, an effect called **perceptual defense.** Any stimulus below the level of conscious awareness is said to be **subliminal.** There is some evidence that **subliminal perception** occurs, but subliminal advertising is largely ineffective.
- The **visible spectrum** consists of electromagnetic radiation in a narrow range. The eye is in some ways like a camera, but ultimately, it is a **visual system,** not a photographic one. Individual cells in the visual cortex of the brain act as **feature detectors** to analyze visual information.
- Four common visual defects, correctable with glasses, are **myopia** (nearsightedness), **hyperopia** (farsightedness), **presbyopia** (loss of accommodation), and **astigmatism.**
- The **rods** and **cones** are **photoreceptors** making up the **retina** of the eye. The rods specialize in night vision, black and white reception, and motion detection. The cones, found exclusively in the **fovea** and otherwise toward the middle of the eye, specialize in color vision, **acuity** (perception of fine detail), and daylight vision. Much **peripheral vision** is supplied by the rods.
- The rods and cones differ in color sensitivity. *Yellowish green* is brightest for cones; *blue-green* for the rods (although they will see it as colorless). Color vision is explained by the **trichromatic theory** in the retina and by the **opponent-process theory** in the visual system beyond the eyes.
- Total **color blindness** is rare, but 8 percent of males and 1 percent of females are red-green color-blind or color-weak. Color blindness is a **sex-linked trait** carried on the *X* chromosome. Color blindness is revealed by the **Ishihara test.**
- **Dark adaptation,** an increase in sensitivity to light, is caused by increased concentration of visual pigments in both the rods and the cones, but mainly by **rhodopsin** recombining in the rods. Vitamin A deficiencies may cause **night blindness.**
- **Sound waves** are the stimulus for hearing. They are transduced by the **eardrum, auditory ossicles, oval window, cochlea,** and ultimately, the **hair cells.** The **frequency theory** and **place theory** of hearing together explain how pitch is sensed. Three basic types of deafness are **nerve deafness, conduction deafness,** and **stimulation deafness.**
- **Olfaction** (smell) and **gustation** (taste) are **chemical senses** responsive to airborne or liquefied molecules. The

lock and key theory partially explains smell. Specific areas on the tongue are more responsive to sweet, salty, sour, and bitter tastes.

• The **somesthetic senses** include the **skin senses, vestibular senses,** and **kinesthetic senses.** The skin senses include touch, pressure, pain, cold, and warmth. Sensitivity to each is related to the number of receptors present.

• Incoming sensations are affected by **sensory adaptation** (a reduction in the number of nerve impulses sent), by **selective attention** (selection and diversion of messages in the brain), and by **sensory gating** (blocking or alteration of messages flowing toward the brain). Selective gating of pain messages apparently takes place in the spinal cord.

• Pain is greatly affected by **anxiety, attention, control** over the stimulus, the **interpretation** placed on an experience, and by **counterirritation.** Pain can therefore be reduced by controlling these factors.

• Various forms of **motion sickness** are related to messages received from the **vestibular system,** which senses gravity and movement. **Sensory conflict theory** blames motion sickness on a mismatch of visual, kinesthetic, and vestibular sensations. Motion sickness can be avoided by minimizing sensory conflict.

Questions for Discussion

1. Is your brain sitting on a laboratory table somewhere? It is theoretically possible that your brain was donated to science some time ago. Let's say that it was preserved and recently reactivated and that a sophisticated computer is artificially generating patterns of nerve activity in the cortex by mimicking normal sensory messages in the nerves. These messages duplicate the sights, sounds, odors, and sensations of sitting in a college classroom. If this were happening—right now—could you tell? Would you be able to discover that you had no body? Defend your answer.

2. William James once said, "If a master surgeon were to cross the auditory and optic nerves, then we would hear lightning and see thunder." Can you explain what James meant?

3. Let's say that you would like to design a system that uses touch to convey "images" to a blind person. How would you proceed? What would be the advantages and disadvantages of using various body areas (hands, back, forehead, and so on)?

4. What changes would be likely to take place if the absolute thresholds for vision and hearing were changed so that we could see infrared and ultraviolet light and hear sounds up to 50,000 cycles per second? (Consider lighting systems, the design of stereo equipment, and so forth.)

5. In Zen Buddhism there is a familiar *koan,* or riddle, that says: "Last night I dreamt I was a butterfly. How do I know today that I am not a butterfly dreaming I am a man?" Can you relate this to the idea that we construct a version of reality out of the more basic world of physical energies surrounding us?

6. Why do you think your voice sounds so different when you hear a tape recording of yourself speaking? (Hint: How else might vibrations from the voice reach the cochlea?)

Chapter 5

Perceiving the World

In This Chapter

Perceptual constancies
Organizing perceptions
Perceiving depth and distance
Perceptual learning
Attention, habituation, and motives
Expectancies and sets

Applications

Perception and objectivity

Exploration

Evaluating extrasensory perception

Chapter Preview

Murder!

The following is a true account. Only the degree of exaggeration has been changed for educational purposes.

I was in a supermarket when a girl suddenly came running around a corner. She looked back and screamed, "Stop! Stop! You're killing him! You're killing my father!" Naturally I was interested! As I quickly retraced her path, I was greeted by a grisly scene. There was a man stretched out on the floor with another on top of him. The guy on top was huge. At 6 feet 6 inches tall and 300 pounds, he looked only half human. He had his victim by the throat and was beating his head against the floor. There was blood everywhere. I decided to do the right thing. I ran. . . .

By the time the store manager and I returned to the "scene of the crime," the police were just arriving. It took quite a while to straighten things out, but here is what happened: The "guy on the bottom" had passed out and hit his head. This caused the cut (actually quite minor) that accounted for the "blood everywhere." The "guy on top" saw the first man fall and was trying to prevent him from further injuring himself. He was also loosening the man's collar.

If I had never returned. I would have sworn in court that I had seen a murder. The girl's description completely determined my own perceptions. This perhaps is understandable. But what I will never forget is the shock I felt when I met the "murderer"—the man I had seen a few moments before, in broad daylight, as a huge, vicious horrible-looking creature. The man was not a stranger. He was a neighbor of mine. I had seen him dozens of times before. I know him by name. He is a rather small man.

The last chapter discussed sensation, the process of bringing information into the nervous system. This chapter is about ***perception,*** *or how we assemble sensations into a usable "picture" or model of the world. As we perceive events, the brain actively selects, organizes, and integrates sensory information. These mental pro-*

cesses are so automatic that we are rarely aware of them. It may, in fact, take drastic misperceptions like that just described to call attention to this marvelous process. Perception creates faces, melodies, works of art, illusions, and, on occasion, "murders" out of the raw material of sensation. Let's see how this takes place.

Survey Questions

- What are perceptual constancies, and what is their role in perception?
- What basic principles do we use to group sensations into meaningful patterns?
- How is it possible to see depth and judge distance?
- What effect does learning have on perception?
- How is perception altered by attention, motives, values, and expectations?
- How reliable are eyewitness reports?
- Is extrasensory perception possible?

Perceptual Constancies—Taming an Unruly World

What would it be like to have your vision restored after a lifetime of blindness? In reality, a first look at the world can be disappointing. A newly sighted person must *learn* to identify objects, to read clocks, numbers, and letters, and to judge sizes and distances (Senden, 1960). Indeed, learning to "see" can be quite frustrating.

Richard Gregory (1977) describes the experiences of Mr. S. B., a 52-year-old cataract patient who had been blind since birth. After an operation restored his sight, Mr. S. B. struggled to use his vision. At first, for instance, he could only judge distance in familiar situations. One day, he was found crawling out of a hospital window to get a closer look at traffic on the street. It's easy to understand his curiosity, but he had to be restrained. His room was on the fourth floor!

Question: Why would Mr. S. B. try to crawl out of a fourth-story window? Couldn't he at least tell distance from the size of the cars?

No, because using size to judge distance requires familiarity with the appearance of objects. Try holding your left hand a few inches in front of your eyes and your right hand at arm's length. The image of your right hand should be about half the size of your left hand. Still, because you have viewed your hands from different distances countless times, you know your right hand did not suddenly shrink. This is called **size constancy:** The perceived size of an object remains the same even though the size of its retinal image changes.

To perceive your hand accurately, you had to draw on past experience. Some perceptions—like seeing a line on a piece of paper—are so basic they seem to be **native** (inborn). But much perception is **empirical,** or based on prior experience (Julesz, 1975). For example, Colin Turnbull (1961) tells of the time he took a Pygmy from the dense rain forests of Africa to the vast African plains. The Pygmy had never before seen objects at a great distance. Hence, the first time he saw a herd of buffalo in the distance, he thought it was a swarm of insects. Imagine his confusion when he was then driven toward the animals. He concluded that witchcraft was being used to fool him because the "insects" seemed to grow into buffalo before his eyes.

Perhaps you have also experienced the failure of size constancy in unfamiliar situations. When viewed from an airplane, houses, cars, and people no longer seem normal in size; instead, they begin to look like toys.

Shape constancy is another interesting effect. Shape constancy can be demonstrated by looking at this page from directly overhead and then from an angle. Obviously, the page is rectangular, but most of the time the image that reaches your eye is distorted. Even though the book's image changes, your perception of its shape remains constant. (For additional examples, see Fig. 5–1.)

Let's say that you are outside in bright sunlight. Beside you is a friend wearing a white blouse. Suddenly a cloud shades the sun. It might seem that the blouse would grow dimmer, but it still appears to be bright white. This happens because the blouse continues to reflect a larger *proportion* of light than nearby objects. The principle of **brightness constancy** states that the apparent brightness

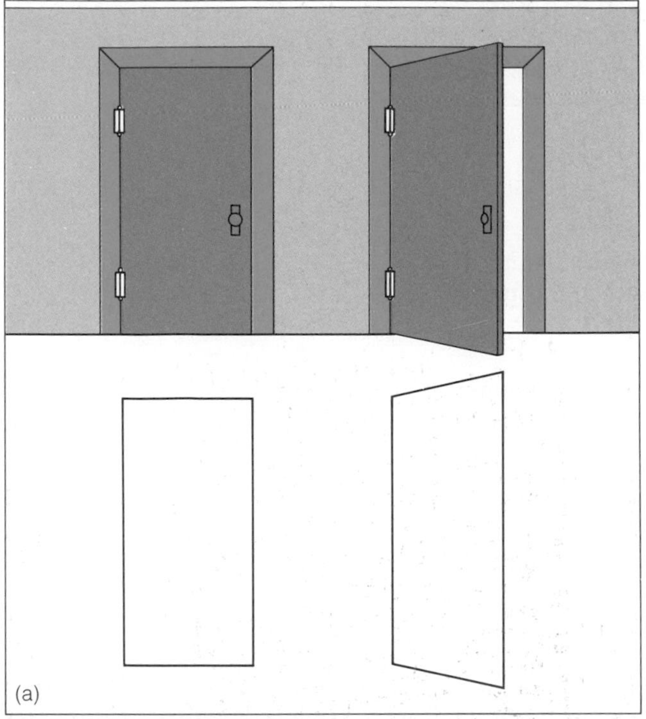

Fig. 5–1 *Shape constancy. (a) When a door is open, its image actually forms a trapezoid. Shape constancy is indicated by the fact that it is still perceived as a rectangle. (b) With great effort you may be able to see this design as a collection of flat shapes. However, if you maintain shape constancy, the distorted squares strongly suggest the surface of a sphere. (From "Spherescapes 1," by Scott Walter and Kevin McMahon, 1983.)*

Fig. 5–2 *A reversible figure-ground design. Do you see two faces in profile or a wineglass?*

of an object stays the same under changing conditions of light.

To summarize, the energy patterns reaching our senses are constantly changing, even when they come from the same object. Size, shape, and brightness constancy rescue us from a confusing world in which objects would seem to shrink and grow, change shape as if they were made of rubber, and light up or fade like neon lamps. Gaining these constancies was only one of the hurdles Mr. S. B. faced in learning to see. In the next section, we will consider some others.

● Perceptual Grouping—Getting It All Together

William James said, "To the infant the world is just a big, booming, buzzing confusion." Like an infant, Mr. S. B. had to find meaning in his visual sensations. He was soon able to tell time from a large wall clock and to read block letters he had known before only from touch. At a zoo, he recognized an elephant from descriptions he had heard. However, handwriting meant nothing to him for more than a year after he regained sight, and many objects remained meaningless until he touched them. Thus, while Mr. S. B. had visual *sensations*, his ability to *perceive* remained limited.

Question: How are sensations organized into meaningful perceptions?

The simplest organization involves grouping some sensations into an object, or *figure*, that stands out on a plainer background. **Figure-ground** organization is probably inborn, since it is the first perceptual ability to appear after cataract patients regain sight (Hebb, 1949). In normal figure-ground perception, only one figure is seen. In **reversible figures,** however, figure and ground can be switched. In Figure 5–2, it is equally possible to see either a wineglass figure on a dark background or two face profiles on a white background. As you shift from one pattern to the other, you should get a clear sense of what figure-ground organization means.

Question: What causes the formation of a figure?

The Gestalt psychologists (see Chapter 1) studied this question in detail. Even if you were seeing for the first time, they concluded, a number of factors would bring some order to your perceptions (Fig. 5–3).

1. Nearness. Stimuli that are near each other tend to be grouped together (see Fig. 5–3a). Thus, if three people

Fig. 5–3 *Perceptual grouping illustrations.*

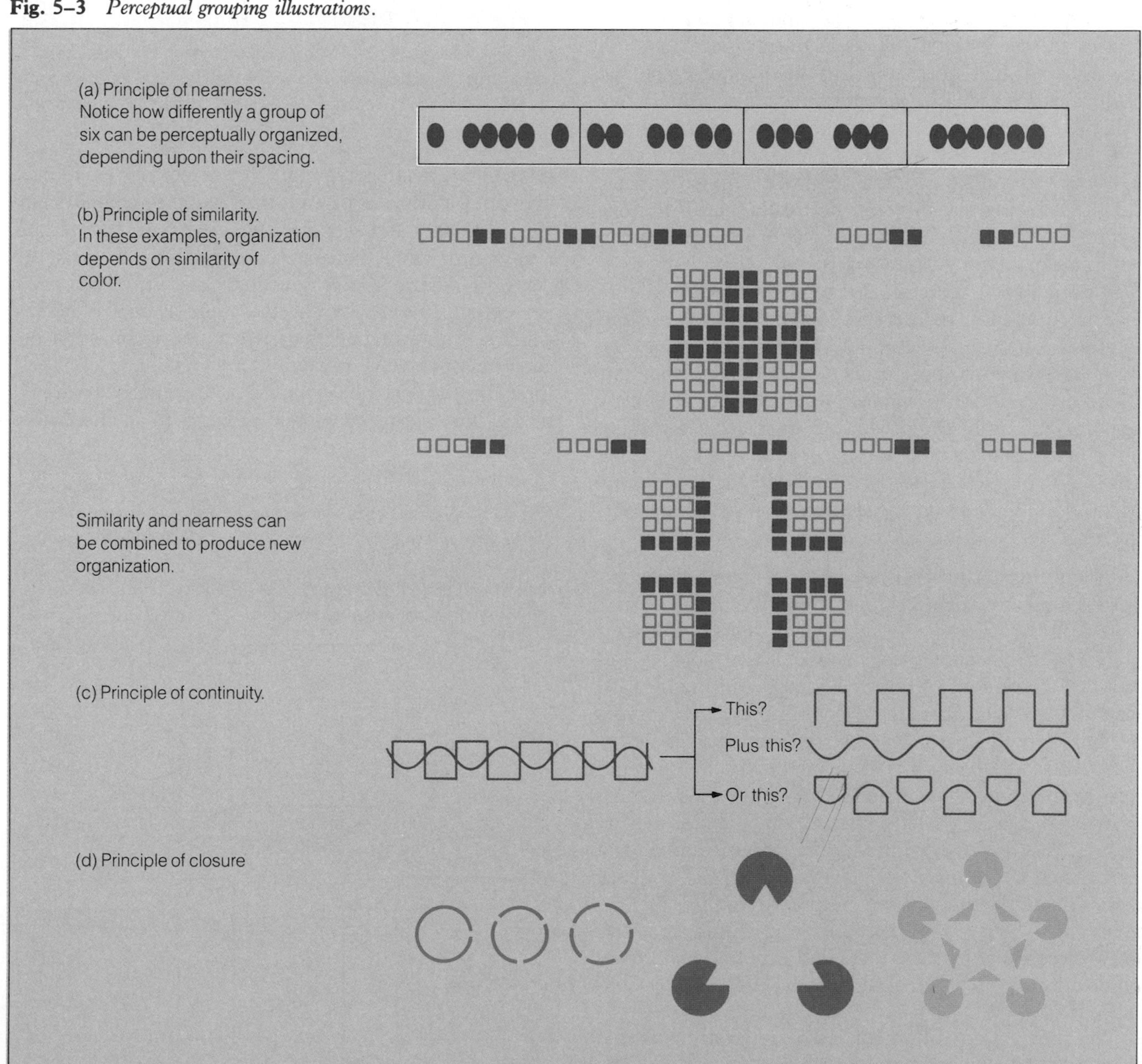

stand near one another and a fourth person stands 10 feet away, the adjacent three will be seen as a group and the distant person an outsider.

2. **Similarity.** "Birds of a feather flock together," and stimuli that are similar in size, shape, color, or form tend to be grouped together (see Fig. 5–3b). For instance, picture two bands marching side by side. If their uniforms differ, the bands will be seen as two separate groups, not as a single large group.

3. **Continuation, or continuity.** Perceptions tend toward simplicity and continuity. In Figure 5–3c, it is easier to visualize a wavy line on a squared-off line than it is to see a complex row of shapes.

4. **Closure.** Closure refers to the tendency to *complete* a figure, so that it has a consistent overall form. Each of the drawings in Figure 5–3d has one or more gaps, yet each is perceived as a recognizable figure. The white "shapes" that appear in the middle of the two right drawings in Figure 5–3d are called **illusory figures** (Parks, 1984). Even young children see these implied shapes, despite knowing that they are "not really there." Illusory figures reveal that our tendency to form shapes—even with minimal cues—is powerful.

5. **Contiguity.** A principle that can't be shown in Figure 5–3 is contiguity, or nearness in time *and* space. Contiguity is often responsible for the perception that one thing has *caused* another (Michotte, 1963). A psychologist friend of the author's demonstrates this principle in class by knocking on his head with one hand while knocking on a wooden table (out of sight) with the other. The knocking sound is perfectly timed with the movements of his visible hand. This leads to the irresistible perception that his head is made of wood.

In addition to these principles, learning and past experience greatly affect perceptual organization. Contrast Mr. S. B.'s immediate recognition of letters to his inability to read handwriting. Also, take a moment and look for the camouflaged animal pictured in Figure 5–4. **Camouflage** patterns are those that break up figure-ground organization. If you had never seen similar animals before, could you have located this one? Mr. S. B. would have been at a total loss to find meaning in such a picture.

In a way, we are all detectives, seeking patterns in what we see. In this sense, a meaningful pattern represents a **perceptual hypothesis,** or guess held until the evidence contradicts it. Have you ever seen a "friend" in the distance, only to have the friend turn into a stranger as you drew closer? Pre-existing ideas and expectations *actively* guide our interpretation of sensations (McBurney & Collings, 1984).

The active nature of organizing perceptions is perhaps most apparent for **ambiguous stimuli** (patterns allowing more than one interpretation). If you look at a cloud, you may discover dozens of ways to organize its contours into fanciful shapes and scenes. Even clearly defined stimuli may permit more than one interpretation. Stare at the design in Figure 5–5 if you doubt the active nature of perception. In some instances, a stimulus may offer such conflicting information that perceptual organization becomes impossible. For example, the tendency to make a three-dimensional object out of a drawing is frustrated by the "three-pronged widget" (Fig. 5–6), an **impossible figure.**

Fig. 5–4 *An example of perceptual organization. Once the camouflaged insect (known as a giant walkingstick) becomes visible, it is almost impossible to view the picture again without seeing it.*

Fig. 5–5 *Necker's cube. Visualize the top cube as a wire box. If you stare at the cube, its organization will change. Sometimes it will seem to project upward, like the lower left cube; other times it will project downward. The difference lies in how the brain interprets the same information.*

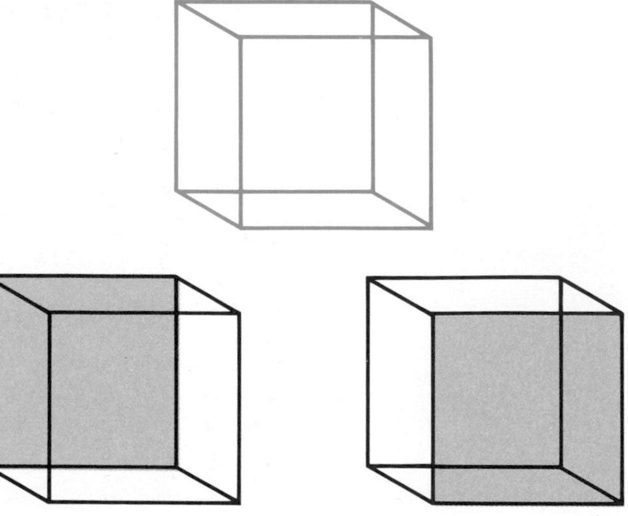

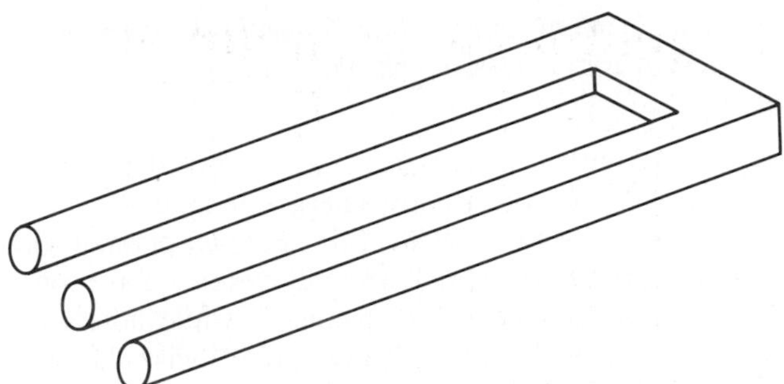

Fig. 5–6 *An impossible figure—the "three-pronged widget."*

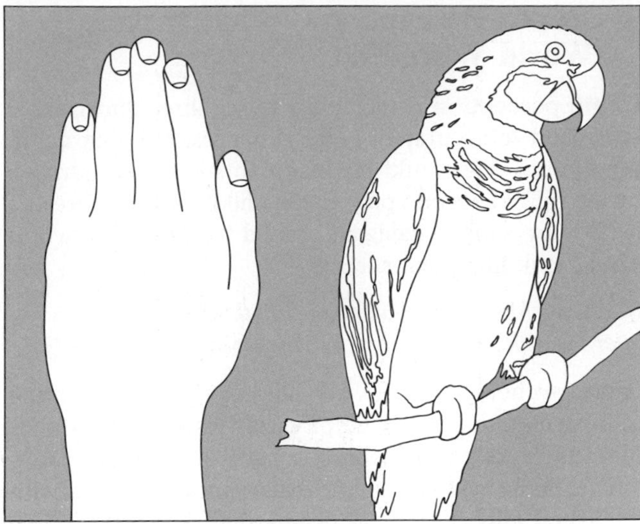

Fig. 5–7 *Stimuli similar to those used by Kennedy (1983) to study the kinds of information universally recognized in drawings. (See text for explanation.)*

Question: Is the ability to understand drawings learned?

Humans almost always appear to understand lines that represent the *edges of surfaces*. We also have no problem with a single line used to depict the *parallel edges* of a narrow object, such as a rope. One thing that we *do not* easily recognize is lines showing color boundaries on the surface of an object (Kennedy, 1983).

To illustrate the last point, let's pay a brief visit to the Songe, a small tribe in Papua New Guinea. Before they were tested, the Songe had never made or seen line drawings—not even doodles scratched on the ground. As a test, the Songe were shown drawings like those in Figure 5–7. When this was done, they easily recognized the hand and the parrot from simple outlines. But lines showing color boundaries confused them. The half-moons on the fingernails, for example, made them think that the nails had been damaged and new ones were growing in. Similarly, they thought that the parrot must have been cut repeatedly. They thought this even though the lines in the drawing match color markings of parrots found in Songe territory (Kennedy, 1983).

One of the most amazing feats of perceptual organization deserves a separate discussion. In the next section, we will explore our capacity to create three-dimensional space from flat retinal images.

Learning Check

Try these questions before reading more.

1. Which among the following are subject to basic perceptual constancy?
a. figure-ground organization *b.* size *c.* ambiguity *d.* brightness *e.* continuity *f.* closure *g.* shape *h.* nearness

2. The first and most basic perceptual organization to emerge when sight is restored to a blind person is
a. continuity *b.* nearness constancy *c.* recognition of numbers and letters *d.* figure-ground

3. At times, meaningful perceptual organization represents a ________________, or "guess," held until the evidence contradicts it.

4. Ambiguous figures have more than one meaningful organization. T or F?

5. The design known as Necker's cube is a good example of an impossible figure. T or F?

6. There is evidence that humans universally recognize line drawings depicting the edges of ________________ and narrow parallel lines.

Answers:

1. *b, d, g* **2.** *d* **3.** hypothesis **4.** T **5.** F **6.** surfaces

Depth Perception—What If the World Were Flat

Depth perception is the ability to see three-dimensional space and to accurately judge distances. Without depth perception, you would be unable to successfully drive a car or ride a bicycle, play catch, shoot baskets, thread a needle, or simply navigate around a room. The world would look like a flat surface.

Question: Mr. S. B. had trouble with depth perception after his sight was restored. Is depth perception learned?

Some psychologists (nativists) hold that depth perception is inborn. Others (the empiricists) view it as learned. Most likely, depth perception is partly learned and partly innate. Some evidence on the issue comes from work with the **visual cliff** (Fig. 5–8). The visual cliff is basically a glass-topped table. On one side a checkered surface lies directly beneath the glass. On the other side, the checkered surface is 4 feet below. This makes the glass look like a tabletop on one side and a cliff, or drop-off, on the other.

To test for depth perception, 6- to 14-month-old infants were placed in the middle of the visual cliff. This gave them a choice of crawling to the shallow side or the deep side. (The glass prevented them from doing any "skydiving" if they chose the deep side.) Most infants chose the shallow side. In fact, most refused the deep side even when their mothers tried to call them toward it (Gibson & Walk, 1960).

Question: If infants were at least 6 months old when they were tested, isn't it possible that they learned to perceive depth?

Yes, it is. However, other tests have shown that human depth perception consistently emerges at about 4 months of age (Aslin & Smith, 1988). For example, psychologist Jane Gwiazada fitted infants with goggles that make some designs stand out three-dimensionally while others remain flat. By watching head movements, Gwiazada could tell when babies first become aware of "3-D" designs. As in other tests, this occurs at age 4 months. The nearly universal emergence of depth perception at this time suggests that it depends more on brain development than it does on individual learning. It is very likely that at least a basic level of depth perception is innate.

Question: Then why do some babies crawl off tables or beds?

As soon as infants become active crawlers, they refuse to cross the deep side of the visual cliff (Campos et al., 1978). But even babies who perceive depth may not be able to catch themselves if they slip. A lack of coordination—not an inability to see depth—probably explains most "crash landings" after about 4 months of age.

Question: How do adults perceive depth?

A number of **depth cues** combine to produce our experience of three-dimensional space. Depth cues are features of the environment and messages from the body

Fig. 5–8 *Human infants and newborn animals refuse to go over the edge of the visual cliff.*

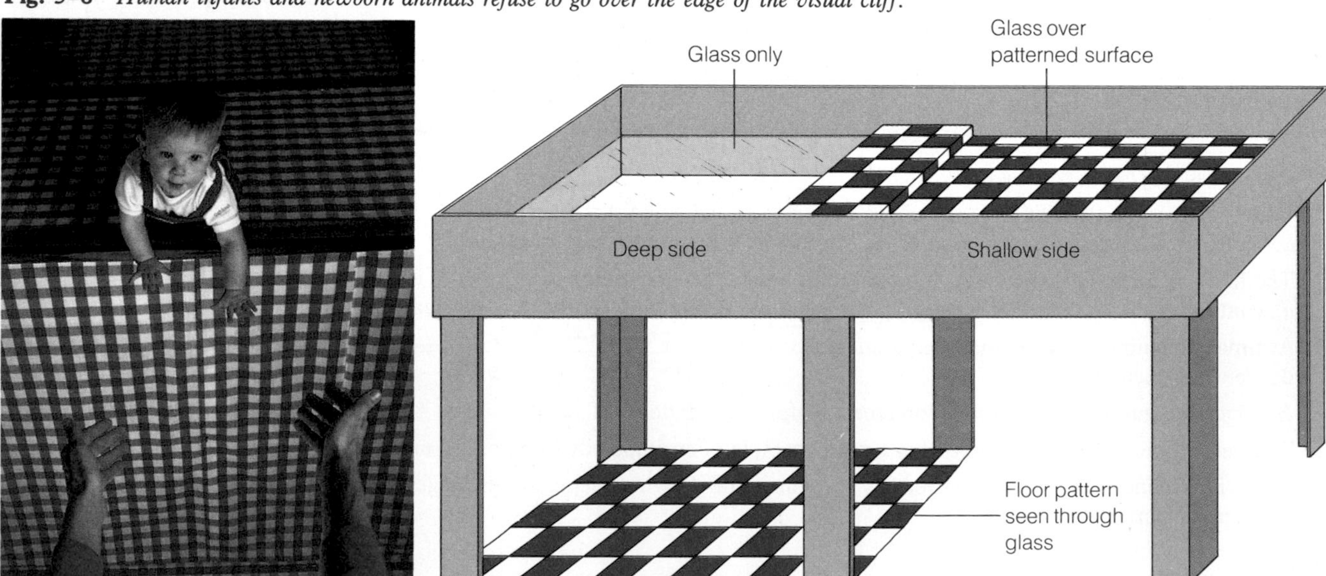

that supply information about distance and space. Some cues will work with just one eye (**monocular cues**), while others require two eyes (**binocular cues**).

Muscular Cues As their name implies, muscular cues come from within the body. One such cue is **accommodation,** a monocular cue for depth perception. You may recall from Chapter 4 that the lens in each eye must bend or bulge to focus nearby objects. Sensations from muscles attached to the lens are channeled back to the brain. Differences in these sensations help us judge distances within about 4 feet of the eyes. Beyond 4 feet, accommodation has a limited effect on depth perception. (It does, however, contribute to an interesting illusion described later in this chapter.) Obviously, accommodation is more important to a watchmaker or a person trying to thread a needle than it is to a basketball player or someone driving an automobile.

A second bodily source of information about depth is **convergence,** a binocular cue. When you look at a distant object, the lines of vision from your eyes are parallel. However, when you look at something 50 feet or less in distance, your eyes must converge (turn in) to focus the object (Fig. 5–9).

You are probably not aware of it, but whenever you estimate a distance under 50 feet (as when you approach a stop sign, play catch, or zap flies with your personal laser), you are using convergence. How? Again, there is a relationship between muscle sensations and distance. Convergence is controlled by a group of muscles attached to the eyeball. These muscles feed information on eye position to the brain to help it judge distance. You can feel convergence by exaggerating it: Focus on your fingertip and bring it toward your eyes until they almost cross. At that point, you can feel the sensations from the muscles that control eye movement.

Fig. 5–9 *The eyes must converge, or turn in toward the nose, to focus close objects.*

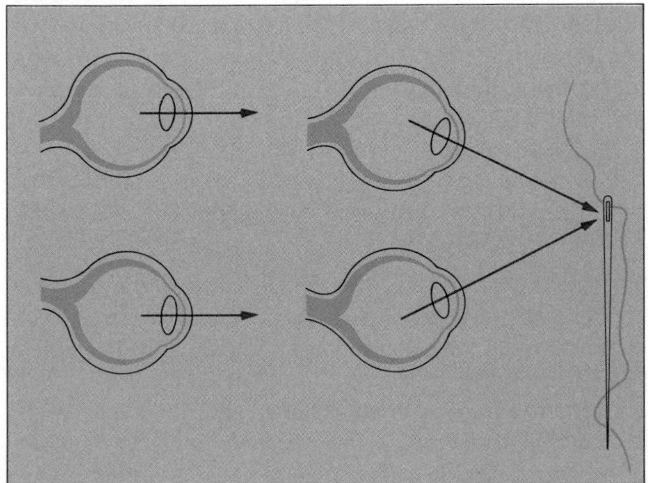

Stereoscopic Vision The most basic source of depth perception is **retinal disparity,** also a binocular cue. Retinal disparity is based on the simple fact that the eyes are about 2½ inches apart. Because of this, each eye receives a slightly different view of the world. When the two images are *fused* into one overall image, **stereoscopic vision** occurs. This produces a powerful sensation of depth (Fig. 5–10).

Retinal disparity can be used to produce 3-D movies by filming with two cameras separated by several inches. Later, both images are simultaneously projected on a screen. Audience members wear glasses that filter out one of the images to each eye. Since each eye gets a separate image, normal stereoscopic vision is duplicated. Try the following demonstration of retinal disparity and fusion.

Totally Tubular

Roll a piece of paper into a tube. Close your left eye. Hold the tube to your right eye like a telescope. Look through the tube at some object in the distance. Place your left hand against the tube halfway down its length and in front of your left eye. Now open your left eye. You should see a "hole" in your hand. You couldn't expect a professional photographer to do a better job blending the two images than your visual system does automatically.

Question: How does retinal disparity produce depth?

Perceiving depth is more than a simple blending of two images, or "pictures," of the world. In Figure 5–10c, you will find two squares of random dots. Notice that they contain no lines, edges, or distinct patterns. Just the same, when these **random dot stereograms** are properly viewed (one to each eye), a center area seems to float above the background. Researcher Bela Julesz believes the designs show that the brain is very sensitive to any **mismatch** of information from the eyes. In this example, depth comes from shifting dots in the center of one square so they do not match dots in the other square (Julesz, 1971; Ross, 1976). To a large extent, three-dimensional space is woven from countless tiny differences between what the right and left eyes see.

Question: If disparity is so important, can a person with one eye perceive depth?

A one-eyed person lacks convergence and retinal disparity, and accommodation is helpful mainly for judging

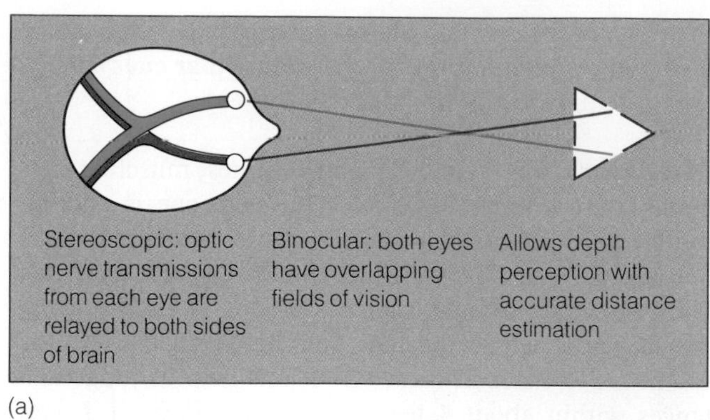

(a)

(b)

(c)

Fig. 5–10 *(a) Stereoscopic vision. (b) The photographs show what the right and left eye would see when viewing a vase. Hold a file card or small piece of paper (4 or 5 inches tall) vertically between the two photos. Place the bridge of your nose on the card so that each eye sees only one photo. Relax your eyes so that they sight along parallel lines, as if looking at something in the distance. Then try to fuse the vases into one image. The third dimension appears like magic. (c) Now do the same with the random dot stereogram, but with your eyes 8 or 10 inches from the page. With luck you will see a diamond shape hovering over the background. (See text for explanation.) Most readers will not be able to get the effect without using a prism to perfectly fuse the right and left dot squares. (Julesz, 1971; reprinted by permission of the University of Chicago Press.)*

short distances. This means that a person with only one eye will have limited depth perception. Try driving a car or riding a bicycle some time with one eye closed. You will find yourself braking too soon or too late, and you will have difficulty estimating your speed. ("But officer, my psychology text said to. . . .") Despite this, you will be able to drive, although it will be more difficult than usual. A person with one eye can even successfully land an airplane—a task that depends strongly on depth perception.

Pictorial Cues for Depth—A Deep Topic

A good movie, painting, or photograph can create a convincing sense of depth where none exists. And, as noted, a one-eyed person can learn to accurately gauge depth.

Question: How is the illusion of depth created on a two-dimensional surface, and how is it possible to judge depth with one eye?

The answers lie in the **pictorial depth cues,** all of which are monocular (they will work with just one eye). These cues supply much of the information present in real three-dimensional scenes (Haber, 1980). To understand how the pictorial cues work, imagine that you are looking outdoors through a window. If you traced everything you saw through the window onto the glass, you would have an excellent drawing, with convincing depth. If you then analyzed what was on the glass, you would find the following features.

Pictorial Depth Cues

1. Linear perspective. This cue is based on the apparent convergence of parallel lines in the environment. If you stand between two railroad tracks, they appear to meet near the horizon. Since you know they are parallel, their convergence implies great distance (Fig. 5–11a).

2. Relative size. If an artist wishes to depict two objects of the same size at different distances, the artist makes the more distant object smaller (Fig. 5–11b). Films such

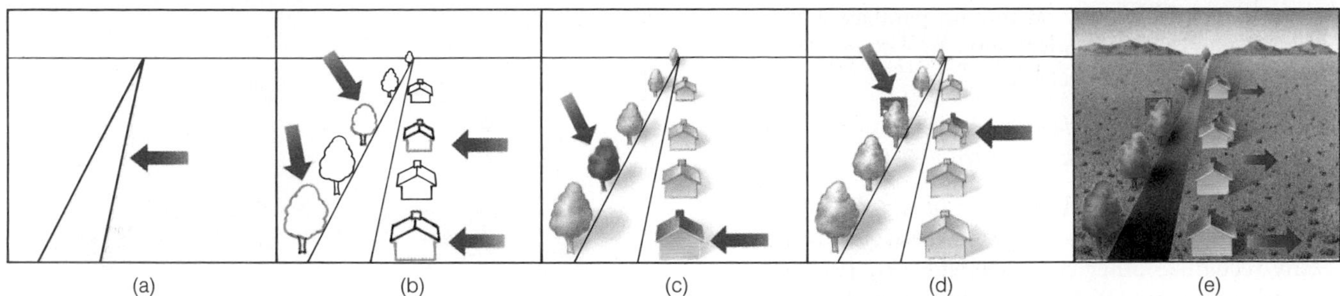

Fig. 5–11 *(a) Linear perspective. (b) Relative size. (c) Light and shadow. (d) Overlap. (e) Texture gradients.*

as *Star Wars* and *Return of the Jedi* created sensational illusions of depth by rapidly changing the image size of planets, space stations, and starships.

3. Light and shadow. Most objects in the environment are lighted in ways that create clear patterns of light and shadow. Copying such patterns of light and shadow can give a two-dimensional design a three-dimensional appearance (Fig. 5–11c).

4. Overlap. Overlap (also know as *interposition*) is a depth cue that occurs when one object partially blocks another object. Hold your hands up and have a friend try to tell from across the room which is nearer. Relative size will give the answer if one hand is much nearer to your friend than the other. But if one hand is only slightly closer than the other, your friend may have difficulty—until you slide one hand in front of the other. Overlap then removes any doubt (Fig. 5–11d).

5. Texture gradients. Changes in texture also contribute to depth perception. If you stand in the middle of a cobblestone street, the street will look coarse near your feet. However, its texture will get smaller and finer if you look into the distance (Fig. 5–11e).

6. Aerial perspective. Smog, fog, dust, and haze add to the apparent distance of an object. Because of aerial perspective, objects seen at great distance tend to be hazy, washed-out in color, and lacking in detail. This is true even in clear air, but it is increasingly the case in our mechanized society. As a matter of fact, aerial haze is often most noticeable when it is missing. If you have traveled the wide open spaces of states such as Colorado or Wyoming, you may have seen mountain ranges that looked only a few miles away, and then were shocked to find that you were actually viewing them through 50 miles of crystal-clear air.

7. Relative motion. Relative motion, also known as *motion parallax* (PAIR-ah-lax), can be seen by looking out a window and moving your head from side to side. Notice that objects near you appear to move a sizable distance as your head moves. In comparison, trees, houses, and telephone poles at a greater distance appear to move slightly in relation to the background. Distant objects like hills, mountains, or clouds don't seem to move at all.

When combined, pictorial cues can create a powerful illusion of depth (Fig. 5–12).

Question: Is motion parallax really a pictorial cue?

Strictly speaking it is not, except in movies, television, or animated cartoons. However, when it is present, depth is almost always perceived. Much of the apparent depth of a good movie comes from the relative motion of objects captured by the camera. People who can only see with

Fig. 5–12 *Pictorial depth. Look closely! The artist has used many of the pictorial depth cues to fool the eye. (M. C. Escher,* Still Life and Street. *© M. C. Escher Heirs c/o Cordon Art, Baarn, Holland. Collection Haags, Gemeentemuseum—The Hague. Reproduced by permission.)*

one eye depend heavily on motion parallax. Often, they make frequent head movements to exaggerate parallax and improve depth perception.

Question: Are pictorial depth cues universal, like the understanding of basic drawings noted earlier?

Not entirely. Some cultures use only selected pictorial cues to represent depth. People in these cultures may not easily recognize other cues (Deregowski, 1972). For example, researcher William Hudson tested members of remote tribes who do not use relative size to show depth in drawings. These people perceive simplified drawings as two-dimensional designs. As you can see in Figure 5–13, they do not assume, as we do, that a larger image means that an object is closer.

Fig. 5–13 *A Hudson test picture. Two-dimensional perceivers assume the hunter is trying to spear the distant elephant rather than the nearby antelope. Some acquaintance with conventions for representing depth in pictures and photographs seems necessary. (From "Pictorial Perception and Culture" by J. B. Deregowski. © 1972 by Scientific American, Inc. All rights reserved.)*

Question: How do the depth perception cues relate to daily experience?

The Moon Illusion Like the bodily depth cues, we constantly use the pictorial cues to gauge depth and judge distances. Cues of both types also combine to produce an intriguing illusion. When the moon is on the horizon, it tends to look as large as a silver dollar. When it is directly overhead, it looks like a dime, very much smaller than it did earlier the same evening. Contrary to what some people believe, the moon's image is not magnified by the atmosphere. If you take a photograph of the moon and measure its image, you will find that it is not larger on the horizon. But the moon *looks* larger when it's low in the sky. This is because the **apparent distance** of the moon is greater when it is near the horizon than when it is overhead.

Question: But if it seems farther away, shouldn't it look smaller?

No. When the moon is overhead, there are few depth cues around it. In contrast, when you see the moon on the horizon, it is behind houses, trees, telephone poles, and mountains. These objects add numerous depth cues, which cause the horizon to seem more distant than the sky overhead (Dember & Warm, 1980).

To better understand the moon illusion, picture two balloons, one 10 feet away and the second 20 feet away. Suppose the more distant balloon is inflated until its image matches the image of the nearer balloon. How do we know the more distant balloon is larger? Because its image is the same size as a balloon that is closer. Similarly, the moon makes the same-size image on the horizon as it does overhead. However, the horizon seems more distant because more depth cues are present. As a result, the horizon moon must be perceived as larger (Rock, 1962).

This explanation is known as the **apparent distance hypothesis.** You can test it by removing depth cues while looking at a horizon moon. Try looking at the moon through a rolled-up paper tube, or make your hands into a "telescope" and look at the next large moon you see. It will immediately appear to shrink when viewed without depth cues.

Question: How exactly does apparent distance change the moon's perceived size?

Researchers recently discovered that the moon illusion is directly related to changes in accommodation (Iavecchia et al., 1983; Roscoe, 1985). Extra depth cues near the horizon cause the eyes to focus on a more distant point than they do when you look overhead. Such changes in accommodation appear to provide the brain with a "yardstick" for judging the size of images, including that of the moon.

Learning Check

If you have difficulty with any of these questions, skim back over the previous material.

1. The visual cliff is used to test for infant sensitivity to linear perspective. T or F?

2. Write an M or a B after each of the following to indicate if it is a monocular or binocular depth cue.

accommodation ____	convergence ____
retinal disparity ____	linear perspective ____
motion parallax ____	overlap ____
relative size ____	stereoscopic mismatch ____

3. Which of the depth cues listed in question 2 are based on muscular feedback? ______________________

4. Interpretation of pictorial depth cues requires no prior experience. T or F?

5. The moon's image is greatly magnified by the atmosphere near the horizon. T or F?

Answers:

1. F **2.** accommodation (M), convergence (B), retinal disparity (B), linear perspective (M), motion parallax (M), overlap (M), relative size (M), stereoscopic mismatch (B) **3.** accommodation or convergence **4.** F **5.** F

Perceptual Learning—What If the World Were Upside Down?

England is one of the few countries in the world where people drive on the left side of the road. In view of this reversal, it is not unusual for visitors to step off curbs in front of cars—after carefully looking for traffic in the *wrong* direction. This problem is so common, in fact, that crosswalks near tourist attractions in London are stenciled with the words, "Look right"! As this example suggests, learning has a powerful impact on perception, something we have already seen in other ways.

Question: How does learning affect perception?

Perceptual Habits One way learning affects perception is through ingrained patterns of organization and attention, referred to as **perceptual habits.** Stop for a moment and look at Figure 5–14. The left face looks somewhat unusual, to be sure. But the distortion seems mild—until the page is turned upside down. Viewed normally, the face looks quite grotesque. Why is there a difference? Apparently, most people have little experience with upside-down faces. Perceptual learning, therefore, has less impact on our perceptions of an upside-down face. With a face in normal position, you know what to expect and where to look.

Before we continue, read aloud the short phrase in Figure 5–15. Did you read "Paris in the spring"? If so, look again. The word *the* appears twice in the phrase. Because of past experience with the English language, good readers often overlook the repeated word. Again, the effects of perceptual learning are apparent.

Magicians make use of perceptual habits when they use sleight of hand to distract observers while performing

Fig. 5–14 *The effects of prior experience on perception. The doctored face looks far worse when viewed right side up, because it can be related to past experience.*

Fig. 5–15

tricks. Another kind of "magic" is related to consistency in the environment. It is usually safe to assume that a room is shaped roughly like a box. This need not be true, however. When viewed from a certain point, a lopsided room can be made to appear square. This is done by carefully distorting the proportions of the walls, floor, ceiling, and windows. One such room, called an **Ames room** after the man who designed it, presents a unique problem for the perceptual habits of an observer (Fig. 5–16).

Since the left corner of the Ames room is farther from a viewer than the right, a person standing in that corner looks very small, whereas one standing in the nearer, shorter right corner looks very large. If a person walks from the left corner of the room to the right, observers are faced with a conflict. They can maintain shape constancy by perceiving the room as square, or they can maintain size constancy by refusing to see the person "grow." Most people choose shape constancy and see people "shrink" and "grow" before their eyes.

As mentioned in the previous chapter, the brain is especially sensitive to **perceptual features** in the environment. At least some of this sensitivity appears to be learned. Colin Blakemore and Graham Cooper of Cambridge University raised kittens in a room with only vertical stripes on the walls. Another set of kittens saw only horizontal stripes. When returned to normal environments, the "horizontal" cats could easily jump onto a chair, but when walking on the floor, they bumped into chair legs. "Vertical" cats, on the other hand, easily avoided chair legs, but they missed when trying to jump to horizontal surfaces. The cats raised with vertical stripes were "blind" to horizontal lines, and the "horizontal" cats acted as if vertical lines were invisible (Lewin, 1974). Other experiments show that there is an actual decrease in brain cells tuned to the missing features (Grobstein & Chow, 1975).

Question: Would it be possible, then, for an adult to adapt to a completely new perceptual world?

Inverted Vision An answer comes from experiments in which people wore lenses that invert visual images. In

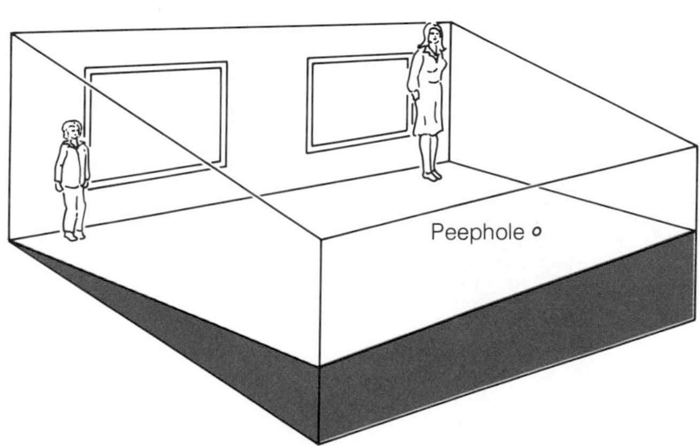

Fig. 5–16 *The Ames room. From the front, the room looks normal; actually, the right-hand corner is very short, and the left-hand corner is very tall. In addition, the left side of the room slants away from viewers. The diagram shows the shape of the room and reveals why people appear to get bigger as they cross the room toward the nearer, shorter right corner.*

one experiment, a subject wore goggles that turned the world upside down and reversed objects from right to left. At first, even the simplest tasks—walking, eating, and so forth—were incredibly difficult (Fig. 5–17). Imagine trying to reach for a door handle and watching your hand shoot off in the wrong direction.

Subjects also reported that head movements made the world swing violently through space, causing severe headaches and nausea. Yet, after several days they began to adapt to inverted vision. Their success, while not complete, was impressive. Such a high degree of adaptation is related to superior human learning abilities. If the eyes of goldfish are surgically turned upside down, the fish swim in circles and rarely adapt (Sperry, 1956).

Question: Did everything turn upright again for the humans?

No. While they wore the goggles, their visual images remained upside down. But subjects learned to perform most routine activities, and their inverted world began to seem relatively normal. In later experiments, subjects wearing inverting lenses were able to successfully drive cars. One subject even flew an airplane after a few weeks of adaptation (Kohler, 1962). These feats are like driving or flying upside down, with right and left reversed. Some ride!

Fig. 5–17 *Inverted vision. Adaptation to complete inversion of the visual world is possible but challenging.*

Active movement in a new visual world seems to be a key to rapid adaptation. In one experiment, people wore glasses that grossly distorted vision. Those who walked on their own adapted more quickly than subjects pushed around in a wheeled cart (Held, 1971). Why does movement help? Probably because commands sent to the muscles can be related to sensory feedback (McBurney & Collings, 1984). Remaining immobile would be like watching a weird movie over which you have no control. There would be little reason for any perceptual learning to occur.

Adaptation Level An important factor affecting perception is the external **context** in which a stimulus is judged. For example, a man 6 feet in height will look "tall" when surrounded by others of average height, and "short" among a group of professional basketball players. In Figure 5–18, the center circle is the same size in both designs. But like the man in different company, context alters the circle's apparent size. The importance of context is also shown by Figure 5–19. What do you see in the middle? If you read across, context causes it to be organized as a 13. Reading down makes it a B.

Fig. 5–18 *Are the center dots in both figures the same?*

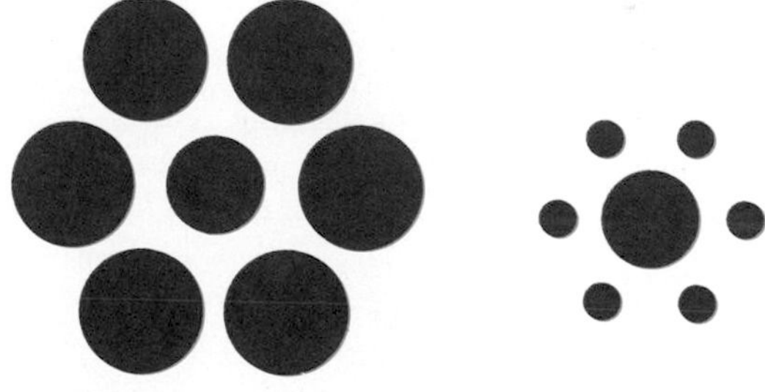

Fig. 5–19 *Context alters the meaning of the middle figure.*

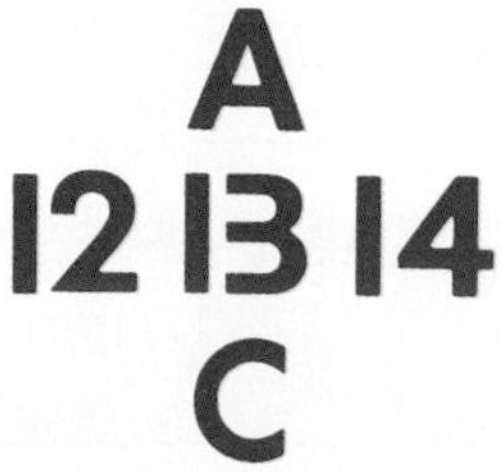

A

12 13 14

C

In addition to external contexts, we all have *internal* **frames of reference,** or standards by which stimuli are judged. If you were asked to lift a 10-pound weight, would you label it light, medium, or heavy? The answer to this question depends on your **adaptation level** (Helson, 1964). This is your own personal "medium point," or frame of reference. Each person's adaptation level is constantly modified by experience. If most of the weights you lift in day-to-day life *average* around 10 pounds, you will call a 10-pound weight medium. If you are a watchmaker and spend your days lifting tiny watch parts, you will probably call a 10-pound weight heavy. If you work as a furniture mover, your adaptation level will exceed 10 pounds, and you will call a 10-pound weight light. (If you are an aging rock star, you will no doubt call everything "heavy," man.)

Illusions Perceptual learning is responsible for a number of **illusions.** In an illusion, length, position, motion, curvature, or direction is consistently misjudged (Gillam, 1980). Illusions differ from **hallucinations** in that illusions distort stimuli that actually exist. People who are hallucinating perceive objects or events that have no external reality (for example, they hear voices that are not there). If you think you see a 3-foot-tall butterfly, you can confirm you are hallucinating by trying to touch its wings. To detect an illusion, it is often necessary to measure a drawing or apply a straight-edge to it.

Illusions are a fascinating challenge to our understanding of perception. On occasion, they also have practical uses. An illusion called **stroboscopic movement** (strobe-oh-SKOP-ik) puts the "motion" in motion pictures. The strobe lights sometimes used on dance floors reverse this illusion. Each time the strobe flashes, it "freezes" dancers in particular positions. However, if the flashes are speeded up sufficiently, normal motion is seen. In a similar way, movies project a rapid series of "snapshots" on the screen, so the gaps in motion are imperceptible.

Question: Can other illusions be explained?

Not in all cases, or to everyone's satisfaction. Generally speaking, size and shape constancy, habitual eye movements, continuity, and perceptual habits combine in various ways to produce the illusions in Figure 5–20. Rather than attempt to explain all of the pictured illusions, let's focus on one deceptively simple example.

Fig. 5–20 *Some interesting perceptual illusions.*

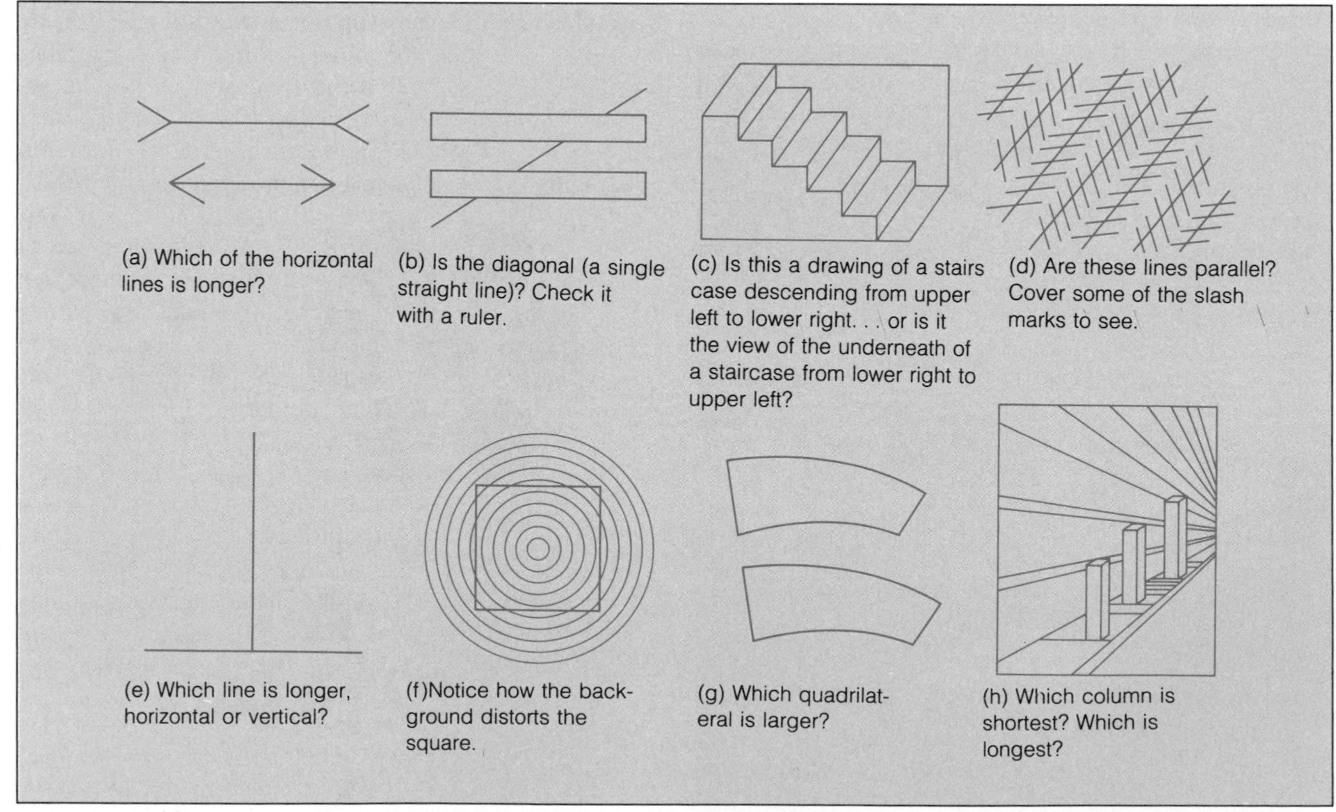

Consider the drawing in Figure 5–20a, the familiar **Müller-Lyer illusion** (MUE-ler-LIE-er). In this illusion, the horizontal line with arrowheads appears shorter than the line with V's on each end. A quick measurement will show that they are the same length. How can we explain this illusion? Evidence suggests it is based on a lifetime of experience with the edges and corners of rooms and buildings. Richard Gregory (1977) believes you see the horizontal line with the V's as if it were the corner of a room viewed from inside (Fig. 5–21). The line with arrowheads, on the other hand, suggests the corner of a room or building seen from outside.

Earlier, to explain the moon illusion, we said that if two objects make images of the same size, the more distant object must be larger. This is known formally as **size-distance invariance.** Gregory believes the same concept explains the Müller-Lyer illusion. That is, if the V-tipped line looks farther away than the arrowhead-tipped line, then you must compensate by seeing the V-tipped line as longer. This explanation of the Müller-Lyer illusion presumes that you have had years of experience with straight lines, sharp edges, and corners—a pretty safe assumption in our culture.

Question: Is there any way to show that past experience causes the illusion?

If we could test someone who saw only curves and wavy lines as a child, we would know if experience with a "square" culture is important. Fortunately, a group of people in South Africa, the Zulus, live in a "round" culture. In their daily lives, Zulus rarely encounter a straight line: Their huts are shaped like rounded mounds and arranged in a circle, tools and toys are curved, and there are no straight roads or square buildings.

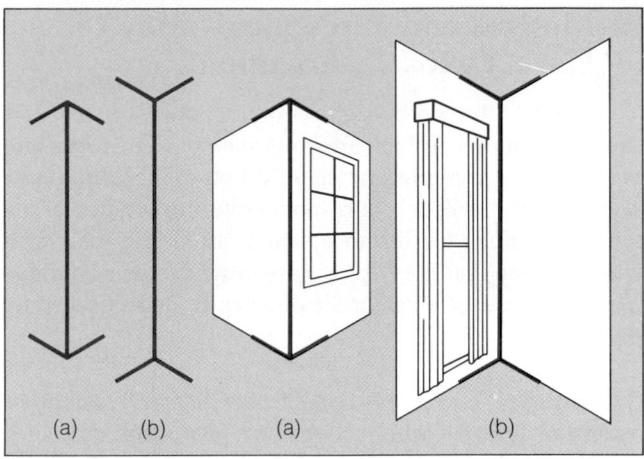

Fig. 5–21 *Why does line (b) in the Müller-Lyer illusion look longer than line (a)? Probably because it looks more like a distant corner than a nearer one. Since the vertical lines form images of the same length, the more "distant" line must be perceived as larger.*

Question: What happens if a Zulu looks at the Müller-Lyer design?

The typical Zulu does not experience the illusion. At most, he or she sees the V-shaped line as *slightly* longer than the other (Gregory, 1977). This seems to confirm the importance of past experience and perceptual habits in determining our view of the world.

Learning Check

1. Perceptual habits may become so ingrained that they lead us to misperceive a stimulus. T or F?
2. Perceptual learning seems to program the brain for sensitivity to important ________________ of the environment.
3. The Ames room is used to test for adaptation to inverted vision. T or F?
4. An important factor in adaptation to inverted vision is
   a. learning new categories *b.* active movement *c.* overcoming illusions *d.* the stroboscopic movement effect
5. Size-distance relationships appear to underlie which two illusions? ________________ and ________________.
6. An adaptation level represents a personal "medium point," or internal ________________ ________________ ________________.

Answers:

1. T 2. features 3. F 4. *b* 5. moon illusion and Müller-Lyer illusion 6. frame of reference

● Motives and Perception—May I Have Your . . . Attention!

You are surrounded by sights, sounds, odors, tastes, and touch sensations. Which are you aware of? The first stage of perception is attention, the selection of incoming messages. There is little doubt about the importance of attention. Think, for instance, about an airline pilot who fails to notice that the flaps are not down before a landing. This error caused a major air disaster at Detroit's airport in 1987.

Attention As you may recall from Chapter 4, **selective attention** refers to the fact that we give some messages priority and put others on hold (Johnston & Dark, 1986). Psychologists have found it helpful to think of selective attention as a sort of *bottleneck*, or narrowing in the information channel linking the senses to perception (Reed, 1988). When one message enters the bottleneck, it seems to prevent others from passing through. This may be why it is very difficult to listen to two people speaking at once. Typically, you can "tune in" one person or the other, but not both.

Have you ever felt overloaded when trying to do several things at once? **Divided attention** often arises from our limited *capacity* for storing and thinking about information. At any moment, you must divide your mental effort among tasks, each of which requires more or less attention. For example, when a person first learns to drive, almost all of his or her attention is needed to steer, brake, shift, and so forth. However, as a skill becomes more automatic, it requires less attention. In driving, greater skill frees mental capacity for other things, such as tuning the car's radio or carrying on a conversation (Reed, 1988).

Question: Are some stimuli more attention-getting than others?

Yes. Very *intense* stimuli usually command attention. Stimuli that are brighter, louder, or larger tend to capture attention: A gunshot in a library would be hard to ignore. Big, bright cars probably get more tickets than small, dull ones. Loud, irritating comedian Don Rickles has made a career out of the first principle of attention.

Repetitious stimuli, repetitious stimuli, repetitious stimuli, repetitious stimuli, repetitious stimuli, repetitious stimuli are also attention-getting. A dripping faucet at night makes little noise by normal standards, but because of repetition, it may become as attention-getting as a single sound many times louder. This effect is used repeatedly, so to speak, in television and radio commercials.

ATTENTION IS ALSO FREQUENTLY RELATED TO contrast OR *change* IN STIMULATION. The contrasting type styles in the preceding sentence draw attention because they are *unexpected*. Norman Mackworth and Geoffrey Loftus (1978) found that people who look at drawings like Figure 5–22 focus first and longest on unexpected objects (the octopus, in this case). Change, contrast, and incongruity are perhaps the most basic sources of attention. We quickly **habituate** (respond less) to predictable and unchanging stimuli.

Question: How does habituation differ from sensory adaptation?

Habituation As described in Chapter 4, *adaptation* decreases the actual number of sensory messages sent to the brain. When messages do reach the brain, the body makes a sort of "What is it?" reaction known as the **orientation response** (OR). An OR is characterized by enlarged pupils, brain wave changes, a short pause in breathing, increased blood flow to the head, and turning toward the stimulus (Dember & Warm, 1979). Have you ever seen someone do a double take? If so, you have observed an orientation response.

Now, think about what happens when you buy a new record album. At first the album holds your attention all the way through. But when the album becomes "old," a whole side may play without your really attending to it. When a stimulus is repeated *without change*, the OR **habituates,** or decreases.

Fig. 5–22 *One of the drawings used by Mackworth and Loftus (1978) to investigate attention. Observers attend to unexpected objects longer than they do to expected objects. In this drawing, observers looked longer at the octopus than they did at a tractor placed in the same spot. What do you think would happen if a tractor were shown upside down or on the roof of the barn?*

Motives Motives also play a role in attention. If you are riding in a car and are hungry, you will notice restaurants and billboards picturing food. If you are running low on gas, your attention will shift to gas stations. Advertisers, of course, know that their pitch will be more effective if it gets your attention. Ads are therefore loud, repetitious, and intentionally irritating. They are also designed to take advantage of two motives that are widespread in our society: *anxiety* and *sex*.

Everything from mouthwash to automobile tires is merchandised using sex as a source of attention. For instance, a recent ad for Triple Sec Liqueur ran in national magazines under the heading "Sec's Appeal." Another liquor ad shows a woman in a seductive velvet dress and says, "Feel the velvet." And what could be more obvious than ads for designer jeans that feature a shapely posterior pointed at the camera? Other ads combine sex with anxiety. Mouthwash, deodorant, soaps, toothpaste, and countless other articles are pushed in ads that play on desires to be attractive or have "sex appeal" and to avoid embarrassment.

In addition to directing attention, motives may alter what is perceived:

> As part of a supposed study of "the dating practices of college students," male volunteers were shown a picture of a female student and asked to give a first impression of how attractive she was. Before making these ratings, each subject read one of two short written passages: one was sexually arousing and the other was not. The important finding was that subjects who read the more arousing passage rated the female as more attractive. (Stephan et al., 1971.)

This result may come as no surprise to you if you have ever been infatuated with someone and then fallen out of love. A person who once seemed highly attractive may look quite different when your feelings change.

Another interesting experiment demonstrates that an emotional stimulus can shift attention away from other information. In this experiment, members of a Jewish organization watched as pictures like Figure 5–23 were flashed on a screen for a split second. Their recognition for symbols at the edge of the figure was impaired when the central item was an emotional symbol like the pictured swastika (Erdelyi & Appelbaum, 1973). This effect probably explains why fans of opposing sports teams often act as if they had seen two completely different games.

Fig. 5–23 *Emotionally significant stimuli influence attention. (Erdelyi & Appelbaum, 1973, p. 50. Reprinted by permission.)*

Perceptual Expectancies—On Your Mark, Get Set

On a piece of paper, draw a circle about 3 inches in diameter. Above and to the left of center, make a large black dot, about ½ inch in diameter. Make another dot above and to the right of center. Now, below the center of the circle, draw an arc, curved upward and about 2 inches long. If you followed these instructions, your reaction might now be, "Oh! Why didn't you just say to draw a happy face?"

Like the happy face drawing, perception seems to proceed in two major ways. In **bottom-up processing,** we analyze information starting at the "bottom" with small units (features) and build upward into a complete perception (Goldstein, 1984). The reverse also seems to occur. Many experiences are organized using one's knowledge of the world. This is called **top-down processing.** In this case, pre-existing knowledge is used to rapidly organize features into a meaningful whole. Both types of processing are illustrated by Figure 5–24. Another good example of top-down processing is found in perceptual expectancies.

Question: What is a perceptual expectancy?

A runner in the starting blocks at a track meet is **set** to respond in a certain way. Likewise, past experience, motives, context, or suggestion may create a **perceptual expectancy** that sets you to perceive in a certain way. If a car backfires, runners at a track meet may jump the gun. As a matter of fact, we all frequently jump the gun when perceiving. In essence, an expectancy is a perceptual hypothesis we are *very likely* to apply to a stimulus—even if applying it is inappropriate.

Perceptual sets often lead us to see what we *expect* to see. For example, let's say you are driving across the desert. You are very low on gas. Finally, you see a sign approaching. On it are the words FUEL AHEAD. You

Fig. 5–24 *This painting by abstract artist Al Held is 9 feet by 9 feet. If you process the painting "bottom-up," all you will see is two small dark geometric shapes. Would you like to try some top-down processing? Knowing the painting's title will allow you to apply your knowledge and see the painting in an entirely different way. The title? It's* The Big N. *Can you see it now? (Courtesy The Museum of Modern Art, New York.)*

relax, knowing you will not be stranded. But as you draw nearer, the words on the sign become FOOD AHEAD. Most people have had similar experiences in which expectations altered their perceptions. To observe preceptual expectancies firsthand, perform the experiment described in Figure 5–25.

Perceptual expectancies are frequently created by *suggestion*. This is especially true of perceiving other people. For example, a psychology professor once arranged for a guest lecturer to teach his class. Half the students in the class were given a page of notes that described the lecturer as a "rather *cold* person, industrious, critical, practical, and determined." The other students got notes describing him as a "rather *warm* person, industrious, critical, practical, and determined" (Kelley, 1950; italics added). Students who received the "cold" description perceived the lecturer as unhappy and irritable and didn't volunteer in class discussion. Those who got the "warm" description saw the lecturer as happy and good-natured, and they actively took part in discussion with him.

Categories Have you ever seen playing cards with a *red* ace of spades or a *black* four of hearts? Psychologist Jerome Bruner used a *tachistoscope* (tack-IS-toh-scope: a device for projecting pictures for very short periods) to flash pictures of cards on a screen. He found that observers misperceived cards that did not fit their knowledge and expectations. For instance, a *red* six of spades would be misperceived as a normal six of hearts (Bruner

Fig. 5–25 *"Young woman/old woman" illustrations. As an interesting demonstration of perceptual expectancy, show some of your friends view I and some view II (cover all other views). Next show your friends view III and ask them what they see. Those who saw view I should see the old woman in view III; those who saw view II should see the young woman in view III. Can you see both? (After Leeper, 1935.)*

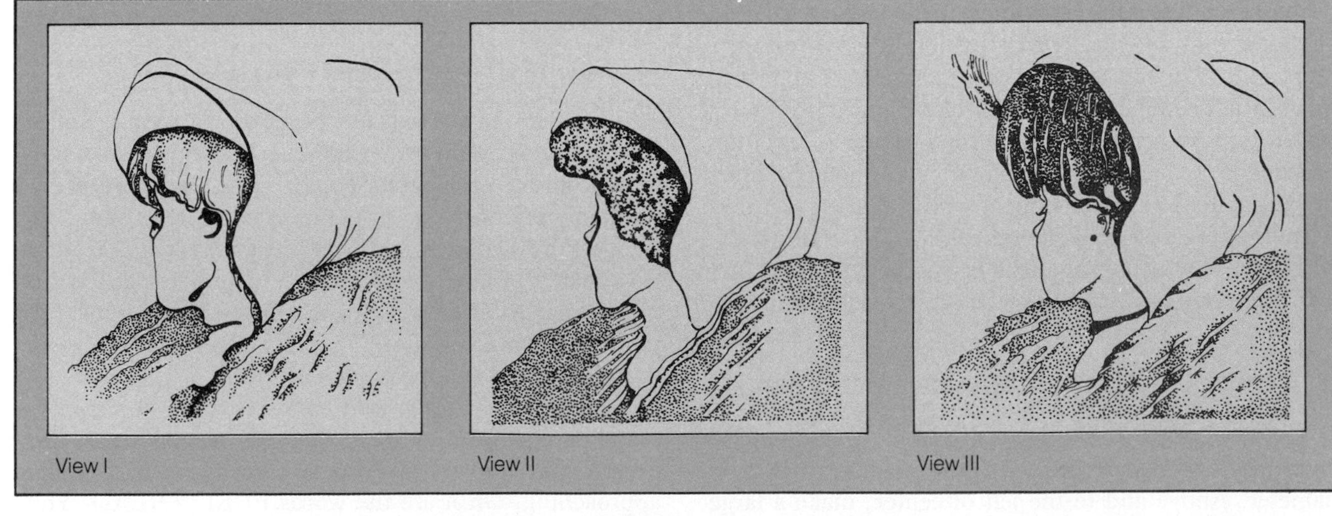

& Postman, 1949). Bruner believes that perceptual learning builds up mental **categories.** Experiences are then "sorted" into these categories. Since observers had no category for a red six of spades, they saw it as a six of hearts. Categories such as "punk," "mental patient," "queer," "honky," "bitch," and so on, are particularly likely to distort perception.

Question: Those are extremes. Does it really make that much difference what you call someone or something?

Perceptual categories, especially those defined by labels, do make a difference. This is especially true in perceiving people, where even trained observers may be influenced. For example, in one study, psychotherapists were shown a videotaped interview. Half of the therapists were told that the man being interviewed was applying for a job. The rest were told that the man was a mental patient. Therapists who thought the man was a job applicant perceived him as "realistic," "sincere," and "pleasant." Those who thought he was a patient perceived him as "defensive," "dependent," and "impulsive" (Langer & Abelson, 1974).

In this chapter, we have moved from basic perceptions of form to the complexities of perceiving people and events. In the Applications section, we will continue this progression with a look at objectivity and eyewitness testimony. After that, an Exploration addresses an interesting question: Is there any evidence that extrasensory perception exists? Before we continue, here's a Learning Check.

Learning Check

1. Selective attention is promoted by all but one of the following. Which does not fit?
a. habituation *b.* contrast *c.* change *d.* intensity

2. The occurrence of an orientation response shows that habituation is complete. T or F?

3. Changes in brain waves and increased blood flow to the head are part of an OR. T or F?

4. Research shows that heightened sexual arousal can cause a person to perceive members of the opposite sex as more physically attractive. T or F?

5. In top-down processing of information, individual features are analyzed and assembled into a meaningful whole. T or F?

6. When a person is prepared to perceive events in a particular way, it is said that a perceptual expectancy or ______________ exists.

7. Perceptual expectancies are greatly influenced by the existence of mental categories and labels. T or F?

Answers:
1. *a* 2. F 3. T 4. T 5. F 6. set 7. T

Applications: Perception and Objectivity—Believing Is Seeing

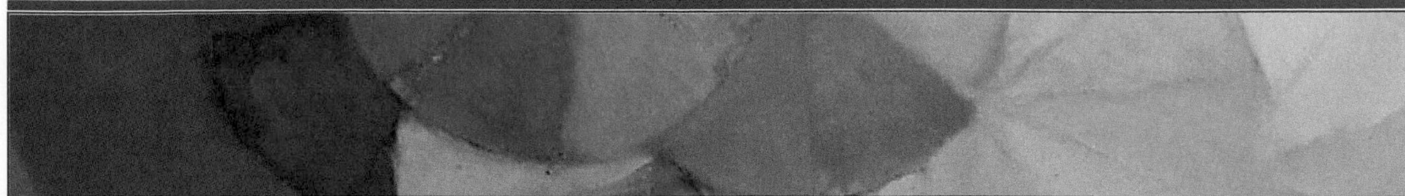

Have you ever seen the sun set? You may think you have. Yet, in reality, we know that the sun does not "set." Instead, our viewing angle changes as the earth turns, until the sun is obscured by the horizon. Want to try the alternative? This evening stand facing the west. With practice, you can learn to feel yourself being swept backward on the rotating surface of the earth as you watch an unmoving sun recede in the distance (Fuller, 1969).

This radical shift in perspective illustrates the limitations of "objective" observation. As with most other perceptions, seeing a "sunset" is an active and creative **reconstruction** of events. As we have seen, perception reflects one's needs, expectations, attitudes, values, and beliefs. In this light, the phrase "seeing is believing," must be modified. Clearly, we see what we believe, as well as believe what we see.

In some cases, subjective perception nurtures the personal vision valued in art, music, poetry, and scientific innovation. Often, though, it is a real liability.

Eyewitness In the courtroom, eyewitness testimony can be a key element in establishing guilt or innocence. The claim, "I saw it with my own eyes," carries a lot of weight with a jury. But to put it bluntly, eyewitness testimony is frequently wrong. In fact, experiments show that a person's confidence in his or her testimony has almost no bearing on its accuracy (Wells & Murray, 1983)! In addition, misleading questions about what a person saw can greatly decrease eyewitness accuracy (Smith & Ellsworth, 1987).

Psychologists are gradually convincing lawyers, judges, and police officers of the fallibility of eyewitnesses (Wells & Loftus, 1984). In one case, a police officer testified that he saw the defendant shoot the victim as both stood in a doorway 120 feet away. A psychologist showed that at that distance, light from the doorway was extremely weak—less than a fifth of that from a candle. To further show that identification was improbable, a juror stood in the doorway under identical lighting conditions. None of the other jurors could identify him. The defendant was acquitted (Buckhout, 1974).

Unfortunately, perception rarely provides an "instant replay" of events. Even in broad daylight, eyewitness testimony is untrustworthy. After a horrible DC-10 airliner crash in Chicago in 1979, 84 pilots who saw the accident were interviewed. Forty-two said the DC-10's landing gear was up, and 42 said it was down! As one investigator commented, the best witness may be a "kid under 12 years old who doesn't have his parents around" (McKean, 1982). Adults, it seems, are easily swayed by their expectations.

Perceptions formed when a person is surprised, threatened, or under stress are especially prone to distortion. This is why witnesses to crimes so often disagree. As a dramatic demonstration of this problem, an assault was staged in which a professor was attacked by an actor. Immediately after the event, 141 witnesses were questioned in detail. Their descriptions were then compared to a videotape made of the staged "crime." The total accuracy score for the group (on features such as appearance, age, weight, and height of the assailant) was only *25 percent* of the maximum possible (Buckhout, 1974).

Question: Wouldn't the victim of a crime remember more than a mere witness?

A revealing experiment found that eyewitness accuracy is virtually the same for witnessing a crime (seeing a pocket calculator stolen) as it is for being a victim (seeing one's own watch stolen) (Hosch & Cooper, 1982). Jurors who place more weight on the testimony of victims may be making a serious mistake. Also, it is worth repeating that witnesses who are confident in their testimony are no more likely to be accurate than those who have doubts.

In many crimes, victims also fall prey to the phenomenon of **weapon focus.** Understandably, victims often fix their entire attention on the knife, gun, or other weapon used by an attacker. In doing so, they fail to perceive details of appearance, dress, or other clues to identity (Loftus, 1979).

Implications How often are everyday perceptions as inaccurate or distorted as those of an emotional eyewitness? The answer we have been moving toward is, very frequently. Bearing this in mind may help you be more tolerant of the views of others and more cautious about your own objectivity. It may also encourage more frequent **reality testing** on your part.

Question: What do you mean by reality testing?

Reality Testing In any situation having an element of doubt or uncertainty, reality testing involves obtaining additional information to check your perceptions. Even simple designs like those in Figure 5–26 are easily misperceived. One of the designs in the drawing is a continuous line; the other is not. Most people cannot see this difference spontaneously. Instead, they must carefully trace and compare the two designs as a check on pure perception (Julesz, 1975).

Psychologist Sidney Jourard once offered a pertinent example of reality testing. One of Jourard's students believed her roommate was stealing from her. The student gradually

Applications

became convinced of her roommate's guilt, but said nothing. As her distrust grew, their relationship turned cold and distant. Finally, at Jourard's urging, she confronted her roommate. The roommate cleared herself immediately and expressed relief when the puzzling change in their relationship was explained (Jourard, 1974). With their friendship reestablished, the true culprit was soon caught. (The cleaning woman did it!)

If you have ever concluded that someone was angry, upset, or unfriendly without checking the accuracy of your perceptions, you have fallen into a subtle trap. Personal objectivity is an elusive quality, requiring frequent reality testing to maintain. At the very least, it pays to ask a person what he or she is feeling when you are in doubt. Undoubtedly, most of us could learn to be better "eyewitnesses" to daily events.

Question: Do some people perceive things more accurately than others?

Perceptual Awareness Humanistic psychologist Abraham Maslow (1969) believed that some people are unusually accurate in perceptions of themselves and of others. Maslow characterized these people as especially alive, open, aware, and mentally healthy. He found that their perceptual styles were marked by immersion in the present, a lack of self-consciousness, freedom from selecting, criticizing, or evaluating, and a general "surrender" to experience. The kind of perception Maslow described is like that of a mother with her newborn infant, a child at Christmas, or two people in love.

Other researchers have tested Zen masters for habituation to repeated stimuli. The results indicate that Zen masters fail to show the expected habituation (Kasamatsu & Hirai, 1966). This finding lends some credibility to claims that Zen masters perceive a tree as vividly after seeing it 500 times as they did the first time.

Attention Whereas the average person has not reached perceptual restriction of the "if you've seen one tree, you've seen them all" variety, the fact remains that most of us tend to look at a tree and classify it into the perceptual category of "trees

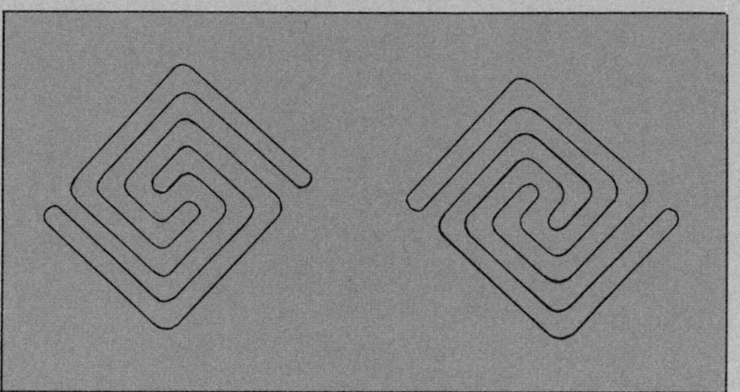

Fig. 5–26 *Limits of pure perception. (Adapted from patterns devised by Marvin L. Minsky and Seymour A. Papert.)*

in general" without really appreciating the miracle standing before us. How then can we bring about a dishabituation of perception (without going through years of meditative discipline)? The deceptively simple answer is: Pay attention.

The following quote summarizes the importance of attention:

> One day a man of the people said to Zen Master Ikkyu:
>
> "Master, will you please write for me some maxims of the highest wisdom?"
>
> Ikkyu immediately took his brush and wrote the word "Attention."
>
> "Is that all?" asked the man. "Will you not add something more?"
>
> Ikkyu then wrote twice running: "Attention. Attention."
>
> "Well," remarked the man rather irritably, "I really don't see much depth or subtlety in what you have just written."
>
> Then Ikkyu wrote the same word three times running: "Attention. Attention. Attention." Half angered, the man demanded, "What does that word 'Attention' mean anyway?"
>
> And Ikkyu answered gently: "Attention means attention." Kapleau, 1966.)

To this we can add only one thought, provided by the words of poet William Blake: "If the doors of perception were cleansed, man would see everything as it is, infinite."

Learning Check

1. Most perceptions can be described as active reconstructions of external reality. T or F?

2. Inaccuracies in eyewitness perceptions obviously occur in "real life," but they cannot be reproduced in psychology experiments. T or F?

3. Accuracy scores for facts provided by witnesses to staged crimes may be as low as 25 percent correct. T or F?

4. Victims of crimes are more accurate eyewitnesses than are impartial observers. T or F?

5. *Reality testing* is another term for dishabituation. T or F?

Answers:

1. T 2. F 3. T 4. F 5. F

Exploration: Extrasensory Perception—Do You Believe in Magic?

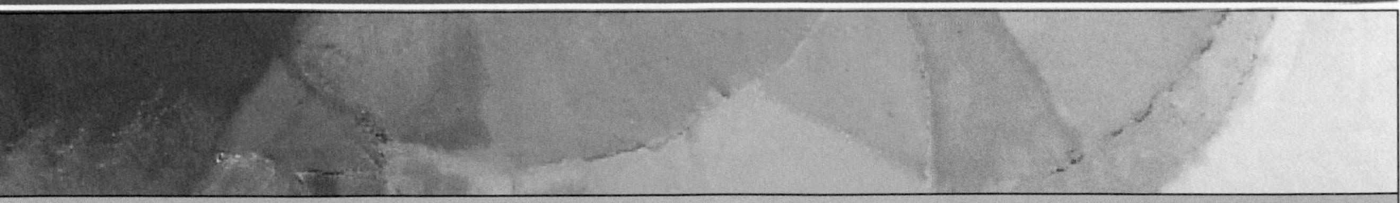

In a quiet laboratory, Uri Geller, a self-proclaimed "psychic," has agreed to demonstrate his claimed abilities to communicate by mental telepathy, to detect hidden objects, and to predict future events. In the course of testing, Geller was supposedly able to select from a row of 10 film canisters the one that contained an object, correctly guess the number that would come up on a die shaken in a closed box 8 out of 8 times, and reproduce drawings sealed in opaque envelopes.

Question: Was Geller cheating, or was he using some ability beyond normal perception?

There is now little doubt that Geller was cheating (Randi, 1980). But how? The answer lies in a discussion of **extrasensory perception (ESP)**—the purported ability to perceive events in ways that cannot be explained by accepted perceptual principles.

Parapsychology

Parapsychology is the study of ESP and other **psi** phenomena (*psi* is pronounced like *sigh*), or events that seem to defy accepted scientific laws. Parapsychologists seek answers to the questions raised by three basic forms that ESP could take. These are:

1. Clairvoyance. The ability to perceive events or gain information in ways that appear unaffected by distance or normal physical barriers.

2. Telepathy. Extrasensory perception of another person's thoughts, or more simply, an ability to read someone else's mind.

3. Precognition. The ability to perceive or accurately predict future events. Precognition may take the form of *prophetic dreams* that foretell the future.

While we are at it, we might as well toss in another purported psi ability:

4. Psychokinesis. The ability to exert influence over inanimate objects by willpower ("mind over matter"). (Psychokinesis cannot be classed as a type of perception, extrasensory or otherwise, but it is frequently studied by parapsychologists.)

Question: Have parapsychologists confirmed the existence of ESP and other psi abilities?

American psychologists as a group remain skeptical about psi abilities. If you doubt ESP, then you should know that some experiments seem to support its existence. If you are among those who believe in ESP, then you should know why the scientific community doubts many of these experiments!

Coincidence Anyone who has ever had an apparent clairvoyant or telepathic experience may find it hard to question the existence of ESP. Yet, the difficulty of excluding *coincidence* makes natural ESP occurrences less conclusive than they might seem. For example, consider a typical psychic experience. During the middle of the night, a woman away for a weekend visit suddenly had a strong impulse to return home. When she arrived, she found the house on fire with her husband asleep inside (Rhine, 1953).

An experience like this is striking, but it does not confirm the existence of ESP. If, by coincidence, a hunch turns out to be correct, it may be *reinterpreted* as a premonition or case of clairvoyance (Marks & Kammann, 1979). If it is not confirmed, it will simply be forgotten. Most people don't realize it, but such coincidences occur so often that we should *expect* them, not consider them strange or mysterious (Alcock, 1981).

The formal study of psi events owes much to the late J. B. Rhine. Rhine established the first parapsychological laboratory at Duke University and spent the rest of his life trying to document ESP. To avoid problems of coincidence and after-the-fact interpretation of "natural" ESP events, Rhine tried to study ESP more objectively. Many of his experiments made use of the **Zener cards** (Fig. 5–27). In a typical clairvoyance test, subjects tried to guess the symbols on the cards as they were turned up from a shuffled deck. Pure guessing in this test will produce an average score of 5 "hits" out of 25 cards.

Unfortunately, some of Rhine's most dramatic early experiments used badly printed Zener cards that allowed the symbols to show faintly on the back. It is also very easy to cheat, by marking cards with a finger-

Exploration

Fig. 5–27 *ESP cards used by J. B. Rhine, an early experimenter in parapsychology.*

nail or by noting marks on the cards caused by normal use. Even if this were not the case, there is evidence that early experimenters sometimes unconsciously gave subjects cues about the cards with their eyes, facial gestures, or lip movements. In short, none of the early studies in parapsychology were done in a way that eliminated the possibility of fraud (Alcock, 1981).

Modern parapsychologists are now well aware of the need for double-blind experiments, maximum security and accuracy in record keeping, meticulous control, and repeatability of experiments (Rhine, 1974a). In the last 10 years, hundreds of experiments have been reported in parapsychological journals, many of them supporting the existence of psi abilities.

Question: Then why do most psychologists remain skeptical about psi abilities?

For one thing, fraud continues to plague the field. Walter J. Levy, who was former director of Rhine's laboratory, was caught faking records, as have some others who got positive results. Even honest scientists have been fooled by various frauds and cheats, so there is reason to remain skeptical and on guard.

Statistics and Chance A major criticism of psi research has to do with inconsistency. For every study with positive results, there are others that fail (Hansel, 1980). It is rare—in fact, almost unheard of—for a subject to maintain psi ability over any sustained period of time (Jahn, 1982; Schmeidler, 1977). ESP researchers consider this "decline effect" an indication that parapsychological skills are very fragile and unpredictable (Rhine, 1977). But critics argue that subjects who only temporarily score above chance have just received credit for a **run of luck.** When the run is over, it is not fair to assume that ESP is temporarily gone. We must count *all* attempts.

To understand the run-of-luck criticism, consider an example. Say that you flip a coin 100 times and record the results. You then flip another coin 100 times, again recording the results. The two lists are compared. For any 10 pairs of flips, we would expect heads or tails to match 5 times. Let's say that you go through the list and find a set of 10 pairs where 9 out of 10 matched. This is far above chance expectation. But does it mean that the first coin "knew" what was going to come up on the second coin? The idea is obviously silly.

Now, what if a person guesses 100 times what will come up on a coin. Again, we might find a set of 10 guesses that matches the results of flipping the coin. Does this mean that the person, for a time, had precognition—then lost it? Parapsychologists tend to believe the answer is yes. Skeptics assume that nothing more than random matching occurred, as in the two-coin example.

Research Methods

Unfortunately, many of the most spectacular findings in parapsychology simply cannot be **replicated** (repeated) (Gardner, 1977; Hyman, 1977). More importantly, improved research methods usually result in fewer positive results. Proponents of parapsychology feel that they can point to experiments that meet all possible criticisms. But in virtually every case, the results cannot be repeated by doubters.

Believers in ESP, such as ex-astronaut Edgar Mitchell, claim that other factors explain negative results: "The scientist has to recognize that his own mental processes may influence the phenomenon he's observing. If he's really a total skeptic, the scientist may well turn off the psychic subject." This may sound convincing, but skeptics consider it unfair. With Mitchell's argument in effect, anyone attempting an objective experiment can only get two results: He or she may find evidence of ESP or be accused of having suppressed it. This makes it impossible to disprove ESP to believers, even if it truly does not exist.

Reinterpretation is also a problem in psi experiments. For example, Mitchell claimed he did a successful telepathy experiment from space. Yet, news accounts never mentioned that on some trials Mitchell's "receivers" scored above chance, while on

Exploration

others they scored *below* chance. The second outcome, Mitchell decided, was also a "success" because it represented intentional "psi missing." But as skeptics have noted, if both high scores and low scores count as successes, how can you lose?

Stage ESP Skeptics and serious researchers in ESP both agree on one point. If psychic phenomena do occur, they cannot be controlled well enough to be used by entertainers. Stage ESP (like stage magic) is based on a combination of sleight of hand, deception, and patented gadgets (Fig. 5–28). A case in point is Uri Geller, a former nightclub magician who "astounded" audiences—and some scientists—from coast to coast with apparent telepathy, psychokinesis, and precognition.

Geller's performance on tests was described earlier. Not mentioned is what University of Oregon Professor Ray Hyman calls the "incredible sloppiness" of these tests. One example is Geller's reproductions of sealed drawings. These, it turns out, were done in a room next to the one where the drawings were made. Original reports of Geller's alleged "ability" failed to mention that there was a hole in the wall between the two rooms, through which Geller might have heard discussions of the pictures being drawn. Also unreported was the fact that Geller's friend Shipi Stang was present at every test. Geller's manager has since testified that Stang frequently acted as Geller's accomplice in trickery (Alcock, 1981). Is it a coincidence that when a picture of a rocket ship was drawn, Stang hummed the theme music from the motion picture *2001: A Space Odyssey*? A similar lack of control pervaded every other test. In the "die in the box" tests, for instance, Geller was allowed to hold the box, shake it, and have the honor of opening it (Randi, 1980; Wilhelm, 1976). Why weren't such pertinent details reported?

Sensational and uncritical reporting of apparent paranormal events is widespread. Hundreds of books, articles, and television programs are produced each year by people who have become wealthy promoting unsupported claims. If a person did have psychic powers, he or she would not have to make a living by entertaining, giving demonstrations, or making personal appearances. A quick trip to the gaming tables of Las Vegas would allow the person to retire for life.

Conclusion After close to 130 years of investigation, it is still impossible to say conclusively whether psi events occur. As we have seen, a close look at psi experiments often reveals serious problems of evidence, procedure, and scientific rigor (Alcock, 1981; Hansel, 1980; Marks & Kammann, 1979; Randi, 1980). Yet, being a skeptic does not

Fig. 5–28 *Fake psychokinesis. (a) The performer shows an observer several straight keys. While doing so, he bends one of the keys by placing its tip in the slot of another key. Normally, this is done out of sight, behind the "psychic's" hand. It is clearly shown here so you can see how the deception occurs. (b) Next, the "psychic" places the two keys in the observer's hand and closes it. By skillful manipulation, the observer has been kept from seeing the bent key. The performer then "concentrates" on the keys to "bend them with psychic energy." (c) The bent key is revealed to the observer. "Miracle" accomplished! (Adapted from Randi, 1983.)*

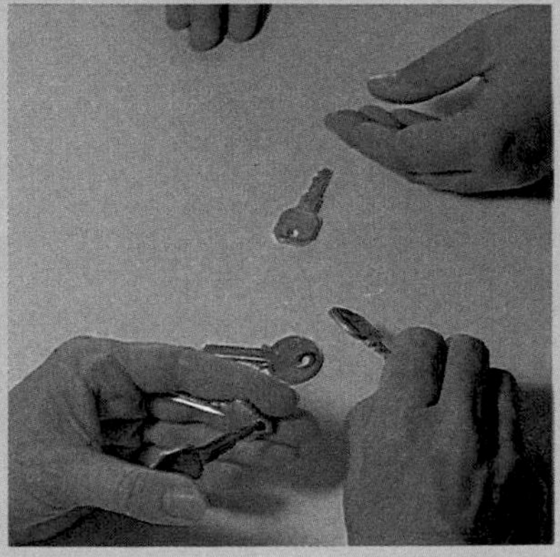

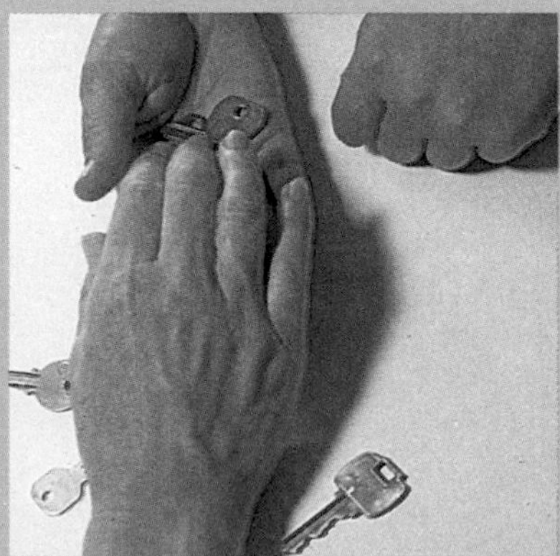

Exploration

mean a person is against something. It means that you are unconvinced. The purpose of this discussion, then, has been to counter the *uncritical* acceptance of psi events that is rampant in the media.

Question: What would it take to scientifically demonstrate the existence of ESP?

Quite simply, a set of instructions that would allow any competent, unbiased observer to produce a psi event under standardized conditions (Moss & Butler, 1978). Undoubtedly, some intrepid researchers will continue their attempts to supply just that. Others remain skeptics, and some consider 130 years of inconclusive efforts reason enough to abandon the concept of ESP (Swets et al., 1988). At the least, it seems essential to be carefully skeptical of evidence reported in the popular press or by researchers who are uncritical "true believers." But then, you already knew I was going to say that, didn't you!

Learning Check

1. Four purported psi events investigated by parapsychologists are clairvoyance, telepathy, precognition, and ____________________.

2. The ____________________ cards were used by J. B. Rhine in early tests of ESP.

3. Natural, or "real life," occurrences are regarded as the best evidence for the existence of ESP. T or F?

4. Skeptics attribute positive results in psi experiments to statistical runs of luck. T or F?

5. Replication rates are very high for ESP experiments. T or F?

Answers:

1. psychokinesis 2. Zener 3. F 4. T 5. F

Chapter Summary

- **Perception** is the process of assembling sensations into a usable mental representation of the world.
- In vision, the image projected on the retina is constantly changing, but the external world appears stable and undistorted because of **size, shape,** and **brightness constancy.**
- The most basic organization of sensations is a division into **figure and ground** (object and background). A number of factors contribute to the organization of sensations. These are **nearness, similarity, continuity, closure, contiguity,** and combinations of the preceding. Basic elements of line drawings appear to be universally recognized.
- A perceptual organization may be thought of as a **hypothesis** held until evidence contradicts it. Perceptual organization shifts for **ambiguous stimuli. Impossible figures** resist stable organization altogether.
- **Depth perception** (the ability to perceive three-dimensional space and judge distances) is present in rudimentary form soon after birth (as shown by testing with the **visual cliff** and other methods).
- Depth perception depends on the **muscular cues** of **accommodation** (bending of the lens) and **convergence** (inward movement of the eyes). **Stereoscopic vision** is created mainly by **retinal disparity** and the resulting overlap and **mismatch** of visual sensations.
- A number of **pictorial cues** also underlie depth perception. These are, **linear perspective, relative size, light and shadow, overlap, texture gradients, aerial haze,** and **relative motion** (motion parallax). All are monocular depth cues (only one eye is needed to make use of them).
- The **moon illusion** is at least partially explained by the **apparent distance hypothesis,** which emphasizes the greater number of depth cues present when the moon is

on the horizon. Changes in accommodation also contribute to the moon illusion.

• The organizing and interpreting of sensations are greatly influenced by **perceptual habits.** Studies of **inverted vision** show that even the most basic organization is subject to a degree of change. **Active movement** speeds adaptation to a new perceptual environment.

• Perceptual judgments are not made in a vacuum. They are almost always related to **context,** or to an internal **frame of reference** called the **adaptation level.**

• One of the most familiar of all illusions, the **Müller-Lyer illusion,** seems to be related to perceptual learning, linear perspective, and **size-distance invariance** relationships.

• **Attention** is **selective,** and it may be **divided** among various activities. Attention is closely related to **stimulus intensity, repetition, contrast, change,** and **incongruity.** Attention is accompanied by an **orientation response.** When a stimulus is repeated without change, the orientation response undergoes **habituation.**

• Personal **motives** and **values** often alter perceptions by changing the evaluation of what is seen or by altering attention to specific details.

• Perceptions may be based on **top-down** or **bottom-up processing** of information. Attention, prior experience, suggestion, and motives combine in various ways to create **perceptual sets,** or **expectancies.** These prepare a person to perceive or misperceive in a particular way. Expectancies are often related to pre-existing mental categories and labels.

• Perception is an active **reconstruction** of events. This is one reason why **eyewitness testimony** is surprisingly unreliable. Eyewitness accuracy is further damaged by **weapon focus.** Perceptual accuracy is enhanced by **reality testing, dishabituation,** and conscious efforts to **pay attention.**

• **Parapsychology** is the study of purported **psi phenomena,** including **clairvoyance, telepathy, precognition,** and **psychokinesis.** Research in parapsychology remains controversial owing to a variety of problems and shortcomings. **Stage ESP** is based on deception and tricks.

Questions for Discussion

1. Return for a moment to the incident described in the Chapter Preview. What perceptual factors were involved in the first version of the "murder"? How did the girl affect what was seen?

2. Do you think your perceptions of an argument or fight with a friend, parent, spouse, or lover are accurate? What perceptual factors might affect your viewpoint?

3. Bicyclists and motorcyclists often complain that automobile drivers act as if cyclists are invisible. What perceptual factors might cause drivers to "look right at" cyclists without seeing them?

4. A professional basketball player is at the free-throw line for the last shot in a tied championship game. What depth cues are available to him? A professional golfer is making the last putt for a $10,000 prize; what depth cues is she using? A pilot is landing at an unfamiliar airport; what cues are available to her? You are looking through a microscope with one eye; what depth cues can you use?

5. Describe a situation you have misperceived. What influenced your perceptions?

6. What role might habituation play in industrial accidents (especially on production lines) and in driving on arrow-straight superhighways? What changes would you make in work procedures or highway design to combat habituation?

7. In view of the Chapter Preview and Applications, how dependable do you think eyewitness testimony is in a courtroom? What factors other than accuracy of original perceptions might contribute to inaccuracies in testimony?

8. If you believe that ESP occurs, what would it take to convince you that it does not? If you do not believe that ESP occurs, what would it take to convince you that it does?

Chapter 6

States of Consciousness

In This Chapter

Normal and altered states of consciousness
Sleep needs and patterns
Stages and types of sleep
Sleep disturbances
Dreams
Hypnosis
Sensory deprivation
Psychoactive drugs
Applications
Exploring and using dreams
Exploration
Perspectives on drug abuse

Chapter Preview

Living Nightmares

January 1959, in New York's Times Square: To raise money for charity, disc jockey Peter Tripp has agreed to go without sleep for 200 hours. All too soon Tripp's fight to stay awake turns brutal. After 100 hours, he begins to have visual hallucinations: He sees cobwebs in his shoes and watches in terror as a tweed coat becomes a suit of "furry worms." When Tripp goes to a hotel to change clothes, a dresser drawer seems to burst into flames.

After 170 hours, Tripp's agony becomes almost unbearable. He struggles with the simplest thought, reasoning, and memory problems. His brain wave patterns look like those of sleep, and he is no longer sure who he is. By the end of 200 hours, Tripp is unable to distinguish between his waking nightmares, hallucination, and reality (Luce, 1965).

The Womb Tank *We shift now to a scene far removed from Peter Tripp's ordeal. Some years ago, physician John Lilly pioneered the use of an unusual* **sensory deprivation** *environment. Subjects in Lilly's experiments wore darkened goggles and floated naked in a tank of body-temperature water (Lilly, 1972). As they drifted weightlessly in this "womblike" environment, subjects were cut off from smell, touch, vision, hearing, and taste sensations.*

Question: What effect does sensory deprivation have?

Under such conditions, subjects often lose track of time and find it hard to concentrate. Some also undergo strange alterations in consciousness. For example, one subject in another experiment screamed in panic, "There is an animal having a long slender body with many legs. It's on the screen, crawling in back of me!" (Heron, 1957).

As you can see, both sleep loss and sensory deprivation have a major impact on consciousness. *In the discussion of consciousness that follows, we will begin with the familiar realms of sleep and dreaming and then move to points beyond.*

Survey Questions

- What is an altered state of consciousness?
- What are the effects of sleep loss or changes in sleep patterns?
- Are there different stages of sleep?
- How does dream sleep differ from dreamless sleep?
- What are the causes of sleep disorders and unusual sleep events?
- Do dreams have meaning?
- How is hypnosis done, and what are its limitations?
- How does sensory deprivation affect consciousness?
- What are the effects of the more commonly used psychoactive drugs?
- Why is drug abuse so widespread?

States of Consciousness—The Many Faces of Awareness

To be conscious means to be aware. **Consciousness** consists of all the sensations, perceptions, memories, and feelings that you are aware of at any given instant. As William James noted, consciousness is an everchanging "stream," or flow of awareness. We spend most of our lives in ordinary **waking consciousness,** which is organized, meaningful, and clear. Waking consciousness is perceived as real, and it is marked by a familiar sense of time and place (Marsh, 1977). But as James also noted, states of consciousness related to fatigue, delirium, hypnosis, drugs, and ecstasy differ markedly from "normal" awareness. All people experience at least some altered states of awareness, such as sleep, dreaming, and daydreaming. In everyday life, changes in consciousness may accompany long-distance running, listening to music, making love, or other circumstances.

Question: It's clear that there are many altered states of consciousness. How are they distinguished from normal awareness?

An **altered state of consciousness** (ASC) is a distinct change in the *quality* and *pattern* of mental activity. Typically, there are shifts in perceptions, emotions, memory, time sense, thinking, feelings of self-control, and suggestibility (Tart, 1975). Definitions aside, most people know when they have experienced an ASC.

Question: Are there other causes of ASCs?

The list of causes is nearly endless. In addition to those already mentioned, we could add: sensory overload (for example, a light show, Mardi Gras crowd, or disco), monotonous stimulation ("highway hypnotism" on long drives is a good example), unusual physical conditions (high fever, hyperventilation, dehydration, sleep loss), sensory deprivation, and many other possibilities. In this chapter we will focus on sleep, dreaming, hypnosis, stimulus deprivation, and the effects of drugs (psychoactive chemicals).

To get right to the questions raised by the Chapter Preview, let's begin with the most familiar altered states of consciousness: sleep and dreaming.

Sleep—A Nice Place to Visit

Each of us will spend some 25 years of life in a strange state of semi-consciousness called sleep. Contrary to common belief, humans are not totally unresponsive during sleep. Studies show that you are more likely to awaken if your own name is spoken instead of another (Webb, 1978). Likewise, a sleeping mother may ignore a jet rumbling overhead, but wake at the slightest whimper of her child. Some people can even do simple tasks while asleep. In one experiment, subjects learned to avoid an electrical shock by touching a switch each time a tone sounded. Eventually, they could do it without waking. (This is much like the basic survival skill of turning off your alarm clock without waking.) Of course, sleep does impose limitations. There is no evidence, for instance, that a person can learn math, a foreign language, or other complex skills while asleep—especially when the snooze takes place in class (Aarons, 1976).

Because of its many contradictions, sleep has always aroused curiosity. What do we know about this daily retreat from the world?

The Need for Sleep

Question: How strong is the need for sleep?

Sleep expert Wilse Webb (1975) calls sleep a "gentle tyrant." Webb considers sleep an **innate biological rhythm** that can never be entirely sidestepped. But if flexibility is needed, sleep will give way temporarily, especially at times of great danger. As comedian Woody Allen put it, "The lion and the lamb shall lie down together, but the lamb will not be very sleepy." You could choose, then, to stay awake for an extended period. But there are limits. Animals prevented from sleeping fall into a coma and die after several days (Kleitman, 1963; Rechtschaffen et al., 1983).

In one set of experiments, animals were placed on treadmills over a pool of water to minimize sleep. Even so, sleep won out. The animals soon began to drift into repeated microsleeps (Goleman, 1982). A **microsleep** is a brief shift in brain activity to patterns normally recorded during sleep. Microsleeps also occur in humans: When you drive, it is well worth remembering that a microsleep can lead to a macro-accident.

Question: How long could a person go without sleep?

Sleep Deprivation With few exceptions, 4 days or more without sleep becomes hell for anyone, but longer sleepless periods are possible. The world record for staying awake is held by Randy Gardner—who at age 17 went 268 hours (11 days) without sleep. Surprisingly, Randy needed only 14 hours of sleep to recover (Dement, 1972). It is usually not necessary to completely replace lost sleep. As Randy found, most symptoms of sleep loss are reversed by a single night's rest.

What are the costs of sleep loss? Age and personality make a big difference. Randy Gardner remained clear-headed to the end of his vigil, whereas Peter Tripp's behavior became quite bizarre. In general, there is little impairment on complex mental tasks after 2 days without sleep. But most people do decline in their ability to pay attention, remain vigilant, and follow simple routines (Webb, 1978).

If you were mildly deprived of sleep, you would probably be able to rouse yourself for more complex or challenging tasks. What usually suffers most is low-level, boring, self-motivated tasks. As Wilse Webb says, "It's not your thinking or memory that goes, it's your will to continue; you would prefer to be asleep" (Goleman, 1982). For a driver, pilot, or machine operator, this may be enough to spell disaster.

Greater sleep loss sometimes causes a temporary **sleep-deprivation psychosis** like Peter Tripp suffered. Common to this reaction are confusion and disorientation, delusions (false or distorted beliefs), and hallucinations. Hallucinations may be visual, like Tripp's "coat of furry worms," or tactile, such as feeling cobwebs on the face. Fortunately, such "crazy" behavior is less common than once thought. Hallucinations and delusions are rarely evident before 60 hours of sleep loss. The most common reactions to extended sleep loss are inattention, staring, trembling hands, drooping eyelids, and an increased sensitivity to pain (Webb, 1978).

Sleep Patterns

Question: Sleep was described as an innate biological rhythm. What does that mean?

Rhythms of sleep and waking are so steady that they continue for many days, even when clocks and light-dark cycles are removed. However, under such conditions, humans eventually shift to a sleep-waking cycle that averages *25 hours,* not 24 (Sulzman, 1983). This finding suggests that external time markers, especially light and dark, help tie our sleep rhythms to a normal 24-hour day (Fig. 6–1). Otherwise, many of us would drift into our own unusual sleep cycles.

Question: What is the normal range of sleep?

According to medical records, there is a man in England who gets by on only 15 minutes to an hour of sleep each night—and feels perfectly fine. However, this is quite rare. Only 8 percent of the population averages 5 hours of sleep or less per night. The majority sleep on a familiar 7- to 8-hour-per-night schedule. It is quite normal, however, to sleep as little as 5 hours per night or as much as 11. Urging everyone to sleep 8 hours would be like advising everyone to wear medium-size shoes. There is one difference worth noting, however: In general, **long sleepers** tend to be daytime "worriers." **Short sleepers,** in contrast, are typically "non-worriers" (Hartmann, 1981). (If you sleep a lot, try not to worry about it!) This difference may reflect sleep's restorative function. That is, people who worry may need more rest each night.

Question: Do elderly people need more sleep?

They may need it, but they seldom get it. As people age they usually sleep less. People over the age of 50 average only 6 hours of sleep a night. In contrast, infants spend up to 20 hours a day sleeping, usually in 2- to 4-hour cycles. As they mature, most children go through a "nap" stage and eventually settle into a steady cycle of sleeping once a day (Fig. 6–2). Some people, of course, maintain the afternoon "siesta" as an adult pattern.

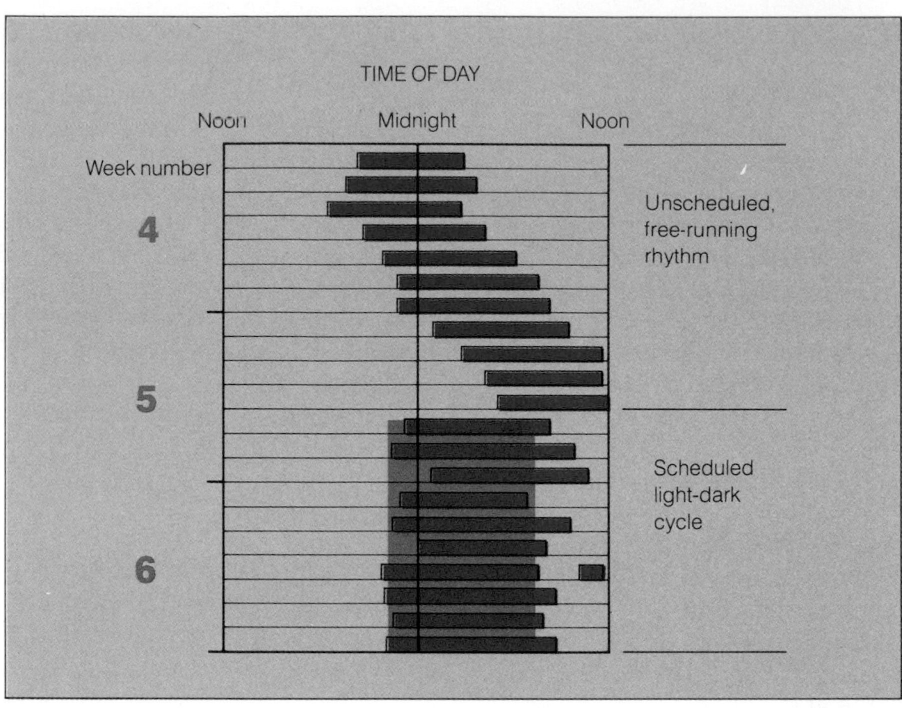

Fig. 6–1 *Sleep rhythms. Bars show periods of sleep during the fourth, fifth, and sixth weeks of an experiment with a human subject. During unscheduled periods, the subject was allowed to select times of sleep and lighting. The result was a sleep rhythm of about 25 hours. Notice how this free-running rhythm began to advance around the clock. When periods of darkness were scheduled (colored area), the rhythm quickly resynchronized with 24-hour days. (Adapted from Czeilser, 1981.)*

It is very tempting to try to reduce sleep time. However, people on *shortened* cycles—for example, 3 hours of sleep to 6 hours awake—often can't get to sleep when the cycle calls for it (Webb, 1978). The underlying sleep rhythm simply won't cooperate. This is why astronauts continue to sleep on their normal earth schedule while in space (Goleman, 1982). Adapting to *longer* than normal days is more promising. Such days can be tailored to match natural **sleep patterns,** which have a ratio of *2 to 1* between time awake and time asleep. One study showed that 28-hour "days" work for some people (Kleitman & Kleitman, 1953). Unfortunately, subjects did poorly on longer 36-hour cycles (24 hours awake and 12 hours asleep) (Webb, 1978). Most people couldn't use the entire 12-hour sleep period, so they repeatedly lost sleep. As with sleep needs, we see again that sleep is a "gentle tyrant." Sleep patterns may be bent and stretched, but they rarely yield entirely to human whims.

Fig. 6–2 *Development of sleep patterns. Short cycles of sleep and waking gradually become the night-day cycle of an adult. (After Williams, 1964.)*

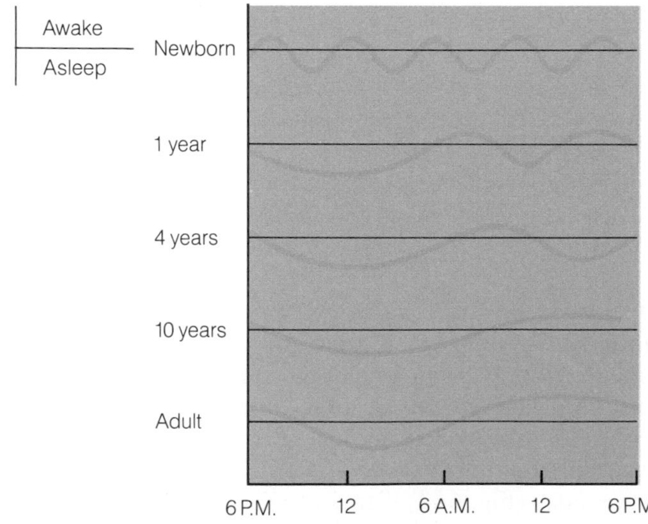

● Stages of Sleep—The Nightly Roller-Coaster Ride

Question: What causes sleep?

Early sleep experts thought that some substance related to fatigue must accumulate in the bloodstream and cause sleep. But studies of Siamese twins (individuals whose bodies are joined at birth) show that this is false. One twin can frequently be observed sleeping while the second is awake (Fig. 6–3). During waking hours, a sleep-promoting chemical collects in the brain and spinal cord, *not* in the blood. If this substance is extracted from one animal and injected into another, the second animal will fall asleep (Pappenheimer, 1976). Notice, however, that this explanation is incomplete. For example, how do we

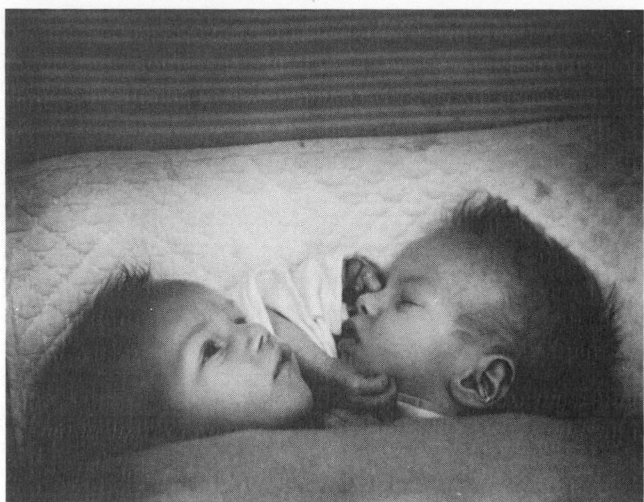

Fig. 6–3 *These Siamese twins share the same blood supply, yet one sleeps while the other is awake. (Photo by Yale Joel, Life Magazine. © 1954 Time, Inc.)*

account for the well-rested student who must fight to stay awake during a boring lecture?

All that can be said for sure is that sleep is *actively* produced by several structures in the brain: the hypothalamus, the reticular formation, and a "sleep center" in the brainstem. Rather than "shutting down" during sleep, the brain changes the *pattern* of its activity, not the amount.

Question: What happens when you fall asleep?

Stages of Sleep

The changes that come with sleep can be measured with an **electroencephalograph** (e-LEK-tro-en-SEF-uh-lo-graf), or brain wave machine, commonly called an **EEG**. The brain gives off tiny electrical signals that can be amplified and recorded. When you are awake and alert, the EEG shows a pattern of small fast waves called **beta** (Fig. 6–4). Immediately before sleep the EEG record shifts to a pattern of larger and slower waves called **alpha.** (Alpha waves also occur when a person is relaxed and thoughts are allowed to drift.) As the eyes close, breathing becomes slow and regular, the pulse rate slows, and body temperature drops.

Stage 1 As you lose consciousness and enter **light sleep,** your heart rate slows even more. Breathing becomes more irregular; the muscles of your body relax. This sometimes triggers a reflex muscle contraction called a **hypnic jerk** (HIP-nik: sleep), which is quite normal. (Have no fear, then, about admitting to your friends that you fell asleep with a hypnic jerk.) Muscle spasms in the legs that occur later, during sleep itself, are called **myoclonus** (MY-oh-KLOE-nus). This problem causes about 15 to 20 percent of all cases of insomnia.

In stage 1 sleep the EEG is made up mainly of small,

Fig. 6–4 *(a) Photograph of an EEG recording session. The man in the background is asleep. (b) Changes in brain wave patterns associated with various stages of sleep. Actually, most wave types are present at all times, but they occur more or less frequently in various sleep stages.*

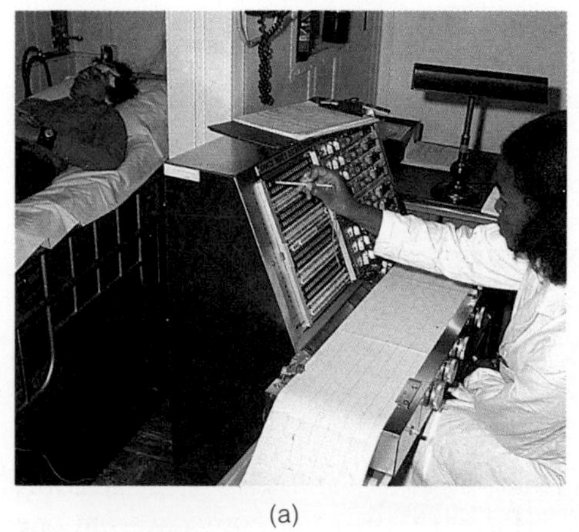

(a)

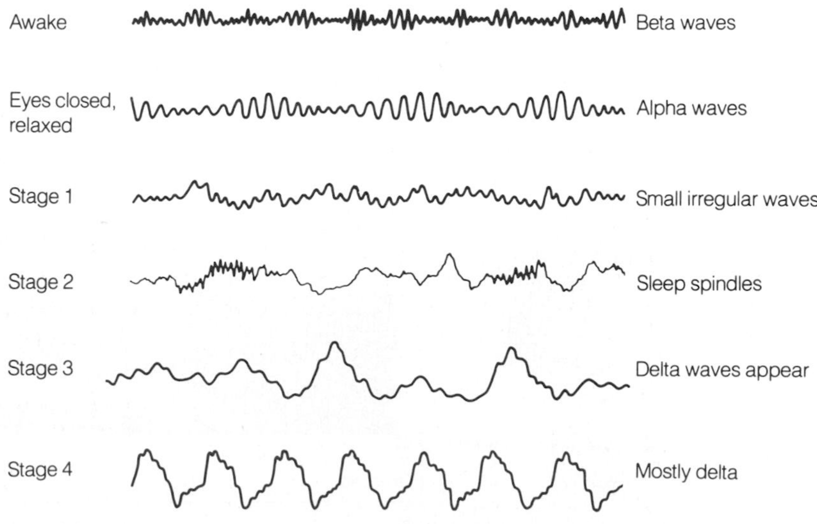

(b)

irregular waves with some alpha. Persons awakened at this time may or may not say they were asleep.

Stage 2 As sleep deepens, the EEG begins to show short bursts of activity called **sleep spindles,** and body temperature drops further (see Fig. 6–4). Sleep spindles seem to mark the true boundary of sleep. Within 4 minutes after spindles appear, the majority of persons who are awakened say they were asleep (Bonnet & Moore, 1982).

Stage 3 In stage 3, a new brain wave called **delta** begins to appear. Delta waves are very large and slow. Delta waves signal deeper sleep and a further loss of consciousness.

Stage 4 **Deep sleep** is reached about an hour after sleep begins. In stage 4 the brain wave pattern becomes almost pure delta waves, and the sleeper is in a state of oblivion. If you sound a loud noise during stage 4, the sleeper will awaken in confusion and may not remember the noise.

After spending some time in stage 4, the sleeper returns (through stages 3 and 2) to stage 1. Further shifts between deeper and lighter sleep occur throughout the night (Fig. 6–5).

Two Basic States of Sleep

If you watch a person who is asleep, you will soon notice that the sleeper's eyes occasionally move under the eyelids. These **rapid eye movements** (or **REMs**) are strongly associated with dreaming (Fig. 6–5). Roughly 85 percent of awakenings made during ongoing REMs produce reports of vivid dreams (Cartwright, 1978). **REM sleep** is also easy to observe in pets, such as dogs and cats. Watch for eye and facial movements and for irregular breathing. (You can forget about your pet iguana, though. Reptiles show no signs of REM sleep.)

The two most basic states of sleep now appear to be REM sleep with its associated dreaming and **non-REM (NREM) sleep,** which occurs mainly during stages 2, 3, and 4 (Cartwright, 1978). NREM sleep is dream-free about 90 percent of the time. It is true that people awakened during NREM sleep sometimes say they were dreaming. However, dreams reported during REM sleep are usually longer, clearer, more detailed, and more "dreamlike" (Foulkes & Schmidt, 1983). Your first period of stage 1 sleep is usually free of REMs and dreams. Stage 1 sleep during the rest of the night is usually accompanied by rapid eye movements.

NREM sleep seems to help us recover from fatigue built up during the day. It increases with exercise or physical exertion (Horne & Staff, 1983). In comparison, REM sleep increases when a person is subjected to added daytime stress. Although REM sleep totals only about 1½ hours per night (about the same as a feature movie), its link with dreaming makes it as important as NREM sleep. REM sleep may rise dramatically when there is a death in the family, trouble at work, a marital conflict, or other emotionally charged events (Hartmann, 1973).

Question: What happens to the body when a person dreams?

REM Sleep and Dreaming REM sleep is a time of high emotion. The heart beats irregularly, and blood pressure and breathing waver. Both males and females

Fig. 6–5 *(a) Average proportion of time adults spend daily in REM sleep and NREM sleep. REM periods add up to about 20 percent of total sleep time. (b) Typical changes in stages of sleep during the night. Notice that dreams mostly coincide with REM periods.*

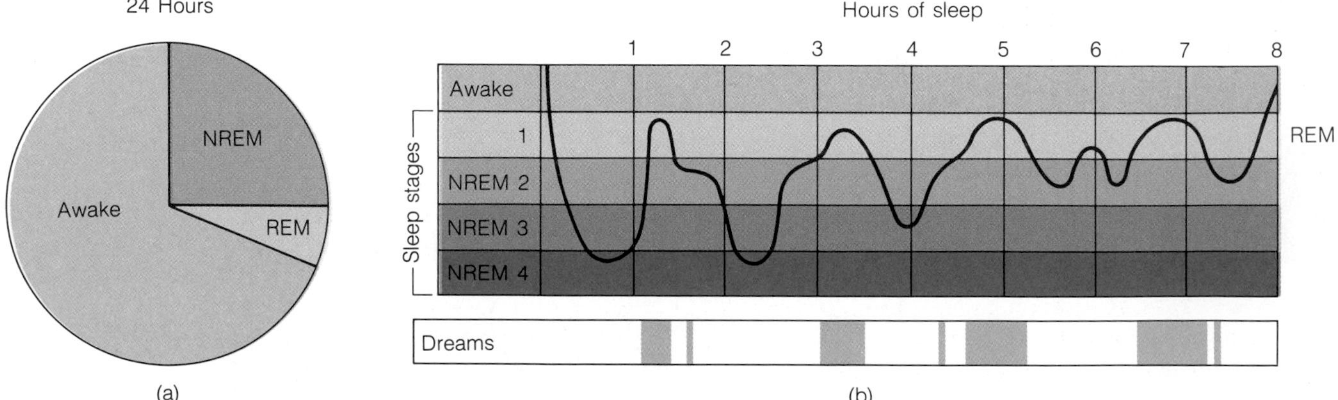

appear to be sexually aroused: Males usually have an erection, and genital blood flow increases in women. This occurs for all REM sleep, so it is not strictly related to erotic dreams. When an erotic dream does occur, evidence of sexual arousal increases (Cartwright, 1978).

With all this emotional activity, you might expect that your muscles would be active during dreaming. The reverse is true, however. During REM sleep the body becomes quite still, as if the person were paralyzed. Imagine for a moment the results of acting out some of your recent dreams. Very likely, REM-sleep paralysis prevents some hilarious—and dangerous—nighttime escapades. Fortunately, changing positions takes place *between* REM periods (De Koninck et al., 1983).

In a moment we will survey some sleep problems—if you are still awake. First, here are a few questions to test your memory of our discussion so far.

Learning Check

1. Altered states of consciousness are defined mainly by changes in patterns of alertness. T or F?

2. A momentary shift in brain activity to a pattern characteristic of sleep is referred to as
a. delta sleep *b.* light sleep *c.* microsleep *d.* deprivation sleep

3. Delusions and hallucinations typically continue for several days after a sleep-deprived individual returns to normal sleep. T or F?

4. Older adults, and particularly the elderly, sleep more than children do because the elderly are more easily fatigued. T or F?

5. Most studies of sleep patterns show a consistent ratio of 2 to 1 between time awake and time asleep. T or F?

6. Rapid eye movements (REMs) indicate that a person is in deep sleep. T or F?

7. Alpha waves are to presleep drowsiness as ________________ ________________ are to stage 4 sleep.

Answers:
1. F 2. *c* 3. F 4. F 5. T 6. F 7. delta waves

Sleep Disturbances—Showing Nightly: Sleep Wars!

Sleep clinics treat thousands of people each year who suffer from sleep disorders or complaints. Let's see what has been learned about a few of the most common problems.

Sleepwalking and Sleeptalking Like many sleep disturbances, sleepwalking is eerie and fascinating. **Somnambulists** (som-NAM-bue-lists) avoid obstacles, descend stairways, climb trees, and on rare occasions may step out of windows or in front of automobiles. The sleepwalker's eyes are usually open, but a blank face, a lack of recognition, and shuffling feet show that the person is still asleep. Children of parents who walk or talk during sleep are likely to have the same problems. This suggests that both disturbances are at least partially hereditary (Abe et al., 1984). A parent who finds a child sleepwalking should gently guide the child back to bed. Awakening a sleepwalker does no harm, but it is not necessary and the sleepwalker often resists.

Question: Does sleepwalking occur during dreaming?

It might seem that sleepwalkers are acting out dreams. But remember that people are usually immobilized during REM sleep. EEG studies have shown that somnambulism occurs during NREM stages 3 and 4. **Sleeptalking** also occurs in NREM stages of sleep and appears to be an outlet for NREM "thinking." A link with the deeper stages of sleep seems to explain why sleeptalking makes little sense and why sleepwalkers are confused and remember little when awakened (DSM-III-R, 1987).

Nightmares and Night Terrors Stage 4 sleep is also the realm of **night terrors.** These severely frightening episodes are quite different from ordinary, garden-variety nightmares (Table 6–1). A **nightmare** is simply a bad dream that takes place during REM sleep. Nightmares are usually brief and remembered in detail. During stage 4 night terrors, a person suffers total panic and may hallucinate frightening dream images into the room itself. The attack may last 15 or 20 minutes. When it is over, the person awakens drenched in sweat, but only vaguely

Table 6–1 Was It a Nightmare or a Night Terror?

	NIGHTMARE	NIGHT TERROR
Stage of sleep	☐ REM	☐ NREM
Activity	☐ Slight or no movement	☐ Violent body movement, sits up, cries out, may run
Emotion	☐ Fear or anxiety	☐ Terror and disorganizing panic
Mental state when awakened	☐ Coherent, can be calmed	☐ Incoherent, disoriented, cannot be calmed, may be hallucinating
Physiological changes	☐ No perspiration	☐ Perspires heavily
Recall	☐ Dream activity usually remembered	☐ Amnesia for episode

(Adapted from Woods & Greenhouse, 1974.)

remembers the terror itself. Since night terrors occur during NREM sleep (when the body is not immobilized), the victim may sit up, scream, get out of bed, or run around the room. Night terrors are most common in childhood, but continue to plague some adults throughout their lives (Kales & Kales, 1973).

Narcolepsy One of the most dramatic sleep problems is **narcolepsy** (NAR-koe-lep-see). Narcoleptics suffer sudden irresistible sleep attacks. These last anywhere from a few minutes to a half hour. The attacks are so overpowering that victims may fall asleep while standing, talking, or even driving. Emotional excitement, especially laughter, commonly triggers narcolepsy. Most victims also suffer from **cataplexy** (CAT-uh-plex-see), a sudden temporary paralysis of the muscles, leading to complete body collapse.

Question: Sudden paralysis sounds like what happens during dreaming. Does that suggest a connection between narcolepsy and REM sleep?

Yes. When monitored on an EEG, narcoleptics tend to fall directly into REM sleep. (Recall that the first REM period normally occurs about 90 minutes after sleep begins.) The narcoleptic's sleep attacks and paralysis seem to occur when REM sleep intrudes into the waking state. Fortunately, narcolepsy is rare. It tends to run in families, which suggests that it too is hereditary. This has been confirmed by breeding several generations of narcoleptic dogs (Guilleminault et al., 1976). (These dogs, by the way, are simply outstanding at learning the trick "Roll over and play dead.") There is no known cure for narcolepsy, but stimulant drugs may cut down the frequency of attacks.

Insomnia While some people sleep when they don't want to, a far greater number have trouble getting enough sleep. About 32 percent of all adults in the United States report some degree of insomnia. About 15 to 20 percent have a serious or chronic problem (Hopson, 1986). **Insomnia** includes difficulty in going to sleep, frequent nighttime awakenings, waking too early, or any combination of these problems.

Americans spend more than one-half billion dollars each year on sleeping pills. There is real irony in this expense. Non-prescription sleeping pills such as *Sominex*, *Nytol*, and *Sleep-eze* have little or no sleep-inducing effect (Kales & Kales, 1973). Even worse are most prescription *sedatives*. These drugs (usually barbiturates) decrease both stage 4 sleep and REM sleep, which drastically lowers sleep quality. In addition, a drug tolerance rapidly builds, so that the initial dosage quits working. Many users become "sleeping-pill junkies" who need an ever greater number of pills to get to sleep. The result is **drug-dependency insomnia,** a serious problem. Victims must be painstakingly withdrawn from their sleeping pills. Otherwise, terrible nightmares and "rebound insomnia" may drive them back to drug use.

Question: If sleeping pills are a poor way to treat insomnia, what can be done?

Actually, there is a new drug called triazolam (try-AS-o-lam) that appears to help in some cases of insomnia (Seidel et al., 1984). However, even triazolam has drawbacks, and it too can cause rebound insomnia on the first few nights after it is withdrawn. Rather than using drugs, it is often far better to learn behavioral techniques to treat insomnia.

Temporary insomnia caused by worry, stress, or excitement usually sets up a cycle in which heightened physical arousal blocks sleep. Then, frustration and anger cause more arousal, which further delays sleep. Delayed sleep causes more frustration, and so on. A good way to beat this cycle is to avoid fighting it. It is usually best to get up and do something useful or satisfying when you have difficulty sleeping (reading a textbook might not be a bad choice of useful activities).

Some insomniacs undergo a drop in blood sugar during the night. The restlessness and hunger this causes can be avoided by having a small snack before sleeping. Also, scientists have discovered that the amino acid **tryptophan** (TRIP-tuh-fan) can help people sleep—especially those who sleep poorly, rather than those who are just slow in getting to sleep (Lindsley et al., 1983). Interestingly, tryptophan can be found in a glass of milk. So grandma was right after all! But she apparently didn't know that an egg-tuna-cottage cheese-soybean-cashew-chicken-turkey-banana sandwich would be even better for inducing sleep. All of the listed foods are also high in tryptophan (Hartmann, 1978; Thompson, 1985).

Question: What about more serious cases of insomnia?

Treatment for **chronic insomnia** usually begins with relaxation training to lower arousal before sleep. (See Chapter 22's Applications section for more information about relaxation.) *Stimulus control* strategies are also helpful. For example, patients are told to strictly avoid doing anything other than sleeping when they go to bed. They are not to study, eat, watch TV, read, or even think in bed. In this way, only sleeping becomes associated with retiring (Bootzin, 1973).

One of the best ways to combat insomnia is also the simplest. Many insomniacs have scattered sleep habits. For these people, adopting a regular schedule (getting up and going to sleep at exactly the same time each day) helps establish a firm body rhythm and greatly improves sleep. (These and other ways of combating insomnia are summarized in Highlight 6–1.)

HIGHLIGHT 6–1
Behavioral Remedies for Insomnia

All of the approaches listed here are effective for treating insomnia (Borkovec, 1982; Hopson, 1986). With a little experimenting, you should be able to find a combination that works for you.

Stimulants Avoid stimulants such as coffee and cigarettes. Remember too that alcohol, while not a stimulant, impairs sleep quality.

Worries Schedule time in the early evening to write down worries or concerns and what you will do about them the next day.

Relaxation Learn a physical or mental strategy for relaxing, such as progressive muscle relaxation (see Chapter 22), meditation (see Chapter 13), or blotting out worries with calming images. Strenuous exercise during the day promotes sleep, but it is usually too stimulating in the evening. Very light evening exercise may be helpful, however.

Stimulus control Link only sleep with your bedroom so that it does not trigger worrying: (1) Go to bed only when you are feeling sleepy. (2) Avoid naps.
(3) Awaken at the same time each morning. (4) Avoid nonsleep activities in bed. (5) Always leave the bedroom if sleep has not occurred within 10 minutes. (6) Do something else when you are upset about not being able to sleep.

Paradoxical intention To remove the pressures of trying to get to sleep, try instead to keep your eyes open (in the dark) and stay awake as long as possible. This allows sleep to overtake you unexpectedly and lowers performance anxiety.

Sleep Apnea Some sage once said, "Laugh and the whole world laughs with you; snore and you sleep alone." Most nightly "wood sawing" is harmless, but it can signal a serious problem. A person who snores loudly, with short silences and loud gasps or snorts, may suffer from **sleep apnea** (AP-nee-ah). In sleep apnea, breathing stops for periods of 20 seconds to 2 minutes. As the need for oxygen becomes intense, the person wakes a little and gulps in air. He or she then settles back to sleep; but soon, breathing stops again. This cycle is repeated hundreds of times a night (Guilleminault, 1979). As you might guess, apnea victims complain of daytime sleepiness known as **hypersomnia** (DSM-III-R, 1987).

Question: What causes sleep apnea?

Some apnea occurs because the brain stops sending signals to the diaphragm to maintain breathing. Another cause is blockage of the upper air passages. In either case, the person can breathe normally during the day, so he or she may be unaware of the problem (Scrima et al., 1982). Apnea should be suspected any time very loud snoring is present. In addition to the misery it causes, apnea seriously endangers health. Persons who suspect they are apneic should seek treatment at a sleep clinic (Hales, 1980).

Sleep apnea is especially dangerous in infancy, when it is suspected as one cause of **sudden infant death syndrome** (SIDS), or "crib death." SIDS is the most frequent cause of death for infants under 1 year of age. Each year it claims 10,000 victims in the United States alone (Naeye,

1980). In the "typical" crib death, a slightly premature or small baby with some signs of a cold or cough is put to bed. A short time later, when parents return to the crib, the child is dead.

Doctors think that some cases of SIDS are caused by apnea due to immature breathing centers in the brainstem (Hales, 1980). Others suspect a defect that stalls the heart during sleep. Sometimes it appears that direct blockage of the nose is responsible. Most infants will cry, flail, and kick if the nose is blocked for a few seconds—responses that can save them if they roll face-down. But a few babies remain passive when breathing is blocked. These infants run a much higher risk of crib death (Lipsett, 1980).

Babies at risk for SIDS must be carefully watched for the first 6 months of life. To aid parents in this task, a special monitor may be used that sounds an alarm when breathing or pulse becomes weak (Naeye, 1980) (Fig. 6–6). The list that follows gives some danger signals for SIDS. Be aware, however, that SIDS can also strike babies who show none of these signs.

Fig. 6–6 *Infants at risk for SIDS are often attached to devices that monitor breathing and heart rate during sleep. An alarm sounds to alert parents if either pulse or respiration falters. (Photo courtesy of Healthdyne, Inc.)*

Some Warning Signs for SIDS

The mother is a teenager or smoker.
The baby is premature.
The baby has an unusual, high-pitched cry.
The baby engages in "snoring," breath-holding, or frequent awakening at night.
The baby breathes mainly through an open mouth.
The baby remains passive when its face rolls into a pillow or blanket.

Dreams—A Separate Reality?

When researchers Nathaniel Kleitman and Eugene Aserinsky discovered REM sleep in 1952, they ushered in a "golden era" of dream inquiry. To conclude our discussion of sleep, let's consider some age-old questions about dreaming.

Question: Does everyone dream? Do dreams occur in an instant?

Most people dream 4 or 5 times a night, but not all people remember their dreams. "Nondreamers" are often shocked by their dreams when first awakened during REM sleep. Dreams are usually spaced about 90 minutes apart. The first dream lasts only about 10 minutes; the last averages 30 minutes and may run as long as 50. Dreams, therefore, occur in real time, not as a "flash" (Cartwright, 1978; Dement, 1960).

Question: How important is dream sleep? Is it essential for normal functioning?

To answer these questions, dream researcher William Dement awakened volunteers each time they entered REM sleep. People kept from dreaming several nights in a row showed an increased tendency to dream. By the fifth night, many had to be awakened 20 or 30 times to prevent REM sleep. When undisturbed sleep was finally allowed, volunteers dreamed extra amounts. This effect, called a **REM rebound,** explains why alcoholics often have horrible nightmares after they quit drinking (Dement, 1960). Alcohol suppresses REM sleep and sets up a powerful rebound effect when it is withdrawn. It's worth remembering that while alcohol may help a person get to sleep, it often greatly reduces sleep quality.

While they were deprived of dream sleep, Dement's volunteers complained of lapses in memory and concentration, and they felt more anxious during the day. For a time, it looked like people deprived of dreaming might go crazy. But sleep researchers now refer to this idea as the "REM myth." Later experiments showed that missing *any* sleep stage can cause a rebound for that stage. In general, daytime disturbances are related to the *total amount* of sleep lost, not to the type of sleep lost (Cartwright, 1978; Johnson et al., 1972).

What, then, is the purpose of REM sleep? There are several interesting possibilities. Early in life, dream sleep may stimulate the developing brain. Newborn babies spend about 50 percent of their sleeping time in REM sleep. This amounts to a hearty 8 or 9 hours a day of dream

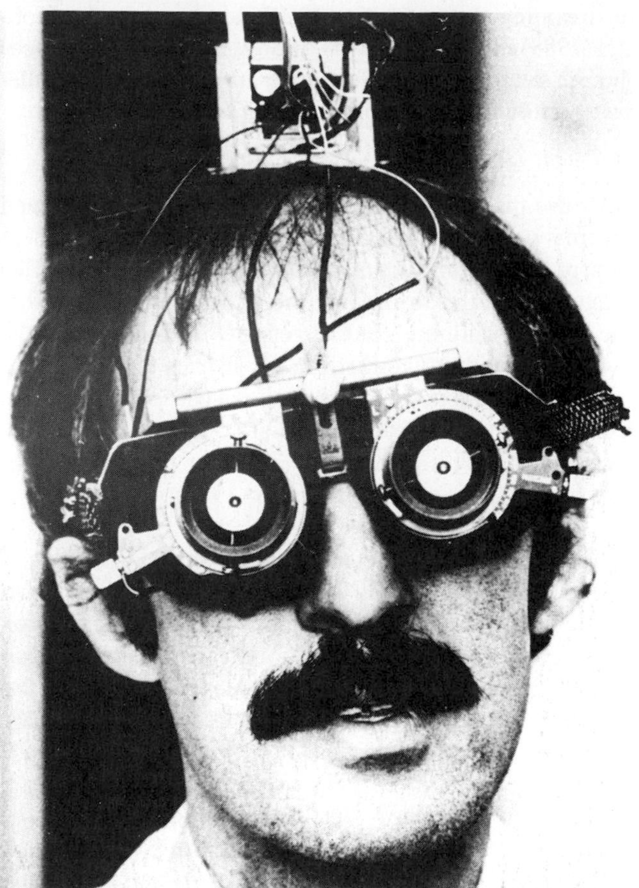

Fig. 6–7 *Dr. John Herman of the University of Texas may look like he just stepped out of the movie Star Wars, but he is actually involved in dream research. Dr. Herman is wearing goggles that electronically monitor eye movements during sleep. Use of such devices has greatly extended our understanding of dreaming.*

time. Premature babies get even more REM sleep (up to 75 percent). By age 5, when the nervous system is more mature, REM time drops to 20 percent, about the same as for an adult (Allison & Van Twyer, 1970; Feinberg & Carlson, 1967).

In adulthood, REM sleep may serve other purposes. For one thing, REM sleep increases after learning, so it may help restore brain chemicals needed for learning and memory (Hartmann, 1981; Stern, 1981). There is further evidence that REM sleep helps sort and integrate memories formed during the day (Evans, 1984). Dreams may prevent sensory deprivation during sleep and aid the processing of emotional events. Although we have much to learn, it seems clear that REM sleep and dreaming are valuable for keeping the brain in good working order.

Dream Worlds

Question: What do people usually dream about?

Calvin Hall, a noted authority on dreams, has collected and analyzed over 10,000 dreams (Hall, 1966; Hall et al., 1982). Hall found that most dreams reflect everyday events. The favorite dream setting is familiar rooms in a house. Action usually takes place between the dreamer and two or three other emotionally important people—friends, enemies, parents, or employers. Dream actions are also mostly familiar: running, jumping, riding, sitting, talking, and watching. About half of the recorded dreams had sexual elements. Dreams of flying, floating, and falling occur less frequently. Hall also found that if you're dreaming more now, you may be enjoying it less. Unpleasant emotions such as fear, anger, and sadness are more frequent in dreams than pleasant emotions.

Question: Do the dreams of men and women differ?

The dreams of men and women (in Western cultures) seem to reflect traditional sex roles. Compared to men, women's dreams are more emotional, less aggressive, less focused on sexual themes, more often indoors, and more often about home and family. Male characters outnumber females in the dreams of both sexes, and men dream more of men than women do (Hall, 1984; Winget & Kramer, 1979). The males in men's dreams are more likely to be rivals or antagonists. Women are more often pursued or endangered in their dreams (Winget & Kramer, 1979).

Dream Theories

Question: How meaningful are dreams?

Most theorists agree that dreams reflect our waking thoughts, fantasies, and emotions (Cartwright, 1978; Winget & Kramer, 1979). Thus, a better question might be, How deep should we dig in interpreting dreams? Some theorists believe that dreams have deeply hidden meanings. Others regard dreams as meaningless. Let's examine both views.

Psychodynamic Dream Theory Sigmund Freud's book *The Interpretation of Dreams* (1900) opened a whole new world of psychological investigation. After analyzing his own dreams, Freud concluded that many dreams represent **wish fulfillment.** Thus, a student who is angry at a teacher may dream of embarrassing the teacher in class; a lonely person may dream of romance; or a hungry child may dream of food.

Although Freud's **psychodynamic** view of dreaming is attractive, there is evidence against it. For example, volunteers in a study of the effects of prolonged starvation showed no particular increase in dreams about food and eating (Keys, 1950). Freud's response, no doubt, would have been that dreams rarely express needs so directly. One of Freud's key insights is that dreams represent thoughts expressed in *images,* or pictures, rather than in words (Globus, 1987).

Freud believed that the conscience relaxes during sleep, allowing dreams to express *unconscious* desires and conflicts in disguised **dream symbols.** For instance, death might be symbolized by a journey, children by small animals, or sexual intercourse by horseback riding or dancing. Similarly, a woman sexually attracted to her best friend's husband might dream of stealing her friend's wedding ring and placing it on her own hand, an indirect symbol of her true desires. (For a discussion of dream analysis in psychotherapy, see Chapter 21.)

Question: Do all dreams have hidden meanings?

Probably not. Even Freud realized that some dreams are trivial or unimportant "day residues," or carryovers from ordinary waking events. Also, you may be relieved to learn that Freud's is not the only approach to dream interpretation.

The Activation-Synthesis Hypothesis At the other end of the scale from Freud stands a radically different view of dreaming offered by scientists Allan Hobson and Robert McCarley (1977). After studying REM sleep in cats, Hobson and McCarley believe that dreams are made in this way: During REM sleep, certain brain cells are activated that normally control eye movements, balance, and actions. However, messages from the cells are blocked from actually reaching the body, so no movement occurs. But the cells continue to tell higher brain areas of their activities. Struggling to interpret this information, the brain searches through stored memories and manufactures a dream. Hobson and McCarley call this explanation of dreaming the **activation-synthesis hypothesis.** Hobson (1988) explains that "the brain is turned on (activated) during sleep and then generates and integrates (synthesizes) its own sensory and motor information."

Question: How does this help explain dream content?

Let's use the classic chase dream as an example. In such dreams we feel we are running but not going anywhere as a pursuer bears down on us. Hobson and McCarley suggest that in such dreams the brain is being told that the body is running, but it gets no feedback from the motionless body to confirm it. As it tries to make sense of this information, the brain creates a chase drama. From this perspective, dreams have no "latent" or hidden meanings. They are merely a different type of thought that occurs during sleep (Hobson, 1988).

A Look Ahead The activation-synthesis hypothesis certainly seems to explain some dream experiences. However, it does not tell us much about how dreams function in the mental life of humans. Many psychologists continue to believe that dreams have deeper meaning (Cartwright, 1978; Globus, 1987; Winget & Kramer, 1979). Moreover, there seems little doubt that dreams can make a difference in our lives: Veteran sleep researcher William Dement once dreamed that he had lung cancer. In the dream a doctor told Dement he would die soon. At the time, Dement was smoking two packs of cigarettes a day. He says, "I will never forget the surprise, joy, and exquisite relief of waking up. I felt reborn." Dement quit smoking the following day (Hales, 1980).

In recent years the idea that dreams can only be interpreted by a professional has given way to acceptance of the personal nature of dream meanings. As a result, many psychologists now urge people to collect and interpret their own dreams. The Applications section in this chapter offers some practical suggestions for doing just that.

Learning Check

1. Night terrors, sleepwalking, and sleeptalking all occur during stage 1, NREM sleep. T or F?
2. Narcolepsy and cataplexy are both associated with ______________ sleep.
3. Sleep ______________ is suspected as one cause of SIDS.
4. Which of the following is *not* a behavioral remedy for insomnia?
   a. daily hypersomnia *b.* stimulus control *c.* progressive relaxation *d.* paradoxical intention
5. The favored setting for dreams is
   a. work *b.* school *c.* outdoors or unfamiliar places *d.* familiar rooms

6. Unpleasant emotions such as fear, anger, and sadness are more frequent in dreams than pleasant emotions. T or F?

7. According to the activation-synthesis model of dreaming, dreams are constructed from ________________ to explain messages received from nerve cells controlling eye movement, balance, and bodily activity.

Answers:
1. F 2. REM 3. apnea 4. *a* 5. *d* 6. T 7. memories

Hypnosis—Look into My Eyes

"Your body is becoming heavy. Your eyes are so tired you can barely keep them open. You feel warm and relaxed and very heavy. You are so tired you can't move. Relax. Sleep, sleep, sleep." These are the last works a book should ever say to you, and the first a professional hypnotist might say.

Hypnosis, like dreaming, has an aura of mystery surrounding it. In reality, hypnosis is not nearly so mysterious as it might seem. **Hypnosis** is an *altered state of consciousness, characterized by narrowed attention and an increased openness to suggestion.* (Not all psychologists agree with this definition. Some regard hypnosis as no more than a blend of conformity, relaxation, imagination, obedience, and suggestion.)

Interest in hypnosis began in the 1700s with Franz Mesmer (whose name is the basis for the term **mesmerize**). Mesmer, an Austrian physician, believed that he could cure diseases by passing magnets over the body. For a time, mesmerism enjoyed quite a following. In the end, however, Mesmer's theories of "animal magnetism" were rejected and he was branded a quack and a fraud. The term *hypnosis* was coined later by an English surgeon named James Braid. The Greek word *hypnos* means "sleep," and Braid used it to describe the hypnotic state. Today we know that hypnosis is *not* sleep, since EEG records during hypnosis are similar to those obtained when a person is awake. Confusion about this point remains because some hypnotists give the suggestion, "Sleep, sleep."

Question: Can anyone be hypnotized?

Approximately 8 people out of 10 can be hypnotized, but only 4 out of 10 will be good hypnotic subjects. People who are imaginative and prone to fantasy are often highly responsive to hypnosis (Lynn & Rhue, 1988). But people who lack these traits may also be hypnotized. If you are willing to be hypnotized, chances are good that you could be. **Hypnotic susceptibility** can be measured by making a series of suggestions and counting the number to which a person responds. A typical hypnotic test is the **Stanford Hypnotic Susceptibility Scale** shown in Table 6–2. (Also see Fig. 6–8.) Notice that the scale progresses from easier to more difficult tasks.

Question: How is hypnosis done? Could anyone be hypnotized against his or her will?

There are as many different hypnotic routines as there are hypnotists. Still, there are certain factors common to

Table 6–2 Stanford Hypnotic Susceptibility Scale

SUGGESTED BEHAVIOR	CRITERION OF PASSING
1. Postural sway	Falls without forcing
2. Eye closure	Closes eyes without forcing
3. Hand lowering (left)	Lowers at least 6 inches by end of 10 seconds
4. Immobilization (right arm)	Arm rises less than 1 inch in 10 seconds
5. Finger lock	Incomplete separation of fingers at end of 10 seconds
6. Arm rigidity (left arm)	Less than 2 inches of arm bending in 10 seconds
7. Hands moving together	Hands at least as close as 6 inches after 10 seconds
8. Verbal inhibition (name)	Name unspoken in 10 seconds
9. Hallucination (fly)	Any movement, grimacing, acknowledgment of effect
10. Eye catalepsy	Eyes remain closed at end of 10 seconds
11. Posthypnotic (changes chairs)	Any partial movement response
12. Amnesia test	Three or fewer items recalled

(Adapted from Weitzenhoffer & Hilgard, 1959.)

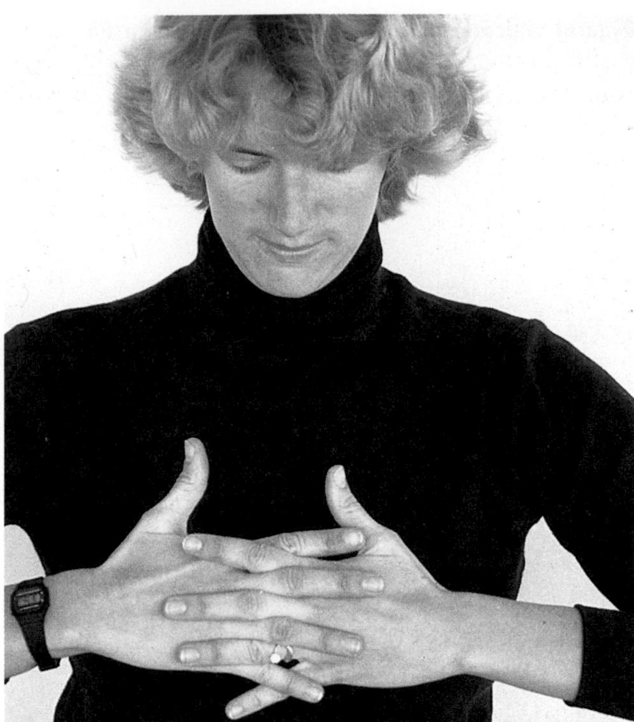

Fig. 6–8 *In one test of hypnotizability, subjects attempt to pull their hands apart after hearing suggestions that their fingers are "locked" together.*

all techniques. They all encourage a person (1) to focus attention on what is being said, (2) to relax and feel tired, (3) to "let go" and accept suggestions easily, and (4) to use vivid imagination (Tart, 1975).

A person in a deep state of hypnosis may relax "reality testing" so that normal "willpower," or self-control, is reduced. But at first, a person must cooperate to become hypnotized. Many theorists believe that all hypnosis is really **self-hypnosis.** In other words, the hypnotist simply acts as a guide to help the person achieve an altered state of awareness that could be reached alone.

Question: What does it feel like to be hypnotized?

You might be surprised at some of your actions during hypnosis, and you might have mild feelings of floating, sinking, anesthesia, or separation from your body. Personal experiences vary widely. However, in all but the deepest hypnosis, people remain aware of what is going on.

A key element in hypnosis is the **basic suggestion effect.** Hypnotized persons feel that suggested actions or experiences are *automatic*—they seem to just "happen" without effort (Kihlstrom, 1985). Here is how one person described his hypnotic session:

> I felt lethargic, my eyes going out of focus and wanting to close. My hands felt real light. . . . I felt I was sinking deeper into the chair. . . . I felt like I wanted to relax more and more. . . . My responses were more automatic. I didn't have to *wish* to do things so much or *want* to do them. . . . I just did them. . . . I felt floating . . . very close to sleep (Hilgard, 1968).

Hypnosis may also cause a *dissociation* or "split" in awareness. To illustrate, researcher Ernest Hilgard asks hypnotized subjects to plunge one hand into a painful bath of ice water. Subjects told to feel no pain say they feel none. The same subjects are then asked if there is any part of their mind that does feel pain. With their free hand, many write, "It hurts," or "Stop it, you're hurting me," while they continue to act pain-free (Hilgard 1977, 1978). One part of the hypnotized person says there is no pain and acts as if there is none. Another part, which Hilgard calls the **hidden observer,** is aware of the pain but remains in the background.

Question: What can be achieved with hypnosis?

Many abilities have been tested for responsiveness to hypnosis. In some cases, the evidence is incomplete or conflicting. Even so, the following conclusions seem justified (Kihlstrom, 1985):

1. Superhuman acts of strength. Hypnosis has no more effect on physical strength than instructions that encourage a subject to make his or her best effort (Barber, 1970).

2. Memory. There is some evidence that hypnosis can enhance memory. However, it also frequently increases the number of false memories as well (Dywan & Bowers, 1983). For this reason, many states now bar persons who have been hypnotized from testifying in court cases. (See Chapter 9 for more information.)

3. Pain relief. Hypnosis can relieve pain (Hilgard & Hilgard, 1983). Therefore, it can be especially useful in situations where chemical painkillers cannot be used or are ineffective. One such situation is control of phantom limb pain. (Phantom limb pains are recurring pains that amputees sometimes feel coming from the missing limb.)

4. Age regression. Through hypnosis, subjects have been "regressed" to childhood. Some theorists feel that regressed subjects are only acting childlike. Doubt is also cast by the fact that age-regressed persons continue to use knowledge they could only have learned as adults. The validity of age regression, therefore, remains doubtful (Kihlstrom, 1985).

5. Sensory changes. Hypnotic suggestions concerning sensations are among the most effective. Given the proper instructions, a person can be made to smell a small bottle of ammonia and respond as if it were a wonderful perfume. It is also possible to alter color vision, hearing sensitivity, time sense, perception of illusions, and many other sensory responses (Kihlstrom, 1985).

Hypnosis seems to have greatest value as a tool for inducing relaxation, as a way of controlling pain (in dentistry and childbirth, for example), and as an adjunct to psychological therapy and counseling. In general, hypnosis is better at changing subjective experience than at modifying behavior, such as smoking or overeating. Hypnotic effects are useful, but seldom amazing (Hilgard, 1974; Rieger, 1976; Williams, 1974).

Stage Hypnosis

On stage the hypnotist intones, "When I count to 3, you will imagine that you are on a train to Disneyland, and growing younger and younger as the train approaches." Responding to these suggestions, grown men and women begin to giggle and squirm like children on their way to a circus.

Question: How do entertainers use hypnosis on stage to get people to do strange things?

They don't. Little or no hypnosis is needed to do a good stage hypnosis act. T. X. Barber, an authority on hypnosis, says that stage hypnotists make use of several features of the stage setting to perform their act (Barber, 1970).

1. Waking suggestibility. We are all more or less open to suggestion, but on stage people are unusually cooperative because they don't want to "ruin the act." As a result, they will readily follow almost any instruction given by the entertainer.

2. Selection of responsive subjects. Participants in stage hypnotism (all *volunteers*) are first "hypnotized" as a group. Thus, anyone who doesn't yield to instructions is eliminated.

3. The hypnosis label disinhibits. Once a person has been labeled "hypnotized," he or she can sing, dance, act silly, or whatever, without fear of embarrassment. On stage, being "hypnotized" takes away personal responsibility for one's actions.

4. The hypnotist as a "director." After volunteers loosen up and respond to a few suggestions, they find that they are suddenly the stars of the show. Audience response to the antics on stage brings out the "ham" in many people. All the "hypnotist" needs to do is direct the action.

5. The stage hypnotist uses tricks. Stage hypnosis is about 50 percent taking advantage of the situation and 50 percent deception. Here is a common deception:

> One of the more impressive stage tricks is to rigidly suspend a person between two chairs. This is astounding only because the audience does not question it. Anyone can do it, as is shown in the photographs and instructions in Figure 6–9. Try it!

To summarize, hypnosis is real, and it can significantly alter private experience. Hypnosis is a useful tool that has been applied in a variety of settings. The TV or nightclub stage, however, is not one of these settings. Stage "hypnotists" entertain; they rarely hypnotize.

Fig. 6–9 *Arrange three chairs as shown. Have someone recline as shown. Ask him to lift slightly while you remove the middle chair. Accept the applause gracefully!*

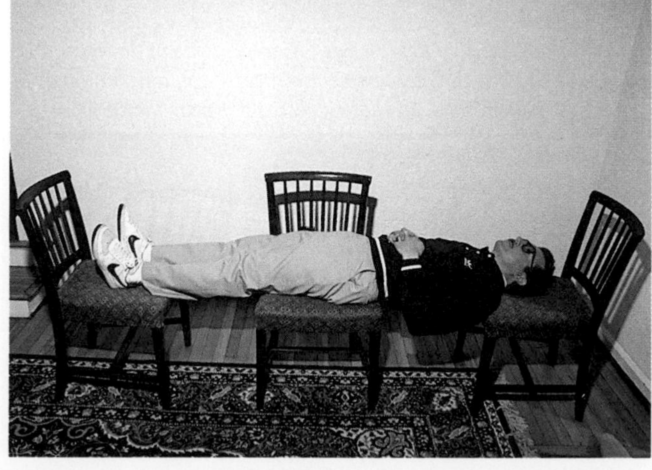

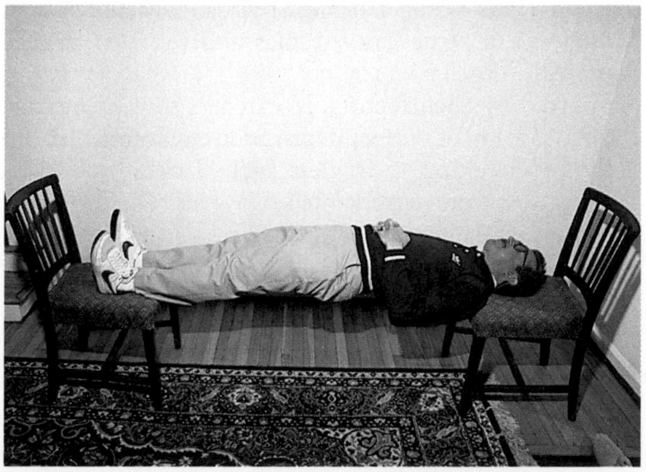

Sensory Deprivation—Life on a Sensory Diet

Throughout history, **sensory deprivation** (SD) has been one of the most widely used means of altering consciousness. Sensory deprivation refers to any major reduction in external stimulation.

Question: What happens when stimulation is greatly reduced?

A hint comes from reports by prisoners in solitary confinement, arctic explorers, high-altitude pilots, long-distance truck drivers, and radar operators. When faced with limited or monotonous stimulation, these people have at times had bizarre sensations, dangerous lapses in awareness, and wildly distorted perceptions. To find out why, D. O. Hebb paid volunteers to undergo sensory deprivation under controlled conditions.

Subjects spent several days lying on their backs in a small cubicle. To prevent vision, they wore darkened goggles. Gloves and cardboard cuffs restricted touch. In the background, a constant hissing noise masked all other sounds. Do these conditions sound interesting? If you were placed in similar circumstances, you might be in for a surprise. Few subjects could take more than 2 or 3 days of sensory deprivation without "pushing the panic button" (Heron, 1957).

Disruptive Effects

Question: What sort of changes take place during sensory deprivation?

As mentioned in the Chapter Preview, a person may misjudge time and have trouble concentrating. After emerging from sensory deprivation, some people experience color distortions, heightened visual illusions, slower reactions, and a brief warping of visual lines and spaces. Volunteers in some early studies also reported strange and vivid images.

Spurred by such reports, researchers soon created an ingenious array of sensory deprivation environments, and volunteers seeking a drugless high flocked to experiments. Most were disappointed, however. We now know that true hallucinations are rare during sensory deprivation (Zubek, 1969b). The fanciful, dreamlike visions that sometimes do occur are actually **hypnogogic images** (hip-no-GAH-jik). Hypnogogic images are similar to those that may occur just before you fall asleep. These images may be vivid and surprising, but they are rarely mistaken for real objects. Hypnogogic images are apparently linked to an increase in the number of *theta waves* produced by the brain. These brain waves, in the 4- to 7-cycle-per-second range, are usually recorded just before sleep. Sensory deprivation also increases their occurrence (Taylor, 1983).

Benefits of Sensory Restriction

In recent years, psychologists have begun to explore the possible benefits of sensory deprivation. Much of this work has involved sensory restriction in small isolation tanks like the one pictured in Figure 6–10.

Question: How could sensory deprivation be beneficial?

Sensory Enhancement One of the most consistent after-effects of sensory deprivation is increased sensory acuity. That is, vision, hearing, touch, and taste are temporarily more sensitive (Suedfeld, 1975; Zubek, 1969b). Some people report using this after-effect to aid creative thinking (Hutchison, 1984). At the very least, it seems that wearing earplugs for a day might be an interesting prelude to hearing a musical concert!

Relaxation As we already noted most people find prolonged sensory deprivation stressful and uncomfortable. Yet, oddly, brief periods of restricted sensation are very relaxing for most people (Forgays & Belinson, 1986; Suedfeld, 1980). An hour or two spent in a flotation tank, for instance, causes a large drop in blood pressure, muscle tension, and other signs of stress. Of course, it could be argued that a warm bath has the same effect. But to date, evidence suggests that brief sensory deprivation is one of the surest ways to induce deep relaxation.

Changing Habits Psychologist Peter Suedfeld has found that sensory deprivation can help people quit

Fig. 6–10 *Sensory isolation chamber. Small flotation tanks like the one pictured have been used by psychologists to study the effects of mild sensory deprivation. Subjects float in darkness and silence. The shallow body-temperature water contains hundreds of pounds of Epsom salts, so that subjects float near the surface.*

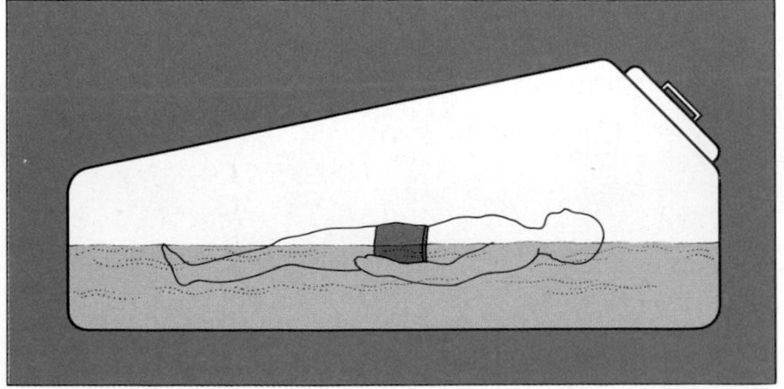

smoking or lose weight. Suedfeld calls his technique **REST,** for restricted environmental stimulation therapy. In one study, Suedfeld tested the effects of standard antismoking messages. These were then compared to the effects of the same messages combined with sensory deprivation. He found that roughly equal numbers of people succeeded in stopping smoking with either treatment. But 3 months later, members of the REST group were smoking 40 percent less than the others (Suedfeld, 1980). Another study found similar benefits for people in a weight-loss program based on sensory deprivation (Borrie & Suedfeld, 1980).

Question: How does sensory deprivation help?

Tape-recorded suggestions to eat less or stop smoking are played for clients while they are isolated in a flotation tank. Suedfeld speculates that deep relaxation makes a person less likely to argue against or otherwise resist suggestions. Also, some mental confusion usually accompanies sensory deprivation. This, he believes, helps unfreeze or "loosen" belief systems. Unfreezing, in other words, may make it easier to bring about lasting changes in beliefs that maintain bad habits.

Prospect After years of being viewed only as a disruptive state, sensory deprivation may yet prove to have other benefits. At the very least, further study of SD should add to our understanding of brainwashing, isolation at remote weather outposts, the after-effects of eye surgery, and the problems of extended space flight. Clearly, there is much yet to be learned from studying "nothingness."

Learning Check

See if you can answer these questions before reading on.

1. The term *hypnotism* was coined by a British surgeon named
   a. Franz Mesmer *b.* James Stanford *c.* T. A. Kreskin *d.* James Braid
2. Only 4 out of 10 people can be hypnotized. T or F?
3. Which of the following can most definitely be achieved with hypnosis?
   a. unusual strength *b.* pain relief *c.* improved memory *d.* sleeplike brain waves
4. Which of the following is not a disruptive effect observed during or immediately after sensory deprivation?
   a. impaired time sense *b.* difficulty concentrating *c.* elevated blood pressure *d.* heightened visual illusions
5. Vivid images during sensory deprivation usually can be best described as
   a. daydreams *b.* hypnogogic *c.* hallucinations *d.* hypodynamic
6. Prolonged periods of sensory deprivation lower anxiety and induce deep relaxation. T or F?

Answers:
1. *d* 2. F 3. *b* 4. *c* 5. *b* 6. F

Drug-Altered Consciousness—The High and Low of It

Alcohol, heroin, amphetamines, barbiturates, marijuana, cocaine, LSD, caffeine, nicotine. . . . The list of mind-altering drugs—legal and illegal—is extensive. The surest way to alter human consciousness is to administer a **psychoactive drug.** A psychoactive drug is a substance capable of altering attention, memory, judgment, time sense, self-control, emotion, or perception (Ludwig, 1966).

Facts about Drugs

Most psychoactive drugs can be placed on a scale ranging from **stimulation** to **depression.** Figure 6–11 shows various drugs and their approximate effects on the central nervous system. A more complete summary of the most frequently abused psychoactive drugs is given in Table 6–3.

Drug dependence falls into two broad categories. When a person compulsively uses a drug to maintain bodily

Table 6–3 Comparison of Psychoactive Drugs

NAME	CLASSIFICATION	MEDICAL USE	USUAL DOSE	DURATION OF EFFECT
Alcohol	Sedative-hypnotic	Solvent, antiseptic	Varies	1–4 hours
Amphetamines	Stimulant	Relief of mild depression, control of appetite and narcolepsy	2.5–5 milligrams	4 hours
Barbiturates	Sedative-hypnotic	Sedation, relief of high blood pressure, hyperthyroidism	50–100 milligrams	4 hours
Caffeine	Stimulant	Counteract depressant drugs, treatment of migraine headaches	Varies	Varies
Cocaine	Stimulant, local anesthetic	Local anesthesia	Varies	Varied, brief periods
Codeine	Narcotic	Ease pain and coughing	30 milligrams	4 hours
Heroin	Narcotic	Pain relief	Varies	4 hours
LSD	Hallucinogen	Experimental study of mental function, alcoholism	100–500 milligrams	10 hours
Marijuana (THC)	Relaxant, euphoriant; in high doses, hallucinogen	Treatment of glaucoma	1–2 cigarettes	4 hours
Mescaline	Hallucinogen	None	350 micrograms	12 hours
Methadone	Narcotic	Pain relief	10 milligrams	4–6 hours
Morphine	Narcotic	Pain relief	15 milligrams	6 hours
Psilocybin	Hallucinogen	None	25 milligrams	6–8 hours
Tobacco (nicotine)	Stimulant	Emetic (nicotine)	Varies	Varies

(Question marks indicate conflict of opinion. It should be noted that illicit drugs are frequently adulterated and thus pose unknown hazards to the user.)
*Persons who inject drugs under nonsterile conditions run a high risk of contracting AIDS, hepatitis, abscesses, or circulatory disorders.
Adapted and updated from *Resource Book for Drug Abuse Education*. NEA, 1969.

Table 6–3 Comparison of Psychoactive Drugs (continued)

EFFECTS SOUGHT	LONG-TERM SYMPTOMS	PHYSICAL DEPENDENCE POTENTIAL	PSYCHOLOGICAL DEPENDENCE POTENTIAL	ORGANIC DAMAGE POTENTIAL
Sense alteration, anxiety reduction, sociability	Cirrhosis, toxic psychosis, neurologic damage, addiction	Yes	Yes	Yes
Alertness, activeness	Loss of appetite, delusions, hallucinations, toxic psychosis	Yes	Yes	Yes
Anxiety reduction, euphoria	Addiction with severe withdrawal symptoms, possible convulsions, toxic psychosis, addiction	Yes	Yes	No
Wakefulness, alertness	Insomnia, heart arrhythmias, high blood pressure	No	Yes	Yes
Excitation, talkativeness	Depression, convulsions	Debated	Yes	Yes
Euphoria, prevent withdrawal discomfort	Addiction, constipation, loss of appetite	Yes	Yes	No
Euphoria, prevent withdrawal discomfort	Addiction, constipation, loss of appetite	Yes	Yes	No*
Insightful experiences, exhilaration, distortion of senses	May intensify existing psychosis, panic reactions	No	No?	No?
Relaxation; increased euphoria, perceptions, sociability	Possible lung cancer, other health risks	No	Yes	Yes
Insightful experiences, exhilaration, distortion of senses	May intensify existing psychosis, panic reactions	No	No?	No?
Prevent withdrawal discomfort	Addiction, constipation, loss of appetite	Yes	Yes	No
Euphoria, prevent withdrawal discomfort	Addiction, constipation, loss of appetite	Yes	Yes	No*
Insightful experiences, exhilaration, distortion of senses	May intensify existing psychosis, panic reactions	No	No?	No?
Alertness, calmness, sociability	Emphysema, lung cancer, mouth and throat cancer, cardiovascular damage, loss of appetite	Yes	Yes	Yes

Adapted and updated from *Resource Book for Drug Abuse Education*. NEA, 1969.

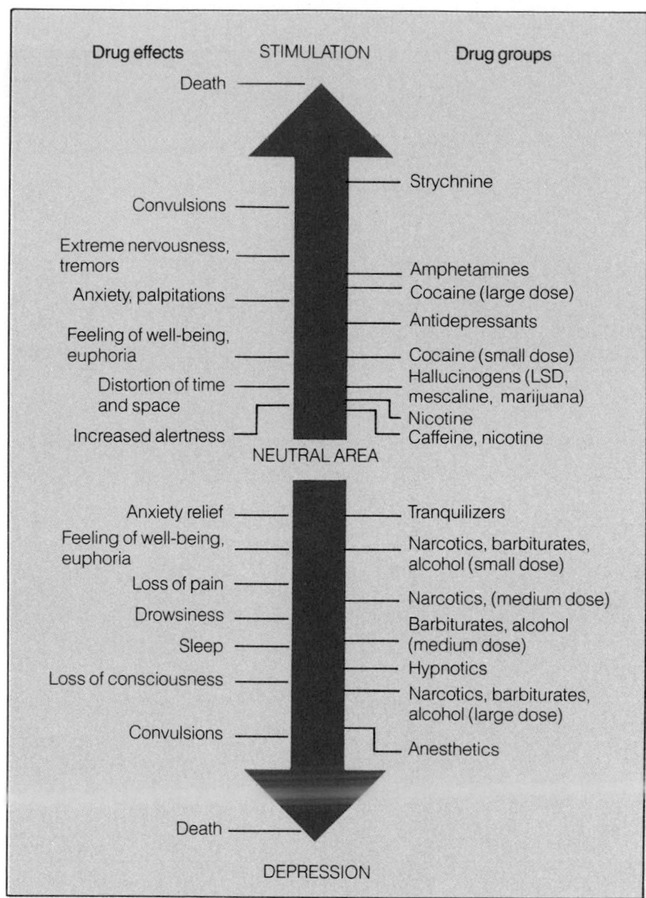

Fig. 6–11 *Spectrum and continuum of drug action. Many drugs can be rated on a stimulation-depression scale according to their effects on the central nervous system. Although LSD, mescaline, and marijuana are listed here, the stimulation-depression scale is less relevant to these drugs. The principal characteristic of hallucinogens is their mind-altering quality.*

comfort, a **physical dependence** (or **addiction**) exists. Physical dependence occurs most often with drugs that cause **withdrawal symptoms.** Withdrawal from drugs such as alcohol, barbiturates, and opiates can be extremely unpleasant. Quitting opiates, for example, causes violent flu-like symptoms of nausea, vomiting, diarrhea, chills, sweating, and cramps (Feldman & Quenzer, 1984). Addiction is often accompanied by a **drug tolerance,** in which the user must take larger and larger doses to get the desired effect.

When a person develops a **psychological dependence,** he or she feels that a drug is necessary to maintain emotional or psychological well-being. Usually, this is based on an intense craving for the drug and its rewarding qualities (Feldman & Quenzer, 1984). Make no mistake, however: Psychological dependence may affect a drug user as powerfully as physical addiction does. This is why some psychologists prefer to define addiction more broadly as any compulsive habit pattern. By this definition, a person who has lost control over his or her drug use, for whatever reason, is addicted (Marlatt et al., 1988).

Note in Table 6–3 that the drugs most likely to lead to physical dependence are alcohol, amphetamines, barbiturates, codeine, heroin, methadone, morphine, and tobacco. Using *any* of the drugs listed in Table 6–3 can result in psychological dependence.

Patterns of Abuse Some drugs, of course, have a higher potential for abuse than others. However, this is only one side of the picture. Often, it is as useful to classify drug-taking *behavior* as it is to rate drugs. For example, some people remain social drinkers for life, whereas others become alcoholics within weeks of taking their first drink. In this sense, drug use can be classified as **experimental** (short-term use based on curiosity), **social-recreational** (occasional social use for pleasure or relaxation), **situational** (use to cope with a specific problem, such as boredom or staying awake for night work), **intensive** (daily use with elements of dependence), or **compulsive** (intense use and extreme dependence) (National Commission of Marihuana and Drug Abuse, 1973). The last three categories of drug-taking tend to be damaging no matter what drug is used. The discussion that follows focuses on the drugs most often abused by college students.

Uppers—Amphetamines, Cocaine, Caffeine, Nicotine

Amphetamines form a large group of synthetic stimulants. Drugs commonly available in this group are *Dexedrine, Methedrine,* and *Benzedrine.* Amphetamines were once widely prescribed to aid weight loss or to combat mild depression. Both practices are now frowned on because patients often become dependent on their legal amphetamines. The only fully legitimate medical uses of amphetamines are to treat narcolepsy and overdoses of depressant drugs. Illicit use of amphetamines is widespread among individuals seeking an easy way to stay awake and by those who think drugs can improve mental or physical performance.

Amphetamines rapidly produce a drug tolerance. Most abusers who begin with 1 or 2 pills a day progress to taking dozens a day to get the same effect. Eventually, some users switch to injecting Methedrine ("speed") directly into the bloodstream. The true speed freak typically goes on binges lasting several days, after which he or she "crashes" from lack of sleep and food.

Question: How dangerous are amphetamines?

Amphetamine use poses many dangers. To stay high, the abuser must take more and more of the drug as the body's tolerance grows. Higher doses can cause nausea, vomiting, high blood pressure, fatal heart arrhythmias, and crippling strokes. Also, it is important to realize that amphetamines speed the use of bodily resources; they do not magically supply energy. Hence, the after-effects of an amphetamine binge can be dangerous and uncomfortable. Possible effects include fatigue, depression, terrifying nightmares, confusion, uncontrolled irritability, and aggression. Repeatedly overextending one's body with stimulants may lead to "considerable weight loss, sores and nonhealing ulcers, brittle fingernails, tooth grinding, chronic chest infections, liver disease, a variety of hypertensive disorders, and in some cases cerebral hemorrhage." (Canadian Government's Commission of Inquiry, 1971.)

Amphetamines can also cause a loss of contact with reality, known as **amphetamine psychosis.** Affected users feel threatened and suffer from paranoid delusions that someone is out to get them. Acting on these delusions, the speed freak may become violent, resulting in self-injury or injury to others (Snyder, 1972).

Cocaine Cocaine is a powerful central nervous system stimulant extracted from the leaves of the coca plant. Its effects are sensations of alertness, euphoria, well-being, power, and boundless energy (Spotts & Shontz, 1980).

Cocaine has a long history of use and misuse. At the turn of the century, dozens of non-prescription potions and cure-alls contained cocaine. It was during this time that Coca-Cola was indeed the "real thing." From 1886 until 1906, when the Pure Food and Drug Act was passed, Coca-Cola contained cocaine (which has since been replaced with caffeine) (Grinspoon & Bakalar, 1977). Today, cocaine is becoming one of the most widely abused drugs. An estimated 4 to 5 million Americans use it at least once a month, and an estimated 30 million have tried it (Hammer & Hazelton, 1984).

Question: How does cocaine differ from amphetamines?

The two are very much alike in their effect on the central nervous system. In fact, when experienced users are given both (in blind testing), they can't tell the difference (Resnick et al., 1977). At high dosages, the main difference is that amphetamine effects may last several hours; cocaine is quickly metabolized, so its effects last only about 15 to 30 minutes (Woods et al., 1987).

Question: How dangerous is cocaine?

Many scientists are beginning to think it is addicting, especially as the number of dependent abusers has continued to grow. But this judgment depends on how addiction is defined. On the one hand, there is little evidence that withdrawal symptoms occur when a person stops taking cocaine (Grinspoon & Bakalar, 1985). Yet, on the other hand, many users report powerful cravings when they try to stop using it (Wilbur, 1986). Cocaine users also show little long-term tolerance. But short-term tolerance is common. That is, later doses have less and less impact during a drug-taking session. Thus, while it remains debatable if cocaine is physically addicting in the classic sense, there is little doubt about its tremendous potential for compulsive abuse (Byck, 1987).

Many authorities now regard cocaine as one of the most dangerous drugs in use today. Even casual or first-time users run a risk because cocaine can cause convulsions, heart attack, or a stroke (Cregler & Mark, 1986; Isner, 1986). The highly publicized death in 1986 of basketball star Len Bias is a case in point.

When rats and monkeys are given free access to cocaine, they find it irresistible. Many, in fact, end up dying of convulsions from self-administered overdoses of the drug (Hammer & Hazelton, 1984). Cocaine increases activity in brain pathways sensitive to the chemical messengers dopamine (DOPE-ah-meen) and noradrenaline (nor-ah-DREN-ah-lin). Noradrenaline arouses the brain, and added dopamine produces a "rush" of pleasure. This combination is so powerfully rewarding that compulsive cocaine use is highly likely. In short, those who use cocaine run a high risk of becoming dependent and compulsive abusers.

Cocaine's rate of abuse would probably be even higher were it not for its absurdly high price. Many authorities estimate that if cocaine were cheaper, 9 out of 10 users would progress to compulsive use. In fact, rock cocaine (or "crack"), which is cheaper, appears to be producing very high abuse rates among those who try it.

Despite its allure, cocaine abuse is no picnic. A survey of 500 cocaine abusers identified a host of complaints, including anxiety, irritability, paranoid thoughts, interpersonal problems, insomnia, headaches, tremors, and nausea (Helfrich et al., 1983; Washton & Gold, 1984). Here are some increasingly serious signs of cocaine abuse (Pursch, 1983).

- **Compulsive use.** If cocaine is available—say, at a party—you will undoubtedly use it. You can't say no to it.
- **Loss of control.** Once you have had some cocaine, you will keep using it until you are exhausted or the cocaine is gone.

• **Disregarding consequences.** You don't care if the rent gets paid, your job is endangered, your lover disapproves, or your health is affected, you'll use cocaine anyway.

It is becoming clear that cocaine's capacity for abuse and social damage rivals that of the decidedly unglamorous drug heroin. Anyone who thinks he or she may be developing a cocaine problem should seek advice at a drug clinic or a Cocaine Anonymous meeting.

Caffeine Caffeine is the most frequently used psychoactive drug in the United States. Caffeine stimulates the brain by blocking chemicals that normally inhibit or slow nerve activity (Julien, 1985). Its effects become apparent with doses as small as 100 to 200 milligrams (the amount found in about 2 cups of brewed coffee). Psychologically, caffeine suppresses fatigue or drowsiness and increases feelings of alertness; some people have a hard time starting a day without it.

How much caffeine did you consume today? It is common to think of coffee as the major source of caffeine, but there are many others. Caffeine is found in tea, many soft drinks (especially colas), chocolate, and cocoa. Over 2000 non-prescription drugs also contain caffeine, including stay-awake pills, cold remedies, and many name-brand aspirin products. Table 6–4 gives the approximate caffeine content of several foods.

Fig. 6–12 *Like other drugs, caffeine is subject to abuse by some users.*

Question: Are there any serious drawbacks to using caffeine?

Serious abuse of caffeine may result in an unhealthy dependence known as **caffeinism** (Levitt, 1977). Insomnia, irritability, loss of appetite, chills, racing heart, and elevated body temperature are all signs of caffeinism (Fig. 6–12). It is not uncommon to find that individuals with these symptoms are drinking 15 or 20 cups of coffee a day. Even in the absence of caffeinism, there are some caffeine-related health risks. Caffeine encourages the development of breast cysts in women, and it may add to insomnia, stomach problems, heart problems, and high blood pressure. Health authorities urge pregnant women to give up caffeine entirely because of a suspected link between caffeine and birth defects. A possible link between caffeine and miscarriages has also been detected (Grady, 1986).

Table 6–4 Average Caffeine Content of Various Foods

Instant coffee (5 ounces), 64 milligrams
Percolated coffee (5 ounces), 108 milligrams
Drip coffee (5 ounces), 145 milligrams
Decaffeinated coffee (5 ounces), 3 milligrams
Black tea (5 ounces), 42 milligrams
Canned iced tea (17 ounces), 30 milligrams
Cocoa drink (6 ounces), 8 milligrams
Chocolate drink (8 ounces), 14 milligrams
Sweet chocolate (1 ounce), 20 milligrams
Colas (12 ounces), 50 milligrams
Soft drinks (12 ounces) 0–52 milligrams

It is customary in our culture to think of caffeine as a nondrug. But as this discussion shows, it is wise to remember that it *is* a drug and use it in moderation.

Nicotine Nicotine is a natural stimulant found mainly in tobacco. Next to caffeine, it is the most widely used psychoactive drug (Julien, 1985).

Question: How does nicotine compare with other stimulants?

Nicotine is a potent drug. It is so toxic that it is sometimes used as an insecticide! In large doses it causes stomach pain, vomiting and diarrhea, cold sweats, dizziness, confusion, and tremors. In very large doses, nicotine may cause convulsions, respiratory failure, and death (Levitt,

1977). For a nonsmoker, 50 to 75 milligrams of nicotine taken in a single dose could be lethal. (Chain-smoking about 17 to 25 cigarettes will produce this dosage.)

Most first-time smokers get sick on 1 or 2 cigarettes. In contrast, a heavy smoker may inhale 40 cigarettes a day without feeling ill. This difference indicates that regular smokers build a tolerance for nicotine (Levitt, 1977).

Question: Is it true that nicotine can be addicting?

A 1988 report by the U.S. Surgeon General concluded that nicotine is addicting. For many smokers, withdrawal from nicotine causes headaches, sweating, cramps, insomnia, digestive upset, irritability, and a sharp craving for cigarettes (Feldman & Quenzer, 1984; Shiffman, 1980). These symptoms may last from 2 to 6 weeks and may be worse than heroin withdrawal. Indeed, relapse patterns are nearly identical for alcoholics, heroin addicts, cocaine abusers, and smokers who try to quit (Brownell et al., 1986; Koop, 1988a).

Question: How serious are the health risks of smoking?

A burning cigarette releases more than 6800 different chemicals. Many of these are potent *carcinogens* (car-SIN-oh-jins: cancer-causing substances). In addition, nicotine itself may be cancer-causing (Bock, 1980). Lung cancer and other cancers caused by smoking are now considered the single most preventable cause of death in the United States. Among men, 97 percent of lung cancer deaths are caused by smoking. For women, 74 percent of all lung cancers are due to smoking, a rate that has risen sharply in recent years. Altogether, smoking is responsible for about one-third of all cancer deaths (Reif, 1981).

If you think smoking is harmless, or the link between smoking and cancer is unproved, you're kidding yourself. As one expert says, "The scientific link between tobacco smoking and cancer is now as firmly established as any link between cause and effect in a human disease is likely to be" (Reif, 1981). By the way, urban cowboys and Skol bandits, similar conclusions apply to smokeless tobacco (chewing tobacco and snuff). Users of smokeless tobacco run a 4 to 6 times higher risk of developing oral cancer. Smokeless tobacco also causes shrinkage of the gums, contributes to heart disease, and probably is as addicting as cigarettes (Christian & McDonald, 1987; Foreyt, 1987).

Smokers, unless they have a death wish, must be getting something out of smoking. Most claim that smoking helps them concentrate, feel sociable, or calm down. But psychologist Stanley Schachter asserts, "The heavy smoker gets nothing out of smoking. He smokes only to prevent withdrawal" (Schachter, 1978). Schachter has shown that smoking does not improve the mood or the performance of heavy smokers compared to nonsmokers. On the other hand, heavy smokers who are *deprived* of nicotine feel worse and perform worse than nonsmokers.

The real reason dinosaurs became extinct

Schachter has also shown that heavy smokers adjust their smoking to keep bodily levels of nicotine constant. Thus, when smokers are given lighter cigarettes, they smoke more. Also, if they are under stress (which speeds the removal of nicotine from the body), they smoke more (Schachter, 1978). The link between stress and nicotine probably explains why students smoke more during stressful periods such as final exams, or at parties, which are also stressful.

Question: Is it better for a person to quit smoking abruptly or taper down gradually?

Many authorities recommend cutting down gradually or at least switching to a low-tar cigarette. But Schachter and others believe it is better to quit cold-turkey rather than to merely cut down or smoke lighter cigarettes. Schachter's work shows that smokers who cut down are in a constant state of withdrawal. This causes irritability and discomfort without really ending smoking. Smokers who switch to lighter cigarettes often end up smoking more to get the same total nicotine input. In doing so, they may expose themselves to more cancer-causing substances than before (Schachter, 1978; Shiffman, 1980). Whichever approach is taken, quitting smoking is not easy. People who try to quit should be prepared to make several attempts before succeeding (Brownell et al., 1986). But the good news is, tens of millions of people have quit.

Downers—Barbiturates and Alcohol

Question: How do downers differ from the stimulant drugs?

The most widely used downers, or depressant drugs, are alcohol and barbiturates. These drugs are so much alike in their effects that barbiturates are sometimes referred to as "solid alcohol." Let's examine the properties of each.

Barbiturates

Barbiturates are **sedative** drugs that depress activity in the brain. Medically, they are used to calm patients or to induce sleep. In mild doses, barbiturates have an effect similar to alcohol intoxication, but an overdose can easily cause coma or death. Barbiturates combined with alcohol are particularly risky. When mixed, the effects of both drugs are multiplied by a **drug interaction** (one drug enhances the effect of another).

Barbiturates are often taken in excess amounts because a first dose may be followed by others as the user becomes uninhibited or forgetful. Marilyn Monroe, Judy Garland, and a number of other well-known personalities have died of barbiturate overdoses. An overdose of barbiturates first causes unconsciousness. Then it so severely depresses the brain centers controlling heartbeat and breathing that death results.

Abuse The most frequently abused downers are short-acting barbiturates such as *Seconal* and *Tuinal*. Closely related to these (and to alcohol) is the non-barbiturate drug *methaqualone* (*Quaalude*, *Sopor*, and *Parest* are its trade names). These drugs seem to be preferred because they take effect quickly, and the rush of intoxication only lasts from 2 to 4 hours. Like the other depressants, repeated use can cause physical dependence and emotional depression. Freddie Prinze, a popular television comedian, was on Quaaludes before he committed suicide.

All too often, the short-acting depressants are gulped down with alcohol or added to a "spiked" punch bowl. This is the combination that left a young woman named Karen Ann Quinlan in a coma that lasted 10 years, ending with her death in 1985. It is no exaggeration to restate that mixing barbiturates with alcohol can be fatal.

Alcohol

Contrary to popular belief, alcohol is not a stimulant. The apparent gaiety at drinking parties is due to alcohol's effect as a central nervous system **depressant.** As Figure 6–13 shows, small amounts of alcohol reduce inhibition and produce feelings of relaxation and euphoria. Larger amounts of alcohol cause ever greater impairment of the brain until the drinker loses consciousness. Alcohol is also not an aphrodisiac. It usually impairs sexual performance, particularly in males. As William Shakespeare observed long ago, drink "provokes the desire, but it takes away the performance."

Abuse Alcohol, America's favorite depressant, breeds this country's biggest drug problem. Over 140 million Americans use alcohol, and an estimated 14 to 18 million of these have a serious drinking problem. A particularly alarming trend is a dramatic increase in alcohol abuse among adolescents and young adults. A recent national survey of college students found that 17 percent (more than 1 out of 6) are heavy drinkers. For college males, the figure was 25 percent, or 1 out of 4 male students (Olmstead, 1984).

Question: What are the signs of alcohol abuse?

Recognizing Problem Drinking Because alcohol abuse is such a common problem, it is important to recognize the danger signals of alcoholism. The progression from a social drinker to a problem drinker to an alcoholic is often subtle. Jellinek (1960) gives these typical steps in the development of a drinking problem.

1. Initial phase. At first, the social drinker begins to turn more often to alcohol to relieve tension or to feel good. Four danger signals in this period that signal excessive dependence on alcohol are:

Increasing consumption. The individual drinks more and more and may begin to worry about his or her drinking.

Morning drinking. Morning drinking is a dangerous sign, particularly when it is used to combat a hangover or to "get through the day."

Regretted behavior. The person engages in extreme behavior while drunk that leaves her or him feeling guilty or embarrassed.

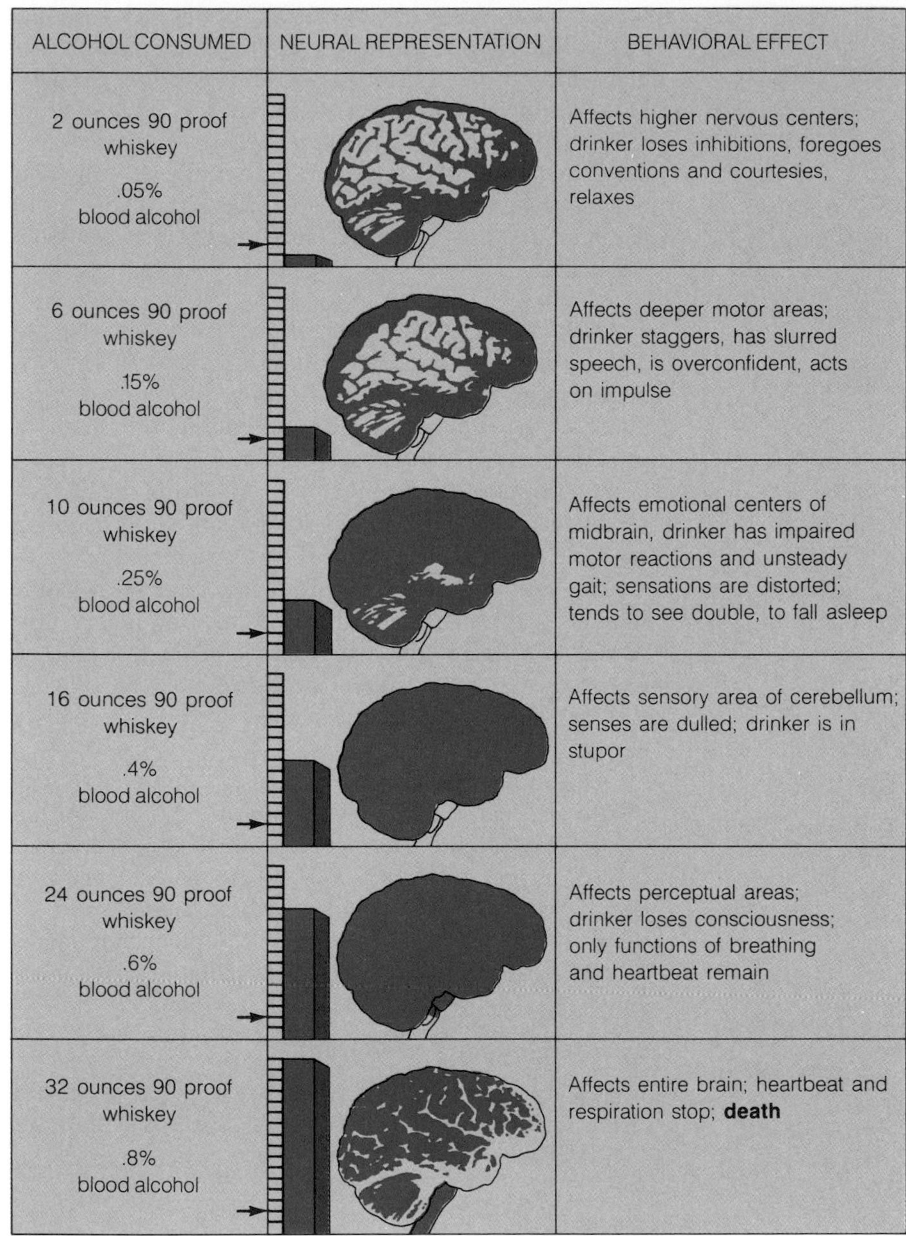

Fig. 6–13 *The behavioral effects of alcohol are related to blood alcohol content and the resulting suppression of higher mental function. Arrows indicate the typical threshold for legal intoxication in the United States. (From Jozef Cohen, Eyewitness Series in Psychology, p. 44. Copyright © by Rand McNally and Company. Reprinted by permission.)*

Blackouts. Abusive drinking may be revealed by an inability to remember what happened during intoxication.

2. Crucial phase. A crucial turning point comes as the person begins to lose control over drinking. At this stage, there is still some control over when and where a first drink is taken. But one drink starts a chain reaction leading to a second and a third, and so on.

3. Chronic phase. At this point, alcoholics drink compulsively and continuously. They rarely eat, they become intoxicated from far less alcohol than before, and they crave alcohol when deprived of it. Work, family ties, and social life all deteriorate. Their self-drugging is usually so compulsive that when given a choice, the bottle comes before friends, relatives, employment, and self-esteem. The alcoholic is an addict.

To add to this summary, Highlight 6–2 may help you form a clearer picture of the development of a drinking problem.

Many social-recreational drinkers could do a far better job of managing their use of alcohol. Almost everyone has been to a party or social gathering spoiled by someone

HIGHLIGHT 6–2
The Development of a Drinking Problem

Early Warnings

You are beginning to feel guilty about your drinking.

You drink more than you used to and tend to gulp your drinks.

You try to have a few extra drinks before or after drinking with others.

You have begun to drink at certain times or to get through certain situations.

You drink to relieve feelings of boredom, depression, anxiety, or inadequacy.

You are sensitive when others mention your drinking.

You have had memory blackouts or have passed out while drinking.

Signals Not To Be Ignored

There are times when you need a drink.

You drink in the morning to overcome a hangover.

You promise to drink less and are lying about your drinking.

You often regret what you have said or done while drinking.

You have begun to drink alone.

You have weekend drinking bouts and Monday hangovers.

You have lost time at work or school because of drinking.

You are noticeably drunk on important occasions.

Your relationship to family and friends has changed because of your drinking.

who drank too much too fast. Those who avoid overdrinking have a better time, and so do their friends. But how do you avoid drinking too much? After all, as one wit once observed, "The conscience dissolves in alcohol." Psychologists Roger Vogler and Wayne Bartz (1982) provide a partial answer.

Vogler and Bartz observe that drinking makes you feel good as long as blood alcohol remains below a level of about 0.05. In this range, people feel relaxed, euphoric, and sociable. At higher levels, they go from moderately intoxicated to thoroughly drunk. Later, as blood alcohol begins to fall, those who overdrink become sick and miserable. Table 6–5 shows the approximate amount per hour that can be consumed without exceeding the 0.05 blood alcohol level. (Even at this level, driving may be affected.) By pacing themselves, those who choose to drink can remain comfortable, pleasant, and coherent during a long party or other event. In short, if you drink, it might be wise to learn your "magic" number from Table 6–5.

Treatment Treatment for alcoholism begins by sobering up the person and cutting off the supply. This phase is referred to as **detoxification.** It frequently produces all the symptoms of drug withdrawal and can be extremely unpleasant for the alcoholic. The next step is to try to restore the alcoholic's health. Continued heavy use of alcohol usually causes severe damage to body organs and the nervous system. Food, vitamins, and medical care cannot fully reverse the damage, but a reasonable state of health can be obtained. When alcoholics have "dried out" and health has been restored, they may be treated with tranquilizers, antidepressants, or psychotherapy. Unfortunately, the success of these procedures has been limited.

One mutual-help approach that has been fairly successful is Alcoholics Anonymous (AA). AA acts on the premise that it takes a former alcoholic to understand and help a current alcoholic. Participants at AA meetings admit that they have a problem, share feelings, and resolve to stay "dry" one day at a time. Other group members provide support for those struggling to end depen-

Table 6–5 Moderated Drinking

YOUR WEIGHT (POUNDS)	APPROXIMATE NUMBER OF DRINKS PER HOUR TO STAY BELOW 0.05 BLOOD ALCOHOL.*
100	0.75
120	1.00
140	1.25
160	1.30
180	1.50
200	1.60
220	1.80

One drink = 12 ounces beer
= 4 ounces wine
= 2.5 ounces brandy
= 1.25 ounces 80 proof liquor

*Table entries are approximate, owing to individual differences in metabolism, recency of meals, and other factors. Estimates are from tables prepared by Vogler and Bartz (1982).

dency. (Cocaine Anonymous and Narcotics Anonymous use the same approach.)

Eighty-one percent of those who remain in AA over 1 year get through the following year without a drink (Sexias, 1981). AA's success rate may simply reflect the fact that members participate voluntarily, meaning they have admitted that they have a serious problem. Sadly, it seems that alcohol abusers will often not face their problems until they have really "hit bottom." If they are willing, though, AA presents a practical approach to the problem.

● Marijuana—What's in the Pot?

If you pick any three Americans at random, one will have tried marijuana at least once (National Institute of Drug Abuse, 1985). More than 18 million Americans may be regular users, which puts marijuana in a league with tobacco and alcohol. **Marijuana** and **hashish** are derived from the hemp plant *Cannabis sativa*. The main active chemical in *Cannabis* is tetrahydrocannabinol, or **THC** for short. THC is a mild **hallucinogen** (hal-LU-sin-oh-jin)—a substance that alters sensory impressions.

There have been no overdose deaths from marijuana use reported in the United States (Carr & Meyers, 1980). However, enough is now known about the effects of marijuana to make it clear that it cannot be considered harmless. Particularly worrisome is the fact that THC accumulates in the body's fatty tissues, especially in the brain and reproductive organs. Even if a person smokes marijuana just once a week, the body is never entirely free of THC (Nahas, 1979a).

Question: Does marijuana produce physical dependence?

Studies of long-term heavy users of marijuana in Jamaica, Greece, and Costa Rica failed to find any physical dependence (Carter, 1980; Rubin & Comitas, 1975; Stefanis et al., 1977). Marijuana's potential for abuse lies primarily in the realm of psychological dependence, not addiction (Fig. 6–14).

Immediate Effects of Marijuana Marijuana's typical psychological effects are a sense of euphoria or well-being, relaxation, altered time sense, and perceptual distortions (Carr & Meyers, 1980). Being stoned on marijuana impairs short-term memory and slows learning—effects that can be a serious problem for frequent users (Nahas, 1979b). All considered, marijuana intoxication is relatively subtle by comparison to a drug such as alcohol (Carter, 1980). Despite this, it is now well established that driving a car or operating machinery while high on marijuana can be extremely hazardous. As a matter of fact, driving under the influence of any intoxicating drug is dangerous.

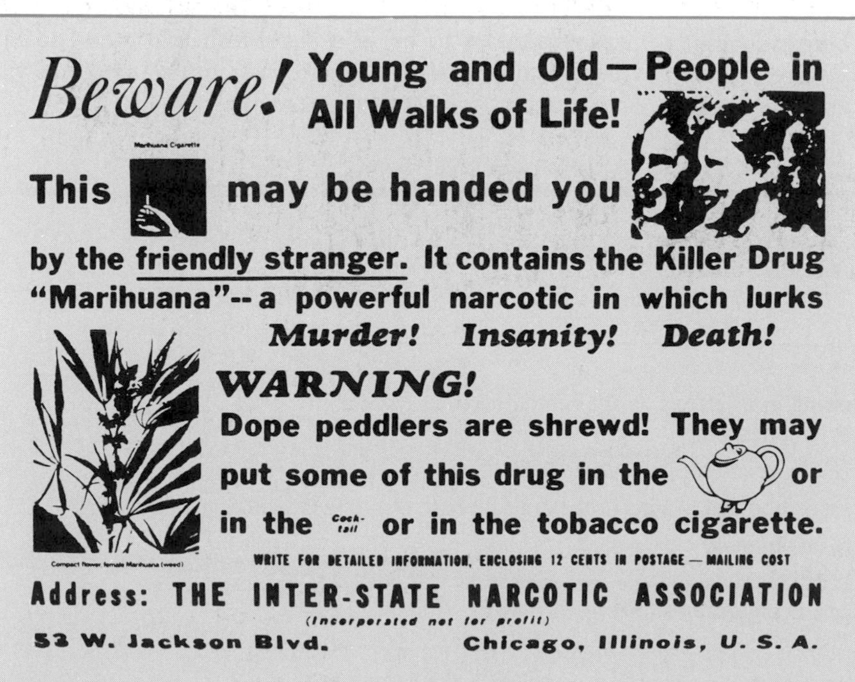

Fig. 6–14 *An outdated anti-marijuana poster demonstrates the kind of misinformation that has long been attached to this drug. Research is beginning to sort out what risks are associated with continued use of marijuana.*

Question: There have been very alarming reports in the press about the dangers of marijuana. Are they accurate?

Dangers of Marijuana Use As one pharmacologist put it, "Those reading only *Good Housekeeping* would have to believe that marijuana is considerably more dangerous than the black plague." Unfortunately, an evaluation of marijuana's risks has been clouded by emotional debate. Let's see if we can make a realistic appraisal.

In the 1970s, it was widely reported that marijuana causes brain damage, genetic damage, and a loss of motivation. These are serious charges, but each has been criticized for being based on poorly done or inconclusive research (Brecher, 1975a; Julien, 1985; NIDA, 1976; Zinberg, 1976). In addition, major studies in Jamaica, Greece, and Costa Rica failed to find any serious health problems or mental impairment in long-term marijuana smokers (Carter, 1980; Rubin & Comitas, 1975; Stefanis et al., 1977). Does this mean that marijuana gets a clean bill of health? Not really. As is true of alcohol, some adults become highly dependent on marijuana. The use of any drug, including marijuana, can seriously impair mental, physical, and emotional development (Nahas, 1979b; Zinberg, 1976).

Health Risks After many years of conflicting information, some of marijuana's health hazards are being clarified. After an extensive review of research, the National Academy of Sciences (1982) concluded that marijuana's long-term effects include several health risks.

1. In regular users, marijuana causes chronic bronchitis and pre-cancerous changes in lung cells. At present, no direct link between marijuana and lung cancer has been proved, but it is suspected. A recent study by Swiss researchers found that marijuana smoke contains 50 percent more cancer-causing hydrocarbons than does tobacco smoke. Some doctors estimate that smoking several "joints" a week is the equivalent of smoking a dozen cigarettes a day (Nahas, 1979a). Other researchers have found that "smokers of only a few joints a day have as much microscopic damage to the cells lining the airways as smokers of more than a pack of cigarettes a day" (Wu et al., 1988).

2. Marijuana temporarily lowers sperm production in males, and some studies show more abnormal sperm in men who use it. This could be a problem for a man who is marginally fertile and wants to have a family.

3. In experiments with female monkeys. THC causes abnormal menstrual cycles and disrupts ovulation. It is not known if the same applies to human females. Other animal studies show that THC causes a higher rate of miscarriages and that it can reach the developing fetus (Nahas, 1979a). As is true for so many other drugs, it appears that marijuana should be avoided during pregnancy.

4. Researcher Herman Friedman has produced direct evidence that THC can suppress the body's immune system, possibly increasing the risk of disease (Turkington, 1986).

When the preceding findings are compared with the studies of veteran marijuana users, it is clear that no one can say with certainty that marijuana is extremely harmful or completely safe. Although much is still unknown, marijuana appears to be in a class with two other potent drugs—tobacco and alcohol. Only future research will tell for sure "what's in the pot."

Learning Check

1. Which of the drugs listed below are known to cause a physical dependence?
a. heroin *c.* codeine *e.* barbiturates *g.* caffeine
b. morphine *d.* methadone *f.* alcohol *h.* amphetamines

2. Amphetamine psychosis is similar to extreme ________________, in which the individual feels threatened and suffers from delusions.

3. Cocaine is very similar to which of the following in its effects on the central nervous system?
a. Quaaludes *b.* codeine *c.* *Cannabis* *d.* amphetamine

4. The combination of ________________ and alcohol can be fatal.

5. One drink starts a chain reaction leading to a second and a third in the crucial phase of problem drinking. T or F?

6. This country's biggest drug problem centers on abuse of
a. marijuana *b.* alcohol *c.* tobacco *d.* cocaine

7. Most experts now acknowledge that marijuana is physically addicting. T or F?

Answers:

1. All but *g* **2.** paranoia **3.** *d* **4.** barbiturates or driving **5.** T **6.** *b* **7.** F

Applications: Exploring and Using Your Dreams

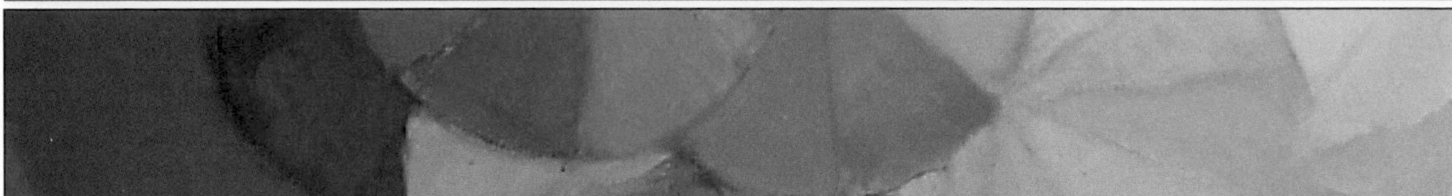

Dreaming is one of the most familiar altered states and also one of the most mysterious. At one time or another almost everyone has had a dream that seemed to have deep meaning. In view of this, it seems appropriate to return to dreaming in this Applications section. Let's start with Freud's approach to dream interpretation.

Interpreting Your Dreams

To unlock dreams, Freud identified four **dream processes** that he believed disguise the hidden meanings of dream images. The first is called **condensation.** Through condensation, a single character in a dream may represent several people at once. A character in a dream that looks like a teacher, acts like your father, talks like your mother, and is dressed like your employer might be a condensation of authority figures in your life.

A second way of disguising dream content is **displacement.** Displacement may cause the most important emotions or actions of a dream to be redirected toward safe or seemingly unimportant images. Thus, a student angry at his parents might dream of accidentally wrecking their car instead of directly attacking them.

A third dream process is **symbolization.** As mentioned earlier, Freud believed that dreams are often expressed in images that are symbolic rather than literal in their meaning. To uncover the meaning of dreams, it helps to ask what feelings or ideas a dream image might symbolize. Let's say, for example, that a student dreams of coming to class naked. A literal interpretation would be that the student is an exhibitionist! A more likely symbolic meaning might be that the student feels vulnerable in the class or is unprepared for a test.

A process called **secondary elaboration** is the fourth method by which the meaning of dreams is disguised. Secondary elaboration is the tendency to make a dream more logical and to add details when remembering it. The fresher a dream memory is, the more useful it is likely to be.

Looking for condensation, displacement, symbolization, and secondary elaboration may help you unlock your dreams. But there are simpler ways to proceed. Dream theorist Calvin Hall (1966, 1974) prefers to think of dreams as plays and the dreamer as a playwright. Hall does admit that the images and ideas in dreams tend to be more primitive than those experienced while awake. Nevertheless, much can be learned by simply considering the **setting, cast of characters, plot,** and **emotions** portrayed in a dream.

Another dream researcher, Rosalind Cartwright (1969, 1978) suggests that dreams are primarily "feeling statements." According to her, the overall **emotional tone** of a dream is a major clue to its meaning. Is the dream comical, threatening, joyous, or depressing? Were you lonely, jealous, frightened, in love, or angry? Cartwright encourages use of everyday dream life as a source of varied experience and personal enrichment and considers dream explorations an avenue for personal growth.

Dream theorist Ann Faraday (1972) also believes in the value of studying one's own dreams. Faraday considers dreams a message *from* yourself *to* yourself. Thus, the way to understand dreams is to remember them, write them down, look for the message they contain, and become deeply acquainted with *your* own symbol system. Here's how.

How To Catch a Dream

1. Before retiring, plan to remember your dreams. Keep a pen and paper or a tape recorder beside your bed.
2. If possible, arrange to awaken gradually without an alarm. Natural awakening is almost always soon after a REM period.
3. If you rarely remember your dreams, you may want to set an alarm clock to go off an hour before you usually awaken. Although less desirable than awakening naturally, this method may let you catch a dream.
4. Upon awakening, lie still and review the dream images with your eyes closed. Try to recall as many details as possible.
5. If you can, make your first dream record (whether by writing or by tape) with your eyes closed. Opening your eyes will disrupt dream recall.
6. Review the dream again and record as many additional details as you can remember. Dream memories disappear quickly. Be sure to describe feelings as well as the plot, characters, and actions of the dream.
7. Put your dreams into a permanent dream diary. Keep dreams in chronological order and review them periodically. This procedure will reveal recurrent themes, conflicts, and emotions. It almost always produces valuable insights.
8. Remember, a number of drugs suppress dreaming (see Table 6–6).

Because each dream has several possible meanings or levels of meaning, there is no fixed way to work with it. Telling the dream to others and discussing its meaning can be a good

Applications

Table 6-6 Effects of Selected Drugs on Dreaming

DRUG	EFFECT ON REM SLEEP
Alcohol	Decrease
Amphetamines	Decrease
Barbiturates	Decrease
Caffeine	None
Cocaine	Decrease
LSD	Slight increase
Marijuana	Slight decrease or no effect
Opiates	Decrease
Valium (benzodiazepam)	Decrease

start. Describing it may help you relive some of the feelings in the dream, and family or friends may be able to offer interpretations you would be blind to yourself. Watch for verbal or visual puns and other playful elements in dreams. If, for example, you dream that you are in a wrestling match and your arm is pinned behind your back, it may mean that you feel someone is "twisting your arm" in real life.

The meaning of most dreams will yield to careful scrutiny and a little detective work. If you still have trouble seeing the meaning of a dream, you may find it helpful to use a technique developed by Fritz Perls. Perls, the originator of Gestalt therapy, considered most dreams a special message about what's missing in our lives, what we avoid doing, or feelings that need to be "reowned." Perls felt that dreams are a way of filling in gaps in personal experience (Perls, 1969).

An approach that Perls found helpful is to "take the part of" or "speak for" each of the characters and objects in the dream. In other words, if you dream about a strange man standing behind a doorway, you would speak aloud to the man, then answer for him. To use Perls' method, you would even speak for the door, perhaps saying something like, "I am a barrier. I keep you safe, but I also keep you locked inside. The stranger has something to tell you. You must risk opening me to learn it."

A particularly interesting dream exercise is to continue a dream as waking fantasy so that it may be concluded or carried on to a more meaningful ending. As the world of dreams and your personal dream language become more familiar, you will doubtless find many answers, paradoxes, intuitions, and insights into your own behavior.

Using Your Dreams

Dream theorist Gordon Globus (1987) believes that some of our most creative moments take place during dreaming. Even unimaginative people, he notes, may create amazing worlds each night in their dreams. For many of us, this rich ability to create is lost in the daily rush of sensory input. How might we tap the creative power of dreams that is so easily lost during waking?

History is full of cases where dreams have been a pathway to creativity and discovery. A striking example is provided by Dr. Otto Loewi, a pharmacologist and winner of a Nobel Prize. Loewi had spent years studying the chemical transmission of nerve impulses. A tremendous breakthrough in his research came when he dreamed of an experiment three nights in a row. The first two nights he woke up and scribbled the experiment on a pad. But the next morning, he couldn't tell what the notes meant. On the third night, he got up after having the dream. This time, instead of making notes he went straight to his laboratory and performed the crucial experiment. Loewi later said that if the experiment had occurred to him while awake he would have rejected it.

Loewi's experience gives some insight into using dreams to produce creative solutions. Inhibitions are reduced during dreaming, which may be especially useful in solving problems that require a fresh point of view.

Being able to take advantage of dreams for problem solving is improved if you "set" yourself before retiring. Before you go to bed, try to think intently about a problem you wish to solve. Steep yourself in the problem by stating it clearly and reviewing all relevant information. Then use the suggestions listed in the previous section to catch your dreams. While this method is not guaranteed to produce a novel solution or a new insight, it is certain to be an adventure.

Lucid Dreaming If you would like to press further into the territory of dreams, you may want to learn lucid dreaming. During a **lucid dream,** the dreamer "wakes" within an ordinary dream and feels capable of normal thought and action. Lucid dreamers know they are dreaming, but they feel fully conscious within the dream world (La Berge, 1981a, 1985).

Stephen La Berge and his colleagues at the Stanford University Sleep Research Center have used a unique approach to show that lucid dreams are real and that they occur during REM sleep. In the sleep lab, lucid dreamers agree to make prearranged signals when they become aware they are dreaming. One such signal is to look up abruptly in a dream, causing a distinct upward eye movement. Another signal is to clench the right and left fists (in the dream) in a prearranged pattern. Corresponding muscle changes in the wrists can then be recorded electrically. Such signals show very clearly that lucid dreaming and voluntary action in dreams is possible (La Berge, 1981b, 1985; La Berge et al., 1981).

Question: How would a person go about learning to have lucid dreams?

Applications

La Berge (1980) found he could greatly increase lucid dreaming by following this simple routine: When you awaken spontaneously from a dream, take a few minutes to try to memorize it. Next, engage in 10 to 15 minutes of reading or any other activity requiring full wakefulness. Then, while lying in bed and returning to sleep, say to yourself, "Next time I'm dreaming, I want to remember I'm dreaming." Finally, visualize yourself lying in bed asleep while in the dream you just rehearsed. At the same time, picture yourself realizing that you are dreaming. Follow this routine each time you awaken (substitute a dream memory from another occasion if you don't awaken from a dream).

Question: Why would anyone want to have more lucid dreams?

Researchers are interested in lucid dreams because they provide a new tool for understanding dreaming. Using subjects who can signal while they are dreaming may make it possible to explore dreams with first-hand data from the dreamer's world itself (La Berge, 1985).

On a more personal level, lucid dreaming can convert dreams into a nightly "workshop" for emotional growth. Consider, for example, a recently divorced woman who kept dreaming that she was being swallowed by a giant wave. Rosalind Cartwright (1978) asked the woman to try swimming the next time the wave engulfed her. She did, with great determination, and the nightmare lost its terror. More importantly, her revised dream made her feel that she could cope with life again.

Learning Check

1. In secondary elaboration, one dream character stands for several others. T or F?
2. Calvin Hall's approach to dream interpretation emphasizes the setting, cast, plot, and emotions portrayed in a dream. T or F?
3. Rosalind Cartwright stresses that dreaming is a relatively mechanical process having little personal meaning. T or F?
4. Both alcohol and LSD cause a slight increase in dreaming. T or F?
5. "Taking the part of" or "speaking for" dream elements is a dream interpretation technique originated by Fritz Perls. T or F?
6. Recent research shows that lucid dreaming occurs primarily during NREM sleep or micro-awakenings. T or F?

Answers:
1. F 2. T 3. F 4. F 5. T 6. F

Exploration: Drug Abuse—Many Questions, Few Answers

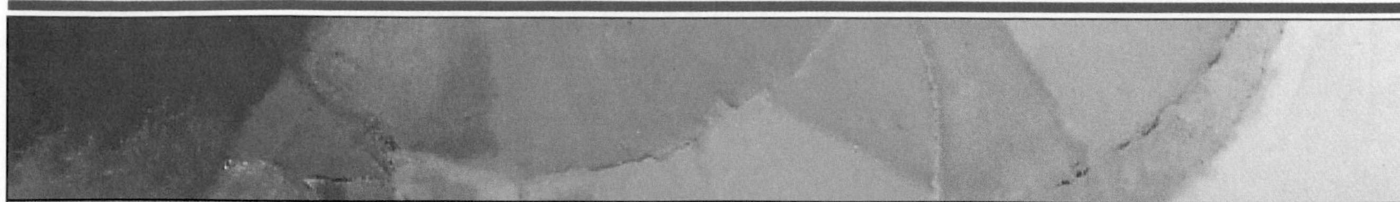

Question: Why do people use drugs?

People seek drug experiences for a variety of reasons, ranging from curiosity and a desire to belong to a group to a search for meaning or an escape from feelings of inadequacy (Lipinski & Lipinski, 1970). The best predictors of adolescent drug use and abuse are peer drug use, parental drug use, delinquency, parental maladjustment, poor self-esteem, social nonconformity, and stressful life changes (Marlatt et al., 1988). For many young people, drug abuse is just one part of a general pattern of problem behavior. This may be why drug intervention programs that teach social skills have been relatively successful (Marlatt et al., 1988).

Many abusers turn to drugs in a self-defeating attempt to cope with life. All of the frequently abused drugs produce immediate feelings of pleasure. The negative consequences follow much later. This combination of immediate pleasure and delayed punishment allows abusers to feel good on demand. In time, of course, most of the pleasure goes out of drug abuse, and the abuser's problems get worse. But if an abuser merely feels *better* (however briefly) after taking a drug, drug-taking can become compulsive (Barrett, 1985).

Closely related to a drug's actual effects are users' beliefs and expectations about drugs. Patterns of drinking alcohol offer a good example of how expectations promote abuse. For example, Brown, Goldman, and Christiansen (1985) studied the expectations people have about drinking. Drinkers were asked about alcohol's effect on general good feelings, sexual performance, social and physical pleasure, self-assertion, relaxation, and feelings of power. The study found that heavy drinkers expect far more positive effects and fewer negative consequences from drinking alcohol than light drinkers do.

There is a widespread tendency to think of drugs as a magic way to produce good feelings by avoiding, minimizing, or escaping negative situations. Some observers believe that drug use is so deeply ingrained in modern society that "we are addicted to addiction. This is to say that, with few exceptions we subscribe to the premise that life cannot be lived without drugs." We are so used to having our own way that we have come to believe "we should be able to will ourselves to be calm, cheerful, thin, industrious, creative—and moreover, to have a good night's sleep" (Farber, 1966). Farber believes that the medical profession, well meaning but misguided, has accepted these premises wholeheartedly and unnecessarily encourages legal drug use. Indeed, one psychologist observed:

> Depression, social inadequacy, anxiety, apathy, marital discord, children's misbehavior, and other psychological and social problems of living are now being redefined as medical problems, to be solved by physicians with prescription pads. (Rogers, 1971.)

Perhaps physicians and the general public alike can be partially excused for placing undue faith in the value of drugs because each group is the target of multimillion-dollar advertising campaigns aimed at encouraging drug use. Even the lowly aspirin is now pushed as a means of relieving "nervous tension." Advertisements directed at physicians encourage overuse of drugs even more blatantly. An ad pictures a distraught mother with a child and asks, "Her kind of pressures last all day . . . shouldn't her tranquilizer?" Another reads:

> School, the dark, separation, dental visits, monsters. The everyday anxiety of children sometimes gets out of hand. A child can usually deal with his anxieties. But sometimes the anxieties overpower the child. Then he needs your help. Your help may include Vistaril.

Drugs, of course, have legitimate uses and have alleviated much suffering. The problem is that drugs strong enough to ease pain, induce sleep, end depression, or otherwise alter consciousness have a high potential for abuse.

Drug abuse in Western nations has reached epidemic proportions in recent years. Problems once restricted to drug-related subcultures and the urban poor are now seen regularly among high school and college students and among the vast middle classes. In the United States, one recent survey found that nearly 40 percent of doctors under age 40 admitted that they use marijuana or

Exploration

cocaine to get high with friends (McAuliffe, 1986)!

Question: What, if anything, should be done about drug abuse?

Prevention Traditional approaches have emphasized limiting drug supplies, strict law enforcement, and legal penalties. Limiting supplies has been relatively successful in the case of some drugs. But drug abuse and the legality of a drug are two separate issues. This distinction becomes clear when it is recognized that one of the most potent, destructive, and potentially dangerous drugs available is alcohol. By the government's own standards, alcohol should be at the top of the list of controlled substances. Yet it is legal.

Facts such as these have led some observers to conclude that anyone who seeks drug-induced consciousness alteration will find a drug, legal or illegal, to achieve it. Psychiatrist Thomas Szasz (1972, 1985) believes that it is futile for the government to attempt to "legislate morality" by regulating what drugs a person chooses to take. Szasz suggests that current drug regulations have an effect similar to the prohibition of alcohol in the United States in the 1920s. That is, they encourage a black market, organized crime, disrespect for the law, and occasional poisonings from adulterated drugs. As Szasz points out, "tobacco is not legally considered a drug, marijuana is, gin is not, but Valium is. . . ."

After an extensive review of research on drugs, drug abuse, and drug laws, the magazine *Consumer Reports* drew the same conclusion and added these recommendations (Brecher, 1972):

—Stop publicizing the horrors of the "drug menace." Scare publicity has functioned not as warnings, but to popularize drugs and as a lure to recreational drug use.
—Stop misclassifying drugs. Our current legal classification system treats alcohol and nicotine—two of the most harmful drugs—essentially as nondrugs, while marijuana is equated with heroin—a shocking and harmful bit of foolishness. Cocaine is still listed as a narcotic when it is clearly a stimulant. A scientifically based legal system must replace the current politically based one.

Whereas it is true that drug *use* is essentially a "victimless crime," the fact remains that *abuse* of drugs—legal or illegal—represents a serious loss in the productivity and mental health of self-drugged citizens.

The point of view expressed by Szasz is obviously controversial. Many, in fact, believe that the answer to drug problems is to be found in stricter penalties and law enforcement. And yet, a sober look at drug abuse makes it clear that some psychoactive drugs are almost always available. In general, Americans tend to overlook the frequency of abuse of legal drugs such as tranquilizers or alcohol and overestimate the misuse of illegal drugs (Drug Abuse Council, 1980).

Although billions of dollars have been spent on drug enforcement, there has been an increase in the overall level of drug use in the United States. Given this fact, some experts believe that prevention through education and early intervention is the answer to drug problems. What do you think?

Learning Check

1. Advertising campaigns directed at physicians tend to overstate the need for treating behavioral problems with drugs. T or F?
2. Heavy drinkers of alcohol learn from experience to expect more negative consequences from alcohol's effects. T or F?
3. Thomas Szasz believes that it is time for the government to take a lead in "legislating morality" with regard to drug use. T or F?
4. Current laws in the United States have been accused of misclassifying some drugs. T or F?
5. The immediate reinforcing effects of drugs and the delayed negative consequences are believed to play a major role in drug abuse. T or F?

Answers:
1. T 2. F 3. F 4. T 5. T

Chapter Summary

• States of awareness that differ from normal, alert, waking consciousness are called **altered states of consciousness** (ASCs). Altered states are associated especially with sleep and dreaming, hypnosis, sensory deprivation, and psychoactive drugs.

• Sleep is an **innate biological rhythm** essential for survival. Higher animals and people deprived of sleep experience involuntary **microsleeps.** Moderate sleep loss mainly affects vigilance and performance on routine or boring tasks. Extended sleep loss can (somewhat rarely) produce a temporary **sleep-deprivation psychosis.**

• **Sleep patterns** show some flexibility, but 7 to 8 hours remains average. The amount of daily sleep decreases steadily from birth to old age. Once-a-day **sleep patterns,** with a 2-to-1 ratio of waking and sleep, are most efficient for most people.

• Sleep occurs in four **stages.** Stage 1 is **light sleep,** and stage 4 is **deep sleep.** The sleeper alternates between stages 1 and 4 (passing through stages 2 and 3) several times each night.

• There are two basic sleep states, **rapid eye movement (REM)** sleep and **non-REM (NREM)** sleep. REM sleep is much more strongly associated with dreaming than non-REM sleep is.

• Dreaming and REMs occur mainly during stage 1. Dreaming is accompanied by emotional arousal but relaxation of the skeletal muscles. People deprived of dream sleep show a **REM rebound** when allowed to sleep without interruption. However, total sleep loss seems to be more important than loss of a single stage.

• **Sleepwalking** and **sleeptalking** occur during NREM sleep. **Night terrors** occur in NREM sleep, whereas **nightmares** occur in REM sleep. **Narcolepsy** (sleep attacks) and **cataplexy** are caused by a sudden shift to stage 1 REM patterns during normal waking hours.

• **Insomnia** may be temporary or chronic. When it is treated through use of drugs, sleep quality is often lowered and **drug-dependency insomnia** may develop. **Behavioral approaches** to managing insomnia have been shown to be effective.

• **Sleep apnea** (interrupted breathing) is one source of insomnia and daytime **hypersomnia** (sleepiness). Apnea is suspected as one cause of **sudden infant death syndrome** (SIDS).

• Most **dream content** is about familiar settings, people, and actions. Dreams more often involve negative emotions than positive emotions. The Freudian, or **psychodynamic,** view is that dreams express unconscious wishes, frequently hidden by **dream symbols.** Many theorists have questioned Freud's view of dreams. For example, the **activation-synthesis model** portrays dreaming as a physiological process.

• **Hypnosis** is an altered state characterized by narrowed attention and increased suggestibility. Hypnosis appears capable of producing relaxation, controlling pain, and altering perceptions. **Stage hypnotism** takes advantage of typical stage behavior and uses deception to simulate hypnosis.

• Extreme or unusual stimulus conditions often induce altered states of consciousness. A prime example is **sensory deprivation.** Prolonged sensory deprivation is stressful and disruptive. However, brief sensory deprivation can enhance sensitivity and relaxation. Sensory deprivation also appears to aid the breaking of long-standing habits.

• A **psychoactive drug** is a substance that affects the brain in ways that alter consciousness. Most psychoactive drugs can be placed on a scale ranging from **stimulation** to **depression.**

• Drugs may cause a **physical dependence** (addiction) or a **psychological dependence,** or both. The physically addicting drugs are heroin, morphine, codeine, methadone, barbiturates, alcohol, amphetamines, tobacco, and possibly cocaine. All psychoactive drugs can lead to psychological dependence.

• Drug use can be classified as **experimental, recreational, situational, intensive,** and **compulsive.** Drug abuse is most often associated with the last three.

• **Stimulant drugs** are readily abused due to the period of depression that often follows stimulation. The greatest risks are associated with **amphetamines, cocaine,** and **nicotine,** but even **caffeine** can be a problem. Nicotine includes the added risk of lung cancer and other health problems.

• **Barbiturates** are depressant drugs whose action is similar to that of alcohol. The overdose level for barbiturates is close to the intoxication dosage, making them dangerous drugs. Mixing barbiturates and alcohol may result in a fatal **drug interaction.**

• **Alcohol** is the most heavily abused drug in common use today. The development of a drinking problem is usually marked by an **initial phase** of increasing consumption, a **crucial phase,** in which a single drink can set off a chain reaction, and a **chronic phase,** in which a person lives to drink and drinks to live.

• **Marijuana** is subject to an abuse pattern similar to alcoholism. Studies of long-term users have failed to find any drastic health changes due to marijuana. However, laboratory studies have implicated marijuana as a possible source of lung cancer and other health problems.

• Dreams may be used to promote self-understanding. Freud held that the meaning of dreams is hidden by **condensation, displacement, symbolization,** and **secondary elaboration.** Hall emphasizes the **setting, cast, plot,** and **emotions** of a dream. Cartwright's view of dreams as **feeling statements** and Perls' technique of **speaking for** dream elements are also helpful. Dreams may be used for **creative problem solving,** especially when dream control is achieved through **lucid dreaming.**

• Drug abuse is related to a variety of factors, especially attempts to cope, the immediate reinforcing qualities of psychoactive drugs, and expectations about the value and effects of drugs. Proposed remedies for drug abuse have ranged from severe punishment to legalization. The search for a solution continues.

Questions for Discussion

1. How would your life change if you needed to sleep 15 hours per day? How would it change if you only needed 2 hours a day? Would you give up sleep if you could?

2. Have you ever gone without sleep for an extended period? If so, what were your reactions? Your greatest difficulties?

3. Describe a recent dream you have had. How does it relate to your daytime experiences and feelings? What additional meanings can you find in it? Do you think that recording your dreams would be worthwhile?

4. Have you ever solved a problem in your dreams? How much control do you have over what you dream?

5. Respond to the statement, "The REM state is not sleep at all; during REM we are paralyzed and hallucinating." Do you agree? If you were dreaming right now, how could you prove it?

6. Do you agree or disagree with the idea that prohibition of drug use leads to adulteration, black markets, organized crime, unwillingness of abusers to seek help, and greater injury through imprisonment than is caused by the drugs themselves? What arguments can you give to support your position?

7. Why do you think there is such a contrast between the laws regulating marijuana and those regulating alcohol and tobacco?

8. In the novel *Brave New World,* Aldous Huxley described an imaginary drug called *soma* that made people feel continuously happy and cooperative. If such a drug existed, what controls would you impose on its use? Why? If a drug that could enhance creativity were discovered, what use would you allow for it? What about a drug to improve memory?

9. If you have ever seen a stage hypnotist or participated in a hypnosis demonstration, how did your experience compare with Barber's analysis of stage hypnosis?

10. Have you ever been in a situation that produced sensory deprivation (such as a commercial "flotation center" or a radar room)? How did you react? Why do you think brief sensory deprivation is restful and longer periods are stressful?

11. Do you think that seeking altered states of consciousness is "natural"? What altered states does our culture accept? About which states is it ambivalent? What altered states does it clearly reject? How do you think such differences developed?

12. In view of their addictive qualities, should advertising be allowed for tobacco and alcohol? Should American tobacco companies be allowed to promote smoking in other countries where there is less public awareness of the health hazards of tobacco?

13. If you had a totally free hand, how would you handle this country's drug abuse problem?

Part Three

Learning and Cognition

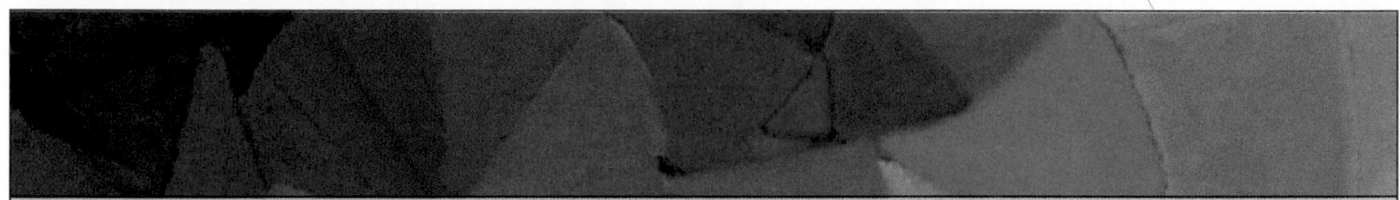

Chapter 7

Conditioning and Learning I

In This Chapter

Learning: antecedents and consequences

Elements of classical conditioning

Emotional conditioning

Operant conditioning

Types of reinforcement

Schedules of reinforcement

Stimulus control

Applications

Conditioning in everyday situations

Exploration

Behavioral self-management

Chapter Preview

What Did You Learn in School Today?

When your aging author was in college, students discovered an interesting "game" that could be played with the plumbing in the dorms. When a toilet was flushed while someone was taking a shower, the cold water pressure dropped suddenly. This caused the shower to become scalding hot. Naturally, the shower victim screamed in terror as his reflexes caused him to leap back in pain. Soon it was further discovered that if several students flushed all *the toilets at once, the effects were multiplied many times over!*

The sound of a flushing toilet has to be one of the world's most uninspiring stimuli. But for a time, a whole flock of college students twitched involuntarily whenever they heard a toilet flush. Their reactions to this formerly neutral stimulus were the result of classical conditioning, *a special type of learning. Details about classical conditioning are explored in this chapter.*

Now consider another learning situation: Let's say that you are at school and that you are "starving to death." Locating a vending machine, you deposit your last quarter to buy a candy bar. You press the button, and . . . nothing happens. Being civilized and in complete control, you press the other buttons, try the coin return, and look for an attendant. Still nothing. Your stomach growls. Being no longer either civilized or self-controlled, you give the machine a little kick (just to let it know how you feel). Then, as you turn away, the machine begins to whirr and out pops a candy bar plus 15 cents change. Once this happens, chances are good that you will repeat the "kicking response" in the future. If it pays off several times more, kicking vending machines may become a regular feature of your behavior. In this case, learning is based on operant conditioning *(also called* instrumental learning*).*

Classical and operant conditioning underlie much human learning. In fact, conditioning reaches into every corner of our lives. You should certainly find it useful to learn more about it. Are you ready to learn more about learning? If so, read on! This chapter and the next explore conditioning and other forms of learning.

Survey Questions

- What is learning? How does it relate to innate behavior?
- What is classical conditioning? Have I been conditioned?
- What is operant conditioning? How does it affect human behavior?
- How are we influenced by conditioning and patterns of reward?
- How is conditioning applied to practical problems?

What Is Learning—Does Practice Make Perfect?

The weaverbird is a curious creature that ties a special grass knot to hold its nest together. How does it learn to make the knot? It doesn't! Weaverbirds raised in total isolation for several generations still tie the knot the first time they build a nest.

Knot tying in the weaverbird is a **fixed action pattern (FAP).** A FAP is an instinctual chain of movements found in almost all members of a species. Like other **innate** (inborn) **behaviors,** fixed action patterns help animals meet major needs in their lives (picture a cat's face-washing routine, for instance). A simpler innate behavior is a **reflex,** such as blinking when your eyelashes are touched. More complicated behaviors, like the maternal instinct in lower animals, combine both fixed action patterns and reflexes.

Question: Do humans have instincts?

Humans do not have instincts as most psychologists define them. (See the Exploration in Chapter 24 for further discussion.) To qualify as instinctual, a behavior must be both complex and "species specific." **Species-specific behaviors** are those that occur in almost all members of a species. Other than reflexes, no human behaviors seem to qualify. However, what humans lack in instinctual "programming" is more than made up for by learning capacity.

Our ability to learn is so advanced that most of our daily activities are either wholly learned or directly affected by learning. Imagine what you would be like if you suddenly forgot everything you had ever learned. What could you do? You would be unable to read, write, or speak. You couldn't feed yourself, find your way home, drive a car, play the bassoon, or "party." Needless to say, you would be totally incapacitated. (Dull, too!)

Question: Learning is obviously important. What's a formal definition of learning?

Learning is a *relatively permanent change in behavior due to reinforcement.* Notice that this definition *excludes* temporary changes caused by motivation, fatigue, maturation, disease, injury, or drugs. Each of these can alter behavior, but none qualifies as learning.

Question: Isn't learning the result of practice?

It depends on what you mean by practice. Repeating a response will not necessarily produce learning—unless some type of *reinforcement* is present. **Reinforcement** refers to any event that increases chances that a response will occur again. Thus, if I want to teach a dog a trick, I could reinforce correct responses by giving the dog some food each time it sits up. Similarly, a child who often gets praise or a hug for picking up toys will learn to be neat. These, of course, are only examples. As we will see later, learning can be reinforced in many ways.

Compare: Learned and Innate Behaviors

Innate behavior A genetically programmed or inborn behavior pattern.

Fixed action pattern (FAP) A genetically programmed sequence of actions that occur mechanically and almost universally in a species.

Reflex An innate, automatic response to a stimulus; for example, an eye blink, knee jerk, or dilation of the pupil.

Species-specific behavior Patterned behavior that is exhibited by all normal members of a particular species (an FAP, for example).

Learning Any relatively permanent change in behavior that can be attributed to experience but not to fatigue, maturation, injury, and so forth.

Antecedents and Consequences Unlocking the secrets of learning begins with noting what happens just before and just after a response. Events before a response are called **antecedents.** Those that follow a response are called **consequences.** Paying careful attention to the "before and after" of learning is a key to understanding it.

In classical conditioning, all the "action" occurs before a response. We begin with a stimulus that already triggers a response. Imagine, for example, that a puff of air (the stimulus) is aimed at your eye. This will automatically make you blink (the response). The blink occurs without any prior learning. Now, assume that we sound a horn (another stimulus) just before each puff of air hits your eye. If the horn and the air puff occur together many times, what happens? Soon, the horn alone will make you blink. Since you didn't blink before when the horn sounded, learning has occurred. Similarly, if your mouth waters each time you eat a sweet roll, you may learn to salivate when you merely *see* a sweet roll.

In classical conditioning, *antecedent events* become *associated* with one another: A stimulus that does not produce a response is linked with one that does. Learning is evident when the new stimulus also begins to elicit (bring forth) responses.

Operant conditioning involves learning that is affected by *consequences*. Each time a response is made, it may be followed by reinforcement, punishment, or nothing. These results determine whether a response is likely to be made again. For example, if you wear a particular shirt or blouse and get lots of compliments (reinforcement), you are likely to wear it more often. If people snicker, insult you, call the police, or scream (punishment), you will probably wear it less often.

Now that you have an idea of what happens in the two basic kinds of learning, let's look at classical conditioning in more detail.

Classical Conditioning—Does the Name Pavlov Ring a Bell?

Question: How was classical conditioning discovered?

At the beginning of the twentieth century, something happened in the lab of the Russian physiologist **Ivan Pavlov** that brought him lasting fame. The event was so unastounding that a lesser man might have ignored it: Pavlov's subjects drooled at him.

Actually, Pavlov was studying digestion. To observe salivation, he placed meat powder or some tidbit on a dog's tongue. After doing this many times, Pavlov noticed that his dogs were salivating *before* the food reached their mouths. Later, the dogs even began to salivate at the mere sight of Pavlov entering the room. Was this misplaced affection? Pavlov knew better. Salivation is normally a reflex (automatic, nonlearned) response. For the animals to salivate at the mere sight of food, some form of learning had to be taking place. Pavlov called this type of learning **conditioning.** Because of its importance in psychology's history, it is now called **classical conditioning** (also known as **respondent conditioning).**

Question: How did Pavlov study conditioning?

Pavlov's Experiment After Pavlov observed that meat powder caused automatic reflex salivation, he began his classic experiments (Fig. 7–1). To begin, he rang a bell.

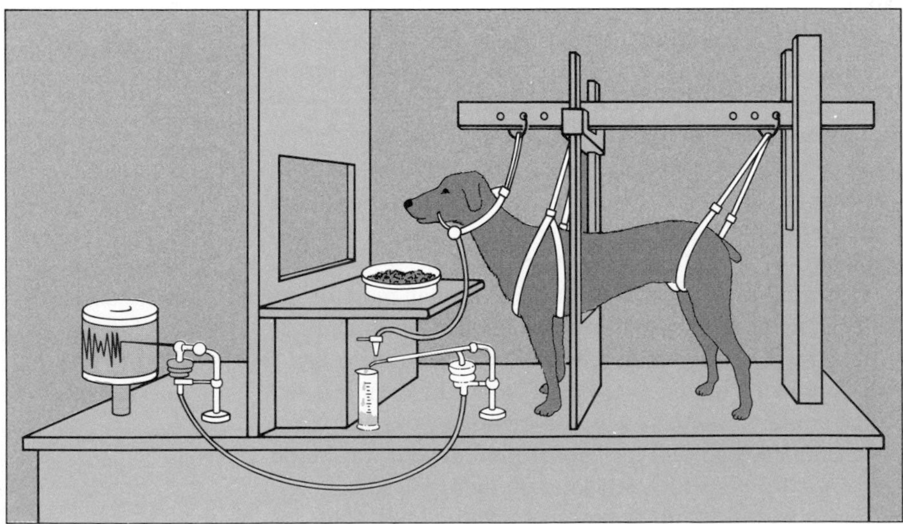

Fig. 7–1 *Pavlov's conditioning apparatus. In Pavlov's early experiments, a tube carried saliva from the dog's mouth to a lever that activated a recording device (far left). The placing of a dish of food in front of the dog was paired with various other stimuli for conditioning.*

Initially, the bell was a *neutral stimulus*. (It did not produce a response.) After Pavlov rang the bell he placed meat powder on the dog's tongue. Each time Pavlov rang the bell, he followed it with meat powder, which always caused salivation. This sequence was repeated many times: bell, meat powder, salivation; bell, meat powder, salivation. Eventually (as conditioning took place), the bell alone began to cause salivation (Fig. 7–2). By association, the bell, which before had no effect, began to produce the same response that food did. This was shown by sometimes ringing the bell alone and observing that the dog salivated.

Psychologists use several terms to describe these events. The bell in Pavlov's experiment starts out as a **neutral stimulus (NS)** (a stimulus that does not evoke a response). In time, the bell becomes a **conditioned stimulus (CS),** that is, a stimulus to which the dog has *learned* to respond. The meat powder is an **unconditioned stimulus (US)** (because the dog does not have to learn to respond to it). Unconditioned stimuli typically produce reflex responses. Since a reflex is "built in," it is called an **unconditioned** (nonlearned) **response (UR).** In Pavlov's study, salivation is the UR. When the bell alone causes salivation, the response can no longer be called a simple reflex. Instead, it is a **conditioned** (learned) **response (CR)** (see Fig. 7–2).

Question: Are all these terms and code letters really necessary?

In a word, yes, because they help us recognize similarities in various instances of classical conditioning. Let's summarize the terms using an earlier example:

Before Conditioning	**Example**
US → UR	Puff of air → eye blink
NS → no effect	Horn → no effect
After Conditioning	**Example**
CS → CR	Horn → eye blink

Now, see if you can apply the terms to explain the effects of the shower and flushing toilet described in the Chapter Preview.

1. What is the unconditioned (nonlearned) response?

____

2. What is the unconditioned stimulus that evokes the response?

____

3. What is the conditioned stimulus?

____

Let's see if you used the terms correctly. The unconditioned, or nonlearned, response was a reflex jump from the hot water. The unconditioned stimulus was the hot water. The conditioned stimulus was the sound of a flushing toilet. That is, the flushing sound was at first neutral. But as a result of conditioning, it began to elicit a reflex.

Elements of Classical Conditioning—Teach Your Little Brother to Salivate

A number of interesting events occur during classical conditioning. To observe them, you could ring a bell, squirt lemon juice into a child's mouth, and condition salivation to the bell. The child's reactions might then be used to explore other aspects of conditioning.

Acquisition During **acquisition,** or training, a conditioned response must be **reinforced,** or strengthened (see Fig. 7–3.) In classical conditioning, reinforcement occurs whenever the CS is followed by, or paired with, an unconditioned stimulus (US). For our child, the bell is the CS; salivating is the UR; and the US is the sour lemon juice. To reinforce salivating to the bell, we must pair the bell with the lemon juice. Conditioning will be most rapid if the US follows *immediately* after the CS. With most reflexes, the optimal delay between CS and US is from ½ second to about 5 seconds (Schwartz, 1984).

Fig. 7–2 *The conditioning procedure.*

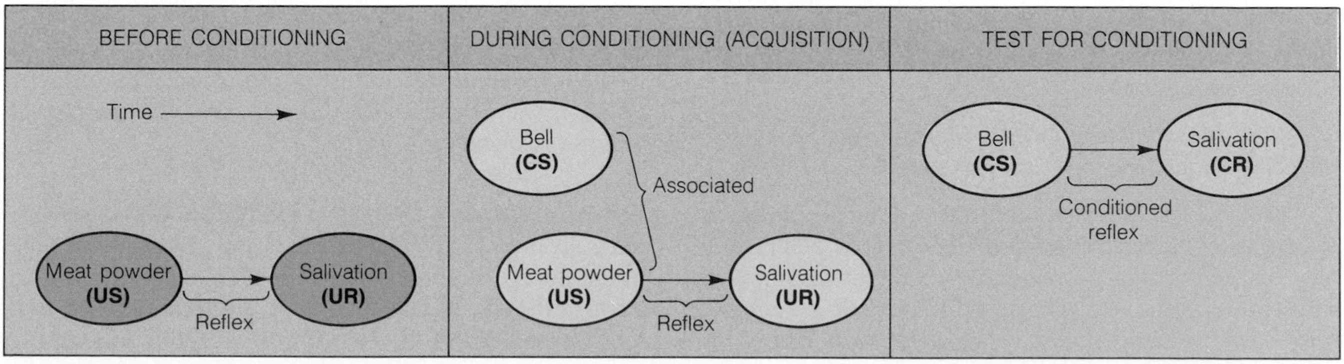

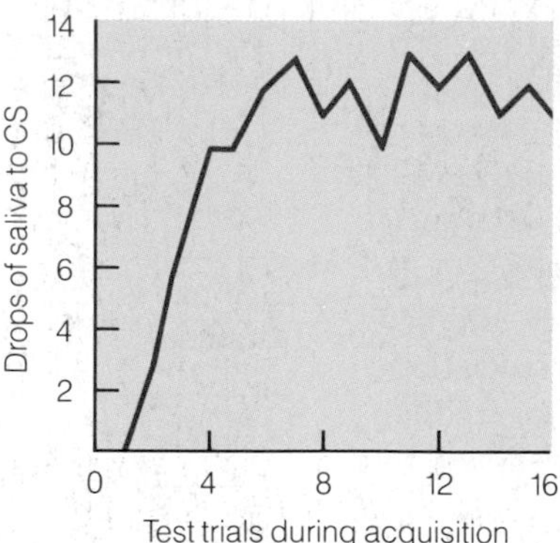

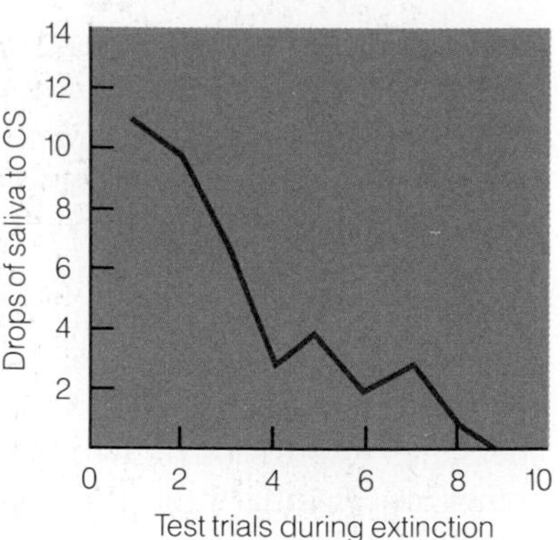

Fig. 7–3 *Acquisition and extinction of a conditioned response. (After Pavlov, 1927.)*

Higher-Order Conditioning Once a response is learned, it can bring about **higher-order conditioning.** In higher-order conditioning, a well-learned CS is used to reinforce further learning. Let's illustrate again with our salivating child. As a result of earlier learning, the bell now produces salivation, without the lemon juice. To go a step further, you could clap your hands and then ring the bell. (No lemon juice would be used.) As before, the child would soon learn to salivate when you clapped your hands. (This little trick could be a real hit with friends and neighbors.)

Through higher-order conditioning, learning can be extended one or more steps beyond the original conditioned stimulus. Many advertisers try to use this effect by pairing images that evoke good feelings (such as people smiling and having fun) with pictures of their products. Obviously, they hope that you will learn, by association, to feel good when you see their products.

Question: After conditioning has occurred, what would happen if the US no longer followed the CS?

Extinction and Spontaneous Recovery If the US never again follows the CS, conditioning will **extinguish.** If the bell (in our example) is rung many times and not followed by lemon juice, the child's tendency to salivate to the ringing of the bell will be *inhibited* (or suppressed). Thus, we see that classical conditioning can be weakened by removing reinforcement (see Fig. 7–3). This process is called **extinction.**

Question: If conditioning takes a while to build up, shouldn't it take time to reverse?

Yes. In fact, several extinction sessions may be necessary to completely reverse conditioning. After the bell is rung until the child quits responding, we might assume that extinction is complete. However, if the bell is rung the next day, the child might respond again at first. This reaction is called **spontaneous recovery.** Spontaneous recovery explains why a person who has been in a terrifying car accident may need many slow, calm rides before fear is completely extinguished.

Generalization Once a person or an animal has learned to respond to a conditioned stimulus, other stimuli *similar* to the CS may also trigger a response. For example, we might find that our conditioned child salivates to the sound of a ringing telephone or doorbell. **Stimulus generalization,** as this effect is called, has been verified many times in studies of both humans and animals (Kimble, 1961).

It is easy to see the value of stimulus generalization. Consider, for instance, the child who burns a finger while playing with matches. Conditioning principles predict that the sight of a lighted match will become a conditioned stimulus for fear. But will the child fear only matches? Because of stimulus generalization, the child should also show a healthy fear of flames from lighters, fireplaces, stoves, and so forth. Fortunately, generalization tends to extend learning to new settings and similar situations. Were it not for this, we would all be far less adaptable.

As you may have guessed, stimulus generalization does have limits. Testing shows that there is a gradual decrease in response as stimuli become less like the original CS (Siegel et al., 1968). In other words, if you condition a person to blink each time you play a particular note on a piano, blinking will decline as you play higher or lower notes. If the notes are *much* higher or lower, the person will not respond at all (Fig. 7–4).

Discrimination Let's consider one more idea with our salivating child (who by now must be ready to hide in the closet). Suppose the child is again conditioned with a bell as the CS. As an experiment, we occasionally sound a buzzer instead of the bell, but never follow it with the

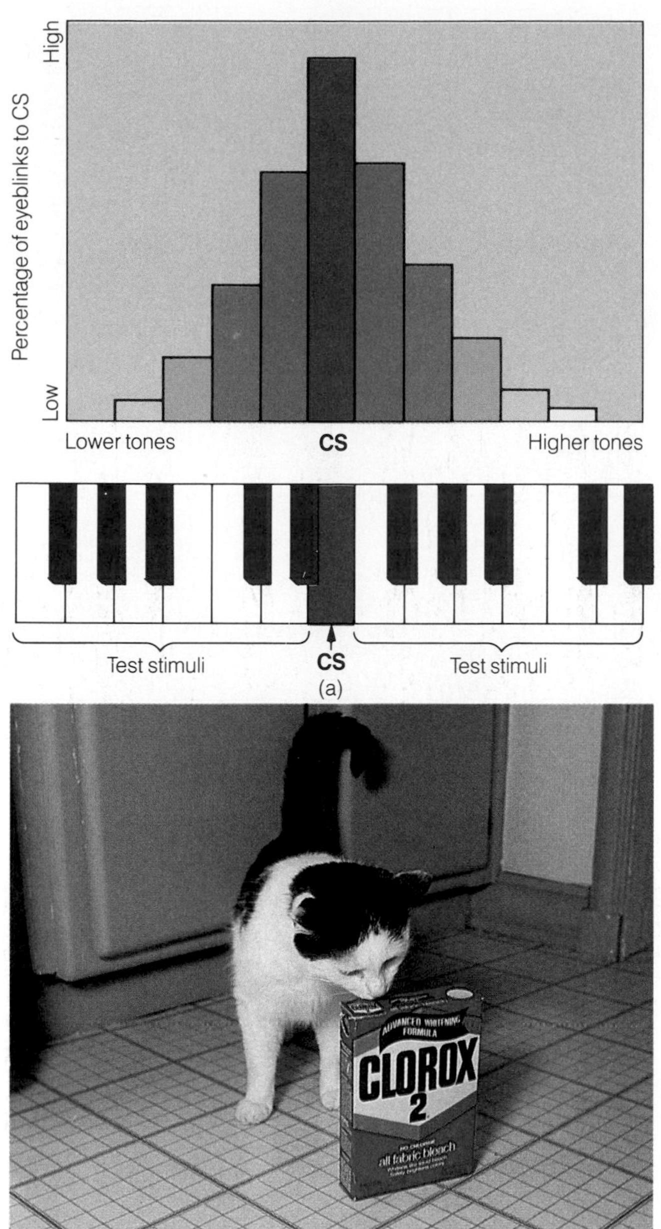

Fig. 7–4 *(a) Stimulus generalization. Stimuli similar to the CS also elicit a response. (b) This cat has learned to salivate when it sees a cat food box. Because of stimulus generalization, it also salivates when shown a similar-looking detergent box.*

US (lemon juice). At first, the buzzer produces salivation (because of generalization). But after hearing the buzzer several times more, the child stops responding to it. The child has now learned to *discriminate,* or respond differently to, the bell and the buzzer. In essence, the child's generalized response to the buzzer has extinguished.

Stimulus discrimination is an important part of learning. As an example, you might remember the feelings of anxiety or fear you had as a child when your mother's or father's voice changed to its you're-about-to-get-swatted tone. Most children quickly learn to discriminate voice tones associated with pain from those associated with praise or affection.

● Classical Conditioning in Humans—An Emotional Topic

Question: How much human learning is based on classical conditioning?

In its simplest form, classical conditioning depends on reflex responses. Recall that a *reflex* is a dependable, inborn stimulus-and-response connection. For example, pain causes reflex withdrawal of various parts of the body. The pupil of the eye reflexively narrows in response to bright lights. Various foods cause salivation. It is entirely possible for humans to associate any of these—or other—reflex responses with a new stimulus. At the very least, you have probably noticed how your mouth waters when you see or smell a bakery. You may even have salivated to pictures of food (a picture of a lemon is great for this).

Of larger importance, perhaps, are the more subtle ways that conditioning affects us. In addition to simple reflexes, more complex *emotional,* or "gut," responses may be conditioned to new stimuli. For instance, if your face reddened as part of your emotional reaction to being punished as a child, you may blush now as an adult when you are embarrassed or ashamed. Or think about associating pain with a dentist's office during your first visit. On later visits, did your heart pound and your palms sweat *before* the dentist began? Many *involuntary,* autonomic nervous system responses ("fight-or-flight" reflexes) are linked with new stimuli and situations by classical conditioning.

Another common example of such conditioning is a **phobia** (FOE-bee-ah). Phobias are fears that persist even when no realistic danger exists. Persons with fears of animals, water, heights, thunder, fire, bugs, or whatever, can often trace their fear to a time when they were frightened, injured, upset, or in pain while exposed to the feared object or stimulus. Reactions of this type, called **conditioned emotional responses (CERs),** are often broadened into phobias by stimulus generalization (Fig. 7–5). In fact, a therapy called **desensitization** is now widely used to *extinguish,* or countercondition, fears, anxieties, and phobias. (Desensitization is described in detail in Chapter 22.)

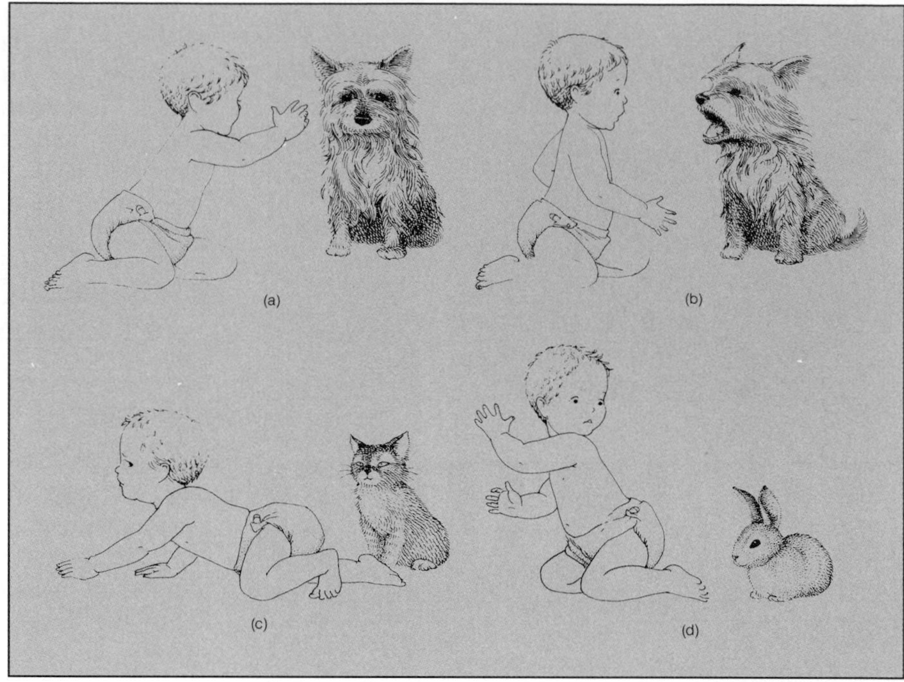

Fig. 7–5 *Hypothetical example of a CER becoming a phobia. Child approaches dog (a) and is frightened by it (b). Fear generalizes to other household pets (c) and later to virtually all furry animals (d).*

Vicarious, or Secondhand, Conditioning Conditioned emotional responses can also be learned indirectly, a fact that adds to their effect on us. One experiment, for example, showed that people will learn to respond emotionally to a light if they merely watch another person get an electric shock each time the light comes on. Even though subjects never directly received a shock, they developed a CER to the light just the same (Bandura & Rosenthal, 1966). Children who learn to fear thunder by watching as their parents react to it have undergone similar conditioning.

Vicarious classical conditioning, as it is called, occurs when we observe the emotional reactions of another person to a stimulus and thereby learn to respond emotionally to the same stimulus. Such learning probably affects feelings in many situations. For example, the film *Jaws* made ocean swimming a conditioned fear stimulus for many viewers. If movies can affect us, we might expect the emotions of parents, friends, and relatives to have even more impact. How, for instance, does a city child learn to fear snakes and to respond emotionally to mere pictures of them? Being told that "snakes are dangerous" may not explain the child's *emotional* response. More likely, such fears are learned by observing others react fearfully when the word *snake* is mentioned or a snake image appears on television. (For another view of CERs, see Highlight 7–1.)

The emotional attitudes we develop toward certain types of food, political parties, minority groups, escalators—whatever—are probably not only conditioned by direct experience but vicariously as well. Parents may do well to look in a mirror if they wonder how or where a child has "picked up" a particular fear or emotional attitude.

Learning Check

Be sure you can answer these questions before continuing.

1. Complex automatic responses known as ______________ help many animals adapt to their environment.
a. conditioned emotional generalizations *b.* unconditioned discriminations *c.* fixed action patterns *d.* releasers

2. Classical conditioning, studied by the Russian physiologist ______________, is also referred to as ______________ conditioning.

3. Classical conditioning is strengthened or reinforced when the ______________ follows the ______________.
a. CS, US *b.* US, CS *c.* UR, CR *d.* CS, CR

HIGHLIGHT 7–1
How Do You Feel About Space Music and Crawly Things?

Undoubtedly, many of our likes, dislikes, and fears are acquired as conditioned emotional responses. For example, in a recent study, college students developed CERs when colored geometric shapes were paired with the theme music from the movie *Star Wars*. The colored shapes were the CS and the music, which presumably made the students feel good, was the US. When tested later, the students gave higher ratings to shapes paired with the pleasant music than to shapes associated with silence (Bierly et al., 1985). As noted before, advertisers try to achieve the same effect by pairing products with pleasant images and music. So do many students on a first date.

Through classical conditioning, it is possible to learn to fear or dislike just about anything. Is it possible, however, that some fears are easier to learn than others (Fig. 7–6)? Martin Seligman's (1972) **prepared fear theory** holds that it is. Seligman believes that we are prepared by evolution to readily develop fears to certain stimuli, such as snakes and spiders. Other common objects are more likely to cause pain or harm (a hammer, light socket, or skis, for example). Even so, phobias are less likely to develop for such objects than for spiders or snakes.

Why should fears of "crawly things" be easier to acquire? According to Seligman's theory, such stimuli posed dangers earlier in human history. Through natural selection, they have become highly effective conditioning stimuli. Experiments in which fear was conditioned to images of spiders, snakes, neutral shapes, and electrical plugs offer some support for Seligman's theory (Hugdahl & Karker, 1981). Maybe with further evolution, humans will develop proper fears of light sockets and skis, too!

Fig. 7–6 *Which of these stimuli do you think would make a better conditioned stimulus for learned fear? Why did you choose as you did?*

Learning Check, continued

4. Training that inhibits (or weakens) a conditioned response is called ______________.

5. When a conditioned stimulus is used to reinforce the learning of another conditioned stimulus, higher-order conditioning has occurred. T or F?

6. Many phobias very likely begin when a CER generalizes to other, similar situations. T or F?

7. Conditioning brought about by observing pain, joy, or fear in others is called ______________ conditioning.

8. A dependable, inborn stimulus-response connection is called
a. an unconditioned stimulus *b.* a CER *c.* a reflex *d.* a reinforcer

Answers:

1. *c* **2.** Pavlov, respondent **3.** *b* **4.** extinction **5.** T **6.** T **7.** vicarious **8.** *c*

Operant Conditioning—Can Pigeons Play Ping-Pong?

As stated earlier, **operant conditioning** concerns how we learn to associate responses with their consequences. The basic principle of operant conditioning (or instrumental learning) is simple: Acts followed by reinforcement tend to be repeated. Pioneer learning theorist Edward L. Thorndike called this the **law of effect.** According to Thorndike, learning is strengthened each time a response is followed by a satisfying state of affairs. Think of the earlier example of the vending machine. Because kicking the machine had the effect of producing food and money, the odds of repeating the "kicking response" increased.

As we have seen, classical conditioning is passive and involuntary. It simply "happens to" the learner when a CS and US are associated. In operant conditioning, the learner actively "operates on" the environment. Thus, operant conditioning refers mainly to learning *voluntary* responses. For example, waving your hand in class to get a teacher's attention is a learned operant response. (See Table 7–1 for a further comparison of classical and operant conditioning.)

The idea that reward affects learning is certainly nothing new to parents (and other trainers of small animals). However, parents, as well as teachers, politicians, supervisors, and even you, may use reward in ways that are haphazard, inexact, or misguided. A case in point is the very term *reward.* To be correct, it is better to say *reinforcer.* Why? Because rewards do not always increase responding. If you try to give licorice candy to a child as a reward for good behavior, it will work only if the child likes licorice. What is reinforcing for one person may not be for another. As a practical rule of thumb, psychologists define an **operant reinforcer** as any event that follows a response and increases its probability.

Acquiring an Operant Response Most laboratory studies of operant learning take place in some form of **conditioning chamber,** also called a Skinner box (after B. F. Skinner, who invented it to study operant conditioning) (Fig. 7–7). A look into a typical Skinner box will clarify the process of operant conditioning.

The Adventures of Mickey Rat

A hungry rat is placed in a small cagelike chamber. The walls are bare except for a metal lever and a tray into which food pellets can be dispensed (see Fig. 7–7).

Frankly, there's not much to do in a Skinner box. This fact increases the chances that our subject will make the response we want to reinforce, which is pressing the bar. Hunger also ensures that the animal will be motivated to seek food and to actively *emit,* or freely give off, a variety of responses. Now let's take another look at our subject.

Further Adventures of Mickey Rat

For a while our subject walks around, grooms, sniffs at the corners, or stands on his hind legs—all typical rat behaviors. Then it happens. He places his paw on the lever to get a better view of the top of the cage. *Click!* The lever depresses, and a food pellet drops into the tray. The rat walks to the tray, eats the pellet, then grooms himself. Up and exploring the cage again, he leans on the lever. *Click!* After a trip to the food tray, he returns to the bar and sniffs it, then puts his foot on it. *Click!* Soon the rat settles into a smooth pattern of frequent bar pressing.

Notice that the rat did not acquire a new skill in this situation. He already had the responses necessary to depress the bar. Reward only alters how *frequently* he presses the bar. In operant conditioning, reinforcement is used to alter the frequency of responses or to mold them into new patterns.

A good example of how operant reinforcement can change behavior is shown in Figure 7–8. The results are from an effort to reduce the number of deviant behaviors performed by children in a special classroom. (Deviant behavior was defined as fighting, crying, and temper tantrums.) As you can see, chaos reigned during the initial,

Table 7–1 Comparison of Classical Conditioning and Operant Conditioning

	CLASSICAL CONDITIONING	OPERANT CONDITIONING
Nature of response	Involuntary, reflex	Spontaneous, voluntary
Reinforcement	Occurs *before* response (conditioned stimulus paired with reinforcing stimulus)	Occurs *after* response (response is followed by reinforcing stimulus or event)
Role of subject	Passive (response is *elicited*)	Active (response is *emitted*)
Nature of learning	Association between antecedent stimuli	Probability of response altered by consequences

Fig. 7–7 *The Skinner box. This simple device, invented by B. F. Skinner, allows careful study of operant conditioning. When the rat presses the bar, a pellet of food or a drop of water is automatically released.*

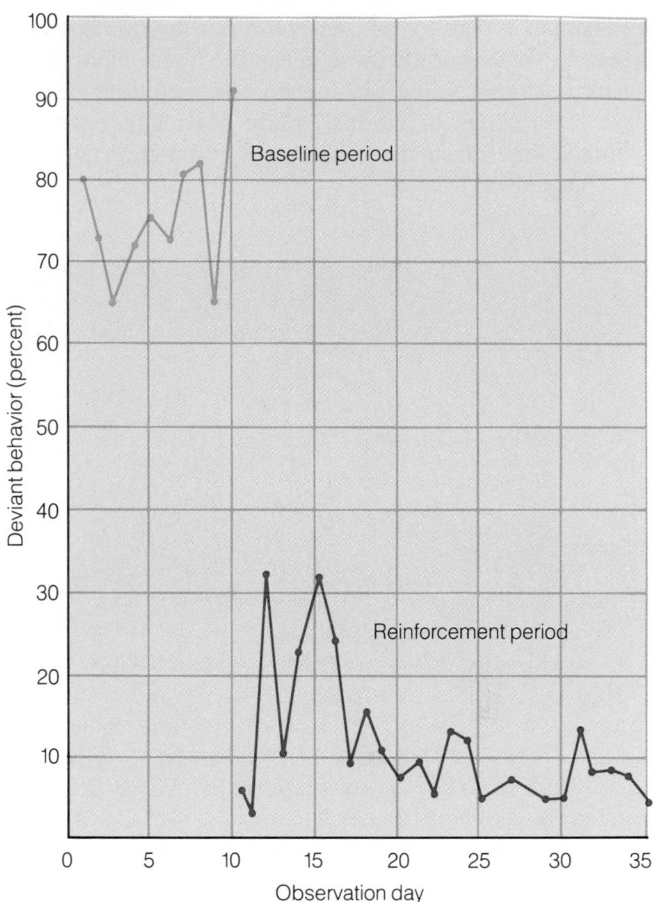

Fig. 7–8 *Reinforcement and human behavior. The amount of deviant behavior engaged in each day by children in a classroom setting is shown. Before reinforcement of good behavior began, disruptive actions were the rule. The effectiveness of reinforcement is indicated by the rapid drop in crying, fighting, and tantrums that occurred. (Adapted from O'Leary & Becker, 1967.)*

baseline period. However, when good behavior (such as paying attention or remaining seated) was reinforced, disruptive actions declined rapidly (O'Leary & Becker, 1967).

To be effective, operant reinforcement must be **response contingent.** That is, it must be given *only* after desired responses. If children like those in the preceding study received reinforcement haphazardly, their behavior wouldn't improve at all. In situations ranging from studying to working hard on the job, contingent reinforcement also affects the *performance* of responses (Fig. 7–9).

Shaping Even in a barren Skinner box, it might be a long time before a rat accidentally pressed the bar and ate a food pellet. We might wait forever for more complicated responses to occur. For example, you would have to wait a long time for a duck to accidentally walk out of its cage, turn on a light, play a toy piano, turn off the light, and walk back to its cage. If this is what you wanted to reward, you would never get the chance.

Question: Then how are the animals on TV and at amusement parks taught to perform complicated tricks?

The answer lies in **shaping,** which is the gradual molding of responses to a final desired pattern. Let's look again at our subject, Mickey Rat.

Mickey Rat Shapes Up

Assume that the rat has not yet learned to press the bar. He also shows no signs of interest in the bar. Instead of waiting for the first accidental bar press, we can shape his behavior patterns. At first, we settle for just getting him to face the bar. Any time he turns toward the bar, he is reinforced with a bit of food. Soon Mickey spends much of his time facing the bar. Next, we reinforce him every time he takes a step toward the bar. When he turns toward the bar, then walks away, nothing happens. But when he faces the bar and takes a step forward, *click!* His responses are being shaped.

By changing the rules about what makes a successful response, we can gradually train the rat to approach the bar and to press it. We can reward responses that come closer and closer to the final desired pattern until it occurs. The principle of shaping, then, is that **successive approximations** (ever closer matches) to the desired response are reinforced. B. F. Skinner once taught two pigeons to play Ping-Pong in this way (Fig. 7–10 and Highlight 7–2).

Shaping applies to humans, too. Let's say, for example, that you want to study more, clean the house more often, or exercise more. Success in each case would be aided if you set a series of gradual, daily goals and rewarded yourself for each small step in the right direction (Watson & Tharp, 1981).

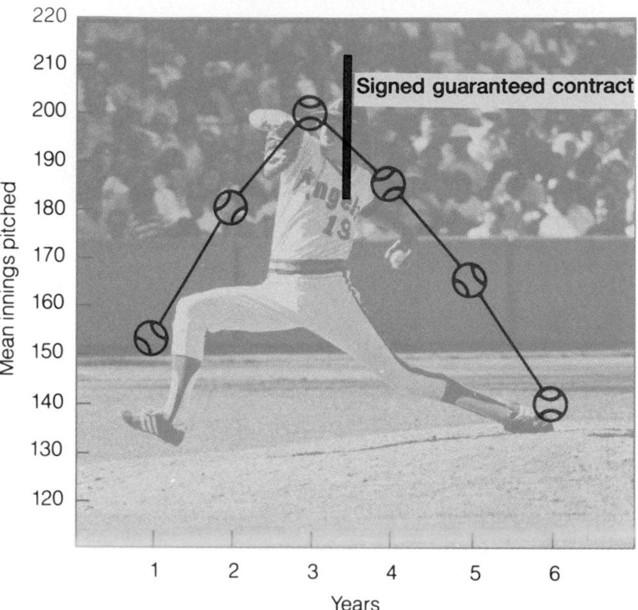

Fig. 7–9 *Mean number of innings pitched by major league baseball players before and after signing long-term guaranteed contracts. The performance of 38 pitchers who signed multiyear contracts for over $100,000 per season is shown. When salary was no longer contingent on good performance, there was a rapid decline in innings pitched and in the number of wins. During the same 6-year period, the performance of pitchers on 1-year contracts remained fairly steady. (Data from O'Brian et al., 1981.)*

Fig. 7–10 *Operant conditioning principles were used to train these pigeons to play Ping-Pong.*

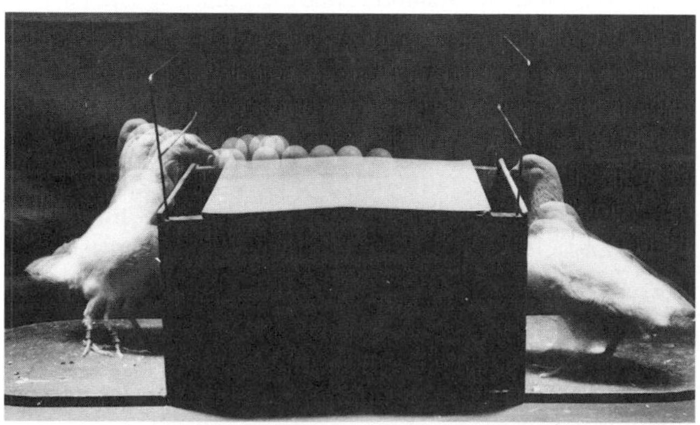

HIGHLIGHT 7–2
Biological Constraints—The Reluctant Raccoon

B. F. Skinner's success in shaping pigeons to play Ping-Pong was aided by the fact that pigeons naturally peck objects. At one time, psychologists assumed that almost any voluntary response could be taught by operant conditioning. But in recent years, it has become clear that some responses are easier to learn than others. This observation suggests that there are a number of **biological constraints,** or limits, to operant learning—especially for animals. For example, two noted psychologists, Keller and Marion Breland, went into business training animals for television shows, zoo displays, and amusement parks. Along with their successes came some revealing failures.

In one instance, the Brelands tried to condition a raccoon to put coins in a piggy-bank for an advertisement. Instead, the raccoon repeatedly rubbed the coins together in a miserly-looking fashion (Breland & Breland, 1961). No amount of reinforcement would change this behavior. The Brelands ran into similar snags with other animals. In each case, an innate behavior pattern hindered learning. They called this problem **instinctive drift:** Learned responses tend to "drift" toward innate ones. The "miserly" behavior of the raccoon was simply an innate food-washing response. In view of such observations, it is wise to remember that the laws of learning operate within a framework of biological limits and possibilities (Adams, 1980).

Extinction You might expect that a rat's bar pressing would immediately stop if food delivery ended. Actually, the rat would stop pressing the bar, but not immediately. Just as acquiring an operant response takes time, so does **operant extinction.** If a learned response is not reinforced, it gradually drops out of behavior. Operant extinction therefore refers to the same general concept as extinction in classical conditioning.

Even after extinction seems complete, there may be a return of the previously reinforced response. If a rat is removed from a Skinner box after extinction and given a short rest, the rat will begin pressing the bar again when returned to the Skinner box.

Question: Does extinction take as long the second time?

If reinforcement is still withheld, bar pressing will extinguish again, usually more quickly. The brief return of an operant response after extinction is another example of *spontaneous recovery* (also mentioned earlier regarding classical conditioning). Spontaneous recovery seems to be very adaptive. The rat responds again in a situation that produced food in the past: "Just checking to see if the rules have changed!"

Operant Reinforcement—What's Your Pleasure?

For humans, an effective operant reinforcer may be anything from an M&M candy to a pat on the back. In categorizing such reinforcers, useful distinctions can be made among *primary reinforcers, secondary reinforcers, generalized reinforcers,* and *prepotent responses.* Operant reinforcers of all types have a large impact on our lives. Let's examine them in more detail.

Primary Reinforcement

Primary reinforcers are natural, or unlearned. Hence, they apply almost universally to a particular species. They are usually of a biological nature and produce comfort, end discomfort, or fill an immediate physical need. Food, water, and sex are obvious primary reinforcers. Every time you open the refrigerator, walk to a drinking fountain, turn up the heat, or make a trip to an ice cream parlor, your actions reflect the effect of primary reinforcement.

In addition to the most obvious examples, there are other less natural primary reinforcers. One of the most unusual (and powerful) is **intra-cranial stimulation** (ICS). ICS involves direct stimulation of "pleasure centers" in the brain (Olds & Fobes, 1981) (Fig. 7–11).

Wiring a Rat for Pleasure

Use of brain stimulation for reward requires the permanent implantation of tiny electrodes in specific areas of the brain. A rat "wired for pleasure" can be trained to press the bar in a Skinner box to deliver electrical stimulation to its own brain. Some rats will press the bar thousands of times per hour to obtain brain stimulation. After 15 or 20 hours of constant pressing, animals sometimes collapse from exhaustion. When they revive, they begin pressing again. If the reward circuit is not turned off, an animal will ignore food, water, and sex in favor of bar pressing.

One shudders to think what might happen if brain implants were easy and practical to do. (They are not.) Every company from *Playboy* to General Motors would have a device on the market, and we would have to keep a closer watch on politicians than usual!

Secondary Reinforcement

In some primitive societies, learning is still strongly tied to food, water, and other primary reinforcers. Most of us, however, respond to a much broader range of rewards and reinforcers. Money, praise, attention, approval, success, affection, grades, and similar rewards, all serve as *learned* or **secondary reinforcers.**

Question: How does a secondary reinforcer gain its ability to promote learning?

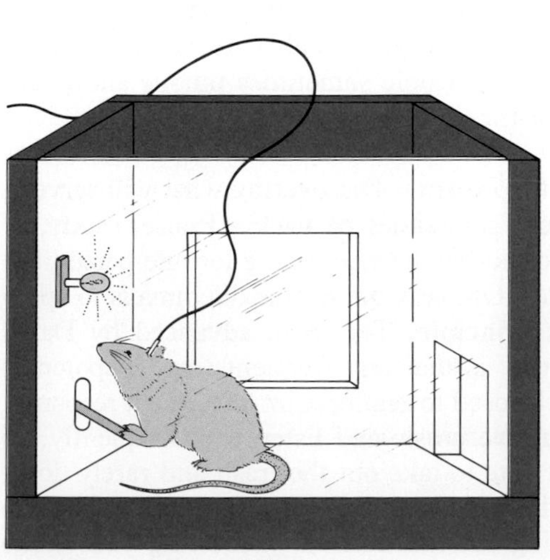
(a)

(b)

Fig. 7–11 *In the apparatus shown in (a), the rat can press a bar to deliver mild electric stimulation to a "pleasure center" in the brain. Humans also have been "wired" for brain stimulation, as shown in (b). (See Chapter 3 for more information on ICS.)*

Some secondary reinforcers are simply associated with a primary reinforcer. This can be shown in the following way.

The Button-Down Rat

A rat caged in a Skinner box has learned through operant conditioning to press the bar for food pellets. Each rewarded bar press is also followed by a brief auditory tone. After a period of training in which bar pressing, food, and the tone are associated, the rat is moved to a new cage. This cage has no bar, but it does have a button mounted on the wall. If the rat pushes the button, the tone sounds, but no food is delivered. Even though no primary reinforcement (food) is given, the rat learns to press the button to turn on the tone. Because it was associated with food, the tone has become a secondary reinforcer.

Tokens Secondary reinforcers that can be *exchanged* for primary reinforcers may gain their value more directly. Printed money obviously has little or no value of its own. You can't eat it, drink it, or sleep with it. However, it can be exchanged for food, water, lodging, and other necessities. In a series of classic experiments, chimpanzees were taught to work for **tokens.**

Chimps were first trained to put poker chips into a "Chimp-O-Mat" vending machine that dispensed a few grapes or raisins for each chip. Once the animals had learned to exchange tokens for food, they would learn new tasks to earn the chips. They also learned to lift a heavy weight to obtain chips. Value of the tokens was maintained by occasionally allowing the chimps to use the "Chimp-O-Mat" to exchange chips for food (Fig. 7–12). (Wolfe, 1936; Cowles, 1937.)

One problem with primary reinforcers is that people and animals receiving them may quickly *satiate* (SAY-she-ate). (To be satiated means to be fully satisfied or to have reduced desire.) If, for example, you want to use candy to reinforce a retarded child for correctly naming things, the child might only show interest while still hungry. A major advantage of tokens is that they do not lose reinforcing value as quickly as primary reinforcers do. That's why tokens (plastic chips, gold stars, and the like) have been useful in work with troubled children, adolescents and adults in special programs, as well as in educating the mentally retarded. (Fig. 7–13.) Tokens are even used at times in ordinary elementary school classrooms. In each case the goal is to provide an immediate, tangible reward as an incentive for learning. Typically, tokens may be exchanged for food, desired goods, special privileges, or trips to movies, amusement parks, and so forth. (See Chapter 22 for more information on the use of tokens in therapy.)

Fig. 7–12 *Poker chips normally have little or no value for chimpanzees, but this chimp will work hard to earn them once he learns that the "Chimp-O-Mat" will dispense food in exchange for them.*

Question: People sometimes hoard money even when all their needs are met. Why is that?

Generalized Reinforcers Interestingly, the chimps working for tokens also tended to hoard them, even when hungry. This and similar observations suggests that money may become a **generalized reinforcer** (a secondary reinforcer that has become largely independent of its link to primary reinforcers). Not only can money be exchanged for primary reinforcers, it may also lead to other secondary reinforcers, such as prestige, attention, approval, status, or power. This property makes its value so general in our society that people sometimes pursue and hoard money just for the sake of having it.

Prepotent Responses Discovering what will serve as a reinforcer can sometimes be tricky. Praise, candy, or a pat on the back may be reinforcing for one person but not for another. One way out of this dilemma is to apply the **Premack principle.** The idea, advanced by David Premack (1965), is that any frequent (or "prepotent") response can be used to reinforce an infrequent response. Let's say you love music and listen to it frequently. In contrast, you hate to take out the trash and rarely do it. If this were the case, listening to music could be used to reinforce taking out the trash. By requiring yourself to take out the trash before turning on music, you would increase the low-frequency response. As another example, access to video games is a very effective reinforcer for managing the behavior of children who often play the games (Buckalew & Buckalew, 1983).

If you are interested in applying reinforcement to change your own behavior (your study habits, for instance), remember that anything you do frequently (watching television, talking with friends, listening to music) can serve as a reinforcer.

Delay of Reinforcement

Reinforcement has its greatest effect on operant learning when the time lapse between a response and its consequences is short. This point can be demonstrated in a simple experiment.

Fig. 7–13. *Reinforcement in a token economy. This graph shows the effects of using tokens to reward socially desirable behavior in a mental hospital ward. Desirable behavior was defined as cleaning, bed making, attending therapy sessions, and so forth. Tokens earned could be exchanged for basic amenities such as meals, snacks, coffee, game-room privileges, or weekend passes. The graph shows more than 24 hours per day because it represents the total number of hours of desirable behavior performed by all patients in the ward. (Adapted from Ayllon & Azrin, 1965.)*

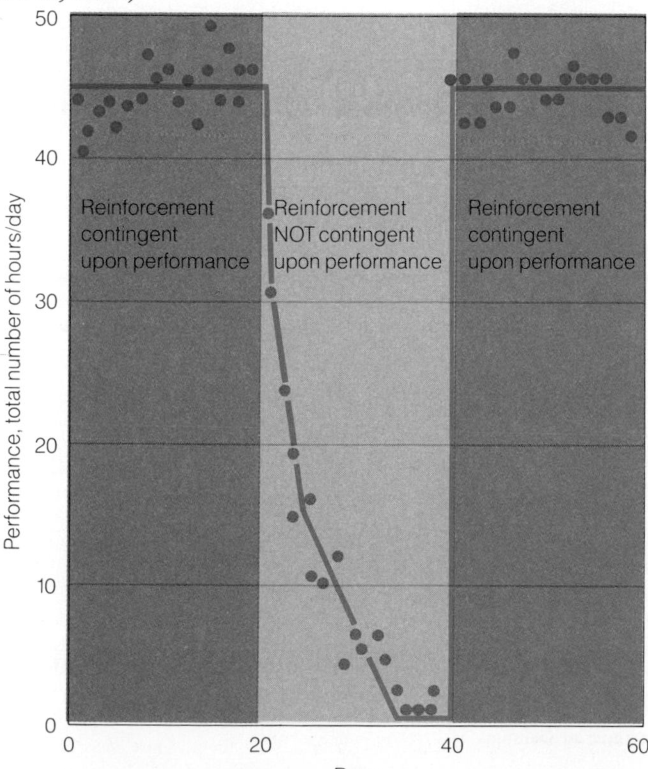

Mickey Rat and Friends Get Delayed

Several groups of rats are trained to press the bar in a Skinner box for a food reward. For some of the animals, a bar press is followed immediately by a food pellet. Other animals are trained with even greater amounts of delay between a bar press and a reward. When the delay reaches about 50 seconds, very little learning occurs. If delivery of the food pellet follows a bar press by more than about 1½ minutes, no learning occurs (Fig. 7–14). (Perin, 1943.)

If you wish to reward either an animal or a person for a correct response, reward will be most effective if it is given *immediately* after the response.

Question: Let's say I work hard all semester in a class to get an A. Wouldn't the delay in reinforcement keep me from learning anything?

No, for several reasons. First, as a human, you can anticipate future reward. Second, you get reinforced by quiz and test grades all through the semester. Third, a single reinforcer can often maintain a long *chain* of responses. A simplified example of **response chaining** is provided by Barnabus, a rat trained by psychologists at Brown University.

The Great Barnabus

By carefully working from the last response to the first, Barnabus was trained to make an ever longer chain of responses to obtain a single food pellet. When in top form, Barnabus was able to climb a spiral staircase, cross a narrow bridge, climb a ladder, pull a toy car with a chain, get into the car, pedal it to a second staircase, climb the staircase, wriggle

Fig. 7–14 *The effect of delay of reinforcement. Notice how rapidly the learning score drops when reward is delayed. Animals learning to press a bar in a Skinner box showed no signs of learning if food reward followed a bar press by more than 100 seconds. (Perin, 1943.)*

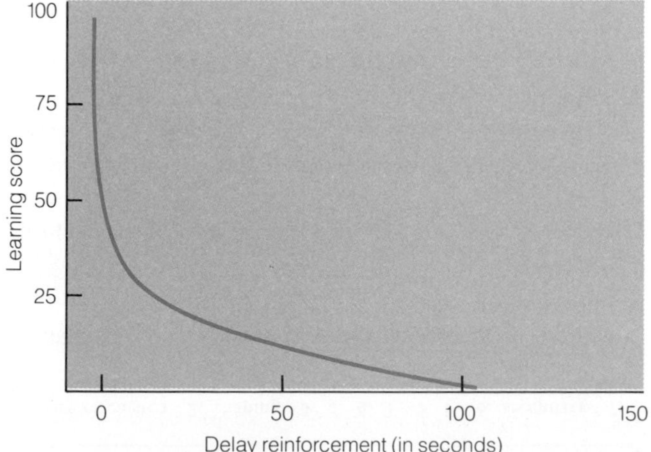

through a tube, climb onto an elevator and descend to a platform, press a lever to receive a food pellet, and . . . start over! (Pierrel & Sherman, 1963.)

Many of the things we do every day involve similar response chains. The long series of events necessary to prepare a meal, for instance, is rewarded by the final eating. A violin maker may spend three months carrying out thousands of steps for the final reward of hearing the first note from an instrument. Tying a shoe is a short but familiar response chain.

Superstitious Behavior Reinforcement affects not only the last response that precedes it, but also other responses occurring shortly before. This helps account for the learning of many human superstitions. If a golfer taps her club on the ground three times and then hits an unusually fine shot, the success of the shot reinforces not only the correct swing but also the three taps. During operant training, animals often develop similar unnecessary responses. If a rat scratches its ear just before its first bar press, it may continue to scratch its ear before each ensuing bar press. A bar press is all that is needed to produce food, but the animal may continue to "superstitiously" scratch its ear each time, as if this were necessary.

Question: But if the superstitious behavior is unnecessary, why does it continue?

Superstitious acts probably *appear* to pay off to the person or animal. For example:

Why Pigeons Shouldn't Gamble

A pigeon has been placed in a Skinner box, where it is allowed to peck at a key three times to obtain food. Then the key is turned off. At random intervals, food falls into the tray as the pigeon continues pecking. *There is no connection between pecking and food,* but there *appears* to be. During 20 testing periods, 20 minutes in length, the pigeon made an average of 2,700 "superstitious" pecks. (Neuringer, 1970.)

Many human superstitions seem to be based on the same pattern. If you get the large half of a wishbone and have good fortune soon thereafter, you may credit the wishbone for your luck (Fig. 7–15). If you walk under a ladder and then break a leg, you may avoid ladders in the future. Each time you avoid a ladder and nothing bad occurs, your superstitious response is reinforced. Belief in magic can also be explained along such lines. Rituals to bring rain, ward off illness, or produce abundant crops very likely earned the faith of participants by occasionally appearing to succeed. Besides, better safe than sorry!

Fig. 7–15 *Many gamblers rely on charms for good luck. Such superstitious behavior occurs because the charm is occasionally associated with reinforcement (winning).*

Learning Check

1. Responses in operant conditioning are ______________, whereas those in classical conditioning are passive, ______________ responses.
2. Changing the rules so that an animal (or person) is gradually trained to respond as desired is called ______________.
3. Extinction in operant conditioning is also subject to ______________ of a response.
   a. successive approximations *b.* shaping *c.* automation *d.* spontaneous recovery
4. Reinforcement in operant conditioning depends on the consequences of a response, or what happens after it is made. T or F?
5. Primary reinforcers are those learned through classical conditioning. T or F?
6. Tokens are basically ______________ reinforcers.
7. Superstitious responses are those that are
   a. shaped by secondary reinforcement *b.* extinguished *c.* prepotent *d.* unnecessary to obtain reinforcement

Answers:

1. voluntary or emitted, involuntary or elicited **2.** shaping **3.** *d* **4.** T **5.** F **6.** secondary **7.** *d*

● Partial Reinforcement—Las Vegas, a Human Skinner Box?

SERENDIPITY (n): to discover one thing while looking for another

B. F. Skinner, so the story goes, was studying operant conditioning when he ran short of food pellets. In order to continue, he arranged for a pellet to reward every other response. Thus began the formal study of **schedules of reinforcement.** Until now, we have treated operant reinforcement as if it were continuous. **Continuous reinforcement** means that a reinforcer follows every response. This is fine for the lab, but it has little to do with the real world. Most of our responses are more inconsistently rewarded. In daily life, learning is usually based on **partial reinforcement,** in which reinforcers do not follow every response. Partial reinforcement may be given in a number of patterns, each of which affects responding. In addition to these specific effects (to be explored in a moment), there is a general effect: *Responses acquired by partial reinforcement are highly resistant to extinction.* For some obscure reason, lost in the lore of psychology, this is called the **partial reinforcement effect.** It applies to both classical and operant conditioning.

Question: How does getting reinforced part of the time make a habit stronger?

If you have ever visited Las Vegas or a similar gambling mecca, you have probably been amused by row after row of people pulling slot machine handles. To gain insight into partial reinforcement effects, imagine that you are making your first visit to Las Vegas. You put a nickel in a slot machine and pull the handle. Twenty-five cents in nickels spills into the tray. Using one of your newly won nickels, you pull the handle again. Again there is a small payoff. Let's say this continues for 15 minutes. Every pull is followed by a payoff. Then, without your knowing it, someone turns off the payoff mechanism. Suddenly, each pull is followed by nothing. Obviously, you would respond several times more before giving up. However, when continuous reinforcement is followed by extinction, the message soon becomes clear: no more payoffs.

Contrast this with partial reinforcement. You begin by placing 5 nickels in the machine without a payoff. You are just about to quit, but decide to play one more. Bingo! The machine returns $2 in change. After this, payoffs continue on a partial schedule; some are large, and some are small. All are unpredictable. Sometimes you hit 2 in a row, and sometimes 20 or 30 pulls go unrewarded. Now let's say the payoff mechanism is turned off again. How many times do you think you would respond this time before your handle-pulling behavior extinguished? Since you have developed the expectation that any play may be "the one," it will be hard to resist just one more play . . . and one more . . . and one more. Also, since partial reinforcement includes long periods of nonreward, it will be harder to discriminate between periods of reinforcement and extinction. It is no exaggeration to say that the partial reinforcement effect has left many people penniless. Even psychologists visiting Las Vegas often get "cleaned out"—and they should know better!

Fig. 7–16 *The one-armed bandit (slot machine) is a dispenser of partial reinforcement.*

Schedules of Partial Reinforcement

The patterns in which partial reinforcement could be given are limitless. Let's consider the four most basic possibilities, which have some interesting effects on us.

Fixed Ratio (FR) What would happen if a reinforcer only followed every other response? Or what if we followed every third, fourth, fifth, or other number of responses with reinforcement? Each of these patterns is a **fixed ratio (FR) schedule.** The ratio of reinforcers to responses is fixed: FR-2 means that every other response is rewarded; FR-3 means that every third response is reinforced, and so forth.

Fixed ratio schedules produce *very high rates of response* (Fig. 7–17). A hungry rat on an FR-10 schedule will

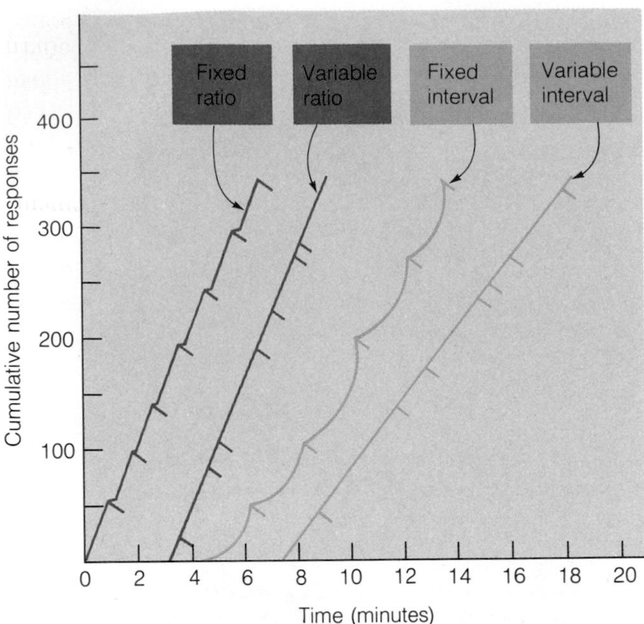

Fig. 7–17 *Typical response patterns for reinforcement schedules. Results such as these are obtained when a cumulative recorder is connected to a Skinner box. The device consists of a moving strip of paper and a mechanical pen that jumps upward each time a response is made. Rapid responding causes the pen to draw a steep line; a horizontal line indicates no response. Small tick marks on the lines show when a reinforcer was given.*

quickly run off 10 responses, pause to eat, and will then run off 10 more. A similar situation occurs when factory or farm workers are paid on a piecework basis. When a fixed number of items must be produced for a set amount of pay, work output is high.

Variable Ratio (VR) A **variable ratio (VR) schedule** is a slight variation on fixed ratio. Instead of reinforcing, for example, every fourth response (FR-4), a person or animal on a VR-4 schedule gets rewarded *on the average* every fourth response. Sometimes a response must be made 2 times to obtain a reinforcer, sometimes 5 times, sometimes 4, and so on. The actual number of responses required varies, but it averages out to 4 (in this example). Variable ratio schedules also produce high response rates.

Question: VR schedules seem less predictable than FR. Does that have any effect on extinction?

Yes. Since reinforcement is less predictable, VR schedules tend to produce greater resistance to extinction than fixed ratio schedules. Playing a slot machine is an example of behavior maintained by a variable ratio schedule. Another would be a child asking for a "treat" at the supermarket. The number of times the child must ask before getting reinforced varies, so the child becomes quite persistent. Golf, tennis, and many other sports are also reinforced on a variable ratio basis: An average of perhaps 1 good shot in 5 or 10 may be all that's needed to create a sports fanatic.

Fixed Interval (FI) In another pattern, reinforcement is given for the first correct response made after a fixed amount of time has passed. Thus, a rat on an FI-30-second schedule has to wait 30 seconds after the last reinforced response before a bar press will pay off again. The rat can press the bar as often as it wants during the interval, but it will not be rewarded. **Fixed interval (FI) schedules** produce *moderate response rates*. These are marked by spurts of activity mixed with periods of inactivity. Animals working on an FI schedule seem to develop a keen sense of the passage of time. For example:

Mickey Rat Takes a Break

Mickey Rat, trained on an FI-60-second schedule, has just been reinforced for a bar press. What does he do? He saunters around the cage, grooms himself, hums, whistles, reads magazines, and polishes his nails. After 50 seconds, he walks to the bar and gives it a press—just testing. After 55 seconds, he gives it two or three presses, but there's still no payoff. Fifty-eight seconds, and he settles down to rapid pressing, 59 seconds, 60 seconds, and he hits the reinforced press. After one or two more presses (unrewarded), he wanders off again for the next interval.

Question: Is getting paid weekly an FI schedule?

Pure examples of fixed interval schedules are rare, but getting paid each week at work does come close. Notice, however, that most people do not work faster just before payday, as an FI schedule predicts. A closer parallel would be having a report due every 2 weeks for a class. Right after turning in a paper, your work would probably drop to zero for a week or more. Then, as the next due date draws near, a work frenzy occurs. Another fixed interval example is checking a Thanksgiving turkey in the oven. Typically, the frequency of checking increases as the time for the turkey to be done draws near (Schwartz, 1984).

Variable Interval (VI) **Variable interval (VI) schedules** are a variation on fixed intervals. Here, reinforcement is given for the first correct response made after a varied amount of time. On a VI-30-second schedule, reinforcement is available after an interval that *averages* 30 seconds. VI schedules produce *slow, steady rates* of response and tremendous resistance to extinction. When you dial a phone number and get a busy signal, reward (getting through) is on a VI schedule. You may have to wait 30 seconds or 30 minutes. If you are like most people, you will doggedly dial over and over again until you get a connection. Success in fishing is also on a VI schedule—which may explain the bulldog tenacity of many anglers (Schwartz, 1984).

Compare: Schedules of Reinforcement

Schedule of reinforcement A rule or plan for determining which responses will be reinforced.

Continuous reinforcement A schedule of reinforcement in which every response is followed by a reinforcer.

Fixed ratio schedule A pattern in which a set number of responses must be made to obtain a reinforcer.

Variable ratio schedule A pattern in which the number of responses required to obtain a reinforcer varies.

Fixed interval schedule A pattern in which reinforcement is given for the first correct response that occurs after a fixed time has passed since the last reinforced response.

Variable interval schedule A schedule in which reinforcement is available after varying time periods.

Stimulus Control—Putting Habits on a Leash

When you are driving, your behavior at intersections is controlled by the red or green light. In similar fashion, many of the stimuli we encounter each day act like stop or go signals that guide responding. This is called **stimulus control.** To state the idea more formally, antecedent stimuli (events that come before a response) also affect operant conditioning. If a response is reinforced in a specific situation, it tends to come under the control of stimuli present in that situation. Notice how this works with our friend Mickey Rat.

Lights Out for Mickey Rat

While learning the bar-pressing response, Mickey has been in a Skinner box illuminated by a bright light. During several training sessions, the light is alternately turned on and off. When the light is on, a bar press will produce food. When the light is off, bar pressing goes unrewarded. We soon observe that the rat presses vigorously when the light is on and ignores the bar when the light is off.

In this example, the light signals what consequences will follow if a response is made. A similar situation would be a child learning to ask for candy when her mother is in a good mood, but not asking at other times. In operant conditioning, stimuli that precede a rewarded response tend to influence *when* and *where* the response will occur. Evidence for stimulus control could be shown in our example by turning the food delivery *on* when the light is *off*. A well-trained rat might never discover that the rules had changed.

Generalization Two important aspects of stimulus control are **generalization** and **discrimination.** Let's return to the example of the vending machine (from the Chapter Preview) to illustrate these concepts. First, generalization.

Question: Is generalization the same in operant conditioning as it is in classical conditioning?

Basically, yes. Responses followed by reinforcement tend to be made again when similar antecedents are present. Assume, for instance, that you have been reliably rewarded for kicking one particular vending machine. Your kicking response tends to occur in the presence of that machine. It has come under stimulus control. Now let's say that there are three other machines on campus identical to the one that pays off. Because they are similar, your kicking response will very likely transfer to them. If each of these machines also pays off when kicked, your kicking response may *generalize* to other machines only mildly similar to the original.

Generalization is further illustrated by the way children use new words. One child studied by psychologist Melissa Bowerman (1977) first used the word *snow* while handling snow outdoors. For a while, however, the child also called each of the following "snow": the white tail of a toy horse, a white toy boat, a white flannel blanket, and spilled milk on the floor. Similar generalization explains why children may temporarily call all men *daddy*—much to the embarrassment of their parents.

Discrimination Meanwhile, back at the vending machine. . . . As stated earlier, to **discriminate** means to respond differently to different stimuli. Because one vending machine reinforced your kicking response, you began kicking other identical machines (generalization). Because these also paid off, you began kicking similar machines (more generalization). If kicking these new machines has no effect, the kicking response that generalized to them will extinguish because of non-reinforcement. Thus, your response to machines of a particular size and color is consistently rewarded, whereas the same response to different machines is extinguished. You have learned to discriminate between antecedent stimuli that signal reward and nonreward. As a result, your response pattern

HIGHLIGHT 7–3
Stimulus Control

The role of discriminative stimuli may be clarified by an interesting feat achieved by Jack, a psychologist friend of the author's. Jack decided to teach his cat to say its name. Here is how he proceeded. First he gave the cat a pat on the back. If the cat meowed in a way that sounded anything like its name, Jack immediately gave the cat a small amount of food. If the cat made this unusual meow at other times, it received nothing. This process was repeated many times each day. By gradual shaping, the cat's meow was made to sound very much like its name. Also, this peculiar meow came under stimulus control: When it received a pat on the back, the cat said its name; without the pat, it remained silent or meowed normally. Psychologists symbolize a stimulus that precedes reinforced responses as an S+. Discriminative stimuli that precede unrewarded responses are symbolized as S− (Schwartz, 1984). Thus, the accompanying diagram summarizes the cat's training.

I should add at this point that I was unaware that Jack had a new cat or that he had trained it. I went to visit him one night and met the cat on the front steps. I gave the cat a pat on the back and said, "Hi Kitty, what's your name?" Imagine my surprise when the cat immediately replied, "Ralph"!

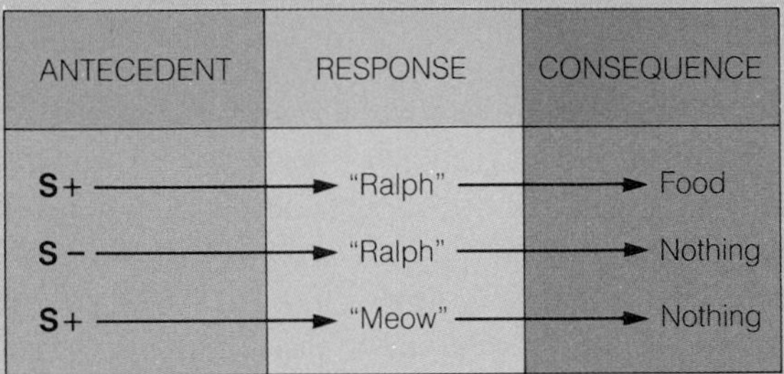

ANTECEDENT	RESPONSE	CONSEQUENCE
S+ →	"Ralph" →	Food
S− →	"Ralph" →	Nothing
S+ →	"Meow" →	Nothing

will shift to match these **discriminative stimuli** (Fig. 7–18).

A discriminative stimulus that most drivers are familiar with is a police car on the freeway. This stimulus is a clear signal that a specific set of reinforcement contingencies applies. As you have probably observed, the presence of a police car brings about rapid reductions in driving speed, lane changes, tail-gating, and, in Los Angeles, gun battles. (Also, see Highlight 7–3.)

Stimulus discrimination is also aptly illustrated by the "sniffer" dogs used at airports and border stations to locate drugs and explosives. Operant discrimination

Fig. 7–18 *Stimulus control. Operant shaping was used to teach Flo, the pictured walrus, first to cover her face (left) and then to douse her trainer. A fish is her reward. Notice the trainer's hand signal, which serves as a discriminative stimulus to control Flo's performance. (Photographs © 1984, Los Angeles Times.)*

training is used to teach these dogs to recognize contraband. During training, the dogs are reinforced only for approaching containers baited with drugs or explosives (Fig. 7–19). Stimulus discrimination clearly has a tremendous impact on human behavior. Learning to recognize different automobile brands, birds, animals, wines, types of music, and even the answers on psychology tests all depend, in part, on operant discrimination learning.

Coming Attractions Some of the examples in this chapter are simplified and a little unrealistic. They were selected to clearly express the basic principles of conditioning. To complete our discussion, the Applications section covers more realistic examples of human and animal learning. After that, an Exploration proposes a personal experiment in applying operant conditioning to your own behavior. Don't miss these coming attractions!

Fig. 7–19 *Operant discrimination training is used to sharpen the skills of "detective" dogs.*

Learning Check

1. Two aspects of stimulus control are ________________ and ________________.
2. Responding tends to occur in the presence of discriminative stimuli associated with reinforcement and tends not to occur in the presence of discriminative stimuli associated with non-reinforcement. T or F?
3. Stimulus generalization refers to making an operant response in the presence of stimuli similar to those that preceded reinforcement. T or F?
4. When a reward follows every response, it is called
   a. continuous reinforcement *b.* fixed reinforcement *c.* ratio reinforcement *d.* controlled reinforcement
5. Partial reinforcement tends to produce slower responding and reduced resistance to extinction. T or F?
6. The schedule of reinforcement associated with playing slot machines and other types of gambling is
   a. fixed ratio *b.* variable ratio *c.* fixed interval *d.* variable interval
7. If you are able to pass a classroom test scheduled every 3 weeks, your studying is reinforced on a ________________ ________________ schedule of reinforcement. If you must study for unannounced pop quizzes, studying is reinforced on a ________________ ________________ schedule. The style of testing that would probably produce the most consistent daily studying is ________________ ________________.

Answers:
1. generalization and discrimination **2.** T **3.** T **4.** *a* **5.** F **6.** *b* **7.** fixed interval, variable interval, variable interval (pop quizzes)

Applications: Managing Behavior—Conditioning in Everyday Situations

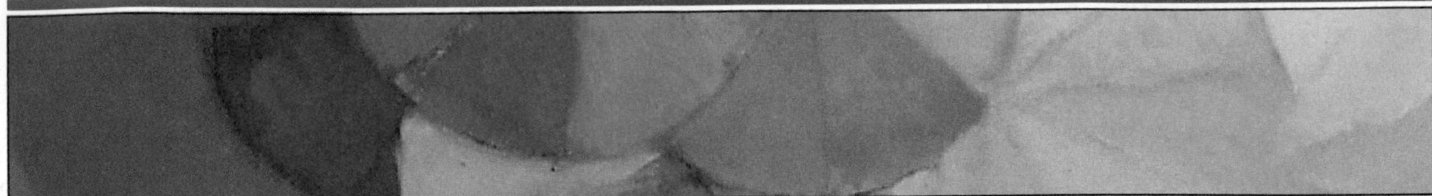

A technology of behavior is emerging. As you will see, conditioning principles have found their way into business, education, industry, and the home. If you understand these principles, you will find frequent uses for them. It is impossible to detail all the possibilities, but a number of examples should extend your understanding. (For more information, also see Chapter 22.)

Conditioning Pets

One of the most common mistakes people make with pets (especially dogs) is hitting them if they do not come when called. Calling the animal then becomes a conditioned stimulus for fear and withdrawal. No wonder the pet disobeys when called on future occasions.

Question: How can conditioning be used to correct this?

An excellent way to train an animal to come when you call is to give a distinctive call or whistle daily during feeding. This makes the signal a discriminative stimulus for reward (food). Effectiveness of the signal is greatly enhanced if it is also used at other times and in other settings and is followed first always, then frequently, then occasionally with a little food. This can be achieved by carrying a few dog biscuits with you during training. (Canned dog food is a little hard on the pockets.) Ultimately, very few "bribes" will be necessary to maintain the effectiveness of the signal if it is conditioned on a partial reinforcement schedule. Later, petting and praise can be substituted for food.

Question: What can be done about an animal that begs at the table?

Pets beg at the table for only one reason: They have been rewarded occasionally for doing so. The problem is usually that the owner finds begging bothersome most of the time and seeks to discourage it by not rewarding it with food. But there is always that time when Fido is just too cute to resist. If the owner gives in then, begging has been reinforced on a partial schedule, which makes it very resistant to extinction. Also, persistence has been reinforced. If you don't want your pets to beg, never give in and reward them. If you want them to beg quietly, reward them after a period of silence, not after a particularly sorrowful plea. Then, gradually extend the length of the silent period.

Conditioning in Business

Most business and industrial applications of reinforcement principles focus on the effects of various bonuses, payment schedules, incentives, commissions, and profit-sharing plans. Before this trend, most people worked for either a straight salary or for an hourly wage. A straight salary can be thought of as a fixed interval schedule of reward. There is little relationship between the amount of effort expended from one paycheck to the next and the amount of pay. This is also partially true of an hourly wage. While it is true that more hours worked means a larger paycheck, an employee gets paid the same amount for an hour of productive work as he or she does for an hour of goofing off. It can be demoralizing to see others do less work and receive the same pay.

With these facts in mind, industrial psychologists have sought to tie pay more directly to work output. The simplest alternative to hourly wages or a salary is payment on a piecework (fixed ratio) basis. If an individual is paid a small amount for each item handled, pound picked, shirt sewed, or whatever, work output tends to be high because more items mean more pay. Piecework pay has something of a bad reputation because some employers pay so little per item that tremendous amounts of work are necessary to earn a reasonable wage. But this need not be the case. For example, employees of a small leather factory in Los Angeles are paid for making a prearranged number of items per week (billfold backs, handbag handles, and so on). Employees are allowed to work as many or as few hours per day as they choose, and they can work at any rate. This allows great flexibility for the workers, and the company pays only for the work it gets.

The most widely used business adaptation of schedules of reinforcement is a combination of hourly wages and incentives for extra effort. Fixed interval rewards (hourly wage or salary) guarantee a basic level of productivity and give workers a secure base pay. Then, in addition, fixed ratio reinforcement (incentives, bonuses, commissions, or profit sharing) tie extra effort to increased pay or other rewards. For example, in one study clerks in a department store were given a chance to earn paid time off by meeting specific goals for selling and stockwork. This strategy brought about a significant improvement

Applications

in their performance, as compared to a control group (Luthans et al., 1981).

Conditioning and Children

Children seem to have an almost limitless craving for attention. This makes attention and approval from parents very powerful reinforcers.

Question: How does that affect a child?

Parents often unknowingly reinforce **negative attention seeking** in children. Generally, children are *ignored* when they are quiet or are playing constructively. They get attention as they get louder and louder, when they yell "Hey Mom!" at the top of their lungs, when they throw a tantrum, show off, or break something. Granted, the attention they get is often a scolding, but it is still attention, and it still reinforces negative attention seeking. To avoid this, parents can ignore children when they seek attention with disruptive behavior. However, if attention seeking declines because it is not reinforced, some other behavior must be rewarded to take its place. Parents report dramatic changes in their children's behavior when they make a special effort to actively praise, attend to, or spend time with their children when the children are quiet or playing constructively.

Question: What can be done about a child who throws tantrums in a store if he or she isn't allowed to buy candy?

Children are realists. If you say, "No, you may not buy candy" and stick to it, the child will get the message. Children can discriminate between what is said in a situation and the *actual* possibility of a reward. Children learn to throw tantrums with one parent but not the other; they learn to discriminate between parents' and grandparents' susceptibility to their requests; and they discriminate between a casual no and an angry no. The problem is that "no" occasionally becomes, "OK, but shut up!" If so, whining or crying has been rewarded on a partial schedule, and it will occur even more frequently in the future. Consistency is the key. If tantrums *never* pay off, they will be abandoned.

Question: But what if the tantrum is really embarrassing? Sometimes parents are willing to do anything to quiet a child.

Beginning a program of nonreward for tantrums may require considerable courage, but it does work. If you don't mind the idea of buying a treat, but dislike the tantrum, try requiring the child to "help" you in some (quiet) way as a condition for receiving the treat. If necessary, walk away from the child and return only when the child has quieted down; or leave the store with the child when a tantrum starts and allow a return to the store only when the child has quieted down.

Conditioning Other Adults

Students seldom realize how much power they have over their teachers. Even tough-skinned veteran teachers are (believe it or not) still human and therefore sensitive to whether or not they are succeeding in class and being accepted by students. This fact can be used in a demonstration of the effects of reward on human behavior.

Shaping a Teacher

For this demonstration, approximately one-half (or more) of the students in a classroom must participate. First, a target behavior should be selected. This should be something like "lecturing from the right side of he room." (Keep it simple; teachers aren't too clever.) Begin training in this way: Each time the instructor turns toward the right side of the room or takes a step in that direction, participating students should look *really* interested. Also, smile, ask questions, lean forward, and make eye contact. If the teacher turns to the left or takes a step in that direction, participating students should lean back, yawn, check out their split ends, close their eyes, or generally look bored. Soon, without being aware of why, the instructor should be spending most of his or her time each class period lecturing from the right side of the classroom.

This trick has been a favorite of psychology graduate students for decades. For a time, one of my professors delivered all of his lectures from the right side of the room while toying with the cords from the venetian blinds. (We added the cords the second week!)

As was pointed out in the discussion of reinforcement with children, attention and approval are powerful rewards for human behavior. This is something to keep in mind when interacting with others.

Question: But how can this be applied?

An excellent example is provided by the work of two educators, Paul S. Graubard and Harry Rosenberg, who taught "incorrigible," "deviant," and "socially outcast" students to use reinforcement on classmates. They cite the example of Peggy, an attractive, intelligent student who was unable to make friends. Peggy encountered so much hostility that she was miserable and unhappy and because of this did poorly in school.

When asked to name three other students she would like to have as friends, Peggy named three students who frequently insulted her. Here is how Peggy began to put into effect the

Applications

reinforcement principles she had learned: She began by ignoring Doris if Doris said anything bad to her. When Doris said anything nice, Peggy complimented her or sat down and asked Doris to join her. Doris soon began to say nice things about Peggy, and to sit by her in class, and for the first time ever, they were able to ride on the bus together without fighting.

Peggy dealt with another student's hostility in the same way. Whenever Elwyn said something bad to her, she turned her back on him. But the first time he walked past her without saying something bad, she gave him a big smile and said, "Hi Elwyn, how are you today?" The authors add that after Elwyn recovered from his initial shock, he grew to be Peggy's best friend (Graubard & Rosenberg, 1974).

Experimental Living In 1948, B. F. Skinner published *Walden Two,* a utopian novel about a model community based on behavioral engineering. Would such a community work? On a small scale, the answer appears to be yes. One such operant community organized at the University of Kansas was quite successful. College students took part in an Experimental Living Project in which 30 men and women shared a large house (Miller, 1976). In this "community," work, leadership, and self-government were tied directly to behavioral principles.

Worksharing provides a good example of the project's operant approach. Basic jobs such as preparing food and cleaning were divided into approximately 100 tasks. Each task was described in terms of its expected end result. Residents performed all of the tasks themselves, and one community member checked daily to see that each job was completed. (This role was rotated periodically.) To maintain job performance, credits were assigned for each of the tasks. At the end of the month, residents who had collected 400 credits got a sizable rent reduction.

This system was very effective in maintaining day-to-day work habits. As anyone who has shared living quarters knows, good intentions are no guarantee that the chores will get done. More importantly, residents rated the project as superior to dormitory living and similar alternatives. Most were highly satisfied with the system (Miller, 1976). The Experimental Living Project is a good example of the possibilities of applying conditioning principles to human behavior.

The examples cited here should give you an idea of the value of understanding conditioning and of applying conditioning principles to everyday problems. Their successful use requires practice, but your efforts are sure to foster a deeper appreciation for their application. Give them a try!

Learning Check

1. Pets who beg for food are often very persistent because they have been rewarded on a schedule of partial reinforcement. T or F?
2. A straight salary can be thought of as fixed interval reinforcement, whereas piecework pay is a fixed ratio schedule. T or F?
3. Negative attention seeking by a child is reinforced when the parent ignores disruptive behavior and praises more desirable responses. T or F?
4. Compliments, attention, and approval can serve as powerful reinforcers of human behavior. T or F?

Answers:

1. T 2. T 3. F 4. T

Exploration: Behavioral Self-Management

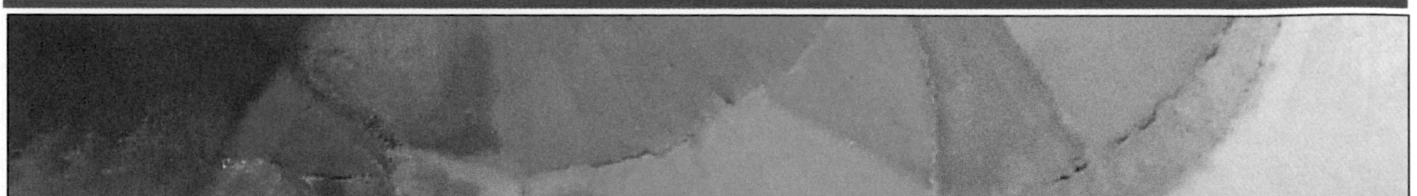

This discussion could be the start of one of the most personal "explorations" in this book. There is now little doubt that self-administered reward affects behavior (Watson & Tharp, 1981). Many people have learned to successfully use self-administered reinforcement to alter or manage their own behavior. At the very least, trying self-management can make you more aware of your behavior and what controls it.

This, then, is an invitation to carry out a self-management project of your own. Would you like to increase the number of hours you spend studying each week? Would you like to exercise more, attend more classes, concentrate longer, or read more books? All these activities and many others can be improved by following the rules described here.

1. **Choose a target behavior.** Identify the activity you want to change.
2. **Record a baseline.** Record how much time you currently spend performing the target activity, or count the number of desired or undesired responses you make each day.
3. **Establish goals.** Remember the principle of shaping and set realistic goals for gradual improvement on each successive week. Also, set daily goals that add up to the weekly goal.
4. **Choose reinforcers.** If you meet your daily goal, what reward will you allow yourself? Daily rewards might be watching television, eating a candy bar, socializing with friends, playing a musical instrument, or whatever you enjoy. Also establish a weekly reward. If you reach your weekly goal, what reward will you allow yourself? A movie? A dinner out? A weekend hike?
5. **Record your progress.** Keep accurate records of the amount of time spent each day on the desired activity.
6. **Reward successes.** If you meet your daily goal, collect your reward. If you fall short, be honest with yourself and skip the reward. Do the same for your weekly goal.
7. **Adjust your plan** as you learn more about your behavior. Overall progress will reinforce your attempts at self-management.

If you have trouble finding rewards, or if you don't want to use the entire system, remember that anything done often can serve as reinforcement (the Premack principle). For example, if you watch television every night and want to study more, make it a rule not to turn on the set until you have studied for an hour (or whatever length of time you choose). Then lengthen the requirement each week.

Here is a sample of one student's plan:

1. *Target behavior:* number of hours spent studying for school
2. *Recorded baseline:* an average of 15 minutes per day for a weekly total of 1¼ hours
3. *Goal for first week:* an increase in study time to 20 minutes per day; weekly goal of 2 hours total study time. *Goal for second week:* 25 minutes per day and 2½ hours per week. *Goal for third week:* 30 minutes per day and 3 hours per week. *Ultimate goal:* to reach and maintain 8 hours per week study time.
4. *Daily reward for reaching goal:* 1 hour of guitar playing in the evening; no playing if the goal is not met. *Weekly reward for reaching goal:* going to a movie or buying a record album.

Self-Recording Even if you find it difficult to give and withhold the rewards in your program, you are likely to succeed. Simply knowing that you are reaching a desired goal can be reward enough. The key to any self-management program therefore becomes accurate record keeping. This concept is demonstrated by a study in which some students in an introductory psychology course recorded study time and graphed their daily and weekly study behavior. Even though no extra rewards were offered, students who were asked to record their study time earned better grades than those who were not required to keep records (Johnson & White, 1971).

Contracting If you try the techniques described here and have difficulty sticking with them, you may want to try **behavioral contracting.** In a behavioral contract, you state a *specific* problem behavior you want to control or a goal you want to achieve. Also state the rewards you

Exploration

will receive, privileges you will forfeit, or punishments you must accept. The contract should be typed and signed by you and a person you trust.

A behavioral contract can be quite motivating, especially when mild punishment is part of the agreement. Here's an example reported by Nurnberger and Zimmerman (1970): A student working on his Ph.D. had completed all requirements but his dissertation, yet for 2 years had not written a single page. A contract was drawn up for him in which he agreed to meet weekly deadlines on the number of pages he would complete. To make sure he would meet the deadlines, he wrote postdated checks. These were to be forfeited if he failed to reach his goal for the week. The checks were made out to organizations he despised (the Ku Klux Klan and American Nazi Party). From the time he signed the contract until he finished his degree, the student's work output was greatly improved.

Getting Help Attempting to manage or alter your own behavior may be more difficult than it sounds. If you feel you need more information, consult either of the books listed below. You will also find helpful advice in the Applications sections of Chapters 8 and 22. If you do try a self-modification project, but find it impossible to reach your goal, be aware that professional advice is available.

For more information, consult:

Watson, D. L., and Tharp, R. G. *Self-directed behavior.* Pacific Grove, CA: Brooks/Cole, 1981.

Williams, R. L., and Long, J. D. *Toward a self-managed life style.* Boston, MA: Houghton Mifflin, 1979.

Learning Check

1. After a target behavior has been selected for reinforcement, it's a good idea to record a baseline so you can set realistic goals for change. T or F?

2. Self-recording, even without the use of extra rewards, can bring about desired changes in target behaviors. T or F?

3. The Premack principle states that behavioral contracting can be used to reinforce changes in behavior. T or F?

4. A self-management plan should make use of the principle of shaping by setting a graduated series of goals. T or F?

Answers:
1. T 2. T 3. F 4. T

Chapter Summary

• **Classical,** or **respondent,** conditioning and **instrumental,** or **operant,** conditioning are two basic types of learning. In classical conditioning, a previously neutral stimulus begins to elicit a response through **association** with another stimulus. In operant conditioning, the frequency and pattern of voluntary responses are altered by their **consequences.**

• Many animals are born with **innate** behavior patterns far more complex than **reflexes.** These are organized into **fixed action patterns** (FAPs), which are stereotyped, **species-specific** behaviors.

• **Learning** is a relatively permanent change in behavior due to experience. Learning due to basic conditioning processes depends on **reinforcement.** Reinforcement increases the probability that a particular response will occur.

• Classical conditioning, studied by **Pavlov,** occurs when a **neutral stimulus** (NS) is associated with an **unconditioned stimulus** (US). The US causes a reflex called the **unconditioned response** (UR). If the NS is consistently paired with the US, it becomes a **conditioned stimulus** (CS) capable of producing a response by itself. This response is a **conditioned** (learned) **response** (CR).

• When the conditioned stimulus is followed by the unconditioned stimulus, conditioning is **reinforced** (strengthened). A well-learned CS can also be used to reinforce further learning in a process known as **higher-order conditioning.** When the CS is repeatedly presented alone, conditioning is **extinguished** (weakened or inhibited). Temporary reappearance of a conditioned response after extinction seems to be complete is called **spontaneous recovery.**

• Through **stimulus generalization,** stimuli similar to the conditioned stimulus will also produce a response. Generalization gives way to **stimulus discrimination** when an organism learns to respond to one stimulus, but not to similar stimuli.

• Conditioning applies to visceral or emotional responses as well as simple reflexes. As a result, **conditioned emotional responses** (CERs) also occur. Irrational fears called **phobias** may be CERs. Conditioning of emotional responses can occur **vicariously** (secondhand) as well as directly.

• Operant conditioning occurs when a voluntary action is followed by a **reinforcer.** Reinforcement in operant conditioning increases the frequency or probability of a response. This result is based on the **law of effect.**

• Complex operant responses can be taught by reinforcing **successive approximations** to a final desired response. This is called **shaping.** It is particularly useful in training animals. However, learning in animals is limited at times by various **biological constraints,** such as **instinctive drift.**

• If an operant response is not reinforced, it may **extinguish** (disappear). But after extinction seems complete, it may temporarily reappear (**spontaneous recovery**).

• **Primary reinforcers** are "natural," physiologically based rewards. **Intra-cranial stimulation** of "pleasure centers" in the brain can also serve as a primary reinforcer.

• **Secondary reinforcers** are learned. They typically gain their reinforcing value by direct association with primary reinforcers or by being subject to exchange for primary reinforcers. **Tokens** and money gain their reinforcing value in this way. Money may be exchanged for so many other reinforcers that it sometimes becomes a **generalized reinforcer. Prepotent,** or frequent, responses can be used to reinforce low-frequency responses.

• **Delay** of reinforcement greatly reduces its effectiveness, but long **chains** of responses may be built up in which a single reinforcer rewards many responses. **Superstitious behaviors** often become part of response chains because they *appear* to be associated with reinforcement.

• Reward, or reinforcement, may be given **continuously** (after every response), or on a **schedule of partial reinforcement.** Partial reinforcement produces greater resistance to extinction. Four of the most basic schedules of reinforcement are **fixed ratio, variable ratio, fixed interval,** and **variable interval.**

• Stimuli that precede a reinforced response tend to control the response on future occasions (**stimulus control**). Two aspects of stimulus control are **generalization** and **discrimination.** In generalization, an operant response tends to occur when stimuli similar to those preceding reinforcement are present. In discrimination, responses are given in the presence of **discriminative stimuli** associated with reinforcement (**S+**) and withheld in the presence of stimuli associated with non-reinforcement (**S−**).

• Operant principles can be readily applied to manage behavior in everyday settings. When managing one's own behavior, **self-reinforcement, self-recording,** and **behavioral contracting** are all helpful.

Questions for Discussion

1. Lately you have been getting a shock of static electricity every time you touch a door handle. You begin to notice a hesitation in your door-opening movements. Can you analyze this situation in terms of classical conditioning?

2. Over the years, balloons have occasionally popped in your face when you were blowing them up. Now you squint and feel tense whenever you blow up a balloon. What kind of conditioning is this? What schedule of reinforcement has contributed to the conditioning? How could you extinguish the response?

3. You are in charge of a group of fifth-grade children that meets regularly for recreation. Other members of the group have excluded a younger girl and a very shy boy from activities. How could you use reinforcement principles to improve this situation? (Include techniques aimed at both the excluded children and the group.)

4. What role has reinforcement had in your selection of a major? Friends? A job? The clothes you wore to school today?

5. From your point of view, what would be the ideal way to be paid at a job? Should pay be weekly, hourly, daily? Should it be tied to work output? Should rewards other than money be offered? If you owned a business, what would you consider the ideal way to pay your employees?

6. How many situations can you list in which rewards are haphazardly or inefficiently applied (for example, tax breaks for people who have children instead of those who don't; better seats for those who take "cuts" in line; and so on)? How would you feel about applying a behavioral engineering approach to such problems?

7. How might operant conditioning principles be used to encourage people to pick up litter (what rewards could be offered, and how might the cost of rewards be kept low)?

8. In what ways could instinctive drift be adaptive for an animal? In what ways could it be maladaptive? Do you think human learning shows signs of any biological constraints?

Chapter 8

Conditioning and Learning II

In This Chapter
Two-factor learning
Feedback
Punishment
Cognitive learning
Observational learning
Biofeedback
Skill learning
Applications
Breaking bad habits
Exploration
Television as a model

Chapter Preview

Mark the Shark

His eyes, driven and blazing, dart from side to side. His left hand beats a frenzied rhythm, looking at times like a videotape on fast-forward. The hand twitches, dances, rises, and strikes, hitting its target again and again. At the same time, his right hand furiously spins in circular motions: a half turn left, a full turn right, a full turn left, another full turn left. The movements are fluid, ceaseless, blindingly quick. All of this is accompanied by incessant body movements, foot shuffling, and a cryptic stream of spoken sounds: "Gnarly!" "Rad!" "Ak!" "Burly!" "Full ollie!" "Yuh!"

Does this describe some strange neurological disorder? Or perhaps it reveals the effects of a powerful new drug? Actually, the passage depicts 10-year-old Mark as he plays his favorite video game, an animated skateboarding adventure!

Mark's mastery of electronic skateboarding, in all its frenetic splendor, is in some ways quite impressive. Try the game yourself and you will find that it's harder than it looks. Mark's skill may well rival that needed to type or to drive a car. How did Mark learn the complex movements needed to excel at this unusual task? After all, he was not rewarded with food or money for correct responses. The answer lies in the fact that Mark's favorite video game provides two key elements that underlie learning: a responsive environment *and* information.

Video games often promote rapid learning (of useless skills, unfortunately). Whenever you move one of the controls on a video game, the machine responds instantly with sounds, animated actions, and a higher or lower score. The machine's responsiveness and the information flow it provides can be very motivating if the player's goal is to win or to master the game. The same dynamic applies to many other learning situations: If you are trying to learn to use a computer, to play a musical instrument, to cook, or to solve math problems, reinforcement comes from knowing that you succeeded at getting a desired result.

In Chapter 7, we discussed learning as if it were fairly mechanical. It is now time to explore learning at a higher level of analysis. An important theme to watch for as you read this chapter is that learning is based on information.

Survey Questions

- In what ways are classical conditioning and operant conditioning alike?
- What is feedback and how does it affect learning?
- What does punishment do to behavior?
- What is cognitive learning? Does learning occur by imitation?
- How are motor skills best learned?
- What can be done to break a bad habit?
- How serious are the effects of television violence?

Conditioning in Perspective—Great Expectations

An ice cream truck approaches with its bell ringing. A boy hears the bell and thinks about ice cream. As he does, his mouth waters. He runs to the truck, buys an ice cream and eats it. What kind of learning is this? If it seems to you that both classical and operant conditioning are present in this example, you are right.

Two-Factor Learning

In the real world, classical and operant conditioning are often intertwined. This is called **two-factor learning.** As you can see in Figure 8–1, the boy's behavior reflects both kinds of learning. As a result of classical conditioning, the boy will salivate each time he hears the truck's bell. Also, the bell is a discriminative stimulus (S+) signaling that reward is available if certain responses are made. When he hears the bell, the boy will run to the truck to buy and eat an ice cream (operant conditioning). The boy's involuntary responses are altered by classical conditioning, while his voluntary behavior is shaped by operant conditioning.

Question: Other than the fact that they often occur together, do operant and classical conditioning have anything in common?

Information At one time, psychologists pictured conditioning as a mechanical "stamping in" of responses. Now, many think of learning in terms of *information processing.* According to this **informational view,** learning creates mental **expectancies** (or expectations) about events. Once acquired, these expectancies alter behavior. For example, researcher Robert Rescorla (1980, 1987) explains classical conditioning this way: The conditioned stimulus reliably precedes the unconditioned stimulus; because it does, the CS *predicts* the US. When the CS is present, the brain *expects* the US to follow. Therefore, the brain prepares the body to respond to the US.

In our example, whenever the boy hears the bell or sees the truck, his mouth waters to prepare for eating ice cream. Similarly, when you are about to get a shot with a hypodermic needle, your muscles tighten and there is a catch in your breathing as your body prepares for pain. Notice that the CS gives valuable *information* about the US before the US appears. Pavlovian conditioning is not a "stupid" process that links any two stimuli that happen to occur together. Rather, conditioning occurs as we seek information about the world (Rescorla, 1988).

If you think about it, operant reinforcers also supply information. In operant conditioning, we learn to *expect* that a certain response will have a certain effect at certain times (Bolles, 1979). From this point of view, reward tells a person or an animal that a response was "right" and worth repeating. Likewise, stimuli or events prior to actions tell what response to make to get a reinforcer. Thus, when the boy hears the bell, he *expects* that running to the truck and paying for an ice cream will lead to eating it. If his expectation changes, his behavior will, too. Picture what would happen if the ice cream truck changed its route and the boy repeatedly ran out to find, instead, a garbage truck with its safety bell ringing. Rapid extinction would follow as the boy's expectancy changed from "bell means ice cream" to "bell means garbage."

The adaptive value of information helps explain why much human learning occurs without obvious reinforcement by food, water, and the like. Humans readily learn responses that merely have a desired effect or that bring a goal closer. Let's explore this idea further.

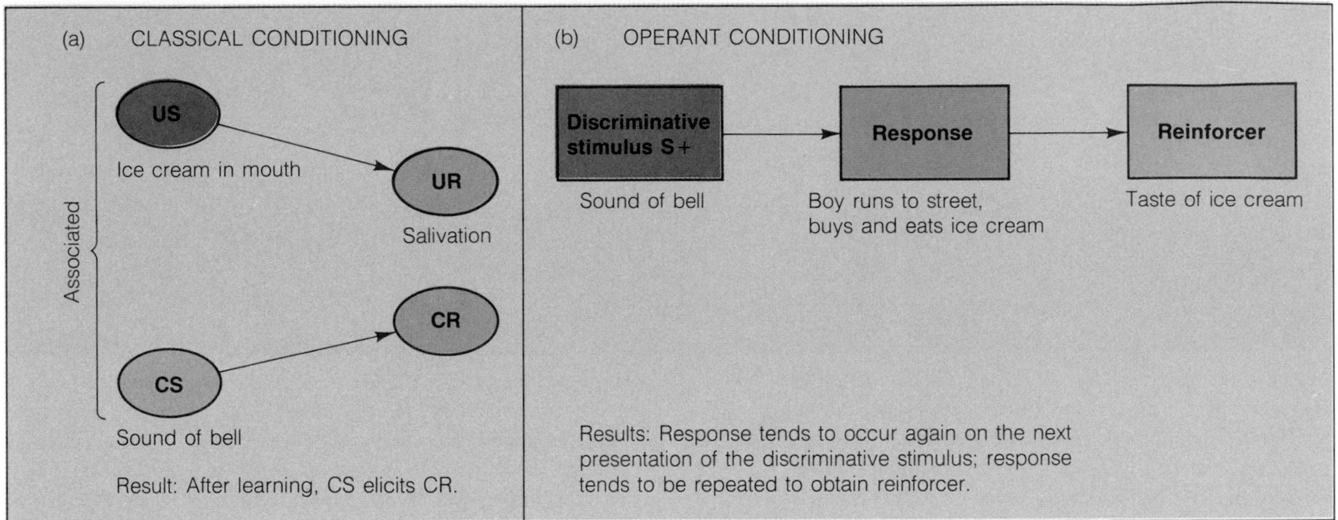

Fig. 8–1 *Two-factor learning.*

Feedback

Imagine that you are asked to throw darts at a target. Each dart must pass over a screen that prevents you from telling if you hit the target. If you threw 1000 darts this way, we would expect little improvement in your performance, because no *feedback* is provided. **Feedback** (information about what effect a response had) is particularly important in human learning. Recall, for instance, that Mark's video game did not explicitly reward him for correct responses. Yet, because it provided feedback, rapid learning took place.

The value of feedback (also called **knowledge of results,** or **KR**) is one of the most useful lessons to be gained from studies of learning. Increased feedback almost always improves learning and performance.

Question: How can feedback be applied?

There are many methods already in wide use. If you want to learn to play a musical instrument, to sing, to speak a second language, or to deliver a speech, tape-recorded feedback can be very helpful. In sports, videotapes are used to improve everything from tennis serves to pick-off moves in baseball. If you would like to make a similar use of feedback, it's worth knowing that taped replays are most helpful when a skilled coach directs attention to key details (Salmoni et al., 1984).

Learning Aids Feedback is valuable in education, too. In recent years, operant learning and feedback have been combined in two interesting ways. These are *programmed instruction* and *computer-assisted instruction.*

Question: How do these techniques make use of feedback?

Feedback is most effective when it is *frequent, immediate,* and *detailed.* **Programmed instruction** teaches students in a format that requires precise answers about information as it is presented. This method gives frequent feedback to keep learners from practicing errors. It also has the advantage of letting students work at their own pace. (The Learning Check that follows this discussion is done in a programmed format so that you can see what one looks like.)

In **computer-assisted instruction (CAI),** students work at individual computer terminals. The computer displays lessons on a screen, and students type answers. In addition to giving immediate feedback, the computer can *analyze each answer.* This allows use of a **branching program** that supplies extra information and asks extra questions when errors are made. The newest CAI programs, which use artificial intelligence programs (see Chapter 10), can even give hints about why an answer was wrong and what is needed to correct it.

Elementary school children seem to do especially well with a "computer tutor" because of the rapid feedback and individualized pacing. Adults, too, benefit from computer-assisted instruction. For example, CAI has been found to speed training in the military and in business (Alessi & Trollip, 1985; Dossett & Hulvershorn, 1983). It also accelerates learning for various college subjects (Kulic et al., 1980). Although the final level of skill or knowledge is no higher than that gained by conventional methods, CAI can save much time and effort (Wexley, 1984).

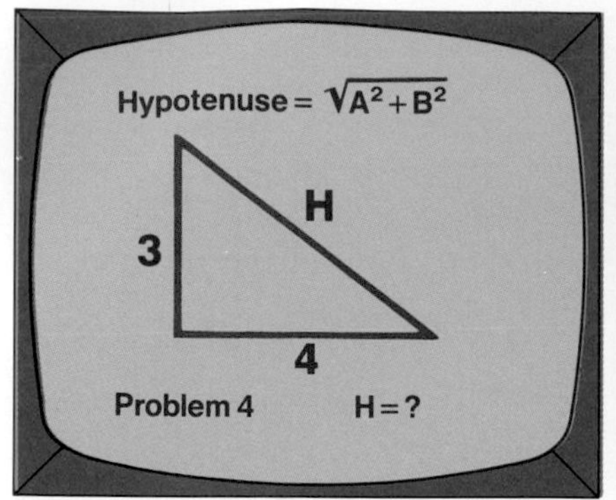

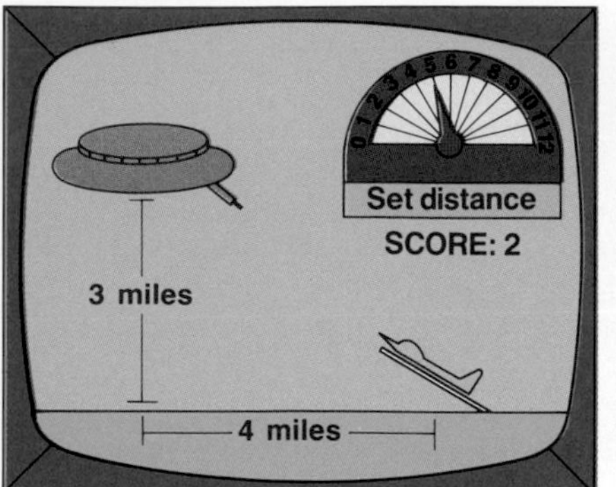

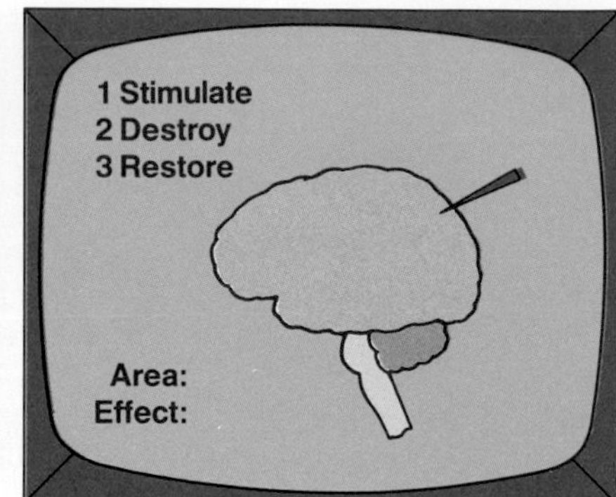

Fig. 8–2 *Computer-assisted instruction. The screen on the left shows a typical drill-and-practice math problem, in which students must find the hypotenuse of a triangle. The center screen presents the same problem as an instructional game to increase interest and motivation. In the game, a child is asked to set the proper distance on a ray gun in the hovering space ship to "vaporize" an attacker. The screen on the right depicts an educational simulation. Here, students place a "probe" at various spots in a human brain. They then "stimulate," "destroy," or "restore" areas. As each area is altered, it is named on the screen, and the effects on behavior are described. This allows students to explore basic brain function on their own.*

The simplest computerized instruction consists of self-paced **drill and practice.** In this format, students answer questions similar to those found in printed workbooks. This has the advantage of instantly providing correct answers. In addition, the computer can give extra KR, such as how fast you worked, your percentage correct, or how your work compared with previous scores (Lepper, 1985).

Higher-level CAI programs include **instructional games** and **educational simulations.** Instructional games use stories, competition with a partner, sound effects, and gamelike graphics to increase interest and motivation (Fig. 8–2). In educational simulations, students face problems in an imaginary situation or "microworld." By seeing the effects of their choices, students discover basic principles of physics, biology, psychology, or other subjects (Lepper, 1985).

Psychologists are only now beginning to fully explore the value and limits of computer-assisted instruction. Nevertheless, it seems likely that their efforts will improve not only education, but our understanding of human learning as well.

Learning Check

To give you an idea of what programmed instruction is like, this Learning Check is presented in a programmed format. To use it, cover the words on the left, and then uncover each answer after you have filled in a blank.

classical	In many learning situations, ________________ and operant conditioning occur simultaneously.
two-	This circumstance is referred to as ________________ factor learning. Often, a reinforcer that
classical	strengthens an operant response also serves as an unconditioned stimulus for ________________
	conditioning. The informational view of learning states that both classical and operant conditioning create
expectancies	mental ________________ that alter behavior. Much human learning is based on informational
knowledge	feedback about the effects a response has had. Feedback is also known as KR or ________________
results	of ________________. Programmed instruction is self-paced and gives immediate
feedback	________________ to the learner. The simplest form of computer-assisted instruction is
drill	________________ and practice.

● Punishment—Putting the Brakes on Behavior

For better or worse, punishment is one of the most popular ways to control behavior. Spankings, reprimands, loss of privileges, fines, jail sentences, firings, failing grades, and the like all reveal widespread use of punishment (Fig. 8–3). Clearly, the story of learning is unfinished without a discussion of punishment. Before we begin, however, a brief return to reinforcement is in order.

Negative Reinforcement Versus Punishment Until now, we have stressed **positive reinforcement,** which occurs when a pleasant or desired event follows a response. But how else could learning be reinforced? The time has come to consider the "flip side" of conditioning: **Negative reinforcement** occurs when a response *ends* or *removes* an *unpleasant* event. Like positive reinforcement, negative reinforcement also increases responding. However, it does so by *ending discomfort*.

Let's say that you have a headache and take an aspirin. Your aspirin taking will be negatively reinforced if the headache stops. Likewise, a rat could be taught to press a bar to get food (positive reinforcement), or the rat could be shocked mildly until it pressed a bar that turned off the shock (negative reinforcement). Either way, bar pressing would increase because it leads to a desired state of affairs (food or an end to pain). Often, positive and negative reinforcement combine. If you are uncomfortably hungry, eating a meal is reinforced by the good-tasting food (positive reinforcement) and by an end to nagging hunger (negative reinforcement).

Many people mistake negative reinforcement for punishment. However, **punishment** is "any event that follows a response and *decreases* its likelihood of occurring again" (Adams, 1980). As noted, negative reinforcement *increases* responding. The difference can be seen in a hypothetical example. Let's say you live in an apartment and your neighbor's stereo is blasting so loudly that your ears hurt. If you pound on the wall and the volume drops (negative reinforcement), future wall pounding will be more likely. But if you pound on the wall and the volume increases (punishment), or if the neighbor comes over and pounds on you (more punishment), pounding on the wall becomes less likely.

As another example, consider a drug addict undergoing withdrawal. Taking the drug temporarily ends painful withdrawal symptoms. Drug taking is therefore negatively reinforced. If, on the other hand, the drug intensified the pain (punishment), the addict would quickly stop taking it.

Question: Isn't it also punishing to have privileges, money, or other positive things taken away for making a particular response?

Yes. Punishment also occurs when a reinforcer or positive state of affairs is removed, such as losing privileges. This second type of punishment is called **response cost** (Cautela & Kearney, 1986). Parents who "ground" their teenage children for misbehavior are applying response cost. Parking tickets and other fines are also based on response cost. For your convenience, Figure 8–4 summarizes what we have covered so far.

Fig. 8–3 *Punishment has long been used to suppress undesirable behavior.*

Edict of Louis XI, King of France
A.D. 1481

"Anyone who sells butter containing stones or other things (to add to the weight) will be put into our pillory, then said butter will be placed on his head until entirely melted by the sun. Dogs may lick him and people offend him with whatever defamatory epithets they please without offense to God or King. If the sun is not warm enough, the accused will be exposed in the great hall of the gaol in front of a roaring fire, where everyone will see him."

Compare: Reinforcement and Punishment

Positive reinforcement Occurs when a response is followed with a reward or other positive event.

Negative reinforcement Occurs when a response is followed with an end to discomfort or with the removal of a negative state of affairs.

Punishment Occurs when a response is followed with pain or an otherwise negative event, such as the removal of a positive reinforcer (response cost).

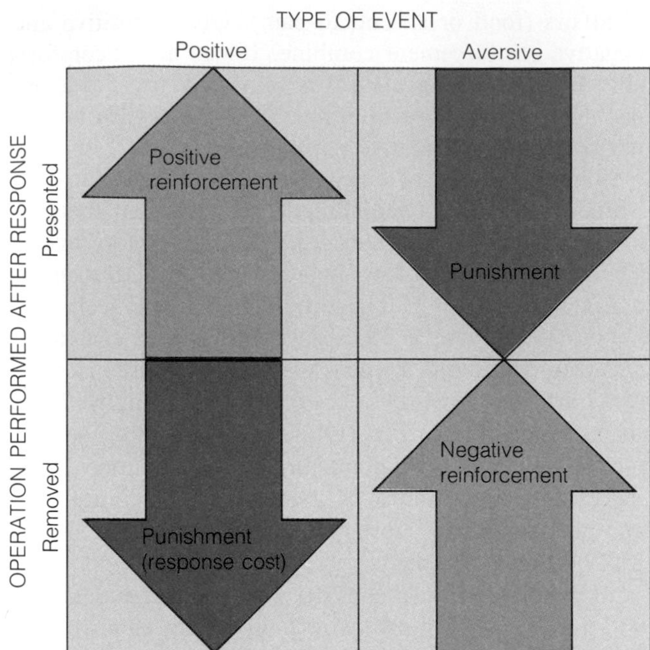

Fig. 8–4 *Types of reinforcement and punishment. The impact of an event depends on whether it is presented or removed after a response is made. Each square defines one possibility: Arrows pointing upward indicate that responding is increased; downward-pointing arrows indicate that responding is decreased. (Adapted from Kazdin, 1975.)*

Variables Affecting Punishment

Question: Reinforcement strengthens a response. Does punishment weaken a response?

Many people assume that punishment stops undesired behavior. Is this always true? Psychologists have learned that the effect of punishment depends greatly on its *timing, consistency,* and *intensity*. Punishment suppresses behavior best when it occurs as the response is being made, or *immediately* afterward (timing), and when it is given *each time* a response occurs (consistency). Thus, a dog that has developed a habit of constantly barking can be effectively (and humanely) punished if water is sprayed on its nose each time it barks. Ten to fifteen such treatments are usually enough to greatly reduce barking. This would not be the case if punishment were applied occasionally or long after the barking stopped. If you discover that your dog dug up and ate a tree while you were gone, it will do little good to punish him hours later. Likewise, the commonly heard childhood threat, "Wait 'til your father comes home, then you'll be sorry," does more to make father an ogre than it does to effectively punish an undesirable response.

Severe punishment can be extremely effective in stopping behavior. If a child sticks a finger in a light socket and gets a shock, that may be the last time the child *ever* tries it. More often, however, punishment only temporarily *suppresses* a response. If the response is still reinforced, punishment may be particularly ineffective. Responses suppressed by **mild punishment** usually reappear later. If a child sneaks a snack from the refrigerator before dinner and is punished for it, the child may pass up snacks for a short time. But since snack sneaking was also rewarded by the sneaked snack, the child will probably try sneaky snacking again, sometime later.

This fact was demonstrated experimentally by slapping rats on the paw as they were bar pressing in a Skinner box. Two groups of well-trained rats were placed on extinction. One group was punished with a slap for each bar press, while the other group was not. It might be expected that the slap would cause bar pressing to extinguish more quickly. Yet, this was not the case, as you can see in Figure 8–5. Punishment temporarily slowed responding, but it did not cause more rapid extinction. Slapping the paws of rats or children has little permanent effect on a reinforced response. It is worth stating again, however, that intense punishment may permanently suppress a response. Experiments show that actions as basic as eating can be suppressed. Animals severely punished while eating may never eat again (Bertsch, 1976).

Question: Then should punishment be used to control behavior?

Using Punishment Wisely Parents, teachers, animal trainers, and the like have three basic tools to control simple learning: (1) *Reinforcement* strengthens responses; (2) *non-reinforcement* causes responses to extinguish; (3) *punishment* suppresses responses. These tools work best in combination. When punishment is mild, as it should be, its value may be limited if reinforcers are still available in the situation. If you choose to use punishment, it is best to also reward an alternate, desirable response. From an informational view, punishment tells a person or an animal that a response was "wrong." However, it does not say what the "right" response is, so it *does not teach new behaviors*. If reinforcement is missing from the formula, punishment becomes less effective.

In a situation that poses immediate danger, such as when a child reaches for something hot or a dog runs into the street, mild punishment may prevent disaster. Punishment in such cases works best when it produces actions *incompatible* with the response you want to suppress. Let's say a child reaches toward a stove burner.

HIGHLIGHT 8–1
If You Must Punish, Here's How

There are times when punishment may be necessary to manage the behavior of an animal, child, or even another adult. If you feel that you must punish, here are some tips to keep in mind.

1. *Don't use punishment at all if you can discourage misbehavior in other ways.* Make liberal use of positive reinforcement, especially praise, to encourage desirable behavior. Also, try extinction first: See what happens if you ignore a problem behavior; or shift attention to a desirable activity and then reinforce it with praise.

2. *Apply punishment during, or immediately after, misbehavior.* Of course, immediate punishment is not always possible. With older children and adults, you can bridge the delay by clearly stating what act you are punishing. If you cannot punish an animal *immediately*, wait for the next instance of misbehavior.

3. *Use the minimum punishment necessary to suppress misbehavior.* Often, a verbal rebuke or a scolding is enough. Avoid harsh physical punishment. (Never slap a child's face, for instance.) Taking away privileges or other positive reinforcers (response cost) is usually best for older children and adults. Frequent punishment may lose its effectiveness, and harsh or excessive punishment has serious negative side effects (see text).

4. *Be consistent.* Be very clear about what you regard as misbehavior. Punish every time the misbehavior occurs. Don't punish for something one day and ignore it the next. If you are usually willing to give a child three chances, don't change the rule and explode without warning after a first offense. Both parents should try to punish their children for the same things and in the same way.

5. *Expect anger from a punished person.* Briefly acknowledge this anger, but be careful not to reinforce it. Be willing to admit your mistake if you wrongfully punish someone or if you punished too severely.

6. *Punish with kindness and respect.* Allow the punished person to retain self-respect. For instance, do not punish a person in front of others, if at all possible. A strong, trusting relationship tends to minimize behavior problems. Ideally, others should *want* to behave well to get your praise, not because they fear punishment.

Would a swat on the bottom serve as effective punishment? Probably so. It would be better, however, to slap the child's outstretched hand so it will be *withdrawn* from the source of danger. For additional tips on using punishment, see Highlight 8–1.

Question: What are the drawbacks of using punishment?

Side Effects of Punishment

The basic problem with punishment is that it is usually *aversive* (painful or uncomfortable). As a result, people

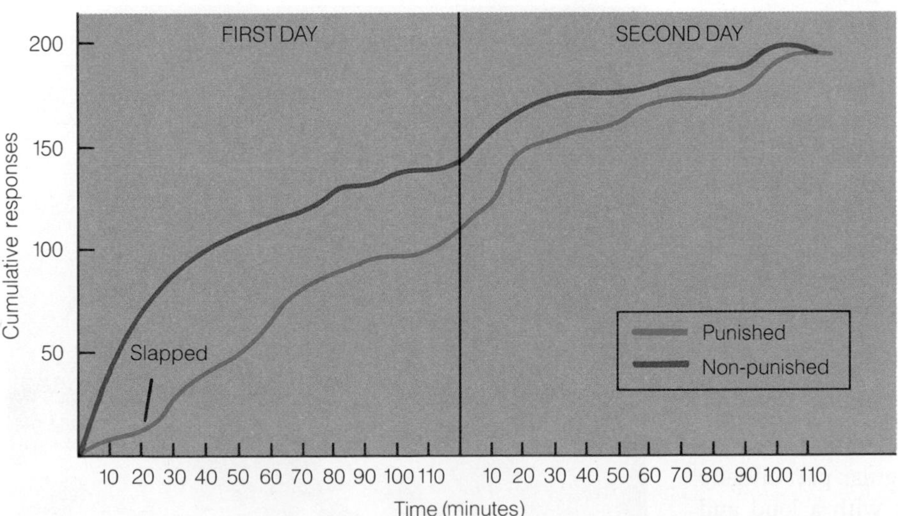

Fig. 8–5 *The effect of punishment on extinction. Immediately after punishment, the rate of bar pressing is suppressed, but by the end of the second day, the effects of punishment have disappeared. (After B. F. Skinner,* The Behavior of Organisms. *© 1938. D. Appleton-Century Co., Inc. Reprinted by permission of Prentice-Hall, Inc.)*

and situations associated with punishment tend, through classical conditioning, to also become aversive (feared, resented, or disliked). This association, perhaps, is why children so often choose school windows to break when other targets are also available. The aversive nature of punishment makes it especially poor to use when teaching children to eat politely or when toilet training them.

Escape and Avoidance A second major problem is that aversive stimuli usually encourage **escape learning** and **avoidance learning.** Escape learning simply reflects the operation of negative reinforcement:

> A dog is placed in a two-compartment cage called a shuttle box. If it is shocked in one of the compartments, it will quickly learn to jump to the second compartment to *escape* the shock. If a buzzer is sounded 10 seconds before the shock is turned on, the dog will soon learn to associate the buzzer with shock. It will then *avoid* pain by jumping *before* the shock begins. (Solomon & Wynne, 1953)

Psychologists theorize that avoidance involves two-factor learning, described earlier. An animal first learns, through classical conditioning, to feel fear in the presence of the buzzer. After that, leaving the compartment as the buzzer sounds reduces fear, which negatively reinforces avoidance. This is operant learning.

Newer automobiles in the United States have an unpleasant buzzer that sounds if the ignition key is turned before the driver's seat belt is fastened. Most drivers quickly learn to fasten the belt to stop the annoying sound. This is an example of escape conditioning. Avoidance conditioning is evident when a driver learns to buckle up before the buzzer sounds (Cautela & Kearney, 1986). However, not everyone reaches this point. The buzzer also stops if you simply wait long enough, which reinforces some drivers for patiently ignoring it.

Once avoidance is learned it is very persistent. The electric shock in a shuttle box can be turned off, and yet the dog will continue to leap from the compartment each time the buzzer sounds. This fact is rather puzzling: If the buzzer is never followed by shock, why doesn't fear of the buzzer extinguish? In informational terms, the dog has learned to expect that the buzzer is followed by shock. If the dog leaves before the shock would normally occur, it gets no new information to change the expectancy (Schwartz, 1984).

Question: How do escape and avoidance learning relate to punishment?

Escape and avoidance learning are a regular part of daily experience. For instance, if you work with a loud and obnoxious person, you may at first escape from conversations with him; later you may learn to avoid him altogether. Each time you sidestep him, your avoidance is reinforced by a sense of relief. In many situations involving frequent punishment, similar desires to escape and avoid are activated. For example, children who run away from punishing parents (escape) may soon learn to lie about their behavior (avoidance) or to spend as much time away from home as possible (also an avoidance response).

Aggression A third problem with punishment is that it can greatly increase *aggression*. Researchers have shown that animals consistently react to pain by attacking whomever or whatever else is around (Azrin et al., 1965). A common example of this effect is the faithful dog that nips its owner during a painful procedure at the veterinarian's office.

We also know that one of the most common responses to frustration is aggression (Fig. 8–6). Generally speaking, punishment is painful, frustrating, or both. Punishment, therefore, sets up a powerful environment for learning aggression. When a child is spanked, the child may feel angry, frustrated, and hostile. What if the child then goes outside and hits a brother, sister, or a neighbor? The danger is that it may feel good because it releases anger and frustration. If so, aggression has been rewarded and will tend to occur again in other frustrating situations. One study found that overly aggressive adolescent boys had been severely punished for aggression at home. Since aggression was suppressed at home, parents were often surprised to learn that their "good boys" were in trouble

Fig. 8–6 *Frustration and aggression are frequent side effects of punishment.*

at school for fighting and other forms of aggression (Bandura & Walters, 1959).

To summarize, the most common error in using punishment is to rely on it alone for training or discipline. The overall emotional adjustment of a child or pet disciplined mainly by reward is usually superior to one disciplined mainly by punishment. Frequent punishment makes a person or an animal unhappy, confused, anxious, aggressive, and fearful of the source of punishment. Children who are punished often by parents or teachers learn not only to dislike parents and teachers, but also to dislike and to avoid the activities associated with punishment (schoolwork or household chores, for instance) (Munn, 1969). It is not entirely unreasonable with 3- to 5-year-old children to occasionally use mild physical punishment (see Chapter 15 Applications). Otherwise, it would seem that the adage "Spare the rod and spoil the child" should at least be changed to "Use the rod sparingly or spoil the child" and perhaps to simply "Spare the rod."

● Cognitive Learning—Beyond Conditioning

Question: Is all learning just a connection between stimuli and responses?

Some learning can be thought of this way. But, as we have seen, even basic conditioning has "mental" elements. As a further example of this fact, assume that you have been conditioned—by pairing a light with shock—to feel fear each time the light comes on. If the shock is then turned off and the light is presented many times, your fear will gradually extinguish. Now, what would happen if you were simply *told* that a shock would not follow the light again? The surprising finding is that your fear would disappear almost immediately (Grings & Lockhart, 1963; Wickens et al., 1963). As a human, you can anticipate future reward or punishment and react accordingly. (You may wonder why this doesn't seem to work when a doctor or dentist says, "This won't hurt a bit." Here's why: They lie!)

There is no doubt that human learning includes a large *cognitive,* or mental, dimension. As humans, we are greatly affected by information, expectations, perceptions, mental images, and the like. Loosely speaking, **cognitive learning** refers to understanding, knowing, anticipating, or otherwise making use of higher mental processes. Cognitive learning extends beyond basic conditioning into the realms of memory, thinking, problem solving, and language. Since these topics are covered in later chapters, our discussion here is limited to a first look at learning beyond conditioning.

Cognitive Maps How do you navigate around the town you live in? Is it fair to assume that you have simply learned to make a series of right and left turns to get from one point to another? It is far more likely that you have developed an overall mental picture of how the town is laid out. This **cognitive map** (internal representation of relationships) acts as a guide even when you must detour or take a new route.

Question: Are animals capable of cognitive learning?

A little psychological "monkey business" shows that they are. In one experiment, chimpanzees watched as a psychologist hid pieces of fruit in a field at various places. Later, the chimps were released into the field. Chimps who watched the hiding found about 12 pieces of fruit each. Control group chimps averaged only 1 find each—mostly by following the informed monkeys and sharing the "fruits of their labors" (Menzel, 1978). Actually, it's not surprising that higher animals are capable of cognitive learning. Even the lowly rat—not exactly a mental giant—learns *where* food is found in a maze, not just which turns to make to reach the food (Tolman, 1946).

In a sense, cognitive maps also apply to other kinds of knowledge. For instance, it could be said that you have been developing a "map" of psychology while reading this book. This may be why students sometimes find it helpful to draw pictures of how they envision concepts fitting together.

Latent Learning Cognitive learning is also revealed by **latent** (hidden) **learning.** That is, learning sometimes occurs without obvious reinforcement and remains hidden until reinforcement is provided.

Mickey Rat II Learns Where the Action Is

Two groups of rats are allowed to explore a maze. Rats in one group find food at the far end of the maze and soon learn to make their way rapidly through the maze when released. Rats in the second group are unrewarded and show no signs of learning. But later, when the same rats are given food, they run the maze as well as the rewarded group. (Tolman & Honzik, 1930)

Although there was no outward sign of it, the unrewarded rats had learned their way around the maze. Their learning, therefore, remained latent at first (Fig. 8–7).

Question: How did they learn if there was no reinforcement?

Apparently, satisfying curiosity can be enough to reward learning (Harlow & Harlow, 1962). In humans, latent learning is probably related to high-level abilities, such as anticipating future reward. For example, if you give

an attractive classmate a ride home, you may make mental notes about how to get to his or her house, even if a date is only a remote future possibility.

Discovery Learning Much of what is meant by cognitive learning is summarized by the word *understanding*. Each of us has, at times, learned ideas by *rote* (repetition and memorization). Although rote learning is efficient, many psychologists believe that learning is more lasting when people *discover* facts and principles on their own (Lepper, 1985). In **discovery learning,** skills are gained by insight and understanding instead of by rote (Bruner, 1968).

Question: As long as learning occurs, what difference does it make?

Figure 8–8 illustrates the difference. Two groups of students were taught to calculate the area of a parallelogram. Some were encouraged to see that a "piece" of a parallelogram could be "moved" to create a rectangle. Later, they were better able to solve unusual problems than were students who simply memorized a rule (Wertheimer, 1959). As this suggests, discovery learning tends to produce better understanding of new problems and situations (Lepper, 1985). In sum, it seems worthwhile to take extra steps to foster insight and deeper understanding, even if learning by discovery takes longer.

Compare: Cognitive Learning and Related Concepts

Cognitive learning Higher-level learning involving thinking, knowing, understanding, and anticipation.

Cognitive map Internal images or other mental representations of an area (maze, city, campus) that underlie an ability to choose alternate paths to the same goal.

Latent learning Learning that occurs without obvious reinforcement and that remains unexpressed until reinforcement is provided.

Discovery learning Learning based on insight or understanding, rather than on a mechanical application of rules.

Observational learning Learning achieved by watching and imitating the actions of another person (a model) or by noting the consequences of those actions.

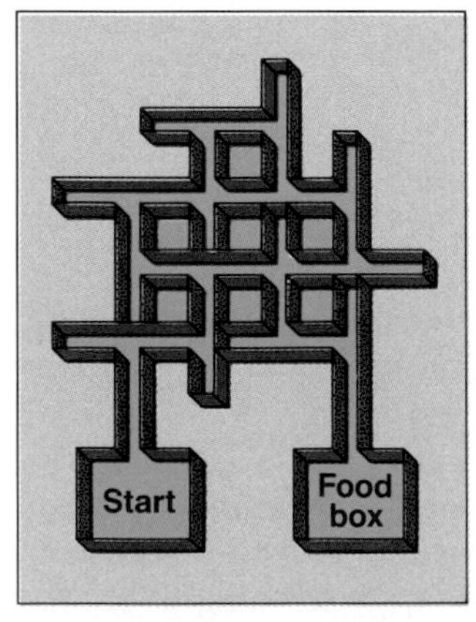

(a)

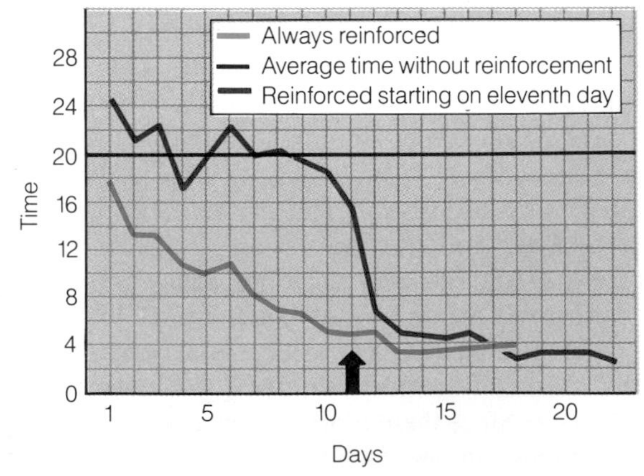

(b)

Fig. 8–7 *Latent learning. (a) The maze used by Tolman and Honzik to demonstrate latent learning by rats. (b) Results of the experiment. Notice the rapid improvement in performance that occurred when food was made available to the previously unreinforced animals. This indicates that learning had occurred, but that it remained hidden or unexpressed. (Adapted from Tolman & Honzik, 1930.)*

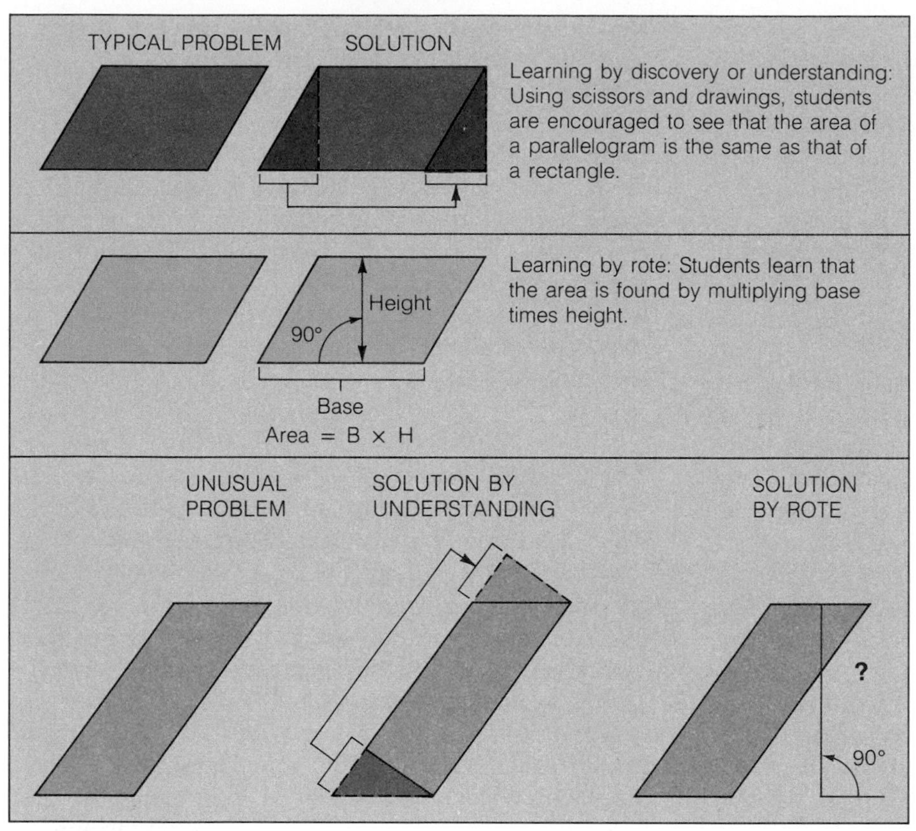

Fig. 8–8 *Learning by understanding and by rote. For some types of learning, understanding may be superior, although both types of learning are useful. (After Wertheimer, 1959.)*

Modeling—Do as I Do, Not as I Say

The class watches intently as a skilled potter pulls a spinning ball of clay into the form of a vase. There is little doubt that many skills are learned by what Albert Bandura (1971) calls **observational learning, modeling,** or simply imitation. The value of learning by observation is obvious: Imagine trying to *tell* someone how to tie a shoe, do a dance step, crochet, or play a guitar. Bandura believes that anything that can be learned from direct experience can be learned by observation. Often, this allows a person to skip the tedious trial-and-error stage of learning.

Question: It seems obvious that we learn by observation, but how does it occur?

Observational Learning

By observing a **model** (someone who serves as an example), a person may (1) learn new responses, (2) learn to carry out or avoid previously learned responses (depending on what happens to the model for doing the same thing), or (3) learn a general rule that can be applied to various situations (Rosenthal & Zimmerman, 1978).

For observational learning to occur, several things must take place. First, the learner must pay *attention* to the model and *remember* what was done. (A beginning auto mechanic might be interested enough to watch an entire tune-up, but unable to remember all the steps.) Next, the learner must be able to *reproduce* the modeled behavior. (Sometimes this is a matter of practice, but it may be that the learner will never be able to perform the behavior. I may admire the feats of world-class gymnasts, but with no amount of practice could I ever reproduce them.) If a model is *successful* at a task or *rewarded* for a response, the learner is more likely to imitate the behavior. In general, models who are attractive, rewarding, admired, or high in status also tend to be imitated. (Bandura & Walters, 1963). Finally, once a new response is tried, normal *reinforcement determines if it will be repeated thereafter*. (Notice the similarity here to latent learning, described earlier.)

Imitating Models Modeling has a powerful effect on behavior. In a classic experiment, children watched an adult attack a large blowup Bo-Bo doll. Some children saw an adult sit on the doll, punch it, hit it with a hammer, and kick it around the room. Others saw a color movie of these actions. A third group saw a cartoon version of the aggression. Later, the children were frustrated (by having some attractive toys taken away from them) and then allowed to play with the Bo-Bo doll. Most imitated the attack they had seen the adult perform (Fig. 8–9). Some even added new aggressive acts of their own! Interestingly, the cartoon was only slightly less effective in encouraging aggression than the live adult model and the filmed model (Bandura et al., 1963).

Question: Then do children blindly imitate adults?

No. Remember that observational learning equips a person to duplicate a response, but whether it is actually imitated depends on whether the model was rewarded or punished for what was done. Nevertheless, research shows that when parents tell a child to do one thing, but model a completely different response, children tend to imitate what the parents *do*, and *not* what they *say* (Bryan & Walbek, 1970). Thus, through modeling, children learn not only attitudes, gestures, emotions, and personality traits, but fears, anxieties, and bad habits as well.

Consider a typical situation. Little Shawn-Erin-Ringo-Jeremy Jones has just been interrupted at play by his little brother. Angry and frustrated, he hits his little brother. This behavior interrupts his father's TV watching. Father promptly spanks little Shawn-Erin-Ringo-Jeremy, saying, "This will teach you to hit your little brother." And it will. Because of modeling effects, it is unrealistic to expect a child to "Do as I say, not as I do." The message the father has given the child is clear: "You have frustrated me; therefore, I will hit you." Is it any wonder that the child does the same when he is frustrated?

Question: Can television serve as a model for observational learning?

There is reason to believe that it can. As a convicted criminal once told *TV Guide* magazine, "TV taught me how to steal cars, how to break into establishments, how to go about robbing people, even how to roll a drunk. Once after having watched 'Hawaii Five-O,' I robbed a gas station. The show showed me how to do it."

In addition to teaching new antisocial actions, television may **disinhibit** dangerous impulses that viewers already have. For example, many TV programs give the message that violence is normal, acceptable behavior. For some people, this message can lower inhibitions against acting out hostile feelings (Berkowitz, 1984). Disinhibition may even extend to self-destructive impulses. There is some evidence that after a television soap opera character commits suicide, real suicides increase among viewers (Phillips, 1982).

The World According to TV Did you know that the world is populated primarily by males, professionals, whites, and members of the middle class? Did you know that women make up only 28 percent of the population; that one-half of all women are teenagers or in their early 20s; that more than one-third are unemployed or have no purpose beyond offering emotional support to men or serving as objects of sexual desire? That minorities are generally service workers, criminals, victims, or students? That over one-half of all villains have accents? That most victims are single women, young boys, or nonwhites? If you watch much TV, these are the impressions you get daily on the tube (Carlson, 1986; Charren & Sandler, 1983; U.S. Commission on Civil Rights, 1977).

It is clear that TV reality does not match the real world. Every day, TV provides an endless stream of bad models. Here are some additional examples:

- Stable, happy marriages are rarely portrayed on TV because they don't make for good plots.
- There are 3 instances of drinking alcohol per hour of prime-time TV; 6 per hour for soap operas. TV characters drink 15 times more alcohol than water.
- Most workers are authority figures, such as police officers, doctors, lawyers, judges, and so on. Children

Fig. 8–9 *A nursery school child imitates the aggressive behavior of an adult model he has just seen in a movie. (Photos courtesy of Albert Bandura.)*

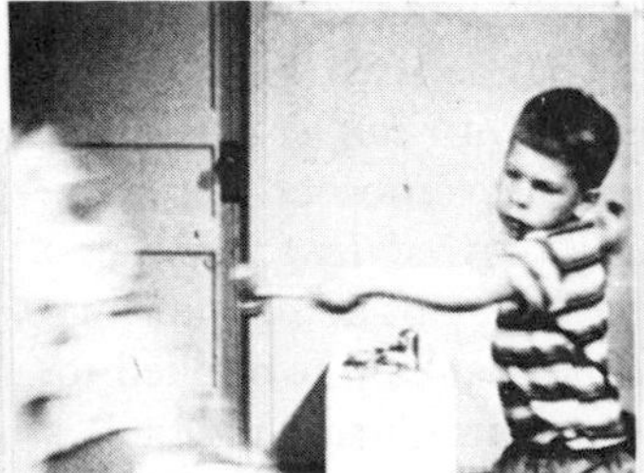

watching TV learn more about coroners and spies than they do about the real world of work (Charren & Sandler, 1983).

• Soap operas average 1.5 mentions of sexual intercourse per hour. During a 6-month period on one series, the show's characters went through 8 divorces and 4 separations. During the same period, 21 couples were living or sleeping together out of wedlock (Brown, 1986).

Televised violence is even more disturbing. In the United States, there are about 188 hours of violent programs per week (Fig. 8–10). Eighty-one percent of all programs contain violence, averaging 5.2 aggressive acts per hour (Huesmann & Eron, 1986). There are more gunshots fired in one evening of American TV than in one year in a medium-sized American city. Eighty-five percent of these shots fail to hit their targets, which makes it seem like violence typically does not end in bloodshed (Charren & Sandler, 1983). More than half of all music videos contain violence, and more than three-fourths of these violent videos include sexual imagery (Brown, 1986). TV law officers more often than not contribute to violence, rather than prevent it (Oskamp, 1984). Murder, robbery, kidnapping, and assault make up 85 percent of TV crimes. In real life, they total about 5 percent. On TV, law officers resolve the majority of criminal investigations with violent acts (Carlson, 1986).

Are the distortions and stereotypes of "TV land" cause for concern? It would seem so. In over 99 percent of all United States households, TV is practically a member of the family. Average TV viewing in America now exceeds 7 hours per day. If forced to choose between having indoor plumbing or television, many families would find it difficult to decide! Clearly, television is a major influence in the lives of most children and many adults (Oskamp, 1984).

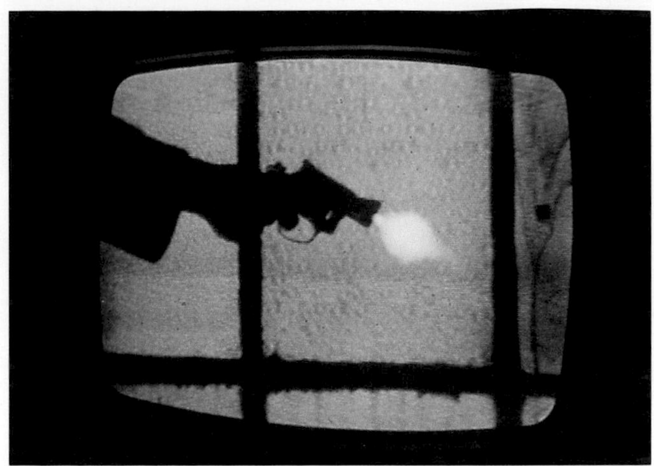

Fig. 8–10 *Televised violence may promote observational learning of aggression.*

Many psychologists are especially concerned about the effects of televised violence on children (see Highlight 8–2). Given the influence of television in Western societies, TV's impact as a model deserves further examination—something we will undertake in this chapter's Exploration.

Learning Check

1. Negative reinforcement increases responding; punishment suppresses responding. T or F?
2. Three factors that greatly influence the effects of punishment are timing, consistency, and ______________.
3. Mild punishment tends to only temporarily ______________ a response that is also reinforced.
   a. enhance *b.* aggravate *c.* replace *d.* suppress
4. Three undesired side effects of punishment are: (1) conditioning of fear and resentment, (2) encouragement of aggression, and (3) the learning of escape or ______________ responses.
5. In humans, extinction of a conditioned response can be influenced by expectation. T or F?
6. An internal representation of relationships is referred to as a ______________ ______________.
7. Learning that suddenly appears when a reward or incentive for performance is given is called
   a. discovery learning *b.* latent learning *c.* rote learning *d.* reminiscence
8. Psychologists use the term ______________ to describe observational learning.
9. If a model is successful, rewarded, attractive, or high in status, his or her behavior is
   a. difficult to reproduce *b.* less likely to be attended to *c.* more likely to be imitated *d.* subject to positive transfer
10. Children who observed a live adult behave aggressively became more aggressive; those who observed movie and cartoon aggression did not. T or F?

Answers:

1. T 2. intensity 3. *d* 4. avoidance 5. T 6. cognitive map 7. *b* 8. modeling 9. *c* 10. F

HIGHLIGHT 8–2
Life After TV: A Natural Experiment

North American children and adults spend the majority of their leisure time watching TV. What effect does this have on behavior? A recent study offers a fascinating look at life with the tube. A team of researchers found a town in northwestern Canada that did not receive TV broadcasts. Discovering that the town was about to get TV, the research team seized a rare opportunity. Tannis Williams and her team carefully tested residents of the town just before TV arrived and again 2 years later. This natural experiment revealed that after TV came to town:

- Reading development among children declined (Corteen & Williams, 1986).
- Children's scores on tests of creativity dropped (Harrison & Williams, 1986).
- Children's perceptions of sex roles became more stereotyped (Kimball, 1986).
- There was a significant increase in both verbal and physical aggression (Fig. 8–11). This occurred for both boys and girls, and it applied equally to children who were high or low in aggression before they began watching TV (Joy et al., 1986).

The last result comes as no surprise. Researchers have consistently found that television has a strong impact on aggression. In view of such findings, it is understandable that Canada, Norway, and Switzerland have restricted the amount of permissible violence on television (Levinger, 1986). Should this country do the same?

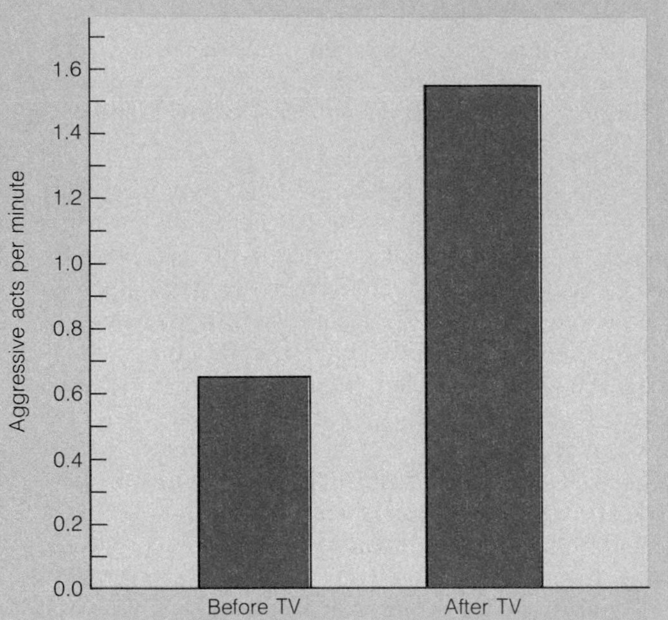

Fig. 8–11 *This graph shows the average number of aggressive acts per minute before and after television broadcasts were introduced into a Canadian town. The increase in aggression after television watching began was significant. Two other towns that already had television were used for comparison. Neither showed significant increases in aggression during the same time period. (Data compiled from Joy et al., 1986.)*

Learning Principles in Action—Biofeedback

Psychologists have discovered that humans can learn to control bodily activities once thought to be involuntary. For years, yoga and Zen masters have shown unusual control over heart rate, blood pressure, oxygen consumption, and temperature of parts of the body. Now we are finding that under the proper conditions, anyone can duplicate these seemingly impossible effects.

Electronic Yoga? By applying the principle of feedback to bodily control, we arrive at **biofeedback.** If I were to say to you, "Raise the temperature of your right hand," you probably couldn't, because you wouldn't know if you were succeeding. To make your task easier, we could attach a sensitive thermometer to your hand. The thermometer could be wired so that an increase in temperature would activate a signal light. Then, all you would have to do is try to keep the light on as much as possible. With practice and the help of biofeedback, you could learn to raise your hand temperature at will.

Question: If you succeed at raising hand temperature, what are you actually doing?

If asked to describe what you did, you might say, "I thought warm thoughts," or, "I just had a feeling when the light was on and I kept trying to recapture that feeling."

The point is that when you are given feedback, you can repeat successful responses, even if they are subtle. Biofeedback promotes learning by converting bodily processes into a clear signal that provides *information* about correct responses.

Question: Of what value is this?

Applications of Biofeedback

Biofeedback holds promise as a way to treat *psychosomatic problems* (illnesses caused mainly by stress or emotional factors) (Fig. 8–12). For example, Elmer and Alyce Green have successfully trained people to prevent migraine headaches with biofeedback. Sensors are taped to patients' hands and foreheads. Patients then learn to redirect blood flow away from the head to their extremities. Since migraine headaches are caused by excessive blood flow to the head, biofeedback equips patients to short-circuit headaches before they develop (Luce & Peper, 1971).

Early successes led many to predict that biofeedback would offer a cure for psychosomatic illnesses, anxiety, phobias, drug abuse, and a long list of other problems. In reality, biofeedback has proved helpful, but not an instant cure. Biofeedback can definitely relieve muscle-tension headaches and migraine headaches (Adler & Adler, 1976; Blanchard et al., 1982; Budzynski, 1977). It shows promise for lowering blood pressure and alleviating irregular heart rhythms (Blanchard et al., 1984; Kristt & Engel, 1975). The technique has even been used with some success to control epileptic seizures (Sterman, 1977).

Fig. 8–12 *Biofeedback training involving muscle tension and blood flow has been used to relieve headaches and to promote relaxation. Here, a biofeedback signal is routed back to the patient through headphones, allowing him to alter bodily activities.*

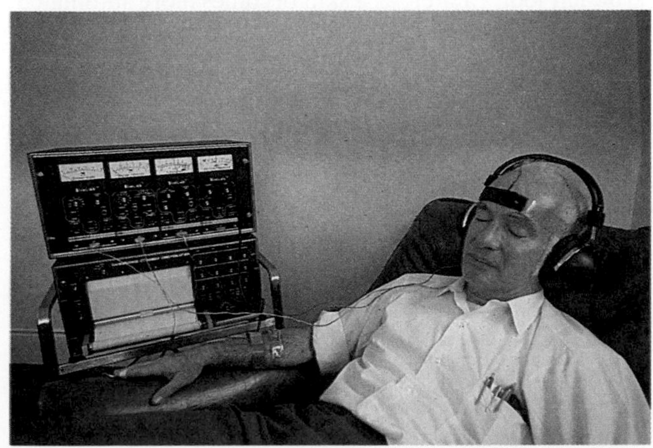

How does biofeedback help with such problems? Some researchers believe that many of its benefits arise from *general relaxation* (Blanchard & Epstein, 1978). Others stress that there is no magic in biofeedback itself. The method simply acts as a "mirror" to help a person perform tasks involving *self-regulation* (Green & Shellenberger, 1986; Norris, 1986). Just as a mirror does not comb your hair, biofeedback does not do anything by itself. It can, however, help people make desired changes in their behavior.

Biofeedback has special promise for the rehabilitation of people suffering from nerve damage, muscular disorders, and stroke (Orne, 1982). For example, Neal Miller (1985) tells of a child with an injury that paralyzed the child's hand. To help the child regain movement, electrodes were attached to the muscles in his arm. Each time the child managed to flex the right muscles, dots appeared on a computer screen. This feedback helped the boy learn to regain use of his hand.

Question: Does biofeedback apply to brain activity?

Alpha Control Alpha waves are one of several brain wave patterns that can be recorded with the EEG (electroencephalograph). Using an EEG, psychologist Joseph Kamiya developed a system that signals subjects with a tone or light whenever they produce alpha waves (Kamiya, 1968). Subjects in early alpha-control studies reported that high levels of alpha were linked with sensations of pleasure, relaxation, passive alertness, or peaceful images.

Some people looked on these findings as a potential avenue to "instant bliss." But more recently, serious questions have been raised about the use of alpha training to promote deep relaxation. Research has shown that for some people, increased alpha output is the product of relaxation; but for others, it occurs at times of *heightened* arousal (Orne & Wilson, 1978). For the moment, it seems that we have not yet reached the age of "electronic yoga." This is especially true of low-cost home "alpha-feedback" machines. These devices are so inaccurate that many "blissed out" users are actually listening to electrical noise from their house wiring, rather than their own brain waves (Beyerstein, 1985).

Learning Principles in Action—Learning Skills Skillfully

A **motor skill** is a series of actions molded into a smooth and efficient performance. Typing, walking, pole-vaulting, shooting baskets, playing golf, driving a car, writing, and skiing are examples of motor skills.

Question: How are motor skills learned?

Many begin as simple response chains. However, as skills improve, we typically develop **motor programs** for them (Blumenthal, 1976). Motor programs are mental plans or models of what a skilled movement should be like. A good example of this kind of learning was provided by a guitarist friend of the author's. The guitarist once cut the first finger of his right hand before a performance. Normally, he did his finger-picking with his thumb and first two fingers. How could he perform with an injured finger? No problem! He used the second and third fingers instead. His musical skills were in his head (as a motor program), not in his fingers (Fig. 8–13).

Question: How do motor programs guide movement?

To perform an action, such as walking, we use feedback from the body and senses to compare our actions to an internal ideal (or program). Such monitoring, plus rapid corrections, is what allows us to walk on ice, sand, rocks, and stairs with no loss of skill. Motor programs also underlie many sports skills. A basketball player, for instance, may never make exactly the same shot twice in a game. This makes it almost impossible to practice every shot that might occur. Instead, the skilled athlete learns a variety of general programs, not a collection of set responses (Klausmeir, 1975).

Fig. 8–13 *Strobe-light photograph of a motor skill. Multiple exposures reveal the complexity of skilled movement. Motor skills are guided by mental plans or programs.*

New skills usually require conscious guidance. Think of when you learned to ride a bicycle. Initially, almost all of your attention was focused on pedaling, steering, balancing, and braking; holding a conversation with another rider or watching the scenery was probably out of the question. However, as motor programs develop, we can pay less attention to specific movements (also see Chapter 5). Eventually, skills become *automated,* or nearly automatic. This frees higher brain centers to make decisions and attend to other information (Singer, 1978). Thus, a skilled biker or skier can enjoy the scenery, a knitter can talk or watch television, and a driver can tune the radio or think about things other than driving.

Skillful Skill Learning

Throughout life, you will face the challenge of learning new motor skills. How can psychology make your learning more effective? Research findings suggest that you should keep in mind the following points for optimal skill learning (Drowatzky, 1975; Gagne & Fleishman, 1959; Klausmeir, 1975; Meichenbaum, 1977; Singer, 1978.):

1. Begin by observing and imitating a *skilled model.* Modeling provides a good mental picture of the skill. At this point, try simply to grasp a visual image of the skilled movement.

2. Learn *verbal rules* to back up motor learning. Such rules are usually most helpful in the early phases of skill learning. When first learning cross-country skiing, for example, it is helpful to say, "left arm, right foot, right arm, left foot." Later, as a skill becomes more automated, internal speech may actually get in the way.

3. Practice should be as *lifelike* as possible so that artificial cues and responses do not become a part of the skill. A competitive diver should practice on the board, not on a trampoline. If you want to learn to ski, try to practice on snow, not straw.

4. Get *feedback* from a mirror, videotape, coach, or observer. Whenever possible, get someone experienced in the skill to direct attention to *correct responses* when they occur.

5. When possible, it is better to practice natural units rather than breaking the task into artificial parts. When learning to type, it is better to start with real words rather than nonsense syllables.

6. Learn to *evaluate* and *analyze* your own performance.

Remember, you are trying to learn a motor program, not just train your muscles. Motor skills are actually very mental.

The last point leads to one more suggestion. Research has shown that merely thinking about or imagining a skilled performance can aid learning (Annett, 1979; Kemeny & Maltzman, 1987). This technique, called **mental practice,** seems to help by refining motor programs. Although mental practice is better than no practice at all, it is still not better than actual practice. Also, the more familiar you are with a skill, the more mental rehearsal helps (Drowatzky, 1975; Meichenbaum, 1977). When you begin to get really good at a skill you are interested in, give mental practice a try. You may be surprised at how effective it can be.

Practice Effects It also helps to know that improving the performance of a motor skill is most rapid when short practice sessions are alternated with rest periods (Fig. 8–14). This pattern, called **spaced practice,** keeps fatigue and boredom to a minimum. It can also prevent the learner from practicing errors when tired. (Perfect practice makes perfect.)

The opposite of spaced practice is **massed practice,** in which little or no rest is given between learning sessions. Notice in Figure 8–14 that massed practice lowers performance during training. As you can also see, both massed and spaced practice produce similar amounts of learning after a short break in training. However, in the long run, skills learned with spaced practice are retained better than those learned by massed practice (Bouzid & Crawshaw, 1987; Drowatzky, 1975). This suggests that you should keep practice sessions short and well spaced if you are learning to type, use a computer, play a musical instrument, juggle, or master some other skill.

Transfer of Training Most skiing enthusiasts are familiar with the "graduated length method." In this approach, the beginning skier learns on short, easily managed skis and moves to longer skis as skill develops. This technique makes intuitive use of positive transfer. **Positive transfer** is said to have taken place when mastery of one task aids mastery of a second task. Another example would be learning to balance and turn on a bicycle before learning to ride a motorcycle or motorscooter.

Question: Is there such a thing as negative transfer?

There is indeed. In **negative transfer,** skills developed in one situation conflict with those required to master a new task. Learning to back a car with a trailer attached is a good example. Normally, when you are backing a car, the steering wheel is turned in the direction you want to go, the same as when moving forward. However, with a trailer attached, the steering wheel must be turned opposite from the direction you want the trailer to go. This situation results in negative transfer, and often creates comical scenes at campgrounds and boat launching ramps.

On a more serious note, many tragic crashes caused by negative transfer finally led to greater standardization of airplane cockpits. Fortunately, negative transfer is usually brief, and it occurs less often than positive transfer (Drowatzky, 1975). Negative transfer is most likely to occur when a new response must be made to an old stimulus. If you have ever encountered a pull-type handle on a door that must be pushed open, you will appreciate this final point.

So far, we have emphasized ways of enhancing learning. To turn things around a bit, the upcoming Applications section describes ways to break bad habits. While you probably have absolutely no bad habits of any kind, you may at least find some hints you can pass on to friends and relatives, who are curiously blind to their own faults.

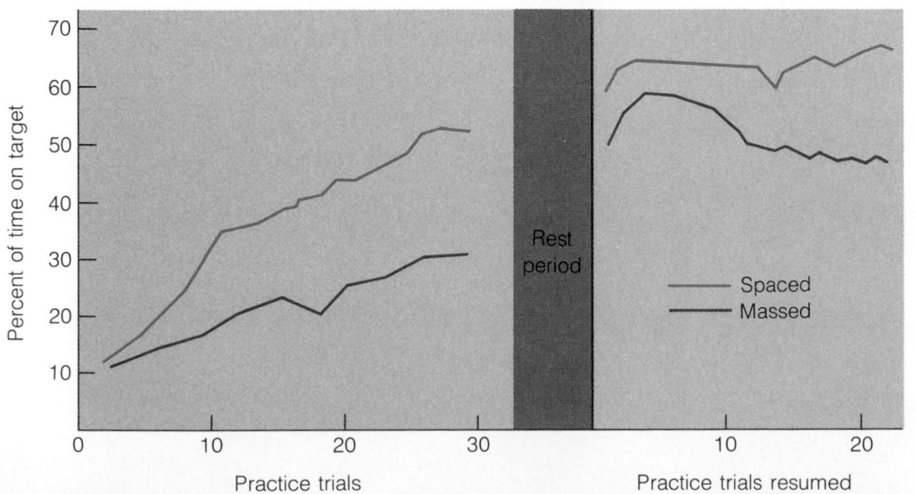

Fig. 8–14 *Performance curves for massed and spaced practice. Subjects learned to keep a pointer on a moving target. During the first learning session, the spaced-practice group performed better. After a rest period, performance was similar for both groups. However, further trials again lowered performance in the massed-practice group. (From Jones & Ellis, 1962.)*

Learning Check

1. Biofeedback is a type of meditation in which the body is made very quiet so that bodily functioning can be detected. T or F?
2. Two major elements of biofeedback training appear to be relaxation and self-regulation. T or F?
3. Biofeedback can definitely relieve
   a. depression *b.* diabetes *c.* stomach ulcers *d.* muscle-tension headaches
4. Joseph Kamiya developed a technique whereby subjects can gain control over the brain's production of ______________ ______________.
5. An important step in the mastery of many motor skills is achieved when the skill becomes
   a. reversible *b.* automated *c.* graduated *d.* fixed
6. Mental models, called ______________ ______________, appear to underlie well-learned motor skills.
7. In motor skill learning, massed practice generally produces performance that is superior to spaced practice. T or F?
8. Learning verbal rules to back up motor learning is usually most helpful in the early stages of acquiring a skill. T or F?

Answers:

1. F **2.** T **3.** *d* **4.** alpha waves **5.** *b* **6.** motor programs **7.** F **8.** T

Applications: Good Ways To Break Bad Habits

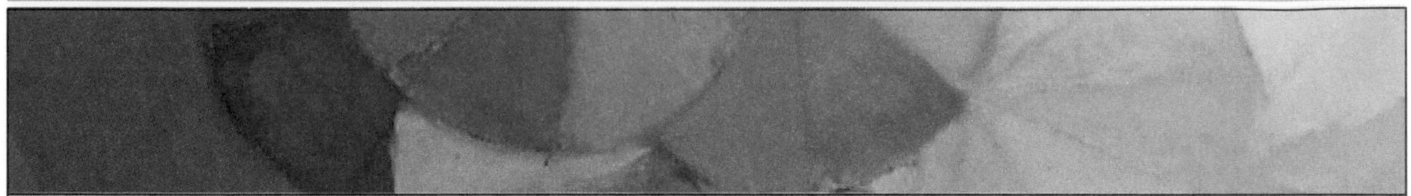

Question: How can I use learning principles to break a bad habit?

The following techniques offer some helpful possibilities. They combine ideas drawn from both this chapter and the preceding chapter.

Extinction

Try to discover what is reinforcing a response and remove, avoid, or delay the reinforcement.

Example: A student has developed a habit of taking longer and longer "breaks" when studying. Almost always, her breaks are lengthened by TV watching.

Comment: Obviously, watching TV is reinforcing more frequent break taking. To improve her study habits, the student could ask her roommate to act as a monitor to remind her that she cannot watch TV until her work is done. Or, she could require 2 hours of study from herself for each ½ hour of TV watching. She could delay reinforcement by making it a rule that she must do the dishes, some ironing, or another chore before turning on the TV.

Example: Pam has a slightly different problem. While reading in the evening, her periods of concentration last only about 15 minutes. They are usually followed by a trip to the kitchen for a snack. In addition to falling behind in her reading, she is gaining weight.

Comment: Snacking is rewarding her impulse to avoid reading. She should do her reading at school or at a library, so that there is a delay between the impulse to eat and the reward of snacking. At home, she should build in delays by keeping only foods that must be prepared to eat or by keeping only staples on hand, so that a separate trip to a store is required for "goodies." Requiring a walk around the block before eating a snack would also help delay reinforcement (Ferster et al., 1962).

Alternate Responses

Try to get the same reinforcement with new responses.

Example: A young mother realized she was yelling at her children more often than she would like. This habit seemed to be reinforced by the periods of relative quiet that followed when she raised her voice.

Comment: To avoid this habit (which is negatively reinforced), she should (as much as possible) ignore her children when they are noisy and should make a special effort to praise them, show approval, and pay attention to them when they are playing quietly and constructively. In this way, both she and the children get the same reinforcers (quite and attention) for new responses.

Example: Frank has been drinking increasing amounts of beer after getting home from work in the evening. He usually feels more relaxed but often drinks too much and gets into arguments with other family members.

Comment: Frank's need to "unwind" and dissipate the frustrations of the workday might be better achieved by participation in an athletic activity, such as jogging, swimming, bowling, handball, and so forth. An organized team sport might ensure that he will actually stick with his substitute activity.

Cues and Antecedents

Avoid or narrow down cues that elicit the bad habit.

Example: A student has begun to notice how much impulse buying he does at the grocery store. As a first step in avoiding this habit, he has begun to shop after he has had a meal because he has observed that hunger is a cue for his food buying.

Comment: He should also make a shopping list and stick to it. That way, he will look only at items he intends to buy and not at impulse items. If he knows that the candy isle is especially dangerous for him, he should avoid it entirely.

Example: A father has noticed that he nags and criticizes his 4-year-old son almost nightly because the boy pours ketchup all over his dinner. He is upset about this and other daily instances of criticizing the boy.

Comment: The father has identified one cue for his excessive criticizing. It could be avoided by giving the boy a small bowl of ketchup to prevent the regular dinner battle. Other cues for nagging can be avoided in similar ways as they are identified (Schmidt, 1976).

Applications

Example: Raul is not ready to give up smoking, but he would like to cut down. He has taken many smoking cues out of his daily routine by removing ashtrays, matches, and extra cigarettes from his house, car, and office. He also has been making an effort to avoid situations in which most of his smoking occurs by staying away from other smokers, taking a walk after meals (leaving his cigarettes at home), and putting a piece of gum in his mouth when he feels nervous.

Comment: To improve his control of smoking, Raul should try narrowing cues. He could begin by smoking only inside buildings, never outside or in his car. He could then limit his smoking to home. Then to only one room at home. Then to one chair at home. If he succeeds in getting this far, he may want to limit his smoking to only one uninteresting place, such as a bathroom, basement, or garage (Goldiamond, 1971).

Response Chains

Break response chains that precede an undesired behavior.

This is another strategy for controlling antecedents. The key idea is to scramble the chain of events that leads up to the undesired response (Watson & Tharp, 1981).

Example: Almost every night, Steve comes home, turns on the television, and drinks two or three colas while he eats nearly a whole bag of cookies or chips. He then takes a shower and changes. By dinner time he has lost his appetite. Steve realizes that he is substituting junk food for dinner. If he does eat dinner, he feels uncomfortably full.

Comment: Steve might solve the problem by simply showering immediately when he gets home or by not turning on the television until after dinner.

Incompatible Responses

Make an incompatible response in the presence of stimuli that usually precede the bad habit.

Example: A sprinter has developed a habit of "jumping the gun" at track meets and is frequently disqualified.

Comment: The sprinter should prepare for meets by remaining in the blocks while his coach fires the starter's pistol several times.

Example: A child has developed the habit of throwing her coat on the floor after coming in the front door. After being scolded, she would hang it up.

Comment: The parents should recognize that scolding has become the cue for hanging the coat up. The girl should not just be scolded, but should be required to put her coat on again, go outside, come in the door, and hang her coat up. Soon, coming in the door will become the cue for hanging the coat up.

Example: June bites her nails so much they are painful and unsightly. She has identified several situations in which she is most likely to bite her nails and would like to break the connection between these and her habit.

Comment: June should make a list of incompatible behaviors she can engage in when she has the urge to bite her nails. These might include putting her hands in her pockets, taking notes in class, sketching pictures, crossing her arms, leaning against something with her hands, chewing gum, playing a musical instrument, or combing her hair (Perkins & Perkins, 1976).

Negative Practice

Use negative practice to associate a bad habit with discomfort.

Example: Rick has a habit of saying "you know" or "uh" too often when speaking.

Comment: In negative practice, a response is repeated until it becomes boring, painful, or produces fatigue. This increases awareness of the habit and tends to discourage its recurrence. Rick should set aside 15 minutes a day and repeat the words "you know" and "uh" over and over while thinking, "I hate the way this sounds when someone else says it." He should repeat the errors until he would really very much like to stop making them.

Feedback

Utilizing feedback is one of the most direct of all approaches to changing bad habits.

Example: Four college students who are renting a house together are concerned about their high utility bills. Also, they would like to make an effort to conserve energy. To date, however, their good intentions have not lowered their electric bill.

Comment: The roommates should keep a daily record of their energy consumption by writing down and posting the numbers shown on their electric meter. A study of families given this kind of daily feedback showed that their energy use was greatly reduced (Palmer et al., 1977).

Putting It All Together

Like the examples we have covered, many problem behaviors respond to changes in the basic elements of learning. If you

Applications

would like to break a bad habit, pay close attention to *antecedents*, the *response* itself, and the *consequences* that follow the behavior. Here's a general plan for breaking a bad habit.

Habit Breaking, Step-by-Step

1. Identify the behavior you want to change. Be specific about what it is you do, say, or think that is undesirable or that bothers you.
2. Identify antecedents. For a week, make notes concerning stimuli that precede the behavior you want to change. Also, try to identify any response chains leading up to the undesired behavior. Include internal behaviors (thoughts) that occur before the undesired response, too.
3. Also note and record what happens immediately after the undesired behavior. Can you identify reinforcers maintaining the bad habit?
4. Write a plan for change, using suggestions from this Applications and the Exploration in Chapter 7. (Also, see Chapter 22 for additional strategies.) Look for ways to delay or remove reinforcers, or find ways to get them by making other (desired) responses. Avoid, narrow down, or remove the antecedent cues you identified. Also, try making incompatible responses to the cues. Scramble or rearrange antecedent response chains. Apply negative practice, if appropriate.
5. Continue to record how often the undesired response occurs, and revise your plan as needed.

The last point is worth emphasizing. As noted in Chapter 7, almost any habit will benefit from simply keeping score. Keep track of the number of times daily that you arrive late to class, smoke a cigarette, watch an hour of TV, drink a cup of coffee, bite your fingernails, swear, or whatever you are interested in changing. A simple tally on a piece of paper will do, or you can get a small mechanical counter like those used to keep golf scores or count calories. Record keeping alone helps break patterns, and the feedback can be motivating as you begin to make progress.

If You Still Have Trouble In this chapter and the preceding one, we have emphasized the application of learning theories to everyday problems. Many simple difficulties can be handled without special training. If, however, you have a really troublesome habit, such as overeating or excessive use of alcohol, cocaine, cigarettes, or marijuana, you may find it most expedient to consult a professional.

Learning Check

1. Removing or avoiding reinforcement of a bad habit can help eliminate it, but delaying reinforcement has no effect. T or F?

2. A mother who praises her children when they are quiet instead of yelling at them when they are noisy has received the same reinforcement for an alternate response. T or F?

3. Restricting smoking to only one room in a house is an example of using feedback to alter a bad habit. T or F?

4. To break the link between an undesired response and various situations in which it occurs, it can be helpful to practice making an incompatible response in the same situations. T or F?

5. In negative practice, we learn to avoid or narrow down cues that elicit a bad habit. T or F?

Answers:
1. F 2. T 3. F 4. T 5. F

Exploration: Modeling and Television—The Tube as Teacher

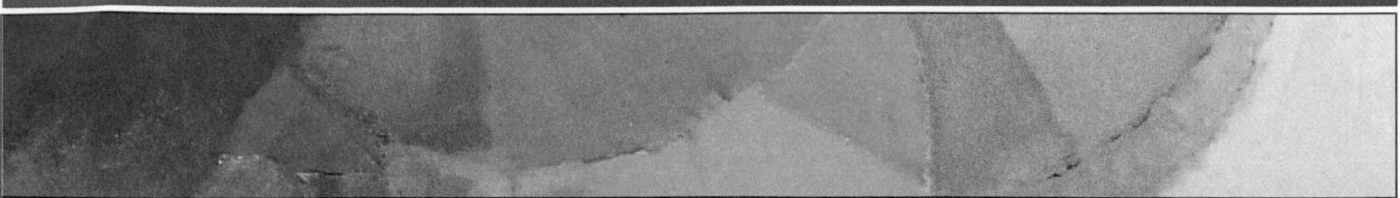

The impact of TV can be found in these figures: By the time the average person has graduated from high school, he or she will have viewed some 15,000 hours of TV, compared with only 11,000 hours spent in the classroom. In that time, such viewers will have seen some 18,000 murders and countless acts of robbery, arson, bombing, torture, and beatings (Oskamp, 1984). It's true that TV programming in the United States has improved somewhat during the last decade. Programs such as "The Bill Cosby Show" have helped bring a needed balance to prime time. Overall, however, violent acts, dynamite blasts, gun battles, high-speed car wrecks, stereotypes, and sexism still prevail (Eron, 1986; Palmer, 1987).

Question: Earlier, the effects of observational learning were described. Do they apply to TV violence?

Television and Aggression Where the effects of TV violence on children are concerned, the answer appears to be yes. At this point, hundreds of studies, involving well over 10,000 children, have been completed. The vast majority point to the same conclusion: "If large groups of children watch a great deal of televised violence, they will be more prone to behave aggressively" (Comstock et al., 1978; Joy et al., 1986; Levinger, 1986; Liebert et al., 1973; National Institute of Mental Health, 1982; Rubinstein, 1978). In other words, not all children will become more aggressive, but many will.

Question: How does TV violence affect children?

As Albert Bandura showed in his Bo-Bo doll study, children may learn new aggressive actions by watching violent or aggressive behavior, or they may learn that violence is "okay." Either way, they are more likely to act aggressively. It is important to remember that younger children do not grasp the nuances of TV plots. A child may simply remember that when good guys were bothered in some way by others, they aggressed. Heroes on TV are as violent as the villains, and they usually receive praise for their violence. TV dramas tend to give the message that violence leads to success and popularity.

Psychologists Rowell Huesmann and Neil Malamuth (1986) believe that habitual aggression is mostly learned during the first 10 years of life. By then, aggression becomes a set style of behavior that is very hard to change. Aggression is most likely to become a child's dominant style if the child's environment provides aggressive models and reinforces aggression. Just as children may learn by observation to throw a baseball, so too may they learn to hit others who bother them.

In addition to encouraging imitation of aggression, TV violence tends to lower sensitivity to violent acts. As anyone who has seen a street fight or a mugging can tell you, TV violence is sanitized and unrealistic. The real thing is gross, ugly, and gut-wrenching. Even when it is graphic, TV violence is viewed in the relaxed and familiar setting of the home. For at least some viewers, this combination diminishes emotional reactions to violent scenes. When Victor Cline and his associates showed a bloody fight film to a group of boys, they found that heavy TV viewers (averaging 42 hours a week) showed much less emotion than those who watched little or no TV (Cline et al., 1972).

Television, it seems, can cause a *desensitization* to violence. In another study, college men saw five R-rated slasher films that depicted violence against women. The men consistently reported lower levels of anxiety when viewing the last film as compared with the first (Lintz et al., 1984). (See Chapter 22 for more on desensitization and Chapter 24 for information on sexual violence in the media.)

Question: Is it fair to say, then, that televised violence causes aggression in viewers, especially children?

No. That would be an exaggeration. Televised violence can make aggression more *likely,* but it does not invariably "cause" it to occur (Freedman, 1984; Levinger, 1986). Many other factors affect the chances that hostile thoughts will be turned into actions (Berkowitz, 1984). Among children, one such factor is the extent to which a child *identifies* with aggressive characters (Huesmann et al., 1983). That's why it is so sad to find TV *heroes* behaving aggres-

Exploration

sively, as well as villains. Youngsters who believe that aggression is an acceptable way to solve problems, who believe that TV portrayals of violence are realistic, and who identify with TV characters are most likely to copy televised aggression (Eron, 1986).

Question: Couldn't TV's impact also be used constructively?

TV as a Positive Model There is no denying TV's tremendous power to inform and to entertain. When these features are combined, as they were in specials such as *Roots* or *Holocaust*, the effect can be quite constructive. Perhaps the best examples of TV as a positive social force are the educational programs "Sesame Street," "The Electric Company," and "Mr. Rogers' Neighborhood." Over 150 research reports have dealt with the impact of these programs. An overwhelming majority of these evaluations are positive. Clearly, television can teach children while holding their interest and attention (Rubinstein, 1978).

As a model for prosocial attitudes and responses, TV could be used to promote helping, cooperation, charity, and brotherhood in the same way that it has tended to stereotype and encourage aggression. Over 200 studies have now shown that prosocial behavior on TV increases prosocial behavior by viewers (Hearold, 1987). To illustrate, children in one experiment watched a TV program that emphasized helping (a "Lassie" episode). Later, these children were more willing than others to help a puppy in distress, even when it meant skipping a chance to win prizes (Rubinstein et al., 1974).

Buffering Television's Impact
Other than pulling the plug, what can parents do about television's negative effects on children? Actually, quite a lot. Children typically model parents' TV viewing habits, and they are guided by parents' reactions to programs. Parents can make a big difference if they do the following (Eron, 1986; Huesmann, 1986; Schneider, 1987).

Parents as TV Guides

1. Limit total viewing time so that television does not dominate your child's view of the world. If necessary, set schedules for when watching TV is allowed.
2. Closely monitor what your child does watch. Change channels or turn off the TV if you object to a program. Be prepared to offer games and activities that stimulate your child's imagination and creativity.
3. Actively seek programs your child will enjoy, especially those that model positive behavior and social attitudes.
4. Watch television with your child so that you can counter what is shown. Help your child distinguish between reality and TV fantasies. Reply to distortions and stereotypes as they appear on screen.
5. Discuss the social conflicts and violent solutions shown on television. Ask your child in what ways the situations are unrealistic and why the violence shown would not work in the real world. Encourage the child to propose more mature, realistic, and positive responses to situations.
6. Show by your own disapproval that violent TV heroes are not the ones to emulate. Remember, children who identify with TV characters are more likely to be influenced by televised aggression.

By following these guidelines you can help children learn to enjoy television without being overly influenced by programs and advertisers.

Think About It Almost since the first TVs blinked to life in living rooms across the country, television has been damned and defended, praised and put down. In view of our discussion, you might want to think about these questions: Why is so much violence shown on TV? Do you think your views or behavior have been influenced by TV? Given what you know about modeling, what changes would you make in TV programming? Would others watch the programs you propose? Would you?

Learning Check

1. Children are most likely to imitate TV characters with whom they identify, but this applies only to characters who are nonviolent. T or F?

2. Heavy exposure to television appears to result in lowered emotional sensitivity to violence. T or F?

3. Psychological research indicates that televised violence causes aggressive behavior in children. T or F?

4. Research indicates that positive actions portrayed on television have little or no effect on viewers. T or F?

Answers:
1. F **2.** T **3.** F **4.** F

Chapter Summary

• Many real-world situations involve **two-factor learning,** a combination of classical conditioning and operant conditioning.
• From an **informational view,** conditioning creates **expectancies,** which alter response patterns. In classical conditioning, the CS creates an expectancy that the US will follow. Learning in operant conditioning is based on the expectation that a response will have a specific effect.
• **Feedback,** or **knowledge of results,** aids learning and improves performance. It is most effective when it is **immediate, detailed,** and **frequent.**
• **Programmed instruction** breaks learning into a series of small steps and provides immediate feedback. **Computer-assisted instruction (CAI)** does the same, but has the added advantage of providing alternative exercises and information when needed. Three variations of CAI are **drill and practice, instructional games,** and **educational simulations.**
• **In positive reinforcement,** reward (a pleasant event) follows a response. In **negative reinforcement,** a response that ends discomfort becomes more likely. **Punishment** decreases responding. Punishment occurs when a response is followed by the onset of an aversive event or by the removal of a positive event **(response cost)**.
• Punishment is most effective when it is **immediate, consistent,** and **intense. Mild punishment** tends only to temporarily suppress responses that are also reinforced or were acquired by reinforcement.
• The undesirable side effects of punishment include the **conditioning of fear** to punishing agents and situations associated with punishment; the learning of **escape** and **avoidance responses;** and the encouragement of **aggression.**
• **Cognitive learning** involves higher mental processes, such as understanding, knowing, or anticipating. Even in relatively simple learning situations, animals and people seem to form **cognitive maps** (internal representations of relationships). In **latent learning,** learning remains hidden or unseen until a reward or incentive for performance is offered. **Discovery learning** emphasizes insight and understanding, in contrast to **rote learning.**
• Much human learning is achieved through observation, or modeling. **Modeling (observational learning)** is influenced by many factors, especially the personal characteristics of the model and the success or failure of the model's behavior. Studies have shown that aggression is readily learned and released by modeling.
• During **biofeedback training,** bodily processes are monitored and converted to a signal that indicates what the body is doing. With practice, biofeedback allows alteration of many bodily activities. It shows promise for the alleviation of some stress-related illnesses. Its long-term effectiveness is still being evaluated. The usefulness of **alpha control** (voluntary control of brain waves) is debatable.
• **Motor skills** are nonverbal response chains assembled into a smooth performance. Motor skills are guided by internal mental models called **motor programs.** Motor skill learning is usually best when practice is **spaced,** rather than **massed.** Depending on the relationship between prior learning and a new task, motor skills may show **positive transfer** or **negative transfer** (carryover to a new situation).
• Bad habits can be managed by controlling the **antecedents** and **consequences** of undesired responses. Helpful strategies focus on **extinction, alternate responses, cues** and **antecedents, response chains, incompatible responses, negative practice,** and **feedback.**
• Televised violence increases the likelihood of aggression by viewers. Television violence models and teaches aggression and **desensitizes** viewers to violence. Television can also promote **prosocial behavior.** By guiding children's viewing and by discussing what is shown, parents can reduce the negative impact of television programs.

Questions For Discussion

1. Can you think of anything that you do that is not affected in some way by learning?
2. How could you include more feedback or more immediate feedback in your study habits?
3. If you could change procedures to enhance learning in an elementary school classroom, what would you do? What changes would you make in a high school classroom.

4. Corporal punishment has been banned in many schools. In your opinion, what would be the pros and cons of banning corporal punishment in homes?

5. Draw a map of your school's campus as you picture it now. Draw a map of the campus as you pictured it after your first visit. How does the second map differ from the first?

6. Describe a behavior you learned by observation. What were the advantages of learning in this way? What were the disadvantages? What changes would have made the model you observed more effective?

7. Choose a bad habit you would like to break. How could you apply the principles discussed in this chapter to breaking the habit?

8. What incompatible responses can you think of that could be performed in public to prevent the following behaviors: smoking, knuckle cracking, swearing, fingernail biting, hand wringing, eyelash plucking?

9. How would you explain the many distortions of commercial television programs? Do you think that people watch television because of such distortions or in spite of them?

10. In your opinion, should TV programs come with a violence rating scale or a rating system like that used for movies? What, if anything, would you suggest be done about the quality of TV programs and the amount of violence they contain?

Chapter 9

Memory

In This Chapter
- Stages of memory
- Short-term memory
- Long-term memory
- Measures of memory
- Exceptional memory
- Theories of forgetting
- Forming memories
- How to improve memory

Applications
- Mnemonic systems

Exploration
- Types of long-term memory

Chapter Preview

"What the Hell's Going On Here?"

February, 1978. Steven Kubacki is cross-country skiing on the ice of Lake Michigan. He stops for a moment, pausing to enjoy the winter solitude. It's cold; colder in fact than he had realized. Steven decides to turn back. In a few minutes comes a new realization: He is lost. Wandering on the ice, he grows numb and very, very tired.

Put yourself in Steven Kubacki's shoes, and you will appreciate the shock of what happened next. Steven clearly recalls wandering lost and alone on the ice. Immediately after that, he remembers waking up in a field. But as he looked around, Steven knew something was wrong. It was spring! The backpack beside him contained running shoes, swimming goggles, and a pair of glasses—all unfamiliar. As he looked at his clothing—also unfamiliar—Steven thought to himself, "What the hell's going on here?" Fourteen months had passed since he left to go skiing (Loftus, 1980). How did he get to the field? Where did the strange gear come from? Steven couldn't say. He had lost over a year of his life to total amnesia.

As Steven Kubacki's amnesia vividly shows, life without memory would be meaningless. Imagine the terror and confusion of having all of your memories wiped out, from birth to the present. You would have no identity, no knowledge, no life history, no recognition of friends or family. Your past would be a total blank. In a very real sense, we are our memories.

This chapter discusses memory and forgetting. As an inquiring person, you should find the information interesting. Also included is a large section on improving memory skills. As a student, you should find this discussion particularly helpful. Almost anyone (including you) can learn to use memory more effectively.

Survey Questions

- How do we store information in memory?
- Is there more than one type of memory?
- How is memory measured?
- What are "photographic" memories?
- What causes forgetting?
- How accurate are everyday memories?
- How can memory be improved?

Stages of Memory—Do You Have a Mind Like a Steel Trap? Or a Sieve?

"A dusty storehouse of facts." That's how many people think of memory. In reality, **memory** is an *active system* that receives, stores, organizes, alters, and recovers information. In some ways memory acts like a computer (Fig. 9–1). Information to be recorded is first **encoded,** or changed into a usable form. This step is like typing data into a computer. Next, information is **stored,** or held in the system. (As we will see in a moment, human memory actually has three separate storage systems.) Finally, memories must be **retrieved,** or taken out of storage, to be useful. To remember something, encoding, storage, and retrieval all must take place.

Question: What are the three separate memory systems just mentioned?

Psychologists have identified three stages of memory. To be stored for a long time, information must pass through all three (Fig. 9–2).

Sensory Memory Let's say a friend asks you to pick up several things at a market. How do you remember them? Incoming information first enters **sensory memory.** Sensory memory holds an exact copy of what is seen or heard for a few seconds or less. For instance, if you look at an object and then close your eyes, an **icon** (EYE-kon), or fleeting image, will persist for about ½ second afterward (Klatzky, 1980). Without sensory memory, a movie would look like a sequence of still pictures. Similarly, information you hear is held as a brief **echo** in sensory memory for up to 2 seconds (Klatzky, 1980). In general, sensory memory holds information just long enough to transfer it to the second memory system.

Short-Term Memory Not everything seen or heard is kept in memory. Let's say a radio is playing in the background as your friend reads you her shopping list. Do you remember what the announcer says too? Probably not, because *selective attention* (discussed in Chapters 4 and 5) determines what information moves on to **short-term memory (STM).** Short-term memories are also brief, but longer than sensory memories. Attending to your friend's words will place the shopping list in short-term memory (while allowing you to ignore the voice on the radio saying, "Buy Burpo Butter").

Question: How are short-term memories encoded?

Short-term memories can be stored as images. But more often, they are stored by *sound,* especially in recalling words and letters (Klatzky, 1980) If you are introduced to Tim at a party and you forget his name, you are more likely to call him by a name that *sounds like* Tim (Jim, for instance) than a name that sounds different, such as Bob or Tod. Your friend with the shopping list will be

Fig. 9–1 *In some ways, a computer acts like a mechanical memory system. Both systems process information, and both allow encoding, storage, and retrieval of data.*

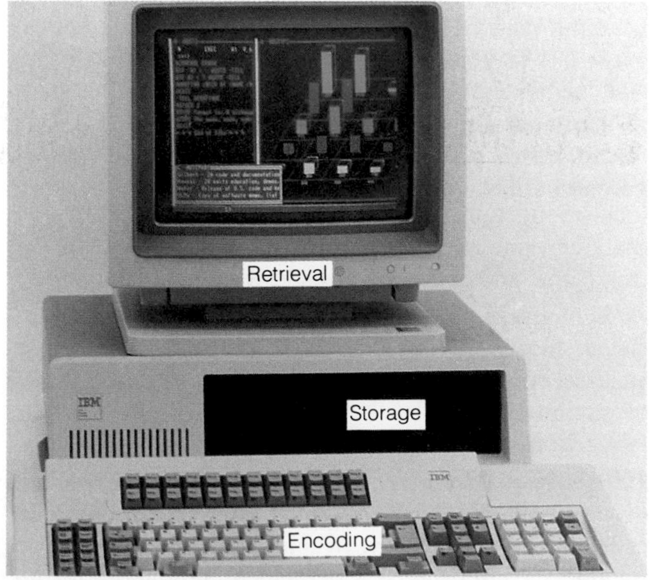

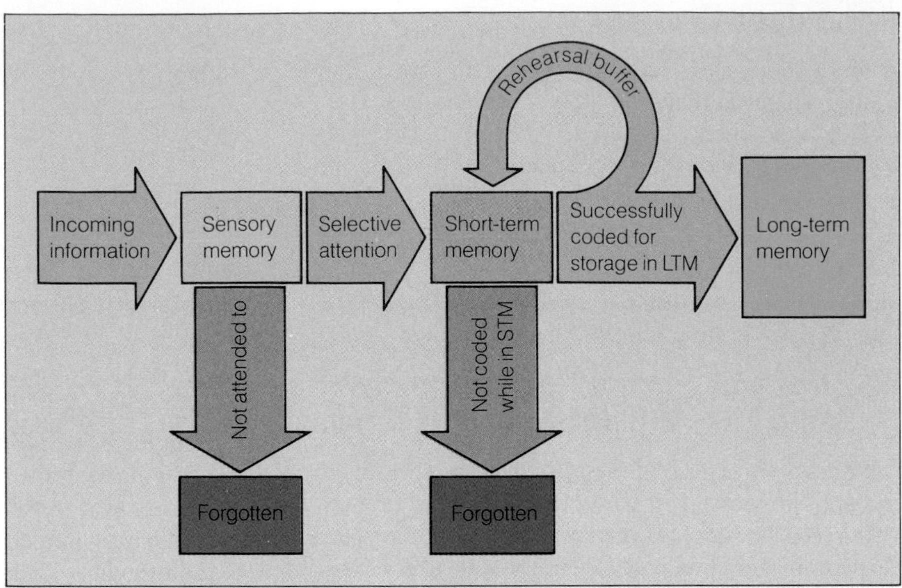

Fig. 9–2 *Memory is thought to involve at least three steps. Incoming information is first held for a second or two by sensory memory. Information selected by attention is then transferred to temporary storage in short-term memory. If new information is not rapidly encoded, or rehearsed, it is forgotten. If it is transferred to long-term memory, it becomes relatively permanent, although retrieving it may be a problem. The preceding is a useful* model *of memory; it may not be literally true of what happens in the brain.*

lucky if you don't bring home peas instead of cheese and soap instead of soup!

Short-term memory acts as a *temporary* storehouse for *small amounts* of information. Unless the information is important, it is quickly "dumped" from STM and forever lost. Short-term memory prevents our minds from collecting useless names, dates, telephone numbers, and other trivia (Miller, 1964). At the same time, it provides a **working memory** where we do much of our thinking. Dialing a phone number, doing mental arithmetic, remembering a shopping list, and the like, all rely on STM (Atkinson & Shriffrin, 1971).

As you may have noticed when dialing a telephone, STM is very sensitive to *interruption*, or *interference* (Adams, 1967). You've probably had this happen with STM: You look up a number and walk to the phone repeating it to yourself. You dial the number and get a busy signal. Returning a few minutes later, you find that you must look up the number again. This time as you are about to dial, someone asks you a question. You answer, turn to the phone, and find that you have forgotten the number.

Question: If short-term memory is brief, easily interrupted, and limited in "size," how do we remember for greater lengths of time?

Long-Term Memory Information that is important or *meaningful* is transferred to the third memory system, called long-term memory. In contrast to STM, **long-term memory (LTM)** acts as a permanent storehouse for information. LTM contains everything you know about the world—from aardvark to zucchini, math to Monopoly, facts to fantasy. And yet, there appears to be no danger of running out of room in LTM. LTM has a nearly limitless storage capacity (Klatzky, 1980).

Question: Are long-term memories also encoded as sounds?

No. Information in LTM is stored on the basis of *meaning* and importance, not by sound. If you make an error in LTM, it will probably be related to meaning. For example, if you are trying to recall the word BARN from a memorized list, you are more likely to mistakenly say SHED or FARM than BORN.

When new information enters STM, it is related to knowledge stored in LTM. This gives the new information meaning and makes it easier to store in LTM. As an example, try to memorize this story:

> With hocked gems financing him, our hero bravely defied all scornful laughter. "Your eyes deceive," he had said, "An egg, not a table, correctly typifies this unexplored planet." Now three sturdy sisters sought proof. Forging along, days became weeks as many doubters spread fearful rumors about the edge. At last from nowhere welcome winged creatures appeared, signifying momentous success. (Adapted from Dooling & Lachman, 1971)

This story emphasizes the impact of meaning on memory. People given the title of the story were able to remember it far better than those not given a title. See if the title helps you as much as it did them. The title is "Columbus Discovers America."

Compare: Memory Systems

Sensory memory The first stage of memory, which holds an explicit and literal record of incoming information for a few seconds or less.

Short-term memory The memory system used to hold small amounts of information for relatively brief time periods.

Working memory Another name for short-term memory, especially as it is used for thinking and problem solving.

Long-term memory Memory system used for the relatively permanent storage of meaningful information.

Dual Memory Most of our daily memory chores are handled by STM and LTM. To summarize their connection, picture short-term memory as a small desk at the front of a huge warehouse full of filing cabinets (LTM). As information enters the warehouse, it is first placed on the desk. Since the desk is small, it must be quickly cleared off to make room for new information. Some items are simply tossed away because they are unimportant. Meaningful or important information is placed in the permanent files (long-term memory).

When we want to use knowledge from LTM to answer a question, the information is returned to STM. Or, in our analogy, a folder is taken out of the files (LTM) and moved to the desk (STM), where it can be used. (Computer users may prefer to think of STM as being like RAM and LTM as being like a hard disk.)

Now that you have a general picture of STM and LTM it is time to explore both in more detail. The discussions that follow should add to your understanding.

Learning Check

Match: **A.** Sensory memory **B.** STM **C.** LTM

1. ________ Working memory

2. ________ Holds information for a few seconds or less

3. ________ Stores an icon or echo

4. ________ Permanent, unlimited capacity

5. ________ Temporarily holds small amounts of information

6. ________ Selective attention determines its contents

7. STM is improved by interruption, or interference, because attention is more focused at such times. T or F?

Answers:

1. B 2. A 3. A 4. C 5. B 6. B 7. F

Short-Term Memory—Do You Know the Magic Number?

Question: How much information can be held in short-term memory?

For an answer, read the following numbers once. Then close the book and write as many as you can in the correct order.

8 5 1 7 4 9 3

This is called a **digit-span test.** If you were able to correctly repeat this series of 7 digits, you have an average short-term memory. Now try to memorize the following list of digits, reading them only once.

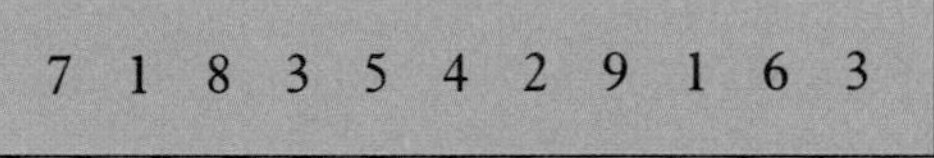

This series was probably beyond your short-term memory capacity. Psychologist George Miller has shown that short-term memory is limited to what he calls the "magic number" **7** (plus or minus 2) **bits** of information (Miller, 1956). A *bit* is a single "piece" of information—a single digit, for example. It is as if short-term memory has 7 "slots" or "bins" into which separate items can be placed.

When all of the "slots" in STM are filled, there is no room for new information (Klatzky, 1980). Picture how this works at a party. Let's say your hostess begins introducing everyone who is there: "Ted, Barbara, Donna, Roseanna, Wayne, Shawn, Linda. . . ." "Stop," you think to yourself. But she continues: "Eddie, Jay, Gordon, Frank, Marietta, Dan, Patty, Glen, Ricky." The hostess leaves, satisfied that you have met everyone. And you spend the evening talking with Ted, Barbara, and Ricky, the only people whose names you remember!

Recoding Before we continue, try your short-term memory again, this time on letters. Read the following letters once, then look away and try to write them in the proper order.

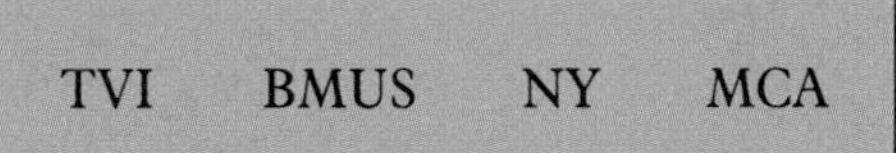

Notice that there are 12 letters, or "bits" of information. This should be beyond the 7-item limit of STM. However, since the letters are presented as 4 groups, or **chunks** of information, many students are able to memorize them.

Question: How does chunking help?

Chunking **recodes** information into larger units. Most often, it does so by taking advantage of units already in LTM. For example, you may have noticed that NY is the abbreviation for New York. If so, the bits N and Y became one chunk. In a memory experiment that used lists like this one, subjects remembered best when the letters were read as familiar meaningful chunks: TV, IBM, USN, YMCA (Bower & Springston, 1970). If you recoded the letters this way, you undoubtedly remembered the entire list.

Chunking suggests that STM holds about 7 of whatever units we are using, be they numbers, letters, words, phrases, or familiar sentences (Klatzky, 1980). Picture STM as a small desk again. Through chunking, we combine several items into one "stack" of information. This allows us to place 7 stacks on the desk, where before there was only room for 7 separate items.

Question: How long do short-term memories last?

Rehearsal Short-term memories appear to weaken and disappear very rapidly. However, a short-term memory can be prolonged by silently repeating it until it is needed. Remembering a telephone number you intend to use only once is often done this way.

Keeping a short-term memory alive by silently repeating it is called **rehearsal.** The longer a short-term memory is rehearsed, the greater its chances of being stored in LTM. What if rehearsal is prevented, so a memory cannot be recycled or moved to LTM? Without rehearsal, STM is incredibly short.

> In one experiment, subjects heard meaningless syllables like XAR followed by a number like 67. As soon as subjects heard the number, they began counting backward by threes (to prevent them from repeating the syllable.) After only 18 seconds of delay, memory scores fell to zero. (Peterson & Peterson, 1959)

After *18 seconds* without rehearsal, the short-term memories were gone forever! Keep this in mind when you get only one chance to hear information you want to remember. For example, if you are introduced to someone, and his or her name slips out of STM, there is no way to retrieve it. To escape this awkward situation you might try saying something like, "I'm curious, how do you spell your name?" But unfortunately, the response is often an icy reply like, "B-O-B S-M-I-T-H, it's really not too difficult." To avoid embarrassment, pay careful attention to the name, repeat it to yourself several times, and try to use it in the next sentence or two—before you lose it.

Long-Term Memory—Where the Past Lives

An electrode was placed at location number 11 on the patient's brain. She immediately said, "Yes, sir, I think I heard a mother calling her little boy somewhere. It seemed to be something happening years ago. It was somebody in the neighborhood where I live." A short time later the electrode was applied to the same spot. Again the patient said, "Yes, I hear the same familiar sounds, it seems to be a woman calling, the same lady" (Penfield, 1958). These statements were made by a woman undergoing brain surgery for epilepsy. Only local anesthetics were used (there are no pain receptors in the brain), so the patient was awake as her brain was electrically stimulated (Fig. 9–3). When activated, some brain areas seemed to produce vivid memories of long-forgotten events.

Question: Does this mean that every experience a person has ever had is recorded in memory?

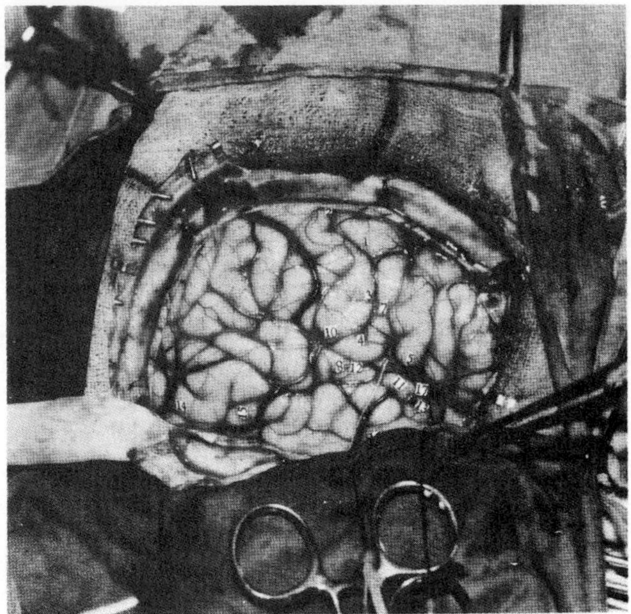

Fig. 9–3 *Exposed cerebral cortex of a patient undergoing brain surgery. Numbers represent points that reportedly produced "memories" when electrically stimulated. A critical evaluation of such reports suggests that they are more like dreams than memories. This fact raises questions about claims that long-term memories are permanent. (From Wilder Penfield,* The Excitable Cortex in Conscious Man, *1958. Courtesy of the author and Charles C Thomas, Publisher, Springfield, Illinois.)*

Permanence Results like those described led neurosurgeon Wilder Penfield to claim that the brain records the past like a "continuous strip of movie film, complete with sound track" (Penfield, 1957). But as you now know, this is an exaggeration. Many events never get past short-term memory. More importantly, in only about 3 percent of cases does brain stimulation produce memorylike experiences. Most reports resemble dreams more than memories, and many are clearly fictional. Memory experts Elizabeth and Geoffrey Loftus have carefully examined Penfield's work as well as research on "truth serums" and hypnosis. They conclude that there is little evidence that long-term memories are absolutely permanent (Loftus & Loftus, 1980). It is probably more accurate to say that long-term memories are *relatively* permanent, or long lasting.

Constructing Memories There is another reason to doubt Penfield's claim. As new long-term memories are formed, older memories are often updated, changed, lost, or *revised* (Cofer, 1975). To illustrate this point, Loftus and Palmer (1974) showed subjects a filmed automobile accident. Afterward, some subjects were asked to estimate how fast the cars were going when they "smashed" into each other. For others the words "bumped," "contacted," or "hit" replaced "smashed." One week later, subjects were asked, "Did you see any broken glass?" Those asked earlier about the cars that "smashed" into each other were more likely to say yes. (No broken glass was shown in the film.) The new information ("smashed") was included in subjects' memories and altered them.

Updating memories is called **constructive processing.** Research shows that gaps in memory, which are common, may be filled in by logic, guesses, or new information (Loftus, 1977, 1980). Indeed, it is possible to have "memories" for things that never happened (such as remembering broken glass at an accident when there was none). People in Elizabeth Loftus' experiments who had these **pseudo-memories** (false memories) were often quite upset to learn they had given false "testimony" (Loftus, 1980).

The updating of long-term memory is a common problem in police work. For example, a witness may select a photo of a suspect from police files or see a photo in the news. Later, the witness identifies the suspect in person (in a lineup or in court). Did the witness really remember the suspect from the scene of the crime? Or was it from the more recently seen photograph? Even if the suspect is innocent, he or she may be "remembered" as the criminal. It is quite possible for a photo to update or *blend* with the original memory. Many tragic cases of mistaken identity have occurred in this way.

Question: Couldn't hypnosis be used to avoid such problems?

News stories often give the impression that it can. Is this true? For an answer, see Highlight 9–1.

Organization Long-term memory may record 1 quadrillion separate bits of information in a lifetime (Asimov, 1967). How is it possible, then, to quickly find specific memories? The answer is that each person's "memory index" is highly organized.

Question: Do you mean that information is arranged alphabetically, as in a dictionary?

Not a chance! If I ask you to name a black and white animal that lives on ice, is related to a chicken, and cannot fly, you don't have to go from aardvark to zebra to find the answer. You will probably only think of black and white birds living in the Arctic. Which of these cannot fly? *Voila,* the answer is penguin.

The arrangement of information in LTM may be based on rules, images, categories, symbols, similarity, formal meaning, or personal meaning (Atkinson & Shiffrin, 1971). In recent years, psychologists have begun to develop a picture of the **structure,** or arrangement, of memories. One example will serve to illustrate this research.

You are given the following two statements, to which you must answer yes or no: *A canary is an animal. A canary is a bird.* Which do you answer more quickly? Collins and Quillian (1969) found that *A canary is a bird* produced a faster yes than *A canary is an animal.* Why should this be so? Collins and Quillian believe that a **network model** of memory explains why. According to them, LTM is organized as a network of linked ideas (Fig. 9–4). When ideas are "farther" apart, it takes a longer chain of associations to connect them. The more two items are separated, the longer it takes to answer. In other words, *canary* is probably close to *bird* in your "memory files." *Animal* and *canary* are farther apart. Remember, though, this has nothing to do with alphabetical order. We are talking about organization based on related meanings.

Psychologists still have much to learn about the nature of long-term memory. For now, one thing stands out clearly: People who have good memories excel at organizing information and making it meaningful (Mandler, 1968). With this in mind, the Applications for this chapter tells how you can use organization and meaning to improve your memory.

● HIGHLIGHT 9–1
Hypnosis, Imagination, and Memory

In 1976, near Chowchilla, California, 26 children were abducted from a school bus and held captive for a ransom. Under hypnosis, the bus driver recalled the license plate number of the kidnappers' van. This memory helped break the case and led to the children's rescue. Such successes seem to imply that hypnosis can improve memory. But does it? Read on, and judge for yourself.

Research has shown that a hypnotized person is more likely than normal to use imagination to fill in gaps in memory. Also, when hypnotized subjects are given false information, they tend to weave it into their memories (Sheehan et al., 1984). It has been shown that "leading" questions asked during hypnosis can alter memories (Sanders & Simmons, 1983). And even when a memory is completely false, the hypnotized person's confidence in it can be unshakable (Laurence & Perry, 1983). Most telling of all is the fact that hypnosis increases false memories more than it does true ones. Eighty percent of the new memories produced by hypnotized subjects in one experiment were *incorrect* (Dywan & Bowers, 1983).

Overall, it can be concluded that hypnosis does not greatly improve memory (Kihlstrom, 1985). Even when hypnosis uncovers more information, there is no way to tell which memories are true and which are false. Clearly, hypnosis is not the "magic bullet" against forgetting that some police investigators hoped it would be.

Learning Check

1. The digit-span test is commonly used to measure LTM. T or F?

2. There is evidence that STM lasts about 18 seconds, without rehearsal. T or F?

3. Information can be held indefinitely in STM by
a. chunking *b.* recoding *c.* networking *d.* rehearsal

4. Constructive processing is often responsible for creating pseudo-memories. T or F?

5. Electrical stimulation of the brain has shown conclusively that all memories are stored permanently, but not all memories can be retrieved. T or F?

6. Memories elicited under hypnosis are more vivid, complete, and reliable than normal. T or F?

7. ______________________ of related information are an example of the structure or organization found in LTM.

Answers:
1. F **2.** T **3.** *d* **4.** T **5.** F **6.** F **7.** Networks

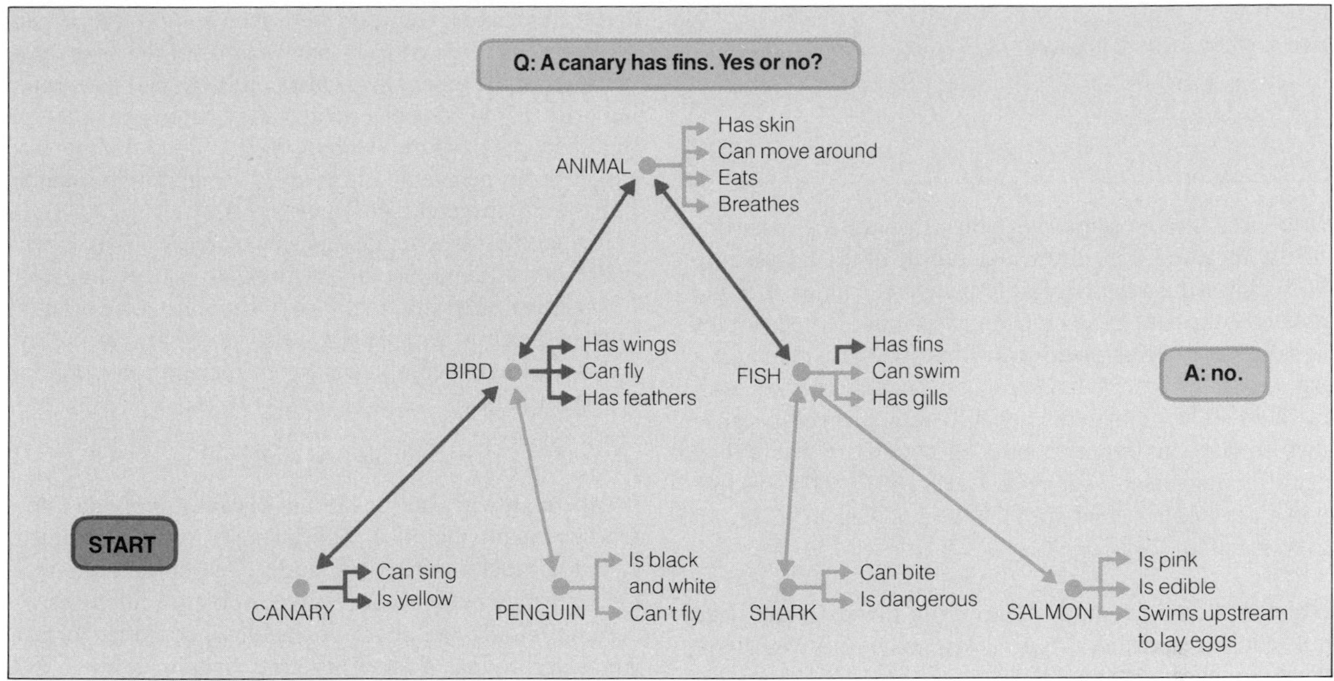

Fig. 9–4 *A hypothetical network of facts about animals shows what is meant by the structure of memory. Small networks of ideas such as this are probably organized into larger and larger units and higher levels of meaning. (Adapted from Collins & Quillian, 1969.)*

Measuring Memory—The Answer Is on the Tip of My Tongue

Initially, it might seem that you either remember something or you don't. But a moment of thought should convince you that this is not always true. For instance, have you ever recognized someone you only saw once before and thought you had completely forgotten? If so, you have used a form of partial memory called *recognition*. Partial memory is also demonstrated by the **tip-of-the-tongue state.** This is the experience of having an answer or a memory just out of reach—on the "tip of your tongue."

In one study of the tip-of-the-tongue state, university students read the definitions of words such as *sextant, sampan*, and *ambergris*. Students who "drew a blank" and couldn't name a defined word were asked to give whatever other information they could about it. Often, they could accurately guess the first and last letter and even the number of syllables of the word they were seeking. They were also able to give words that sounded like or meant the same thing as the defined word (Brown & McNeill, 1966). A related finding is that people can often tell beforehand if they are likely to remember something (Nelson, 1987). This ability is based on a state called **the feeling of knowing.** Feeling-of-knowing reactions are easy to observe on television game shows, where they occur just before contestants are allowed to answer.

Because memory is not an all-or-nothing event, there are several ways of measuring it. Three commonly used **memory tasks** are *recall, recognition*, and *relearning*. Let's see how they differ.

Recall What is the name of the first song on your favorite record album? Who won the World Series last year? Who wrote the *Gettysburg Address?* If you can answer these questions you are demonstrating recall. To **recall** means to supply or reproduce facts or information. Tests of recall often require *verbatim* (word-for-word) memory. If you study a poem or a speech until you can recite it without looking, you are recalling it. If you complete a fill-in-the-blank question, you are using recall. When you take an *essay* exam and provide facts and ideas without prompting, you are also using recall, even though you didn't learn your essay verbatim. Essay tests tend to be difficult because they offer few cues to aid memory.

The order in which information is memorized has an interesting effect on recall. To experience it, try to memorize the following list, reading it only once:

BREAD, APPLES, SODA, HAM, COOKIES, RICE, LETTUCE, BEETS, MUSTARD, CHEESE, ORANGES, ICE CREAM, CRACKERS, FLOUR, EGGS

If you are like most people, you will have the most difficulty recalling items from the middle of the list. Figure 9–5 shows the results of a similar test. Notice that the greatest number of errors is found for middle items. This is called the **serial position effect.** The last items on a list appear to be remembered best because they are still in STM. The first items are also remembered because they entered an "empty" short-term memory where they could be rehearsed (Tarpy & Mayer, 1978). The middle items are neither held in STM nor moved to LTM, so they are often lost.

Recognition If you tried to write down all the facts you could remember from a class taken last year, you might conclude that you had learned very little. However, a more sensitive test based on **recognition** could be used. For instance, you could be given a *multiple-choice* test on facts and ideas from the course. Since multiple-choice tests only require you to recognize the correct answer, we would probably find evidence of considerable learning.

Recognition memory can be amazingly accurate for pictures, photographs, or other visual input. One investigator showed subjects 2560 photographs at a rate of one every 10 seconds. Subjects were then shown 280 pairs of photographs. One in each pair was from the first set of photos and the other was similar but new. Subjects could tell with 85 to 95 percent accuracy which photograph they had seen before (Haber, 1970). This finding may explain why people so often say, "I may forget a name, but I never forget a face."

Recognition is usually superior to recall. This is why police departments use photographs or a lineup to identify criminal suspects (Fig. 9–6). Witnesses who disagree in their recall of a suspect's height, weight, age, or eye color often agree completely when recognition is all that is required.

Question: Is recognition always superior?

It depends greatly on the kind of **distractors** used. These are false items included with an item to be recognized. If the distractors are very similar to the correct item, memory may be poor. A reverse problem sometimes occurs when only one choice looks like it could be correct. This can produce a **false positive,** or false sense of recognition. For example, there have been instances in which witnesses described a criminal as black, tall, or young. Then a lineup was held in which a suspect was the only black among whites, the only tall suspect, or the only

Fig. 9–5 *The serial position effect. The graph shows the percentage of subjects correctly recalling each item in a 15-item list. Recall is best for the first and last items. (Data from Craik, 1970.)*

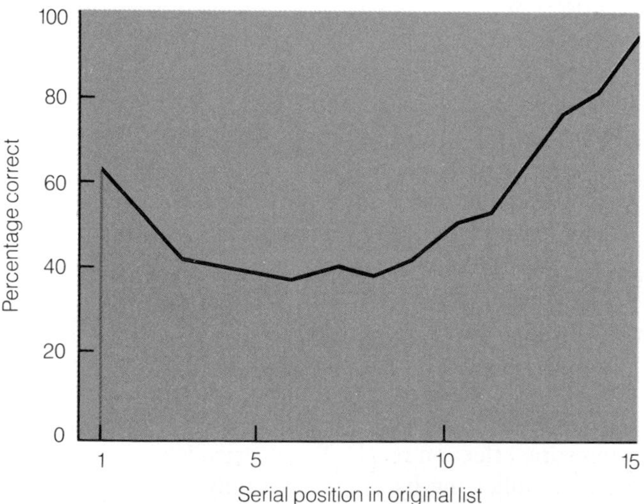

Fig. 9–6 *Police lineups make use of the sensitivity of recognition memory.*

young person (Loftus, 1980). Under such circumstances a false identification is very likely.

Relearning In a classic experiment on memory, a psychologist read a short passage in Greek to his son. This was done daily when the boy was between 15 months and 3 years of age. At age 8, the boy was asked if he remembered the Greek passage. He showed no evidence of recall. He was then given selections from the passage he heard and selections from other Greek passages. Could he recognize the one he heard as an infant? "It's all Greek to me!" he said, indicating no recognition (and drawing a frown from everyone in the room).

Had the psychologist stopped, he might have concluded that no memory of the Greek remained. However, the child was then asked to memorize the original quotation and others of equal difficulty. This time his earlier learning became evident. The boy memorized the passage he had heard in childhood 25 percent faster than the others (Burtt, 1941). As this experiment suggests, relearning is typically the most sensitive measure of memory.

When a person is tested by **relearning,** how do we know a memory still exists? As with the boy described, relearning is measured by a **savings score.** Let's say it takes you 1 hour to memorize all the names in a telephone book. (It's a small town.) Two years later, you relearn them in 45 minutes. Because you "saved" 15 minutes, your savings score would be 25 percent (15 divided by 60 times 100). Savings of this type are a good reason for studying a wide range of subjects. It may seem that time spent learning algebra, history, or a foreign language is wasted because so much is lost within a year or two. But if you ever need such information, you will find you can relearn it in far less time.

Redintegration There is a fourth way in which memories may be revealed. Imagine finding a picture taken on your sixth birthday or tenth Christmas. As you look at the photo, one memory leads to another, which leads to another, and another. (Picture this as following some of the "branches" of your memory network.) Soon you have unleashed a flood of seemingly forgotten details. This process is called **redintegration** (ruh-DIN-tuh-GRAY-shun). Many people find that such memories are also touched off by distinctive odors out of the past—from a farm visited in childhood, Grandma's kitchen, the seashore, a doctor's office, the perfume or after-shave of a former lover, and so on. The key idea in redintegration is that one memory serves as a cue to trigger another. As a result, an entire past experience may be reconstructed from one small recollection. Such memories usually involve personal experience rather than formal learning.

Compare: Ways to Retrieve Memories

Recall To supply or reproduce memorized information with a minimum of external cues.

Recognition Memory in which previously learned material is correctly identified as that which was seen before.

Relearning Learning again something that was previously learned; used as a measure of memory for prior learning.

Redintegration The process of reconstructing an entire complex memory after first observing or remembering only a part of it.

Eidetic Imagery—Picture This!

Question: What is a photographic memory? How is it different from the types of memory already described?

Eidetic (eye-DET-ik) **imagery,** known informally as photographic memory, occurs when a person has visual images clear enough to be "scanned" or retained for at least 30 seconds. Eidetic imagery occurs most often in childhood, with about 8 children out of 100 having eidetic images (Haber, 1969).

In one series of tests, children were shown a picture from *Alice in Wonderland* (Fig. 9–7). To test your eidetic imagery, look at the picture and read the instructions there. Now, let's see how much you remember. Can you say (without looking again) which of Alice's apron strings is longer? Are the cat's front paws crossed? How many stripes are on the cat's tail? After the picture was removed from view, one 10-year-old boy was asked what he saw. He replied, "I see the tree, gray tree with three limbs. I see the cat with stripes around its tail." Asked to count the stripes, the boy replied, "There are about 16" (a correct count!). The boy then went on to describe the remainder of the picture in striking detail (Haber, 1969).

Don't be disappointed if you didn't do too well when you tried your eidetic skills. Most eidetic imagery disappears during adolescence and becomes quite rare by adulthood (Haber, 1974). Actually, this change may not be too much of a loss. The majority of eidetic memorizers have no better long-term memory than average.

Internal Images Eidetic images are "projected" out in front of a person. Many psychologists believe that a second type of imagery is also used in memory. Can you remember how many doors there are in your house or apartment? To answer a question like this, many people form **internal images** of each room and count the doorways they "see."

Kosslyn, Ball, and Reisler (1978) found an interesting way to show that memories do exist as images. Subjects first memorized a sort of treasure map similar to the one shown in Figure 9–8a. They were then asked to picture a black dot moving from one object, such as the tree, to another, such as the hut at the top of the island. Did subjects really form an image to do this task? It seems they did. As shown in Figure 9–8b, the time it took to "move" the dot was directly related to actual distances on the map.

Some people may have such vivid internal images that they too have "photographic memory." A notable example was reported by A. R. Luria (1968) in his book, *The Mind of a Mnemonist*. Luria studied a man (Mr. S) who had practically unlimited memory for visual images. Mr. S could remember almost everything that ever happened to him with incredible accuracy. When Luria tried to test Mr. S's memory by using longer and longer lists of words or numbers, he discovered that no matter how long the list, Mr. S was able to recall it without error. Psychologists used to think that such exceptional memory was a biological gift and could not be learned. However, recent research has raised questions about this conclusion (see Highlight 9–2).

Fig. 9–7 *Test picture like that used to identify children with eidetic imagery. To test your eidetic imagery, look at the picture for 30 seconds. Then look at a blank surface and try to "project" the picture on it. If you have good eidetic imagery, you will be able to see the picture in detail. Return now to the text and try to answer the questions there. (Redrawn from an illustration in Lewis Carroll's* Alice in Wonderland.*)*

Fig. 9–8 *(a) "Treasure map" similar to the one used by Kosslyn, Ball, and Reisler (1978) to study images in memory. (b) This graph shows how long it took subjects to move a visualized spot various distances on their mental images of the map. (See text for explanation.)*

(a)

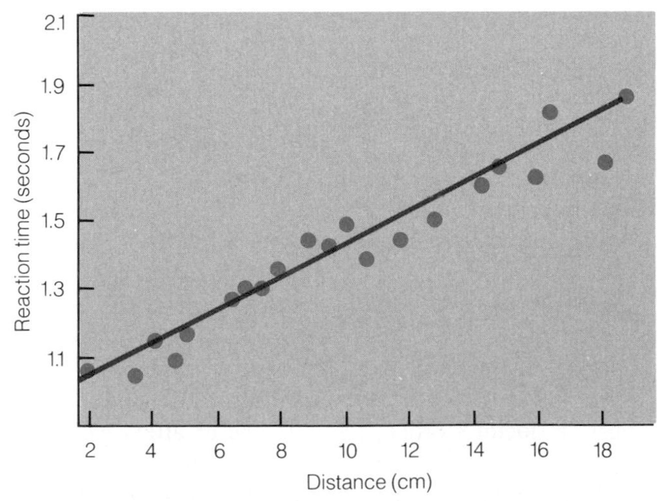

(b)

● HIGHLIGHT 9–2
Can Exceptional Memory Be Learned?

At first, a student volunteer we will call Steve could remember 7 digits—a typical score for a college student. Could he improve with practice? For 20 months, psychologist William Chase guided Steve as he practiced memorizing ever longer lists of digits. Ultimately, Steve was able to memorize around 80 digits, like this sample:

92842048050842268953990190252912807999706
60657471731060108058526972602635733213 5

How did Steve reach such lofty heights of memory? He worked by chunking digits into meaningful groups containing 3 or 4 digits each. Steve's avid interest in long-distance running helped greatly. For instance, to him the first 3 digits above represented 9 minutes and 28 seconds, a good time for a 2-mile run. When running times wouldn't work, Steve used other associations, such as ages or dates, to chunk digits (Ericsson & Chase, 1982).

Chase and psychologist Anders Ericsson believe that Steve's performance shows that exceptional memory is merely a learned extension of normal memory. They believe this is true even of people who have phenomenal memories like Mr. S (the man studied by Luria and described earlier). As further evidence, they note that Steve's short-term memory did not improve during his months of practice. For example, he could still memorize only 7 consonants. Steve's phenomenal memory for numbers grew as he figured out ways to encode digits so he could rapidly store them in LTM.

The idea that Mr. S had a normal memory is, perhaps, open to debate. Mr. S could memorize, with equal ease, strings of digits, meaningless consonants, mathematical formulas, and poems in foreign languages. His memory was so powerful that he had to devise ways to *forget*—such as writing information on a piece of paper and then burning it.

In sum, there is evidence that exceptional memory can be learned. It's an open question, however, about whether some exceptional memories, like Mr. S's, are based on unusually vivid images or other rare abilities.

As fantastic as it might sound to a struggling student, Mr. S's memory caused great difficulty. He remembered so much that he could not separate important facts from trivia. For instance, if he were tested on the contents of this chapter after reading it, he might remember not only every word, but all the images each word made him think of and all the sights, sounds, and feelings that occurred as he was reading. Finding the answer for a specific question, writing a logical essay, or even understanding a single sentence, therefore, was very difficult for him.

Learning Check

Unless you have a memory like Mr. S's, it might be a good idea to see if you can answer these questions before reading on.

1. Four common techniques for measuring or demonstrating memory are

____________________ ____________________

____________________ ____________________

2. Multiple choice tests primarily require ____________________ memory.

3. Essay tests require ____________________ of facts or ideas.

4. As a measure of memory, a savings score is associated with
a. recognition *b.* eidetic images *c.* relearning *d.* reconstruction

5. Children with eidetic imagery typically have no better than average long-term memory. T or F?

Answers:

1. recall, recognition, relearning, redintegration 2. recognition 3. recall 4. c 5. T

Why We, Uh, Let's See; Why We, Uh . . . Forget!

Question: Why are some memories lost so quickly? For example, why is it hard to remember information a week or two after taking a test in class?

Generally speaking, most forgetting occurs immediately after memorization. In a famous set of experiments, **Herman Ebbinghaus** (1885) tested his own memory at various times after learning. Ebbinghaus wanted to be sure he would not be swayed by prior learning, so he memorized **nonsense syllables.** These are meaningless 3-letter words such as GEX, CEF, and WOL. The importance of using meaningless words is shown by the fact that VEL, FAB, and DUZ are no longer used on memory tests. Subjects who recognize these words as detergent names find them very easy to remember.

By waiting various lengths of time before testing himself, Ebbinghaus constructed a **curve of forgetting** (Fig. 9–9). Owing to the great care Ebbinghaus took in his work, these findings remain valid today. Notice that forgetting is rapid at first and is then followed by a slow decline. As a student, you should note that forgetting is minimized when there is little delay between review and taking a test. However, don't take this as a reason for cramming. The error most students make is to cram *only*. If you cram, you don't have to remember for very long, but you may not learn enough in the first place. If you use short, daily study sessions and, in addition, review intensely before a test, you will get the benefit of good preparation and a minimum time lapse.

Question: The Ebbinghaus curve shows less than 30 percent remembered after only 2 days have passed. Is forgetting really that rapid?

No, not always. Meaningful information is not lost nearly as quickly as nonsense syllables. For example, tests show that students of Spanish forget an average of 30 percent of their vocabulary during the first 3 years after they stop studying. After this early decline, however, little more forgetting occurs during the next 20 years (Bahrick, 1984). Thus, the forgetting of well-learned meaningful information takes place slowly. In fact, as learning grows stronger, some knowledge may become nearly permanent. (This idea is discussed further in the Exploration section.)

"I'll never forget old, old . . . oh, what's his name?" Forgetting is both frustrating and embarrassing. Why *do* we forget? The Ebbinghaus curve gives a general picture of forgetting, but it doesn't explain it. For explanations we must search further.

Encoding Failure

Whose head is on a U.S. penny? Which way is it facing? What is written at the top of a penny? Can you accurately draw and label a penny? In an interesting experiment, Nickerson and Adams (1979) asked a large group of students to draw a penny. Few could. Well then, could the students at least recognize a drawing of a real penny among fakes? (See Figure 9–10.) Again, few could.

The most obvious reason for forgetting is also the most

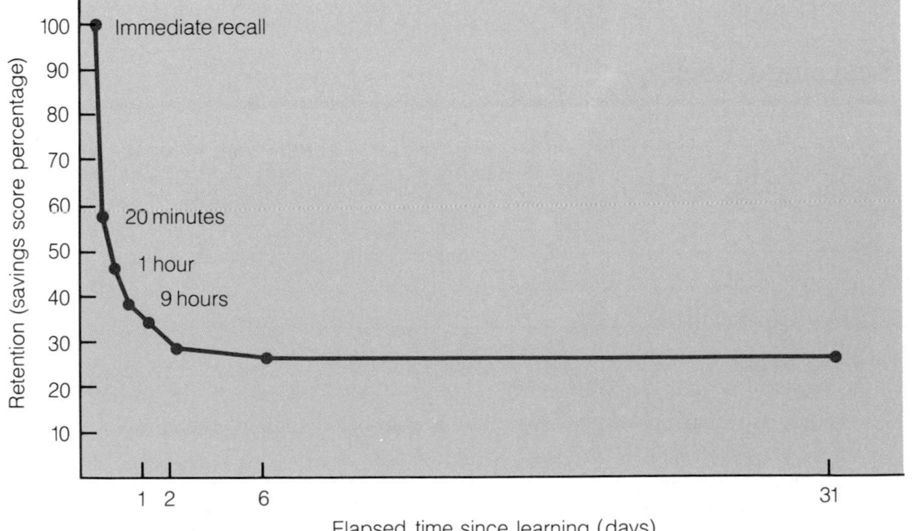

Fig. 9–9 *The curve of forgetting. This graph shows the amount remembered (measured by relearning) after varying lengths of time. Notice how rapidly forgetting occurs. Material learned was nonsense syllables. Meaningful information is not forgotten so quickly. (After Ebbinghaus, 1885.)*

Fig. 9–10 *Some of the distractor items used in a study of recognition memory and encoding failure. Penny A is correct but was seldom recognized. Pennies G and J were popular wrong answers. (Adapted from Nickerson & Adams, 1979.)*

commonly overlooked. In many cases we "forget" because a memory was never formed in the first place. Obviously, few of us ever encode the details of a penny. If you are bothered by frequent forgetting, it is wise to ask yourself, "Have I been storing the information in the first place?"

Decay

One view of forgetting holds that **memory traces** (changes in nerve cells or brain activity) fade, weaken, or **decay** over time. Decay appears definitely to be a factor in the loss of sensory memories. Such fading also applies to short-term memory. Information stored in STM seems to initiate a brief flurry of activity in the brain that quickly dies out (Shiffrin & Cook, 1978). Short-term memory therefore operates like a "leaky bucket": New information constantly pours in, but it rapidly fades away and is replaced by still newer information (Miller, 1956).

Disuse Is it possible that the decay of memory traces also explains long-term forgetting? That is, could long-term memory traces fade from **disuse** and eventually become so weak they cannot be retrieved? As tempting as this theory may be, there are reasons to doubt it. One reason already mentioned is the recovery of seemingly forgotten memories through redintegration. Another is that disuse fails to explain why some unused memories fade, while others are carried for life. A third contradiction will be recognized by anyone who has spent time with the elderly. People growing senile may become so forgetful that they can't remember what happened a week ago. Yet at the same time your Uncle Oscar's recent memories are fading, he may have vivid memories of trivial and long-forgotten events from the past. "Why, I remember it as clearly as if it were yesterday," he will say, forgetting that the story he is about to tell is one he told earlier the same day. In short, disuse alone does not adequately explain long-term forgetting.

Question: If decay and disuse don't fully explain forgetting, what does?

There are several additional possibilities. Let's briefly consider each.

Cue-Dependent Forgetting

Often, memories appear to be *available*, but not accessible. An example is having an answer on the "tip of your tongue." You know the answer is there, but it remains just "out of reach." This situation indicates that many memories are "forgotten" because **cues** present at the time of learning are absent when the time comes to retrieve information. For example, if you were asked, "What were you doing on Monday afternoon of the third week in September two years ago?" your reply might be, "Come on. How should I know?" However, if you were reminded, "That was the day the courthouse burned," or "That was the day Mary had her automobile accident," you might remember immediately. The presence of such cues almost always enhances memory (Fig. 9–11). In theory, memory will be best if you study in the same room where you will be tested. Since this is often impossible, it may be wise to vary your study environment so that memories are not tied too strongly to a particular place (Smith, 1985).

State-Dependent Learning Nearly everyone has heard the story about the drunk who misplaced his wallet and had to get drunk again to find it. Although this tale

Fig. 9–11 *Because of the many cues they provide, photographs often bring back numerous memories.*

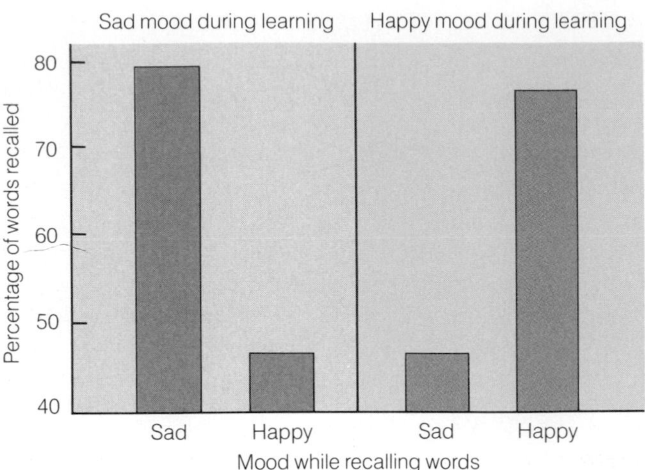

Fig. 9–12 *The effect of mood on memory. Subjects best remembered a list of words when their mood during testing was the same as their mood when they learned the list. (Adapted from Bower, 1981.)*

is often told as a joke, it is not too far-fetched. The *bodily state* that exists during learning can be a strong cue for later memory (Overton, 1985). For this reason, information learned under the influence of a drug is best remembered when the drugged state occurs again—an effect known as **state-dependent learning.**

A similar effect may apply to emotional states. For instance, Gordon Bower (1981) found that people who learned a list of words while in a happy mood recalled them better when they were again happy. People who learned while they felt sad remembered best when they were sad (Fig. 9–12). The link between emotional cues and memory could explain why couples who quarrel often end up remembering—and rehashing—old arguments.

Interference

Further understanding of forgetting comes from an experiment in which college students learned lists of nonsense syllables. After studying, students in one group slept for 8 hours and were then tested for memory of the lists. A second group remained awake for 8 hours and went about business as usual. When members of the second group were tested, they remembered *less* than the group that slept (Fig. 9–13). This difference is based on the fact that new learning can **interfere** with previous learning (Shiffrin, 1970). Such interference seems to apply to both short-term and long-term memories (Klatzky, 1980). As you may recall from Chapter 8, it also applies to motor skills in the form of negative transfer.

It is not completely clear if new memories alter existing memory traces or if they make it harder to "locate" (retrieve) earlier memories. In any case, there is no doubt that interference is a major cause of forgetting (Johnson & Hasher, 1987). College students who memorized 20 lists of words (one list each day) were able to recall only 15 percent of the last list. Students who learned only one list remembered 80 percent (Underwood, 1957) (Fig. 9–14.)

Fig. 9–13 *The amount of forgetting after a period of sleep or of being awake. Notice that sleep causes less memory loss than activity that occurs while one is awake. (After Jenkins & Dallenbach, 1924.)*

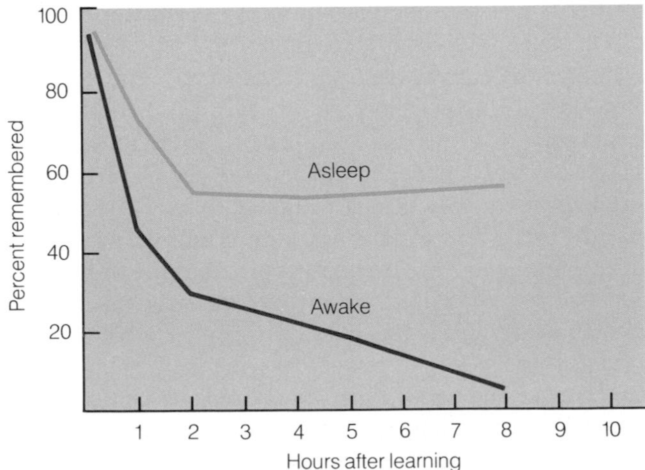

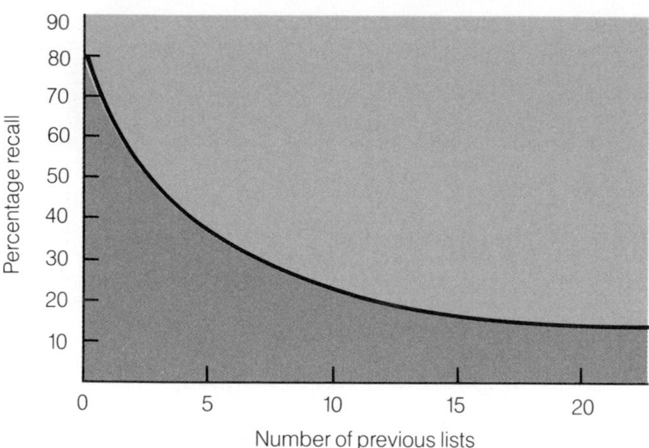

Fig. 9–14 *Effects of interference on memory. A graph of the approximate relationship between percentage recalled and number of different word lists memorized. (Adapted from Underwood, 1957.)*

Order Effects The sleeping college students remembered more because **retroactive** (RET-ro-AK-tiv) **interference** was held to a minimum. Retroactive interference refers to the tendency for new learning to inhibit retrieval of old learning. Avoiding new learning prevents retroactive interference from occurring. This fact doesn't exactly mean you should hide in your closet after you study for an exam. However, you should avoid studying other subjects until the exam. Sleeping after study can help you retain memories, and reading, writing, or even watching TV may cause interference.

Retroactive interference is easily demonstrated in the laboratory by this arrangement:

Experimental group:	Learn A	Learn B	Test A
Control group:	Learn A	Rest	Test A

Imagine yourself as a member of the experimental group. In task A, you learn a list of telephone numbers. In task B, you learn a list of Social Security numbers. How do you do on a test of task A (the telephone numbers)? If you do not remember as much as the control group that learns *only* task A, then retroactive interference has occurred. The second thing learned has interfered with memory of the first thing learned; the interference went "backward," or was "retroactive" (Fig. 9–15).

Proactive (pro-AK-tiv) **interference** is a second basic source of forgetting. Proactive interference occurs when prior learning inhibits recall of later learning. A test for proactive interference would take this form.

Experimental group:	Learn A	Learn B	Test B
Control group:	Rest	Learn B	Test B

If the experimental group remembers less than the control group on a test of task B, then learning task A has interfered with memory of task B.

Question: Then proactive interference goes "forward"?

Yes. For instance, if you cram for a psychology exam and then later the same night cram for a history exam, your memory for the second subject studied (history) will be less accurate than if you had studied only history. (Because of retroactive interference, your memory for psychology would probably also suffer.) The greater the similarity in the two subjects studied, the more interference takes place. The moral, of course, is don't procrastinate in preparing for exams.

Repression

Take a moment from reading and scan over the events of the last few years of your life. What kinds of things

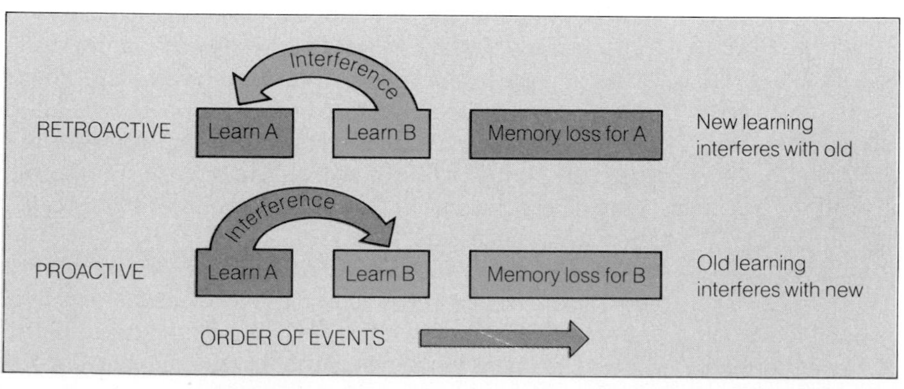

Fig. 9–15 *Retroactive and proactive interference. The order of learning and testing shows whether interference is retroactive (backward) or proactive (forward).*

most easily come to mind? Many people find that they tend to remember happy, positive events better than disappointments and irritations (Linton, 1979). A clinical psychologist would call this tendency **repression,** or motivated forgetting. Through repression, painful, threatening, or embarrassing memories are held out of consciousness by forces within one's personality. The forgetting of past failures, upsetting childhood events, the names of persons you dislike, or appointments you don't want to keep, may indicate repression.

Question: If I try to forget a test I have failed, am I repressing it?

No. Repression can be distinguished from **suppression,** an active attempt to put something out of one's mind. By not thinking about the test, you have merely suppressed a memory. If you choose to, you can remember the test. Clinicians consider true repression an *unconscious* event. When a memory is repressed, we are unaware that forgetting has even occurred. (See Chapter 12 for more information on repression.)

Flashbulb Memories

Why are some traumatic events vividly remembered while others are repressed? Psychologists Roger Brown and James Kulik (1977) use the term **flashbulb memories** to describe lasting images that are frozen in memory at times of personal tragedy, accident, or other significant events. Depending on your age, you may have a flashbulb memory for the Pearl Harbor attack, the assassination of John F. Kennedy, or the space shuttle disaster. An interesting quality of such memories is that they often focus primarily on how you reacted to the event (Rubin, 1985). One reason such memories can be so vivid is that the hormones adrenaline and ACTH are secreted at times of emotion or stress. Both substances have been shown to enhance memory, possibly by altering brain chemistry (Gold, 1987; McGaugh, 1983).

Incidentally, not all flashbulb memories are negative. In general, vivid memories are most likely when an event is surprising, important, or emotional (Rubin, 1985). Table 9–1 lists some memories that had "flashbulb" clarity for at least 50 percent of a group of college students. How vivid are the memories they trigger for you?

Table 9–1 Bright Flashes of Memory

Memory Cue	Percentage of Students With Flashbulb Memories
A car accident you were in or witnessed	85
When you first met your college roommate	82
The night of your high school graduation	81
The night of your senior prom (if you went or not)	78
An early romantic experience	77
A time you had to speak in front of an audience	72
When you first got your college admissions letter	65
Your first date—the moment you met him/her	57
When President Reagan was shot in Washington	52

(From Rubin, 1985.)

Memory Formation—Some "Shocking" Findings

One possibility overlooked in our discussion of forgetting is that memories may be lost as they are being formed. For example, a head injury may cause a "gap" in memories preceding the accident. **Retrograde amnesia,** as this is called, involves forgetting events that occurred *before* an injury or the onset of disease. (In contrast, **anterograde amnesia** involves forgetting events that occur *after* an injury or trauma.) Retrograde amnesia can be understood if we assume that it takes a certain amount of time to move information from short-term to long-term memory. The forming of a long-term memory is called **consolidation** (John, 1967). You can think of consolidation as being somewhat like writing your name in wet concrete. Once the concrete is set, the information (your name) is fairly lasting, but while it is setting, it can be wiped out (amnesia) or scribbled over (interference).

Consider a classic experiment on consolidation, in which a rat is placed on a small platform. The rat steps down to the floor and receives a painful electric shock. After one shock, the rat can be returned to the platform repeatedly, but it will not step down. Obviously, the rat remembers the shock. Would it remember if consolidation were disturbed?

Interestingly, one way to prevent consolidation is to give a different kind of shock called **electroconvulsive shock (ECS)** (Jarvik, 1964). ECS is a mild electric shock to the brain. It does not harm the animal, but it does destroy any memory that is being formed. If each painful shock (the one the animal remembers) is followed by ECS (which wipes out memories during consolidation), the rat will step down over and over. Each time, ECS will erase the memory of the painful shock. (ECS has been employed as a psychiatric treatment for severe depression in humans. Used in this way, electroshock therapy also causes memory loss. See Chapter 20 for details.)

Question: What would happen if ECS were given several hours after the learning?

Recent memories are more easily disrupted than older memories (Gold, 1987). If enough time is allowed to pass between learning and ECS, the memory is unaffected. Apparently, consolidation is already completed. This is why people with head injuries usually only lose memories from immediately before the accident, while older memories remain intact (Baddeley, 1976). Likewise, you would forget more if you studied, stayed awake 8 hours, and then slept 8 hours than you would if you studied, slept 8 hours, and were then awake for 8 hours. Both cases involve the passage of 16 hours. However, in the second instance forgetting is reduced because more consolidation takes place before interference begins.

Question: Can memory be improved with drugs?

Drugs and Consolidation The possibility of chemically improving memory has long intrigued psychologists. We have known for some time that various stimulating drugs speed up consolidation if given just after learning (McGaugh, 1983). Note, however, that this only reduces the time during which interference can take place; it does not magically improve memory. Also, the drugs involved (metrazol, strychnine, nicotine, caffeine, and amphetamine) must be given in carefully controlled dosages. If the dosage is too high by even a small amount, memory will be *disrupted* (McGaugh, 1970).

Question: What effect does alcohol have on memory?

Memory losses are common when a person overindulges in alcohol. This may be due, in part, to state-dependent learning. At higher levels of intoxication, alcohol seems to directly impair encoding and consolidation of memories. A person suffering an alcohol blackout may lose anywhere from a few minutes to several hours of memory (Loftus, 1980). Research makes it clear that studying while drunk is an excellent way to *lower* test scores (Birnbaum et al., 1978).

Question: What part of the brain causes consolidation?

From STM to LTM Actually, many areas of the brain are responsible for memory, but the **hippocampus** is of particular importance. This structure, buried deep within the brain, seems to act as a sort of "switching station" between short-term and long-term memory.

Humans who have had hippocampal damage show a striking inability to store new memories. A patient described by Brenda Milner is typical. Two years after an operation that affected the hippocampus, a 29-year-old patient continued to give his age as 27 and reported that it seemed that the operation had just taken place (Milner, 1965). His memory of events before the operation remained clear, but he found forming new long-term memories almost impossible. (He suffered, in other words, from anterograde amnesia.) When his parents moved to a new house a few blocks away on the same street, he could not remember the new address, and he read the same magazines over and over again without finding them familiar. If you were to meet this man, he would seem fairly normal, since he still has short-term memory. But if you were to leave the room and return 15 minutes later, he would act as if he had never seen you before (Milner, 1965). Years ago his favorite uncle died, but he suffers the same grief anew each time he is told of the death. Lacking the ability to form new lasting memories, he lives eternally in the present.

The Brain and Memory Somewhere within the 3-pound mass of the human brain lies all we know: zip codes, faces of loved ones, history, favorite melodies, the taste of an apple, and much, much more. Where is this information? Karl Lashley, a pioneering brain researcher, set out in the 1920s to find an **engram,** or memory trace. Lashley taught animals to run mazes and then removed parts of their brains to see how memory of the maze changed. After 30 years, he had to concede defeat: Engrams are not located in any one area of the brain. It mattered little which part of the brain's cortex he removed. Only the *amount* removed correlated to memory loss.

Question: Then how are memories recorded in the brain?

Scientists studying simple animals are beginning to identify the exact ways in which individual nerve cells record information. There is now much evidence that learning alters the electrical activity, structure, and chemistry of the brain (McGaugh, 1983). For example, Eric Kandel and his colleagues have studied learning in the marine snail *Aplysia* (Fig. 9–16). Kandel has found that learning in *Aplysia* occurs when certain nerve cells in a circuit alter the amount of transmitter chemicals they release (Kandel,

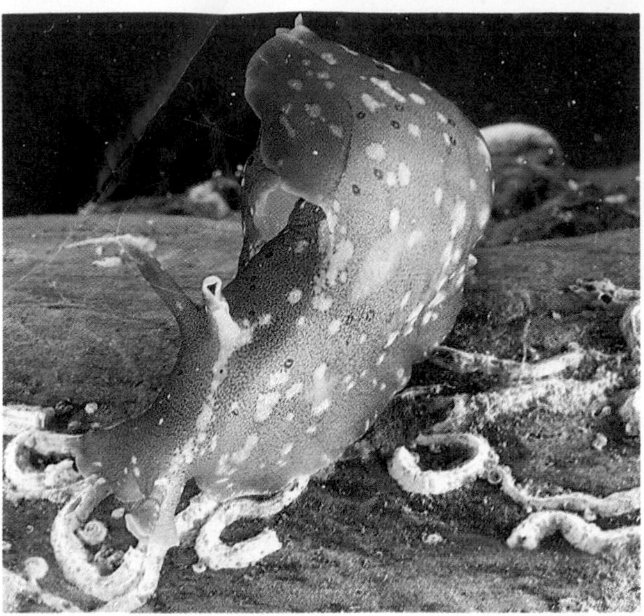

Fig. 9–16 *An* Aplysia. *The relatively simple nervous system of this sea animal allows scientists to study memory as it occurs in single nerve cells.*

1976). Such changes determine which circuits get strengthened and which become weaker. It has also been shown that an increase in receptor cites for transmitter chemicals occurs during learning (Lynch & Baudry, 1984).

On the basis of such breakthroughs, scientists are now studying a bewildering array of chemicals and brain processes that affect memory (McGaugh, 1983). If this research succeeds, it may be possible to help the millions of persons who suffer from memory impairment. Will researchers ever produce a "memory pill" for those with normal memory? Some neuroscientists are confident that memory can be and will be artificially enhanced. At present, however, the possibility of something like a "physics pill" or a "math pill" seems especially remote.

Learning Check

1. According to the Ebbinghaus curve of forgetting, we forget slowly at first and then a rapid decline occurs. T or F?

2. Which explanation seems to account for loss of short-term memories?
a. decay *b.* disuse *c.* repression *d.* interference

3. When memories are available but not accessible, forgetting may be cue-dependent. T or F?

4. When learning one thing makes it more difficult to recall another, forgetting may be caused by ______________.

5. You are asked to memorize long lists of telephone numbers. You learn a new list each day for 10 days. When tested on list 3, you remember less than a person who only learned the first three lists. Your larger memory loss is probably due to
a. disuse *b.* retroactive interference *c.* regression *d.* proactive interference

6. Repression is thought of as a type of motivated forgetting, T or F?

7. Retrograde amnesia results when consolidation is speeded up. T or F?

8. Researchers have clearly established that engrams are stored in the hippocampus. T or F?

Answers:
1. F **2.** *a* and *d* **3.** T **4.** interference **5.** *b* **6.** T **7.** F **8.** F

● How to Improve Your Memory—Keys to the Memory Bank

While you're waiting around for the development of a memory pill, let's focus on some ways of improving your memory right now.

Knowledge of Results Learning proceeds best when feedback, or knowledge of results, allows you to check to see if you are learning. Feedback also helps you identify material that needs extra practice. In addition, knowing that you have remembered or answered correctly can be rewarding. A prime means of providing feedback for yourself when studying is *recitation.*

Recitation Recitation means repeating to yourself what you have learned. If you are going to remember something, eventually you will have to retrieve it. Recitation forces you to practice retrieving information as you are learning. When you are reading a text, you should stop frequently and try to remember what you have just read by summarizing it aloud. Completing the Learning Checks in this text is a form of recitation. If you haven't been using them, you're missing a good way to enhance your memory. It's also a good idea to recite on your own. In one experiment, the best memory score of all was earned by a group of students who spent 80 percent of their time reciting and only 20 percent reading (Gates, 1968). Maybe students who talk to themselves aren't crazy after all.

Overlearning Numerous studies have shown that memory is greatly improved when study is continued beyond bare mastery. In other words, after you have learned material well enough to remember it once without error, you should continue studying. Overlearning is your best insurance against going blank on a test because of nervousness or anxiety.

Selection The Dutch scholar Erasmus said that a good memory should be like a fish net: It should keep all the big fish and let the little ones escape. If you boil down the paragraphs in most textbooks to one or two important terms or ideas, your memory chores will be more manageable. Practice careful and selective marking in your texts, and use marginal notes to further summarize ideas. Most students mark their texts too much instead of too little. If everything is underlined, you haven't been selective.

Spaced Practice Spaced practice is generally superior to massed practice (Rea & Modigliani, 1987). By improving attention and consolidation, three 20-minute study sessions can produce more learning than 1 hour of continuous study. Perhaps the best way to make use of this principle is to *schedule* your time. If most students were to keep a totally honest record of their weekly activities, they would probably find that very few hours were spent really studying. To make an effective schedule, designate times during the week before, after, and between classes when you will study particular subjects. Then treat these times just as if they were classes you had to attend.

Organization Assume that you must memorize the following list of words: *north, man, red, spring, woman, east, autumn, yellow, summer, boy, blue, west, winter, girl, green, south*. This rather difficult list could be reorganized into *chunks* as follows: *north-east-south-west, spring-summer-autumn-winter, red-yellow-green-blue, man-woman-boy-girl*. This simple reordering made the second list much easier to learn when college students were tested on both lists (Deese & Hulse, 1967). In another experiment, students who made up stories using long lists of words to be memorized learned the lists better than those who didn't (Bower & Clark, 1969). Organizing class notes and outlining chapters can be helpful when studying. It may even be helpful to outline your outlines, so that the overall organization of ideas becomes clearer and simpler.

Whole versus Part Learning If you had to memorize a speech, would it be better to try to learn it from beginning to end or in smaller parts like paragraphs? Generally, it is better to practice whole packages of information rather than smaller parts. This is especially true for fairly short, organized information. An exception is that learning parts may be better for extremely long, complicated information. Try to study the largest *meaningful* amount of information possible at one time.

For very long or complex material, try the *progressive part method*. In this approach, you break a learning task into short sections. At first, you study part A until it is mastered. Next, you study parts A and B; then A, B, and C; and so forth. This is a good way to learn the lines of a play, a long piece of music, or a poem. After the material is learned, you should also practice it by starting at points other than A (at C, D, or B, for example). This helps prevent getting "lost" or going blank in the middle of a performance.

Serial Position Whenever you must learn something in *order*, be aware of the *serial position effect*. As you will recall, this is the tendency to make the most errors in remembering the middle of a list. If you are introduced to a long line of people, the names you are likely to forget will be those in the middle, so you should make an extra effort to attend to them. The middle of a list, poem, or speech should also be given special attention and extra practice.

Sleep Remember that sleeping after study reduces interference. Since you obviously can't sleep after every study session or study everything just before you sleep, your study schedule (see Spaced Practice) should include ample breaks between subjects. Using your breaks and free time in a schedule is as important as living up to your study periods.

Review If you have spaced your practice and overlearned, review will be like icing on your study cake. Reviewing shortly before an exam cuts down the time during which you must remember details that may be important for the test. When reviewing, hold the amount of new information you try to memorize to a minimum. It may be realistic to take what you have actually learned and add a little more to it at the last minute by cramming. But remember that more than a little new learning may interfere with what you already know.

Cues The best cues for remembering are those that were present during encoding (Reed, 1988). For example, students in one study had to recall a list of 600 words. As they read the list (which they did not know they would be tested on), the students gave three other words closely related in meaning to each listed word. In a test given later, the words each student supplied were used as cues to jog his or her memory. The students recalled an astounding 90 percent of the original word list (Mantyla, 1986). This shows why it often helps to *elaborate* information as you learn. When you study, try to use new names, ideas, or terms in several sentences. Also, form images that include the new information, and relate it to knowledge you already have. Your goal should be to knit meaningful cues into your memory code to help you retrieve information when you need it.

Using a Strategy To Aid Recall Successful recall is usually the result of a planned *search* of memory (Reed, 1988). For example, one study found that students were most likely to recall names that eluded them if they made use of partial information (Read & Bruce, 1982, cited by Reed, 1988). The students were trying to answer questions such as, "He is best remembered as the scarecrow in the Judy Garland movie *The Wizard of Oz*." (The answer is Ray Bolger.) Partial information that helped students remember included impressions about the length of the name, letter sounds within the name, similar names, and related information (such as the names of other characters in the movie). A similar helpful strategy is to go through the alphabet, trying each letter as the first sound of a name or word you are seeking.

Using a variety of cues, even partial ones, opens more paths to a memory. Highlight 9–3 gives further hints for recapturing context and jogging memories. After that, the Applications section covers some of the most powerful memory techniques of all.

HIGHLIGHT 9–3
Memory Detectives

You may not think of yourself as a "memory detective," but active probing often helps improve recall. A case in point is the *cognitive interview,* a technique used to jog the memory of eyewitnesses. The cognitive interview was created by R. Edward Geiselman and Ron Fisher to help police detectives. When used properly, it produces 35 percent more correct information than standard questioning (Geiselman et al., 1986).

By following four simple steps, you can apply cognitive principles to your own memory. The next time you are searching for a "lost" memory—one that you know is in there somewhere—try the following search strategies.

1. Say or write down *everything* you can remember that relates to the information you are seeking. Don't worry about how trivial any of it seems; each bit of information you remember can serve as a cue to bring back others.

2. Try to recall events or information in different orders. Let your memories flow out backward or out of order, or start with whatever impressed you the most.

3. Recall from different viewpoints. Review events by mentally standing in a different place. Or try to view information as another person would remember it. When taking a test, for instance, ask yourself what other students or your professor would remember about the topic.

4. Mentally put yourself back in the situation where you learned the information. Try to mentally re-create the learning environment or relive the event. As you do, include sounds, smells, details of weather, nearby objects, other people present, what you said or thought, and how you felt as you learned the information (Fisher & Geiselman, 1987).

These strategies help re-create the context in which information was learned, and they provide multiple memory cues. If you think of remembering as a sort of "treasure hunt," you might even learn to enjoy the detective work.

Learning Check

1. To improve memory, it is reasonable to spend as much or more time reciting as reading. T or F?
2. Organizing information while studying has little effect on memory because long-term memory is already highly organized. T or F?
3. The progressive part method of study is best suited to long and complex learning tasks. T or F?
4. Sleeping immediately after studying is highly disruptive to the consolidation of memories. T or F?
5. As new information is encoded and rehearsed, it is helpful to elaborate on its meaning and connect it to other information. T or F?

Answers:
1. T **2.** F **3.** T **4.** F **5.** T

Applications: Mnemonics—Memory Magic

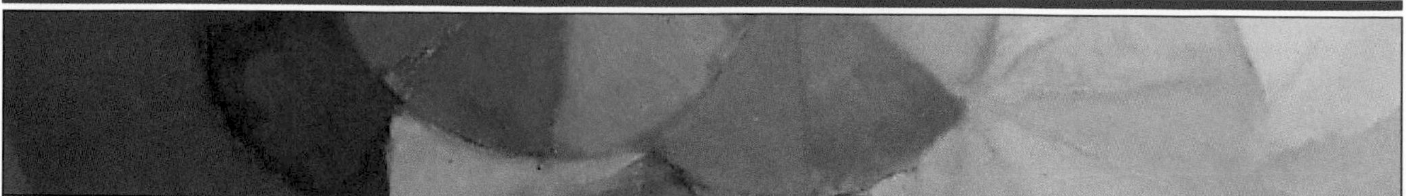

Question: Some stage performers use memory as part of their acts. Do they have eidetic imagery?

Various "memory experts" entertain by giving demonstrations in which they memorize the names of everyone at a banquet, the order of all the cards in a deck, long lists of words, or other seemingly impossible amounts of information. Such feats may seem like magic, but if they are, you can have a magic memory too. These tricks are performed through the use of **mnemonics** (nee-MON-iks). A mnemonic is any kind of memory system or aid.

Some mnemonic systems have become so common that almost everyone knows them. If you are trying to remember how many days there are in a month, you may find the answer by reciting, "Thirty days hath September. . . ." Physics teachers often help their students remember the colors of the spectrum by giving them the mnemonic "Roy G. Biv": **R**ed, **Or**ange, **Y**ellow, **G**reen, **B**lue, **I**ndigo, **V**iolet. The budding sailor who has trouble telling port from starboard may remember that port and left both have four letters or may remind himself, "I *left* port." And what beginning musician hasn't remembered the notes represented by the lines and spaces of the musical staff by learning "F-A-C-E" and "**E**very **G**ood **B**oy **D**oes **F**ine."

Mnemonic techniques are ways of avoiding *rote* learning (learning by simple repetition). The superiority of mnemonic learning as opposed to rote learning has been demonstrated many times. For example, Bower (1973) asked college students to study 5 different lists of 20 unrelated words. At the end of a short study session, subjects were asked to recall all 100 items. Subjects using mnemonics remembered an average of 72 items, whereas a control group using simple, or rote, learning remembered an average of 28.

Stage performers rarely have a naturally superior memory. Instead, they make extensive use of memory systems to perform their feats. Few of these systems are of practical value to you as a student, but the principles underlying mnemonics are. By practicing mnemonics you should be able to greatly improve your memory with little effort.

Here, then, are the basic principles of mnemonics:

1. Use mental pictures. There are at least two kinds of memory, *visual* and *verbal*. Visual pictures, or images, are generally easier to remember than words. Turning information into mental pictures is therefore very helpful (Kroll et al., 1986; Paivio, 1969).

2. Make things meaningful. Transferring information from short-term to long-term memory is aided by making it meaningful. If you encounter technical terms that have little or no immediate meaning for you, *give* them meaning, even if you have to stretch the term to do so. (This point is clarified by the examples following this list.)

3. Make information familiar. Connect it to what you already know. Another way to get information into long-term memory is to connect it to information already stored there. If some facts or ideas in a chapter seem to stay in your memory easily, associate other more difficult facts with them.

4. Form bizarre, unusual, or exaggerated mental associations. Forming images that make sense is better in most situations (Reed, 1988). However, when associating two ideas, terms, or especially mental images, you may sometimes find that the more outrageous and exaggerated the association, the more likely you are to remember it later. Bizarre images can make stored information more *distinctive* and therefore easier to recall.

A sampling of typical applications of mnemonics should make these four points clear to you.

Example 1 Let's say you have 30 new vocabulary words to memorize in Spanish. You can proceed by rote memorization (repeat them over and over until you begin to get them), or you can learn them with little effort by using the **keyword method** (Pressley et al., 1980). To remember that the word *pajaro* (pronounced PA-ha-ro) means bird, you can link it to a "key" word in English: *Pajaro* (to me) sounds like "parked car-o." Therefore, to remember that *pajaro* means bird, I will visualize a parked car jam-packed full of birds. I will try to make this image as vivid and exaggerated as possible, with birds flapping and chirping and feathers flying everywhere. Similarly, for the word *carta* (which means "letter"), I will imagine a shopping *cart* filled with postal letters. If you link similar keywords and images for the rest of the list, you may not remember them all, but you will get most without any more practice. As a matter of fact, if you have formed the *pajaro* and *carta* images just now, it is going to be almost impossible for you to ever see these words again without remembering what they mean.

Question: What if I think that pajaro *means "parked car" when I take my Spanish test?*

This is why you should form one or two extra images so that the important feature (bird, in this case) is repeated.

Example 2 Let's say you have to learn the names of all the bones and muscles in the human body for biology. You are trying to remember that the jawbone is the *mandible*. This one is easy because you can associate it to a *man nibbling*, or maybe

Applications

you can picture a *man dribbling* a basketball with his jaw (make this image as ridiculous as possible). If the muscle name *latissimus dorsi* gives you trouble, familiarize it by turning it into *"the ladder misses the door, sigh."* Then picture a ladder glued to your back where the muscle is found. Picture the ladder leading up to a small door at your shoulder. Picture the ladder missing the door. Picture the ladder sighing like an animated character in a cartoon.

Question: This seems like more to remember, not less; and it seems like it would cause you to misspell things.

Mnemonics are not a complete substitute for normal memory; they are an aid to normal memory. Mnemonics are not likely to be helpful unless you make extensive use of *images.* Your mental pictures will come back to you easily. As for misspellings, mnemonics can be thought of as a built-in hint in your memory. Often, when taking a test, you will find that the slightest hint is all you need to remember correctly. A mnemonic image is like having someone leaning over your shoulder who says, "Psst, the name of that muscle sounds like 'ladder misses the door, sigh.' " If misspelling continues to be a problem, try to create memory aids for spelling, too.

Here are two more examples to help you appreciate the flexibility of a mnemonic approach to studying.

Example 3 Your art history teacher expects you to be able to name the artist when you are shown slides as part of exams. You have seen many of the slides only once before in class. How will you remember them? As the slides are shown in class, make each artist's name into an object or image. Then picture the object *in* the paintings done by the artist. For example, you can picture Van Gogh as a *van* (automobile) *going* through the middle of each Van Gogh painting. Picture the van running over things and knocking things over. Or, if you remember that Van Gogh cut off his ear, picture a giant bloody ear in each of his paintings.

Example 4 If you have trouble remembering history, try to avoid thinking of it as something from the dim past. Picture each historical personality as a person you know right now (a friend, teacher, parent, and so on). Then picture these people doing whatever the historical figures did. Also, try visualizing battles or other events as if they were happening in your town, or make parks and schools into countries. Use your imagination.

Question: How can mnemonics be used to remember things in order?

Here are three techniques that are helpful:

1. Form a chain. To remember lists of ideas, objects, or words in order, trying forming an exaggerated association (mental image) connecting the first item to the second, then the second to the third, and so on. To remember the following short list in order—*elephant, doorknob, string, watch, rifle, oranges*—picture a full-sized *elephant* balanced on a *doorknob* playing with a *string* tied to him. Picture a *watch* tied to the string, and a *rifle* shooting *oranges* at the watch. This technique can be used quite successfully for lists of 20 or more items. Try it next time you go shopping and leave your list at home.

2. Take a mental walk. Ancient Greek orators had an interesting way to remember ideas in order when giving a speech. Their method was to take a mental walk along a familiar path. As they did, they associated topics with the images of statues found along the walk. You can do the same thing by "placing" objects or ideas along the way as you mentally take a familiar walk.

3. Use a system. Many times, the first letter or syllables of words or ideas can be formed into another word that will serve as a reminder of order. "Roy G. Biv" is an example. As an alternative, learn the following: 1 is a bun, 2 is a shoe, 3 is a tree, 4 is a door, 5 is a hive, 6 is sticks, 7 is heaven, 8 is a gate, 9 is a line, 10 is a hen. To remember a list in order, form an image associating bun with the first item on your list. For example, if the first item is *frog* picture a "frog-burger" on a bun to remember it. Then, associate shoe with the second item, and so on.

If you have never used mnemonics, you may still be skeptical, but give this approach a fair trial. Most people find they can greatly extend their memory through the use of mnemonics. But remember, mnemonics only supplement the memory tips given earlier; they do not replace them. Like most things worthwhile, remembering takes effort.

Learning Check

1. Memory systems and aids are referred to as ______________.

2. Which of the following is least likely to improve memory?
a. using exaggerated mental images *b.* forming a chain of associations *c.* turning visual information into verbal information *d.* associating new information to information that is already known or familiar

3. Picturing your knee moaning as it tries to remember something could serve as a mnemonic for the term mnemonic. T or F?

4. Bower's 1973 study showed that, in general, mnemonics only improve memory for related words or ideas. T or F?

Answers:
1. mnemonics 2. c. 3. T 4. F

Exploration: How Many Types of Memory Are There?

As we have seen, *memory* is an umbrella term that includes both short-term and long-term memory. Beyond this, it is becoming clear that more than one type of long-term memory exists. Let's probe a little further into the mysteries of memory.

Skill Memory and Fact Memory A curious thing happens to many people who develop amnesia. A patient like the one described by Brenda Milner (1965) (see earlier discussion) may be unable to learn a telephone number, an address, or a person's name. And yet, this particular patient, like many such patients, could learn the frustrating task of drawing while watching his hands reversed in a mirror. Likewise, amnesiac patients may learn to complete complex puzzles in the same amount of time as normal subjects (McKean, 1983) (Fig. 9–17). These and other observations have led many psychologists to conclude that long-term memories fall into at least two categories. One of these might be called **procedural memory** (or skill memory). The other is sometimes called **fact memory.**

Procedural memory includes basic conditioned responses and response chains like those involved in typing, solving a puzzle, or swinging a golf club. Memories such as these can be fully expressed only as actions. It is likely that skill memories register in "lower" brain areas, especially the cerebellum, and that they appeared early in the evolution of the brain (Tulving, 1985). They appear to represent the more basic "automatic" elements of conditioning, learning, and memory.

Fact memory is the ability to learn specific information, such as names, faces, words, dates, and ideas. This is the memory that a person with amnesia lacks and that most of us take for granted. Some psychologists believe that fact memory can be further divided into two other types, called semantic and episodic memory (Tulving, 1985).

Semantic Memory Most of our basic *factual knowledge* about the world is almost totally immune to forgetting. The names of objects, the days of the week or months of the year, simple math skills, the seasons, words and language, and other general facts are all quite lasting. Such facts make up a part of LTM called **semantic memory.** Semantic memory serves as a mental dictionary or encyclopedia of basic knowledge.

Episodic Memory Semantic memory has no connection to times or places. It would be rare, for instance, to remember when and where you first learned the names of the seasons. In contrast, **episodic memory** (ep-ih-SOD-ik) is "autobiographical." It records life events (or "episodes") day after day, year after year. Can you remember your seventh birthday? Your first date? An accident you witnessed? The first day of college? Ideas you have read in this text? What you had for breakfast 3 days ago? All are episodic memories.

Question: Are episodic memories as lasting as semantic memories?

In general, episodic memories are

Fig. 9–17 *The tower puzzle. In this puzzle, all the colored disks must be moved to another post, without ever placing a larger disk on a smaller one. An amnesia patient learned to solve the puzzle in 31 moves, the minimum possible. Even so, each time he began, he protested that he did not remember ever solving the puzzle before and that he did not know how to begin. Evidence like this suggests that skill memory is distinct from fact memory.*

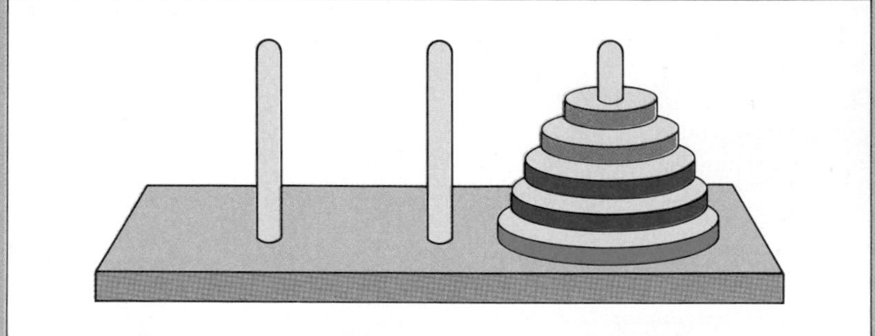

Exploration

more easily forgotten than semantic memories. (Flashbulb memories, described earlier, are an exception.) This is because new information constantly pours into episodic memory. Stop for a moment and remember what you did last summer. That was an episodic memory. Notice that you now remember that you just remembered something. You have a new episodic memory in which you remember that you remembered while reading this text! It's easy to see how much we ask of our memory system.

How Many Types of Memory? In answer to the question posed by the title of this Exploration, it is very likely that 3 kinds of long-term memories exist: procedural, semantic, and episodic. However, the relationship among these is still actively debated (Johnson & Hasher, 1987). Although the debate continues, and other types of memory may be discovered in the future (Tulving, 1985, 1986), it appears that some pieces of the puzzle called memory are falling into place.

Learning Check

1. Procedural memories are stored in STM, whereas factual memories are stored in LTM. T or F?
2. Semantic memories and episodic memories are both fact memories. T or F?
3. Episodic memories are almost totally immune to forgetting. T or F?
4. Episodic memories are largely autobiographical. T or F?
5. In general, semantic memories are more easily forgotten than episodic memories. T or F?

Answers:
1. F 2. T 3. F 4. T 5. F

Chapter Summary

- **Memory** is an active, computer-like system that **encodes, stores,** and **retrieves** information.
- Humans appear to have three interrelated memory systems. These are **sensory memory, short-term memory** (STM, also called **working memory**), and **long-term memory** (LTM).
- Sensory memory is exact, but very brief. Through **selective attention,** some information is transferred to STM.
- STM has a capacity of about **7 bits** of information, but this can be extended by **chunking,** or **recoding.** Short-term memories are brief and very sensitive to **interruption,** or **interference;** however, they can be prolonged by **rehearsal.**
- LTM functions as a general storehouse of information, especially *meaningful* information. Long-term memories are *relatively permanent*, or lasting. LTM seems to have an almost *unlimited storage* capacity.
- LTM is subject to **constructive processing,** or ongoing revision and updating. LTM is highly *organized* to allow retrieval of needed information. The pattern, or **structure,** of memory **networks** is the subject of current memory research.
- **Hypnosis** may improve memory to a small degree, but it also increases the number of **false memories** reported.
- The **tip-of-the-tongue state** shows that memory is not an all-or-nothing event. Memories may therefore be revealed by **recall, recognition, relearning,** or **redintegration.**
- In recall, memory proceeds without *explicit cues,* as in an *essay* exam. Recall of listed information often reveals a **serial position effect** (middle items on the list are most subject to errors). A common test of recognition is the *multiple-choice* question, which requires selection of a correct answer. In relearning, "forgotten" material is learned

again, and memory is indicated by a **savings score.** In redintegration, memories are **reconstructed** as each memory serves as a cue for the next memory.
• **Eidetic imagery** (photographic memory) occurs when a person is able to project an image onto a blank surface. Such images allow brief, nearly complete recall in some children. Eidetic imagery is rarely found in adults. However, many adults have **internal memory images,** which can be very vivid.
• **Exceptional memory** can be learned by finding ways to directly store information in LTM. Learning has no effect on the limits of STM. Some people may have exceptional memories that exceed what can be achieved through learning.
• Forgetting and memory were extensively studied by **Herman Ebbinghaus,** whose **curve of forgetting** shows that forgetting is most rapid immediately after learning. This is one reason why **periodic review** can be helpful in studying.
• **Failure to encode** information is a common cause of "forgetting." Forgetting in sensory memory and STM probably reflects **decay** of **memory traces** in the nervous system. Decay or **disuse** of memories may also account for some LTM loss, but much forgetting cannot be explained in this way.
• Often, forgetting is **cue-dependent.** That is, information is stored and *available* but not *accessible*, because the cues necessary to retrieve it are missing. The power of cues to trigger memories is revealed by **state-dependent learning** and the link between moods and memory.
• Much forgetting in both STM and LTM can be attributed to **interference** of memories with one another. When recent learning interferes with retrieval of prior learning, **retroactive interference** has occurred. If old learning interferes with new learning, **proactive interference** has occurred.
• **Repression** is the forgetting of painful, embarrassing, or traumatic memories. Repression is thought to be unconscious, in contrast to **suppression,** which is a conscious attempt to avoid thinking about something.
• **Retrograde amnesia** and the effects of electroconvulsive shock (ECS) may be explained by the concept of **consolidation.** Consolidation theory holds that **engrams** (permanent memory traces) are formed during a critical period after learning. Until they are consolidated, long-term memories are easily destroyed. The **hippocampus** is a brain area that has been linked with consolidation of memories.
• The search within the brain for engrams has now settled on changes in individual nerve cells. The best-documented changes are alterations in the amounts of **transmitter chemicals** released by the cells and the number of **receptor cites** on each cell.
• Memory can be improved by using **feedback** and **recitation,** by **overlearning,** by **selecting** and **organizing** information, and by using **spaced practice,** the **progressive part method,** and active **search strategies.** Effects of **serial position, sleep, review, cues,** and **elaboration** should also be kept in mind when studying or memorizing.
• **Mnemonic systems** use mental images and unusual associations to link new information with familiar memories already stored in LTM. Such strategies give information personal meaning and make it easier to recall.
• **Fact memories** seem to differ from **procedural memories.** Fact memories may be further categorized as **semantic memories** or **episodic memories.** The properties and relationships among types of memory are currently being debated.

Questions for Discussion

1. What type of classroom testing do you prefer? Why? What would you consider an ideal way to be tested? ("Never" does not count as an answer!)

2. Would you like to have a memory like the man studied by A. R. Luria? What would be the advantages and disadvantages of such a memory? Mr. S could not recognize faces. Can you explain why? If, as an adult, you retained eidetic memory, how would you use it?

3. If you were forced to give up either STM or LTM, which would you choose? Think carefully about your answer.

4. We have seen that there are several reasons for forgetting. Which does the use of mnemonics most directly combat? How would you minimize the other major causes of forgetting?

5. You must study French, Spanish, psychology, and

biology in one evening, and you have little time for breaks. What do you think would be the best order in which to study these subjects so as to minimize interference? Why?

6. If scientists perfect a drug that improves memory, do you think it should be widely available? Would you want to try it? If a drug were perfected that could cause selective forgetting of memories, would you support its use for victims of rape, assault, disaster, or a horrifying accident?

7. What mnemonic strategies have you used in studying? Which have been most helpful? How could a person with limited mental imagery use mnemonics?

8. What have you done to cope with remembering longer zip codes?

9. Describe a case of mistaken identity you have seen in the news. What aspect of memory contributed to the mistake?

10. In view of the text's discussion, do you think memories that occur during hypnosis should be allowed as evidence in court? One expert has suggested videotaping sessions during which witnesses or victims are questioned under hypnosis. If such tapes were available to juries, do you think testimony based on hypnosis would be more trustworthy? Why or why not?

Chapter 10

Cognition and Creativity

In This Chapter
What is cognition?
Animal intelligence
Mental imagery
Concepts
Language
Problem solving
Insight and creativity
Intuition
Applications
Improving thinking
Exploration
Artificial intelligence

Chapter Preview

Chess, Anyone?

David Levy was in trouble. It was the fourth game of a 6-game chess match, and Levy was trying a new strategy. If he lost the match, Levy would forfeit $2500 of his own money. Game 1 was a tie. Levy won games 2 and 3. Now, in game 4, he was locked in a sharp tactical battle, and he was losing. What was wrong? In the earlier games Levy had relied on the kind of wide-open maneuvering that had made him an International Master. In contrast, his opponent's strength was a powerful short-term, or tactical, style of play. Maybe "powerful" isn't the right word. Unbeatable is closer to the truth, as Levy soon learned. For the moment, David Levy had met his match. He watched silently as the robot arm of Chess 4.7 made its final move, winning game 4.

Chess 4.7 is a computer program. It once won the Minnesota Open Chess Tournament—against humans. However, David Levy, the reigning Scottish champion, proved to be a tougher opponent. After losing game 4, Levy quickly returned to his original style of play—and won the match (Ehara, 1980). For all their raw power, computers are only able to plan 5 or 6 chess moves in advance (by considering over 1 billion possibilities). They don't make mistakes in the short run, but they can be beaten by strategy and foresight.

David Levy's victory symbolizes one of the most unique of all human capacities, the ability to think intelligently and creatively. We know how computers "think" because we created them. But how do we explain David Levy's creativity and problem-solving ability? Or yours? Thinking, problem solving, and creativity are the challenging topics of this chapter.

Survey Questions

- What is the nature of thought?
- Do animals think?
- What basic units are used in thinking, and how do they differ?
- How do concepts and language influence thought?
- Can animals be taught to use language?
- What do we know about problem solving and creativity?
- How accurate is intuition?
- Can creativity be learned?
- What is artificial intelligence?

What Is Thinking?—It's All in Your Head!

Thinking takes many forms, including daydreaming, fantasizing, problem solving, and reasoning (to name but a few). Stated more formally, **thinking,** or **cognition,** refers to the mental manipulation of images, concepts, words, rules, symbols, and precepts. How do psychologists study thinking? The challenge is similar to figuring out how a computer works by repeatedly asking, "I wonder what would happen if I did this?" But in **cognitive psychology** the "computer" is the brain, and thinking is the "programming" we seek to understand.

Although an ability to think is not limited to humans, imagine trying to teach an animal to match the feats of Shakuntala Devi, who holds the "world record" for mental calculation. Devi once multiplied two 18-digit numbers (7,686,369,774,870 times 2,465,099,745,779) in her head, giving the answer in 28 seconds (Morain, 1988). (That's 18,947,668,177,995,426,773,730 if you haven't already figured it out yourself.)

Question: To what extent are animals capable of thought?

Most pet owners can readily supply stories of apparent thinking in animals. A friend might say, "Wow, you should have seen Studebaker figure out how to get into the closet where I hid the dog food." Are animals actually thinking in such situations? In a rudimentary sense they are. At its most basic, thinking is the **internal representation** of a problem or situation. (Picture a chess player who mentally tries out several possible moves before actually touching a chess piece.)

Animals demonstrate internal representation in **delayed response problems.** For example, a hungry animal could be allowed to watch as food is hidden under one of three goal boxes. After a delay, the animal is released. Can it select the correct box? If the delay is brief, the answer is yes. At times, animal behavior implies far higher levels of thought. In fact, German psychologist Wolfgang Köhler (VOOLF-gong KEAR-ler) believed that animals such as chimpanzees are capable of insight.

Insight is a sudden mental reorganization of the elements of a problem that makes the solution obvious. To test for insight, Köhler challenged Sultan, his brightest chimp, with a **multiple-stick problem.** In this problem, several sticks of increasing length were arranged between the cage and a banana (Fig. 10–1). To reach the banana, Sultan had to use the first stick to retrieve the second

Fig. 10–1 *Psychologist Wolfgang Köhler believed that the solution of a multiple-stick problem revealed a capacity for insight in chimpanzees.*

stick (which was longer than the first). The second stick could then be used to get an even longer stick, which could then be used to reach the banana (Köhler, 1925).

When confronted with this problem, Sultan looked at the banana, then at the sticks . . . then at the banana. Picking up the first stick, Sultan smoothly and without further hesitation solved the problem and raked in the banana.

Psychologists have long debated whether Köhler's chimps actually displayed insight. More recently, however, David Premack (1983) found added evidence of insightful problem solving by a chimp. In one fascinating experiment, Premack showed a chimpanzee a videotape of an actor jumping up and down below a bunch of bananas. The chimp was then shown several still photographs of the actor in various positions. From these, the chimp chose a photograph of the actor stepping up onto a chair. Note that this choice makes sense only if the chimp understood that the actor was trying to reach the bananas.

In recent years evidence for animal intelligence and thinking ability has continued to grow—but not without controversy (see Highlight 10–1).

Some Basic Units of Thought In the Chapter Preview, we used chess playing as an example of human thought. Let's briefly consider another chess example. Chess Grand Master Miguel Najdorf once simultaneously played 45 chess games, while *blindfolded*. It is estimated that over 3600 different positions arose during the evening of the exhibition (Hearst, 1969).

How did Najdorf perform his feat? Like most people,

HIGHLIGHT 10–1
How Intelligent Are Animals?

Evidence for the idea that animals are capable of intelligent thought is varied and, to many researchers, convincing:

- Monkeys can learn to select, from among three objects, the one that differs from the other two.
- When a container of sugar water is moved a set distance farther from a beehive each day, the bees begin to go to the new location *before* the water is moved.
- Pigeons can learn to select photographs of humans from a group of photos that includes various objects.
- A chimpanzee is allowed to see itself in a mirror. It is then anesthetized, and a red spot is placed on its forehead. When it awakens and looks in the mirror, it tries to rub away the colored spot.

Do such examples really demonstrate thinking by animals? Some psychologists say yes; some say no. What would it take, then, to verify animal thinking? Psychologist Donald Griffin suggests that we must observe behavior that is *versatile* and *appropriate* to changing circumstances. He also believes that thinking is implied by actions that appear to be planned with an awareness of likely results. As one example, sea otters select suitably sized rocks and use them to hammer shellfish loose for eating. They then use the rock to open the shell (Fig. 10–2).

Fig. 10–2 *Does the seemingly intelligent behavior of sea otters and other animals reflect thinking ability, instinct, or conditioning? The evidence remains inconclusive, so psychologists disagree.*

As convincing as such examples may seem, they have been challenged. For instance, Epstein, Lanza, and Skinner have conditioned pigeons to duplicate seemingly insightful behavior like that claimed for higher animals. David Premack, however, replies that the pigeons only achieved the *appearance* of thinking, because their behavior was strongly guided by reinforcement.

As stated before, it seems reasonable to assume that animals do think. However, debate is sure to continue about the limits of their intelligence and about whether specific examples demonstrate thinking, instinct, or conditioning. (Sources: Epstein et al., 1981; Griffin, 1984; Herrnstein, 1979; Premack, 1983; Rose, 1984.)

he probably used the following basic *units of thought:* (1) **images,** (2) **muscular responses,** (3) **concepts,** and (4) **language,** or **symbols.** All four ways of representing information may be combined in complex thinking. Indeed, in some situations people need all the help they can get. To accomplish their mental feats, blindfolded chess players rely on visual images, muscular sensations involving "lines of force," concepts ("Game 2 is an English opening"), and the special notational system, or "language," of chess (Hearst, 1969).

In a moment we will explore the units of thought identified here. Be aware, however, that thinking involves attention, pattern recognition, memory, decision making, intuition, knowledge, and more. This chapter is only a sample of what cognitive psychologists study.

Compare: Four Ways To Mentally Represent Information

Image Most often, a mental representation that has picturelike qualities; an icon.

Muscular imagery Internal representations of events in terms of generated, remembered, or imagined muscular sensations.

Concept A generalized idea representing a category or class of objects or events grouped together on some basis.

Language A body of words, or symbols, and rules for combining them that is used for communication and thought and is understood by a sizable community.

Mental Imagery—Does a Frog Have Lips?

A survey of 500 people found that 97 percent have visual images and 92 percent have auditory images. Over 50 percent had imagery that included movement, touch, taste, smell, and pain (McKellar, 1965). When we speak of images, we usually think of mental "pictures." But as you can see, images may involve the other senses as well. For example, your image of a bakery may include its delicious odor, as well as its appearance. Some people even have a rare form of imagery called **synesthesia** (sin-es-THEE-zyah). For these individuals, images cross normal sensory barriers (Marks, 1978). For instance, a synesthetic individual listening to music may experience a burst of colors or tastes as well as sound sensations. Despite such variations, it is generally accepted that most people use images to think and to solve problems.

In recent years Stephen Kosslyn and other researchers have added greatly to our understanding of mental imagery. For instance, Kosslyn (1983) discovered that mental images are not flat like photographs. To sample Kosslyn's work, think about the following question: Does a frog have lips and a stubby tail? Unless you often kiss frogs, you will probably tackle this question by using mental images. To answer, most people report that they picture a frog, "look" at its mouth, and then **mentally rotate** the frog to check its tail (Kosslyn, 1983). Mental images, then, are not necessarily flat, and they can be moved about as needed (Fig. 10–3).

Question: How are images used to solve problems?

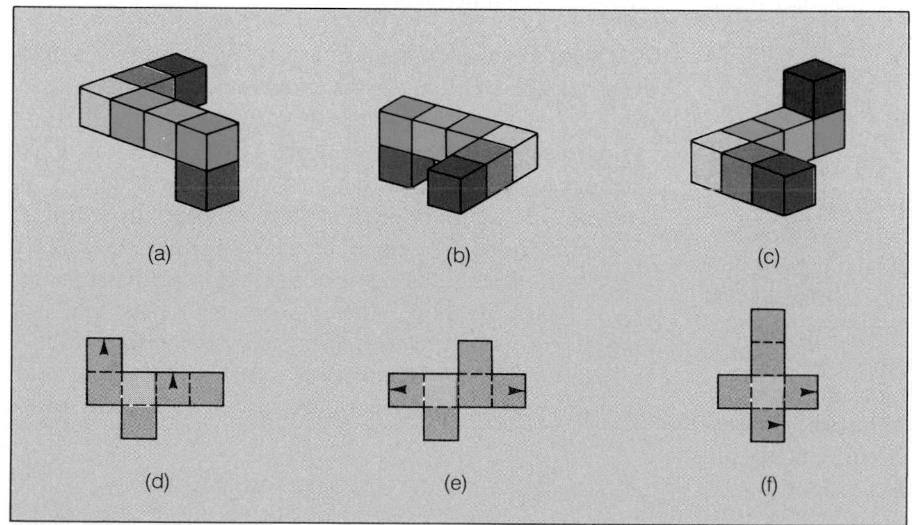

Fig. 10–3 *Imagery in thinking.* (Top) *Subjects were shown a drawing similar to* (a) *and drawings of how* (a) *would look in other positions, such as* (b) *and* (c). *Subjects could recognize* (a) *after it had been "rotated" from its original position. However, the more* (a) *was rotated in space, the longer it took to recognize it. This result suggests that subjects actually formed a three-dimensional image of* (a) *and rotated the image to see if it matched. (Shepard, 1975.)* (Bottom) *Try your ability to manipulate mental images: Each of these shapes can be folded to make a cube; in which do the arrows meet? (After Kosslyn, 1985.)*

Stored images can be used to bring prior experience to bear on problem solving. If you were asked the question, "How many uses can you think of for an old automobile tire?" you might begin by picturing all the uses you have already seen. To generate more original solutions, **created images** may be used. Research shows that people who have good imaging ability tend to score higher on tests of creativity (Shaw & Belmore, 1983). Thus, an artist may completely picture a proposed sculpture before beginning work.

Does the "size" of a mental image make any difference in thinking? To find out, first picture a cat sitting beside a housefly. Now try to "zoom in" on the cat's ears so you see them clearly. Next, picture a rabbit sitting beside an elephant. How quickly can you "see" the rabbit's front feet? Did it take longer than picturing the cat's ears?

When a rabbit is pictured with an elephant, the rabbit's image must be small because the elephant is large. Using such tasks, Kosslyn (1975) found that the smaller an image is, the harder it is to "see" its details. To put this finding to use, try forming over-sized images of things you want to think about. For example, to understand electricity, picture the wires as large pipes with electrons the size of golf balls moving through them; to understand the human ear, explore it (in your mind's eye) like a large cave; and so forth.

Muscular Imagery

Question: How do muscular responses relate to thinking?

It is surprising to realize that we think with our bodies as well as our heads. Jerome Bruner (1966) believes that we often represent things in a kind of **muscular imagery** created by actions or *implicit* (unexpressed) actions. For example, people who "talk" with their hands are using gestures to help themselves think as well as to communicate. A great deal of information is contained in *kinesthetic sensations* (feelings from the muscles and joints). As a person talks, these sensations help structure the flow of ideas (Horowitz, 1970). If you try to tell a friend how to knead bread dough, you may find it impossible to resist moving your hands as you describe the proper motion.

Most thinking is accompanied by muscular tension and **micromovements** throughout the body. In one classic study, a subject was asked to imagine that he was hitting a nail with a hammer. As he did, a burst of activity was recorded in the muscles of his unmoving arm (Jacobson, 1932). If you would like to demonstrate the link between muscular activity and thinking, ask a friend who was in a sports event to describe what occurred. Along with a description, you will probably get an "instant replay" of the high points!

Concepts—I'm Positive, It's a Whatchamacallit.

A **concept** is an idea that represents a class of objects or events. Concepts are powerful tools because they allow us to think more *abstractly,* free from distracting details. Imagine, for instance, that you have shown a 5-year-old child 2 big toy frogs and 4 little frogs. You then ask the child, "Are there more frogs or more baby frogs?" When Markman and Seibert (1976) asked kindergarten children the same question, most erred and said, "More baby frogs." The researchers then brought the concept of a *family* into the problem ("This is a family of frogs. Are there more frogs or more baby frogs?") Adding the concept dramatically reduced the children's thinking errors.

Question: How are concepts learned?

Concept formation is the process of classifying information into meaningful categories. At its most basic, concept formation involves experience with **positive** and **negative instances** of the concept. This is not as simple as it might seem. Imagine a child learning the concept of *dog*.

Dog Daze

A child and her father go for a walk. At a neighbor's house, they see a medium-sized dog. The father says, "See the dog." As they pass the next yard, the child sees a cat and says, "Dog!" Her father corrects her, "No, that's a *cat*." The child now thinks, "Aha, dogs are large and cats are small." In the next yard, she sees a Pekingese and says, "Cat!" "No, that's a dog," replies her father.

The child's confusion is understandable. At first she might even mistake a Pekingese for a dust mop. However, with more positive and negative instances, the child will eventually recognize everything from Great Danes to Chihuahuas as examples of the same category—dogs.

As adults, we more often acquire concepts by learning or forming **rules.** For example, a *triangle* must be a closed shape with three sides made of straight lines. Rule learning is generally more efficient than examples, but examples remain important (Rosenthal & Zimmerman, 1978). It is unlikely that memorizing a series of rules would allow an uninitiated listener to accurately categorize *punk, new wave, fusion, salsa, heavy metal,* and *rap* music.

Question: Are there different kinds of concepts?

Yes, several general types of concepts have been identified. A **conjunctive concept** refers to a class of objects having more than one feature in common. Conjunctive concepts are sometimes called "and" concepts: To belong to the concept class, an item must have "this feature *and* this feature *and* this feature." For example, a *motorcycle* must have two wheels *and* an engine *and* handle bars.

Relational concepts classify objects on the basis of their relationship to something else or by the relationship between features of an object. *Larger, above, left, north,* and *upside down* are all relational concepts. Another example is *sister,* which is defined as "a female considered in her relation to another person having the same parents."

Disjunctive concepts refer to objects that have at least one of several possible features. These are "either-or concepts." To belong, an item must have "this feature *or* that feature *or* another feature." For example, in the game of baseball, a *strike* is *either* a swing and a miss *or* a pitch down the middle *or* a foul ball. The either-or quality of disjunctive concepts makes them difficult to learn.

When you think of the concept *bird,* do you make a mental list of features that birds have? Probably not. In addition to rules and features, most people also use **prototypes,** or ideal models, to identify concepts (Rosch, 1977). A robin, for instance, is a model bird, whereas an ostrich is not. What this tells us is that not all examples of a concept are equally representative. For example, which of the drawings in Figure 10–4 best represents a cup? At some point, a cup that is made taller or wider becomes a vase or a bowl. How do we know when the line is crossed? Probably, we mentally compare objects to an "ideal" cup, like number 5. The upshot is that identifying concepts is difficult when we cannot come up with a prototype relevant to what we see. What, for example, are the objects shown in Figure 10–5?

Generally speaking, concepts have two types of meaning. The **denotative meaning** of a word or concept is its exact definition. The **connotative meaning** is its emotional or personal meaning. For example, the denotative meaning of the word *naked* (having no clothes) is the same for a nudist as it is for a movie censor, but we could expect their connotations to differ.

Question: Can you give a clearer statement of what a connotative meaning is?

Researcher Charles Osgood (1952) used a method called the **semantic differential** to measure connotative meaning (Fig. 10–6). When words or concepts are rated on a series of scales, most of their connotative meaning boils down to the dimensions *good-bad, strong-weak,* and *active-passive.* (Sounds like a good movie title, doesn't it: *The Good the Bad the Strong the Weak the Active and the Passive.*) Because concepts vary on these dimensions, words or phrases with roughly the same denotative meaning may have very different connotations. For example, I am *conscientious;* you are *careful*; he is *nit-picking*!

Fig. 10–4 *When does a cup become a bowl or a vase? Deciding if an object belongs to a conceptual class is aided by relating it to a prototype, or ideal example. Subjects in one experiment chose number 5 as the "best" cup. (After Labov, 1973.)*

Fig. 10–5 *Use of prototypes in concept identification. Even though its shape is unusual, item* (a) *can be related to a model (an ordinary set of pliers) and thus recognized. But what are items* (b) *and* (c)*? If you don't recognize them, look ahead to Fig. 10–7. (After Bransford & McCarrell, 1977.)*

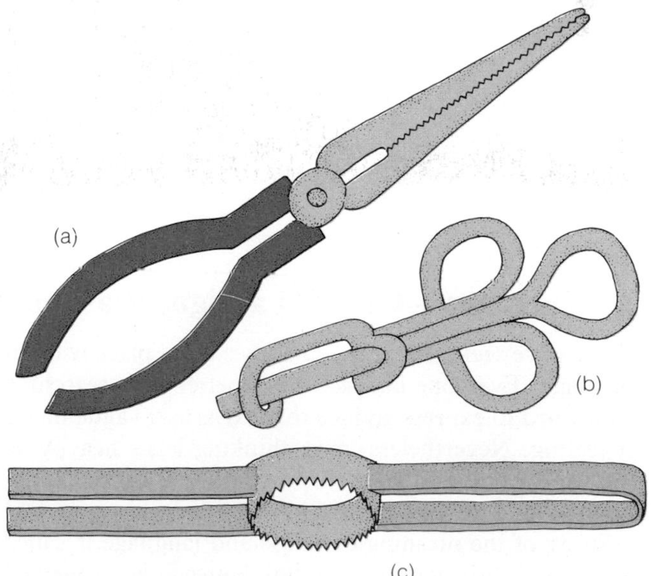

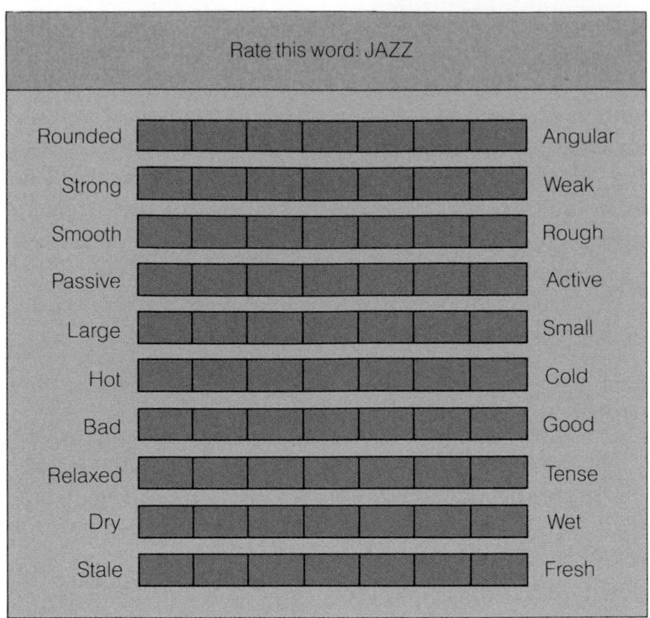

Fig. 10–6 *This is an example of Osgood's semantic differential. The connotative meaning of the word* jazz *can be established by rating it on the scales. Mark your own rating by placing dots or X's in the spaces. Connect the marks with a line; then have a friend rate the word and compare your responses. It might be interesting to do the same for* rock and roll, disco, *and* classical. *You also might want to try the word* psychology. *(From C. E. Osgood. Copyright © 1952 American Psychological Association. Reprinted by permission.)*

Learning Check

1. There is evidence that chimpanzees are capable of insightful solutions to problems, but some psychologists remain unconvinced that true thinking is involved. T or F?

2. List four basic units of thought:

____________________ ____________________

____________________ ____________________

3. Synesthesia is the use of kinesthetic sensations as a vehicle for thought. T or F?

4. Our reliance on imagery in thinking means that problem solving is impaired by micromovements. T or F?

5. Humans appear capable of forming three-dimensional images that can be moved or rotated in mental space. T or F?

6. A *mup* is defined as anything that is small, blue, and hairy. *Mup* is a ____________________ concept.

7. The connotative meaning of the word *naked* is "having no clothes." T or F?

Answers:

1. T **2.** images, muscular responses, concepts, and language or symbols (others could be listed) **3.** F **4.** F **5.** T **6.** conjunctive **7.** F

● Language—Give Us a Sign, Washoe

As we have seen, thinking sometimes takes place without language. Everyone has had the experience of searching for a word to express an idea that exists as a vague image or feeling. Nevertheless, most thinking leans heavily on language, because it allows the world to be **encoded** into symbols that are easy to manipulate.

Study of the meaning of words and language is called **semantics.** It is here that the link between language and thought becomes most evident. Suppose, on an intelligence test, you were asked to circle the word that does not belong in this series:

SKYSCRAPER CATHEDRAL
TEMPLE PRAYER

If you circled prayer, you answered as most people do. Now try another problem, again circling the odd item:

CATHEDRAL PRAYER
TEMPLE SKYSCRAPER

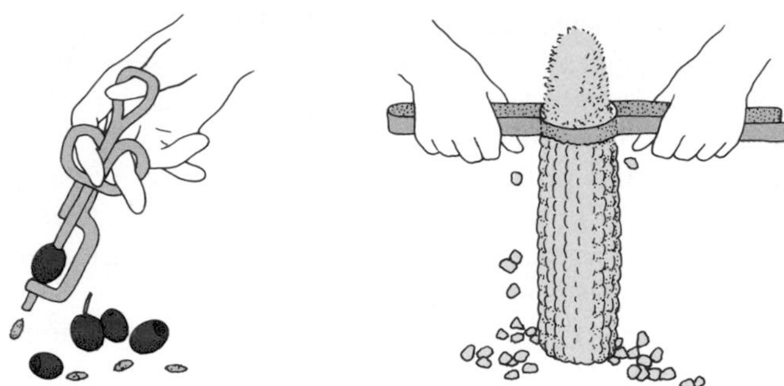

Fig. 10–7 *Context can substitute for a lack of appropriate prototypes in concept identification.*

Had you seen only this question, you probably would have circled skyscraper. There is a subtle change in meaning caused by reordering the words (Judson & Cofer, 1956, cited by Mayer, 1977).

Semantic problems often arise when a word has dual, or unclear, meaning: Does the sentence "Tom was seated by the waiter" mean that the waiter gave Tom a seat or that Tom was seated beside the waiter? Choice of words may directly influence thinking by shifting meaning: Has one country's army "invaded" another? Or "effected a protective incursion"? Is the city reservoir "half full" or "half empty"? Would you rather eat "prime beef" or "dead cow"?! (See Fig. 10–8.)

Question: What does it take to make a language?

The Structure of Language

First of all, a language must provide *symbols* that can stand for objects and ideas. The symbols we call words are built out of **phonemes** (FOE-neems: basic speech sounds) and **morphemes** (MOR-feems: speech sounds collected into meaningful units, such as syllables or words). For instance, in English, the sounds *m, b, w,* and *a* cannot form a syllable *mbwa*. In Swahili, they can. The units of speech can be arranged in countless ways. Consider the possibilities with just four morphemes *reach, to, able,* and *un*. From these, we can make *able to, unable to, reach to, to reach, able to reach, unable to reach, reachable, unreachable, reachable to, unreachable to, unto, unto Able.*

As a second point, a language must have a **grammar,** or set of rules, for making sounds into words and words into sentences. One part of grammar, known as **syntax,** consists of rules for word order in sentences. Syntax is important because rearranging words almost always changes the meaning of a sentence: "Dog bites man" versus "Man bites dog."

Traditional grammar is concerned with "surface" language—the sentences we actually speak. The revolutionary ideas of linguist Noam Chomsky focus instead on the unspoken rules we use to change core ideas into various sentences. Chomsky (1968) argues that we do not learn all the sentences we might ever say. Rather, we actively *create* them by applying **transformation rules.** For example, the core sentence "Dog bites man" can be transformed to the following patterns (and others as well):

Past: The dog bit the man.
Passive: The man was bitten by the dog.
Negative: The dog did not bite the man.
Question: Did the dog bite the man?

Children show evidence of using transformation rules when they form sentences such as "I runned home." The child has applied the past tense rule to the irregular verb *to run.*

The third, and perhaps most essential, characteristic of language is that it is **productive.** The great strength of any true language is that it can produce new thoughts

Fig. 10–8 *The Stroop interference task. Test yourself by naming the colors in the top two rows as quickly as you can. Then name the colors of the* ink *used to print the words in the bottom two rows (do not read the words themselves). The greater difficulty of naming colors in the bottom rows shows how intimately thought is linked to language. The meaning of words has a powerful impact on our response to them (After Tzeng & Wang, 1983.)*

or ideas. Because words do not resemble the things they represent, words can be rearranged to produce an infinite variety of meaningful sentences (Bruner, 1966). Some are silly: "Please don't feed me to the goldfish." Some are profound: "We hold these truths to be self-evident, that all men are created equal." In either case, it is the productive quality of language that makes it such a powerful tool for thought.

Question: Do animals use language?

Animals do communicate. The cries, gestures, and mating calls of animals have broad meanings immediately understood by other animals of the same species (Premack, 1983). For the most part, however, natural animal communication is quite limited. Even apes and monkeys make only a few dozen distinct cries, which carry messages such as "attack," "flee," or "food here." More importantly, animal communication seems to lack the productive quality of human language. For example, when a monkey gives an "eagle distress call," it means something like, "I see an eagle." The monkey has no way of saying, "I don't see an eagle," or "Thank heavens that wasn't an eagle," or "That sucker I saw yesterday was some huge eagle" (Glass et al., 1979).

Question: Could an animal be taught to use language?

Psychologists have made several interesting attempts to teach animals to use language. Let's consider some of their successes and failures.

Talking Chimps Early attempts to teach chimps to talk were a dismal failure. The world record was held by Viki, a chimp who could say only 4 words (*mama, papa, cup,* and *up*) after 6 years of intensive training (Fleming, 1974; Hayes, 1951). (Actually, all four words sounded something like a belch.) Then there was a breakthrough. Beatrice Gardner and Allen Gardner of the University of Nevada, Reno, used operant conditioning and imitation to teach a female chimp named Washoe to use **American Sign Language (ASL).** ASL is a set of hand gestures used by the hearing impaired (each gesture stands for a word).

Washoe's communication skills blossomed rapidly as her "vocabulary" grew. Soon she began to put together primitive sentence strings like "Come-gimme sweet," "Out please," "Gimme tickle," and "Open food drink." She now has a vocabulary of about 240 signs and can construct 6-word sentences. She even communicates with other chimpanzees using sign language, and she is "teaching" her adopted son Loulis to use signs (Gardner & Gardner, 1969; Rose, 1984).

Some critics are skeptical about Washoe's abilities, since her arrangement of "words" is somewhat haphazard. Children quickly learn the difference between word orders like "Give me candy" and "Me give candy." An answer to this criticism comes from the work of David Premack (1970), who taught a female chimp named Sarah to use 130 "words" consisting of plastic chips arranged on a magnetized board (Fig. 10–9).

From the beginning of her training, Sarah was required to use proper word order. She has learned to answer questions, to label things "same" or "different," to classify objects by color, shape, and size, and to construct compound sentences (Premack & Premack, 1983). One of her most outstanding achievements is the use of sentences involving **conditional relationships:** "If Sarah take apple, then Mary give Sarah chocolate." "If Sarah take banana, then Mary no give Sarah chocolate."

Question: Can it be said with certainty that the chimps understand such interchanges?

Most researchers working with chimps believe that they have indeed communicated with them. Especially striking are the chimp's spontaneous responses. Washoe once "wet" on psychologist Roger Fouts' back while riding

Fig. 10–9 *After reading the message "Sarah insert apple pail banana dish" on the magnetic board, Sarah performed the actions as directed. (From "Teaching Language to an Ape" by Ann J. Premack and David Premack. Copyright © 1972 by Scientific American, Inc. All rights reserved.)*

on his shoulders. When Fouts asked, with some annoyance, why she had done it, Washoe signed, "It's funny!"

Some of the most convincing evidence on language comprehension by an animal has come from work by Penny Patterson. Patterson has trained a gorilla named Koko to use over 300 signs. Patterson regards conversations held about *past events* and *feelings* as a strong sign of Koko's comprehension (Patterson et al., 1987). For example, 3 days after Koko bit Patterson, the following conversation took place:

Me: "What did you do to Penny?"
Koko: "Bite."
Me: "You admit it?"
Koko: "Sorry bite scratch. Wrong bite."
Me: "Why bite?"
Koko: "Because mad."
Me: "Why mad?"
Koko: "Don't know."
(Adapted from Patterson, 1978)

Such interchanges are impressive. But communication and actual language use are two different things. Several psychologists have recently expressed doubt that apes can really use language. For one thing, the chimps rarely "speak" without prompting. Many of their seemingly original sentences turn out to be responses to questions or imitations of signs the teacher made. Also, it appears that the apes may be simply performing chains of *operant responses* to get food or other "goodies" (Savage-Rumbaugh et al., 1979; Terrace, 1985). By using such responses, the apes then manipulate their trainers to get what they want.

You might say that the critics believe that the apes have made monkeys out of their trainers. However, psychologists Roger and Debbi Fouts recently countered such criticism. An analysis they performed of some 6000 conversations between chimps showed that only 5 percent had anything to do with food. The Fouts also videotaped conversations between chimps that took place when no humans were present to cue them (Fouts et al., 1984). So, maybe the chimps will make monkeys out of the critics. Although the issue is far from resolved, such research promises to unravel some of the mysteries of language learning. In fact, it has already been helpful for teaching language to aphasic children (children with serious language impairment) (Huges, 1974).

Problem Solving—Getting an Answer in Sight

A good way to start a discussion of problem solving is to solve a problem. Give this one a try.

> A famous ocean liner (the *Queen Ralph*) is steaming toward port at 20 miles per hour. It is 50 miles from shore when a sea gull takes off from its deck and flies toward port. At the same instant, a speedboat leaves port at 30 miles per hour. The bird flies back and forth between the speedboat and the *Queen Ralph* at a speed of 40 miles per hour. How far will the bird have flown when the two boats pass?

If you don't immediately see the answer to this problem, read it again. (The answer is revealed shortly in Insightful Solutions.)

We all do a tremendous amount of problem solving every day. Problem solving can be as commonplace as figuring out how to make a nonpoisonous meal out of leftovers or as significant as developing a cure for cancer. In either case, we begin with an awareness that an answer probably exists and that by proper thinking, a solution can be found. A number of different approaches to problem solving can be identified.

Mechanical Solutions

Mechanical solutions may be achieved by **trial and error** or by **rote.** If I forget the combination to my bike lock, I may be able to discover it by trial and error. In an era of high-speed computers, many trial-and-error solutions are best left to machines. A computer could generate all possible combinations of the five numbers on my lock in a split second.

When a problem is solved by rote, thinking is guided by a learned set of rules. If you have a good background in mathematics, you may have solved the problem of the bird and the boats by rote. (I hope you didn't. There is an easier solution.)

Solutions by Understanding

Many problems cannot be solved mechanically or by habitual modes of thought. In this case, a higher level of thinking based on **understanding** is necessary. A classic series of studies on thinking of this type was performed by German psychologist Karl Duncker (1945). Duncker gave college students this problem:

> Given an inoperable stomach tumor and rays which at high intensity will destroy tissue (both healthy and diseased), how can the tumor be destroyed without damaging surrounding tissue? (Students were also shown the sketch in Fig. 10–10.)

Question: What did this problem show about problem solving?

Duncker asked the students to think aloud as they worked and found that there were two phases to successful problem solving. First, students had to discover the **general**

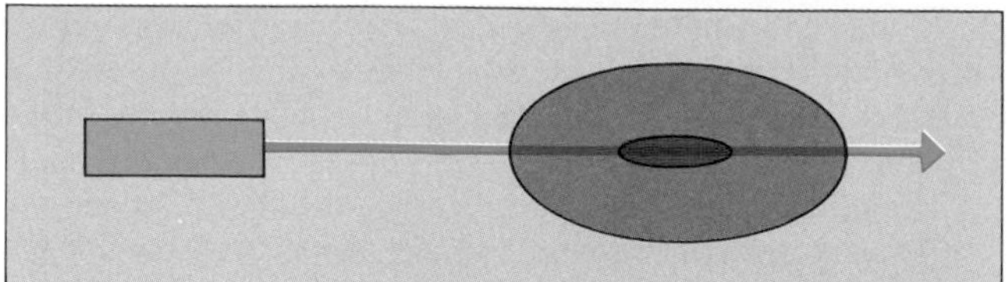

Fig. 10–10 *A schematic representation of Duncker's tumor problem. The dark spot represents a tumor surrounded by healthy tissue. How can the tumor be destroyed without injuring surrounding tissue? (After Duncker, 1945.)*

properties of a correct solution. This phase was complete when they realized that the intensity of the rays had to be lowered on their way to the tumor. Then, in the second phase, they proposed a number of **functional** (workable) **solutions** and selected the best one. (One correct solution is to focus weak rays on the tumor from several angles. Another solution is to rotate the person's body so that the exposure of healthy tissue is minimized.)

Compare: Solutions by Understanding

General solution A solution that correctly states the requirements for success but not in sufficient detail for further action.

Functional solution A detailed, practical, and workable solution.

At this point, it might help to summarize with a more familiar example. Almost everyone who has tried the Rubick's cube puzzle begins at the mechanical, *trial-and-error* level. If you want to take the easy route, printed instructions are available that give the steps for a *rote* solution. In time, those who persist begin to *understand* the *general properties* of the puzzle. After that, they can solve it consistently.

Heuristics "You can't get there from here." Or so it often seems when facing a problem. Solving problems often requires a strategy. If the number of alternatives is small, a **random search strategy** may work. This is another example of trial-and-error problem solving in which all possibilities are tried. Imagine, for example, that you are traveling and decide to look up an old friend, J. Smith, in a city you are visiting. You open the phone book and find 47 J. Smiths listed. Of course, you could dial each number until you find the right one. "Forget it," you say to yourself. "Is there any way I can narrow the search?" "Oh, yeah! I remember hearing that Janet lives by the beach." Then you take out a map and call only the numbers with addresses near the waterfront (Ellis & Hunt, 1983).

The approach used in this example is a **heuristic** (hew-RIS-tik) or problem-solving strategy. Typically, heuristics reduce the number of alternatives that a thinker must consider. In more complex problem solving, heuristics do not guarantee success, but they certainly help. Here are some strategies that often work:

- Try to identify how the current state of affairs differs from the desired goal. Then find steps that will reduce the difference.
- Try working backward from the desired goal to the starting point or current state.
- If you can't reach the goal directly, try to identify an intermediate goal or subproblem that at least gets you closer.
- Represent the problem in other ways, with graphs, diagrams, or analogies, for instance.
- Generate a possible solution and test it. Doing so may eliminate many alternatives, or it may clarify what is needed for a solution.

Ideal Problem Solving Perhaps the most valuable heuristic of all is having a *general* thinking strategy. Psychologist John Bransford and his colleagues list five steps that they believe lead to effective problem solving: *i*dentify, *d*efine, *e*xplore, *a*ct, and *l*ook and *l*earn (Bransford et al., 1986; Bransford & Stein, 1984). Notice that the first letters of the steps spell *ideal*.

To apply the ideal thinking strategy, you should *identify* the problem, *define* it clearly, and then *explore* possible solutions and relevant knowledge. Next, you must *act* by trying a possible solution or hypothesis. Finally, you should *look* at the results and *learn* from them. Of course, each attempted solution may identify further subproblems. These can again be tackled with the "ideal" steps until a final satisfactory solution is found.

Insightful Solutions

Köhler's apes, you may recall, sometimes seemed to show *insight* in solving problems. With humans, we say that insight has occurred when an answer suddenly appears after a period of unsuccessful thought. An insight is usually so *rapid* and *clear* that we often wonder how such an "obvious" solution could have been missed.

Let's return now to the problem of the boats and the bird. The best way to solve it is by insight. Because the boats will cover the 50-mile distance in exactly 1 hour, and the bird flies 40 miles per hour, the bird will have flown 40 miles when the boats meet. No math is necessary if you have insight into this problem.

In a recent experiment, college students rated how "warm" (close to an answer) they felt while solving insight problems. Students who had insights usually jumped directly from "cold" to the correct answer. In contrast, those who gradually felt "warmer" and then "very warm" usually gave wrong answers (Metcalfe, 1986). The surprising message in this study is that you may be headed for a mistake if an insight is *not* rapid.

Question: What, really, does it mean to have an insight?

The Nature of Insight Psychologists Robert Sternberg and Janet Davidson (1982) have studied people as they solve problems that require insight or "leaps of logic." According to them, insight involves three abilities. The first is **selective encoding,** which refers to selecting information that is relevant to a problem, while ignoring distractions. For example, consider the following problem:

> If you have white socks and black socks in your drawer, mixed in the ratio of 4 to 5, how many socks will you have to take out to make sure of having a pair of the same color?

A person who fails to recognize that "mixed in a ratio of 4 to 5" is irrelevant information will be less likely to come up with the correct answer of 3 socks.

Insight also relies on **selective combination;** or bringing together seemingly unrelated bits of useful information. Try this sample problem:

> With a 7-minute hourglass and an 11-minute hourglass, what is the simplest way to time the boiling of an egg for 15 minutes?

The answer requires using both hourglasses in combination. First, the 7-minute and the 11-minute hourglasses are started running. When the 7-minute hourglass runs out, it's time to begin boiling the egg. At this point, 4 minutes remain on the 11-minute hourglass. Thus, when it runs out it is simply turned over. When it runs out again, 15 minutes will have passed.

A third source of insights is **selective comparison.** This is the ability to compare new problems with old information or with problems already solved. A good example is the hat rack problem, in which subjects must build a structure that can support an overcoat in the middle of a room. Subjects are given only two long sticks and a C-clamp to work with. The solution, shown in Figure 10–11, is to clamp the two sticks together so that they are wedged between floor and ceiling. If you were given this problem, you would be more likely to solve it

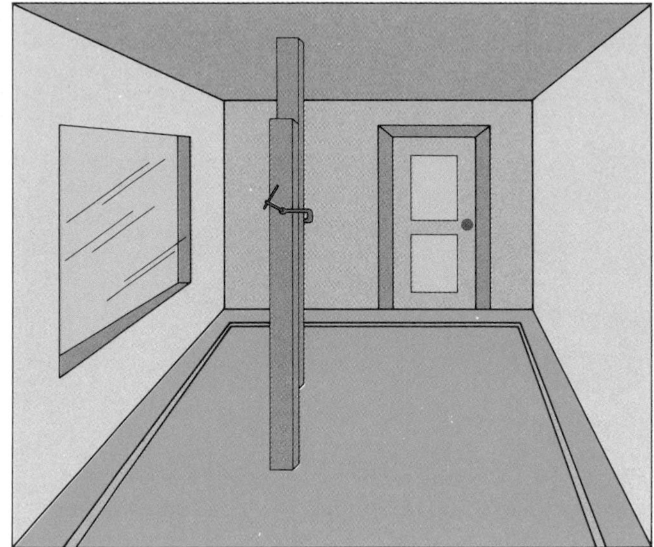

Fig. 10–11 *Solution to the hat rack problem.*

if you first thought of the way pole lamps are wedged between floor and ceiling.

Fixations The ease with which problems are solved is related to a variety of factors. One of the most important barriers to problem solving is called **fixation.** Fixation is the tendency to get "hung up" on wrong solutions or to become blind to alternatives. A prime example of fixation is **functional fixedness.** Functional fixedness is the inability to see new uses (functions) for familiar objects or for objects that have been used in a particular way. If you have ever used a dime as a screwdriver, you've overcome functional fixedness.

Question: How does functional fixedness affect problem solving?

Karl Duncker, who coined the term *functional fixedness,* performed a clever study to demonstrate it. Duncker challenged students to mount a candle on a vertical board so that the candle could burn normally. Duncker gave each student 3 candles, some matches, some cardboard boxes, some thumbtacks, and other items. Half of Duncker's subjects received these items *inside* the cardboard boxes. The others were given all the items, including the boxes, spread out on a tabletop.

Duncker found that when the items were in the boxes, solving the problem was very difficult. This is because the boxes were seen as *containers,* not as items that might be part of the solution. (If you haven't guessed the solution, check Fig. 10–12.) Undoubtedly, we could avoid

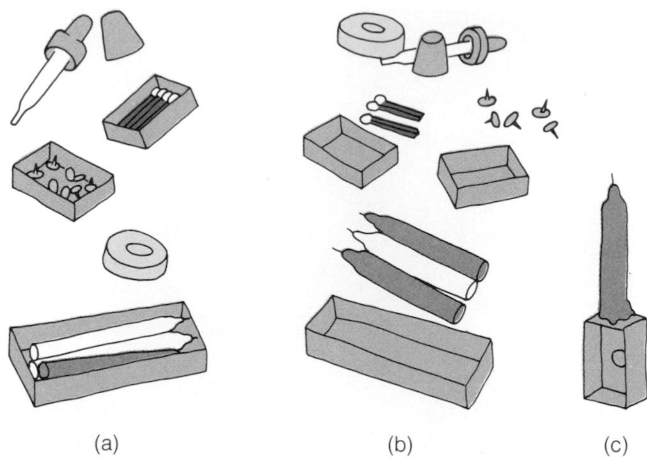

Fig. 10–12 *Materials for solving the candle problem were given to subjects in boxes* (a) *or separately* (b). *Functional fixedness caused by condition* (a) *interfered with solving the problem. The solution to the problem is shown in* (c).

HIGHLIGHT 10–2
Common Barriers to Creative Thinking

1. Emotional barriers: Inhibition and fear of making a fool of oneself, fear of making a mistake, inability to tolerate ambiguity, excessive self-criticism.
2. Cultural barriers: Values that hold that fantasy is a waste of time; that playfulness is for children only; that reason, logic, and numbers are good; that feelings, intuitions, pleasure, and humor are bad or have no value in the serious business of problem solving.
3. Learned barriers: Conventions about uses (functional fixedness), meanings, possibilities, taboos.
4. Perceptual barriers: Habits leading to a failure to identify important elements of a problem.

many fixations if we took a more flexible approach to categorizing the world (Langer & Piper, 1987). For instance, creativity could be facilitated in Duncker's container problem by saying, "This *could be* a box," instead of, "This *is* a box."

Functional fixedness is just one of the mental blocks that prevent insight. Here's an example of another: How would you remove a $5 bill placed below a stack of precariously balanced objects (without touching or moving the objects)? A good answer is to split the bill at the edge and tear it in half, gently pulling from opposite ends. Many people fail to see this solution because they have learned not to destroy money (Adams, 1980). Notice again the impact of placing something in a category, in this case, "things of value" (which should not be destroyed). Other mental blocks and fixations are listed in Highlight 10–2.

Learning Check

Before you read more, it might be a good idea to see if you can answer these questions.

1. True languages are ________________ because they can be used to generate new possibilities.

2. The basic speech sounds are called ________________; the smallest meaningful units of speech are called ________________.

3. One of the chimpanzee Sarah's most outstanding achievements has been the construction of sentences involving
a. negation *b.* conditional relationships *c.* adult grammar *d.* unprompted questions

4. Critics consider "sentences" constructed by apes to be simple ________________ responses having little meaning to the animal.

5. Insight refers to rote, or trial-and-error, problem solving. T or F?

6. The first phase in problem solving by understanding is to discover the general properties of a correct solution. T or F?

7. Problem-solving strategies that guide the search for solutions are called ________________.

8. A common element underlying insight is that information is encoded, combined, and compared
a. mechanically *b.* by rote *c.* functionally *d.* selectively

9. The term *fixation* refers to the point at which a helpful insight becomes fixed in one's thinking. T or F?

Answers:

1. productive **2.** phonemes, morphemes **3.** *b* **4.** operant **5.** F **6.** T **7.** heuristics **8.** *d* **9.** F

Creative Thinking—Fluency, Flexibility, and Originality

As we have noted, problem solving may be the result of thinking that is mechanical, insightful, or based on understanding. To this we can add that thought may be **inductive** (going from specific facts or observations to general principles) or **deductive** (going from general principles to specific situations). Thinking may also be **logical** (proceeding from given information to new conclusions on the basis of explicit rules) or **illogical** (intuitive, associative, or personal).

Question: What distinguishes creative thinking from more routine problem solving?

Creative thinking involves all these styles of thought (in varying combinations) *plus* fluency, flexibility, and originality (Guilford, 1950). The meaning of these terms can be illustrated by returning to an earlier example. Let's say that you would like to find a creative use (or uses) for the millions of automobile tires discarded each year. The creativity of your suggestions could be rated in this way: **Fluency** is defined as the total number of suggestions you are able to make. **Flexibility** is defined as the number of times you shift from one class of possible uses to another. **Originality** refers to how novel or unusual your suggestions are. By totaling the number of times you showed fluency, flexibility, and originality, we could rate the creativity of your thinking on this problem. Speaking more generally, we would be rating your capacity for **divergent thinking** (Wallach, 1985). (See Highlight 10–3.)

Divergent thinking is the most widely used measure of creative problem solving. In routine problem solving or thinking, there is one correct answer, and the problem is to find it. This leads to **convergent thought** (lines of thought converge on the correct answer). **Divergent thinking** is the reverse, in which many possibilities are developed from one starting place (Wallach, 1985).

Compare: Two Major Styles of Thinking

Divergent thought Thinking that produces many ideas or alternatives; a major element in original or creative thought.

Convergent thought Thinking directed toward discovery of a single established correct answer; conventional thinking.

There are several tests of divergent thinking. In the **Unusual Uses Test,** a person is asked to think of as many uses for an object (such as the tires just mentioned) as possible. In the **Consequences Test,** the object is to answer a question such as, "What would be the results if everyone suddenly lost the sense of balance and were unable to stay in an upright position?" Subjects try to list as many reactions as possible. In the **Anagrams Test,** subjects are given a word such as *creativity* and asked to make as many new words as possible by rearranging the letters. Each of these tests can be scored for fluency, flexibility, and originality. (For an example of other tests

HIGHLIGHT 10–3
Daydreams, Fantasy, and Creativity

Has your reading of this chapter been interrupted by a daydream? Clinical psychologist Jerome Singer (1974) found that most people daydream sometime each day. What do we know about this unique form of thought?

Content Two of the most common daydream plots are the **conquering hero** and the **suffering martyr** themes. In a conquering hero fantasy, the daydreamer gets the starring role as a famous, rich, or powerful person: a celebrity, athlete, musician, famous surgeon, brilliant lawyer, or magnificent lover. Themes such as these seem to reflect needs for mastery and escape from the frustrations of everyday life. Suffering martyr daydreams center on feelings of being neglected, hurt, rejected, or unappreciated by others. In such fantasies, others end up regretting their past actions and realizing what a *wonderful person* the daydreamer was all along.

Benefits Daydreams often fill a need for stimulation during routine or boring tasks. They also improve our ability to delay immediate pleasures so that future goals can be achieved. And in everyday terms, fantasy can be an outlet for frustrated impulses. If you have a momentary urge to kill the fool in front of you on the highway, substituting fantasy for action may avert disaster (Biblow, 1973).

Perhaps the greatest value of fantasy is its contribution to creativity. In the imaginative realm of fantasy, nothing is impossible—a quality allowing for tremendous fluency and flexibility of thought. For most people, fantasy and daydreaming are associated with positive emotional adjustment, lower levels of aggression, and greater mental flexibility or creativity (Singer, 1974). Perhaps this is why Albert Einstein, one of the world's most celebrated thinkers, was, in his own words, "disorderly and a dreamer."

of divergent thought, see Fig. 10–13.) Tests of divergent thinking apparently tap something quite different from intelligence. Generally there is little correlation between such tests and IQ test scores (Wallach, 1985).

Question: Isn't creativity more than divergent thought? What if a person comes up with a large number of useless answers to a problem?

A good question. Divergent thought is definitely an important part of creative thinking, but there is more to it. To be creative, the solution to a problem must be more than novel, unusual, or original. It must also be useful or meaningful, and it must meet the demands of the problem (MacKinnon, 1962). This is the dividing line between a "harebrained scheme" and a "stroke of genius" (Figs. 10–14 and 10–15). In other words, the creative person brings reasoning and critical thinking to bear on novel ideas once they are produced (Snow, 1986).

Question: Is there any pattern to creative thinking?

Stages of Creative Thought A good summary of the sequence of events in creative thinking proposes five stages that usually occur:

1. Orientation. As a first step, the problem must be defined and important dimensions identified.
2. Preparation. In the second stage, creative thinkers saturate themselves with as much information pertaining to the problem as possible.
3. Incubation. Most major problems produce a period during which all attempted solutions will have proved futile. At this point, problem solving may proceed on a subconscious level: While the problem seems to have been set aside, it is still "cooking" in the background.
4. Illumination. The stage of incubation is often ended by a rapid insight or series of insights. These produce the "Aha!" experience, often depicted in cartoons as a light bulb appearing over the thinker's head.
5. Verification. The final step is to test and critically evaluate the solution obtained during the stage of illumination. If the solution proves faulty, the thinker reverts to the stage of incubation.

Of course, creative thought is not always so neat. Nevertheless, the stages listed are a good summary of the most typical sequence of events.

You may find it helpful to attach the stages to the

Fig. 10–13 *Some tests of divergent thinking. Creative responses are more original and more complex. [*(a) *after Wallach & Kogan, 1965;* (b) *after Barron, 1958.]*

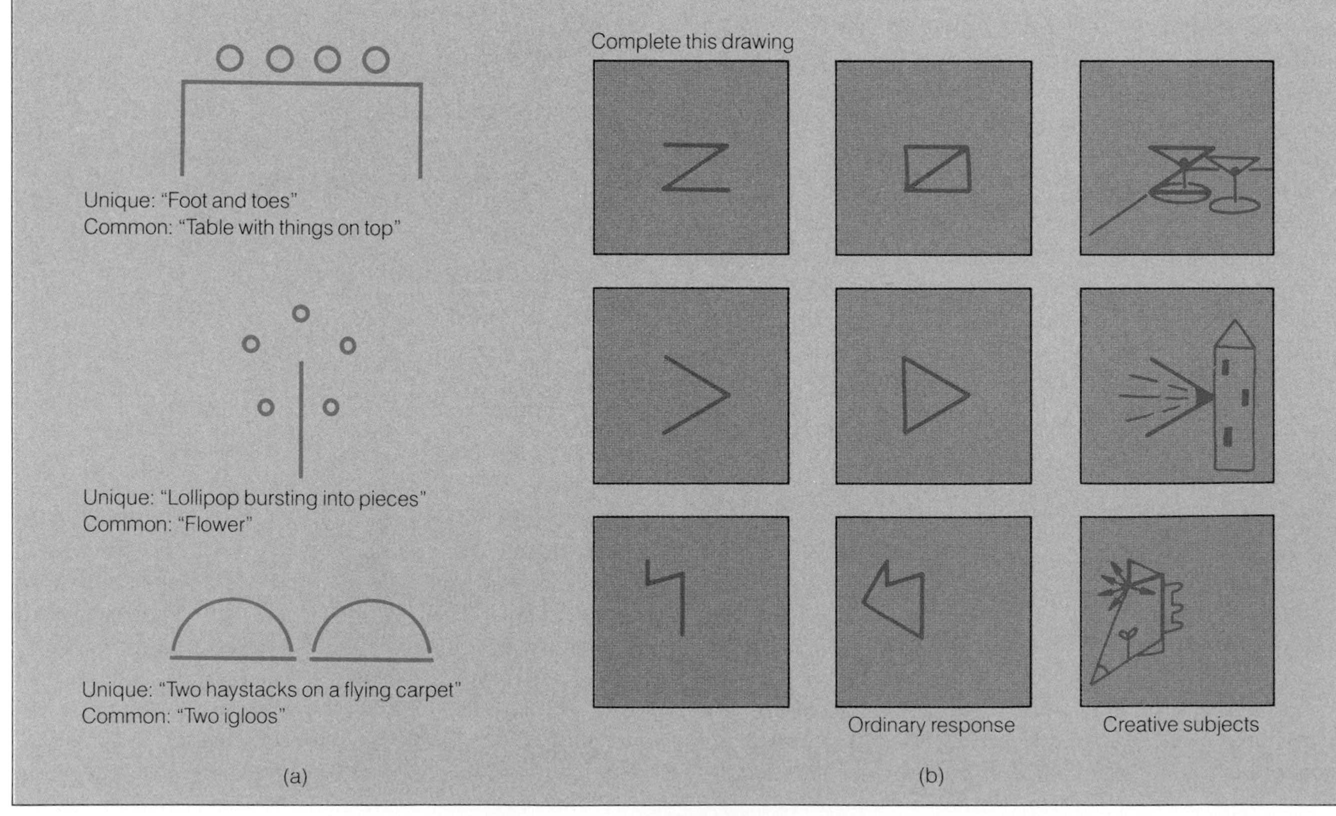

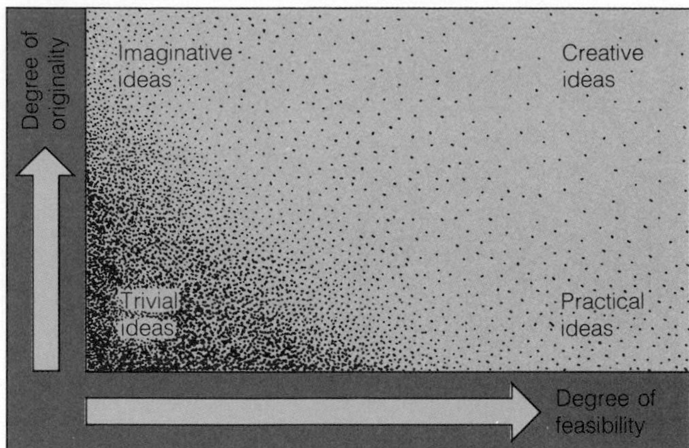

Fig. 10–14 *Creative ideas combine originality with feasibility. (Adapted from McMullan & Stocking, 1978.)*

following more or less true story. Legend has it that the king of Syracuse (a city in ancient Greece) once suspected that his goldsmith had substituted cheaper metals for some of the gold in a crown and had pocketed the difference. Archimedes, a famous mathematician and thinker, was given the problem of discovering whether the king had been cheated.

Archimedes began by defining the problem (*orientation*): "How can I determine what metals have been used in the crown without damaging it?" He then checked all known methods of analyzing metals (*preparation*). All involved cutting or melting the crown, so he was forced to temporarily set the problem aside (*incubation*). Then one day as he stepped into his bath, Archimedes suddenly knew he had the solution (*illumination*). He was so excited he is said to have run naked through the streets shouting "Eureka, eureka!" (I have found it, I have found it!).

Fig. 10–15 *Hat-tipping device. According to the patent, it is for "automatically effecting polite salutations by the elevation and rotation of the hat on the head of the saluting party when said person bows to the person or persons saluted." In addition to being original or novel, a creative solution must fit the demands of the problem. Is this a creative solution to the "problem" of hat tipping?*

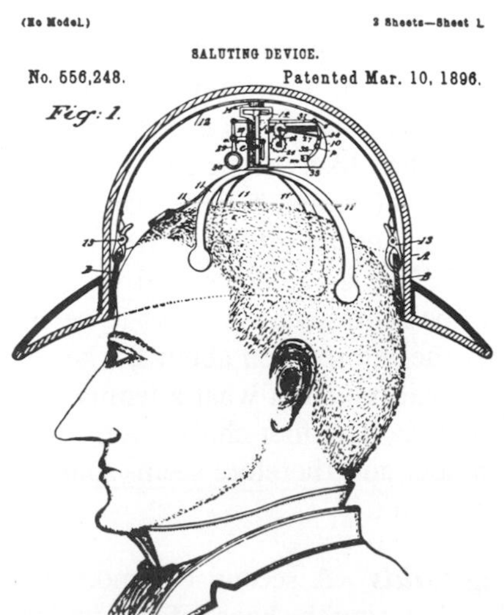

On observing his own body floating in the bath, Archimedes realized that different metals of equal weight would displace different amounts of water. A pound of brass, for example, occupies more space than a pound of gold, which is denser. All that remained was to test the solution (*verification*). Archimedes placed an amount of gold (equal in weight to that given the goldsmith) in a tub of water. He marked the water level and removed the gold. He then placed the crown in the water. Was the crown pure gold? If it was, it would raise the water to exactly the same level. Unfortunately, the purity of the crown and the fate of the goldsmith are to this day unknown!

Question: What makes a person creative?

The Creative Personality According to the popular stereotype, highly creative people are eccentric, introverted, neurotic, socially inept, unbalanced in their interests, and frequently, on the edge of madness. Although some well-known artists and musicians cultivate a public image to fit the stereotype, there is little truth in it. Studies by psychologist Donald MacKinnon paint a very different picture of the creative person. After extensive testing of creative writers, architects, mathematicians, and scientists, MacKinnon (1968) and others have drawn these conclusions:

1. At any given level of IQ, some people are creative and some are not. For people of normal or above normal intelligence, there is little correlation between creativity and IQ (Nelson & Crutchfield, 1970; Taylor, 1978).
2. Creative people usually have a greater than average range of knowledge and interests, and they are more fluent in combining ideas from various sources.
3. Creative people have an openness to experience. They accept irrational thoughts and are uninhibited about their feelings and fantasies.
4. MacKinnon's subjects enjoyed symbolic thought, ideas, concepts, and possibilities. They tended to be interested in truth, form, and beauty, rather than in recognition or success. Their creative work was an end in itself.
5. Highly creative people value independence and have a preference for complexity. However, they are unconventional and nonconforming primarily in their work; otherwise they do not have particularly unusual, outlan-

dish, or bizarre personalities. Indeed, most creative personalities resemble the profile in Highlight 10–4.

Question: Can creativity be learned?

Most of what we know about creativity remains preliminary. Nevertheless, it is beginning to look as if some creative thinking skills can be taught. In the Applications section of this chapter you will find a brief discussion of some helpful strategies.

At the same time that irrational, intuitive thought may contribute to creative problem solving, it can also lead to thinking errors. The next sections tells how this can happen.

HIGHLIGHT 10–4
Creativity Profile

The following qualities have repeatedly been found to characterize creative individuals:

1. An unusual awareness of people, events, and problems
2. A high degree of verbal fluency
3. Flexibility with numbers, concepts, media, and in social situations
4. Originality of ideas and expressions; a sense of humor
5. An ability to abstract, organize, and synthesize
6. A high energy/activity level
7. Persistence at tasks of interest
8. Impatience with routine or repetitive tasks
9. A willingness to take risks
10. A vivid and spontaneous imagination; in childhood, this may take the form of "fibbing" or imaginary companions

(Source: Meeker, 1978)

Intuition—Mental Short Cut? Or Dangerous Detour?

Problem 1 An epidemic breaks out and 600 people are about to die. Doctors have two choices. If they give drug A, 200 lives will be saved. If they give drug B, there is a one-third chance that 600 people will be saved, and a two-thirds chance that none will be saved. Which drug should they choose?

Problem 2 Again, 600 people are about to die, and doctors must make a choice. If they give drug A, 400 people will die. If they give drug B, there is a one-third chance that no one will die, and a two-thirds chance that 600 will die. Which drug should they choose?

Most people choose drug A for the first problem and drug B for the second. This is fascinating because the two problems are identical. The only difference is that the first is stated in terms of lives saved, the second in terms of lives lost. Yet, even people who realize that their answers are contradictory find it difficult to change them (Kahneman & Tversky, 1972, 1973).

Intuition As the example shows, we often make decisions on the basis of intuition rather than logic. Doing so may provide quick answers, but it can also be misleading and sometimes disastrous. Two noted psychologists, Daniel Kahneman (KON-eh-man) and Amos Tversky (tuh-VER-ski), have spent nearly 20 years studying how people make decisions and predictions in the face of uncertainty. They have found, to put it bluntly, that human judgment is often seriously flawed (Kahneman et al., 1982). Understanding the thinking errors they have identified may help you to avoid them. Let's explore some common errors.

Representativeness One very common pitfall in judgment is illustrated by the following question:

Which is more probable?

A. Boris Becker will lose the first set of a tennis match but win the match.

B. Boris Becker will lose the first set.

Tversky and Kahneman (1982) found that most people regard statements like A as more probable than B. However, this intuitive answer overlooks an important fact: The likelihood of two events occurring together is lower than the probability of either alone. (For example, the probability of getting one head when flipping a coin is one-half, or .5. The probability of getting two heads when flipping two coins is one-fourth, or .25.) Therefore, A is less likely to be true than B.

Tversky and Kahneman believe that such faulty conclusions are based on an intuitive error called **representativeness.** That is, a choice is given greater weight if it seems to be representative of what we already know. Thus, the information about Becker is compared to a mental model of what a tennis pro's behavior should be like. The first choice seems to better represent this model and therefore seems more likely, even though it isn't.

Underlying Odds A second common error in judgment involves ignoring the **base rate,** or underlying probability of an event. In one experiment, for instance, subjects were told that they would be given descriptions of 100 people—70 lawyers and 30 engineers. Subjects were then asked to guess, without knowing anything about a person, whether he or she was an engineer or a lawyer. All correctly stated the probabilities as 70 percent for lawyer and 30 percent for engineer. Subjects were then given this description:

> Dick is a 30-year-old man. He is married with no children. A man of high ability and high motivation, he promises to be quite successful in his field. He is well liked by his colleagues.

Notice that the description gives no new information about Dick's occupation. He could still be either an engineer or a lawyer. Therefore, the odds should again be estimated as 70–30. However, most people changed the odds to 50–50. Intuitively, it seems that Dick has an equal chance of being either an engineer or a lawyer. But this guess completely ignores the underlying odds.

Perhaps it is fortunate that we do at times ignore underlying odds. Were this not the case, how many people would get married in the face of a 50 percent divorce rate? Or how many would start high-risk businesses? On the other hand, people who smoke, drink and then drive, or skip wearing auto seat belts ignore rather high odds of injury or illness. In many high-risk situations, ignoring base rates is the same as thinking you are an exception to the rule.

Framing Perhaps the most general conclusion from Kahneman and Tversky's work is that the way a problem is stated, or **framed,** affects decisions (Tversky & Kahneman, 1981). As the first example in this discussion revealed, people often give different answers to the same problem stated in slightly different ways. Usually, the *broadest* way of framing or stating a problem produces the most rational decisions. However, people often state problems in increasingly narrow terms until a single, seemingly "obvious" answer emerges. For example, to select a career, it would be wise to consider pay, working conditions, job satisfaction, needed skills, future employment outlook, and many other factors. Instead, such decisions are often narrowed to thoughts such as, "I like to write, so I'll be a journalist," "I want to make good money and law pays well," or "I can be creative in photography." Framing decisions so narrowly greatly increases the risk of making a poor choice.

Conclusion We have discussed only some of the intuitive errors made in the face of uncertainty. The study of intuitive decision making is rapidly finding application to medical diagnosis, business decisions, military strategy, investing and finance, international relations, and more. In each area, people are learning to think twice before they decide. With practice, you, too, can learn to spot errors like those described. Remember, short cuts to answers often short-circuit clear thinking—a point we will explore further in the upcoming Applications section.

Learning Check

1. Fluency, flexibility, and originality are characteristics of
a. convergent thought *b.* deductive thinking *c.* creative thought *d.* trial-and-error solutions

2. List the typical stages of creative thinking in their correct order:
______ ______ ______
______ ______

3. An ability to organize, abstract, and synthesize ideas blocks creativity; these are noncreative qualities. T or F?

4. To be creative, an original idea must also be practical or feasible. T or F?

5. Intelligence and creativity are highly correlated; the higher a person's IQ, the more likely he or she is creative. T or F?

6. Kate is single, outspoken, and very bright. As a college student, she was deeply concerned with discrimination and other social issues and participated in several protests. Which statement is more likely to be true?
a. Kate is a bank teller. *b.* Kate is a bank teller and a feminist.

7. The probability of two events occurring together is lower than the probability of either one occurring alone. T or F?

8. Usually, the broadest way of ______ a problem yields the most rational decisions.

Answers:
1. *c* **2.** orientation, preparation, incubation, illumination, verification **3.** F **4.** T **5.** F **6.** *a* **7.** T **8.** framing

Applications: Steps to Better Thinking and Problem Solving

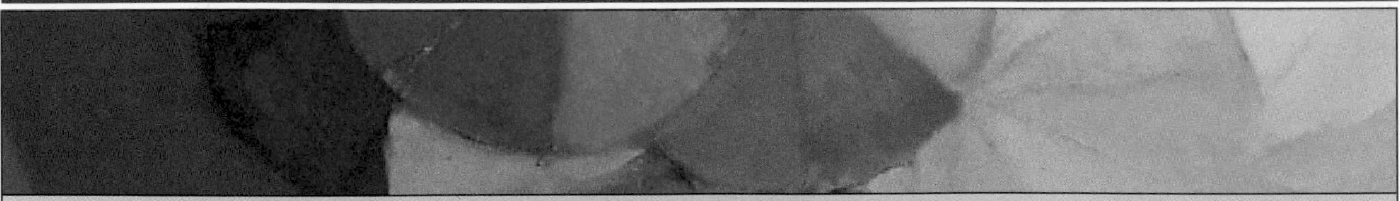

At one time or another, we all experience difficulties in thinking and problem solving. The following should alert you to some of the more common problems.

Rigid Mental Set Try the problems pictured in Figure 10–16. If you have difficulty, try asking yourself what assumptions you are making. The problems are designed to demonstrate the limiting effects of a mental set. (The answers to these problems, along with an explanation of the sets that prevent their solution, are found on p. 276.) In addition to the assumptions and mental sets we bring to a problem, problems themselves may produce a disruptive set. A simple example is the following: The name Polk is pronounced "poke," the world *folk* is prounced "foke," and the white of an egg is pronounced ________________. Here is another example: See if you can unscramble each set of letters to make a word that uses all the letters:

MEST ________________
LFAE ________________
DUB ________________
STKAL ________________
OTOR ________________
LTEPA ________________

Now try a new list:

FINEK ________________
OPONS ________________
KROF ________________
PUC ________________
SDIH ________________
LTEPA ________________

Did you notice that the last problem was the same in each case? Many people don't and end up solving the problem twice. To complete the first list (*stem, leaf, bud, stalk, root*), the item LTEPA is usually unscrambled as *petal*. In the second list (*knife, spoon, fork, cup, dish*), LTEPA becomes *plate* for many people.

Now that you have been forewarned about the danger of faulty assumptions, see if you can correctly answer the following questions.

1. Argentines do not have a fourth of July. T or F?
2. How many birthdays does the average person have?

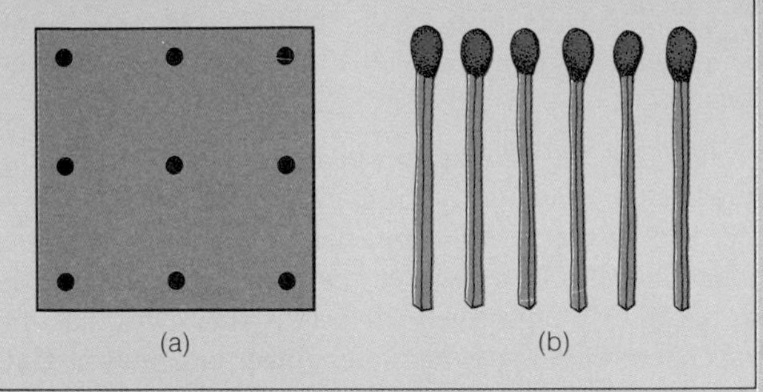

Fig. 10–16 (a) *Nine dots are arranged in a square. Can you connect them by drawing four continuous straight lines without lifting your pencil from the paper?* (b) *Six matches must be arranged to make 4 triangles. The triangles must be the same size, with each side equal to the length of one match. (The solutions to these problems appear on p. 276.)*

3. A farmer had 19 sheep. All but 9 died. How many sheep did the farmer have left?
4. It is not unlawful for a man living in Winston-Salem, North Carolina, to be buried west of the Mississippi River. T or F?
5. Some months have 30 days, some have 31. How many months have 28 days?
6. I have 2 coins that together total 55 cents. One of the coins is not a nickel. What are the 2 coins?
7. It would be far better to have an elephant eat you than a gorilla. T or F?

These questions are designed to cause thinking errors. Here are the answers:

1. F. Of course they have a fourth of July. What would they do, go from the third to the fifth? **2.** One, celebrated each year. **3.** Nineteen—9 alive and 10 dead. **4.** F. It is against the law to bury a living man anywhere. **5.** All of them. **6.** A half-dollar and a nickel. One of the coins is not a nickel, but the other one is! **7.** F. It would be better to have the elephant eat the gorilla. (Read it again.)

If you got caught on any of the questions, consider it an additional reminder of the value of actively challenging the assumptions you are making in any instance of problem solving.

Applications

Problems with Logic A major thinking difficulty centers on the process of *logical reasoning*. Simple sequences of logical thought can be arranged as a set of *premises* (assumptions) and a *conclusion*. This format is called a **syllogism.** A syllogism can be evaluated for the *validity* of its reasoning and for the *truth* of its *conclusion*. It is entirely possible to draw true conclusions using faulty logic or to draw false conclusions using valid logic. The following examples show how this is possible.

Syllogism I

All humans are mortal. **(Major premise)**
All women are humans. **(Minor premise)**
Therefore, all women are mortal. **(Conclusion)**

Comment: As you can see from Figure 10–17, the logic of this syllogism is valid. Since our premises are true, this means the conclusion is true. The diagram shows all women included within the boundaries of mortals.

Syllogism II

All women are humans.
All humans are mortal.
Therefore, all mortals are women.

Comment: In this example, the conclusion drawn is false because the reasoning is invalid. The diagram for Syllogism I shows that all mortals are not women. Notice how little the syllogism has to be changed to produce a false conclusion. Now consider Syllogism III.

Syllogism III

All psychologists are weird.
Mary is a psychologist.
Therefore, Mary is weird.

Comment: In this case the reasoning is valid, but the conclusion is false because the first premise is false. All psychologists are *not* weird. (Honest!) Now let's consider one more syllogism.

Fig. 10–17

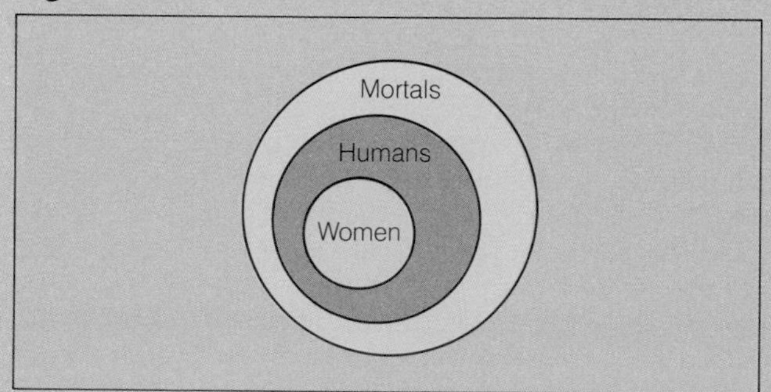

Syllogism IV

All ducks have wings.
All birds have wings.
Therefore, all ducks are birds.

Comment: This syllogism shows the importance of paying close attention to logic. The reasoning appears to be valid, since the conclusion is true, but substitute *bats* or *airplanes* for *ducks* and see how the conclusion reads. It is a good idea to get in the habit of questioning the logic used by politicians, advertisers, and psychologists, too, for that matter.

Over-simplification It may be an over-simplification to say so, but over-simplification is another basic source of thinking errors. There are two types of over-simplification that are particularly troublesome. The first is **all-or-nothing thinking.** Classifying things as absolutely right or wrong, good or bad, acceptable or unacceptable, or honest or dishonest prevents appreciation of the complexity of most life problems.

The second problem is thinking in terms of **stereotypes.** Stereotypes are particularly troublesome when human relationships are involved (see Chapter 24). An overly simplified, inaccurate, or rigid picture of men, blacks, women, conservatives, liberals, police officers, or any other group of people leads to muddled thinking about individual members of the group. Try to look for this and the other errors in your own thinking habits.

Enhancing Creativity—Brainstorms

Thomas Edison once explained his creativity by saying, "Genius is 1 percent inspiration and 99 percent perspiration." Many studies of creativity show that "genius" owes as much to persistence and dedication as it does to inspiration (Hunt, 1982). Once it is recognized that creativity can be hard work, then something can be done to enhance it. Here are some suggestions on how to begin (from Hayes, 1978, and indicated sources).

1. Define the problem broadly. Whenever possible, enlarge the definition of a problem. For instance, assume your problem is: Design a better doorway. This is likely to lead to ordinary solutions. Why not change the problem to: Design a better way to get through a wall? Now your solutions will be more original. Best of all might be to state the problem as: Find a better way to define separate areas for living and working. This could lead to truly creative solutions (Adams, 1980).

Let's say that you are the leader of a group interested in designing a new can opener. Wisely, you ask the group to think about *opening* in general, rather than about can openers.

Applications

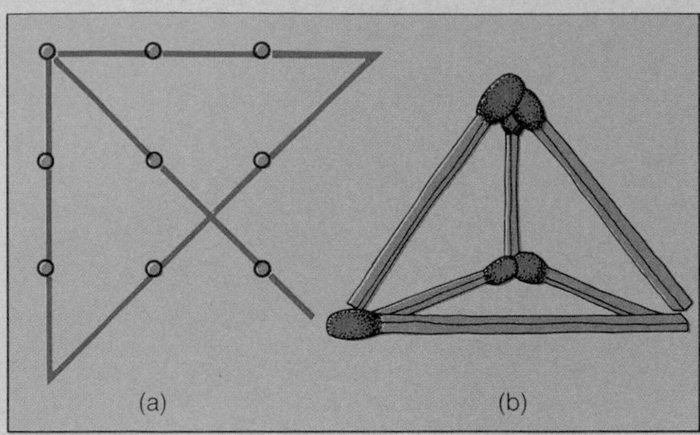

Fig. 10–18 *Problem solutions.* (a) *The dot problem can be solved by extending the lines beyond the square formed by the dots. Most people assume incorrectly that they may not do this.* (b) *The match problem can be solved by building a three-dimensional pyramid. Most people assume that the matches must be arranged on a flat surface.*

This was just the approach used in developing the pop-top can. As the design group discussed the concept of opening, one member suggested that nature has its own openers, like the soft seam on a pea pod. Instead of a new can-opening tool, the group invented the self-opening can (Stein, 1974) (Fig. 10–19).

2. Create the right atmosphere. A variety of experiments show that people make more original, spontaneous, and imaginative responses when exposed to others (models) doing the same (Amabile, 1983). If you want to become more creative, spend more time around creative people. This is the premise underlying much education in art, theater, dance, and music.

3. Allow time for incubation. Trying to hurry or to force a problem's solution may simply encourage fixation on a dead end. In one experiment, subjects were asked to list as many consequences as possible that would follow if people no longer needed to eat. Most subjects rapidly produced several ideas and then ran dry. After working for a time, some subjects were interrupted and required to do another task for 20 minutes. Then they turned to the original question. The interruption improved their scores, even though they worked no longer than the control group (Fulgosi & Guilford, 1968).

Fig. 10–19

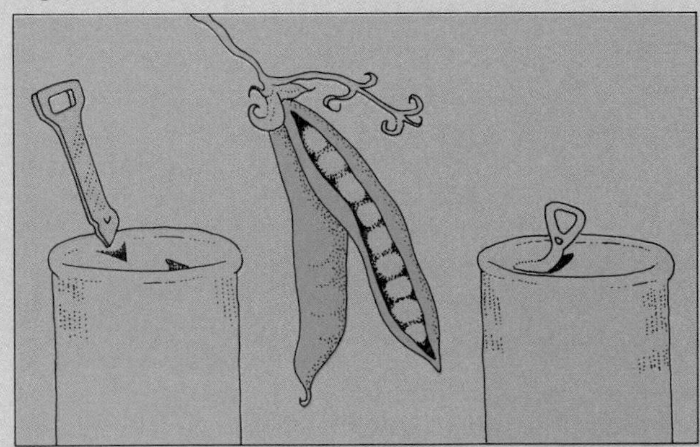

4. Seek varied input. Remember, creativity requires divergent thinking. Rather than digging deeper with logic, you are attempting to shift your mental "prospecting" to new areas. As an example of this strategy, Edward de Bono (1970) recommends that you randomly look up words in the dictionary and relate each to the problem. Often this activity will trigger a fresh perspective or open a new avenue. For instance, let's say you are asked to come up with new ways to clean oil off a beach, and you draw a blank. Following de Bono's suggestion, you would read the following randomly selected words, relate each to the problem, and see what thoughts are triggered: *weed, rust, poor, magnify, foam, gold, frame, hole, diagonal, vacuum, tribe, puppet, nose, link, drift, portrait, cheese, coal.*

5. Look for analogies. As the principle of selective comparison (described earlier) suggests, many "new" problems are really old problems in new clothing. Representing a problem in a variety of ways is often the key to solution. Most problems become easier to solve when they are effectively represented. For example, consider this problem:

> Two backpackers start up a steep trail at 6 A.M. They hike all day, resting occasionally, and arrive at the top at 6 P.M. The next day they start back down the trail at 6 A.M. On the way down they stop several times and vary their pace. They arrive back at 6 P.M. On the way down, one of the hikers, who is a mathematician, tells the other that she has realized that they will pass a point on the trail at exactly the same time as they did the day before. Her nonmathematical friend finds this hard to believe, since on both days they have stopped and started many times and changed their pace. The problem: Is the mathematician right?

Perhaps you will see the answer to this problem immediately. If not, think of it this way: What if there were two pairs of backpackers, one going up the trail, the second coming down, and both hiking on the *same day?* It becomes obvious that the two pairs of hikers will pass each other at some point on the trail. Therefore, they will be at the same place at the same time. The mathematician was right (adapted from Hayes, 1978).

6. Delay evaluation. Various studies suggest that people are most likely to be creative when they are given the freedom to play with ideas and solutions without having to worry about whether they will be evaluated. In the first stages of creative thinking, it is important to avoid criticizing your efforts. Wor-

Applications

rying about the correctness of solutions tends to inhibit creativity (Amabile, 1983). This idea is expanded in the discussion that follows.

An alternative approach to enhancing creativity is called brainstorming. Although brainstorming is a group technique, it can be applied to individual problem solving as well.

Brainstorming The essence of brainstorming is that *production* and *criticism* of ideas are kept separate. To encourage divergent thinking in group problem solving, participants are encouraged to produce as many ideas as possible without fear of criticism or evaluation. Only after a brainstorming session is complete are ideas reconsidered and evaluated (Haefele, 1962). As ideas are freely generated, an interesting **cross-stimulation effect** takes place in which one participant's ideas trigger ideas from others. The four basic rules for successful brainstorming are:

1. Criticism of an idea is absolutely barred. All evaluation is to be deferred until after the session.
2. Modification or combination with other ideas is encouraged. Don't worry about giving credit for ideas or keeping them neat. Mix them up!
3. Quantity of ideas is sought. In the early stages of brainstorming, quantity is more important than quality. Try to generate lots of ideas.
4. Unusual, remote, or wild ideas are sought. Let your imagination run amok!

Question: How is brainstorming applied to individual problem solving?

The essential point to remember is to *suspend judgment*. Ideas should first be produced without regard for logic, organization, accuracy, practicality, or any other evaluation. In writing an essay, for instance, you would begin by writing ideas in any order, the more the better, just as they occur to you. Later you would go back and reorganize, rewrite, and criticize your efforts.

As an aid to following rules 2, 3, and 4 of the brainstorming method, you might find this checklist helpful for encouraging original thought. It can be used to see if you have overlooked a possible solution (adapted from Parnes, 1967).

Creativity Checklist

1. Redefine. Consider other uses for all elements of the problem. (This is designed to alert you to fixations that may be blocking creativity.)
2. Adapt. How could other objects, ideas, procedures, or solutions be adapted to this particular problem?
3. Modify. Imagine changing anything and everything that could be changed.
4. Magnify. Exaggerate everything you can think of. Think on a grand scale.
5. Minify. What if everything were scaled down? What if all differences were reduced to zero? "Shrink" the problem down to size.
6. Substitute. How could one object, idea, or procedure be substituted for another?
7. Rearrange. Break the problem into pieces and shuffle them.
8. Reverse. Consider reverse orders, and opposites, and turn things inside out.
9. Combine. This one speaks for itself.

By making a habit of subjecting a problem to each of these procedures, you should be able to greatly reduce the chances that you will overlook a useful, original, or creative solution.

Learning Check

1. In evaluating a syllogism, it is possible to draw a true conclusion with faulty logic, or a false conclusion with valid logic. T or F?
2. Stereotyping is an example of over-simplification in thinking. T or F?
3. Exposure to creative models has been shown to enhance creativity. T or F?
4. In brainstorming, each idea is critically evaluated as it is generated. T or F?
5. Defining a problem broadly produces a cross-stimulation effect that can inhibit creative thinking. T or F?

Answers:
1. T 2. T 3. T 4. F 5. F

Exploration: Artificial Intelligence

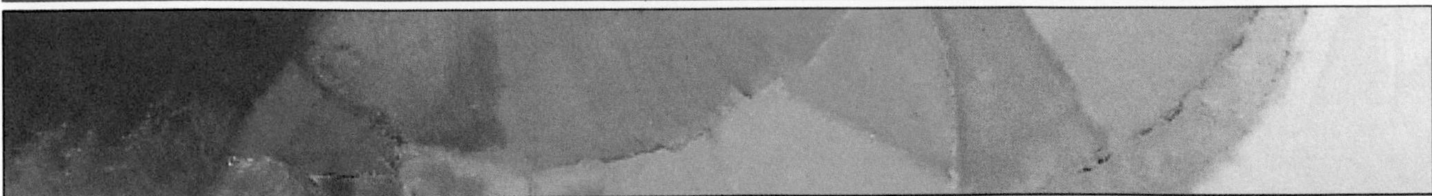

It's been a long time since Johann Sebastian Bach, the eighteenth-century German composer, last wrote any music. But listeners can be forgiven if they briefly mistake music created by Kemal Ebcioglu for Bach's work. In 1988, Ebcioglu devised a computer program that writes harmonies remarkably similar to Bach's. Ebcioglu analyzed Bach's music and came up with 350 rules that govern the harmonization process. The resulting program displays what is known as *artificial intelligence.* Its compositions sound like reasonably good classical music. This shows the power of artificial intelligence. Small but glaring defects in the music and a certain lack of inspiration reveal its shortcomings (Maugh, 1988)

Artificial intelligence (AI) refers to computer programs capable of doing things that require intelligence when done by people (Best, 1986). Artificial intelligence is based on the fact that many tasks—from harmonizing music to medical diagnosis—can be reduced to a set of rules applied to a body of information. AI is valuable in situations where speed, vast memory, and persistence are required. In fact, AI programs are better at some tasks than humans.

AI and Cognition

Artificial intelligence provides a way to probe some of the oldest questions about the mind, such as how we comprehend language, make decisions, and solve problems. Increasingly, cognitive psychologists are using AI as a research tool in two basic ways.

In **computer simulations,** programs are used to simulate human behavior, especially problem solving. Here, the computer acts as a "laboratory" for testing models of cognition. If a computer program behaves as humans do (including making the same errors), then the program may be a good model of how we think (Mayer, 1983).

Expert systems are programs that display advanced knowledge of a specific topic or skill. Expert systems have demystified some areas of human ability by converting complex skills to clearly stated rules that a computer can follow. Expert systems have been created to predict the weather, to analyze geological formations, to diagnose disease, to tell when to buy and sell stocks, to play chess, to read text, to do psychotherapy, and to perform many other tasks.

Experts and Novices Working with artificial intelligence has helped especially to clarify differences between novices and experts. Research on chess masters, for example, shows that their skills are based on specific **organized knowledge** and **acquired strategies.** In other words, becoming a star performer does not come from some general strengthening of the mind. Master chess players don't necessarily have better memories than beginners (except for chess positions). And, typically, they don't explore more moves ahead than lesser players.

What does set master players apart is their ability to recognize *patterns* that suggest what lines of play should be explored next (Best, 1986). This helps eliminate a large number of possible moves. The chess master, therefore, does not waste time exploring unproductive pathways. Experts are better able to see the true nature of problems and to define them in terms of general principles (Rabinowitz & Glaser, 1985).

Expertise also allows more **automatic processing,** or fast, fairly effortless thinking based on experience with similar problems. Automatic processing frees attention and "space" in short-term memory that can be used to work on the problem. At the highest skill levels, expert performers tend to rise above a reliance on rules and plans. Their decisions, thinking, and actions become rapid and fluid. Thus, when a chess master recognizes a pattern on the chessboard, the most desirable tactic comes to mind almost immediately (Dreyfus & Dreyfus, 1986).

Limitations What the preceding tells us is that experts in one area do not automatically become better problem solvers elsewhere. Nor do they become generally smarter (Bransford et al., 1986). The same conclusion applies to artificial intelligence. Expert systems have been hailed as a possible remedy for hu-

● Exploration

man errors in tasks such as air traffic control, the operation of nuclear power plants, and the control of weapons systems. However, the truth is that expert systems are "idiot geniuses." They are very adept within a narrow range of problem solving, but they are "stone stupid" at everything else.

Eventually, AI may lead to robots that recognize voices and that speak and act "intelligently" (Best, 1986). But cognitive scientists are becoming aware that machine "intelligence" is ultimately "blind" outside its underlying set of rules. In contrast, human cognition is much more flexible. For example, u cann understnd wrds thet ar mizpeld. Computers are very literal and easily stymied by such errors.

Humans are able to take into account exceptions, context, and interpretations as they think. We also make commitments and take responsibility for our actions. A rule-driven expert system processes information without regard for the meaning of actions. Expert systems may never be able to anticipate the infinite number of possible events that could occur. As a result, their actions might be disastrous in unanticipated situations (Denning, 1988).

Clearly, artificial intelligence will play an increasingly visible role in cognitive research and in our lives. However, it is not likely to soon replace the human touch in many areas. Although Bach might have been fascinated by AI, it is doubtful that his musical magic will be eclipsed by a machine.

Learning Check

1. Two aspects of artificial intelligence are computer simulations and automatic processing. T or F?
2. Computer simulations are often used to test models of human cognition. T or F?
3. Organized knowledge, acquired strategies, and automatic processing are all characteristics of human expertise. T or F?
4. Expert systems can be described as broadly intelligent because their rules and heuristics apply to almost any problem-solving situation. T or F?

Answers:
1. F 2. T 3. T 4. F

Chapter Summary

- Thinking is the manipulation of **internal representations** of external stimuli or situations.
- Animals reveal a capacity for thought when they solve **delayed response problems** and in some cases problems that appear to require understanding or **insight.** Some psychologists remain unconvinced about such abilities, however.
- Four basic units of thought are **images, concepts, muscular responses,** and **language.**
- Most people have internal images of one kind or another. Images may be **stored** or **created.** Sometimes they cross normal sense boundaries in a type of imagery called **synesthesia.** Images used in problem solving may be three-dimensional, and their size may change.
- **Muscular images** are created by memory of actions or by **implicit actions. Kinesthetic sensations** and **micromovements** seem to help structure the flow of thought for many people.
- A **concept** is a generalized idea of a class of objects or events. **Concept formation** may be based on **positive** and **negative instances** or more commonly, on **rule learning.** In practice, concept identification frequently makes use of **prototypes,** or general models of the concept class. Concepts may be classified as **conjunctive** ("and" concepts), **disjunctive** ("either-or" concepts), or **relational.**
- The **denotative** meaning of a word or concept is its dictionary definition. **Connotative** meaning is personal

or emotional. Connotative meaning can be measured with the **semantic differential.**

- Language allows events to be **encoded** into **symbols** for easy mental manipulation. Thinking in language is influenced by meaning. The study of meaning is called **semantics.**
- Language carries meaning by combining a set of symbols according to a set of rules **(grammar),** which includes rules about word order **(syntax).** A true language is **productive** and can be used to generate new ideas or possibilities.
- Animal communication is relatively limited because it lacks symbols that can be rearranged easily. Attempts to teach chimpanzees systems such as **American Sign Language** suggest to some that primates are capable of language use. Others question this conclusion.
- The solution to a problem may be arrived at **mechanically** (by **trial and error** or by **rote** application of rules), but mechanical solutions are frequently inefficient or ineffective except where aided by computer.
- Solutions by **understanding** usually begin with discovery of the **general properties** of an answer. Next comes proposal of a number of **functional solutions.**
- Problem solving is frequently aided by **heuristics.** These are strategies that typically narrow the search for solutions. The **ideal strategy** is a general heuristic.
- When understanding leads to a rapid solution, it is said that **insight** has occurred. Three elements of insight are **selective encoding, selective combination,** and **selective comparison.**
- Insight and other problem solving can be blocked by **fixation. Functional fixedness** is a common fixation, but **emotional blocks, cultural values, learned conventions,** and **perceptual habits** are also problems.
- Creative thinking requires **divergent** thought, characterized by **fluency, flexibility,** and **originality.** To be creative, a solution must be useful or meaningful as well as original. **Fantasy** is a source of much divergent thinking.
- Five stages often seen in creative problem solving are **orientation, preparation, incubation, illumination,** and **verification.** Not all creative thinking fits this pattern.
- Studies suggest that the **creative personality** has a number of identifiable characteristics, most of which contradict popular stereotypes. There appears to be little or no correlation between IQ and creativity.
- Intuitive thinking often leads to errors. Wrong conclusions may be drawn when an answer seems highly **representative** of what we already believe is true. Another problem is ignoring the **base rate** (or **underlying probability**) of an event. Clear thinking is usually aided by stating or **framing** a problem in broad terms.
- **Rigid mental set, faulty logic,** and **over-simplification** are major sources of thinking errors. Various strategies, including **brainstorming,** tend to enhance creative problem solving.
- Two principal areas of **artificial intelligence** research are **computer simulations** and **expert systems.** Both are helping scientists explore the nature of human thought, knowledge, and expertise.

Questions for Discussion

1. If you suddenly lost your ability to mentally represent external problems, what changes would you have to make in your behavior?

2. In your opinion, are chimps that are trained to use hand signs really using language? Why or why not?

3. Describe a time when you have used imagery to solve a problem. What are the advantages and disadvantages of imagery in comparison to other modes of thought?

4. How do differences in connotative meaning contribute to arguments and misunderstandings? Do you think connotative meaning could or should be standardized?

5. The text implies that animals communicate, but do not use language in the human sense. Do you agree? Can you give an example of animal communication that qualifies as a language?

6. Think of the most creative person you know. What is that person like? How does he or she differ from your less creative acquaintances?

7. In your opinion, should measures of divergent or creative thinking be used to select students for college admission? Why or why not?

8. What effects would you expect the following to have on fantasy: television; highly realistic toys; free or unstructured time; high levels of stress or anxiety; skits, role taking, or acting; sensory deprivation; sensory overload?

9. Can you provide a real-life example of each of Kahneman and Tversky's concepts (representativeness, base rates, and framing)?

10. To what kinds of tasks do you think artificial intelligence should be applied? Would you be comfortable with computerized medical diagnosis, for instance? What about the launch of a nuclear attack?

Part Four

Motivation, Adjustment, and Health

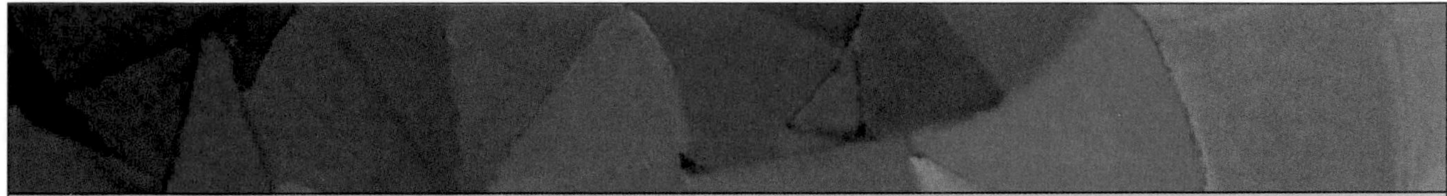

Chapter 11

Motivation

In This Chapter

Chapter Preview

Flight of the *Gossamer Albatross*

What would it feel like to pedal *an airplane over the English Channel? Cyclist Bryan Allen found out the hard way by serving as pilot and "engine" for the first human-powered flight from England to France. Allen pedaled a delicate aircraft, the* Gossamer Albatross, *in a grueling 3-hour flight. The flight took Allen to the limits of endurance as he fought head winds, thirst, leg cramps, and exhaustion. The following excerpts are from Allen's (1979) account:*

> 6:59 A.M. At last, word comes over the radio . . . "We have France in sight—four miles to go. . . ."
>
> Four miles or four hundred. I'm fading now and know it. Gradually the head winds have been building up . . . I talk to myself . . . Don't give up now, you *can* do it! As I waver between hope and despair, the radio crackles again:
>
> "Altitude six inches, six inches; get it up, you've got to get it up!"
>
> 7:29 A.M. One mile. Less distance than I had flown *Gossamer Condor* two years before for the original Kremer prize. Then, however, there were no head winds or turbulence, no thirst, no cramps. . . . Despite the cramps, I struggle back up to five feet. "Against all hope," I repeat to myself, "against all hope."
>
> 7:36 A.M. Four hundred yards to shore. . . . One hundred yards now. I am running on reserves I never knew I had. . . .

Motivation *This chapter is about the goals, needs, and motives that underlie Bryan Allen's behavior—and your own. Bryan Allen's final burst of effort ("I am running on reserves I never knew I had") is but one example of highly motivated behavior—behavior ranging from eating and drinking to feats like Allen's historic flight. How do we explain such diversity? The answer is by considering a broad sweep of ideas—from "feeding systems" in the brain to Abraham Maslow's concept of self-actualization. The pages that follow are an introduction to some of the most interesting and useful of these ideas.*

Survey Questions

- Are there different types of motives?
- What causes hunger? Thirst? Overeating?
- In what ways are pain avoidance and the sex drive unusual?
- How does arousal relate to motivation?
- How are motives learned?
- Are some motives more basic than others?
- What is intrinsic motivation?
- Can psychology be applied to dieting?
- What causes eating disorders?

● Motivation—Forces That Push and Pull

We move. We seek different goals, some more vigorously than others. The same goal may be pursued for different reasons, or different goals may be pursued for the same reasons. We use the concept of motivation to explain each of these basic aspects of behavior. To be more specific, **motivation** refers to "the dynamics of behavior, the process of initiating, sustaining, and directing activities of the organism" (Goldenson, 1970).

Question: Can you clarify that?

Yes. Let's relate the concept of motivation to a simple sequence of activity:

> Liz is studying (psychology, of course) in the library. She begins to feel hungry and has difficulty concentrating. Her stomach growls. She grows restless and decides to buy an apple from a vending machine. The machine is empty, so she goes to the cafeteria. Closed. She returns to the library, packs up her books, and drives home, where she prepares a meal and eats. At last her hunger is satisfied, and she again resumes studying.

Liz's food seeking was *initiated* by her bodily need for food; it was *sustained* because her need was not immediately met; and her activities were *directed* by possible sources of food. Notice too that her food seeking was *terminated* by achieving her goal.

A Model of Motivation Many motivated activities can be thought of as beginning with a **need.** The need that initiated Liz's search was a depletion of necessary substances within the cells of her body. Needs cause a psychological state or feeling called a **drive** to develop. (The drive was hunger, in Liz's case.) Drives activate a **response** (or a series of actions) designed to attain a **goal** that will satisfy the need. Meeting the need temporarily ends the motivational sequence. Thus, a simple model of motivation can be shown in this way:

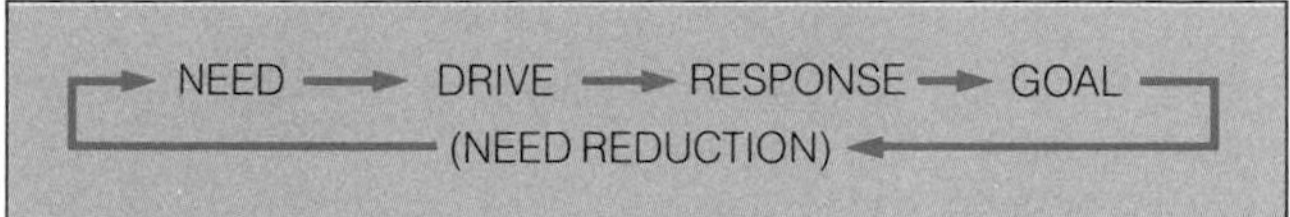

Question: Why use the terms need *and* drive? *Aren't they the same thing?*

Both terms are necessary because the strength of needs and drives can differ. If you were to begin fasting, your bodily need for food would increase daily, but you would probably be less "hungry" on the seventh day of fasting than you were on the first. Your need steadily increases, but the hunger drive comes and goes.

Before we assume that we have a complete model of motivation, let us observe Liz's eating behavior on another occasion:

> For dinner, Liz has just eaten soup, salad, a large steak, a large baked potato, one-half of a loaf of bread, two pieces of cheesecake, and four cups of coffee. After the meal she remarks about her discomfort from overeating. Soon after, Liz's roommate arrives with a strawberry pie. Liz exclaims that strawberry pie is her favorite dessert and proceeds to eat three good-sized pieces and has a cup of coffee to wash them down.

Is this hunger? Certainly we can believe that Liz's extra-large meal was enough to satisfy her biological needs for food.

Question: How does this change the model of motivation?

The story illustrates that motivated behavior can be energized by the "pull" of external stimuli, as well as by the "push" of internal needs. The pull exerted by a goal is called its **incentive value.** Some goals are so desirable (strawberry pie, for example) that they motivate behavior in the absence of internal need. Other goals are so low in incentive value that they will be rejected even though they might meet the internal need. Fresh, live grubworms, for instance, are considered a delicacy in some parts of the world, but it is doubtful that the average American could eat one no matter how hungry he or she might be.

Compare: Basic Concepts of Motivation

Motivation Mechanisms within an organism that activate behavior or direct it toward some goal.

Need A specific state within the organism that may energize behavior to satisfy the need; needs are often related to the depletion of essential body substances.

Drive The psychological expression of motivation derived from an internal need state or a valued goal; for example, hunger, thirst, or a drive for material success.

Goal The target or objective of a motivated and directed chain of behaviors.

Incentive value The value a goal holds for a person or an animal above and beyond the goal's ability to fill a need.

In most instances, it is helpful to recognize that actions are energized by both internal needs *and* external incentives. In addition, a strong state of need may make a less attractive incentive into a desirable goal. You may never have eaten a grubworm, but chances are good that you have eaten some pretty horrible leftovers when the refrigerator was bare. Incentives also help account for motives that do not seem to have any identifiable internal need, such as drives for success, status, or approval (Fig. 11–1).

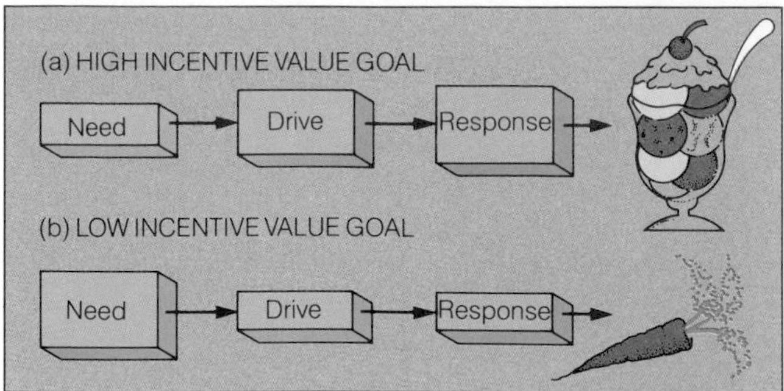

Fig. 11–1 *Needs and incentives interact to determine drive strength* (top). (a) *Moderate need combined with a high-incentive goal produces a strong drive.* (b) *Even when a strong need exists, drive strength may be moderate if a goal's incentive value is low. It is important to remember, however, that incentive value lies "in the eye of the beholder"* (photo). *No matter how hungry, few people would be able to eat the pictured grubworms.*

Types of Motives For the purpose of study, motives can be divided into three major categories:

1. **Primary motives** are based on biological needs that must be met for survival. The most important primary motives are hunger, thirst, pain avoidance, and the need for air, sleep, elimination of wastes, and regulation of body temperature. Primary motives are innate.

2. **Stimulus motives** also appear to be innate, but they are not necessary for survival of the organism. Their purpose seems to be to provide the nervous system with useful information and stimulation. The stimulus motives include activity, curiosity, exploration, manipulation, and physical contact.

3. **Learned, or secondary, motives** account for the great diversity of human activities suggested by the Chapter Preview. Behavior like Bryan Allen's flight over the English Channel is probably best understood in terms of learned motives or goals. Many secondary motives are related to acquired needs for power, affiliation (the need to be with others), approval, status, security, and achievement. The important motives of fear and aggression also appear to be subject to learning.

Primary Motives and Homeostasis—Keeping the Home Fires Burning

How important is food in your life? Water? Sleep? Air? Temperature regulation? For most of us, satisfying these biological needs is so habitual we tend to overlook how much of our behavior they actually direct. But exaggerate any of these needs through famine, shipwreck, poverty, near-drowning, or exposure, and their powerful grip on behavior becomes evident. We are, after all, still animals in many ways.

Biological drives are essential because they maintain **homeostasis** (HOE-me-oh-STAY-sis), or bodily equilibrium (Cannon, 1932).

Question: What is homeostasis?

The term *homeostasis* means "standing steady," or "steady state." Within the body there are "ideal" levels for body temperature, for concentration of various chemicals in the blood, for blood pressure, and so forth. When the body deviates from these ideal levels, automatic reactions restore equilibrium. You might find it helpful to think of the homeostatic mechanism as being similar in operation to a *thermostat* set at a particular temperature.

A (Very) Short Course on Thermostats

If room temperature falls below the level set on a thermostat, the heat is automatically turned on to warm the room. When the heat equals or slightly exceeds the ideal temperature, it is automatically turned off. In this way room temperature is maintained in a state of equilibrium hovering around the ideal level.

In the human body the first reactions to disequilibrium are also automatic. For example, if you become too hot, blood flow to body surfaces is increased and perspiring begins, thus lowering body temperature. We become aware of the need to maintain homeostasis only when driven by continued disequilibrium to seek shade, warmth, food, or water.

Since hunger is one of the most interesting and better understood of the primary drives, we will examine it in detail before we discuss biological drives in general. Before reading more you may find it helpful to complete the Learning Check that follows.

Learning Check

1. Motives ________________, sustain, and ________________ activities.
2. Needs provide the ________________ of motivation, whereas incentives provide the ________________.

Classify the following needs or motives by placing the correct letter in the blank.

A. Primary motive **B.** Stimulus motive **C.** Secondary motive

3. ____ curiosity
4. ____ status
5. ____ sleep
6. ____ thirst
7. ____ achievement
8. ____ physical contact
9. The maintenance of bodily equilibrium is called thermostasis. T or F?
10. A goal high in incentive value may create a drive in the absence of any internal need. T or F?

Answers:
1. initiate, direct **2.** push, pull **3.** B **4.** C **5.** A **6.** A **7.** C **8.** B **9.** F **10.** T

Hunger—Pardon Me, That's Just My Hypothalamus Growling

Question: What causes hunger?

When you feel hungry, you probably associate a desire for food with sensations from your stomach. This, sensibly enough, is where the search for hunger began. In an early study, Cannon and Washburn (1912) decided to see if the contractions of an empty stomach cause hunger. To do this, Washburn trained himself to swallow a balloon. Once it was in his stomach, the balloon was inflated through an attached tube so that stomach contractions could be recorded (Fig. 11–2). Cannon and Washburn observed that when Washburn's stomach contracted, he felt "hunger pangs." They concluded that hunger is nothing more than stomach contractions.

Fig. 11–2 *In Cannon's early study of hunger, a simple apparatus was used to simultaneously record hunger pangs and stomach contractions. (After Cannon, 1934.)*

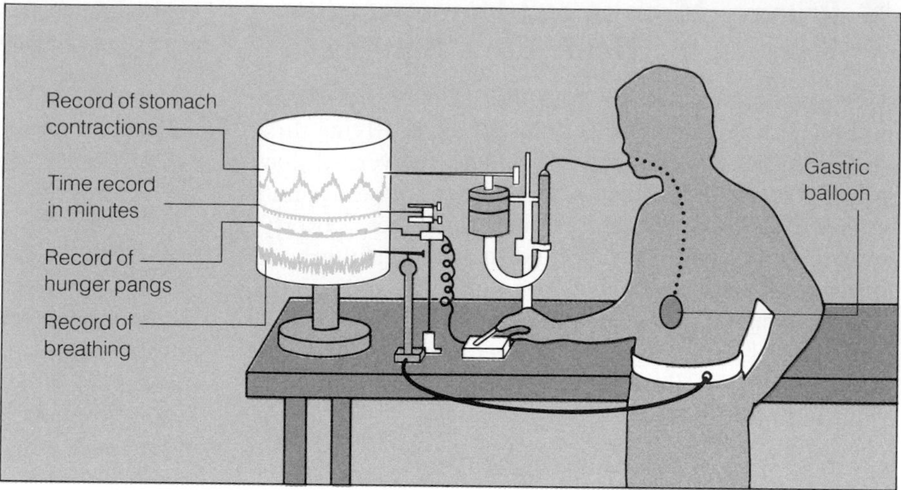

Later research contradicted this conclusion. Perhaps you already guessed that something more than the stomach is involved in hunger. Many people experience hunger as an overall feeling of weakness or shakiness that does not seem to be associated with the stomach. And, while eating *is* limited when the stomach is distended (full), it can be shown that the stomach is not essential for experiencing hunger.

Question: How has that been demonstrated?

For one thing, cutting the sensory nerves from the stomach (so that the stomach sensations can no longer be felt) does not abolish hunger in animals. Even more convincing is the fact that many people have had their stomachs removed surgically. These people continue to feel hungry and to eat regularly. It would seem that some *central* factor must be the cause of hunger. One important element now appears to be the level of sugar in the blood. If insulin is injected in a human, it produces **hypoglycemia** (HI-po-gli-SEE-me-ah: low blood sugar) and stimulates feelings of hunger and stomach contractions (Hoyenga & Hoyenga, 1984). Strange as it may seem, the liver may also affect hunger.

Question: The liver?

Yes, the liver. Evidence suggests that the liver responds to a lack of bodily "fuel" by sending nerve impulses to the brain, thus triggering the desire to eat (Friedman & Stricker, 1976).

Question: What part of the brain controls hunger?

When you are hungry, many brain areas are affected, so no single "hunger center" exists. However, one area of importance is the **hypothalamus** (HI-po-THAL-ah-mus), a small structure near the base of the brain (Fig. 11–3).

Cells in the hypothalamus are sensitive to levels of sugar (and perhaps other substances) in the blood. The hypothalamus also receives messages from the liver and the stomach (Hoyenga & Hoyenga, 1984). These messages appear to combine to produce hunger. One area of the hypothalamus seems to be part of a **feeding system** in the brain. If the *lateral hypothalamus* is activated electrically, even a well-fed animal will immediately begin eating. (The term *lateral* simply means the sides of the hypothalamus.) If the same area is destroyed, the animal

Fig. 11–3 *Location of the hypothalamus in the human brain.*

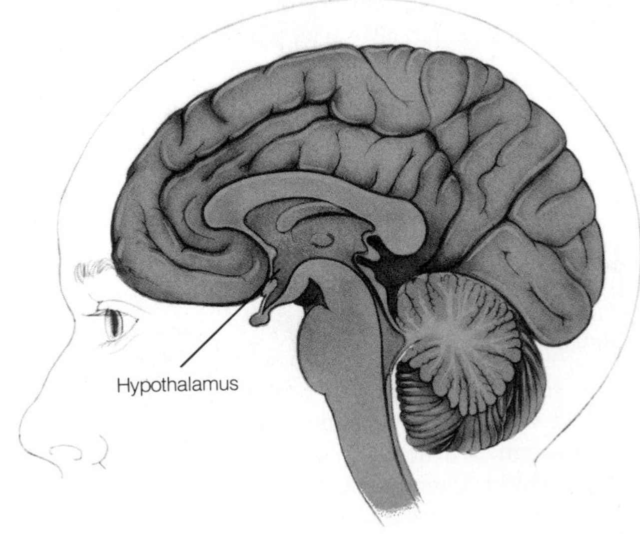

will refuse to eat and will die if not force-fed (Anand & Brobeck, 1951).

A second area within the hypothalamus seems to be part of a **satiety system** (or "stop system") for eating. If the *ventromedial hypothalamus* is destroyed, dramatic overeating results. (*Ventromedial* refers to the bottom middle of the hypothalamus.) Rats with such damage overeat to the point of total obesity. Some balloon up to weights of 1000 grams or more and get so large that they can barely move (Fig. 11–4). A normal rat weighs about 180 grams. To picture this weight change in human terms, envision someone you know who weighs 180 pounds growing to a weight of 1000 pounds.

Like the brain itself, hunger is very complex. While it is clear that the hypothalamus plays a role in hunger, it is worth stating again that scientists have been unable to locate simple "hunger control centers." The effects of damage to the hypothalamus, for example, may simply reflect the fact that a large amount of sensory and motor activity passes through this area (Thompson, 1985).

It should come as no surprise that there is more to hunger than simple "start" and "stop" systems in the brain. Evidence suggests that fat stored in the body also influences hunger. The body acts as if there is a **set point** for the *proportion* of body fat that is maintained (LeMagnen, 1980). That is, the set point acts like a "thermostat" for body fat. Your personal set point is the weight you maintain when you are making no effort to gain or lose weight. When your body goes below its set point, you are likely to feel hungry most of the time (Friedman & Stricker, 1976).

Fig. 11–4 *Damage to the hunger satiety system in the hypothalamus can produce a very fat rat, a condition called hypothalamic* hyperphagia *(overeating). This rat weights 1080 grams. (The pointer has gone completely around the dial and beyond.) (Photo courtesy of Neal Miller.)*

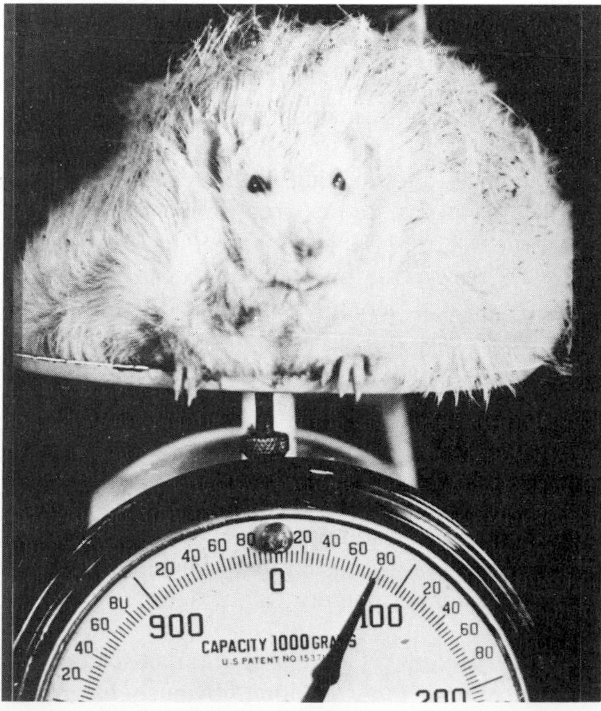

Question: Do people have different set points?

Yes. The set point appears to be partly inherited and partly determined by early feeding patterns. Adopted children whose birth parents are overweight are much more likely to be overweight themselves (Stunkard et al., 1986). This shows that a person's genes greatly influence adult weight. Also, the set point may be lastingly altered when a child is overfed. If a weight problem begins in childhood, the person will, as an adult, have *more* fat cells and *larger* fat cells in the body. If the person does not become overweight until adulthood, his or her fat cells will be larger, but their number usually does not increase. Thus, when a weight problem begins in childhood, it is much more difficult to control.

Question: Why do people overeat?

Obesity Set points are only one piece in a complex puzzle that scientists are still trying to solve. Their search is fueled by the fact that obesity is a major health risk and, for many, a source of social stigma and low self-esteem (Brownell, 1982) (Fig. 11–5).

Perhaps if eating were controlled only by internal needs, fewer people would overeat. As noted earlier, however, the sight or aroma of food often makes people want to eat, even when they do not feel hungry. It seems that many people are sensitive to **external eating cues** (signs and signals linked with food) (Rodin, 1978). If you are sensitive to external cues, you are most likely to eat when food is attractive, highly visible, and easy to obtain (Schachter & Rodin, 1974).

Even the time of day can influence eating. In one intriguing experiment, subjects were allowed to nibble on some crackers while waiting in a room. On the wall was a clock that could be adjusted to run fast or slow. When obese subjects were led to believe it was closer to mealtime than it actually was (fast clock), they ate more crackers than when they thought dinnertime was farther away than it actually was (slow clock). Subjects of normal weight *decreased* their eating when they thought it was closer to mealtime (Schachter & Gross, 1968). When the clock read

Fig. 11–5 *Professional football player William (Refrigerator) Perry has received much notoriety because of his size and his good humor about it. However, when Perry arrived at training camp in 1988 weighing 377 pounds, he admitted that he had a problem and entered a program for eating disorders. Obesity can be a serious health problem and is ultimately no laughing matter.*

5 minutes after 6, the reaction of fat subjects seems to have been, "Hmm, dinner time, I must be hungry!"

Question: Does that mean that people who are overweight are more sensitive to external eating cues?

Until recently, the obese were thought to be "externally cued eaters." Lean people, in contrast, were assumed to be better attuned to internal hunger signals. Unfortunately, this idea proved too simple. People of all weights can be found who are unusually sensitive to external eating cues, so this is not strictly a problem of the obese (Rodin, 1981). Just the same, eating cues do appear to be a factor in some overeating. For example, psychologist Judith Rodin found that externally responsive girls were most likely to gain weight at a 2-month summer camp (Rodin, 1978).

It is highly likely that **diet** also contributes to overeating. Placing animals on a "supermarket" diet, for instance, can lead to gross obesity. In one experiment, rats were given meals of chocolate chip cookies, salami, cheese, bananas, marshmallows, milk chocolate, peanut butter, and fat. Rats on this diet gained almost 3 times as much weight as controls that ate only standard laboratory rat chow (Sclafani & Springer, 1976). (Rat chow is a dry mixture of several bland foods. If you were a rat, you'd probably eat more cookies than rat chow, too!) We humans also appear to be sensitive to dietary content. In general, *sweetness,* high *fat content,* and *variety* tend to encourage overeating (Ball & Grinker, 1981). It seems that our culture may provide the worst possible kinds of foods for those with a tendency toward obesity.

It is tempting to assume that fatness comes from constant overeating, but this is a myth. Studies by Albert Stunkard (1980) and Judith Rodin (1978) show that overeating occurs mainly when a person is gaining weight. Once excess weight is gained, it can be maintained with a normal diet. An added problem is that as people gain weight, many reduce their activity level and burn fewer calories. As a result, some overweight persons may continue to gain weight while consuming fewer calories than their slimmer neighbors (Ball & Grinker, 1981).

Question: Is it true that people also overeat when they are emotionally upset?

Yes. People with weight problems are just as likely to eat when they are anxious, angry, bored, or distressed as when hungry (Bruch, 1973; Hoyenga & Hoyenga, 1984). Furthermore, unhappiness often accompanies obesity in our fat-conscious culture (Rodin, 1978). The result is a pattern of overeating that leads to emotional distress and still more overeating, making weight control extremely difficult.

To summarize, overeating is the result of a complex interplay of internal and external influences, diet, emotions, genetics, exercise, and many other factors (Rodin, 1978). To answer the question we began with, people become obese in different ways and for different reasons. Clearly, scientists are still a long way from winning the "battle of the bulge." (For another perspective on overeating, see Highlight 11–1.)

Other Factors in Hunger

As research on overeating suggests, "hunger" is affected by more than bodily needs for food. Let us consider some additional factors of interest.

Cultural Factors Learning to think of some foods as desirable and others as revolting obviously has much to

● HIGHLIGHT 11–1
The Paradox of Yo-Yo Dieting

If dieting works, why are hundreds of "new" diets published each year? The answer is that while dieters do lose weight, most regain it soon after the diet ends. Indeed, many people experience a rebound that can push weight higher than before the diet began. Why should this be so? Many theorists now believe that dieting (starving) alters the physiology of the body.

In effect, dieting causes the body to become highly efficient at *conserving* calories and storing them as fat (Bennet & Gurin, 1982). Any diet may have this effect, but "yo-yo dieting," or repeated weight loss and gain, is especially troublesome. Frequent **weight cycling** caused by dieting tends to slow the body's **metabolic rate** (the rate at which energy is used up). This makes it harder to lose weight each time a person diets and easier to regain weight when the diet ends (Brownell et al., 1986; Brownell, 1988).

Apparently, evolution prepared us to save energy when food is scarce and to stock up on fat when food is plentiful. Briefly starving yourself, therefore, may have little lasting effect on weight. To avoid ineffectively bouncing between feast and famine requires a permanent change in basic eating habits—a topic we will return to in this chapter's Applications.

do with eating habits. In America we would never consider eating the eyes out of the steamed head of a monkey, but in some parts of the world this dish is considered a real delicacy. By the same token, our willingness to consume large quantities of meat, to eat cows, and to cook fish would be considered barbaric in many cultures. Thus, **cultural values** greatly affect the incentive value of various foods.

Taste Even tastes for "normal" foods may vary considerably. One experiment demonstrated that the hungrier a person is, the more pleasant a sweet food tastes (Cabanac & Duclaux, 1970). It is also interesting to note that a **taste aversion** can be easily learned if a food causes sickness or if it is eaten just before nausea is caused by something else (Nachman, 1970). Not only will such foods be avoided, they too can become nauseating. A friend of the author's, who once became ill after eating a cheese Danish (well, actually, *several*), has never again been able to come face to face with this delightful pastry.

Question: If getting sick occurs long after eating, how does it become associated with the food eaten?

A good question. Taste aversions are a type of classical conditioning. And as stated in Chapter 7, a long delay between the CS and US usually prevents conditioning. For this reason psychologists theorize that there is a biological tendency to associate an upset stomach with food eaten earlier. Such learning usually helps protect both animals and people (Garcia et al., 1974). Yet, sadly, many human cancer patients suffer taste aversions long after the nausea of their drug treatment has passed (Bernstein, 1978).

If you like animals, you will be interested in an imaginative approach to an age-old problem. In many parts of the country, predators are poisoned, trapped, or shot on sight by livestock owners. These practices have virtually extinguished the timber wolf, and in some areas the coyote faces a similar end. How might the coyote be saved without an unacceptable loss of livestock?

In a now classic experiment, coyotes were given lamb tainted with lithium chloride. Coyotes who took the bait rapidly became nauseated and vomited. After one or two such treatments, they developed **bait shyness**—a lasting distaste for the tainted food (Gustavson & Garcia, 1974). If applied consistently, taste aversion conditioning might solve many predator-livestock problems at less expense than traditional methods (Fig. 11–6). (Perhaps this technique would even be used to protect roadrunners from the Wiley Coyote!)

Taste aversions may also help people avoid severe nutritional imbalances. For example, if you went on a fad diet and ate only grapefruit, you would eventually begin to feel ill. In time, associating your discomfort with grapefruit could create an aversion to it and restore some balance to your diet.

One classic study on **self-selection feeding** found that human infants ate a balanced diet when given a free choice of foods (Davis, 1928). Since the infants sometimes went on food jags, the overall balance of their eating may have been due in part to the process just described. It should be noted, however, that the "wisdom of the body" is quite limited. Babies in the study were only allowed to choose from fresh, unseasoned, unsweetened foods. If candy had been a choice, the infants might have gorged themselves on it (Story & Brown, 1987). We humans seem to have an innate preference for sweet and fatty foods—juicy steaks and fried chicken, cookies, cakes, and so on (Katahn, 1984). Thus, an appetite for candy and junk food can easily override the weaker tendency to eat a balanced diet.

Fig. 11–6 *Like humans and other animals, coyotes develop taste aversions when food is associated with nausea.*

Primary Motives Revisited—Thirst, Sex, and Pain

Patterns similar to those observed in the control of hunger also apply to most other primary motives. For example, thirst is only partially related to dryness of the mouth and throat. When drugs are used to keep the mouth constantly wet or dry, thirst and water intake remain normal. Like hunger, thirst appears to be controlled through the hypothalamus, where separate *thirst* and *thirst satiety* systems are found. Also like hunger, thirst is strongly affected by individual learning and by cultural values.

Thirst You may not have noticed, but there are actually two kinds of thirst. **Extracellular thirst** occurs when water is lost from the fluids surrounding the cells of your body. Bleeding, vomiting, diarrhea, sweating, and drinking alcohol cause this type of thirst (Houston, 1985). When a person loses both water and minerals in any of these ways—especially by perspiration—a slightly salty liquid may be more satisfying than plain water.

Question: Why would a thirsty person want to drink salty water?

The reason is that before the body can retain water, minerals lost through perspiration (mainly salt) must be replaced. In lab tests, animals greatly prefer salt water after salt levels in their bodies are lowered (Stricker & Verbalis, 1988). Similarly, some nomadic peoples of the Sahara Desert prize blood as a beverage, probably because of its saltiness. (Maybe they should try Gatorade?)

A second type of thirst occurs when you eat a salty meal. In this instance your body does not lose fluid. Instead, *excess* salt causes fluid to be drawn out of cells. As the cells "shrink," **intracellular thirst** is triggered. Thirst of this type is best quenched by plain water.

The drives for food, water, air, sleep, and elimination are all fairly similar in that they are generated by a combination of activities in the body and the brain, are modified by learning and culture, and are influenced by external factors. Two of the primary drives are unlike the others. These are the sex drive and the drive to avoid pain. Each differs from the other primary drives in some interesting ways.

Question: How is the drive to avoid pain different?

Pain Drives such as hunger, thirst, and sleepiness come and go in a fairly regular cycle each day. Pain avoidance, by contrast, is an **episodic drive** (ep-ih-SOD-ik). That is, it occurs in distinct episodes, since it is aroused only when damage to the tissues of the body takes place. Most of the primary drives cause a person to actively seek a desired goal (food, drink, warmth, and so forth). The goal of the pain avoidance drive is the elimination of pain.

It may surprise you to discover that the drive to avoid pain is partly learned. This fact was demonstrated by a study in which dogs were totally isolated (in special cages) from the normal bumps, bites, and other pains of puppyhood. As adults, the dogs reacted strangely to pain. For example, when a lighted match was held near their noses, many pushed toward it as if they felt no pain (Melzack & Scott, 1957). Apparently, the dogs had not learned the meaning of pain or how to avoid it.

Human pain avoidance is also affected by learning. Some people, for instance, feel they must be "tough" and not show any discomfort; others complain loudly at the smallest ache or pain. As you might expect, the first attitude raises pain tolerance, and the second lowers it (Klienke, 1978). Such attitudes explain why members of some societies endure cutting, burning, whipping, tatooing, and piercing of the skin that would agonize the typical member of our society.

The Sex Drive Sexual motivation is quite unusual compared with other biological motives. In fact, many psychologists do not think of sex as a primary motive because sex (contrary to anything your personal experience might suggest) is not necessary for *individual* survival. It is necessary, of course, for *group* survival among humans and other creatures.

In lower animals the sex drive is directly related to the action of bodily hormones. Females of the lower species are interested in mating only when their fertility cycle is in the stage of **estrus,** or "heat" (caused by secretion of the hormone **estrogen** into the bloodstream). Hormones are important in the male animal as well. In most lower animals, castration will abolish the sex drive. But in contrast to the female, the normal male animal is always ready to mate. His sex drive is primarily aroused by the behavior of a receptive female. In animals, mating is therefore closely tied to the fertility cycle of the female.

Question: How much do hormones affect the sex drive in humans?

The link between hormones and the sex drive grows weaker as we ascend the biological scale. Hormones do affect the human sex drive, but only to a limited degree. For example, one careful study found no connection between female sexual activity and the monthly menstrual cycle (Udry & Morris, 1977). In humans, mental, cultural, and emotional factors determine sexual expression. However, our liberation from hormones is not total. Human males show a loss of sex drive after castration, and some women lose sexual desire when using birth control pills (McCauley & Ehrhardt, 1976).

Human sexual behavior and attitudes are discussed in detail in Chapter 25. For now it is enough to note that the sex drive is largely **non-homeostatic.** In humans, the sex drive can be aroused at virtually any time by almost anything. It therefore shows no clear relationship to deprivation (the amount of time since the drive was last satisfied). True, an increase in desire may occur as time passes. But on the other hand, recent sexual activity does not prevent sexual desire from occurring again. The sex drive is also unusual in that its arousal is as actively sought as its reduction.

The non-homeostatic quality of the sex drive can be shown in this way: An animal is allowed to copulate until it seems to have no further interest in sexual behavior. Then a new sexual partner is provided. Immediately, the animal resumes sexual activity. This pattern is called the *Coolidge effect* after former U.S. president Calvin Coolidge. What, you might ask, does Calvin Coolidge have to do with the sex drive? The answer is found in the following story.

When touring an experimental farm, Coolidge's wife reportedly asked if a rooster mated just once a day. "No ma'am," she was told, "he mates dozens of times each day." "Tell that to the president," she said, with a faraway look in her eyes. When President Coolidge reached the same part of the tour, his wife's message was given to him. His reaction was to ask if the dozens of matings were with the same hen. No, he was told, different hens were involved. "Tell *that* to Mrs. Coolidge," the president is said to have replied.

Learning Check

1. Systems for the control of hunger and thirst are linked with the ______________ of the brain.
2. The hunger satiety system in the hypothalamus signals the body to start eating when it receives signals from the liver or detects changes in blood sugar. T or F?
3. Varied diets containing high levels of sweets and fats tend to encourage overeating only for people who tend to eat when they are anxious. T or F?
4. Bait shyness occurs when
   a. a specific hunger develops
   b. the set point for body fat is altered
   c. the hypothalamus is activated electrically
   d. a taste aversion is formed
5. People who diet frequently tend to benefit from practice: They lose weight more quickly each time they diet. T or F?
6. Thirst may be either intracellular or ______________.
7. Pain avoidance is an ______________ drive.
8. Sexual behavior in animals is largely controlled by estrogen levels in the female and the occurrence of estrus in the male. T or F?

Answers:

1. hypothalamus 2. F 3. F 4. *d* 5. F 6. extracellular 7. episodic 8. F

Stimulus Drives—Skydiving, Horror Movies, and the Fun Zone

It is sometimes said that curiosity killed the cat, but nothing could be further from the truth. Drives for **exploration, manipulation,** or simply for **curiosity** seem to aid survival for most animals. As mentioned earlier, such drives might be explained by the life-and-death necessity of keeping track of sources of food, danger, and other important details of the environment. However, the curiosity drives seem to go beyond such needs.

Monkey Business

In an experiment, monkeys confined to a dimly lit box learned to perform a simple task in order to open a window that allowed them to view the outside world (Butler & Harlow, 1954). In a similar experiment, monkeys quickly learned to solve a mechanical puzzle made up of interlocking metal pins, hooks, and hasps (Butler, 1954) (Fig. 11–7). In both situations, no external reward was offered for exploration or manipulation.

The monkeys described seemed to work for the sheer fun of it. An interest in video games, chess, puzzles, Rubick's cube, and the like offers a human parallel. Curiosity—the drive to *know*—also seems to be powerful in humans. Scientific investigation, intellectual curiosity, and other advanced activities may be an extension of this basic drive.

Closely related to curiosity is the drive for sensory stimulation. It is now well established that humans and animals demand and actively seek stimulation (Reykowski, 1982). As discussed in Chapter 6, people who have undergone prolonged or severe **sensory deprivation**—for example, prisoners, arctic explorers, radar operators, and truck drivers—often report sensory distortions and disturbed thinking. The nervous system seems to require varied, patterned stimulation to respond normally (Suedfeld, 1975).

Fig. 11–7 *Monkeys happily open locks that are placed in their cage. Since no reward is given for this activity, it provides evidence of the existence of stimulus needs. (Photo courtesy of Harry F. Harlow.)*

The drive for stimulation can even be observed in infants. When babies are shown patterns of varying complexity (Fig. 11–8), they spend more time looking at complex patterns than at simpler ones (Berlyne, 1966). Indeed, human infants seem to have an almost limitless appetite for stimulation. By the time a child can walk, there are few things in the home that have not been tasted, touched, viewed, handled, or in the case of toys, destroyed!

Question: Are stimulus drives homeostatic?

Arousal Theory

Some psychologists would argue that they are not. However, by relating drives for stimulation to the concept of homeostasis, we get a useful model for understanding many human activities. This position, called the **arousal theory** of motivation, assumes that there is an ideal level of arousal for various activities and that individuals behave in ways that keep arousal near this ideal level (Hebb, 1966).

Fig. 11–8 *Berlyne studied curiosity in infants by showing them these designs. Babies looked first at the more complex patterns on the right. (From* Science, *153:25–33. Copyright © 1966 by the American Association for the Advancement of Science.)*

other time zone travelers often make errors or perform poorly when their body rhythms are disturbed by jet lag (Rader & Hicks, 1987). If you travel great distances east or west, the peaks and valleys of your circadian rhythms will be out of phase with the sun and clocks. For example, you might find that your period of peak arousal occurs at 4 A.M., while your low point falls during the middle of the day. Shift work has the same effect, causing lower efficiency, as well as fatigue, irritability, upset stomach, nervousness, depression, and a decline in mental agility (Akerstedt et al., 1982).

Question: How fast do people adapt to such time shifts?

For major time zone shifts (5 hours or more), it can take from several days to 2 weeks to resynchronize. Adaptation to jet lag is slowest when you stay indoors (in a hotel room, for instance), where you can continue to sleep and eat on "home time." Getting outdoors, where you must sleep, eat, and socialize on the new schedule, tends to speed adaptation (Moore-Ede et al., 1982).

The *direction* of travel also affects adaptation. If you fly west, adapting is relatively easy, taking an average of 4 to 5 days. If you fly east, adapting takes 50 percent longer, or more (Fig. 11–11). Why is there a difference? The answer is that when you fly east, the sun comes up earlier (relative to your "home" time). As you fly west, it comes up later. You may recall from Chapter 6 that the sleep-waking rhythm naturally runs longer than 24 hours. For this reason, most people find that it is easier to "advance" (stay up later and sleep in) than it is to shift backward.

When you travel east, you must go to sleep during your former afternoon and get up when your body thinks it is the middle of the night. Likewise, work shifts that "rotate" backward (night, evening, day) are more disruptive than those that advance (day, evening, night). If work shifts must change, those lasting only 3 days are less disruptive than week-long shifts (Williamson & Sanderson, 1986). Best of all are work shifts that do not change: Even continuous night work is less disruptive than changing shifts.

Question: What does all of this have to do with those of us who are not shift workers or world travelers?

There are few college students who have not at one time or another "burned the midnight oil," especially for final exams. During this or any other strenuous period, it is wise to remember the effects of disturbed body rhythms. Any major deviation from your regular schedule is likely to cost more than it's worth. Often, you can accomplish

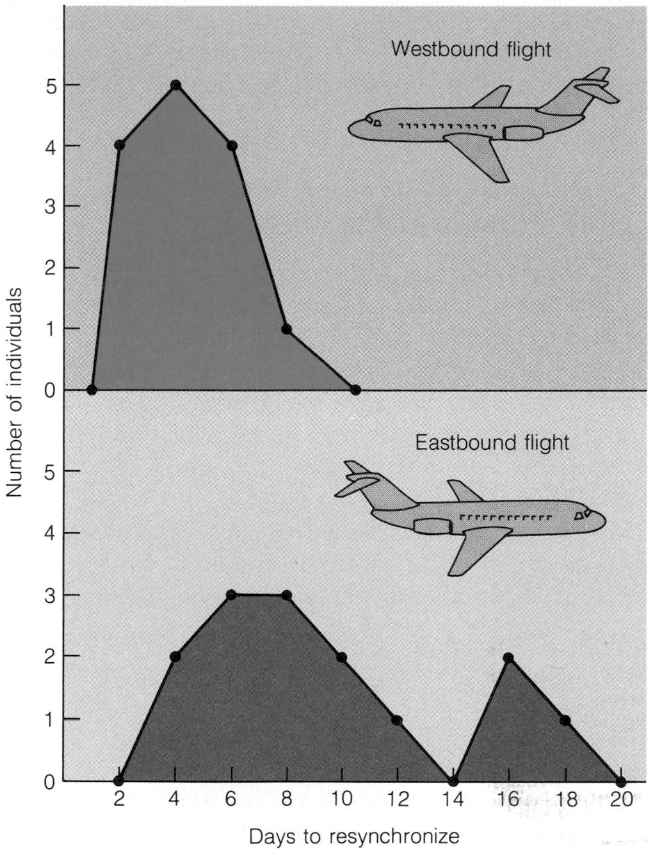

Fig. 11–11 *Time required to adjust to air travel across 6 time zones. The average time to resynchronize was shorter for westbound travel than for eastbound flights. (Data from Beljan et al., 1972; cited by Moore-Ede et al., 1982.)*

as much during 1 hour in the morning as you could have in 3 hours of work after midnight. The 2-hour difference in efficiency might as well be spent sleeping. If you feel you must depart from your normal schedule, do it gradually over a period of days.

In general, if you can anticipate an upcoming body rhythm change (when traveling, before finals week, or when doing shift work), it is best to **preadapt** yourself to your new schedule beforehand. Before traveling, for instance, you should go to sleep 1 hour later (or earlier) each day until your sleep cycle matches the time at your destination. If you are unable to do that, it at least helps to fly early in the day when you fly east. When you fly west, it is better to fly late. (Remember, the *E* in *east* matches the *E* in *early*.)

Question: Are circadian rhythms related to biorhythms?

No. Evidence suggests that biorhythm theory, which is promoted commercially, is a false system. The reasons for this conclusion are explained in Highlight 11–2.

Learned Motives—Cheap Thrills and the Pursuit of Excellence

Many motives are acquired directly. It is easy enough to see that praise, money, success, pleasure, and similar reinforcers affect our goals and desires. But how do people learn to enjoy activities that are at first painful or frightening? Why do people climb rocks, jump out of airplanes, run marathons, take sauna baths, or swim in frozen lakes? For an answer, let's examine a related situation.

When a person first tries a drug such as heroin, he or she feels a "rush" of pleasure. However, as the drug wears off, a period of discomfort or craving occurs. The easiest way to end the discomfort is to take another dose of the drug—as most drug users quickly learn. But in time, habituation takes place; the drug stops producing pleasure, although it will end discomfort. At the same time, the after effects of the drug grow more painful. At this point, the drug user has acquired a powerful new motive. In a vicious cycle, heroin relieves discomfort, but it guarantees that the withdrawal will occur again in a few hours.

Opponent-Process Theory Psychologist Richard L. Solomon (1980) offers an intriguing explanation for drug addiction and other learned motives. According to his **opponent-process theory,** if a stimulus causes strong emotion, such as fear or pleasure, an opposite emotion tends to occur when the stimulus ends. For example, if you are in pain, and the pain ends, you will feel a pleasant sense of relief. If you feel pleasure, as in the case of drug use, and the pleasure ends, it will be followed by craving

HIGHLIGHT 11–2
Biorhythms—Fact or Fallacy?

Owing to its popularity, you have probably heard of biorhythm theory. Perhaps you have been curious about it. What does biorhythm theory claim? What evidence is there to support it? Is there any value to having your biorhythms charted?

Biorhythm Theory Biorhythm theory states that we are all subject to 3 cycles: a physical cycle lasting 23 days, an emotional cycle of 28 days, and a 33-day intellectual cycle. The first half of each cycle is supposedly positive (made up of good days) and the second half negative. According to the theory, all 3 cycles begin at birth and continue throughout life. When a cycle changes from positive to negative, it is termed a "critical day." When all 3 cycles line up on critical days, the chances for disaster or accident are supposedly quite high.

Biorhythm theory is often promoted with case histories of celebrities who made serious errors, had accidents, or performed exceptionally well when biorhythms were "working for or against" them. What the promoters usually overlook, however, is all the cases that don't fit (Louis, 1978).

Save Your Money Some of the logical problems with biorhythm theory may have already occurred to you. Why should the 3 cycles begin at birth? After all, the fetus is alive before birth. Are we to believe, as well, that a cesarean birth can change a person's entire life? Or that being born a few days earlier or later can make a lifelong difference? And why should the cycles last exactly 23, 28, and 33 days for everyone on earth?

The strongest evidence against biorhythm theory comes from attempts to match cycles with outcomes. For instance, one researcher compared 100 no-hit baseball games pitched in the major leagues to biorhythm charts for the pitchers. The result? He found no connection between cycles and these performances (Louis, 1978). In Canada, the Workers' Compensation Board of British Columbia studied over 13,000 occupational accidents. The outcome? Accidents are no more likely to occur on "critical" days than at any other time (Nelson, 1976). Other studies have found absolutely no correlation between aviation accidents and pilots' biorhythms, or between biorhythms and recovery from surgery, time of death, or the scores of golf pros (Holmes et al., 1980; Wolcott et al., 1977).

In summary, the evidence is strongly against biorhythm theory. If you fail a test, have an accident, lose a game, insult your boss, or dissolve your marriage, don't look to a biorhythm chart for the explanation.

or discomfort. If you are in love and feel good when you are with your lover, you will be uncomfortable when he or she is absent.

Question: What happens if the stimulus is repeated?

Solomon assumes that when a stimulus is repeated, our response to it habituates, or gets weaker. First time skydivers, for instance, are almost always terrified. But with repeated jumps, fear lessens, until finally the skydiver feels a "thrill" instead of terror. In contrast, emotional after effects get stronger with repetition. After a first jump, beginning parachutists experience a brief but exhilarating sense of relief. After many such experiences, seasoned skydivers can get a "rush" of euphoria that lasts for hours after a jump (Fig. 11–12). With repetition, the pleasurable after effect gets stronger and the initial "cost" (pain or fear) gets weaker. The opponent-process theory thus explains how skydiving, rock climbing, ski jumping, and other hazardous pursuits become reinforcing. If you are a fan of horror movies or of carnival rides, your motives may be based on the same effect.

Fig. 11–12 *A sport parachutist takes the plunge. The typical emotional sequence for a first jump is: anxiety before, terror during, and relief after the jump. After many jumps the emotional sequence becomes: eagerness before, a thrill during, and exhilaration after a jump. The new sequence strongly reinforces skydiving.*

Social Motives

Competition and achievement are highly valued in Western culture. In less industrialized nations, the desire to achieve may be minimal. Some of your friends are more interested than others in success, money, possessions, status, love, approval, grades, dominance, power, or belonging to groups. In each case, we are referring to differences in **social motives** or goals. Social motives are acquired in complex ways through socialization and cultural conditioning. The behavior of outstanding artists, scientists, athletes, educators, and leaders is best understood in terms of such learned needs, particularly the need for achievement.

The Need for Achievement The **need for achievement (nAch)** is not the only social motive of importance, but it is certainly prominent. To many people, being "motivated" means being interested in achievement. In other chapters, we will investigate the motives behind aggression, love, affiliation, and seeking approval. For now, let us focus on the need for achievement.

The need for achievement can be defined as a desire to meet some *internalized standard of excellence* (McClelland, 1961). The person with high needs for achievement strives to do well in any situation in which evaluation takes place.

Question: Is that like the aggressive businessperson who strives for success?

Not necessarily. Needs for achievement may lead to material wealth and prestige, but a person who is a high achiever in art, music, science, or amateur athletics may be striving for excellence without concern for material reward. The need for achievement differs from a **need for power,** which is a desire to have *impact* or control over others (McClelland, 1975). People with strong needs for power want their importance to be visible: They buy expensive possessions, read flashy magazines, and try to exploit relationships.

David McClelland (1958, 1961) and a number of other psychologists have been interested in the effects of high or low needs for achievement. Using a simple measure of nAch, McClelland found that he could predict the behavior of high and low achievers in many situations. In one study, for example, the occupations of college graduates were compared with scores on a need-for-achievement test given in their sophomore year. Fourteen years after graduation, those who scored high in nAch were found more often in careers involving an element of risk and responsibility than were those with low nAch scores (McClelland, 1965). Interestingly, scores for achievement motivation have declined for students in recent years (Lueptow, 1980). Some psychologists believe that this may help account for the dramatic decline in *Scholastic Aptitude Test (SAT)* scores observed in the last decade (Hoyenga & Hoyenga, 1984).

Characteristics of Achievers In front of you are five targets placed at various distances from where you are standing. You are given a beanbag to toss at the target of your choice. Target A, anyone can hit; target B, most people can hit; target C, some people can hit; target D, very few people can hit; target E is rarely if ever hit. If you hit A, you will receive $2; B, $4; C, $8; D, $16; and E, $32. You get only one toss. Which one would you choose? McClelland's research suggests that if you have a high need for achievement, you will select C or perhaps D.

Those high in nAch are *moderate* risk takers. When faced with a problem or challenge, persons high in nAch avoid goals that are too easy because they offer no sense of satisfaction. They also avoid long shots because there is no hope of success or because if success occurs, it will be due to luck rather than skill. Persons low in nAch select either sure things or impossible goals. Either way, there is no risk of personal responsibility for failure.

Fig. 11–13 *The person with high needs for achievement strives to do well in any situation in which evaluation takes place.*

Desires for achievement and calculated risk taking are converted into successful performances of tasks in many situations. People high in nAch do better on various tasks in the laboratory. They are more likely to complete difficult tasks. They earn better grades in high school and college, and they tend to excel in their chosen occupations. College students high in nAch tend to attribute success to their own ability, and failure to insufficient effort (Kleinke, 1978). Thus, high nAch students are more likely to renew their efforts when faced with a poor performance. When the going gets tough, high achievers get going.

Fear of Success Have you ever hidden your talents in favor of blending into a group? Have you ever backed off from "winning" in sports or school? Have you ever "played dumb" with friends? Everyone has probably done so at times. Each of these actions involves an avoidance, or fear, of success (see Highlight 11–3). Obviously, fearing success can stifle efforts to achieve.

Why would anyone avoid success? Most often because: (1) success can require a stressful shift in self-concept; (2) many people fear rejection when they stand out in a group; and (3) some people fear the extra demands of being a "successful person" (Tresemer, 1977). All three reasons are illustrated by a secretary who quit when she was offered a job as a supervisor. When asked why she quit, she said it was because she didn't want to be a "career woman," because she feared her former friends in the office would reject her, and because she disliked telling others what to do.

Question: Do fears of success occur mainly in women?

Both men and women appear to be equally subject to success fears (Kearney, 1985). But in our culture there is often an extra conflict for women. By adulthood, many men and women have learned to consider it "unfeminine" for a woman to excel (de Charms & Muir, 1978). Understandably, then, successful women are most often those who define achievement as an acceptable feminine quality (Kleinke, 1978). Perhaps the women's movement and changing attitudes will help remove this unnecessary stumbling block for future generations of talented and aspiring women.

The Key to Success? What does it take to achieve extraordinary success? Educational psychologist Benjamin Bloom did an interesting study of America's top performers in six fields: concert pianists, Olympic swimmers, sculptors, tennis players, mathematicians, and re-

> **HIGHLIGHT 11–3**
> **Who's Afraid of a Little Success?**
>
> With which of the following statements do you agree?
>
> 1. I am happy only when I am doing better than others.
> 2. Achievement commands respect.
> 3. It is extremely important for me to do well in all things that I undertake.
> 4. Often, the cost of success is greater than the reward.
> 5. I believe that successful people are often sad and lonely.
> 6. I think success has been emphasized too much in our culture.
>
> (Source: Zuckerman & Allison, 1976)
>
> Agreement with the first three statements shows a positive attitude toward success. People who agree with the last three statements tend to avoid success. It might seem that avoiding success is always undesirable. In reality, an overemphasis on achievement can be as big a handicap as avoidance of success. Our society is notorious for its successful but unhappy workaholics. In the final analysis, a truly successful life strikes a balance between achievement and other needs.

search neurologists. Bloom (1985) found that drive and determination, not great natural talent, led to success in the lives of the high achievers he studied.

Development of Bloom's subjects began when parents exposed the child to music, swimming, scientific ideas, and so forth, "just for fun." At first, many of the children were quite ordinary in their skills. One Olympic swimmer, for instance, remembers repeatedly losing races as a 10-year-old. At some point, however, the children began to get recognition for their abilities and pursued them more actively. Before long, parents noticed the child's rapid progress and sought out a more expert instructor or coach. After more successes and encouragement, the youngsters began "living" for their talent. Most spent many hours each day practicing their skills. This continued for many years before they reached truly extraordinary heights of achievement.

The upshot of Bloom's work is that talent is nurtured by dedication and hard work. It appears that this is most likely to happen when parents give their wholehearted support to a child's special interest and when they place emphasis on doing one's best at all times. Other studies of child prodigies and eminent adults also show that intensive practice and expert instruction are common ingredients of high achievement (Wallach, 1985). The old belief that "talent will out" of its own accord is largely a myth.

Motives in Perspective—A View from the Pyramid

As you may recall from Chapter 1, humanistic psychologist Abraham Maslow defined self-actualization as the full development of personal potential. As a sidelight to his work on self-actualization, Maslow proposed that there is a **hierarchy** (or ordering) of human needs. By this he meant that some needs are more basic or powerful than others. Think for a moment about the needs that influence your behavior. Which seem strongest? Which do you spend the most time and energy satisfying? Now look at Maslow's hierarchy (Fig. 11–14). Note that physiological needs are at the bottom. Since these are necessary for survival, they tend to be prepotent, or dominant over the higher needs. It could be said, for example, that "to a starving person, food is god."

Maslow believed that higher needs are expressed only when the prepotent physiological needs are satisfied. This is also true of needs for safety and security. Until there is a basic amount of order and stability in meeting the lower needs, a person may have little interest in higher pursuits. A person who is extremely thirsty, for instance, might have little interest in writing poetry or making small talk about the weather. For this reason, Maslow

Fig. 11–14 *Maslow believed that lower needs in the hierarchy are dominant. Basic needs must be satisfied before growth motives are fully expressed. Desires for self-actualization are reflected in various meta-needs (see text).*

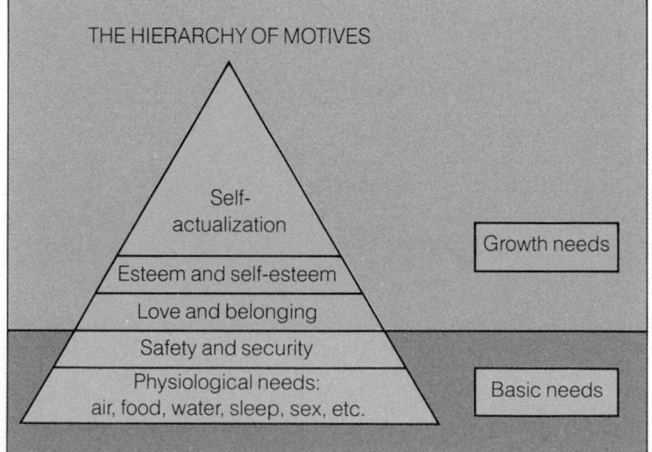

described the first two levels of the hierarchy as **basic needs.** Higher needs, or **growth needs,** include love and belonging (family, friendship, caring), needs for esteem and self-esteem (recognition and self-respect), and self-actualization needs (Fig. 11–15). Although Maslow believed that a desire for self-actualization is universal, he placed it at the top of the hierarchy. This placement indicates that he viewed it as fragile and easily interrupted by lower needs.

Question: How are needs for self-actualization expressed?

Maslow called the less powerful but humanly important actualization motives **meta-needs** (Maslow, 1970). These are listed in Table 11–1. According to Maslow, there is a tendency to move up the hierarchy to the meta-needs. A person whose survival needs are met, but whose meta-needs are unfulfilled, falls into a "syndrome of decay" and experiences despair, apathy, and alienation. Mere survival and creature comforts, in other words, are usually not enough to make a full and satisfying life.

Maslow's hierarchy is not well documented by research, and questions can be raised about it. How, for instance, do we explain the use of fasting as a means of social protest? How has the meta-need for justice overcome the more basic need for food? (Perhaps the answer is that fasting is temporary and self-imposed.) Despite such objections, Maslow's views have been widely influential as a way of understanding and appreciating the rich interplay of human motives. Rather than being a scientific theory, Maslow's hierarchy represents a philosophical viewpoint.

Fig. 11–15 *Wheelchair athletes engage in vigorous competition. Maslow considered such behavior an expression of the need for self-actualization.*

Table 11–1 Maslow's List of Meta-Needs

Meta-needs are seen as an expression of tendencies for self-actualization, the full development of personal potential.

1. Wholeness (unity)
2. Perfection (balance and harmony)
3. Completion (ending)
4. Justice (fairness)
5. Richness (complexity)
6. Simplicity (essence)
7. Aliveness (spontaneity)
8. Beauty (rightness of form)
9. Goodness (benevolence)
10. Uniqueness (individuality)
11. Playfulness (ease)
12. Truth (reality)
13. Autonomy (self-sufficiency)
14. Meaningfulness (values)

Question: Did Maslow believe that many people are motivated by meta-needs?

Maslow estimated that only about 1 person in 10 is primarily motivated by self-actualization needs. Most are more concerned with esteem, love, or security. Perhaps this is because incentives and rewards in our society are slanted to encourage conformity, uniformity, and security in schools, jobs, and relationships. When was the last time you met a meta-need?

Intrinsic and Extrinsic Motivation

Some people cook for a living and consider it hard work. Others cook for pleasure and dream of opening a restaurant. For some people, carpentry, gardening, writing, photography, or jewelry making is fun. For others, the same activities are drudgery they must be paid to do. How can the same activity be "work" for one person and "play" for another?

When you undertake an activity for enjoyment, to demonstrate competence, or to gain skill, your motivation is usually *intrinsic.* **Intrinsic motivation** occurs when there is no obvious external reward or ulterior purpose behind your actions. The activity is an end in itself. Intrinsic motivation is closely related to the higher levels of Maslow's hierarchy. In contrast, **extrinsic motivation** stems from obvious external factors, such as pay, grades, rewards, obligations, and approval. Most of the activities we think of as "work" are extrinsically rewarded.

Turning Play into Work It might seem that increasing extrinsic incentives would strengthen motivation, but this is not always the case. Research with children shows that excessive rewards can undermine spontaneous interest (Ross et al., 1976). For instance, children lavishly rewarded for drawing with Magic-Markers (felt-tip pens) later showed little interest in playing with them (Greene & Lepper, 1974). Apparently, "play" can be turned into "work" by *requiring* a person to do something he or she would otherwise enjoy. A similar effect occurred when adult college students were rewarded for working on puzzles (Daniel & Esser, 1980).

The reverse effect also holds: People are more likely to be creative when they are intrinsically motivated than when extrinsic rewards are stressed. On the job, the *quantity* of work may be increased by salaries and bonuses. However, the *quality* of work is tied more to intrinsic factors, such as interest, freedom of action, and constructive feedback (Amabile, 1983; Kohn, 1987). When a person is intrinsically motivated, a certain amount of challenge, surprise, and complexity makes a task rewarding. When extrinsic motivation is stressed, complexity, surprise, and challenge just become barriers to reaching a goal (Pittman & Heller, 1987).

Question: How can the concept of intrinsic motivation be applied?

Motivation can't always be intrinsic. Nor should it be. Not every worthwhile activity is intrinsically satisfying. In addition, extrinsic motivation is often needed if we are to develop enough skill or knowledge for an activity to become intrinsically rewarding. This effect can be observed in learning to read, to play a musical instrument, or to enjoy a sport. At first, external encouragement or incentives may be needed to get a person to the level of ability needed for intrinsic motivation to occur.

So, both extrinsic and intrinsic motivation are necessary. But extrinsic motivation should not be overused. Greene and Lepper (1974) summarize: (1) If there is no intrinsic interest in an activity to begin with, there is nothing to lose by using extrinsic rewards; (2) if needed skills are lacking, extrinsic rewards may be necessary to begin; (3) extrinsic rewards may focus attention on an activity so that real interest can develop—this is especially true for motivating learning in children; (4) if extrinsic rewards or incentives are to be used, they should be as small as possible, used only when absolutely necessary, and faded out as soon as possible. A good rule of thumb to remember is that the more complex an activity is, the more it is hurt by extrinsic reward (Kohn, 1987). By following these rules, you can avoid taking spontaneous interest and satisfaction out of motivation for others, especially children.

Learning Check

1. Exploration, manipulation, and curiosity provide evidence for the existence of ____________________ drives.
2. People who score high on the SSS tend to be extroverted, independent, and individuals who value change. T or F?
3. When a task is complex, the ideal level of arousal is ____________________; when a task is simple, the optimal level of arousal is ____________________.
4. The overall relationship between arousal and efficiency can be described as
   a. non-homeostatic *b.* a negative correlation *c.* an inverted U function *d.* an SSS score
5. The need for achievement can be described as a desire to meet an internalized ____________________ of ____________________.
6. People with high nAch are attracted to "long shots" and "sure things." T or F?
7. Fears of success are common in men, but occur less often for women. T or F?
8. According to Maslow, meta-needs are the most basic and prepotent sources of human motivation. T or F?
9. Intrinsic motivation is often undermined in situations in which obvious external rewards are applied to a naturally enjoyable activity. T or F?

Answers:
1. stimulus **2.** T **3.** low, high **4.** *c* **5.** standard, excellence **6.** F **7.** F **8.** F **9.** T

Applications: Behavioral Dieting—Fat Chance for a Slim Future

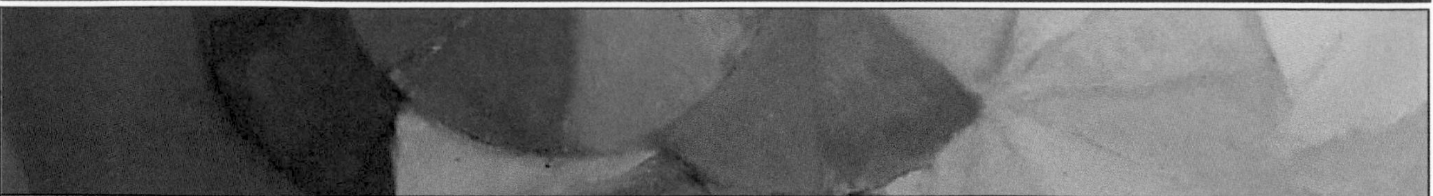

The goal of the previous discussion was to help you better understand a number of basic motives. In this section, we will consider an application of motivational research by looking at psychological techniques for weight control.

Question: What can be done to control weight?

The basic approach for years has been to "diet," that is, to restrict food intake drastically for a brief period. This, of course, is perfectly sensible in theory: You must eat less to lose weight. As noted earlier, however, most people who lose weight by dieting regain it rapidly. And as the Exploration that follows points out, there may be other risks in dieting as well.

What is really needed if one wishes to lose weight is to overhaul *eating habits* and to control *cues* for eating. The person who succeeds in changing eating habits can expect a permanent weight reduction. This approach, called **behavioral dieting,** is greatly superior to simple dieting for weight control. The following list summarizes several behavioral techniques that have proved helpful (compiled from Kiell, 1973; Lake, 1973; Mayer, 1968; Trotter, 1974; and noted sources).

1. Begin any weight control program with a physical checkup. About 5 percent of all weight problems are physical.
2. Learn your eating habits by observing yourself and keeping a "diet diary." Begin by making a complete record of your eating habits for 2 weeks. Record when and where you eat, what you eat, and the feelings and events that occur just before and after eating. How do others around you respond to your eating? Is a roommate, relative, or spouse encouraging you to overeat?
3. Count calories, but don't starve yourself. To lose, you must eat less, and calories allow you to keep an accurate record of your food intake.
4. Develop techniques to control the act of eating. Begin by taking smaller portions. Carry to the table only what you plan to eat. Put all other food away before leaving the kitchen. Eat slowly, finish one mouthful before taking another, count your mouthfuls, and leave food on your plate. Generally, avoid eating alone, since you're less likely to overeat in front of others. (One exception is eating at social events where food is plentiful and you are urged to eat. Another is eating with someone else who is overeating. In either case, eating may be facilitated.)
5. Learn to weaken your personal eating cues. When you have learned when and where you do most of your eating, avoid these situations. Try to restrict your eating to one room, and do not read, watch TV, study, or talk on the phone while eating. Require yourself to interrupt what you are doing in order to eat. Be especially aware of the "night eating syndrome." Most calories are consumed late in the day or at night. Keep food out of sight and find things to do to keep yourself busy during this dangerous period.
6. Avoid snacks. Buy low-calorie foods that require preparation, and fix only a single portion at a time. If you have an impulse to snack, set a timer for 20 minutes and see if you are still hungry then. Delay the impulse to snack several times if possible. Dull your appetite by filling up on raw carrots, bouillon, water, coffee, or tea.
7. Exercise. Physical activity burns calories. Stop saving steps and riding elevators. Add activity to your routine in every way you can think of. Contrary to popular opinion, regular exercise does not increase appetite. For reasons that are not well understood, exercise lowers the body's set point for fat storage (Bennett & Gurin, 1982). Many psychologists are now convinced that no diet can succeed for long without an increase in exercise (Katahn, 1984). Burning as little as 200 extra calories a day can play a major role in preventing regain of weight (Foreyt, 1987b).
8. Get yourself committed to weight loss. Involve as many people in your program as you can. Formal programs such as Overeaters Anonymous or Take Off Pounds Sensibly can be a good source of social support (Foreyt, 1987b).
9. Make a list of rewards you will receive if you change your eating habits and punishments that will occur if you don't. You may find it helpful to set up specific rewards (see Chapter 22 for more details). Don't reward yourself with food!
10. Chart your progress daily. Record your weight, the number of calories eaten, and whether you met your daily goal. (Set realistic goals by cutting down calories gradually. Losing about a pound per week is realistic, but remember, you are changing habits, not just losing weight.) Take pride in your successes. Post your chart in a prominent place. This feedback on your progress is possibly the most important of all the techniques.
11. Beware of relapses. Try to identify specific high-risk situations in which you are likely to overeat. Then form a plan using the principles already described to help you cope with the risk of relapse (Foreyt, 1987b). It also helps to tell yourself

Applications

that a single overeating incident does not mean that you have "blown it." Faltering should be interpreted as an isolated slip, not as a sign that you might as well give up (Marlatt & Gordon, 1985).

12. Set a "threshold" for weight control. A study of Weight Watchers members found that those who successfully maintained their weight loss had a regain limit of 3 pounds or less. In other words, if they gained more than 2 or 3 pounds, they immediately began to make corrections in their diet and exercise (Brownell et al., 1986).

Be patient with this program. It takes years to develop eating habits. You can expect it to take at least several months to change them. If you are unsuccessful at losing weight with these techniques, you might find it helpful to seek the aid of a psychologist familiar with behavioral weight-loss techniques.

Learning Check

1. According to behavioral dieting specialists, about 45 percent of all weight problems are physical. T or F?
2. In addition to burning calories, physical exercise can lower the body's set point. T or F?
3. For behavioral dieting, you should maintain a diet diary and chart your progress, but you should avoid the trap of counting calories. T or F?
4. Those who successfully control their weight are willing to admit to themselves that they have "blown it" if they deviate from their diet. T or F?

Answers:
1. F 2. T 3. F 4. F

Exploration: Anorexia and Bulimia—Hungering for Control

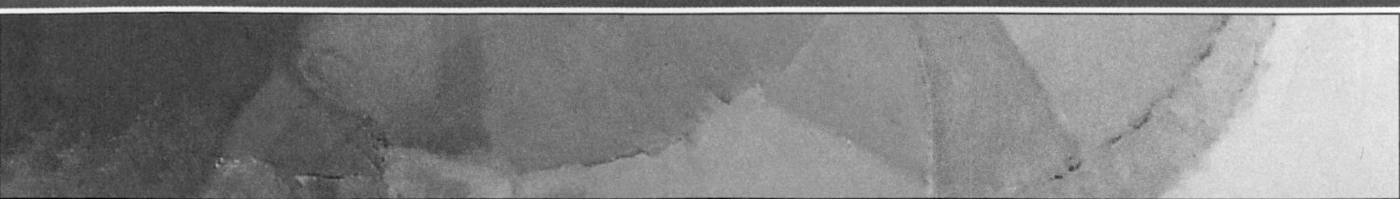

Under the sheets of her hospital bed Krystal looks like a "starved skeleton." If her self-destructive course cannot be changed, Krystal may die of malnutrition. How could things go so desperately wrong with a motive as basic as hunger? Recent attempts to understand problems like Krystal's provide a fascinating look at motivation gone awry.

Eating Disorders

Serious cases of undereating like Krystal's are called **anorexia nervosa** (AN-or-EX-yah ner-VOH-sah). Victims of anorexia, who are mostly adolescent females (5 percent are male), suffer devastating weight loss from self-inflicted starvation. The problem affects as many as 1 in 100 females between ages 12 and 18.

Question: Do anorexics lose their appetite?

Anorexia nervosa is not a simple loss of desire for food. Many anorexics continue to feel hunger and struggle to starve themselves. The problem can best be described as a *relentless pursuit of excessive thinness.* Persons who suffer from anorexia nervosa have an obsessive fear of gaining weight. Often, the problem starts with normal dieting that gradually begins to dominate the person's life. In time, anorexics suffer physical weakness, absence of menstrual cycles, and a dangerous risk of infection. About 5 to 18 percent die of malnutrition or related health problems. The death of singer Karen Carpenter is a case in point. Some victims of anorexia nervosa realize the harmfulness of their excessive dieting, but they feel powerless to stop.

Bulimia nervosa (bue-LIHM-ee-yah), also known as the binge-purge syndrome, is a second major eating disorder. Bulimics gorge on food, then induce vomiting or take laxatives to avoid gaining weight. Like anorexia, bulimia is far more prevalent in women than in men. A recent study of college women found that 5 percent (1 out of 20) are bulimic (Hart & Ollendick, 1985).

In a culture that values slimness, bulimia may seem relatively harmless. However, like anorexia nervosa, binging and purging can cause serious health problems. Typical risks include sore throat, hair loss, muscle spasms, kidney damage, dehydration, tooth decay, swelling of the salivary glands, menstrual irregularity, loss of sex drive, and even heart attack.

Recognizing Trouble

Question: Could a person be both anorexic and bulimic?

Yes. Close to 50 percent of anorexics are also bulimic. It is not unusual, for instance, for the parents of anorexics to plead with them to eat more. However, if she gives in to such coaxing, the anorexic may just disappear into the bathroom to secretly vomit.

Although they are related, anorexia and bulimia are separate problems. Anorexic individuals suffer a weight loss of at least 15 percent of their original body weight. Some anorexics lose weight by fasting and dieting. Those who are also bulimic alternate between gorging and purging. Either way, weight loss is severe for anorexics. In contrast, persons who are only bulimic may be from any weight group, from thin to heavy. Most, in fact, are only slightly below average weight.

Of the two disorders, bulimia is harder to detect because weight often remains nearly normal, and binging and purging can be hidden. However, bulimia is indicated if any *three* of the following conditions are present: binge eating; hiding the amount eaten during a binge; gorging on food, followed by self-induced vomiting or abdominal pain; repeated attempts to lose weight by severe dieting; use of vomiting, laxatives, or diuretics to lose weight; frequent weight changes of more than 3 pounds; awareness that one's eating is abnormal, coupled with an inability to change; anxiety or depression following binges.

Question: What causes anorexia and bulimia?

Causes Both anorexics and bulimics have exaggerated fears of becoming fat and unrealistic views of what constitutes normal size. Anorexics, especially, have distorted body images. Most overestimate their body size by 25 percent or more and continue to see themselves as "fat," when in fact they are wasting away.

Anorexics are usually described as

Exploration

"perfect" daughters—helpful, considerate, conforming, and obedient. Many are would-be high achievers who frantically try to be "perfect" in one area—to have complete control over their weight and to be perfectly slim. The thought of gaining weight fills them with terror. They literally feel that they are losing control.

Bulimics also seem to be concerned with control. For them, however, maintaining control is an ongoing struggle. Bulimics are obsessed with thoughts of weight, food, eating, and ridding themselves of food. Most appear to believe that what is fat is bad, what is thin is beautiful, and what is beautiful is good. As a result, they feel guilt, shame, self-contempt, and anxiety after a binge. For many, vomiting reduces the anxiety triggered by a binge. This makes purging highly reinforcing.

Dieting Recent research suggests that dieting may actually encourage binging. Most bulimics, for instance, go through a period of "normal" dieting before they begin to purge too.

Question: How does dieting contribute to binging?

Psychologists Janet Polivy and Peter Herman have found that dieters eat *more* after first eating a large meal than if they ate nothing beforehand. It is as if dieters are barely able to keep the brakes on eating. When they feel that they have "broken" their diet, the suppressed urge to eat is released and a binge follows. This effect can occur even when dieters are merely *told* that they ate a high-calorie meal (that was actually low in calories). Thus, as long as dieters *believe* they are "in control" and their diet is intact, they eat with restraint. But when they believe that their diet has been violated, they can no longer control eating and tend to gorge themselves. In short, societal pressures to diet and the link between dieting and binging may be contributing to an increase in bulimia.

Treatment In almost all cases, a person with anorexia nervosa or bulimia nervosa will need professional help to restore normal eating. Treatment for anorexia usually begins with admitting the person to a hospital. There, a carefully controlled diet is used to restore weight and health. As a second step, the client enters counseling to work on the personal conflicts and family issues that led to weight loss. For bulimia, psychologists have had some success with behavioral counseling that includes careful self-monitoring of food intake and work on extinguishing the urge to vomit after eating.

Although much progress is being made in treating eating disorders, most anorexics do not seek help, and many actively resist it. Bulimics will sometimes seek treatment, but usually not until their eating habits become intolerable. In either case, it may take strong urging by family or friends to get victims into treatment. With this in mind, it is worth emphasizing again that anorexia nervosa and bulimia are serious, health-threatening problems that rarely disappear on their own. (Sources: DSM-III-R, 1987; Moore, 1981; Polivy & Herman, 1985; Rosen & Leitenburg, 1982; Schlessier-Stroop, 1984.)

Learning Check

1. Anorexia nervosa is also known as the binge-purge syndrome. T or F?
2. A person can suffer from both anorexia nervosa and bulimia nervosa at the same time. T or F?
3. Anorexics underestimate their body size by 25 percent or more. T or F?
4. A dieter who eats a large meal will typically eat more soon afterward than will a dieter who did not eat before. T or F?

Answers:
1. F 2. T 3. F 4. T

Chapter Summary

• Motives **initiate, sustain,** and **direct** activities. Motivation typically involves the sequence: **need, drive, goal,** and **goal attainment** (need reduction).

• Behavior can be activated either by **needs** (push) or by **goals** (pull). The attractiveness of a goal and its ability to initiate action are related to its **incentive value.**

• Three principal types of motives are **primary motives** (based on biological survival needs), **stimulus motives** (which serve needs for activity, exploration, manipulation, and so forth), and **secondary motives** (activated by learned needs and valued goals). Most primary motives operate to maintain **homeostasis.**

• Hunger is influenced by a complex interplay of factors. These include fullness of the stomach, blood sugar levels, metabolism in the liver, and fat stores in the body. The most direct control of eating is effected by the **hypothalamus,** which has areas that act like **feeding** and **satiety** systems.

• Other factors influencing hunger are the body's **set point,** external **eating cues,** the attractiveness and variety of **diet, emotions,** learned **taste preferences** and **taste aversions,** and **cultural values.**

• Like hunger, thirst and other basic motives are affected by a number of bodily factors, but are primarily under the central control of the hypothalamus. Thirst may be either **intracellular** or **extracellular.**

• Pain avoidance is an unusual primary drive because it is **episodic** as opposed to **cyclic.** Pain avoidance and pain tolerance are partially learned. The sex drive is also unusual in that it is **non-homeostatic** (both increases and decreases in drive level are actively sought).

• The stimulus motives include drives for **exploration, manipulation, change,** and **sensory stimulation.** Stimulus motives appear to be innate because they operate independent of other rewards.

• Drives for stimulation are partially explained by **arousal theory,** which states that an ideal level of bodily arousal will be maintained if possible. The desired level of arousal or stimulation varies from person to person. Stimulus needs have been measured with the *Sensation-Seeking Scale* (SSS).

• Optimal performance on a task usually occurs at *moderate* levels of arousal. This relationship is described by an **inverted U function.** An added qualification, known as the **Yerkes-Dodson law,** states that for simple tasks the ideal arousal level is higher, and for complex tasks it is lower.

• **Circadian rhythms** of bodily activity are closely tied to sleep, activity, and energy cycles. Time zone travel and shift work can seriously disrupt sleep and bodily rhythms. Traveling east intensifies jet lag, and backward shift rotations are more upsetting than forward rotations. **Preadapting** to new time schedules can minimize these effects. Biorhythm theory is a false system unrelated to circadian rhythms.

• **Social motives** are learned through socialization and cultural conditioning. Such motives account for much of the diversity of human motivation. **Opponent-process theory** explains the operation of some acquired motives.

• One of the most prominent and intensely studied social motives is the **need for achievement (nAch).** Achievement striving differs from the **need for power.** High nAch is correlated with success in many situations, with occupational choice, and with *moderate* risk taking. There is evidence that at times, both men and women experience a **fear of success.**

• Maslow's **hierarchy of motives** categorizes needs as **basic** and **growth-oriented.** Lower needs in the hierarchy are assumed to be **prepotent** (dominant) over higher needs. Self-actualization, the highest and most fragile need, is reflected in **meta-needs.**

• Higher needs in Maslow's hierarchy are closely related to the concept of **intrinsic motivation.** In many situations, **extrinsic motivation** (that which is induced by obvious external rewards) can reduce intrinsic motivation, enjoyment, and creativity.

• Because of the limitations of traditional dieting, changing basic eating patterns and habits is usually more effective. **Behavioral dieting** brings about such changes by use of self-control techniques.

• **Anorexia nervosa** (self-inflicted starvation) and **bulimia nervosa** (gorging and purging) are two prominent eating disorders. Both problems tend to involve conflicts about self-image, self-control, and anxiety.

Questions for Discussion

1. Which of the primary drives do you consider the strongest? Why? Which occupies the greatest amount of your time and energies? How could the strength of the primary drives be determined for animals?
2. Discuss some of the factors that contribute to overeating at Thanksgiving or a similar feast.
3. The sex drive is not essential for individual survival, and it can be easily interrupted by any of the other primary drives. Why do you think so much energy is directed toward sexuality in our culture?
4. In what ways have you observed the stimulus motives at work in human behavior? Does learning contribute to curiosity or needs for stimulation?
5. Does the American emphasis on competition (in your opinion) encourage achievement or discourage it? (Consider the effects, for example, when only one person can be considered the "winner" in many situations.)
6. How could you apply the concept of incentives to improve your motivation to study?
7. In *Lady Windermere's Fan,* playwright Oscar Wilde said, "In this world there are only two tragedies. One is not getting what one wants, and the other is getting it. The last is the real tragedy." What do you think Wilde meant? Where does your motivation come from?
8. If you had a guaranteed income, would you "work?" What do you think you would spend your time doing? For how long? What, if anything, does this reveal about sources of intrinsic motivation?
9. How has our culture contributed to eating problems such as obesity, anorexia nervosa, and bulimia? In some cultures, a degree of fatness is considered desirable as a hedge against starvation. Do we label people "fat" when they are perfectly healthy?

Chapter 12

Emotion

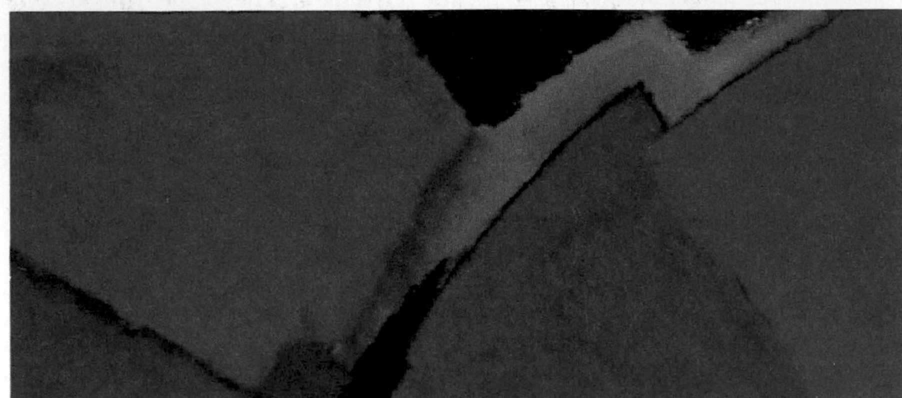

In This Chapter

- Elements of emotion
- Fight-or-flight reactions
- Sudden death and lying
- Developing emotions
- Emotional expression
- Theories of emotion
- Coping with emotion
- Defense mechanisms
- Learned helplessness

Applications

- Coping with depression

Exploration

- Types of love

Chapter Preview

Voodoo Death

Few events are more bizarre than sudden death caused by "voodoo" or "magic." Yet, many scientists have witnessed this strange spectacle. Here is an account of what happens in one tribe when a man discovers that he has been cursed by an enemy:

> He stands aghast, with his eyes staring at the treacherous pointers, with his hands lifted as though to ward off the lethal medium. . . . His cheeks blanch and his eyes become glassy and the expression of his face becomes horribly distorted. . . . His body begins to tremble and the muscles twist involuntarily. He sways backwards and falls to the ground. . . . From this time onwards he sickens and frets, refusing to eat and keeping aloof from the daily affairs of the tribe. Unless help is forthcoming in the shape of a countercharm, death is only a matter of a comparatively short time. (Basedow, 1925; cited in Cannon, 1942).

At first glance, voodoo deaths seem to require belief in the power of magic. Actually, all they require is belief in the power of emotion. Walter Cannon (1942), a well-known physiologist, studied many voodoo deaths and concluded that they are explained by changes in the body that accompany strong emotion. Specifically, he believed that the fear of cursed victims is so intense that it causes a heart attack or other bodily disaster.

More recent research suggests that Cannon's explanation was only partly correct. It now appears that such deaths are caused not by fear itself, but by the body's delayed reaction to fear. Normally, the parasympathetic nervous system reverses the bodily changes caused by strong emotion. For example, during intense fear, heart rate is dramatically increased; to counteract this increase, the parasympathetic system later slows the heart. It is now believed that the cursed person's emo-

tional response is so intense that the parasympathetic nervous system overreacts and slows the heart to a stop (Seligman, 1974).

There is more to this story (as we will see later in this chapter). For now, it is enough to say that emotions are not only the spice of life. For some, they may be the spice of death as well.

Survey Questions

- What causes emotion?
- What happens to the body during emotion?
- Can "lie detectors" really detect lies?
- How do emotions develop?
- How accurately are emotions expressed by "body language" and the face?
- How do psychologists explain emotions?
- What do we know about coping with threatening situations, helplessness, and depression?
- What is the nature of love?

Dissecting an Emotion—How Do You Feel?

If a mad scientist were to replace your best friend's brain with a sophisticated computer, how would you know that something was different? One of the first telltale signs might be the absence of emotion. Emotion adds greatly to the meaning of life and the depth of caring in our relationships.

Have you ever waited until someone was in a good mood to ask for a favor? If so, you are aware that emotions have a powerful influence on behavior. On the plus side, for example, it is easier to make decisions when you are in a good mood (Isen & Means, 1983). Likewise, people who are feeling happy are more likely to help others in need (O'Malley & Andrews, 1983). It is equally apparent, however, that emotions also have a negative impact. Hate, anger, contempt, disgust, and fear all disrupt behavior and relationships.

The root of the word **emotion** means "to move," and emotions do indeed move us. First, the body is physically aroused during emotion. Such bodily stirrings are what cause people to say they were "moved" by a play, a funeral, or an act of kindness. Second, we are often motivated, or moved to take action, by emotions such as fear, anger, or joy. Underlying all this, perhaps, is the fact that emotions are linked to such basic **adaptive behaviors** as attacking, retreating, seeking comfort, helping others, reproducing, and the like (Plutchik, 1980). Again, we must realize that human emotions can be disruptive, as in having stage fright or choking up in an athletic contest. But more often, emotions aid survival. This seems to be why emotional reactions have been retained throughout evolution.

Most people closely identify a pounding heart, sweating palms, and "butterflies" in the stomach with emotion. This observation is valid since **physiological changes** within the body are a major element of fear, anger, joy, and other emotions. These include changes in heart rate, blood pressure, perspiration, and other bodily stirrings. (More on this in a moment.) Most of these reactions are caused by release of **adrenaline** into the bloodstream. Adrenaline is a hormone that stimulates the sympathetic nervous system, which in turn activates the body.

Emotional expressions, or outward signs of what a person is feeling, are another major element of emotion. For example, when you are intensely afraid, your hands tremble, your face contorts, and your posture becomes tense and defensive. Emotion is also revealed by marked shifts in voice tone or modulation. Other signs of emotion range from shrill rage to the surprisingly subdued last words on flight recorders after air disasters (a common last word is "Damn," spoken calmly). Such emotional expressions are particularly important because they communicate emotion from one person to another (Fig. 12–1). A final major element of emotion consists of **emotional feelings,** or a person's private emotional experience. This is the part of emotion with which we are typically most familiar.

Fig. 12–1 *How accurately do facial expressions reveal emotion? After you have guessed what emotion these people are feeling, turn to p. 316.*

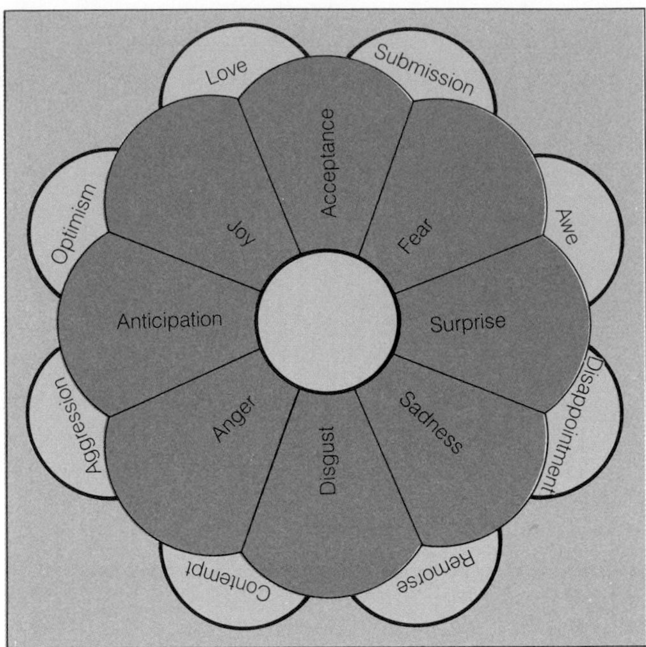

Fig. 12–2 *Primary and mixed emotions. In Robert Plutchik's model, there are eight primary emotions, as listed in the inner areas. Adjacent emotions may combine to give the emotions listed around the perimeter. Mixtures involving more widely separated emotions are also possible. (Adapted from Plutchik, 1980.)*

Compare: Four Elements of Emotion

Adaptive behaviors Actions that aid humans and animals in their attempts to survive and adapt to changing conditions.

Physiological changes in emotion Changes in bodily activities (especially involuntary responses) and general arousal that accompany emotional states.

Emotional expression Any behavior that gives an outward sign that an emotion is occurring, especially those signs that communicate the presence of emotion to others.

Emotional feelings The private, subjective experience of having an emotion.

Question: Are some emotions more basic than others?

Based on his research, Robert Plutchik (1980) believes there are eight **primary emotions: fear, surprise, sadness, disgust, anger, anticipation, joy,** and **acceptance** (receptivity). If the list seems too short, it's because each listed emotion can vary in *intensity*. Anger, for instance, may vary from rage to simple annoyance.

One of Plutchik's most interesting ideas concerns the mixing of primary emotions. As shown in Figure 12–2, each pair of adjacent emotions can be mixed to yield a third, more complex emotion. Other mixtures are also possible. For example, a child about to eat a stolen cookie may feel both joy and fear. The result? Guilt—as you may recall from your own childhood. Likewise, jealousy could be a mixture of love, anger, and fear.

Later we will attempt to put all the elements of emotion together into a single picture. But first, we need to look more closely at physiological arousal and emotional expressions.

Physiology and Emotion—Arousal, Sudden Death, and Lying

To a large degree, the physical aspects of emotion are innate, or built into the body. The physical reactions of an African Bushman frightened by a wild animal and an urbane city dweller frightened by a prowler are quite similar. Reactions to unpleasant emotions are especially consistent. The most typical are muscle tension, a pounding heart, irritability, dryness of the throat and mouth, sweating, butterflies in the stomach, frequent urination, trembling, restlessness, sensitivity to loud noises, and a large number of internal reactions (Shaffer, 1947). These reactions are nearly universal because they are caused by the **autonomic nervous system (ANS).** As you may recall from Chapter 3, the reactions of the ANS are *automatic* and not normally under voluntary control. There are two divisions of the ANS, one called the **sympathetic branch** and the other the **parasympathetic branch.**

Question: What do these do during emotion?

Fight or Flight

The sympathetic branch prepares the body for emergency action—for "fighting or fleeing"—by arousing a number of bodily systems and inhibiting others. (Sympathetic nervous system effects are listed in Table 12–1.) These changes have a purpose. Sugar is released into the bloodstream for quick energy, the heart beats faster to distribute blood to the muscles, digestion is temporarily inhibited, blood flow in the skin in restricted to reduce bleeding, and so forth. Most sympathetic reactions increase the chances that a person or an animal will survive an emergency. (To learn about an interesting sidelight of sympathetic arousal, see Highlight 12–1.)

The parasympathetic branch generally reverses emotional arousal and calms and relaxes the body. After a period of high emotion, the heart is slowed, the pupils return to normal size, blood pressure drops, and so forth. In addition to restoring balance, the parasympathetic system helps build up and conserve bodily energy.

The parasympathetic system responds much more slowly than the sympathetic system. This is why increased heart rate, muscle tension, and other signs of arousal do not fade for 20 or 30 minutes after you experience an intense emotion, such as fear. Moreover, after a strong emotional shock, the parasympathetic system may overreact and lower blood pressure too much. This is why people sometimes become dizzy or faint at the sight of blood and other such shocks (Kleinknecht, 1986)

Sudden Death As noted, the parasympathetic system may overreact during intense fear. This reaction is called a **parasympathetic rebound.** When it is severe it can sometimes cause death. Voodoo curses are not the only cause of such deaths. There is evidence that in times of war, combat can be so savage that some soldiers literally die of fear (Moritz & Zamcheck, 1946). Even in civilian life such deaths apparently are possible. In one case, a terrified young woman was admitted to a hospital because she felt she was going to die. A backwoods midwife had predicted that the woman's two sisters would die before their sixteenth and twenty-first birthdays. Both died as predicted. The midwife also predicted that this woman would die before her twenty-third birthday. She was found dead in her hospital bed the day after she was admitted. It was two days before her twenty-third birthday (Zimbardo, 1975). The woman was an apparent victim of her own terror.

Question: Is the parasympathetic nervous system always responsible for such deaths?

Table 12–1 Autonomic Nervous System Effects

Organ	Parasympathetic System	Sympathetic System
Pupil of eyes	Constricts to diminish light	Dilates to increase light
Tear glands Mucous membrane of nose and throat Salivary glands	Stimulate secretion	Inhibit secretion, cause dryness
Heart Blood vessels	Slowing of heart; constriction of blood vessels	Acceleration of heart; dilation of blood vessels to increase blood flow
Lungs, windpipe	Constrict bronchi of lungs to relax breathing	Dilate bronchi to increase breathing
Esophagus Stomach Abdominal blood vessels	Stimulate secretion and movement	Inhibit secretion and movement, divert blood flow
Liver	Liberate bile	Retains bile
Pancreas	———	Releases blood sugar
Intestines	Stimulate secretion	Inhibit secretion
Rectum Kidney Bladder	Excitation, expulsion of feces and urine	Inhibition, retention of feces and urine
Skin blood vessels	Dilate, increase blood flow	Constrict; skin becomes cold and clammy
Sweat glands	Inhibited	Stimulated to increase perspiration
Hair follicles	Relaxed	Tensed to make hair stand on end

HIGHLIGHT 12–1
Emotion—The Eyes Have It

Question: Is there any truth to the idea that the eyes can reveal emotion?

The eyes have long been considered "windows on the soul" and indicators of emotion. If you doubt someone's word, you may ask them to "look you in the eye." Many seasoned poker players claim to have detected a bluff by watching the eyes of their opponents. Psychologist Eckhard Hess (1975) believes that in such instances we are mainly interested in the size of a person's *pupils*. As shown in Table 12–1, emotion affects the pupils. Specifically, *arousal, interest,* or *attention* can activate the sympathetic nervous system and cause the pupils to dilate (enlarge).

Dilation of the pupils can occur during both pleasant and unpleasant emotions (Woodmansee, 1970). Despite this fact, most people tend to interpret *large* pupils as a sign of pleasant feelings and *small* pupils as a sign of negative feelings. To illustrate, Hess (1975) showed two photos of an attractive young woman to a group of men. In one photograph the woman's pupils were large. In the other they were small. The men consistently described the woman with large pupils as "soft," "feminine," or "pretty." The same woman, with small pupils, was described as "hard," "selfish," and "cold" (Fig. 12–3).

Fig. 12–3 *Select the face you think looks more attractive, warm, or friendly. Research by Eckhard Hess (1975) suggests you will choose the face on the left because the pupils of the eyes are larger.*

This effect, of course, does not apply only to women. In another experiment, subjects were introduced to two individuals of the opposite sex and asked to choose one as a partner for the experiment. One person in each pair had been given eye drops to dilate his or her pupils, and the other had not. Subjects of both sexes tended to select the person with the larger pupils as a partner. (Perhaps at long last we know why the bad guys in movies always have beady eyes!)

Probably not. In the case of older persons or those with heart problems, the direct effects of sympathetic activation may be enough to bring about heart attack and collapse. For example, at a memorial concert honoring the late Louis Armstrong, his widow was stricken with a heart attack as she played the final chord of "St. Louis Blues." Psychiatrist George Engel (1977) has studied hundreds of similar occurrences and concludes that many lead to death. He found that almost half of all sudden deaths are associated with the extremely traumatic disruption of a close relationship, such as the anniversary of the death of a loved one. Recently widowed men, for instance, have a sudden death rate 40 percent higher than married men of the same age. Clearly, relationships are one of the most potent sources of human emotional response.

Lie Detectors

Because bodily changes caused by the ANS are good indicators of emotion, several ways of measuring them have been developed. One use of such measures is the "lie detector." If you have never taken a lie detector test, there is a chance that you will someday. Of course, this doesn't mean you are likely to become a criminal. It simply reflects the fact that many businesses use lie detectors to check the honesty of employees. This practice must be questioned for two reasons: First, the lie detector's accuracy is doubtful; and second, such testing is often a serious invasion of privacy (Lykken, 1981).

Question: What is a lie detector? Do lie detectors really detect lies?

The lie detector is more accurately called a **polygraph** (Fig. 12–4). A polygraph (the word means "many writings") is a device that draws a record of changes in **heart rate, blood pressure, breathing rate,** and the **galvanic skin response (GSR).** (The GSR is recorded from the surface of the hand by electrodes that measure skin conductance or, more simply, sweating.) The polygraph is popularly known as a lie detector because it is used by the police. In reality, the polygraph is not a lie detector at all. As critic David Lykken (1981) points out, there is

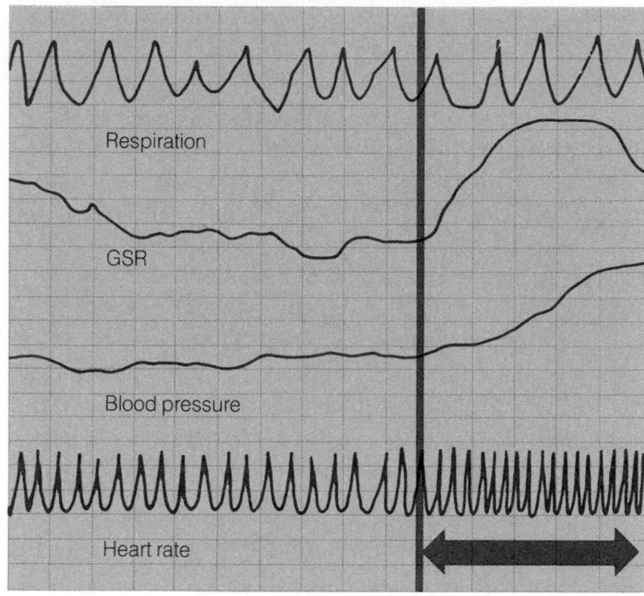

Fig. 12–4 (a) *A typical polygraph includes devices for measuring heart rate, blood pressure, respiration, and galvanic skin response. Pens mounted on the top of the machine make a record of bodily responses on a moving strip of paper.* (b) *Changes in the area marked by the arrow indicate emotional arousal. If such responses appear when a person answers a question, he or she may be lying, but other causes of arousal are also possible.*

no unique "lie response" that everyone gives when not telling the truth. The machine only records *general emotional arousal*—it can't tell the difference between lying and fear, anxiety, or excitement.

When attempting to detect a lie, the polygraph operator begins by asking **irrelevant** (nonemotional) **questions** ("What is your name?" "What did you have for lunch?" and so forth). This establishes a "baseline" for normal emotional responsiveness. Then **relevant questions** can be asked: "Did you murder Hensley?" A person who lies will presumably become anxious or emotional when answering relevant questions.

Question: Wouldn't a person be nervous just from being questioned?

Yes, but to minimize this problem, a skilled polygraph examiner asks a *series* of questions with critical items mixed among them. An innocent person may respond emotionally to the whole procedure, but only a guilty person is supposed to show increased response to key questions. For example, a suspected bank robber might be shown several pictures and asked, "Was the teller who was robbed this person? Was it this person?" (Lykken, 1974).

As an alternative, subjects may be asked **control questions** that can be compared with critical questions (Saxe et al., 1985). Control questions are designed to make almost anyone anxious: "Have you ever stolen anything from a place you worked?" Typically, control questions are very difficult to answer truthfully with an unqualified no. In theory they allow the examiner to see how a person reacts to doubt or misgivings. The person's reaction to critical questions can then be compared with his or her response to control questions.

Even when questioning is done properly, lie detection may be inaccurate. For example, in August 1978, Floyd Fay was convicted of murdering his friend Fred Ery. To prove his innocence, Fay volunteered to take a lie detector test, which he failed. Fay spent 2 years in prison before the real killer confessed to the crime. Psychologist David Lykken (1981) has documented three such cases in which innocent people spent from 1 to 5 years behind bars after being convicted on the basis of polygraph evidence.

Question: If Floyd Fay was innocent, why did he fail the test?

Put yourself in his place, and it's easy to see why. Imagine the examiner asking, "Did you kill Fred?" Since you knew Fred, and you are a suspect, it's no secret that this is a critical question. What would happen to *your* heart rate, blood pressure, breathing, and perspiration under such circumstances?

Proponents of lie detection claim from 90 to 95 percent accuracy. But in one laboratory experiment, accuracy was lowered to 25 percent by subjects who thought exciting or upsetting thoughts during questioning (Smith, 1971). Similarly, the polygraph may be thrown off by self-inflicted pain, by tranquilizing drugs, or by people who can lie without anxiety (Waid & Orne, 1982). Worst of all, the test's most common error is to label an innocent person guilty, rather than a guilty person innocent (Lykken, 1981). To avoid such errors the polygraph would have to be extremely accurate—more accurate, in fact, than even its most enthusiastic backers claim it is now (Murphy, 1987). In field studies involving real crimes and criminal suspects, an average of approximately 1 innocent person in 5 was rated as guilty by the lie detector (Saxe et al., 1985). In some instances, these false positives reached 75 percent, or 3 persons out of 4.

In 1988, the U.S. Congress passed a law strictly limiting the use of lie detector tests for job applicants and employees of private businesses. However, this has not totally ended the use of the polygraph. In the event of a theft, a test can be given if (1) the employee has access to the stolen property, (2) the employer has a "reasonable suspicion" that the worker is involved, and (3) the employer has described in writing details of the incident and evidence supporting the suspicion. The fact remains, then, that you could be given a lie detector test. Should this occur, the best advice is to remain calm; then actively challenge the outcome if the machine wrongly questions your honesty.

Learning Check

See if you can correctly answer these questions.

1. Many of the physiological changes associated with emotion are caused by secretion of the hormone
a. atropine *b.* adrenaline *c.* attributine *d.* amoduline

2. Emotional ________________ often serve to communicate a person's emotional state to others.

3. Awe, remorse, and disappointment are among the primary emotions listed by Robert Plutchik. T or F?

4. Emotional arousal is closely related to activity of the ________________ nervous system.

5. The sympathetic system prepares the body for "fight or flight" by activating the parasympathetic system. T or F?

6. The parasympathetic system inhibits digestion and raises blood pressure and heart rate. T or F?

7. What bodily changes are measured by a polygraph? ________________

8. The polygraph is really an ________________ detector.

9. The pupils of the eyes dilate during pleasant emotions and constrict during unpleasant emotions. T or F?

Answers:

1. *b* **2.** expressions **3.** F **4.** autonomic **5.** F **6.** F **7.** heart rate, blood pressure, breathing rate, galvanic skin response **8.** arousal or emotion **9.** F

Development and Expression of Emotions—Feeling Babies and Talking Bodies

Question: How soon do emotions develop?

Even the basic reactions of **anger, fear,** and **joy**—which appear to be unlearned—take time to develop. General **excitement** is the only emotional response newborn infants clearly express. However, as any parent can tell you, the emotional life of a baby blossoms rapidly. One researcher (Bridges, 1932) observed a large number of babies and found that all the basic human emotions appear before age 2. Bridges found that there is a consistent order in which emotions appear and that the first basic split is between pleasant and unpleasant emotions (Fig. 12–5).

More recent research suggests that even by the end of the first year, babies can express happiness, surprise, fear, anger, sadness, disgust, and interest (Saarni, 1982). This is an important development because it contributes to a fascinating interplay of emotions between infants and adults. For example, when new parents see and hear a crying baby, they feel annoyed, irritated, disturbed, or unhappy. In addition, their blood pressure and perspiration increase (Frodi et al., 1978). Such reactions encourage parents to tend to a baby's needs, thus increasing its chances for survival.

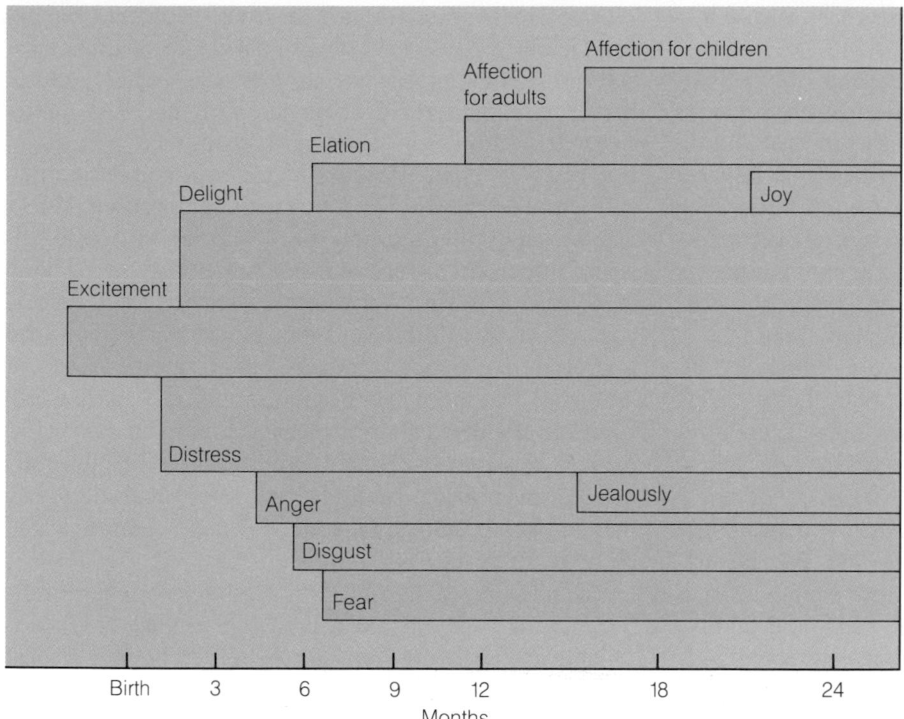

Fig. 12–5 *In the human infant, emotions are rapidly differentiated from an initial capacity for excitement. (After K.M.B. Bridges, 1932. Reprinted by permission of the Society for Research in Child Development, Inc.)*

Question: Does the order of emotions that Bridges observed apply to children of all cultures?

Development of the ability to express emotion is probably related to maturation of the brain, since children of all cultures show a similar pattern (Greenberg, 1977). Babies the world over, it seems, rapidly become capable of letting others know what they like and dislike. (Prove this to yourself sometime by driving a baby buggy.)

Emotional Expression

Are human emotional expressions a carryover from more primitive and animal-like stages of human evolution? Charles Darwin thought so. Darwin (1872) observed that tigers, monkeys, dogs, and humans all bare their teeth in the same way during rage. Darwin believed that emotional expressions were retained during the course of human evolution because communicating feelings to others is an aid to survival (Fig. 12–6).

Question: Are emotional expressions the same for all people?

The most basic expressions appear to be fairly universal. Children who are born deaf and blind have little opportunity to learn emotional expressions from others. Even

Fig. 12–6 *The "yawn" of this baboon is actually a threat. Emotional expressions allow dominance relationships among animals to be maintained with little actual fighting.*

so, they use the same facial gestures as others to display joy, sadness, disgust, and so on (Knapp, 1978). In fact, the gestures of such children may be one of the few examples of "pure" emotional expression. By adulthood, most people have learned to carefully control facial expression so that many gestures become unique to various cultures. Among the Chinese, for example, sticking out the tongue is a gesture of surprise, not of disrespect or teasing. Despite such differences, facial expressions of *fear, surprise, sadness, disgust, anger,* and *happiness* are recognized by people of all cultures (Ekman, 1980). Notice that this covers most of the primary emotions listed earlier in the chapter. It's also nice to note that a smile is the most universal and easily recognized facial expression of emotion (Boucher & Carlson, 1980).

Body Language If a friend approached you and said, "Hey, ugly, what are you doing?" would you be offended? Probably not, because such expressions are usually accompanied with a big grin. The facial and bodily gestures of emotion speak a language all their own and add an additional message to what is said verbally. The study of communication through body movement, posture, gestures, and facial expressions is called **kinesics** (kih-NEEZ-iks) and informally referred to as body language.

Question: What kinds of messages are sent with body language?

Fig. 12–7 *Facial and bodily gestures do not always allow an observer to accurately "read" emotion. The agonized expression on the face of Frank De Vito is deceptive. Mr. De Vito and his wife have just learned that he has won $1 million in the New Jersey state lottery.*

Most of the popular books on body language (for example, Fast, 1970) tend to list particular meanings for gestures. For instance, a woman who stands rigidly, crosses her arms over her chest, or sits with her legs tightly crossed is supposedly sending a "hands off" message. But researchers in the field of kinesics emphasize that gestures are rarely this fixed in meaning (Swensen, 1973). The message might simply be, "This room is cold." It is also important to realize that gestures vary in meaning in different cultures. What, for instance, does it mean if you touch your thumb and first finger together to form a circle? In America it means "Everything is fine" or "A-okay." In France and Belgium it means "You're worth zero." In Southern Italy it means "You're an ass!" (Ekman et al., 1984). Thus, when the layer of culturally defined meanings is removed, it is more realistic to say that an overall **emotional tone** is usually communicated by body language.

The most expressive and frequently noticed part of the body is the face. Physiologists estimate that the face is capable of producing some 20,000 different expressions. Most of these are **facial blends,** involving a mixture of two or more basic expressions. Imagine, for example, that you just received an F on an unfair test. Quite likely, your eyes, eyebrows, and forehead would show anger, while your mouth would express sadness (Knapp, 1978).

Most of us believe we can fairly accurately tell what others are feeling by observing facial expressions. If thousands of facial blends occur, how do we make such judgments? The answer seems to lie in the fact that facial expressions can be boiled down to basic dimensions of **pleasantness-unpleasantness, attention-rejection,** and **activation** (or arousal) (Schlosberg, 1954). By smiling when giving a friend a hard time, you add the emotional message of pleasantness and acceptance to the verbal insult and change its meaning. As they say in movie Westerns, it makes a big difference to "Smile when you say that, partner."

Other emotional feelings are telegraphed by the body. The most general seem to be **relaxation** or **tension,** and **liking** or **disliking.** Relaxation is expressed by casually positioning the arms and legs, leaning back (if sitting), and spreading the arms and legs. Liking is expressed mainly by leaning toward a person or object (Mehrabian, 1969) (Fig. 12–8). Thus, body positioning can reveal feelings that would normally be concealed. Who do you "lean toward"?

Imagine that you are standing 30 yards from a classroom in which test grades are being announced. As students file out, do you think you could tell—without the aid of facial expressions—who got an A and who got an

Fig. 12–8 *Emotions are often unconsciously revealed by gestures and body positioning.*

F? Actually, your task might not be too difficult. Research suggests that overall *posture* can also indicate one's emotional state. Specifically, when a person is successful, his or her posture is likely to be more erect (Weisfeld & Beresford, 1982) (Fig. 12–9). It remains debatable whether this tendency is a product of evolution or is simply learned. In any case, standing tall with pride and slumping with dejection do seem to be consistent patterns.

Question: Does body positioning or movement ever reveal lying or deception?

Fig. 12–9 *Posture and success. These drawings show the end points of a 5 point rating scale used to measure erectness of posture. Success by human subjects in various situations was found to be reflected by erect posture. (Adapted from Weisfeld & Beresford, 1982.)*

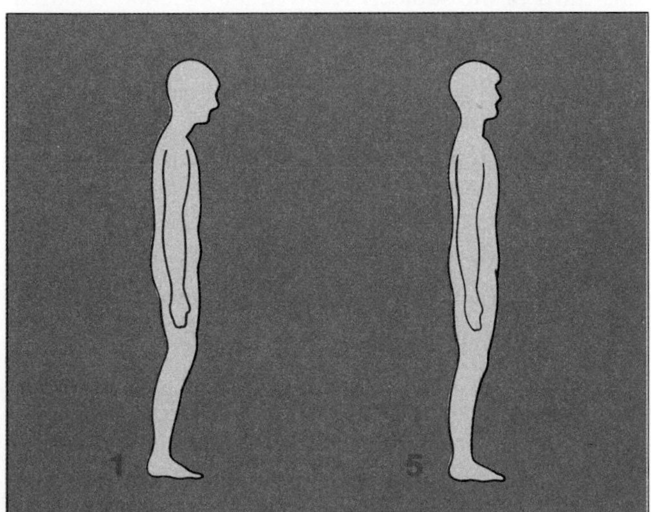

If you know a person well, you may be able to detect deception from expressive changes (Ekman & Friesen, 1975). But don't count on it. Most people learn to maintain careful control over their facial expressions. A good example is smiling so you won't hurt someone's feelings when you have received a disappointing gift. Because of such control, deception is often best revealed by the lower body (Ekman & Friesen, 1975). Even a good con artist may be too busy attending to his or her words and face to control the bodily clues revealed in Highlight 12–2.

● Theories of Emotion—Several Ways To Fear a Bear

Question: Is it possible to explain what takes place during emotion? How are arousal, behavior, cognition, expression, and feelings interrelated?

Various theories of emotion offer different answers to these questions. Let's investigate some of the most prominent views.

The James-Lange Theory (1884–1885)

Common sense tells us that we see a bear, feel fear, become aroused, and run (and sweat and yell). But psychologists have questioned this order of events. In the 1880s, American psychologist William James (the functionalist) and Danish physiologist Carl Lange proposed that common sense had it backward. According to James and Lange, bodily arousal (such as increased heart rate) does not follow a feeling such as fear. Instead, they argued, *emotional feelings follow bodily arousal.* Thus, we see a bear, run, are aroused, and *then* feel fear as we become aware of our bodily reactions.

To support this line of thought, James pointed out that we often do not experience an emotion until after reacting. For example, imagine that you are driving and that a car suddenly pulls out in front of you. You swerve and skid to an abrupt halt at the side of the road. Only after you have come to a stop do you notice your pounding heart, rapid breathing, and tense muscles—and recognize your fear.

The Cannon-Bard Theory (1927)

American physiologist Walter Cannon and his student Phillip Bard found a number of reasons to question the James-Lange theory. While agreeing that the body becomes stirred up during emotion, Cannon (1932) and Bard proposed that emotional feelings and bodily arousal

HIGHLIGHT 12-2
Behavioral Lie Catching

The salesman swears that he is giving you "the buy of a lifetime." If you can't touch his tongue to a hot knife, how else can you tell if he's lying? Most people assume that shifty eyes and squirming are clear signs of lying. But Paul Ekman (1986) has found that neither of these clues increases when a person is fibbing. Also contrary to what you might expect, nervous movements that involve touching one's own body (rubbing, grooming, scratching, twisting hair, rubbing hands, biting lips, stroking the chin, and so on) are not consistently related to lying.

On the other hand, the gestures people use to *illustrate what they are saying* may reveal lying. These gestures, called **illustrators,** tend to *decrease* when a person is telling a lie. In other words, persons who usually "talk with their hands" may be much less animated when they are lying.

Other movements, called **emblems,** can also reveal lying. Emblems are gestures that have clear meanings within a particular culture. Some examples are the thumbs-up sign, the A-Okay sign, the middle-finger insult, a head nod for yes, and a head shake for no. Emblems tend to *increase* when a person is lying. More importantly, they often reveal true feelings contrary to what the liar is saying. For example, a person might smile and say, "Yes, I'd love to try some of your homemade candied pig's feet" while slowly shaking her head from side to side.

Among the best clues to lying are the signs of strong emotion produced by the ANS. These include blinking, blushing, blanching, pupil dilation, rapid or irregular breathing, perspiration, frequent swallowing, speech errors, and a louder, higher-pitched voice. All of these clues are hard for the liar to censor. But remember, such clues are like the polygraph: They reveal emotions, such as guilt, fear, anxiety, or apprehension; they do not always mean a person is lying.

There are other telltale mistakes that liars make involving the body, face, faked emotion, and speech. If you would like to learn more about lie catching, consult Paul Ekman's book, *Telling Lies*. But remember, good liars can fool most people most of the time—and that's no lie.

are both organized in the brain. In their theory, seeing a bear activates the thalamus, which in turn alerts both the cortex and the hypothalamus for action. The cortex is responsible for emotional feelings and emotional behavior. The hypothalamus is responsible for arousing the body. Thus, if the bear is seen as dangerous, bodily arousal, running, and feelings of fear will all be generated *at the same time* by brain activity.

Schachter's Cognitive Theory of Emotion (1971)

The previous theories are mostly concerned with physical responses. Stanley Schachter realized that cognitive (mental) factors also enter into emotion. According to Schachter, emotion occurs when a particular *label* is applied to general physical *arousal*. Schachter assumes that when we are aroused, we have a need to interpret our feelings. Assume, for instance, that someone sneaks up behind you on a dark street and says, "Boo!" No matter who the person is, your body will be aroused (pounding heart, sweating palms, and so on). If the person is a total stranger, you may interpret this arousal as fear; if the person is a close friend, the arousal may be labeled as surprise or delight. The label (such as anger, fear, or happiness) applied to bodily arousal is influenced by past experience, the situation, and the reactions of others.

Support for the cognitive theory of emotion comes from an experiment in which subjects watched a slapstick movie (Schachter & Wheeler, 1962). Before viewing the movie, one-third of the subjects received an injection of adrenaline, one-third got a placebo injection, and the remaining subjects were given a tranquilizer. Subjects who received the adrenaline rated the movie funniest and showed the most amusement while watching it. In contrast, those given the tranquilizer were least amused, and the placebo group fell in between.

According to the cognitive theory of emotion, individuals who received adrenaline had a stirred-up body, but no explanation for the way they were feeling. Consequently, they became happy when the movie implied that their arousal was due to amusement. This and similar experiments make it clear that emotion is much more than just an agitated body. Perception, experience, attitudes, judgment, and many other mental factors also affect emotion. Schachter would predict, then, that if you met a bear, you would be aroused. If the bear seemed unfriendly, you would interpret your arousal as fear, and if the bear offered to shake your hand, you would be happy, amazed, and relieved!

Attribution We now move from slapstick movies and fear of bear bodies to appreciation of bare bodies. Researcher Stuart Valins (1967) has added an interesting wrinkle to Schachter's theory of emotion. According to Valins, arousal can be attributed to various sources—a process that alters perceptions of emotion. To demonstrate such **attribution,** Valins (1966) showed male college students a series of slides of nude females. While watching the slides, each subject heard an amplified heartbeat that he believed was his own. In reality, subjects were listening to a recorded heartbeat carefully designed to beat *louder* and *stronger* when some (but not all) of the slides were shown.

After viewing the slides, each subject was asked to say which slide he found most attractive. Students exposed to the false heartbeat consistently rated slides paired with a "pounding heart" as the most attractive. In other words, when a student saw a slide and heard his heartbeat become more pronounced, he attributed his "emotion" to the slide. His interpretation seems to have been, "Now that one I like!" His next reaction, perhaps, was "But why?" More recent research suggests that subjects persuade themselves that the slide really is more attractive in order to explain their apparent arousal (Truax, 1983).

Question: That seems somewhat artificial. Does it really make any difference what arousal is attributed to?

Yes. To illustrate how attribution works in the "real world," consider what happens when parents interfere with the budding romance of a son or daughter. Often, trying to break up a young couple's relationship *intensifies* their feelings for one another. Parental interference adds frustration, anger, and fear or excitement (as in seeing each other "on the sly") to the couple's feelings. Since they already care for one another, they are likely to attribute all this added emotion to "true love" (Walster, 1971).

Attribution theory predicts that you are most likely to "love" someone who gets you stirred up emotionally, even when fear, anger, frustration, or rejection is part of the formula. Thus, if you want to successfully propose marriage, take your intended to the middle of a narrow, windswept suspension bridge over a deep chasm and look deeply into his or her eyes. As your beloved's heart pounds wildly (from being on the bridge, not from your irresistible charms), say, "I love you." Attribution theory predicts that your companion will conclude, "Oh wow, I must love you, too."

Fig. 12–10 *Which theory of emotion best describes the reaction of these people? Given the complexity of emotion, each theory appears to possess an element of truth.*

The preceding is not as farfetched as it may seem. In an ingenious study, a female experimenter interviewed men in a park, some on a swaying suspension bridge 230 feet above a river and others on a solid wooden bridge just 10 feet above the ground. After the interview, each subject was given the experimenter's telephone number, so he could "find out about the results" of the study if he wanted to. Men interviewed on the suspension bridge were much more likely to give the "lady from the park" a call (Dutton & Aron, 1974). Apparently, these men experienced heightened arousal, which they interpreted as attraction to the experimenter—a clear case of love at first fright! (Love is discussed further in this chapter's Exploration.)

The Facial Feedback Hypothesis

Schachter added thinking and interpretation (cognition) to our view of emotion, but the picture still seems incomplete. What about emotional expressions? How do they influence emotion? As Charles Darwin observed, the face seems very central to emotion. Is it really just an "emotional billboard"?

Psychologist Carrol Izard (1977) was among the first to suggest that the face does, indeed, affect emotion.

According to Izard and others, emotional activity causes innately programmed changes in facial expression. The face then provides cues to the brain that help us determine what emotion we are feeling (Strongman, 1987). This idea is known as the **facial feedback hypothesis.** Stated another way, it says that having facial expressions and becoming aware of them is what leads to emotional experience. Exercise, for instance, arouses the body, but this arousal is not experienced as emotion because it does not trigger emotional expressions.

Psychologist Paul Ekman takes the idea one step further. Ekman believes that "making faces" can actually cause emotion. In one study, he and his colleagues carefully guided subjects as they arranged their faces, muscle by muscle, into expressions of surprise, disgust, sadness, anger, fear, and happiness (Fig. 12–11). At the same time, subjects' bodily reactions were monitored.

Contrary to what might be expected, "making faces" brought about changes in the autonomic nervous system, as reflected by heart rate and skin temperature. In addition, each facial expression produced a different pattern of activity. An angry face, for instance, raised heart rate and skin temperature, whereas disgust lowered heart rate and skin temperature (Ekman et al., 1983).

It appears, then, that not only do emotions determine expressions, but expressions may determine emotions. This could explain an interesting effect you have probably observed. When you are feeling "down," forcing yourself to smile will sometimes be followed by an actual improvement in your mood (Laird, 1974, 1984).

A Contemporary Model of Emotion

Current thought holds that each of the theories we have described is partly true. James and Lange were right that feedback from arousal and behavior adds to emotional experience. However, Cannon and Bard were right about the timing of events. Schachter showed that cognition is important. Today, psychologists are increasingly aware that the way a situation is **appraised** greatly affects the course of emotion (Strongman, 1987). (Appraisal refers to evaluating the personal meaning of a stimulus: Is it good/bad, threatening/supportive, relevant/irrelevant, and so on?) However, Schachter's theory tends to overlook the role of other parts of emotion, such as facial expressions. Also, the theory doesn't seem to fit all circumstances. For example, how can a child who hasn't learned to label emotion have an emotion?

In recent years, many new theories of emotion have appeared. Rather than pick one "best" theory, let's put the main points of several theories together in a single **contemporary model of emotion** (Fig. 12–12).

Imagine that a large snarling dog has just lunged at you with its teeth bared. A modern view of emotion goes something like this: An *emotional stimulus* (the dog) is *appraised* (judged) as a threat or other cause for emotional response. (You think to yourself, "Uh oh, big trouble!") Your emotional appraisal gives rise to *ANS arousal* (your heart pounds and your body becomes stirred up). The appraisal also releases *innate emotional expressions* (your face twists into a mask of fear and your posture becomes

Fig. 12–11 *Facial feedback and emotion. Participants in Ekman's study formed facial expressions like those normally observed during emotion. When they did this, emotion-like changes took place in their bodily activity. (After Ekman et al., 1983.)*

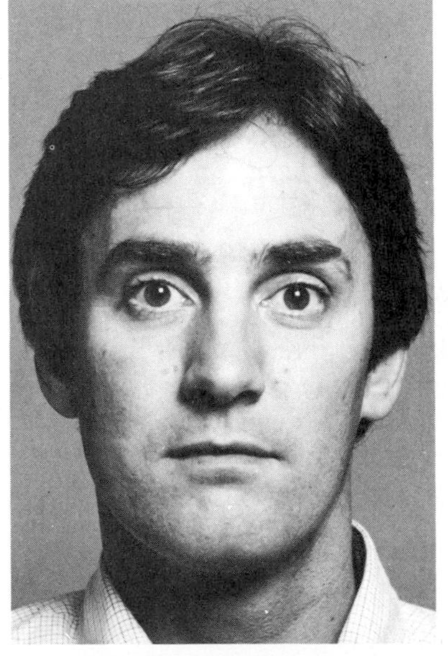

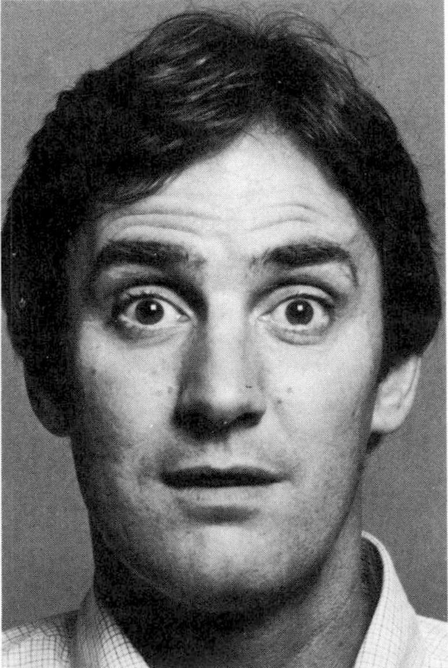

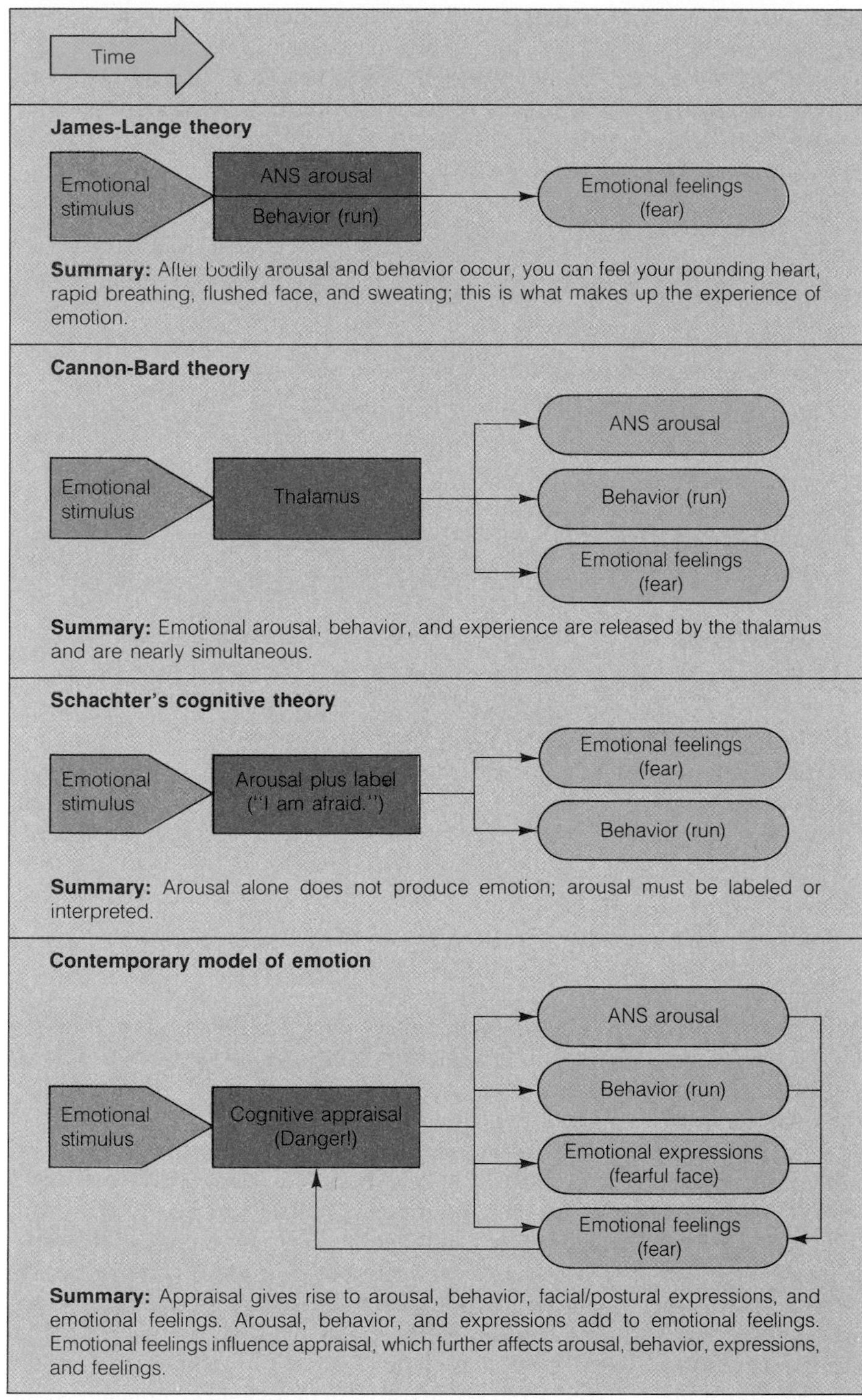

Fig. 12–12 *Theories of emotion.*

tense). At the same time, the appraisal leads to *adaptive behavior* (running from the dog). It also causes a change in consciousness that you recognize as the subjective experience of fear. (The intensity of this *emotional feeling* is directly related to the amount of ANS arousal.)

Each element of emotion—the ANS arousal, adaptive behavior, subjective experience, and emotional expression—may feed back into your appraisal and alter it. In other words, this feedback changes your thoughts, judgments, or perceptions of emotion. Such changes further alter all of the other reactions, which again alter the appraisal or interpretation of events. Thus, emotion may blossom, change course, or diminish as it proceeds. Note too that the original emotional stimulus can be external, like the attacking dog, or internal, such as a memory of being chased by a dog, rejected by a lover, or praised by a friend. This is why mere thoughts and memories can make us fearful, sad, or happy (Strongman, 1987).

In the next section we will look further at the impact of emotional appraisal, especially as it relates to coping with a threat. Before we continue, you might want to appraise your learning with the questions that follow.

Learning Check

1. The first recognizable emotional response in a newborn baby is fear. T or F?

2. The pattern of emotional development in human infants varies greatly from one culture to another. T or F?

3. Charles Darwin held that emotional expressions aid survival for animals. T or F?

4. A formal term for "body language" is ______________.

5. Which three dimensions of emotion are communicated by facial expressions?
a. pleasantness-unpleasantness *b.* complexity *c.* attention-rejection
d. anger *e.* curiosity-disinterest *f.* activation

6. According to the James-Lange theory, emotional experience precedes physical arousal and emotional behavior. (We see a bear, are frightened, and run.) T or F?

7. The Cannon-Bard theory of emotion says that bodily arousal and emotional experience occur ______________.

8. According to Schachter's cognitive theory, bodily arousal must be labeled or interpreted for an emotional experience to occur. T or F?

9. Subjects in Valin's false heart rate study attributed increases in their heart rate to the action of a placebo. T or F?

10. As you try to wiggle your ears, you keep pulling the corners of your mouth back into a smile. Each time you do, you find yourself giggling. Which of the following provides the best explanation for this reaction?
a. attribution *b.* the Cannon-Bard theory *c.* appraisal *d.* facial feedback

Answers:

1. F **2.** F **3.** T **4.** kinesics **5.** *a, c, f* **6.** F **7.** simultaneously **8.** T **9.** F **10.** *d*

Coping with Emotion—"Am I Okay or in Trouble?"

Situation: You have been selected to give a speech to 300 people. Or, a doctor tells you that you must undergo a dangerous and painful operation. Or, the one true love of your life walks out the door. What would your emotional response to these events be? How do you cope with an emotional threat? According to Richard Lazarus (1975, 1981, 1984), there are two important steps in coping with a threatening situation. The first is a **primary appraisal,** in which you decide if a situation is relevant or irrelevant, positive or threatening. In essence, this appraisal answers the question, "Am I okay or in trouble?" (Lazarus & Folkman, 1984). Then you make a **secondary appraisal,** during which you assess your resources and choose a way to meet the threat or challenge. ("What can I do about this situation?")

The emotional effects of appraising a threatening situation were demonstrated in a fascinating experiment by Joseph Spiesman and his associates (1964). The study used a graphic film called *Subincision* to stimulate emotional responses in volunteers. Subincision is a ritual used to initiate adolescent boys into manhood in a tribe of Australian Aborigines. The filmed procedure begins with three or four adults holding a boy down to prevent escape. Then a crude and obviously painful operation is performed in which the adolescent's penis is slit on the underside for its entire length. To add insult to injury, the operation is performed with a sharpened flint stone. Needless to say, most viewers respond emotionally to the gory details of this film.

The film was shown in four different versions to test the emotional effects of different appraisals. The first had no sound track. The second, emphasized the painful and traumatic aspects of the operation. The third treated the operation in an intellectual and distant way. The fourth glossed over the threatening aspects of the operation and denied that it was painful.

Question: Did the sound tracks affect emotional reactions?

Recordings of heart rate and GSR showed quite clearly that appraisal of a situation affects emotional response. The film emphasizing pain produced more emotion than the silent film did. On the other hand, the intellectual and denial sound tracks reduced emotion. The way a situation is "sized up" therefore becomes very important to coping with it. Public speaking, for instance, can be appraised as an intense threat or as a challenge and a chance to perform. Emphasizing the threat—by imagining failure, rejection, or embarrassment—obviously invites disaster.

Coping with Threat After a person makes a secondary appraisal, his or her coping attempts can be either problem-focused or emotion-focused (Lazarus & Folkman, 1984). **Problem-focused coping** is aimed at managing or altering the distressing situation itself. In **emotion-focused coping,** the person tries instead to control his or her emotional reaction.

Question: Couldn't both types of coping occur together?

Yes. Sometimes the two types of coping aid one another. Say, for example, that a woman feels anxious as she steps to the podium to give a speech. If she does some deep breathing to reduce her anxiety (emotion-focused coping), she will be better able to glance over her notes to improve her delivery (problem-focused coping). Highlight 12–3 describes some strategies (of both types) that may help you cope better with taking tests, an often threatening situation.

It is also possible, unfortunately, for the two types of coping to clash or impede one another. If you have to make a difficult decision, for instance, you may suffer unbearable emotional distress. In such circumstances, there is a temptation to make a quick and ill-advised choice, just to end the emotional suffering. Doing so may allow you to cope with your emotions, but it shortchanges problem-focused coping (Lazarus & Folkman, 1984). Coping effectively is a major topic in its own right. In the next chapter we will discuss additional reactions to stressful, threatening, and emotional situations.

THE FAR SIDE By GARY LARSON

"The fuel light's on, Frank! We're all going to die! ... Wait, wait. ... Oh, my mistake—that's the intercom light."

Psychological Defense—Mental Karate?

Threatening situations are often accompanied by an unpleasant emotion know as **anxiety.** A person who is anxious feels tense, uneasy, apprehensive, worried, and vulnerable. This can lead to emotion-focused coping that is *defensive* in nature. Since anxiety is unpleasant and uncomfortable, we are usually motivated to avoid it. Anxiety caused by stressful situations or by our own shortcomings and limitations may be lessened by the use of **psychological defense mechanisms.**

Question: What are psychological defense mechanisms and how do they reduce anxiety?

A defense mechanism is any technique used to avoid, deny, or distort sources of threat or anxiety. Defense mechanisms are also used to maintain an idealized self-image so that we can comfortably live with ourselves. Many of the defenses were first identified by Sigmund Freud, who assumed they operated *unconsciously.* Often, unconscious defensiveness creates large "blind spots" in awareness, as when an extremely stingy person fails to recognize that he or she is a tightwad. Everyone has at one time or another used such defenses. Let's consider

HIGHLIGHT 12–3
Coping with Test Anxiety

When taking tests, do you often feel extremely tense and anxious? Spend much of your time worrying about whether you will pass? "Go blank," even when you know the answer? Feel hurried, inadequate, or panicked?

If you answered yes to most of these questions, you probably have a high level of test anxiety. **Test anxiety** refers to a combination of heightened *physiological arousal* (uneasiness, tension, sweating, pounding heart, nervousness) and *excessive worry* during test taking. This combination—worry plus arousal—tends to distract students with a rush of upsetting thoughts and feelings (Mueller & Thompson, 1984).

Worries, Worries "I'm not sure about any of these answers. I must be stupid. I can't do this. I'll never pass. Look how much time is gone already. What if I flunk?" Worries like these arise when a test is appraised as a threat. Such worries are the real heart of test anxiety because they directly interfere with thinking about the test (Eysenck, 1984; Salame, 1984). Some test-anxious students actually spend as much time worrying as they do working on the test.

Treating Test Anxiety

In recent years, psychologists have become relatively successful in treating test anxiety. Let's see what can be learned from their efforts.

Preparation The most direct antidote for test anxiety is *hard work.* Many test-anxious students simply study too little and too late for exams (Becker, 1982). And, paradoxically, the more a student expects to fail, the less he or she is likely to study. Thus, one solution for test anxiety is to *overprepare* by studying well in advance of the "big day." Students who are well prepared score higher, worry less, and are less likely to become overly aroused (Lazarus & Folkman, 1984).

Relaxation Learning to relax can also help lower test anxiety (Ricketts & Galloway, 1984). Students interested in learning self-relaxation skills should look ahead to Chapter 22, where a relaxation technique is described. Test anxiety is also lowered by support from others (Sarason, 1981). If you tend to be overly anxious during tests, you may find it helpful to discuss the problem with your professor. Preparing for the test with a supportive friend or classmate can also help.

Rehearsal Some students find that nervousness during tests can be lessened by carefully *rehearsing* how they will cope with upsetting events. Before taking a test, imagine yourself going blank, running out of time, or feeling panicked. Then calmly plan how you will handle each situation—by keeping your attention on the task, by focusing on one question at a time, and so forth (Watson & Tharp, 1981).

Restructuring Thoughts Because worries are such a major part of test anxiety, changing self-defeating thinking patterns can be the best solution of all (Wise & Haynes, 1983). Test-anxious students often benefit from listing the kinds of distracting and self-defeating thoughts they have during exams. They then work on learning to counter their worries with calming, rational replies. (These are called *coping statements*; see Chapter 13 for more information.)

Let's say, for example, that a student thinks, "I'm going to fail this test and all my friends will think I'm stupid." To counter this upsetting thought, he or she might say, "If I prepare well and control my worries, I will probably pass the test. Even if I don't, it won't be the end of the world. My friends will still like me, and I can try to improve on the next test."

Students who cope well with testing typically take a practical attitude and try to do the best they can, even under trying circumstances. With practice, most students can learn to be less testy at test time.

some of the most common. (A more complete listing is given in Table 12–2.)

Denial One of the most basic defense mechanisms is **denial.** Denial means to protect oneself from an unpleasant reality by refusing to accept it or believe it. Denial is closely linked with death, illness, and similar painful and threatening experiences. For instance, if you were told that you had only 3 months to live, how would you react? Your first thoughts might be "Aw, come on, someone must have mixed up the X-rays" or "The doctors must be mistaken" or simply "It can't be true!" Similar denial and disbelief are common reactions to the unexpected death of a friend or relative: "It's just not real. I don't believe it. I just don't believe it!"

Table 12–2 Psychological Defense Mechanisms

Compensation	Counteracting a real or imagined weakness by emphasizing desirable traits or seeking to excel in other areas
Denial	Protecting oneself from an unpleasant reality by refusing to perceive it
Fantasy	Fulfilling unmet desires in imagined achievements or activities
Intellectualization	Separating emotion from a threatening or anxiety-provoking situation by talking or thinking about it in impersonal terms
Isolation	Separating contradictory thoughts or feelings into "logic-tight" mental compartments so that they do not come into conflict
Projection	Attributing one's own feelings, shortcomings, or unacceptable impulses to others
Rationalization	Justifying one's own behavior by giving reasonable and rational but false reasons for it
Reaction formation	Preventing dangerous impulses from being expressed by exaggerating opposite behavior
Regression	Retreating to an earlier level of development or to earlier, less demanding habits or situations
Repression	Preventing painful or dangerous thoughts from entering consciousness
Sublimation	Working off unmet desires or unacceptable impulses in activities that are constructive

Repression Freud noticed that his patients had tremendous difficulty recalling shocking or traumatic events from childhood. It seemed that powerful forces were holding these painful memories from awareness. Freud called this **repression.** Apparently, we protect ourselves by repressing thoughts or impulses that are painful or threatening. Feelings of hostility toward a loved one, the names of disliked people, and past failures and embarrassments are common targets of repression.

Reaction Formation **Reaction formation** is a defense in which impulses are not only repressed, but are also held in check by exaggerated opposite behavior. For example, a mother who unconsciously resents her children may, through reaction formation, become absurdly overprotective and overindulgent. Her real thoughts of "I hate them" and "I wish they were gone" are replaced by "I love them" and "I don't know what I would do without them." The mother's hostile impulses are traded for "smother" love, so that she won't have to admit her dislike of her children. The basic idea in a reaction formation is that the individual acts out an opposite behavior to block threatening impulses or feelings.

Regression In its broadest meaning, **regression** refers to any return to earlier, less demanding situations or habits. Most parents who have a second child have to put up with at least some regression by the older child. Threatened by a new rival for attention, an older child may regress to childish speech, bed-wetting, or infantile play after the new baby arrives. However, regression is usually less severe. The child at summer camp who gets homesick and longs for the security of familiar surroundings is undergoing mild regression. An adult who throws a temper tantrum or a married adult who "goes home to mother" is also regressing.

Projection **Projection** is an unconscious process that protects us from the anxiety that would occur if we were to discern our own faults or unacceptable traits. A person who is *projecting* tends to see his or her own shortcomings or unacceptable impulses in others. Projection lowers anxiety by exaggerating negative traits in others while directing attention away from one's own failings.

The author once worked for a greedy shop owner who cheated many of his customers. This same man considered himself a pillar of the community and a good Christian. How did he justify to himself his greed and dishonesty? He believed that everyone who entered his store was bent on cheating *him* any way they could. In reality, few, if any, of his customers shared his motives, but he projected his own greed and dishonesty onto them.

Rationalization Every teacher is familiar with this strange phenomenon: On the day of an exam, an incredible wave of disasters sweeps through the city. An amazing number of mothers, fathers, sisters, brothers, aunts, uncles, grandparents, friends, relatives, and pets become ill or die. Motors suddenly fall out of automobiles. Books are lost or stolen. Alarm clocks go belly up and ring no more.

The making of excuses comes from a natural tendency to explain one's behavior. When the explanation offered is reasonable, rational, and convincing—but not the real reason—we say a person is *rationalizing*. **Rationalization** provides us with reasons for behavior we ourselves find somewhat questionable. Here is a typical example of rationalization. A student who fails to turn in an assignment made at the beginning of the semester explains:

> My car broke down 2 days ago and I couldn't get to the library until yesterday. Then I couldn't get all the books I needed because some were checked out, but I wrote what I could. Then last night, as the last straw, the ribbon in my typewriter broke, and since all the stores were closed, I couldn't finish the paper on time.

If asked why he left the assignment until the last minute (the real reason for its being late), the student would probably offer another set of rationalizations. If these are questioned, the student may become emotional as he is forced to see himself without the protection of his rationalizations.

Question: All of the defense mechanisms described seem pretty undesirable. Do they have a positive side?

People who overuse defense mechanisms become less adaptable, because they consume great amounts of emotional energy to control anxiety and to maintain an unrealistic self-image. Defense mechanisms do have value, however. Often, they help keep us from being overwhelmed by immediate threats. This can provide time for learning to cope in a more effective manner with continuing threats and frustrations. If you recognize some of your own behavior in the descriptions here, it is hardly a sign that you are hopelessly defensive. As noted earlier, most people make occasional use of defense mechanisms.

Two defense mechanisms that have a decidedly more positive quality are *compensation* and *sublimation*.

Compensation **Compensatory reactions** are defenses against feelings of inferiority. A person who has a defect or weakness (real or imagined) may go to unusual lengths to overcome the weakness or to compensate for it by excelling in other areas. One of the pioneers of "pumping iron" in America is Jack LaLanne. LaLanne made a successful career out of body building in spite of the fact that he was thin and sickly as a young man. Or perhaps it would be more accurate to say *because* he was thin and sickly. There are dozens of examples of compensation at work. A childhood stutterer may excel in debate at college. Franklin D. Roosevelt's outstanding achievements in politics came after he was stricken with polio. As a child, Helen Keller was unable to see or hear, but she became an outstanding thinker and writer. Doc Watson, Ray Charles, Stevie Wonder, Ronnie Milsap, and a number of other well-known musicians are blind.

Sublimation **Sublimation** (sub-lih-MAY-shun) is defined as working off frustrated desires (especially sexual desires) in activities that are constructive and accepted by society. Freud believed that art, music, dance, poetry, scientific investigation, and other creative activities can serve to rechannel sexual energies into productive behavior. Freud also felt that almost any strong desire can be sublimated. For example, a very aggressive person may find social acceptance as a professional soldier, boxer, or football player (Fig. 12–13). Greed may be refined into a successful business career. Lying may be sublimated into storytelling, creative writing, or politics.

Sexual motives appear to be the most easily and widely sublimated. Freud would have had a field day with such modern pastimes as surfing, motorcycle riding, drag racing, and dancing to or playing rock music, to name but a few. People enjoy each of these activities for a multitude of reasons, but it is hard to overlook the rich, sexual symbolism apparent in each.

Fig. 12–13 *For some players—and fans—football probably allows sublimation of aggressive urges.*

Learned Helplessness—Is There Hope?

Question: What would happen if a person's defenses failed or if the person appraised a threatening situation as hopeless?

Bruno Bettelheim (1960), who survived imprisonment in Nazi concentration camps, has described a reaction he calls "give-up-itis." Many of the prisoners felt so helpless that they developed a "zombie-like" detachment that made them into "walking corpses." Martin Seligman (1974) has described a similar reaction in Vietnam prisoner of war camps. Seligman reports the case of a young marine who had adapted unusually well to the stresses of being a POW. His health was apparently related to a promise made by his captors that if he would cooperate, he would be released on a certain date. As the date approached, his spirits soared. Then came a devastating blow. He had been deceived. There was never any intention of releasing him. He immediately lapsed into a deep depression, refused to eat or drink, and died shortly thereafter.

Examples such as these are admittedly extreme, but they show once again the power of emotions. Recent attempts to understand such events have focused on the concept of **learned helplessness.**

Learned helplessness has been studied in the laboratory with animals tested in a shuttle box (Fig. 12–14). If placed in one side of a divided box, dogs will quickly learn to leap to the other side to escape an electric shock. If they are given a warning before the shock occurs (for example, a light that dims), most dogs learn to avoid the shock by leaping the barrier before the shock arrives. This is true of most dogs, but not those who have learned to feel helpless.

Question: How is a dog made to feel helpless?

Before being tested in the shuttle box, some dogs are placed in a harness (from which they cannot escape) and are given several painful shocks. The animal is helpless to prevent these shocks (Overmier & Seligman, 1967). When placed in the shuttle box, these dogs react to the first shock by crouching, howling, and whining. None try to escape. They helplessly resign themselves to their fate. After all, they have already learned that there is nothing they can do about the shocks.

Similar effects occur when humans fail or when they receive punishment they cannot predict or prevent (Fox & Oakes, 1984). However, where humans are concerned, attributions (remember attribution?) have a large effect on helplessness. Persons who are made to feel helpless in one situation are more likely to act helpless in other situations if they attribute their failure to *lasting, general* factors. An example would be concluding "I must be stupid" after failing to solve a series of puzzles. In contrast, attributing failure to specific factors in the original situation ("I'm not too good at puzzles" or "I wasn't really interested") tends to prevent learned helplessness from spreading (Alloy et al., 1984; Anderson et al., 1984).

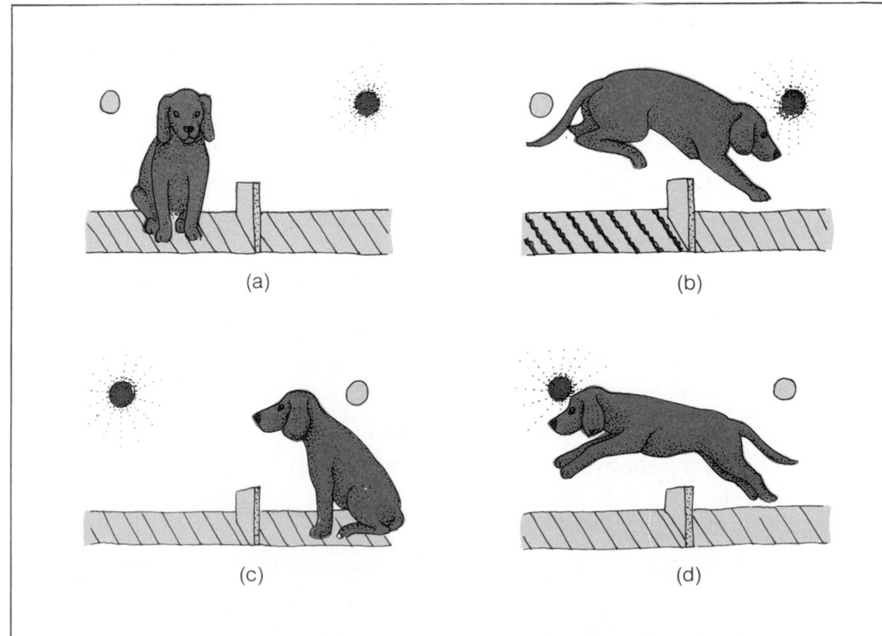

Fig. 12–14 *In the normal course of escape and avoidance learning, a light dims shortly before the floor is electrified* (a). *Since the light does not yet have meaning for the dog, the dog receives a shock (noninjurious, by the way) and leaps the barrier* (b). *Dogs soon learn to watch for the dimming of the light* (c) *and to jump before receiving a shock* (d). *Dogs made to feel "helpless" rarely even learn to escape shock, much less to avoid it.*

Question: What does learned helplessness have to do with emotion?

Depression Seligman and his associates have drawn attention to the similarities between learned helplessness and depression. Symptoms that occur in both depression and learned helplessness include feelings of powerlessness and hopelessness, decreased activity, lowered aggression, loss of sexual drive and appetite, and, in humans, a tendency to see oneself as failing, even when this is not the case (Miller et al., 1977).

Depression is one of the most widespread emotional problems, and it undoubtedly has many causes (see Chapter 19). However, Seligman has made a good case for learned helplessness as a factor in at least some cases of depression and hopelessness. For example, Seligman (1972) describes the fate of Archie, a 15-year-old boy. For Archie, school is an unending series of shocks and failures. Other students treat him as if he's stupid; in class he rarely answers questions because he doesn't know some of the words. He feels knocked down every direction he turns. These may not be electric shocks, but they are certainly psychological "shocks," and Archie has learned to feel helpless to prevent them. When he leaves school, his chances of success will be poor. He has learned to passively endure whatever shocks life has in store for him.

Question: Does Seligman's research give any clues about how to "unlearn" helplessness?

Hope With dogs, one effective technique is to forcibly drag them away from the shock into the "safe" compartment. After this is done several times, the animals regain "hope" and feelings of control over the environment. Just how this can be done with humans is a question for further research. It seems obvious, however, that someone like Archie would benefit from an educational program that would allow him to "succeed" repeatedly. This prediction is backed up by other animal experiments. When animals are given **mastery training,** they become more resistant to learned helplessness (Volpicelli et al., 1983). For example, animals that first learned to successfully escape shock were more persistent later in trying to escape inescapable shock. In effect, they wouldn't give up, even when the situation was hopeless.

Such findings suggest that we might even be able to "immunize" people against helplessness and depression by giving them experience at mastering seemingly impossible challenges. The Outward Bound schools, in which people pit themselves against the rigors of mountaineering, white-water canoeing, and wilderness survival, might serve as a model for such a program.

As a final note, the value of hope should not be overlooked. As fragile as this emotion seems to be, it is a powerful antidote to depression and helplessness. As an individual, you may find hope in religion, nature, human companionship, or even technology. Wherever you find it, remember its value: Hope is among the most important of all human emotions.

Learning Check

1. In the model of coping proposed by Richard Lazarus, choosing a means of meeting a threat is done during the ______________ appraisal.
2. According to Lazarus, coping with threatening situations can be both problem-focused and ______________ -focused.
3. Most people are aroused when taking a test, but those subject to test anxiety are especially prone to excessive worrying. T or F?
4. The more that students expect to fail a test, the more they tend to study for it. T or F?
5. Mentally rehearsing ways to calmly deal with anticipated test-taking problems can help lower test anxiety. T or F?
6. The psychological defense known as denial refers to the natural tendency to explain or justify one's actions. T or F?
7. Fulfilling frustrated desires in imaginary achievements or activities defines the defense mechanism of
   a. compensation *b*. isolation *c*. fantasy *d*. sublimation
8. In compensation, one's own undesirable characteristics or motives are attributed to others. T or F?
9. Of the defense mechanisms, two that are considered relatively constructive are
   a. compensation *b*. denial *c*. isolation *d*. projection
   e. regression *f*. rationalization *g*. sublimation
10. Depression in humans is similar to ______________ ______________ observed in animal experiments.

Answers:

1. secondary **2.** emotion **3.** T **4.** F **5.** T **6.** F **7.** *c* **8.** F **9.** *a*, *g* **10.** learned helplessness

Applications: Coping with Depression—A Problem for Everyone

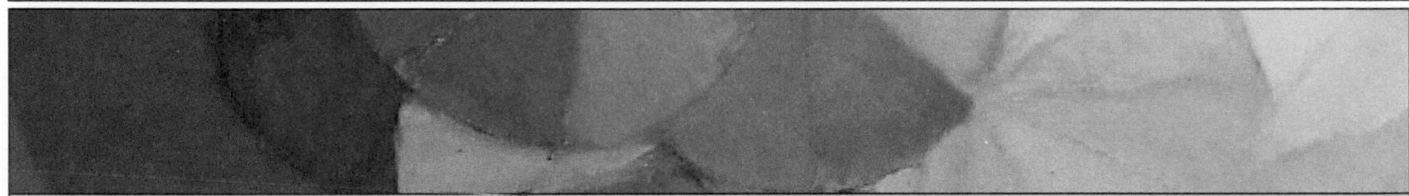

Studies show that during the school year, up to 78 percent of students at American colleges suffer some of the symptoms of depression. At any given time, roughly one-quarter of the student population is experiencing such symptoms (Beck & Young, 1978). In a more recent survey, college students reported that they got depressed from 1 to 2 times a month. These episodes lasted from a few hours to several days (Snyder & Smith, 1985). Why should so many students be "blue"? A variety of problems typically contribute to such depressive feelings. Here are some of the most common:

1. Stresses from the increased difficulty of college work and pressures to make a career choice often leave students feeling that they are missing out on fun or that all their hard work is meaningless.
2. Isolation and loneliness are common when a student leaves his or her support group behind. Before, family, a circle of high school friends, and often an intimate boyfriend or girlfriend could be counted on for support or encouragement.
3. Problems with studying and grades frequently trigger depression. Many students enter college with high aspirations and little former experience with failure. At the same time, many lack basic skills necessary for academic success.
4. A fourth common cause of college depression is the breakup of an intimate relationship, either with a former boyfriend or girlfriend or with a newly formed college romance (Beck & Young, 1978).

Recognizing Depression Most people know, obviously enough, when they are "down." Aaron Beck, an authority on depression, suggests you should assume that more than a minor fluctuation in mood is involved when five conditions exist:

1. You have a consistently negative opinion of yourself.
2. You engage in frequent self-criticism and self-blame.
3. You place negative interpretations on events that usually wouldn't bother you.
4. The future looks bleak and negative.
5. You feel that your responsibilities are overwhelming.

Question: What can be done to combat depression?

Combating Depression Beck and Greenberg (1974) suggest you should begin by making a *daily schedule* for yourself. Try to schedule activities to fill up every hour during the day. It is best to start with easy activities and progress to more difficult tasks. Check off each activity as it is completed. In this way, you will begin to break the self-defeating cycle of feeling helpless and falling further behind (depressed students spend much of their time sleeping). A series of small accomplishments, successes, or pleasures may be all that you need to get going again. However, if you are lacking skills needed for success in college, ask for help in getting them. Don't remain "helpless."

Beck and Greenberg also believe that feelings of worthlessness and hopelessness are supported by self-critical or negative thoughts. They recommend writing down such thoughts as they occur, especially those that immediately precede feelings of sadness. After you have collected these thoughts, write a rational answer to each. For example, the thought "No one loves me" should be answered with a list of those who do care. (See Chapter 22 for more information on this point.)

Attacks of the "college blues" are common and should be distinguished from more serious cases of depression. Severe depression is a serious problem that can lead to suicide or a major impairment of emotional functioning.

Question: How can mild depression be distinguished from more serious problems?

This is a rather difficult judgment to make because it is related to many psychological dimensions. Practically speaking, a useful answer can be found in a list of 10 "danger signals" compiled by the National Association for Mental Health to help people distinguish normal depression from reactions that require professional help.

Danger Signals for Depression

1. A general and lasting feeling of hopelessness and despair.
2. Inability to concentrate, making reading, writing, and conversation difficult. Thinking and activity are slowed because the mind is absorbed by inner anguish.
3. Changes in physical activities such as eating, sleeping, and sex. Frequent physical complaints with no evidence of physical illness.
4. Loss of self-esteem, which brings on continual questioning of personal worth.
5. Withdrawal from others due to immense fear of rejection.
6. Threats or attempts to commit suicide, viewed as a way out of a hostile environment and a belief that life is worthless.
7. Hypersensitivity to words and actions of others and general irritability.

Applications

8. Misdirected anger and difficulty in handling most feelings. Self-directed anger because of perceived worthlessness may produce general anger directed at others.

9. Feelings of guilt in many situations. A depressed person assumes he or she is wrong or responsible for the unhappiness of others.

10. Extreme dependency on others. Feelings of helplessness and then anger at the helplessness.

No single item (except number 6) necessarily indicates dangerous depression, but if several are observed, it should be assumed that it would be wise to seek professional help. Also, the points made here pertain only to very mild depression. When depression is more severe it becomes a major mental health problem, as discussed in Chapter 20.

Learning Check

1. Frequent self-criticism and self-blame are a natural consequence of having high aspirations for success in college. T or F?
2. At any given time, close to one-half of the college student population suffers symptoms of depression. T or F?
3. To break a cycle of depression and helplessness, Beck and Greenberg suggest it is best to get difficult tasks out of the way first. T or F?
4. Countering negative, self-critical thoughts only calls attention to them and makes depression worse. T or F?
5. General irritability and sensitivity to the actions of others are frequently signs of depression. T or F?

Answers:

1. F 2. F 3. F 4. F 5. T

Exploration: Love—Stalking an Elusive Emotion

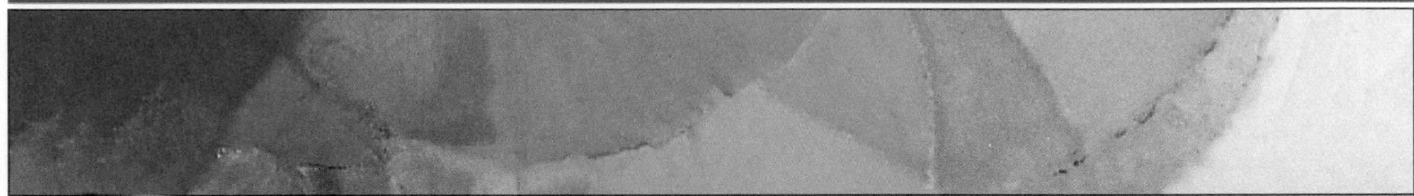

Love is one of the most intense of all human experiences. Moreover, at one time or another, most people must ask themselves, "Is this love or lust?" "Is it real or infatuation?" "What am I really feeling?" All of which raises the question, What is love? Think, for instance, about the different ways we love our parents, friends, and spouses or lovers.

Question: How do various kinds of love differ from one another?

This is the question that recently led psychologist Robert Sternberg to propose his **triangular theory of love.** Although the theory is still preliminary, it may help you think more clearly about your own loving relationships.

Love Triangles

According to Sternberg (1986, 1987), love is made up of **intimacy, passion,** and **commitment.** As you can see in Figure 12–15, each factor can be visualized as one side of a triangle. Notice also that the 3 elements can combine to produce 7 different types of love. We will return to these types in a moment, but first let's briefly explore love's 3 "ingredients."

Intimacy A relationship has intimacy, or closeness, if affection, sharing, communication, and support are present. Intimacy grows steadily at first, but in time it levels off. After it does, people in long-term relationships may gradually lose sight of the fact that they are still very close and mutually dependent.

Passion Passion refers mainly to *physiological arousal.* This arousal may be sexual, but it includes other sources too. As discussed earlier in this chapter, arousal, no matter what its cause, may be interpreted as passion in a romantic relationship (Bersheld & Walster, 1974b). This is probably why passionate love often occurs against a backdrop of danger, adversity, or frustration—especially in soap operas and romance novels! Passion is the primary source of love's *intensity.* It's not surprising, then, that romance inspires the strongest feelings of love. In contrast, love for siblings is least intense (Sternberg & Grajeck, 1984).

Commitment The third side of the love triangle consists of your decision to love another person and your degree of long-term commitment to them. Commitment starts at zero before you meet a person and it grows steadily as you get acquainted. Like intimacy, commitment tends to level off. However, it may waver up and down with a relationship's good times and bad times. Commitment drops rapidly when a relationship is in serious trouble.

Fig. 12–15 *Sternberg's triangular theory of love.*

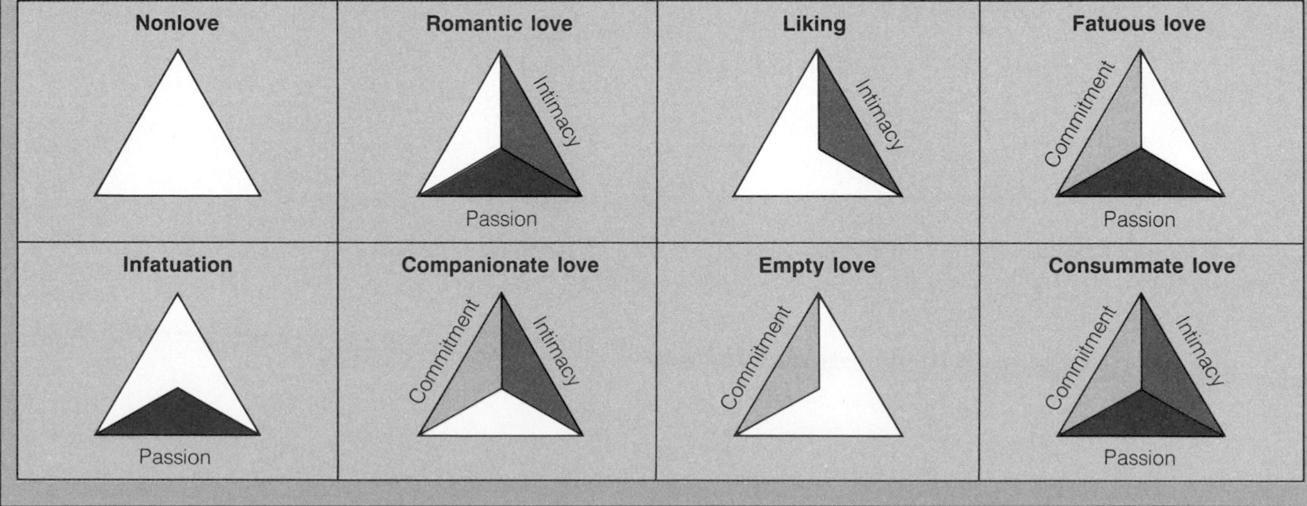

Exploration

Seven Flavors of Love

The presence or absence of intimacy, passion, and/or commitment produces 8 triangles. The first defines **nonlove,** a total absence of all three elements.

In **liking,** you feel close to a person and communicate well with her or him. However, you do not feel any passion or deep commitment to the person. A likeable classmate might fall into this category.

Romantic love mixes intimacy (closeness and sharing) with passion (often in the form of physical attraction). Despite its intensity, romantic love does not involves much commitment at first. Think, for example, of a summer romance that ends in a relatively easy parting of ways.

Fatuous love describes commitments made rapidly on the basis of physical attraction (passion), but without much emotional intimacy. Fatuous love is of the boy-meets-girl-and-they-get-married-a-month-later type. Relationships started this way risk failure because lovers make a commitment before they really get to know each other well.

Infatuation is an even more superficial form of love. In this case, a person is inflamed with passion, but shares no intimacy or commitment with the beloved. In time, of course, infatuation may lead to more lasting kinds of love.

Companionate love refers to affection and deep attachment that is built on respect, shared interests, and firm friendship. Companionate love is lower-key emotionally. However, it is steady and long-term and tends to grow in time. Companionate love is the "kind of affection we feel for those with whom our lives are deeply intertwined" (Walster & Walster, 1978).

Couples sometimes reach a point where there is little passion or intimacy left in their relationship. If they stay together merely out of commitment or habit, they experience **empty love.**

Consummate love occurs when two people are passionate, committed to one another, and emotionally close. Complete, balanced love of this kind occurs only in very special relationships.

How Do I Love Thee? The categories described here are certainly not the last word on love. Undoubtedly, other kinds of love also exist. In addition, Sternberg's theory may place too much emphasis on passion. In most relationships, intimacy and commitment are a bigger part of love than passion is (Clark & Reis, 1988).

Our culture also tends to place much emphasis on passion as the main basis for "falling" in love. However, this overlooks the fact that the passionate, breathless stage of love typically lasts only about 6 to 30 months (Walster & Walster, 1978). What happens when this period ends? Quite often, people separate.

There is a degree of danger in expecting to live forever on a romantic cloud. People who are primarily caught up in passionate love may neglect to build a more lasting relationship. Rather than downplaying companionate love, it is helpful to realize that lovers must also be friends. In fact, consummate love is basically a blending of romantic love and companionate love.

You may be tempted to match the love triangles with your own relationships. If you do apply the theory, remember that relationships vary greatly and that few are perfect (Trotter, 1986). In another study, Sternberg and Michael Barnes (1986) found that relationships are generally satisfying if you think the other person feels about you the way you would *like* for her or him to feel about you.

In the 1970s, some politicians belittled the study of love as "unscientific." But in a world often wracked by violence, hatred, and despair, what could be more important than understanding the elusive state we call love?

Learning Check

1. Essentially, all types of love can be described as a passion for another person. T or F?
2. According to Sternberg's theory, all forms of love involve commitment to another person or to a relationship. T or F?
3. Passion is the primary element of infatuation. T or F?
4. Fatuous love can be defined as commitment based on passion but lacking in intimacy. T or F?
5. The passionate stage of love usually lasts only 6 to 30 weeks. T or F?

Answers:
1. F 2. F 3. T 4. T 5. F

Chapter Summary

• Emotions were probably retained in evolution because they are linked to many basic **adaptive behaviors.** Other major elements of emotion are **physiological changes** in the body, **emotional expressions** (outward signs of emotion), and **emotional feelings** (subjective emotional experience).

• The following are considered to be **primary emotions:** *fear, surprise, sadness, disgust, anger, anticipation, joy,* and *acceptance.* Other emotions seem to represent mixtures of the primaries.

• Physical changes associated with emotion are caused by the action of **adrenaline,** a hormone released into the bloodstream, and by activity in the **autonomic nervous system** (ANS).

• The **sympathetic branch** of the ANS is primarily responsible for arousing the body, the **parasympathetic branch** for quieting it. Sudden death due to prolonged and intense emotion is probably related to a **parasympathetic rebound.** Heart attacks caused by sudden intense emotion are more likely due to sympathetic arousal.

• The **polygraph,** or "lie detector," measures emotional arousal by monitoring *heart rate, blood pressure, breathing rate,* and the *galvanic skin response (GSR).* The accuracy of the lie detector has been challenged by many researchers.

• Emotions develop from the **generalized excitement** observed in newborn babies. Three of the basic emotions—*fear, anger,* and *joy*—may be unlearned. Basic emotional expressions, such as smiling, frowning, or baring one's teeth when angry, also appear to be unlearned. **Facial expressions** appear to be central to emotion. As a result, some psychologists consider them a carryover from earlier stages of evolution.

• Body gestures and movements (body language) also express feelings, mainly by communicating **emotional tone** rather than specific universal messages. Three dimensions of facial expressions are **pleasantness-unpleasantness, attention-rejection,** and **activation.** The formal study of body language is know as **kinesics.** Lying can sometimes be detected from changes in **illustrators** or **emblems** and from signs of **general arousal.**

• The **James-Lange theory** of emotion says that emotional *experience* follows the bodily reactions of emotion. In contrast, the **Cannon-Bard theory** says that bodily reactions and emotional experience occur at the same time and that emotions are organized in the brain.

• Schacter's **cognitive theory** of emotion emphasizes the importance of *labels,* or interpretations, applied to feelings of bodily arousal. Also important is the process of **attribution,** the effect of associating bodily arousal with a particular person, object, or situation.

• The **facial feedback hypothesis** holds that sensations and information from emotional expressions help define what emotion a person is feeling.

• Contemporary views of emotion place greater emphasis on the effects of **cognitive appraisals** of situations. Also, all of the elements of emotion are seen as interrelated and interacting.

• The **primary appraisal** of a situation greatly affects the emotional response to it. Fear reactions, in particular, are related to an appraisal of threat. During a **secondary appraisal,** some means of coping with a situation is selected. Coping may be either **problem-focused** or **emotion-focused.**

• Anxiety, threat, or feelings of inadequacy frequently lead to the use of psychological **defense mechanisms.** A large number of defense mechanisms have been identified, including *compensation, denial, fantasy, intellectualization, isolation, projection, rationalization, reaction formation, regression, repression,* and *sublimation.*

• The concept of **learned helplessness** has been used to explain the failure to cope with threatening situations and as a model for understanding **depression. Mastery training** acts as one major antidote to helplessness.

• **Depression** is a major, and surprisingly common, emotional problem. Actions and thoughts that counter feelings of helplessness tend to reduce depression.

• Sternberg's **triangular theory** describes love as a combination of **passion, intimacy,** and **commitment.** Combinations of these three factors produce **nonlove, liking, infatuation, romantic love, fatuous love, companionate love, empty love,** and **consummate love.**

Questions For Discussion

1. Do you consider yourself more emotional or less emotional than average? What role has learning played in the development of your emotional life? (Consider the influence of family, friends, and culture.)

2. In what ways have emotions contributed to your enjoyment of life? In what ways have they caused problems for you?

3. There is an element of truth to each of the theories

of emotion. What parts of each seem to apply best to your own emotions?

4. What would be the advantages and disadvantages of being emotionless? (You might use Mr. Spock from "Star Trek" as a model for answering this question.)

5. In your opinion, what added limits, if any, should be placed on the use of lie detection devices by businesses? By the military? By government?

6. Did you learn "body language" from your parents? How similar are your facial and hand gestures to theirs?

7. The defense mechanisms listed in this chapter were described in psychodynamic terms, that is, in terms of the balance of forces within the personality. Can you advance a learning theory explanation for any of the defenses? (*Hint:* Think in terms of avoidance learning and the rewards connected with defensive responses.)

8. What are the advantages and disadvantages of using defense mechanisms? Do you think it would be possible for a person to be completely free of defense mechanisms?

9. In what ways do schools, parents, and the government encourage feelings of helplessness? In what ways do they (or could they) add to feelings of confidence, competence, or "hope"?

10. An atmosphere of competition and evaluation pervades many schools. How might this contribute to test anxiety? Do you think that the amount of testing done in schools should be increased or decreased? What alternatives would you propose if testing were decreased?

11. How do you define love? Do you believe that Sternberg's theory captures the essence of love? Why do you think our culture places so much emphasis on passion as the basis for falling in love? What are the consequences of this emphasis?

Chapter 13

Health, Stress, and Coping

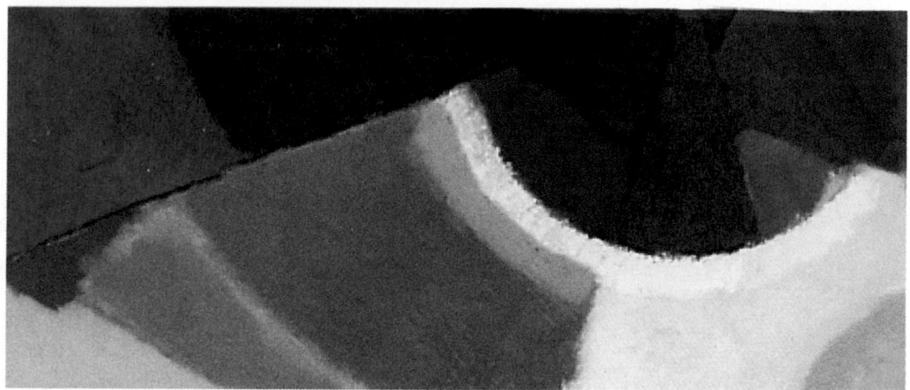

In This Chapter
Stress
Frustration
Conflict
Stress and health
General adaptation syndrome
Health psychology
Behavioral risk factors
Health-promoting behaviors
Applications
Stress management
Exploration
Meditation and relaxation

Chapter Preview

How To Build a Human Time Bomb

When he was arrested, John was sitting atop a 3-ton bulldozer, staring into space. Behind him lay a mile-long path of destruction: John had cut a broad, straight path through yards, roads, and fields. The path led back to his house where the dozer was usually kept. Why did he do it? John explained that his father had denied him use of the family car that morning. Hours later, his anger exploded.

Question: What would cause someone to react so drastically to a family disagreement?

In John's case, the answer is that he was frustrated*—very frustrated! Perhaps you have been as frustrated as John must have been when he climbed into the driver's seat. For example, picture yourself looking for a parking space in a crowded lot. Imagine that you are late for a test and have already been delayed by an irritating traffic jam. After 15 minutes of frantic searching, you finally spy an empty space, but as you start toward it, a Volkswagen darts around the corner and into "your" space. A car behind you begins to honk impatiently. Your car's radiator boils over. In such a situation, you might be seized by a colossal desire to run over anything in sight—other cars, pedestrians, lampposts, trees, and flower beds. Few people actually carry out such impulses, but the feeling is common. Aggressive urges frequently accompany frustration.*

Question: Is frustration the same as anger?

No. Frustration *can be defined as a negative emotional state that occurs when one is prevented from reaching a goal. John's desire to use the family car was blocked by his father. Similarly, in the imaginary parking lot, the goal of finding a parking space was blocked by the presence of other cars.*

Frustration is just one of many causes of stress *that we will investigate in this chapter. Stress occurs whenever a challenge or a threat forces a person to* adjust *or* adapt. *Stress is a normal part of life. But when stress is severe or prolonged it can do tremendous damage to one's health. In the first part of this chapter we will look closely at what stress is and how it affects us. Later, we will explore other factors that affect health and well-being. And finally, we will look at effective ways of coping with stress.*

Survey Questions

- What is the nature of stress?
- What kinds of factors determine the severity of stress?
- What causes frustration, and what are typical reactions to it?
- Are there different types of conflict? How do people react to conflict?
- How is stress related to health and disease?
- What is health psychology?
- Aside from stress, what other behavioral factors affect health? What can be done to promote health?
- What are the best strategies for managing stress?
- Is meditation useful for coping with stress?

Stress—Thrill or Threat?

It is common to assume that stress is always bad or that a complete lack of stress is ideal. However, as stress researcher Hans Selye (1976) observed, "To be totally without stress is to be dead." As stated in the Chapter Preview, **stress** occurs anytime we must adjust or adapt to the environment. Naturally, unpleasant events such as work pressures, marital problems, or financial troubles produce stress. But so do travel, sports, a new job, mountain climbing, dating, and other pleasant activities. Even if you aren't a thrill seeker, a healthy lifestyle may include a fair amount of stress.

Your body's **stress reaction** begins with the same autonomic nervous system arousal that occurs during emotion. If you were standing at the top of a wind-whipped ski jump for the first time, and you found it stressful, we would observe a rapid surge in your heart rate, blood pressure, respiration, muscle tension, and other ANS responses. *Short-term* stresses of this kind can be uncomfortable, but they rarely do any damage. (Your landing might be another matter, however.) Later in this chapter we will describe *long-term* physical changes that accompany prolonged stress. These changes can do much harm.

Question: Other than when it is long-lasting, why is stress sometimes damaging and sometimes not?

Stress reactions are more complex than once thought. Let's examine some of the chief factors that determine whether or not stress is harmful.

When Is Stress a Strain It goes almost without saying that some events are more likely to act as **stressors** than others. Police officers, for instance, suffer from an unusually high rate of stress-related diseases. The threat of injury or death, coupled with periodic confrontations with drunk or belligerent citizens, takes a toll. A major factor here is the *unpredictable* nature of police work. An officer who stops to issue a traffic ticket never knows if a cooperative citizen or an armed fugitive is waiting in the car.

An interesting experiment involving three groups of rats shows how a lack of predictability adds to stress. In the experiment, one group was given shocks preceded by a warning tone. A second group got shocks without warning. The third group received no shocks, but heard the tone. After a few weeks, an autopsy was performed on the rats. The animals that received no shocks had no stomach ulcers. Those receiving unpredictable shocks had severe ulcers. Those given predictable shocks showed little or no ulceration (Weiss, 1972).

Pressure is another element in stress, especially job stress. **Pressure** occurs when activities must be speeded up, when deadlines must be met, when extra work is added unexpectedly, or when a person must work near maximum capacity for long periods. Most students who have survived final exams are familiar with the effects of pressure.

Question: What if I set deadlines for myself? Does it make a difference where the pressure comes from?

Yes. People generally feel more stress in situations over which they have little **control.** For example, DeGood (1975) subjected male college students to an unpleasant shock-avoidance task. Some subjects were allowed to select their own rest periods, while others rested at times selected for them. Subjects allowed to control their own rest periods showed lower stress levels (as measured by blood pressure) than those given no choice (Fig. 13–1). Notice that being unable to control stressors is very similar to the conditions that cause learned helplessness, described in Chapter 12.

The evidence we have reviewed indicates that when emotional "shocks" are *intense* or *repeated, unpredictable, uncontrollable,* and linked to *pressure,* stress will be magnified and damage is likely to result. At work, chronic stress sometimes results in **burnout,** a pattern of emotional exhaustion described in Highlight 13–1.

Appraising Stressors As important as *external* events may be, they are not the whole story where stress is concerned. As you have probably noted, some people are

Fig. 13–1 *Assembly line work can be quite stressful, because employees have little control over the pace of work.*

HIGHLIGHT 13–1
Burnout—The High Cost of Caring

A young nurse realizes with dismay that she has changed from a caring person at work to a cynic who has "lost all patience with her patients" and wishes they would "go somewhere else to be sick." Reactions like this are clear signs of job burnout, a condition that exists when an employee is physically, mentally, and emotionally drained (Farber, 1983). What does it mean to be "burned out"? Psychologist Christina Maslach (1982) has identified three aspects of the problem.

First of all, burnout involves *emotional exhaustion.* Affected persons are fatigued, tense, and apathetic, and they suffer from various physical complaints. They feel "used up" and have an "I don't give a damn anymore" attitude toward work. A second aspect of burnout is *depersonalization,* or detachment from others. "Burned-out" workers coldly treat clients as if they were objects and find it difficult to care about them. The third aspect of burnout is a feeling of *reduced personal accomplishment.* Workers who have burned out do poor work and feel helpless, hopeless, or angry. Their self-esteem suffers and they yearn to change jobs or careers.

Burnout may occur in any job, but it is a marked problem in emotionally demanding helping professions, such as nursing, teaching, social work, counseling, or police work (Farber, 1983).

The irony of burnout is that the same work that tends to produce it can also be highly challenging and rewarding. If our society wishes to keep caring, committed people in the helping professions, several changes may be needed. A good start might include redesigning jobs, workloads, and responsibilities to create a better balance between demands and satisfactions. Building stronger social support systems at work could also help. A good example is the growing use of support groups by nurses and other care-givers. Such groups allow workers to give and receive emotional support as they talk about feelings, problems, and stresses (Sully, 1983). Ultimately, however, the best solution may be for each of us to show greater understanding of the stresses felt by those whose work requires caring about the needs of others.

stressed by events that others view as a thrill or a challenge. Ultimately, stress depends on how a situation is perceived. I have a friend who would find it stressful to listen to five of his son's rock albums in a row. He has a son who would find it stressful to listen to one of his father's opera albums. To know if a person is stressed, we must know what meaning the person places on events. As you may recall from Chapter 12, whenever a stressor is appraised as a *threat,* an especially powerful stress reaction follows (Lazarus et al., 1985).

What does it mean to feel threatened by a stressor? Certainly, in most day-to-day situations it does not mean that you think your life is in danger. Threat has more to do with the idea of control. As psychologist Michael Gazzaniga says, "Animals and people are particularly prone to stress when they can't—or think they can't—control their immediate environment" (Gazzaniga, 1988). In short, a *perceived lack of control* is just as important as actual lack of control in causing us to feel threatened.

Your personal sense of control in any situation comes from believing that you can reach desired goals. Or, to state it another way, it is threatening for a person to feel that he or she lacks *competence* to cope with a particular demand (Bandura, 1986; Woolfolk & Richardson, 1978). Thus, the intensity of the body's stress reaction often depends on what we think and tell ourselves about stressors. This is why it can be valuable to train yourself to think in ways that avoid triggering the body's stress response (Gazzaniga, 1988). (Some strategies for controlling upsetting thoughts are described in this chapter's Applications section.)

We will soon return to another look at stress and its effects. But first, let's examine two major (and all too familiar) causes of stress: frustration and conflict.

● Frustration—Blind Alleys and Lead Balloons

Question: What causes frustration?

Obstacles of many kinds cause frustration. A useful distinction can be made between *external* and *personal* sources of frustration. **External frustration** is based on conditions outside of the individual that impede progress toward a goal. All of the following are external frustrations: getting stuck with a flat tire; having a marriage proposal rejected; finding the cupboard bare when you go to get your poor dog a bone; finding the refrigerator bare when you go to get your poor tummy a T-bone; finding the refrigerator gone when you return home; being chased out of the house by your starving dog. In other words, external frustrations are based on *delay, failure, rejection, loss,* and other direct blocking of motives.

Notice that external obstacles can be either *social* (slow drivers, tall people in theaters, people who cut into lines) or *nonsocial* (stuck doors, a dead battery, rain on the day of the game). If you ask 10 of your friends what has frustrated them recently, most will probably mention someone's behavior ("My sister wore one of my dresses when I wanted to wear it," "My supervisor is unfair," "My history teacher grades too hard"). As social animals, we humans are highly sensitive to social sources of frustration.

Frustration usually increases as the **strength, urgency,** or **importance** of a blocked motive increases. An escape artist submerged in a tank of water and bound with 200 pounds of chain would become *quite* frustrated by the jamming of a trick lock. Remember too that motivation becomes stronger as we near a goal. As a result, frustration is more intense when a person runs into an obstacle very close to a goal. If you've ever missed an A grade by 2 points, you were probably very frustrated. If you've missed an A by 1 point—well, frustration builds character, right?

A final factor affecting frustration is summarized by the old phrase "the straw that broke the camel's back." The effects of *repeated* frustrations can accumulate until a small irritation sets off an unexpectedly violent response. The boy who bulldozed the countryside (see Chapter Preview) probably had been frustrated many times before by his father.

Personal frustrations are based on personal characteristics. If you are 4 feet tall and aspire to be a professional basketball player, you very likely will be frustrated. If you want to go to medical school, but can earn only D grades, you will likewise be frustrated. In both examples, frustration is actually based on personal limitations. Yet, failure may be *perceived* as externally caused. We will return to this point in the Applications section. In the meantime, let's look at some typical reactions to frustration.

Reactions to Frustration

Aggression is one of the most persistent and frequent responses to frustration (Miller, 1941). The frustration-aggression link is so common, in fact, that experiments are hardly necessary to show it. A glance at almost any newspaper will provide examples such as the one that follows.

Justifiable Autocide

Burien, Washington (AP)—Barbara Smith committed the assault, but police aren't likely to press charges. Her victim was a 1964 Oldsmobile which failed once too often to start.

When Officer Jim Fuda arrived at the scene, he found one beat-up car, a broken baseball bat and a satisfied 23-year-old Seattle woman.

"I feel good," Ms. Smith reportedly told the officer. "That car's been giving me misery for years and I killed it."

Question: Does frustration always cause aggression? Aren't there other reactions?

Although the connection is strong, frustration does not always provoke aggression. Later, in Chapter 24, we will explore factors that influence when and where aggression is likely to occur. For now, it is enough to note that aggression is not usually the first, or only, reaction to frustration. More often, frustration is met first with **persistence.** This is characterized by more **vigorous efforts** and more **variable responses.** For example, if you put your last quarter in a vending machine and find that pressing the button has no effect, you will probably press harder and faster (vigorous effort). Then you will press all the other buttons (varied response). Persistence may help you get *around* a barrier in order to reach your goal. However, if the machine *still* refuses to deliver, or return your quarter, you may become aggressive and kick the machine (or at least tell it what you think of it).

Persistence can be very adaptive. Overcoming a barrier ends the frustration and allows the need or motive to be satisfied. The same is true of aggression that removes or destroys a barrier. Picture a small band of primitive humans, parched by thirst but separated from a water hole by a menacing animal. It is easy to see that attacking the animal may ensure their survival. In modern society such direct aggression is seldom acceptable. If you find a long line at the drinking fountain, aggression is hardly an appropriate response. Because direct aggression is disruptive and generally discouraged, it is frequently *displaced.*

Question: How is aggression displaced? Does displaced aggression occur often?

Directing aggression toward a source of frustration may be impossible, or it may be too dangerous. If you are frustrated by your boss at work or by a teacher at school, the cost of direct aggression may be too high (losing your job or failing a needed class). Instead, the aggression may be displaced, or *redirected,* toward whomever or whatever is available.

Targets of **displaced aggression** tend to be safer, or less likely to retaliate, than the original source of frustration. Bulldozing the countryside when the real source of frustration was one's father is a clear case of displaced aggression. Sometimes long *chains* of displacement occur, in which one person displaces aggression to the next. For instance, a businesswoman who is frustrated by high taxes reprimands an employee, who swallows his anger until he reaches home and then yells at his wife, who in turn yells at the children, who then tease the dog. The dog chases the cat, who later knocks over the canary cage.

Psychologists attribute much hostility and destructiveness in our society to displaced aggression. A disturbing example is the finding that when unemployment increases, so does child abuse (Steinberg et al., 1981). A pattern known as **scapegoating** is particularly damaging. A scapegoat is a person who has become a habitual target of displaced aggression. A tragic example of scapegoating on a large scale is the fact that in the United States between 1880 and 1930 there was a strong correlation between the price of cotton and the number of lynchings of blacks in the South. As the price of cotton went down (and frustration increased), the number of lynchings increased (Dollard et al., 1939). Despite recent progress,

Fig. 13–2 *Frustration and reactions to it.*

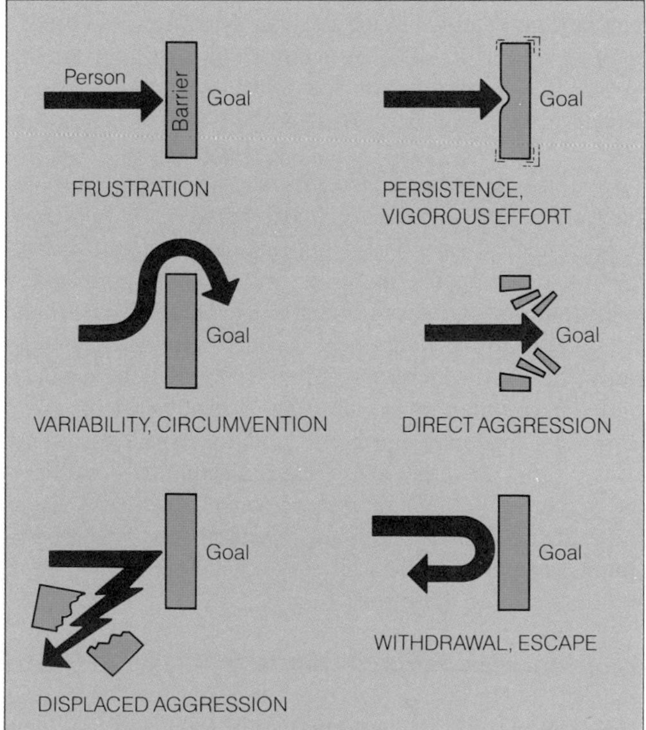

many minority groups continue to suffer from hostility based on scapegoating. Think, for example, about the hostility that was expressed toward Arabic persons in the United States at the time when Americans were being held hostage in Iran.

Question: I have a friend who dropped out of school to hitchhike around the country. He seemed very frustrated before he quit. What type of response to frustration is this?

Another major reaction to frustration is **escape,** or **withdrawal.** It is stressful and unpleasant to be frustrated. If other reactions do not reduce feelings of frustration, a person may try to escape. Escape may mean actually leaving a source of frustration (dropping out of school, quitting a job, leaving an unhappy marriage), or it may mean *psychologically* escaping. Two common forms of psychological escape are *apathy* (pretending not to care) and the *use of drugs* such as alcohol, marijuana, or narcotics. (See Fig. 13–2 for a summary of common reactions to frustration.)

● Conflict—Yes-No-Yes-No-Yes-No-Yes-No-Yes-No . . . Well, Maybe

Conflict occurs whenever a person must choose between *incompatible* or *contradictory* needs, desires, motives, wishes, or external demands. Choosing between college and work, marriage and single life, or study and failure are conflicts many students face. There are four basic forms of conflict. As we will see, each has its own effects and characteristics (Lewin, 1935) (see Figs. 13–3 and 13–4.)

Approach-Approach Conflicts The simplest conflict comes from having to choose between two *positive,* or desirable, alternatives. Choosing between tutti-frutti-coconut-mocha-champagne-ice and orange-marmalade-peanut butter-coffee-swirl at the ice cream parlor may throw you into a temporary conflict. However, if you really like both choices, your decision will be quickly made. Even when more important decisions are at stake, **approach-approach conflicts** tend to be the easiest to resolve. The old fable about the mule that died of thirst and starvation while standing between a bucket of water and a bucket of oats is obviously unrealistic. When both options are positive, the scales of decision are easily tipped one direction or the other.

Avoidance-Avoidance Conflicts Being forced to choose between two *negative,* or undesirable, alternatives creates an **avoidance-avoidance conflict.** A person in an avoidance conflict is caught between "the devil and the deep blue sea" or between "the frying pan and the fire." In real life, avoidance-avoidance conflicts involve such dilemmas as choosing between studying and failure, unwanted pregnancy and abortion, the dentist and tooth decay, or a monotonous job and poverty.

Question: Suppose I don't object to abortion. Or suppose that I consider any pregnancy sacred and not to be tampered with?

Like many other stressful situations, these examples can be defined as conflicts only on the basis of personal needs and values. If a woman wants to end a pregnancy and does not object to abortion, she experiences no conflict. If she would not consider abortion under any circumstances, there is no conflict.

Double avoidance conflicts often have a "damned if you do, damned if you don't" quality. In other words, both choices are negative, but *not choosing* may be impossible or equally undesirable. To illustrate, imagine the plight of a person trapped in a hotel fire 20 stories from the ground. Should the person jump from the window and almost surely die on the pavement? Or should the person try to dash through the flames and almost surely die of smoke inhalation and burns? When faced with a choice such as this, it is easy to see why people often *freeze,* finding it impossible to decide or take action. A trapped individual may first think about the window, approach it, and then back away after looking down 20 stories. Next, the person may try the door and again back away as heat and smoke billow in. In actual disasters of this sort, people are often found dead in their rooms, victims of an inability to take action.

Indecision, inaction, and freezing are not the only reactions to double avoidance conflicts. Since avoidance conflicts are stressful and rarely solved, people sometimes pull out of them entirely. This reaction, called *leaving the field,* is another form of escape. It may explain the behavior of a student the author knew who could not attend school unless he worked. However, if he worked he could not earn passing grades. His solution after much conflict and indecision? He joined the navy.

Approach-Avoidance Conflicts Approach-avoidance conflicts are also difficult to resolve. Since people seldom escape them, they are in some ways more troublesome than avoidance conflicts. A person in an **approach-avoidance conflict** is "caught" by being attracted to, and repelled by, the same goal or activity. Attraction keeps the person in the situation, but its negative aspects cause turmoil and distress. For example, a high school student arrives to pick up his date for the first time. He

Fig. 13–3 *Three basic forms of conflict.*

Fig. 13–4 *Conflict diagrams. As shown by the colored areas in the graphs, desires to approach and to avoid increase near a goal. The effects of these tendencies are depicted below each graph. The "behavior" of the ball in each example illustrates the nature of the conflict above it. An approach conflict* (left) *is easily decided. Moving toward one goal will increase its attraction (graph) and will lead to a rapid resolution. (If the ball moves in either direction, it will go all the way to one of the goals.) In an avoidance conflict* (center), *tendencies to avoid are deadlocked, resulting in inaction. In an approach-avoidance conflict* (right), *approach proceeds to the point where desires to approach and avoid cancel each other. Again, these tendencies are depicted (below) by the action of the ball. (Graphs after Miller, 1944.)*

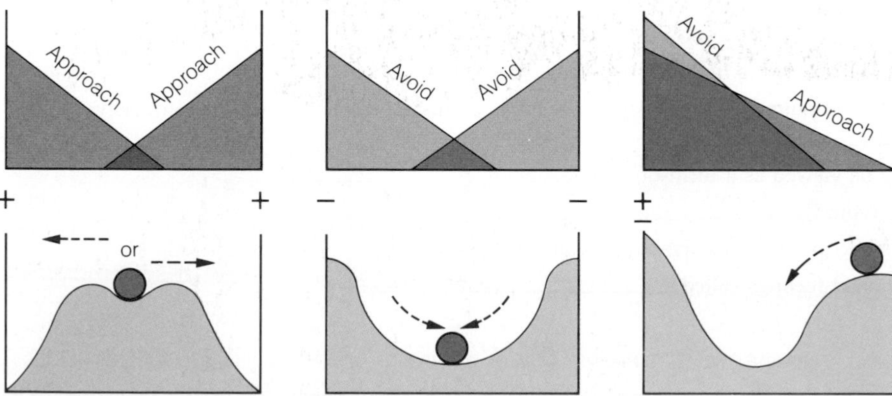

is met at the door by her father, who is a professional wrestler—7 feet tall, 300 pounds, and entirely covered with hair. The father gives the boy a crushing handshake and growls that he will break him in half if the girl is not home on time. The student considers the girl attractive and has a good time. But does he ask her out again? It depends on the relative strength of his attraction and his fear. Almost certainly he will feel *ambivalent* about asking her out again, knowing that another encounter with her father is involved.

Ambivalence (mixed positive and negative feelings) is a central characteristic of approach-avoidance conflicts. Ambivalence is usually translated into *partial approach* (Miller, 1944). Since our student is still attracted to the girl, he may spend time with her at school and elsewhere. But he may not actually date her again. Some more realistic examples of approach-avoidance conflicts are planning marriage to someone your parents strongly disapprove of, wanting to be an actor but suffering stage fright, wanting to buy a car but not wanting to make monthly payments, wanting to eat when overweight, and wanting to go to school but hating to study. Many of life's important decisions have approach-avoidance dimensions.

Question: Aren't real-life conflicts more complex than the ones described here?

Yes. In reality, conflicts are rarely as clear-cut as those described. People in conflict are usually faced with several dilemmas at once, so several types of conflict are intermingled. The fourth type of conflict moves us closer to this realistic state of affairs.

Double Approach-Avoidance Conflicts You are offered two jobs: One has good pay but poor hours and dull work; the second has interesting work and excellent hours, but low pay. Which do you select? This situation is more typical of the choices we must usually make. It offers neither completely positive nor completely negative options. It is, in other words, a **double approach-avoidance conflict,** in which each alternative has both positive and negative qualities.

As with single approach-avoidance conflicts, people faced with double approach-avoidance conflicts feel ambivalent about each choice. This causes them to **vacillate,** or waver, between the alternatives. Just as you are about to choose one such alternative, its undesirable aspects tend to loom large. So, what do you do? You swing back toward the other choice. If you have ever been romantically attracted to two people at once—each having qualities you like and dislike—then you have probably experienced vacillation.

On a day-to-day basis, most double approach-avoidance conflicts are little more than an annoyance. When they involve major life decisions, such as choosing a career, school, mate, job, or whether to have children, they add greatly to the amount of stress experienced.

Learning Check

Be sure you can answer these questions before continuing.

1. Greater perceived control over a source of stress is usually associated with a reduction in the amount of stress experienced. T or F?
2. Emotional exhaustion, depersonalization, and reduced accomplishment are characteristics of job ________________.
3. Delays, rejections, and losses may be thought of as ________________ frustrations.
4. Which of the following is *not* a common reaction to frustration?
   a. ambivalence *b.* aggression *c.* displaced aggression *d.* persistence
5. ________________ can be thought of as a type of displaced aggression.
6. Sampson Goliath is 7 feet tall and weighs 300 pounds. He has failed miserably in his aspirations to become a jockey. The source of his frustration is mainly ________________.
7. As a reaction to frustration, apathy may be viewed as a form of ________________.
8. The easiest type of conflict to resolve is typically an ________________ conflict.
9. Inaction and freezing are most characteristic of avoidance-avoidance conflicts. T or F?
10. Approach-avoidance conflicts produce mixed feelings called ________________.

Answers:
1. T **2.** burnout **3.** external **4.** *a* **5.** Scapegoating **6.** personal **7.** escape **8.** approach-approach **9.** T **10.** ambivalence

Stress and Health—Unmasking a Hidden Killer

At the University of Washington, Dr. Thomas Holmes and his associates confirmed something long suspected: Stressful events can reduce the body's natural defenses against disease. Stress, therefore, can increase the likelihood of illness (Holmes & Masuda, 1972). Holmes found that disaster and sorrow often precede illness. More surprising is the finding that almost any major *change* in one's life requires adjustment and may increase susceptibility to accidents and illness.

Question: How would I know if I were subjecting myself to too much stress?

Life Change Units Holmes and his associates developed a rating scale to estimate the health hazards faced when stresses add up. Their **Social Readjustment Rating Scale (SRRS)** is reprinted in Table 13–1. Notice that the effect of life events is expressed in **life change units (LCUs).**

As you read the scale, notice too that a positive life event may be as costly as a disaster. Marriage rates 50 life change units, even though it is usually a happy event. Notice also that many items read "Change in. . . ." This means that an improvement in life conditions can be as costly as a decline.

To use the scale, add up the LCUs for all life events you have experienced during the last year and compare the total to the following standards:

0–150: No significant problems
150–199: Mild life crisis (33 percent chance of illness)
200–299: Moderate life crisis (50 percent chance of illness)
300 or over: Major life crisis (80 percent chance of illness)

According to Holmes, there is a high chance of illness or accident in the near future when one's LCU total exceeds 300 points.

A more conservative rating of stress can be obtained by totaling LCU points for only the previous 6 months.

Table 13–1 Social Readjustment Rating Scale (SRRS).
The SRRS lists significant life events and offers a rating of their contribution to susceptibility to illness.

RANK	LIFE EVENT	LIFE CHANGE UNITS	RANK	LIFE EVENT	LIFE CHANGE UNITS
1	Death of spouse	100	22	Change in responsibilities at work	29
2	Divorce	73	23	Son or daughter leaving home	29
3	Marital separation	65	24	Trouble with in-laws	29
4	Jail term	63	25	Outstanding personal achievement	28
5	Death of a close family member	63	26	Spouse begins or stops work	26
6	Personal injury or illness	53	27	Begin or end school	26
7	Marriage	50	28	Change in living conditions	25
8	Fired at work	47	29	Revision of personal habits	24
9	Marital reconciliation	45	30	Trouble with boss	23
10	Retirement	45	31	Change in work hours or conditions	20
11	Change in health of family member	44	32	Change in residence	20
12	Pregnancy	40	33	Change in school	20
13	Sex difficulties	39	34	Change in recreation	19
14	Gain of new family member	39	35	Change in church activities	19
15	Business readjustment	39	36	Change in social activities	18
16	Change in financial state	38	37	Take out loan less than $20,000	17
17	Death of close friend	37	38	Change in sleeping habits	16
18	Change to different line of work	36	39	Change in number of family get-togethers	15
19	Change in number of arguments with spouse	35	40	Change in eating habits	15
20	Take out mortgage or loan for major purchase	31	41	Vacation	13
			42	Christmas	12
21	Foreclosure of mortgage or loan	30	43	Minor violations of the law	11

Adapted with permission from "Social readjustment rating scale," by T. H. Holmes and R. H. Rahe, *Journal of Psychosomatic Research,* 1967. Reprinted with permission from Pergamon Press, Ltd.

Studies of U.S. Navy personnel produced the figures shown here for 6-month totals (Rahe, 1972).

LCUs	Average number of illnesses reported for 6-month period
0–100	1.4
300–400	1.9
500–600	2.1

Question: Many of the listed life changes don't seem relevant to young adults or college students. Does the SRRS apply to these people?

The SRRS tends to be more appropriate for older, more established adults. However, research has shown that the health of college students is also affected by stressful events, such as entering college, changing majors, or the breakup of a steady relationship (Martin et al., 1975).

The SRRS is not a foolproof way to rate stress, and some studies have failed to confirm the LCU-illness link (Schless, 1977; Weinberger, 1987). It is also debatable whether positive life events are always stressful (Feuerstein et al., 1986). Perhaps the most important criticism of the scale is based on a point made earlier: People differ greatly in their reactions to the same event. For such reasons, the SRRS is, at best, only a rough index of stress. Nevertheless, a high LCU score should be taken seriously. If your score goes much over 300, an adjustment in your activities or lifestyle may be needed. Remember, "To be forewarned is to be forearmed."

Question: There must be more to stress than major life changes. Isn't there a link between ongoing stresses and health?

The Hazards of Hassles In addition to their immediate impact, major life changes often create a kind of "ripple effect." That is, countless daily frustrations and irritations spring from the original event. In addition, many of us face ongoing stresses at work or at home that do not involve major life changes. In view of these facts, psychologist Richard Lazarus and his associates studied the impact of minor but frequent stresses. Lazarus (1981) aptly refers to such stresses as **hassles,** or **microstressors.** Hassles are defined as distressing daily annoyances. They range from traffic jams to losing classroom notes; from an argument with a roommate to an employer's unrealistic demands.

In a year-long study, Lazarus had 100 men and women keep track of the frequency and severity of the hassles they endured. Subjects in the study also filled out questionnaires about their physical and mental health. As Lazarus had suspected, frequent and severe hassles turned out to be better predictors of day-to-day emotional and physical health than major life events were. However, major life events did predict changes in health 1 or 2 years after the events took place. It appears that daily hassles are closely linked to immediate health. Major life changes have more of a long-term impact.

In follow-up work, Lazarus and others have found that the personal importance of hassles affects the amount of stress they produce (Lazarus et al., 1985). Hassles that are viewed as central to one's self-worth are many times more likely to cause trouble. For many people, central hassles are linked to work, family, and relationships. But as psychologist Rand Gruen notes, "Taking care of paper work or being organized can be central for some people" (Fisher, 1984). This observation again emphasizes that stress occurs in people, not in the environment. Stress is always related to personality, values, perceptions, and personal resources.

Question: What can be done about a high LCU score or feeling excessively hassled?

A good response is to use stress management skills. For serious problems, stress management should be learned directly from a therapist or at a stress clinic. When ordinary stresses are involved, there is much you can do on your own. This chapter's Applications section will give you a start. In the meantime, take it easy!

Psychosomatic Disorders

As we have seen, chronic or repeated stress can damage physical health, as well as upset emotional well-being (Selye, 1976). Prolonged stress reactions are related especially to a large number of psychosomatic (SIKE-oh-so-MAT-ik) illnesses. Most people recognize that stomach ulcers are stress-related, but so are many other illnesses. In **psychosomatic disorders** (*psyche*: mind; *soma*: body), psychological factors are associated with actual damage to tissues of the body. Psychosomatic problems, therefore, are *not* the same as *hypochondria*. **Hypochondriacs** (HI-po-KON-dree-aks) *imagine* that they suffer from diseases. There is nothing imaginary about a bleeding ulcer. A severe case could be fatal. The person who says, "Oh it's *just* psychosomatic" misunderstands the seriousness of stress-related diseases.

Question: What diseases are psychosomatic? Who gets them?

The most common problems are gastrointestinal and respiratory (ulcers and asthma, for example), but there are many others. Included are problems such as eczema (skin rash), hives, migraine headaches, rheumatoid arthritis, hypertension (high blood pressure), colitis (ulceration of the colon), and heart disease. Actually, these are only the major problems. Lesser health complaints are also frequently stress-related. Typical examples include muscle tension, headaches, neckaches, backaches, indigestion, constipation, fatigue, insomnia, and sexual dysfunction (Brown, 1980; Hurst et al., 1979). It is estimated that at least half of all patients who see a doctor have a psychosomatic disorder or an illness that is complicated by psychosomatic symptoms.

It would be a mistake to assume that stress is the sole cause of psychosomatic diseases. Usually, several factors combine to produce damage. These include hereditary differences, specific organ weaknesses, and learned reactions to stress. Personality also enters the picture. To a degree, there are "ulcer personalities," "asthma personalities," and so on. The best documented of such patterns is the "cardiac personality"—a person prone to heart disease.

Fig. 13–5 *Individuals with Type A personalities feel a continuous sense of anger, irritation, and hostility.*

Type A Two noted cardiologists, Meyer Friedman and Ray Rosenman, offer a glimpse at how some people create unnecessary stress. On the basis of a long-term study of heart problems, Friedman and Rosenman (1974) classified people into two categories: **Type A personalities** (those who run a high risk of heart attack) and **Type B personalities** (those who are unlikely to have a heart attack). Friedman and Rosenman then did an 8-year follow-up, finding more than twice the rate of heart disease in Type A's than in Type B's (Rosenman et al., 1975).

Question: What is the Type A personality like?

Type A people are hard-driving, ambitious, highly competitive, achievement-oriented, and striving (Fig. 13–5). Type A people believe that with enough effort they can overcome any obstacle, and they "push" themselves accordingly. In tests of physical capacity (on a treadmill), Type A's work very close to their limits of endurance, but say they are less fatigued than Type B people do (Glass, 1977). Type A's don't know when to quit!

Perhaps the most telltale signs of a Type A personality are *time urgency* and chronic *anger* or *hostility*. Type A's seem to chafe at the normal pace of events. They hurry from one activity to another, racing the clock in self-imposed urgency. As they do, they feel a constant sense of frustration and anger. Feelings of anger and hostility, in particular, are strongly related to increased risk of heart attack (Lenfant & Schweizer, 1985).

Question: Some news reports have stated that Type A behavior is not a factor in heart attacks. Why is that?

It's true that some recent studies have failed to show a link between Type A behavior and heart attacks (Case et al., 1985). However, many researchers believe it is possible that these studies did not accurately classify people as Type A's and Type B's in the first place. There is also growing evidence that anger or hostility may be more important than other aspects of Type A behavior (Chesney & Rosenman, 1985; Friedman & Booth-Kewley, 1987; Wright, 1988). Beyond this, hundreds of studies *have* supported the validity of the Type A concept. At this point, it still seems that Type A's would be wise to take their increased health risks seriously.

Question: How are Type A people identified?

Many of the destructive habits of Type A people are summarized in the short self-identification test presented in Table 13–2. If most of the list applies to you, you may be a Type A.

A recent large-scale study of heart attack victims found that modifying Type A behavior significantly reduces the rate of repeat heart attacks (Friedman et al., 1984). Since our society places a premium on achievement, competition, and mastery, it is not surprising that many people develop Type A personalities. The best way to avoid the self-made stress this causes is to adopt behavior that is the opposite of that listed in Table 13–2 (Suinn, 1982). It is entirely possible to succeed in life without sacrificing your health in the process. (For additional hints on com-

Table 13–2 Characteristics of the Type A Person

Check the items that apply to you.

Do you:

______	Have a habit of explosively accentuating various key words in ordinary speech even when there is no need for such accentuation?
______	Finish other persons' sentences for them?
______	*Always* move, walk, and eat rapidly?
______	Quickly skim reading material and prefer summaries or condensations of books?
______	Become easily angered by slow-moving lines or traffic?
______	Feel an impatience with the rate at which most events take place?
______	Tend to be unaware of the details or beauty of your surroundings?
______	Frequently strive to think of or do two or more things simultaneously?
______	Almost always feel vaguely guilty when you relax, vacation, or do absolutely nothing for several days?
______	Tend to evaluate your worth in quantitative terms (number of A's earned, amount of income, number of games won, and so forth)?
______	Have nervous gestures or muscle twitches, such as grinding your teeth, clenching your fists, or drumming your fingers?
______	Attempt to schedule more and more activities into less time and in so doing make fewer allowances for unforeseen problems?
______	Frequently think about other things while talking to someone?
______	Repeatedly take on more responsibilities than you can comfortably handle?

Shortened and adapted from Meyer Friedman and Ray H. Rosenman, *Type A behavior and your heart* (New York: Alfred A. Knopf, 1974).

bating Type A behavior, consult Friedman and Rosenman, *Type A behavior and your heart*.)

Question: How do Type A people who do not develop heart disease differ from those who do?

Hardy Personality For the last 10 years, psychologists Salvatore Maddi and Suzanne Kobasa (1984) have studied people who have what they call a **hardy personality.** Such people seem to be unusually resistant to stress. Maddi and Kobasa's studies began with a comparison of two groups of managers at a large utility company. All of the managers held high-stress positions. Yet, some tended to get sick after stressful events, while others were rarely ill. How did the people who were thriving differ from their "stressed-out" colleagues? Both groups seemed to have traits typical of the Type A personality, so that wasn't the explanation. They were also quite similar in most other respects. The main difference was that the hardy group seemed to hold a world view that consisted of the following:

1. They had a sense of personal *commitment* to self, work, family, and other stabilizing values.
2. They felt that they had *control* over their lives and their work.
3. They had a tendency to see life as a series of *challenges*, rather than as a series of threats or problems.

These traits seemed to allow the hardy personality to transcend stresses. Some aspects of this research have been criticized, and further study is needed on the nature of hardiness (Hull et al., 1987). But the message is clear that a willingness to commit yourself to active coping can do much to change stress into a healthy challenge.

A very basic question remains unanswered in our discussion of stress. How does stress, and our response to it, translate into bodily damage? The answer seems to lie in the body's defense against stress, a pattern known as the *general adaptation syndrome*.

The General Adaptation Syndrome

Study of the **general adaptation syndrome** (G.A.S.) began when Canadian physiologist Hans Selye (1976) noticed that the first symptoms of almost any disease or trauma (poisoning, infection, injury, or stress) are almost identical. After more research, Selye concluded that the body responds in the same way to any stress, be it infection, failure, embarrassment, adjustment to a new job, trouble at school, or a stormy romance.

Question: What pattern does the body's response to stress take?

The G.A.S. consists of three stages: an *alarm reaction,* a *stage of resistance,* and a *stage of exhaustion* (Selye, 1976).

In the **alarm reaction,** the body mobilizes its resources to cope with added stress. The pituitary gland secretes a hormone that causes the adrenal glands to step up their output of adrenaline and noradrenaline. As these hormones are dumped into the bloodstream, some bodily processes are speeded up and others are slowed so that bodily resources are applied where they are needed.

We should all be thankful that our bodies instantly and automatically respond to emergencies. But brilliant as this automatic emergency system is, it can also cause problems (Wilson, 1986). In the first phase of the alarm reaction, people have such symptoms as headache, fever, fatigue, sore muscles, shortness of breath, diarrhea, upset stomach, loss of appetite, and lack of energy. Notice that these are also the symptoms of being sick, of stressful travel, of high-altitude sickness, of final exam week, and (possibly) of falling in love!

Soon the body's defenses are stabilized, and symptoms of the alarm reaction disappear. Physically, the body has made adjustments to resist stress. However, the outward appearance of normality comes at a high cost. During the **stage of resistance,** the body is better able to cope with the original source of stress (Fig. 13–6), but its resistance to other stresses is lowered. For example, animals placed in an extremely cold environment become more resistant to the cold, but more susceptible to infection. It is during the stage of resistance that the first signs of psychosomatic disorders begin to appear.

If stress continues, the **stage of exhaustion** may be reached. In this stage the body's resources are exhausted and the stress hormones are depleted. Unless a way of relieving stress is found, the result will be a psychosomatic disease, a serious loss of health, or complete collapse.

The stages of the G.A.S. may sound melodramatic if you are young and healthy or if you have never endured prolonged stress. However, stress should not be taken lightly. When Selye examined animals in the later stages of the G.A.S., he found enlargement and discoloration of their adrenal glands, intense shrinkage of the thymus, spleen, and lymph nodes, and deep bleeding stomach ulcers (Cox, 1978). In addition to such direct effects, stress can disrupt the body's **immune system,** making people more vulnerable to illness (Jemmott & Locke, 1984) (see Highlight 13–2).

Fig. 13–6 *The General Adaptation Syndrome. During the initial alarm reaction to stress, resistance falls below normal. It rises again as bodily resources are mobilized, and it remains high during the stage of resistance. Eventually, resistance falls again as the stage of exhaustion is reached. (From* The stress of life *by Hans Selye. Copyright © 1956, 1976 by Hans Selye. Used by permission of McGraw-Hill Book Company.)*

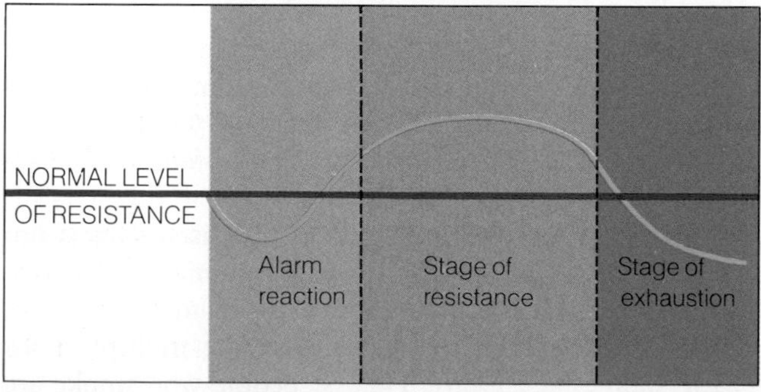

● HIGHLIGHT 13–2
Stress and the Immune System

Health experts are beginning to uncover fascinating evidence that the body and the brain work together as a kind of "health care system." It is now becoming clear that the body's immune system is regulated, in part, by the brain (Ader, 1981; Schwartz, 1984). Because of this link, stress, upsetting thoughts, and emotions may affect the immune system in ways that increase susceptibility to disease (Gazzaniga, 1988; McCabe & Schneiderman, 1984; Schwartz, 1984). (By the way, this area of research is called *psychoneuroimmunology*. Try dropping that into a conversation some time if you want to observe a stress reaction!)

Interestingly, control again appears to be an important factor in how stress affects us. For instance, one recent study found that the immune system's response was suppressed in rats given inescapable shocks. However, rats given escapable shocks did not show this effect (Laudenslager et al., 1983). Another study found that the immune system was weakened in students during stressful major exam times (Jemmott et al., 1983). Findings such as these suggest that part of the link between stress and illness may be traced to changes in the immune system. This is probably why the "double whammy" of getting sick when you are trying to cope with stress is so common.

Learning Check

1. Holmes' SRRS appears to predict long-range changes in health, whereas the frequency and severity of daily hassles is closely related to immediate ratings of health. T or F?

2. Ulcers, migraine headaches, and hypochondria are all frequently psychosomatic disorders. T or F?

3. Evidence is beginning to suggest that the most important feature of the Type A personality is a sense of time urgency rather than feelings of anger and hostility. T or F?

4. Which of the following is *not* classified as a psychosomatic disorder?
a. hypertension *b.* colitis *c.* eczema *d.* thymus

5. A sense of commitment, challenge, and control characterizes the hardy personality. T or F?

6. The first stage of the G.A.S. is called the ________________ reaction.

7. Most outward symptoms of stress disappear during the stage of ________________.

8. Suppression of the immune system is lessened when a person realizes he or she has no control over stressful events. T or F?

Answers:

1. T 2. F 3. F 4. *d* 5. T 6. alarm 7. resistance 8. F

Health Psychology—Here's to Your Good Health

Most people agree that health is important—especially their own. Yet, almost one-half of all deaths in the United States are primarily due to unhealthy behavior or lifestyles. A new specialty called **health psychology** aims to do something about it. The core of this approach is the use of psychological principles to promote health and to prevent illness (Matarazzo, 1984). Psychologists working in the allied field of **behavioral medicine** apply psychological knowledge to medical problems. Their interests include the control of pain, adjustment to chronic illness, adherence to doctors' instructions, psychosomatic disease, and similar topics (Feuerstein et al., 1986).

Behavioral Risk Factors

Around the turn of the century, people primarily died from infectious diseases and accidents. Today, people generally suffer and die from "lifestyle" illnesses, such as heart disease, stroke, lung cancer, and similar problems (Patton et al., 1986). Clearly, some behaviors and lifestyles promote health, whereas others increase the likelihood of illness and death (Matarazzo, 1984).

Question: What kinds of behavior are you referring to as unhealthy?

Although some causes of poor health are beyond our control, health psychologists have identified a number of major **behavioral risk factors** that *can* be controlled. One reason that we have paid so much attention to stress in this chapter is because it plays a key role in many health problems. This is also why stress management is a major activity in health psychology (Feuerstein et al., 1986). In addition to stress, each of the following behavioral factors increases the chances of accident, disease, and early death: untreated high blood pressure, cigarette smoking, abuse of alcohol or other drugs, overeating, underexercise, Type A behavior, and driving at excessive speeds (Matarazzo, 1984; Miller, 1983).

Lifestyle In your mind's eye, fast-forward an imaginary film of your life all the way to old age. Do it twice—once with a lifestyle including a large number of behavioral risk factors, and the second time without them. It should be obvious that when countless small risks add up, they dramatically raise the chance of illness. If you smoke, picture a lifetime's worth of cigarette smoke blown through your lungs in a week or a day. If you drink, take a lifetime of alcohol's assaults on the brain, stomach, and liver and squeeze them into a month: Your body would be poisoned, ravaged, and soon dead. If you eat a high-fat, high-cholesterol diet, fast-forward a lifetime of heart-killing plaque building up in your arteries (Fig. 13–7).

Although it may sound like it, this discussion is not meant to be a sermon. It is merely a reminder that risk factors do make a difference. To make matters worse, unhealthy lifestyles almost always create multiple risks (Feuerstein et al., 1986). That is, people who smoke are

Fig. 13–7 *In the long run, behavioral risk factors and lifestyles do make a difference in health and life expectancy.*

also likely to drink excessively. Those who overeat usually do not get enough exercise, and so on (Matarazzo, 1984).

Health-Promoting Behaviors

To help prevent disease and promote well-being, health psychologists first try to remove behavioral risk factors. All the medicine or surgery in the world may not be enough to restore health without such changes in behavior. We all know someone who has had a heart attack or lung disease and who can not or will not change the habits that have contributed to their illness (Matarazzo, 1984).

Beyond this, psychologists are also interested in increasing behaviors that actively promote health. Health-promoting behaviors include such obvious practices as getting regular exercise, maintaining a balanced diet, and managing stress. Health-promoting behaviors can also be as simple as using seat belts in a car—a practice that greatly ups life expectancy!

Common sense suggests that basic health practices should extend a person's life. But do they? A major study done in Alameda County, California, provides an answer (Belloc, 1973; Belloc & Breslow, 1972; Breslow & Enstrom, 1980). In this study, nearly 7000 people were given a detailed health questionnaire that focused on 7 basic health practices. In ensuing years the health and death records of these people were closely watched. Before we discuss the results, you might find it interesting to check the items listed here that apply to you.

Basic Health-Promoting Behaviors

1. I get 7 to 8 hours of sleep a night.
2. I am currently at or near the ideal weight for my height.
3. I have never smoked cigarettes.
4. I use alcohol moderately or not at all.
5. I get regular physical exercise.
6. I eat breakfast almost every day.
7. I never or rarely eat between meals.

The authors of this study found that men who engaged in all 7 health practices had a death rate almost 4 times lower than that of men who engaged in 0 to 3 practices. The comparable death rate for women who engaged in all 7 practices was 2 times lower than that for women who engaged in 0 to 3 practices. To state the results another way, a 45-year-old male who regularly engages in only 3 of the behaviors has a remaining life expectancy of about 22 years. A man of the same age who maintains 6 or 7 of the health practices has a remaining life expectancy of 33 years. That's a 50 percent increase in life expectancy.

Later work has shown that the first 5 practices are the most important for predicting health. You should note, however, that these are not the only elements of a healthy lifestyle. They are just the ones investigated in this particular study (Matarazzo, 1984).

Prevention and Health Campaigns Smoking has been called "the largest preventable cause of death in the U.S." (Lichtenstein & Brown, 1982). It is clearly the single most lethal behavioral risk factor (Matarazzo, 1984). As such, smoking provides a good example of the behavioral possibilities for preventing illness.

Question: What have health psychologists done to lessen the risks?

A Way to Change Your Habits:

SELF MONITORING

Before you can make any changes, you need to know how much of something you are already doing, such as smoking, eating or exercising.

We have all known people who kept gaining weight on their diets while swearing up and down that they never eat. Their problem was that they were not keeping track of how much they were really eating.

Here are the steps to help you find out what you are doing. Just keeping track may help you decide to make a change.

STEP 1:
Decide which habit you want to watch.

CAUTION: *Keep track of only one habit at a time. You should not try to quit smoking, lose weight and increase your exercise all at the same time.*

Fig. 13–8 *The page shown here is reproduced from a booklet prepared as part of a public health campaign conducted in southern Arizona. Such campaigns promote health by calling attention to psychological risk factors and by telling what to do about them. (From Marques et al., 1982.)*

● HIGHLIGHT 13–3
Have a Heart

A good example of a community health campaign in action is the Stanford Heart Disease Prevention Program (Meyer et al., 1980). In the Stanford project, a media campaign about risk factors in heart disease—smoking, diet, and exercise—was combined with special group "workshops" for high-risk individuals. The program's success can be seen in the fact that after 2 years, the number of smokers decreased by 17 percent in two test communities. Compare this figure with the 12 percent *increase* observed in similar, untreated communities.

Such progress may seem modest, but it is, in fact, worthwhile, cost-effective, and highly promising (Foreyt, 1987; Miller, 1983). Overall, results of the project show a 15 percent reduction in risk of heart disease in the target cities (Farquhar et al., 1984). All you have to do is picture someone you love staying healthy or living longer to appreciate the value of such efforts.

Recent attempts to "immunize" youths against pressures to start smoking provide a glimpse of health psychology in action. The smoker who says, "Quitting is easy, I've done it dozens of times" states a basic truth—giving up smoking is very difficult. In fact, only 1 smoker in 10 has long-term success. Thus, the best way to deal with smoking may be to prevent it before it becomes a lifelong habit. In one prevention program, junior high students were given "standard" information on the unhealthy effects of smoking. Then, to add to the program's impact, the students *role played* ways to resist pressures from peers, adults, and cigarette advertisements. Follow-up checks indicated that students who did the role playing were only half as likely to begin smoking as were students in a control group (Hurd et al., 1980).

In addition to small projects like the one described, health psychologists have had some success with **community health campaigns.** These are education projects designed to lessen a combination of major risk factors (see Highlight 13–3 and Fig. 13–8).

The work we have reviewed here has drawn new attention to the fact that each of us has a personal responsibility for maintaining and promoting health (Patton et al., 1986). In the Applications section that follows, we will return to the topic of stress for a look at what you can do to better manage and cope with this major health risk. But first, the following Learning Check may help you maintain a healthy grade on your next psychology test.

Learning Check

1. Adjustment to chronic illness and the control of pain are topics that would more likely be of interest to a specialist in ____________ ____________ rather than to a health psychologist.
2. With respect to health, which of the following is *not* a major behavioral risk factor?
   a. overexercise *b.* cigarette smoking *c.* Type A behavior *d.* high blood pressure
3. Eating breakfast almost every day and rarely eating between meals proved to be the two most important health-promoting behaviors in the Alameda County study. T or F?
4. Health psychologists tend to prefer ____________ rather than later modification of habits (like smoking) that become difficult to break once they are established.
5. Many of the links between stress, emotion, and health are now believed to be related to changes in the activity of the body's ____________ system.

Answers:
1. behavioral medicine **2.** *a* **3.** F **4.** prevention **5.** immune

Applications: Stress Management

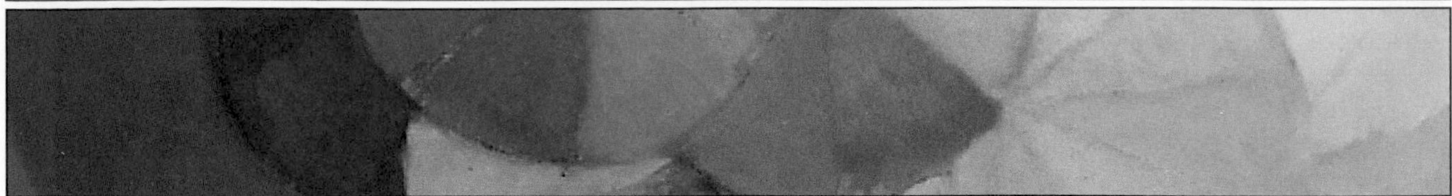

The simplest way of coping with stress is to modify or remove its source—by leaving a stressful job, for example. Obviously, this is often impossible, which is why learning to manage stress is so important.

As shown in Figure 13–9, stress triggers *bodily effects, upsetting thoughts,* and *ineffective behavior*. Also shown is the fact that each element worsens the others in a vicious cycle. Indeed, the basic idea of the "Stress Game" is that once it begins, *you lose*—unless you take action to break the cycle. The information that follows tells how. (Stress management techniques are derived from Davis et al., 1980; Meichenbaum, 1977; Woolfolk & Richardson, 1978; and other sources as indicated.)

Bodily Reactions

Much of the immediate discomfort of stress is caused by the body's fight-or-flight emotional response. The body is ready to act, with tight muscles and a pounding heart. When action is prevented, we merely remain "uptight." A sensible remedy is to learn a reliable, drug-free way of relaxing.

Exercise Because stress prepares the body for action, its effects can be dissipated by using the body. Any full-body exercise can be effective. Swimming, dancing, jumping rope, yoga, most sports, and especially walking are valuable outlets. Be sure to choose activities that are vigorous enough to relieve tension, yet enjoyable enough to be done repeatedly. Exercising for stress management is most effective when it is done daily.

Meditation Many stress counselors recommend meditation for quieting the body and promoting relaxation. We will consider meditation techniques and their effects in the upcoming Explorations section. For now, it is enough to note that meditation is easy to learn—taking an expensive commercial course is unnecessary. Also be aware that listening to or playing music, taking nature walks, enjoying hobbies, and the like can be meditations of sorts.

Progressive Relaxation Progressive relaxation refers to a method in which people learn to relax systematically, completely, and by choice. To learn the full technique, consult Chapter 22 of this book. The basic idea is to tighten all the muscles in a given area of the body (the arms, for instance) and then voluntarily relax them. By first tensing and relaxing each area of the body, you can learn to be highly aware of how muscle tension feels. Then when each area is relaxed, the change is more noticeable and more controllable. In this way it is possible, with practice, to greatly reduce tension.

Ineffective Behavior

Stress is often made worse by our response to it. The following suggestions may help you deal with stress more effectively.

Slow Down Remember that stress can be self-generated. Try to deliberately do things at a slower pace—especially if your pace has speeded up over the years. Tell yourself, "What counts most is not if I get there first, but if I get there at all" or, "My goal is distance, not speed."

Organize Disorganization creates stress. Try to take a fresh look at your situation and get organized. Setting priorities can be a real stress fighter. Ask yourself what's really important and concentrate on the things that count. Learn to let go of trivial but upsetting irritations. And above all, when you are feeling stressed, remember to K.I.S.: **K**eep **I**t **S**imple.

Strike a Balance Work, school, family, friends, interests, hobbies, recreation, community, church—there are many important elements in a satisfying life. Damaging stress often comes from letting one element—especially work or school—get blown out of proportion. Your goal should be quality in life, not quantity. Try to strike a balance between challenging "good stress" and relaxation. Remember, when you are "doing nothing," you are actually doing something very important: Set aside time for "me acts" such as loafing, browsing, puttering, playing, and napping.

Recognize and Accept Your Limits Many of us set unrealistic and perfectionistic goals. Given that no one can ever be perfect, this attitude leaves many people feeling inadequate, no matter how well they have performed. Set gradual, achievable goals for yourself. Also, set realistic limits on what you try to do on any given day. Learn to say no to added demands or responsibilities.

Seek Social Support Recent studies have shown that close, positive relationships with others facilitate good health and morale (Cobb, 1976). One reason for this is that support from family and friends serves as a buffer to cushion the impact of

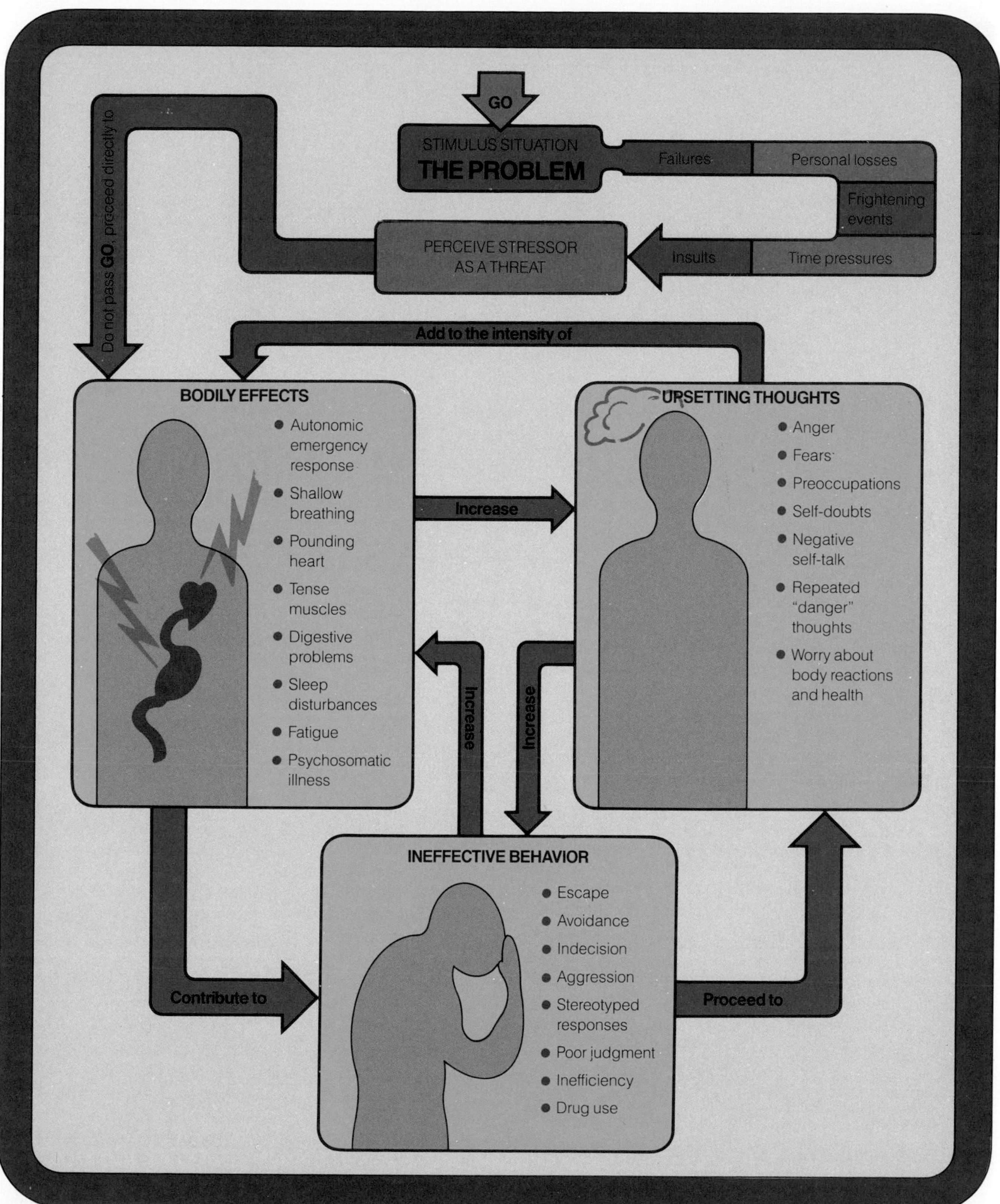

Fig. 13–9 *The stress game.* (Adapted from Rosenthal and Rosenthal, 1980.)

Applications

stressful events (Paradine et al., 1981). Talking out problems and expressing tensions can be incredibly helpful. If things really get bad, seek help from a therapist, counselor, or clergyman (please note that bartender is not on the list).

Upsetting Thoughts

Assume you are taking a test. Suddenly you realize that you are running short of time. If you say to yourself, "Oh no, this is terrible, I've blown it now," your body's response will probably be sweating, tenseness, and a knot in your stomach. On the other hand, if you say, "I should have watched the time, but getting upset won't help now, I'll just take one question at a time," your stress level will be much lower.

As stated earlier, stress is greatly affected by the views we take of events. Physical symptoms and a tendency to make poor decisions are increased by negative thoughts or "self-talk." In many cases what you say to yourself can be the difference between coping and collapsing.

Coping Statements Donald Meichenbaum of the University of Waterloo, Canada, has popularized a technique called **stress inoculation.** In it, clients learn to fight fear and anxiety with an internal monologue of positive **coping statements.** First, clients learn to identify and monitor **negative self-statements.** Negative, self-critical thoughts are a problem because they tend to directly elevate physical arousal (Schuele & Wiesenfeld, 1983). To counter this effect, clients learn to replace negative statements with coping statements from a supplied list. Eventually they are encouraged to make their own lists.

Question: How are coping statements applied?

Coping statements are used to block out, or counteract, negative self-talk in stressful situations. Before giving a short speech, for instance, you would replace "I'm scared," "I can't do this," "My mind will go blank and I'll panic," or "I'll sound stupid and boring" with "I'll give my speech on something I like," or "I'll breathe deeply before I start my speech," or "My pounding heart just means I'm psyched up to do my best." Additional examples of coping statements follow.

Preparing for Stressful Situation

I'll just take things one step at a time.
If I get nervous I'll just pause a moment.
Tomorrow I'll be through it.
I've managed to do this before.
What exactly do I have to do?

Confronting the Stressful Situation

Relax now, this can't really hurt me.
Stay organized, focus on the task.
There's no hurry, take it step by step.
Nobody's perfect, I'll just do my best.
It will be over soon, just be calm.

Meichenbaum cautions that saying the "right" things to yourself may not be enough to improve stress tolerance. You must practice this approach in actual stress situations. Also, it is important to develop your own personal list of coping statements by finding what works for you. Ultimately, the value of learning this, and other stress management skills, ties back into the idea that much stress is self-generated. Knowing that you can manage a demanding situation is in itself a major antidote for stress.

Coping with Frustration and Conflict

A psychologist studying frustration placed rats on a small platform at the top of a tall pole. Then he forced them to jump off the platform toward two elevated doors, one locked and the other unlocked. If the rat chose the correct door, it swung open and he landed safely on another platform. If he chose the locked door, he bounced off it and fell into a net far below.

The problem of choosing the open door was made unsolvable and very frustrating by randomly alternating which door was locked. After a time, most rats adopted a stereotyped response. That is, they chose the same door every time. This door was then permanently locked. All the rat had to do was jump to the other door to avoid a fall, but time after time the rat bounced off the locked door (Maier, 1949).

Question: Isn't this an example of persistence?

No. Persistence that is not *flexible* can become "stupid," stereotyped behavior like that of a rat on a jumping stand. It is important when dealing with frustration to know when to quit and establish a new direction. Here are some suggestions to help you avoid needless frustration:

1. Try to identify the source of your frustration. Is it external or personal?
2. Is the source of frustration something that can be changed? How hard would you have to work to change it? Is it under your control at all?
3. If the source of your frustration can be changed or removed, are the necessary efforts worth it?

The answers to these questions help determine if persistence will be futile. There is value in learning to accept gracefully those things that cannot be changed.

It is also important to distinguish between *real* barriers and

Applications

imagined barriers. All too often we create our own imaginary barriers. For example:

> Anita wants a part-time job to earn extra money. At the first place she applied, she was told that she didn't have enough "experience." Now she complains of being frustrated because she wants to work but cannot. She needs "experience" to work, but can't get experience without working. She has quit looking for a job.

Is Anita's need for experience a real barrier? Unless she applies for *many* jobs it is impossible to tell if she has overestimated its importance. For her the barrier is real enough to prevent further efforts, but with persistent looking she might locate an "unlocked door." If a reasonable amount of persistence does show that experience is essential, it might be obtained in other ways—through temporary volunteer work, for instance.

Question: How can I handle conflicts more effectively?

Most of the suggestions just made also apply to conflict. However, here are some additional things to remember when you are in conflict or must make a difficult decision:

1. Don't be hasty when making important decisions. Take time to collect information and to weigh pros and cons. Hasty decisions are often regretted. Even if you do make a faulty decision, it will trouble you less if you know that you did everything possible to avoid a mistake.

2. Try out important decisions *partially* when possible. If you are thinking about moving to a new town, try to spend a few days there first. If you are choosing between colleges, do the same. If classes are in progress, sit in on some. If you want to learn to skin-dive, rent equipment for a reasonable length of time before buying.

3. Look for workable compromises. Again it is important to get all available information. If you think that you have only one or two alternatives and they are undesirable or unbearable, seek the aid of a teacher, counselor, minister, or social service agency. You may be overlooking possible alternatives these people will know about.

4. When all else fails, make a decision and live with it. Indecision and conflict exact a high cost. Sometimes it is best to select a course of action and stick with it unless it is very obviously wrong after you have taken it.

In class you may want to describe some of the frustrations and conflicts you have experienced and how you handled them. Prepare to discuss frustrations and conflicts you have resolved unusually effectively or that you might have handled better. Do you have some additional hints to share with other students?

Learning Check

1. Exercise, meditation, and progressive relaxation are considered effective ways of countering negative self-statements. T or F?

2. Research shows that social support from family and friends has little effect on the health consequences of stress. T or F?

3. One element of stress inoculation is training in the use of positive coping statements. T or F?

4. Stereotyped responding can be particularly troublesome in coping with frustration. T or F?

Answers:

1. F 2. F 3. T 4. T

Exploration: Meditation—The Twenty-Minute Vacation

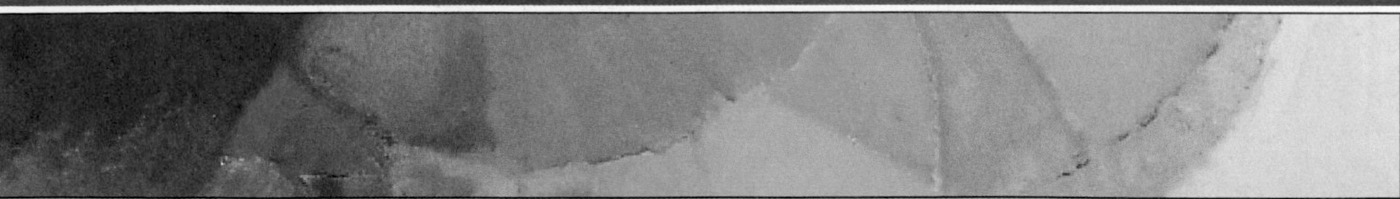

Meditation refers to a family of mental exercises designed to focus attention in a way that interrupts the typical flow of thoughts, worries, and analysis (Shapiro, 1984; Wilson, 1986). Meditation takes many forms and has many meanings in various cultures. Here we are interested in meditation as a self-control strategy for lowering physical and mental arousal. People who regularly use meditation as a stress reduction technique often report less daily physical arousal and anxiety. Even if meditation is not practiced daily, it may be a useful technique for interrupting worries and fearful thinking (Wilson, 1986).

Meditation takes two major forms. In **concentrative meditation,** attention is given to a single focal point, such as an object, a thought, or one's own breathing. In contrast, **receptive meditation** is "open," or expansive. That is, attention is widened to include a nonjudgmental awareness of one's total subjective experience and presence in the world (Walsh, 1984). An example of this type of meditation is losing all self-consciousness while walking in the wilderness with a quiet and receptive mind. Although it may not seem so, receptive meditation is regarded as more difficult to attain than concentrative meditation (Smith, 1986). For this reason, we will discuss concentrative meditation as a practical self-control method.

Question: How is concentrative meditation done?

Concentrative Meditation The basic idea in concentrative meditation is to sit still and quietly focus on some external object or on a repetitive internal stimulus such as a word or your own breathing (Wilson, 1986). In one experiment, college students were instructed to concentrate on breathing:

> While you are sitting, let your breath become relaxed and natural. Let it set its own pace and depth if you can. Then focus your attention on your own breathing: the movements of your belly, not your nose and throat. Do not allow extraneous thoughts or stimuli to pull your attention away from your breathing. This may be hard to do at first, but keep directing your attention back to it. Turn everything else aside if it comes up. (Maupin, 1965)

Not all subjects responded to this exercise, but at the end of a 2-week period, those who did reported experiences of deep concentration, pleasant bodily sensations, and extreme detachment from outside worries and distractions.

An alternative approach you may want to try involves the use of a **mantra.** Mantras are smooth, flowing words that are easily repeated. Instead of focusing on breathing, you can silently repeat a mantra. Two widely used mantras are "om" and "om mani padme hum." Like breathing, a mantra is basically used as a focus for attention. If other thoughts arise during meditation, one should return attention to the mantra as often as necessary to maintain meditation.

The Relaxation Response A principal claim of many commercial meditation courses is that they offer a mantra tailored to the needs of each individual. But medical researcher Herbert Benson found that the physical benefits of meditation are the same no matter what word is used. These include lowered heart rate, blood pressure, muscle tension, and other signs of stress.

Benson believes that the core of meditation is the **relaxation response.** By this he means an innate physiological pattern that opposes activation of the body's fight-or-flight mechanisms. Benson feels, quite simply, that most of us have forgotten how to relax deeply. Subjects in his experiments have had considerable success in producing the relaxation response by following these instructions:

> Sit quietly in a comfortable position. Close your eyes. Deeply relax all your muscles, beginning at your feet and progressing up to your face. Keep them deeply relaxed.
>
> Breathe through your nose. Become aware of your breathing. As you breathe out, say the word "one" silently to yourself.
>
> Do not worry about whether you are successful in achieving a deep level of relaxation. Maintain a passive attitude and permit relaxation to occur at its own pace. Expect distracting thoughts. When these distracting thoughts occur, ignore them and continue repeating "one." (Adapted from Benson, 1977)

Question: What effects does medita-

Exploration

tion have, other than producing relaxation?

Effects of Meditation Many extravagant claims have been made about meditation. For example, members of the Transcendental Meditation (TM) movement have stated that 20 minutes of meditation is as restful as a full night's sleep. This, however, is simply not true. One recent study, for instance, found that merely "resting" for 20 minutes produces the same bodily effects as meditation (Holmes, 1984; Holmes et al., 1983). Long-term meditators have also claimed improvement in memory, alertness, creativity, and intuition. Again, such claims must be judged cautiously. Most are based on personal testimonials or poorly controlled studies. Contrary to such claims, a study by Warrenburg and Pagano (1983) found no improvement in verbal, musical, or spatial skills that could be linked to TM.

Before you dismiss meditation, however, let's explore a little further. A thorough review of studies on meditation leads to a number of interesting conclusions (Pagano & Warrenburg, 1983).

As already stated, meditation does reliably elicit the relaxation response. The fact that other activities will do the same does not cancel the value of meditation as a way to control relaxation. Also, it is important to remember that relaxation is mental as well as physical. As a stress control technique, meditation may be a good choice for people who find it difficult to "turn off" upsetting thoughts when they need to relax (Smith, 1986).

Regular meditators consistently report lower levels of day-to-day stress and a greater sense of well-being. This effect appears to be genuine. It cannot be explained as a placebo effect or the result of who chooses to learn meditation. It is interesting to note, however, that similar stress reduction occurs when people set aside time daily to engage in other restful activities. Muscle relaxation, positive daydreaming, and even leisure reading can bring similar benefits.

There is some evidence that those who meditate regularly react more strongly to stressful stimuli during laboratory testing. However, they recover faster than non-meditators and say they felt less stressed.

As you can see, the effects of meditation are positive and beneficial, but far from magical. In fact, it must be concluded that many activities will elicit the relaxation response. Benson (1975) believes that the following elements are the key to producing the relaxation response:

1. A quiet environment
2. Decreased muscle tension
3. A mental device (such as a repeated word) that helps shift thoughts away from ordinary, rational concerns
4. A passive attitude toward whether you are "succeeding" at becoming relaxed

Summary To summarize, recent research suggests that concentrative meditation is only one of several ways to elicit the relaxation response. For many people, sitting quietly and "resting" can be as effective. However, if you are the type of person who finds it difficult to ignore upsetting thoughts, then concentrative meditation might be a better way to promote relaxation. More important than the method you choose, however, is a willingness to set aside time each day to intentionally relax. Meditation and similar techniques provide a valuable, stress-lowering "time-out" from the normal clamor of thoughts and worries—something almost everyone could use in our fast-paced society.

Learning Check

1. The focus of attention in concentrative meditation is "open," or expansive. T or F?
2. Mantras are words said silently to oneself to end a session of meditation. T or F?
3. Research conducted by Herbert Benson indicates that careful selection of a mantra is necessary to obtain the physical benefits of meditation. T or F?
4. The most immediate benefit of meditation appears to be its capacity for producing the relaxation response. T or F?

Answers:
1. F 2. F 3. F 4. T

Chapter Summary

- **Stress** occurs when demands are placed on an organism to adjust or adapt.
- Stress is more damaging in situations involving *pressure*, a *lack of control, unpredictability* of the stressor, and *intense* or *repeated* emotional shocks. Stress is intensified when a situation is perceived as a *threat* and when a person does not feel *competent* to cope with it. In work settings, prolonged stress, especially when associated with caregiving, can lead to **burnout.**
- **Frustration** is the negative emotional state that occurs when progress toward a goal is blocked. Sources of frustration may be usefully classified as *external* or *personal.*
- External frustrations are based on *delay, failure, rejection, loss* and other direct blocking of motives. Personal frustration is related to *personal characteristics* over which one has little control. Frustrations of all types become more intense as the *strength, urgency,* or *importance* of the blocked motive increases.
- Major behavioral reactions to frustration include *persistence, more vigorous responding, circumvention, direct aggression, displaced aggression* (including *scapegoating*), and *escape,* or *withdrawal.*
- **Conflict** occurs when one must choose between contradictory alternatives. Four major types of conflict are **approach-approach** (choice between two desirable alternatives), **avoidance-avoidance** (both alternatives are negative), **approach-avoidance** (a goal or activity has both positive and negative aspects), and **double approach-avoidance** (both alternatives have advantages and disadvantages).
- Approach-approach conflicts are usually the easiest to resolve. Avoidance conflicts are difficult to resolve and are characterized by *inaction, indecision, freezing,* and a *desire to escape* (called *leaving the field*). People usually remain in approach-avoidance conflicts, but fail to fully resolve them. Approach-avoidance conflicts are associated with *ambivalence* and *partial approach. Vacillation* (a wavering between alternatives) is probably the most common reaction to double approach-avoidance conflicts.
- Work with the *Social Readjustment Rating Scale* indicates that an accumulation of **life changes** can increase susceptibility to accident or illness. However, immediate psychological and mental health is more closely related to the intensity and severity of daily annoyances, or **hassles.**
- When stress is intense or prolonged (especially when associated with negative emotional response), it may cause damage in the form of ulcers and other *psychosomatic* problems. **Psychosomatic** (mind-body) **disorders** have no connection to **hypochondria,** the tendency to imagine that one has some terrible disease.
- People with **Type A personalities** are competitive, striving, and frequently angry or hostile, and they have a chronic sense of time urgency. These characteristics—especially anger and hostility—combine to double the chances of heart attack. People who have traits of the **hardy personality** seem to be resistant to stress, even if they also have Type A traits.
- The body reacts to stress in a series of stages called the **general adaptation syndrome** (G.A.S.). The stages of the G.A.S. are **alarm, resistance,** and **exhaustion.** The pattern of bodily reactions and changes in resistance observed in the G.A.S. follows closely the pattern observed in the development of psychosomatic disorders. In addition, stress may lower the body's immunity to disease.
- **Health psychologists** are interested in behavior that helps maintain and promote health. Studies of health and illness have identified a number of **behavioral risk factors** and **health-promoting behaviors.** Health psychologists have pioneered efforts to *prevent* the development of unhealthy habits and to improve well-being through **community health campaigns.**
- A sizable number of coping skills can be applied to manage stress. Most of these focus on one of three areas: *bodily effects, ineffective behavior,* and *upsetting thoughts.*
- **Concentrative meditation** is a self-control technique that can be used to reduce stress. Two major benefits of meditation are its ability to interrupt anxious thoughts and its ability to elicit the **relaxation response.**

Questions for Discussion

1. How could you reduce conflict or avoid an unfortunate decision in the following situations: choosing a school to attend, choosing a major, deciding about marriage, choosing a job, buying a car?

2. Calculate your life change score. If your score is elevated, what could you do to reduce the chances of illness? If it is low, what could you do to put more excitement in your life?! Can you see any relationship between periods of illness you have had and the number of life changes or hassles that preceded them?

3. What do you consider the most prominent sources of stress in our society? What do you think should or could be done to combat these stresses?

4. Over a decade ago, journalist Alvin Toffler predicted that large numbers of people would become victims of "future shock." According to Toffler, future shock is a condition of shattering stress and disorientation brought on by overly rapid social change. In your view, is there any truth to the idea that we are "future-shocked" or that we may be in the near future?

5. Explain why you agree or disagree with the following statement (attributed to Professor P. T. Barnumand-bailey Circuits): "Television is the opiate of the people. If all the TV tubes in the United States suddenly went blank, the mental health of the nation would crumble because people could no longer escape their problems by watching television."

6. How could you best deal with the following sources of frustration: delays, losses, lack of resources, failure, rejection?

7. In view of the relationship between smoking and health, should the government continue to give a large yearly subsidy to tobacco growers? Why or why not?

8. Why do you think the relationship between behavioral risk factors and health is so widely ignored? How important is health to you? How do your acquaintances rationalize their unhealthy behaviors? How do you?

Part Five

Human Development and Personality

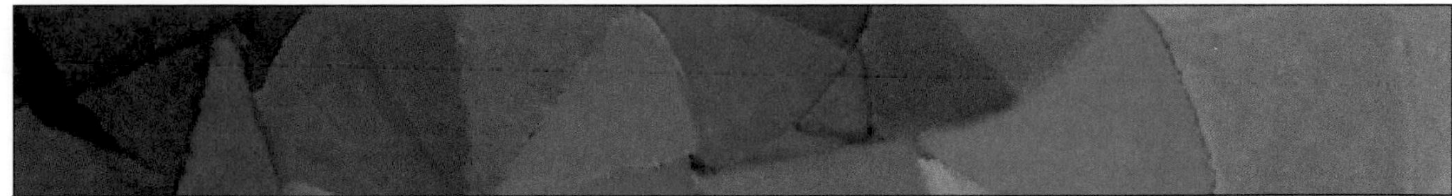

Chapter 14

Child Development

In This Chapter

Chapter Preview

Alien Minds

You may not have noticed. Not everyone has. There are alien creatures among us. More arrive daily. They look a lot like you and me, but they're smaller, and they think differently. Their speech is strange. They ask many questions. It's obvious they are trying to understand how we live. Their goal is to inhabit the planet earth in our place. Who are these creatures? Where are they from? You need not be alarmed: They come not from outer space, but from inner space. They are the product of life perpetuating life. They are children.

Studying children helps answer the question, How did I become the person I am today? This makes the study of children rewarding, but there is another reason for interest: A child's understanding of the world is qualitatively *different from yours and mine. Entry into a child's circle of awareness has much of the intrigue of meeting a person from another culture. It might even be compared to encountering an alien mind. In short, children are extremely interesting creatures and a tremendous amount of psychological research has focused on them.*

Question: What branch of psychology studies children?

The study of children is the heart of **developmental psychology.** *However, you should recognize that developmental psychologists are interested in every stage of life from "the womb to the tomb." Developmental psychology can be described as the* study of progressive changes in behavior and abilities from conception to death. *With a definition like this, it's clear that developmental psychology includes many topics—so many in fact, that some appear in other chapters.*

In this chapter, we will discuss a number of general topics and principles of development, including the far-reaching events in the first years of life. The next chapter covers development viewed over an entire life span. It also gives special attention to problems often encountered at various points in life. Perhaps learning about development will contribute to your own development. Find out by reading more!

Survey Questions

- What can newborn babies do?
- How aware are infants of their surroundings?
- How do heredity and environment affect development?
- How important are parenting styles?
- Of what significance is a child's emotional attachment to parents?
- How do children acquire language and thinking abilities?
- How do children develop morals and values?
- What are the effects of a poor early environment?
- What can be done to enhance early development?
- How have sex selection, genetic counseling, and the like, affected parents and children?

The Newborn Baby—The Basic Model Comes with Options

At birth the human **neonate** (NEE-oh-NATE: *neo:* new; *nate:* born) is completely helpless and will die if not cared for. Newborn babies cannot lift their heads, turn over, or feed themselves. Does this mean they are inert and unfeeling? Definitely not! Neonates can see, hear, smell, taste, and respond to pain and touch. Although their senses are less acute at birth, babies are immediately responsive to their surroundings. Neonates will, in fact, follow a moving object with their eyes and will turn in the direction of sounds.

A number of adaptive *reflexes* can also be observed in the newborn. An object pressed in the neonate's palm will be grasped with surprising strength. The **grasping reflex** is so strong that many infants can hang from a raised bar, like little trapeze artists. Very likely, the grasping reflex improves an infant's chances of survival by helping to prevent falling. Another adaptive reflex can be demonstrated by touching a baby's cheek. Immediately the baby will turn toward your finger, as if searching for something.

Question: How is such turning adaptive?

The **rooting reflex,** as this is called, helps the infant to find a bottle or breast. Then, when a nipple touches the infant's mouth, the **sucking reflex** helps the baby obtain needed food. At the same time, food rewards nursing, which rapidly increases in vigor during the first days after birth. Thus, we see that learning begins immediately in the newborn.

The **Moro reflex** is also interesting. If a baby's head is allowed to drop, or if the baby is startled by a loud noise, the infant will make movements similar to an embrace. These movements have been compared to the ones used by baby monkeys to cling to their mothers. (It is left to the reader's imagination to decide if there is any connection.)

We are tempted to think of newborn babies as mere bundles of reflexes. But infants can respond in ways that are more subtle than was once imagined. For example, Andrew Meltzoff and Keith Moore (1977, 1983) have found that babies are born mimics. Figure 14–1 shows Meltzoff as he sticks out his tongue, opens his mouth, and purses his lips at a 20-day-old girl. Will the baby imitate him? Videotapes made of babies tested in this way confirmed that they imitate adult facial gestures. As early as 9 months of age, infants can also imitate other actions and they can repeat them the next day (Meltzoff, 1988). Such mimicry is obviously an aid to rapid learning in infancy.

Question: How much intelligence does a newborn have?

Child psychologist Jerome Bruner (1984) believes that babies are smarter than most people think, Bruner cites an experiment in which 3- to 8-week-old babies showed signs of understanding that a person's voice and body are connected. If babies heard their mother's voice coming from where she was standing, they remained calm. If her

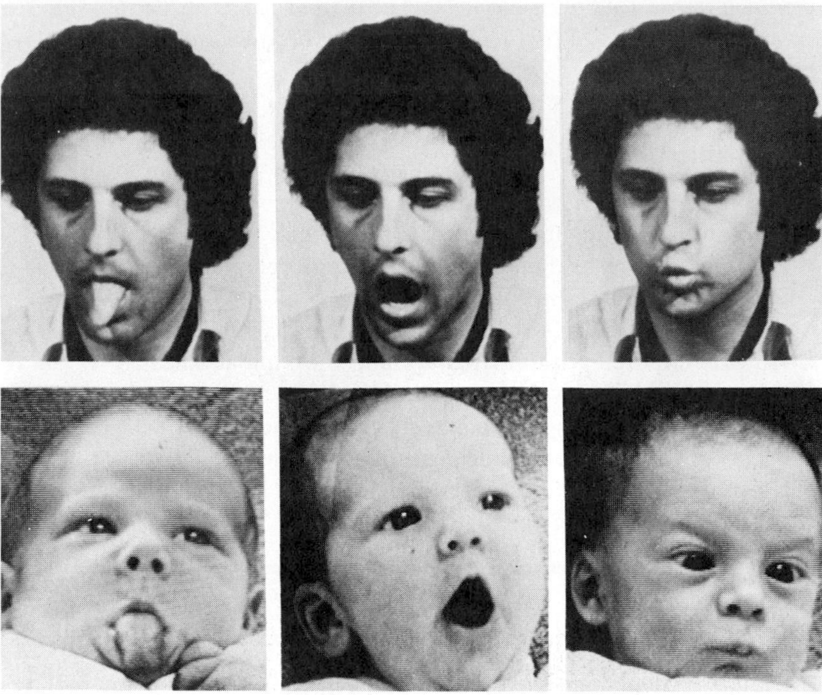

Fig. 14–1 *Infant imitation. In the top row of photos, Andrew Meltzoff makes facial gestures at an infant. The bottom row records the infant's responses. Videotapes of Meltzoff and of tested infants helped ensure objectivity. (Photos courtesy of Andrew N. Meltzoff.)*

voice came from a loudspeaker several feet away, the babies became agitated and began to cry. Bruner believes that this and similar experiments show that the human mind is quite active from birth onward.

Another look into the private world of infants can be drawn from tests of their vision.

Question: How is it possible to test a baby's vision?

Working with infants always requires imagination because they cannot talk. To test infant vision, Robert Fantz (1963) invented a device called a **looking chamber** (Fig. 14–2a). A child is placed on his or her back inside the chamber, facing a lighted area above. Next, 2 objects are placed in the chamber. By observing the movements of the infant's eyes and the images they reflect, it is possible to tell what the infant is looking at.

Fantz found that 3-day-old babies prefer complex patterns, such as checkerboards and bull's-eyes, to simpler colored rectangles. Other researchers have learned that infants are more excited by circles and curves and that they will look longer at red and blue than at other colors (Fig. 14–2b) (Bornstein, 1975; Ruff & Birch, 1974). Findings such as these demonstrate (as a friend of the author's once put it) that "There really is a person inside that little body."

Of possibly greater interest is the finding that infants will spend more time looking at a human face pattern than at a scrambled face or a colored oval (Fig. 14–2c). When real human faces were used, Fantz found that familiar faces were preferred to unfamiliar faces. However, preference for the familiar reverses at about age 2. At that time, unusual objects begin to hold greater interest for the child. For instance, Jerome Kagan (1971) showed 3-dimensional face masks to 2-year-olds and found they were fascinated by a face with eyes on the chin and a nose in the middle of the forehead. Kagan believes that their interest came from a need to understand why the scrambled face differed from what they had come to expect.

Maturation

Early development of the abilities we have described closely parallels maturation. **Maturation** refers to physical growth and development of the body—especially the nervous system. Maturation underlies the *orderly sequence* observed in the unfolding of many basic abilities, particularly motor abilities, such as crawling and walking.

While the *rate* of maturation varies from child to child, the *order* is almost universal. For instance, the strength and coordination a child needs to sit without support appears before that needed for crawling. Therefore, infants the world over typically sit before they crawl (and crawl before they stand, stand before they walk, and so on) (Fig. 14–3).

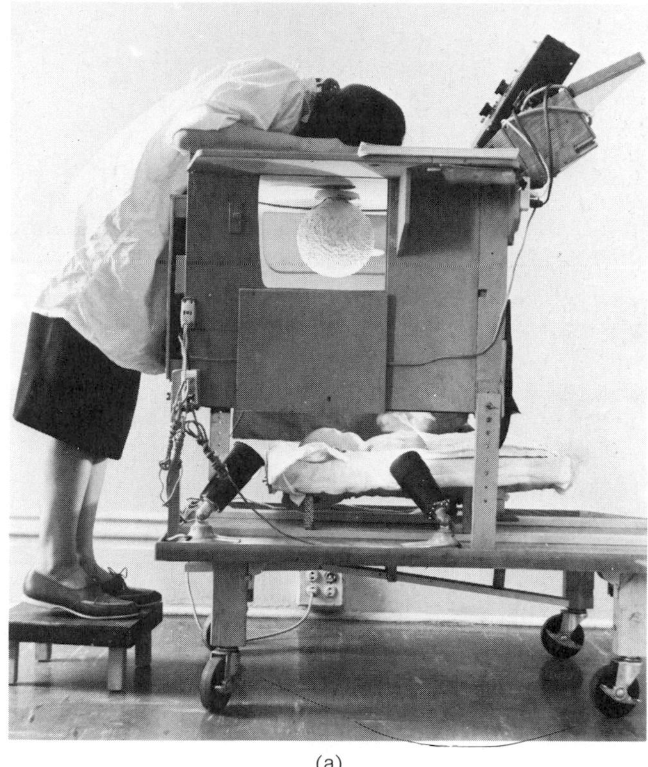

(a)

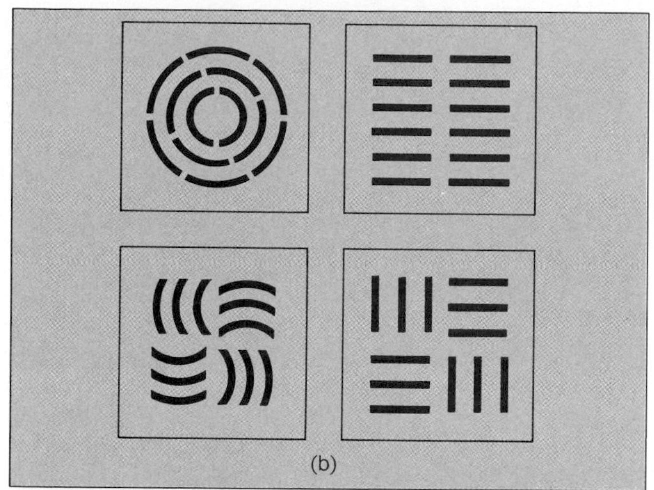

(b)

(c)

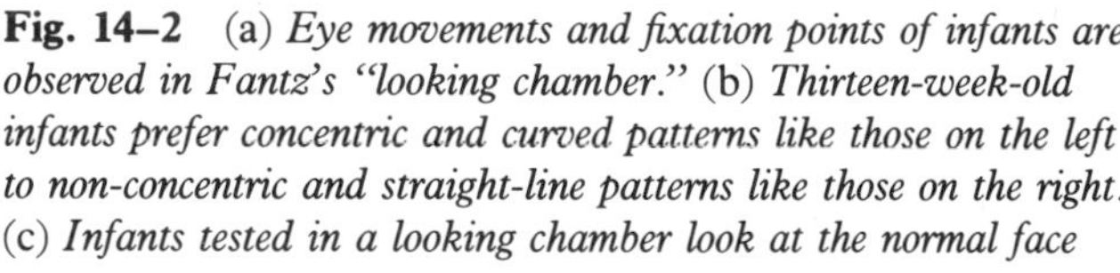

Fig. 14–2 (a) *Eye movements and fixation points of infants are observed in Fantz's "looking chamber."* (b) *Thirteen-week-old infants prefer concentric and curved patterns like those on the left to non-concentric and straight-line patterns like those on the right.* (c) *Infants tested in a looking chamber look at the normal face longer than at the scrambled face and at both faces longer than at the design on the right. (Photo courtesy of David Linton. Drawing from "The Origin of Form Perception" by Robert L. Fantz. Copyright © 1961 by Scientific American, Inc. All rights reserved.)*

Question: What about my weird cousin Emo who never crawled?

Like cousin Emo, a few children substitute rolling, creeping, or shuffling for crawling. A very few move directly from sitting to standing and walking (Robson, 1984). Even so, an orderly sequence of motor development remains evident. In general, increased muscular control in infants proceeds from *head to toe,* and from the *center* of the body *to the extremities.*

Readiness Maturation often creates a condition of **readiness** for learning. The principle of readiness (also known as the **principle of motor primacy**) states that until the necessary physical structures are mature, no amount of practice will be sufficient to establish a skill. It is impossible, for instance, to teach children to walk or to use a toilet before they have matured enough to control the necessary muscles. Parents who try to force children to learn skills for which they are not yet ready invite failure. They also run a risk of needlessly frustrating the child.

Question: Then are there definite ages at which children become ready to learn particular skills?

No. Readiness is not an all-or-nothing state. Training that comes too early will be unsuccessful; training that is only a little early may succeed, but it will be inefficient; and training when a child is maturationally ready produces rapid learning.

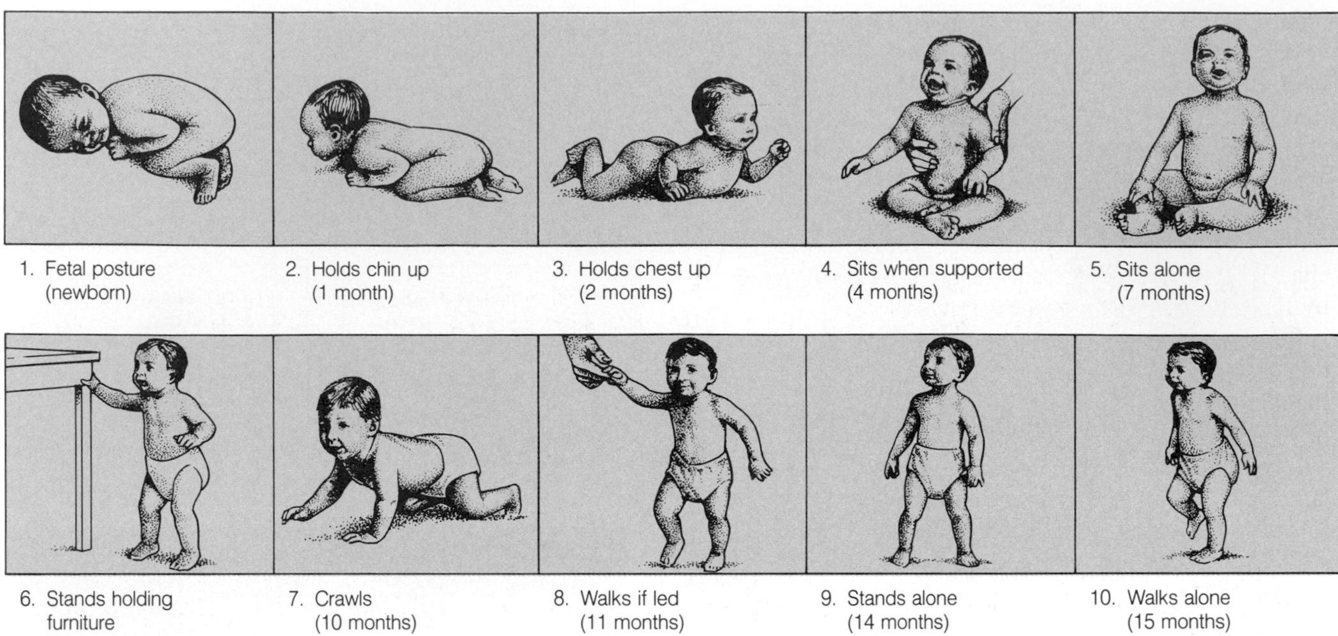

Fig. 14–3 *Motor development. Most infants follow an orderly pattern of motor development. Although the order in which children progress is similar, there are large individual differences in the ages at which each ability appears. The ages listed are averages for American children. It is not unusual for many of the skills to appear 1 or 2 months earlier than average or several months later (Frankenberg & Dodds, 1967).*

Many parents are anxious to see their children progress, and there is always a temptation to try to hurry a child along. However, it is valuable to recognize that much needless grief can be avoided by respecting a child's personal rate of growth. Consider, for instance, the eager parents who toilet train an 18-month-old child in 10 trying weeks of false alarms and accidents. Had the parents waited until the child was 24 months old, they might have succeeded in just 3 weeks. A recent study found that parents may control when toilet training starts, but maturation tends to determine when it will be completed (Martin et al., 1984). (Around 30 months is average for completion.) So why fight nature? (The wet look is in.)

Perhaps the most striking aspect of the human infant is the dazzling speed with which he or she is transformed from a helpless baby to an independent person. Early growth is extremely rapid. By the third year of life, the child stands, walks, talks, explores, and has a unique personality. At no other time after birth does development proceed more rapidly. During this period there is a fascinating interplay of forces shaping the child's development, the most important of which are heredity and environment.

Heredity and Environment—The Nature of Nurture and the Nurture of Nature

Question: Which has a greater effect on development, heredity or environment?

For many years psychologists debated—sometimes heatedly—the relative importance of nature versus nurture in determining behavior. The potent effects of **heredity** (nature) certainly cannot be denied. At the moment of conception, when a sperm and an ovum (egg) unite, an incredible number of personal features and growth patterns are determined. It is estimated that the genetic information carried in each human cell would fill thousands of 1000-page books—and that's in fine print!

Question: How does heredity operate?

Heredity The nucleus of every cell in the body contains 46 threadlike structures called **chromosomes** that transmit the coded instructions of heredity. **Genes** are smaller areas on chromosomes. Each gene carries instructions that affect a particular process or personal characteristic. Genes are made up of **DNA,** deoxyribonucleic acid (dee-OX-see-RYE-bo-new-KLEE-ik). DNA is a long, ladderlike chemical molecule that is made up of smaller molecules. The order of these smaller molecules, or organic bases, acts as a code for genetic information. There are at least 100,000 genes in every human cell, and perhaps more. In some cases, a single gene is responsible for a particular inherited feature, such as eye color. Most characteristics, however, are **polygenetic,** or determined by many genes working in combination.

Genes may be dominant or recessive. When a gene is **dominant,** the trait it controls will be present every time the gene is present. When a gene is **recessive,** it must be paired with a second recessive gene before its effect will be expressed. Some examples should make this relationship clearer. We receive one-half of our chromosomes (and genes) from each parent. If you were to get a brown-eye gene from your father and a blue-eye gene from your mother, you would be brown-eyed, because brown-eye genes are dominant.

Question: If brown-eye genes are dominant, how is it that two brown-eyed parents sometimes have a blue-eyed child?

If each parent has 2 brown-eye genes, the couple's children can only be brown-eyed. But what if each parent has 1 brown-eye gene and 1 blue-eye gene? In this case the parents would both have brown eyes, but there is 1 chance in 4 that their children will get 2 blue-eye genes and have blue eyes (Fig. 14–4).

Sex is also genetically determined—in this case by 2 specialized chromosomes. A child who inherits two ***X* chromosomes** will be a female. An *X* chromosome paired with a ***Y* chromosome** yields a male. The woman's ovum always provides an *X* chromosome, since she has 2 *X*'s in her own genetic makeup. In contrast, one-half of the male's sperm carry *X* chromosomes and the other half *Y*'s. This has effects beyond determining sex, since some traits are **sex-linked,** or carried by recessive genes on the *X* chromosome. An example is color blindness, which is carried on an *X* chromosome and given from mother to son. (In a few instances, sex-linked traits are carried on a *Y* chromosome. However, this is exceedingly rare.)

Nature Hereditary instructions carried by the chromosomes influence development throughout life by affecting the sequence of growth, the timing of puberty, and the course of aging. The broad outlines of the **human growth sequence** are therefore universal. They extend from conception to senescence (aging) and death, as Table 14–1 shows. In addition, heredity determines eye color, skin color, and susceptibility to some diseases. It underlies maturation and the orderly sequence of motor development. Heredity also exerts considerable influence over body size and shape, height, intelligence, athletic potential, personality traits, and a host of other details (Fig. 14–5). Score 1 for those who favor heredity as the more important factor in development!

Nurture Does the preceding mean that **environment** (nurture) takes a back seat in development? Definitely not. As Aldous Huxley (1965) pointed out, humans today are physically very similar to cave dwellers who lived 20,000 or 30,000 years ago. A bright baby born today could become almost anything—a computer programmer, an engineer, or a biochemist who likes to paint in water colors, for instance. But an Upper Paleolithic baby could not possibly have grown into anything except a hunter or food gatherer. Score 1 for the environmentalists!

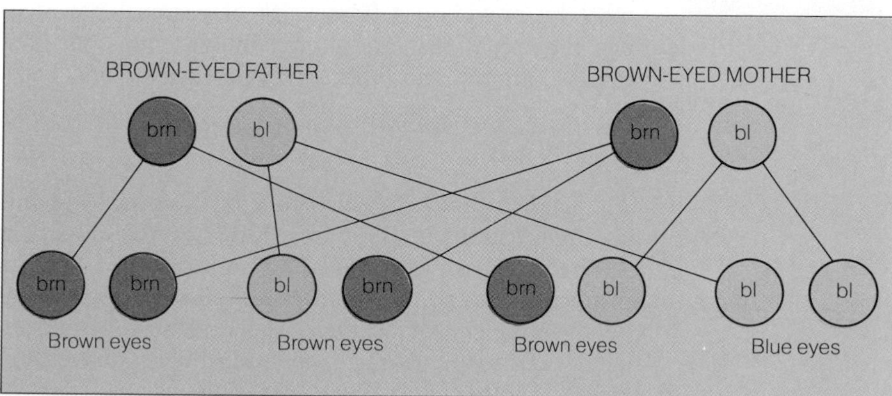

Fig. 14–4 *Gene patterns for children of brown-eyed parents, each with 1 brown-eye gene and 1 blue-eye gene. Since the brown-eye gene is dominant, only 1 child in 4 will be blue-eyed.*

Table 14–1 Human Growth Sequence

PERIOD*	DURATION (APPROXIMATE)	DESCRIPTIVE NAME
Germinal period	First two weeks after conception	Zygote
Embryonic period	2–8 weeks after conception	Embryo
Fetal period	From 8 weeks after conception to birth	Fetus
Neonatal period	From birth to a few weeks after birth	Neonate
Infancy	From a few weeks after birth until child is walking securely; some children walk securely at less than a year, while others may not be able to until age 17–18 months	Infant
No designated name for this period	From about 15–18 months until about 2–2½ years	Toddler
No specific name; sometimes called "run-about years"	From age 2–3 to about age 6	Preschool child
Middle years of childhood	From about age 6 to about age 12	No specific name
Pubescence	Period of about 2 years before puberty	No specific name
Puberty	Point of development at which biological changes of pubescence reach a climax marked by sexual maturity	No specific name
Adolescence	From the beginning of pubescence until full social maturity is reached (difficult to fix duration of this period)	Adolescent
Adulthood Young adulthood (19–25) Adulthood (26–40) Maturity (41 plus)	From adolescence to death; sometimes subdivided into other periods as shown at left	Adult
Senescence	No defined limit that would apply to all people; extremely variable; characterized by marked physiological and psychological deterioration	Adult (senile), "old age"

Table courtesy of Tom Bond.
*Note: There is no exact beginning or ending point for the various growth periods. The ages are approximate, and each period may be thought of as blending into the next.

Fig. 14–5 *Identical twins. Twins who share identical genes (identical twins) demonstrate the powerful influence of heredity. Even when they are reared apart, identical twins are strikingly alike in motor skills, physical development, and appearance (Horn et al., 1976).*

Nature-Nurture Interactions The outcome of this debate (we have only viewed an opening round) is recognition that *both* heredity and environment are important. The two are, in fact, inseparable. As a person grows, there is a constant interplay, or *interaction,* between the forces of nature and nurture. Heredity shapes development by providing a framework of personal potentials and limitations that are altered by learning, nutrition, disease, culture, and other environmental factors.

Question: How soon after birth do hereditary differences appear?

They appear immediately. From birth onward, infants are unique individuals. Jerome Kagan (1969) found that newborn babies differ noticeably in activity, irritability, distractibility, and other aspects of **temperament.** (Temperament refers to the physical foundations of personality, such as prevailing mood, sensitivity, and energy levels.) Another study found that babies can be separated into 3 major categories. *Easy children* (about 40 percent of those observed) are relaxed and agreeable. *Difficult children* (about 10 percent) are moody, intense, and easily angered. *Slow-to-warm-up children* (about 15 percent) are restrained and unexpressive, or shy. The remaining children do not fit neatly into any single category (Thomas & Chess, 1977, 1986). (Perhaps we should call them "generic" children?)

Because of inborn differences in readiness to smile, cry, vocalize, reach out, or pay attention, babies rapidly become *active participants* in their own development—especially their social development. Growing infants alter parents' behavior at the same time they are changed by it. For example, Amy is an easy baby who smiles frequently and is easily fed. This encourages touching, feeding, and affection from her mother. The mother's responses, in turn, reward Amy and cause more smiling and other positive reactions. A dynamic *relationship* has been established between mother and child.

Consistent differences in temperament can be detected for at least the first 2 years of life (Matheny et al., 1984). Yet by age 10, children's personalities show little connection to irritability, activity, or attentiveness observed in infancy (Kagan, 1976). Such findings emphasize again that environmental forces continue to modify inborn potentials with each passing year.

To summarize, we might say that three factors combine to determine a person's **developmental level** at any stage of life. These are *heredity, environment,* and the individual's *own behavior,* each tightly interwoven with the others.

Learning Check

1. If an infant is startled, it will make movements similar to an embrace. This is known as the
   a. grasping reflex *b.* rooting reflex *c.* Moro reflex *d.* adaptive reflex
2. After age 2, infants tested in a looking chamber show a marked preference for familiar faces and simpler designs. T or F?
3. As a child develops there is a continuous ______________ between the forces of heredity and environment.
4. Which of the following represents a correct sequence?
   a. zygote, fetus, embryo, neonate, infant *b.* zygote, embryo, neonate, fetus, infant
   c. embryo, zygote, fetus, neonate, infant *d.* zygote, embryo, fetus, neonate, infant
5. "Slow-to-warm-up" children can be described as restrained, unexpressive, or shy. T or F?
6. The orderly sequence observed in the unfolding of many basic responses can be attributed to ______________.
7. The principle of motor primacy is also known as ______________.
8. DNA contains a code made up of dominant and recessive chromosomes. T or F?

Answers:
1. *c* 2. F 3. interaction 4. *d* 5. T 6. maturation 7. readiness 8. F

Early Environment—As the Twig Is Bent

Environment obviously begins to modify development immediately after birth, but the prenatal environment is also important. Normally we think of the **intrauterine environment** of the womb as highly protected and stable. In general, it is, but a number of conditions can affect development before birth.

Prenatal Influences

During embryonic and fetal development, it is quite possible for the effects of environment to reach the seemingly well-protected interior of the womb. If a mother's health or nutrition is poor, if she contracts certain diseases, such as German measles or syphilis, uses drugs, or is exposed to X-rays or atomic radiation, the fetus may be harmed. The resultant damage is referred to as a **congenital problem** (Fig. 14–6). Congenital problems (or "birth defects," as they are sometimes called) are different from **genetic problems,** which are inherited. (You will find more information on genetic problems in this chapter's Exploration.)

Question: How is it possible for the embryo or the fetus to be harmed?

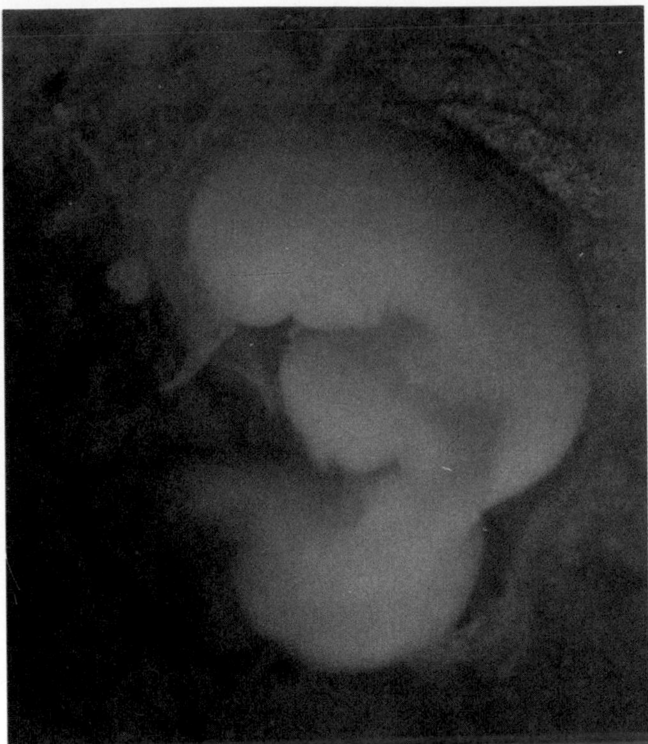

Fig. 14–6 *Due to the rapid growth of basic structures, the developing fetus is sensitive to a variety of diseases, drugs, and sources of radiation. This is especially true during the first trimester (3 months) of gestation.*

Effects of Drugs As you might know, there is no direct intermixing of blood between the mother and the unborn child. Nevertheless, some substances—especially drugs—do reach the fetus. If the mother is addicted to morphine, heroin, or methadone, the infant may be born with a drug addiction. Most common prescription drugs—many of them capable of producing fetal malformations—also reach the fetus.

Even a partial listing of troublesome drugs underscores the need for caution in drug use during pregnancy. Potentially damaging substances include general anesthetics, cortisone, tetracycline, excessive amounts of vitamins A, D, B_6, and K, cocaine, some barbiturates, opiates, tranquilizers, synthetic sex hormones, and possibly even caffeine and aspirin (Cox, 1984); Jacobson et al., 1984).

Question: What about alcohol and tobacco?

Repeated heavy drinking by a pregnant woman can produce a pattern known as the **fetal alcohol syndrome.** Affected infants have low birth weight, a variety of bodily defects and facial malformations, and many are mentally retarded. Miscarriages and premature births are also common (Matarazzo, 1984). There is increasing evidence that even modest use of alcohol during pregnancy can be damaging (Streissguth et al., 1984).

Alcohol appears to cause severe oxygen loss to the rapidly developing fetus, producing irreversible brain damage (Matarazzo, 1984). The *maximum* amount a pregnant woman should drink on any day is 1 ounce of hard liquor, or 1 glass of wine, or 2 glasses of beer (Furey, 1982). During the first 3 months of pregnancy, frequent drinking of even such small amounts of alcohol may cause damage. Considering the risks, the best advice for pregnant women is to entirely avoid drinking alcohol.

Smoking also has an adverse effect on prenatal development. Smoking can elevate or lower the heart rate of the unborn child, and a mother who smokes heavily is more likely to miscarry. Heavy smokers run a higher risk of premature birth and tend to give birth to underweight babies. Both premature birth and low birth weight increase the chances of infant sickness and death after birth (Cox, 1984). The infant death rate immediately before, during, or after birth is 27 percent higher if a woman smokes during pregnancy (Matarazzo, 1984). A pregnant woman who smokes 2 packs of cigarettes a day blocks off about 25 percent of the oxygen supply to the fetus.

Birth

More than ever before, parents can choose how their child will be born. Should it be a conventional hospital birth? Should they try natural childbirth? Should the father be present for the birth? In recent years, researchers have carefully probed the effects of such choices. Let's briefly explore what they have learned.

Conventional Delivery Until recently, **medicated births** in hospital delivery rooms were the rule in Western nations. In such births, the mother is assisted by a physician and given drugs to relieve pain. The drugs used range from local analgesics (painkillers) to general anesthetics that cause a loss of consciousness. Increasingly, doctors and parents have come to realize that general anesthesia during birth has major drawbacks. For one thing, drugs dull or block the mother's awareness of birth. They also reduce oxygen flow to the fetus, and they can cause the infant to be born partially anesthetized. For such reasons, babies whose mothers were given heavy doses of anesthetic tend to lag in muscular and neural development (Brackbill, 1979).

In the last 5 years, there has been a marked move away from the use of general anesthesia during birth. Nevertheless, some form of painkiller is used in 95 percent of all deliveries in the United States. Certainly, mothers should not feel guilty if they need a painkiller during childbirth. However it appears wise to use as few drugs as possible.

Prepared Childbirth What can parents do to minimize the discomfort of birth while giving their babies the best possible start in life? Many psychologists are convinced that **natural,** or **prepared, childbirth** is the answer. The most widely used approach to natural childbirth is the *Lamaze method* (la-MAHZ), developed by French physician Ferdinand Lamaze.

Couples begin learning the Lamaze method during pregnancy. Part of the training explains what will happen physically during birth. Women who thoroughly understand what is happening in their bodies tend to have fewer fears and less anxiety. Couples are also taught methods of breathing and muscular control to minimize pain during birth. Another important element is training the father or a friend to give support to the mother during childbirth.

Natural childbirth typically shortens labor and minimizes pain. In addition, it treats birth as a celebration of life, rather than a medical problem or a disease. Accordingly, parents are more likely to experience birth as a time of great happiness when natural childbirth is used *and* the father is present (Tanzer & Block, 1976). (Should the celebration extend to the baby? See Highlight 14–1 for a discussion of "gentle birth.")

Question: How important is it for fathers to participate in the birth process?

For most parents, the emotional intensity of birth magnifies its impact. A father may form memories at the time of his child's birth that will be with him for life. Such memories can make a difference in the father's willingness to care for the child or in his reaction when the child angers him. Researchers have found that fathers generally make a better transition to parenthood when they participate in the preparation for childbirth (Grossman et al., 1980). But while participation in the birth itself is valuable for fathers, it is apparently not essential. The father's *attitude* toward the birth of his child is probably more

HIGHLIGHT 14—1
Gentle Birth

From the warm and protected confines of the womb, a baby is forcefully thrust into a cold, noisy world. The new arrival is greeted with glaring lights, booming voices, cutting of the umbilical cord, and weighing on a cold scale. According to French obstetrician Frederick Leboyer (leh-BOY-a), these events make birth a needlessly traumatic experience.

Leboyer (1975) advocates a system of **gentle birth** that he claims is pleasant for both mother and baby. Delivery takes place in a silent, dimly lit room. Immediately after birth, the baby is placed on the mother's abdomen and massaged. After several minutes of soothing, the umbilical cord is cut and the baby is bathed in warm water. Leboyer believes that this approach is superior to conventional birth procedures, which he regards as "violent" and "cruel."

From a medical standpoint, some of Leboyer's methods can be risky. A darkened delivery room, for instance, may delay detection of a "blue baby" or other complications. Still, gentle birth appeals to many parents, and thousands of babies have been delivered by the Leboyer method.

A second point to consider is that birth is inherently traumatic. A degree of stress during birth may be normal and perhaps even desirable. There is some evidence that babies born by cesarean section (surgical birth) have a lower survival rate.

Leboyer claims that gentle births produce children who are happier, healthier, more relaxed, and more emotionally stable. However, evidence in support of this claim is not very convincing. It is true that during the first 15 to 20 minutes after birth, Leboyer babies are more relaxed than other newborns (Oliver & Oliver, 1978). From that point on, however, Leboyer-delivered babies do not differ in any measurable way from conventionally delivered babies (Nelson et al., 1980). Even if the Leboyer babies did differ, could we conclude that gentle birth is beneficial? What if parents who choose gentle births tend to be more loving or attentive? If this were the case, the later emotional health of their infants might have nothing to do with birth itself.

Undoubtedly, parents should use the method of delivery that makes them most comfortable, and many parents regard gentle birth as a desirable alternative. At this point, however, it appears that gentle births may be done more for parents than for babies!

important. A recent study found that fathers who *wanted* to be present during delivery showed greater interest in their infants during the first year and were more likely to help care for the baby (Grossman & Volkmer, 1984). This was true whether or not the father was actually able to attend the birth.

Many hospitals now have homelike **birthing rooms** that allow fathers to room-in (Fig. 14–7). This allows them to participate in the birth and to share in caring for the newborn. At the same time, it ensures that prompt medical attention is available in the event of any birth complications. Even traditional delivery rooms are allowing fathers to be present during birth, either as observers or to coach the mother through labor and childbirth. In some cases the father cuts the umbilical cord and gives the infant its first bath. Babies are now less often rushed off to a nursery. In many hospitals the baby spends its first night with the parents in the birthing room. Clearly, such changes are making birth more psychologically rewarding for mother, father, and baby.

Maternal and Paternal Influences

In later years a child's environment expands to include the effects of culture, subculture, family, school, television, and peers. Immediately after birth and for the first few years, however, the most important influences come from an infant's caregivers. The quality of mothering and fathering is therefore of prime importance.

One revealing study of **maternal influences** began with the selection of children who were unusually competent ("A" children) or who had a low degree of competence ("C" children). As increasingly younger children were observed, it became apparent that A and C patterns were already set by age 3.

Fig. 14–7 *Changing attitudes toward childbirth have encouraged mothers and fathers to actively prepare for birth and to participate more fully in caring for the newborn.*

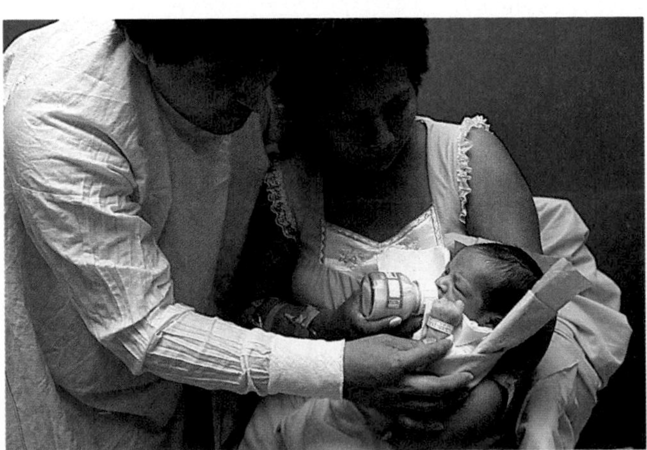

To learn how this was possible, researchers visited homes and observed children under 3 and their mothers (White & Watts, 1973). The **caregiving styles** that were observed ranged from the "super mother" to the "zoo-keeper mother." Super mothers went out of their way to provide educational experiences for their children and allowed their children to initiate some activities. This caregiving style produced an A child, competent in most areas of development. At the other end of the spectrum, zoo-keeper mothers gave their children good physical care, but interacted with them very little. Their child care routines were rigid and highly structured. The result was C children who tended to approach problems inflexibly (Pines, 1969).

Optimal caregiving is also related to the **goodness of fit** between parents and children (Chess & Thomas, 1986). For instance, a slow-to-warm-up child who has impatient parents may have more difficulty adjusting than if the same child had easy-going parents. A similar point is made by a study that found that children's intellectual abilities at age 6 can be predicted, to some extent, by their mothers' *responsiveness* to them during infancy (Coates & Lewis, 1984). Effective mothers, it seems, are sensitive to their children's needs. Put another way, effective mothers alter their own behavior to meet their children's changing needs at each stage of development.

Taken together, such findings support two beliefs long held by developmental psychologists. First, mothering *does* make a difference. Second, early development has lasting effects on a person.

Question: Aren't you overlooking the effects of fathering?

Yes. Fathers also add significantly to an infant's social and intellectual growth. In fact, fathers make a unique contribution to development by interacting with the infant in ways that differ from those typical of mothers. Recent studies of **paternal influences** have shown that the father's main role tends to be that of a *playmate* for the infant (Fig. 14–8). Fathers typically spend 4 or 5 times as much time playing with their infants as they do in caregiving (Parke & Sawin, 1977).

It might seem that the father's role as a playmate makes him less important in the child's development. Not so. From birth of the child onward, fathers pay more visual attention to the child than do mothers. They are much more tactile (lifting, tickling, and handling the baby), more physically arousing (engaging in rough-and-tumble play), and more likely to engage in unusual play (imi-

Fig. 14–8 *Fathering typically makes a contribution to early development that differs in emphasis from mothering.*

tating baby, for example) (Crawley & Sherrod, 1984; Parke & Sawin, 1977). Mothers speak to the infant more, play more conventional games (such as peekaboo), and as previously noted, spend more time in caregiving activities (Fig. 14–9). Such differences in mothers' and fathers' behavior continue until at least middle childhood (Russell & Russell, 1987).

Thus, from the first days of life, infants get very different views of males and females. Females, who offer comfort, nurturance, and verbal stimulation, also tend to be close at hand. Males come and go, and when they are present, action, exploration, and risk taking prevail (Herbert & Greenberg, 1983). It's no wonder, then, that maternal and paternal caregiving styles appear to have a major impact on children's sex role development (Biller, 1982; Siegal, 1987).

Social Development—Baby, I'm Stuck On You

Infants are social creatures from the day they are born. Their ability to imitate adults and their interest in the human face, described earlier, are good examples of their sensitivity to others. Also, as the preceding discussion shows, children's relationships with their parents strongly influence their social and personal development.

Two major elements of early social development are infants' growing self-awareness and their increased awareness of others.

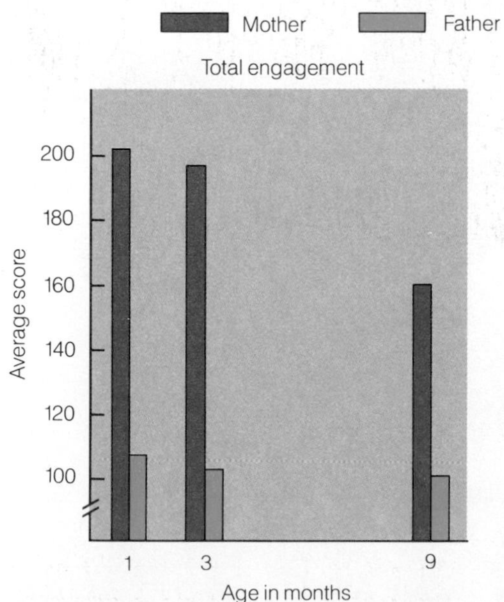

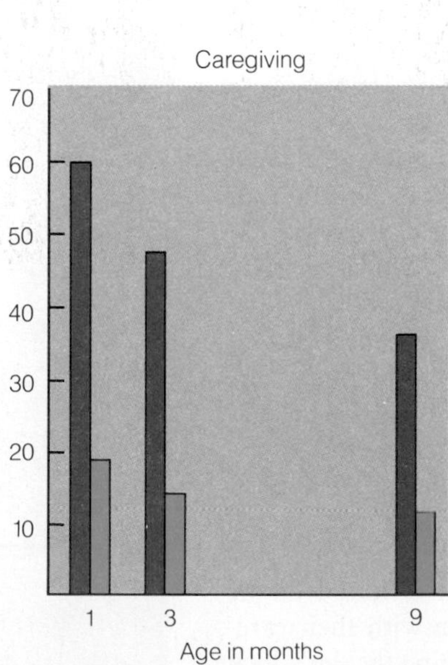

Fig. 14–9 *Mother-infant and father-infant interactions. These graphs show what occurred on routine days in a sample of 72 American homes. The graph on the left records the total amount of contact parents had with their babies, including such actions as talking to, touching, hugging, or smiling at the infant. The graph on the right shows the amount of caregiving (diapering, washing, feeding, and so forth) done by each parent. Note that in both cases mother-infant interactions greatly exceed father-infant interactions. (Adapted from Belsky et al., 1984.)*

Self-Awareness When you look in a mirror, you recognize the image looking back as your own—except, perhaps, early on Monday mornings. At what age did this sense of recognition first develop? Like many other events in development, **self-awareness** depends on maturation of the nervous system.

Question: How is self-awareness demonstrated in a baby?

In an experiment that must have been fun to do, mothers of children 9 to 24 months old secretly rubbed a spot of rouge on their child's nose. Each child was then placed in front of a mirror for testing. The question was, When would the child realize that the red spot was on his or her nose, indicating recognition of the mirror image? The probability that a child would touch his or her nose was very low at 9 months. However, it jumped dramatically through the second year. In an even stronger test of self-recognition, infants were shown their own videotaped images on a TV screen. Most infants had to be 15 months old before they could recognize their own images (Lewis & Brooks-Gunn, 1979). Increased self-awareness, then, closely parallels the human growth sequence (Kagan, 1976). When coupled with an increased awareness of others, self-awareness begins to form the core of social development.

Social Referencing At about the same time that self-awareness develops, infants become increasingly aware of others. Have you ever noticed how adults sometimes glance at the facial expressions of others to decide how to respond to them? **Social referencing** of this sort can also be observed in babies. By 12 months of age, most babies *reference* (glance at) their mothers when placed in an unfamiliar situation.

In a recent study of social referencing, babies were placed on a visual cliff. (A visual cliff is pictured in Chapter 5.) The deep side of the cliff was just high enough so that the babies were tempted to cross it, but did not. Most babies placed on the edge of the cliff repeatedly looked at their mothers. As they did, the mothers made faces at them. (All for science, of course.) When the mothers posed faces of joy or interest, most babies crossed the deep side of the cliff. When they posed fear or anger, few babies crossed (Sorce et al., 1985). Thus, by the end of their first year, infants are aware of the facial expressions of others and seek guidance from them (Klinnert, 1984). Again, we see the roots of an important social skill.

The real core of social development is found in the emotional attachments that babies form with their caregivers. Before we consider this topic directly, let's look at some related animal behavior to see what we can learn from it.

Critical Periods and Imprinting

Question: Why do experiences early in life often have such lasting effects?

Part of the answer lies in the existence of critical periods for acquiring particular behaviors. A **critical period** is a time of increased sensitivity to environmental influences (both positive and negative). Often, certain events must occur during a critical period for a person or an animal to develop normally. To illustrate, Konrad Lorenz, an ethologist who studied animal behavior, once became curious about why baby geese follow their mother. The obvious explanation seemed to be, "It's instinctive," but Lorenz showed otherwise.

Mother Lorenz

Normally, the first large moving object a baby goose sees is its mother. Lorenz hatched geese in an incubator, so the first moving object they saw was Lorenz. From then on, these baby geese followed Lorenz. They even reacted to his call as if he were their mother (Fig. 14–10). (Lorenz, 1937)

Imprinting It can be seen that the response pattern of "mother-goose following" is not automatic. It is estab-

Fig. 14–10 *"Mother" Lorenz leads his charges. The goslings have imprinted on Lorenz because he was the first moving object they saw after they hatched.*

lished during a critical period by the essential experience of seeing a large moving object. The rapid and early learning of a permanent behavior pattern of this type is called **imprinting.**

In most birds, the critical period for imprinting is very brief. For instance, Hess (1959) found that if ducklings are not allowed to imprint on their mother or some other object within 30 hours after hatching, they never will. (Ducklings have been imprinted on decoys, rubber balls, wooden blocks, and other unlikely objects.) In many animals, imprinting and other events taking place during critical periods have lifelong consequences (Lorenz, 1962).

Revenge of the Jackdaw

Imprinting normally serves to attach a young animal to its mother. It also guides the selection of a mate of the same species at sexual maturity. In another of Lorenz's experiments, a jackdaw (European starling) imprinted on him. When the bird reached sexual maturity, Lorenz became the object of its mating ritual. Part of this ritual involves stuffing worms into the mouth of the intended mate—as a surprised Lorenz learned while asleep on the lawn one day. When Lorenz refused its gift, the jackdaw stuffed a worm in Lorenz's ear. (Showing, perhaps, that it's not nice to fool Mother Nature!)

Attachment

Question: Does imprinting occur in humans?

True cases of imprinting are limited to birds and some other animals (Hess, 1959). However, human infants do form an **emotional attachment** to their *primary caregivers* (usually parents), and there is a critical period (roughly the first year of life) during which this must occur for healthy development (Bowlby, 1969, 1973).

A direct sign that an emotional bond has been formed appears when infants are around 8 to 12 months of age. At that time, babies display **separation anxiety** (crying and signs of fear) when their parents leave them alone or leave them with strangers (Kagan, 1976). It is interesting to note that infants who spend much time with their grandmothers show nearly as strong an attachment to them as they do to their mothers (Myers et al., 1987). For many children, such attachments may be part of the first step in broadening social relationships to others.

Attachment can have quite an effect on early development. Infants who are securely attached to their parents later show more resiliency, curiosity, problem-solving ability, and social competence in preschool (Parke & Asher, 1983).

Question: Does daycare for young children interfere with the quality of attachment?

For the most part, it seems that it does not. For one thing, separation anxiety normally disappears when parting with parents becomes a routine event. In addition, studies of daycare effects have concluded that "*high-quality* non-maternal care does not appear to have harmful effects on the preschool child's maternal attachment, intellectual development, social-emotional behavior, or physical health" (Etaugh, 1980; Tephy & Elardo, 1984). This conclusion applies until daycare exceeds 20 or more hours a week. Then there often are some signs of insecurity in children's relationships with their mothers (Belsky & Rovine, 1988). Some insecurity is especially likely if the child is firstborn and under 1 year of age and if the mother works full-time (Barglow et al., 1987). Aside from such considerations, the key ingredient for secure attachment is a mother who is accepting and sensitive to her baby's signals and rhythms (Belsky et al., 1984).

In recent years, a major controversy has raged over whether attachment is influenced by events that occur immediately after birth. For your interest, Highlight 14–2 offers a discussion of "mother-infant bonding."

Motherless Monkeys Research with rhesus monkeys suggests that like imprinting, infant attachments can have lasting effects. Harry Harlow (1966, 1967) has shown that baby monkeys separated from their mothers and raised in isolation become troubled adult animals. Among other things, these motherless monkeys never develop normal sexual behaviors, and they make very poor mothers if mated. They are coldly rejecting or indifferent to their babies and may brutalize or injure them. It has been suggested that human parents who abuse, reject, or physically injure their children may be displaying a similar pattern. Most abusive parents were themselves rejected or mistreated as children. In addition, some psychologists believe that antisocial behavior can often be traced to a lack of attachment in infancy (Magid, 1988). Children with severe attachment problems do not learn to trust and care about others. As a result, many are cruel, angry, and self-destructive.

Meeting a baby's **affectional needs** is every bit as important as meeting more obvious needs for food, water, and physical care. All things considered, one of the most important developments in the first year of life appears to be creation of a bond of trust and affection between the infant and at least one other person (see Chapter 15). Parents are sometimes afraid of "spoiling" a baby with too much attention, but for the first year or two this is nearly impossible. As a matter of fact, a later capacity to experience warm and loving relationships may depend on it.

HIGHLIGHT 14–2
Mother-Infant Bonding—A Touching Debate

In one hospital ward, new mothers are given traditional contact with their infants: a glimpse after birth and 30-minute visits every 4 hours for feeding. In a second ward; "extended-contact group" mothers are given their babies for 1 hour during the first 3 hours after birth and for an extra 5 hours of contact each afternoon for the first 3 days after delivery. Does extra contact have any effect?

An initial series of studies reported by Marshall Klaus and John Kennel (1982) seemed to suggest that there are lasting benefits to close early contact between a mother and her infant. According to Klaus and Kennel, there is a sensitive period in the first hours after an infant's birth. Therefore, mother-child pairs who spend extra time together form a stronger **emotional bond** to one another. This is especially true, they believe, if skin-to-skin touching is part of early contact.

Klaus and Kennel have reported that "bonded" babies are more alert and responsive, as well as healthier and brighter than those denied extra contact. However, the majority of recent, more carefully done studies have failed to support the idea that extended early contact is crucial to the mother-infant bond (Myers, 1984). Critics also point out that adopted children, premature babies, and babies born by cesarean section (surgical birth) all develop normal, affectionate bonds with their mothers. Even Klaus and Kennel now acknowledge that it is unlikely that something as important as emotional attachment would depend *solely* on the first few hours of life (Klaus & Kennel, 1984). Humans are highly adaptable, and there are many opportunities for attachment during the first year of life.

Advocates of bonding continue to believe that early mother-infant contact can be beneficial. Even those experts who doubt that early contact makes a difference agree that allowing mother, father, and infant to be together during the first few hours is humane and natural. So, while most evidence suggests that early contact is not necessary, it is undoubtedly a positive, emotionally satisfying experience.

Learning Check

1. The intrauterine environment is so protected that it has little effect on a person's development. T or F?
2. The "super mother" goes out of her way to provide educational experiences, but accepts the child as he or she is. T or F?
3. Patterns of paternal behavior typically differ little from maternal caregiving patterns. T or F?
4. Clear signs of self-awareness or self-recognition are evident in most infants by the time they reach 8 months of age. T or F?
5. Social ______________ of parents' facial expressions is evident in infants by the time they are 1 year old.
6. A duckling can be imprinted after the critical period has passed if special attention is given to its affectional needs. T or F?
7. The development of separation anxiety in an infant corresponds to the formation of an attachment to parents. T or F?
8. Research has shown conclusively that mother-infant contact immediately after birth is essential for optimal development. T or F?

Answers:
1. F 2. T 3. F 4. F 5. referencing 6. F 7. T 8. F

Language Development—Fast-Talking Babies

There's something almost miraculous about a baby's first words. As infants, how did we manage to leap into the world of language? As will soon be apparent, social development provides a foundation for language learning. But before we explore that connection, let's begin with a survey of language development.

Language Acquisition The development of language is closely tied to maturation. As any parent can tell you, babies can cry from birth on. By 1 month of age, the infant can control crying enough to use it as an attention-getting device, and parents can tell the nature of the infant's needs from the tone of the crying. Around 6 to 8 weeks of age, babies begin **cooing** (the repetition of vowel sounds like "oo" and "ah").

By the time a child is 6 months old, the nervous system has matured enough to allow the child to grasp objects, to smile, laugh, sit up, and to **babble.** In the babbling stage, consonant sounds are added to produce a continuous outpouring of repeated language sounds. The influence of environment at this stage is indicated by the fact that babbling increases when parents talk to the child (Mussen et al., 1979).

At about 1 year of age, the child can stand alone for a short time and can respond to words such as *no* or *hi.* Soon afterward, the first connection between words and objects is formed, and children may address their parents as "Mama" or "Dada." Between the ages of 1½ and 2 years, children become able to stand and walk alone. By this time their vocabulary may include from 24 to 200 words. At first there is a **single-word stage,** during which the child says things such as "go," "juice," or "up" (Bloom & Lahey, 1978). Soon after, words are arranged in simple 2-word sentences called **telegraphic speech:** "Want Teddy," "Mama gone." From this point on, growth of the child's vocabulary and language skills proceeds at a phenomenal rate. By first grade, the child can understand around 8000 words and use about 4000.

The Roots of Language

In a fascinating study, researchers Louis Sander and William Condon (1974) filmed newborn infants as the babies listened to various sounds. A later frame-by-frame analysis of the films showed something astonishing: Infants move their arms and legs in synchrony to the rhythms of human speech. Random noise, rhythmic tapping, or disconnected vowel sounds will not produce this "language dance." Only the natural rhythms of speech have this effect.

Why would day-old infants "dance" to speech but not other sounds? One possibility is that language recognition is innate. Linguist Noam Chomsky (1968, 1975) has long claimed that humans have a **biological predisposition** to develop language. According to Chomsky, language organization is inborn, much like a child's ability to coordinate walking. If such inborn language recognition does exist, it may explain why children around the world use a limited number of patterns in their first sentences. Typical patterns include the following (Mussen et al., 1979):

Identification:	"See Kitty."
Nonexistence:	"Allgone milk."
Possession:	"My doll."
Agent-Action:	"Mama give."
Negation:	"Not ball."
Question:	"Where doggie?"

Question: Does Chomsky's theory explain why language develops so rapidly?

Perhaps. But many psychologists feel that Chomsky underestimates the importance of learning (Bruner, 1983). **Psycholinguists** (specialists in the psychology of language) have recently shown that language is not magically "switched on" by adult speech. Imitation of adults and rewards for correctly using words (as when a child asks for a cookie) are also a part of language learning. More important, parents and children begin to communicate long before the child can speak. Months of shared effort precede the child's first word (Miller, 1977). From this point of view, the filmed infants' behavior reflects a readiness to interact *socially* with parents, not innate language recognition.

Question: How do parents communicate with infants before they can talk?

Early Communication Parents go to a great deal of trouble to get babies to smile and vocalize (Fig. 14–11). In doing so, they quickly learn to change their actions to keep the infant's attention, arousal, and activity at optimal levels (Brazelton et al., 1974). A familiar example is the "I'm-Going-to-Get-You Game." In it, the adult says, "I'm gonna getcha. . . . I'm gonna getcha. . . . I'm gonna getcha. . . . Gotcha!" Through such games, adults and babies come to share similar rhythms and expectations (Stern, 1982). Soon a system of shared **signals** is created. Touching, vocalizing, gazing, and smiling help lay a foundation for later language use. Specifically, these signals establish a pattern of "conversational" **turn taking** (Bruner, 1983; Snow, 1977).

Mother	*Ann*
	(smiles)
"Oh what a nice little smile!"	
"Yes, isn't that nice?"	
"There."	
"There's a nice little smile."	(burps)
"Well, pardon you!"	
"Yes, that's better, isn't it?"	
"Yes."	(vocalizes)
"Yes."	(smiles)
"What's so funny?"	

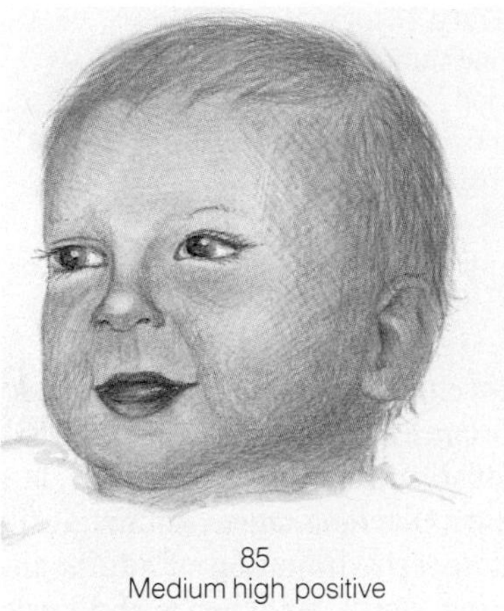

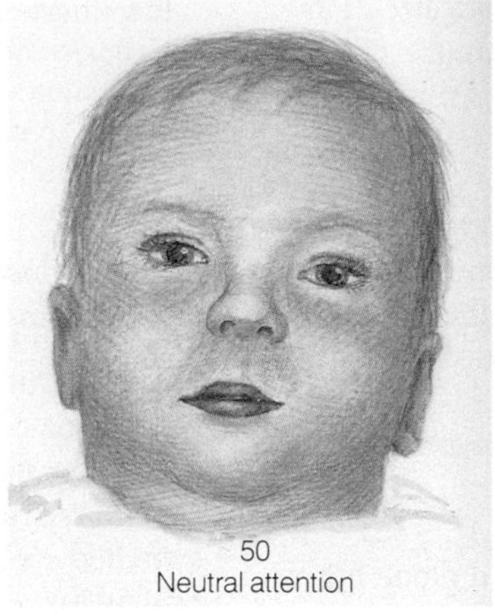

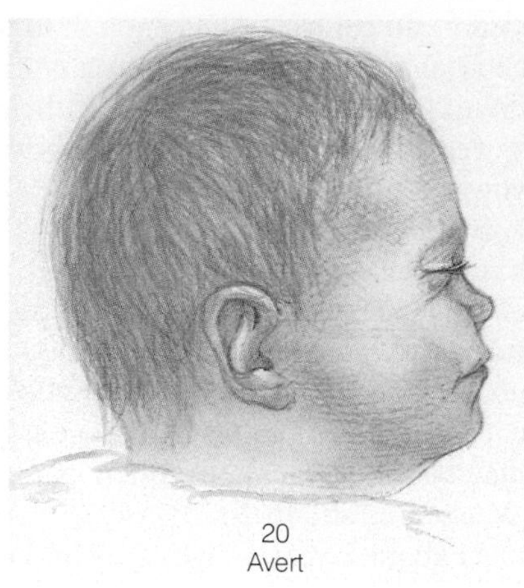

Fig. 14–11 *Infant engagement scale. These samples from a 90-point scale show various levels of infant engagement, or attention. Babies participate in prelanguage "conversations" with parents by giving and withholding attention and by smiling, gazing, or vocalizing. (From Beebe et al., 1982.)*

From the outside, such exchanges may look meaningless. In reality, they represent real communication. A baby's vocalizations and attention provide a way of interacting emotionally with parents (Stern et al., 1975). Even infants as young as 3 months make more speechlike sounds when an adult engages them in a turn-taking pattern of interaction (Bloom et al., 1987). (For another perspective on turn taking, see Fig. 14–12.)

In summary, some elements of language may be innate, but a full flowering of speech requires careful cultivation. Now that we have our subjects (babies) talking, let's move on to a broader view of intellectual development.

Cognitive Development—How Do Children Learn To Think? How Do Children Think To Learn?

Question: How different is a child's understanding of the world from that of an adult?

Generally speaking, a child's thinking is less abstract than an adult's. Children use fewer generalizations, categories, or principles. They also tend to base their understanding of the world on particular examples, tangible sensations, and material objects.

An indication of the concrete nature of thinking in very young infants is their failure to recognize the permanence of objects. Older children and adults realize that an object

Fig. 14–12 *This graph shows the development of turn taking in games played by an infant and his mother. For several months Richard responded to games such as peekaboo and "hand-the-toy-back" only when his mother initiated action. At about 9 months, however, he rapidly began to initiate action in the games. Soon, he was the one to take the lead about one-half of the time. Learning to take turns and to direct actions toward another person underlie basic language skills. (From Bruner, 1983.)*

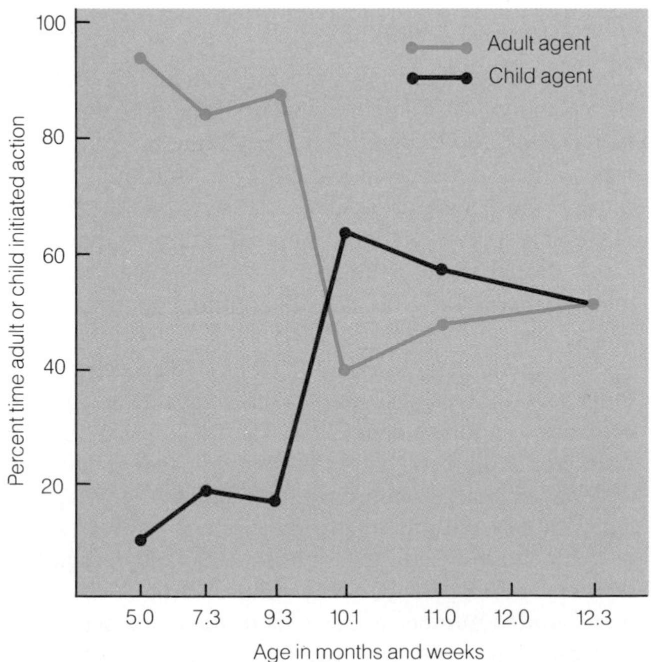

that is out of sight still exists. With a very young child, "out of sight" can literally mean "out of mind." If a ball rolls behind something while a 4- or 5-month-old infant is playing with it, the child behaves as if the ball has ceased to exist and stops looking for it.

Long after children have discovered the permanence of objects, their thinking remains concrete in other ways. For example, before age 6 or 7, children are unable to make *transformations*. If you show a child a short, wide glass full of milk and a tall, narrow glass (also full), the child will tell you that the taller glass contains more milk. Children will tell you this even if you allow them to watch as you pour milk from the short glass into an empty, tall glass. They are not bothered by the apparent transformation of the milk from a smaller to a larger amount (Fig. 14–13). They respond only to the fact that *taller* seems to mean *more*. After about age 7, children are no longer fooled by this situation. Perhaps this is why 7 has been called the "age of reason." From age 7 on, we see a definite trend toward more abstract thought (Elkind, 1968).

Fig. 14–13 *Children under age 7 intuitively assume that a volume of liquid is increased when it is poured from a short, wide container into a tall, thin one.*

Question: Is there any pattern to the growth of intellect in childhood?

According to the Swiss psychologist and philosopher Jean Piaget (1951, 1952) there is.

Piaget's Theory of Cognitive Development

Piaget (pea-ah-JAY) believed that all children pass through a series of distinct stages in intellectual development (Fig. 14–14). Many of his ideas came from observing his own children as they solved various thought problems. (It is tempting to imagine that Piaget's illustrious career was launched one day when his wife said to him, "Watch the children for a while, will you, Jean?") Piaget's many observations convinced him that intellect grows through processes that he called *assimilation* and *accommodation*.

Assimilation refers to using existing patterns in new situations. Let's say that a plastic hammer is Benjamin's favorite toy. Benjamin uses the hammer properly and loves to pound on blocks with it. For his birthday Benjamin gets an oversize toy wrench. If he uses the wrench for pounding, it has been assimilated to an existing mental structure.

In *accommodation*, existing ideas are modified to fit new requirements. For instance, a younger child might think

Fig. 14–14 *Jean Piaget—philosopher, psychologist, and keen observer of children.*

that a dime is worth less than a (larger) nickel. As the child begins to spend money, he or she will be forced to alter ideas about what "more" and "less" mean. Thus, new situations are assimilated to existing ideas, and new ideas are created to accommodate new experiences.

Piaget's theories have had a profound effect on our thinking about children. The following is a brief summary of what he found.

The Sensorimotor Stage (0–2 Years) In the first 2 years of life, a child's intellectual development is largely *nonverbal.* The child is mainly concerned with learning to coordinate *purposeful* movements with information from the senses. Also important at this time is gradual emergence of the concept of **object permanence.** By about age 1½, the child begins to actively pursue disappearing objects. By age 2, the child can anticipate the movement of an object behind a screen. For example, when watching an electric train, the child looks ahead to the end of a tunnel, rather than staring at the spot where the train disappeared.

In general, developments in this stage indicate that the child's conceptions are becoming more *stable.* Objects cease to appear and disappear magically, and a more orderly and predictable world replaces the confusing and disconnected sensations of infancy.

The Preoperational Stage (2–7 Years) During the preoperational period, the child is developing an ability to think *symbolically* and to use language. But the child's thinking is still very **intuitive.** (Do you remember thinking as a child that the sun and moon followed you when you took a walk?) In addition, the child's use of language is not as sophisticated as it might seem. Children have a tendency to confuse words with the objects they represent. If the child calls a toy block a "car" and you use it to make a "train," the child may be upset. To children, the name of an object is as much a part of the object as its size, shape, and color. This seems to underlie a preoccupation with name calling. To the preoperational child, an insulting name may hurt as much as "sticks and stones." Consider, for instance, one rather protected youngster who was angered by her older brother. Searching for a way to retaliate against her larger and stronger foe, she settled on, "You panty-girdle!" It was the worst thing she could think of saying.

During the preoperational stage, the child is also quite **egocentric,** or unable to take the viewpoint of other people. The child's ego seems to stand at the center of his or her world. To illustrate, show a child a 2-sided mirror. Then hold it between the two of you so the child can see herself in it. If you ask her what she thinks *you* can see, she imagines that you can see *her* reflected image instead of your own. The concept of egocentrism helps us to understand why children can seem exasperatingly selfish or uncooperative at times. A child who blocks your view by standing in front of a television set assumes that you can see if he can. If you ask him to move so you can see, he may move so that he can see better!

The Concrete Operational Stage (7–11 Years) An important development during this stage is mastery of the concept of **conservation.** Children have learned the concept of conservation when they understand that rolling a ball of clay into a "snake" does not increase the amount of clay and that pouring liquid from a tall, narrow glass into a shallow dish does not reduce the amount of liquid. In each case, the volume remains the same despite a change in shape or appearance. The original amount is conserved (see Fig. 14–13).

During the concrete operational stage, a child's thoughts begin to include the concepts of time, space, and number. Categories and principles are used, and the child can think logically about concrete objects or situations. These abilities explain why children stop believing in Santa Clause when they reach the stage of concrete operations. Because of their ability to conserve, they come to realize that Santa's sack couldn't hold that many toys or that it would be impossible to visit everyone's house in one evening (Fehr, 1976). Similarly, Charles Croll (1986) found that 65 percent of children aged 5 to 7 believe that the Tooth Fairy is real. Around the ages of 7 to 8, however, most children begin to realize that this is a fantasy.

Another important development at this time is the ability to reverse thoughts or operations. Lack of reversibility is illustrated by the following conversation with a 4-year-old boy still in the preoperational stage (Phillips, 1969).

> "Do you have a brother?"
> "Yes."
> "What's his name?"
> "Jim."
> "Does Jim have a brother?"
> "No."

Reversibility of thought allows children in the concrete operational stage to recognize that if $4 \times 2 = 8$, then 2×4 does, too. Younger children must memorize each relationship separately. Thus, a child may know that $4 \times 9 = 36$, but may not realize that 9×4 also equals 36.

The Formal Operations Stage (11 Years and Up) Sometime after about the age of 11, the child begins to break away from concrete objects and specific examples. Thinking is based more on abstract principles. Children can think about their thoughts, and they become less egocentric. The older child or adolescent also gradually becomes able to consider hypothetical possibilities (see Highlight 14–3). For example, if you ask a younger child, "What do you think would happen if it suddenly became possible for people to fly?" the child might respond, "But people can't fly." Older children are able to consider the possibilities and to discuss their implications.

During the stage of formal operations, full adult intellectual ability is attained. The older adolescent is capable of inductive and deductive reasoning and can comprehend math, physics, philosophy, psychology, and other abstract systems. From this point on, improvements in intellectual ability are based on gaining knowledge, experience, and wisdom, rather than on gains in basic thinking capacity.

Piaget Today Piaget's theory is a valuable "road map" for understanding how children think. But some research suggests that intellectual growth is not as strictly age-and-stage-related as Piaget claimed. Today, many psychologists are convinced that Piaget gave too little credit to the effects of learning (Harris, 1986). For example, children of pottery-making parents can correctly answer questions about the conservation of clay at an earlier age than Piaget would have predicted (Bransford et al., 1986). According to learning theorists, children continuously gain specific knowledge; they do not undergo stagelike increases in general mental ability (Carey, 1986).

Numerous studies do show that children make swift mental gains at about the ages Piaget stated. In fact, researchers have recently found evidence that cycles of brain growth occur at times that correspond with Piaget's stages (Thatcher et al., 1987). Thus, the truth may lie somewhere between Piaget's stage theory and modern learning theory. At the very least, further study is likely to refine and amend the ideas that grew from Piaget's fateful decision to "watch the children for awhile."

● HIGHLIGHT 14–3
Monopoly à la Piaget

Piaget's stages of cognitive development may be easier to remember if we relate them to a single example. What would happen at each stage if we played a game of *Monopoly* with the child?

Sensorimotor stage:	The child puts houses, hotels, and dice in mouth and plays with "Chance" cards.
Preoperational stage:	The child plays *Monopoly*, but makes up own rules and cannot understand instructions.
Concrete operational stage:	The child understands basic instructions and will play by the rules, but is not capable of hypothetical transactions dealing with mortgages, loans, and special pacts with other players.
Formal operations stage:	The child no longer plays the game mechanically; complex and hypothetical transactions unique to each game are now possible.

Learning Check

Match each item with one of the following stages.

A. Sensorimotor **B.** Preoperational **C.** Concrete operational **D.** Formal operations

1. ____ egocentric thought
2. ____ abstract or hypothetical thought
3. ____ purposeful movement
4. ____ intuitive thought
5. ____ conservation
6. ____ reversibility
7. ____ object permanence
8. ____ nonverbal development
9. Assimilation refers to applying existing thought patterns or knowledge to new situations. T or F?

10. The development of speech and language usually occurs in which order?
a. crying, cooing, babbling, telegraphic speech *b.* cooing, crying, babbling, telegraphic speech
c. babbling, crying, cooing, telegraphic speech *d.* crying, babbling, cooing, identification

11. Prelanguage turn taking and social interactions would be of special interest to a psycholinguist. T or F?

Answers:
1. B 2. D 3. A 4. B 5. C 6. C 7. A 8. A 9. T 10. *a* 11. T

● Moral Development—Growing a Conscience

A person with a terminal illness is in great pain. She is pleading for death. Should extraordinary medical efforts be made to keep her alive? If a friend of yours desperately needed to pass a test and asked you to help him cheat, would you do it? These are *moral* questions, or questions of conscience. How are moral values acquired? Psychologist Lawrence Kohlberg (1981a) believed that they are learned, in part, as children develop the ability to think and reason.

Question: What did he base this belief on?

Moral Dilemmas To study moral development, Kohlberg posed *moral dilemmas* to children of different ages. The following is one of the dilemmas he used (Kohlberg, 1969, adapted).

> A woman was near death from cancer, and there was only one drug that might save her. It was discovered by a druggist who was charging 10 times what it cost him to make the drug. The sick woman's husband could only pay $1000, but the druggist wanted $2000. He asked the druggist to sell it cheaper or to let him pay later. The druggist said no. So the husband became desperate and broke into the store to steal the drug for his wife. Should he have done that? Was it wrong or right? Why?

Each child was asked what action the husband should take. By classifying reasons given for each choice, Kohlberg identified three levels of moral development

At the first, **preconventional** level, moral thinking is determined by the consequences of actions (punishment, reward, or an exchange of favors). In the second, **conventional** level of moral development, actions are directed by a desire to conform to the expectations of others or to socially accepted rules and values. The third, **postconventional** level represents advanced moral development. Behavior at this level is directed by self-accepted moral principles. In addition to the 3 major levels, Kohlberg identified 6 stages of moral development (Table 14–2). In time, Kohlberg found it necessary to combine stages 5 and 6 because it proved difficult, in practice, to separate them (Kohlberg, 1981b). He remained firm in his belief, however, that morality develops in preconventional, conventional, and postconventional phases.

Question: Does everyone eventually reach the last level?

Kohlberg and his associates found that people advance through the stages at different rates and that many people fail to reach the "principled" postconventional stage. The preconventional stages (1 and 2) are most characteristic of young children and delinquents. Conventional group-oriented morals of stages 3 and 4 are characteristic of older children and most of the adult population. Kohlberg estimated that postconventional morality, representing self-direction and higher principles, is achieved by only about 20 percent of the adult population.

Morality in the Real World To illustrate the importance of moral development, let us compare two very different individuals. First let's apply Kohlberg's analysis to statements attributed to Nazi officer Adolf Eichmann, accused of sharing responsibility for the deaths of millions of Jews in Germany during World War II:

> In actual fact, I was merely a little cog in the machinery that carried out the directives of the German Reich [stage 1]. It was really none of my business [stage 2]. Yet what is there to "admit"? I carried out my order [stage 1]. (Kohlberg, 1969)

Compare this to the words of Mahatma Gandhi, the famous leader who protested British rule of India. Gandhi once addressed a British court:

> I had to either submit to a system which I considered had done irreparable harm to my country, or incur the risk. . . . I am here, therefore, to invite and cheerfully submit to the highest penalty that can be inflicted upon me for what in law is a deliberate crime and what appears to me to be the highest duty of a citizen.

Gandhi, like other great leaders (Lincoln, Martin Luther King, Bishop Tutu), was clearly operating at a postconventional level of morality in his political life.

Table 14–2 Kohlberg's Stages of Moral Development

PRECONVENTIONAL
Stage 1: Punishment orientation. Actions are evaluated in terms of possible punishment, not goodness or badness; obedience to power is emphasized. *Example:* "He shouldn't steal the drug because he could get caught and sent to jail" (avoiding punishment).
Stage 2: Pleasure-seeking orientation. Proper action is determined by one's own needs; concern for the needs of others is largely a matter of "You scratch my back and I'll scratch yours," not of loyalty, gratitude, or justice. *Example:* "It won't do him any good to steal the drug because his wife will probably die before he gets out of jail" (self-interest).
CONVENTIONAL
Stage 3: Good boy/good girl orientation. Good behavior is that which pleases others in the immediate group or which brings approval; the emphasis is on being "nice." *Example:* "He shouldn't steal the drug because others will think he is a thief. His wife would not want to be saved by thievery" (avoiding disapproval).
Stage 4: Authority orientation. In this stage the emphasis is on upholding law, order, and authority, doing one's duty, and following social rules. *Example:* "Although his wife needs the drug, he should not break the law to get it. Everyone is equal in the eyes of the law, and his wife's condition does not justify stealing" (traditional morality of authority).
POSTCONVENTIONAL
Stage 5: Social-contact orientation. Support of laws and rules is based on rational analysis and mutual agreement; rules are recognized as open to question, but are upheld for the good of the community and in the name of democratic values. *Example:* "He should not steal the drug. The druggist's decision is reprehensible, but mutual respect for the rights of others must be maintained" (social contract).
Stage 6: Morality of individual principles. Behavior is directed by self-chosen ethical principles that tend to be general, comprehensive, or universal; high value is placed on justice, dignity, and equality. *Example:* "He should steal the drug and then inform the authorities that he has done so. He will have to face a penalty, but he will have saved a human life" (self-chosen ethical principles).

Moral development is a promising topic for further study. As an example, consider the work of psychologist Carol Gilligan.

Justice or Caring? Gilligan (1982) has pointed out that Kohlberg's system is concerned mainly with the ethics of *justice*. Based on studies of women who faced real-life dilemmas, Gilligan argues that there is also an ethic of *caring* and responsibility. As one illustration, Gilligan presented the following story to 11- to 15-year-old American children.

The Porcupine and the Moles

> Seeking refuge from the cold, a porcupine asked to share a cave for the winter with a family of moles. The moles agreed. But because the cave was small, they soon found they were being scratched each time the porcupine moved about. Finally, they asked the porcupine to leave. But the porcupine refused, saying, "If you moles are not satisfied, I suggest that you leave."

Gilligan found that boys who read this story tended to opt for justice in resolving the dilemma: "It's the moles' house. It's a deal. The porcupine leaves." In contrast, girls tended to look for solutions that would keep all parties happy and comfortable, such as "Cover the porcupine with a blanket."

Gilligan's point is that male psychologists have, for the most part, defined moral maturity in terms of justice and autonomy. From this perspective, women's concern with relationships can look like a weakness rather than a strength. (A woman who is concerned about what pleases or helps others would be placed at stage 3 in Kohlberg's system.) But Gilligan believes that caring is also a major element of moral development and she suggests that males may lag in achieving it.

Whatever the outcome of such debates, research on moral development seems highly worthwhile. Many of the problems facing us today—over-population, environmental destruction, crime, prejudice—are essentially problems of individual conscience.

We have now examined development in several major areas. To conclude our discussion, the next section describes the effects of *deprivation* and *enrichment*. These are conditions that can affect nearly all facets of a child's early years.

Deprivation and Enrichment—A Practical Definition of Tender Loving Care

News item: "Wild Child Raised by Apes Found in Africa." Over the years there have been several reported discoveries of "feral children." These are children who supposedly have grown up in the care of animals and who act like animals when found. Actually, there is little documented evidence that such children have existed, but we needn't go this far afield for proof of the destructive effects of early **deprivation.**

Compare: Deprivation and Enrichment

Deprivation In development, the loss or withholding of normal stimulation, nutrition, comfort, love, and so on; a condition of lacking.

Enrichment In development, any attempt to make a child's environment more novel, complex, and perceptually or intellectually stimulating.

There are many confirmed cases of children who have spent the first 5 or 6 years of life in closets, attics, and other restricted environments. When discovered, these children are usually mute, severely retarded, and emotionally damaged. Some suffer from **deprivation dwarfism**—stunted growth associated with isolation, rejection, or general deprivation in the home environment (see boxed news excerpt). Special efforts to teach such children to speak and behave normally often meet with limited success. Examples such as this, as well as the earlier discussion of attachment, suggest that in many ways all of infancy is a *relatively critical period* in development.

"Closet Child" Now with Loving Parents

LONG BEACH (AP)—Becky's story began to unfold when the Sheriff's Department responded to a tip like hundreds of others. They found Becky in urine-soaked clothes, asleep on a hard cot in her parents' bedroom.

"She was almost like an animal," one of the deputies reported.

Her world then was the bedroom and its closet, in which she was kept for untold hours. Now Becky lives in a spacious foster home.

Since Becky's rescue, she has gained 12 pounds and grown 6 inches. But she is still a mite, for she weighed only 24 pounds and stood only 32 inches tall last April.

When she was found, Becky couldn't even crawl; now she walks. Then, she knew only a few words—now she speaks in sentences. She is, except for the hurt in her eyes, like almost any toddler.

But Rebecca is no toddler. She is 9 years old, and her pediatrician says she may never catch up.

Question: What aspects of deprivation are responsible for the damage done?

One of the earliest hints came when psychoanalyst René Spitz (1945) compared two groups of infants. One group was made up of healthy and lively babies in an institution Spitz called the "nursery." Spitz studied a second group of babies in a "foundling home" who suffered from a condition he called **hospitalism.** This is a pattern of deep depression marked by weeping and sadness and long periods of immobility or mechanical rocking. A lack of normal responsiveness to other humans is also typical of the problem. The foundling home had an unusually high rate of infant deaths, and development of the living babies was severely retarded.

Spitz compared conditions at the two institutions and found some striking differences. At the nursery, each baby had a separate attendant. At the foundling home, there were 8 babies to a nurse. In view of this, Spitz considered the "wasting away" of the foundling home babies a result of their lack of dependable "mother figures."

Question: In other words, the babies failed to form an attachment to an adult, right?

Yes. Recent work shows that a lack of attachment is a major element in early deprivation. For example, making living conditions better for a group of children in a Canadian institution failed to reverse their declining mental health. The children improved only when they were placed with caring foster parents or adoptive parents (Flint, 1978).

A second major factor in many cases of deprivation is a lack of **perceptual stimulation.** All of the "wasted" babies that Spitz studied were well cared for physically. However, they were kept in bare rooms in cribs with white sheets hung on the sides. The infants could see only the blank ceiling, and their only contact with others came during a few brief periods each day when they were quickly fed or changed. To put it mildly, there was *nothing happening* for these children: no change, no input, no cuddling, no attention, and most of all, no stimulation. This was deprivation in the fullest sense of the word.

Early Stimulation

Experiments with animals have confirmed the destructive effects of a lack of stimulation in infancy. For example, Harry Harlow separated infant rhesus monkeys from their mothers at birth. The real mothers were replaced with **surrogate** (artificial) **mothers.** These were essentially dummies of approximately the same size and shape as real monkeys. Some of the surrogates were made of cold, unyielding wire, and others were covered with soft terry cloth (Fig. 14–15). When the infants were given a choice between the two mothers, they consistently chose to spend most of their time clinging to the cuddly terry-cloth mother. This was true even when a bottle was mounted in the wire mother, making it the source of food.

The "love" and attachment displayed toward the cloth mothers was identical to that shown toward natural mothers. When frightened by rubber snakes, wind-up toys, and other "fear stimuli," the infant monkeys ran to their cloth mothers and clung to them for security (Harlow & Zimmerman, 1958). Harlow concluded that one of the most important dimensions of early stimulation is **contact comfort,** supplied by touching, holding, and stroking an infant. Harlow's findings may be inconclusive for humans, but other findings back them up. For example, one researcher found that just 20 minutes of extra touching a day could accelerate the development of infants in an institution (Casler, 1965).

Fig. 14–15 *An infant monkey clings to a cloth-covered surrogate mother. Baby monkeys become attached to the cloth "contact-comfort" mother but not to a similar wire mother. This is true even when the wire mother provides food. (Photo courtesy of Harry Harlow, University of Wisconsin Primate Laboratory.)*

For many psychologists, contact comfort is part of the rationale for advocating breast feeding of infants. Breast feeding almost guarantees that a baby will receive an adequate amount of touching and handling, and it appears to aid attachment (Jensen et al., 1981). In addition, breast-feeding mothers product **colostrum** (kuh-LOSS-trum) rather than milk for the first few days after birth. Colostrum is a fluid rich in proteins that carries antibodies from the mother to the newborn and helps prevent certain infectious diseases.

Question: What about the mother who can't breast-feed or who prefers not to?

The advantages of breast feeding are not overriding. If a mother is aware of the importance of touching and cuddling, bottle feeding is in no way psychologically inferior to breast feeding. In fact, a mother's warmth or coldness, relaxation or tension, and acceptance or rejection are more important than the choice of breast or bottle (Heinstein, 1963). As mentioned earlier, being sensitive to a baby's feeding rhythms and needs seems to be the key to promoting healthy infant attachment (Ainsworth, 1979).

Contact comfort may also underlie the tendency of many children to become attached to inanimate objects, such as blankets or stuffed toys. This does not appear to be a cause for alarm, however. A recent study of 2- to 3-year-old "blanket-attached" children found that they were no more insecure than others (Passman, 1987). (So, maybe Linus is okay after all.)

Enrichment If too little stimulation limits development, can an abundance of stimulation enhance it? Many attempts to answer this question have made use of **enriched environments.** Enriched environments are deliberately made more novel, complex, and richly stimulating. Enriched environments for infants may be the "soil" from which brighter children grow. To illustrate, let us begin with an experiment in which rats were raised in an enriched environment (Kretch et al., 1962).

Building Bigger and Better Brains

To begin, infant rats were divided into 2 groups. One group was raised in *stimulus-poor* conditions. These animals were housed in adequate but unstimulating cages. The cages had gray walls, and they contained nothing to explore or investigate. The second group was housed in a sort of "rat wonderland." The walls of the *stimulus-enriched* environment were decorated with colored patterns, and the cage was filled with platforms, ladders, and cubbyholes to be explored. When the

> rats reached adulthood, their ability to learn mazes was tested. The stimulated rats dramatically out-performed their deprived relatives. In addition, later tests showed that the stimulated rats had brains that were larger and heavier, with a thicker cortex.

It is a long leap from rats to people, but it is hard to overlook an increase in brain size caused by sensory stimulation. If stimulation can enhance the "intelligence" of a lowly rat, it is reasonable to assume that human infants also benefit from stimulation.

Question: Is there any evidence that this is actually the case?

As might be expected, it is much harder to demonstrate that such things occur in humans. In Chapter 18 you will find a full discussion of the effects of environment on intelligence. For now, let us examine two examples of enrichment applied to humans.

Infants like to reach out and touch things, but normally it takes about 5 months after birth for this skill to develop. In an experiment done at a state hospital, newborn infants were given several kinds of extra stimulation each day for several months (White & Held, 1966). Each child in the stimulus enrichment condition was handled an extra 15 minutes daily. Each was placed in a position that allowed visual exploration outside the crib. White crib sheets were replaced by patterned sheets with colorful animal designs. A collection of bright and colorful objects was hung over each child's crib. As limited as these changes may seem, they caused **visually directed reaching** to occur an average of 6 weeks early. This may not sound like an earth-shaking improvement in adult terms, but to an infant it is a substantial acceleration in development.

The preceding is only one of many experiments showing a positive relationship between stimulation and improvements in various abilities—particularly those that might be labeled "intellectual." One of the most encouraging examples of the benefits of enrichment is Program Head Start. The goal of Head Start is to prepare disadvantaged children for school by providing intellectual stimulation and helping them "learn to learn." Studies of Head Start and similar **early childhood education programs** show real improvements in later school performance. This is especially true for the most needy children (Scarr & Weinberg, 1986). There is little question that these programs enrich the lives of many children.

Summary Most people recognize that babies need lots of "tender loving care" where their physical needs are concerned. But as the previous discussion shows, a complete definition of tender loving care should include a baby's psychological needs as well. In general, the effects of deprivation and enrichment appear to apply to *all* of the categories of development discussed earlier. It would be a good idea to place perceptual and intellectual stimulation, affectionate touching, and personal warmth high on any list of infant needs.

Learning Check

1. According to Kohlberg, the conventional level of moral development is marked by a reliance on outside authority. T or F?
2. Self-interest and avoiding punishment are elements of postconventional morality. T or F?
3. About 80 percent of all adults function at the postconventional level of moral reasoning. T or F?
4. Gilligan regards gaining a sense of justice as the principal basis of moral development. T or F?
5. Harlow's "motherless monkeys" became attached to the wire surrogate mother if it fed them. T or F?
6. René Spitz attributed hospitalism to an absence of perceptual stimulation. T or F?
7. Bottle feeding prevents a mother from providing an adequate amount of contact comfort for an infant. T or F?
8. Early childhood education programs can be characterized as attempts to enrich the environments of deprived children. T or F?

Answers:

1. T 2. F 3. F 4. F 5. F 6. F 7. F 8. T

Applications: Making the Most of a Magic Time of Life

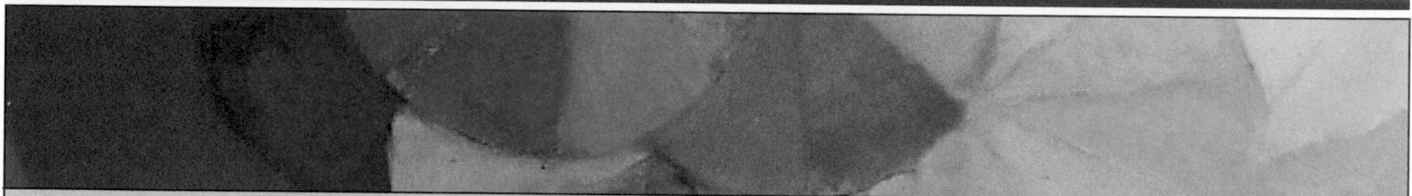

Many applications of the ideas presented in this chapter are self-evident. A few bear additional emphasis or extension.

Maturation It is valuable to remember that individual differences in maturation rates are the rule in human development. Aware parents recognize the difference between the **statistical child** and the **particular child.** Developmental norms specifying ages at which particular abilities appear are based on *averages*. There is always a wide range of normal variation around each average. Thus, it is reasonable to expect plateaus, reversals, and periods of rapid advancement in the development of a particular child. This applies not only to the emergence of motor skills, such as crawling and walking, but also to language development and the stages of cognitive development described by Piaget. In all areas of development, a child's uniqueness should be respected. This means resisting the temptation to compare the child with others—particularly in the child's presence. Each child is an individual and should be judged as such.

Enrichment

As we have noted, babies need stimulation. By keeping this need in mind, parents can do much to provide opportunities for varied sensory experience during infancy. A baby should be surrounded by colors, music, people, and things to see, taste, smell, and touch. Babies are not vegetables. It makes perfect sense to talk to infants, to take them outside, to hang mobiles over their cribs, or to rearrange their rooms now and then. Also, the more time babies spend interacting with parents, the faster they develop language and thinking abilities (Clarke-Stewart & Koch, 1983). Most parents could put far more imagination into enriching an infant's surroundings than they typically do.

Question: Can enrichment be overdone?

The answer depends more on the *quality* of enrichment than on its quantity. Remember that the goal in enrichment is to create a world that *responds* to the infant—not one that bombards the infant with stimuli.

Responsiveness The concept of **responsiveness,** mentioned earlier, applies to toys and objects, as well as to parents' behavior. Toys that respond to a child's actions, such as balls, rattles, mirrors—even a spoon and a pie tin—help speed infant learning. Experiences that allow children to see cause-and-effect results from their own behavior are particularly effective. As psychologist Paul Chance points out, the most expensive toys tend to be the least responsive. The least responsive toy available is probably a $500 color television, while one of the most responsive is a $1 rubber ball (Chance, 1982).

Many authorities are concerned about parents who try to push their children's intellectual development in a misguided attempt to produce "super babies." It's worth stating again that forcing a barrage of stimuli, flash cards, exercises, and the like, on infants is not enriching. Parents who approach play and learning as if their preschooler were on the fast track for Harvard are filling their own needs at the expense of the child (Alvino et al., 1985). True enrichment is responsive to the child's curiosity and interests. It does not make the child feel pressured to perform.

Question: Is enrichment useful only during infancy?

Definitely not. An enriched, responsive environment is beneficial at any stage of childhood. As a matter of fact, Jerome Kagan has reported that stimulation in later childhood can have a greater effect on intellect than previously thought.

Kagan studied babies who were raised in darkened huts in an isolated Guatemalan village. Without the benefit of even a moderate amount of stimulation, these children were severely retarded by age 2. Yet by age 11 they had become beautiful children—gay, alert, and active (Kagan & Klein, 1973). The rich stimulation of village life during later childhood was enough to reverse the effects of early deprivation.

Question: In general, what kinds of experiences are most likely to encourage intellectual development?

Piaget Revisited

Piaget's theory suggests that the ideal is to provide experiences that are only slightly novel, unusual, or challenging. Remember, a child's intellect develops mainly through accommodation. As old concepts and thinking habits become obsolete, they are discarded or adapted to fit new demands.

To stretch a child's intellect, demands must be made, but experiences that are too far beyond the familiar may cause frustration and withdrawal. Therefore, gradually expanding

Applications

beyond a child's current level of comprehension is usually most productive. Effective parents typically follow a sort of *one-step-ahead strategy* when adapting their instruction to their infants' current level of ability (Heckhausen, 1987).

Parents can contribute greatly to intellectual growth through their attitudes toward a child's *investigation* or exploration of the world. The child who repeatedly hears, "Don't touch that" (chair, handle, trash, radio, pencil, flower) or "I told you not to" (go up there, play with that, leave this spot, get dirty, and so forth) may become passive and intellectually dulled (Carew et al., 1976). Placing virtually all common objects off limits for a child is a serious mistake.

In addition, Piaget's work shows the importance of relating to a child on the right level. If you give a physical explanation when a very young child asks, "Why does the sun come up in the morning?" You may have missed the point. Answering in terms of the child's egocentric viewpoint is often more likely to be meaningful. An answer such as, "So that you will know it's time to get up" is completely satisfactory for a young child. Later, explanations can be made increasingly abstract and accurate.

It is also valuable to remember that children are newcomers to language. Many of the "silly" things children say have meanings that become apparent only to the adult patient enough to look for them. For example, language expert S. I. Hayakawa (1965) relates the following incident:

> Once when our little girl was 3 years old, she found the bath too hot and said, "Make it warmer." It took me a moment to figure out that she meant, "Bring the water more nearly to the condition we call warm." It makes perfectly good sense if you look at it that way. (From "The Use and Misuse of Language" by S. I. Hayakawa. In R. E. Farson, Ed., *Science and Human Affairs*. Palo Alto, California: Science and Behavior Books, 1965.).

Intellectual growth is encouraged when children feel free to express their ideas and when they feel understood.

Question: Are there any guidelines for relating to children at their own level?

In a delightful book entitled *Using Psychology*, psychologist Morris Holland offers some suggestions about how best to relate to children at different stages of intellectual development. The following points are drawn from his discussion (Holland, 1975).

1. **Sensorimotor stage (0–2).** Active play with a child is most effective at this stage. Encourage explorations in touching, smelling, and manipulating objects. Peekaboo is a good way to establish the permanence of objects.
2. **Preoperational stage (2–7).** Although children are beginning to talk to themselves and act out solutions to problems, touching and seeing things will continue to be more useful than verbal explanations. Concrete examples will also have more meaning than generalizations. The child should be encouraged to classify things in different ways. Learning the concept of conservation may be aided by demonstrations involving liquids, beads, clay, and other substances.
3. **Concrete operational stage (7–11).** Children in this stage are beginning to use generalizations, but they still require specific examples to grasp many ideas. Expect a degree of inconsistency in the child's ability to apply concepts of time, space, quantity, and volume to new situations.
4. **Formal operations stage (11–adult).** At this point, it becomes more realistic to explain things verbally or symbolically to a child. Helping the child to master general rules and principles now becomes productive. Encourage the child to create hypotheses and to imagine how things could be.

Keeping this general outline in mind should help you adjust to the changing patterns of intellect displayed by developing children.

Learning Check

1. The idea that the particular child is different from the "statistical child" applies to language development and cognitive skills, but not to motor development. T or F?
2. In his study of a Guatemalan village, Kagan found that a stimulating environment can sometimes reverse severe early deprivation. T or F?
3. To promote accommodation, it is best to provide information or experiences only moderately beyond a child's current level of comprehension. T or F?
4. Playing peekaboo is a good way to help the sensorimotor child master the concept of conservation. T or F?

Answers:
1. F 2. T 3. T 4. F

Exploration: The Brave New World of Genetics and Reproduction

In his famous novel, *Brave New World,* Aldous Huxley described a futuristic society in which "baby factories" produce thousands of duplicate humans to do society's labor. Huxley, writing in the 1930s, envisioned a future in which biological engineering would be used for sinister and totalitarian ends. Now that the future has arrived, we find instead that some of the possibilities Huxley anticipated have made it possible for previously infertile couples to have children. And yet, as is often true, new solutions create new problems. In this Exploration we will briefly describe some recent developments in medicine and genetics that raise interesting social, psychological, and ethical questions.

Biological Engineering

In the recent past, adoption was the only alternative for couples with untreatable infertility. Now, such couples have an array of new options. Let's investigate two that are of special interest.

Artificial Insemination If her husband is sterile, a woman can undergo **artificial insemination.** In this procedure, sperm from an anonymous donor are used to impregnate the woman. Donors are selected so that their eye and hair color, height, and so on, match as closely as possible the husband's. For obvious emotional reasons, some of the husband's sperm are sometimes mixed with the donor sperm so that it is impossible to tell who was actually the father.

Test-Tube Babies A technique called **in vitro fertilization** has recently made it possible for some infertile couples to bear children who share both the mother's and father's genes. To produce a "test-tube" baby, egg cells are surgically collected from the mother's ovary. The egg cells are then placed in a petri dish containing nutrients, and the father's sperm cells are added. After an egg cell is fertilized and begins dividing, it is implanted in the mother's womb, where it develops normally. In a new variation on in vitro fertilization, an unrelated woman may donate an egg cell to the infertile couple. The egg cell is then fertilized with the husband's sperm and implanted in the wife's uterus. Infertile couples who are considering this technique should be warned, however. The average first-time success rate is only 6 percent, and the cost ranges from $4000 to $6000.

Questions and Controversies

The procedures outlined here raise a number of practical, emotional, moral, and even religious issues. Many will no doubt occur to the reader. A few that may not are listed here.

Many donors for artificial insemination are used repeatedly. One clinic reported that a single donor fathered 50 babies. What if this donor harbored a genetic disease or defect? What if children fathered by the same donor were to meet and marry? Since they would be half brother and sister, their offspring would run a high risk of having genetic defects. What rules of testing and record keeping should apply to artificial insemination by donor?

Many scientists believe that handling egg cells for in vitro fertilization may increase the risk of deformities in the newborn. If a child is born with a defect, is the physician responsible? What if more than one egg is fertilized? Should it be donated to another infertile couple? Would letting it die constitute an abortion? Should in vitro fertilization be allowed if the man and woman are not married?

Sex Selection Another recent development that may have an impact on parenthood is the possibility of selecting an infant's sex prior to conception. The procedure involves separating *X*- and *Y*-bearing sperm and then artificially fertilizing the egg cell with all male-producing or all female-producing sperm.

Currently, sex selection techniques cannot *guarantee* to produce a child of the desired sex. Sex selection is also relatively expensive (about $400), and some couples may be discouraged by the need for artificial insemination. A further worry is that two-thirds of all childless American couples say they would prefer to have a boy as a first child. If large numbers of couples select their children's sex, would there be an excess of male births?

Exploration

Genetics and Parenthood

In recent years, having children has also been influenced by improved understanding of human genetics. Increasingly, it has become possible to combat troubles that "run in the family." It is now possible to identify a large number of genetic disorders, such as sickle-cell anemia, hemophilia, cystic fibrosis, muscular dystrophy, albinism, and some forms of mental retardation.

Genetic Counseling Prospective parents who suspect that they may be carriers of genetic disorders may seek **genetic counseling.** By examining the family history of each prospective parent, and in some cases by directly mapping chromosomes, geneticists can calculate the risk of a genetic disorder (Rowley, 1984).

Question: What can a couple do if the risk of a genetic defect is high?

Knowing the risks, parents can choose not to have a child; or, if the odds are in their favor, they may elect to take the chance. Even when there is a reasonable likelihood of genetic disorder, some couples elect to have children, but then have a test performed during pregnancy to detect the presence or absence of the genetic defect. Such prenatal testing is done by **amniocentesis** (AM-nee-oh-SEN-tee-sis), which involves taking a sample of amniotic fluid from the mother's womb. This procedure allows determination of fetal sex and the detection of many genetic defects.

Amniocentesis is usually done at about the fifteenth week of pregnancy. Thus, when a serious genetic defect is detected, couples who do not object to abortion can terminate the pregnancy. Parents who consider abortion unacceptable still have the advantage of forewarning so that they may prepare the best possible care for the child.

The Future

Recent advances in biology and genetics and the exploding knowledge about how DNA controls heredity will quite likely bring about profound changes in the human condition. Let's sample some of the possibilities.

Eugenics It is probably true that domestic plants and animals have been improved more in the past 50 years than in the previous 5000. This improvement has been accomplished primarily through **eugenics** (you-JEN-iks), or selective breeding for desirable characteristics. Some extremists have already proposed that eugenics be applied to humans. But the very idea is loaded with ethical problems. How would we decide what characteristics are desirable? And who would decide who can have children and who cannot? In practice, it is unlikely that widespread human eugenics will ever be practiced. On the other hand, the steady use of genetic counseling could have a eugenic effect on future generations.

Genetic Engineering In the future it may become possible to remove defective genes and replace them with normal ones. Could such genetic engineering also be used to produce beauty, intelligence, resistance to aging, or superhuman athletic potential? In theory yes, but practically speaking, probably not. Literally thousands of genes affect such qualities, not to mention the effects of environment. For this reason, limited genetic engineering involving one or two genes may soon become possible, but tampering with genes on a major scale is not likely in the near future. **Cloning,** the production of an entire organism from a single cell, is also likely to remain science fiction (where humans are concerned) for the immediate future.

Gene Cards One authority on genetic engineering and genetic defects predicts that people will one day carry a "gene identity card" based on blood tests made during childhood. These would show what hereditary diseases a person is predisposed to, or which problems may be passed on in childbearing when combined with the gene pattern of a mate (Milunsky, 1977).

Rapid advances in techniques that affect heredity and conception have an important place in the understanding of behavior. And as we have seen, such changes raise a number of important psychological and ethical questions. Some additional questions of interest are provided in the Questions for Discussion that conclude this chapter.

● Exploration

Learning Check

1. The procedure known as in vitro fertilization involves fertilizing a woman with donor sperm. T or F?
2. Test-tube babies are produced by fertilizing an egg cell outside of the body. T or F?
3. Current sex selection procedures can consistently produce male offspring, but they cannot guarantee female babies. T or F?
4. Amniocentesis is primarily used to select sex before birth. T or F?
5. The term *eugenics* refers to the production of an entire organism from a single cell. T or F?

Answers:
1. F 2. T 3. F 4. F 5. F

Chapter Summary

• The human **neonate** has a number of *adaptive reflexes,* including the **grasping, rooting, sucking,** and **Moro reflexes.** Neonates show immediate evidence of learning and of appreciating the consequences of their actions.
• Tests in a **looking chamber** reveal a number of visual preferences in the newborn. The neonate is drawn to complex, circular, curved, red or blue designs. Human face patterns are also preferred, especially familiar faces. In later infancy, interest in the unfamiliar emerges.
• **Maturation** of the body and nervous system underlies the orderly *sequence* of motor, cognitive, and language development. The *rate* of maturation, however, varies from person to person. Many early skills are subject to the principle of **readiness** (or **motor primacy**).
• The *nature-nurture controversy* concerns the relative contributions to development of **heredity** (nature) and **environment** (nurture). Hereditary instructions are carried by the **chromosomes** and **genes** in each cell of the body. Most characteristics are **polygenetic** and reflect the combined effects of **dominant** and **recessive** genes. Heredity influences a large number of personal characteristics and programs the general **human growth sequence.**
• Heredity is also involved in differences in **temperament** present at birth. Most infants reliably fall into one of three temperament categories: *easy* children, *difficult children, and slow-to-warm-up* children.
• Most psychologists accept that heredity and environment are inseparable and *interacting* forces. A child's **developmental level** therefore reflects *heredity, environment,* and the effects of the child's *own behavior.*
• **Prenatal development** is subject to environmental influences in the form of diseases, drugs, radiation, and the mother's diet, health, and emotions. Prenatal damage to the fetus may cause **congenital problems,** or "birth defects."
• Healthy children are produced by both **conventional birth** and by **natural (prepared) childbirth.** However, prepared births do have the advantage of minimizing the use of anesthetics. The father's presence at birth appears to be desirable, although his attitude toward birth may be of more basic importance. There is little evidence that **gentle birth** has any lasting advantages, although parents may prefer it for other reasons.
• Studies of parents and their children suggest that **caregiving styles** have a substantial impact on emotional and intellectual development. Whereas mothers typically emphasize caregiving, fathers tend to function as a playmate for the infant.
• **Self-awareness** and **social referencing** are elements of early social development. A variety of **critical periods** exist in development, as illustrated by **imprinting** in animals. **Emotional attachment** of human infants to their caregivers is a critical early event. Infant attachment is reflected by **separation anxiety.** Although the issue is debated, it is doubtful that immediate *mother-infant contact* is crucial for forming lasting emotional bonds.
• **Language development** proceeds from control of **crying,** to **cooing,** then **babbling,** the use of **single words,** and then to **telegraphic speech.**
• The underlying patterns of telegraphic speech suggest a *biological predisposition* to acquire language. This innate predisposition is augmented by learning. **Prelanguage communication** between parent and child involves *shared rhythms,* nonverbal *signals,* and *turn taking.*

• The intellect of a child is *less abstract* than that of an adult. Jean Piaget theorized that intellectual growth occurs through a combination of **assimilation** and **accommodation.** He also held that children go through a fixed series of **cognitive stages.** The stages and their approximate age ranges are: **sensorimotor (0–2), preoperational (2–7), concrete operational (7–11),** and **formal operations (11–adult).**
• Lawrence Kohlberg theorized that **moral development** passes through a series of stages revealed by moral reasoning. These stages can be grouped into **preconventional, conventional,** and **postconventional** levels of morality. Some psychologists have questioned whether measures of moral development should be based only on a morality of justice.
• Early *perceptual, intellectual,* and *emotional* **deprivation** seriously retards development. Even physical growth may be affected, as is the case in **deprivation dwarfism.**
• Research on deprivation suggests that perceptual stimulation is essential for normal development. Work with subhuman primates (monkeys) has also pointed to **contact comfort** as an important source of infant stimulation and attachment. Deliberate **enrichment** of the environment in infancy has a beneficial effect on development.
• Wise parents recognize the difference between the **statistical child** and a **particular child.** Effective enrichment is *responsive* to a child's interests and needs, and it takes into account the child's level of cognitive development.
• Many recent developments in genetics and reproduction raise ethical and social questions. Examples of such developments are **artificial insemination, in vitro fertilization, sex selection techniques, amniocentesis, eugenics,** and **cloning.**

Questions for Discussion

1. Should humans try to control their own heredity? Who would decide what characteristics should be developed? Who would get them? For what purpose? Would you endorse use of genetic engineering to delay or prevent aging?

2. If pre-selection of the sex of a child becomes possible, what effect would you predict on the *long-term* ratio of males to females born? (Currently, 106 males are born for every 100 females.) Why do you make this prediction? What are its implications? (If the population became roughly 70 percent male, the birth rate and population growth would slow dramatically.)

3. Which do you think would produce a better decision by prospective parents receiving genetic counseling: to be told that "There is a 1 percent chance of having a child with a chromosome abnormality" or to be given the same information this way: "You must realize that either it will or it will not happen"?

4. What are your thoughts on the practical and ethical questions that follow. Should children conceived by donor artificial insemination or by donor egg be told about their parentage? Should records be kept that would allow them to find their donor fathers or mothers if some extraordinary need were to arise? What would be the psychological impact of knowing that you were conceived in vitro?

5. In view of the importance of infant attachment and the participation of fathers in child care, what changes would you recommend in maternity and paternity leaves from work? Would you change the traditional division of labor in maternal and paternal roles? Why or why not?

6. What is your reaction to the following statement, made by anthropologist Margaret Mead? "Fathers are a biological necessity but a social accident."

7. In what ways is it accurate to treat children as "little adults"? In what ways is it inaccurate? What is the value of children in society?

8. How many ways can you think of for an infant to reward its mother and for the mother to reward the infant?

9. What types of toys would you select for an infant or young child? Do you think simple toys or elaborate toys would be best? Why? Would your choice change for an older child? Why?

10. How has heredity affected your development? How has environment affected you? How would child rearing be different if parents had to teach children to walk or to talk?

11. How did you answer Kohlberg's moral dilemma about the husband who stole a drug for his sick wife? Do you think your answer reflects the role of moral reasoning in your personality?

12. Do you think the "draft dodgers," antiwar activists, or conscientious objectors of the 1960s were acting in self-interest or at higher levels of morality? What level of morality would you say Oliver North was operating at preceding the Iran-Contra scandal of 1988? What level of moral reasoning is most frequently displayed by the characters in TV dramas, comedies, or commercials?

Chapter 15

From Birth to Death: Life-Span Development

In This Chapter
Erikson's stages of life
Problems of childhood
Serious childhood problems
Adolescence and puberty
Adult development
Aging
Death and dying
Applications
Parenting
The problem of child abuse
Exploration
New perspectives on death

Chapter Preview

Life with Billy

By the time he was 5, Billy resembled a parent's worst nightmare. Billy threw uncontrollable temper tantrums and never seemed to sleep. He had not learned to talk. He got into closets and tore up his mother's dresses and urinated on her clothes. He smashed furniture and spread soap powder and breakfast food all over the floors. He attacked his mother at every opportunity, once going for her throat with his teeth. He tried to stuff his baby brother in a toy box. When Billy's parents bought him a doll they called by the baby's name, they began finding the doll pushed head down in the toilet bowl.

Billy refused to eat anything but cold, greasy hamburgers from a certain drive-in. To get through a week, his parents were forced to buy the hamburgers by the sack and hide them around the house, so Billy wouldn't eat them all at once. When his parents went out driving they had to detour around drive-ins to prevent Billy from frothing at the mouth and trying to jump out the window (Moser, 1965). Billy, you may note, was not an average 5-year-old.

Question: What was his problem?

Billy was an autistic *child. His problem is rare. Few children get off to as bad a start in life as Billy. Nevertheless, each of us faces certain challenges and problems on the path to healthy development. Some obstacles, such as toilet training or establishing an identity, can be considered universal. Others are specialized problems. In either case, the challenges of development extend far beyond childhood and into old age.*

In this chapter we will examine development from a life-span perspective. Life-span psychologists study both continuity *and* change *in behavior during a lifetime (Baltes, 1987). As you read this chapter, be alert for information pertinent to your own life. Watch for Billy, too. You'll meet him again later in the chapter.*

Survey Questions

- What are the typical tasks and dilemmas of childhood, adolescence, adulthood, and old age?
- What are some of the more serious childhood problems?
- In what ways is adolescent development especially challenging?
- What happens psychologically during adulthood and aging?
- How do effective parents rear their children?
- In what ways are attitudes toward death changing?

The Cycle of Life—Rocky Road or Garden Path?

If you pride yourself on being one of a kind, you have good reason. There is no such thing as a "typical person" or a "typical life." Nevertheless, there are certain broad similarities in the universal **life stages** of infancy, childhood, adolescence, young adulthood, middle adulthood, and old age. Each stage confronts a person with a new set of **developmental tasks** to be mastered. These are skills that must be acquired or personal changes that must take place for optimal development. Examples are learning to read in childhood, adjusting to sexual maturity in adolescence, and establishing a vocation as an adult (Havighurst, 1979).

In an influential book entitled *Childhood and Society* (1963), personality theorist Erik Erikson suggests that we face a specific **psychosocial dilemma,** or "crisis," at each stage of life. According to Erikson, resolving each dilemma creates a new balance between a person and the social world. An unfavorable outcome throws us off balance and makes it harder to deal with later crises. A string of "successes" produces healthy development and a satisfying life. Those who are plagued with unfavorable outcomes may experience life as a "rocky road."

Question: What are the major developmental tasks and life crises?

This is a broad question requiring an extended answer. Read on!

Stage One, First Year of Life: Trust Versus Mistrust During the first year of life, children are completely dependent on others. Erikson believes that a basic attitude of **trust** or **mistrust** is formed at this time. Trust is established when babies are given adequate warmth, touching, love, and physical care. Mistrust is caused by inadequate or unpredictable care and by parents who are cold, indifferent, or rejecting. Basic mistrust may later cause insecurity, suspiciousness, or inability to relate to others. Notice that basic trust is encouraged by the same conditions that help babies become securely attached to their parents (see Chapter 14).

Stage Two, 1–3 Years: Autonomy Versus Shame and Doubt In stage 2, children's growing self-control is expressed by climbing, touching, exploring, and a general desire to do things for themselves. Parents help foster a sense of **autonomy** by encouraging children to try new skills. However, the child's crude efforts often result in spilling, falling, wetting, and other "accidents." Thus, parents who *ridicule* their children, or *overprotect* them, may cause them to feel **shame** and to **doubt** their abilities.

Stage Three, 3–5 Years: Initiative Versus Guilt In stage 3, the child moves from simple self-control to an ability to take initiative. Through play the child learns to plan, undertake, and carry out a task. Parents reinforce **initiative** by giving the child the freedom to play, to ask questions, to use imagination, and to choose activities (Fig. 15–1). Children may be emotionally handicapped by parents who criticize severely, prevent play, or discourage questions. In this case, children learn to feel **guilty** about the activities they initiate.

Stage Four, 6–12 Years: Industry Versus Inferiority Many of the events of middle childhood are symbolized by that fateful day when you first entered school. With dizzying speed your world expanded beyond your family, and you faced a whole series of new challenges.

Erikson describes the elementary school years as the child's "entrance into life." In school, children begin to learn skills valued by society, and success or failure can have lasting effects on their feelings of adequacy. Children learn a sense of **industry** if they win praise for building, painting, cooking, reading, studying, and other productive activities. If a child's efforts are regarded as messy, childish, or inadequate, feelings of **inferiority** result. For the first time, teachers, classmates, and adults outside the

Fig. 15–1 *According to Erikson, children aged 3 to 5 learn to plan and initiate activities through play.*

home become as important as parents in shaping attitudes toward oneself.

Stage Five, Adolescence: Identity Versus Role Confusion Adolescence is a turbulent time for many persons in our culture. Caught between childhood and adulthood, the adolescent faces some unique problems. Erikson considers a need to answer the question, "Who am I?" the primary task during this stage of life. Mental and physical maturation brings to the individual new feelings, a new body, and new attitudes (Fig. 15–2). The adolescent must build a consistent **identity** out of self-perceptions and relationships with others. Conflicting experiences as a student, friend, athlete, worker, son or daughter, lover, and so forth, must be integrated into a unified sense of self (more on this later). According to Erikson, persons who fail to develop a sense of identity suffer from **role confusion,** an uncertainty about who they are and where they are going.

Question: What does Erikson believe is the major conflict in early adulthood?

Stage Six, Young Adulthood: Intimacy Versus Isolation In stage 6, the individual experiences a need to achieve an essential quality of **intimacy** in his or her life. After establishing a stable identity, a person is pre-

Fig. 15–2 *Dramatic differences in physical size and maturity are found in adolescents of the same age. The girls pictured are all 13, the boys 16. Maturation that occurs earlier or later than average can affect the "search for identity." (From "Growing Up" by J. M. Tanner. Copyright © September 1973 by Scientific American, Inc. All rights reserved.)*

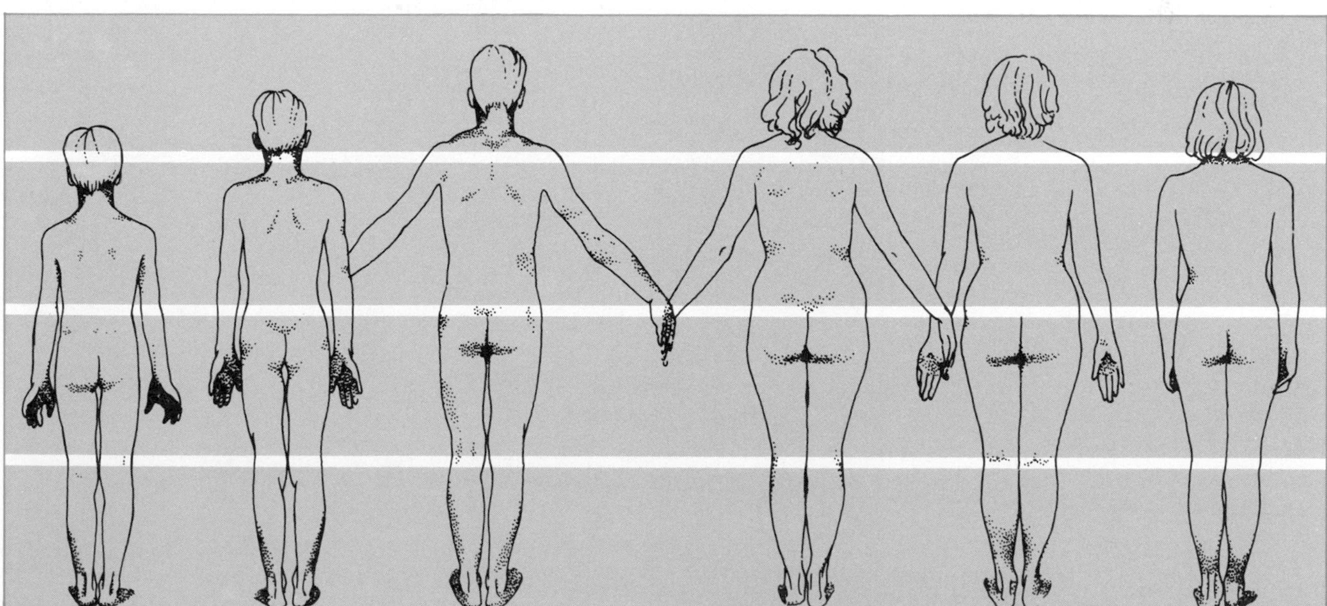

pared to share meaningful love or deep friendship with others. By "intimacy," Erikson means an ability to care about others and to share experiences with them. In line with Erikson's view, 75 percent of college-age men and women rank a good marriage and family life as their primary adult goal (Bachman & Johnson, 1979). And yet, marriage or sexual involvement is no guarantee that intimacy will prevail: Many adult relationships remain superficial and unfulfilling. Failure to establish intimacy with others leads to a deep sense of **isolation.** The person feels alone and uncared for in life. This circumstance often sets the stage for later difficulties.

Stage Seven, Middle Adulthood: Generativity Versus Stagnation. According to Erikson, an interest in guiding the next generation is the main source of balance in mature adulthood. This quality, called **generativity,** is expressed by caring about oneself, one's children, and the future (Fig. 15–3). Generativity may be achieved by guiding one's own children or by helping other children (as a teacher, clergyman, or coach, for example). It may also be achieved through productive or creative work. In any case, a person's concern and energies must be broadened to include the welfare of others and of society as a whole. Failure in this is marked by a **stagnant** concern with one's own needs and comforts. Life loses meaning, and the person feels bitter, dreary, and trapped.

Question: What does Erikson see as the conflicts of old age?

Stage Eight, Late Adulthood: Integrity Versus Despair Because old age is a time of reflection, a person must be able to look back over the events of a lifetime with a sense of acceptance and satisfaction. According to Erikson, the previous seven stages of life become the basis for successful aging. The person who has lived richly and responsibly develops a sense of **integrity.** This allows the person to face aging and death with dignity. If previous life events are viewed with regret, the elderly person falls into **despair.** In this case, there is a feeling that life has been a series of missed opportunities, that one has failed, and that it is too late to reverse what has been done. Aging and the threat of death then become a source of fear and depression.

In squeezing the events of a lifetime into a few pages, we must ignore countless details. Although much is lost, the net effect is a clearer picture of an entire life cycle. Is Erikson's description, then, an exact map of your future? Probably not. Still, the dilemmas we have discussed reflect major psychological events in the lives of many people. Knowing about such events may allow you to anticipate typical trouble spots in life. You may also be better prepared to understand the problems and feelings of friends and relatives at various stages in the life cycle.

Having completed our whirlwind birth-to-death tour, we will revisit several life stages for a closer look at some of their challenges, milestones, tasks, and problems. Before we begin, it might be a good idea to complete the Learning Check that follows.

Fig. 15–3 *According to Erikson, an interest in future generations characterizes optimal adult development.*

Learning Check

Since Erikson's eight life stages are scattered through the previous pages, you might find it helpful to summarize them. Complete this do-it-yourself summary to check your recall of the stages. Compare your answers with those given at the end of this Learning Check to make sure you have a correct summary.

Stage	Crisis	Favorable outcome
First year of life	**1.** ________ vs. **2.** ________	Faith in the environment and in others
Ages 1–3	Autonomy vs. **3.** ________	Feelings of self-control and adequacy
Ages 3–5	**4.** ________ vs. guilt	Ability to begin one's own activities
Ages 6–12	Industry vs. **5.** ________	Confidence in productive skills, learning how to work
Adolescence	**6.** ________ vs. role confusion	An integrated image of oneself as a unique person
Young adulthood	Intimacy vs. **7.** ________	Ability to form bonds of love and friendship with others
Middle adulthood	Generativity vs. **8.** ________	Concern for family, society, and future generations
Late adulthood	**9.** ________ vs. **10.** ________	Sense of dignity and fulfillment, willingness to face death

Answers:

1. trust **2.** mistrust **3.** shame or doubt **4.** initiative **5.** inferiority **6.** identity **7.** isolation **8.** stagnation **9.** integrity **10.** despair

Problems of Childhood—Why Parents Get Gray Hair

Can you remember a time in your childhood when your actions led to a disaster or a near disaster? It shouldn't be hard. It's a wonder that many of us survive childhood at all. Where I grew up, digging underground tunnels, wriggling down chimneys, hopping on trains, jumping off houses, crawling through storm drains, making bombs—and worse—were common childhood adventures.

Question: If initiative and industry are important in childhood, what limits should parents place on a child's freedom to explore the world?

An answer is provided by psychologist Diana Baumrind (1980), who has studied the effects of three major styles of parenting. According to Baumrind, each style tends to have a different effect on children's behavior. See if you recognize the styles she describes.

Authoritarian parents view children as having few rights but adultlike responsibilities. The authoritarian parent tends to demand strict adherence to rigid standards of behavior. The child is expected to stay out of trouble and to accept without question what the parents regard as right or wrong behavior. The children of such parents typically are obedient and self-controlled. But they also tend to be emotionally stiff, withdrawn, apprehensive, and lacking in curiosity.

Overly permissive parents view children as having few responsibilities but rights similar to adults. Such parents require little responsible behavior from their children. Rules are not enforced, and the child usually gets his or her way. This tends to produce dependent, immature children who misbehave frequently. Such children are aimless and tend to "run amok."

Baumrind describes **effective parents** as those who balance their own rights with those of their children. Such parents are *authoritative* but not authoritarian. That is, they control their children's behavior, but they are also loving and caring. Effective parents approach discipline in a way that is firm and consistent, not harsh or rigid. In general, they encourage the child to act responsibly. This parenting style produces children who tend to be competent, self-controlled, independent, assertive, and inquiring. Thus, by balancing freedom and restraint, effective parents help children become responsible adults.

As an added guide to parenting, it may help to remember that stress is a normal part of life—even in childhood. Certainly this does not mean that parents should go out of their way to stress a child. However, it does suggest that children need not be completely shielded from stressful stimulation. **Overprotection** (sometimes called "smother love") can be as damaging as overly stressing a child or being overly strict or permissive.

Most children do a good job of keeping stress at comfortable levels when *they* initiate an activity (Murphy & Moriarty, 1976) (Fig. 15–4). At a public swimming pool, for instance, some children can be observed making death-defying leaps from the high dive, while others stick close to the wading area. If no immediate danger is present, it is reasonable to let children get stuck in trees, make themselves dizzy, squabble with neighborhood children, and so forth. Getting into a few scrapes can help prepare a child to cope with later stresses. Just think, if your author hadn't crawled through a few storm pipes, his adult interest in plumbing the depths of the psyche might have gone down the drain.

Question: How can you tell if a child is being subjected to too much stress?

Normal Childhood Problems Child specialists Chess, Thomas, and Birch (1965) have listed a number of difficulties experienced at times by almost every child. These can be considered normal reactions to the unavoidable stress of growing up.

Fig. 15–4 *Most children do a good job of keeping stress at comfortable levels when they initiate an activity.*

1. All children experience occasional **sleep disturbances,** including wakefulness, frightening dreams, or a desire to get into their parents' bed.
2. **Specific fears** of the dark, dogs, school, or a particular room or person are also common.
3. Most children will be **overly timid** at times, allowing themselves to be bullied by other children into giving up toys, a place in line, and the like.
4. Temporary periods of **general dissatisfaction** may occur, when nothing pleases the child.
5. Children also normally display periods of **general negativism** marked by tantrums, refusal to do anything requested, or a tendency to say no on principle.
6. Another normal problem is **clinging,** in which children refuse to leave the side of their mothers or to do anything on their own.
7. Development does not always advance smoothly. Every child will show occasional **reversals** or **regressions** to more infantile behavior.

An additional problem common to the elementary school years is **sibling rivalry.** It is normal for a certain amount of jealousy, rivalry, and even hostility to develop between brothers and sisters. Some sibling conflict may even be constructive. A limited amount of aggressive give-and-take between siblings provides an opportunity to learn emotional control, self-assertion, and good sportsmanship (Bank & Kahn, 1982). Parents can help keep such conflicts within bounds by not "playing favorites" and by resisting the temptation to compare one child with another.

Parents should also expect some **rebellion** from their children. Most school-age children rebel at times against the rules and limitations of the adult world. For many children, being with peers offers a chance to "let off steam" by doing some of the things the adult world forbids. It is normal for children to be messy, noisy, hostile, or destructive to a moderate degree.

It is important to keep in mind that "normal problems" can signal a more serious disturbance if they worsen or last for long periods. Problems of a more serious nature are identified in the following section.

Significant Childhood Problems—Off to a Bad Start

Although severe emotional disturbances affect only a minority of children, the number involved is larger than most people realize.

Question: What is the nature of these problems?

Toilet-Training Disturbances Difficulty sometimes centers on toilet training or bowel and bladder habits. The two most common problems are **enuresis** (EN-you-REE-sis: lack of bladder control) and **encopresis** (EN-coh-PREE-sis: lack of bowel control). Enuresis is more common than encopresis and many times more common among males than females. Both wetting and soiling can be a means of expressing frustration or pent-up hostility.

Parents should not be overly alarmed by some delays in toilet training or by a few "accidents." As mentioned in Chapter 14, 30 months is the average age for completing toilet training. It is not unusual, however, for some children to take 6 months longer. Even when problems persist, they may be purely physical. Many bed-wetters, for instance, have difficulty because they become extremely relaxed when asleep. These children can be helped by limiting the amount they drink during the evening. They should also use the toilet before going to bed, and they can be rewarded for "dry" nights. Understanding, tact, and sympathy can do much to alleviate mild disturbances. Where more serious problems exist, parents should seek professional help.

Feeding Disturbances Feeding disturbances take a variety of forms. The disturbed child may vomit or refuse food for no reason or may drastically overeat or undereat. **Overeating** is sometimes encouraged by a parent who feels unloved and compensates by showering the child with "love" in the form of food. Some parents overfeed simply because they consider a fat baby healthy or desirable. Whatever the case, overfed children develop eating habits and conflicts that have lifelong consequences.

As described in Chapter 11, serious cases of *undereating*, or self-starvation, are called **anorexia nervosa** (AN-or-REX-yah ner-VOH-sah: nervous loss of appetite). The victims of anorexia nervosa are mostly adolescent females. In addition to the causes described in Chapter 11, anorexia may reflect conflicts about maturing sexually. By starving themselves, adolescent girls can limit figure development and prevent menstruation (Palazolli, 1978). This delays the time when they must face adult responsibilities.

Another childhood eating difficulty is called **pica** (PIE-ka). Some children go through a period of intense appetite during which they eat or chew on all sorts of inedible substances. The two most common substances are plaster and chalk. But some children try to eat things like buttons, rubber bands, mud, or paint flakes. The latter can be quite dangerous because some paint contains lead, which is highly poisonous.

Speech Disturbances The two most common speech problems are **delayed speech** and **stuttering.** A serious delay in learning to talk can be a serious handicap. An example is Tommy, who at age 5 was still talking in telegraphic speech: "Me go. Outdoor. Mama in car now. Dink Tommy cup" (Van Riper & Emerick, 1984). Delayed speech is sometimes caused by too little intellectual stimulation in early childhood. Other possible causes are parents who discourage the child's attempts to grow up, childhood stresses, mental retardation, and emotional disturbances.

In the past, stuttering was held to be a psychological disturbance, and many parents were made to feel guilty about their child's speech problem. Now, researchers believe that stuttering is usually of physical origin. For example, stuttering is 4 times more common in males than in females, and it seems to be at least partially inherited (Sheehan & Costley, 1977). However, learned fears, anxieties, and speech patterns probably add to the problem as well (Van Riper & Emerick, 1984).

Stuttering is most likely to occur when a person fears that he or she is going to stutter. Thus, parents must be careful not to add to a child's anxiety and frustration by being angry or critical. If a child begins speech therapy before adolescence, there is a chance that stuttering will disappear. In some cases, it may even disappear on its own. But if it doesn't disappear, or isn't treated, stuttering can become a lifelong problem.

Learning Disorders Soon after Gary entered school, he became shy and difficult. Gary's teacher suspected a learning disability, and a specialist confirmed it. **Learning disabilities** include problems with thinking, perception, language, attention, or activity levels. Gary's specific problem was **dyslexia** (dis-LEX-yah), an inability to read with understanding. Because of it, he often felt confused and "stupid" in class, although his intelligence was normal.

The causes of dyslexia are not known at present. However, researchers suspect that it is related to brain dominance. As you may recall from Chapter 3, the left side of the brain is usually dominant over the right in language ability. In a minority of people, the right brain is language dominant or shares language ability with the left brain. People with shared or reversed dominance of this sort seem to be more prone to language disorders, including dyslexia (Durden-Smith & DeSimone, 1984; Marx, 1983).

One of the most significant learning disorders is **hyperactivity.** The hyperactive child is constantly in motion and cannot concentrate (Fig. 15–5). The child talks rapidly, cannot sit still, rarely finishes work, acts on impulse, and cannot pay attention. Hyperactivity occurs in 3 to 5

Fig. 15–5 *The hyperactive child's inability to hold still and pay attention can seriously disrupt learning.*

percent of American children, with 5 times as many boys as girls being affected (Varley, 1984). Unless it is carefully managed, hyperactivity can severely limit a child's ability to learn (Mannuzza et al., 1988).

Question: What causes hyperactivity?

The most widely held theory is that hyperactivity is the result of **minimal brain dysfunction (MBD).** Experts who support this theory link hyperactivity to a lag in brain maturation or to undetected damage to the brain. Physicians typically use stimulant drugs to control hyperactivity. (Stimulants help the child to pay attention longer.) On one hand, such drugs do appear to lessen excessive activity (Solanto, 1984). On the other hand, psychologists have objected to this blanket use of powerful drugs, which they regard as dangerous and unnecessary (Havighurst, 1976).

Question: What kind of treatment do they suggest?

Some researchers have found **behavior modification** as effective as drug treatment (Gadow, 1985; Pelham, 1977). Behavior modification is the application of learning principles to human problems (see Chapter 22 for more information). The basic idea is to find times when the hyperactive child is calm and attentive and to reward the child for such behavior. When children are taught self-control in this way, improvements are more lasting than they are with drug treatment alone (Franks, 1987).

Childhood Autism Childhood **autism** (AW-tiz'm) is a problem that affects 1 in 2500 children, boys 4 times more often than girls. Autism is one of the most severe childhood problems. The autistic child is locked into a private world and appears to have no need for affection or contact with others. Autistic children do not even seem to know or care who their parents are.

In addition to being extremely isolated, the autistic child may throw gigantic temper tantrums—sometimes including self-destructive behavior such as head banging. Sadly, many well-meaning parents unintentionally reward such behavior with attention and concern (Edelson, 1984). Many autistic children are mute. If they speak at all, autistic children often infuriatingly parrot back everything said, a response known as **echolalia** (EK-oh-LAY-li-ah). These children also engage in frequent repetitive actions such as rocking, flapping their arms, or waving their fingers in front of their eyes. Additionally, they may show no response to an extremely loud noise (sensory blocking) or they may spend hours watching a water faucet drip (sensory "spin-out") (Ferster, 1968; Rimland, 1978).

Question: Do parents cause autism?

At one time experts blamed parents for autism. It is now recognized that autism is caused by congenital defects in the nervous system (Schopler, 1978). This is why even as babies, autistic children are aloof and do not cuddle or mold to their parents' arms. Recent research suggests that the defect may lie in the cerebellum, which affects attention and motor activity (Courchesne et al., 1988).

Question: Can anything be done for an autistic child?

Even with help, only about 1 autistic child in 4 approaches normalcy. Nevertheless, almost all autistic children can make progress with proper care (Schopler, 1978). When treatment is begun early, behavior modification has been particularly successful.

Do you remember the child described in the Chapter Preview? Billy was one of the first patients in a pioneering program designed by psychologist Ivar Lovaas. Billy was selected for the program because of his unusual appetite for hamburgers. Teaching Billy to talk illustrates one aspect of his treatment. It began with his learning to blow out a match—making a sound like "who." Each time he made the "who" sound, Billy was rewarded with a bite of his beloved hamburgers. Next he was rewarded for babbling meaningless sounds. If he accidentally said a word, he was rewarded. After several weeks, he was able to say words such as *ball, milk, mama,* and *me.* By this painstaking process, Billy was eventually taught to talk. Notice that this process is basically an example of **operant shaping,** discussed in Chapter 7.

In a behavior modification program, each of an autistic child's maladaptive behaviors is altered using reward and punishment. In addition to food, therapists are finding that sensory stimulation, such as tickling or music, is often very reinforcing for the autistic child (Rincover & Newsom, 1985). And strangely enough, researchers have found that following actions such as head banging and hand biting with punishment can bring a swift end to self-destructive behavior (Haywood et al., 1982). When such efforts are combined with parental involvement in treatment at home, considerable progress can be made (Short, 1984).

Autism and other severe childhood problems are a monumental challenge to the ingenuity of psychologists, educators, and parents. However, great strides have been made in the last few years. There is reason to believe that in the future even more help will be available to children who get a bad start in life.

Learning Check

See if you can answer these questions before you continue reading.

1. Occasional reversals and regressions to more infantile behavior are sure signs that a significant childhood problem exists. T or F?
2. Sleep disturbances and specific fears can be a sign of significant childhood problems when they are prolonged or exaggerated. T or F?
3. A moderate amount of sibling rivalry is considered normal. T or F?
4. Encopresis is the formal term for lack of bladder control. T or F?
5. The hyperactive child is lost in his or her own private world. T or F?
6. According to Diana Baumrind's research, effective parents are authoritarian in their approach to their children's behavior. T or F?

Answers:

1. F 2. T 3. T 4. F 5. F 6. F

Adolescence—The Best of Times, the Worst of Times

Adolescence is a time of change, exploration, exuberance, and youthful searching. It is also a time of worry and problems, especially in today's world. It might even be fair to describe adolescence as "the best of times, the worst of times." Just in case you weren't taking notes in junior high, let's survey problems and challenges of this colorful chapter of life.

Adolescence and Puberty

Adolescence refers to the period during which we move from childhood to acceptance as an adult. This change is recognized in almost all cultures. However, the length of adolescence varies greatly from culture to culture (Siegel, 1982). For example, most 14-year-old girls in America live at home and go to school. In contrast, many 14-year-old females in rural villages of the Near East are married and have children (Santrock, 1984). In our culture, 14-year-olds are adolescents. In others, they may be adults.

Many people confuse adolescence with puberty. But as you can see, the culturally defined period of adolescence differs from puberty, which is a *biological* event. **Puberty** refers to rapid physical growth, coupled with hormonal changes that bring sexual maturity. Interestingly, the peak **growth spurt** during puberty occurs earlier for girls than for boys (Fig. 15–6). This difference accounts for the 1- to 2-year period when girls tend to be taller than boys. (Remember going to dances where the girls towered over the boys?) For girls the onset of puberty typically occurs between 11 and 14 years of age. For most boys the age range is 13 to 16 years (Kaluger & Kaluger, 1984).

Compare: Adolescence and puberty

Adolescence The socially defined period between childhood and adulthood.

Puberty The biologically defined period during which a person matures sexually and becomes capable of reproduction.

When you were going through puberty, did you ever spend *hours* preparing to attend a party, dance, or other social event? If you did, you weren't alone. Puberty tends to dramatically increase body awareness and concerns about physical appearance (Siegel, 1982). Beyond this, about one-half of all boys and one-third of all girls report being dissatisfied with their appearance during early adolescence (Rosenbaum, 1979). In many instances, such feelings are related to the *timing* of puberty. Girls who are temporarily "too tall," boys who are "too small," and both boys and girls who lag in sexual development are likely to be upset about their bodies.

Question: How much difference does the timing of puberty make?

Early and Late Maturation Because puberty involves so many rapid changes, it can be stressful for just about anyone. When puberty comes unusually early or late, its impact may be magnified—for both good and bad.

For boys, maturing early is generally beneficial. Typically, it enhances their self-image and gives them an advantage socially and athletically (Petersen, 1987). For such reasons, early-maturing boys tend to be more poised, relaxed, dominant, self-assured, and popular with their peers (Santrock, 1984; Siegel, 1982). Many late-maturing boys are anxious about being behind in development. However, after they catch up they tend to be more eager, talkative, self-assertive, and tolerant of themselves than average maturers.

For girls, the advantages of early maturation are less clear-cut. In elementary school, developmentally advanced girls tend to have *less* prestige among peers. Presumably, this is because they are larger and heavier than their classmates. By junior high, however, early development leads to *greater* peer prestige and adult approval. In contrast, later-maturing girls have the possible advantage of usually growing taller and thinner than early-maturing girls. Other relevant findings are that early-maturing girls date sooner and are more independent and more active in school; they are also more often in trouble at school (Siegel, 1982).

As you can see, there are costs and benefits associated with both early and late puberty. One added cost of early maturation is that it may force premature identity formation (Siegel, 1982). When a teenager begins to look like an adult, he or she may be treated like an adult. Ideally, this change can encourage greater maturity and independence. But what happens when a person is treated as an adult before he or she is emotionally ready? Then the search for identity may end too soon, leaving the person with a distorted, poorly formed sense of self (see Highlight 15–1).

Fig. 15–6 *The typical rate of growth for boys and girls. Notice that growth in early adolescence equals that for ages 1 to 3. Note too the earlier growth spurt for girls.*

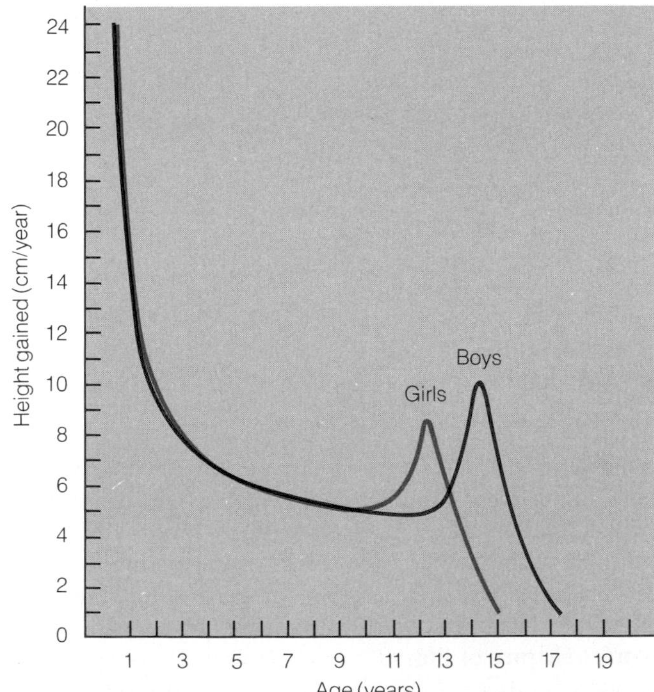

● HIGHLIGHT 15–1
Hurried into Adulthood

Psychologist David Elkind (1981) believes that many parents are hurrying their children's development. Elkind is concerned about parents who try to raise their babies' IQs, force them to "read" flash cards, or have them swimming and doing gymnastics before they are 3 months old. Such pushing, he believes, partly explains why more children have recently begun to show serious stress symptoms. Moreover, hurried children are turning into hurried teenagers—urged by parents and media alike to grow up fast. Elkind believes that too many teenagers are left without the guidance, direction, and support they need to become healthy adults (Elkind, 1984).

Elkind's main point is that today's teenagers have adulthood thrust on them too soon. Violence, drug abuse, X-rated movies, youth crime, teenage pregnancy, divorce and single-parent families, date rape, aimless schools—all this, and more, strikes Elkind as evidence that there is no place for teenagers in today's society.

According to Elkind, the traditional **social markers** of adolescence have all but disappeared. (Markers are signs that tell where a person stands socially—such as a driver's license or a wedding ring.) As an example, Elkind notes that clothing for children and teenagers is increasingly adultlike. Girls, especially, are urged to wear seductive clothing and revealing swimsuits.

Clearly, Elkind is stating a clinical opinion, not a hard fact. It's possible that his view will prove exaggerated—indeed, much of what he says is debatable. Nevertheless, his portrayal of hurried adolescents as "all grown up with no place to go" is highly thought provoking.

Search for Identity

As discussed earlier, many psychologists regard identity formation as a key task of adolescence. To be sure, problems of identity occur at other times too. But in a very real sense, puberty signals that the time has arrived to begin forming a new, more mature image of oneself. Answering the question, "Who am I?" is also spurred by cognitive development. After adolescents have attained the stage of formal operations, they are better able to ask questions about their place in the world and about morals, values, politics, social relationships, and private thoughts. Then, too, being able to think about hypothetical possibilities allows the adolescent to contemplate the future and ask more realistically, "Who will I be?" (Coleman et al., 1977).

David Elkind has noted another interesting pattern in adolescent thought. According to Elkind (1984), many teenagers are preoccupied with **imaginary audiences.** That is, they act like others are as aware of their thoughts and feelings as they are themselves. Sometimes this leads to painful self-consciousness—as in thinking that *everyone* is staring at a bad haircut you just received. The imaginary audience also seems to underlie attention-seeking "performances" involving outlandish dress or behavior. In any case, adolescents become very concerned with controlling the impressions they make on others (Santrock, 1984). For many, being "on stage" in this way helps define the shape of an emerging identity.

Question: What effects do parents have on identity formation?

Parents and Peers The adolescent search for identity often results in increased conflict with parents. However, this is not necessarily a problem. Some conflict with parents is probably necessary for growth of a separate identity. A complete lack of conflict may mean that the adolescent is afraid to seek independence (Siegel, 1982). Actually, there is usually a good deal of agreement between adolescents and their parents on basic topics such as religion, marriage, and morals. The largest conflicts tend to be over more superficial differences regarding styles of dress, manners, social behavior, and the like. In general, adolescents tend to overestimate differences between themselves and their parents (Lerner & Shea, 1982).

In high school, were you a jock, preppy, brain, hacker, surfer, cowboy, punk, mod, warthog, dervish, gargoyle, or aardvark? (Well, okay, I made up the last four—the rest are real.) Increased identification with peer groups is quite common during adolescence. To an extent, membership in such groups gives a measure of security and a sense of identity apart from the family. Beyond this, group membership provides practice in belonging to a social network. Children tend to see themselves more as members of families and small friendship groups, not as members of society as a whole. Therefore, gaining a broader, member-of-society perspective can be a major step toward adulthood (Kohlberg, 1976) (Fig. 15–7).

Question: But aren't groups also limiting?

Yes, they are. Conformity to peer values peaks in early adolescence, but it remains strong at least through high school (Newman, 1982). Throughout this period there is always a danger of allowing group pressure to foreclose personal growth (Newman & Newman, 1987). By the

Fig. 15–7 *Membership in friendship groups and cliques helps adolescents build an identity apart from their relationship to parents. However, over-identification with a clannish group that rejects anyone who looks or acts different can limit personal growth.*

end of high school, many adolescents have not yet sufficiently explored various interests, values, vocations, skills, or ideologies on their own. Perhaps this is why many students view moving on to work or college as a chance to break out of earlier roles—to expand or reshape personal identity. For many who choose college, the effect may be more a matter of placing further changes in identity on hold. By doing so, college students keep open the possibility of changing majors, career plans, personal style, and so on. Typically, commitment to an emerging adult identity grows stronger in later college years (Santrock, 1984).

The search for identity we have discussed here may be intensified during adolescence, but it does not end there. In the next section we will move on into early adulthood for a look at further developments. Before you read more, here's a chance to check your memory.

Learning Check

1. In most societies, adolescence begins with the onset of puberty and ends with its completion. T or F?
2. Early-maturing boys tend to experience more clear-cut advantages than do early-maturing girls. T or F?
3. According to David Elkind, the traditional markers of adolescence and adulthood have been blurred. T or F?
4. The imaginary audience refers to conformity pressures that adolescents believe adults apply to them. T or F?

Answers:
1. F 2. T 3. T 4. F

Challenges of Adulthood—Charting Life's Ups and Downs

After a "settling down" period somewhere in the 20s, adult development is uniform and uninteresting, right? Wrong! A fairly predictable series of challenges is associated with development from adolescence to old age.

Question: What personality changes and psychological developments can a person look forward to in adulthood?

Further study has added important detail to the events discussed by Erikson. One of the most informative accounts is based on clinical work by Roger Gould, a psychiatrist interested in adult personality. Gould's research (1975) reveals that the most common patterns for American adults are as follows.

Ages 16–18: Escape from Dominance Ages 16 to 18 are marked by a struggle to escape from parental dominance. Efforts to do so cause considerable anxiety about the future and conflicts about continuing dependence on parents.

Ages 18–22: Leaving the Family The majority of people break away from their families in their early 20s. Leaving home is usually associated with building new friendships with other adults. These friends serve as substitutes for the family and as allies in the process of breaking ties.

Ages 22–28: Building a Workable Life The trend in the mid-20s is to seek mastery of the real world. Two dominant activities are striving for accomplishment (seeking competence) and reaching out to others. Note that the second activity corresponds to Erikson's emphasis on seeking intimacy at this time. Married couples in this age group tend to place a high value on "togetherness."

Ages 29–34: Crisis of Questions Around the age of 30 many people experience a minor life crisis. The heart of this crisis is a serious questioning of what life is all about. Assurance about previous choices and values tends to waver. Unsettled by these developments, the person actively searches for a style of living that will bring meaning to the second half of life. Marriages are particularly vulnerable during this time of dissatisfaction. Extramarital affairs and divorces are common symptoms of the "crisis of questions."

Ages 35–43: Crisis of Urgency People of age 35 to 43 are typically beginning to become more aware of the reality of death. Having a limited number of years to live begins to exert pressure on the individual. Intensified attempts are made to succeed at a career or to achieve one's life goals. Generativity, in the form of nurturing, teaching, or serving others, helps alleviate many of the anxieties of this stage.

Ages 43–50: Attaining Stability The urgency of the previous stage gives way to a calmer acceptance of one's fate in the late 40s. The predominant feeling is that the die is cast and that former decisions can be lived with. Those who have families begin to appreciate their children as individuals and ease up on their tendency to extend their own goals to their children's behavior.

Age 50 and Up: Mellowing After age 50, a noticeable mellowing occurs. Emphasis is placed on sharing day-to-day joys and sorrows. There is less concern with glamor, wealth, accomplishment, and abstract goals. Many of the tensions of earlier years give way to a desire to savor life and its small pleasures.

Question: Where does the midlife crisis fit in?

A Midlife Crisis? It is clear that difficulty at the midpoint of life is not universal. Many people thrive during this period and have no special problems. However, psychologist Daniel Levinson carried out an in-depth study of adult lives that shows what a "midlife crisis" looks like if one does occur. Levinson (1978, 1986) identifies 5 periods during adulthood when people typically make major transitions (Table 15–1). A **transition period** ends one life pattern and opens the door to new possibilities (Levinson, 1986). Levinson found that most of his subjects (all males) went through a period of instability, anxiety, and change between the ages of 37 and 41 as they approached the midlife transition. (Notice that this corresponds closely to Gould's crisis-of-urgency period.)

Roughly one-half of all the men studied by Levinson defined the midlife period as a sort of "last chance" to achieve their goals. Such goals were often stated as a key event—for example, attaining a supervisory position, achieving a certain income, becoming a full professor or shop steward, and so forth. For these individuals, the midlife period is stressful, but manageable. A second pattern involved a serious midlife decline, often based on having chosen a dead-end job or lifestyle. In some cases, it meant that subjects had achieved material success but they felt that what they were doing was pointless. In a third pattern, a few hearty individuals appeared to be "breaking out" of a seriously flawed life structure. For them, a decision to "start over" was typically followed by 8 to 10 years of rebuilding.

Thus, it can be seen that the midlife crisis, if it takes place at all, can be both a danger and an opportunity. Ideally, it is a time of reworking old identities, of achieving long-sought goals, of finding one's own truths, and of preparing for later maturity and aging (Barrow & Smith, 1979). It is also important to emphasize again that many people's lives differ greatly from the generalized summaries given here. Adult development is complex, and each person's path through life is unique.

Middle Age When individuals reach their 40s and 50s, declining vigor, strength, and youthfulness make it clear that more than one-half of their time is gone. At the same time, greater stability comes from letting go of the "impossible dream" (Sheehy, 1976). That is, there is an increased attempt to be satisfied with the direction one's life has taken and to accept that hoped-for life goals may no longer be possible.

Table 15–1 Three Views of Developmental Challenges

Erikson	Gould	Levinson
CHILDHOOD		
Trust/mistrust (1) Autonomy/shame, doubt (1–3) Initiative/guilt (3–5) Industry/inferiority (6–12)		
ADOLESCENCE		
Identity/confusion (12–18)	Escape from dominance (16–18)	Early adulthood transition (17–22)
EARLY ADULTHOOD		
Intimacy/isolation	Leaving the family (18–22) Building a workable life (22–28) Crisis of questions (29–34)	Age 30 transition (28–33)
MIDDLE ADULTHOOD		
Generativity/self-absorption	Crisis of urgency (35–43) Attaining stability (43–50) Mellowing (50+)	Midlife transition (40–45) Age 50 transition (50–55)
LATE ADULTHOOD		
		Late adult transition (60–65)
OLD AGE		
Integrity/despair		

For most women during this era, **menopause** represents the first real encounter with aging. At menopause, monthly menstruation ends, and a woman is no longer able to bear children. In menopause, the level of the hormone estrogen drops—sometimes causing drastic changes in mood or appearance and also sometimes causing physical symptoms such as "hot flashes" (a sudden uncomfortable sensation of heat).

Some women find menopause as difficult to adjust to as adolescence, and many experience anxiety, irritability, or depression at this time. Most post-menopausal women, however, report that menopause was not as bad as they expected and that much of their anxiety came from not knowing what to expect (Mussen et al., 1979).

Question: Do men go through similar changes?

Males do not undergo any physical change that is directly comparable to menopause. Just the same, some authorities now believe that 40- to 60-year-old males often pass through a **climacteric** (kly-MAK-ter-ik), or significant physiological change (Zaludek, 1976). During the climacteric, decreases in male hormone output may cause psychological symptoms similar to those experienced by women in menopause. However, men remain fertile at this time, and many of their symptoms (depression, anxiety, irritability) are more likely related to self-doubts caused by declining vigor and changing physical appearance.

After the late 50s, the problems an individual faces in maintaining a healthy and meaningful life are complicated by the inevitable process of aging. How unique are the problems of older people, and how severely do they challenge the need to maintain integrity and personal comfort? We will look at some answers in the next section.

Aging—Will You Still Need Me When I'm 64?

In 1978, students at Long Beach City College in California elected Pearl Taylor their spring festival queen. Ms. Taylor had everything necessary to win: looks, intelligence, personality, and campus-wide popularity. At about the same time, citizens of Raleigh, North Carolina, elected Isabella Cannon as their mayor.

Question: What's so remarkable about these events?

Not too much, really, except that Pearl was 90 years old when elected, and Isabella was 73 (Barrow & Smith, 1979). Both are part of the graying of America. Currently, some 30 million Americans are over the age of 65. By the year 2020, some 50 million persons, or *1 out of every 5*, will be 65 years of age or older. These figures make the elderly the fastest-growing segment of society. Understandably, psychologists have become increasingly interested in aging.

Question: What is life like for the aged?

There are large variations in aging. Most of us have known elderly individuals at both extremes: those who are active, healthy, and satisfied and whose minds are clear and alert; and those who are confused, childlike, dependent, or senile. Despite such variations, some generalizations can be made.

Aging **Biological aging** is a gradual process that begins quite early in life. Peak functioning in most physical capacities reaches a maximum by about 25 to 30 years of age. Thereafter, gradual declines occur in muscular strength, flexibility, circulatory efficiency, speed of response, sensory acuity, and other functions.

Question: So people are "over the hill" by 30?

Hardly! Prime abilities come at different ages for different activities. Peak performances for professional football and baseball players usually occur in the mid-20s; for professional bowlers, the mid-30s; for artists and musicians, the 50s; and for politicians, philosophers, business or industrial leaders, and others, the early 60s.

For those who are still young, the prospect of aging physically may be the greatest threat of old age (see Highlight 15–2). However, it is wrong to believe that most elderly people are sickly, infirm, or senile. Only about 5 percent of those over 65 years old are in nursing homes. As for the possibility of a mental slide, physician Alex Comfort (1976) comments, "The human brain does not shrink, wilt, perish, or deteriorate with age. It normally continues to function well through as many as 9 decades." As a **gerontologist** (jer-ON-TOL-o-jist: one who studies aging), Comfort estimates that only 25 percent of the disability of old people is medically based. The remaining 75 percent is social, political, and cultural.

Comfort's view is backed by studies of the intellectual capacities of aging individuals. Little overall decline occurs in intelligence test scores with aging. Although it is true that **fluid abilities** (those requiring speed or rapid learning) may decline, **crystallized abilities,** such as vocabulary and stored-up knowledge, actually improve—at least into the 70s (Baltes & Schaie, 1974). The general intellectual decline attributed to old age is largely a myth.

● HIGHLIGHT 15–2
Biological Aging—How Long Is a Lifetime?

Whatever the biological causes of aging, humans seem to grow, mature, age, and die within a set time. The length of our lives is limited by a boundary called the **maximum life span.** Humans, like other animals, appear to live a limited number of years, even under the best of circumstances. Estimates of the average human life span place it around 95 to 110 years (Botwinick, 1984).

For most people, **life expectancy** (the actual number of years the average person lives) is shorter than a life span. In the 1800s the average life expectancy was 36 years. Now, average life expectancy for American males is 72 years, and for females it is 79 years. With improved health care, life expectancy should move even closer to the maximum life span.

At present there is no known way to extend the human life span. On the other hand, there is every reason to believe that life expectancy can be increased. If you would personally like to add to a new, higher average, here are some deceptively simple rules for living a long life (Coni et al., 1984):

1. Do not smoke.
2. Use alcohol in moderation or not at all.
3. Avoid becoming overweight.
4. If you suffer from high blood pressure, have it treated.
5. Remain socially and economically active in retirement.
6. Exercise regularly throughout life.

To this we can add: Get married (married persons live longer), learn to manage stress, and choose long-lived parents!

Question: What kind of person adjusts most successfully to aging?

Activity and Disengagement Two principal theories have been proposed to explain successful adjustment to the physical and social changes of aging. **Disengagement theory** assumes that it is normal and desirable for people to withdraw from society as they age (Cumming

& Henry, 1961). According to this theory, elderly persons welcome disengagement since it relieves them of roles and responsibilities they have become less able to fulfill. Likewise, society benefits from disengagement as younger persons with new energy and skills fill positions vacated by aging individuals.

Certainly we have all known people who disengaged from society as they grew older. Nevertheless, disengagement theory can be criticized for describing successful aging as a retreat. While disengagement may be common, it is not necessarily ideal.

Question: What does the second theory say?

A second view of optimal aging is provided by **activity theory,** a sort of "use-it-or-lose-it" view that assumes activity is the essence of life for people of all ages. Activity theory predicts that people who remain active physically, mentally, and socially will adjust better to aging (Havighurst, 1961).

Proponents of activity theory believe that aging persons should maintain the activities of their earlier years for as long as possible. If a person is forced to give up particular roles or activities, it is recommended that these activities or roles be replaced with others. In so doing, the aging person is able to maintain a better self-image, greater satisfaction, and more social support—resulting in more successful aging.

Question: Which theory is correct?

The majority of studies on aging support the *activity theory,* although there have been exceptions (Barrow & Smith, 1979). At the same time, some people do seek disengagement, so neither theory is absolutely "correct." Actually, successful aging probably requires a combination of activity and disengagement. For example, one researcher found that the elderly tend to disengage from activities that are no longer satisfying while maintaining those that are (Brown, 1974). In the final analysis, it seems that life satisfaction in old age depends mainly on how much time we spend doing things we find meaningful (Horn & Meer, 1987) (Fig. 15–8).

Ageism In one way or another, you have encountered ageism. **Ageism** refers to discrimination or prejudice on the basis of age. It applies to people of all ages and can oppress the young as well as the old. For instance, a person applying for a job may just as likely be told, "You're too young," as "You're too old." In some societies ageism is based on respect for the elderly. In Japan, for instance, aging is seen as positive, and increased age brings increased status and respect (Kimmel, 1988). In most Western nations, however, ageism tends to have a negative impact on older individuals. Usually, it is expressed as an aversion, hatred, or rejection of the elderly. As Alex Comfort (1976) points out, the concept of "oldness" is often used to expel people from useful work. According to Comfort, retirement is frequently just another name for dismissal and unemployment.

Another facet of ageism is stereotyping of the aged. Popular stereotypes of the "dirty old man," "meddling old woman," "senile old fool," and the like, help perpetuate the myths underlying ageism. Contrast such im-

Fig. 15–8 *Social centers and exercise programs for senior citizens are a direct expression of the benefits predicted by activity theory. Remaining active may also give older persons a feeling of* control *over their lives. As discussed in Chapters 12 and 13, feelings of control contribute to mental and physical well-being.*

ages to those associated with youthfulness: The young are perceived as fresh, whole, attractive, energetic, active, emerging, appealing, and so forth. Even positive stereotypes can be a problem. If older people are perceived as financially well-off, wise, or experienced, it can blind others to the real problems of the elderly (Gatz & Pearson, 1988). The important point, then, is to realize that there is a tremendous diversity among the elderly—ranging from the infirm and senile, to aerobic-dancing grandmothers.

Question: What can be done about ageism?

One of the best ways to combat ageism is to counter stereotypes with facts. For example, studies show that in many occupations older workers perform better at jobs requiring *both* speed and skill (Giniger et al., 1983). Gradual slowing with age is a reality. But often, it is countered by experience, skill, or expertise (Schaie, 1988). One study, for example, showed that older typists responded slower on reaction-time tests than younger typists. Nevertheless, there was no difference in the actual typing speeds of younger and older typists (Salthouse, 1987).

Taking a broader view, Bernice Neugarten (1971) examined the lives of 200 people between the ages of 70 and 79. Neugarten found that 75 percent of these people were satisfied with their lives after retirement. Neugarten's findings also countered other myths about aging.

1. Old persons generally do not become isolated and neglected by their families. Most *prefer* to live apart from their children.
2. Old persons are rarely placed in mental hospitals by uncaring children.
3. Old persons who live alone are not necessarily lonely or desolate.
4. Few elderly persons ever show signs of senility or mental decay, and few ever become mentally ill.

In short, most of the elderly studied by Neugarten were integrated, active, and psychologically healthy. Findings such as these call for an end to the forced obsolescence of the elderly. As a group, older people represent a valuable source of skill, knowledge, and energy that we can no longer afford to cast aside. As we face the challenges of this planet's uncertain future, we need all the help we can get!

● Death and Dying—The Curtain Falls

DEAR ABBY: Do you think about dying much?

CURIOUS

DEAR CURIOUS: No, it's the last thing I want to do.

Death is a topic of importance to us all. The statistics on death are very convincing: One out of one dies. In spite of this, there tends to be a conspiracy of silence surrounding the topic of death. As a result, most of us are poorly informed about a process that is as basic as birth.

We have seen in this chapter that it is valuable to understand major trends in the course of development. With this in mind, let us now explore emotional responses to death, the inevitable conclusion of every life.

Fears of Death

Fears of death are not so extensive as might be supposed. In a poll of 1500 adults, only about 4 percent showed evidence of directly fearing their own death (Kastenbaum & Aisenberg, 1972). It might seem that as people grow older they would become more fearful of death. However, a study of individuals ranging in age from 30 to 82 years found no overall differences in death anxiety associated with age (Conte et al., 1982). However, those fears that do exist apparently change with age. Hall (1922) found that younger individuals fear the occurrence of death, whereas old people fear the circumstances of death.

These findings seem to indicate a general lack of death fears, but there is another possibility. It may be more accurate to say that they reflect a deeply ingrained denial of death. The mere fact that death has been something of a taboo subject suggests that underlying fears do exist. When *Psychology Today* surveyed its readers on the subject of death, less than one-third said they grew up in families where death was openly discussed (Shneidman, 1971). The average person's exposure to death consists of the artificial and unrealistic portrayals of death on TV. By the time the average person is 17 years old, he or she will have witnessed roughly 18,000 TV deaths. With few exceptions these will have been *homicides*, not deaths due to illness or aging (Oskamp, 1984).

Reactions to Impending Death

A more direct account of emotional responses to death comes from the work of Elizabeth Kübler-Ross (1975). Kübler-Ross is a thanatologist (THAN-ah-TOL-oh-jist: one who studies death) who spent hundreds of hours at the bedsides of the terminally ill. She found that dying persons tend to display several emotional reactions as they prepare for death. Five basic reactions are described here.

1. Denial and isolation. A typical first reaction to impending death is an attempt to deny its reality and to isolate oneself from information confirming that death is really going to occur. Initially the person may be sure that "It's all a mistake," that lab reports or X-rays have been mixed up, or that a physician is in error. This may proceed to attempts to ignore or avoid any reminder of the situation.

2. Anger. Many dying individuals feel anger and ask, "Why me?" As they face the ultimate threat of having everything they value stripped away, their anger can spill over into rage or envy toward those who will continue living. Even good friends may temporarily evoke anger because their health is envied.

3. Bargaining. In another common reaction the terminally ill bargain with themselves or with God. The dying person thinks, "Just let me live a little longer and I'll do anything to earn it." Individuals may bargain for time by trying to be "good" ("I'll never smoke again"), by righting past wrongs, or by praying that if they are granted more time they will dedicate themselves to their religion.

4. Depression. As death draws near and the person begins to recognize that it cannot be prevented, feelings of futility, exhaustion, and deep depression may set in. The person recognizes that he or she will be separated from friends, loved ones, and the familiar routines of life, and this causes a profound sadness.

5. Acceptance. If death is not sudden, many people manage to come to terms with dying and accept it calmly. The person who accepts death is neither happy nor sad, but at peace with the inevitable. Acceptance usually signals that the struggle with death has been resolved. The need to talk about death ends, and silent companionship from others is frequently all that is desired.

Not all terminally ill persons display all these reactions, nor do they always occur in this order. Individual styles of dying vary greatly, according to emotional maturity, religious belief, age, education, the attitudes of relatives, and so forth. Generally, there does tend to be a movement from initial shock, denial, and anger toward eventual acceptance of the situation. However, some people who seem to have accepted death may die angry and raging against the inevitable. Conversely, the angry fighter may let go of the struggle and die peacefully. In general, one's approach to dying will mirror his or her style of living (DeSpelder & Strickland, 1983).

It is best not to think of Kübler-Ross' list as a fixed series of stages to go through in order. It is an even bigger mistake to assume that someone who does not show all the listed emotional reactions is somehow deviant or immature (Shneidman, 1987). Rather, the list describes typical and appropriate reactions to impending death. It is also interesting to note that many of the same reactions accompany any major loss, be it divorce, loss of a home due to fire, death of a pet, or loss of a job.

Question: How can I make use of this information?

First, it can help both the dying individual and survivors recognize and cope with periods of depression, anger, denial, and bargaining. Second, it helps to realize that close friends or relatives of the dying person may feel many of the same emotions before or after the person's death because they, too, are facing a loss.

Perhaps the most important thing to recognize is that the dying person may have a need to share feelings with others and to discuss death openly. Too often, the dying person feels isolated and separated from others by the wall of silence erected by doctors, nurses, and family members. Adults tend to "freeze up" with a dying person, saying things such as, "I don't know how to deal with this."

Understanding what the dying person is going through may make it easier for you to offer support at this important time. A simple willingness to be with the person and to honestly share his or her feelings can help bring dignity, acceptance, and meaning to death.

Bereavement After a friend or relative has died, a period of grief typically follows. Grief is a natural and normal reaction to death as survivors adjust to loss.

Grief tends to follow a predictable pattern (Parkes, 1979; Schulz, 1978). Grief usually begins with a period of **shock** or numbness. For a brief time, the bereaved remain in a dazed state in which they may show little emotion. Most find it extremely difficult to accept the reality of their loss. This phase usually ends by the time of the funeral, which unleashes tears and bottled-up feelings of despair (Fig. 15–9).

Initial shock is followed by sharp **pangs of grief.** These are episodes of painful yearning for the dead person and, sometimes, anguished outbursts of anger. During this period the wish to have the dead person back is intense. Often, mourners continue to think of the dead person as alive. They may hear his or her voice and see the deceased vividly in dreams. During this period, agitated distress alternates with silent despair, and suffering is acute.

The first powerful reactions of grief gradually give way to weeks or months of **apathy, dejection,** and **depression.** The person faces a new emotional landscape with a large gap that cannot be filled. Life seems to lose much of its meaning, and a sense of futility dominates the person's outlook. The mourner is usually able to resume work or other activities after 2 or 3 weeks. However, insomnia, loss of energy and appetite, and similar signs of depression may continue.

Little by little, the bereaved person accepts what cannot be changed and makes a new beginning. Pangs of grief may still occur, but they are less severe and less frequent. Memories of the dead person, though still painful, now include positive images and nostalgic pleasure. At this point, the person can be said to be moving toward **resolution.**

As was true of approaching death, individual reactions to grief vary considerably. In general, however, a month or two typically passes before the more intense stages of grief have run their course. As you can see, grief allows survivors to discharge their anguish and to prepare to go on living.

Question: Is it true that suppressing grief leads to more problems later?

It has long been assumed that suppressing grief may later lead to more severe and lasting depression. However, there is little evidence to support this idea. A lack of intense grief does not usually predict later problems (Wortman & Silver, 1987). Bereaved persons should work through their grief at their own pace and in their own way—without worrying about whether they are grieving too much or too little. Some additional suggestions for coping with grief follow.

Coping with Grief

- Face the loss directly and do not isolate yourself.
- Discuss your feelings with relatives and friends.
- Do not block out your feelings with drugs or alcohol.
- Allow grief to progress naturally; neither hurry nor suppress it. (Coni et al., 1984)

Fig. 15–9 *As cultural rituals, funerals encourage a release of emotion and provide a sense of closure for survivors, who must come to terms with the death of a loved one.*

The subject of death brings us full circle in the cycle of life. In the upcoming Applications section, we will return to the topic of parenting, a process that deeply links the lives of adults and children.

Learning Check

Check your comprehension with these questions.

1. Building a workable life tends to be the dominant activity during which age range?
   a. 18–22 *b.* 22–28 *c.* 29–34 *d.* 35–43
2. Levinson's description of the "midlife crisis" corresponds roughly to Gould's
   a. escape from dominance *b.* crisis of questions *c.* crisis of urgency *d.* settling down period
3. The average male experiences the menopause between the ages of 45 and 50. T or F?
4. Many indications of biological aging start to become evident as early as the mid-20s. T or F?
5. An expert on the problems of aging is called a ____________________.
6. The activity theory of optimal aging holds that aging individuals should restrict their activities and withdraw from former community activities. T or F?
7. After age 65, a large proportion of older people show significant signs of senility, and most require special care. T or F?
8. In the reaction that Kübler-Ross describes as bargaining, the dying individual asks, "Why me?" T or F?
9. A dazed state of shock or numbness is typical of the first phase of grief. T or F?
10. Most evidence supports the idea that suppressing grief leads to later problems, such as severe depression. T or F?

Answers:
1. *b* 2. *c* 3. F 4. T 5. gerontologist 6. F 7. F 8. F 9. T 10. F

Applications: Parenting—The World's Most Important Job

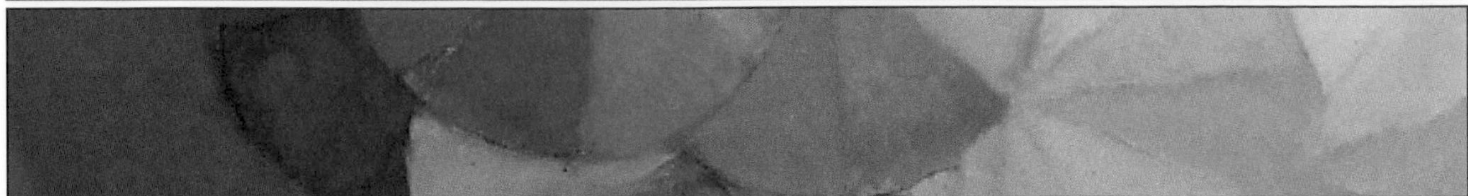

Raising children draws many of the problems of development into a single arena. When parenting is effective, both adult and child benefit. When parents fail to give their children a good start in life, everybody suffers—the child, the parents, and society as a whole. Healthy development requires emotional and social competence as well as intellectual ability. In addition to the skills needed for achievement, effective parents give their children a capacity for love, joy, and fulfillment.

Question: What can parents do to promote healthy development in their children?

Much of the answer can be found in two key areas of parent-child relationships. These are communication and discipline. In each area, parents can set an example of tolerance, understanding, and acceptance that goes beyond their traditional role as mere dispensers of "dos" and "don'ts."

Rearing Children

No psychologist would deny that love is essential for healthy development, but *discipline* can be equally important. Parents with unmanageable, delinquent, or unhappy children often can honestly claim that they have given them lots of love. Yet, when parents fail to provide a framework of guidelines for behavior, children become antisocial, aggressive, and insecure. As noted earlier in this chapter, overly permissive parents—those who allow themselves to be dominated or manipulated—create lifelong patterns of self-serving behavior in their children.

Question: Does this mean that discipline should be strict and unbending?

No. Recall that authoritarian parents also have undesirable effects on their children. Families do not need to be run like a military boot camp. Effective discipline is authoritative yet sensitive. The goal is to socialize a child without undue frustration and without destroying the bond of love and trust between parent and child. One 22-year-long study found that children whose parents are critical, harsh, or authoritarian often become self-absorbed adults. They also have a higher-than-average record of violence and substance abuse (Dubow et al., 1987).

Question: How can a balance be maintained?

Many experts are advocating a style of child rearing that recognizes a child's psychological needs. Discipline should give children freedom to express their deepest feelings through speech and actions. This does not mean freedom to do entirely as one pleases. It means that the child has room to move about freely within well-defined limits. Of course, individual parents may choose limits that are more "strict" or less "strict." But this choice is less important than the consistency of parental standards. Consistent discipline gives a child a sense of security and stability; inconsistency makes the child's world seem unreliable and unpredictable.

Question: How can limits best be maintained?

Parents tend to base discipline on one or more of the following techniques: power assertion, withdrawal of love, or child management (Coopersmith, 1968; Hoffman, 1977).

Power assertion refers to physical punishment or to a show of force in which parents take away toys or privileges. As an alternative, some parents use **withdrawal of love** by refusing to speak to a child, by threatening to leave, by rejecting the child, or by otherwise acting as if the child is temporarily unlovable. **Management techniques** combine praise, recognition, approval, rules, reasoning, and the like, to encourage desirable behavior. Each of these approaches can effectively control a child's behavior, but their side effects differ considerably.

Question: What are the side effects?

Power-oriented techniques—particularly harsh or severe physical punishment—are associated with fear, hatred of parents, and a lack of spontaneity and warmth. Severely punished children also tend to be defiant, rebellious, and aggressive (Patterson, 1982).

Withdrawal of love, which is a major middle-class mode of discipline, produces children who tend to be self-disciplined. We might say that such children have developed a good conscience. They are often described as "model" children or as unusually "good." But as a side effect, they are also frequently anxious, insecure, and dependent on adults for approval.

Management techniques also have their limitations. Most important is the need to carefully adjust them to a child's level of understanding. Younger children may not always see the connection between rules, explanations, and their own behavior. In spite of this limitation, management techniques

Applications

receive a big plus in an important area of child development. Psychologist Stanley Coopersmith (1968) has found a direct connection between parental styles of discipline and a child's **self-esteem.**

Question: What is self-esteem?

Self-esteem refers to a quiet confidence that comes from regarding oneself as a worthwhile person. Many theorists consider high self-esteem essential for emotional health. Individuals with low self-esteem have a low estimation of their value as people.

In direct studies of children, Coopersmith found that low self-esteem is related to the use of physical punishment or withholding of love. High self-esteem, in contrast, was related to management techniques that emphasized clear and consistent discipline coupled with high parental interest and concern for the child. Thus, it seems best for parents to minimize physical punishment and to avoid unnecessary withdrawal of love.

Question: Are you saying that physical punishment and withdrawal of love should not be used?

Effective parents use each of the three major types of discipline at one time or another, and each has its place. Coopersmith's findings simply suggest that physical punishment and withdrawal of love should be used with caution. In using these two forms of punishment, parents should observe the following guidelines (also see Chapter 8):

1. Parents should separate disapproval of the act from disapproval of the child. Instead of saying, "I'm going to punish you because *you are bad,*" say, "I'm upset about *what you did.*"
2. Punishment should never be harsh or injurious to a child. Don't physically punish a child while you are angry. Also remember that giving a child the message "I don't love you right now" can be more painful than any spanking.
3. Punishment is most effective when it is administered immediately. This statement is especially true for younger children.
4. Spanking and other forms of physical punishment are not particularly effective for children under age 2. The child will only be confused and frightened. Spankings also become less effective after age 5 because they tend to humiliate the child and breed resentment.
5. Reserve physical punishment for situations that pose an immediate danger to the younger child, for example, when a child runs into the street.
6. Remember too that it is usually more effective to reinforce children when they are being good than it is to punish them for misbehavior.

After age 5, management techniques are the most effective form of discipline, especially techniques that emphasize communication.

Communication Between Parent and Child

When clear communication is maintained between parent and child, many discipline problems can be avoided before they develop. Dr. Haim Ginott (1965) has suggested that it is essential to make a distinction between a child's feelings and a child's behavior. Since children (and parents, too) do not choose how they will feel, it is important to allow free expression of feelings.

The child who learns to regard some feelings as "bad," or unacceptable, is being asked to deny a very real part of his or her experience. Ginott encourages parents to teach their children that all feelings are appropriate; it is only actions that are subject to disapproval. Many parents are unaware of just how often they block communication and the expression of feelings in their children. Consider this typical conversation excerpted from Ginott's book (1965):

Son: I am stupid, and I know it. Look at my grades in school.
Father: You just have to work harder.
Son: I already work harder and it doesn't help. I have no brains.
Father: You are smart, I know.
Son: I am stupid, I know.
Father: (loudly) You are not stupid!
Son: Yes, I am!
Father: You are not stupid. Stupid!

By debating with the child, the father misses the point that his son *feels* stupid. It would be far more helpful for the father to encourage the boy to talk about his feelings.

Question: How could he do that?

He might say, "You really feel that you are not as smart as others, don't you? Do you feel this way often? Are you feeling bad at school?" In this way, the child is given a chance to express his emotions and to feel understood. The father might conclude the conversation by saying, "Look, son, in my eyes you are a fine person. But I understand how you feel. Everyone feels stupid at times."

Communication with a child can also be the basis of effective discipline. Thomas Gordon (1970), a child psychologist who has developed a program called Parent Effectiveness Training (PET), offers a useful suggestion. Gordon believes that parents should send "I" messages to their children, rather than "you" messages.

Question: What's the difference?

Applications

"You" messages take the form of threats, name-calling, accusing, bossing, lecturing, or analyzing. Generally, "you" messages tell children what's "wrong" with them.

An "I" message is a form of communication that tells children what effect their behavior has had on you. To illustrate the difference, consider this example. After a hard day's work, Susan wants to sit down and rest awhile. She begins to relax with a newspaper when her 5-year-old daughter starts banging loudly on a toy drum. Most parents would respond with a "you" message:

> "You go play outside this instant." (bossing)
> "Don't ever make such a racket when someone is reading." (lecturing)
> "You're really pushing it today, aren't you?" (accusing)
> "You're a spoiled brat." (name-calling)
> "I'm going to swat you!" (threatening)

Gordon suggests sending an "I" message such as, "I am very tired, and I would like to read. I feel upset and can't read when you make so much noise." This forces the child to accept responsibility for the effects of her actions. If this doesn't curb misbehavior, the consequences can also be stated as an "I" message: "I would like for you to stop banging on that drum; otherwise, please take it outside." If the child continues to bang on the drum inside the house, then she has caused the toy to be put away. If she takes it outside, she has made a decision to play with the drum in a way that respects her mother's wishes. In this way, both parent and child have been allowed to maintain a sense of self-respect, and a needless clash has been averted.

Only two additional points on communicating with children need be noted. They are: "Listen more than you talk"; and "Live the message you wish to communicate."

Child Abuse

Sadly, no account of parenting would be complete without a brief discussion of child abuse. Much as we might like to believe otherwise, child abuse is widespread. Estimates on the number of children who are physically abused by parents range from 3.5 percent to 14 percent. Even if the lower figure is right, that would mean that 1.7 million children are physically battered each year in the United States (Browne, 1986). In about one-third of all cases of physical abuse, the child is seriously injured. Every year hundreds of children are killed by their own parents.

Question: What are abusive parents like?

Characteristics of Abusive Parents Abusive parents are usually young (under 30) and from lower-income levels. However, professionals who treat child abuse see parents of all ages and income levels.

Abusive parents often have a high level of stress and frustration in their lives. Typical problems include loneliness, marital discord, unemployment, drug abuse, divorce, family violence, heavy drinking, and work anxieties (Giovannoni & Becerra, 1979). Some parents are aware that they are mistreating a child but are unable to stop. Other abusive parents literally hate their children or are disgusted by them. The child's sloppiness, diapers, crying, or needs are unbearable to the parent. Often these parents expect the child to love them and make them happy. When the child (who is usually under 3 years old) cannot meet these unrealistic demands, the parent reacts with lethal anger. A recent study uncovered a striking fact about abusive mothers: In addition to being highly reactive to stress, abusive mothers are more likely to believe that their children are acting *intentionally* to annoy them (Bauer & Twentyman, 1985).

As mentioned previously, the core of much child abuse is a cycle of violence that flows from one generation to the next. The best recent estimate is that roughly 30 percent of all parents who were abused as children will mistreat their own children (Kaufman & Zigler, 1987). Such parents simply never learned to love, communicate with, or discipline a child.

When does the cycle of violence begin? Sad to say, it shows up almost immediately:

> **Abusive Toddlers**
>
> In a recent study, abused 1- to 3-year olds were observed as they interacted with playmates. The question of interest was, How do abused children react when another child is crying or distressed? In almost every instance, abused children responded to distress with fear, threats, or physical assault. (Main & George, 1985)

In short, abused children rapidly become abusive children, and later many become abusive adults.

Question: What can be done about child abuse?

Preventing Child Abuse Many public agencies now have teams to identify battered or neglected children. However, legal "cures" for child abuse are not very satisfying. The courts can take custody of a child, or the parents may voluntarily agree to place the child in a foster home. Foster care can be an improvement, but it may also further traumatize the child. In some cases the child is allowed to remain with the parents, but under court supervision. Even then, there is a chance of further injury unless the parents get help.

Self-help groups staffed by former child abusers and concerned volunteers are a major aid to parents. One such group is Parents Anonymous, a national organization of parents de-

Applications

termined to help each other stop abusing children. Local groups set up networks of members that parents can call in an abuse crisis or when they feel one coming on. Parents also learn how to curb violent impulses and how to cope with their children. Such training may be especially effective when carried out at home, where abuse usually occurs (Nomellini & Katz, 1983).

Another way of preventing child abuse is by changing attitudes. Despite newspaper and TV coverage of the problem, many parents believe it is their "right" to slap or hit their children. A survey of parents found that physical punishment is widely accepted in this country. Even hitting a child with a leather strap or a wooden stick was rated as only "moderately serious" (Giovannoni & Becerra, 1979). A child had to be "banged against a wall" or "hit in the face with a fist" before the parents considered the act abusive. As the authors of the survey put it, the public attitude appears to be, "It's all right to hit your child, but not too hard; in fact it's all right to hurt your child—but not too badly."

To face the problem squarely, we must realize that the line between acceptable discipline and child abuse is blurred. As a society we seem to say, "Violence is okay if the child isn't injured; if the child is injured, then it's child abuse." Of course, when the child is injured, it's too late to take back the violence. By condoning punishment that borders on being abusive, we greatly raise the chances of injury. The best solution to physical abuse, then, may lie in rethinking our attitudes toward physical punishment and toward the rights of children.

Learning Check

1. According to the text, effective discipline gives children freedom within a structure of consistent and well-defined limits. T or F?
2. Coopersmith found that high self-esteem in childhood is related to discipline based on either management techniques or withdrawal of love. T or F?
3. Spankings and other physical punishment are most effective for children under the age of 2. T or F?
4. Authoritarian parents view children as having few rights but many responsibilities. T or F?
5. Approximately 30 percent of all parents who were abused as children mistreat their own children. T or F?

Answers:
1. T 2. F 3. F 4. T 5. T

Exploration: Approaching Death—New Pathways

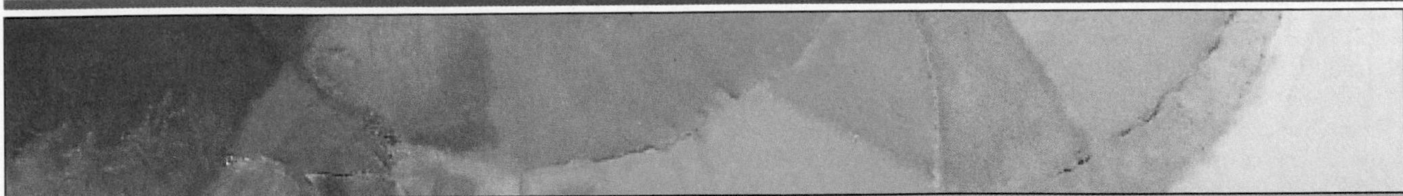

In 1967, H. Bedford, a psychology professor from Glendale, California, died at the age of 73. His body was immediately frozen—submerged in liquid nitrogen—making him the first person in the United States to try to cheat death by cryonic suspension (Keeffe, 1977). Mr. Bedford's story is only one indication of changing attitudes toward dying.

For some, death is a sudden tragedy. For others, it is a long-wished-for release. Whatever the case, death—the last phase of life—is something we all must face. It therefore behooves each of us to know something about death. In this section we will add to our earlier discussion of death by considering four departures from traditional approaches to dying. These are the hospice movement, passive euthanasia, active euthanasia, and cryonics.

Hospice At the beginning of this century most people died at home. Today, in the United States more than 70 percent of all deaths take place outside the home, most often in either a hospital or a nursing home (Fulton, 1979). Just as some people have begun to question traditional funeral practices (embalming, viewing, elaborate and expensive caskets and ceremonies), many are now beginning to question treatment of the terminally ill. Too often, dying persons are isolated, frightened, in pain, and stripped of control over their final days of life. The hospice concept was created to counter this situation.

A **hospice** is basically a hospital for the terminally ill, modeled after a pioneering English facility. The goal of the hospice is to give specialized care to the dying individual and to improve the quality of life in the person's final days. The first hospice was created in recognition of dying individuals' needs to be included, to know that someone still cares, to maintain control over their lives, and to have a say in their own dying. In operation, the first hospices presented a striking contrast to the grim wards for the terminally ill found in many hospitals.

Question: How is a hospice different?

First, there are lots of people present. A hospice offers support, counseling, guidance, and companionship from volunteers, other patients, staff, clergy, and counselors. Friendship and kindness are expressed toward patients so that when the time comes to die, they know they will be remembered with respect and love.

Second, the atmosphere differs markedly from that of a traditional hospital. A hospice attempts to provide pleasant surroundings, an atmosphere of intentional informality, and a sense of continued living for patients. Unlimited around-the-clock visits are permitted by relatives, friends, children, and even pets. Patients receive constant attention, play games, make day trips, have predinner cocktails if they choose, enjoy entertainment, and visit with volunteers. In short, life goes on for them.

A third aspect of hospice care is the freedom of choice allowed to patients. Patients decide about their own diets, about whether or not they will use painkilling drugs, and about whether or not they want to continue medical care. Patients may also choose freedom from intolerable pain. This is usually achieved by providing them with Brompton's mixture, a combination of cherry syrup and morphine. The dosage of morphine in a Brompton's "cocktail" is small enough so that the person does not become euphoric or groggy; it simply relieves pain.

At present most larger cities in the United States have hospices. Their success has been such that they are likely to be added to many more communities. At the same time, treatment for the terminally ill has drastically improved in hospitals—largely a result of the pioneering efforts in the hospice movement.

A Right to Die? The "right to die" concept might be better stated as a right to live in peace and comfort until death. Much of the recent interest in this issue has focused on the Karen Ann Quinlan case. In 1975, Karen lapsed into a coma after suffering an overdose of drugs and alcohol. After doctors said she would never recover, Karen's parents began a legal fight to turn off the respirator and other devices being used to prolong her life. In 1976, the New Jersey Supreme Court issued a landmark decision giving permission to

Exploration

the parents to order removal of Karen's life-support equipment. Despite the doctors' prediction, Karen continued to live for another 10 years. Karen died in 1985 at the age of 31.

Is there a right to die? Doctors and other medical personnel are legally and morally bound to prolong and preserve life, and in most states relatives and guardians cannot legally give permission for removal of life-supporting equipment. One way out of this dilemma that is gaining support is the **living will.** The intent of a living will is to free the terminally and irreversibly ill from a slow and cruel death, allowing death with dignity. The will is made out when the person is still healthy, and states that, in the event of irreversible illness, the person does not want to have life sustained by medical machines or heroic measures. A living will is not yet binding in most states, but it does make clear the wishes of terminally ill persons unable to speak for themselves. The following excerpt is from one widely used living will.

A Living Will

If at such a time the situation should arise in which there is no reasonable expectation of my recovery from extreme physical or mental disability, I direct that I be allowed to die and not be kept alive by medications, artificial means or "heroic measures." I do, however, ask that medication be mercifully administered to me to alleviate suffering even though this may shorten my remaining life. (Reprinted with permission from Concern for Dying, 250 West 57th Street, New York, NY, 10017.)

Euthanasia The right to die won for Karen Quinlan by her parents may be thought of as **passive euthanasia** (YOU-tha-NAY-zyah), in which death is allowed to occur but is not actively caused. In **active euthanasia,** or "physician-assisted suicide," steps would be taken at a patient's request to deliberately hasten death, perhaps by administering drugs that induce death painlessly. Both forms of euthanasia present ethical dilemmas for physicians, who are trained to keep patients alive. On the other hand, doctors are also sworn to *humane* treatment. With the second point in mind, proponents of euthanasia believe that it is a basic human right to die with dignity and a minimum of discomfort. To a degree, passive euthanasia is already practiced in the United States. Should active euthanasia ever become legal (many people find the idea totally unacceptable), it might also become possible for next of kin to request euthanasia for an incapacitated individual.

There are several arguments against euthanasia. The case of Karen Delahanty of Avon, Connecticut, provides a good starting point. After a head-on automobile accident, Karen entered a coma from which doctors predicted she would never recover. One year later she miraculously regained consciousness. What if euthanasia had been carried out?

Other questions that arise, in addition to unexpected recovery, include: What guarantee is there that the choice of euthanasia would be made freely and without pressure? Can family members be trusted to make a correct decision? Would they feel guilt afterward? What about the medical personnel involved; how would they respond emotionally to "mercy killing"? No doubt you can think of other objections.

Cryonics To complete our brief sampling of new approaches to death, let's return to cryonics. Cryonics involves freezing a person's body immediately after death. The idea is to keep the person frozen until medical science perfects ways to thaw, restore, and revive the person. Those who have been placed in **cryonic suspension** obviously are gambling that if they are revived, a cure will exist for whatever killed them.

Question: Does freezing actually work?

Cryonic suspension must be viewed as a symbolic attempt to cheat death or perhaps as an emotional hedge against the finality of death. At this point, cryonic suspension is impractical because freezing does serious damage to the body (Vogel, 1988). The ice crystals formed by freezing and unfreezing the human brain would almost surely turn it to mush—wiping out most or all of the memories stored there. If a person frozen at death were ever to be successfully revived, that person would have no identity and perhaps no understanding of where he or she was or why he or she was there. Such persons would, in most cases, be quite old. (To date, most of the persons who have been frozen have been middle-aged or older.) Another problem is the great expense of maintaining cryonic capsules for many years. (Aging LSD guru Tim Leary has arranged to have only his head frozen—he can't afford the whole-body treatment.) And in California (where else?), a case has already surfaced where careless operators of a cryonics service allowed a number of bodies to defrost.

Whereas it is true that for a few pioneering souls there is clearly "ice after death," immortality, it would seem, does not yet fall within the province of technology.

Exploration

Learning Check

1. The goal of a hospice is to freeze persons who have died of diseases that might one day become curable. T or F?
2. In passive euthanasia, death is allowed to occur but is not actively induced. T or F?
3. Cryonic suspension is a type of passive euthanasia. T or F?
4. Active euthanasia is now legal in most states, providing that the terminally ill patient has signed a living will. T or F?

Answers:
1. F 2. T 3. F 4. F

Chapter Summary

• According to Erikson, each life stage provokes a specific **psychosocial crisis.** In order of occurrence, these are: *trust versus mistrust, autonomy versus shame and doubt, initiative versus guilt, industry versus inferiority, identity versus role confusion, intimacy versus isolation, generativity versus stagnation,* and *integrity versus despair.* In addition to the dilemmas identified by Erikson, we recognize that each life stage requires successful mastery of certain **developmental tasks.**

• Three major parental styles are *authoritarian, permissive,* and *effective (authoritative).* When judged by its effects on children, authoritative parenting appears to be most effective.

• Few children grow up without experiencing some of the normal problems of childhood, including **negativism, clinging, specific fears, sleep disturbances, general dissatisfaction, regression, sibling rivalry,** and **rebellion.**

• Significant problems affect about 1 child in 10. Major areas of difficulty are *toilet training* (including **enuresis** and **encopresis**); *feeding disturbances,* such as **overeating, anorexia nervosa** (self-starvation), and **pica** (eating nonfood substances); *speech disturbances* **(delayed speech, stuttering);** and *learning disorders* (**dyslexia, hyperactivity,** and other problems). **Childhood autism** is representative of some of the more severe problems that can occur. Some cases of hyperactivity and autism are being treated successfully with **behavior modification.**

• **Adolescence** is a culturally defined social status. **Puberty** is a biological event. *Early maturation* is beneficial mostly for boys; its effects are mixed for girls. One danger of early maturation is *premature identity formation.* Adolescent identity formation is accelerated by cognitive development and influenced by parents and peers.

• Certain relatively consistent events mark adult development in our society. These range from escaping parental dominance in the late teens to a noticeable acceptance of one's lot in life during the 50s. Some research indicates that a *midlife crisis* affects many people in the 37–41 age range. Adjustment to later middle age is often complicated for women by **menopause** and for men by a **climacteric.**

• Both the *number* and *proportion* of older people in the population has grown. **Biological aging** begins between 25 and 30, but peak performance in a particular pursuit may come at various points throughout life. Intellectual decline is quite limited, at least through one's 70s.

• **Gerontologists** have proposed two major theories of successful aging. The **disengagement theory** holds that withdrawal from society is necessary and desirable in old age. The **activity theory** counters that optimal adjustment to aging is tied to continuing activity and involvement. There is an element of truth to each, but the activity theory has received more support.

• **Ageism** refers to prejudice, discrimination, and stereotyping on the basis of age. It affects people of all ages, but is especially damaging to older people. Most ageism is based on stereotypes, myths, and misinformation.

• Typical emotional reactions to impending death are

denial, anger, bargaining, depression, and **acceptance. Bereavement** also brings forth a typical series of reactions, ranging from shock to final acceptance.

• Effective parental discipline tends to emphasize **child management techniques** (especially communication), rather than **power assertion** or **withdrawal of love. Child abuse** is a major problem for which few solutions currently exist. Roughly 30 percent of all abused children become abusive adults.

• New approaches to death include the **hospice** movement, **living wills,** and **cryonic suspension.** A continuing controversy concerns the ethics of **passive euthanasia** and **active euthanasia.**

Questions for Discussion

1. Describe an incident from your own childhood that you consider growth-promoting. Describe an incident that set you back or had a negative effect on you. How do these incidents differ?

2. Were you physically punished as a child? What is your attitude toward physical punishment now? Would you use physical punishment on your own children?

3. In what ways do parents add to the conflicts of young adults who are seeking independence?

4. Do you know a person who seems to have "flunked" one or more of Erikson's developmental stages? What effect has this had on the person's subsequent development?

5. Anthropologist Margaret Mead has charged, "We have become a society of people who neglect our children, are afraid of our children." Do you agree?

6. Do we need a "children's liberation movement" to establish the civil rights of children? (Keep in mind that few parents show their children the courtesy they show strangers.)

7. How common do you think it is to experience a "midlife crisis"? Would you expect people of other cultures to experience a similar crisis? People born in various decades have very different life experiences. How much do you think this affects patterns of development and the likelihood of problems at midlife?

8. When and how would you prefer to die? If you had a terminal illness, would you want to be told? Do you think sudden death or death with forewarning would be better?

9. Should passive euthanasia be allowed? Should active euthanasia be allowed? What are the arguments for and against each? Do you think a "living will" is a good idea? Why or why not?

10. If you could choose to remain a particular age, which would you choose? Why? What are your attitudes toward aging?

11. How general are the emotional stages of death described by Kübler-Ross? Do they describe the reactions of people you know who have died?

12. Why do you think dying individuals so often feel isolated? How could the emotional needs of dying persons be better served than they are now in hospitals and nursing homes?

Where to Write for Information

• **Anorexia Nervosa** National Association of Anorexia Nervosa and Associated Disorders, Box 271, Highland Park, Illinois 60035.

• **Autism** The National Society for Autistic Children, 101 Richmond St., Huntington, West Virginia 25701; or, Autism Society of America, Suite C1017, 1234 Massachusetts Ave., NW, Washington, D.C. 20005.

• **Child Abuse** Parents Anonymous, 22330 Hawthorne Blvd., Torrance, California 90505.

• **Hospice** The National Hospice Organization, 301 Tower Suite 506, 301 Maple Ave. West, Vienna, Virginia 22180.

• **Hyperactivity** Department of Health, Education, and Welfare, Office of the Secretary, Secretary's Committee on Mental Retardation, Washington, D.C. 20201.

• **Learning Disorders** National Association for Children with Learning Disabilities, 5225 Grace St., Pittsburgh, Pennsylvania 15236.

• **Living Will** Concern for Dying, 250 West 57th St., New York, New York 10019.

Chapter 16

Dimensions of Personality

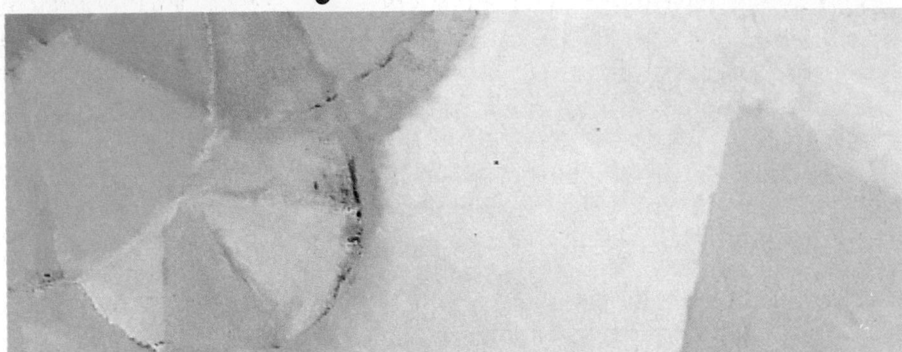

In This Chapter

Defining personality
Traits, types, self-concept, and theories
Trait theories
Birth order and personality
The androgyny debate
Assessing personality
Interviews, observation, and situational tests
Personality questionnaires
Projective tests
Sudden murderers

Applications

Understanding shyness

Exploration

Genetics, twins, and personality

Chapter Preview

The Hidden Essence

Rural Colorado. The car lurched over the last few yards of brain-jarring ruts. Before us stood an ancient farmhouse, a hulking monument to neglect. Annette was out of the house—hooting and whooping—before we had stopped.

If anyone was suited for a move to the "wilds" of Colorado, it was Annette, the "terror of Tenth Street." Still, it was hard to imagine a more radical change. After separating from her husband, she had traded housewifery in the city for survival in the hinterlands. Survival, by the way, is no exaggeration. Annette was working as a ranch hand and as a lumberjack (lumberjill?), trying to make it alone through some hard winters.

So radical were the changes in Annette's life, I must confess I expected just as radical a change in her. She was, on the contrary, more her "old self" than ever.

Perhaps you have had a similar experience. After several years of separation it is always intriguing to see an old friend. Often you will be struck at first by ways in which the person has changed. Soon, however, you will probably be pleased to discover how superficial such changes really are. Under it all there is a core that ties the semistranger before you to the person you once knew. It is exactly this core of consistency that psychologists have in mind when they use the term personality.

The Extra Dimension *Despite our advanced technology, the human dimension still determines success or failure in many situations. Errors in human judgment contributed significantly to the* Challenger *spacecraft disaster. Similarly, it is often said that the most dangerous part of an automobile is "the nut at the wheel." Without doubt, personality touches many aspects of our daily lives. Selecting a mate, choosing friends, getting along with co-workers, voting for a president, and numerous other activities raise questions about personality. But what is personality? How does it differ from temperament, character, or attitudes? How stable are personality characteristics? These and related questions are the concerns of this chapter.*

Survey Questions

- How do psychologists use the term *personality*?
- Are some personality traits more basic or important than others?
- Does birth order have any effect on personality?
- What is psychological androgyny (and is it contagious)?
- How do psychologists measure personality?
- What causes shyness? What can be done about it?
- How much does heredity influence personality?

Do You Have Personality?

"Jim's not handsome, but he has a great personality." "My father's business friends think he's a nice guy, but they should see him at home where his real personality comes out." "It's hard to believe they're sisters. They have such opposite personalities."

It's obvious from such statements that we all frequently use the term *personality*. But when asked, many people seem hard-pressed to define personality. Most simply end up saying something about "charm," "charisma," or "style." If you use *personality* in such ways, you are giving it a different meaning than psychologists do. To a psychologist, it makes little sense to ask, "Do I have personality?" or to proclaim, "She has lots of personality." In psychological terms, everyone has personality.

Question: Then how do psychologists use the term?

Since personality is a *hypothetical construct,* psychologists give it different meanings. (Hypothetical constructs are explanatory concepts that are not directly observable.) Most, however, regard **personality** as a person's *unique and enduring behavior patterns*. In other words, personality refers to the consistency in who you are, have been, and will become. It also refers to the special blend of talents, attitudes, values, hopes, loves, hates, and habits that makes each of us a unique person.

Question: How is that different from the way most people use the term?

Many people confuse personality with **character.** The term *character* implies that a person has been *judged* or *evaluated,* not just described. If, by saying someone has "personality," you mean the person is friendly, outgoing, and attractive, you are really referring to what is considered good character in our culture. But in some cultures it is deemed good for a person to be fierce, warlike, and cruel. So, while everyone in a particular culture has personality, not everyone has character—or at least, not good character. (Do you know any good characters?)

Personality can also be distinguished from **temperament.** As mentioned in Chapter 14, temperament is the "raw material" from which personality is formed. Temperament refers to the hereditary aspects of one's emotional nature: sensitivity, strength and speed of response, prevailing mood, and changes in mood (Allport, 1961).

Fig. 16–1 *Does this man have personality? Do you?*

As you may recall, differences in temperament are apparent from birth onward.

Psychology Looks at Personality

Psychologists use a large number of concepts to explain personality. It might be wise, therefore, to start with a few key terms. These ideas should help you keep your bearings as you read this chapter and the next.

Traits We use the idea of traits every day in talking about the personalities of friends and acquaintances. For instance, my friend Dan is *sociable, orderly,* and *intelligent.* His sister Andrea is *shy, sensitive,* and *creative.* In general, psychologists think of **traits** as *lasting qualities* within a person that are inferred from observed behavior. If you see Dan talking to strangers—first at a supermarket and later at a party—you might deduce that he is "sociable." You might then predict from this trait that he will also be sociable at school or at work. As you can see, we often use traits to predict future behavior from past behavior (Rowe, 1987). Traits also imply some consistency in behavior. As an example, think about how little the personality traits of your best friends have changed in the last 5 years.

Types Have you ever asked the question, "What type of person is she (or he)?" before meeting someone new? An interest in personality *types* is quite natural. A **personality type** represents a category of individuals who have a number of traits or characteristics in common (Potkay & Allen, 1986). Informally, it is quite common to speak of various personality types. Your own thinking might include the executive type, the athletic type, the motherly type, the Yuppie type, the strong silent type, and so forth.

Question: How valid is it to speak of personality "types"?

Over the years, psychologists have proposed various ways to categorize personalities. Consider the idea, first advanced by Swiss psychiatrist Carl Jung (yung), that a person is either an **introvert** (shy, self-centered person) or an **extrovert** (bold, outgoing person). These terms are so widely used that you may think of yourself and your friends as being one or the other. However, the wildest, wittiest, most party-loving "extrovert" you know is introverted at times, and extremely introverted persons are assertive and sociable in some situations. In short, two categories (or even several) are often inadequate to fully describe differences in personality.

Even though types tend to oversimplify personality, they do have value. Most often, types are used by psychologists as a shorthand way of labeling people who share similar personality traits. You might recall from Chapter 13, for instance, that classifying people as Type A or Type B personalities may help predict their chances of suffering a heart attack. Similarly, you will read in Chapter 19 about unhealthy personality types such as the paranoid personality, the dependent personality, and the antisocial personality.

Self-Concept Another way of understanding personality is to focus on a person's self-concept. The rough outlines of your own self-concept would be revealed by this request: "Please tell us about yourself." In other words, a **self-concept** is a person's *perception* of his or her own personality traits. It consists of all your ideas and feelings about who you are (Potkay & Allen, 1986).

Many psychologists believe that self-concepts have a major impact on behavior. We creatively build our self-concepts out of daily experience. Then we slowly revise them as we have new experiences. Once a stable self-concept exists, it tends to shape our subjective world by guiding what we attend to, remember, and think about (Markus & Nurius, 1986).

An individual's self-concept can greatly affect personal adjustment—especially when the self-concept is *inaccurate* or *inadequate* (Potkay & Allen, 1986). As an example, imagine a student who thinks she is stupid, worthless, and a failure, despite having completed 3 years of college with good grades. With such a negative self-concept, the student will probably be depressed or anxious no matter how well she does. Problems of this type are explored further in the next chapter.

Personality Theories Personality is so complex that we might easily become lost without a guiding framework for understanding it. How do the observations we make about personality fit together? Can we explain and predict behavior from our knowledge of personality? How does personality develop? Why do people become emotionally unhealthy? How can they be helped? To answer such questions, psychologists have created a fascinating array of theories. A **personality theory** is a system of assumptions, ideas, and principles proposed to explain personality. In this chapter you will find two examples of trait theories of personality. The next chapter is devoted entirely to more elaborate theories offered by thinkers such as Sigmund Freud, B. F. Skinner, and Carl Rogers.

Compare: Core Concepts of Personality

Personality An individual's unique and relatively unchanging psychological characteristics and behavior patterns.

Character A subjective evaluation of personality, particularly with regard to a person's desirable or undesirable qualities.

Temperament The physical foundation of personality, including prevailing mood, sensitivity, energy levels, and so forth.

Traits Relatively permanent and enduring patterns of behavior that a person displays in most situations.

Personality types Categories used to describe personality, with each category representing a collection of related traits.

Self-concept Knowledge of one's own personality traits; a collection of beliefs, ideas, and feelings about one's own identity.

Personality theory An interrelated system of concepts and principles used to understand and explain personality.

● HIGHLIGHT 16–1 Extroverted Study Habits

Where do you prefer to study in the library? The answer may reveal a basic trait of your personality.

As we noted, splitting people into introverted and extroverted *types* is an oversimplification. On the other hand, many psychologists regard one's *degree* of introversion/extroversion as one of several important personality *traits*. Viewed in this way, a person's level of introversion/extroversion can have interesting links to behavior.

One recent study found that students scoring high in extroversion chose study locations that provided more chances for socializing and that had higher noise levels (Campbell & Hawley, 1982). In the campus library at Colgate University (where the study was done), you can find extroverted students in the second floor lounge. Or, if you prefer, more introverted students can be found studying in the carrels on the first and third floors!

● The Trait Approach—Describe Yourself in 18,000 Words or Less

Now that you are oriented, let's take a deeper look at personality. How many words can you think of to describe the personality of a close friend? You should have little trouble making a long list: Over 18,000 English words refer to personal characteristics (Allport & Odbert, 1936). As stated earlier, **traits** are *relatively permanent and enduring qualities* that a person shows in most situations (see Highlight 16–1). For example, if you are usually optimistic, reserved, and friendly, these qualities might be considered stable traits of your personality.

Question: What if I am sometimes pessimistic, uninhibited, or shy?

The first three qualities are still traits as long as they are most *typical* of your behavior. Let's say Ima Student approaches most situations with optimism, but has a habit of expecting the worst each time she takes a test. If her pessimism is limited to this situation or to a few others, it is still accurate and useful to describe her as an optimistic person.

In general, the trait approach attempts to identify traits that best describe a particular individual. Take a moment to check the traits in Table 16–1 that you feel describe your personality. Are the traits you checked of equal importance? Are some stronger or more basic than others? Do any overlap? For example, if you checked "dominant," did you also check "confident" and "bold"? Answers to these questions would interest a **trait theorist.** To understand personality, trait theorists attempt to classify traits and to discover which are most basic.

Table 16–1 Adjective Checklist

Check the traits you feel are characteristic of your personality. Are some more basic than others?

aggressive	organized	ambitious
confident	loyal	generous
warm	bold	cautious
sensitive	mature	talented
sociable	busy	funny
dominant	dull	accurate
humble	uninhibited	future-oriented
thoughtful	serious	helpful
orderly	anxious	conforming
liberal	curious	optimistic
meek	neighborly	passionate
kind	compulsive	honest
cheerful	emotional	good-natured
clever	calm	reliable
jealous	religious	nervous

Question: Are there different kinds of traits?

Classifying Traits Psychologist Gordon Allport (1961), who was deeply interested in personality, identified several kinds of traits. **Common traits** are those shared by most members of a culture. Common traits show how people from a particular nation or culture are similar, or which traits the culture emphasizes. In American culture, for example, competitiveness is a fairly common trait. Among the Hopi of Northern Arizona, it is a relatively rare trait. Of course, common traits tell us little about individuals. While many people are competitive in American culture, each person may rate high or low in this trait. Even if we study only highly competitive personalities, we must also consider each person's unique qualities, or **individual traits.**

If the difference between common traits and individual traits is unclear, consider this analogy: If you were going to buy a pet dog, you would want to know the general characteristics of a particular breed (its common traits). In addition, you would want to know about the "personality" of a specific dog before selecting it (its individual traits).

Allport also made distinctions between **cardinal traits, central traits,** and **secondary traits.** A cardinal trait is so basic that all of a person's activities can be traced to the trait's existence. It is said, for instance, that an overriding factor in the life of Albert Schweitzer was "reverence for every living thing." Likewise, Abraham Lincoln's personality was dominated by the cardinal trait of honesty. According to Allport, few people have cardinal traits.

Question: How do central and secondary traits differ from cardinal traits?

Central traits are the basic building blocks of personality. Allport found that a surprisingly small number of central traits are enough to capture the essence of a person. College students asked to write a short description of someone they knew well mentioned an average of only 7.2 central traits (Allport, 1961).

In contrast, secondary traits are less consistent and less important aspects of a person. For this reason, any number of secondary traits could be listed in a personality description. Your own secondary traits include such things as food preferences, attitudes, political opinions, musical tastes, and so forth. In Allport's terms, a personality description might therefore include the following.

Name: Jane Doe
Age: 22
Cardinal traits: None
Central traits: Possessive, autonomous, artistic, dramatic, self-centered, trusting
Secondary traits: Prefers colorful clothes, likes to work alone, politically liberal, always late . . .

Source Traits A second major approach to the study of traits is illustrated by the work of Raymond B. Cattell (1965). Cattell was dissatisfied with merely classifying traits. Instead, he wanted to reach deeper into personality to learn how traits are organized and interlinked.

Cattell began by studying features that make up the visible portions of personality. He called these **surface traits.** Through the use of questionnaires, direct observation, and life records, Cattell assembled data on the surface traits of a large number of people. He then noted that surface traits often appear in *clusters,* or groups. In fact, some traits appeared together so often that they seemed to represent a single more basic trait. Cattell called such underlying personality characteristics **source traits.**

Question: How do source traits differ from Allport's central traits?

The main difference is that Allport classified traits subjectively, whereas Cattell used a statistical technique called **factor analysis** to reduce surface traits to source traits. Factor analysis uses correlations to identify traits that are interrelated. Using this approach, Cattell developed a list of 16 underlying source traits. He considers this the basic number necessary to describe an individual personality.

Cattell's source traits are measured by a test called the *Sixteen Personality Factor Questionnaire* (often referred to as the 16 PF). Like many tests of its type, the 16 PF can be used to produce a **trait profile.** A trait profile presents a graph of a person's scores for each trait. Trait profiles can be very helpful for obtaining a "picture" of an individual personality or for making comparisons between the personalities of two or more persons (Fig. 16–2).

Before you read the next section, take a moment to answer the questions in Highlight 16–2. Doing so will add to your understanding of a long-running controversy in the psychology of personality.

Traits, Consistency, and Situations

For many years, psychologists debated the relative importance of personality traits and external circumstances in determining behavior. There is now little doubt that personality traits show a degree of consistency over long periods of time (Conley, 1984; Moss & Susman, 1980). And yet, *situations* also exert a powerful influence on our behavior. For instance, it would be unusual to find some-

HIGHLIGHT 16–2
How Do You View Personality?

The questions that follow may help you gain insight into the assumptions you make about personality. Answer true or false for each statement.

1. My friends' actions are fairly consistent from day to day and in different situations. T or F?
2. Whether a person is honest or dishonest, kind or cruel, a hero or a coward, depends mainly on circumstances. T or F?
3. Most people that I have known for several years have pretty much the same personalities now as they did when I first met them. T or F?
4. The reason that people in some professions (such as teachers, lawyers, or doctors) seem so much alike is because their work requires that they act in particular ways. T or F?
5. One of the first things I would want to know about a potential roommate is what the person's personality is like. T or F?
6. I believe that immediate circumstances usually determine how people act at any given time. T or F?
7. To be comfortable in a particular job, a person's personality must match the nature of the work. T or F?
8. Almost anyone would be polite at a wedding reception; it doesn't matter what kind of personality the person has. T or F?

Now count the number of times you marked true for the odd-number items. Do the same for the even-numbered items. If you agreed with most of the odd-numbered items, you tend to view behavior as strongly influenced by personality traits or lasting personal dispositions. If you agreed with most of the even-numbered items, you view behavior as strongly influenced by external situations and circumstances. If the number of times you answered true is nearly equal for odd and even items, you place equal weight on traits and situations as sources of behavior. This is the view now held by many personality psychologists.

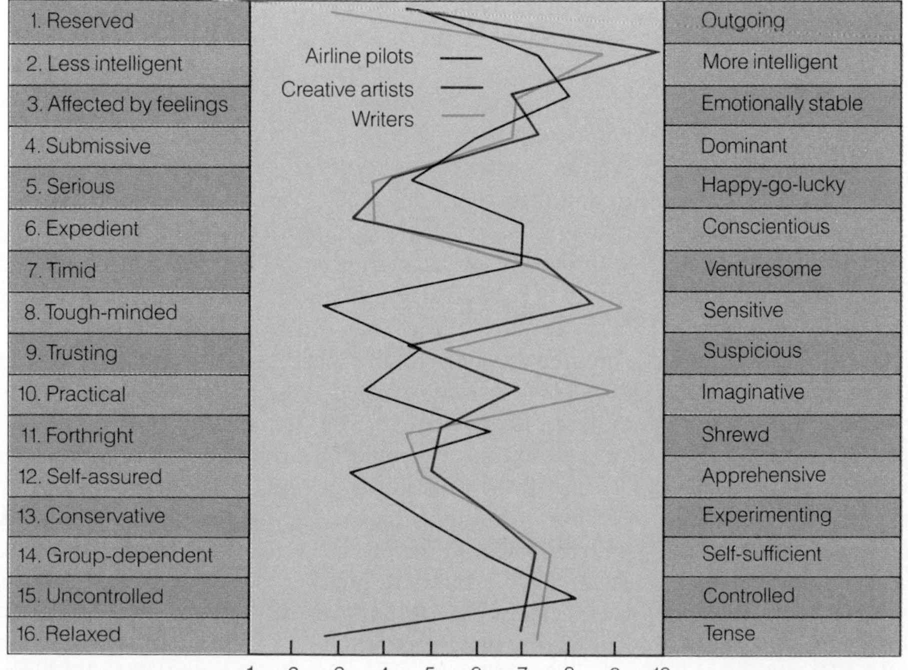

Fig. 16–2 *The 16 source traits measured by Cattell's 16 PF are listed beside the graph. Scores can be graphed as a profile for an individual or a group. The profiles shown here are group averages for airline pilots, creative artists, and writers. Notice the similarity between artists and writers and the difference between these two groups and pilots. (After Cattell, 1973.)*

one reading a book at a football game or dancing at a movie. Likewise, few people sleep in roller coasters or laugh at funerals. On the other hand, your personality traits may help predict whether you choose to read a book, go to a movie, or attend a football game in the first place. In view of such observations, most psychologists now agree that traits *interact* with situations to determine behavior (Loevinger & Knoll, 1983). (This point is discussed further in Chapter 17.)

To illustrate what is meant by **trait-situation interactions,** imagine what would happen if you moved from a church to a classroom to a party to a football game. As the setting changed, your behavior would probably become more loud and boisterous. This change would demonstrate situational effects on behavior. Yet, at the same time, your personality traits would also be apparent: If you were quieter than average in class, you would probably be quieter than average in the other settings, too (Rorer & Widiger, 1983).

The concept of traits allows us to address some interesting questions about personality. Let's take a moment to explore two intriguing examples of trait research.

Birth Order—Personality By Position?

Without exception you are one of the following: the oldest or only child in your family, a middle child, or the youngest. If you had it to do over again, which would you choose to be? Your answer could depend on the personality traits you would most like to have. Birth order, or **ordinal position,** in a family can leave an imprint on personality.

Question: What traits are associated with birth order?

Firstborn/Later-born The clearest differences are between **firstborn** and **later-born** children. Firstborn children seem to have a higher chance of achieving eminence than later-born persons. Freud, Kant, Beethoven, Dante, Einstein, and an unexpectedly large number of other high-achieving men and women were firstborn children (Harris, 1964). Firstborns have better high school and college grade averages. More firstborns become National Merit Scholars, and more are medical students or graduate students. Most U.S. astronauts were firstborn (Harris, 1964; Hilton, 1967). In short, firstborns tend to be high achievers—responsible, hardworking, and disciplined persons with high levels of pride and self-esteem (Howarth, 1980).

Before you congratulate yourself on being a firstborn or lament that you are not, consider this: Firstborns are also shyer, more conforming, and more likely to be anxious or neurotic than later-born persons (Howarth, 1980; Schachter, 1959).

Question: What are the strengths of later-born persons?

Later-born persons tend to excel in social relationships. They are affectionate, friendly, and at ease with others. Youngest children also tend to be more original and creative than first borns. For such reasons, later-borns are typically more popular with their peers. They also display better social skills when interacting with strangers (Ickes & Turner, 1983).

Question: How does birth order influence personality?

Parental Attitudes The answer seems to lie in the "emotional set" that parents bring to each child. Because they are the first on the scene, oldest children often get more attention, praise, and concern than later children. The first child is talked to more, punished more, and gets more stimulation and affection than later-born children do (Belsky et al., 1984). The firstborn is also more likely to be a planned child and is breast-fed longer (Sears et al., 1957).

Such patterns seem to benefit the firstborn, who come to think of themselves as important persons. High parental expectations for the firstborn are then translated into high self-expectations. For example, women business executives who have excelled in traditional, male-dominated occupations tend be firstborn children. Although the connection is open to interpretation, it may be that these firstborn women were especially encouraged to achieve by their parents (Hoyenga & Hoyenga, 1984).

A principal drawback of being firstborn is that new parents are more anxious and inconsistent. As a result, firstborns develop higher levels of anxiety and a tendency to conform to adult values. Parents consistently report that they used lighter discipline and were more relaxed with second or later children. The youngest child in a family is particularly prone to be pampered and to have fewer responsibilities than did older brothers and sisters. Another way of saying this is that firstborn children tend to become parent-oriented, whereas later-borns tend to be more peer-oriented (Markus, 1981).

At this point, it should be emphasized that birth-order effects can be stated only as broad patterns. Being a first or later-born child does not mean that your personality will invariably fit the profiles we have outlined. Countless factors, including the number of children in a family, their sex, and age differences, and the age of the parents, can modify birth-order effects. For example, a third child who is born 4 or 5 years after the last previous child may get nearly as much attention from parents as the firstborn did. Nevertheless, when large samples of people are considered, small birth-order effects do emerge (Ernst & Angst, 1983; Sutton-Smith, 1982).

Compared to birth-order effects, growing up as a male or a female has many times more impact on personality. What does it mean to have "masculine" or "feminine" traits? To find out, let's explore a second area of interesting research.

Psychological Androgyny—Are You Masculine, Feminine, or Androgynous?

Are you aggressive, ambitious, analytical, assertive, athletic, competitive, decisive, dominant, forceful, independent, individualistic, self-reliant, and willing to take risks? If so, you are quite "masculine." Are you affectionate, cheerful, childlike, compassionate, flatterable, gentle, gullible, loyal, sensitive, shy, soft-spoken, sympathetic, tender, understanding, warm and yielding? If so, then you are quite "feminine."

Question: What if I have traits from both lists?

Then you may be **androgynous** (an-DROJ-ih-nus). The two lists just given are from the work of psychologist Sandra Bem. Using lists of various traits, Bem constructed the **Bem Sex Role Inventory (BSRI),** a list of 20 "masculine" traits (self-reliant, assertive, and so forth), 20 "feminine" traits (affectionate, gentle), and 20 neutral traits (truthful, friendly). Next, Bem and her associates gave the BSRI to thousands of people, asking them to say whether or not each trait applied to them. Of those surveyed, 50 percent fell into traditional masculine or feminine categories; 15 percent scored higher on traits of the opposite gender; and 35 percent were androgynous, getting high scores on both the masculine and feminine items.

Question: You haven't said yet what it means to be androgynous. Is it having both male and female traits?

Psychological Androgyny The word **androgyny** (an-DROJ-ih-nee) literally means "man-woman." Androgyny sounds as if it might have something to do with androids, asexuality, or sex-change operations, but it actually refers to having both masculine and feminine traits.

Bem's interest in androgyny stems from her belief that our complex society requires flexibility with respect to sex roles. She believes that it is right, and more than ever necessary, for men to be gentle, compassionate, sensitive, and yielding and for women to be forceful, self-reliant, independent, and ambitious—*as the situation requires*. In short, Bem feels that more people should be androgynous (Fig. 16–3).

Adaptability In an interesting series of experiments, Bem and her associates tried to show that androgynous individuals are more adaptable and less hindered by sex roles or images of what is appropriate "masculine" or "feminine" behavior. For example, in one experiment Bem gave people the choice of performing either a "masculine" activity (oil a hinge, nail boards together, and so forth) or a "feminine" activity (prepare a baby bottle, wind yarn into a ball, and so on). Masculine men and feminine women consistently chose sex-appropriate activities, even when the opposite choice paid more!

Bem's conclusion from a number of studies is that rigid sex roles can seriously restrict behavior, especially for men (Bem, 1974, 1975a, 1975b, 1981). She believes that masculine males have great difficulty expressing warmth, playfulness, and concern—even when these qualities are appropriate—because they view such traits as "feminine." Likewise, feminine women have trouble being independent and assertive, even when these qualities are called for.

Fig. 16–3 *Androgynous individuals adapt easily to both traditionally "masculine" and "feminine" situations.*

In the years since Bem's first studies, androgyny has been variously supported, attacked, and debated. Now, as the dust begins to settle, the picture looks like this:

- Having "masculine" traits primarily means that a person is independent and assertive. Scoring high in "masculinity," therefore, is related to high self-esteem and to success in many situations.
- Having "feminine" traits primarily means that a person is nurturant and interpersonally oriented. People who score high in "femininity," therefore, tend to experience greater social closeness with others and more happiness in marriage.

In sum, there are advantages to possessing both "masculine" and "feminine" traits, whatever one's gender may be (Spence, 1984).

Many people, of course, remain comfortable with traditional views of masculinity and femininity. Nevertheless, personality researchers have done much to show that "masculine" traits and "feminine" traits can exist in the same person and that androgyny can be a highly adaptive balance.

Learning Check

1. ________________ refers to the hereditary aspects of a person's emotional nature.
2. The term ________________ refers to the presence or absence of desirable personal qualities.
   a. personality *b.* source trait *c.* character *d.* temperament
3. A system that classifies all people as either introverts or extroverts is an example of a ________________ approach to personality.
4. An individual's perception of his or her own personality constitutes that person's ________________.
5. According to Allport, few people have ________________ traits.
6. Central traits are those shared by most members of a culture. T or F?
7. Cattell believes that clusters of ________________ traits reveal the presence of underlying ________________ traits.
8. Cattell's personality questionnaire provides ratings on 16 surface traits. T or F?
9. The Bem Sex Role Inventory is used to identify source traits in androgynous individuals. T or F?
10. Whereas firstborn persons tend to be high achievers, later-born persons tend to excel in social skills. T or F?

Answers:
1. Temperament **2.** *c* **3.** type **4.** self-concept **5.** cardinal **6.** F **7.** surface, source **8.** F **9.** F **10.** T

Personality Assessment—Psychological Yardsticks

One of the greatest values of the trait approach is the refinement it has brought to personality measurement and testing. To study traits, psychologists have found it helpful to create ways of assessing personality. The results have been of tremendous value in research, industry, education, and clinical work.

Question: How is personality "assessed"?

Psychologists use **interviews, observation, questionnaires,** and **projective tests** to measure personality. Each method is a refinement of more informal ways of judging individuals. Each way of assessing personality has limitations (described later). For this reason, they are often used in combination.

At one time or another, you have probably "sized up" a potential date, friend, or employer by engaging in conversation (interview). Perhaps you have asked a friend, "When I am delayed I get angry. Do you?" (questionnaire). Maybe you watch your professors when they are angry or embarrassed to learn what they are "really" like (observation). Or possibly you have noticed that when you say, "I think people feel . . .," you may be expressing your own feelings (projection). Let's see how psychologists apply each approach to probe personality.

The Interview

A very direct way to learn about personality is to engage a person in conversation. An interview is described as **unstructured** if the conversation is informal and the interviewee determines what subjects are discussed. In a **structured** interview, the interviewer obtains information by asking a series of planned questions.

Question: How are interviews used?

Interviews are used to identify personality disturbances; to select persons for employment, college, or special programs; and to study the dynamics of personality. Interviews also provide information for counseling or therapy. For instance, a counselor might ask a depressed person, "Have you ever contemplated suicide? What were the circumstances?" The counselor might then follow by asking, "How did you feel about it?" or, "How is what you are now feeling different from what you felt then?"

In addition to providing information, interviews make it possible to observe a person's tone of voice, hand gestures, posture, and facial expressions. Such "body language" cues are important because they may radically alter the message conveyed, as when a person claims to be "completely calm," but trembles uncontrollably.

Limitations Interviews give rapid insight into personality, but they are subject to certain limitations. For one thing, interviewers can be swayed by preconceptions. A person identified as a "housewife," "college student," "high school athlete," "punk," or "ski bum" may be misjudged because of an interviewer's attitude toward a particular lifestyle. Second, an interviewer's own personality may influence the interviewee's behavior, thus accentuating or distorting some of the interviewee's characteristics.

A third problem is the **halo effect.** The halo effect is a tendency to generalize a favorable or unfavorable impression to unrelated details of personality (Fig. 16–4). A person who is likeable or physically attractive may be rated more mature, intelligent, or adjusted than he or she actually is. The halo effect is something to keep in mind when interviewing for employment. First impressions do make a difference.

Even with their limitations, interviews are a respected method of personality assessment. In many cases, interviews are an essential step to additional personality testing and to counseling or therapy.

Direct Observation and Rating Scales

Are you fascinated by bus depots, airports, subway stations, or other public places? Many people relish a chance to observe the behavior of others. When used as an assessment procedure, direct observation is a simple extension of this natural interest in "people watching." For instance, a psychologist might arrange to observe a disturbed child playing with other children. Does the child remain withdrawn from others? Does she become hostile or aggressive without warning? By careful observation, the psychologist will identify personality characteristics and clarify the nature of the child's problems.

Fig. 16–4 *What is your impression of the person wearing the black jacket? Interviewers are often influenced by the halo effect (see text).*

Question: Wouldn't observation be subject to the same problems of misperception as an interview?

Yes. Misperceptions can be a difficulty. For this reason, **rating scales** are sometimes used (Table 16–2). Rating scales limit the chance that some traits will be overlooked while others are exaggerated. Perhaps they should be standard procedure for choosing a roommate, spouse, or lover!

An alternative to rating scales is to do a **behavioral assessment.** In this case, observers record how often various *actions* occur, not what traits they think a person has. For example, psychologists working with hospitalized mental patients may find it helpful to record the frequency of patients' aggression, self-care, speech, and unusual behaviors (Alevizos & Callahan, 1977).

Behavioral assessments are not strictly limited to visible behavior. They can also be helpful in probing thought processes. In one study, for example, students high in math anxiety were asked to think aloud while doing math problems. Then their thoughts were analyzed to pinpoint the causes of their anxiety (Blackwell et al., 1985).

Situational Testing A specialized form of direct observation is called **situational testing.** Situational tests are based on the premise that the best way to learn how a person reacts to certain types of situations is to simulate those situations. Situational tests expose a person to frustration, temptation, pressure, boredom, or other conditions capable of revealing personality characteristics.

Question: How are situational tests done?

An interesting current example of situational testing is the "Shoot–Don't Shoot" training provided by many police departments (Fig. 16–5). At times, police officers must make split-second decisions about using their guns. A mistake may be fatal. In the Shoot–Don't Shoot Test, actors play the part of armed juveniles or criminals. As various high-risk scenes are acted out live or on videotape, officers must decide to shoot or hold fire. A newspaper reporter who once took the test (and failed it) gives this account (Gersh, 1982):

> I judged wrong. I was killed by a man in a closet, a man with a hostage, a woman interrupted when kissing her lover, and a man I thought was cleaning a shotgun. . . . I shot a drunk who reached for a comb, and a teenager who pulled out a black water pistol. Looked real to me.

In addition to the training it provides, the Shoot–Don't Shoot Test uncovers police cadets who lack the good judgment needed to carry a gun out on the street.

Table 16–2 Sample Rating Scale Items

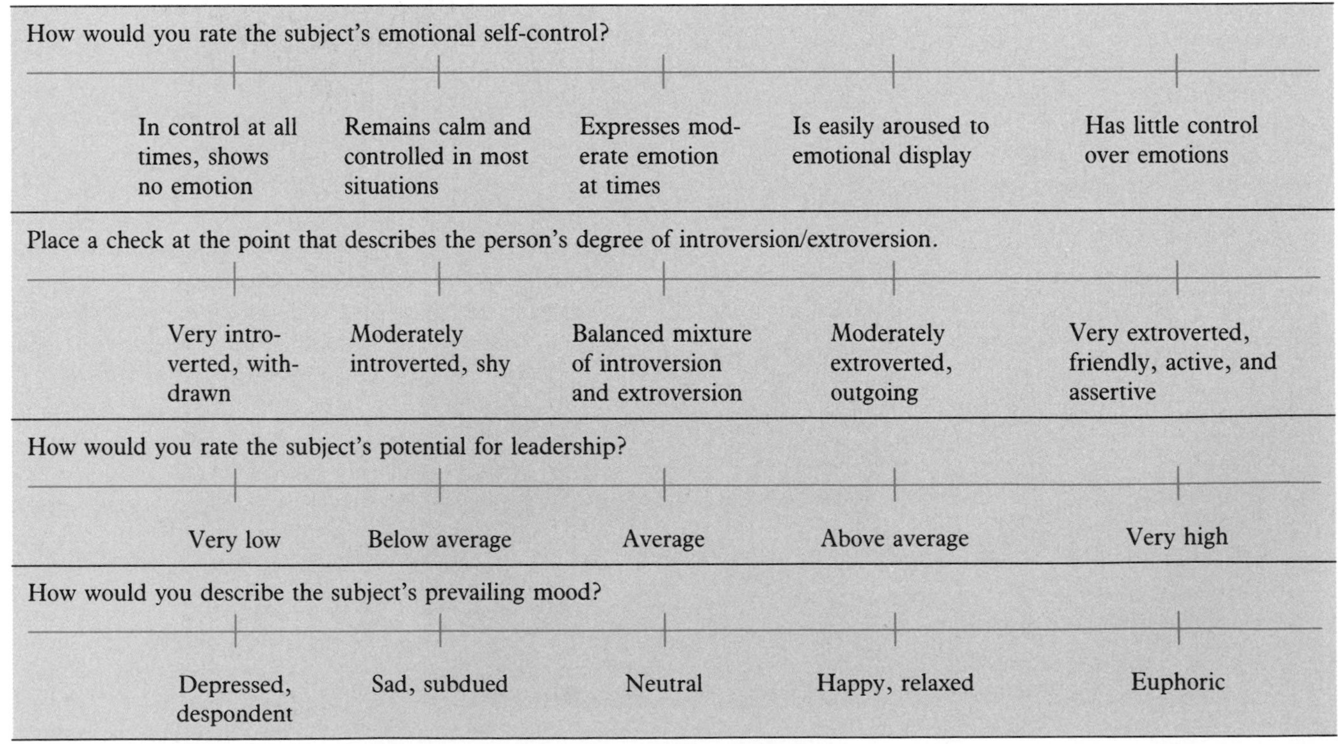

How would you rate the subject's emotional self-control?

In control at all times, shows no emotion	Remains calm and controlled in most situations	Expresses moderate emotion at times	Is easily aroused to emotional display	Has little control over emotions

Place a check at the point that describes the person's degree of introversion/extroversion.

Very introverted, withdrawn	Moderately introverted, shy	Balanced mixture of introversion and extroversion	Moderately extroverted, outgoing	Very extroverted, friendly, active, and assertive

How would you rate the subject's potential for leadership?

Very low	Below average	Average	Above average	Very high

How would you describe the subject's prevailing mood?

Depressed, despondent	Sad, subdued	Neutral	Happy, relaxed	Euphoric

Fig. 16–5 *A police officer undergoes a Shoot–Don't Shoot Test. Variations on this situational test are used by a growing number of police departments. All officers must score a passing grade.*

Personality Questionnaires

Most **personality questionnaires** are paper-and-pencil tests requiring people to answer questions about themselves. As measures of personality, questionnaires are more *objective* than interviews or observation. Questions, administration, and scoring are all standardized so that scores are unaffected by the opinions or prejudices of the examiner. (See Chapter 18 for more information on test standardization.)

Many personality tests have been developed, including tests such as the *Guilford-Zimmerman Temperament Survey,* the *California Psychological Inventory,* the *Allport-Vernon Study of Values,* the *16 PF,* and many more. One of the best-known and most widely used objective tests of personality is the *Minnesota Multiphasic Personality Inventory (MMPI).* The MMPI is composed of 550 items to which a subject must respond "true," "false," or "cannot say." Items include statements such as the following.

Everything tastes the same.
There is something wrong with my mind.
I enjoy animals.
Whenever possible I avoid being in a crowd.
I have never indulged in any unusual sex practices.
Someone has been trying to poison me.
I daydream often.*

*Reproduced by permission. Copyright 1943, renewed 1970 by the University of Minnesota. Published by The Psychological Corporation, New York, NY. All rights reserved.

Question: How can these items show anything about personality? For instance, what if a person has a cold so that "everything tastes the same"?

For an answer to this question (and a little bit of fun), see Highlight 16–3.

The MMPI measures 10 major aspects of personality (listed in Table 16–3). After the MMPI is scored, results are charted as an **MMPI profile** (Fig. 16–6). By com-

Table 16–3 MMPI Subscales

1. **Hypochondriasis** (HI-po-kon-DRY-uh-sis). Exaggerated concern about one's physical health.
2. **Depression.** Feelings of worthlessness, hopelessness, and pessimism.
3. **Hysteria.** The presence of physical complaints related to emotional disturbances (psychosomatic problems).
4. **Psychopathic deviate.** Emotional shallowness in relationships and a disregard for social and moral standards.
5. **Masculinity/femininity.** One's degree of traditional "masculine" aggressiveness or "feminine" sensitivity.
6. **Paranoia.** Extreme suspiciousness and feelings of persecution.
7. **Psychasthenia** (psych-as-THEE-nee-ah). The presence of irrational fears (phobias) and compulsive (ritualistic) actions.
8. **Schizophrenia.** Emotional withdrawal and unusual or bizarre thinking and actions.
9. **Hypomania.** Emotional excitability, manic moods or behavior, and excessive activity.
10. **Social introversion.** One's tendency to be socially withdrawn.

HIGHLIGHT 16–3
Personality Tests: A Roast and a Rationale

Humorist Art Buchwald (1965) once lampooned personality questionnaires by writing his own test. The following is a sample of his items. Answer "Yes," "No," or "Don't bother me, I can't cope!"

I would enjoy the work of a chicken flicker.
My eyes are always cold.
Frantic screams make me nervous.
I believe I smell as good as most people.
Most of the time I go to sleep without saying good-bye.
I use shoe polish to excess.
The sight of blood no longer excites me.

More recently, psychologist Carol Sommer added the following gems to Buchwald's list.

I salivate at the sight of mittens.
As an infant I had very few hobbies.
Spinach makes me feel alone.
Dirty stories make me think about sex.
I stay in the bathtub until I look like a raisin.
I like to put chameleons on plaid cloth.
I never finish what I

Such questions may seem ridiculous, but they are not very different from the real thing. How, then, do the items on tests such as the MMPI reveal anything about personality? The answer is that a single item tells nothing about personality. For example, a person who agrees that "Everything tastes the same" might simply have a cold. It is only through *patterns* of response that personality dimensions are revealed.

Items on the MMPI were selected for their ability to correctly identify persons with particular psychiatric problems. For instance, if a series of items is consistently answered in a particular way by depressed persons, it is assumed that others who answer the same way are also prone to depression. As silly as the gag items in the preceding lists may seem, it is possible that some could actually work in a legitimate test. But before an item could become part of a test, it would have to be shown to correlate highly with some trait or dimension of personality.

paring a person's profile to scores produced by normal adults, a psychologist can identify various personality disorders.

Question: How accurate is the MMPI?

The accuracy of the MMPI or any other personality questionnaire rests on the assumption that people are willing to tell the truth about themselves. Because of the importance of this assumption, the MMPI has additional **validity scales** to detect attempts of subjects to "fake good" (make themselves look good) or "fake bad" (make it look like they have problems). Other scales help adjust final scores that are affected by personal defensiveness or by tendencies to exaggerate shortcomings and troubles.

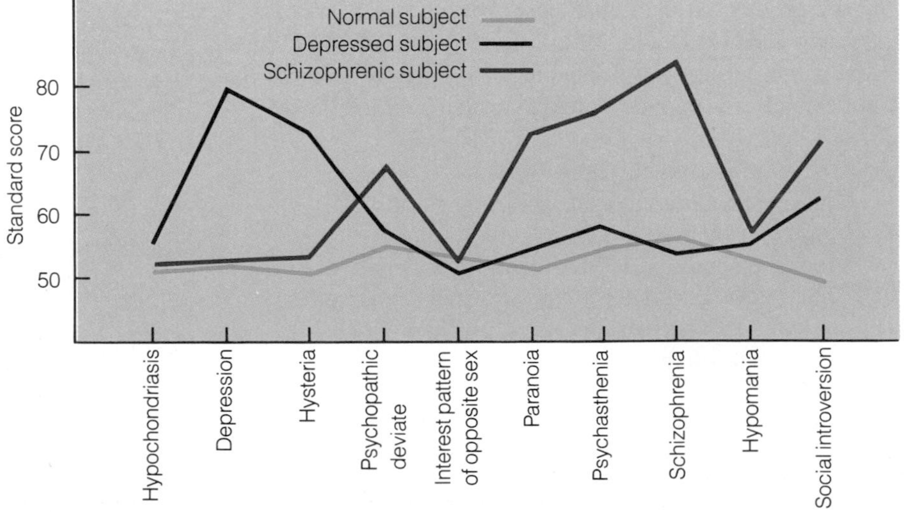

Fig. 16–6 *An MMPI profile showing hypothetical scores indicating normality, depression, and psychosis.*

Unfortunately, the validity scales alone are not enough to ensure accuracy. If MMPI scores were used as the only basis for classifying a person as neurotic (overly anxious), severely depressed, or schizophrenic, a large number of normal people would be incorrectly labeled (Cronbach, 1970). Fortunately, such judgments usually take into account information from interviews or other sources.

Most psychologists are well aware of the limitations of psychological tests. If psychologists were the only persons giving these tests, there would be few problems. However, many organizations, including businesses, routinely use personality tests, and errors or abuses sometimes occur. With this in mind, you should be aware that the U.S. Supreme Court handed down a decision limiting the use of tests as conditions of employment or promotion. If you think a test was unfair, you may have a case.

Projective Tests of Personality—Inkblots and Hidden Plots

Projective tests take a very different approach to personality than the techniques already discussed. Interviews, observation, rating scales, and inventories typically identify overt, observable traits. By contrast, projective tests attempt to uncover deeply hidden or *unconscious* wishes, thoughts, and needs.

As a child, you may have delighted in finding faces and objects in cloud formations. Or perhaps you have learned something about your friends' personalities from their reactions to movies or paintings. If so, you will have some insight into the rationale for projective tests. A **projective test** provides *ambiguous stimuli* that subjects are asked to describe or make up stories about. Describing an unambiguous stimulus (a picture of an automobile, for example) tells little about your personality. But when you are faced with an unstructured stimulus or situation, you must organize and interpret what you see in terms of your own life experiences. Everyone sees something different in a projective stimulus, and what is perceived can reveal the inner workings of one's personality.

Because projective tests have no right or wrong answers, the ability of subjects to fake or "see through" such tests is greatly reduced. Moreover, projective tests can be a rich source of information, since responses are not restricted to simple true/false or yes/no answers.

Question: Is the inkblot test a projective technique?

The Rorschach Inkblot Test The inkblot test, or *Rorschach* (ROR-shock), is one of the oldest and most widely used projective tests. Developed by Swiss psychologist Hermann Rorschach in the 1920s, it consists of a set of 10 standardized inkblots. These vary in color, shading, form, and complexity.

Question: How does the test work?

First, subjects are shown each blot and asked to describe what they see in it (Fig. 16–7). Later the psychologist may return to a blot, asking a subject to identify specific sections of it, to elaborate on previous descriptions, or to suggest a completely new story about it. Obvious differences in content—such as "blood dripping from a dagger" versus "flowers blooming in a field"—are important for identifying personal conflicts and fantasies. But surprisingly, content is considered less important than what parts of the inkblot are used to form an image and how the image is organized. These factors allow a

Fig. 16–7 *Inkblots similar to those used on the Rorschach. What do you see?*

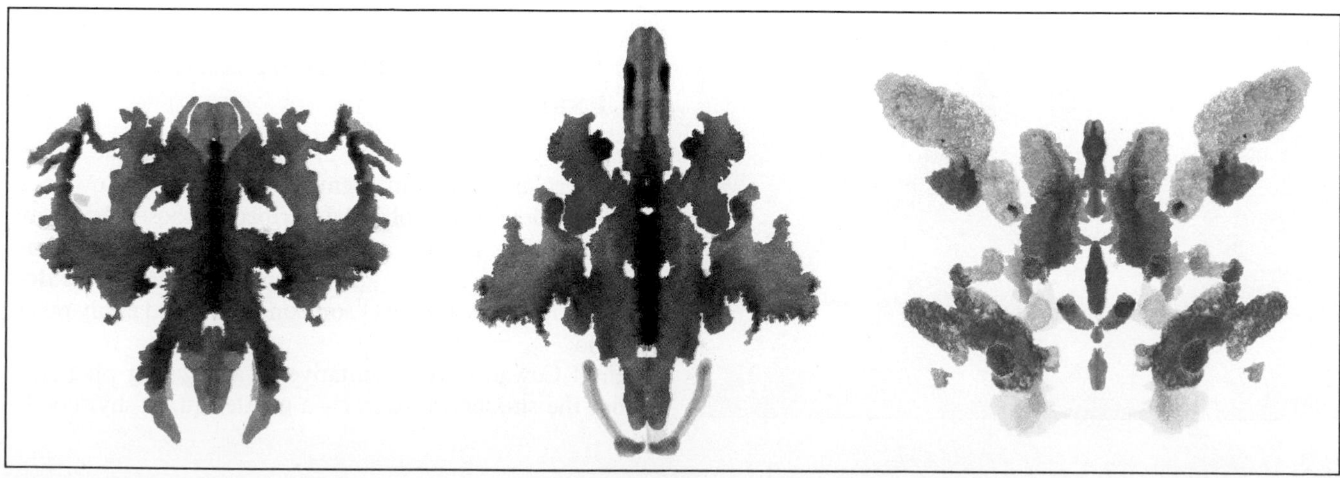

psychologist to view the ways in which a person perceives the world and to detect disorders in personality functioning.

The Thematic Apperception Test Another popular projective test is the *Thematic Apperception Test (TAT)* developed by Harvard psychologist and personality theorist Henry Murray.

Question: How does the TAT differ from the Rorschach?

The TAT consists of 20 sketches depicting various scenes and life situations (Fig. 16–8). The subject is shown each sketch and is asked to make up a story about the people in it. Later, the subject is shown each sketch a second or, perhaps, a third time and asked to elaborate on previous stories or to construct new stories for each.

Scoring of the TAT is restricted to analyzing the content of the stories. In particular, the psychologist is concerned with what the basic issues are in each story: Interpretation focuses on how people feel, how they interact, what events led up to the incidents depicted in the sketch, and how the story will end. The psychologist might also count the number of times the central figure in each story is angry, overlooked, apathetic, jealous, or threatened. For example, here is a story written by a student to describe Figure 16–8.

> The girl has been seeing this guy her mother doesn't like. The mother is telling her that she better not see him again. The mother says, "He's just like your father." The mother and father are divorced. The mother is smiling because she thinks she is right. But she doesn't really know what the girl wants. The girl is going to see the guy again, anyway.

Fig. 16–8 *This is a picture like those used for the Thematic Apperception Test. If you wish to simulate the test, tell a story that explains what led up to the pictured situation, what is happening now, and how the action will end.*

Question: How accurate are projective tests?

Limitations of Projective Testing Although projective tests have been popular with clinical psychologists, their *validity* is considered lowest among tests of personality. (A test is valid when it measures what it claims to measure; see Chapter 18 for more information.) Because of the subjectivity involved in scoring, *objectivity* (consistency) of judgments among different users of the TAT and Rorschach is also low. Note that after the subject interprets an ambiguous stimulus, the scorer must interpret the subject's (sometimes) ambiguous responses. In a sense, the interpretation of a projective test may be a projective test for the scorer!

Despite the drawbacks of projective tests, many psychologists attest to their value, especially as part of a **battery** (group) of tests and interviews. It is said that in the hands of a skillful and experienced clinician, projective tests can detect major conflicts and aid in setting goals for therapy. Moreover, since projective tests are unstructured, they may be more effective for getting clients to talk about anxiety-provoking topics than are the direct questions of inventories and interviews.

● Sudden Murderers—A Research Example

Personality studies provide us with clues to some of the most perplexing human events. Consider Fred Cowan, a model student in school and described by those who knew him as quiet, gentle, and a man who loved children. Despite his size (6 feet tall, 250 pounds), Fred was described by a co-worker as "someone you could easily push around."

Fred Cowan is representative of a puzzling phenomenon: the sudden murderer—a gentle, quiet, shy, good-natured person who explodes without warning into violence (Lee et al., 1977). Two weeks after he was suspended from his job, Fred returned to work determined to get even with his supervisor. Unable to find the man, he killed four co-workers and a policeman before taking his own life.

Question: Isn't such behavior contrary to the idea of personality traits?

It might seem that sudden murderers are newsworthy simply because they seem to be such unlikely candidates for violence. On the contrary, research conducted by Melvin Lee, Philip Zimbardo, and Minerva Bertholf suggests that sudden murderers explode into violence *because* they are shy, restrained, and inexpressive, not in spite of it. These researchers studied prisoners at a California prison. Ten were inmates whose homicide was an unexpected first offense. Nine were criminals with a record of habitual violence prior to murder. Sixteen were inmates convicted of nonviolent crimes.

Question: Did the inmates differ in personality makeup?

Lee and his associates administered a battery of tests to the inmates. Included were the MMPI, a test measuring shyness, an adjective checklist, and personal interviews with each inmate. As expected, the sudden murderers were passive, shy, and overcontrolled (restrained) individuals. The habitually violent inmates were "masculine" (aggressive), undercontrolled (impulsive), and less likely to view themselves as shy than the average person (Lee et al., 1977).

Interviews and other observations have revealed that quiet, overcontrolled individuals are likely to be especially violent if they ever lose control. Their attacks are usually triggered by a minor irritation or frustration, but the attack reflects years of unexpressed feelings of anger and belittlement. When sudden murderers finally release the strict controls they have maintained on their behavior, a furious and frenzied attack ensues. Usually, it is totally out of proportion to the offense against them, and often they have amnesia for some or all of their violent actions.

In comparison, the previously violent murderers showed very different reactions. Although they killed, their violence was moderate—usually only enough to do the necessary damage. Typically, they felt they had been cheated or betrayed and that they were doing what was necessary to remedy the situation or to maintain their manhood (Lee et al., 1977).

This brief example illustrates how some of the concepts and techniques discussed in this chapter can be applied to further our understanding. The Applications section that follows should add balance to your view of personality. Don't be shy. Read on!

Learning Check

1. Planned questions are used in a ______________ interview.
2. The halo effect is the tendency of an interviewer to influence what is said by the interviewee. T or F?
3. Which of the following is considered the most objective measure of personality?
   a. rating scales *b.* personality questionnaires *c.* projective tests *d.* TAT
4. Situational testing allows direct ______________ of personality characteristics.
5. A psychotic person would probably score highest on which MMPI scale?
   a. depression *b.* hysteria *c.* schizophrenia *d.* hypomania
6. The use of ambiguous stimuli is most characteristic of
   a. interviews *b.* projective tests *c.* personality inventories *d.* direct observation
7. The content of one's responses to the MMPI is considered an indication of unconscious wishes, thoughts, and needs. T or F?
8. Doing a behavioral assessment requires direct observation of the person's actions or a direct report of the person's thoughts. T or F?
9. A surprising finding is that sudden murderers are usually overcontrolled, very masculine, and more impulsive than average. T or F?

Answers:
1. structured **2.** F **3.** *b* **4.** observation **5.** *c* **6.** *b* **7.** F **8.** T **9.** F

● Applications: Shrinking Violets and Bashful Beaux—Understanding Shyness

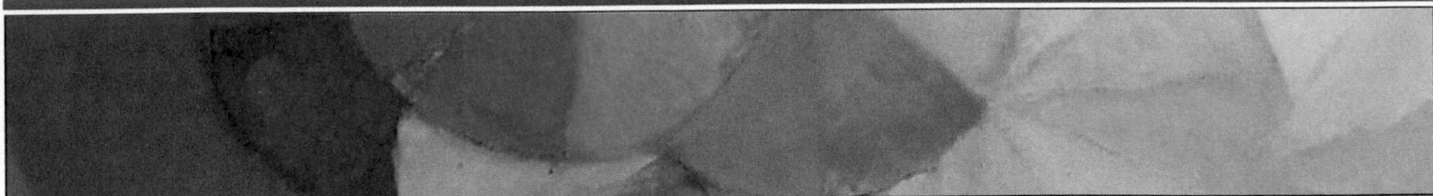

Do you:

Find it hard to talk to strangers?
Lack confidence with people?
Feel uncomfortable in social situations?
Feel nervous with people who are not close friends?

If so, you may be part of the *40 percent* of college students who consider themselves shy. If you are shy, it may help to know that many others are too. However, three-fourths of those who are shy say they don't like it (Zimbardo et al., 1978). As a personality trait, **shyness** refers to a tendency to avoid others, as well as feelings of social inhibition (uneasiness and strain when socializing) (Buss, 1980). Shy persons fail to make eye contact, retreat when spoken to, speak too quietly, and display little interest or animation in conversations.

Question: What causes shyness?

Elements of Shyness To begin with, shy persons often lack **social skills.** Many simply have not learned how to meet others or how to start a conversation and keep it going. **Social anxiety** is also a factor in shyness. Almost everyone feels nervous in some social situations (such as meeting an attractive stranger). Typically, this is a reaction to *evaluation fears* (fears of being embarrassed, ridiculed, or rejected or of seeming inadequate). In general, however, evaluation fears are more frequent or intense for shy persons. A third problem for shy persons is a **self-defeating bias** in their thinking. Specifically, shy persons almost always blame themselves when a social encounter doesn't go well (Girodo, 1978).

Situational Causes of Shyness Shyness is most often triggered by *novel* or *unfamiliar* social situations. A person who does fine with family or close friends may become shy and awkward when meeting a stranger. Shyness is also magnified by formality, by meeting someone of higher status, by being noticeably different from others, or by being the focus of attention (as in giving a speech) (Buss, 1980; Pilkonis, 1977).

Question: Don't most people become cautious and inhibited in such circumstances?

Yes. That's why we need to see how the personalities of shy and nonshy persons differ.

Dynamics of the Shy Personality There is a tendency to think that shy persons are wrapped up in their own feelings and thoughts. But surprisingly, researchers Jonathan Cheek and Arnold Buss (1979) found no connection between shyness and **private self-consciousness** (attention to inner feelings, thoughts, and fantasies). Instead, they discovered that shyness is linked to **public self-consciousness.**

Persons who rate high in public self-consciousness are intensely aware of themselves as *social objects* (Buss, 1980). They are concerned about what others think of them, and they feel that others are evaluating them. They worry about saying the wrong thing or appearing foolish. With such concerns, many shy persons think that they are being rejected even when they are not. In public, they may feel "naked" or as if others can "see through them." Such feelings trigger anxiety or outright fear during social encounters, leading to awkwardness and inhibition (Buss, 1986).

As mentioned, almost everyone feels anxious in at least some social situations. But there is a key difference in the way shy and nonshy persons *label* this anxiety. Shy persons tend to consider their social anxiety a *lasting personality trait*. Shyness, in other words, becomes part of their self-concept. In contrast, nonshy persons believe that *external situations* cause their occasional feelings of shyness. When nonshy persons feel anxiety or "stage fright," they assume that almost anyone would feel as they do under the same circumstances (Zimbardo et al., 1978).

Labeling is important because it affects *self-esteem*. In general, nonshy persons tend to have higher self-esteem than shy persons. This is because nonshy persons give themselves credit for their social successes and they recognize that failures are often due to circumstances. In contrast, shy people blame themselves for social failures and never give themselves credit for successes (Buss, 1980; Girodo, 1978).

Question: What can be done to reduce shyness?

Overcoming Shyness

Visitors to China frequently marvel at the almost total lack of shyness among the Chinese. In America, many children seem to "outgrow" shyness as they gain social skills and wider social experience. Some adults overcome shyness with the aid of a shyness clinic or similar program. Each of these observations suggests that shyness is open to change. If you are shy and would like to change, the information that follows may offer

Applications

a starting point. Even if you are not shy, some of the ideas should be useful to you.

Shy Beliefs While directing a shyness clinic, psychologist Michel Girodo (1978) observed that shyness is often maintained by unrealistic or self-defeating beliefs. Here's a sample of such beliefs.

1. *If you wait around long enough at a social gathering, something will happen.*
Comment: This is really a cover-up for fear of starting a conversation. For two people to meet, at least one has to make an effort, and it might as well be you.
2. *Other people who are popular are just lucky when it comes to being invited to social events or asked out.*
Comment: Except for times when a person is formally introduced to someone new, this is false. People who are more active socially typically make an effort to meet and spend time with others. They join clubs, invite others to do things, strike up conversations, and generally leave little to luck.
3. *The odds of meeting someone interested in socializing are always the same, no matter where I am.*
Comment: This is another excuse for inaction. It pays to seek out situations that have a higher probability of leading to social contract, such as clubs, teams, and school events.
4. *If someone doesn't seem to like you right away, they really don't like you and never will.*
Comment: This belief leads to much needless shyness. Even when a person doesn't show immediate interest, it doesn't mean the person dislikes you. Liking takes time and opportunity to develop.

Unproductive beliefs like the preceding can be replaced with statements such as the following.

1. I've got to be active in social situations.
2. I can't wait until I'm completely relaxed or comfortable before taking a social risk.
3. I don't need to pretend to be someone I'm not; it just makes me more anxious.
4. I may think other people are harshly evaluating me, but actually I'm being too hard on myself.
5. I can set reasonable goals for expanding my social experience and skills.
6. Even people who are very socially skillful are never successful 100 percent of the time. I shouldn't get so upset when an encounter goes badly. (Adapted from Girodo, 1978)

Social Skills

Learning social skills takes practice. There is nothing "innate" about knowing how to meet people or start a conversation. Social skills can be directly practiced in a variety of ways. It can be helpful, for instance, to get a tape recorder and listen to several of your conversations. You may be surprised by the way you pause, interrupt, miss cues, or seem disinterested. Similarly, it can be useful to look at yourself in a mirror and exaggerate facial expressions of surprise, interest, dislike, pleasure, and so forth. By such methods, most people can learn to put more animation and skill into their self-presentation. (For a discussion of related skills, see the section on self-assertion in Chapter 24.)

Opening Lines A recent study of 200 men and women found that 90 percent of them agreed that when trying to meet somebody new, either a man or a woman can approach the other. It appears that whether you're a man or a woman, you have the option of beginning a conversation. If you do take the initiative, what's the best way to begin? In a study reported by psychologist Chris Kleinke (1986), 1000 men and women rated a collection of typical "opening lines." An analysis of these statements revealed that they fell into three categories: *direct, innocuous* (mild or harmless) and *cute-flippant.* The examples that follow illustrate each category (adapted from Kleinke, 1986).

Direct

I feel a little embarrassed about this, but I'd like to meet you.
Since we're both sitting alone, would you care to join me?
That's a very pretty (sweater, jacket, skirt) you have on.

Innocuous

Hi.
Would you watch my books for a minute?
It's beautiful today, isn't it.
Can you give me directions to ______________?

Cute-Flippant

Do you think I deserve a break today?
I play the field, and I think I just hit a home run.
Your place or mine?
I'm easy. Are you?

By a large margin, both men and women preferred opening lines that were direct or innocuous. Cute or flippant statements were least liked, especially by women. The kinds of opening lines so often used by male and female characters in the movies appear to be duds in real life.

Conversation One of the simplest ways to make better conversation is by learning to ask questions. A good series of questions shifts attention to the other person and shows you are interested. Nothing fancy is needed. You can do fine with questions such as, "Where do you (work, study, live)?" Do you like (dancing, travel, music)?" How long have you (been at this school, worked here, lived here)?" After you've broken

Applications

the ice, the best questions are often those that are *open-ended* (Girodo, 1978):

"What parts of the country have you seen?" (as opposed to: "Have you ever been to Florida?")
"What's it like living on the west side?" (as opposed to: "Do you like living on the west side?")
"What kinds of food do you like?" (as opposed to: "Do you like Chinese cooking?")

It's easy to see why open-ended questions are helpful. In replying to open-ended questions, people often give "free information" about themselves. This extra information can be used to ask other questions or to lead into other topics of conversation.

This brief sampling of ideas is no substitute for actual practice. Overcoming shyness requires a real effort to learn new skills and test old beliefs and attitudes. It may even require the help of a counselor or therapist. At the very least, a shy person must be willing to take social risks. Breaking down the barriers of shyness will always include some awkward or unsuccessful encounters. Nevertheless, the rewards are powerful: human companionship and personal freedom.

Learning Check

1. Surveys show that 14 percent of college students consider themselves shy. T or F?

2. Social anxiety and evaluation fears are seen almost exclusively in shy individuals; the nonshy rarely have such experiences. T or F?

3. Unfamiliar people and situations most often trigger shyness. T or F?

4. Public self-consciousness plus a tendency to label oneself as shy are major characteristics of the shy personality. T or F?

5. Changing personal beliefs and practicing social skills can be helpful in overcoming shyness. T or F?

Answers:

1. F 2. F 3. T 4. T 5. T

Exploration: Identical Twins—Twin Personalities?

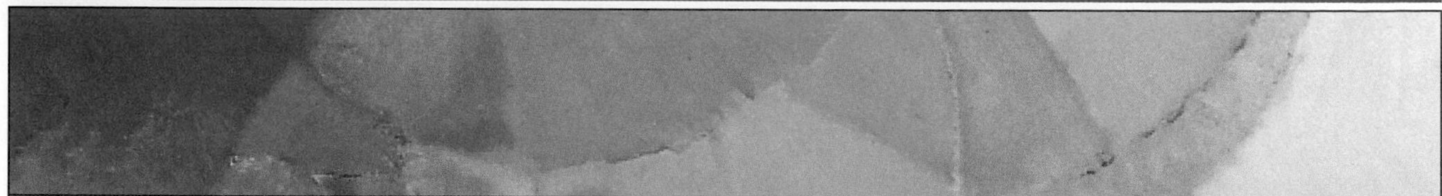

Some breeds of dogs have reputations for being friendly, aggressive, intelligent, calm, or emotional. Such differences fall in the realm of **behavioral genetics**—the study of inherited *behavioral* traits. Just as physical features are inherited, so too are many behavioral traits. For instance, selective breeding of animals can lead to striking differences in social behavior, emotionality, learning ability, aggression, activity, and other behaviors (Sprott & Staats, 1975).

Question: To what extent do such findings apply to humans?

Genetic studies of humans rely mainly on comparisons of identical twins and other close relatives. Such studies, of course, are less conclusive than work done with animals. Nonetheless, they show that intelligence, some mental disorders, temperament, and other complex qualities are influenced by heredity. (For specific examples of behavioral genetic research, see Chapters 14, 18, and 20.) In view of findings like these, we also might wonder, Do genes affect personality?

Question: Wouldn't comparing the personalities of identical twins help answer the question?

It would indeed—especially if the twins were separated at birth or soon after.

The Minnesota Twins Over the past several years, psychologists at the University of Minnesota have been studying twins who grew up in separate homes. At the university, reunited twins take a wide range of medical and psychological tests. The tests probe each twin's brain waves, physical capacities, health, diet, IQ, tastes, fears, fantasies, dreams, personality traits, ambitions, and more (Fig. 16–9).

These tests, and work by others, indicate that identical twins are much alike, even when they are reared apart (Bouchard et al., 1981). Like all identical twins, the reunited twins are astonishingly similar in appearance and voice quality. Observers are also struck by how often the twins display identical facial gestures, hand movements, and nervous tics, such as nail biting or finger tapping.

On many of the physical tests, the results for reunited twins are so similar that they might have been produced by the same person on different days. As we will see in Chapter 18, identical twins, even when reared apart, have highly correlated IQ scores. Separated twins also tend to share similar talents. If one twin excels at art, music, dance, drama, or athletics, the other is likely to also—despite wide differences in childhood environment (Farber, 1981).

All of these observations make it clear that heredity has a sizable effect on each of us. Where personality is concerned, similarities also exist, but they are not as strong. For instance, identical twins frequently dif-

Fig. 16–9 *Reunited identical twins Terry and Margaret undergo lung function tests at the University of Minnesota. Researchers collected a wide range of medical and psychological data for each set of twins.*

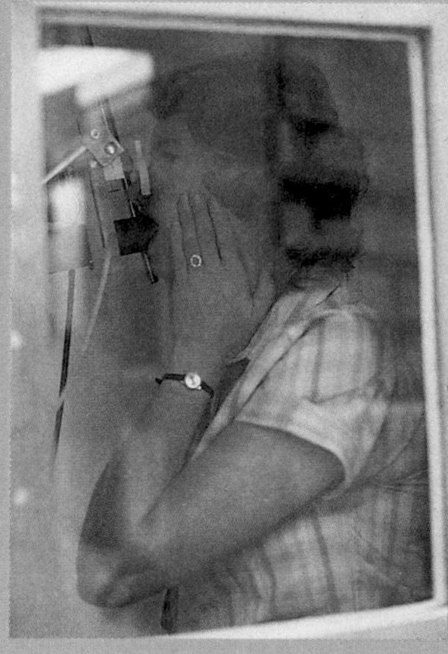

Exploration

fer in dominance and extroversion. That is, one twin is usually more extroverted or dominant than the other (Farber, 1981). Because of such differences, personality profiles for separated twins may have much in common, but they are usually far from identical.

All told, it seems reasonable to conclude that there is a genetic factor in personality (Farber, 1981). However, it is relatively small in comparison to the great physical similarity of identical twins (Scarr et al., 1981). This modest conclusion contrasts sharply with reports of twin studies in the popular press. The impression created there has been one of overwhelming genetic control of behavior.

Question: For example?

The "Jim Twins" Many of the reunited twins who participated in the Minnesota study displayed similarities far beyond what one would expect on the basis of heredity. A good example is provided by the "Jim twins," James Lewis and James Springer. These two reunited twins, like the others tested, had the same height and weight and very similar speech patterns, mannerisms, and posture.

The similarities, however, did not stop there. Both Jims had married and divorced women named Linda. Both had undergone police training. Both had named their firstborn sons James Allan. Both drove Chevrolets and vacationed at the same beach each summer. Both listed carpentry and mechanical drawing among their hobbies. Both had built circular benches around trees in their yards. And so forth (Holden, 1980).

Counterpoint Such coincidences may seem amazing at first. But the astute reader will realize that they have little to do with genetics. In the first place, many such coincidences are quite common. It would not be unusual, for instance, for two unrelated people to drive the same make of car. The odds of this occurring for a Chevrolet are 1 in 7 (Nelson, 1982).

Question: That might be true for some similarities. But what about the Jim twins' shared hobbies, police training, and so on?

As a second point, it is important to realize that unlikely similarities also occur for unrelated persons. Consider, for example, two women who discovered that they had the same maiden names and that they shared a Social Security number. Both women were born on the same day and both were named Patricia Ann Campbell. After the women learned of one another's existence, they also discovered the following similarities. They both had fathers named Robert. They both had worked as bookkeepers. They both had two children of the same age. They both had studied cosmetology and enjoyed oil painting. They both had married military men. And so on ("Fate," 1983).

Such similarities are not really so surprising. Two adults of the same age and sex are likely to have had many experiences in common. This is true because they live in the same historical time and choose from a similar range of societal options. In fact, one recent study compared twins with unrelated pairs of students of the same age and sex. The unrelated pairs were almost as alike as twins are with respect to political beliefs, musical interests, religious preferences, jobs held, hobbies, favorite foods, and so on (Wyatt et al., 1984).

The preceding brings us to a last point. Imagine that you were separated at birth from a twin brother or sister. If you were reunited with your twin today, what would you do? Quite likely, you would spend the next several days in almost nonstop conversation. And what would this conversation center on? Almost certainly, you would compare every imaginable detail of your lives.

Under such circumstances we could virtually guarantee that you and your twin would compile a long list of similarities. ("Wow! I use the same brand of toothpaste you do!") Yet, two unrelated persons of the same age and sex could probably rival your list—*if* they were as motivated to find similarities.

In short, much of the seemingly "astounding" coincidences shared by reunited twins may be a special case of the fallacy of positive instances, described in Chapter 1. Similarities blaze brightly in the memories of reunited twins, while differences are ignored.

Summary The points we have covered do not deny that personality is influenced by heredity. A variety of studies suggest that heredity may be responsible for as much as 40 to 50 percent of the variation in some personality traits (Loehlin et al., 1988). But even if this estimate holds up (and many psychologists think it is too high), our discussion suggests that some people have gone overboard in ascribing personal prefer-

Exploration

ences, interests, and specific behaviors to heredity.

There is always a danger in overstating the role of heredity in human behavior. Doing so can easily lead to racist or sexist attitudes. For this reason, it is wise to remember that we do not inherit specific behavioral traits. Rather, we inherit certain potentials and general ways of reacting to the environment. These, in turn, can be greatly altered by experience (Farber, 1981). We are not—thank goodness—genetically programmed robots whose behavior is "wired in" for life.

Learning Check

1. Behavioral genetics is the study of how heredity influences behavioral traits and patterns. T or F?
2. Contrary to earlier research, the Minnesota study found relatively low correlations among IQ scores of reunited identical twins. T or F?
3. Research with identical twins has shown that heredity is the single most powerful influence on adult personality. T or F?
4. A large amount of evidence now indicates that genes strongly influence personal preferences and interests, but not personality traits. T or F?

Answers:
1. T 2. F 3. F 4. F

Chapter Summary

• **Personality** is made up of one's unique and enduring behavior patterns. **Character** is personality evaluated, or the possession of desirable qualities. **Temperament** refers to the hereditary and physiological aspects of one's emotional nature.

• Personality **traits** are lasting personal qualities that are inferred from behavior. Traits imply a degree of personal consistency and help predict future behavior. Personality **types** group people into categories on the basis of shared traits or similar characteristics. Although type systems tend to oversimplify personality, they remain useful at times. Behavior is influenced by **self-concept,** which is a perception of one's own personality traits. **Personality theories** combine interrelated assumptions, ideas, and principles to explain personality.

• **Trait theories** attempt to specify qualities of personality that are most lasting or characteristic of a person. Allport makes useful distinctions between **common traits** and **individual traits** and between **cardinal, central,** and **secondary traits.**

• A second trait approach, developed by Cattell, attributes visible **surface traits** to the existence of underlying **source traits.** Cattell identified 16 source traits by use of a statistical method called **factor analysis.**

• Cattell's source traits are measured by the *Sixteen Personality Factor Questionnaire* (16 PF). Like other trait measures, the outcome of the 16 PF may be graphically presented as a **trait profile.**

• Traits appear to **interact** with **situations** to determine behavior. Neither factor alone fully explains our actions.

• A variety of research suggests that birth order, or **ordinal position** in a family, can influence personality development. **Firstborn** and only children tend to be high achievers, but they are also shyer, more conforming, and more anxious. **Later-born** persons are more likely to excel in social skills.

• Research conducted by Bem and others indicates that roughly one-third of all persons are **androgynous.** Psychological androgyny (possessing both masculine and feminine traits) appears related to greater adaptability or flexibility in behavior.
• Accurate **personality assessment** is of great importance to psychologists. Techniques typically used to measure personality are **interviews, observation, questionnaires,** and **projective tests.**
• **Structured** and **unstructured interviews** provide much information, but they are subject to interviewer bias and misperceptions. The **halo effect** (a tendency to generalize first impressions) may also lower the accuracy of an interview.
• **Direct observation,** sometimes involving **situational tests, behavioral assessment,** or the use of **rating scales,** allows evaluation of a person's actual behavior.
• **Personality questionnaires,** such as the *Minnesota Multiphasic Personality Inventory (MMPI),* are objective, but their accuracy and validity are open to question.
• **Projective tests** ask a subject to project thoughts or feelings to an ambiguous stimulus or unstructured situation. *The Rorschach,* or inkblot test, is a well-known projective technique. A second is the *Thematic Apperception Test (TAT)*. The validity and objectivity of projective tests are quite low. Nevertheless, projective techniques are considered useful by many clinicians, particularly as part of a **test battery.**
• **Shyness** is a combination of social inhibition and social anxiety. It is marked by heightened **public self-consciousness** and a tendency to regard one's shyness as a lasting trait. Shyness can be lessened by changing self-defeating beliefs and by improving social skills.
• Studies of separated identical twins suggest that heredity contributes significantly to adult personality traits. However, many of the sensational correspondences reported for separated twins are likely based on coincidence and selective memory.

Questions For Discussion

1. Are birth-order effects an example of personality typing? To what extent do they oversimplify matters?
2. Have you ever been interviewed or given a personality test? How accurate did you consider the resulting assessment of personality?
3. Under what circumstances would you consider a personality test an invasion of privacy? Do you think it is acceptable for personality tests to be used to select job applicants?
4. If you could select only three personality traits, which would you consider most basic? Why?
5. If you were selecting candidates for an extended space flight, how would you make your choices? What could you do to improve the accuracy of your judgments of candidates' personalities?
6. Do you think that there is such a thing as "national character"? That is, do all Germans, all French, all Americans, all Canadians, and so forth, have some traits that are common to their national group?
7. Do you know anyone who seems to have a cardinal trait? What do you think are the central traits of your personality? Secondary traits?
8. Do you think that animals have personalities? Defend your answer.
9. Can you name any public personalities (entertainers, politicians, athletes, artists, musicians) who seem to be androgynous? Are any of your friends or acquaintances androgynous? Do you agree or disagree with Bem's assertion that these people are more adaptable?
10. Why do you think that media coverage of reunited twins has exaggerated the role of genetics in human behavior and personality?

Chapter 17

Theories of Personality

In This Chapter

- Psychoanalytic theory
- Freudian view of development
- Neo-Freudian theories
- Learning theories
- Behavioristic view of development
- Humanistic theories
- Humanistic view of development
- Comparison of theories
- **Applications:** Self-actualization
- **Exploration:** Self-monitoring

Chapter Preview

Eels, Cocaine, Hypnosis, and Dreams

One of his earliest scientific discoveries was the location of the testes in an eel. Later he obtained some cocaine and began to study its value as a medicine. He was soon convinced it was a wonder drug. He proclaimed, "I took coca again and a small dose lifted me to heights in a wonderful fashion. I am just now busy collecting the literature for a song of praise to this magical substance" (Jones, 1953). But his praise quickly ended when he prescribed cocaine to aid a friend addicted to morphine. Instead of improving, the friend became dependent on both drugs. His next interest was hypnosis, but he abandoned it when it did not meet his needs. At age 44, criticized and virtually unknown in intellectual circles, he published his first book. It was a masterwork entitled The Interpretation of Dreams *(1900). Less than 1000 copies were sold.*

Question: Who are you talking about?

The hero of this little essay is no less than the best known of all personality theorists—Sigmund Freud. Volume after volume followed Freud's initial work until he had built a theory of personality that deeply influenced modern thought. Other theorists owe a debt to his pioneering efforts.

As there are dozens of personality theories, it is possible to introduce only a few of the most influential. For clarity, we will confine ourselves to three broad perspectives: (1) psychodynamic theories, *(2)* behavioristic theories, *and (3)* humanistic theories. *Psychodynamic theories focus on the inner workings of personality, especially internal conflicts and struggles. Behavioristic theories place greater importance on the external environment and on the effects of conditioning and learning. Humanistic theories stress subjective experience and personal growth.*

Survey Questions

- How do psychodynamic theories explain personality?
- What do behaviorists emphasize in their approach to personality?
- How do humanistic theories differ from other perspectives?
- According to each major viewpoint (psychodynamic, behavioristic, and humanistic), what childhood events shape adult personality?
- What can be done to promote self-actualization?
- Are you high or low in self-monitoring, and how does it affect your behavior?

Psychoanalytic Theory—Id Came to Me in a Dream

Psychoanalytic theory, the best-known psychodynamic approach, grew out of the clinical study of disturbed individuals. Sigmund Freud, a Viennese physician, became interested in personality when he realized that many of his patients' problems seemed to lack physical causes. As Freud once commented, "My life has been aimed at one goal only; to infer or to guess how the mental apparatus is constructed and what forces interplay and counteract in it." Starting about 1890 and continuing until he died in 1939, Freud evolved a theory of personality that is more complex than a short sketch can show. We will consider only its main features.

Question: How did Freud view personality?

The Structure of Personality

Freud viewed personality as a dynamic system directed by three structures: the **id,** the **ego,** and the **superego.** Each of these is a complex system in its own right. According to Freud, most behavior involves the activity of all three.

The Id The id is made up of innate biological instincts and urges present at birth. It is self-serving, irrational, impulsive, and totally **unconscious.** The id operates on the **pleasure principle,** meaning that pleasure-seeking urges of all kinds are freely expressed. If everyone's personality were solely under control of the id, the world would be chaotic beyond belief.

Freud thought of the id as a well of energy for the entire **psyche** (sie-KEY), or personality. This energy, called **libido** (lih-BEE-doe), flows from the **life instincts** (called **Eros**). According to Freud, libido promotes survival, underlies sexual desires, and is expressed whenever we seek pleasure. Freud also described a **death instinct (Thanatos),** which he said is responsible for aggressive and destructive urges (Fig. 17–1). Freud offered humanity's long history of wars and violence as evidence of such urges. Most id energies, then, are aimed at a discharge of tensions related to sex and aggression.

The Ego The ego is sometimes described as the "executive," because it directs energies supplied by the id. The id is like a blind king or queen whose power is awesome but who must rely on others to carry out orders. The id can only form mental images of things it desires. (This is called "primary process thinking.") The ego wins power to direct behavior by relating the desires of the id to external reality.

Question: Are there other differences between the ego and the id?

Yes. Recall that the id operates on the pleasure principle. The ego, in contrast, is guided by the **reality principle.** That is, the ego delays action until it is practical or appropriate. The ego is the system of thinking, planning, problem solving, and deciding. It is in conscious control of the personality.

Question: What is the role of the superego?

The Superego The superego acts as a judge or censor for the thoughts and actions of the ego. One part of the superego, called the **conscience,** reflects all actions for which a person has been punished. When standards of the conscience are not met, you are punished internally by *guilt* feelings. A second part of the superego is the **ego ideal.** The ego ideal reflects all behavior one's parents approved of or rewarded. The ego ideal is a source of goals and aspirations. When its standards are met, *pride* is felt. By these processes, the superego acts as an "internalized parent" to bring behavior under control. In Freudian terms, a person with a weak superego will be a delinquent, criminal, or antisocial personality. In contrast, an overly strict or harsh superego may cause inhibition, rigidity, or unbearable guilt.

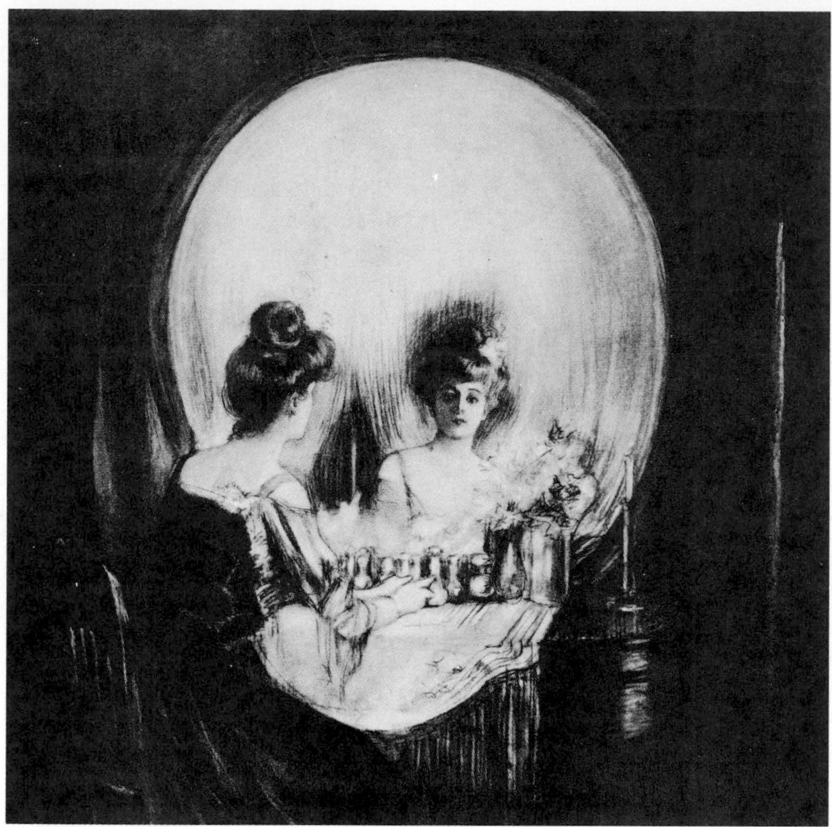

Fig. 17–1 *Freud considered personality an expression of two conflicting forces, life instincts and the death instinct. Both are symbolized in this drawing by Allan Gilbert. (If you don't immediately see the death symbolism, stand farther from the drawing.)*

The Dynamics of Personality

Question: How do the id, ego, and superego interact?

It is important to recognize that Freud did not picture the id, ego, and superego as parts of the brain or as "little people" running the human psyche. In reality, they are separate and conflicting mental processes. Freud theorized a delicate balance of power among the three. For example, the demands of the id for immediate pleasure often clash with the superego's moral restrictions. Perhaps an example will help clarify the role of each part of the personality.

Freud in a Nutshell

Let's say you are sexually attracted to someone. The id clamors for immediate satisfaction of its sexual desires, but is opposed by the superego (which finds the very thought of sexual behavior shocking). The id says, "Go for it!" The superego icily replies, "Never even think that again!" And what does the ego say? The ego says, "I have a plan!"

Of course, this is a drastic simplification, but it does capture the core of Freudian thinking. To reduce tension, the ego could begin actions leading to friendship, romance, courtship, and marriage. If the id is unusually powerful, the ego may give in and attempt a seduction. If the superego prevails, the ego may be forced to *displace* or *sublimate* sexual energies to other activities (sports, music, dancing, push-ups, cold showers). According to Freud, internal struggles and rechanneled energies typify most personality functioning.

Question: Is the ego always caught in the middle?

Basically yes, and the pressures on it can be intense. In addition to meeting the conflicting demands of the id and superego, the overworked ego must deal with external reality. According to Freud, you feel anxiety when your ego is threatened or overwhelmed. Impulses from the id cause **neurotic anxiety** when the ego can barely keep them under control. Threats of punishment from the superego cause **moral anxiety.** Each person develops habitual ways of calming these anxieties, and many resort to using *ego-defense mechanisms* to lessen internal conflicts (see Chapter 12).

Levels of Awareness A major principle of psychoanalytic theory and other psychodynamic theories is that behavior often expresses unconscious (or hidden) internal forces. The **unconscious** contains repressed memories and emotions, plus the instinctual drives of the id. Interestingly, modern scientists are beginning to find brain areas that seem to have the kinds of unconscious effects that Freud described. Especially important are areas linked with emotion and memory—such as the hippocampus in the limbic system (Reiser, 1985; Wilson, 1985).

Even though they are beyond awareness, unconscious thoughts, feelings, or urges may slip into behavior in disguised or symbolic form. For example, if you meet someone you would like to know better, you may unconsciously leave a book or a jacket at the person's house to ensure another meeting.

Question: Earlier you said that the id is completely unconscious. Are the actions of the ego and superego unconscious?

At times, yes, but they also operate on two other levels of awareness (Fig. 17–2). The **conscious** level includes everything we are aware of at a given moment, including thoughts, perceptions, feelings, and memories. The **preconscious** contains material that can be easily brought to awareness. If you stop to think about a time when you felt angry or rejected, you will be moving this memory from the preconscious to the conscious level of awareness.

The operation of the superego gives another sign of the levels of awareness. At times we consciously try to live up to moral codes or standards. Yet, at other times a person may feel guilty without knowing why. Psychoanalytic theory credits the second kind of guilt to unconscious workings of the superego. Freudian psychology holds that events that are truly unconscious cannot be easily brought to awareness or directly known by the individual.

Fig. 17–2 *The approximate relationship between the id, ego, and superego, and the levels of awareness.*

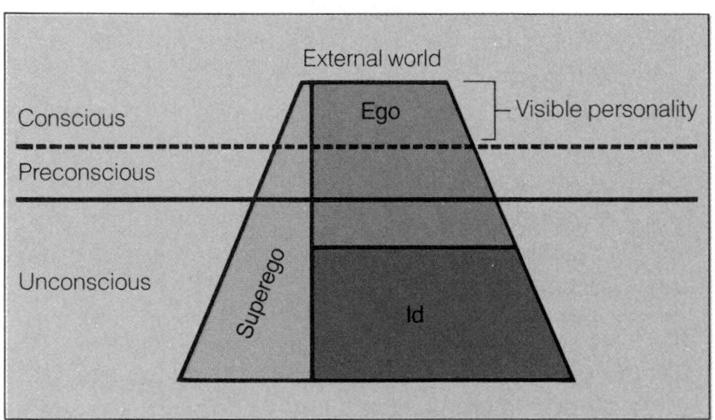

In view of the large number of terms used in psychoanalytic theory, Table 17–1 summarizes what we have covered so far.

Personality Development

Every society must **socialize** its children by teaching them language, customs, rules, roles, and morals. The job of preparing children to take part in society is typically placed in the hands of parents. This pattern is convenient and fateful. While carrying out socialization, parents leave traces of their own personality in their children.

Question: How does this occur? What factors are most influential in the development of adult personality?

Each theory offers a different version of the important events in forming personality. Let's continue with a look at the psychoanalytic viewpoint.

A Freudian Fable? Freud theorized that the core of personality is formed before age 6 in a series of **psychosexual stages.** His account holds that childhood urges for erotic pleasure have lasting effects on development. Freud's emphasis on infantile sexuality is one of the most controversial aspects of his thinking. However, Freud used the term *sex* very broadly to refer to several different physical sources of pleasure.

Freud identified four psychosexual stages: the **oral, anal, phallic,** and **genital.** At each stage, a different part of the body becomes a child's primary **erogenous zone** (an area capable of producing pleasure). Each area then serves as the main source of pleasure, frustration, and self-expression. Freud believed that many adult personality traits can be traced to **fixations** in one or more of the stages.

Question: What is a fixation?

A fixation is an unresolved conflict or emotional hang-up caused by overindulgence or by frustration. A description of the psychosexual stages shows why Freud considered fixations important.

The Oral Stage During the first year of life, most of an infant's pleasure comes from stimulation of the mouth. If a child is overfed or frustrated, oral traits may be created. Adult expressions of oral needs include gum chewing, nail biting, smoking, kissing, overeating, and alcoholism (Fig. 17–3).

Question: What if there is an oral fixation?

Fixation early in the oral stage produces an **oral-dependent** personality. Oral-dependent persons are gullible (they

Table 17–1 Some Key Psychoanalytic Terms

Psychoanalytic theory Freudian theory of personality that emphasizes unconscious forces and internal conflicts in its explanations of behavior.

Id According to Freud, the most primitive part of personality, which remains unconscious, supplies energy to other parts of the psyche, and demands immediate gratification.

Pleasure principle The principle under which the id operates, consisting of a desire for immediate satisfaction of wishes, desires, or needs.

Psyche The mind, mental life, and personality as a whole.

Libido In Freudian theory, the force, primarily pleasure-oriented, that energizes the subparts of personality.

Eros Freud's name for the "life instincts" postulated by his theory.

Thanatos The death instincts postulated by Freud.

Ego The executive portion of personality in Freudian theory, which is charged with directing rational, realistic behavior.

Reality principle The principle by which the ego functions, involving a delay of action (or gratification) until it is appropriate.

Superego In Freudian theory, an internalization of parental values and societal standards.

Conscience In Freudian theory, the part of the superego that causes guilt when its standards are not met.

Ego ideal In Freudian theory, a part of the superego representing ideal behavior; a source of pride when its standards are met.

Neurotic anxiety Apprehension that occurs when the ego must struggle to maintain control over id impulses.

Moral anxiety Apprehension felt when one's thoughts, impulses, or actions conflict with standards enforced by the superego.

Unconscious In Freudian theory, the region of the mind that is beyond awareness, especially impulses and desires not directly known to a person.

Conscious Region of the mind that includes all mental contents (thoughts, images, feelings, memories, and so on) that a person is aware of at any given moment.

Preconscious The area of the mind that contains information that is not currently in consciousness, but that can be voluntarily brought to awareness.

Fig. 17–3 *Was Freud's ever-present cigar a sign of an oral fixation?*

swallow things easily!) and passive and need lots of attention (they want to be mothered). Frustrations later in the oral stage may cause aggression, often in the form of biting. Fixation here creates an **oral-aggressive** adult who likes to argue ("biting sarcasm" is their forte!), is cynical, and exploits others.

The Anal Stage Between the ages of 1 and 3, the child's attention shifts to the process of elimination. When parents attempt toilet training, the child can gain approval or express rebellion or aggression by "holding on" or "letting go." Therefore, harsh or lenient toilet training may lock such responses into personality. Freud described the **anal-retentive** (holding-on) personality as obstinate, stingy, orderly, and compulsively clean. The **anal-expulsive** (letting-go) personality is disorderly, destructive, cruel, or messy.

The Phallic Stage Adult traits of the **phallic personality** are vanity, exhibitionism, sensitive pride, and narcissism (self-love). Freud theorized that such traits develop between the ages of 3 and 6. At this time, increased sexual interest causes the child to be physically attracted to the parent of the opposite sex. In males this attraction leads to an **Oedipus conflict.** In it, the boy feels rivalry with his father for the affection of the mother.

Freud believed that the male child feels threatened by the father (specifically, the boy fears castration). To ease his anxieties, the boy must **identify** with the father. Their rivalry ends when the boy seeks to become more like his father. As he does, he begins to accept the father's values and to form a conscience.

Question: What about the female child?

In a parallel to the Oedipus conflict, called the **Electra conflict,** the girl loves her father and competes with her mother. However, according to Freud, the girl identifies with the mother more gradually. This, he said, is less effective in creating a conscience. Freud believed that females already feel castrated. Because of this, they are less driven to identify with their mothers than boys are with their fathers. This particular part of Freudian thought has been thoroughly (and rightfully) rejected by modern feminists. It is probably best understood as a reflection of the male-dominated times in which Freud lived.

Latency According to Freud there is a period of *latency* from age 6 to puberty. Latency is not actually a stage. Rather, it is a time during which psychosexual development is interrupted. Freud's belief that psychosexual development is "on hold" at this time is hard to accept. Nevertheless, Freud saw latency as a relatively quiet time compared to the stormy first 6 years of life.

The Genital Stage At puberty, an upswing in sexual energies activates all the unresolved conflicts of earlier years. This upsurge, according to Freud, is the reason why adolescence can be such a trying time, filled with emotion and turmoil. The genital stage begins at puberty. It is marked, throughout adolescence, by a growing capacity for mature and responsible social-sexual relationships. The genital stage ends with heterosexual love and the realization of full adult sexuality.

Critical Comments As bizarre as Freud's developmental theory might seem, it has been influential for several reasons. First, it pioneered the idea that the first years of life help shape adult personality. Second, it identified feeding, toilet training, and early sexual experiences as critical events in personality formation. Third, Freud was among the first to propose that development proceeds through a series of stages. (Erik Erikson's psycho*social* stages, described in Chapter 15, are a modern offshoot of Freudian thinking.)

Question: Is the Freudian view of development widely accepted?

Despite its contributions, few psychologists wholeheartedly embrace Freud's theory. In some cases Freud was clearly wrong. His portrayal of the elementary school years (latency) as free from sexuality and unimportant for personality development is hard to believe. His idea of the role of a stern or threatening father in the development of a strong conscience in males has also been challenged. Studies show that a son is more likely to develop a strong conscience if his father is affectionate and accepting, rather than stern and punishing (Mussen et al., 1969; Sears et al., 1957). Freud also overemphasized sexuality in personality development; other motives and cognitive factors are of equal importance. Many more criticisms could be listed, but the fact remains that there is an element of truth to much of what Freud said.

Psychodynamic Theories—Freud's Descendants

Freud's ideas quickly attracted a brilliant following. Just as rapidly, the importance Freud placed on instinctual drives and sexuality caused many to disagree with him. Those who stayed close to the core of Freud's thinking are now referred to as **neo-Freudians** (*neo* means "new"). Some of the better-known neo-Freudians are Karen Horney, Anna Freud (Freud's daughter), Otto Rank, and Erich Fromm. Other early followers of Freud broke away more completely and created their own opposing theories. This group includes people such as Alfred Adler, Harry Sullivan, and Carl Jung.

Question: How did the thinking of these people differ from Freud's ideas?

The full story of other psychodynamic theories must await your first course in personality. For now, let's sample three views. The first represents an early rejection of Freud's thinking (Adler). The second embraces most but not all of Freud's theory (Horney). The third involves a carryover of Freudian ideas into a related but unique theory (Jung).

Alfred Adler (1870–1937) Adler broke away from Freud because he disagreed with Freud's emphasis on the unconscious, on instinctual drives, and on the importance of sexuality. Adler believed that we are *social* creatures governed by social urges, *not* by biological instincts. In Adler's view, the main driving force in personality is a **striving for superiority.** This striving, he said, is a struggle to overcome imperfections, an upward drive for competence, completion, and mastery of shortcomings.

Question: What motivates "striving for superiority"?

Adler believed that everyone experiences **feelings of inferiority.** This occurs mainly because we begin life as small, weak, and relatively powerless children surrounded by larger and more powerful adults. Feelings of inferiority may also come from our personal limitations. The struggle for superiority arises from such feelings.

While everyone strives for superiority, each person tries to **compensate** for different limitations, and each chooses a different pathway to superiority. Adler believed that this situation creates a unique **style of life** (or personality pattern) for each individual. According to Adler the core of each person's style of life is formed by age 5. (Adler also believed that valuable clues to a person's style of life are revealed by the earliest memory that can be recalled. You might therefore find it interesting to search back to your earliest memory and contemplate what it tells you.) However, later in his life, Adler began to emphasize the existence of a **creative self.** By this he meant that humans *create* their personalities through choices and experiences.

Karen Horney (1885–1952) As a neo-Freudian, Karen Horney (HORN-eye) remained faithful to most of Freud's ideas. Yet, at the same time, she altered or rejected some ideas and added many of her own. Horney also resisted Freud's more mechanistic, biological, and instinctive ideas. For example, as a woman, Horney rejected Freud's claim that "anatomy is destiny." This view, woven into Freudian psychology, held that males are dominant or superior to females. Horney was among the first to challenge the obvious male bias in Freud's thinking.

Horney also disagreed with Freud about the cause of neurosis. Freud held that neurotic (anxiety-ridden) individuals are struggling with forbidden id drives that they fear they cannot control. Horney's view was that a core of **basic anxiety** occurs when people feel isolated and helpless in a hostile world. These feelings, she believed, are rooted in childhood. Basic anxiety then causes troubled individuals to exaggerate a single mode of interacting with others.

Question: What do you mean by "mode of interacting"?

According to Horney, each of us can move **toward** others (by depending on them for love, support, or friendship), we can move **away** from others (by withdrawing, acting like a "loner," or being "strong" and independent), or we can move **against** others (by attacking, competing with, or seeking power over them). Horney believed that emotional health reflects a balance in moving toward, away from, and against others. In her view, emotional problems tend to lock people into overuse of only one of the three modes—an insight that remains valuable today.

Carl Jung (1875–1961) Carl Jung (yung) was a student of Freud's, but the two parted ways as Jung began to develop his own ideas. Like Freud, Jung called the conscious part of the personality the ego. However, he further noted that between the ego and the outside world we often find a **persona,** or "mask." The persona is the "public self" presented to others when people adopt particular roles or when they hide their deeper feelings. As mentioned in the previous chapter, actions of the ego may reflect attitudes of **introversion** (in which energy is mainly directed inward), or of **extroversion** (in which energy is mainly directed outward).

Question: Was Jung's view of the unconscious the same as Freud's?

Jung used the term **personal unconscious** to refer to what Freud simply called the unconscious. The personal unconscious is a storehouse for personal experiences, feelings, and memories that are not directly knowable. But Jung departed from Freud and also proposed a deeper **collective unconscious** shared by all humans. Jung believed that from the beginning of time, all humans have had experiences with birth, death, power, god figures, mother and father figures, animals, the earth, energy, evil, rebirth, and so on. According to Jung, such universals create **archetypes** (AR-KEH-types: original ideas or patterns).

Archetypes, found in the collective unconscious, are unconscious images that cause us to respond emotionally to *symbols* of birth, death, energy, animals, evil, and the like. Jung believed that he detected symbols of such archetypes in the art, religion, myths, and dreams of every culture and age. Let us say, for instance, that a man dreams of dancing with his sister. To Freud, this would probably be a sign of hidden incestuous feelings. To Jung, the image of the sister might represent an unexpressed feminine side of the man's personality, and the dream might represent the cosmic dance that intertwines "maleness" and "femaleness" in all lives.

Question: Are some archetypes more important than others?

Two particularly important archetypes are the **anima** (representing the female principle) and the **animus** (representing the male principle). Each person has both an anima and an animus. For full development, Jung thought it is essential for both the "masculine" and "feminine" side of personality to be expressed. The presence of the anima in males and the animus in females also enables us to relate to members of the opposite sex.

Jung regarded the **self archetype** as the most important of all. The self archetype represents unity. Its existence causes a gradual movement toward balance, wholeness, and harmony within the personality. Jung felt that we become richer and more completely human when a balance is achieved between the conscious and unconscious, the anima and animus, thinking and feeling, sensing and intuiting, the persona and the ego, introversion and extroversion.

Question: Was Jung talking about self-actualization?

Essentially, he was. Jung was the first to use the term *self-actualization* to describe a striving for completion and unity. He believed that the self archetype is symbolized in every culture by **mandalas** (magic circles) of one kind or another (Fig. 17–4).

Jung's theory may not be scientific but clearly he was a man of genius and vision. If you would like to know more about Jung and his ideas, a good starting place is his autobiography, *Memories, Dreams, Reflections*.

Fig. 17–4 *Jung regarded circular designs as symbols of the self-archetype and representations of unity, balance, and completion within the personality.*

Learning Check

1. List the three divisions of personality postulated by Freud. ______________________.
2. Which division is totally unconscious? ______________
3. Which division is responsible for moral anxiety? ______________
4. Freud proposed the existence of a death archetype known as Thanatos. T or F?
5. Freud's view of personality development is based on the concept of ______________ stages.
6. Arrange these stages in the proper order: phallic, anal, genital, oral.

____

7. Freud considered the anal-retentive personality to be obstinate and stingy. T or F?

Match:

8. ___ striving for superiority	**A.** Freud
9. ___ basic anxiety	**B.** Adler
10. ___ pleasure principle	**C.** Horney
11. ___ collective unconscious	**D.** Jung
12. ___ anima	

Answers:

1. id, ego, superego **2.** id **3.** superego **4.** F **5.** psychosexual **6.** oral, anal, phallic, genital **7.** T **8.** B **9.** C **10.** A **11.** D **12.** D

Learning Theories of Personality—Habit I Seen You Somewhere Before?

Question: How do behaviorists approach personality?

According to some critics, as if people are robots like R2D2 of *Star Wars* fame. Actually, the behaviorists position is not nearly as mechanistic as some critics would have us believe, and its value is well established. For one thing, behaviorists have shown repeatedly that children can *learn* things like kindness, hostility, generosity, or destructiveness (Bandura & Walters, 1963; Hoffman, 1975). But what does this have to do with personality? Everything, according to the behavioral viewpoint.

The behaviorist position is that personality is no more (or less) than a collection of learned behavior patterns. Personality, like other learned behavior, is acquired through classical and operant conditioning, observational learning, reinforcement, extinction, generalization, and discrimination (Fig. 17–5). When Mother says, "It's not nice to make mud pies with Mommy's blender. If we want to grow up to be a big girl, we won't do it again, will we?" she serves as a model and in other ways shapes her daughter's personality.

Strict **learning theorists** reject the idea that personality is made up of consistent traits. They would assert, for instance, that there is no such thing as a trait of "honesty" (Bandura, 1973; Mischel, 1968).

Fig. 17–5 *Freud believed that aggressive urges are "instinctual." In contrast, behavioral theories assume that personal characteristics such as aggressiveness are learned. Is this boy's aggression the result of observational learning, harsh punishment, or prior reinforcement?*

Question: Certainly, some people are honest while others are not. How can honesty not be a trait?

A learning theorist would agree that some of the people you know are honest *more often* than others. But knowing this does not allow us to predict for certain whether a person will be honest in a specific situation. It would not be unusual, for example, to find that a person honored for returning a lost wallet had cheated on a test or broken the speed limit. If you were to ask a learning theorist, "Are you an honest person?" the reply might be, "In what situation?"

By drawing our attention to **situational determinants** of behavior, learning theorists have not entirely removed the "person" from personality. Walter Mischel (1973) agrees that some situations strongly affect behavior (for instance, an escaped lion walks into the supermarket; you accidentally sit on a lighted cigarette; you find your lover in bed with your best friend). Other situations are trivial and have little impact. Thus, external events *interact* with each person's unique learning history to produce behavior in any given situation. As discussed in Chapter 16, trait theorists also believe that situations affect behavior. But in their view, situations interact with *traits*. So, in essence, learning theorists favor replacing the concept of "traits" with "past learning" to explain behavior.

Question: How do learning theorists view the structure of personality?

Behavior = Personality The behavioral view of personality can be illustrated with an early theory proposed by John Dollard and Neal Miller (1950). In their view, **habits** make up the structure of personality. As for the dynamics of personality, Dollard and Miller believe that habits are governed by four elements of learning: **drive, cue, response,** and **reward.** A *drive* is any stimulus strong enough to goad a person to action (such as hunger, pain, lust, frustration, fear). *Cues* are signals from the environment that guide *responses* so they are most likely to bring about *reward* or reinforcement.

Question: How does that relate to personality?

An example may clarify this viewpoint. Let's say a child is frustrated by an older brother who takes a toy from her. The child could make any of several responses. She could throw a temper tantrum, hit her brother, tell Mother, and so forth. The response she chooses is guided by available cues and the previous effects of each response. If telling Mother has paid off in the past, and the mother is present, telling again may be her immediate response.

If a different set of cues exists (if Mother is absent or if the older brother looks particularly menacing), the girl may select some other response. To an outside observer, the child's actions seem to reflect her personality. To the learning theorist, they are a direct reaction to the combined effects of drive, cue, response, and reward.

Question: Doesn't this analysis leave out a lot?

Yes. Learning theorists first set out to provide a simple, clear model of personality. But in recent years they have had to face a fact that they originally tended to overlook. The fact is: People think. The new breed of behavioral psychologists—who include perception, thinking, and other mental events in their views—are called **social learning theorists.** (The label *social* is used because they also stress social relationships and modeling.)

Social Learning Theory The "cognitive behaviorism" of social learning theory can be illustrated by three concepts proposed by Julian Rotter (1975). They are: the psychological situation, expectancy, and reinforcement value. Let's examine each.

Someone trips you. How do you respond? Your response probably depends on whether you think it was planned or an accident. It is not enough to know the setting in which a person responds. We also need to know the person's **psychological situation,** that is, how the person *interprets* or *defines* the situation. Here's another example. Let's say you score low on an exam. Do you consider it a challenge to work harder, a sign that you should drop the class, or an excuse to get drunk? Again, your interpretation is important.

An **expectancy** refers to your anticipation that making a response will lead to reinforcement. To continue the example, if working harder has paid off in the past, it is a likely reaction to a low test score. But according to Rotter, behavior is not automatic. To predict your response, we would also have to know if you *expect* your efforts to pay off in the present situation. In fact, expected reinforcement may be more important than actual past reinforcement. And what about the *value* you attach to grades, school success, or personal ability? Rotter's third concept, **reinforcement value,** states that humans attach different values to various activities or rewards. This, too, must be taken into account to understand personality.

One more idea deserves mention here. At times, we all evaluate our actions and may reward ourselves with special privileges or treats when the evaluation is positive (Fig. 17–6). With this in mind, social learning theory adds the concept of **self-reinforcement** to the behavioristic view. Thus, habits of self-praise and self-blame become an important part of personality. In fact, self-reinforcement can be thought of as the behaviorist's counterpart to the superego (see Highlight 17–1).

Radical Behaviorism As you have probably noted, social learning theory is only moderately behavioristic. A more extreme view of personality is held by radical behaviorist B. F. Skinner, who has said, "Intelligent peo-

Fig. 17–6 *Through self-reinforcement, we reward ourselves for personal achievements and other "good" behavior.*

● HIGHLIGHT 17–1 Self-Reinforcement

The following statements, adapted from a scale developed by Elaine Heiby (1983), will add to your understanding of self-reinforcement. Check those that apply to you.

- ☐ I often think positive thoughts about myself.
- ☐ I frequently meet standards that I set for myself.
- ☐ I try not to blame myself when things go wrong.
- ☐ I usually don't get upset when I make mistakes because I learn from them.
- ☐ I can get satisfaction out of what I do even if it's not perfect.
- ☐ When I make mistakes, I take time to reassure myself.
- ☐ I don't think talking about what you've done right is too boastful.
- ☐ Praising yourself is healthy and normal.
- ☐ I don't think I have to be upset every time I make a mistake.
- ☐ My feelings of self-confidence and self-esteem stay pretty steady.

People who agree with all or most of the preceding statements tend to have high rates of self-reinforcement. And, as the last item suggests, high rates of self-reinforcement are related to high self-esteem. The reverse is also true: Numerous studies have shown that mildly depressed college students tend to have low rates of self-reinforcement (Heiby, 1983).

It is not known if low self-reinforcement leads to depression, or the reverse. But in any case, learning to be more self-reinforcing appears to lessen depression (Fuchs & Rehm, 1977). From a behavioral viewpoint, there is value in learning to be "good to yourself."

ple no longer believe that men are possessed by demons . . . but human behavior is still commonly attributed to indwelling agents" (Skinner, 1971). For Skinner, the term *personality* is a fiction we invent to pretend we have explained behavior that is actually controlled by the environment. Skinner believes that everything a person does is ultimately based on past and present rewards and punishments. Perhaps Skinner's point of view has been shaped by his environment.

Again, we have discussed a large number of terms in our look at behavioral views of personality. To help you learn them, the terms are summarized in Table 17–2.

Table 17–2 Behavioral Concepts of Personality

Behavioral personality theory Any model of personality that emphasizes observable behavior, the relationship between stimuli and responses, and the impact of learning.

Learning theorist With regard to personality, a psychologist interested in the ways that learning principles shape and explain personality.

Situational determinants Immediate conditions (for example, rewards and punishments) in a given situation that determine what behavior is likely to occur, independent of the actor's personality traits.

Habit A deeply ingrained, learned pattern of response.

Drive Any stimulus (especially an internal stimulus such as hunger) strong enough to goad a person into action.

Cue External stimuli or signs that guide responses, especially those that signal the likely presence or absence of reinforcement.

Response Any behavior, either observable or internal.

Social learning theory An approach that combines behavioral principles, cognition (perception, thinking, anticipation), social relationships, and observational learning to explain personality.

Psychological situation A situation as it is perceived and interpreted by an individual, not as it exists objectively.

Expectancy One's anticipation or expectation concerning the effect some response will have, especially regarding reinforcement.

Reinforcement value The subjective value a person attaches to a particular activity or reinforcer.

Self-reinforcement Praising oneself or giving oneself a special treat or reward for having made a particular response (such as completing a school assignment).

Radical behaviorism An approach that avoids any reference to thoughts or other internal processes; radical behaviorists are interested strictly in relationships between stimuli and responses.

Question: How do learning theorists account for personality development?

Behavioristic View of Development

Many of Freud's major points can be restated in terms of modern learning theory. Miller and Dollard (1950) agree with Freud that the first 6 years are crucial for personality development, but for different reasons. Rather than thinking in terms of psychosexual urges and fixations, they ask, "What makes early learning experiences so lasting in their effects?" Their answer is that childhood is a time of urgent and tearing drives, powerful rewards and punishments, and crushing frustrations. Also important is **social reinforcement** based on the effects of attention and approval from others. These forces combine to shape the core of personality.

Critical Situations Miller and Dollard consider four developmental situations to be of critical importance. These are (1) **feeding,** (2) **toilet** or **cleanliness training,** (3) **sex training,** and (4) learning to express **anger** or **aggression.**

Question: Why are these of special importance?

Feeding serves as an illustration. If children are fed when they cry, they are encouraged to actively manipulate their parents. The child allowed to cry without being fed learns to be passive. Thus, a basic active or passive orientation toward the world may be created by early feeding experiences. Feeding can also affect later social relationships, because the child learns to associate people with satisfaction and pleasure or with frustration and discomfort.

Toilet and cleanliness training can be a particularly strong source of emotion for both parents and children. Parents are usually aghast the first time they find a child smearing feces about with gay abandon. Their reaction is often sharp punishment. For the child, the result is frustration and confusion. Many attitudes toward cleanliness, conformity, and bodily functions are formed at such times. Studies also show that severe, punishing, or frustrating toilet training can have undesirable effects on personality development (Sears et al., 1957). Toilet and cleanliness training therefore demand patience and a sense of humor.

Question: What about sex and anger?

When, where, and how a child learns to express anger and aggression are of obvious importance. So, too, is expression of sexual behavior. Both types of experiences can leave an imprint on personality. Specifically, permissiveness for sexual and aggressive behavior in childhood is linked to adult needs for power (McCelland & Pilon, 1983). This link probably occurs because permitting such behaviors allows children to get pleasure from asserting themselves.

Sex training also involves learning "male" and "female" behaviors—which creates an even broader basis for shaping personality.

Becoming Male or Female From birth onward, children are identified as boys or girls and encouraged to learn sex-appropriate behavior. According to social learning theory, *identification* and *imitation* contribute greatly to personality development in general and to sex training in particular. **Identification** refers to the child's emotional attachment to admired adults, especially to those the child depends on for love and care. Identification typically encourages **imitation,** a desire to be like the valued and admired adult (Fig. 17–7). Many "male" or "female" traits come from children's conscious or unconscious attempts to imitate the behavior of a same-sex parent with whom they identify.

Question: If children are around parents of both sexes, why don't they imitate behavior typical of the opposite sex as well as of the same sex?

You may recall from Chapter 8 that Albert Bandura and others have shown that learning takes place vicariously as well as directly (Bandura, 1965). This means that we can learn without direct reward by observing and remembering the actions of others. But the actions we choose to imitate depend on their outcome. For example, boys and girls have equal chances to observe adults and other

Fig. 17–7 *Adult personality is influenced by identification with parents.*

children acting aggressively. However, girls are less likely than boys to imitate aggressive behavior because they rarely see female aggression rewarded or approved. Thus, many arbitrary "male" and "female" qualities are passed on at the same time sexual identity is learned.

A study of preschool children by Lisa Serbin and Daniel O'Leary (1975) found that teachers are 3 times more likely to pay attention to boys who are aggressive or disruptive than to girls acting the same way. Boys who hit other students or who broke things typically got loud scoldings and became the center of attention for the whole class. When teachers responded to disruptive girls, they gave brief, soft rebukes that others couldn't hear. Since we know that attention of almost any kind reinforces children's behavior, it is clear that the boys were being encouraged to be active and aggressive. Serbin and O'Leary found that girls got the most attention when they were within arm's reach, more or less clinging to the teacher.

It's easy to see that the teachers were unwittingly encouraging the girls to be submissive, dependent, and passive. Similar differences in reinforcement probably explain why males are responsible for much more aggression in society than females are. Rates of murder and assault, for example, are consistently higher for men (Deaux, 1985).

Learning Check

1. Learning theorists believe that personality "traits" really are ________________ acquired through prior learning. They also emphasize ________________ determinants of behavior.
2. Dollard and Miller consider cues the basic structure of personality. T or F?
3. To explain behavior, social learning theorists include mental elements, such as ________________ (the anticipation that a response will lead to reinforcement).
4. Self-reinforcement is to behavioristic theory as superego is to psychoanalytic theory. T or F?
5. The radical behaviorist view of personality is represented by
   a. Neal Miller *b.* Abraham Maslow *c.* B. F. Skinner *d.* Carl Rogers
6. Which of the following is *not* a "critical situation" in the behaviorist theory of personality development?
   a. feeding *b.* sex training *c.* language training *d.* anger training
7. Social learning theories emphasize identification and ________________.

Answers:

1. habits, situational **2.** F **3.** expectancies **4.** T **5.** *c* **6.** *c* **7.** imitation

Humanistic Theory—A Peek at Peak Experiences

Humanism is a reaction to the pessimism of psychoanalytic theory and the mechanism of learning theory. At its core is a new image of what it means to be human. Humanists reject the Freudian view of personality as a battleground for biological instincts and unconscious forces. Instead, they view **human nature** as inherently *good* and they seek ways to allow our positive potentials to emerge. Humanists also oppose the mechanical, "thing-like" overtones of the behaviorist viewpoint. We are not, they say, merely a bundle of moldable responses; rather, we are creative beings capable of **free choice.** To a humanist, the person you are today is largely the product of all of your previous choices. The humanistic viewpoint also places greater emphasis on immediate **subjective experience,** rather than on prior learning. Humanists believe that there are as many "real worlds" as there are people. To understand behavior, we must learn how a person subjectively views the world—what is "real" for her or him.

Question: Who are the major humanistic theorists?

There are many psychologists whose theories fall within the humanistic tradition. Of these, the best known are Carl Rogers (1902–1987) and Abraham Maslow (1908–

1970). Since Maslow's idea of self-actualization was introduced in Chapter 1, let's begin with a more detailed look at this facet of his thinking.

Maslow and Self-Actualization

Psychologists have tended to study human problems more than human strengths. An exception to this can be found in Abraham Maslow's studies of people living unusually effective lives. Maslow became interested in people who seemed to be using almost all of their talents and potentials. How were they different from the average person? To find an answer, Maslow began by studying the lives of great men and women, such as Albert Einstein, William James, Jane Adams, Eleanor Roosevelt, Abraham Lincoln, John Muir, and Walt Whitman. From there he moved on to directly study artists, writers, poets, and other creative individuals.

Along the way, Maslow's thinking changed radically. At first he studied only people of obvious creativity or high achievement. However, it eventually became clear that a housewife, carpenter, clerk, or student could live creatively and make full use of his or her potentials. Maslow referred to this tendency as *self-actualization* (Maslow, 1954) (see Highlight 17–2).

Question: Maslow's choice of self-actualizing people seems pretty subjective. Is it really a fair representation of self-actualization?

Although Maslow tried to investigate self-actualization empirically, his choice of people for study was subjective. Undoubtedly there are many ways to reach full development of personal potential. Maslow's primary contribution was to draw attention to the *possibility* of continued personal growth. Maslow considered self-actualization an ongoing process, not a simple end point to be attained only once.

Carl Rogers' Self Theory

Like Freud, Carl Rogers based his theory on clinical experience. Unlike Freud, who portrayed the normal per-

HIGHLIGHT 17–2
Characteristics of Self-Actualizers

In his studies, Maslow found that **self-actualizers** shared a great number of similarities. Whether famous or unknown, academically distinguished or uneducated, rich or poor, self-actualizers tended to fit this profile:

1. Efficient perceptions of reality. Subjects were able to judge situations correctly and honestly and were very sensitive to the fake and dishonest.

2. Comfortable acceptance of self, others, nature. Subjects were able to accept their own human nature with all its shortcomings. The shortcomings of others and the contradictions of the human condition were also accepted with humor and tolerance.

3. Spontaneity. Maslow's subjects extended their creativity into everyday activities. They tended to be unusually alive, engaged, and spontaneous.

4. Task centering. Most subjects had a mission to fulfill in life or some task or problem outside of themselves to pursue. Humanitarians such as Albert Schweitzer or Mother Teresa represent this quality.

5. Autonomy. Subjects were free from dependence on external authority or other people. They tended to be resourceful and independent.

6. Continued freshness of appreciation. The self-actualizer seems to constantly renew appreciation of life's basic goods. A sunset or a flower will be experienced as intensely the one-thousandth time as it was the first. There is an "innocence of vision," like that of an artist or child.

7. Fellowship with humanity. Maslow's subjects felt a deep identification with others and the human situation in general.

8. Profound interpersonal relationships. The interpersonal relationships of self-actualizers are marked by deep, loving bonds.

9. Unhostile sense of humor. This refers to the wonderful capacity to laugh at oneself. It also refers to the kind of humor a man like Abraham Lincoln had. Lincoln probably never made a joke that hurt anybody. His wry comments were a gentle prodding at human shortcomings.

10. Peak experiences. All of Maslow's subjects reported the frequent occurrence of **peak experiences.** These were marked by feelings of ecstasy, harmony, and deep meaning. Subjects reported feeling at one with the universe, stronger and calmer than ever before, filled with light, beautiful and good, and so forth. In short, self-actualizers feel safe and unanxious, accepted, loved, loving, and alive.

sonality as "adjusted" to internal conflict, Rogers saw greater possibility for inner harmony. The **fully functioning person,** he said, is one who has achieved an openness to feelings and experiences and has learned to trust inner urges and intuitions (Rogers, 1961). Rogers believed that this attitude is most likely to occur when a person receives ample amounts of love and acceptance from others.

Personality Structure and Dynamics Rogers' theory of personality centers on the concept of the **self,** a flexible and changing perception of personal identity that emerges from the **phenomenal field** (Fig. 17–8).

Question: What is the phenomenal field?

The phenomenal field is the person's total *subjective* experience of reality. The self is made up of those experiences identified as "I" or "me" that are separated from "not-me" experiences. Much human behavior can be understood as an attempt to maintain consistency between one's **self-image** and one's actions. For example, individuals who think of themselves as kind and considerate will act that way in most situations.

Fig. 17–8 *Humanists consider self-image a central determinant of behavior and personal adjustment.*

Question: Let's say I know a person who thinks she is kind and considerate, but she really isn't. How does this fit Rogers' theory?

According to Rogers, experiences that match the self-image are **symbolized** (admitted to consciousness) and contribute to gradual changes in the self. Information or feelings inconsistent with the self-image are said to be **incongruent.** It is incongruent, for example, to think of yourself as a considerate person if others frequently mention your rudeness. It is also incongruent to pretend you are kind when you are feeling callous or to say you are not angry when you are seething inside.

Experiences seriously incongruent with the self-image can be threatening, and they are often distorted or denied conscious recognition. Blocking, denying, or distorting experiences prevents the self from changing and creates a gulf between the self-image and reality. As the self-image grows more unrealistic, the **incongruent person** becomes confused, vulnerable, dissatisfied, or seriously maladjusted (Fig. 17–9). (For more information, also see Chapter 19.)

When your self-image is consistent with what you really think, feel, do, and experience, you are best able to actualize your potentials. Rogers also considered it essential to have congruence between the self-image and the **ideal**

Fig. 17–9 *Incongruence occurs when there is a mismatch between any of these three entities: the ideal self (the person you would like to be), your self-image (the person you think you are), and the true self (the person you actually are). Self-esteem suffers when there is a large difference between one's ideal self and self-image. Anxiety and defensiveness are common when the self-image does not match the true self.*

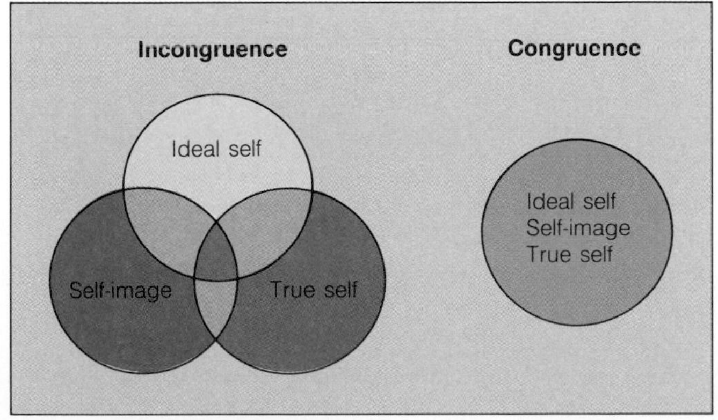

self. The ideal self is similar to Freud's ego ideal. It is an image of the person you would most like to be. (For another perspective, see Highlight 17–3.)

Question: Is it really incongruent not to live up to one's ideal self?

Rogers was aware that we never fully attain our ideals, but the greater the gap between the way you see yourself and the way you would like to be, the greater the tension and anxiety experienced. The Rogerian view of personality can therefore be summarized as a process of maximizing potentials by accepting information about oneself as realistically and honestly as possible. In accord with Rogers' thinking, researchers have found that people with a close match between their self-image and ideal self tend to be socially poised, confident, and resourceful. Those with a poor match tend to be anxious, insecure, and lacking in social skills (Gough et al., 1983).

HIGHLIGHT 17–3
Possible Selves

Your ideal self is only one of many personal identities you may have pondered. Psychologists Hazel Markus and Paula Nurius (1986) believe that each of us harbors images of many **possible selves.** These selves include the person we would most like to become (the ideal self), as well as other selves we could become or are afraid of becoming.

Possible selves translate our hopes, fears, fantasies, and goals into specific images of who we *could* be. Thus, a beginning law student might picture herself as a successful attorney; the husband in a troubled marriage might picture himself as a divorcee; and a person on a diet might imagine both slim and grossly obese possible selves. Such self-images tend to direct future behavior. They also give meaning to current behavior and help us evaluate it. For example, the unhappy spouse might be moved by upsetting images of his "divorcee self" to try saving the marriage.

Even day-to-day decisions may be guided by possible selves. Purchasing clothes, a car, cologne, membership in a health club, and the like may be influenced by images of a valued future self. Of course, identities are not all equally possible. As Markus and Nurius point out, almost everyone over age 30 has probably felt the anguish of realizing that some cherished possible selves will never be realized.

Humanistic View of Development

Why do mirrors, photographs, tape recorders, and the reactions of others hold such fascination and threat for most people? Carl Rogers' theory suggests it is because they provide information about one's self. The development of a self-image depends greatly on information

Table 17–3 Some Key Humanistic Terms

Humanism An approach to psychology that focuses on human experience, problems, potentials, and ideals.

Subjective experience Reality as it is perceived and interpreted, not as it exists objectively; personal, private, nonobjective experience.

Self-actualization The full development of personal potential.

Self-actualizer One who is living creatively and making full use of his or her potentials.

Task centering Focusing on the task at hand, rather than on one's own feelings or needs.

Autonomy A freedom from dependence on external authority or the opinions of others.

Peak experiences Temporary moments of self-actualization, marked by feelings of ecstasy, harmony, and deep meaning.

Fully functioning person Rogers' term for persons living in harmony with their deepest feelings, impulses, and intuitions.

Self A continuously evolving conception of one's personal identity.

Phenomenal field A person's total subjective experience of reality; his or her private psychological world.

Self-image Total subjective perception of oneself, including an image of one's body and impressions of one's personality, capabilities, and so on.

Symbolization In Rogers' theory, the process of admitting an experience to awareness.

Incongruence A mismatch or inconsistency; in Rogers' theory, experiences that are inconsistent with one's self-image are said to be incongruent.

Incongruent person A person who has a distorted or inaccurate self-image.

Ideal self An idealized image of oneself (the person one would like to be) that, optimally, closely matches one's overall self-image.

from the environment. It begins with a sorting of perceptions and feelings: my body, my toes, my nose, I want, I like, I am, and so on. Soon, it expands to include self-evaluation: I am a good person, I did something bad just now, and so forth.

Question: How does development of the self contribute to later personality functioning?

Rogers' believed that positive and negative evaluations by others cause children to develop internal standards of evaluation called **conditions of worth.** In other words, we learn that some actions win our parents' love and approval, whereas others are rejected.

Learning to evaluate some experiences or feelings as "good" and others as "bad" is directly related to a later capacity for self-esteem, positive self-evaluation, or **positive self-regard,** to use Rogers' term. To think of yourself as a good, lovable, worthwhile person, your behavior and experiences must match your internal conditions of worth. The problem is that this can cause incongruence by leading to the denial of many true feelings and experiences.

To put it simply, Rogers regarded many adult adjustment problems as an attempt to live by the standards of others. He believed that congruence and self-actualization are encouraged by replacing conditions of worth with **organismic valuing.** Organismic valuing is a direct, gut-level response to life that avoids the filtering and distortion of incongruence. It is the ability to trust one's own feelings and perceptions—to become one's own "locus of evaluation." Organismic valuing is most likely to develop, Rogers felt, when children (or adults) receive "unconditional positive regard" from others. That is, when they are "prized" just for being themselves, without any conditions or strings attached.

Learning Check

1. Humanists view human nature as basically good, and they emphasize the effects of subjective learning and unconscious choice. T or F?
2. Maslow used the term ______________________ to describe the tendency of certain individuals to fully use their talents and potentials.
3. According to Rogers, a close match between the self-image and the ideal self creates a condition called incongruence. T or F?
4. Markus and Nurius describe alternative self-concepts that a person may have as "possible selves." T or F?
5. Rogers' theory considers acceptance of conditions of ______________________ a troublesome aspect of development of the self.
6. According to Maslow, a preoccupation with one's own thoughts, feelings, and needs is characteristic of self-actualizing individuals. T or F?

Answers:
1. F 2. self-actualization 3. F 4. T 5. worth 6. F

Personality Theories—Overview and Comparison

Question: Which personality theory is right?

Each theory has added to our understanding of personality by meaningfully organizing observations of human behavior. Nevertheless, none of the major theories can be fully proved or disproved. (If a theory could be proved true, it would no longer be a theory. It would be a law.) At the same time that theories are neither true nor false, their implications or predictions may be. The best way to judge a theory, then, is in terms of its *usefulness* for explaining behavior, for stimulating research, and for suggesting ways of treating psychological disorders. Each theory has fared differently in these areas.

Psychoanalytic Theory By present standards, psychoanalytic theory seems to over-emphasize sexuality and biological instincts. These distortions were corrected somewhat by the neo-Freudians, but problems remain. One of the most telling criticisms of Freudian theory is that it can explain any psychological event *after* it has occurred. But beforehand, it offers little help in predicting future behavior. For this reason, many psychoanalytic concepts are difficult or impossible to test.

Behavioristic Theory Learning theories have provided a good framework for personality research. Of the three major perspectives, the behaviorists have made the best effort to rigorously test and verify their ideas. They have, however, been criticized for understating the impact that temperament, emotion, and subjective experience have on personality. To a degree, social learning theory is an attempt to answer such criticisms.

Humanistic Theory A great strength of the humanists is the light they have shed on positive dimensions of personality. As Maslow (1968) put it, "Human nature is not nearly as bad as it has been thought to be. It is as if Freud supplied us with the sick half of psychology and we must now fill it out with the healthy half." Despite their contributions, the humanists can be criticized for using imprecise concepts that are difficult to measure or study objectively. Even so, humanistic thought has encouraged many people to seek greater self-awareness and personal growth.

Summary In the final analysis, we need the concepts of all three perspectives (and those discussed in the previous chapter) to adequately explain personality. There is an element of truth to each view, and a balanced picture emerges only when all are considered. Table 17–4 provides a final overview of the three principal theories we have discussed.

Table 17–4 Comparison of Three Views of Personality

	PSYCHOANALYTIC THEORY	BEHAVIORISTIC THEORY	HUMANISTIC THEORY
View of human nature	Negative	Neutral	Positive
Is behavior free or determined?	Determined	Determined	Free
Principal motives	Sex and aggression	Drives of all kinds	Self-actualization
Personality structure	Id, ego, superego	Habits	Self
Role of unconscious	Maximized	Practically non-existent	Minimized
Conception of conscience	Superego	Self-reinforcement	Ideal self, valuing process
Developmental emphasis	Psychosexual stages	Critical learning situations: identification and imitation	Development of self-image
Barriers to personal growth	Unconscious conflicts; fixations	Maladaptive habits; pathological environment	Conditions of worth; incongruence

Applications: The Search for Self-Actualization

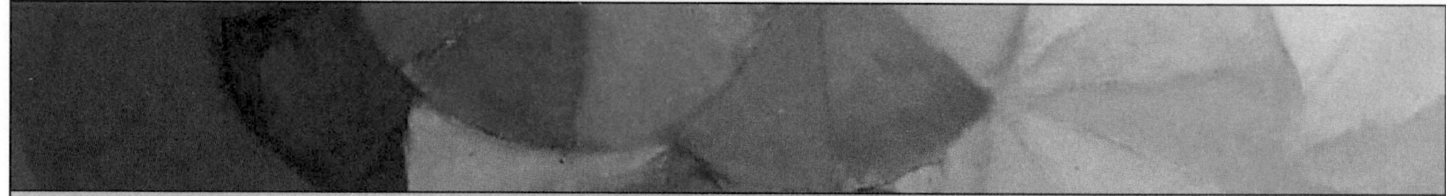

> Some people fear finding themselves alone—and so they don't find themselves at all.
>
> André Gide

> What a man can be, he must be. This need we may call self-actualization.
>
> Abraham Maslow

Self-actualization is a concept that has appeared several times in this book. Perhaps you have been attracted to the promise it holds for personal growth. Self-actualizers lead rich, creative, and fulfilling lives.

Question: What steps can be taken to promote self-actualization?

Promoting self-actualization is more difficult than might be imagined. Many people are caught in a struggle for survival or security and never get a chance to develop their potentials fully. Others show little interest in personal growth or in the qualities Maslow described. Moreover, Maslow made few specific recommendations about how to proceed. Nevertheless, a number of helpful suggestions can be gleaned from his writings (Maslow, 1954, 1967, 1971).

Steps Toward Self-Actualization

There is no magic formula for leading a more creative life. Knowing or even imitating the traits of unusually effective people cannot be counted on to promote self-actualization. Self-actualization is primarily a *process,* not a goal or an end point. As such, it requires hard work, patience, and commitment. Here are some ways to begin.

Be Willing To Change Begin by asking yourself, "Am I living in a way that is deeply satisfying to me and which truly expresses me?" If not, be prepared to make changes in your life. Indeed, ask yourself this question often and accept the need for continual change.

Take Responsibility You can become an architect of self by acting as if you are personally responsible for every aspect of your life. Shouldering responsibility in this way is not totally realistic, but it helps end the habit of blaming others for your own shortcomings. This attitude is illustrated by a young woman who realized in a counseling session, "I can't depend on someone else to give me an education. I'll have to get it myself" (Rogers, 1962).

Examine Your Motives Self-discovery involves an element of risk. To learn your strengths, limitations, and true feelings, you must be willing to go out on a limb, speak your mind, and take some chances. Fears of failure, rejection, loneliness, or disagreement with others are a tremendous barrier to personal change. If most of your behavior seems to be directed by a desire for safety or security, it may be time to test the limits of these needs. Try to make each life decision a choice of growth, not a response to fear or anxiety.

Experience Honestly and Directly Wishful thinking is another barrier to personal growth. Self-actualizers trust themselves enough to accept all kinds of information without distorting it to fit their fears and desires. Try to see yourself as others do. Be willing to admit, "I was wrong" or, "I failed because I was irresponsible." This basic honesty can be extended to perception in general. Try to experience the world as you did when you were a child: fully, vividly, and directly. Try to see things as they are, not as you would like them to be.

Make Use of Positive Experiences As a "rule of thumb," growth-promoting activities usually "feel good." Perhaps you have felt unusually alert and alive when expressing yourself through art, music, dance, writing, or athletics. Or perhaps life seems especially rich when you are alone in nature, surrounded by friends, or helping others. Whatever their source, Maslow considered peak experiences temporary moments of self-actualization. Therefore, you might actively repeat activities that have caused feelings of awe, amazement, exaltation, renewal, reverence, humility, fulfillment, or joy.

Be Prepared To Be Different Maslow felt that everyone has a potential for "greatness," but most fear becoming what they might. Much of this fear is related to the fact that actualizing potentials may place you at odds with cultural expectations or with others who are important in your life. As part of personal growth, be prepared to be unpopular when your views don't agree with others. Trust your own impulses and feelings; don't automatically judge yourself by the standards of others. Accept your uniqueness. As one young woman put it, "I've always tried to be what others thought I should be, but now I'm wondering whether I shouldn't just see that I am what I am" (Rogers, 1962).

Applications

Get Involved Maslow found with few exceptions that self-actualizers tend to have a mission or "calling" in life. For these people, "work" is not done just to fill deficiency needs, but to satisfy higher yearnings for truth, beauty, brotherhood, and meaning. Many of the things you do may be motivated by more commonplace needs, but you can add meaning to these activities by endeavoring to work hard at whatever you do. Get personally involved and committed. Turn your attention to problems outside yourself.

Slow Down Try to avoid hurrying or over-scheduling your time. Self-awareness takes time to develop, and a certain amount of leisure is essential for contemplation and self-exploration. Time pressures tend to force a person to rely compulsively on old habits.

Start a Journal Although this suggestion does not come from Maslow's writings, it is a valuable means of promoting self-awareness. Many people find that a journal provides the kind of information necessary to make growth-oriented life changes. A journal should include a description of significant events in your daily life. In addition, thoughts, feelings, fears, wishes, frustrations, and dreams should be recorded. Some find it useful to write dialogues in their journal in which they speak to parents, teachers, lovers, objects, and so forth. Review and reread your journal periodically. You will find that it is easier to learn from an event after it has "cooled off" and you can view it objectively.

Assess Your Progress Since there is no final point at which one becomes self-actualized, it is important to gauge your progress frequently and to renew your efforts. Boredom is a good sign you are in need of change. If you feel bored at school, at a job, or in a relationship, consider it a challenge or an indication that you have not taken responsibility for personal growth. A situation is only as "boring" as you allow it to be. Almost any activity can be used as a chance for self-exploration if it is approached creatively.

What To Expect As we have already noted, growth-promoting activities are usually personally satisfying.

Question: Are there other signs that one is moving in the right direction?

Yes. There should be a noticeable improvement in the quality of your daily life and a greater acceptance of yourself and others. You should feel more confident and should carry out daily routines with less strain or conflict. These changes do not happen overnight, and your first steps toward self-actualization may be threatening at the same time they are exhilarating. Positive changes can also be quite subtle. An idea of what to expect is provided by the words of Henry David Thoreau. After he had spent 2 years in the wilderness at Walden Pond, Thoreau had this to say about his experience:

> I learned this, at least, by my experiment: that as one advances confidently in the direction of his dreams, and endeavors to live the life which he has imagined, he will meet with a success unexpected in common hours. He will put some things behind, will pass an invisible boundary; new universal and more liberal laws will begin to establish themselves around and within him. . . . The laws of the universe will appear less complex, and solitude will not be solitude, nor poverty, poverty, nor weakness, weakness.

Learning Check

1. In his writings, Maslow emphasized that self-actualization is a process, not a goal or end point. T or F?

2. Making fuller use of personal potentials requires learning to live up to the expectations of others. T or F?

3. Maslow described peak experiences as temporary moments of self-actualization. T or F?

4. A major characteristic of self-actualizers is their interest in status and personal recognition. T or F?

5. According to Maslow, wishful thinking and distorted self-perceptions are barriers to self-actualization. T or F?

Answers:

1. T 2. F 3. T 4. F 5. T

Exploration: Self-Monitoring—Which Me Do You See?

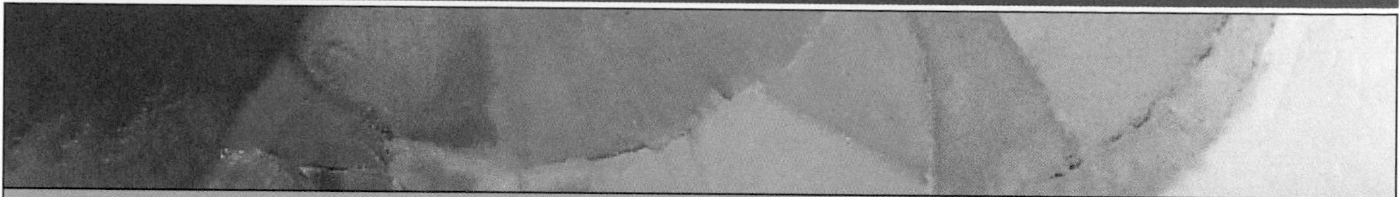

As you walk into the room, you face a dilemma that challenges party-goers everywhere: On the left, a conversation is taking place between three similar people—a film lover, an art lover, and a music lover. On the right side of the room, a mixed group has formed, including a member of the peace movement, a military "hawk," and a shy person. Which group do you join? Your answer may depend on whether you are high or low in *self-monitoring*) (Snyder & Harkness, 1984).

Self-monitoring refers to how much people *monitor* (observe, regulate, and control) the image of themselves that they display to others in public. Some of us are **high self-monitors,** who are very sensitive to situations and expectations. It is as if high self-monitors ask, "Who does this situation want me to be, and how can I be that person?" In contrast, **low self-monitors** are less interested in controlling the impression they make. Such people seek to faithfully express what they really think and feel. It is as if they want to know, "Who am I, and how can I be me in this situation?" (Snyder, 1987).

The Public Self Self-monitoring has been extensively studied by psychologist Mark Snyder. In general, persons high in self-monitoring take a flexible approach to defining themselves. They are very interested in their public "image." Low self-monitors, on the other hand, try to accurately present their beliefs and principles no matter what the situation is. Snyder believes that the way people define what they regard as "me" has an impact on their lives and behavior.

To return to the party, Snyder and Harkness (1984) found that in similar situations high self-monitors preferred to join clearly defined groups. At the party, for example, they could strike a "cultured" pose if they joined the first group. However, the second group would put them in a difficult position: Any image they projected could offend at least one member of the group. Such group differences had far less impact on low self-monitors. Basically, they chose whichever group had someone with whom they could identify.

Question: How can you tell if you are high or low in self-monitoring?

High or Low? To measure this characteristic, Snyder developed the *Self-Monitoring Scale.* Although the entire scale cannot be reprinted here, the items that follow are examples of statements that separate highs from lows.

High Self-Monitors

I would probably make a good actor.
I'm not always the person I appear to be.
I guess I put on a show to impress and entertain others.

Low Self-Monitors

I have never been good at games like charades or improvisational acting.
In a group, I am rarely the center of attention.
At a party, I let others keep the jokes and stories going.

If you are still not sure what your self-monitoring style is, the following comparisons may be helpful. Each difference has been verified in studies of self-monitoring (Snyder, 1987).

- **Highs** are keenly interested in the actions of others and in trying to "read" their motives, attitudes, and traits. Presumably, high self-monitors do this so that they will know how to present themselves to a particular person, such as a date.
- **Lows** seek to match their public behavior to their private attitudes, feelings, and beliefs. Lows tend to speak their mind no matter who is listening.

- **Highs** are flexible and adaptable, and they display different behavior from situation to situation.
- **Lows** change little from situation to situation. They value a match between who they believe they are and what they do. Lows do not want to change opinions to please others or win their favor.

- **Highs** tend to declare who they are by listing their roles and memberships (student, post office employee, member of the school orchestra, third-ranking player on the tennis team, and so on).
- **Lows** identify themselves in terms of their beliefs, emotions, values, and personality.

- **Highs** choose friends who are skilled or knowledgeable in various

Exploration

areas. They also tend to have specific friends for specific activities.

- **Lows** have friends who tend to all be alike in basic ways. No matter what the activity, they prefer to get together with the same friends.

- **Highs** are concerned with outer appearances. They choose their clothes, hair style, jewelry, and so forth, to project an image.
- **Lows** have a wardrobe that is less varied; they do not have to look different as often as high self-monitors do.

- **Highs** initiate dating based mainly on the date's appearance. (In the personals column, their ads are the ones that emphasize appearance.)
- **Lows** are more interested in a potential date's personality.

- **Highs** believe it is possible to love two people at the same time.
- **Lows** believe that there is only one real love for a person.

- **Highs** prefer jobs where their role is very clearly defined.
- **Lows** prefer jobs where they can "just be themselves."

Implications As you can see, there are advantages and disadvantages to being either high or low in self-monitoring. In general, high self-monitors are adaptable and present themselves well in social situations. However, they tend to reveal little about their private feelings, beliefs, and intentions. This, plus gaps between their attitudes and actions, may have a negative effect on relationships. The primary drawback to being low in self-monitoring is a tendency to be unresponsive to the demands of different situations. Low self-monitors want to "just be themselves," even when adjustments in self-presentation would make them more effective.

One True Self? Is there a single "true self" that underlies the many roles we play in daily life? Studies of self-monitoring raise questions about the idea that each person has a "true self." High self-monitors, in particular, act as if they have many selves. For these people, controlling the image they impart is a way of life, at parties, in meetings, in classes, and elsewhere. The "public self" of high self-monitors may nor may not be backed by a perceived "real me" on the inside. In many cases, it may be better to try to understand the self *in action* by looking at the ways people define themselves. Just as the answer to the question "Who am I?" varies for each person, the answer to the question "Do I have a single true self?" may vary, too.

Do you have a single true self? Give the question some thought the next time you go to a party!

Learning Check

1. Self-monitoring refers to how much people compare their self-image to the image others hold of them. T or F?
2. Low self-monitors tend to ask, "Who does this situation want me to be?" T or F?
3. In social situations, high self-monitors prefer clearly defined groups that do not create self-presentation conflicts. T or F?
4. A low self-monitor would probably agree with the statement, "I usually prefer to wear my most comfortable clothes, no matter what the occasion is." T or F?
5. "Handsome Tom Cruise look-alike seeking slim fashion-model type fox for flights of fancy." This ad would most likely be placed by a person high in self-monitoring. T or F?

Answers:
1. F 2. F 3. T 4. T 5. T

Chapter Summary

• Like other **psychodynamic** approaches, Sigmund Freud's **psychoanalytic theory** emphasizes unconscious forces and conflicts within the personality. In his theory, personality is made up of the **id, ego,** and **superego. Libido,** derived from the life instincts, is the primary energy running the personality. Conflicts within the personality may cause **neurotic anxiety** or **moral anxiety** and motivate use of **ego-defense mechanisms.** The personality operates on three levels; the **conscious, preconscious,** and **unconscious.**

• The Freudian view of personality development is based on a series of **psychosexual stages:** the **oral, anal, phallic,** and **genital** stages. **Fixation** at any stage can leave a lasting imprint on personality.

• Some of Freud's followers, known as **neo-Freudians,** altered and updated his theories. Others have developed related but separate psychodynamic theories.

• Alfred Adler proposed a more **social view** of personality, emphasizing **feelings of inferiority** and a **striving for superiority.** Striving for superiority and **compensation** for limitations creates a unique **style of life,** which is further altered by the **creative self.**

• Karen Horney countered some of Freud's male-oriented thinking and contended that emotional disturbances are rooted in **basic anxiety.** Basic anxiety can cause an overuse of one of the three modes of relating to others: moving **toward, away from,** or **against** them.

• Carl Jung broke away from Freud to develop his own theory, which includes such unique concepts as the **persona, extroversion** and **introversion,** the **personal unconscious,** and the **collective unconscious.** His most controversial ideas pertain to the existence of **archetypes,** such as the **anima** and **animus** and the **self archetype.**

• **Behavioral theories** of personality emphasize learning, conditioning, and immediate effects of the environment. **Learning theorists** generally reject the idea of stable personality "traits," preferring instead to stress the effects of **prior learning** and **situational determinants** of behavior.

• Learning theorists John Dollard and Neal Miller consider **habits** the basic core of personality. Habits express the combined effects of **drive, cue, response,** and **reward.**

• **Social learning theory** adds cognitive elements, such as perception, thinking, and understanding, to the behavioral view of personality. Such elements are exemplified by Julian Rotter's concepts of the **psychological situation, expectancies,** and **reinforcement value.** Some social learning theorists treat "conscience" as a case of **self-reinforcement.**

• The behavioristic view of personality development holds that **social reinforcement** in four situations is critical. The **critical situations** are **feeding, toilet** or **cleanliness training, sex training,** and **anger** or **aggression training. Identification** and **imitation** are of particular importance in sex training.

• **Humanistic theory** emphasizes **subjective experience** and needs for **self-actualization.** Abraham Maslow's study of **self-actualizers** showed that they have a variety of characteristics in common, ranging from efficient perceptions of reality to frequent peak experiences.

• Carl Rogers' theory views the **self** as an entity that emerges from the **phenomenal field.** Experiences that match the **self-image** are **symbolized** (admitted to consciousness), while those that are **incongruent** are excluded. The **incongruent person** has a highly unrealistic self-image. The **congruent,** or **fully functioning,** person is flexible and open to experiences and feelings.

• In the development of personality, humanists are primarily interested in the emergence of a **self-image** and in **self-evaluations.** As parents apply **conditions of worth** to children's behavior, thoughts, and feelings, children begin to do the same. Internalized conditions of worth then contribute to incongruence and interrupt the **organismic valuing process.**

• Self-actualization can be viewed as an ongoing **process** of personal growth, rather than a destination. In this sense, self-actualization may be actively pursued at any point in life.

• People vary in their desire to control the impression they make on others. **High self-monitoring** persons try hard to fit their public image to various situations. **Low self-monitors** are interested in accurately expressing their feelings, beliefs, and values, regardless of the situation. High self-monitoring raises questions about whether a single "true self" exists for all people.

Questions For Discussion

1. Can you describe an action you performed recently that seems to represent operation of the id, ego, or superego? How would a behaviorist or a humanist interpret the same event?

2. Can you cite a behavior or an experience that seems to support the existence of the unconscious or of unconscious motivation?

3. Can you cite observations that support Freud's scheme of psychosexual stages? Can you cite observations that contradict it?

4. Is "Mr. Clean" an anal-retentive?

5. As a child, whom did you identify with? What effect did this have on your personality?

6. Freud thought that adolescent males who clash with adult male authority figures (teachers, ministers, policemen, and so forth) are experiencing a carryover of the Oedipus conflict. What do you think?

7. What experiences have you had that have contributed to personal growth? What experiences set you back or were otherwise negative in their effects? Which personality theory best explains the differences between these experiences?

8. The film *Close Encounters of the Third Kind* culminates with a visit to earth by a magnificent round spaceship. The ship opens to reveal childlike creatures who have come to take a chosen few to a new life among the stars. What archetypal symbols are represented by these images? Can you think of other films, works of art, or images that seem to symbolize Jungian archetypes?

9. Presently, what are the most prominent "possible selves" you visualize? How have these self-images influenced your behavior?

10. Most people pay at least some attention to managing the impression they make on others. Do you think that preoccupation with one's public self (high self-monitoring) means that a person has no single "true self"? Or, could it be that the thought "I like to look good to others" is a core element of the person's true self-image?

Chapter 18

Intelligence

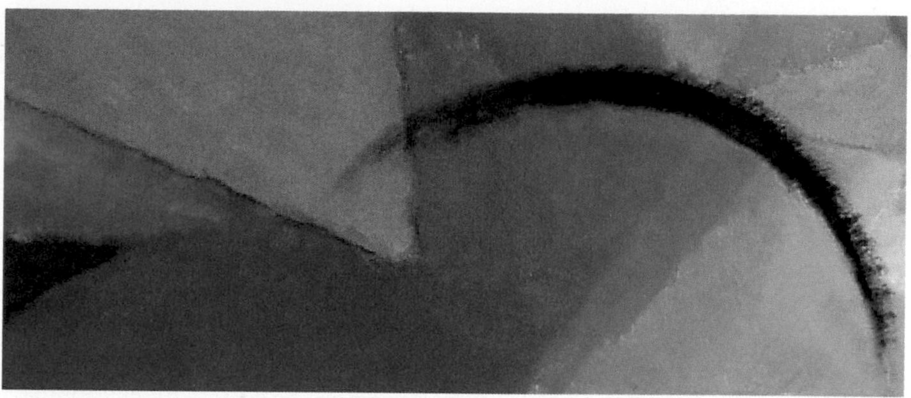

In This Chapter

Defining intelligence
Qualities of good tests
Intelligence tests
The concept of IQ
Variations in IQ
The mentally gifted
Mental retardation
Heredity and environment
Applications: IQ in perspective
Exploration: The Larry P. case

Chapter Preview

What Day Is It?

Ask George in which recent years April 21 fell on a Sunday. Without hesitation, he will answer "1985, 1974, 1968, 1963, 1957, 1946." Surprisingly, this gives only the slightest hint of his ability. If encouraged, George will go back as far as 1700—with complete accuracy! His calendar calculations cover a range of at least 6000 years. With equal ease he can identify February 15, 2002, as a Friday or August 28, 1591, as a Wednesday.

Question: Is he a genius?

George's abilities are all the more amazing in view of the fact that he is mentally retarded and cannot add, subtract, multiply, or divide even simple numbers (Horwitz et al., 1965). George's strange talent is an example of the savant syndrome, *in which an island of brilliance is found in a sea of retardation. The savant syndrome occurs when a person of subnormal intelligence shows highly developed mental ability in one or more very limited areas.*

Question: How could George be retarded and have this ability both at the same time?

The striking contrast between George's general retardation and his unusual mental ability is a fitting introduction to the challenge psychologists face in trying to define and measure intelligence. Quite frankly, we are still searching for answers to questions like these: Is intelligence a general trait or a collection of specific skills? Is intelligence determined by the genetic "wheel of fortune" or is it nurtured by environment? Is it possible to construct an intelligence test that is fair to all people? How important is intelligence for "success"? Because our understanding of intelligence is rapidly changing, we cannot hope to give final answers.

For the sake of clarity, this chapter is divided into two parts. First, we will assume that intelligence can *be measured, and we will use test results as a way to answer questions about intelligence. Later, we will consider questions that have been raised about intelligence tests and the meaning of their results.*

Survey Questions

- How do psychologists define intelligence?
- What are the qualities of a good psychological test?
- What are typical IQ tests like?
- How do IQ scores relate to gender, age, and occupation?
- What does IQ tell us about genius?
- What causes mental retardation?
- Does heredity or environment have the greatest effect on intelligence?
- Are IQ tests fair to all racial and cultural groups?

Defining Intelligence—Intelligence Is . . . It's . . . You Know, It's . . .

Like so many important concepts in psychology, intelligence cannot be observed directly: It has no mass, occupies no space, and is invisible. Nevertheless, we feel certain it exists. Consider the following two individuals:

> When she was 14 months old, Anne H. wrote her own name. She taught herself to read at age 2. At age 5, she astounded her kindergarten teacher by walking into class with a stack of encyclopedias—which she proceeded to read. At 10 she breezed through an entire high school algebra course in 12 hours.

> At age 10 Billy A. can write his name and can count, but he has trouble with simple addition and subtraction problems and finds multiplication impossible. He has been held back in school twice and is still incapable of doing the work his 8-year-old classmates find easy. His teachers have suggested placing him in a special educational program for slow learners.

Anne is considered a genius; Billy, a slow learner. There seems little doubt that they differ in intelligence.

Question: Wait! Anne's ability is obvious, but how do we know that Billy isn't just lazy?

This dilemma is one that **Alfred Binet** faced in 1904. The minister of education in Paris had given Binet the task of finding a way to distinguish slower students from the more capable (or the capable but lazy). In a flash of brilliance, Binet and an associate created a test made up of "intellectual" questions and problems. Next, they learned which questions an average child could answer at each age. Children low in intellectual ability were identified by below-par scores on the test.

Binet's approach gave rise to modern intelligence tests. At the same time, it launched 80 years of debate that has often been heated and at times bitter. Part of the debate is related to the basic difficulty in defining intelligence.

Question: Is there an accepted definition of intelligence?

Most psychologists would probably agree with David Wechsler's general description of **intelligence** as the *global capacity to act purposefully, to think rationally, and to deal effectively with the environment*. To add to the definition, Table 18–1 shows results from a recent survey of 1020 experts on intelligence. At least three-quarters of this group agreed that the listed elements are important parts of intelligence (Snyderman & Rothman, 1987).

Beyond this, there is so much disagreement that many psychologists simply accept an **operational definition** of intelligence (Fig. 18–1). (We define a concept operationally by specifying what procedures will be used to measure it.) By selecting test items, a psychologist is saying in a very direct way, "This is what I mean by intelligence." A test that measures memory, reasoning, and verbal fluency offers a very different definition of intelligence than one that measures strength of grip, shoe size, length of the nose, or the person's best Pac-Man score.

Reliability and Validity Suppose that a deranged psychologist, Professor Ike Q. Tester, decides to write an intelligence test (the *I. Q. Tester IQ Test*). As a concerned citizen, there are two questions you should ask about Tester's test: "Is it *reliable?*" and "Is it *valid?*"

Question: What does reliability refer to?

A reliable bathroom scale gives the same weight on several successive weighings. For a test to be **reliable,** it must

Table 18–1 Important Elements of Intelligence

DESCRIPTION	PERCENT OF AGREEMENT
Abstract thinking or reasoning	99.3
Problem-solving ability	97.7
Capacity to acquire knowledge	96.0
Memory	80.5
Adaptation to one's environment	77.2

(Adapted from Snyderman & Rothman, 1987)

yield the same score, or close to the same score, each time it is given to the same individual. In other words, the scores should be consistent and highly correlated. It is easy to see that a test has little value if it is unreliable. Imagine a medical test for pregnancy, for instance, that gives positive and negative responses for the same woman on the same day.

To check the reliability of the *I. Q. Tester IQ Test,* we could administer it to a large group of people. Then each person could be tested again a week later to establish *test-retest reliability*. Reliability is also sometimes measured by comparing the score on one-half of the test items to the score on the other half (*split-half reliability*). Likewise, if Tester offered two versions of the test, we could correlate scores on one to scores on the other for each person (*equivalent-forms reliability*).

By comparing such scores, we find that the Tester test is quite reliable. In fact, the scores are identical each time the test is given: Everyone scores zero (except Professor Tester, who scores 100 percent and thereby proclaims himself the only human with any intelligence). So, let's concede to Tester that his test is reliable (but for the wrong reasons). A more important question then becomes, Is the test valid?

Obviously, we have been playing with a silly example. A test has **validity** when it measures what it claims to measure. By no stretch of the imagination could a test of intelligence be valid if the person who wrote it is the only one who can pass it.

Question: How is validity established?

Validity is usually demonstrated by comparing test scores to actual performance. This is called *criterion validity*. A test of legal aptitude, for example, might be validated by comparing scores on the test to grades in law school. If high scores correlate with high grades or some other standard of success, the test may be considered valid. Unfortunately, many tests you will encounter, such as those found in magazines or offered by commercial self-improvement courses, have little or no validity.

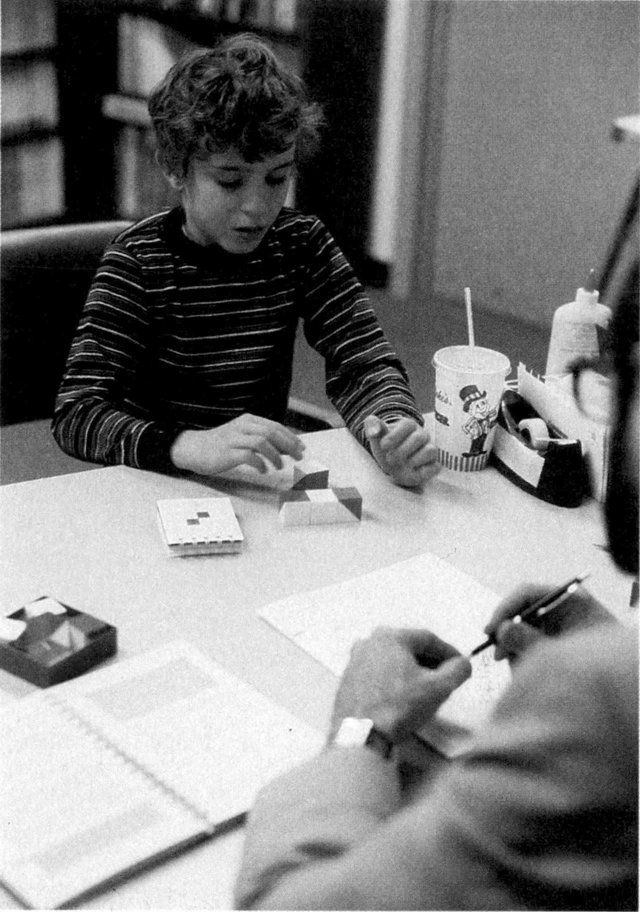

Fig. 18–1 *Modern intelligence tests are widely used to measure intellectual abilities. When properly administered, such tests provide an operational definition of intelligence.*

Tester's Last Stand Let's return to Professor Tester for a final point. Although he admits that his test has problems, Professor Tester claims that at least it is **objective.** Is he right? Actually, he might be. If the test gives the same score when corrected by different people, it is objective. However, objectivity is not enough to guarantee a fair test. To be useful, a psychological test must also be *standardized.*

Test **standardization** refers to two things. First, it means that standard procedures are used in giving the test to all people. That is, the instructions, answer forms, amount of time to work, and so forth, are the same for all test takers. Second, it means finding the **norm,** or average score, made by a large group of people like those for whom the test was designed. Without standardization, it would be unfair to compare the scores of people taking a test on different occasions. And without norms, there would be no way to tell if a score is high, low, or average.

Later in this chapter we will address the question of whether intelligence tests are valid. For now, let's take a practical approach by examining some widely used standardized tests and the meaning of their scores.

● Testing Intelligence—The IQ and You

American psychologists quickly saw the value of Binet's test. In 1916, **Lewis Terman** and others at Stanford University revised it for use in this country. After several more revisions, the **Stanford-Binet Intelligence Scale** is still widely used. The Stanford-Binet assumes that intellectual ability in childhood improves as age increases. As a result, the Stanford-Binet is really a graded set of more difficult tests, one for each age group.

The age-ranked questions of the Stanford-Binet allow a person's **mental age** to be measured. For example, at ages 8 or 9, very few children can define the word *connection*. At age 10, 10 percent can. At age 13, 60 percent can. In other words, the ability to define *connection* indicates mental ability equal to that of the average 13-year-old and gives a mental age of 13 (on this single item). Table 18–2 is a sample of items that persons of average intelligence can answer at various ages.

Mental age is a good measure of actual ability, but it says nothing about whether overall intelligence is high or low. To know the meaning of mental age, **chronological age** (age in years) must also be considered. Mental age can then be related to actual age to yield an **IQ,** or **intelligence quotient.** When the Stanford-Binet was first used in the United States, IQ was defined as mental age (MA) divided by chronological age (CA) and multiplied by 100:

$$\frac{\mathbf{MA}}{\mathbf{CA}} \times 100 = \mathbf{IQ}$$

An advantage of the IQ is that intelligence can be compared among children with different chronological and

Table 18–2 Sample Items from the Stanford-Binet Intelligence Scale

2 years old	On a large paper doll, points out the hair, mouth, feet, ears, nose, hands, and eyes. When shown a tower built of four blocks, builds one like it.
3 years old	When shown a bridge built of three blocks, builds one like it. When shown a drawing of a circle, copies it with a pencil.
4 years old	Fills in the missing word when asked, "Brother is a boy; sister is a ____." "In daytime it is light; at night it is ____." Answers correctly when asked, "Why do we have houses?" "Why do we have books?"
5 years old	Defines *ball, hat,* and *stove.* When shown a drawing of a square, copies it with a pencil.
9 years old	Answers correctly when examiner says, "In an old graveyard in Spain they have discovered a small skull which they believe to be that of Christopher Columbus when he was about 10 years old. What is foolish about that?" Answers correctly when asked, "Tell me the name of a color that rhymes with head." "Tell me a number that rhymes with tree."
Adult	Can describe the difference between laziness and idleness, poverty and misery, character and reputation. Answers correctly when asked, "Which direction would you have to face so your right hand would be toward the north?"

(Terman & Merrill, 1960)

mental ages. For instance, a 10-year-old child with a mental age of 12 has an IQ of 120:

$$\frac{(\text{MA})\ 12}{(\text{CA})\ 10} \times 100 = 120\ (\text{IQ})$$

A second child having a mental age of 12, but with a chronological age of 12, would have an IQ of 100:

$$\frac{(\text{MA})\ 12}{(\text{CA})\ 12} \times 100 = 100\ (\text{IQ})$$

The IQ shows that the younger child is brighter than his 12-year-old friend, even though their intellectual skills are actually the same. Notice that IQ equals 100 when MA = CA. An IQ score of 100 is therefore defined as average intelligence.

Question: Then does a person with an IQ score below 100 have below-average intelligence?

Not unless the IQ is far below 100. An IQ of 100 is the *mathematical* average (or mean) for such scores. *Average intelligence* is usually defined as any score from 90 to 109. The important point is that IQ scores will be over 100 when mental age is higher than age in years (Fig. 18–2), while IQ scores below 100 occur when age in years exceeds mental age. An example of the second situation would be a 15-year-old with an MA of 12:

$$\frac{12}{15} \times 100 = 80\ (\text{IQ})$$

The preceding calculations are offered to give you insight into the meaning of IQ scores. However, there is no longer any need to calculate IQs for many modern tests. Instead, a **deviation IQ** score is used. To find a deviation IQ, we determine how far above or below average a person's score is, relative to others taking the test. (For more information, see Appendix B.) Tables supplied with the test are then used to convert a person's *relative standing* in the group to an IQ score. This approach avoids certain troublesome errors that occur when IQ is calculated directly.

Fig. 18–2 *With a score of 230, Marilyn Mach vos Savant has the highest IQ ever officially recorded. When she was only 7 years and 9 months old, vos Savant could answer questions that the average 18-year-old can answer. At ages 8, 9, and 10, she got perfect scores on the Stanford-Binet scale. Now in her early 40s, she is capitalizing on her celebrity by giving lectures and writing books (Lemley, 1986).*

Compare: Terms Used To Define IQ

Mental age: A measure of mental ability defined in terms of the average capabilities of individuals at each age; that is, mental ability apart from age in years.

Chronological age: One's age in years.

Intelligence quotient (IQ): An index of intelligence defined as a person's mental age divided by his or her chronological age and multiplied by 100.

Deviation IQ: An IQ obtained statistically from a person's relative standing in his or her age group; that is, how far above or below average the person's score is relative to other scores.

Question: How old do children have to be before their IQ scores become stable?

Stability of IQ IQ scores are not very dependable until about age 6 (Honzik, 1983). The correlation between IQ scores obtained at age 2 and those obtained at age 18 is only .31. (Recall that a perfect correlation is 1.00, and a correlation of 0.00 occurs when scores are unrelated.) With increasing age, IQs become more reliable. The average change (median change) in IQ on retesting is roughly 5 points in either direction. However, children may show small ups and downs in tested intelligence as they dèvelop. No typical pattern exists, and in some cases changes in IQ of 15 points or more may take place. Overall, though, changes are usually quite small after middle childhood.

Question: How much does aging affect the IQ?

Since IQ reflects education, maturity, and experience, as well as native intellectual capacity, test scores show a small gradual increase until about age 40 (Eichorn et al., 1981). This trend, of course, is an average. Some people show fairly large gains in IQ, whereas others experience sizable losses. How do the two groups differ? In general, persons who show the largest IQ gains were exposed to stimulating intellectual experiences during early adulthood. Those who decline most typically suffer from chronic illness, drinking problems, or unstimulating lifestyles (Honzik, 1984).

Some studies of IQ have recorded slow declines after middle age, while others indicate little or no change due to aging (Schaie, 1980). As you may recall from Chapter 15, these contradictory results can be explained in this way: When general information or comprehension is emphasized, there is little decline in IQ until advanced age; however, test items requiring speed, rapid insight, or perceptual flexibility show earlier losses and a rapid decline after middle age (Baltes & Schaie, 1974). Overall, age-related losses are small for most healthy, well-educated individuals (Schaie, 1980).

Perhaps the most intriguing link between IQ and aging is the observation that impending death may be signaled by marked changes in brain function. Certain intellectual skills have been shown to decline abruptly about 5 years before death. This **terminal decline** in IQ can be measured even when the person appears to be in good health (Jarvik et al., 1973; Suedfeld & Piedrahita, 1984).

Question: Is the Stanford-Binet the only intelligence test?

The Wechsler Test A widely used alternative to the Stanford-Binet is the **Wechsler Adult Intelligence Scale–**

Table 18–3 Sample Items Similar to Those Used on the WAIS–R

Verbal Subtests	**Sample Items**
Information	How many wings does a bird have? Who wrote *Paradise Lost*?
Digit span	Repeat from memory a series of digits, such as 3 1 0 6 7 4 2 5, after hearing it once.
General Comprehension	What is the advantage of keeping money in a bank? Why is copper often used in electrical wires?
Arithmetic	Three men divided 18 golf balls equally among themselves. How many golf balls did each man receive? If 2 apples cost 15¢, what will be the cost of a dozen apples?
Similarities	In what way are a lion and a tiger alike? In what way are a saw and a hammer alike?
Vocabulary	This test consists simply of asking, "What is a ____?" or "What does ____ mean?" The words cover a wide range of difficulty or familiarity.
Performance Subtests	**Description of Item**
Picture arrangement	Arrange a series of cartoon panels to make a meaningful story.
Picture completion	What is missing from these pictures?
Block design	Copy designs with blocks (as shown at right).
Object assembly	Put together a jigsaw puzzle.
Digit symbol	(see below)

1	2	3	4
X	III	I	0

Fill in the symbols:

3	4	1	3	4	2	1	2

(Courtesy of The Psychological Corporation.)

Revised, or **WAIS-R.** This test also has a form for use with children, called the **Wechsler Intelligence Scale for Children–Revised (WISC-R).**

The Wechsler tests are generally similar to the Stanford-Binet, but differ in some important ways. The WAIS-R is specifically designed to test adult intelligence. Also, both the WISC-R and the WAIS-R rate **performance** (nonverbal) intelligence in addition to **verbal** intelligence. The Stanford-Binet only gives one overall IQ, whereas the Wechsler tests can be broken down to reveal strengths and weaknesses in various areas. The intellectual skills revealed by the Wechsler tests and some sample test items are listed in Table 18–3.

Compare: Two Types of Intelligence Measured by the WAIS-R

Performance intelligence: Intelligence as demonstrated in solving puzzles, assembling objects, completing pictures, and performing other nonverbal tasks.

Verbal intelligence: Intelligence as revealed by answering questions involving vocabulary, general information, arithmetic, and other language- or symbol-oriented tasks.

Group Tests Both the Stanford-Binet and the Wechsler tests are **individual intelligence tests** that must be given by a trained specialist. Other tests of intelligence are designed for use with large groups of people. **Group intelligence tests** are usually in paper-and-pencil form. Typically, they require test takers to read, to follow instructions, and to solve problems of logic, reasoning, mathematics, or spatial skills. The first group intelligence test was the *Army Alpha,* developed for use in rating World War I military inductees. As you can see in Table 18–4, intelligence testing has come a long way since then.

If you're wondering if you have ever taken an intelligence test, the answer is probably yes. The *Scholastic Aptitude Test (SAT),* the *American College Test (ACT),* and the *College Qualification Test (CQT)* are all group tests that can be used to estimate intelligence as well as a person's chances for success in college.

Table 18–4 Items from the Army Alpha Subtest on "Common Sense"

The *Army Alpha* was given to World War I army recruits in the United States as a way to identify potential officers. In these sample questions, note the curious mixture of folk wisdom, scientific information, and moralism (Kessen & Cahan, 1986). Other parts of the test were more like modern intelligence tests.

1. If plants are dying for lack of rain, you should
   - ☐ water them
   - ☐ ask a florist's advice
   - ☐ put fertilizer around them
2. If the grocer should give you too much money in making change, what is the right thing to do?
   - ☐ buy some candy for him with it
   - ☐ give it to the first poor man you meet
   - ☐ tell him of his mistake
3. If you saw a train approaching a broken track, you should
   - ☐ telephone for an ambulance
   - ☐ signal the engineer to stop the train
   - ☐ look for a piece of rail to fit in
4. Some men lose their breath on high mountains because
   - ☐ the wind blows their breath away
   - ☐ the air is too rare
   - ☐ it is always cold there
5. We see no stars at noon because
   - ☐ they have moved to the other side of the earth
   - ☐ they are much fainter than the sun
   - ☐ they are hidden behind the sky

Learning Check

Check your comprehension before you continue reading.

1. The first successful intelligence test was developed by ______________________.
2. If we define intelligence by writing a test, we are using
   a. a circular definition *b.* an abstract definition *c.* an operational definition *d.* a chronological definition
3. Place an R or a V after each operation to indicate if it would be used to establish the reliability or the validity of a test.
   a. Compare score on one-half of test items to score on the other half. ( )
   b. Compare scores on test to grades, performance ratings, or other measures. ( )
   c. Compare scores from the test after administering it on two separate occasions. ( )
   d. Compare scores on alternate forms of the test. ( )

4. IQ was originally defined as ____ × 100.

5. The ability to answer general information and comprehension questions shows the most rapid decline during aging. T or F?

6. The WAIS-R is a group intelligence test. T or F?

7. Establishing norms and uniform procedures for administering a test are elements of standardization. T or F?

8. Scores on modern intelligence tests are based on one's deviation IQ (relative standing among test takers) rather than on the ratio between mental age and chronological age. T or F?

Answers:

1. Alfred Binet **2.** *c* **3.** *a.* (R), *b.* (V), *c.* (R), *d.* (R) **4.** MA/CA **5.** F **6.** F **7.** T **8.** T

Variations in Intelligence—The Numbers Game

Based on scores from a large number of randomly selected people, IQ ranges have been classified as shown in Table 18–5. A look at the percentages reveals a definite pattern. The distribution of IQs approximates a **normal** (bell-shaped) **curve,** in which the majority of scores fall close to the average, with far fewer at the extremes. Figure 18–3 shows this characteristic of measured intelligence.

Question: On the average, do males and females differ in intelligence?

Sex IQ does not give a definite answer to this question because intelligence test items are selected to be equally difficult for both sexes. It seems safe to assume that men and women do not differ in overall intelligence, and no significant IQ difference has been found. However, tests like the WAIS-R allow a comparison of the intellectual strengths and weaknesses of men and women. Here a difference does emerge: Women perform better on test items that require verbal ability, vocabulary, and rote learning; men are best at items that require visualization of spatial relationships and arithmetic reasoning (Wechsler, 1958).

It is important to realize that such differences are small and based on *averages*. Many women are better than men at math, and many men are better than women at verbal skills. Scores for men and women overlap so much that it is impossible to predict if any one individual will be good or bad at math or language simply from knowing his or her gender (Sapolsky, 1987).

Table 18–5 Distribution of Adult IQ Scores on WAIS–R

IQ	DESCRIPTION	PERCENT
Above 130	Very superior	2.2
120–129	Superior	6.7
110–119	Bright normal	16.1
90–109	Average	50.0
80–89	Dull normal	16.1
70–79	Borderline	6.7
Below 70	Mentally retarded	2.2

(Wechsler, 1958)

Question: How do IQ scores relate to success in school, jobs, and other undertakings?

School and Occupation IQ differences of a few points tell little about intellectual potential. But when a broader range of scores is considered, meaningful differences emerge. The correlation between IQ and school grades is .50—a sizable association. If measured intelligence were the only factor affecting grades, the association might be even higher. However, motivation, special talents, off-campus educational opportunities, and many other factors influence school grades and success.

Interestingly, IQ is not as good a predictor of out-of-school achievements such as art, music, creative writing, dramatics, science, and leadership. Tests related to creativity, such as tests of ideational fluency, are much more strongly related to such achievements (Wallach, 1985).

As you might expect, there is also a relationship between IQ and job classification. Persons holding white-collar, professional positions average higher IQs than those in blue-collar occupational settings. For example, accountants average about 120 in IQ and miners about 90 (Anastasi & Foley, 1958). It is important to note, however, that there is a range of IQ scores in all occupations. Many people of high intelligence, because of choice or circumstance, can be found in "low-ranking" jobs (Fig. 18–4).

It is tempting to interpret the link between IQ and occupation as evidence that professional jobs require more intelligence. This interpretation is dangerous because IQ tests require the same types of mental gymnastics needed for success in school. Since higher-status jobs often require an academic degree, the apparent connection between IQ and job status may be misleading. Selection procedures for professional jobs appear to be biased in favor of a particular type of intelligence, namely, the kind measured by intelligence tests.

When IQs are extreme—below 70 or above 140—influences on adjustment and one's potential for success become unmistakable. Only about 3 percent of the population fall in these ranges, but this translates to millions of people who have exceptionally high or low IQs. Discussions of the mentally gifted and mentally retarded follow.

Fig. 18–4 *John Kirtley has an IQ score of 174, yet he prefers to do custodial work, feeling that his unusual intellect would be "used" by his employers if he pursued a technical occupation.*

● The Mentally Gifted—Is Genius Next to Insanity?

Question: How high is the IQ of a genius?

Only about 1 percent of the population scores above 140 on IQ tests. A person scoring this high is at least "gifted," and depending on the standards used, he or she may be considered a "genius." However, some psychologists reserve the term *genius* for even higher IQs or for other qualities, such as exceptional creativity or insight (Sternberg & Davidson, 1983).

Are high IQ scores in childhood associated with later ability? To directly answer this question, Lewis Terman selected 1500 children with IQs of 140 or more. By following the development of this gifted group into adulthood, Terman countered a number of popular misconceptions about genius.

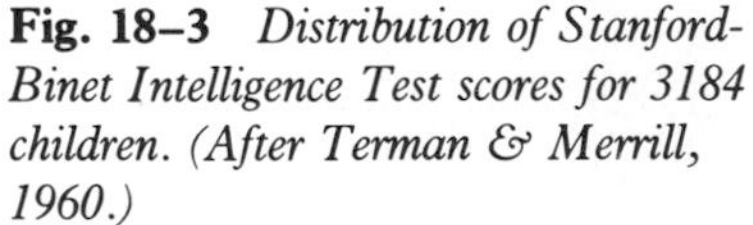

Fig. 18–3 *Distribution of Stanford-Binet Intelligence Test scores for 3184 children. (After Terman & Merrill, 1960.)*

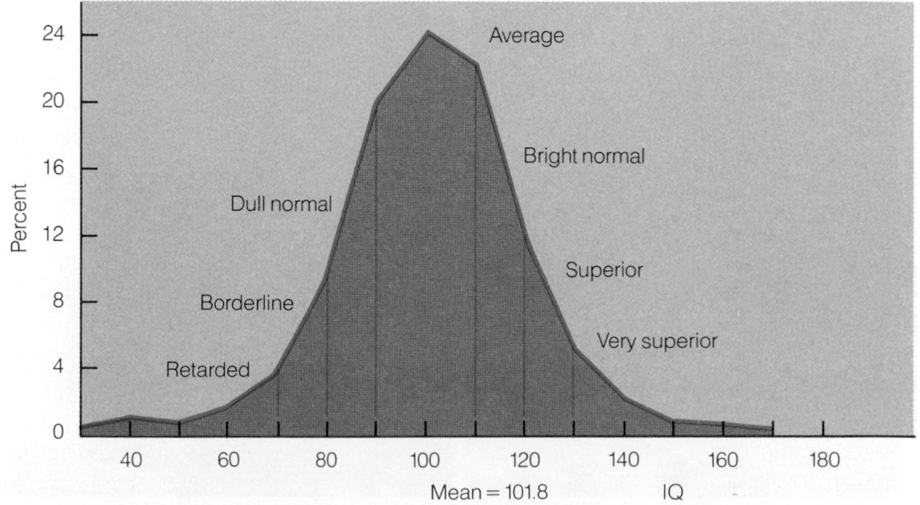

Misconception: The gifted tend to be peculiar, socially backward people.
Fact: On the contrary, Terman's gifted subjects were socially well adjusted and showed above-average leadership capacity.
Misconception: "Early ripe means later rot": The gifted tend to fizzle out as adults.
Fact: This is false. When retested as adults, Terman's subjects again scored in the upper IQ ranges.
Misconception: The very bright are usually physically inferior "eggheads" or weaklings.
Fact: This is also a misconception. As a group, the gifted were above average in height, weight, and physical appearance.
Misconception: The highly intelligent person is more susceptible to mental illness ("Genius is next to insanity").
Fact: Terman demonstrated conclusively that the gifted have better than average mental health records, indicating a greater *resistance* to mental illness. However, the very intelligent (IQ of over 180) may have social and behavioral adjustment problems as children (Janos & Robinson, 1985).
Misconception: Intelligence has nothing to do with success, especially in practical matters.
Fact: The later success of Terman's subjects was the most striking finding of the study. Far more of them than average had completed college, earned advanced degrees, and held professional positions. As a group, the gifted had produced dozens of books, thousands of scientific articles, and hundreds of short stories and other publications (Terman & Oden, 1959). As noted earlier, IQ scores are not generally good predictors of real-world success. However, when scores are in the gifted range, the likelihood of outstanding achievement does seem to be higher.

Question: Were all of the gifted children superior as adults?

No. Remember that high IQ reveals *potential*, not achievement. A high IQ is no guarantee of success. Some of the gifted had committed crimes, were unemployable, or were poorly adjusted.

Question: How did the more successful subjects differ from the less successful?

A recent follow-up found that the highly successful subjects were more *persistent* and *motivated* to succeed (Feldman, 1982). The meaning of this finding is clear: As one educator put it, "No one is paid to sit around being capable of achievement—what you do is always more

Fig. 18–5 *It is wise to remember that there are many ways in which a child may be gifted. Many schools now offer Gifted and Talented Education programs for students with a variety of special abilities—not just for those who score well on IQ tests.*

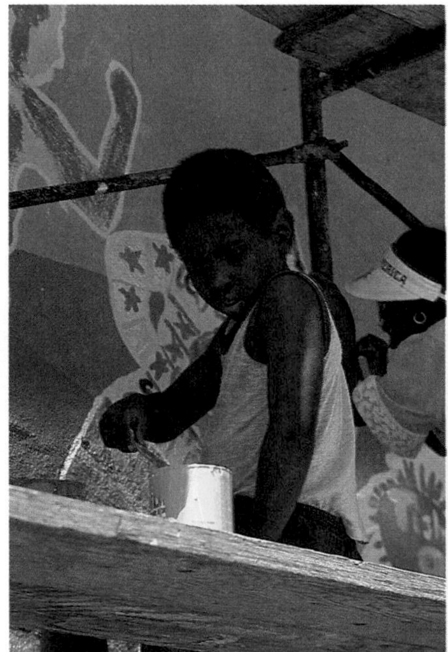

important than what you should be able to do" (Whimbey, 1980). There are a lot of people walking around with high IQs who have accomplished very little.

Question: How might a parent spot an unusually bright child?

Early signs of giftedness include a tendency to seek out and identify with older children and adults; an early fascination with explanations and problem solving; talking in complete sentences as early as 2 or 3 years of age; an unusually good memory; precocious talent in art, music, or number skills; an early interest in books, along with early reading (often by age 3); showing of kindness, understanding, and cooperation toward others (Alvino et al., 1985).

Notice that this list contains behavior other than straight "academic" intelligence. Children may be gifted in ways other than having a high IQ (Sternberg & Davidson, 1985). In fact, if artistic talent, mechanical aptitude, musical aptitude, athletic potential, and so on, were considered, 19 out of 20 children could be labeled "gifted" in some respect (Fig. 18–5) (Feldman & Bratton, 1972). It may therefore be a mistake to identify giftedness primarily with IQ (Alvino et al., 1985). Such limited definitions of giftedness may shortchange many children with special talents or potentials (see Highlight 18–1).

Being gifted in the sense of having a high IQ is not without its problems, particularly in childhood. The gifted child may become bored in a classroom designed for average children. Boredom can lead to behavioral problems or to clashes with teachers who consider the gifted child a show-off or smart aleck. The extremely bright child may also find classmates less stimulating than older children or adults (Alvino et al., 1985). In recognition of these problems, many school systems now provide special Gifted and Talented Education (GATE) programs and classes for gifted children. Such programs combine classroom enrichment with fast-paced instruction (Horowitz & O'Brien, 1986).

● Mental Retardation—A Difference That Makes a Difference

A person with mental abilities far below average is termed **mentally retarded** or **developmentally disabled.** An IQ of approximately 70 or below is regarded as the dividing line for retardation. However, a person's ability to perform **adaptive behaviors** (such as dressing, eating, communicating, shopping, and working) also figures into evaluating retardation (DSM-III-R, 1987; Haywood et al., 1982).

● HIGHLIGHT 18–1
Frames of Mind—Seven Intelligences?

At an elementary school, a student who is two grades behind in reading shows his teacher how to solve a difficult computer programming problem. In a nearby room, one of his classmates, who is poor in math, plays an intricate piece of music on a piano. Both of these children show clear signs of intelligence. And yet, each might score below average on a traditional IQ test. Such observations have convinced many psychologists that it is time to forge new, broader definitions of intelligence. Their basic goal is to better predict "real-world" success—not just the likelihood of success in school (Sternberg, 1985).

One such psychologist is Howard Gardner of Harvard University. Gardner (1985) theorizes that there are actually 7 different kinds of intelligence. These include abilities in language, logic and math, visual and spatial thinking, music, bodily-kinesthetic skills (such as dance or athletics), intrapersonal skills (self-knowledge), and interpersonal skills (leadership, social abilities). Most of us are probably strong in only a few types of intelligence. In contrast, geniuses like Albert Einstein seem to be able to use all of the intelligences, as needed, to solve problems.

If Gardner's theory is correct, traditional IQ tests measure only a part of real-world intelligence—namely, linguistic, logical-mathematical, and spatial abilities. A further implication is that our schools may be wasting a lot of human potential. For example, some children might find it easier to learn math or reading if these topics were tied into art, music, dance, drama, and so on.

Not all psychologists agree with Gardner's broader definition of intelligence. His view, in fact, is at odds with studies that suggest that scores on IQ tests mainly reflect an underlying "general intelligence" or general ability factor (often referred to as *g*) (Canavan et al., 1986). This *g-factor* is said to explain the high correlations found among scores on various tests of intellectual ability and achievement. Gardner's reply would probably be that such correlations only show how narrowly traditional tests define intelligence. Whether or not he is right, it seems likely that in the future, intelligence will not be so strongly equated with IQ.

Below an IQ of 70, the severity of retardation is classified as shown in Table 18–6. The listed IQ ranges are approximate because IQ scores normally vary a few points. The terms in the right-hand column are listed only to give you a general impression of each IQ range. Unless they are used cautiously, such terms can needlessly limit the educational goals of retarded persons (DSM-III-R, 1987).

Question: Are the retarded usually placed in institutions?

No. Total care is only necessary for the **profoundly** retarded. Many of these individuals live within the community in group homes or with their families. The **severely** and **moderately** retarded are capable of mastering basic language skills and routine self-help skills. Many become self-supporting by working in *sheltered workshops* (special simplified work environments). The **mildly** retarded (about 85 percent of all those affected) benefit from carefully structured and supervised education. As adults, they are capable of living alone and may marry (although they tend to have difficulties with many of the demands of adult life).

It is important to realize that the developmentally disabled have no handicap where feelings are concerned. They are sensitive to rejection and easily hurt by teasing or ridicule. Likewise, they respond warmly to love and acceptance. Professionals working with the retarded emphasize their rights to self-respect and to a place in the community. This is especially important during childhood, when the support of others adds greatly to the person's chances of becoming a well-adjusted member of society (Fig. 18–6).

Fig. 18–6 *This youngster is a participant in the Special Olympics—an athletic event for the mentally retarded. It is often said of the Special Olympics that "everyone is a winner—participants, coaches, and spectators."*

Question: What causes mental retardation?

Causes of Retardation

About 50 percent of all cases of mental retardation are *organic,* or related to physical disorders, including **birth injuries** (such as a lack of oxygen), **fetal damage** (from maternal drug abuse, disease, or infection), **metabolic disorders** (such as cretinism and phenylketonuria, discussed in the next section), and **genetic abnormalities** (DSM-III-R, 1987). Severe levels of retardation are likely to be associated with one or more such biological abnormalities.

Table 18–6 Levels of Mental Retardation

IQ RANGE	DEGREE OF RETARDATION	EDUCATIONAL CLASSIFICATION
50–55 to 70	Mild	Educable
35–40 to 50–55	Moderate	Trainable
20–25 to 35–40	Severe	Dependent
Below 20–25	Profound	Life-support

(DSM-III-R, 1987; Robinson & Robinson, 1976)

Family Environment In 30 to 40 percent of cases, no known biological problem can be identified. In many such cases the degree of retardation is mild, in the 50 to 70 IQ range, and quite often other family members are also mildly retarded. **Familial retardation,** as this is called, occurs most often in very poor households. In some such homes, nutrition, early stimulation, medical care, intellectual stimulation, and emotional support are inadequate. This suggests that familial retardation is based largely on an impoverished environment. Thus, many cases of retardation might be prevented by better nutrition, education, and early childhood enrichment programs.

To conclude our discussion, let's briefly return to organic retardation for a look at several distinctive problems.

Phenylketonuria (PKU) Phenylketonuria (FEN-ul-KEET-uh-NURE-ee-ah) is a genetically induced lack of an important enzyme. Lack of the enzyme causes the buildup of phenylpyruvic acid (a destructive chemical) within the body. If PKU goes untreated, severe retardation typically occurs by age 3 (Kopp & Parmelee, 1979). PKU is now easily detected in babies by medical testing during the first month of life. It can usually be controlled by a special diet low in foods containing substances the child's body can't handle.

Microcephaly Microcephaly (MY-kro-SEF-ah-lee) means small-headedness. The microcephalic suffers a rare abnormality in which the skull is extremely small or fails to grow. The brain is forced to develop in a limited space, causing severe retardation that usually requires the individual to be placed in an institution. The microcephalic is typically affectionate, well behaved, and easy to work with.

Hydrocephaly Hydrocephaly (HI-dro-SEF-ah-lee: water on the brain) is caused by a buildup of cerebrospinal fluid within brain cavities. Pressure from this fluid can damage the brain and greatly enlarge the head. Hydrocephaly is not uncommon—about 8000 babies are born with the problem each year in the United States. Thanks to new medical procedures, most of these infants now will lead normal lives. Treatment involves surgically implanting a tube that drains fluid from the brain into the abdomen. If this is done within the first 3 months of life, retardation can usually be avoided.

Cretinism Cretinism (KREET-un-iz-um) is a form of retardation that develops in infancy due to an insufficient supply of thyroid hormone. In some parts of the world, cretinism is caused by too little iodine in the diet (iodine is necessary for normal thyroid function). Widespread use of iodized salt makes this cause of the condition rare in the industrialized nations. Cretinism causes stunted physical and intellectual growth that cannot be corrected unless detected early. Fortunately, it is easily and routinely detected in infancy and may be treated by thyroid hormone replacement.

Down Syndrome The disorder known as Down syndrome causes moderate to severe retardation and a shortened life expectancy (usually around 40 years) in 1 out of 800 babies. Distinctive features of this problem, once referred to as mongolism, are almond-shaped eyes, a slightly protruding tongue, stubby hands, a stocky build, and sometimes a deep crease on the palm of the hand. It is now known that Down children also have an extra chromosome. That is, cells in the child's body have 47 chromosomes, instead of the usual 46. This condition results from flaws in the parents' egg or sperm cells. Thus, while Down syndrome is *genetic,* it is not usually *hereditary* and does not "run in the family."

A very significant factor in Down syndrome appears to be the age of parents at the time of conception. The reproductive cells of older men and women are more prone to errors during cell division, which raises the odds that an extra chromosome will be present. Mothers in their early 20s have about 1 chance in 2000 of giving birth to a Down syndrome baby. At age 40, the odds increase to about 1 in 105. By age 48, the risk reaches 1 in 12. Recent research has determined that the age of the father is also linked to increased risk. In about 25 percent of cases, the father is the source of the extra chromosome (de la Cruz & Muller, 1983).

These rather significant changes in risk should be considered in family planning. There is no "cure" for Down syndrome. However, these children are usually loving and responsive, and they can make progress in a caring environment. Experts working with Down syndrome children emphasize that they can do most of the things that other children can do, only slower (Pueschel et al., 1978). There is evidence that Down children continue to learn and make slow mentai progress well into adulthood (Berry et al., 1984). The best hope for Down syndrome victims therefore lies in specially tailored educational programs that enable them to lead fuller lives.

Learning Check

1. The distribution of IQs approximates a ______________________ (bell-shaped) curve.
2. The association between IQ and high-status professional jobs shows that such jobs require more intelligence. T or F?
3. Women tend to excel on test items that require verbal ability, vocabulary, and rote learning. T or F?
4. Only about 6 percent of the population score above 140 on IQ tests. T or F?

5. An IQ score below 90 indicates mental retardation. T or F?
6. Many cases of mental retardation without known organic causes appear to be ______________.
7. According to Howard Gardner's theory, the three basic human intelligences are linguistic skills, logic, and spatial skills. T or F?

Match:

8.	____ PKU	**A.**	Too little thyroid hormone
9.	____ Microcephaly	**B.**	Very small brain
10.	____ Hydrocephaly	**C.**	47 chromosomes
11.	____ Cretinism	**D.**	Lack of an important enzyme
12.	____ Down Syndrome	**E.**	Excess of cerebrospinal fluid
		F.	Caused by a lack of oxygen at birth

Answers:
1. normal **2.** F **3.** T **4.** F **5.** F **6.** familial **7.** F **8.** D **9.** B **10.** E **11.** A **12.** C

Heredity and Environment—Super Rats and Family Trees

Question: Is intelligence inherited?

This seemingly simple question is loaded with controversy. Some psychologists believe that intelligence is strongly affected by heredity. Many others feel that environment is dominant. Let's examine some of the evidence for each view.

In a classic study of genetic factors in learning, Tryon (1929) managed to breed separate strains of "maze-bright" and "maze-dull" rats (animals that were extremely "bright" or "stupid" at learning mazes). After several generations of breeding, the slowest "super rat" outperformed the best "dull" rat. This and other studies of **eugenics** (selective breeding for desirable characteristics) suggest that some traits are highly influenced by heredity.

Question: That may be true, but is maze-learning really a measure of intelligence?

No, it isn't. Tryon's study seemed to show that intelligence is inherited, but later researchers found that the "bright" rats were simply more motivated by food and less easily distracted during testing (Whimbey, 1980). When they weren't chasing after rat chow, the "bright" rats were no more intelligent than the supposedly dull rats. Because of such problems, animal studies cannot tell us with certainty how heredity and environment affect intelligence. Let's see what human studies reveal.

Most people are aware that there is a moderate similarity in the intelligence of parents and their children, or between brothers and sisters. As Figure 18–7 shows, the similarity in IQ scores among relatives grows in proportion to their closeness on the family tree.

Question: Does that indicate that intelligence is hereditary?

Not necessarily. Brothers, sisters, and parents share similar environments as well as similar heredity. To separate heredity and environment, we need to make some selected comparisons.

Twin Studies Notice in Figure 18–7 that the IQ scores of fraternal twins are more alike than those of ordinary siblings. **Fraternal twins** come from 2 separate eggs fertilized at the same time. Thus, they are no more genetically alike than ordinary siblings. Why then, should the twins' IQ scores be more similar? The reason is environmental: Parents treat twins more alike than ordinary siblings, resulting in a closer match in IQs.

More striking similarities are observed with **identical twins,** who develop from a single egg and have *identical* genes. At the top of Figure 18–7 you can see that identical twins who grow up in the same family have highly correlated IQs. This is what we would expect with identical heredity and highly similar environments. Now, let's consider what happens when identical twins are reared apart. As you can see, the correlation drops, but only from .86 to .72. Psychologists who emphasize genetics believe that figures like these show that adult intelligence is from 55 to 75 percent hereditary (DeFries et al., 1987; Lykken, 1987).

Question: How do environmentalists interpret the figures?

Environmentalists point out that some separated twins

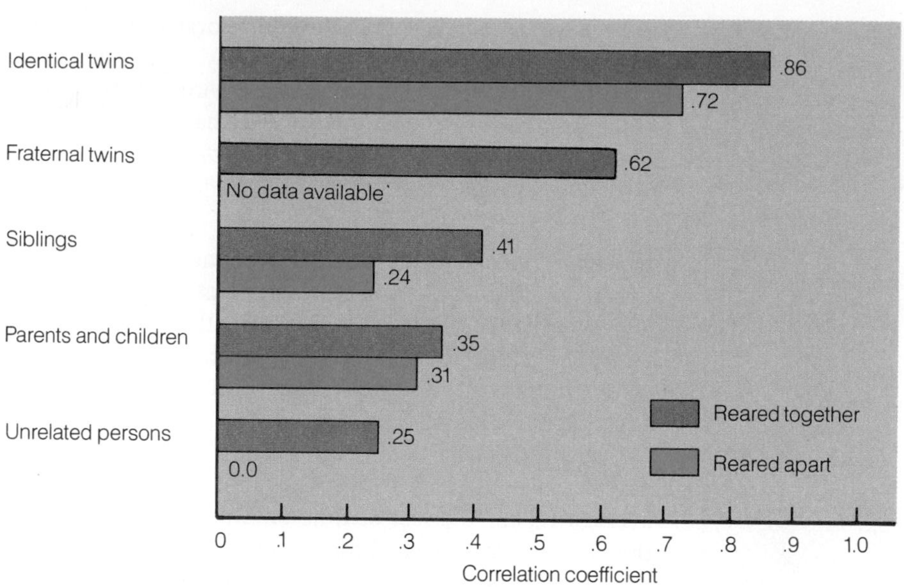

Fig. 18–7 *Approximate correlations between IQ scores for persons with varying degrees of genetic and environmental similarity. Notice that the correlations grow smaller as the degree of genetic similarity declines. Also note that a shared environment increases the correlation in all cases. (Estimates from Bouchard, 1983; Henderson, 1982.)*

differ by as much as 20 IQ points. In every case where this occurs there are large educational and environmental differences between the twins (Whimbey, 1980). Also, separated twins are almost always placed in homes socially and educationally similar to their biological parents. This fact would tend to inflate apparent genetic effects by making the separated twins' IQs more alike (Kamin, 1981).

Strong evidence for an environmental view of intelligence comes from families having one adopted child and one biological child. As Figure 18–8, shows, parents contribute genes *and* environment to their biological child. With an adopted child, they contribute only environment. If intelligence is highly genetic, the IQs of biological children should be more like their parents' IQs than are the IQs of adopted children. However, two studies show that children reared by the same mother resemble her in IQ to the same degree. It does not matter whether or not they share her genes (Horn et al., 1979; Kamin, 1981; Weinberg, 1977). Also, trans-racially adopted children are as similar in IQ to their adoptive brothers and sisters as biologically related siblings are (Scarr & Weinberg, 1983).

Fig. 18–8 *Comparison of an adopted child and a biological child reared in the same family. (After Kamin, 1981.)*

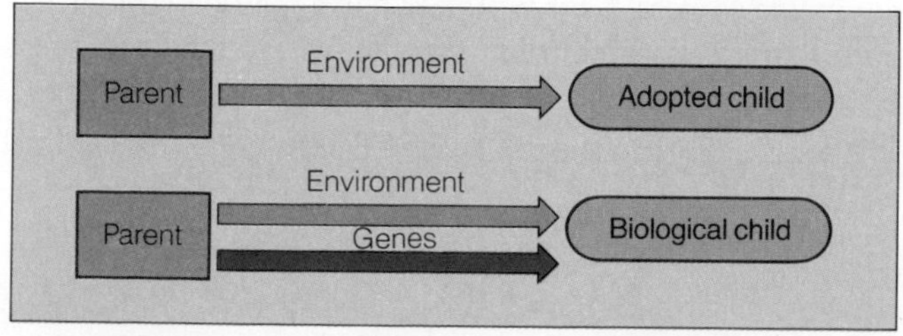

Question: How much can environment alter intelligence?

IQ and Environment In one study, striking increases in IQ occurred in 25 children who were moved from an orphanage to more stimulating environments. The children, all considered mentally retarded and unadoptable, were moved to an institution where they received personal attention from adults. Later, these supposedly retarded children were adopted by parents who gave them love, a family, and a stimulating environment. The IQs of the children showed an average gain of 29 points. For one child, the increase was an amazing 58 points. A second group of initially less "retarded" children who remained in the orphanage *lost* an average of 26 IQ points (Skeels, 1966)!

More recently, data from 14 nations have shown average IQ gains of from 5 to 25 points during a single generation (the last 30 years) (Flynn, 1987). These IQ boosts, averaging 15 points, have occurred in far too short a time for genetics to explain them. It is more likely that the gains reflect some as yet unidentified environmental force, such as improved education or other advantages. This and the related studies are an encouraging indication that intelligence can be raised by an improved environment. (Also, see Highlight 18–2.)

The Family Size Controversy Some environmental effects may be more subtle than the previous examples

HIGHLIGHT 18–2
Can Intelligence Be Taught?

The traditional answer to the question, "Can intelligence be taught?" is "No." Coaching, for instance, has little positive effect on aptitude and intelligence test scores (Kulik et al., 1984). But is a brief period of coaching a fair test of the modifiability of intelligence? Apparently not. There is increasing evidence that extended, in-depth training in thinking skills can increase tested intelligence (Whimbey, 1980).

At the forefront of such efforts is Israeli psychologist Reuven Feuerstein (FOY-er-shtine). Feuerstein and his colleagues have developed a program they call Instrumental Enrichment. The program involves hundreds of hours of guided problem solving. The emphasis throughout is on remedying the kinds of gaps and flaws in thinking that lower IQ scores (Feuerstein et al., 1980). Feuerstein and other researchers have shown that such training can, in fact, raise IQ scores (Haywood et al., 1982; Messerer et al., 1984).

Another major attempt to improve cognitive skills is now under way in Venezuela. For the last 6 years, over 400 seventh-grade students have taken special classes in reasoning, problem solving, decision making, inventiveness, and other thinking skills. The program was designed by a team of American psychologists, who report that "the course had sizable, beneficial effects on students" (Herrnstein et al., 1986).

The difficulty with such training, however, is that it is very time-consuming. In recognition of this problem, psychologists are now writing computer programs to teach problem solving, effective thinking, and other elements of intelligence (Pellegrino, 1985). With our growing understanding of how people think, and with the tireless aid of computers, it may indeed become common in schools to "teach intelligence."

indicate. Psychologist Robert Zajonc (ZYE-onz) believes that IQ tends to decline as family size grows. That is, the brightest children come from the smallest families. In addition, the brightest children are, on the average, those who are born first in a family (Zajonc, 1975; Zajonc & Markus, 1975). It is also interesting that average SAT scores declined in the United States during a period when family size increased (Zajonc, 1986). How can these observations be explained? According to Zajonc's **confluence model,** each arriving baby temporarily lowers the "average intellectual level" in a family. This, he says, makes large families less stimulating environments. (Have you ever tried to have an intellectual chat with a baby?)

Question: If I am the last child from a large family, how should I take these findings?

Not too seriously! Critics of the confluence model believe that large families do not by themselves affect a child's intelligence. Any link to IQ *averages,* they say, may be related to the fact that nation-wide, large families are more common among couples with low social and educational advantages (Rodgers, 1988).

Even if Zajonc is right, the average IQ score for the older of two children is only 10 points higher than the average IQ for the last of nine children. Differences of this amount may mean little in terms of what a person can actually do. Also, later-born children may excel in other ways (see Chapter 16). Later-borns, for instance, usually have excellent social skills, leading to greater popularity among peers and schoolmates. And as a final point, there is evidence that birth-order differences in IQ may disappear by age 17 (McCall, 1984).

Summary To sum up, few psychologists seriously believe that heredity is not a factor in intelligence, and all acknowledge that environment affects it. Estimates of the impact of each factor continue to vary. But ultimately, both camps agree that improving social conditions and education can raise intelligence.

There is probably no limit to how far *down* intelligence can go in a poor environment, but heredity may impose some limits on how far up IQ can go, even under ideal conditions (Scarr-Salapatek, 1971). It is telling, nevertheless, that gifted children tend to come from homes where parents encourage intellectual exploration, answer their children's questions, and spend time with their children (Horowitz & O'Brien, 1986; Janos & Robinson, 1985).

As a final summary, it might help to think of inherited intellectual potential as a rubber band that is stretched by outside forces. A long rubber band may be stretched more easily, but a shorter one can be stretched to the same length if enough force is applied (Stern, 1956). Of course, a superior genetic gift may allow for a higher maximum IQ. Yet, in the final analysis, intelligence reflects development as well as potential, nurture as well as nature.

Learning Check

1. Selective breeding for desirable characteristics is called ______________________.
2. The closest similarity in IQs would be observed for
   a. parents and their children
   b. identical twins reared apart
   c. fraternal twins reared together
   d. siblings reared together
3. Most psychologists believe that intelligence is 90 percent hereditary. T or F?
4. Except for slight variations during testing, IQ cannot be changed. T or F?
5. Environmental effects are probably more capable of lowering IQ than of raising it. T or F?
6. According to the research of Robert Zajonc, children in large families provide extra stimulation for one another, thereby increasing intelligence. T or F?

Answers:

1. eugenics **2.** *b* **3.** F **4.** F **5.** T **6.** F

Applications: Intelligence in Perspective—Are Intelligence Tests Intelligent?

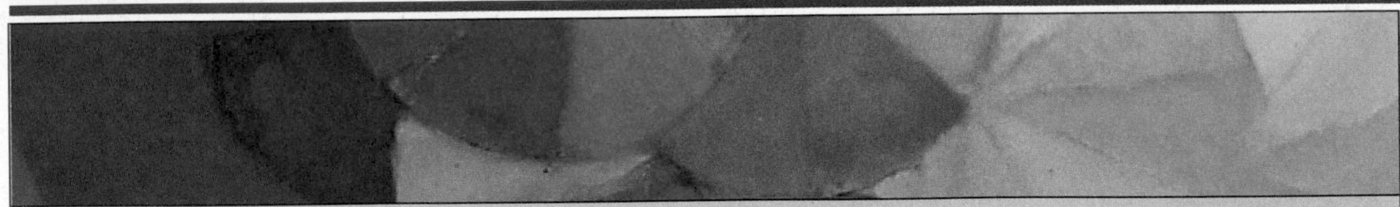

Almost everyone is curious about how they would score on an intelligence test. If you would like to get a rough estimate of your IQ, take the following self-administered test.

Dove Counterbalance Intelligence Test

Time limit: 5 minutes
Circle the correct answer.

1. T-bone Walker got famous for playing what?
a. trombone *b.* piano *c.* T-flute
d. guitar *e.* "hambone"

2. A"gas head" is a person who has a
a. fast-moving car *b.* stable of "lace"
c. "process" *d.* habit of stealing cars
e. long jail record for arson

3. If you throw the dice and 7 is showing on the top, what is facing down?
a. 7 *b.* snake eyes *c.* boxcars
d. little joes *e.* 11

4. Cheap chitlings (not the kind you purchase at a frozen-food counter) will taste rubbery unless they are cooked long enough. How soon can you quit cooking them to eat and enjoy them?
a. 45 minutes *b.* 2 hours
c. 24 hours *d.* 1 week (on a low flame)
e. 1 hour

5. Bird or Yardbird was the jacket jazz lovers from coast to coast hung on
a. Lester Young *b.* Peggy Lee
c. Benny Goodman *d.* Charlie Parker
e. Birdman of Alcatraz

6. A "handkerchief head" is
a. a cool cat *b.* a porter *c.* an Uncle Tom
d. a hoddi *e.* a preacher

7. Jet is
a. an East Oakland motorcycle club
b. one of the gangs in West Side Story
c. a news and gossip magazine
d. a way of life for the very rich

8. "Bo Diddly" is a
a. game for children *b.* down-home cheap wine
c. down-home singer *d.* new dance
e. Moejoe call

9. Which word is most out of place here?
a. splib *b.* blood *c.* gray
d. spook *e.* black

10. If a pimp is uptight with a woman who gets state aid, what does he mean when he talks about "Mother's Day"?
a. second Sunday in May
b. third Sunday in June
c. first of every month
d. none of these
e. first and fifteenth of every month

11. How much does a "short dog" cost?
a. 15¢ *b.* $2 *c.* 35¢
d. 5¢ *e.* 86¢ plus tax

12. Many people say that "Juneteenth" (June 19) should be made a legal holiday because this was the day when
a. the slaves were freed in the United States
b. the slaves were freed in Texas
c. the slaves were freed in Jamaica
d. the slaves were freed in California
e. Martin Luther King was born
f. Booker T. Washington died

13. If a man is called a "blood," then he is a
a. fighter *b.* Mexican-American
c. Negro *d.* hungry hemophile
e. red man or Indian

14. What are the Dixie Hummingbirds?
a. a part of the KKK
b. a swamp disease
c. a modern gospel group
d. a Mississippi Negro paramilitary strike force
e. deacons

15. The opposite of square is
a. round *b.* up *c.* down
d. hip *e.* lame

Answers: 1. *d* 2. *c* 3. *a* 4. *c* 5. *d* 6. *c* 7. *c* 8. *c* 9. *c* 10. *c* 11. *c* 12. *b* 13. *c* 14. *c* 15. *d*

If you scored 14 on this exam, your IQ is approximately 100, indicating average intelligence. If you scored 11 or less, you are mentally retarded. With luck and the help of a special educational program, we may be able to teach you a few simple skills!

Applications

Race and IQ

Question: Isn't this test a little unfair?

No, it is *very* unfair. It was written by black sociologist Adrian Dove as "a half serious attempt to show that we're just not talking the same language." Dove tried to slant his test as much in favor of urban black culture as he believes the typical intelligence test is biased toward a white middle-class background. (Because of its age, the test is probably now also unfair for anyone under 30.)

Dove's test is a thought-provoking reply to the fact that black children in the United States score an average of about 15 points lower on standardized IQ tests than white children. By reversing the bias, Dove has shown that intelligence tests are not equally valid for all groups. As Kagan (1973) says, "If the Wechsler and Binet scales were translated into Spanish, Swahili, and Chinese and given to every 10-year-old in Latin America, East Africa, or China, the majority would obtain IQ scores in the mentally retarded range."

Certainly we cannot believe that children of different cultures are all retarded. The fault must lie in the test. To minimize this problem, some psychologists have tried to develop **culture-fair tests** that do not disadvantage certain groups. (For a sample of culture-fair test items, see Fig. 18–9.)

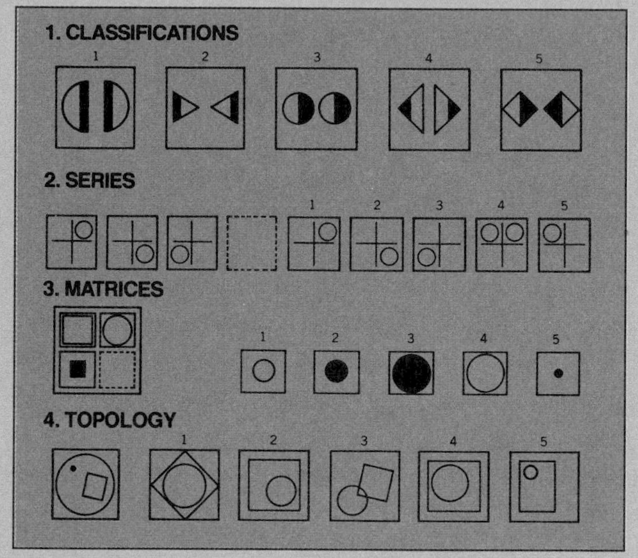

Fig. 18–9 *Sample items from a culture-fair test. 1. Which pattern is different from the remaining four? (Number 3.) 2. Which of the five figures on the right would properly continue the three on the left—that is, fill the blank? (Number 5.) 3. Which of the figures on the right should go in the square on the left to make it look right? (Number 2.) 4. At left, the dot is outside the square and inside the circle. In which of the figures on the right could you put a dot outside the square and inside the circle? (Number 3.) (Courtesy of R. B. Cattell.)*

Biased tests are not the only IQ issue blacks have confronted. Arthur Jensen, writing in the *Harvard Educational Review,* once claimed that the lower IQ scores of blacks can be primarily attributed to "genetic heritage." Before we go any further, it is important to note that few psychologists support Jensen. Soon after Jensen made his genetic claim, psychologists responded with a number of counter-arguments.

First, it is no secret that as a group, blacks in the United States are more likely than whites to live in environments that are physically, educationally, and intellectually impoverished. As one critic notes, test scores are meaningless if they result from unequal educational opportunity. Further, it is tragic if those scores are then used to deny further educational opportunities (Grover, 1983).

Second, the gap in IQ between blacks and whites is small enough to be closed by environment. Jensen's reply to this claim was that special educational programs such as Head Start have proved incapable of narrowing the IQ gap. But it is essentially ridiculous to expect that a brief summer program or a few hours a day are enough to counteract the differences in educational and environmental advantages of blacks and whites.

Third, Jensen ignores the point made by the Dove Test. The assumptions, biases, and content of standard IQ tests do not allow meaningful comparisons between ethnic, cultural, or racial groups (Garcia, 1977). As Leon Kamin (1981) says, "The important fact is that we cannot say which sex (or race) might be more intelligent, because we have no way of measuring 'intelligence.' We have only IQ tests."

Kamin's point is that the makers of IQ tests decided in advance to use test items that would give men and women equal IQ scores. It would be just as easy to put together an IQ test that would give blacks and whites in this country equal scores. Differences in IQ scores are not a fact of nature, but a decision by the test makers. This is why whites do better on IQ tests written by whites, and blacks do better on IQ tests devised by blacks. Another example of this fact is an intelligence test made up of 100 words selected from the *Dictionary of Afro-American Slang*. Williams (1975) gave the test to 100 black and 100 white high school students in St. Louis and found that the black group averaged 36 points higher than the white group.

Perhaps the most devastating criticism of Jensen is that his logic is faulty. Consider this example: Corn comes in different varieties selectively bred to grow to a certain height. If we plant tall and short varieties side by side in the same field, we

Applications

will observe a genetically determined difference in their height at maturity. But what if we take corn (all the same variety) and plant half in a fertile field and half in poor soil? Again we observe a difference in maximum height, but this time it is clearly a mistake to assume that it is genetically caused.

Only when black children are raised in exactly the same surroundings as white children can hereditary factors be clearly assessed. Along this line, one revealing study looked at the fate of black children adopted by white families. These children had IQ scores averaging 106, which is comparable to the national average for white children (Scarr-Salapatek & Weinberg, 1975). It is not clear if the black children were actually "brighter" as a result of this experience or if they were just better prepared to take a "white" test. The fact remains, however, that when an equal opportunity for intellectual development can close the IQ gap, then narrow genetic views of IQ differences must be abandoned.

Questioning the Concept of IQ—Beyond the Numbers Game

Blacks are not the only segment of the population with reason to question the validity of intelligence testing and the role of heredity in determining intelligence. The clarifications won by blacks extend to others as well.

Consider the 9-year-old child confronted with this question on an intelligence test: "Which of the following does not belong with the others? Roller skates, airplane, train, bicycle." If the child fails to answer "airplane," does it reveal a lack of intelligence? It can be argued that an intelligent choice could be based on any of these alternatives: Roller skates are not typically used for transportation; an airplane is the only non-land item; a train can't be steered; a bicycle is the only item with just two wheels (Sheils & Monroe, 1976). The parents of a child who misses this question may have reason to be angry, since educational systems tend to classify children and then make the label stick.

Recent court decisions have led some states to outlaw the use of intelligence tests in public schools (see the Exploration section). Criticism of intelligence testing has also come from the academic community. Harvard University psychologist David McClelland (1973) believes that IQ is of little value in predicting real competence to deal effectively with the world. McClelland concedes that IQ predicts school performance, but when he compared a group of college students with straight A's to another group with poor grades, he found no differences in later career success.

Standardized Testing In addition to IQ tests, 400 to 500 million standardized multiple-choice tests are given in schools and workplaces around the nation each year. Many, like the *Scholastic Aptitude Test,* may determine whether a person is admitted to college. Other tests—for employment, licensing, and certification—directly affect the lives of thousands by qualifying or disqualifying them for jobs.

Widespread reliance on standardized intelligence tests and aptitude tests raises questions about the relative good and harm they do. On the positive side, tests can open opportunities as well as close them. A high test score may allow a disadvantaged youth to enter college, or it may identify a child who is bright but emotionally disturbed. Test scores may also be fairer and more objective than arbitrary judgments made by admissions officers or employment interviewers. Also, tests *do* accurately predict academic performance. The fact that academic performance *does not* predict later success may call for an overhaul of college course work, not an end to testing.

On the negative side, mass testing can occasionally exclude people of obvious ability. In one case, a student who was seventh in his class at Columbia University and a member of Phi Beta Kappa was denied entrance to law school because he had low scores on the Law School Admissions Test. Other complaints relate to the frequent appearance of bad or ambiguous questions on standardized tests, overuse of class time to prepare students for the tests (instead of teaching general skills), and in the case of intelligence tests, the charge that tests are often biased.

What should we make of the positive and negative aspects of standardized testing? Robert Glaser says we should remember that tests are "limited tools for limited purposes." Glaser (1977) also says that tests are now used primarily to *select* people. In schools they could instead be used to *adapt* instruction to the strengths, weaknesses, and needs of each student—thereby increasing the chances of success.

Conclusion

An application of the preceding discussion to your personal understanding of intelligence can be summarized in this way: Intelligence tests are a two-edged sword; we have learned much from their use, yet they have the potential to do great harm. In the final analysis, it is important to remember—as Howard Gardner has pointed out—that creativity, motivation, physical health, mechanical aptitude, artistic ability, and numerous other qualities not measured by intelligence tests contribute to achievement of life goals. Also remember that IQ is not intelligence. IQ is an index of intelligence (as narrowly defined by a particular test). Change the test and you change the score. An IQ is not some permanent number stamped on the forehead of a child that forever determines potential.

Let us end on an optimistic note. As discussed earlier in Highlight 18–2, some psychologists and educators are seeking ways to teach necessary intellectual skills to all children. In some cases their success has been striking. One experiment

Applications

divided 40 children from extremely disadvantaged (slum) families into 2 groups. Children in the control group received no extra attention or training. Beginning shortly after birth, the experimental group was given a wide variety of stimulation to develop perceptual, motor, and language abilities. At age 2, the children in the experimental group were placed in small classes with other children and several teachers. Each child received lots of teacher attention and exposure to a broad range of topics and thinking exercises. When tested at age 5½, the average IQ for the control group was about 95; the average for the experimentals was 124 (reported by Whimbey, 1980). These results should be encouraging to everyone interested in the fulfillment of human potentials.

Learning Check

1. The WAIS-R, Stanford-Binet, and Dove Test are all culture-fair intelligence scales. T or F?
2. Jensen's claim that heredity accounts for racial differences in average IQ ignores environmental differences and the cultural bias inherent in standard IQ tests. T or F?
3. IQ scores predict school performance. T or F?
4. IQ is not intelligence; it is one index of intelligence. T or F?

Answers:
1. F 2. T 3. T 4. T

● Exploration: The Larry P. Case—"Six-Hour Retardates"

The case: *Larry P. vs. the California State Superintendent of Education.*

The issue: Larry P. is one of 6 black children who claimed that biased IQ test scores were wrongly used to place them in classes for the educable mentally retarded (EMR).

The outcome: In a landmark decision, a federal judge ruled that IQ test scores alone can no longer be used for EMR placement.

The ruling has virtually eliminated IQ testing in California schools. It is likely to do the same in many other states. The bare facts of the Larry P. case only hint at the interesting issues it raised. Testimony during the trial brought out the following:

For Larry P.: All 6 youngsters suing the state had scored below 75 on standardized IQ tests. But they scored from 17 to 35 points higher when retested by psychologists who used language and examples the children were familiar with.

For the State: Experts admitted that IQ test questions can be easier for some groups than for others. However, they held that IQ tests accurately predict school performance and are therefore valid.

For Larry P.: Witnesses pointed out that EMR assignments are almost always permanent. They also described the devastating effects of placing a child of normal intelligence in an EMR class. One researcher found that other students commonly refer to EMR students with cruel nicknames. EMR students are not expected to progress beyond the third- to fifth-grade level. Thus, by the time of graduation, a child of normal intelligence would be hopelessly behind other students. After graduation, EMR students find it difficult to get jobs, because they have been labeled "retarded."

For the State: Defense experts claimed that IQ tests help prevent mistakes in EMR assignments—for example, by revealing the true potential of a child who might be considered "slow" by a biased teacher. They also defended the EMR program as an effort to help less able students.

For Larry P.: Roughly twice as many black and Hispanic children are found in EMR classes than would be expected based on the percentage of blacks and Hispanics in the general population. This fact suggests a defect in the tests, not in the children (Ristow, 1978).

Ignorance vs. Stupidity In the end, the judge ruled that IQ tests violate federal anti-discrimination laws. He was convinced, he said, that they are based mainly on verbal tasks that are unfair to children whose home environment does not provide practice in formal English or verbal skills. He further held that "if tests suggest that a young child is probably going to be a poor student, the school cannot, on that basis alone, deny that child the opportunity to develop and improve the academic skills necessary for success in our society" (from *Psychology Today*, Feb. 1980).

Supporters of the Larry P. decision believe that it affirms the rights of disadvantaged children, whose ignorance—a lack of knowledge—has been mistaken for stupidity—a lack of intelligence. One such supporter is Jane Mercer, a sociologist who gave key testimony in the case.

Six-hour Retardates Mercer testified that the more a child's family is like the average white Anglo middle-class norm, the better the child scores on IQ tests. Mercer believes that schools often label children retarded when actually the children only lack culturally tied knowledge (Mercer, 1977). Mercer has found that many black or Hispanic EMR students show abundant signs of normal intelligence. A child who does poorly in the classroom or on an IQ test may function perfectly well at home and in the community. Mercer refers to such children as "6-hour retardates"—youngsters who are "retarded" only during the school day. *Question: If standardized IQ tests cannot be used to assess student abilities, what can?*

SOMPA Mercer and her associate June Lewis think they have an answer. They call it SOMPA, which stands for System of Multicultural Pluralistic Assessment. SOMPA is not a new test. Rather, it's a different way of looking at children.

Question: How does SOMPA differ from standard IQ tests?

Exploration

SOMPA combines three ways of assessing a child. First, it looks for any medical problems that may be causing low school performance. Next, the child's behavior outside the classroom is evaluated to avoid the mistake of creating a "6-hour retardate" on the basis of a test score. Third, SOMPA assumes that when everything else is held constant (educational advantages at home, especially), the child who has learned the most probably has the most "learning potential." Off-campus environments, however, are not equal. SOMPA therefore assumes that true potential can be masked by a child's cultural background. To avoid this problem, SOMPA compares each child's WISC-R score with that of children from similar backgrounds (Mercer, 1977).

To show how SOMPA works, Mercer offers an example. Maria Gonzales is 7. She lives with her mother, father, and 5 brothers and sisters in an inner-city barrio. Maria's mother and father both grew up in rural Mexico, where the mother finished fourth grade and the father second grade. Maria's family speaks only Spanish.

The average score for a child like Maria—with a background so different from core Anglo culture—is about 85. Maria's score on the WISC-R was 114, almost 30 points above this average. Mercer estimates Maria's real learning potential at 133. If her family had been more like the middle-class norm, Maria's score of 114 would have been accepted as accurate. Considering her age and background, Maria's performance on the WISC-R is truly outstanding (Mercer, 1977). Maria is probably a gifted child whose potential should not be wasted.

More IQ Controversy In December 1986, Judge Robert Peckham, who issued the original opinion, reiterated the California IQ test ban. In fact, he added to it, saying, "The prohibition on IQ tests goes further and prohibits any use of an IQ test as part of an assessment which could lead to special education placement or services, even if the test is only part of a comprehensive assessment plan" (Landers, 1986). This directive appears to eliminate even alternatives like SOMPA for evaluating children.

Understandably, the Larry P. decision remains controversial. Some psychologists object to the courts making educational decisions. Others point out that they must now resort to nonstandard alternative measures. Many of these alternatives are subjective and open to potential abuse. It may become easier, for instance, to rid classrooms of "problem children—late bloomers, troublemakers, quirky learners—who may not be intellectually deficient, but just in need of more attention and understanding. Without IQ tests, how can such children be identified?

A typical reply from critics of IQ testing is that an IQ gives little information about the cause of a low score. It therefore tells little about what corrective action should be taken. To improve mental ability, IQ scores are not needed. The purpose of school is to help children learn and develop skills needed in adjusting to life and work (Baumeister, 1987).

If you were the judge, how would you rule? If you were a school psychologist, how would you feel about using IQ tests or alternatives such as SOMPA? In your opinion, what role should IQ tests have in a democratic society?

Learning Check

1. The basic issue of the Larry P. case was whether children's IQs are lowered by placement in EMR classes. T or F?
2. Before the Larry P. case, placement in EMR classes was almost always done on the basis of group IQ test scores. T or F?
3. SOMPA is designed to obtain IQ scores from an assessment of a child's physical health and social functioning. T or F?
4. In the SOMPA system, IQ scores are compared to norms for children of similar cultural and social backgrounds. T or F?
5. According to the latest ruling, IQ tests can be used for educational placement in California schools only when they are part of a comprehensive assessment plan. T of F?

Answers:

1. F 2. T 3. F 4. T 5. F

Chapter Summary

• **Intelligence** refers to one's general capacity to act purposefully, think rationally, and deal effectively with the environment. In practice, intelligence is **operationally defined** by the creation of intelligence tests.

• To be of any value, a psychological test must be **reliable** (give consistent results). A worthwhile test must also have **validity,** meaning that it measures what it claims to measure. Widely used intelligence tests are **objective** (they give the same result when scored by different people) and **standardized** (the same procedures are always used in giving the test, and **norms** have been established so that scores can be interpreted).

• The first practical intelligence test was assembled by **Alfred Binet.** A modern version of Binet's test is the **Stanford-Binet Intelligence Scale.** A second major intelligence test is the **Wechsler Adult Intelligence Scale–Revised (WAIS-R).** The WAIS-R measures both **verbal** and **performance** intelligence. Intelligence tests have also been produced for use with groups. Group tests include the *Army Alpha* (historically) and the SAT, the ACT, and the CQT.

• Intelligence is expressed in terms of an **intelligence quotient (IQ).** IQ is defined as **mental age** (MA) divided by **chronological age** (CA) and then multiplied by 100. An "average" IQ of 100 occurs when mental age equals chronological age.

• IQ scores become fairly stable at about age 6, and they become increasingly reliable thereafter. On the average, IQ scores continue to gradually increase until middle age. Later intellectual declines are slight for most people until their 70s. Shortly before death, a more significant **terminal decline** in intelligence is often observed.

• The distribution of IQ scores approximates a **normal curve.** There are no overall differences between males and females in tested intelligence, but intellectual strengths exist for each. IQ is related to school grades and job status. The second association may be somewhat artificial.

• People with IQs in the **gifted** or "genius" range of above 140 tend to be superior in many respects. By criteria other than IQ, a large proportion of children might be considered gifted or talented in one way or another. Intellectually gifted children often have difficulties in average classrooms and benefit from special accelerated programs.

• The terms **mentally retarded** and **developmentally disabled** are applied to those whose IQ falls below 70 or who lack various **adaptive behaviors.** Further classifications of retardation are: **mild** (50–55 to 70), **moderate** (35–40 to 50–55), **severe** (20–25 to 35–40), and **profound** (below 20–25). Chances for educational success are related to the degree of retardation.

• About 50 percent of the cases of mental retardation are **organic,** being caused by birth injuries, fetal damage, metabolic disorders, or genetic abnormalities. The remaining cases are of undetermined cause. Many of these cases are thought to be the result of **familial retardation,** a generally low level of educational and intellectual stimulation in the home, coupled with poverty and poor nutrition.

• Five specialized forms of organic retardation are **phenylketonuria (PKU), microcephaly, hydrocephaly, cretinism,** and **Down syndrome.**

• Studies of **eugenics** in animals and familial relationships in humans demonstrate that intelligence is partially determined by **heredity.** However, **environment** is also important, as revealed by changes in tested intelligence induced by stimulating environments. There is increasing evidence that some elements of intelligence can be taught. Intelligence therefore reflects the combined effects of both heredity and environment in the development of intellectual abilities.

• Traditional IQ tests often suffer from a degree of **cultural bias.** For this and other reasons, it is wise to remember that IQ is merely an **index** of intelligence and that intelligence is narrowly defined by most tests.

• The use of standard IQ tests for educational placement of students (especially into special education classes) has been prohibited by law in some states. Whether this is desirable and beneficial to students is currently being debated.

Questions For Discussion

1. In what ways do you think our society encourages the development of different intellectual skills in males and females?

2. Do you know your IQ? Would you like to know it? Why or why not?

3. What advantages or disadvantages would you expect to be associated with knowing your own IQ? With having a teacher know your IQ? With having your parents know your IQ?

4. How might public education be restructured to encourage full intellectual development for all children? How might grading be changed to reflect broader definitions of intelligence?

5. How would you feel about the application of eugenics to human reproduction? Can you think of circumstances under which you would or would not consider it acceptable?

6. The debate over the relative importance of heredity and environment in determining intelligence has raged for decades. Why do you think the debate has lasted so long and attracted so much interest? If the heritability of IQ could be known with certainty, what difference would it make?

7. An organization called the Repository for Germinal Choice in Escondido, California, serves as a sperm bank for Nobel Prize winners and others possessing high IQs. Dozens of babies have now been produced by artificial insemination from the sperm bank. Do you regard this as wise or unwise, ethical or unethical, foolish or inspired?

Part Six

Abnormal Behavior and Therapies

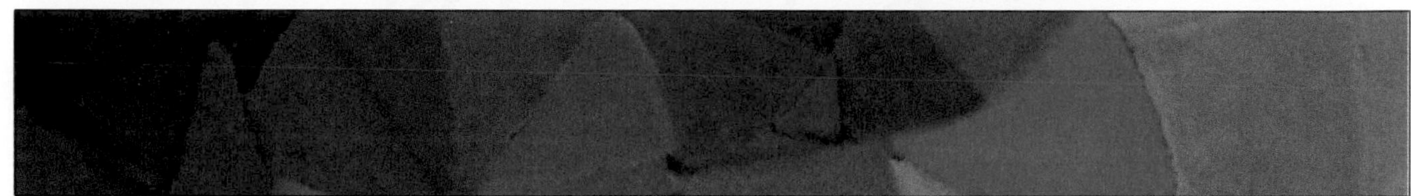

Chapter 19

Maladaptive Behavior: Deviance and Disorder

In This Chapter

Defining psychopathology
Normal and abnormal behavior
Personality disorders
Sexual deviance
Adjustment disorders
Anxiety disorders
Dissociative disorders
Somatoform disorders
Theories of maladjustment
Depression

Applications

Suicide and its prevention

Exploration

The insanity defense

Chapter Preview

Catch-22: A Practical Definition of "Crazy"

"Can't you ground someone who's crazy?"

"Oh, sure, I have to. There's a rule saying I have to ground anyone who's crazy."

"Then why don't you ground me? I'm crazy. Ask Clevinger."

"Clevinger? Where is Clevinger? You find Clevinger and I'll ask him."

"Then ask any of the others. They'll tell you how crazy I am."

"They're crazy."

"Then why don't you ground them?"

"Why don't they ask me to ground them?"

"Because they're crazy, that's why."

"Of course they're crazy," Doc Daneeka replied. "I just told you they're crazy, didn't I? And you can't let crazy people decide whether you're crazy or not, can you?"

Yossarian looked at him soberly and tried another approach.

"Is Orr crazy?"

"He sure is," Doc Daneeka said.

"Can you ground him?"

"I sure can. But first he has to ask me to. That's part of the rule."

"Then why doesn't he ask you to?"

"Because he's crazy," Doc Daneeka said. "He has to be crazy to keep flying combat missions after all the close calls he's had. Sure, I can ground Orr. But first he has to ask me to."

"That's all he has to do to be grounded?"

"That's all. Let him ask me."

"And then you can ground him?" Yossarian asked.

"No. Then I can't ground him."

"You mean there's a catch?"

"Sure there's a catch," Doc Daneeka replied. "Catch-22. Anyone who wants to get out of combat duty isn't really crazy."

There was only one catch and that was Catch-22, which specified that a concern for one's own safety in the face of dangers that were real and immediate was the process of a rational mind. Orr was crazy and could be grounded. All he had to do was ask; and as soon as he did, he would no longer be crazy and would have to fly more missions. Orr would be crazy to fly more missions and sane if he didn't, but if he was sane he had to fly them. If he flew them he was crazy and didn't have to; but if he didn't want to he was sane and had to. Yossarian was moved very deeply by the absolute simplicity of this clause of Catch-22 and let out a respectful whistle.

"That's some catch, that Catch-22," he observed.

"It's the best there is," Doc Daneeka agreed.*

This excerpt from Joseph Heller's novel Catch 22 *captures the ambiguities presented by the classic question, What is normal? In the 1800s, doctors and nonprofessionals alike used such terms as "crazy," "insane," "cracked," and "lunatic" quite freely. The "insane" were thought of as bizarre and definitely different from you or me.*

Today our understanding of emotional disorders is growing ever more sophisticated. Drawing the line between normal and abnormal can be done only by weighing some complex issues. In this chapter and the next we will summarize major psychological problems and their characteristics.

Survey Questions

- How is normality defined, and what are the major psychological disorders?
- What is a personality disorder?
- Is the term *neurosis* still used?
- What problems result when a person suffers high levels of anxiety?
- What causes depression? What can be done about it?
- Why do people commit suicide? Can suicide be prevented?
- What role does the concept of insanity play in criminal trials?

Psychopathology—Defining Major Psychological Problems

In 1978, William Milligan was accused of being the "university rapist" who attacked four women near Ohio State University. At his trial, psychiatrists testified that Milligan had 9 separate personalities. The rapist was assumed to have been a personality identified as an "18-year-old lesbian" named Adelena.

Unlike the *Catch-22* excerpt, William Milligan's problem is not fictional. It is but one hint of the magnitude of mental health problems in this country. Here are the facts on psychopathology in the United States:

- 1 out of every 100 persons will become so severely disturbed as to require hospitalization at some point in his or her lifetime.
- Some 3 to 6 percent of the aged suffer from organic psychoses.
- Each year, some 12 percent of the population experience an anxiety-related disorder.
- 1 out of every 8 school-age children is seriously maladjusted.
- 10 to 20 percent or more of all adults will suffer a major depression in their lifetime.
- Each year over 2 million persons are admitted or readmitted to out-patient services or psychiatric treatment in general hospitals.

A large variety of problems fall into the general category of *psychopathology*. **Psychopathology** may be defined as the *inability to behave in ways that foster the well-being of the individual and ultimately of society*. This definition covers not only obviously maladaptive behavior, such as drug addiction, compulsive gambling, or loss of contact with reality, but also any behavior that interferes with personal growth and self-fulfillment (Carson et al., 1988). Clearly, mental health problems are extensive.

Psychological problems are grouped into broad categories of maladaptive behavior. The most widely used system of classification is found in the *Diagnostic and Statistical Manual of Mental Disorders (DSM-III-R)*. The purpose of the manual is to provide a common language for therapists, researchers, social agencies, and health workers. DSM-III-R helps professionals diagnose and classify problems and aids in the selection of appropriate therapies. If you were to glance through the manual, you would find a wide range of disorders described, including those listed in Table 19–1. It is not possible here to discuss all of the listed problems. (However, many are

Table 19–1 Major DSM-III-R Categories

Disorders Usually First Evident by Adolescence
- Disruptive behavior disorders
  - Example: Hyperactivity
- Anxiety disorders of childhood or adolescence
  - Example: Separation anxiety
- Eating disorders
  - Example: Anorexia nervosa
- Gender identity disorders
  - Example: Transsexualism
- Tic disorders
  - Example: Transient tic disorder
- Elimination disorders
  - Example: Functional enuresis (wetting)
- Speech disorders
  - Example: Stuttering

***Developmental Disorders**
- *Mental retardation*
  - *Example: Mild mental retardation*
- *Pervasive developmental disorders*
  - *Example: Autism*
- *Specific developmental disorders*
  - *Example: Academic skills disorder*

Organic Mental Disorders
- Dementia
  - Example: Alzheimer's disease
- Psychoactive substance-induced organic mental disorders
  - Example: Alcohol withdrawal
- Organic mental disorders associated with a known physical condition
  - Example: Delirium from a head injury

Psychoactive Substance Use Disorders
- Example: Cocaine dependence

Schizophrenia
- Example: Catatonic schizophrenia

Delusional (Paranoid) Disorders
- Example: Jealous delusional disorder

Psychotic Disorders Not Elsewhere Classified
- Example: Brief reactive psychosis

Mood Disorders
- Bipolar disorders
  - Example: Manic bipolar disorder
- Depressive disorders
  - Example: Major depression

Anxiety Disorders
- Example: Panic disorder

Somatoform Disorders
- Example: Conversion disorder

Dissociative Disorders
- Example: Multiple personality disorder

Sexual Disorders
- Paraphilias
  - Example: Voyeurism
- Sexual dysfunctions
  - Example: Premature ejaculation

Sleep Disorders
- Dyssomnias
  - Example: Insomnia
- Parasomnias
  - Example: Sleepwalking

Factitious Disorders (faked disability or illness)
- Example: Factitious disorder

Impulse Control Disorders Not Elsewhere Classified
- Example: Kleptomania

Adjustment Disorders
- Example: Adjustment disorder with depressed mood

***Personality Disorders**
- *Example: Antisocial personality*

*Italicized disorders are not classed as primary clinical syndromes. Developmental and personality disorders may be problems by themselves or they may be combined with other disorders.

covered in other chapters.) The following descriptions give an overview of some of the major disorders. Most of these, and some not mentioned here, are discussed in more detail in this chapter and the next.

Psychotic disorders are among the most severe forms of psychopathology, and they often lead to hospitalization. In psychosis there is a retreat from shared views of reality. The person can no longer tell what is fantasy or hallucination and what is real. In addition, there is usually a major loss of ability to control thoughts and actions. If you look again at Table 19–1, you will see that the only mention of psychosis is the listing "Psychotic Disorders Not Elsewhere Classified." Be aware, however, that schizophrenia, delusional disorders, and some severe mood disorders are forms of psychosis.

Organic mental disorders are problems caused by brain pathology; that is, by senility, drug damage, diseases of the brain, injuries, the toxic effects of poisons, and so on. Organic disorders are often accompanied by such symptoms as severe emotional disturbances, impairment of thinking, memory loss, personality changes, and delirium. Psychotic features are also possible in this category.

Psychoactive substance use disorders are defined as abuse or dependence on mood- or behavior-altering drugs, such as alcohol, barbiturates, opiates, cocaine, amphetamines, hallucinogens, marijuana, and tobacco. Problems in this category center on damaged social or occupational functioning and an inability to stop using the drug (Fig. 19–1).

Mood disorders primarily involve disturbances in affect, or emotion. Individuals suffering from mood disorders may be *manic,* meaning agitated, euphoric, and hyperactive, or they may be *depressed.* In either case, extremes of mood are intense or long lasting, and depressed individuals run a high risk of suicide. Milder mood disorders are discussed in this chapter. More severe mood problems, which often include psychosis, are covered in the next chapter.

Anxiety disorders may take the form of *phobias* (irrational fears of objects, activities, or situations), *panic* (in which the person suffers sudden unexplainable feelings of total panic), *generalized anxiety* (chronic and persistent anxiety), or *post-traumatic stress disorder* (high anxiety that surfaces after an extremely distressing event). A pattern known as *obsessive-compulsive* behavior is also associated with anxiety (more on this later).

Somatoform disorders (so-MAT-oh-form) are indicated when a person has physical symptoms that mimic physical disease or injury (paralysis, blindness, or chronic pain, for example) for which there is no identifiable cause. The assumption in such cases in that psychological factors underlie the symptoms.

Dissociative disorders include cases of sudden temporary *amnesia* and instances of *multiple personality* like William Milligan displayed. Also included are frighten-

Fig. 19–1 *The self-portraits shown here were painted by Andy Wilf between 1978 and 1981. During that time, Wilf is said to have increasingly abused drugs and alcohol. This dramatic series of images is a record of his self-destructive descent into a private hell. The third painting shows a shrouded skull—and foretells the artist's fate. Wilf died of a drug overdose early in 1982. Drug abuse is but one of the many psychopathologies, or "problems in living," psychologists seek to alleviate. (Courtesy of Ulrike Kantor, Ulrike Kantor Gallery.)*

ing episodes of *depersonalization*. Depersonalization refers to feelings of being outside one's body, of behaving like a robot, or of being in a dream world.

Personality disorders are deeply ingrained, unhealthy personality patterns. Such patterns are usually apparent by adolescence and continue throughout most of adult life. They include paranoid (overly suspicious), narcissistic (self-loving), dependent, compulsive, and antisocial personality types, as well as others.

Sexual disorders include *gender identity disorders* (where a person's sexual identity does not match his or her physical gender), *transsexualism* (a persistent discomfort about one's sex and a desire to change to the opposite sex), and a wide range of deviations in sexual behavior known as *paraphilias* (fetishism, voyeurism, and so on). Also found in this category are a variety of *sexual dysfunctions* (problems in sexual desire or sexual response; see Chapter 25).

Question: Shouldn't neurosis be included in the list?

The former *Diagnostic and Statistical Manual* (DSM-II) listed neurosis as a disorder, but the new, revised version (DSM-III-R) discourages use of the term. Why? Because the label *neurosis* tends to lump together too many separate problems. Behavior once considered "neurotic" is now classified as an anxiety, somatoform, or dissociative disorder (or in some cases as a mild mood disorder). Many professionals continue to use the term *neurosis* to loosely refer to problems associated with excessive anxiety. It still makes sense to separate such "neurotic" problems from psychosis, because they do not involve a major loss of contact with reality.

Question: Is psychosis the same as insanity?

No. Psychosis is a *psychiatric* term that describes a particular type of psychopathology. **Insanity** is a *legal* term. Persons who are declared "insane" are not legally responsible for their actions and can be involuntarily committed to a mental hospital. Legally, insanity is usually established by the testimony of psychologists and psychiatrists who serve as **expert witnesses** in a court of law (Carelli, 1982). (See this chapter's Exploration for further discussion of insanity.)

Normality—What Is Normal?

To classify certain behaviors or certain people as psychologically unhealthy raises the age-old issue of what is normal. Defining normality can be a tricky business. We might begin by saying that **subjective discomfort** is characteristic of psychopathology; that is, the unhealthy personality will be marked by unhappiness, anxiety, depression, or other signs of emotional upset.

Question: But couldn't a person be psychotic without feeling subjective discomfort?

Yes. A problem with this definition is that a person's behavior might be quite maladaptive without causing personal discomfort. A psychotic person displaying obviously bizarre and maladjusted behavior might feel "on top of the world." It could be said, also, that a *lack* of discomfort may reveal a problem. If you were to show no signs of grief or depression in response to the death of a friend or loved one, we might suspect psychopathology. In practice, subjective discomfort accounts for most instances in which a person voluntarily seeks professional help.

Some psychologists have tried to pin down normality more objectively by using **statistical definitions.** For example, since we know that anxiety is a characteristic of several milder disorders, we could devise a test to learn how many people show low, medium, or high levels of anxiety. Usually, the results of such a test will form a **normal** (bell-shaped) **curve** (Fig. 19–2). (Normal in this case is a statistical concept referring only to the shape of the curve.) Notice that most people score in the center region of such a curve. Those people who deviate from the average by being anxious all the time (high anxiety) might be considered abnormal. Incidentally, a person who never feels anxiety might also be considered abnormal.

Question: Then a statistical definition of abnormality tells us nothing about the meaning of a deviation from the norm?

Right. It is as statistically "abnormal" (unusual) for a person to score above 145 on an IQ test as it is to score below 55, but only in the second case would we consider the score "abnormal" or undesirable.

Another major problem with statistical definitions is the question of *where to draw the line* between normality and abnormality. To take a new example, we could obtain the average frequency of sexual intercourse for persons of a particular age, sex, and marital status. Obviously, a person who feels driven to seek sexual release dozens of times a day has a problem. But as we move back toward the norm, we face the statistical problem of drawing lines. How often must an otherwise normal behavior occur before it becomes abnormal?

Social nonconformity may also serve as a basis for judging normality. Abnormal behavior can sometimes be viewed as a failure in *socialization*. In this case, the individual may not have adopted the usual minimum rules

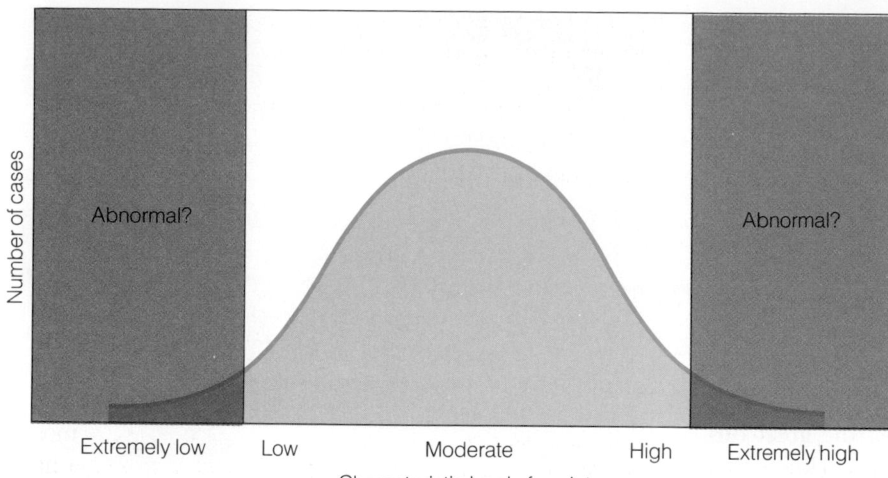

Fig. 19–2 *The number of people displaying a personal characteristic may help define what is statistically abnormal.*

for social conduct or may have learned to engage in socially destructive or self-destructive behavior. This type of nonconformity must be carefully distinguished from that shown by highly creative individuals or by those who have a unique lifestyle (Fig. 19–3). It should be noted also that strict adherence to social norms is no guarantee of mental health. In some cases, psychopathology takes the form of rigid conformity.

Before any behavior can be defined as normal or abnormal, we must consider the **context** in which it occurs. Is it normal to stand outside and water a lawn? It depends on whether or not it is raining. Is it abnormal for a grown man to remove his pants and expose himself to another man or woman in a place of business? It depends on whether the other person is a bank clerk or a doctor! Almost any imaginable behavior can be considered normal in some context, as the following example indicates.

> In mid-October, 1973, an airplane carrying a rugby team called the Old Christians crashed in the snow-capped Andes of South America. Incredibly, 16 of the 45 people who had been aboard at the time of the crash survived 73 days in deep snow and subfreezing temperatures. They were forced to use extremely grim measures to do so—they ate the bodies of those who had died in the crash. (Adapted from *Time*, Jan. 8, 1973)

Culture is one of the most influential contexts in which any behavior is judged. In some cultures it is considered normal to believe that plants and trees are inhabited by

Fig. 19–3 *Social nonconformity does not automatically indicate psychopathology.*

spirits, or to defecate or urinate in public, or to appear naked in public. In our culture each of these behaviors would be considered unusual or abnormal. Cultural differences can also be more subtle. There is, in other words, a high degree of **cultural relativity** in perceptions of normality and abnormality (see Highlight 19–1). Still, all known cultures classify people as abnormal if they either fail to communicate with others or are consistently unpredictable in their actions.

Question: If abnormality is so hard to define, how are judgments of psychopathology made?

It should be clear at this point that all definitions of abnormality are **relative.** Yet, in spite of the great difficulty of formally defining abnormality, we do know that psychological disturbances occur and that they must be identified.

In practice, the judgment that a person needs help usually occurs when the person *does something* (hits a person, hallucinates, stares into space, collects rolls of toilet paper, and so forth) that *annoys* or *gains the attention* of a person in a *position of power* (an employer, teacher, parent, spouse, or the person himself or herself), who then *does something* about it. (A police officer may be called, the person may be urged to see a psychologist, a relative may start commitment proceedings, or the person may voluntarily seek help.)

The sections that follow continue our discussion by describing in greater detail some of the problems already mentioned. A full discussion of schizophrenia and other more severe problems is reserved for the next chapter. Before you read further, see if you can answer these questions.

● HIGHLIGHT 19–1
Women, Culture, and "Madness"

Many more women than men are treated for psychological problems. Why?

- As a result of cultural training, women may be more willing than men to reveal distress and to seek help for their problems.
- Because women are often denied power, responsibility, and independence in our society, they may more often feel depressed, anxious, or hopeless—for good reason.
- There may be a damaging male bias to traditional concepts of normality.

The third possibility is perhaps the most controversial. According to psychologist Marcie Kaplan (1983) and others, DSM-III-R has a distinct male bias. Kaplan believes that women are penalized both for conforming to female stereotypes and for ignoring them. If a woman is independent, aggressive, and unemotional, she may be considered "unhealthy." Yet, at the same time, a woman who is vain, emotional, irrational, and dependent on others (all "feminine" traits in our culture) may be classified as a histrionic or dependent personality.

For the most part, DSM-III-R is a highly useful system. Nevertheless, Kaplan's criticism helps illustrate the subtle influence that culture may have on perceptions of normality.

Learning Check

1. Amnesia, multiple personality, and depersonalization are possible problems in
   a. mood disorders *b.* somatoform disorders *c.* psychosis *d.* dissociative disorders
2. Which among the following is *not* a major psychological problem listed in DSM-III-R?
   a. mood disorders *b.* personality disorders *c.* insanity *d.* anxiety disorders
3. A major difference between psychotic disorders and anxiety disorders (or other milder problems) is that in psychosis the individual has lost contact with reality as shown by the presence of ________ or ________.
4. Statistical definitions of abnormality successfully avoid the limitations of other approaches. T or F?
5. One of the most powerful contexts in which judgments of normality and abnormality are made is
   a. the family *b.* occupational settings *c.* religious systems *d.* culture

Answers:
1. *d* **2.** *c* **3.** delusions, hallucinations **4.** F **5.** *d*

Personality Disorders—Blueprints for Maladjustment

As stated earlier, personality disorders are deeply ingrained maladaptive personality patterns. For example, the paranoid personality is overly suspicious, mistrusting, hypersensitive, guarded, and distrustful of the honesty of others. Persons having narcissistic personalities are preoccupied with their own self-importance: They need constant admiration and they are absorbed in fantasies of power, wealth, brilliance, beauty, and love. The dependent personality is marked by an extreme lack of self-confidence; others are allowed to run the person's life, and the person places his or her own needs second to others. The case described in Highlight 19–2 captures the flavor of a severe personality disorder.

The list of personality disorders is long (Table 19–2), so let us focus on a single frequently misunderstood problem: the antisocial personality.

Question: What are the characteristics of an antisocial personality?

Antisocial Personality The individual with an **antisocial personality** (sometimes referred to as a *sociopath* or *psychopath*) typically has a long history of conflict with society. Antisocial persons are irresponsible, impulsive, selfish, lacking in judgment and morals, and unable to learn from experience. They are also incapable of deep feelings, including guilt, shame, fear, loyalty, and love. In short, the sociopath is poorly socialized, has a general disregard for the truth, and seems to lack a conscience (DSM-III-R, 1987).

Question: Are sociopaths dangerous?

Many sociopaths are delinquents or criminals who may pose a threat to the general public. Studies show that more than 65 percent of all persons with antisocial personalities have been arrested, usually for crimes such as

HIGHLIGHT 19–2
Judy—A Borderline Personality

"Get out of here and leave me alone so I can die in peace," Judy screamed at her nurses. Although only 42 years old and normally very attractive, Judy looked old, disheveled, and haggard in the seclusion room of the psychiatric hospital. On one of her arms, long dark red marks mingled with the scars of previous suicide attempts. Judy once bragged to her therapist that her record was 67 stitches. Today, the nurses had to strap her into restraints to keep her from gouging her eyes out. She was given a sedative and slept for 12 hours. She woke calmly and asked for her therapist—even though this latest incident was ostensibly triggered by his canceling her morning appointment and rescheduling it for the same afternoon.

Judy has a borderline personality disorder. Although she is capable of working, Judy has repeatedly lost jobs because of her turbulent relationships with others. At times she can be friendly and a real charmer. At other times she is extremely unpredictable, moody, and even suicidal. Being a friend to Judy means accepting a burden that is nearly unbearable at times. The cancellation of an appointment, special dates that are forgotten, a wrong turn of phrase—these and similar small incidents may trigger Judy's anger or, worse yet, a suicide attempt. Judy's only hope lies in intensive, long-term therapy.

Table 19–2 Personality Disorders and Typical Degree of Impairment

Moderate Impairment

Dependent: Unhealthy submissiveness and dependence on others

Histrionic: Excessive emotion and attention-seeking behavior

Narcissistic: Exaggerated self-importance and desire for constant admiration

Antisocial: Irresponsible and antisocial behavior

High Impairment

Obsessive-compulsive: Perfectionism and inflexibility

Passive aggressive: Passive resistance to performing tasks or doing things others request

Schizoid: Limited emotion and a lack of interest in close relationships with others

Avoidant: Discomfort in social situations, fear of evaluation, timidity

Severe Impairment

Borderline: Extremely unstable self-image, relationships, and moods

Paranoid: A pervasive tendency to interpret the actions of others as demeaning or threatening

Schizotypal: Extremely odd behavior and thought patterns, but not actively psychotic

From DSM-III-R, 1987 and Millon, 1981.

robbery, vandalism, or rape. However, sociopaths are rarely the crazed murderers that have been portrayed on TV and in movies. In fact, many sociopaths create a good first impression and are frequently described as charming. Their lying, self-serving manipulation and lack of dependability only gradually become evident to their "friends." Many successful businesspeople, entertainers, politicians, and other seemingly normal persons reveal sociopathic leanings by coldly using others for their own ends.

Question: What causes sociopathy?

People with antisocial personalities usually have a childhood history of emotional deprivation and neglect. As mentioned in Chapter 15, some psychologists believe that infants who fail to form a healthy emotional attachment to a caregiver later may be prone to antisocial behavior (Magid, 1988). Adult sociopaths also display some subtle physical problems. For example, they produce unusual brain wave patterns suggesting under-arousal of the brain (Hare & Cox, 1978). This condition may explain why many sociopaths are thrill seekers. Quite likely, they are searching for stimulation strong enough to overcome their chronic under-arousal and "boredom" (Carson et al., 1988).

Another interesting finding comes from psychological testing in which adult sociopaths must learn to avoid an electric shock. Under these and similar circumstances, they show much less anxiety than normal (Hare & Cox, 1978). Those with antisocial personalities might therefore be described as *emotionally cold*. They simply do not feel normal pangs of conscience, guilt, or anxiety. This coldness seems to account for an unusual ability to calmly lie, cheat, steal, or manipulate others.

Question: Can sociopathy be treated?

Antisocial personality disorders are rarely treated with success. All too often, sociopaths manipulate therapy like any other situation. If it is to their advantage to act "cured," they will do so, but they return to former patterns of behavior at the first opportunity. There is, however, some evidence that antisocial behavior declines somewhat after age 30.

Sexual Deviance—Trench Coats, Whips, Leathers, and Lace

Sexual deviance implies a departure from accepted standards of proper behavior. By the most strict standards (including the law in some states), any sexual activity other than face-to-face heterosexual intercourse between married adults is "deviant." But public standards are often at odds with behavior found privately acceptable. By private standards, large numbers of people regard oral sex, masturbation, and premarital sex as perfectly normal.

From a psychological point of view, the mark of true sexual deviations is that they are compulsive, bizarre, and destructive. Typically, they cause guilt, anxiety, or discomfort for one or both participants. Deviations fitting this definition are related to a wide variety of behaviors, including **pedophilia** (sex with children), **incest** (sex with blood relatives), **fetishism** (sexual arousal associated with inanimate objects), **exhibitionism** (displaying the genitals to unwilling viewers), **voyeurism** (viewing the genitals of others), **transvestic fetishism** (achieving sexual arousal by wearing clothing of the opposite sex), **sexual sadism** (deriving sexual pleasure from inflicting pain), **sexual masochism** (desiring pain as part of the sex act), and **frotteurism** (sexually touching or rubbing against a nonconsenting person, usually in a public place such as a subway).

Sexual deviance is a highly emotional subject, and many misconceptions exist about it. Two of the most misunderstood problems are exhibitionism and pedophilia. Check your understanding against the information that follows.

Exhibitionism Exhibitionism is a common problem. Roughly 35 percent of all sexual arrests are for "flashing." Exhibitionists are typically male and married, and most come from strict and repressive backgrounds. Exhibitionists have the highest repeat rate among sexual offenders. Most of them feel a deep sense of inadequacy, which produces a compulsive need to prove their "manhood" by frightening women. While exhibitionists are usually harmless, those who approach closer than arm's reach may be dangerous (Sue et al., 1981). In general, a woman confronted by an exhibitionist can assume that his goal is to shock and alarm her. By becoming visibly upset she actually encourages him (Hyde, 1984).

Child Molestation Child molesters, who also are usually males, are often pictured as despicable perverts lurking in dark alleys. In fact, most are married, and two-thirds are fathers. Many are rigid, passive, puritanical, or religious. In one-half to two-thirds of all cases of molestation, the offender is a friend, acquaintance, or relative of the child. Molesters are also often thought of as child rapists. But most molestations rarely exceed fondling (Sue et al., 1981).

Question: How serious are the effects of a molestation?

The impact varies widely and is affected by how long the abuse lasts and whether genital sexual acts are involved (Freize, 1987). Many authorities believe that a single incident of fondling is unlikely to cause severe psychological harm to a child. For most children the event is frightening, but not a lasting trauma. This is why parents are urged not to overreact to such incidents or to become hysterical. Doing so only further frightens the child (Wilson et al., 1984). This does not mean, however, that parents should ignore hints from a child that a molestation may have occurred. Here are some hints of trouble that parents should watch for.

Recognizing Signs of Child Molestation

1. The child fears being seen nude (for instance, during bathing), when such fears were absent before.
2. The child develops physical complaints, such as headaches, stomachaches, and other stress symptoms.
3. The child displays anxiety, fidgeting, shame, or discomfort when any reference to sexual behavior occurs.
4. The child becomes markedly emotional and irritable.
5. The child engages in hazardous risk taking, such as jumping from high places or riding a bicycle dangerously in traffic.
6. The child reveals self-destructive or suicidal thoughts, self-blame.
7. The child shows a loss of self-esteem or self-worth.

(Adapted from Frederick, 1987)

Repeated molestations, those that involve force or threats, and incidents that exceed fondling can leave lasting emotional scars. As adults, many victims of incest or molestation develop sexual phobias. For them, lovemaking may evoke vivid and terrifying memories of the childhood victimization (Frederick, 1987; Jehu, 1984). Serious harm is especially likely to occur if the molester is someone the child deeply trusts. Molestations by parents, close relatives, teachers, youth leaders, and similar persons can be quite damaging (Freize, 1987). In such cases professional counseling is often needed.

Rape As the preceding discussion suggests, the picture of sexual deviance that most often emerges is one of sexual inhibition and immaturity. Quite often, some relatively infantile sexual expression (like exhibitionism or pedophilia) is selected because it is less threatening than normal sexuality. Rapists are a notable exception to this pattern, however. Rapists often inflict more violence on their victims than is necessary to achieve their goal.

Most authorities no longer think of rape as a sexual act. Rather, it is an act of brutality or aggression based on the need to debase others. Many rapists are antisocial personalities who impulsively take what they want without concern for the feelings of the victim or guilt about their deed. Others harbor deep-seated resentment or outright hatred of women. However, the problem may reach far deeper (see Highlight 19–3).

Quite often, the rapist's goal is not strictly sexual intercourse: It is to attack, subordinate, humiliate, and degrade the victim. Typical after-effects for the victim include rage, guilt, depression, loss of self-esteem, shame, sexual adjustment problems, and in many cases, a lasting

● HIGHLIGHT 19–3
Sex Role Stereotyping and Rape

A number of writers have suggested that rape is in some ways related to sex role socialization. That is, many people learn to believe that women should not show direct interest in sex. Men, on the other hand, are taught to take the initiative and to persist in attempts at sexual intimacy—even when the woman says no.

Psychologists James Check and Neil Malamuth believe that such attitudes create a "rape-supportive culture." In their view, rape is only an extreme expression of a system that condones coercive (forced) sexual intimacy. They point out, for instance, that the single most used cry of rapists to their victims is, "You know you want it." And afterward, "There now, you really enjoyed it, didn't you."

To test the hypothesis that stereotyped images contribute to rape, male college students were classified as either high or low in sex role stereotyping. Each student then read one of three stories: The first described voluntary intercourse; the second depicted stranger rape; and the third described acquaintance rape (forced intercourse on a date).

As predicted, college males high in sex role stereotyping were more aroused by the rape stories. Their arousal patterns, in fact, were similar to those found among actual rapists. Moreover, a chilling 44 percent of those tested indicated they would consider rape—especially if they could be sure of not being caught (Check & Malamuth, 1983).

In another study of rape, over half of a sample of adults agreed with the statement, "A woman who goes to the home or apartment of a man on the first date implies she is willing to have sex" (Burt, 1980). In view of such attitudes—and the continuing widespread belief that when a woman says no she means yes—it is little wonder that rape occurs every 6 minutes in the United States. Perhaps the time has come for our culture to make it clear that no means no.

mistrust of male-female relationships (Freize, 1987). The impact is so great that most women who successfully ward off a rape attempt are just as depressed as rape survivors (Bart & O'Brien, 1985). Any man who doubts the seriousness of rape should imagine himself mistakenly placed in jail, where he is violently raped (sodomized) by other inmates. There is no pleasure in rape for victims of either sex. It is truly a despicable crime.

Learning Check

1. Which of the following personality disorders is associated with an inflated sense of self-importance and a constant need for attention and admiration?
   a. narcissistic *b.* antisocial *c.* paranoid *d.* manipulative
2. Over one-half of all persons with antisocial personalities have been arrested. T or F?
3. Antisocial personality disorders are difficult to treat, but there is typically a decline in antisocial behavior after adolescence. T or F?
4. The formal term for child molesting is
   a. sadism *b.* pedophilia *c.* frotteurism *d.* fetishism
5. What percentage of arrests for sexual offenses involve exhibitionism? ________________
6. Rape is primarily an act of brutality or aggression, rather than an exclusively sexual act. T or F?

Answers:
1. *a* 2. T 3. F 4. *b* 5. 35 percent 6. T

Anxiety-Based Disorders—When Anxiety Rules

Imagine for a moment the feeling of waiting to take an important test for which you are unprepared; or waiting to give a speech to a large audience of strangers; or being followed by a police car while you are driving. You have almost certainly felt **anxiety** in one of these situations. As you may have noticed, the physical reactions that accompany anxiety are similar to those felt in fear. Anxiety is similar to fear, except that anxiety is a response to an *unclear or ambiguous threat*. For instance, what we commonly call "stage fright" is actually anxiety, because an audience poses no real threat to safety (except, perhaps, at extremely bad talent shows). Compared to anxiety, fear is more focused and intense. Typically, it is the result of a specific, identifiable threat (Kleinknecht, 1986).

Disruptive Anxiety We all occasionally feel anxiety, and at times of great stress, anxiety may be intense. But anxiety that is out of proportion to a situation may reveal a problem:

> A college student appeared at the counseling center with a complaint that he was deathly afraid of examinations. He had previously been involved in a confrontation with an instructor whom he accused of having administered an unfair test in that there was not enough time to answer all the questions. He soon realized that the time limit had not been long enough because he had wasted most of his time in attempting to control his anxieties. He had already skipped two other examinations by remaining in bed petrified with his fears of failure. (Adapted from Suinn, 1975)*

The student just described shows signs of having a disruptive emotional problem, but one that does not involve a loss of contact with reality. As mentioned earlier, such problems were once called neuroses. Now they are classified separately as anxiety disorders, dissociative disorders, and somatoform disorders. In general, these problems involve the following features:

- High levels of anxiety and/or restrictive, self-defeating behavior patterns
- A tendency to use elaborate defense mechanisms or avoidance responses to maintain minimal functioning
- Pervasive feelings of stress, insecurity, inferiority, unhappiness, and dissatisfaction with life

In short, affected persons struggle to preserve control, but remain ineffective and accomplish little.

Question: If fear and anxiety are normal emotions, when do they signal a problem?

*From *Fundamentals of Behavior Pathology* by R. M. Suinn. Copyright © 1975. Reprinted by permission of John Wiley & Sons, Inc. Additional Suinn quotes in this chapter and the next are from the same source.

The simplest answer is that a problem exists when anxiety becomes intense or persistent enough to prevent a person from doing what he or she wants or needs to do. Anxiety, fears, and phobias are probably the most common psychological disturbances today. More than 10 percent of the adult population are so affected by these disturbances that they could be diagnosed as having an anxiety disorder (Kleinknecht, 1986).

Question: Do such problems cause a "nervous breakdown"?

Adjustment Disorders Anxiety-based problems seriously disrupt people's lives and almost always cause misery. However, they rarely bring about a total "breakdown." Actually, the term *nervous breakdown* has no formal meaning. Also, "nervous breakdown" seems to imply some sort of disease of the nervous system. But there is nothing physically wrong with the nerves of an anxious or emotionally troubled individual. What many people have in mind when they use the term is properly called an **adjustment disorder.**

Adjustment disorders occur when life stresses push people beyond their ability to cope effectively. Examples of such stresses are prolonged unemployment, extreme marital strife, and chronic physical illness. The presence of an adjustment disorder is signaled by extreme irritability, sleep disturbances, loss of appetite, physical complaints, and apathy, anxiety, or depression. Often, these problems are successfully treated with rest, sedation, supportive counseling, and a chance to "talk through" fears and anxieties.

Question: How is an adjustment disorder different from an anxiety disorder?

The outward symptoms can be similar. However, adjustment disorders typically disappear when life circumstances improve. This shows their link to stressful events.

Anxiety Disorders

In most anxiety disorders, the person's distress seems greatly out of proportion to the situation. Consider, for example, the following description of Ethel B:

> She was never completely relaxed, and complained of vague feelings of restlessness, and a fear that something was "just around the corner." Although she felt that she had to go to work to help pay the family bills, she could not bring herself to start anything new for fear that something terrible would happen on the job. She had experienced a few extreme anxiety attacks during which she felt "like I couldn't breathe, like I was sealed up in a transparent envelope. I thought I was going to have a heart attack. I couldn't stop shaking." (Suinn, 1975)

Distress like Ethel B's is a key element in anxiety disorders. Many psychologists believe that it also underlies dissociative and somatoform disorders, where maladaptive behavior serves to reduce anxiety and personal discomfort. To deepen your understanding, let's examine several related anxiety-based disorders. (A list of anxiety disorders is provided in Table 19–3.)

Generalized Anxiety Disorder The essential feature of a **generalized anxiety disorder** is at least 6 months of unrealistic or excessive anxiety and worry (DSM-III-R, 1987). The discomfort felt in this disorder is sometimes described as **free-floating anxiety,** because the anxiety is so general and related to many different worries. Affected individuals typically complain of sweating, racing heart, clammy hands, dizziness, upset stomach, rapid breathing, and other symptoms of autonomic nervous system activity. They also are continually preoccupied by worries, which makes them irritable and unable to concentrate. Typical worries involve adequacy at work, acceptance by others, desertion by a loved one, feelings of inferiority, and anticipation of disasters such as failure and injury or death of close relatives (Wilson, 1986).

Question: Was Ethel B's problem a generalized anxiety disorder?

No. The added presence of *anxiety attacks* indicates she suffered from **panic disorder.**

Panic Disorder In this very disturbing pattern, continuous tension, worry, and anxiety occasionally explode into *sudden, unexpected* episodes of intense panic. During a panic attack, affected individuals experience heart palpitations or chest pain, choking or smothering sensations, vertigo, feelings of unreality, trembling, and fears of dying, going crazy, or losing control during the attack (DSM-III-R, 1987). Many believe that they are having a heart

Table 19–3 Anxiety Disorders

Anxiety Disorders
Generalized anxiety disorder
Panic disorder
Simple phobia
Social phobia
Agoraphobia
Obsessive-compulsive disorder
Post-traumatic stress disorder

DSM-III-R, 1987.

attack, are going insane, or are about to die. Needless to say, individuals showing this pattern are unhappy and uncomfortable much of the time.

Compare: Anxiety and Panic

Generalized anxiety disorder The person is in a chronic state of tension and worries about work, relationships, ability, or impending disaster; he or she thinks about withdrawing from threatening situations, procrastinates, and copes poorly.

Panic disorder The person is in a chronic state of tension, and he or she also has brief moments of *intense* anxiety; the person worries mainly about losing control (having an anxiety attack) and is very quick to use avoidance to lower anxiety.

Phobic Disorders As stated earlier, phobias are exaggerated, irrational fears that persist even when there is no real danger (Kleinknecht, 1986). In **phobic disorders,** persistent fears, anxiety, and avoidance are focused on various objects, activities, or situations (Fig. 19–4). Affected persons recognize that their fear is unreasonable and excessive, but they cannot control it. For a phobic disorder to exist, the person's fear must disrupt his or her daily life.

Phobias fall into three main categories. These are *simple phobias, social phobias,* and *agoraphobia* (Wilson, 1986). (See the Compare box for definitions.) The following list gives some examples of simple phobias.

Astraphobia—fear of lightning
Arachnephobia—fear of spiders
Acrophobia—fear of heights
Claustrophobia—fear of closed spaces
Hemophobia—fear of blood
Nyctophobia—fear of darkness
Pathophobia—fear of disease
Zoophobia—fear of animals

These, of course, are only a few of the possibilities. Simple phobias may be attached to nearly any object or situation.* Almost everyone has a few mild phobias: Fears of heights, closed spaces, or bugs and crawly things are common. A phobic disorder differs from such garden-variety fears in that it produces overwhelming anxiety that may cause vomiting, wild climbing and running, or fainting. Phobic persons are so threatened that they will go to almost any length to avoid the feared object or situation.

Compare: Three Principal Types of Phobias

Simple (or specific) phobia Fear of specific types of objects or situations and avoidance of such objects or situations.

Social phobia Fear of social situations in which one can be observed, evaluated, embarrassed, or humiliated by others; avoidance of certain social situations, such as eating, writing, blushing, or speaking in public.

Agoraphobia Fear of having an anxiety attack and losing control in public places or unfamiliar situations; fear of leaving the house and familiar surroundings.

Question: Are some phobias more common than others?

The most disruptive problem is **agoraphobia** (ah-go-rah-FOBE-ee-ah). One expert estimates that 1 out of every 100 people has agoraphobia severe enough to restrict his or her life to a serious degree (Hardy, 1976).

Agoraphobia often starts after a stressful life event, such as an interpersonal conflict (Last et al., 1984). In many instances, this triggers a panic attack that seems to come from nowhere (Kleinknecht, 1986). (In many cases, persons suffering from agoraphobia also have panic disorder.) Soon after, the agoraphobic person begins to develop an intense fear of leaving the familiar setting of the home. Typically, he or she begins to find ways of avoiding areas of insecurity—such as crowds, open roads, super-

Fig. 19–4 *For a person with a strong fear of snakes (ophidiophobia), merely looking at this picture may be unsettling.*

*Obviously, by combining the appropriate root word with the word *phobia,* any number of unlikely fears can be named. Some are *acarophobia,* a fear of itching; *zemmiphobia,* fear of the great mole rat; *phobiaphobia,* fear of fear; *arachibutyrophobia,* fear of peanut butter sticking to the roof of the mouth, and *hippopotomonstrosesquipedaliophobia,* fear of long words!

markets, automobiles, and so on (Zane & Milt, 1984). As a result, agoraphobics depend heavily on others to carry out everyday tasks and to maintain a semblance of a normal life. Some agoraphobics are literally housebound and never leave the security of their homes (DSM-III-R, 1987).

Obsessive-compulsive Disorder **Obsessions** are images or thoughts that intrude into consciousness against a person's will. You have probably experienced a mild obsessional thought in the form of some song or stupid commercial jingle that is repeated over and over in your mind. This may be irritating, but it is certainly not disturbing in any major sense. True obsessions are so disturbing that they cause anxiety or extreme discomfort. The most common obsessions are about violence (such as poisoning one's spouse or stabbing a child), about being "dirty" or "unclean," about whether one has performed some action (such as turning off the stove), and about committing immoral acts (Wilson, 1986).

Obsessions usually give rise to **compulsions.** These are irrational acts a person feels driven to repeat (Fig. 19–5). Often, the compulsive act helps control or block out anxiety caused by the obsession. For example, a minister who finds profanities popping into his mind might take up compulsively counting his heartbeat to prevent himself from thinking "dirty" words.

Fig. 19–5 *The severe obsessions and compulsions of billionarie Howard Hughes led him to live as a recluse for over 20 years. Hughes had an intense fear of contamination. To avoid infection, he constructed sterile, isolated environments in which his contact with people and objects was strictly limited by complicated rituals. Before handling a spoon, for instance, Hughes had his attendants wrap the handle in tissue paper and seal it with tape. A second piece of tissue was then wrapped around the first before he would touch it (Hodgson & Miller, 1982). A spoon prepared as Hughes required is shown at right.*

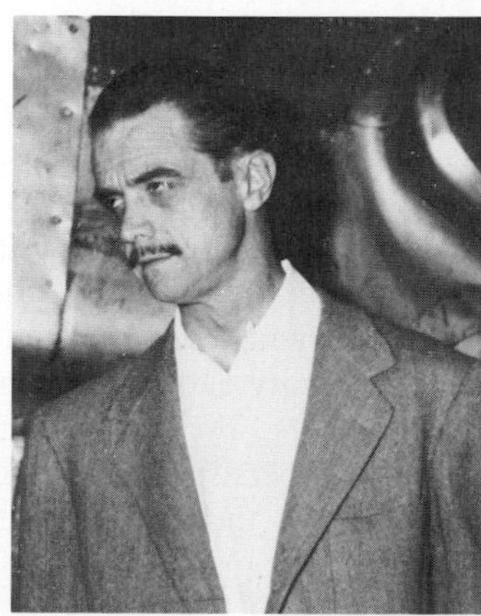

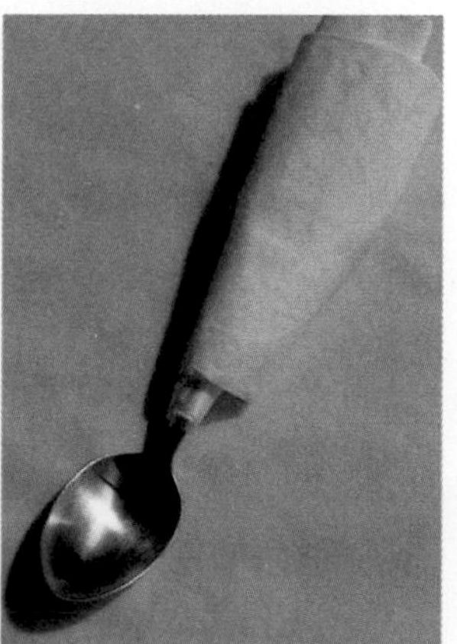

Many people with compulsions can be classified as *checkers* or *cleaners* (Kleinknecht, 1986). Thus, a person who feels guilty or unclean because of a conflict about masturbation might be driven to wash his hands hundreds of times a day. And a young mother who repeatedly has an image of a knife plunging into her infant might count all the knives in the house several times a day and check repeatedly to see that they are locked away.

Of course, not all obsessive-compulsive disorders are so dramatic. Many simply involve extreme orderliness and rigid routine. Compulsive attention to detail and rigid adherence to procedures and rules make the highly anxious person feel more secure by keeping activities totally structured and under control. Notice, too, that when such patterns are long-standing, but less intense, they may be classified as a personality disorder.

Post-traumatic Stress Disorder Most anxiety disorders are relatively lasting patterns. As such, they have little connection to the actual degree of threat. A notable exception is found in **post-traumatic stress disorder (PTSD).** This problem occurs when stresses *outside the range of normal human experience* cause a significant psychological and emotional disturbance (DSM-III-R, 1987). Such reactions frequently follow sudden disasters, such as floods, tornadoes, earthquakes, or serious accidents (Fig. 19–6). Research shows that PTSD also affects many political hostages, combat veterans, prisoners of war, and victims of terrorism, violent crime, child molestation, or rape (Frederick, 1987).

Characteristic symptoms of PTSD include repeatedly reliving the traumatic event, avoiding stimuli associated with the event, and a numbing of emotions. Also common are insomnia, nightmares, guardedness, an inability to concentrate, irritability, and explosions of anger or aggression. Reactions like these may surface long after the stress has passed—as has happened to many veterans of the Vietnam War.

Compare: Adjustment Disorder and PTSD

Adjustment disorder Stressor is usually moderate and within the range of common experience; stress is ongoing and produces anxiety and physical symptoms.

PTSD Stressor is outside the range of common experience and would produce fear and anxiety in anyone who experienced it; person mentally relives the trauma and feels anxious after the event.

Fig. 19–6 *In the aftermath of natural disasters, some survivors suffer from post-traumatic stress reactions. For some, the flare-up of anxiety and distress may occur months or years after the stressful event is over.*

Dissociative Disorders

A dissociative reaction is marked by striking episodes of *amnesia, fugue,* or *multiple personality.* **Amnesia** is the inability to recall one's name, address, or past. **Fugue** (sounds like "fewg") involves fleeing to escape extreme conflict or threat. Dissociations are often triggered by highly traumatic events, as the following case illustrates (Braun, 1986):

> An American soldier in the Vietnam War wandered into the countryside and ambushed Vietcong soldiers without any memory of his actions. His fugue and amnesia were triggered when he discovered the dead body of a Vietnamese child he had adopted. Later, in therapy, he was able to remember the incident: "After 15 years in the Army, he was all I had. It's all my fault! It's all my fault! If I had just taken you over to the hooch, you wouldn't be there, man! It's not fair. They ain't gotta kill kids." (Spiegel, 1986)

It can easily be seen that forgetting one's identity or fleeing unpleasant situations can serve as a defense against intolerable anxiety.

Multiple personality is a relatively rare condition in which two or more separate personalities exist in an individual. (Note that multiple personality is *not* schizophrenia. Schizophrenia is a form of psychosis, as discussed in the next chapter.) One of the most dramatic examples of multiple personality ever recorded is described in the book *Sybil* (Schreiber, 1973). Sybil had 16 different personalities. Each personality had a distinct voice, vocabulary, and posture. One personality could play the piano (not Sybil), but the others could not.

When a personality other than Sybil was in control, Sybil experienced a "time lapse" or memory blackout. For example, as a child she once "awoke" as a fifth-grader and couldn't understand why she was not in her third-grade classroom. When she was asked to do a multiplication problem, she couldn't begin. Two years of her life were missing, and the personality that had inhabited her body had learned multiplication, but Sybil had not.

Sybil's amnesia and alternate personalities developed during childhood when she was regularly beaten, locked in closets, perversely tortured, sexually abused, and almost killed. Sybil's first dissociations allowed her to escape by creating another person who would suffer torture in her place. Multiple personality often begins with similar unbearable childhood experiences. In later years, Sybil continued the pattern by developing additional personalities to defend against new stresses.

Therapy for multiple personality is often aided by hypnosis, which allows contact with the various personalities. The goal of therapy is *integration* and *fusion* of the various personalities into a single, balanced entity (Braun, 1986). Fortunately, multiple personality is far rarer in real life than it is in TV dramas!

Somatoform Disorders

Perhaps you have known someone, particularly someone prone to anxiety, who seems to be continually distracted by fears of having a serious disease. Usually such individuals are preoccupied with bodily functions, such as their heartbeat or digestion, or with minor physical problems such as a small sore or an occasional cough. Often, they have a complicated medical history and have, over the years, consulted numerous doctors. Typically, their unwarranted fear of having a disease persists despite the fact that there is no medical basis for their complaints (DSM-III-R, 1987).

Question: Are you describing hypochondria?

Yes. In **hypochondriasis** (HI-po-kon-DRY-uh-sis), the person has multiple physical complaints for which medical attention is sought, but for which no clear physical cause can be found. **Somatoform pain** is a related problem in which the person is disabled by pain that has no identifiable physical basis. A rarer form of somatoform disorder (or "body-form" disorder) is called a *conversion reaction.*

Question: How does a conversion reaction differ from hypochondriasis?

Conversion reactions occur when anxiety or severe emotional conflicts are "converted" into symptoms that actually disturb physical functioning or closely resemble physical disability. **Conversion disorders** are usually quite dramatic. For instance, a soldier might become deaf or lame or develop "glove anesthesia" just before a battle.

Question: What is "glove anesthesia"?

"Glove anesthesia" is a loss of sensitivity in the areas of the skin that would normally be covered by a glove. Glove anesthesia shows that conversion symptoms often contradict known medical facts. The system of nerves in the hands does not form a glove-like pattern and could not cause the observed symptoms. Conversion reactions are also revealed by a disappearance of symptoms when the victim is asleep, hypnotized, or anesthetized (Fig. 19–7).

The physical symptoms of a conversion disorder usually serve to excuse the person from a threatening situation. In one case, a college student who had a minor traffic accident awakened the following morning with a numbness in his legs and found himself unable to move them. A conversion reaction was suspected when it was noted that he did not seem at all disturbed by his inability to walk. This sign is referred to as *belle indifference.* Investigation revealed that his parents were pressuring him to stay in school (although he wanted to quit) and that he was not prepared for his final exams. If he failed his exams, he expected to be drafted (Suinn, 1975).

A final note of interest: Conversion disorders probably account for many of the so-called miracle cures attributed to faith healers or medical quacks. Persons with conversion symptoms who firmly believe they are being helped may undergo a miraculous cure, but they usually develop new symptoms later.

Fig. 19–7 (left) *"Glove" anesthesia is a conversion reaction involving loss of feeling in areas of the hand that would be covered by a glove* (a). *If the anesthesia were physically caused, it would follow the pattern shown in* (b). (right) *To test for organic paralysis of the arm, an examiner can suddenly extend the arm, stretching the muscles. A conversion reaction is indicated if the arm pulls back involuntarily. (Adapted from Weintraub, 1983.)*

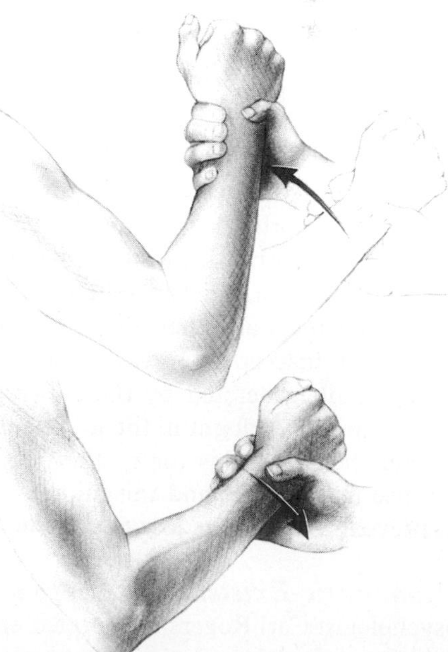

(a)

(b)

Learning Check

We have discussed problems from four major categories of DSM-III-R, as listed below. See if you can correctly match specific disorders with items on the right, by placing letters in the blanks.

______ **1.** Adjustment disorders	**A.** Disturbing thoughts, rigid routine, mechanical behavior
	B. Hypochondriasis, psychogenic pain, conversion reactions
Anxiety disorders:	**C.** Free-floating anxiety, anxiety attacks
______ **2.** Generalized anxiety disorder	**D.** Persistent, irrational fears
______ **3.** Panic disorder	**E.** Emotional distress linked with ongoing life stresses
______ **4.** Phobic disorders	**F.** Amnesia, fugue, multiple personality
______ **5.** Obsessive-compulsive disorders	**G.** Chronic worry and extreme nervousness having no external source
______ **6.** Post-traumatic stress disorder	**H.** Triggered by stresses outside the normal range of experience
______ **7.** Dissociative disorders	
______ **8.** Somatoform disorders	

Answers:
1. E 2. G 3. C 4. D 5. A 6. H 7. F 8. B

Three Theories—Pathways to Anxiety and Disorder

Question: What causes the problems described in the preceding discussion?

At least three major psychological perspectives on the causes of dissociative, anxiety, and somatoform disorders can be identified. These are (1) the *psychodynamic* approach, (2) the *humanistic-existential* approach, and (3) the *behavioral* approach.

Psychodynamic Approach Freud was the first to propose an explanation for what was then known as neurosis. According to Freud, disturbances like those we have described represent a raging conflict between subparts of the personality—the id, ego, and superego.

Freud particularly emphasized that intense anxiety can be caused by forbidden id impulses for sex or aggression that threaten to break through into behavior. It is as if the person is in a constant state of fear that the ego will be overwhelmed and that the person may do something "crazy" or unacceptable. Also important in the Freudian view is guilt generated by the superego in response to these impulses. Caught in the middle, the ego eventually is overwhelmed. This forces the person to adopt rigid defense mechanisms and misguided, inflexible behavior to prevent a disastrous loss of control.

Humanistic-Existential Approaches Humanistic psychologist Carl Rogers interpreted emotional disorders as the end product of a faulty **self-image** (Rogers, 1959). Rogers believed that anxious individuals have built up unrealistic mental images of themselves. This leaves them vulnerable to contradictory information. Let's say, for example, that an essential part of a student's self-image is the idea that she is highly intelligent. If the student does poorly in school, she may deny or distort her perceptions of herself and her perceptions of the situation. Rigid use of defense mechanisms, a conversion reaction, anxiety attacks, or similar symptoms may result from threats to one's self-image. These symptoms in turn become new threats that provoke further distortions. We have, in other words, a classic example of a vicious cycle of maladjustment and anxiety that feeds on itself once started.

Some psychologists take a more existential view and stress that unhealthy anxiety reflects a loss of *meaning* in one's life. According to them, we must show *courage* and *responsibility* in our choices if life is to have meaning. Too often, they say, we give in to "existential anxiety" and back away from life-enhancing choices. Existential anxiety is the unavoidable anguish that comes from knowing that we are personally responsible for our lives. Hence, we have a crushing need to choose wisely and courageously as we face life's empty and impersonal void.

From the existential view, people who are unhappy and anxious are living in "bad faith." That is, they have collapsed in the face of the awesome responsibility to choose a meaningful existence. In short, they have lost their way in life.

Behavioral Approach Behaviorists generally assume that the "symptoms" we have discussed are learned, just as other behaviors are. You might recall from Chapter 8, for instance, that phobias can be acquired through classical conditioning. Similarly, anxiety attacks may reflect conditioned emotional responses that are generalized to new situations. As another example, the hypochondriac's "sickness behavior" may be reinforced by the sympathy and attention he or she gets.

One point that all theorists agree on is that disordered behavior is ultimately self-defeating and paradoxical. A paradox is a contradiction. The contradiction in self-defeating behavior is that it makes the person more miserable in the long run, but its immediate effect is to temporarily lower anxiety.

Question: But if the person becomes more miserable in the long run, how does the pattern get started?

The behavioral explanation is that self-defeating behavior begins with avoidance learning (described earlier, in Chapter 8). Here's a quick review of avoidance learning to refresh your memory:

> An animal is placed in a special cage. After a few minutes a light comes on, followed a moment later by a painful shock. Quickly, the animal escapes into a second chamber. After a few minutes, a light comes on in this chamber, and the shock is repeated. Soon the animal learns to avoid pain by moving before the shock occurs. Once an animal learns to avoid the shock, it can be turned off altogether. A well-trained animal may avoid the nonexistent shock indefinitely.

The same analysis can be applied to disordered human behavior. A behaviorist would say that the powerful reward of *immediate relief* from anxiety keeps self-defeating avoidance behavior alive. This view, known as the **anxiety reduction hypothesis,** seems to explain why the behavior patterns we have discussed often look very "stupid" to outside observers.

There is probably a core of truth to each of the three explanations. For this reason, understanding anxiety disorders, dissociation, or somatoform disorders may be aided by combining parts of all three perspectives. Each viewpoint also suggests a different approach to treatment. Because there are many possibilities, a full discussion of therapy is found later, in Chapters 21 and 22.

Depression—On the Dark Side of the Mood

Nobody loves you when you're down and out—or so it seems. Psychologists have gradually come to realize that **mood disorders** are among the most serious of all. In terms of sheer numbers, studies show that in Europe and the United States, between 10 and 20 percent of the adult population has had a major depressive episode at some time (DSM-III-R, 1987). Roughly 25 percent of all cases treated by private psychiatrists and psychologists are for depression (Marmon, 1975).

Question: Don't mood disorders also include manic behavior?

Yes. But depression is by far the most common problem. In depressive disorders, sadness and despondency are exaggerated, prolonged, or unreasonable. Indications of a depressive disorder are sadness, hopelessness, inability to feel pleasure or to take interest in anything, fatigue, limited movement, sleep and eating disturbances, feelings of worthlessness, an extremely negative self-image, and often, recurrent thoughts of suicide. If a person is depressed more days than not for at least 2 years, the problem is termed **dysthymia** (dis-THY-me-ah). If depression alternates with periods when the person's mood is elevated, expansive, or irritable, the problem is called **cyclothymia** (SIKE-lo-THY-me-ah) (DSM-III-R, 1987).

In serious cases of depression, it becomes impossible for a person to function at work or at school. Sometimes, depressed individuals cannot even feed or clothe themselves. When depression and/or mania is even more severe, the person may become psychotic and lose touch with reality. (Problems of this type are discussed in the next chapter.)

Question: How are depressive disorders different from milder, more normal feelings of depression?

If a loved one dies or a person suffers a major failure, loss, or setback, a period of mourning or depression is to be expected. Depression at such times represents an emotional adjustment that is completed within a reasonable time. When someone is continuously or intensely depressed, we must look for causes that go beyond the apparent triggering incident. In many such **reactive depressions,** we find that the person was unprepared to cope with a major loss due to a previous series of disappointments. For example, after his car is stolen and he fails a class, a college student learns that his girlfriend back home has become engaged to someone else. The student stops eating regularly, withdraws from friends, and neglects studying. In other instances, the person is simply emotionally dependent or immature. In any case, the triggering incident for depression is often merely the "last straw" that reveals an underlying emotional disturbance.

Question: How is depression explained?

Depression and other mood disorders have resisted adequate explanation and treatment. Some scientists are focusing on the biology of mood changes. These researchers are interested in brain chemicals and transmitter substances, electrolytes, serotonin and noradrenaline levels, and so forth. Their findings are complex and inconclusive, but progress has been made. For example, the chemical *lithium carbonate* can be effective for treating some cases of depression, particularly those also showing manic behavior (Feldman & Quenzer, 1984). Others have sought psychological explanations. Psychoanalytic theory, for instance, holds that depression is caused by repressed anger that is displaced and turned inward as self-blame and self-hate (Isenberg & Schatzberg, 1976). As discussed in Chapter 12, behavioral theories of depression emphasize learned helplessness (Abramson et al., 1985).

Adequate understanding and treatment of depression is a challenge to the ingenuity of psychologists, psychiatrists, and other investigators. It is to their credit that this major source of human misery has recently become the target of intensified research (see Highlight 19–4). While we await the outcome of their efforts, a problem remains: Thousands of depressed people commit suicide each year. What can be done about it? This chapter's Applications section provides some answers.

A Final Note—You're Okay, Really! It is your author's hope that you will not fall prey to the psychological equivalent of "medical student's disease" after reading this chapter. Medical students, it seems, have a predictable tendency to notice in themselves the symptoms of each dreaded disease they study. As a psychology student you may have noticed what seem to be abnormal tendencies in your own behavior. If so, don't panic. In the majority of instances, this only shows that pathological behavior is an *exaggeration* of normal defenses and reactions, not that your behavior is abnormal.

HIGHLIGHT 19–4
Postpartum Depression

Two weeks after the birth of her child. Cheryl realized something was wrong. She could no longer ignore that she was extremely irritable, fatigued, tearful, and depressed. "Shouldn't I be happy?" she wondered. "What's wrong with me?"

Many women are surprised to learn that they face an increased risk of depression after giving birth. The two most common forms of the problem are **maternity blues** and **postpartum depression.** (The term *postpartum* refers to the time period following childbirth.)

An estimated 50 to 80 percent of all women undergo a temporary disturbance in mood that usually lasts from 24 to 48 hours after childbirth. These "third-day maternity blues" are marked by crying, fitful sleep, tension, anger, and irritability. For most women, this reaction is a normal part of adjusting to childbirth. Their depression is brief and relatively mild. For some women, however, the maternity blues can be the beginning of a more lasting depression. As many as 20 percent (1 in 5) of all women who give birth may develop a mild to moderate depressive disorder. Typical signs of postpartum depression are mood swings, despondency, feelings of inadequacy, and feeling unable to cope with the new baby. Depression of this kind may last anywhere from 2 months to about a year.

Predicting postpartum depression is difficult. However, the risk is increased by high levels of anxiety during pregnancy and by negative attitudes toward child rearing. The occurrence of stressful life events before birth is also a major factor. Because giving birth and adjusting to parenthood can both be stressful, it may be that any added problems push women toward depression.

Psychologists are still studying the best ways to prevent and treat postpartum depression. Presently, the amount of social support a woman receives seems to be an important part of the problem. That is, women who become depressed are also likely to perceive their husbands as unsupportive. Efforts to educate prospective parents about the risk of postpartum depression and the value of mutual support may prove helpful. (Source: Hopkins et al., 1984)

Learning Check

1. The humanistic explanation of anxiety disorders and related problems emphasizes the importance of faulty self-image. T or F?
2. According to the behavioral view, anxious, self-defeating behavior is explained by ________________ learning.
3. Freud's original psychodynamic explanation of "neurosis" was based on the anxiety reduction hypothesis. T or F?
4. Learned helplessness is emphasized by ________________ theories of depression.
   a. humanistic *b.* biological *c.* behavioristic *d.* psychoanalytic
5. The drug lithium carbonate has been shown to be an effective treatment for anxiety disorders. T or F?
6. The existential explanation of unhealthy anxiety is based on a conflict between subparts of the personality. T or F?

Answers:

1. T 2. avoidance 3. F 4. c 5. F 6. F

Applications: Suicide: Life in Balance

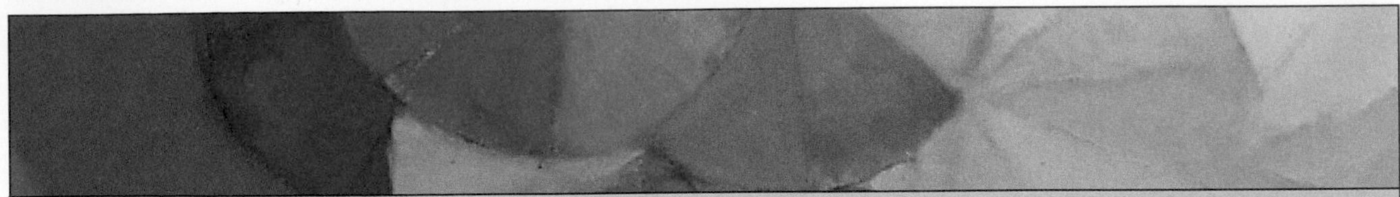

"Suicide: A permanent solution to a temporary problem."

By the time you finish reading this page, someone in the United States will have attempted suicide. Suicide is a disturbing and widely misunderstood problem. It ranks as the seventh cause of death in the United States. Roughly 1 person out of 100 attempts suicide during his or her life. Given these figures, it seems likely that you will sooner or later be affected by the suicide attempt of a friend, relative, neighbor, or co-worker. Check your knowledge of suicide against the following information.

Question: What factors affect suicide rates?

Season Suicide rates vary greatly, but some general patterns emerge. Contrary to popular belief. Suicide rates are lower on major holidays such as Christmas, rather than higher (Phillips & Wills, 1987). For reasons not clearly understood, the peak actually comes in May (Zung & Green, 1974).

Sex Men have the questionable honor of being better at suicide than women. Three times as many men as women *complete* suicide, but women make more attempts (Shneidman, 1987). More men than women die by suicide because they typically use a gun or an equally fatal method. Women most often attempt a drug overdose—a method that leaves greater chance of help arriving before death occurs (Lester, 1972).

Age Age is also a factor in suicide. Suicide rates gradually rise during adolescence. They then sharply increase during young adulthood (ages 20–24). From then until age 84, the rate continues to gradually rise with advancing age (Shneidman, 1987). As a result, more than half of all suicides are committed by individuals over 45 years old. However, there has been a steady increase in the total number of suicides by adolescents and young adults as this age group grows in size (Parachini, 1986). Part of this increase comes from the ranks of college students, where suicide is the leading cause of death. Contrary to popular belief, the most dangerous time for student suicide is the beginning (first 6 weeks) of a semester, not during final exams.

School is a factor in some suicides, but only in the sense that suicidal students were not living up to their own extremely high standards. Many were good students. Other important factors in student suicide are chronic health problems (real or imagined) and interpersonal difficulties (some suicides are rejected lovers, but others are simply withdrawn and friendless people) (Seiden, 1966).

Of special concern to psychologists is the recent dramatic increase in adolescent suicides. At present, about 5000 teenagers and young adults commit suicide each year in the United States. This total—about 13 deaths per day—is double the number reported 10 years ago. Also distressing is the fact that an increasing number of youths employ such highly lethal methods as shooting themselves to commit suicide.

Income Some professions, such as medicine and psychiatry, have higher than average suicide rates. Overall, however, suicide is quite democratic. It is equally a problem of the rich and the poor (Labovity & Hagedorn, 1971).

Marital Status An additional factor in suicide is marital status. Marriage (when successful) may be the best natural guard against suicidal impulses. The highest suicide rates are found among the divorced, the next highest rates occur among the widowed, lower rates are recorded for single persons, and married individuals have the lowest rates of all.

Question: Why do people try to kill themselves?

Immediate Causes The best explanation for suicide may simply come from a look at the conditions that precede it. Usually there is a history of interpersonal troubles with family, in-laws, or a lover or spouse. Often there may be drinking problems, sexual adjustment problems, or job difficulties (Humphrey et al., 1972).

A combination of factors such as these lead to severe depression and a preoccupation with death as the "answer" to the person's suffering. There is usually a break in communication with others that causes the person to feel isolated and misunderstood. Self-image becomes very negative. The person feels worthless and helpless and wants to die (Lester, 1972).

A long history of such conditions is not always necessary to produce a desire for suicide. People who attempt suicide are not necessarily "mentally ill." Anyone may temporarily reach a state of depression severe enough to attempt suicide. Most dangerous for the average person are times of divorce, separation, failure, and bereavement. Each can create what seems like an intolerable situation and can motivate an intense desire for escape.

Applications

The causes of increased adolescent suicide remain unclear. As with adults, there is often a backdrop of problems with drugs, depression, school, peers, family, divorced parents, or the breakup of a romance. However, many victims come from stable and affluent homes. Some experts suggest that many cases of adolescent suicide result from unrealistic expectations. For example, parents may create feelings of despair by pressuring their children to meet impossibly high standards.

Even without parental pressure, teenagers may expect the impossible of themselves in school, sports, romance, or progress toward a future career. Extremely high expectations and an unusual degree of sensitivity to hurt and disappointment can bring self-esteem to rock bottom over even the smallest "failure" (Mack, 1986; Serban, 1982). Again, the outcome is feelings of helplessness, hopelessness, and a desire to escape.

Preventing Suicide—You Can Help

Question: Is it true that people who talk about or threaten suicide are rarely the ones who try it?

No. This is one of the major fallacies about suicide. Of every 10 potential suicides, 8 give warning beforehand (Rudestam, 1971; Shneidman et al., 1965). A person who threatens suicide should be taken seriously. A potential suicide may say nothing more than, "I feel sometimes like I'd be better off dead." Warnings may also come indirectly. If a friend gives you a favorite ring and says, "Here, I won't be needing this any more," or comments, "I guess I won't get my watch fixed—it doesn't matter anyway," it may be a plea for help (Shneidman, 1980).

Question: Is it true that suicide can't be prevented, that the person will find a way to do it anyway?

No. The decision to attempt suicide usually comes when a person is alone, depressed, and unable to view matters objectively. You *should* intervene if someone seems to be threatening suicide.

It is estimated that about two-thirds of all suicide attempts fall in the "to be" category. That is, they are made by people who do not really want to die. Almost a third more are characterized by a "to be or not to be" attitude. These people are *ambivalent* or undecided about dying.

Only about 3 to 5 percent of cases represent individuals who definitely want to die. Most people, therefore, are relieved when someone comes to their aid (Shneidman et al., 1965). Remember that suicide is almost always a cry for help and that you *can* help. As suicide expert Edwin Shneidman (1987) puts it, "Suicidal behavior is often a form of communication, a cry for help born out of pain, with clues and messages of suffering and anguish and pleas for response."

Question: What is the best thing to do if someone hints they are thinking about suicide?

It helps to know some of the common characteristics of suicidal thoughts and feelings. Edwin Shneidman (1987) has identified several.

1. **Escape.** Everyone at times feels like running away from an upsetting situation. Running away from home, quitting school, abandoning a marriage—these are all departures. Suicide, of course, is the ultimate escape. It helps when suicidal persons see that the natural wish for escape doesn't have to be expressed by ending it all.
2. **Unbearable psychological pain.** Emotional pain is what the suicidal person is seeking to escape. A goal of anyone hoping to prevent suicide should be to reduce the pain in any way possible. Ask the person, "Where does it hurt?"
3. **Frustrated psychological needs.** Often, suicide can be prevented if a distraught person's frustrated needs can be identified and eased. Is the person deeply frustrated in his or her search for love, achievement, trust, security, or friendship?
4. **Constriction of options.** The suicidal person feels helpless and decides that death is the *only* solution. The person has narrowed all his or her options solely to death. The rescuer's goal, then, is to help broaden the suicidal person's perspective. Even when all the choices are unpleasant, suicidal persons can usually be made to see that their *least unpleasant option* is better than death.

Knowing these patterns will give some guidance in talking to a suicidal person. In addition, suicide expert David Lester (1971b) suggests that your most important task may be to establish *rapport* with the person. You should offer support, acceptance, and legitimate caring.

Remember that a suicidal person feels misunderstood. You should therefore try to accept and understand the feelings the person is expressing. Shneidman (1987) gives the example of a college senior who made straight A's for 3½ years and then received a B. The student became deeply depressed and was determined to kill himself. His friends pointed out that he still had a 3.98 grade average. But by talking about grades they missed the point. The student's problem was the loss of his perfect record. It would be better to say, "I understand your desire for perfect performance. That grade must seem devastating." Acceptance should also extend to the idea of suicide itself. It is completely acceptable to ask, "Are you thinking of suicide?"

Establishing communication with suicidal persons may be enough to carry them through a difficult time. You may also find it helpful to get day-by-day commitments from them to meet for lunch, share a ride, and the like. Let the person know you *expect* her or him to be there. Such commitments, even

Applications

though small, can be enough to tip the scales when a person is alone and thinking about suicide.

Don't end your efforts too soon. One of the most dangerous times for suicide is when a person suddenly seems to get better after a severe depression. Many experts agree that this often means that the person has finally made the decision to end it all. The improvement in mood is deceptive because it comes from an anticipation that suffering is at an end (Lester & Lester, 1971).

Crisis Intervention There are over 300 centers for suicide prevention in the United States, and most sizeable cities have mental health crisis intervention teams. Both services have staff trained to talk with suicidal persons over the phone. Give a person who seems to be suicidal the number of one of these services to place near a phone. Urge the person to call you or the other number if he or she becomes frightened or impulsive.

The preceding applies mainly to persons who are having mild suicidal thoughts. If a person actually threatens suicide, you must act more quickly. Ask how the person plans to carry out the suicide. A person who has a *concrete, workable plan,* and the means to carry it out, should be asked to accompany you to the emergency ward of a hospital.

If a person seems on the verge of attempting suicide, don't worry about overreacting. Call the police, crisis intervention, or a rescue unit. Needless to say, you should call immediately if a person is in the act of attempting suicide or if a drug has already been taken. The majority of suicide attempts come at temporary low points in a person's life and may never be repeated. Get involved—you may save a life!

Suicide—A Summary of Facts

The following is a list of useful facts to know about suicide:

1. More men than women commit suicide; but women make more attempts.

2. College students are most likely to attempt suicide during the first part of the school quarter or semester.

3. Many people temporarily become depressed enough to contemplate suicide. Those who would attempt suicide are not all psychotic or suffering from lasting mental illness.

4. Suicide strikes both the rich and the poor.

5. A person who is suicidal once may never again become suicidal. Preventing suicide is well worth the effort.

6. Most potentially suicidal persons give warning.

7. People who talk about suicide *do* often attempt it.

8. The majority of people (two-thirds) who attempt suicide do not really want to die, and most of the remainder are ambivalent about dying.

9. A *sudden* improvement in mood after a suicidal depression can mean that the person has decided to carry out a suicide attempt.

10. Four major characteristics of the suicidal state are (1) psychological pain, (2) frustrated needs, (3) a desire to escape, and (4) constricted options.

11. Suicide can often be prevented by the efforts of family, friends, and mental health professionals.

Learning Check

1. More women use guns in their suicide attempts than do men. T or F?

2. While the overall suicide rate has remained about the same, there has been a decrease in adolescent suicides. T or F?

3. Suicide is equally a problem of the rich and the poor. T or F?

4. The highest suicide rates are found among the divorced. T or F?

5. The majority (two-thirds) of suicide attempts fall in the "to be" category. T or F?

Answers:
1. F 2. F 3. T 4. T 5. T

Exploration: Psychology and the Law—The "Twinkie Defense"

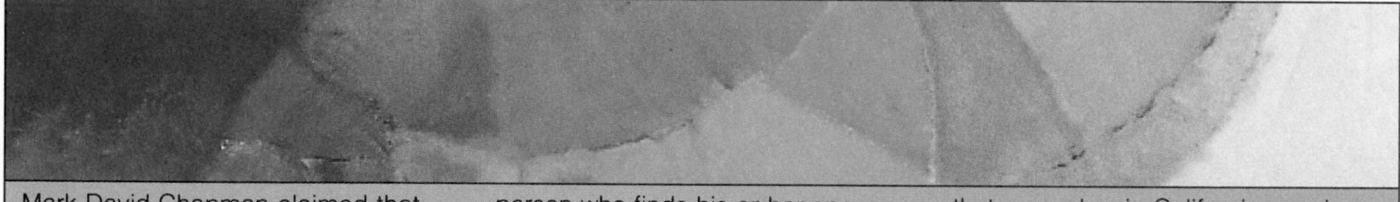

Mark David Chapman claimed that devils forced him to kill former Beatle John Lennon. In court, his lawyer asserted that Chapman was "not guilty by reason of insanity." However, at mid-trial Chapman decided to plead guilty to second-degree murder. His reason? He said that God had visited him in his cell and told him to confess.

Chapman's case was one of thousands each year that mingle law, psychiatry, psychology, and public opinion. For over 130 years, the **insanity defense** has bedeviled the courts and raised difficult legal, moral, and psychological questions.

Question: What exactly is the insanity defense?

Insanity The insanity defense entered Western law as the **M'Naghten rule.** In 1843, the English House of Lords ruled on the case of Daniel M'Naghten, a "madman" who attempted to kill a member of parliament, but murdered another man instead. The court held that a defendant—in this case M'Naghten—must understand the wrongfulness of his or her actions to be held responsible for them. Persons suffering from "mental disease or other defects" that prevent them from knowing right from wrong are "insane." In the U.S. legal system, the taking of life by an insane person is not murder.

Defendants may also claim they knew their act was wrong, but they had an **irresistible impulse** they could not control. An example is the person who finds his or her spouse in a stranger's arms and kills in a jealous rage. A related defense claims **diminished capacity** to control actions or to know right from wrong. A person who commits a crime while under the influence of drugs might make this plea.

The Twinkie Defense The problems posed by the insanity defense are vividly shown by three recent cases. In Oakland, California, a jury declared Darlin June Cromer sane in the racial killing of a 5-year-old boy. This was the verdict, despite the fact that one psychiatrist testified that Cromer was "the most psychotic person" he'd ever seen. Cromer was sentenced to life in prison (Einstein, 1981).

On the opposite side of the Bay, Dan White admitted killing San Francisco Mayor George Moscone and Supervisor Harvey Milk. However, White's lawyer convinced the jury that White acted with diminished capacity. The defense claimed, among other things, that White was deranged from eating too much "junk food"—an argument that became known as the "Twinkie Defense." (For those unschooled in junk food, a Twinkie is a small sponge cake with a sugary cream filling.)

Testimony in the trial established that White planned the murders beforehand and carefully avoided security guards to reach his victims. White received a 7-year jail sentence. (He was paroled in 1984.) The verdict so outraged many citizens that a new law in California now bans claims of "diminished capacity" (Tierney, 1982). In yet another case, "Vampire Killer" Richard Chase was convicted of killing 6 people and drinking the blood of some of his victims. Chase was declared sane.

These cases point to the inconsistencies of a system that allows people who appear sane to be judged insane, and apparently insane people to be judged sane.

Question: How is sanity determined?

Expert Testimony The most sensational criminal trials involving insanity have a typical pattern: Defense psychiatrists interview the defendant and then testify that he or she was insane at the time of the crime; prosecution psychiatrists examine the defendant and testify to his or her sanity. After these **expert witnesses** contradict one another's testimony, it's up to the jury to decide who is right.

But more often, this "battle of the experts" never takes place. In 4 out of 5 cases, prosecutors, defense attorneys, medical experts, and judges agree *before* trial that the defendant is mentally ill (Bower, 1984). Thus, if a person really is psychotic, in most cases experts agree fairly readily.

Opinion, Please The preceding brief discussion raises several interesting questions.

1. The states of Montana, Idaho, and Utah have banned the insanity plea, but in most states it remains intact. Several other states now allow only a

Exploration

"guilty, but mentally ill" plea. In your opinion, should questions of sanity be considered in criminal trials? Should the insanity defense be allowed?

Before you answer, you should know that pleas of insanity are actually relatively rare, being used in only about 1 out of every 500 court cases. In only about 2 percent of these cases does the insanity defense succeed. Nationally, this amounts to about 100 cases a year in the United States (Carelli, 1982).

More important, a verdict of innocence by reason of insanity does not set a person free. In most states, it requires automatic commitment to a mental hospital. Thereafter, the law places the burden of proof on patients. To be released, they must show that they are no longer a danger to themselves or others. Moreover, in some cases, persons declared "insane" have been hospitalized longer than they would have been imprisoned for a criminal conviction.

Then again, critics of the insanity defense point out that insane offenders are now held for an average of about 2 years (Bower, 1984). In some instances, the public may rightly ask if justice has been served.

2. Should the courts accept pleas of diminished capacity? Before you answer this question, think about the "guilt" of a severely retarded person or someone with a brain tumor who commits a crime.

3. In your opinion, who should decide if a person should be committed? Should it be a judge? A jury? A psychiatrist? A psychologist? Who should decided when an "insane" person can be released? Should a person have the right to refuse treatment? What if the person committed a crime?

Before answering, it may be useful to know that psychiatric predictions of violent behavior are largely inaccurate. Follow-ups of arrests and mental hospital records show that from two-thirds to nine-tenths of the time, experts are *wrong* in forecasting violence (Loftus & Monahan, 1980). At present, there is no way to accurately predict which individuals are likely to be dangerous to themselves or to others.

As you can see, there are no easy answers to the preceding questions. Nevertheless, when the issues are "madness," personal freedom, criminal responsibility, and justice, everyone has an opinion. What's yours?

Learning Check

1. Daniel M'Naghten was a lawyer who defended a member of the British House of Lords who was accused of murder, but who pleaded insanity. T or F?
2. In a court of law, the insanity defense is based on the premise that persons who are mentally defective cannot be held fully responsible for their actions. T or F?
3. A person who committed a crime while suffering from a mind-altering reaction to a prescription medicine might have some success in claiming innocence due to diminished capacity. T or F?
4. In every state in the United States, insanity can be used as a legal defense as long as expert witnesses are willing to testify that the defendant was insane at the time of the crime. T or F?
5. Psychiatric predictions of future violence are correct only in about one-tenth to one-third of all forecasts. T or F?

Answers:

1. F 2. T 3. T 4. F 5. T

Chapter Summary

• Mental or emotional disturbances are a major health problem. Major categories of **psychopathology** are described in the *Diagnostic and Statistical Manual of Mental Disorders (DSM-III-R)*. Major problems discussed in this chapter and the next include *psychotic disorders, organic mental disorders, psychoactive substance use disorders, mood disorders, anxiety disorders, somatoform disorders, dissociative disorders, personality disorders, and sexual disorders.*

• Traditionally, a distinction has been made between milder, *nonpsychotic disorders* and *psychoses*—problems involving loss of contact with reality. **Insanity** is a legal term defining the ability to know right from wrong and whether or not one may be held responsible for one's actions.

• Formal definitions of normality usually take into account all or most of the following: *subjective discomfort, statistical definitions* (or *norms*), *social nonconformity,* and the *cultural,* or *situational, context* of behavior. There are problems with each definition in that all are *relative* standards. In practice, judgment of normality is a social act influenced by many factors.

• **Personality disorders** are deeply ingrained maladaptive personality patterns. A frequently misunderstood personality disorder is *sociopathy,* or **antisocial personality.** Antisocial persons seem to lack a *conscience*. They are emotionally unresponsive and manipulative, and they have shallow interpersonal relationships.

• Definitions of **sexual deviance** are highly subjective. Many "sexually deviant" behaviors are acceptable in private or in some cultures. Deviations that often cause difficulty are **pedophilia, incest, fetishism, voyeurism, exhibitionism, transvestic fetishism, sexual sadism, sexual masochism,** and **frotteurism.** Exhibitionists are rarely dangerous and can best be characterized as sexually inhibited and immature. The effects of **child molestation** vary greatly, depending on the severity of the molestation and the child's relationship to the molester. **Forcible rape** is primarily a violent crime of aggression rather than a sex crime. There is evidence that rape is related to stereotyped attitudes toward male and female sex roles.

• Anxiety disorders, dissociative disorders, and somatoform disorders are characterized by *high levels of anxiety, rigid defense mechanisms,* and *self-defeating behavior patterns*. The term *nervous breakdown* has no formal meaning. However, "emotional breakdowns" do correspond somewhat to **adjustment disorders,** in which the person is overwhelmed by ongoing life stresses.

• **Anxiety disorders,** characterized by excessive anxiety or anxiety-based behaviors, include **generalized anxiety disorder** (chronic anxiety and worry), **panic disorder** (anxiety attacks, panic, free-floating anxiety), **phobic disorders** (irrational fears), **post-traumatic stress disorder** (emotional disturbance triggered by severe stress), and **obsessive-compulsive disorders** (obsessions and compulsions).

• **Dissociative disorders** may take the form of **amnesia** (loss of memory and personal identity), **fugue** (flight from familiar surroundings), or **multiple personality** (development of two or more distinct personalities).

• **Somatoform disorders** center on physical complaints that mimic disease or disability. **Hypochondriasis** is a groundless preoccupation with imagined disease for which the person seeks medical attention. **Somatoform pain** refers to discomfort for which there is no identifiable physical cause. In **conversion disorders,** actual symptoms of disease or disability develop, but they are psychological in origin.

• Three broad types of explanation for anxious, disordered behavior are: (1) the **psychodynamic** approach, emphasizing unconscious conflicts within the personality; (2) the **humanistic** approach, emphasizing the effects of a *faulty self-image,* and the related **existential** approach, which stresses a loss of meaning in one's life; and (3) the **behavioral** approach, which emphasizes the effects of previous learning, particularly *avoidance learning*.

• **Depressive disorders** primarily involve disturbances of mood or emotion, producing *manic* (agitated, elated, hyperactive) or *depressive* (sad, apathetic, suicidal) states. Depression is the most common mood disorder. Long-lasting, though relatively moderate, depression is called **dysthymia.** Chronic, though moderate, swings in mood between depression and elation are called **cyclothymia. Reactive depressions** are often triggered by external events; however, they are more intense or prolonged than normal. Biological, psychoanalytic, and behavioral theories of depression have been proposed. Research on the causes and treatment of depression continues.

• Suicide is statistically related to such factors as age, sex, and marital status. However, in individual cases the potential for suicide is best identified by a *desire to escape, unbearable psychological pain, frustrated psychological needs,* and a *constriction of options*. Suicide can often be prevented by the efforts of family, friends, and mental health professionals.

• In Western law, the **insanity defense** evolved from the **M'Naghten rule.** Insanity is closely related to claims of **diminished capacity** or claims that a person had an **irresistible impulse.** Inconsistencies in the application of the insanity defense have fueled debate about its validity.

Questions for Discussion

1. What effect might living in different parts of town, membership in different ethnic groups, or growing up in a different culture have on perceptions of "normality?"
2. Can you think of a behavior that would be considered "abnormal" under any possible set of circumstances?
3. How might your perception of a person change if you knew he or she were an "ex-mental patient"?
4. To what extent does "maladjusted" or "sick" mean "different from me"?
5. Are standards of "normality" in our society broad enough to accommodate varying lifestyles?
6. In what ways might our ultra-competitive society contribute to the development of a sociopathic personality?
7. There is no doubt that sexual abuse of children is widespread. How do you think our society should approach the problem of protecting children?
8. Why do you think American veterans of the Vietnam War have experienced an elevated rate of PTSD? How did their combat experience and treatment upon returning home differ from that experienced by veterans of other wars?

Chapter 20

Major Mental Disorders

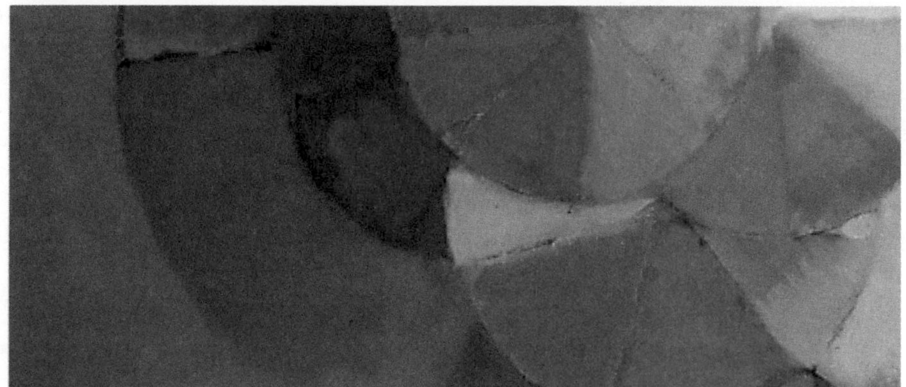

In This Chapter

The nature of psychosis

Delusional disorders

Major mood disorders

Schizophrenia

Causes of schizophrenia

Chemotherapy, ECT, and psychosurgery

Community mental health

Applications

Dangers of psychiatric labeling

Exploration

The politics of mental illness

Chapter Preview

Psychosis—"Losing It"

I'm a man 36 years of age, that in 1956–57 they changed the flag of the United States of America once by adding Alaska as a State to the Union and thus paving the way for Hawaii to become a state in 1959. That of course, gives me the *"capacity of the flag itself"* and therefore like any Congressional Medal of Honor winner, gives me the *"capacity of the President of the United States of America. . . ."*

In 1955–56 civil authorities . . . some "small time" politicians got together on me and sand-bagged me brainwashed me and bugged me with a *"short-wave* Radio grid center, with an ultra-violet cross grid" called a "bug." Its sole purpose is to use a person's senses against himself so as to perjure and distort him to no end of humiliation . . . they vibrate your nerves physically with it and never ceases.

I'd been there several months before they gave me "ground privileges" and once on the grounds they started frequencing my time all the more, vibrating the back of my neck, first flicking it to the front of my face, like a "whip" or a cat of 9 tails. (Suinn, 1975)

These excerpts were taken from a letter written by a man suffering a psychosis. They illustrate some of the severe disturbances in thinking, behavior, speech, and emotions that occur in psychosis.

Psychosis reflects a loss of contact with reality. The following comments, made by several psychotic patients, illustrate what is meant by a "split" from reality (Torrey, 1988):

Everything is in bits. You put the picture up bit by bit into your head. It's like a photograph that's torn in bits and put together again. If you move it's frightening.

I tried sitting in my apartment and reading. . . . I read one paragraph ten times, could make no sense of it whatever, and shut the book.

I felt I had the power to determine the weather, which responded to my inner moods, and even to control the movement of the sun.

> I like talking to a person but not in audible words. I try to force my thoughts into someone. I concentrate on how they move.
>
> Last week I was with a girl and suddenly she seemed to get bigger and bigger, like a monster coming nearer and nearer.

What is psychosis really like? What causes it? What can be done about it? For answers to these and related questions, read on.

Survey Questions

- What are the general characteristics of psychosis?
- How do delusional disorders, schizophrenia, and psychotic mood disorders differ?
- What causes schizophrenia?
- How are psychotic disorders treated?
- Is psychiatric labeling damaging?
- What does it mean to be "crazy"? What should be done about it?

Psychosis—Life in the Shadow of Madness

Psychosis—a major loss of contact with shared views of reality—is among the most serious of all mental problems.

Question: What is psychosis like?

A person who is psychotic undergoes a number of striking changes in thinking, behavior, and emotion. The following descriptions identify some of the major features of psychoses (psycho**sis,** singular; psycho**ses**, plural).

Presence of Delusions **Delusions** are false beliefs that a person continues to hold even when the facts contradict them. Individuals with the psychotic delusion that they are Jesus Christ will not be disturbed if they cannot walk on water or perform miracles. Some common types of delusion are: (1) *depressive* delusions, in which people feel that they have committed horrible crimes or sinful deeds; (2) *somatic* delusions, such as belief that one's body is "rotting away" or that it is emitting foul odors; (3) delusions of *grandeur,* in which individuals think they are extremely important persons; (4) delusions of *influence,* in which people feel they are being controlled or influenced by others or by unseen forces; (5) delusions of *persecution,* in which people feel that others are "out to get them"; and (6) delusions of *reference,* in which unrelated events are given personal significance (as when it is assumed that a newspaper article or a television program is giving a special personal message to the person) (DSM-III-R, 1987). If you reread the opening quote of the Chapter Preview, you will find evidence of delusions of grandeur, influence, and persecution.

Hallucinations and Sensory Changes **Hallucinations** are sensory experiences that occur in the absence of a stimulus. The most common psychotic hallucination is hearing voices. These voices may be familiar, they may be answered, and frequently they are insulting. More rarely, psychotic individuals may also feel "insects crawling under the skin," taste "poisons" in their food, or smell "gas" their "enemies" are using to "get" them. Sensory changes may bring about extreme sensitivity to heat, cold, pain, or touch. Anesthesia, a loss of normal sensitivity, is also possible.

Disturbed Emotions Emotions may swing violently between the extremes of elation and depression, or the psychotic person may be hyperemotional, depressed, emotionally "flat," or apathetic. In instances of **flat affect,** there are almost no signs of emotion. Typically, the person's voice is monotonous and the face is frozen in a blank expression.

Personality Disorganization or Disintegration Major disturbances such as those just described—as well as added problems in thought, speech, memory, actions, and attention—bring about *personality disintegration* and a break with reality. As a result, serious impairment almost always occurs in work, social relations, and self-care. When psychotic disturbances and a shattered personality are evident for weeks or months (often including a period of deterioration, an active phase, and a residual phase), then the person has suffered a psychosis (DSM-III-R, 1987).

Question: How could a person function with such problems?

Actually, the preceding description is somewhat exaggerated. It is rare to find all these changes occurring at once. As a matter of fact, you would probably find a trip to a psychiatric ward disappointing if you expected to see flamboyant, dramatic, or bizarre behavior. Extremely psychotic behavior typically occurs in brief *episodes*. The symptoms of psychosis come and go and much of the time may be quite subtle (Fig. 20–1).

Question: Does psychosis occur without warning?

No. Usually there are signs of impending trouble. A recent study of psychotic patients found that symptoms such as insomnia, emotional changes, or feeling "high" signaled a coming crisis for most of them (Brier & Strauss, 1983). In fact, most of the patients were aware of their symptoms and tried to fight off the psychosis.

Even after a psychotic break, people are not totally unresponsive to their surroundings. In one interesting experiment, psychotic patients were interviewed in two ways. Some were told that the purpose of the interview was to determine if they were "ready for discharge." In this group, patients who were known to like the hospital acted very bizarre and disturbed during the interviews. A second group was told that the interview was to decide which patients should be given "open ward" privileges. In this case, disturbed patients suddenly became amazingly free of symptoms (Braginsky & Braginsky, 1967).

This experiment shows that some psychotic symptoms can be thought of as a primitive form of communication. By their actions, many patients are saying, "I need help," or, "I can't handle it any more." This becomes more evident when it is realized that an almost universal symptom of psychosis is difficulty in communicating verbally with others. Psychotic speech tends to be garbled and chaotic. Sometimes it sounds like no more than a "word salad," as the following example illustrates:

> The lion will have to change from dogs into cats until I can meet my father and mother and we dispart from rats. . . . It's all over for a squab true tray and there ain't no squabs, there ain't no men, there ain't no music, there ain't nothing besides my mother and my father who stand alone upon the Island of Capri where is no ice. Well it's my suitcase sir. (Rodgers, 1982)

Question: Are there different types of psychosis?

A psychosis based on known brain pathology related to disease, gunshot wound, accident, or some other physical cause is termed an **organic psychosis.** A psychosis based on unknown causes or psychological factors is called a **functional psychosis.** The possible causes of functional psychoses are explored later in this chapter.

Organic Psychosis One example of organic psychosis is **general paresis** (pah-REE-sis), which occurs in some cases of untreated syphilis. In advanced stages, syphilis attacks brain cells and gradually brings about a deterioration in behavior. A common sign of general paresis is a loss of inhibition. This can lead to inappropriate comments, shocking profanity, and obscenity—the "dirty old man" syndrome.

A second source of organic psychosis that gives special

Fig. 20–1 *A scene in a state mental hospital.*

cause for alarm is poisoning by lead and mercury (Fig. 20–2). Although relatively rare, such poisoning can damage the brain and cause hallucinations, delusions, and a loss of emotional control. A particularly dangerous situation is found in many old buildings, which are painted with old-style leaded paints. Children who eat this paint may become psychotic or retarded. Other more subtle sources of lead can also be a problem. For example, children who live near busy streets may absorb lead by breathing automobile exhaust. Testing shows that this can lead to difficulties in thinking and attention at school (Yule et al., 1984). Another hidden source of lead is old drinking fountains in schools. Many are contaminated by lead solder or lead-lined coolers (Kemp, 1988).

Senile dementia (duh-MEN-sha) is probably the most common organic problem. In senile dementia, we see major disturbances in memory, reasoning, judgment, impulse control, and personality. This combination usually leaves the person confused, suspicious, apathetic, or withdrawn (Davies, 1988). Senile dementia is closely associated with physical deterioration of the brain. The most common cause of senile dementia is Alzheimer's disease (see Highlight 20–1). Other common causes are circulatory problems, repeated strokes, or general shrinkage and atrophy of the brain.

Three major types of functional psychoses are *delusional disorders*, *psychotic mood disorders*, and *schizophrenia*. Information on each is provided in the following sections. (Remember, too, that a general category called *psychotic disorders not elsewhere classified* also exists.)

Fig. 20–2 *The Mad Hatter, from Lewis Carroll's* Alice in Wonderland. *History provides numerous examples of psychosis caused by toxic chemicals. Carroll's Mad Hatter character is modeled after an occupational disease of the eighteenth and nineteenth centuries. In that era, hatmakers were heavily exposed to mercury used in the preparation of felt. Consequently, many suffered brain damage and became psychotic, or "mad" (Kety, 1979).*

HIGHLIGHT 20–1
Alzheimer's Disease

Alzheimer's disease (ALLS-hi-merz) is one of the most fearsome and devastating problems of aging. The senility it causes afflicts about 5 to 10 percent of all people over age 65, or about 2 million Americans at present.

Alzheimer's victims at first have difficulty remembering recent events. Then they slowly become more disoriented, suspicious, and confused. In time, they lose the ability to work, cook, drive, or use tools. As their condition worsens, victims can no longer read, write, and calculate. Eventually they are mute, bedridden, and unable to walk, sit up, or smile (Roach, 1985).

Researchers are urgently seeking the causes of Alzheimer's disease. It is now known that highly selective damage to nerve cells in the brain is probably to blame. Especially important is the presence of unusual webs and tangles in nerve cells leading to and from the hippocampus—an area important for learning and memory (see Chapter 3) (Hayman et al., 1984). Important changes also take place in an area called the nucleus basalis and in chemicals necessary for carrying messages within the brain (Coyle et al., 1983; Katzman, 1988).

By the year 2000 it is estimated that 1 out of every 10 adults over 65 will be a victim of Alzheimer's disease (Shodell, 1984). Yet, there is now no established treatment (Davies, 1988). Understandably, efforts to find a cure for Alzheimer's disease are expanding. For some of us, such efforts may prove to be a race against time.

Delusional Disorders—An Enemy Behind Every Tree

People with **delusional disorders** usually do not suffer from hallucinations, emotional excesses, or personality disintegration. Even so, their break with reality is unmistakable. The main feature of this problem is the presence of deeply held false beliefs. The content of such delusions may involve grandiosity, jealousy, persecution, bodily complaints, or romantic attraction (Table 20–1).

The most common delusional disorder, often called **paranoid psychosis,** centers on delusions of persecution.

Table 20–1 Delusional Disorders

Erotomanic type: Marked by erotic delusions that one is loved by another, especially by someone famous or of higher status.
Grandiose type: Delusion that one has some great, unrecognized talent, knowledge, or insight or a special relationship with an important person or with God, or that one is a prominent person (who, if alive, is regarded as an imposter).
Jealous type: An all-consuming, unfounded belief that one's spouse or lover is unfaithful.
Persecutory type: Delusion that one is being conspired against, cheated, spied on, followed, poisoned, maligned, or harassed.
Somatic type: Belief that one's body is diseased or infested with insects or parasites, or that it is emitting foul odors, or that parts of the body are misshapen or defective.

(DSM-III-R, 1987)

Many self-styled reformers, crank letter writers, "communist hunters," and the like, suffer paranoid delusions. Paranoid individuals often believe that they are being cheated, spied on, followed, poisoned, harassed, or plotted against. Usually they are intensely suspicious, believing they must be on guard at all times.

The evidence such people find to support their beliefs is usually unconvincing to others. Every detail of the paranoid's existence is woven into a personal version of "what's really going on." Buzzing during a telephone conversation may be interpreted as "someone listening"; a stranger who comes to the door asking for directions may be seen as "really trying to get information"; and so forth.

Persons suffering paranoid delusions are rarely treated, because it is almost impossible for them to accept that they need help. Anyone who suggests that they have a problem simply becomes part of the "conspiracy" to "persecute" them.

Paranoid persons frequently lead lonely, isolated, and humorless lives dominated by constant suspicion and hostility. While they are not necessarily dangerous to others, they can be. A person who believes that "the Mafia" is slowly closing in on him may be moved to violence by his irrational fears. If a stranger came to the door with his hand in his coat pocket, he could become the target of a paranoid attempt at "self-defense."

Because the topics we will consider next involve several new terms and ideas, let's stop for a quick Learning Check before proceeding.

Learning Check

1. A person who wrongly believes that his or her body is "rotting away" is suffering from
   a. depressive delusions *b.* somatic delusions *c.* delusions of grandeur *d.* delusions of persecution
2. Persons suffering from psychoses are almost totally unresponsive to their surroundings. T or F?
3. A psychosis caused by lead poisoning would be termed a *functional* disorder. T or F?
4. Hallucinations and personality disintegration are the principal features of paranoid psychosis. T or F?
5. In *flat affect,* a sensory experience—such as hearing voices—occurs in the absence of a stimulus. T or F?
6. Alzheimer's disease is thought to be caused by lead poisoning of the hippocampus. T or F?

Answers:
1. *b* 2. F 3. F 4. F 5. F 6. F

Major Mood Disorders—Peaks and Valleys

About 14 percent of patients admitted to mental hospitals suffer from major mood disorders. Mood disorders were first introduced in the previous chapter. To help you relate that discussion to this one, Table 20–2 shows how mood disorders are classified by DSM-III-R.

Major mood disorders are marked by lasting extremes of emotion. Usually, one of the following patterns predominates. In **bipolar disorders,** persons go "up" or "down" emotionally. The individual may be continuously loud, elated, hyperactive, and energetic *(manic type)*, or the person may swing between mania and deep depression *(mixed type)*. Even when a person is sad and guilt-ridden, the problem is considered a bipolar disorder *(de-*

Table 20–2 DSM-III-R Classification of Mood Disorders

Bipolar Disorders	Depressive Disorders
Bipolar disorder	Major depression
Mixed	Single episode
Manic	Recurrent
Depressed	
	*Dysthymia
*Cyclothymia	

*Discussed in Chapter 19.

pressed type) if the person has ever been manic before (DSM-III-R, 1987). The person who only goes "down" emotionally suffers from a **unipolar disorder.** If severe depression occurs without any history of mania, it is called a **major depression.**

Major mood disorders can be limited primarily to emotional extremes. Quite often, however, persons with major mood disorders also have psychotic symptoms. This combination of mood disorder and a break with reality is called an **affective psychosis.**

Question: How do such problems differ from other types of psychosis?

Manic individuals throw themselves into fits of activity characterized by extreme distractibility, rapid shifts in thoughts ("flights of ideas"), constant talking, and restless movement. In advanced stages, manic behavior becomes more and more incoherent, agitated, and out of control. Eating or sleeping may be ignored until manic individuals push themselves into states of total delirium. (This behavior accounts for public images of the "raving maniac.") The following brief excerpt from a case history illustrates manic-psychotic behavior:

> Her husband had returned home to find her twirling around the living room bizarrely draped in her wedding gown tied with a bath towel and wearing a lamp shade. She gaily greeted him, laughed with an ear-piercing shrillness, and invited him to stay for the exciting "coming-out" party she was giving. Strewn on the table were a thousand handwritten invitations signed with a flourish and addressed to such dignitaries as the president of the United States, the justices of the Supreme Court, the emperor of Japan. She made incessant noises: singing her own ballads, shouting mottoes, which she devised, reciting limericks, making rhyming sounds, and yelling obscenities. (Suinn, 1970)

Depressive reactions show a reverse pattern in which feelings of failure, sinfulness, worthlessness, and total despair are dominant. The person becomes extremely subdued or withdrawn and may be intensely suicidal. Depressive reactions pose a serious threat to survival. Suicide attempted during a psychotic depression is rarely a simple "plea for help." Usually, the person intends to succeed and may give no prior warning (Fig. 20–3).

Manic and depressive states often appear to be related in bipolar disorders. That is, when manic behavior occurs, it may still be a reaction to depression. The manic person seeks to escape feelings of worthlessness and depression in an unending rush of activity.

Question: How do major mood disorders differ from the affective disorders described in Chapter 19?

The major mood disorders described in this chapter usually involve more severe emotional changes. Also, of course, the person's emotional excesses are often accompanied by psychotic delusions and hallucinations. As a further distinction, major mood disorders and affective psychoses more often appear to be **endogenous** (en-DODGE-

Fig. 20–3 *In a depressive psychosis, suicidal impulses can be intense and despair total.*

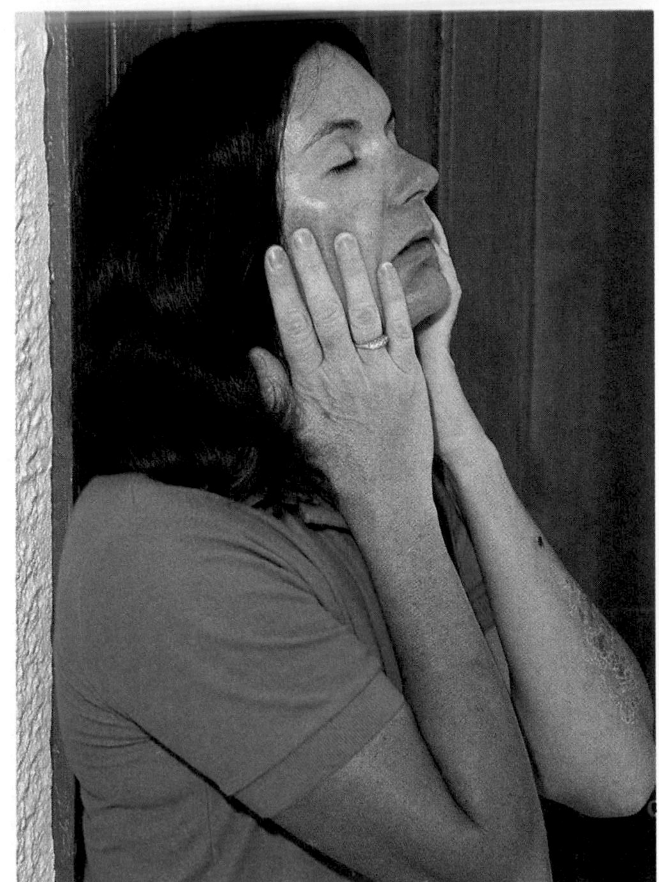

eh-nus: produced from within) rather than a reaction to external events. As you might guess, this implies that *genetics* has a role in causing major mood disorders, especially bipolar disorders (Nurnberger & Gershon, 1982). Among children of depressed parents, for example, the rate of depression is higher even if the children are adopted (Dunner, 1985). The psychological causes discussed in the preceding chapter are also important. But for major mood disorders, biological factors seem to play a larger role. (For an interesting look at another cause of depression, see Highlight 20–2).

HIGHLIGHT 20–2
Feeling sad? It Could Be SAD.

Unless you have experienced a winter of "cabin fever" in the far North, you may be surprised to learn that the rhythms of the seasons underlie some depressions. Researcher Norman Rosenthal has recently found that some people suffer depression only during the fall and winter months. Almost anyone can get a little depressed when days are short, dark, and cold. But when a person's symptoms are lasting and disabling, the problem is called **seasonal affective disorder (SAD)** (Rosenthal et al., 1984).

Starting in the fall, people with SAD sleep longer but more poorly. During the day they feel tired and drowsy and they tend to overeat. With each passing day they become more sad, anxious, irritable, and socially withdrawn. Although their depressions are usually only moderately severe, many victims of SAD face each winter with a sense of foreboding. SAD affects 4 times more women than men, and most victims show signs of suffering from a bipolar disorder.

The causes of SAD are still a mystery. Some experts believe it may be related to an increased release of melatonin during the winter. This hormone is secreted by the pineal gland to regulate the body's response to changing light conditions. What is known is that many SAD patients can be helped by extra doses of bright light. This treatment, which is called **phototherapy,** involves exposing SAD patients to several hours of very bright, full-spectrum fluorescent light each day. Phototherapy has relieved depression within 3 to 7 days for 80 percent of those treated (Hellekson & Rosenthal, 1987). For many SAD sufferers a hearty dose of light appears to be the next best thing to vacationing in the tropics.

Schizophrenia—Shattered Reality

Approximately half of all people admitted to mental hospitals are diagnosed as *schizophrenic*. **Schizophrenia** (SKIT-soh-FREE-nee-uh) is a major health problem. One person in 100 will become schizophrenic. Most schizophrenics are young adults, but schizophrenia can occur at any age.

Question: Does a schizophrenic person have two personalities?

Schizophrenia does not refer to having more than one personality. Recall from the previous chapter that multiple personality is a nonpsychotic, dissociative disorder. (Also, see Highlight 20–3.) The word *schizophrenia* does mean "split-mind," but this refers to a split between thought and emotion.

HIGHLIGHT 20–3
"Schizophrenic" Confusion

"David was so warm and friendly yesterday, but today he's as cold as ice. He's so schizophrenic sometimes that I don't know how to react." Such statements illustrate how often the term *schizophrenic* is misused. As you know, even a person who displays two or more personalities (a dissociative disorder) is not "schizophrenic." Neither, of course, is a person like David, whose behavior is merely inconsistent.

On a more technical level, schizophrenia is often confused with a personality disorder that resembles it somewhat. Recall from Chapter 19 that personality disorders are maladaptive personality patterns. One such pattern is known as the **schizotypal personality.** Starting in adolescence, affected persons slowly become isolated and emotionally withdrawn. They are typically seen as listless and apathetic, and they are often considered "odd," "shiftless," or eccentric. Their behavior at times may be markedly peculiar (collecting garbage, eating cigarette butts, talking to themselves, and so forth).

Problems of this type do resemble some aspects of schizophrenia. But the schizotypal personality, like other personality disorders, does not involve a psychotic "break with reality." Many individuals with a schizotypal personality simply live colorless and isolated lives on the fringes of society as vagrants, eccentrics, derelicts, or prostitutes.

In schizophrenia, emotions may become blunted, or flat, or they may be very inappropriate. For example, a schizophrenic person may smile or giggle when told his mother has died, or may describe her death with no visible emotion. In addition, schizophrenia is characterized by withdrawal from contact with others and a loss of interest in external activities; a breakdown of personal habits and ability to deal with daily events; and the delusions, hallucinations, and thought abnormalities found in other types of psychosis.

Schizophrenic delusions can be particularly bizarre. They often include the idea that the person's thoughts and actions are being controlled, that his or her thoughts are being broadcast so others can hear them, that thoughts have been "inserted" into the person's mind, or that thoughts have been removed.

Question: Is there more than one type of schizophrenia?

Schizophrenia may ultimately turn out to be a whole group of related disturbances. For now, we can identify four major subtypes of schizophrenia (Table 20–3).

Table 20–3 Types of Schizophrenia

Disorganized type: Schizophrenia marked by incoherence, grossly disorganized behavior, bizarre thinking, and flat or grossly inappropriate emotions.

Catatonic type: Schizophrenia marked by stupor, rigidity, unresponsiveness, posturing, mutism, and, sometimes, agitated, purposeless behavior.

Paranoid type: Schizophrenia marked by a preoccupation with delusions or by frequent auditory hallucinations related to a single theme, especially grandeur or persecution.

Undifferentiated type: Schizophrenia in which there are prominent psychotic symptoms, but none of the specific features of catatonic, disorganized, or paranoid types.

(DSM-III-R, 1987)

Disorganized Schizophrenia The disorder known as **disorganized schizophrenia** (also called hebephrenic schizophrenia) comes as close as any true psychiatric problem does to matching the stereotyped images of "insanity" seen in movies and on television. In disorganized schizophrenia, personality disintegration is almost complete. The result is silliness, laughter, and bizarre or obscene behavior (Fig. 20–4), as shown by this intake interview of a patient:

Dr. I am Dr. ____. I would like to know something more about you.
Patient You have a nasty mind. Lord! Lord! Cat's in a cradle.

Fig. 20–4 *In disorganized schizophrenia, behavior is marked by silliness, laughter, and bizarre or obscene behavior.*

Dr. Tell me, how do you feel?
Patient London's bell is a long, long dock. Hee! Hee! (Giggles uncontrollably.)
Dr. Do you know where you are now?
Patient D____n! S____t on all you who rip into my internals! The grudgerometer will take care of you all! (Shouting) I am the Queen, see my magic, I shall turn you all into smidgelings forever!
Dr. Your husband is concerned about you. Do you know his name?
Patient (Stands, walks to and faces the wall) Who am I, who are we, who are you, who are they, (turns) I . . . I . . . I . . . I! (makes grotesque faces.)

Edna was placed in the women's ward where she proceeded to masturbate. She always sat in a chosen spot and in a chosen way, with her feet propped under her. Occasionally, she would scream or shout obscenities. At other times she giggled to herself. She was known to attack other patients. She began to complain that her uterus was attached to a "pipeline to the Kremlin" and that she was being "infernally invaded" by Communism (Suinn, 1975).

Disorganized schizophrenia typically develops in early adolescence or young adulthood and it is often preceded by serious personality disorganization in earlier years. Chances of improvement are limited, and social impairment is usually extreme (DSM-III-R, 1987).

Catatonic Schizophrenia The catatonic person seems to be in a state of total panic. This brings about a stuporous condition in which odd positions may be held for hours or even days. Sometimes, a condition called *waxy flexibility* occurs. While in this state, the catatonic person can be arranged into any position, like a mannequin. These periods of immobility may be similar to the tendency to "freeze" at times of great emergency or panic. There is evidence that catatonic individuals are struggling desperately to control their inner turmoil. One sign of this is the fact that stupor may occasionally give way to agitated outbursts or violent behavior. The following excerpt describes a **catatonic episode:**

> Manuel appeared to be physically healthy upon examination. Yet he did not regain his awareness of his surroundings. He remained motionless, speechless, and seemingly unconscious. One evening an aide turned him on his side to straighten out the sheet, was called away to tend another patient, and forgot to return. Manuel was found the next morning, still on his side, his arm tucked under his body, as he had been left the night before. His arm was turning blue from lack of circulation but he seemed to be experiencing no discomfort. Further examination confirmed that he was in a state of waxy flexibility. (Suinn, 1975)

Notice that in addition to his other problems, Manuel was unable to talk. *Mutism,* along with a marked decrease in responsiveness to the environment, makes the catatonic patient difficult to "reach." Fortunately, this bizarre form of schizophrenia has become rare in Europe and North America (DSM-III-R, 1987).

Paranoid Schizophrenia Paranoid schizophrenia is the most common form of schizophrenic disorder. **Paranoid schizophrenia,** like a paranoid delusional disorder, centers around delusions of grandeur and persecution. However, in paranoid schizophrenia, we see personality disintegration that is not evident in paranoid (delusional) psychosis. The paranoic schizophrenic also experiences hallucinations and has delusions that are more bizarre, fragmented, and unconvincing than those seen in a delusional disorder.

Thinking that their minds are being controlled by God, the government, or "cosmic rays from space," or that someone is trying to poison them, paranoid schizophrenics may feel forced into violence to "protect" themselves. Do you remember James Huberty, who brutally murdered 21 people at a McDonald's restaurant in San Ysidro, California, in 1984? Some observers believe that Huberty was a paranoid schizophrenic who felt persecuted and cheated by life. Shortly before he announced to his wife that he was "going hunting humans," Huberty had been hearing hallucinated voices.

Undifferentiated Schizophrenia The three types of schizophrenia just described occur most often in textbooks. In reality, there is considerable overlap among the types. A real patient may shift from one pattern of behavior to another at different times. Many patients, therefore, are simply classified as suffering from **undifferentiated schizophrenia.**

The diagnosis of schizophrenia is fairly subjective and open to considerable error (McCabe, 1976) (see this chapter's Applications). All things considered, however, there is no doubt that schizophrenia is real or that it is a major challenge to medical and psychological researchers.

The Causes of Schizophrenia—An Unsolved Riddle

Former British Prime Minister Winston Churchill once described a question that perplexed him as "a riddle wrapped in a mystery inside an enigma." The same words might be used to describe the causes of schizophrenia, the most common and devastating of the psychoses.

Question: What do we know about the causes of schizophrenia?

Environment Some experts suspect that early **psychological trauma** may contribute to the later development of schizophrenia. Case studies of schizophrenia often show that its victims were exposed to violence, sexual abuse, death, divorce, or separation in childhood. In general, there seems to have been a greater than average degree of stress in the childhood of those who are schizophrenic (Mirsky & Duncan, 1986). An unanswered question is why early trauma leaves some individuals emotionally crippled and others not (Fig. 20–5).

Many psychologists theorize that a **disturbed family environment** is another risk factor in schizophrenia. For example, one intriguing theory is that schizophrenia is an escape from unsolvable emotional conflicts. British psychiatrist Ronald Laing (1967, 1970) has claimed that the families of schizophrenics frequently engage in **double-bind communication.** A double-bind message is one that places the listener in a "no-win" situation. Thus, the mother of a schizophrenic patient might issue this typical double-bind message: "You don't really love me; you're

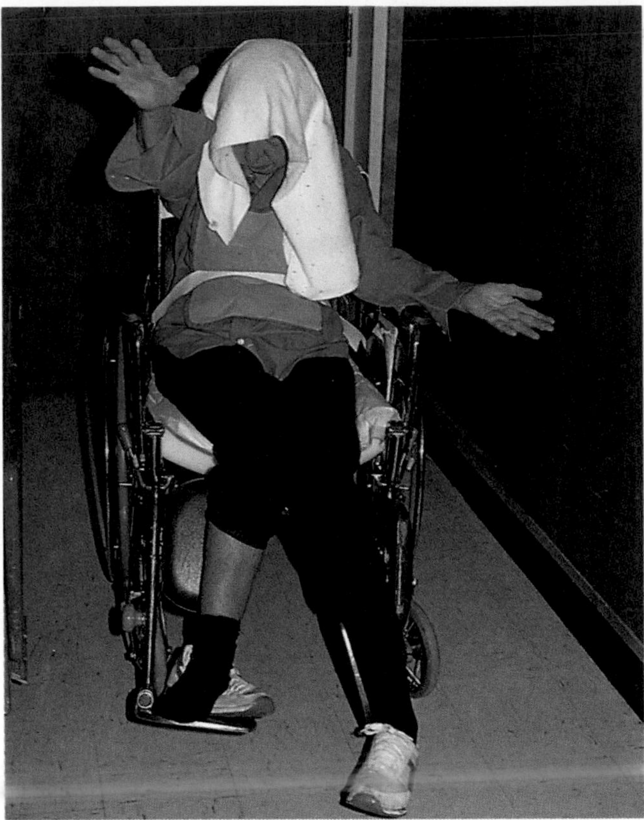

Fig. 20–5 *Can the catatonic's rigid postures and stupor be understood in terms of abnormal body chemistry? Environment? Heredity?*

only pretending you do." This statement asks for a show of love but makes showing love impossible. It wouldn't be surprising if the patient responded in a "crazy" or agitated way.

Support for such views comes from a recent 15-year follow-up study of disturbed adolescents. The study found that the chance of developing schizophrenia was related to patterns of deviant communication in families (Goldstein, 1985). The families of persons most likely to become disturbed interacted in ways that were laden with confusion, conflict, guilt, prying, criticism, negativity, and emotional attacks.

Although they are attractive, environmental explanations alone are not enough to account for schizophrenia (Torrey, 1988). For example, when the children of schizophrenic parents are raised away from their chaotic home environment, they are still likely to become psychotic (Page, 1971).

Question: Does that mean that heredity is a factor in schizophrenia?

HIGHLIGHT 20–4
The Genain Sisters—Trouble Times Four

By the time the Genain quadruplets reached high school, they began to act strangely. Hester broke light bulbs and tore buttons off her clothes. By age 20, Nora moaned at meals and complained that the bones in her neck were slipping. At night she stood on her knees and elbows in bed until they bled. At age 22, Iris quit her job, complaining that "I am pinned down. Someone wants to fight and I don't want to." Soon after, she "went to pieces." She screamed, drooled at meals, and talked of hearing voices. Myra, who was the fourth identical quad, panicked easily and couldn't be reassured, but did not actually break down until age 24 (Rosenthal, 1963).

In addition to sharing identical heredity, the Genain sisters—Nora, Iris, Myra, and Hester—have something else in common: All four became schizophrenic before age 25. The women, who are now in their 50s, have been in and out of mental hospitals all their lives.

You may be immediately tempted to assume that the Genain quads' psychoses were caused by heredity. However, it would be a mistake to overlook the nightmarish family life in which the girls grew up. Mr. Genain was an alcoholic who hounded, spied on, terrorized, and sexually molested the girls.

For the most part, Mrs. Genain was curiously blind to her husband's actions and offered the girls little support. Instead, she added her own bizarre thinking and sexual preoccupations to the family's already warped relationships. To put it mildly, the girls' mother and father failed spectacularly as parents.

In the final analysis, it seems that both heredity and an unhealthy environment led to the Genain sisters' problems (Carson et al., 1988). Further support for this conclusion comes from the fact that Myra, the least ill of the four, was her mother's favorite. Myra also was the only sister able to keep some distance from her father.

In sum, it appears that heredity may set higher or lower thresholds for psychosis. Whether a person "crosses the line" and become actively disturbed, however, may depend on the kind of stresses he or she is exposed to.

Heredity Evidence for heredity as a factor in schizophrenia has been growing ever stronger in recent years (Loehlin et al., 1988). It now appears that some individuals inherit a *potential* for developing schizophrenia.

Question: How can that be shown?

Here is a prime example: If one identical twin becomes schizophrenic (remember, identical twins have identical genes), then the other twin has a *46 percent* chance of also becoming schizophrenic (Nicol & Gottesman, 1983). There is even a case on record of 4 identical quadruplets *all* developing schizophrenia (Rosenthal & Quinn, 1977). (See Highlight 20–4.)

Question: What about other family relationships?

If *both* parents are schizophrenic, a child again has a 46 percent chance of developing the disorder. Persons with a brother or sister and one parent who are schizophrenic run a 17 percent risk themselves. Persons with a schizophrenic brother or sister have a 10 percent chance of also becoming schizophrenic. For *fraternal* twins the chance of mutual schizophrenia is about 14 percent (Nicol & Gottesman, 1983). These figures can be compared to the risk of developing schizophrenia for the population in general, which is 1 percent (Fig. 20–6). Comparisons such as these, and a variety of other studies, have shown that schizophrenia is more common among close relatives than among distant relatives and that it tends to run in families (Gottesman & Shields, 1982).

Question: How could someone inherit a susceptibility to schizophrenia?

Brain Chemistry LSD, PCP ("angel dust"), and similar drugs produce effects that partially mimic the symptoms of psychosis. Also, the same drugs (phenothiazines) that are effective in treating an LSD overdose are effective in the treatment of schizophrenia (Mandell et al., 1972). Such similarities have suggested to many scientists that psychosis may be based on **biochemical abnormalities** that cause the brain to produce some substance similar to a *psychedelic* (mind-altering) drug. At present, one of the most likely candidates is **dopamine** (DOPE-ah-meen), an important chemical messenger in the brain (Fig. 20–7).

Question: How does dopamine fit into the picture?

By far the most exciting discovery in recent years is the close link between dopamine and schizophrenia. Many researchers now believe that schizophrenia is directly related to overactivity in brain dopamine systems (Barchas et al., 1978; Nicol & Gottesman, 1983).

Early hints of a dopamine-psychosis link came when researchers noted that large doses of amphetamines (speed) produce symptoms that are almost identical to paranoid schizophrenia. Amphetamines, it turns out, also raise brain dopamine levels. Another piece of the puzzle fell into place when it was discovered that all major *antipsychotic* drugs *block* the action of dopamine at receptor areas in the brain (Iversen, 1979).

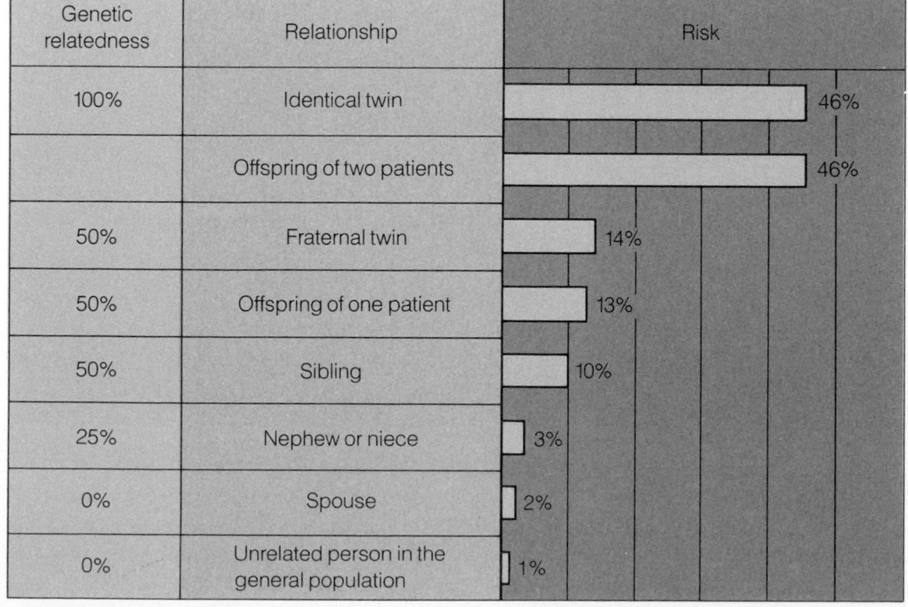

Fig. 20–6 *Lifetime risk of developing schizophrenia is related to how closely a person is genetically related to a schizophrenic individual. A shared environment also increases the risk (Nicol & Gottesman, 1983). (Data from Gottesman & Shields, 1982.)*

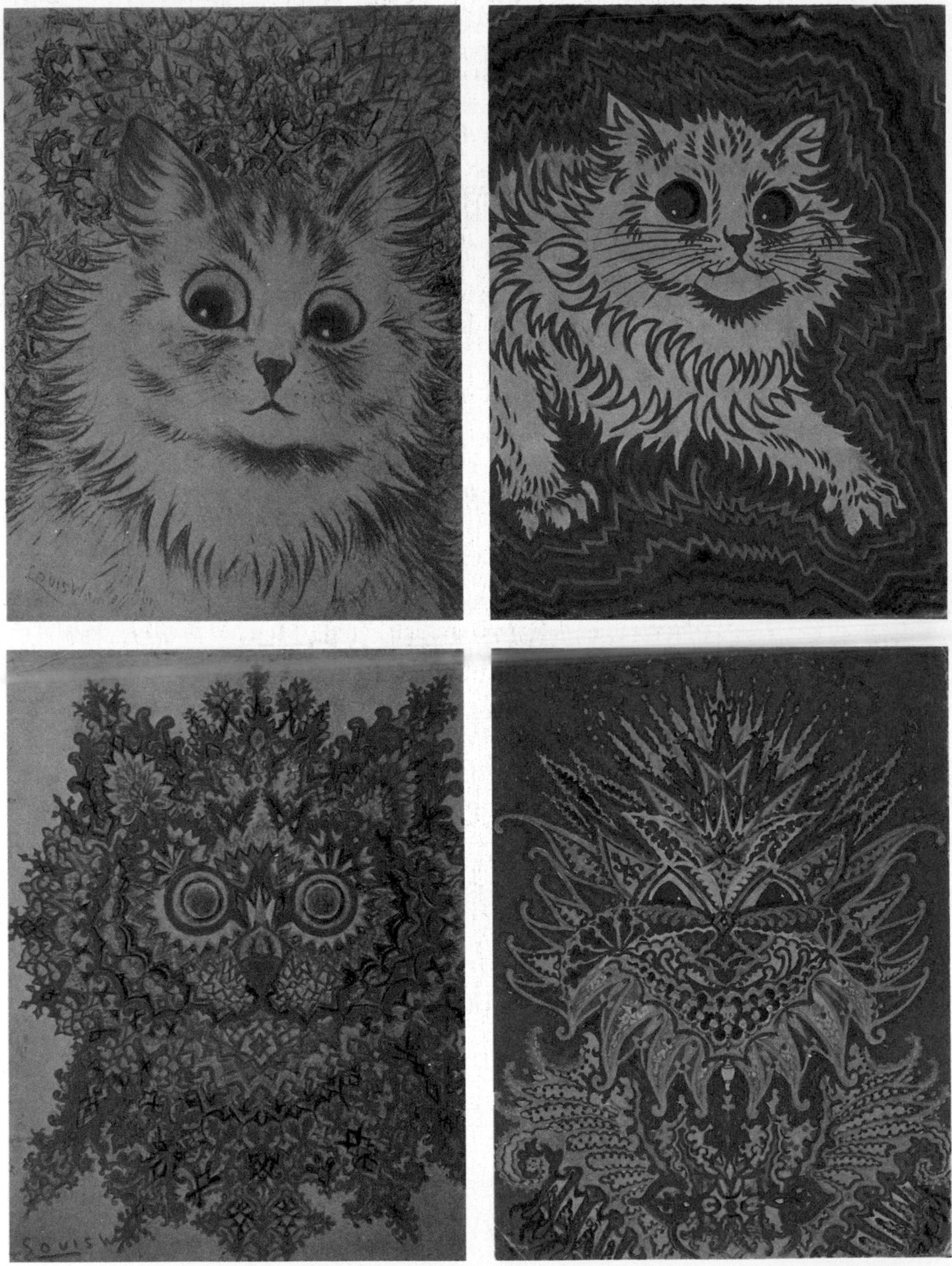

Fig. 20–7 *This series of paintings by Louis Wain reflects a troubled personality. Wain was a British illustrator who became schizophrenic in middle age. As Wain's psychosis progressed, his cat paintings became highly abstract and fragmented. In many ways, Wain's paintings resemble the perceptual changes caused by psychedelic drugs such as mescaline and LSD. Recent research suggests that psychosis may, in fact, be the result of mind-altering changes in brain chemistry. (Derik Bayes/Courtesy Guttman-Maclay* Life *Picture Service.)*

Question: Then is schizophrenia a "dopamine high"?

For a time it seemed so. But no extra or abnormal amounts of dopamine could be found in the brains of schizophrenics (Davis, 1978). So much for the dopamine theory!

But wait. Our story is not over. In a dramatic breakthrough, a team of researchers at the University of Toronto, Canada, found nearly *double* the normal number of dopamine receptors in the brains of schizophrenics. These extra receptors exist in especially large numbers in the limbic system (a major emotional system of the brain) (Lee & Seeman, 1980).

Many scientists now believe that dopamine activation triggers a flood of unrelated thoughts, feelings, and perceptions and directly accounts for the voices, hallucinations, delusions, and other disturbances of schizophrenia (Iversen, 1979). Because of the extra receptors, schizophrenics may get psychedelic effects from normal levels of dopamine in the brain. The implication of this, and of related research on other brain chemicals, is that schizophrenics may be on a sort of drug trip caused by their own bodies (Bushbaum & Haier, 1982; Thompson, 1985).

The Schizophrenic Brain Medical researchers have long hoped for a way to directly observe the schizophrenic brain. Two new medical techniques are now making it possible. One, called a **CT scan,** provides an X-ray picture of the brain. (CT stands for computed tomography, or computer-enhanced X-ray images.) Figure 20–8 shows a CT scan of the brain of John Hinkley, Jr. Hinkley, you may recall, shot President Ronald Reagan and three other men in 1981. In the ensuing trial, Hinkley was judged insane.

As you can see, Hinkley's brain differed from the norm. Specifically, it had wider surface fissuring and enlarged ventricles (fluid-filled spaces within the brain). Similar changes, which are normal in older people, are found in about 1 out of 10 young schizophrenics. Although the meaning of such changes is still in doubt, the CT scan promises to aid in diagnosing schizophrenia and to provide new information on its causes (McKean, 1982).

A second new technique, called a **PET scan,** provides an image of brain *activity*. (PET stands for positron emission tomography.) To make a PET scan, a radioactive

Fig. 20–8 (left) *CT scan of would-be presidential assassin John Hinkley, Jr., taken when he was 25. The X-ray image shows widened fissures in the wrinkled surface of Hinkley's brain.* (right) *CT scan of a normal 25-year-old's brain. In most young adults the surface folds of the brain are pressed together too tightly to be seen. As a person ages, surface folds of the brain normally become more visible. Pronounced brain fissuring in young adults may be a sign of schizophrenia, chronic alcoholism, or other problems (McKean, 1982).*

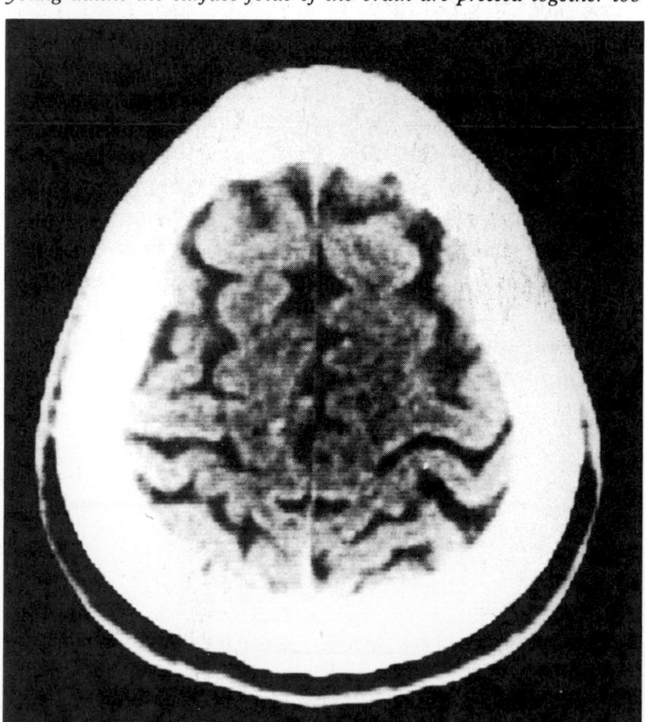

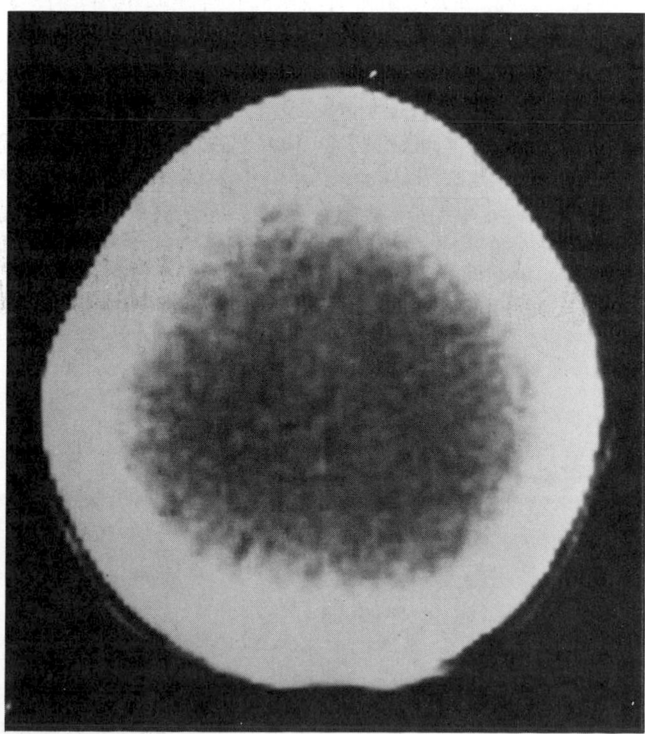

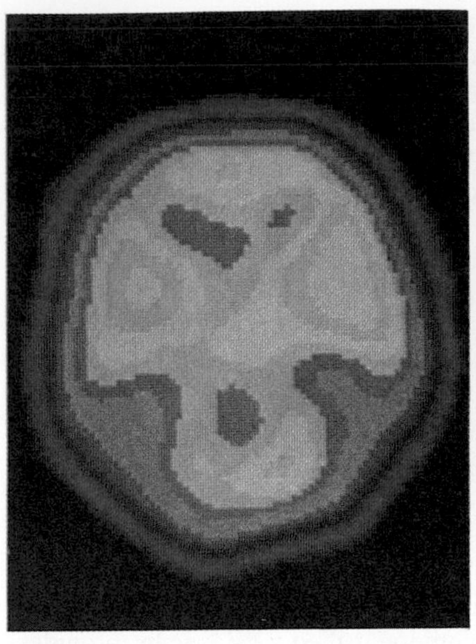

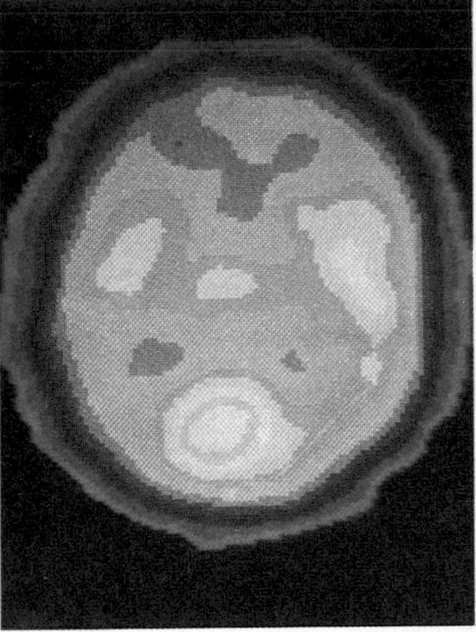

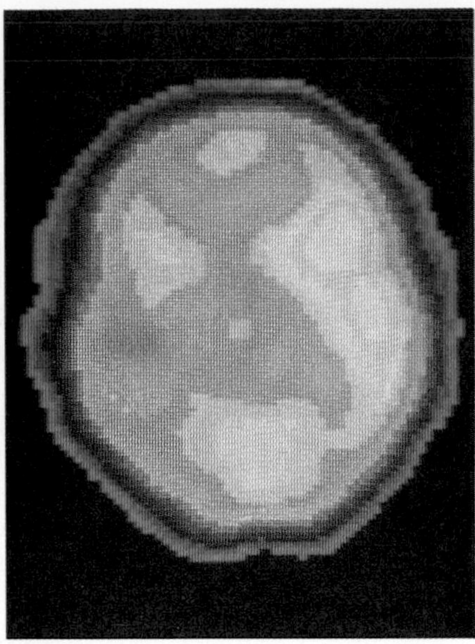

Fig. 20–9 *Positron emission tomography produces PET scans of the human brain. In the scans shown here, red, pink, and orange indicate lower levels of brain activity; white and blue indicate higher activity levels. Notice that activity in the schizophrenic brain is quite low in the frontal lobes (top area of each scan). Activity in the manic-depressive brain is low in the left brain hemisphere and high in the right brain hemisphere. Researchers are trying to identify consistent patterns like these to aid diagnosis of mental disorder.*

sugar solution is injected into a vein. When the sugar reaches the brain, a device measures how much is used in each area. This information is then translated into a colored map, or scan, of brain activity (Fig. 20–9). Researchers are already finding patterns in such scans that are consistently linked with schizophrenia, affective disorders, and other problems. Some researchers believe that in the future PET scans will be routinely used to accurately diagnose schizophrenia (Landis, 1980). For now, PET scans show that there is a clear difference in schizophrenic brain activity.

Summary In summary, the emerging picture of psychosis takes this general form: *Anyone* subjected to enough stress may be pushed to a psychotic break, but some people inherit a difference in brain chemistry or brain structure that makes them more susceptible. Thus, the right combination of inherited potential and environmental stress brings about important changes in brain chemicals or generates mind-altering substances in the body (Gottesman & Shields, 1982).

Ultimately, distinctions between organic and functional psychoses may be dropped, and treatment of major disturbances may become more chemical than psychological. But for now, psychosis remains "a riddle wrapped in a mystery inside an enigma." Let us hope the recent advances that we have so briefly explored are as promising as they appear to be.

Learning Check

Match the following:

______	**1.** Schizotypal personality	**A.** Manic or depressive behavior
______	**2.** Disorganized schizophrenia	**B.** Mutism, odd postures, immobility
______	**3.** Catatonic schizophrenia	**C.** Nonpsychotic disorder
______	**4.** Paranoid schizophrenia	**D.** Silliness, bizarre behavior, personality disintegration
______	**5.** Major mood disorders	**E.** Delusions of grandeur or persecution

6. Major mood disorders, especially bipolar disorders, often appear to be endogenous. T or F?
7. Ronald Laing attributes psychotic behavior to emotional conflicts created by
   a. manic parents *b.* schizoaffective interactions *c.* psychedelic interactions *d.* double-bind communication
8. The ______________ ______________ of a schizophrenic person runs a 46 percent chance of also becoming psychotic.
9. Abnormally high numbers of noradrenaline receptors have been found in the brains of schizophrenics. T or F?
10. Enlarged surface fissures and ventricles, as revealed by CT scans, are found only in the brains of chronic schizophrenics. T or F?
11. The acronym SAD stands for schizotypal affective disorder. T or F?

Answers:
1. C **2.** D **3.** B **4.** E **5.** A **6.** T **7.** *d* **8.** identical twin **9.** F (dopamine receptors) **10.** F **11.** F

Treatment—Medical Approaches

Question: Is psychosis incurable? If a person's symptoms temporarily disappear, can an unexpected relapse occur?

An organic psychosis cannot be "cured" in the usual sense, but it may be controlled with drugs and other techniques. With functional psychoses the outlook is still rather negative, but many people are *permanently* cured. It is wrong to fear "former mental patients" or to exclude them from work, friendships, or other social situations. A psychotic episode does not inevitably lead to a lifelong maladjustment, but too often it leads to unnecessary rejection based on groundless fears.

Question: What can be done about psychosis?

Two basic forms of treatment can be distinguished. The first, called **psychotherapy,** can be described as two people talking about one person's problems. Psychotherapy is a special relationship between a counselor or psychologist and a person in trouble. Psychotherapy may be applied to anything from a brief crisis to a full-scale psychosis. Because approaches vary greatly, a complete discussion of psychotherapy is found in the next two chapters.

A second major approach to treatment is **somatic** (bodily) **therapy.** The main somatic treatments are *chemotherapy, electroconvulsive therapy,* and *psychosurgery.* Somatic therapy is often done in the context of psychiatric *hospitalization.* All the somatic approaches have a medical slant, and they are mostly used to treat psychoses. For these reasons, somatic therapy is an appropriate conclusion to our discussion here.

Drugs The atmosphere in mental hospitals changed radically in the mid-1950s with the widespread adoption of chemotherapy (CHEM-oh-therapy). **Chemotherapy** is the use of drugs or chemical substances to alleviate the symptoms of emotional disturbance. Drugs may relieve the anxiety attacks and other discomforts of nonpsychotic disorders, but they are more frequently used to combat psychosis. Drugs such as Thorazine are credited with emptying mental hospitals, reducing the hospital population from a peak of 560,000 to fewer than 200,000 patients in barely a generation.

Question: What types of drugs are used in chemotherapy?

The three major classes of drugs are *minor tranquilizers, major tranquilizers (antipsychotics),* and *energizers.* **Minor tranquilizers** calm anxious or agitated persons; **energizers** improve the mood of depressed individuals; and **antipsychotics** control hallucinations and other symptoms of psychosis.

Question: Are drugs a valid approach to treatment?

Drugs have greatly improved the chances for recovery from a psychiatric disorder. They have shortened the length of hospital stays and they have made it possible for more individuals to be returned to the community where they may be treated on an "out-patient" basis.

Few experts would argue for a return to the conditions that existed before chemotherapy became available. But there are some drawbacks. First of all, drugs generally do not *cure* mental illness—they only temporarily relieve symptoms. Such relief may allow patients to benefit more fully from psychotherapy and other attempts to help them, but drugs alone may not remove underlying problems. As a matter of fact, patients may separate temporary improvement caused by a drug from improvement they consider genuine. As one patient told the author, "The drugs made me talk more and seem happy, but I knew I really wasn't."

The extensive use of drugs also raises the issue of balancing benefits against possible adverse side effects. For example, as many as 10 percent of patients taking major tranquilizers for long periods develop *tardive dyskinesia* (TAR-div dis-cah-NEE-zyah). This is a neurological condition in which patients develop rhythmic facial and mouth movements, as well as unusual movements of the arms ("fly-catching" motions, for instance) and restless movements of other parts of the body (Feldman & Quenzer, 1984).

Perhaps the most valid criticism of chemotherapy is the simple observation that is easily overused. Apparently, the temptation to reach for the prescription pad is great. Most observers agree that too many drugs are being given to too many people. Researcher David Rosenhan (whose work is described in the Applications section) believes that drugs often are not merely given at therapeutic levels. Rather, they are sometimes used to keep patients docile and easy to manage. Many critics believe that the locks that came off the doors of old-style institutions have been replaced at times by "chemical locks." In the long run, concern over the side effects and the overuse of drugs may temper the popularity of chemotherapy. But where psychosis is concerned, drugs are usually helpful and will remain a major mode of treatment.

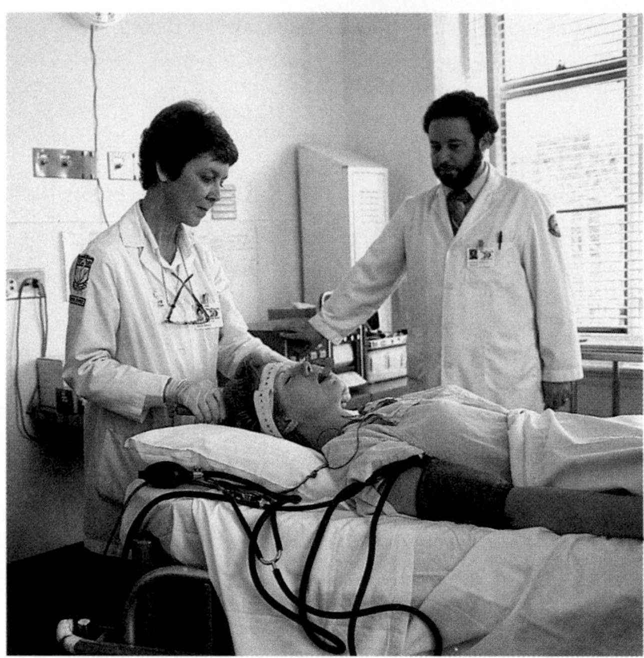

Fig. 20–10 *In electroconvulsive therapy, electrodes are attached to the head, and a brief electrical current is passed through the brain. ECT is used in the treatment of severe depression.*

Shock **Electroconvulsive therapy (ECT)** is a rather drastic medical treatment for depression. In the usual ECT session, a 150-volt electrical current is passed through the brain for slightly less than a second (Fig. 20–10). The current triggers a convulsion and causes the patient to lose consciousness for a short time. Muscle relaxants and sedative drugs are given before ECT to soften its impact. Treatments are given in a series of 6 to 8 sessions spread over 3 to 4 weeks.

Question: How does shock help?

Actually, it is the seizure activity that is believed to be helpful. Proponents of ECT claim that shock-induced seizures alter the biochemical balance in the brain, bringing an end to severe depression and suicidal behavior (Frankl, 1977). Others have charged that ECT works only by confusing patients so they can't remember why they were depressed (Kohn, 1988).

Many people consider ECT a distasteful procedure, and not all professionals support its use. In fact, experts are engaged in a heated debate concerning the value of ECT and the seriousness of its side effects. Critics claim that ECT causes permanent memory losses and occasional brain damage (Friedberg, 1977). Proponents of ECT argue that detailed brain scans show no evidence of damage (Kohn, 1988). Also, it has been reported recently that if electrodes are applied to only one side of the head, memory loss is greatly reduced (Rosenberg & Pettinati, 1984). However, ECT done in this way may not end depression (Kohn, 1988; Sackheim et al., 1987).

Those who support ECT view it as being like any other medical treatment: It involves calculated risks (Fink, 1977; Weiner, 1984). As is true of chemotherapy, the major problem with ECT seems to lie in overuse and misuse. Some patients have had hundreds of shock treatments and have suffered damage in the process.

What, then, can be said about ECT? Most experts seem to agree on the following: (1) At best, ECT produces only temporary improvement—it gets the patient out of a bad spot, but it must be combined with other treatments; (2) ECT does cause permanent memory losses in many patients; and (3) ECT should be used only as a last resort after drug therapy has failed (Kohn, 1988). All told, ECT is still considered by many to be a valid treatment for selected cases of depression—especially when it rapidly ends wildly self-destructive or suicidal behavior.

Surgery The most extreme biological treatment is **psychosurgery,** a general term applied to any surgical alteration of the brain. The best-known psychosurgery is the *lobotomy*. In the **prefrontal lobotomy** and related techniques, the frontal lobes are surgically disconnected from the other areas of the brain. The original goal of this procedure was to calm a person who had not responded to any other type of treatment.

When the lobotomy was first introduced in the 1940s, there were enthusiastic claims for its success. But later studies suggested that some patients were calmed, some showed no noticeable change, and some became "vegetables." Lobotomies also produced a high rate of undesirable side effects, such as seizures, extreme lack of emotional response, and even stupor (Barahal, 1958; Valenstein, 1980). As such problems became apparent, the lobotomy was abandoned.

Question: To what extent is psychosurgery used now?

Psychosurgery is still considered a valid treatment by many neurosurgeons. However, most now use sophisticated **deep lesioning** techniques. In this approach, small target areas are destroyed in the brain's interior. The appeal of deep lesioning is that it can have fairly specific effects. For instance, a patient with uncontrollable aggressive impulses may be calmed by psychosurgery (Valenstein, 1980).

It is worth remembering that all forms of psychosurgery are *irreversible*. A drug can be given or taken away. You can't take back psychosurgery. Many critics argue that psychosurgery should be banned altogether. Others continue to report success with psychosurgical procedures (Mitchell-Heggs et al., 1976). All things considered, it is perhaps most accurate, even after decades of use, to describe psychosurgery as an experimental technique (Perkoff, 1980).

Hospitalization Somatic therapy, psychotherapy, and other techniques may require a special setting or special control for a period of time. Traditionally, this has meant a trip to a psychiatric hospital or state institution. **Hospitalization** by itself may be considered a form of treatment since it removes a troubled individual from situations that may be provoking or maintaining the problem. At its best, the hospital is a sanctuary—a controlled environment in which diagnosis, support, refuge, and psychotherapy are provided (Bachrach, 1984). At worst, an institution can be a brutalizing experience that leaves a person less prepared to face the world than before (Fig. 20–11).

In the last 20 years the resident population in large mental hospitals throughout the United States has been reduced by two-thirds. This reduction is based, in part, on policies designed to improve the odds that hospitalization will be constructive.

Fig. 20–11 *Depending on the quality of the institution, hospitalization may be a refuge or a brutalizing experience. Many state "asylums" or mental hospitals are antiquated and in need of drastic improvement.*

Hospitals are ideally used as a last resort after other forms of treatment within the community have been exhausted. Research indicates that most psychiatric patients do as well with short-term hospitalization (3 to 4 weeks) as they do with longer (3- to 4-month) periods (Glick et al., 1979). In view of this, hospital stays are now held to a minimum through the use of *revolving-door* policies, in which patients are released as soon as possible and readmitted only if necessary. Also, modern hospitals provide recreation and rehabilitation to help end an old problem: Formerly, many patients became so "institutionalized" that they had difficulty returning to the community. Also helpful are halfway houses and voluntary support groups that ease the patient's return to the community.

Question: How successful have such policies been?

In truth, their success has been limited. Many states have welcomed a reduction in mental hospital populations as a way to save money. The upsetting result is that many chronic patients are being discharged to a lonely existence in hostile communities without adequate care. A large percentage of homeless persons interviewed recently at an emergency shelter had psychiatric problems. (Bassuk et al., 1984). In short, critics point out that the revolving door also turns inward. Patients who move from hospitalization to unemployment and social isolation all too often must return for further treatment (Goering et al., 1984; Torrey, 1988).

Large mental hospitals may no longer be warehouses for society's unwanted, but many former patients are no better off consigned to bleak lives in nursing homes, single-room hotels, or board-and-care homes (Bassuk & Gerson, 1978). Ironically, high-quality psychological and psychiatric care is available in almost every community. As much as anything, a simple lack of sufficient funding prevents large numbers of people from getting the care they need. It would be especially helpful if better rehabilitation programs were offered as a follow-up treatment (Goering et al., 1984).

Community Mental Health Programs—Hope and Help for Many

The creation of community mental health centers has been a bright spot in the area of mental health care. **Community mental health centers** attempt to shift emphasis away from hospitalization and seek new answers to mental health problems by providing short-term treatment, out-patient care, and special crisis or emergency services (Spielberger & Stenmark, 1985).

If it is like most, the primary aim of the mental health center in your community is to directly aid troubled citizens. The second goal of mental health centers is *prevention*. Consultation, education, and crisis intervention are used to end or prevent problems before they become serious. Also, some centers attempt to raise the general level of mental health in target areas by combating problems such as unemployment, delinquency, and drug abuse.

Question: How have community mental health centers fared in meeting their goals?

In practice, they have concentrated much more on providing clinical services than they have on prevention (Bloom & Parad, 1977). This situation appears to be primarily the result of wavering government support (translation: money). Overall, community mental health centers have succeeded in making mental health services more accessible than ever before. Many of their programs are made possible by **paraprofessionals,** individuals who work under the supervision of more highly trained staff. Some paraprofessionals are ex-addicts, ex-alcoholics, or ex-patients who have "been there." Many more are persons (paid or volunteer) who have skills in tutoring, crafts, or counseling or who are simply warm, understanding, and skilled at communication. There is a severe shortage of people working in mental health care. The contributions of paraprofessionals will undoubtedly continue to grow. A career as a paraprofessional should not be overlooked by students planning to work in the field of mental health (see Appendix A).

Learning Check

1. The use of chemotherapy has required longer hospital stays since drugs can only be given under hospital supervision. T or F?
2. ECT is a modern form of chemotherapy. T or F?
3. Electroconvulsive therapy is used mainly as a treatment for depression. T or F?
4. Tardive dyskinesia is a possible complication in long term use of
   a. major tranquilizers *b.* energizers *c.* minor tranquilizers *d.* ECT
5. Currently, the frontal lobotomy is the most widely used form of psychosurgery. T or F?
6. Psychosurgery can be reversed if it is unsuccessful. T or F?
7. Whenever possible, the community mental health movement emphasizes prevention of mental health problems. T or F?
8. Research indicates that relatively short periods of psychiatric hospitalization are as beneficial as long-term hospital stays. T or F?

Answers:

1. F 2. F 3. T 4. *a* 5. F 6. F 7. T 8. T

Applications: On Being Sane in Insane Places

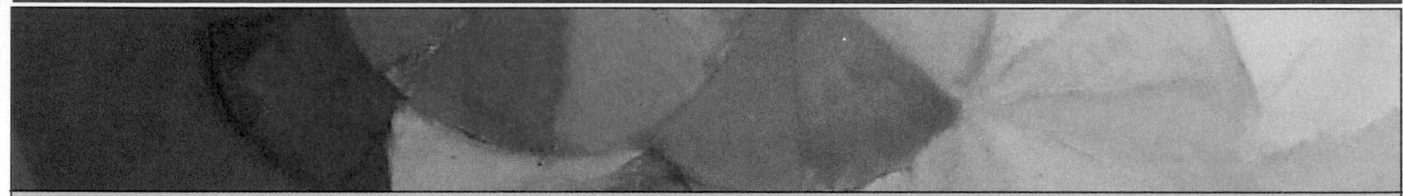

Question: Suppose someone were committed to a psychiatric hospital by accident. Would the staff notice? Would the person be able to get out?

David Rosenhan of Stanford University set out to answer these questions and another: How accurately do psychiatric hospitals distinguish between people who are psychotic and those who are healthy?

To find out, Rosenhan and several colleagues had themselves committed (Rosenhan, 1973). Entrance to mental hospitals was gained by faking only one symptom. Rosenhan and the others complained of hearing voices that said "empty," "hollow," and "thud." In 11 out of 12 tries, they were admitted with a diagnosis of "schizophrenia."

Pseudo-Patients After being admitted, these "pseudo-patients" dropped all pretense of mental illness. Yet, even though they acted completely normal, none of the researchers was ever recognized by hospital *staff* as a phony patient. Other patients were not so easily fooled. It was not unusual for a real patient to say to one of the researchers, "You're not crazy, you're checking up on the hospital!" or, "You're a journalist."

Rosenhan and the others spent from 1 to 7 weeks in hospitals before being discharged. The hospitals ranged from very modern and plush to ancient and shoddy. No matter how good the facilities or how good the hospital's reputation, Rosenhan found some disturbing conditions. Contact between staff and patients was very limited and sometimes marked by fear or hostility. It was found that attendants and staff only spent an average of 11 percent of their time out of the "cage," the glassed-in central compartment in the ward.

It was not unusual for the morning attendants to wake patients with a hostile call of: "Come on, you m____ f____s, out of bed!" When patients tried to talk with staff, they were often ignored or received strange replies. One pseudo-patient approached a psychiatrist and politely asked when he might get grounds privileges. The doctor's reply was, "Good morning, Dave. How are you today?"

Rosenhan found that therapy other than drugs was very limited. Daily contact of patients with psychiatrists, psychologists, or physicians averaged about 7 minutes. On the other hand, the researchers were given a total of 2100 pills to swallow. (Only 2 of these were actually taken, the rest being pocketed or flushed down the toilet.)

Nonpersons Patients tended to be treated as nonpersons. A nurse unbuttoned her uniform to adjust her bra in front of a room full of male patients. She was not being sexy; she just didn't consider the patients men. Patients would often be discussed by the staff while the patient was standing nearby. It was as if patients were invisible.

A situation that sums up Rosenhan's findings better than any other is his note-taking. Rosenhan began taking notes by carefully jotting things on a small piece of paper hidden in his hand. He learned quickly that hiding was totally unnecessary. He was soon walking around with a clipboard and note pads, recording observations and collecting data.

No one questioned this behavior. Note-taking was simply seen as a symptom of his "illness." As a matter of fact, Rosenhan found that anything he did was ignored. When a staff member manhandled a patient (as happened occasionally), Rosenhan would be right there—taking notes on the whole incident!

Labels These observations clarify the failure of staff members to detect the fake patients. Because they were seen in the context of a mental ward and because they had been labeled schizophrenic, anything the pseudo-patients did was seen as a symptom of their "illness."

To return to the original hypothetical question about talking your way out of an accidental commitment, it should be clear that it could be quite futile to say, "Look, this is all a mistake. I'm not crazy. You've got to let me out." The response might very well be, "Have you had these paranoid delusions for long?"

Many mental health professionals found Rosenhan's findings hard to believe. This led to a follow-up study, in which the staff of another hospital was warned that one or more pseudo-patients were going to try to gain admission over the next 3 months. Thus alerted, the staff at this hospital tried to identify fake incoming patients. Among 193 candidates, 41 were labeled fakes by at least one staff member, and 19 more were labeled "suspicious." This only served to confirm Rosenhan's original findings, since he never sent any patients—fake or otherwise—to this hospital!

It is an important final note that all of the normal people who served as pseudo-patients in the original studies were discharged as schizophrenics "in remission" (temporarily free of symptoms). In other words, the label that prevented hos-

Applications

pital staff from seeing the normality of the researchers stayed with them when they left. Psychiatrist Karl Menninger (1964) has commented on a similar situation:

> A label can blight the life of a person even after his recovery from mental illness. A young doctor I knew suffered for a time from some anxiety and indecision. He consulted a psychiatrist and soon recovered. Unfortunately, a "tentative" diagnosis of schizophrenia got abroad—I don't know how—and the young doctor's professional career was seriously impaired. He was injured, not by mental illness but by a word.

Observations such as these are not a total condemnation of psychiatric hospitals. Many of the conditions Rosenhan uncovered will be found in any hospital or other large institution. But Rosenhan's findings do carry an important message for professionals and non-professionals alike: Labels can be dangerous. As Stoller (1967) has said:

> When a person is labeled—neurotic, psychotic, executive, teacher, salesman, psychologist—either by himself or by others, he restricts his behavior to the role and even may rely upon the role for security. This diminishes the kind of experiences he is likely to have. Indeed, it is those groups whose members have shared labels—be it schizophrenic or executive—which are hardest to help move into intimate contact.

Implications The terms reviewed in this and the previous chapter can, and do, aid communication about human problems. But if used carelessly, they may do great damage. Everyone has felt or acted "crazy" during brief periods of stress or high emotion. A person whose adjustment problems extend over a longer period of time is different from you or me only in the severity of his or her difficulty.

It is therefore more productive to label problems than to label people. Think of the difference in impact between saying, "He is experiencing a serious emotional disturbance" and saying, "He is a psychotic." Which statement would you choose to have said about yourself?

It is also important to realize that a severely disturbed person will appreciate being treated normally. Rosenhan's research makes it clear that people are not helped by being thrust into the patient role. One former patient's comments clarify this last point:

> After I got back from the hospital, my friends tried to *act* like nothing had changed. But I could tell they weren't being honest. For instance, a friend invited me to dinner and everything went fine until I dropped my fork. Both my friend and his wife jumped up and stared at me like they thought I might explode. I was quite embarrassed.

Learning Check

1. In the majority of their attempts, Rosenhan's pseudo-patients were admitted to mental hospitals after complaining only that they were hearing voices. T or F?
2. Although they were often detected by professional staff members, the normality of the pseudo-patients was never recognized by other patients. T or F?
3. During a short hospital stay, one pseudo-patient was denied psychiatric drugs even though he requested them. T or F?
4. Rosenhan found that almost anything pseudo-patients said or did was interpreted as a symptom of their "illness." T or F?
5. When they were alerted that a number of pseudo-patients might try to gain entry, hospital staff members were able to more accurately detect the fakes. T or F?

Answers:
1. T 2. F 3. F 4. T 5. F

Exploration: Who Is "Crazy" and What Should Be Done about It?

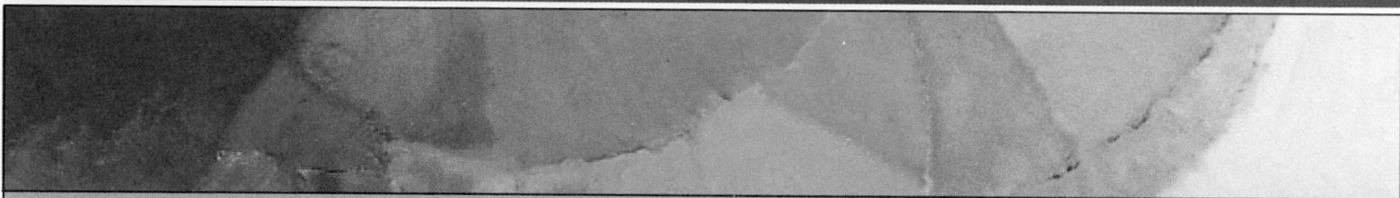

The best-known critic of traditional psychiatric treatment for "mental illness" is psychiatrist Thomas Szasz (pronounced "saz"). Szasz (1966, 1983, 1987) believes that mental illness is a myth. Szasz charges that traditional medical concepts of diseases have been wrongly applied to emotional problems. The *medical model,* as it is called, treats such problems as "diseases" with "symptoms" that can be "cured."

Szasz believes that brain diseases eventually may be found, but that they are not empirically demonstrated as yet (Szasz, 1983). He thus regards "mental illness" as just an idea used when trying to deal with disturbing behavior. If "mental patients" starve themselves, attack members of their families, commit arson or theft, kill themselves, or kill prominent persons, what does psychiatry do? It pardons them (says they are not responsible for their actions) and imprisons them (commits them to a mental hospital for "treatment"). Or, it says they are sane, responsible, and guilty of a crime. In this case they are imprisoned in jail. Szasz believes that labels such as *psychosis* are used mainly to transform people from being responsible for their actions to being non-responsible "patients" who need pity and therapy.

Another of Szasz's points is that "mental illness" and all its categories are merely descriptions of the unlimited variety of human behavior. The labels used to classify mental illness do not explain anything. They are merely applied to behaviors that violate social or psychiatric norms. Thus, the concept of mental illness is used to deal with persons whose behavior creates a *social disturbance* or violates social rules. If a person acts in a way that "offends" society and a law exists against such acts, the person may be jailed. If no law exists, the person may be "treated." In this sense, the distinction between madness and badness, or mental illness and criminality, is a *moral judgment,* not a medical reality.

In light of such thinking, Szasz and a number of other experts prefer to view emotional disturbances as "problems in living." This view makes the goal of therapy "change" rather than "cure" and changes "patients" to "clients." It has also led Szasz to question the handling of the civil rights of psychiatric "patients." Szasz estimates that 90 percent of all patients in mental hospitals are there involuntarily. He sees this as a serious mistake. To commit people because they *might* be dangerous to themselves is indefensible by Szasz's standards.

According to Szasz, the only legitimate reason for depriving a person of freedom is for being "dangerous to others," but then only if the person has broken the law by committing violence or by threatening to do so. Szasz considers the disturbed no more dangerous than a randomly selected group of citizens. He therefore rejects involuntary commitment as "punishment without trial, imprisonment without limit, and stigmatization without hope of redress" (1969).

Point and Counterpoint Szasz does not assert that bizarre behavior is normal. His position is merely that it cannot be explained or sensibly treated using a strict medical model. Szasz's critics reply that advances in neuroscience increasingly call his ideas into question. Certainly, a brain damaged by disease, accident, or drugs can lead to illness, including mental or emotional illness. Szasz's reply is that clearly demonstrated brain abnormalities still apply to only a small percentage of all cases of psychopathology.

It is undoubtedly a mistake to assume that the findings of David Rosenhan and the visions of people such as Szasz justify abandoning the tremendous advances in mental health care found in current approaches. All societies have classified some of their members into categories analogous to our term "mentally ill." The social problems created by "crazy" behavior will not vanish by changing the words used to describe it. Rosenhan and Szasz do, however, raise serious questions about civil rights and involuntary commitment. As a final bit of food for thought, consider the following incident, recorded by a reporter visiting a large state mental hospital:

> A thin man, old and dry, stopped the guide and said, "When the hell you gonna get me a suit and let me outa

Exploration

here? How about it? . . ." The guide said something indefinite and the man walked away, nodding. This was the section for killers, I had been told, so I asked what the thin man had done. "He painted a horse." "He what?" "He painted a horse." "What's wrong with that?" "It was in a field. A live horse. He was drunk and somebody bet him he couldn't make a horse look like a zebra, I think, so he painted it and they put him here. For being drunk probably." "How long has he been in?" "Thirty-seven years. By the time they got around to letting him out he really was crazy. . . . For his own good we just can't let him go out of here."*

*Bruce Jackson, "Our prisons are criminal," *New York Times Magazine*, September 22, 1973, pp. 54–57.

On what basis should we as a society involuntarily commit people? How often would ending involuntary commitment mean freedom to wander lost and neglected on the streets, without family, friends, or hope? What do you think is the right way to deal with "crazy" behavior?

Learning Check

1. Szasz has argued that it is inappropriate to apply a medical or disease model to what he terms "problems in living." T or F?

2. Szasz points out that most people in mental hospitals are there voluntarily. T or F?

3. Psychosis is the only disorder that Szasz recognizes as a legitimate mental disease. T or F?

Answers:
1. T 2. F 3. F

Chapter Summary

• **Psychosis** is a break in contact with reality that is marked by **delusions, hallucinations, sensory changes, emotional disturbances,** and in some cases, **personality disintegration.**

• Psychotic symptoms, as well as lesser problems in thought, speech, memory, and attention, tend to be most prominent during short *episodes* of increased disturbance. There is evidence that some such symptoms are partially under voluntary control.

• An **organic psychosis** is based on known injuries or diseases of the brain. Other problems of unknown origin are termed **functional psychoses.** Three common causes of organic psychosis are *untreated syphilis* **(general paresis),** *poisoning,* and **senile dementia** (especially **Alzheimer's disease**).

• A diagnosis of **delusional disorder** is almost totally based on the presence of delusions concerning grandeur, persecution, infidelity, romantic attraction, or physical disease. The most common delusional disorder is paranoid psychosis. Because they often have intense and irrational delusions of persecution, paranoids may be violent if they believe they are threatened.

• **Major mood disorders** (affective disorders) involve extremes of mood or emotion. When accompanied by psychotic symptoms, they may be called **affective psychoses. Bipolar disorders** combine mania and depression and occur in **manic, depressed,** and **mixed** types. **Major depressions** involve extreme sadness and despondency, but no evidence of mania.

• **Schizophrenia** is the most frequently occurring psychosis. It is distinguished by a split between thought and emotion, delusions, hallucinations, and communication difficulties. Several subtypes of schizophrenia have been identified. They should not be confused with **schizotypal personality disorder,** which involves gradual withdrawal into isolation from others and odd, apathetic behavior.

• **Disorganized schizophrenia** is marked by extreme personality disintegration and silly, bizarre, or obscene behavior. Social impairment is usually extreme.

• **Catatonic schizophrenia** is associated with *stupor, mu-*

tism, and odd postures. Sometimes violent and agitated behavior also occurs.

- In **paranoid schizophrenia** (the most common subtype), outlandish delusions of grandeur and persecution are coupled with psychotic symptoms and personality breakdown.
- **Undifferentiated schizophrenia** is the term used to indicate a lack of clear-cut patterns of disturbance.
- Current explanations of schizophrenia emphasize a combination of *environmental stress, inherited susceptibility,* and *biochemical abnormalities* in the body or brain. One popular environmental theory is that schizophrenics are subjected to unsolvable emotional dilemmas created by **double-bind communication.** A better case can be made for the importance of *early trauma* and *disturbed family environments* as underlying factors in schizophrenia. In addition, studies of twins and other close relatives strongly support a *genetic view* of schizophrenia. Recent biochemical studies have focused on abnormalities in brain transmitter substances, especially **dopamine** and its receptor sites.
- Three **somatic** approaches to treatment of psychosis are **chemotherapy** (use of drugs), **electroconvulsive therapy (ECT)** (brain shock for the treatment of depression), and **psychosurgery** (surgical alteration of the brain). All three techniques are capable of producing serious side effects, and all are controversial to a degree (because of questions about effectiveness and the cost/benefit ratio).
- **Hospitalization** is often associated with the administration of somatic therapy, and it is also considered a form of treatment. Prolonged hospitalization is now discouraged by revolving-door admissions policies and by an emphasis on providing care within the community. As long as community care remains poor, however, repeated hospitalization is likely.
- A development in mental health care that seeks to avoid or minimize hospitalization is the creation of **community mental health centers.** Community mental health centers also have as their goal the prevention of mental health problems through education, consultation, and **crisis intervention.**
- David Rosenhan's use of *pseudo-patients* to study mental hospitals suggests that problems in diagnosis exist and that *psychiatric labeling* can affect our perceptions of others' behavior.
- Thomas Szasz has raised challenging questions about the nature of abnormal behavior and its relationship to personal responsibility and civil rights.

Questions for Discussion

1. What positive and negative roles do mental institutions play in society?

2. Is Szasz justified in his appraisal of mental institutions as simply prisons by another name?

3. Do you think Szasz is unrealistically romantic in his approach to mental illness, or is he the wave of the future?

4. Under what circumstances would you consider it reasonable for a stranger to be involuntarily committed? A friend? A close relative? Yourself?

5. In your opinion, how could a person experiencing a severe "problem in living" be most effectively helped?

6. Should a mental patient have the right to refuse medication? To demand legal counsel and alternative medical opinions? To refuse to work in a mental hospital or to choose the work that will be done? To communicate by phone, letter, or in person with anyone at any time? To keep personal property (including drugs, matches, pocketknives, and other potentially harmful materials)? To request an alternative to legal commitment to a mental hospital? To be represented by an independent "advocate" who is not on the hospital staff?

7. In view of what you know about the causes of psychosis, how valid do you consider the medical model of mental illness? What are the advantages and disadvantages of such a model? What are the advantages and disadvantages of a psychological model?

8. If the genetic component is large in major problems such as schizophrenia and mood disorders, should we try genetically to identify individuals at risk when no sure treatments are available? Should people who are close relatives of affected persons receive special counseling?

9. In 1982, residents of Berkeley, California, voted on a referendum to ban the use of ECT within city limits. Do you think that the use of certain psychiatric treatments or procedures should be controlled by law? Why or why not?

10. The parents of John Hinkley (who attempted to assassinate President Reagan) have complained that "The comedian Robin Williams has great fun making sick jokes about 'crazies' like our son John, but does he joke about muscular dystrophy or cancer? Of course not." Do you agree or disagree with the point they are making?

Chapter 21

Insight Therapy

In This Chapter

Psychotherapy overview
Origins of therapy
Psychoanalysis
Short-term dynamic therapy
Client-centered therapy
Existential therapy
Gestalt therapy
Group therapies
Transactional analysis
Common elements of therapy

Applications

Seeking professional help
How to help others

Exploration

Computer therapy

Chapter Preview

Quiet Terror on a Spring Afternoon

The warm California sun shone brightly. A light breeze danced inland from the ocean. Outside my office window an assortment of small birds sang to a beautiful spring day. I could hear them between Susan's frightened sobs.

As a psychologist, I see many students with personal problems. Still, I was somewhat surprised to see Susan at my office door. Her excellent work in class and her healthy, casual appearance left me unprepared for her first words. "I feel like I'm losing my mind," she said. "Can I talk to you?"

In the next hour, Susan sketched the features of her own personal hell. Her calm exterior hid a world of overwhelming fear, anxiety, and depression. She had lost several part-time jobs because at each one she began to fear her co-workers and the customers so much that she could barely bring herself to speak to them. Her absenteeism and embarrassing interchanges with customers would gradually lead to her dismissal.

At school Susan felt "different" and was sure that other students could tell she was "weird." Several disastrous romances had left her terrified of men. Lately she had become so depressed that she had begun to think frequently of suicide. At times she became so terrified for no apparent reason that her heart pounded wildly and she felt that she was about to lose control of herself completely.

Susan's visit to my office was an important turning point. Emotional conflicts had made her existence a living nightmare. At a time when she was becoming her own worst enemy, Susan had realized that she needed the help and support of another person. In Susan's case, that person was a talented psychologist to whom I referred her. By combining various forms of psychotherapy, the psychologist was able to help Susan come to grips with her emotions and return a healthy balance to her personality.

This chapter and the next discuss psychological methods used to alleviate problems like Susan's. Here, we will describe therapies that emphasize the value of gaining insight *into personal problems. In the next chapter, we will focus on* behavior therapy *and* cognitive therapy, *which are used to directly change troublesome thoughts and behaviors.*

Survey Questions

- How did modern psychotherapies develop?
- Is Freudian psychoanalysis still used?
- What are the characteristics of humanistic therapies?
- Can psychotherapy be done with groups of people? What are group therapies like?
- What do various therapies have in common?
- How would a person go about finding professional help?
- What can be done to help a troubled friend?

Psychotherapy—Getting Better by the Hour

Humpty-Dumpty sat on a wall.
Humpty-Dumpty had a great fall.
All the King's horses and all the King's men
Couldn't put Humpty together again.

In our age of stress, conflict, and anxiety, who will put you together again, and how will they do it? Actually, the odds are that you will *not* experience a life-impairing emotional problem like Susan's, but if you did, what kind of help is available? In most cases, the answer is some form of *psychotherapy*.

Question: What is psychotherapy?

Psychotherapy is any psychological technique used to facilitate positive changes in a person's personality, behavior, or adjustment. The psychotherapist has many approaches to choose from: psychoanalysis, desensitization, Gestalt therapy, logotherapy, client-centered therapy, reality therapy, transactional analysis, behavior modification—to name but a few.

Due to a recent explosive growth in the number of therapies, some confusion may exist about how they differ. To begin, it may help to recognize that psychological problems are complex, and the best approach for a particular person or problem will not always be the same. Also, psychotherapies vary widely in emphasis, as described in Table 21–1.

Myths Popular accounts tend to depict psychotherapy as a complete personal transformation—a sort of "major overhaul" of the psyche. But this ignores the realities of solving human problems. As clinical psychologist Bernie Zilbergeld (1983) points out, therapy is *not* equally effective for all problems. Chances of improvement are fairly good for phobias, low self-esteem, some sexual problems, and marital conflicts. More complex problems, however, can be difficult to treat. Also, contrary to what many people think, therapy usually does not bring about dramatic changes in behavior or an end to personal problems. For many people, therapy's major benefit is that it provides comfort, support, and a way to make constructive changes.

In short, it is often unrealistic to expect psychotherapy to undo a person's entire past history. Yet, even when problems are severe, therapy may help a person gain a new perspective or learn behaviors to better cope with life (Carson et al., 1988). Psychotherapy can be hard work for both client and therapist. But when it succeeds, there are few activities more rewarding.

As a final point, you should also realize that psychotherapy need not be undertaken only to solve a psychological problem or crisis. Some therapies are designed to encourage personal growth and enrichment for people who are already functioning effectively.

Origins of Therapy—Bored Skulls and Hysteria on the Couch

The history of treatment for psychological problems gives ample reason for appreciating the humanity of modern therapies. Archeological findings dating to the Stone Age suggest that most primitive approaches were marked by

Table 21–1 Dimensions of Therapy

The term *psychotherapy* most often refers to verbal interaction between trained mental health professionals and their clients. Many therapists also use learning principles to directly alter troublesome behaviors, as described in Chapter 22.

The terms listed here describe basic aspects of various therapies. Notice that more than one term may apply to a particular therapy. For example, it would be possible to have a directive, action-oriented group therapy or a non-directive, individual, insight-oriented therapy.

Individual therapy	A therapy involving only one client and one therapist
Group therapy	A therapy session in which several clients participate at the same time
Insight therapy	Any psychotherapy whose goal is to lead clients to a deeper understanding of their thoughts, emotions, and behavior
Action Therapy	Any therapy designed to bring about direct changes in troublesome thoughts, habits, feelings, or behavior
Directive therapy	Any approach in which the therapist provides strong guidance
Non-directive therapy	A style of therapy in which clients assume responsibility for solving their own problems; the therapist assists, but does not guide or give advice
Time-limited therapy	Any therapy begun with the expectation that it will last only a certain limited number of sessions

fear and superstitious belief in demons, witchcraft, and magic. One of the more dramatic "cures" practiced by primitive "psychotherapists" was a process called **trepanning** (treh-PAN-ing; also sometimes spelled *trephining*). A hole was bored, chipped, or bashed into the skull of the patient, presumably to relieve pressure or release evil spirits. Actually, trepanning may have simply been an excuse to kill people who were unusual, since many of the "patients" didn't survive the "treatment."

During the Middle Ages, treatment for the mentally ill in Europe focused on **demonology.** Abnormal behavior was attributed to supernatural forces such as possession by the devil or the curses of witches and wizards. As treatment, **exorcism** was used to drive out the evil. For the fortunate, exorcism was a religious ritual. More often, it took the form of physical torture to make the body an inhospitable place for the devil to reside (Fig. 21–1).

One explanation for the rise of demonology may lie in a condition called **ergotism** (AIR-got-ism). In the Middle Ages, rye fields were often infested with ergot fungus (Fig. 21–2). Ergot, we now know, is a natural source of LSD and other mind-altering chemicals. Eating bread made from tainted grain can cause symptoms that might easily be interpreted as possession, bewitchment, or madness. Pinching sensations, convulsions, muscle twitches, facial spasms, delirium, and visual hallucinations are all common reactions to ergot poisoning (Kety, 1979; Matossian, 1982). Thus, many of the "patients" of demonology may have been doubly victimized.

The idea that the emotionally disturbed are "mentally ill" and that they should be treated compassionately emerged after 1793. This was the year **Philippe Pinel** changed the Bicêtre Asylum in Paris from a squalid "madhouse" into a mental hospital by personally unchaining the inmates. Although almost 200 years have passed since Pinel began humane treatment for the emotionally disturbed, the process of improving conditions in psychiatric hospitals and of changing public attitudes toward psychotherapy continues today.

Increased acceptance of the value of psychotherapy is a positive sign, but public attitudes toward the disturbed still tend to be colored by suspicion and fear. Perhaps as more people take part in psychotherapy as a growth experience, it will become more widely understood.

Question: When was psychotherapy developed?

The first true psychotherapy was developed around the turn of the century by Sigmund Freud. As a physician in Vienna, Freud was intrigued by the cases of **hysteria** he encountered (physical symptoms such as paralysis or numbness without known physical cause). As you may recall, such problems are now called *somatoform disorders* (see Chapter 19). Slowly Freud became convinced that the symptoms of hysteria were only the tip of the iceberg and that deeply hidden unconscious conflicts (frequently sexual in nature) were to blame. Based on this insight, Freud went on to develop his own comprehensive form of therapy. Since **psychoanalysis,** as Freud called his technique, is the "granddaddy" of most modern psychotherapies, let us examine it in some detail.

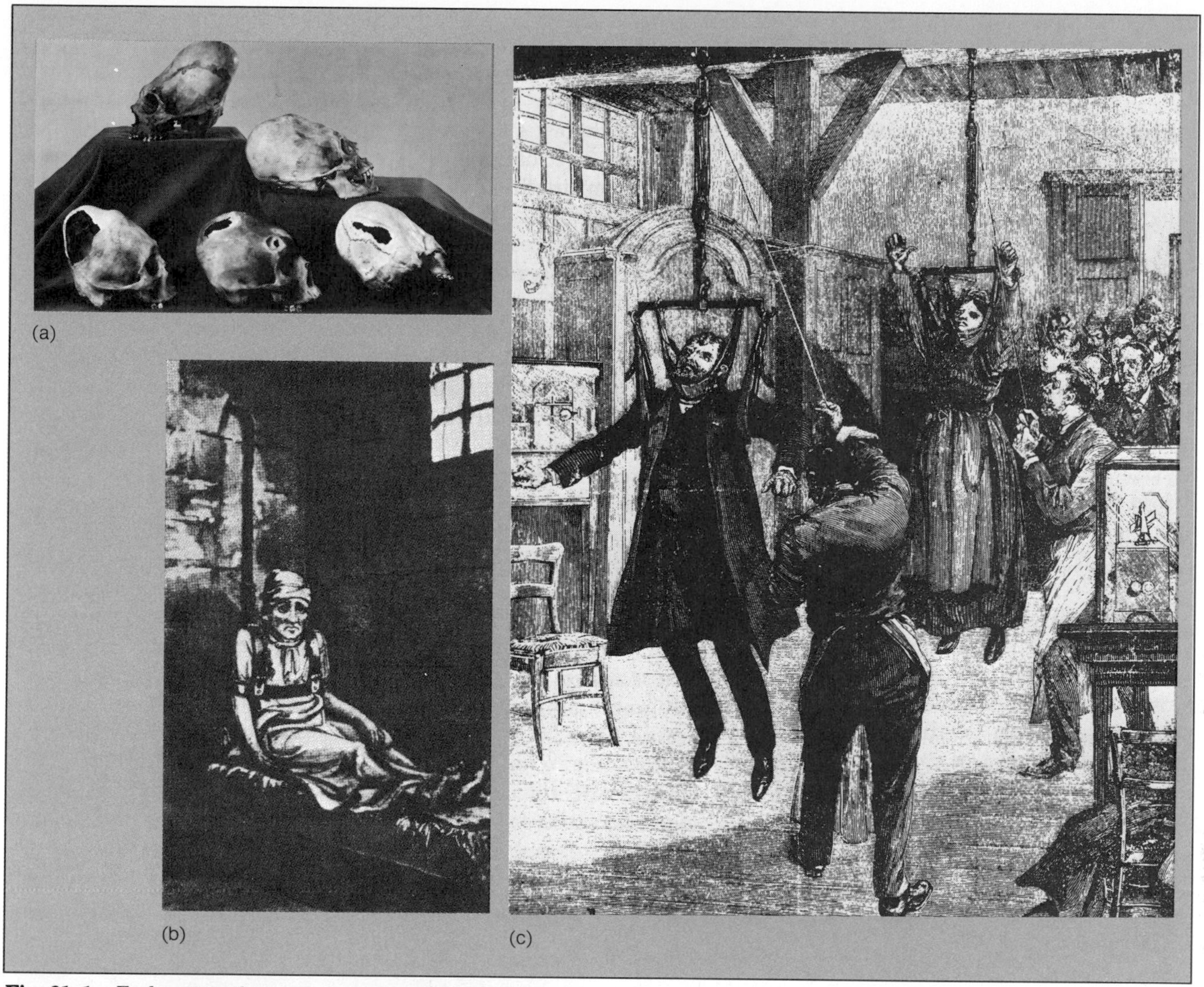

Fig. 21–1 *Early approaches to the treatment of mental illness. (a) Primitive "treatment" for mental disorder sometimes took the form of boring a hole in the skull. (b) Many early asylums were no more than prisons with inmates held in chains. (c) One late nineteenth-century "treatment" was based on swinging the patient in a harness—presumably to calm the patient's nerves.*

Psychoanalysis—Expedition into the Unconscious

Question: Isn't psychoanalysis the therapy where the patient lies on a couch?

Freud's patients usually reclined on a couch during therapy, while Freud sat out of sight taking notes and offering interpretations. This arrangement was selected to encourage relaxation and a free flow of thoughts and

Fig. 21–2 *Two ears of rye infested with ergot fungus (dark areas). The psychedelic effects of the fungus may explain some cases of "possession" in medieval Europe and "bewitchment" in colonial New England.*

images from the unconscious (Fig. 21–3). It is the least important of several characteristics of psychoanalysis and has been abandoned by many modern analysts.

Question: How did Freud treat emotional problems?

Freud's theory stressed that repressed memories, motives, and conflicts—particularly those stemming from instinctual drives for sex and aggression—were the cause of neurosis. Although unconscious and repressed, these factors remain active in the personality, forcing the person to develop rigid ego-defense mechanisms and to devote excessive amounts of time and energy to compulsive and self-defeating behavior. Freud relied on four basic techniques to uncover the unconscious roots of neurosis (Freud, 1949):

1. Free association. During psychoanalysis, the patient must say whatever comes to mind without regard for whether it makes sense or is painful or embarrassing. Thoughts are allowed to move freely from one association to the next.

2. Dream analysis. The purpose of free association is to lower defenses so that unconscious material may emerge. Freud also considered dreams an unusually good way to tap the unconscious. Freud referred to dreams as "the royal road to the unconscious" because he felt that forbidden desires and unconscious feelings are more freely expressed in dreams. He distinguished between the **manifest** (obvious, visible) **content** and the **latent** (hidden) **content** of dreams.

To appreciate fully the unconscious message of a dream, Freud sought to reveal its latent meaning by interpreting **dream symbols.** Let's say a young husband reports a dream in which he pulls a pistol from his waistband and aims at a target while his wife watches. The pistol repeatedly fails to discharge, and the man's wife laughs at him. Freud might see this as an indication of repressed feelings of sexual impotence, with the gun serving as a disguised image of the penis.

3. Analysis of resistance. When free associating or describing dreams, the patient may *resist* talking about or thinking about certain topics. Such resistances are said to reveal particularly important unconscious conflicts. As the analyst becomes aware of resistances, he or she brings them to the patient's awareness so they can be dealt with realistically.

4. Analysis of transference. The individual undergoing psychoanalysis may transfer feelings to the therapist that relate to important past relationships with others. At times the patient may act as if the analyst were a rejecting father, an unloving or overprotective mother, or a former lover. This is considered a prime opportunity to help the patient undergo an emotional re-education. As the patient re-experiences repressed emotions, the therapist can help the patient recognize and understand them.

Question: Is psychoanalysis still used?

Traditional psychoanalysis called for 3 to 5 therapy sessions a week for up to 7 years. Because of the huge amount of time and money this requires, psychoanalysts have

Fig. 21–3 *Pioneering psychotherapist Sigmund Freud in his office.*

become relatively rare. Today, most therapists who use psychoanalytic theory have switched to doing **short-term dynamic therapy.** In this approach, therapists rely on direct interviewing to more rapidly uncover unconscious conflicts (Davanloo, 1980). They also seek to actively provoke emotional reactions that lower defenses and provide insights. By such means, the length of therapy has been shortened considerably (Been & Sklar, 1985; Trujillo, 1986).

The development of newer, more streamlined dynamic therapies is in part due to questions about the effectiveness of traditional psychoanalysis. One critic, H. J. Eysenck (1967), went so far as to suggest that psychoanalysis simply takes so long that there is a **spontaneous remission** of symptoms (improvement due to the mere passage of time).

How seriously should this criticism be taken? It is true that problems ranging from hyperactivity to anxiety improve with the passage of time. However, more recent work affirms that psychoanalysis is usually better than no treatment at all (Bergin & Suinn, 1975). The value of Eysenck's critique and of others that followed is that they encouraged psychologists to try new ideas and techniques. Researchers began to ask: "When psychoanalysis works, why does it work? What procedures are essential, and which are unnecessary?" Based on intuition, personal philosophy, clinical experience, and the personality theory they find most acceptable, modern psychotherapists have given surprisingly varied answers to these questions. Following sections will acquaint you with some of the therapies currently in use.

Learning Check

See if you can answer the following questions. If you miss any, review the previous sections.

Match:

____ **1.** Directive therapies **A.** Change behavior
____ **2.** Action therapies **B.** Place responsibility on client
____ **3.** Insight therapies **C.** The client is guided strongly
____ **4.** Non-directive therapies **D.** Seek understanding

5. Pinel is famous for his use of exorcism. T or F?

6. Freud developed trepanning. T or F?

7. A spontaneous remission of symptoms means that psychotherapy has succeeded. T or F?

8. In psychoanalysis, an emotional attachment to the therapist by the patient is called
a. free association *b.* manifest association *c.* resistance *d.* transference

Answers:
1. C 2. A 3. D 4. B 5. F 6. F 7. F 8. d

Humanistic Therapies—Restoring Human Potential

The goal of traditional psychoanalysis is adjustment. Freud was actually quite conservative in his claims: Any of his patients, he said, could expect only to change their "hysterical misery into common unhappiness"! The humanistic therapies outlined in upcoming sections are generally more optimistic. Most assume that it is possible for people to live rich and rewarding lives and to make full use of their potential. Psychotherapy is seen as a means of giving natural tendencies toward mental health a chance to emerge.

Question: What is client-centered therapy? How is it different from psychoanalysis?

Client-Centered Therapy Psychoanalysts delve into childhood, dreams, and the unconscious. Psychologist Carl Rogers (1902–1987) found it more productive to explore *conscious* thoughts and feelings (Fig. 21–4). The psychoanalyst tends to take a position of authority from which he or she offers interpretations of what is "wrong" with the patient or of what dreams or childhood experiences "mean." Rogers believed that what is right or valuable for the therapist may not be right and valuable

Fig. 21–4 *Psychotherapist Carl Rogers, who originated client-centered therapy.*

for the client. (Rogers preferred the term *client* to *patient* because "patient" implies a person is "sick" and needs to be "cured.") **Client-centered therapy** (also called person-centered therapy) is *non-directive*. The client is the center of a process of personal growth. He or she determines what will be discussed during each session.

Question: If the client runs things, what does the therapist do?

The therapist's job is to create an "atmosphere of growth" by maintaining four basic conditions.

First, the therapist offers the client **unconditional positive regard.** In other words, the client is accepted *totally*. The therapist refuses to react with shock, dismay, or disapproval to anything the client says or feels. Total acceptance by the therapist is the first step to self-acceptance by the client.

Second, the therapist attempts to achieve genuine **empathy** for the client by trying to see the world through the client's eyes and by trying to feel some part of what he or she is feeling.

As a third essential condition, the therapist strives to be **authentic** in his or her relationship with clients. The therapist must not hide behind a professional role. Rogers believed that phony fronts and facades destroy the growth atmosphere sought in client-centered therapy (see Highlight 21–1).

Fourth, the therapist does not make interpretations, propose solutions, or offer advice. Instead, the therapist **reflects** the client's thoughts and feelings. By repeating or restating what the client has said or by telling the client what emotion he or she seems to be displaying, the therapist serves as a psychological "mirror" in which clients learn to see themselves more clearly and realistically. Rogers believed that a person armed with a realistic self-image and with a new level of self-acceptance will gradually discover solutions to life problems.

Existential Therapy According to the existentialists, "being in the world" (existence) creates deep and unavoidable conflicts. Each of us, they say, must deal with the realities of death. We must face the fact that each person creates his or her private world by making choices. We must overcome the isolation of living on a vast and

HIGHLIGHT 21–1
Carl Rogers on Personal Growth

Like other humanistic psychologists, Carl Rogers (1980) believed deeply that there is a natural human urge to seek health and self-growth. Rogers' belief is vividly expressed by the following words:

> I remember that in my boyhood the bin in which we stored our winter's supply of potatoes was in the basement, several feet below a small window. The conditions were unfavorable, but pale white sprouts . . . would grow two or three feet in length as they reached toward the light of the distant window. The sprouts were, in their bizarre, futile growth, a sort of desperate expression of the directional tendency I have been describing. . . . In dealing with clients whose lives have been terribly warped, in working with men and women on the back wards of state hospitals, I often think of those potato sprouts. . . . The clue to understanding their behavior is that they are striving, in the only ways that they perceive as available to them, to move toward growth, toward becoming. To healthy persons, the results may seem bizarre and futile but they are life's desperate attempt to become itself. This potent constructive tendency is an underlying basis of the person-centered approach.

indifferent planet. We must confront feelings of meaninglessness.

Question: What do these concerns have to do with psychotherapy?

Like client-centered therapy, **existential therapy** tries to promote self-knowledge and self-actualization. However, there are important differences. Client-centered therapy seeks to uncover a "true self" hidden behind an artificial screen of defenses. In contrast, existential therapy emphasizes the idea of **free will.** That is, through *choices* one can *become* the person he or she wants to be.

Existential therapy attempts to restore meaning and vitality to life so that the individual has the *courage* to make rewarding and socially constructive choices. Typically, existential therapy focuses on the "ultimate concerns" of human existence. These include the inescapable givens of **death, freedom, isolation,** and **meaninglessness** (Yalom, 1980).

Question: What does an existential therapist do?

One example of existential therapy is Victor Frankl's **logotherapy.**

Frankl (1955) developed his approach on the basis of experiences in a Nazi concentration camp. In the camp, Frankl observed the breakdown of countless prisoners as they were stripped of all hope and human dignity. Frankl felt that those who survived with their sanity did so because they had managed to hang on to a sense of *meaning* (logos). In some cases this was nothing more than the ultimate human freedom—the freedom to choose one's own attitude in any set of circumstances.

Like most existential therapists, Frankl uses a flexible approach centered around **confrontation.** The person is challenged to examine the quality of his or her existence and choices and to *encounter* the unique, intense, here-and-now interaction of two human beings. When existential therapy is successful, it brings about a reappraisal of what's important in life. Indeed, some clients experience an emotional rebirth not unlike that seen in people who have survived a close brush with death. Logotherapy is regarded as successful when clients regain a strong sense of purpose and meaning in life (Dyck, 1987).

Gestalt Therapy Gestalt therapy, which is most often associated with Frederick (Fritz) Perls (1969), is built around the idea that perception, or *awareness,* becomes disjointed and incomplete in the maladjusted individual. The Gestalt approach is more directive than either client-centered therapy or existential therapy, and it places a special emphasis on immediate experience.

Compare: Three Insight Therapies

Client-centered therapy A non-directive therapy based on drawing insights from conscious thoughts and feelings; emphasizes accepting one's true self.

Existential therapy An insight therapy that focuses on the elemental problems of existence, such as death, meaning, choice, and responsibility; emphasizes making courageous life choices.

Gestalt therapy An approach that focuses on immediate experience and awareness to help clients rebuild thinking, feeling, and acting into connected wholes; emphasizes the integration of fragmented experiences.

Question: What does Gestalt mean?

The German word **Gestalt** means "whole," or "complete." The Gestalt therapist seeks to help the individual rebuild thinking, feeling, and acting into connected wholes. This is achieved by expanding personal awareness, by accepting responsibility for one's thoughts, feelings, and actions, and by filling in gaps in experience.

Question: What do you mean by gaps in experience?

Gestalt therapists believe that we often shy away from expressing or "owning" upsetting feelings. This creates a gap in self-awareness that may become a barrier to personal growth. For example, a person who feels anger after the death of a parent might go for years without expressing it. This and similar threatening gaps may block emotional health.

Working either one-to-one or in a group setting, the Gestalt therapist encourages the individual to become more aware of his or her immediate experience. Rather than discussing *why* he or she feels guilt, anger, fear, or boredom, the client is encouraged to have these feelings in the "here and now" and to become fully aware of them. The therapist helps promote awareness by drawing attention to the client's posture, voice, and eye or hand movements. The client may also be asked to exaggerate a vague feeling until it becomes clear. Gestalt therapists believe that expressing such feelings allows people to "take care of unfinished business" and break through emotional impasses.

In all his writings, Perls' basic message comes through clearly: Emotional health comes from knowing what you *want* to do, not dwelling on what you *should* do, *ought* to do, or *should want* to do. Another way of stating this idea is that emotional health comes from taking full responsibility for one's feelings and actions. For example, it means changing "I can't" to "I won't," or "I must" to "I choose to."

Question: How does Gestalt therapy help people discover their real wants?

Above all else, Gestalt therapy emphasizes *present* experience. Clients are urged to stop intellectualizing and talking *about* feelings. Instead they learn to: live now; live here; stop imagining; experience the real; stop unnecessary thinking; taste and see; express rather than explain, justify, or judge; give in to unpleasantness and pain just as to pleasure; surrender to being as you are (Naranjo, 1970).

Learning Check

See if you can answer the following questions.

Match:

______	**1.** Client-centered therapy	**A.** Meaning
______	**2.** Gestalt therapy	**B.** Unconditional positive regard
______	**3.** Existential therapy	**C.** Gaps in awareness
______	**4.** Logotherapy	**D.** Choice and becoming

5. The Gestalt therapist tries to *reflect* a client's thoughts and feelings. T or F?

6. Client-centered therapy is directive. T or F?

7. Confrontation and encounter are concepts of existential therapy. T or F?

Answers:
1. B 2. C 3. D 4. A 5. F 6. F 7. T

Group Therapy—People Who Need People

Question: Is group therapy just individual therapy with more than one person?

Most psychotherapies can be adapted for use in groups. Psychologists first tried working with groups as a practical response to the need for more therapists than were available. To their surprise, group therapy not only worked, it also offered some special advantages (Fig. 21–5).

In group therapy, a person can *act out* or directly experience problems. Doing so often produces insights that might not occur from merely talking about problems. In addition, other group members with similar problems can offer support and useful input. Groups also help form a bridge between therapy and real-life problems by providing a situation that is more realistic than the protected atmosphere of individual therapy. For reasons such as these, a number of specialized groups and techniques have emerged. Because they range from Alcoholics Anonymous to marriage encounter, we will sample only a few representative approaches. (The largest group therapy of all may be on your radio—see Highlight 21–2.)

Psychodrama One of the first group approaches was developed by Jacob L. Moreno (1953), who called his technique **psychodrama.** In psychodrama, an individual **role plays** (acts out) dramatic incidents resembling those that cause problems in real life. For example, a disturbed teenager might act out a typical family fight, with the therapist playing his father and with other patients playing his mother, brothers, and sisters. It was Moreno's belief that insights and the emotional relearning from these enactments transfer to real-life situations. Therapists using psychodrama often find **role reversals** especially helpful (Leveton, 1977). For instance, the teenager just described would be asked to role play his father or mother to better understand their feelings.

Family Therapy Family relationships are the source of great pleasure, and all too often, of great pain for many people. In **family therapy,** husband, wife, and children work as a group to resolve the problems of each family member. Family therapy tends to be brief and focused on specific problems, such as frequent fights or a depressed teenager (Berman, 1982).

Family therapists believe that problems are rarely lim-

● HIGHLIGHT 21–2
"Psych Jockeys"

By now, you have probably heard a phone-in radio psychologist. On a typical program, callers describe problems arising from child abuse, loneliness, love affairs, phobias, sexual adjustment, or depression. The radio psychologist then offers reassurance, advice, or suggestions for getting help.

Talk-radio psychology may seem harmless, but it raises some important questions. For instance, is it reasonable to give advice without knowing anything about a person's background? Might the advice do harm? What good can a psychologist do in 3 minutes?

In defense of themselves, radio psychologists point out that listeners may learn solutions to their own problems by hearing others talk. Many also stress that their work is educational, not therapeutic. And certainly, for some callers, a radio psychologist may be the only person willing to listen to their problem.

The real issue seems to be the question of when advice becomes therapy. The American Psychological Association has taken the position that media psychologists should discuss only problems of a general nature, instead of actually counseling a person. For example, if a caller complains about insomnia, the radio psychologist should talk about insomnia in general, not probe the caller's personal life (Schommer, 1984).

By giving information and advice, radio psychologists probably do help some listeners. Even so, a good guide for anyone tempted to call a radio psychologist might be "let the consumer beware." Or, to use an analogy, how much confidence would you have in a physician who would make a diagnosis over the phone?

ited to a single family member: A problem for one is considered a problem for all. Thus, family members work together to improve communication, to change destructive patterns, and to see themselves and each other in new ways.

Question: Does the therapist work with the whole family at once?

The family therapist treats the family as a unit, but may not meet with the entire family at each session. If a family crisis is at hand, the therapist may first try to identify the most resourceful family members, who can help solve the immediate problem. The therapist and family members may then work on resolving more basic conflicts and on improving family relationships.

Group Awareness Training During the 1960s and 1970s, the human potential movement led many people to become interested in personal growth experiences. Often,

Fig. 21–5 *A group therapy session. Group members offer mutual support while sharing problems, insights.*

their interest was expressed by participation in sensitivity training or encounter groups.

Question: What is the difference between sensitivity groups and encounter groups?

Sensitivity groups tend to be less confrontive than encounter groups. Participants in sensitivity groups take part in exercises that gently enlarge awareness of oneself and others. For example, in a "trust walk," participants expand their confidence in others by allowing themselves to be led about while blindfolded.

In **encounter groups** more intense emotion and communication may take place. Here, the emphasis is on tearing down defenses and false fronts through discussion that can be brutally honest (Stoller, 1972). Because there is a danger of hostile confrontation and psychological damage, encounter group participation is safest when members are carefully screened and when a trained leader guides the group.

In business settings, psychologists still use the basic principles of sensitivity and encounter groups—truth, self-awareness, and self-determination—to improve employee relationships. Specially designed encounter groups for married couples are also widely held (Schutz, 1986). However, in the last decade there has been a shift away from public participation in sensitivity and encounter groups. Instead, hundreds of thousands of people have taken part in various forms of **large-group awareness training** (Finkelstein et al., 1982). Lifespring, Actualizations, est, and similar commercial programs are well-known examples. Like the smaller groups that preceded them, large-group trainings combine psychological exercises, confrontation, new viewpoints, and group dynamics to promote personal change.

Question: Are sensitivity, encounter, and awareness groups really psychotherapies?

Judging from the glowing testimonials given by many participants, such groups must fill some need not met by society or traditional psychotherapy. However, there is, at present, little evidence that these experiences are truly therapeutic (Finkelstein et al., 1982). Many of the claimed benefits may simply result from a kind of **therapy placebo effect** related to positive expectations, a break in daily routine, and an excuse to act differently. The importance of such factors is easily illustrated: Participants in a weekend "retreat" that featured nothing more than volleyball, charades, and ballroom dancing also reported enhanced mental health (McCardel & Murray, 1974)! Kurt Back (1972) may have summarized it best when he said, "Encounter groups may comfort, but they do not cure anything." For some the experience is positive, for some negative, and for many it is merely a diversion.

● Transactional Analysis—Different Strokes for Different Folks

Transactional Analysis (TA) is a therapy that blends humanistic thought with some updated elements of psychoanalysis. TA teaches people a model of behavior to use in becoming more aware of themselves and their *interactions* with others—especially those involving various "games." Because TA emphasizes relationships, it is often conducted as a group therapy.

Question: How does TA enhance awareness?

TA is based on a relatively simple scheme proposed by Eric Berne (1961, 1964). Berne said that the personality has three basic parts, or **ego-states,** known as the *Parent*, the *Adult*, and the *Child*. These can be distinguished from one another by distinct behaviors, words, tones, gestures, attitudes, and expressions.

Ego-States The **Child** is a carryover from youth. The Child can be primitive, impulsive, demanding, creative, playful, or manipulative. The Child tends to say things such as "I want," "I need," "I won't" or simply, "Wow." In addition to this perpetual Child, Berne says we carry another product of our past in the form of the Parent ego-state. The **Parent** is an internal record of all the messages received from parents or other authorities as one's personality developed. The Parent can be evaluative and restrictive or nurturing and allowing. It is activated whenever you judge or nurture yourself or another person. The Parent makes such statements as "You should," "You ought to," "That's good," "You can do it," "That's bad," "Try harder," and "Why didn't you?"

Although Berne denied it, it is easy to see that the three ego-states are an updated version of Freud's concepts of the id, ego, and superego: The Child corresponds to the id, the Adult to the ego, and the Parent to the superego. According to TA, people get into trouble when they use an inappropriate ego-state. TA teaches people how to develop each ego-state and helps them decide when to use it. The **Adult** is a mature and rational decision-making part of the personality. With the adult in charge, an individual can explore alternatives and their consequences and decide which ego-state is needed. TA gives people a thinking strategy with which to explore alternatives and decide what changes they wish to make, especially in *relationships* with others.

Question: How does the ego-state analysis apply to relationships?

Transactions The Parent-Adult-Child analysis can be extended to interactions between two people. That is, a message can be sent from any of the ego-states in one person to any of the ego-states in another. TA holds that trouble comes in relationships when *crossed* or *ulterior transactions* (exchanges) occur. Figure 21–6a represents an Adult-to-Adult transaction, such as, "What time is it?" "It's one o'clock." Communication continues because the expected response was received. But what if the reply is Parent-to-Child, such as, "Why don't you just forget about the time and see if you can get some work done for a change?" Now communication breaks down, or is "crossed" (Fig. 21–6b).

Question: What happens in an ulterior transaction?

In an ulterior transaction the exchange *appears* to take place on one level, but actually takes place on another. For example, the apparent Adult-to-Adult question, "Isn't it getting late?" might carry with it the unspoken (ulterior) cue, "Hey, why don't we quit early tonight?" The reply, "Yeah, it's getting late," might have nothing to do with the time; it may instead be a Child-to-Child reply, "Yeah, let's go play, the supervisor won't know if we leave early."

Games Ulterior transactions may sound harmless enough, but they form the basis of **games,** which are indirect ways of communicating. For example, one spouse might ask another, "How much money is in the checking account?" in such a way that the real message is, "What are you trying to do, put us in the poorhouse?" Games keep people from being close and honest, and at worst they may be physically or emotionally destructive. By the way, the most common game in marriage is, "If it weren't for you" (I would be doing all the things I pretend I want to do but am afraid to try). A major goal of TA is to teach people more direct and creative ways of living, by exploring alternatives to games.

Psychotherapy—An Overview

Question: How effective is psychotherapy?

Judging the outcome of therapy is tricky. Nevertheless, there is evidence that therapy is beneficial. In surveys of hundreds of studies of psychotherapy, a modest but consistent positive effect for therapy was found to exist (Shapiro & Shapiro, 1982; Smith & Glass, 1977). These findings, of course, are based on averages: For some people therapy was tremendously helpful; for others it was unsuccessful; overall it was effective for more people than not. Speaking more subjectively, one real success—in which a person's life is lastingly changed for the better—can be worth the frustration of several cases in which little progress is made.

It is common to think of therapy as a long, slow process. But this is not always the case. Recent research reveals that most people can expect improvement in a reasonably brief time. An analysis of over 2400 patients found that about 50 percent felt better after only 8 therapy sessions. After 26 sessions, roughly 75 percent had improved (Howard et al., 1986) (Fig. 21–7). The typical "dose" of therapy is 1 hourly session per week. This means that the majority of patients had improved after 6 months of therapy, and half felt better in just 2 months. Keep in mind that people often suffer for several years before seeking help. In view of this, such rapid improvement is impressive.

Question: What do psychotherapies have in common?

The therapies we have sampled are but a few of the approaches in use. One author, writing in 1959, counted at least 36 major systems of psychotherapy (Harper, 1959).

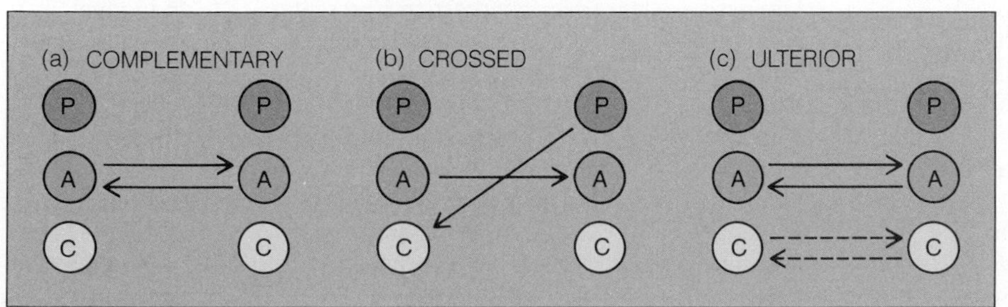

Fig. 21–6 *Basic TA transactions.*

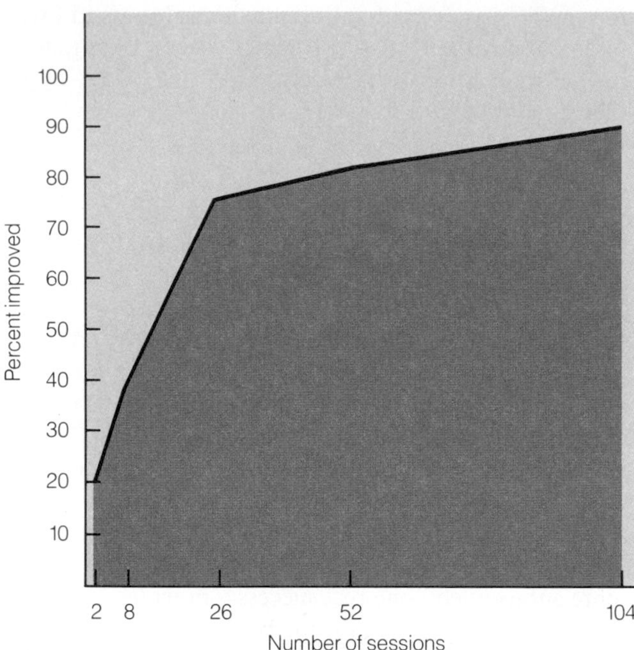

Fig. 21–7 *The dose-improvement relationship in psychotherapy. This graph shows the percentage of patients who improved after varying numbers of therapy sessions. Notice that the most rapid improvement took place during the first 6 months of once-a-week sessions. (From Howard et al., 1986.)*

The count could easily exceed 200 today. The examples cited in this chapter were selected because they represent some of the basic variations in philosophy or techniques and because they offer ideas that may be of immediate use to you. For a summary of the major differences among psychotherapies, see Table 21–2. To add to your understanding, let us briefly summarize what all of the techniques have in common.

All the psychotherapies we have discussed include some combination of the following goals: insight, resolution of conflicts, an improved sense of self, a change in unacceptable patterns of behavior, better interpersonal relations, and an improved picture of oneself and the world. To accomplish these goals, psychotherapies offer the following:

1. Therapy provides a *caring relationship* between client and therapist, sometimes called the *therapeutic alliance* (Stiles et al., 1986). *Emotional rapport* based on warmth, friendship, understanding, acceptance, and empathy forms the basis for this relationship. The therapeutic alliance unites the client and therapist in working together to solve the client's problems.
2. Therapy offers a *protected setting* in which emotional *catharsis* (release) can take place. Therapy provides a sanctuary in which the client is free to express fears, anxieties, and personal secrets without fear of rejection or loss of confidentiality.
3. All therapies to some extent offer an *explanation* or *rationale* for the suffering the client has experienced, and they propose a line of action that if followed will end this suffering.
4. Therapy also provides clients with a *new perspective* about themselves and their situation (Stiles et al., 1986).

These basic foundations of psychotherapy are some of the more valuable concepts in this chapter. Together, they offer a useful perspective for meeting the challenge of helping a troubled friend or relative. More specific suggestions on this point will be found in the discussion that concludes the Applications section of this chapter.

Table 21–2 Comparison of Psychotherapies

	INSIGHT OR ACTION?	DIRECTIVE OR NON-DIRECTIVE?	TIME ORIENTATION	INDIVIDUAL OR GROUP?
Psychoanalysis	Insight	Directive	Past	Individual
Short-term dynamic	Insight	Directive	Past and present	Individual
Client-centered	Insight	Non-directive	Past and present	Individual
Existential	Insight	Both	Present and future	Individual
Gestalt	Insight	Directive	Present	Both
Transactional analysis	Both	Directive	Past and present	Both
Psychodrama	Insight	Directive	Present	Group
Family	Both	Directive	Present	Group
Behavior modification*	Action	Directive	Present	Both
Cognitive*	Action	Directive	Present	Individual
Rational-emotive*	Action	Directive	Present	Individual

*Discussed in Chapter 22.

Learning Check

1. In psychodrama, people attempt to form meaningful wholes out of disjointed thoughts, feelings, and actions. T or F?
2. Most large group awareness trainings make use of Gestalt therapy. T or F?
3. There are no dangers in participating in an encounter group. T or F?
4. Which therapy places great emphasis on role playing?
   a. psychodrama *b.* TA *c.* family therapy *d.* encounter
5. The Adult is a mature and rational decision-making part of the personality. T or F?
6. According to TA, destructive psychological games are based on ____________________ transactions.
7. Emotional ____________________ (release) in a protected setting is an element of most psychotherapies.

Answers:
1. F 2. F 3. F 4. *a* 5. T 6. ulterior 7. catharsis

Applications: Seeking Professional Help—When, Where, and How?

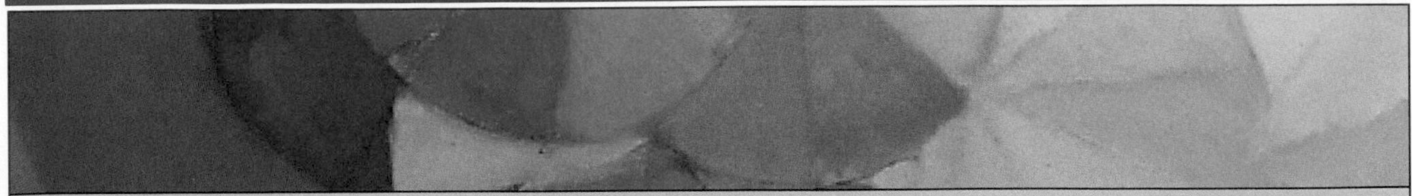

Question: How would I know if I should seek professional help at some point in my life?

Although there is no simple answer to this question, the following guidelines may be helpful.

1. If your level of psychological discomfort (unhappiness, anxiety, or depression, for example) becomes comparable to a level of physical discomfort that would cause you to see a doctor or dentist, you should consider seeing a psychologist or a psychiatrist.
2. Another sign that should influence your decision is the occurrence of significant changes in observable behavior, such as the quality of your work (including schoolwork), your rate of absenteeism, your use of drugs (including alcohol), or your relationships with others who are important to you.
3. Perhaps you have at some time urged a friend or relative to seek professional help and were then dismayed because they refused to recognize the extent of their problem. If *you* find friends or relatives making a similar suggestion, recognize that they may be seeing things more objectively than you.
4. If you have persistent or disturbing suicidal thoughts or impulses, you should seek help immediately.

Question: If I wanted to talk to a therapist, how would I find one?

1. *The yellow pages.* Psychologists are listed in the telephone book under "Psychologist" or in some cases under "Counseling Services." Psychiatrists are generally listed as a subheading under "Physicians." Counselors are typically found under the heading "Marriage and Family Counselors." These listings will usually put you in touch with individuals in private practice.
2. *Community or county mental health centers.* Most counties and many cities in the United States now offer public mental health services. (These are listed in the phone book.) Most public mental health centers provide counseling and therapy services directly and can make referrals to private therapists.
3. *Mental health associations.* Many cities have mental health associations organized by concerned citizens. Groups such as these usually keep listings of qualified therapists and of other services and programs in the community.
4. *Colleges and universities.* If you are a student, don't overlook counseling services offered by a student health center or special student counseling facilities.
5. *Newspaper advertisements.* Some psychologists advertise their services in newspapers. Also, low-cost "outreach" clinics occasionally try to make their presence known to the public by advertising. In either case, you should carefully inquire into a therapist's training and qualifications. Without the benefit of a referral from a trusted person, it is wise to be cautious.

Question: How would I know what kind of a therapist to see? How would I pick one?

The choice between a psychiatrist and a psychologist is somewhat arbitrary. Both are trained to do psychotherapy, and whereas a psychiatrist can administer somatic therapy and prescribe drugs, a psychologist can work in conjunction with a physician if such services seem indicated. Fees for psychiatrists are usually higher, averaging about $90 an hour. Psychologists average about $70 an hour.

With fees in mind, your decision may be influenced by whether you have health insurance that will cover the expense. If fees are a problem, keep in mind that many individual therapists charge on a sliding scale, or ability-to-pay basis, and that community mental health centers almost always charge on a sliding scale.

Some communities now have counseling services staffed by sympathetic paraprofessional counselors, whose fees are much lower. There is a natural tendency, perhaps, to doubt the abilities of paraprofessionals. However, many studies have shown that paraprofessional counselors are often as effective as professionals (Hattie et al., 1984). Group therapy is also much less expensive because the therapist's fee is divided among several people. You can usually get information about the training and qualifications of a therapist simply by asking. A reputable therapist will be glad to reveal his or her background. If you have any doubts, credentials may be checked and other helpful information can be obtained from local branches of any of the following organizations. You can also write to the addresses listed here.

The National Association for Mental Health
1800 N. Kent St.
Rosslyn, VA 22209

Applications

The American Psychiatric Association
1700 18th St. N.W.
Washington, DC 20009

The American Psychological Association
1200 17th St. N.W.
Washington, DC 20036

The American Association of Humanistic Psychology
7 Hartwood Dr.
Amherst, NY 14226

The question of how to pick a particular therapist remains. The best way is to start with one short consultation with a respected psychiatrist or psychologist or with a counselor at a mental health center. This will allow the person you consult to evaluate the nature of your difficulty and recommend an appropriate type of therapy or a therapist who is likely to be helpful. As an alternative, you might ask the person teaching this course for a referral.

Question: How would I know whether or not to quit or ignore a therapist?

A balanced look at psychotherapies suggests that all *techniques* are about equally successful (Gomes-Schwartz et al., 1978; Stiles et al., 1986). However, all *therapists* are not equally successful. Far more important than the approach used are the therapist's personal qualities (Luborsky et al., 1986). The most consistently successful psychotherapists are those who are willing to use whatever method seems most helpful for a client. They are also marked by personal characteristics of warmth, integrity, sincerity, and empathy (Frank, 1973; Katz, 1972; Knight, 1949).

It is perhaps most accurate to say that at this stage of development, psychotherapy is an art, not a science. Since the *relationship* between a client and therapist is the therapist's most basic tool, you must trust and easily relate to a therapist for therapy to be effective. Clients who like their therapist are generally more successful in therapy (Gomes-Schwartz et al., 1978). There is always a temptation to avoid facing up to personal problems. With this in mind, you should give a therapist a fair chance and not give up too easily. But don't hesitate to change therapists or to terminate therapy if you lose confidence in the therapist or if you don't relate well to the therapist as a person.

Becoming a Community Mental Health Resource—How To Help

Question: What can be done to help a friend or relative who has a temporary personal problem or emotional crisis?

Everyone is occasionally faced with the task of comforting a troubled friend. For the majority of such upsets, any caring, emotionally stable, empathic person can aid effectively. For example, Carl Rogers (1980) cited hotline volunteers who with minimal training sometimes "use skill and judgment that would make a professional green with envy." But how can you best give support? Jerome Frank (1973), Carl Rogers (1957), and others appear to agree about two essential conditions for aiding constructive change. These are:

1. An unconditional acceptance of the troubled person, an unshakable positive regard for him or her as a human.
2. A capacity to communicate to the person an understanding of the discomfort he or she is feeling.

We may call the second quality *empathy*, the ability to enter another person's private world, to understand feelings, and to share psychological pain. Because empathy and true caring cannot be faked, your support at times of crisis can be more valuable than anything the best-trained professional can offer. John O. Stevens (1971) has summarized:

> The way to really help someone is not to help him do anything but become more aware of his own experience—his feelings, his actions, his fantasies—and insist that he explore his own experience more deeply and take responsibility for it, no matter what that experience is.

Question: I'm still not sure exactly what is best to do when a friend wants to talk about a problem.

Several points may be kept in mind when "counseling" a friend. (Also, see Table 21–3.)

Active Listening People frequently talk "at" each other without really listening. A person with problems needs to be

Table 21–3 Helping Behaviors

To help another person gain insight into a personal problem, it is valuable to keep the following comparison in mind.

Behaviors That Help	Behaviors That Hinder
Active listening	Probing painful topics
Acceptance	Judging/moralizing
Reflecting feelings	Criticism
Open-ended questioning	Threats
Supportive statements	Rejection
Respect	Ridicule/sarcasm
Patience	Impatience
Genuineness	Placing blame
Paraphrasing	Opinionated statements

Adapted from Kottler & Brown, 1985.

Applications

heard. Make a sincere effort to listen to and understand the person. Try to accept the person's message without judging it or immediately leaping to conclusions (Kottler & Brown, 1985). Let the person know you are listening through eye contact, posture, your tone of voice, and your replies (Ivey & Galvin, 1984).

Clarify the Problem People who have a clear idea of what is wrong in their lives are in a better position to discover solutions. Try to understand the problem from the person's point of view. As you do, check your understanding often. For example, you might ask, "Are you saying that you feel depressed just at school? Or in general?" Remember, a problem well defined is often half solved.

Focus on Feelings Feelings are neither right nor wrong. By focusing on feelings you can avoid making the person defensive. Passing judgment on what is said prevents the free outpouring of emotion that is the basis for catharsis. For example, a friend confides that he has failed a test. Perhaps you know that he studies very little. If you say, "Maybe if you studied a little more you would do better," he will probably become defensive or hostile. Much more can be accomplished by saying, "You must feel very frustrated" or simply, "How do you feel about it?" Remember too that feelings are often revealed by facial gestures, tone of voice, and movements (Ivey & Galvin, 1984).

Avoid Giving Advice Many people mistakenly think that they must solve others' problems for them. Remember that your goal is to provide understanding and support, not solutions (Egan, 1984). Of course, it is reasonable to give advice when you are asked for it, but beware of the trap of the "Why don't you . . .? Yes, but . . ." game. According to Berne (1964), this "game" follows a pattern: Someone says, "I have this problem." You say, "Why don't you do thus and so?" The person replies, "Yes, but . . ." and then gives several reasons why your suggestion won't work. If you make a new suggestion, the reply will once again be, "Yes, but . . ." because the person either knows more about his or her personal situation than you do or because he or she has reasons for avoiding your advice. The student described earlier knows he needs to study. His problem is to understand why he doesn't *want* to study.

Accept the Person's Frame of Reference W. I. Thomas said, "Things perceived as real are real in their effect." Try to resist the temptation to contradict the person with your point of view. Since we all live in different psychological worlds, there is no "correct" view of a life situation. A person who feels that his or her point of view is understood feels freer to examine it objectively and to question it.

Reflect Thoughts and Feelings One of the best things you can do when "counseling" a friend is to give feedback by simply restating what is said. This is also a good way to encourage a person to talk. If your friend seems to be at a loss for words, *restate* or *paraphrase* his or her last sentence. Here's an example.

Friend: I'm really down about school. I can't get interested in any of my classes. I flunked my Spanish test, and somebody stole my notebook for psychology.
You: You're really upset about school, aren't you?
Friend: Yeah, and my parents are hassling me about my grades again.
You: You're feeling pressured by your parents?
Friend: Yeah, damn.
You: It must make you angry to be pressured by them.

As simple as this sounds, it is very helpful to someone trying to sort out feelings. Try it. If nothing else, you'll develop a reputation as a fantastic conversationalist!

Silence Studies show that counselors tend to wait longer before responding than do people in everyday conversations. Pauses of 5 seconds or more are not unusual, and interrupting is rare. Listening patiently lets the person feel unhurried and encourages her or him to speak freely (Goodman, 1984).

Questions Because your goal is to encourage free expression, *open questions* tend to be the most helpful (Goodman, 1984). A *closed question* is one that can be answered yes or no. Open questions call for an open-ended reply (see Chapter 16). Say, for example, that a friend tells you, "I feel like my boss has it in for me at work." A closed question would be, "Oh yeah? So, are you going to quit?" Open questions, such as, "Do you want to tell me about it?" or "How do you feel about it?" are more likely to be helpful.

Maintain Confidentiality Your efforts to help will be wasted if you fail to respect the privacy of someone who has confided in you. Put yourself in the person's place. Don't gossip.

These guidelines are not an invitation to play "junior therapist." Professional therapists are trained to approach serious problems with skills far exceeding those described here. Also, formal therapy provides a protected and confidential arena for problem solving. The point of this discussion is that each of us can supply two of the greatest mental health resources available at any cost: friendship and honest communication.

Applications

Learning Check

1. Persistent emotional discomfort is a clear sign that professional psychological counseling should be sought. T or F?
2. Community mental health centers rarely offer counseling or therapy themselves; they only do referrals. T or F?
3. In many instances, a therapist's personal qualities have more of an effect on the outcome of therapy than does the type of therapy used. T or F?
4. To aid a troubled friend, you should focus on facts rather than feelings, and you should critically evaluate what the person is saying to help him or her grasp reality. T or F?
5. One danger of giving advice is the tendency for the interchange to slip into the "Yes, but" game. T or F?

Answers:
1. T 2. F 3. T 4. F 5. T

Exploration: A Therapist Named Eliza

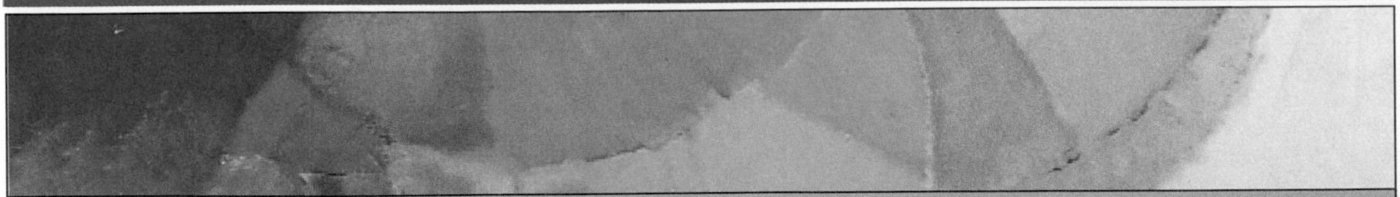

Psychotherapists differ widely in personal style and choice of techniques. The following is a somewhat unusual example of how therapy can act as a "psychological mirror" for a troubled person.

C: Men are all alike.
T: In what way?
C: They're always bugging us about something or other.
T: Can you think of a specific example?
C: Well, my boyfriend made me come here.
T: Your boyfriend made you come here?
C: He says I'm depressed much of the time.
T: I am sorry to hear you are depressed.
C: It's true. I am unhappy.
T: Do you think coming here will help you not to be unhappy?
C: I need some help, that much seems certain.
T: What would it mean to you if you got some help?
C: Perhaps I could learn to get along with my mother.
T: Tell me more about your family.
C: My mother takes care of me.
T: Who else in your family takes care of you?
C: My father.
T: Your father?
C: You are like my father in some ways.
T: What resemblance do you see?
C: You are not very aggressive but I think you don't want me to notice that.
T: What makes you think I am not very aggressive?
C: You don't argue with me.
T: Why do you think I don't argue with you?
C: You are afraid of me.
T: Does it please you to believe I am afraid of you?
C: My father is afraid of everybody.
T: What else comes to mind when you think of your father?
C: Bullies.
T: Does that have anything to do with the fact that your boyfriend made you come here?

Notice how the therapist helped the client see a possible link between her feelings for her father and her boyfriend. This insight is particularly interesting because her therapist was a computer. What you just read is part of a "conversation" held with a computer program named Eliza developed by computer scientist Joseph Weizenbaum (1966).

Question: Is Weizenbaum serious about having a computer act as a therapist?

Actually, Weizenbaum opposes use of computers as therapists for real clients. From the beginning, Weizenbaum has said that computers must never replace human relationships (Williams, 1984). But other psychologists believe otherwise. Supporters point out that computerized therapy would have the advantages of low cost, convenience, consistency, and dependability (Alexander, 1978).

Critics view experimentation with computerized therapy as "dehumanizing technology" and note that when a computer says, "I understand," it is meaningless. They also point out that computers would miss nonverbal messages contained in a glance, a gesture, laughter, or tears.

On the other hand, many people find it helpful to keep a journal of their thoughts and feelings to get a clearer picture of themselves. There is also evidence that tape recording your thoughts on a problem—and then listening to the tape—can contribute to self-awareness (Snider et al., 1984). In similar fashion, a computer "therapist" might provide a helpful sounding board for sorting out feelings and alternatives. At the very least, computer therapy might make a type of "personal education" available to large numbers of people, particularly those unable to afford traditional therapy.

Even with its possible advantages, talking with a computer has proved only mildly therapeutic at best (Williams, 1984). The limitations of computer therapy are aptly illustrated by the following interchange between a journalist and Eliza (Gorman, 1985):

D: I would like to know what you think of your patients.
E: Do you wish to would like to know what me?
D: You talk like a chimpanzee.
E: Oh, I talk like a chimpanzee?
D: Yes, and not as well as some.
E: You seem quite positive.

Exploration

D: Do you wish to would like to know what you—what kind of nonsense is that?

E: You like to think I wish to would like to know what you—don't you?

Therapy is essentially a trusting relationship between people. A computer may be able to simulate some of the speech patterns of human therapists, but they fail miserably at intuition (Joyce, 1988). It appears that in psychotherapy, as in all aspects of life, there is no substitute for human understanding, empathy, and trust.

Learning Check

1. Computer scientist Joseph Weizenbaum has urged psychologists to try Eliza with real clients. T or F?

2. It is probably accurate to say that computer therapy has no value for promoting personal awareness. T or F?

3. Computer therapy would have the advantages of consistency, convenience, and low cost. T or F?

4. Virtually all psychologists regard computer therapy as dehumanizing. T or F?

Answers:

1. F 2. F 3. T 4. F

Chapter Summary

• **Psychotherapies** may be classified as **insight** therapies, **action** therapies, **directive** therapies, **non-directive** therapies, and combinations of these. Behavior therapy and cognitive behavior therapy are major action-oriented approaches. Therapies may be conducted either individually or in groups, and they may be time-limited.

• Primitive approaches to mental illness were often misguided and based on superstition. **Trepanning** involved boring a hole in the skull. **Demonology,** used in the Middle Ages, attributed mental disturbance to supernatural forces and prescribed **exorcism** as the cure. In some instances, the actual cause of bizarre behavior may have been **ergot poisoning.** More humane treatment began in 1793 with the work of *Philippe Pinel* in Paris.

• Freud's **psychoanalysis** was the first formal psychotherapy. Psychoanalysis seeks a release of repressed thoughts and emotions from the unconscious. The psychoanalyst uses the techniques of **free association, dream analysis,** and analysis of **resistance** and **transference** to reveal health-producing insights.

• Some critics have argued that traditional psychoanalysis has received credit for *spontaneous remissions* of symptoms. However, psychoanalysis has been shown to be better than no treatment at all. Also, **short-term dynamic therapy** (which relies on psychoanalytic theory but is brief and focused) is as effective as other major therapies.

• **Client-centered** (or **person-centered**) **therapy** is non-directive and is dedicated to creating an atmosphere of growth. *Unconditional positive regard, empathy, authenticity,* and *reflection* are combined to give the client a chance to solve his or her own problems.

• **Existential therapies,** such as Frankl's **logotherapy,** focus on the end result of the choices one makes in life. Clients are encouraged through *confrontation* and *encounter* to exercise *free will* and to take responsibility for their choices. The goal of existential therapy is to reestablish meaning in one's life.

• **Gestalt therapy** emphasizes immediate awareness of thoughts and feelings. Its goal is to rebuild thinking, feeling, and acting into *connected wholes* and to help clients break through emotional blocks.

• **Group therapy** may be a simple extension of individual methods or it may be based on techniques developed specifically for groups. In **psychodrama,** individuals enact roles and incidents resembling their real-life problems. In **family therapy,** the family group is treated as a unit.

• Although they are not literally psychotherapies, sensitivity and encounter groups attempt to encourage positive personality change. **Sensitivity groups** tend to be non-confrontive, their emphasis being on self-awareness, trust, and communication. In **encounter groups,** participants actively tear down false fronts and defenses. In recent years, commercially offered **large-group awareness trainings** have become popular. However, the therapeutic benefits of such programs are questionable.

• In **transactional analysis (TA),** people learn to apply the *P-A-C* (Parent-Adult-Child) *analysis* to their own behavior and to that of others. By placing the Adult in control, people learn to draw on the strengths of each **ego-state.** They also learn to recognize **complementary, crossed,** and **ulterior transactions** and to avoid **games.**

• Outcome studies of psychotherapy show that it is generally effective. The majority of clients show improvement within 6 months of beginning therapy. However, there are large differences in how various individuals respond to therapy.

• All psychotherapies offer a *caring relationship, emotional rapport,* a *protected setting, catharsis, explanations* for the client's problems, and a *line of action* to follow in alleviating them.

• Sources of psychological help exist in most communities. A competent and reputable therapist can usually be located through a *referral.* Providing *empathy* is a major way to support a troubled friend. Other points to keep in mind are to *listen actively,* try to help the person *clarify the problem, focus on feelings,* avoid giving *unwanted advice,* accept the person's *perspective, reflect* thoughts and feelings, be *patient* during silences, use *open questions* when possible, and maintain *confidentiality.*

• **Computer therapy** offers the benefits of low cost and complete confidentiality. It can provide feedback and other educational experiences that aid constructive personal change. However, computer therapy is no substitute for the insight, intuition, and caring provided by human therapists.

Questions for Discussion

1. What preconceptions did you have about psychotherapy? Has your understanding of therapy changed? Has your attitude changed?

2. Do you agree with existential therapist Rollo May that there has been a loss of individual freedom, faith, and meaning in today's society? Why or why not?

3. Which form of psychotherapy do you find the most attractive? Why?

4. What psychological services are available in your area? Would you know how to find or make use of them? What factors would affect your decision to seek help?

5. Describe a time when you helped someone resolve a personal problem. Describe a time when you were unsuccessful in helping. What factors seemed to make the difference?

6. Do you think it would be right for a therapist to allow a person to make suicide an "existential choice" or an expression of "free will"?

7. What advantages and disadvantages would you anticipate in working with a computer therapist?

8. Which style of therapy would you expect a computer program to most closely duplicate? If a computer were programmed to provide help for a limited problem such as test anxiety, would you find computer therapy more acceptable?

9. In your opinion, are radio psychologists engaged in education or therapy? Is talk-show psychology ethical? What value is there for listeners and callers in talking with a radio psychologist?

10. Psychotherapy is based on trust and confidentiality. Do you think that therapists should be legally required to report dangerous thoughts or fantasies revealed by clients? If a therapist misjudges the seriousness of a client's intent to do harm, should the therapist be held legally responsible? Why or why not?

Chapter 22

Behavior Therapy

In This Chapter
Behavior modification
Aversion therapy
Desensitizing fears
Operant principles
Extinction
Token economies
Cognitive behavior therapy
Rational-emotive therapy
Applications
Covert sensitization
Thought stopping
Covert reinforcement
Reducing fears
Exploration
Self-directed behavior change

Chapter Preview

Behavior Therapy and the Twilight Zone

Five times a day, for several days, Brooks Workman stopped what she was doing and vividly imagined opening a soft drink can. She then pictured herself bringing the can to her mouth and placing her lips on it. Just as she was about to drink, hordes of roaches poured out of the can and scurried into her mouth—writhing, twitching, and wiggling their feelers (Williams & Long, 1979).

Question: Why would anyone imagine such a thing?

Brooks Workman's behavior is not as strange as it sounds. Her goal was self-control: Brooks felt that she was drinking too many colas and she wanted to cut down. The method she chose (called covert sensitization*) is a form of* behavior therapy *(Cautela & Kearney, 1986). Behavioral approaches include* **behavior modification** *(the use of learning principles to change behavior) and* **cognitive behavior therapy** *(the use of learning principles to change upsetting thoughts and beliefs).*

The list of possible applications for behavioral approaches is long. It is almost certain that you will discover a useful technique for self-improvement in this chapter. But before we begin, here is something to think about.

The Twilight Zone? *Pretend for a moment that you work for the telephone company and that you have been sent to repair a phone. Picture a professional building similar to those in which your doctor and dentist are found. Inside the front door is an office bustling with quiet activity. Through the windows of side offices you see pairs of clients and therapists. You ask where the broken phone is. A secretary tells you it is in the opposite end of the building and asks you to fol-*

low. The secretary opens a door on your left. As you step through it, your mind reels.

In confusion you rapidly scan your surroundings. You are in a tavern! In the dim light you see a bar and heavily padded stools. Behind the counter, a bartender polishes glasses in front of a large mirror and a row of bottles. Lighted displays advertising beer glow softly from the wall, and music flows from an unseen speaker.

Catching sight of the secretary again, you wind your way through the tables and hurry to a door on the opposite side of the room. Once again you are in an ordinary office. But over your shoulder you see the bartender close the door behind you, and the strains of music die abruptly with a click of the latch.

What's happening here? Was it a hallucination? A movie set? A modern version of Alice in Wonderland*? A hideout for the CIA? For an answer, read further.*

Survey Questions

- How are learning principles applied in aversion therapy?
- Can behavior therapy be used to treat phobias, fears, and anxieties?
- What role does reinforcement play in behavior modification?
- Can behavior therapy change thoughts and emotions?
- How are behavioral principles applied to everyday problems?

Behavior Modification—Animal, Vegetable, or Mineral?

In the previous chapter, we discussed therapies based on *insight,* or self-awareness. Here we will consider more *action-oriented* approaches. Behavior therapists believe that insight, or deep understanding of one's problems, is often unnecessary for improvement. Instead, behavior therapists try to directly alter troublesome thoughts and actions.

Brooks Workman (described in the Chapter Preview) didn't need to probe into her past or her emotions and conflicts; she simply wanted to break her habit of drinking too many colas. Even when serious problems are at stake, techniques like the one she used have proved valuable. Behavior therapy has helped people to stop drinking, smoking, hiccuping, stuttering, and molesting children. Behavior modification can be used to lose weight or to increase eating in the pathologically underweight. It has improved study habits, work output in factories, and speech in retarded and disturbed children, and it has increased the amount of time psychotic patients will go without hallucinating. Also, through behavior modification, people have conquered fears of heights, snakes, public speaking, sexual intimacy, and automobiles.

Question: In general, how does behavior therapy work?

Behavior therapy is based on one basic assumption: People have *learned* to be the way they are. Consequently, if they have learned responses that cause problems, then they can change them or *relearn* more appropriate responses. Broadly speaking, *behavior modification* refers to any attempt to use the learning principles of *classical (respondent) conditioning* and *operant conditioning* to change human behavior.

Question: How does classical conditioning work? I'm not sure I remember.

Classical conditioning was described in Chapter 7. It is the type of learning first studied by Russian scientist Ivan Pavlov. Here is a brief review of Pavlov's principles:

> A neutral stimulus is followed by an *unconditioned stimulus (US)* that consistently produces an unlearned reaction, called the *unconditioned response (UR)*. Eventually, the previously neutral stimulus begins to produce this response directly. The response is then called a *conditioned response (CR)*, and the stimulus becomes a *conditioned stimulus (CS)*. Thus, for a child, the sight of a hypodermic needle (CS) is followed by an injection (US), which causes anxiety or fear (UR). Eventually, the sight of a hypodermic (the conditioned stim-

ulus) may produce anxiety or fear (a conditioned response) *before* the child gets an injection.

Question: What does classical conditioning have to do with behavior modification?

Classical conditioning can be used to associate discomfort with a bad habit. Psychologists call discomfort used in this way an *aversion*. An aversion may be used to combat an undesirable habit, as in the case of the woman who wanted to drink fewer colas. When more powerful forms of this approach are used, it is called *aversion therapy*.

Aversion Therapy—A Little Pain Goes a Long Way

Imagine that you are eating an apple. Suddenly you discover that you just bit a large green worm in half. You vomit. Months pass before you can eat an apple again without feeling ill. You now have a *conditioned aversion* to apples.

Question: How is a conditioned aversion used in therapy?

In **aversion therapy,** an individual learns to associate a strong aversion (or negative emotional response) to an undesirable habit such as smoking, drinking, or gambling. Aversion therapy has been used to cure hiccups, sneezing, stuttering (Goldiamond, 1965), vomiting (Lang & Melamed, 1969), and bed-wetting (Wickes, 1958), and it is used in the treatment of fetishism, transvestism, and other "maladaptive" sexual behaviors (Fuastman, 1976). To see how aversion therapy can help people quit smoking, see Highlight 22–1.

An excellent example of aversion therapy is provided by the work of Roger Vogler and his associates (1977). Vogler works with alcoholics who have been unable to stop drinking. For many clients, aversion therapy is a last chance. They have often been threatened with desertion by relatives and friends, have lost their jobs, and have tried Alcoholics Anonymous, psychotherapy, detoxification, vitamin therapy, and even Antabuse therapy. (Antabuse is a drug that causes an alcoholic to become violently nauseated after he or she drinks.) Here is a typical aversion procedure:

> While drinking an alcoholic beverage, painful (although non-injurious) electric shocks are delivered to the client's hand. From the client's point of view, the shocks are unpredictable; he or she never knows for sure when one is due. Most of the time, however, the shocks come as the client is beginning to take a drink of alcohol (Fig. 22–1).

HIGHLIGHT 22–1
Puffing Up an Aversion

The fact that nicotine is toxic makes it easy to create an aversion to smoking. Behavior therapists have found that electric shock, nauseating drugs, and similar aversive stimuli are not required to make smokers uncomfortable. All that is needed is for the smoker to smoke—rapidly and for a long time.

Rapid smoking is the most widely used aversion therapy for smoking (Lichtenstein, 1982). In this method, subjects are told to smoke continuously, taking a puff every 6 to 8 seconds. Rapid smoking continues until the smoker is miserable and can stand it no more. By then, most people are thinking, "I never want to see another cigarette for the rest of my life."

Studies suggest that rapid smoking is one of the most effective behavior therapies for smoking (Tiffany et al., 1986). Research also indicates that the health risks of rapid smoking are small (Hall et al., 1984). Nevertheless, anyone tempted to try rapid smoking should realize that it is very unpleasant. Without the help of a therapist, most people quit too soon for the procedure to succeed. (An alternative method that is more practical is described in the Applications section of this chapter.)

The most basic problem with rapid smoking—as with other stop-smoking methods—is that about one-half of those who quit smoking begin again (Hall et al., 1984). Relapse is especially likely for smokers who have strong withdrawal symptoms (O'Connell & Martin, 1987). During at least the first year after quitting, there is no "safe point" after which relapse becomes less likely (Swan & Denk, 1987).

Because the "evil weed" calls so strongly to former smokers, support from a stop-smoking group or a close, caring person can make a big difference. Former smokers who get encouragement from others are much more likely to stay smoke-free (Lichtenstein, 1982). In contrast, former smokers whose social groups include many smokers are more likely to begin smoking again (Mermelstein, 1986).

This *response-contingent* (or response-connected) shock obviously takes the pleasure out of drinking. Shocks also cause the alcohol abuser to develop a conditioned aversion to drinking. Normally, the misery caused by alcohol abuse comes long after the act of drinking—too late to have

Fig. 22–1 *Aversion therapy for drinking. The sights, smells, and tastes of drinking are associated with unpleasant electric shocks applied to the hand.*

much effect. But if we can link the sight and smell of alcohol with *immediate* discomfort, then drinking can come to make the individual very uncomfortable.

Question: But can't the person tell when it is "safe" to drink and when it is not?

Transfer, or *generalization,* of aversion conditioning to the "real world" is a problem. With this in mind, Vogler constructed in his office a vivid re-creation of a "friendly neighborhood tavern," complete with a bar, tables, soft lights, music, and a bartender. Also provided are a "living room," a "bedroom," and a "kitchen." Clients undergo aversion therapy in a setting as much like the normal site of their drinking as possible, and carryover of the averison training is improved.

Actually, aversion therapy is used as a last resort, even for problems as serious as alcohol abuse. Vogler and his associates also train alcoholics to discriminate blood alcohol levels (so clients can tell how drunk they are). They teach alcoholics alternatives to drinking and offer education programs on alcohol abuse as well as general counseling (Vogler et al., 1977). They have also added an interesting twist to their aversion therapy: Alcohol abusers are videotaped as they go from sober to drunk. Later, they watch the videotaped drinking bout and see themselves with slurred speech, dropping cigarette ashes in their drinks and saying stupid and belligerent things. Most react with shame and embarrassment when they see the tapes. Apparently, few people have any idea how unattractive they are when drunk.

To add to the effect, the bartender is trained to provoke clients into becoming argumentative and obnoxious. Presumably, this is not too hard to do by the time the client is saying, "I am 'masshhhed' " (Vils, 1976). In the videotape self-confrontation held later, grossly drunken behaviors are replayed until the client says, "Okay, okay, I've seen enough." Seeing themselves as obnoxious drunks adds to the aversion people feel for drinking, and it increases their determination to quit.

Question: I'm not sure I'm comfortable with the idea of treating humans this way.

People are often disturbed (shocked?) by such methods. It must be emphasized that clients usually volunteer for aversion therapy because it helps them overcome a destructive habit. Indeed, commercial aversion programs for overeating, smoking, and alcohol abuse have attracted large numbers of willing customers.

When psychologists use aversion therapy, they often back it up with supportive counseling. Also, for mild problems, such as nail biting, a person may not have to undergo pain at all. Merely watching a trained actor (who *appears* to get electric shocks while biting his nails) can effectively curb the problem (Rosenthal et al., 1978). Last, and most importantly, aversion therapy can be justified by its long-term benefits. As behaviorist Donald Baer puts it, "A small number of brief, painful experiences is a reasonable exchange for the interminable pain of a lifelong maladjustment" (Baer, 1971).

Desensitization—Who's Afraid of a Big, Bad Hierarchy?

Assume that you are a swimming instructor who wants to help a child overcome fear of the high diving board. How might you proceed? Directly forcing a terrified child off the high board could be a psychological disaster. Obviously, a better approach would be to begin by teaching the child to dive off the edge of the pool. Then the child could be taught to dive off the low board, followed by a platform 6 feet above the water and then an 8-foot platform. As a last step, the child could try the high board.

This *ordered set of steps* is called a **hierarchy.** The hierarchy allows the child to undergo *adaptation.* Gradually, the child adapts to the high dive and overcomes fear, much as one adapts to the cool water of a swimming pool on a hot day. When the child has overcome the fear, a psychologist would say that **desensitization** (dee-SEN-sih-tih-ZAY-shun) has occurred (Fig. 22–2).

Desensitization is also based on the principle of **reciprocal inhibition,** a term coined by Joseph Wolpe (1974). In reciprocal inhibition, one emotional state is used to prevent the occurrence of another. For instance, it is impossible to be anxious and relaxed at the same time. If we have managed to get our subject onto the high board in a relaxed state, anxiety and fear responses will be inhibited. Repeated times on the high board should cause fear in the situation to disappear. Again we would say that the person has been *desensitized.* In general, desensitization (that is, a reduction in fears) is usually brought about by gradually approaching a feared stimulus while maintaining complete relaxation.

Question: What is desensitization used for?

Desensitization is primarily used to help people unlearn or countercondition phobias or strong anxieties. Almost everyone has a phobia or two. Many people fear heights, snakes, public speaking, spiders, and so forth. Usually these cause little difficulty because the individual carefully avoids fear-producing situations. However, consider the following: a teacher with stage fright, a student with test anxiety, a salesperson who fears people, an aspiring pole-vaulter who fears heights, or a newlywed with a fear of sexual intimacy. Each may be hampered enough by fears or anxieties to seek aid.

Question: How is desensitization done?

Desensitization usually involves three steps. First, the client and the therapist *construct a hierarchy.* This is a list of fear-provoking situations involving the phobia and ranging from the least disturbing situation to the most disturbing one. Second, the client is taught *exercises that produce total relaxation* (described in this chapter's Applications section). Once the client is relaxed, he or she proceeds to the third step by trying to *perform the least disturbing item* on the list. For a fear of heights (acrophobia), this might be: "(1) Stand on a chair." The first item is repeated until no anxiety is felt. Any change from complete relaxation is a signal to clients that they must repeat the relaxation process before continuing. Slowly, clients move up the hierarchy: "(2) Climb to the top of a small stepladder"; "(3) Look down a flight of stairs"; and so on, until the last item is performed without fear: "(20) Fly in an airplane."

Question: I understand how some fears can be desensitized by gradual approach—as in the case of the child on the high dive. But how would a therapist use desensitization to combat fear of sexual intimacy?

For a person with a fear of heights, the steps of the hierarchy might be acted out. Often, however, acting out is totally impractical. In some cases, this problem can be

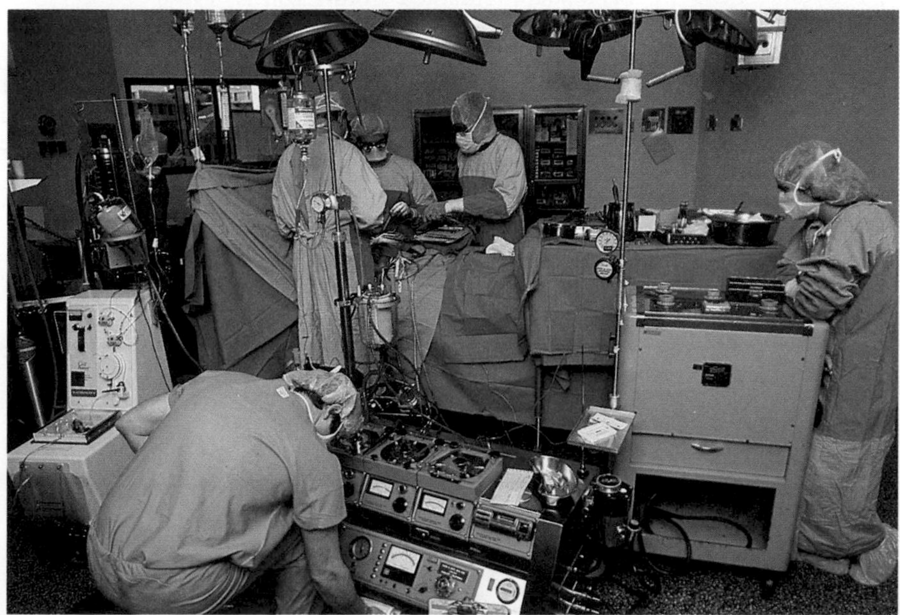

Fig. 22–2 *A case of natural desensitization. Doctors and nurses learn to remain calm at the sight of blood because of their frequent exposure to it.*

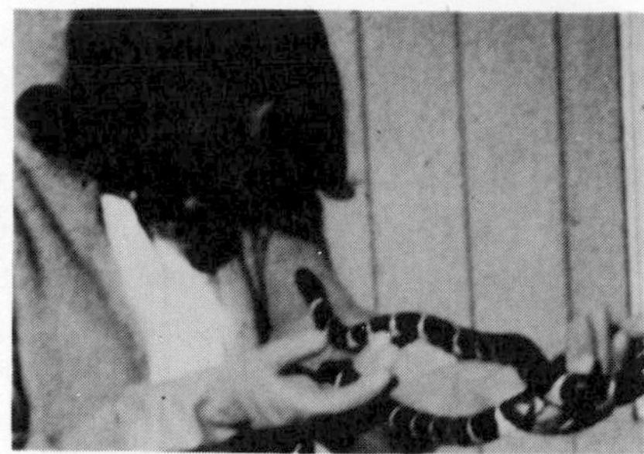

Fig. 22–3 *Treatment of a snake phobia by vicarious desensitization. The photographs show models interacting with snakes. To overcome their own fears, phobic subjects observed the models. (Bandura et al., 1969. Photos courtesy of Albert Bandura.)*

handled by having clients observe models (live or filmed) who are performing the feared behavior (Fig. 22–3). If such **vicarious desensitization** is not practical, there is yet another alternative. Fortunately, desensitization works almost as well when a person *vividly imagines* each step in the hierarchy. If the steps can be visualized without anxiety, fear in the actual situation is reduced.

Here is a sample of the hierarchy imagined by a 24-year-old married woman to overcome the fear and disgust she felt for sexual intercourse. (Some steps are left out to shorten the list.)

1. Dancing with and embracing husband while fully clothed.
2. Being kissed on cheeks and forehead.
3. Being kissed on lips.
4. Sitting on husband's lap, both fully dressed.
5. Husband kisses neck and ears.
6. Husband caresses hair and face.

•
•
•

17. Having intercourse in bed in the dark.
18. Having intercourse in the nude in a dining room or living room.
19. Changing positions during intercourse.
20. Having intercourse in the nude while sitting on husband's lap. (Adapted from Lazarus, 1964)

Mrs. A was able to imagine the last steps in this hierarchy without experiencing anxiety after a 3-month period of desensitization. Accordingly, she and her husband reported that their sexual and marital adjustments were greatly improved.

Learning Check

Before continuing, see if you can answer these questions. If not, review the preceding sections.

1. What two types of conditioning are used in behavior modification? ____________ and ____________

2. Shock, pain, and discomfort play what role in conditioning an aversion?
a. conditioned stimulus *b.* unconditioned response *c.* unconditioned stimulus *d.* conditioned response

3. If shock is used to control drinking, it must be ____________-contingent.

4. A potential problem with aversion therapy is transfer of the aversion to settings outside the clinic or laboratory. T or F?

5. The ordered series of steps used in desensitization make up a ____________ of feared situations.

6. What two principles underlie desensitization? ________________ and ________________

7. When desensitization is carried out through the use of live or filmed models, it is called
a. cognitive therapy *b.* flooding *c.* covert desensitization *d.* vicarious desensitization

8. The three basic steps in desensitization are: Construct a hierarchy, flood the person with anxiety, and imagine relaxation. T or F?

Answers:
1. classical (or respondent), operant **2.** *c* **3.** response **4.** T **5.** hierarchy **6.** adaptation, reciprocal inhibition **7.** *d* **8.** F

Operant Principles—All the World Is a . . . Skinner Box?

Question: Aversion therapy and desensitization are forms of behavior modification based on classical conditioning. Where does operant conditioning fit in?

The principles of operant conditioning have been developed by B. F. Skinner and other psychologists mostly through laboratory research with animals. The operant principles most frequently used by behavior therapists to deal with *human* behavior are:

1. Positive reinforcement. An action that is followed by reward will occur more frequently. If children whine and get attention, they will whine more frequently. If you get A's in your psychology class, you may become a psychology major.
2. Nonreinforcement. An action that is not followed by reward will occur less frequently.
3. Extinction. If a response is not followed by reward after it has been repeated many times, it will go away. After winning 3 times, you pull the handle on a slot machine 30 times more without a payoff. What do you do? You go away. So does the response of handle pulling (for that particular machine, at any rate).
4. Punishment. If a response is followed by discomfort or an undesirable effect, the response will be suppressed (but not necessarily extinguished).
5. Shaping. Shaping means rewarding actions that are closer and closer approximations to a desired response. If a response is complicated, it may never occur and thus may never be rewarded. If I want to reward a retarded child for saying "ball," I may begin by rewarding the child for saying anything that starts with a *b* sound.
6. Stimulus control. Responses tend to come under the control of the situation in which they occur. If I set my clock 10 minutes fast, I can get to work on time in the morning. My departure is under the stimulus control of the clock, even though I know it is fast.
7. Time out. A time-out procedure usually involves removing the individual from a situation in which reinforcement occurs. Time out prevents reward from following an undesirable response; it is a variation of nonreinforcement. For example, children who fight with each other can be sent to separate rooms and allowed out only when they are able to behave more calmly (Olson & Roberts, 1987). (For a more thorough review of operant principles, return to Chapter 7.)

As simple as these principles may seem, they have been used very effectively by behavior modification specialists to overcome difficulties in work, home, school, and industrial settings. Let's see how.

Nonreinforcement and Extinction—Time Out in the Attention Game

An extremely overweight mental patient had a persistent and disturbing habit: She stole food from other patients. No one could persuade her to stop stealing or to diet. For the sake of her health, a behavior therapist assigned her a special table in the ward dining room. If she approached any other table, she was immediately removed from the dining room. Since her attempts to steal food went unrewarded, they rapidly disappeared. Additionally, any attempt to steal from others usually resulted in the patient's missing her own meal (Ayllon, 1963).

Question: What operant principles did the therapist in this example use?

The therapist used *nonreward* to produce *extinction*. The most frequently occurring human behaviors lead to some form of reward. An undesirable response can be eliminated by *identifying* and *removing* the rewards that maintain it. But people don't always do things for food, money, or other obvious rewards. Most of the rewards maintaining human behavior are more subtle. *Attention, approval,* and *concern* are common yet powerful reinforcers for humans (Fig. 22–4).

For instance, in a classroom, we often find that misbehaving children are surrounded by others who giggle and pay attention to them. If seating is rearranged so that the disruptive children are surrounded by less responsive students, misbehavior decreases. Attention from a teacher (even scolding) can also be a reinforcer. An experiment showed that when teachers paid extra attention to classroom misbehavior, it increased. It increased even when the attention took the form of saying things such as "Sit down!" When misbehaving children were *ignored* and attention was given to children who were *not* misbehaving, misbehavior decreased (Madsen et al., 1968).

Question: How are nonreward and extinction applied in therapy?

Nonreward and extinction can eliminate many problem behaviors. Frequently, difficulties center around a limited number of particularly disturbing responses. A typical strategy used in institutions is called *time out*. Time out means refusing to reward maladaptive responses, usually by refusing to play the *attention* game. Another form of time out is to remove an individual immediately from the setting in which an undesirable response occurs, so that the response will not be rewarded. For example:

> Fourteen-year-old Josh periodically appeared in the nude in the activity room of a training center for disturbed juveniles. This behavior always generated a great deal of attention from staff and other patients. Usually Josh was returned to his room and confined there. During this "confinement," he often missed doing his usual chores. As an experiment he was placed on time out. The next time he appeared nude, counselors and other staff members greeted him normally and then ignored him. Attention from other patients rapidly subsided. Sheepishly he returned to his room and dressed.

Reinforcement and Token Economies—The Target Is Health

This section might be called "Throwing a Lifeline to the Unreachable." A distressing problem faced when dealing with the severely disturbed is how to "break through" to a patient who cannot, or will not, communicate. Mental patients sometimes spend years in hospitals without noticeable improvement.

Question: What can be done in such circumstances?

An approach that has been widely used is based on *tokens*. **Tokens** are *symbolic* rewards that can be exchanged for real rewards. (As you may recall from Chapter 7, tokens are secondary reinforcers.)

Tokens may be printed slips of paper, plastic "poker" chips, check marks, points, or gold stars. Whatever form they take, tokens serve as rewards because they may be exchanged for candy, food, cigarettes, recreation, or other privileges, such as private time with a therapist, outings, or using the stereo. Tokens are being used in mental

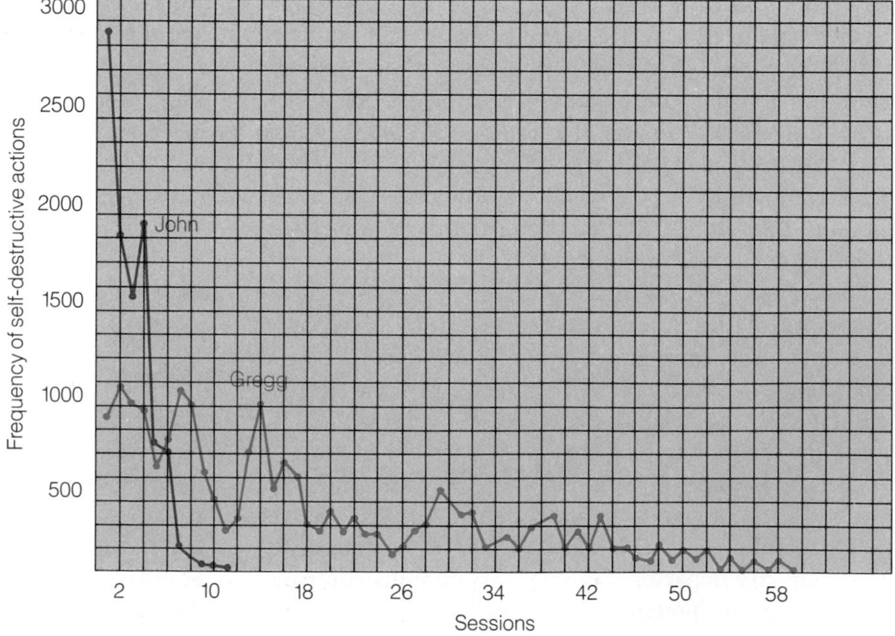

Fig. 22–4 *This graph shows extinction of self-destructive behavior in two autistic boys. Before extinction began, the boys received attention and concern from adults for injuring themselves. During extinction, self-damaging behavior was ignored. (Adapted from Lovaas & Simons, 1969.)*

hospitals, halfway houses for drug addicts, schools for the retarded, programs for delinquents, and ordinary classrooms. Their use is usually associated with dramatic improvements in behavior and overall adjustment.

By using tokens, a therapist can *immediately* reward a positive response. This allows a therapist to use operant shaping to influence behavior directly instead of vaguely urging patients to "get themselves together." For maximum impact, the therapist selects specific **target behaviors** for improvement and then reinforces them with tokens. For example, a mute mental patient might first be given a token each time he or she says a word. Next, tokens may be given for speaking a complete sentence. Later, the patient could gradually be required to speak more often, then to answer questions, and eventually to carry on a short conversation in order to receive tokens. In this way, patients who have not spoken more than a few words for months or years have been returned to the world of normal communication.

Full-scale use of tokens in an institutional setting produces a **token economy.** In a token economy, patients are rewarded with tokens for a wide range of socially desirable or productive activities. They must *pay* tokens for privileges and for engaging in problem behavior (Fig. 22–5). For example, tokens are given to patients who get out of bed, dress themselves, take required medication, arrive for meals on time, and the like. Work at constructive activity, such as gardening, cooking, or custodial duties, may also earn tokens. Patients must *exchange* tokens for meals and for private rooms, movies, passes, off-ward activities, and other privileges. Patients are *charged* tokens for staying in bed, disrobing in public, talking to themselves, fighting, crying, and similar target behaviors.

The effect of a token economy can be a radical change in patients' overall adjustment and morale. Patients have an incentive to change and they are held responsible for maladaptive habits and actions. Many "hopelessly" retarded, mentally ill, and delinquent people have been returned to a productive life by means of token economies.

Question: Wouldn't there be a problem with a lack of generalization of improvements brought about by a token economy?

Yes. Lack of generalization can again be a problem. To minimize this, patients are praised and given *social* recognition when they receive tokens. Each time a token is given, the therapist says something like, "That was very good," or "You're doing so well."

By the time they are ready to leave the program, patients may be earning tokens on a weekly basis for maintaining sane, responsible, and productive behavior (Binder, 1976). Typically, the most effective token economies are

Fig. 22–5 *Shown here is a token used in one token economy system; also pictured is a list of credit values for various activities. Tokens may be exchanged for items or for privileges listed on the board. (Photographs courtesy of Robert P. Liberman.)*

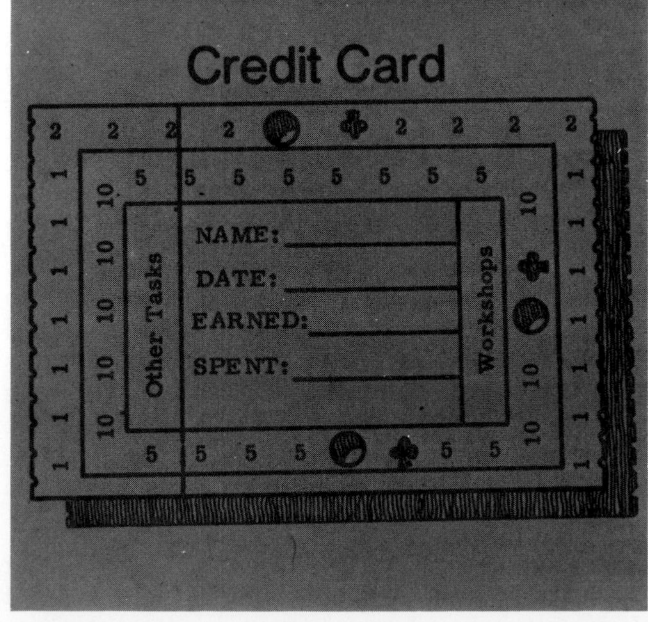

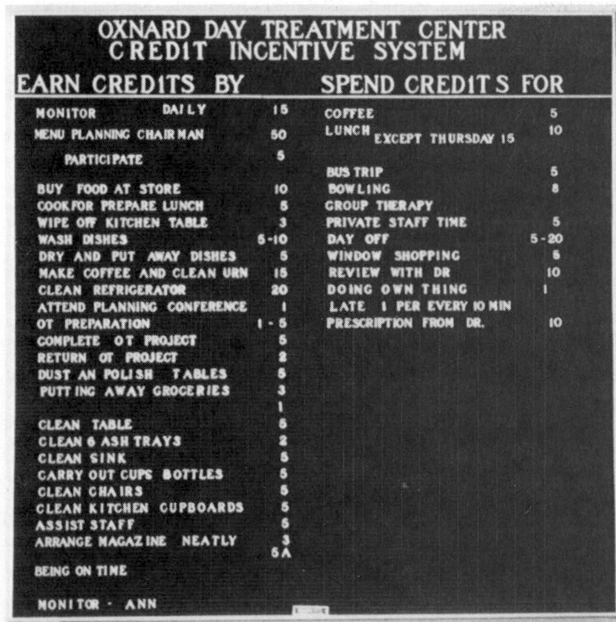

those that gradually switch from tokens to *social rewards* such as recognition and approval (Lieberman et al, 1976). Such rewards are what patients will receive when they return to family, friends, and community.

Cognitive Behavior Therapy—Think Positive!

Question: How would a behavior therapist treat a problem like depression? None of the techniques described seem to apply.

As we have discussed, behavior therapists usually try to change troublesome actions. However, in recent years a new breed of therapist has appeared. **Cognitive behavior therapists,** as they are called, are interested in thoughts, as well as visible behavior. Rather than looking only at actions, cognitive therapists try to learn what people think, believe, and feel. They then help clients change *thinking patterns* that lead to trouble (Meichenbaum, 1977).

Cognitive Therapy for Depression

Cognitive therapy has been especially effective for treating depression. As you may recall from Chapter 12, Aaron Beck believes that negative, self-defeating thoughts underlie depression. According to Beck, depressed persons see themselves, the world, and the future in negative terms. Beck (1985) believes this occurs because of several major distortions in thinking. The first is **selective perception:** If five good things happen during the day and three bad things, the depressed person will focus only on the bad. **Overgeneralization** is a second thinking error underlying depression. An example would be considering yourself a total failure, or completely worthless, if you were to lose a job or fail one class. To complete the picture, Beck says that depressed persons tend to *magnify* the importance of undesirable events, and they engage in **all-or-nothing thinking** (seeing each event as completely good or bad, right or wrong, successful or a failure) (Beck, 1985).

Question: What do cognitive behavior therapists do to alter such patterns?

Cognitive therapists make a step-by-step effort to correct negative thoughts that lead to depression or similar problems. At first, clients are taught to recognize and keep track of their own thoughts. The client and therapist then look for ideas and beliefs that cause depression, anger, avoidance, and so forth. For example, here's how a therapist might challenge all-or-nothing thinking (Burns & Persons, 1982):

> **Patient:** I'm feeling even more depressed. No one wants to hire me, and I can't even clean up my apartment. I feel completely incompetent!
> **Therapist:** I see. The fact that you are unemployed and have a messy apartment proves that you are completely incompetent?
> **Patient:** Well . . . I can see that doesn't add up.

Next, clients are asked to gather information to test their beliefs. For instance, a depressed person might list his or her activities for a week. The list is then used to challenge all-or-nothing thoughts, such as "I had a terrible week" or "I'm a complete failure." With more coaching, clients learn to alter thoughts in ways that improve their moods, actions, and relationships.

In an alternate approach, the cognitive therapist looks for an *absence* of effective coping skills and thought patterns, not for the *presence* of self-defeating thinking (Meichenbaum, 1977). The aim is to teach clients how to cope with anger, depression, shyness, stress, and similar problems. Stress inoculation, which was described in Chapter 13, is a good example of this approach.

Cognitive behavior therapy is a promising and rapidly expanding specialty. Before we leave the topic, let's explore one more widely used form of cognitive therapy.

Rational-Emotive Therapy

According to Albert Ellis (1962, 1973), the basic idea of **rational-emotive therapy (RET)** is as easy as ABC. Ellis assumes that people become unhappy and develop self-defeating habits because of unrealistic or faulty *beliefs*.

Question: How are beliefs important?

Ellis analyzes problems in this way: The letter A stands for an **activating experience,** which the person assumes to be the cause of C, an emotional **consequence.** For instance, a person who is rejected (the activating experience) feels depressed, threatened, or hurt (the consequence). Rational-emotive therapy shows the client that the true cause of difficulty is what comes between A and C: In between is B, the client's irrational and unrealistic **beliefs.** In this example, the unrealistic belief leading to unnecessary suffering is: "I must be loved and approved by almost everyone at all times" (Table 22–1). RET holds that events cannot *cause* us to have feelings. We feel as we do because of our beliefs and expectations (Kottler & Brown, 1985).

Ellis (1979, 1987) believes that most irrational beliefs come from three core ideas, each of which is unrealistic:

1. I *must* perform well and be approved of by significant others. If I don't, then it is awful, I cannot stand it, and I am a rotten person.

Table 22–1 Ten Irrational Beliefs

1. I must be loved and approved by almost every significant other person in my life.
2. I should be completely competent and achieving in all ways to be a worthwhile person.
3. Certain people I must deal with are thoroughly bad and should be severely blamed and punished for it.
4. It is awful and upsetting when things are not the way I would very much like them to be.
5. My unhappiness is always caused by external events; I cannot control my emotional reactions.
6. If something unpleasant might happen, I should keep dwelling on it.
7. It is easier to avoid difficulties and responsibilities than to face them.
8. I should depend on others who are stronger than I am.
9. Because something once strongly affected my life, it will do so indefinitely.
10. There is always a perfect solution to human problems, and it is awful if this solution is not found.

(Adapted from Rohsenow & Smith, 1982)

2. You *must* treat me fairly. When you don't, it is horrible, and I cannot bear it.
3. Conditions *must* be the way I want them to be. It is terrible when they are not, and I cannot stand living in such an awful world.

It's easy to see that such beliefs can lead to much grief and needless suffering in a less than perfect world. Rational-emotive therapists are very directive in their attempts to change a client's irrational beliefs and "self-talk." The therapist may directly attack clients' logic, challenge their thinking, confront them with evidence contrary to their beliefs, and even assign "homework" for the clients. Here, for instance, are some examples of statements that dispute irrational beliefs (after Kottler & Brown, 1985):

- "Where is the evidence that you are a loser just because you didn't do well this one time?"
- "Who said the world should be fair? That's your rule."
- "What are you telling yourself to make yourself feel so upset?"
- "Is it really terrible that things aren't working out as you would like? Or is it just inconvenient?"

RET has been criticized by some as superficial and argumentative, but Ellis' basic insight has considerable merit. For instance, one study found that having irrational beliefs like those listed in Table 22–1 is related to feelings of anger and unhappiness (Rohsenow & Smith, 1982). Many of us would probably do well to give up our irrational beliefs. Improved self-acceptance and a better tolerance of daily annoyances are the benefits of doing so (Ellis, 1987).

The value of cognitive approaches is further illustrated by three techniques (*covert sensitization, thought stopping,* and *covert reinforcement*) described in the Applications section that follows. See what you think of them.

Learning Check

1. Behavior modification programs aimed at extinction of an undesirable behavior typically make use of what operant principles?
a. punishment and stimulus control
b. punishment and shaping
c. nonreinforcement and time out
d. stimulus control and time out
2. Attention can be a powerful ______________ for humans.
3. Token economies depend on the time-out procedure. T or F?
4. An advantage of tokens is that they can be used to ______________ ______________ a desired response.
5. Tokens are used at first to change specific actions called ______________ ______________.
6. Tokens basically allow the operant shaping of desired responses. T or F?
7. According to Beck, selective perception, overgeneralization, and ______________ thinking are cognitive habits that underlie depression.
8. RET teaches people to change the antecedents of irrational behavior. T or F?

Answers:
1. *c* **2.** reinforcer **3.** F **4.** immediately reinforce **5.** target behaviors **6.** T **7.** all-or-nothing **8.** F

Applications: Self Management—Applying Behavioral Principles to Yourself

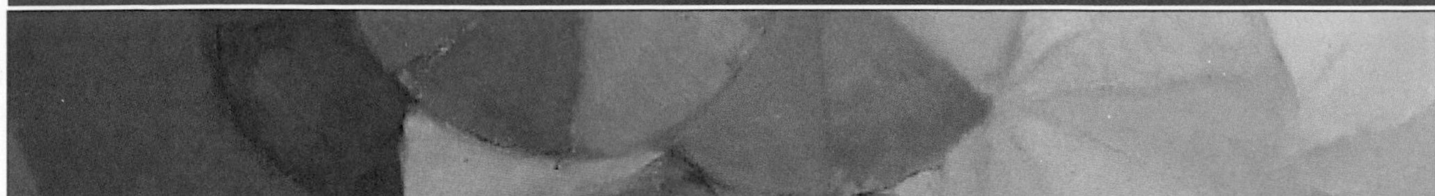

"Throw out the snake oil, ladies and gentlemen, and throw away your troubles. Doctor B. Havior Modification is here to put an end to all human suffering."

True? Well, not quite. Behavior therapy is not a cure-all. Its effective use is often quite complicated and requires a great deal of experience and expertise. Also, there are times when therapists regard insight therapy as more appropriate than behavior therapy. Still, behavior therapy offers a straightforward solution to many problems.

It would be a serious mistake to presume that you could effectively apply the principles of behavior therapy to major personal problems. As mentioned elsewhere in this book, professional help is available and should be sought when a significant problem exists. For lesser difficulties there is a good chance that you might succeed in modest attempts to apply the principles of behavior modification to yourself. Let us see how this might be done.

Covert Reward and Punishment—Boosting Your "Willpower"

"Have you ever decided to quit smoking cigarettes, watching television too much, eating too much, drinking too much, or driving too fast?"

"Well, one of those applies. I have decided several times to quit smoking."

"When have you decided?"

"Usually after I am reminded of how dangerous smoking is—like when I heard that my uncle had died of lung cancer. He smoked constantly."

"If you have decided to quit 'several times,' I assume you haven't succeeded."

"No, the usual pattern is for me to become upset about smoking and then to cut down for a day or two."

"You forget the disturbing image of your uncle's death, or whatever, and start smoking again."

"Yes, I suppose if I had an uncle die every day or so, I might actually quit!"

The use of electric shock to condition an aversion seems remote from everyday problems. Even naturally aversive actions are difficult to apply to personal behavior. As mentioned earlier, for instance, rapid smoking is difficult for most smokers to carry out on their own. And what about a problem like overeating? It would be difficult indeed to eat enough to create a lasting aversion to overeating.

In view of such limitations, psychologists have developed an alternative procedure that can be used to curb smoking, overeating, and other habits (Cautela & Bennett, 1981; Cautela & Kearney, 1986).

Covert Sensitization Obtain six 3 × 5 cards and on each write a brief description of a scene related to the habit you wish to control. The scene should be so *disturbing* or *disgusting* that thinking about it would temporarily make you very uncomfortable about indulging in the habit. For smoking, the cards might read:

- I am in a doctor's office. The doctor looks at some reports and tells me I have lung cancer. He says a lung will have to be removed and sets a date for the operation.
- I am in bed under an oxygen tent. My chest feels caved in. There is a tube in my throat. I can barely breathe.
- I wake up in the morning and smoke a cigarette. I begin coughing up blood.

Other cards would continue along the same line.

For overeating, the cards might read:

- I am at the beach. I get up to go for a swim and I overhear people whispering to each other, "Isn't that fat disgusting?"
- I am at a store buying clothes. I try on several things that are too small. The only things that fit look like rumpled sacks. Salespeople are staring at me.
- And so forth.

The trick, of course, is to get yourself to imagine or picture vividly each of these disturbing scenes *several times* a day. Imagining the scenes can be accomplished by placing them under *stimulus control*. Simply choose something you do *frequently* each day (such as getting a cup of coffee or getting up from your chair). Next make a rule. Before you can get a cup of coffee or get up from your chair, or whatever you have selected as a cue, you must take out your cards and *vividly picture* yourself engaging in the action you wish to curb (eating or smoking, for example). Then *vividly picture* the scene described on the top card. Imagine the scene for 30 seconds.

After visualizing the top card, move it to the bottom so the cards are rotated. Make up new cards each week. The scenes can be made much more upsetting than the samples given

Applications

here. The samples are toned down to keep you from being "grossed out."

Covert sensitization can also be used directly in situations that test your self-control. A person trying to lose weight, for instance, might be able to turn down a tempting dessert in this way: The person should look at the dessert and visualize maggots crawling all over it. If this image is made as vivid and nauseating as possible, losing your appetite is almost a certainty. If you want to apply this technique to other situations, be aware that vomiting scenes are especially effective. Covert sensitization may sound as if you are "playing games with yourself," but it can be a great help if you want to cut down on a bad habit (Cautela & Kearney, 1986). Try it!

Thought Stopping As discussed earlier, behavior therapists have begun to realize that thoughts, like visible responses, can also cause trouble. Think of times when you have repeatedly "put yourself down" mentally or when you have been preoccupied by needless worries, fears, or other negative and upsetting thoughts. If you would like to gain control over such thoughts, recent experiments show how it can be done.

The simplest thought-stopping technique makes use of mild punishment to suppress upsetting mental images and internal "talk." Simply place a large, flat rubber band around your wrist. As you go through the day, apply this rule: Each time you catch yourself thinking the upsetting image or thought, pull the rubber band away from your wrist and snap it. You need not make this terribly painful. Its value lies in drawing your attention to how often you form negative thoughts and in interrupting the flow of thoughts. Strong punishment is not required.

Question: It seems like this procedure might be abandoned rapidly. Is there an alternative?

A second thought-stopping procedure requires only that you interrupt upsetting thoughts each time they occur. Begin by setting aside time each day during which you will deliberately think the unwanted thought. As you begin to form the thought, shout "stop!" aloud, with conviction. (Obviously, you should choose a private spot for this part of the procedure!)

Repeat the thought-stopping procedure 10 to 20 times for the first two or three days. Then switch to shouting "stop!" covertly (to yourself) rather than aloud. Thereafter, thought stopping can be carried out throughout the day, whenever upsetting thoughts occur (adapted from Williams & Long, 1979). After several days of practice, you should be able to stop unwanted thoughts whenever they occur.

Covert Reinforcement Earlier we discussed how punishing images can be linked to undesirable responses, such as smoking or overeating, to decrease their occurrence. Many people also find it helpful to covertly *reinforce* desired actions. For example, suppose your target behavior is, once again, not eating dessert. If this were the case, you could do the following (Cautela & Bennett, 1981; Cautela & Kearney, 1986):

> Imagine that you are standing at the dessert table with your friends. As dessert is passed, you politely refuse and feel good about staying on your diet.

These images would then be followed by imagining a pleasant, reinforcing scene:

> Imagine that you are your ideal weight. You look really slim in your favorite color and style. Someone you like says to you, "Gee, you've lost weight. I've never seen you look so good."

For many people, of course, actual direct reinforcement (as described in the Chapter 7 Exploration) is the most powerful way to alter behavior. Nevertheless, covert or "visualized" reinforcement can have similar effects. To make use of covert reinforcement, choose one or more target behaviors and rehearse them mentally. Then follow each rehearsal with a vivid rewarding image.

Applying Desensitization—Overcoming Common Fears

You have prepared for 2 weeks to give a speech in a large class. As your turn approaches, your hands begin to tremble and perspire. Your heart pounds and you find it difficult to breathe. You say to your body, "Relax!" What happens? Nothing!

Relaxation The key to desensitization is relaxation. To inhibit fear, one must *learn* to relax. Here is a method for achieving deep-muscle relaxation.

> Tense the muscles in your right arm until they tremble. Hold them tight for about 5 seconds and then let go. Allow your hand and arm to go limp and to relax completely. Repeat the procedure. Releasing tension two or three times will allow you to feel whether or not your arm muscles have relaxed. Repeat the tension-release procedure with your left arm. Compare it with your right arm. Repeat until the left arm is equally relaxed. Apply the tension-release technique to your right leg; to your left leg; to your abdomen; to your chest and shoulders. Clench and release your chin, neck, and throat. Wrinkle and release your forehead and scalp. Tighten and release your mouth and face muscles. As a last step, curl your toes and tense your feet. Then release.

Practice relaxation with the tension-release method until you can achieve complete relaxation quickly (5 to 10 minutes).

After you have practiced relaxation once a day for a week or two, you will begin to be able to tell when your body (or a group of muscles) is tense. Also, you will begin to be able

Applications

to relax on command. As an alternative, you might want to try imagining a very safe, pleasant, and relaxing scene. Some people find such images as relaxing as the tension-release method (Crits-Christoph & Singer, 1984). Once you have learned to relax, the next step is to identify the fear you would like to control and construct a *hierarchy*.

Procedure for Constructing a Hierarchy Make a list of situations (related to the fear) that make you anxious. Try to list at least 10 situations. Some should be very frightening and others only mildly frightening. Write a short description of each situation on a separate 3 × 5 card. Place the cards in order from the least disturbing situation to the most disturbing. Here is a sample hierarchy for a student afraid of public speaking:

1. Being given an assignment to speak in class
2. Thinking about the topic and the date the speech must be given
3. Writing the speech; thinking about delivering the speech
4. Watching other students speak in class the week before the speech date
5. Rehearsing the speech alone; pretending to give it to the class
6. Delivering the speech to my roommate; pretending my roommate is the teacher
7. Reviewing the speech on the day it is to be presented
8. Entering the classroom; waiting and thinking about the speech
9. Being called; standing up; facing the audience
10. Delivering the speech

Using the Hierarchy When you have mastered the relaxation exercises and have the hierarchy constructed, set aside time each day to work on reducing your fear. Begin by performing the relaxation exercises. When you are completely relaxed, visualize the scene on the first card (the least frightening scene). If you can *vividly* picture and imagine yourself in the first situation twice *without a noticeable increase in muscle tension,* proceed to the next card. Also, as you progress, relax yourself between cards.

Each day, stop when you reach a card that you cannot visualize without tension after making three attempts. Each day, begin one or two cards before the one on which you stopped the previous day. Continue to work with the cards until you can visualize the last situation without experiencing tension (techniques are based on Wolpe, 1974).

Don't be discouraged if you are unable to relax completely while imagining the upsetting scenes. Research shows that in many instances your fear will still lessen after repeated exposure to the feared situations (Kleinknecht, 1986).

By using this approach you should be able to reduce the fear or anxiety associated with things such as public speaking, entering darkened rooms, asking questions in large classes, heights, talking to members of the opposite sex, and taking tests. Even if you are not always able to reduce a fear, you will have learned to place relaxation under voluntary control. This alone is valuable because controlling unnecessary tension can increase energy and efficiency.

Learning Check

1. Covert sensitization and thought stopping combine aversion therapy and cognitive therapy. T or F?
2. Like covert aversion conditioning, covert reinforcement of desired responses is also possible. T or F?
3. Exercises that bring about deep-muscle relaxation are an essential element in covert sensitization. T or F?
4. Items in a desensitization hierarchy should be placed in order from the least disturbing to the most disturbing. T or F?
5. The first step in desensitization is to place the visualization of disturbing images under stimulus control. T or F?

Answers:
1. T 2. T 3. F 4. T 5. F

Exploration: Self-Directed Behavior Change—A Case Study

By now it should be clear that behavioral principles are highly useful for solving personal problems. To conclude, let's explore a final example of behavior therapy in action. The case study summarized here was done by psychologists Scott Hamilton and David Waldman (1983). Hamilton and Waldman's study concerns Al, a 20-year-old student enrolled in a psychology course.

Case Study Many psychology students now learn self-control methods like those described earlier. As class projects, most students modify target behaviors such as studying, exercise, eating, and the like. Al's project was different. Al had a 4-year history of moderate to severe depression. Previously, Al had tried to alleviate his depression through group therapy and other efforts. However, Al continued to engage in frequent self-criticism and negative thinking, which almost always made him depressed.

Al's depression was worsened by overgeneralization. He often spent hours torturing himself with distorted thoughts such as, "I'm *stupid* and a *total failure* because my grades are bad." Because Al's problem was more serious than most, it was selected for analysis as a case study.

Self-Modification Procedures

Baseline During an initial 18-day period, Al recorded how often he had negative thoughts and how intense they were. This was done to determine his baseline level of depressive thinking.

Behavioral Intervention Because Al's depression was so closely linked to negative thoughts, his first plan focused on solving the problems he worried about most. These included studying too little, low grades, poor time scheduling, and a lack of career goals.

Al set up a program in which he earned points for seeking out career information, meeting daily study goals, maintaining a time schedule, and so forth. Al also made a list of reinforcing activities. He allowed himself to engage in these activities only in exchange for points earned by constructive behavior.

Cognitive Behavioral Intervention As you can see in Figure 22–6, Al's reinforcement system did not consistently lessen his depressive thinking. In view of this, Al dropped the reinforcement system after 2 weeks and concentrated on directly changing his depressive thoughts.

Al's cognitive program had three elements. First, he kept a record of events and thoughts that immediately preceded his becoming depressed. He then re-evaluated the event and restated his thoughts about it in a more rational form. Second, he administered daily covert reinforcement to himself. This took the form of reading written, positive statements about himself while engaging in pleasant activities. The third element of Al's program involved setting aside times each day when he would relax and mentally rehearse coping with stressful situations. At such times, Al tried to imagine the worst possible turn of events and to picture himself dealing with them calmly.

Results and Follow-Up As shown in Figure 22–6, Al's cognitive behavioral program significantly reduced the frequency of his depressive thoughts. Both Al and his peers reported that he was less depressed. This improvement was still evident 6 months later.

Question: Why didn't the behavioral part of Al's program work?

Hamilton and Waldman report that Al's point system did eliminate many of the sources of his self-critical thoughts, such as insufficient studying. However, new depressive thoughts (about his appearance and love life, for instance) began to replace the old worries. In Al's case it proved more effective to directly attack his depressive thinking.

Conclusion Al's case may be unusual. Perhaps others would not be as successful as he was in changing their own thinking patterns. It is worth saying again that for major problems it is advisable to seek guidance from a professional therapist. Nevertheless, Al's success is a tribute to the value of behavioral and cognitive therapies.

Exploration

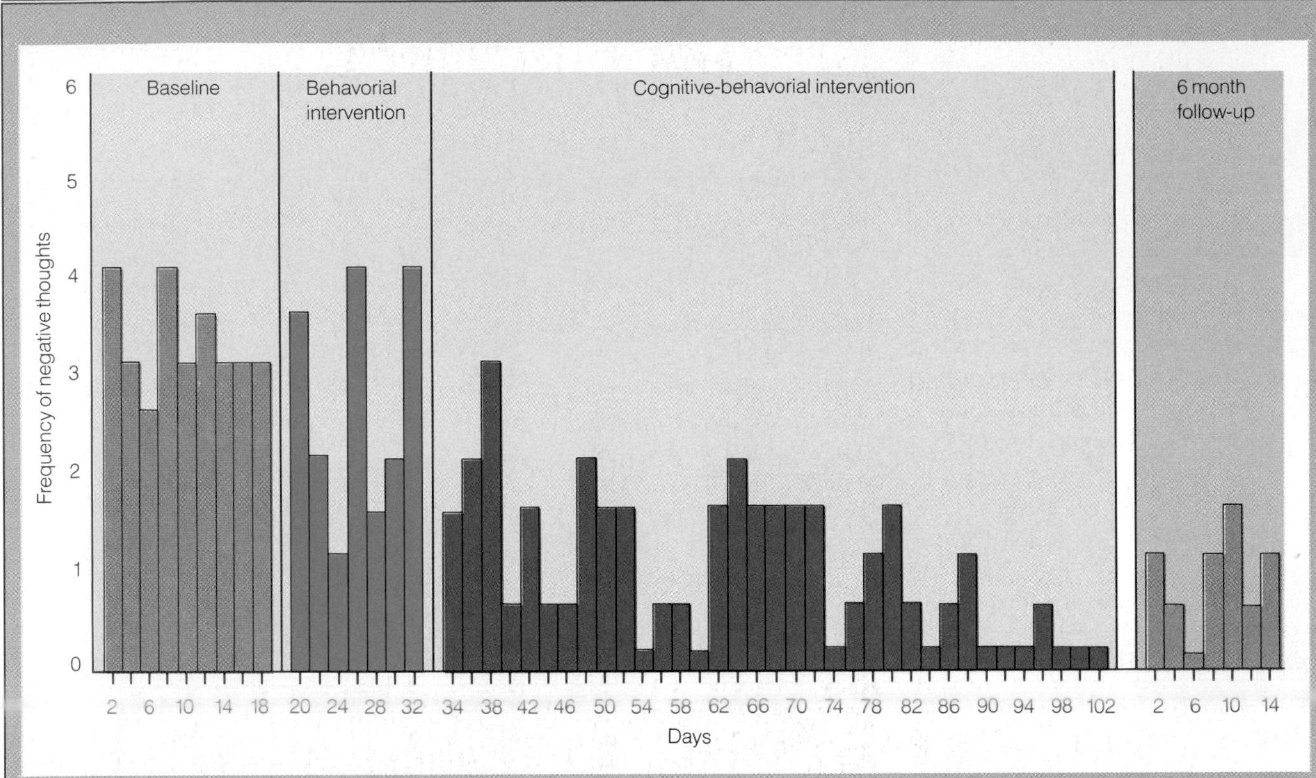

Fig. 22–6 *This graph shows the average frequency of Al's negative thoughts for 2-day intervals. Note the significant reduction that occurred during the cognitive behavioral period of his program. Notice also that Al's improvement was still evident 6 months later. (Data from Hamilton & Waldman, 1983.)*

To Control or Not To Control?

Obviously, if you *voluntarily* use behavioral principles to change your own behavior, problems of control and personal freedom are avoided. But what about when behavior modification is used by some people to change the behavior of others?

When behavior therapy was first developed, many observers feared that it would be used to control people against their will. By now, most fears of behavior therapy have faded. For one thing, it is now clear that *all* psychotherapies modify behavior in one way or another. And for another, studies show that behavior therapists are rated just as "warm" and caring as traditional therapists (Staples et al., 1975).

Behavior Therapy: Are You for or Against It? One area remains in which there is controversy concerning behavior modification. Some critics still object to its use with "captive" groups. Examples of this situation are found in schools, prisons, mental institutions, geriatric hospitals, factories, and so forth.

Proponents of behavior modification believe that it has no peer in areas such as classroom management, work with the retarded, child discipline, treatment for obesity, phobias, sexual dysfunction, and the like. They also argue that many mental patients are serving virtual life sentences in state hospitals. In view of the demonstrated effectiveness of behavioral techniques, they consider it unethical to *withhold* treatment.

The proper place for behavior control in a free society is a complex issue. Where do you stand on the use of behavior modification?

Exploration

Learning Check

1. Al began his program by recording the frequency of his depressive thoughts. This was done so that he could tell when his thoughts got down to the baseline. T or F?
2. Al's plan for reinforcing his own desirable behavior is an example of operant conditioning. T or F?
3. According to Figure 22–6, Al was able to greatly reduce the frequency of his depressive thoughts by reinforcing desirable behavior. T or F?
4. Voluntary use of behavioral principles to change one's own behavior typically does not compromise personal freedom. T or F?

Answers:
1. F 2. T 3. F 4. T

Chapter Summary

• **Behavior therapists** use various types of **behavior modification,** therapy techniques that apply the learning principles of **operant** and **classical conditioning,** to bring about positive changes in human behavior.
• Classical (or respondent) conditioning, the pairing of a **conditioned stimulus** (CS) and an **unconditioned stimulus** (US), can be used to condition an **aversion** when the US causes pain or discomfort.
• In **aversion therapy,** the sights, sounds, odors, and motions of a maladaptive response or bad habit (such as smoking or drinking) are associated with pain or other aversive events. Thus, the undesirable response becomes linked with an aversion that inhibits the response.
• Classical conditioning also underlies **desensitization,** a technique used to overcome fears and anxieties. In desensitization, gradual **adaptation** and **reciprocal inhibition** break the link between fear and particular situations. Typical steps in desensitization are: Construct a **fear hierarchy;** learn to produce total relaxation; and perform items on the hierarchy (from least to most disturbing).
• Desensitization may be carried out with real settings and situations in the environment, or it may be carried out by *vivid imagination* of the fear hierarchy. Desensitization is also effective when it is administered **vicariously,** that is, when clients watch **models** perform the feared responses.
• Behavior modification also makes use of operant principles. The most commonly used principles are **positive reinforcement, nonreinforcement, extinction, punishment, shaping, stimulus control,** and **time out.** Through the application of these principles, behavior modification is used to extinguish undesirable responses and to promote constructive behavior.
• Nonreward can be used to produce extinction of troublesome behaviors. Often this is done by simply *identifying* and *eliminating* reinforcers, particularly *attention* and *approval.*
• In the application of positive reinforcement and operant shaping, symbolic rewards known as **tokens** are often used. Tokens allow *immediate reinforcement* of selected **target behaviors** so that rapid shaping is possible.
• Full-scale use of tokens in an institutional setting produces a **token economy.** In a token economy, responsibilities, goods, services, and privileges are assigned values, and tokens are earned and exchanged. Toward the end of a token economy program, patients are shifted to **social rewards** such as recognition and approval.
• **Cognitive behavior therapy** is a new specialty that emphasizes changing thought patterns that underlie emotional or behavioral problems. Its goals are to correct distorted thinking and/or teach improved coping skills.
• In a variation of cognitive therapy called **rational-emo-**

tive therapy (RET), clients learn to recognize and challenge their own **irrational beliefs.** In the **ABC analysis** of RET, changing beliefs (B) alters the emotional consequences (C) that appear to be unleashed by activating events (A).

• Cognitive behavioral techniques can be an aid to managing one's own behavior. In **covert sensitization,** aversive images are used to discourage unwanted behavior. **Thought stopping** uses mild punishment to prevent upsetting thoughts. **Covert reinforcement** is a way to encourage desired responses by mental rehearsal. *Desensitization* pairs relaxation with a hierarchy of upsetting images to lessen fears.

Questions for Discussion

1. How do you think an insight-oriented therapist would have approached Al's depression (discussed in the Exploration)? What advantages and disadvantages do you see in the behavioral approach? What do you think would be the limitations of self-directed behavior change?

2. Under what conditions would you condone the use of behavior modification? When would you oppose it?

3. Based on the techniques described, would you cooperate with a therapist who wanted to use behavior therapy? Are there some techniques you find acceptable and others not?

4. Select a bad habit you would like to break or a positive behavior you would like to encourage, and explain how you might use a behavioral or cognitive behavioral technique to alter your behavior.

5. Some critics have charged that the use of tokens in the classroom encourages students to expect artificial rewards. Behavior therorists reply that explicit rewards are better than inconsistent rewards such as praise and attention. What are the advantages and drawbacks represented by each position?

6. How do you feel about the use of behavior modification in prisons and psychiatric hospitals? Is behavior therapy any different from the involuntary administration of tranquilizers or other drugs? Why or why not?

7. Some states have tried at times to ban the use of aversive therapy techniques for severely disturbed people. Do you think that such treatment decisions should or should not be limited by law?

Part Seven

Self and Society

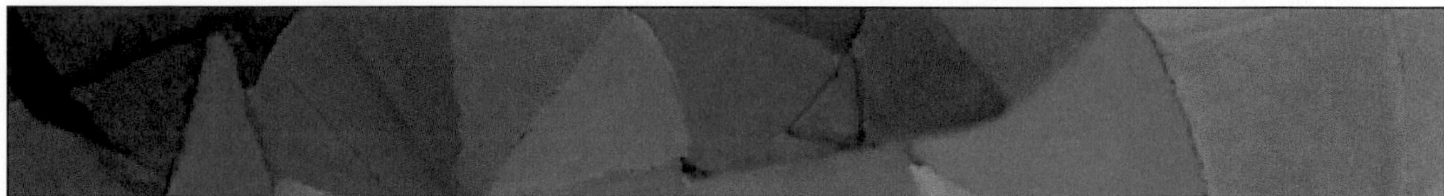

Chapter 23

Social Psychology I

In This Chapter

Group membership
Personal space
Attribution theory
Needs for affiliation
Interpersonal attraction
Conformity
Social power
Obedience
Compliance
Applications
Self-assertion
Exploration
Social traps

Chapter Preview

The Social Animal

To live alone, one must be either an animal or a god.
Aristotle

No man is an Iland, intire of itselfe.
John Donne

Your assignment is this: You have been given a written message and the name, address, and occupation of the person who should receive it. This "target person" lives over 1500 miles away in a city you have never visited. You are allowed to move the message through the mail, but you may send it only to a first-name acquaintance. That person, in turn, must mail the message only to one of his or her first-name acquaintances. The message is to be moved in this manner until it reaches the target person, whom the previous person must know by name.

Sound impossible? Social psychologist Stanley Milgram and his associates asked a number of people to try moving a message in this way. Amazingly, about 1 message in 5 made it. Even more amazing was the number of people needed to complete a chain between two strangers separated by half a continent. The average number of "links" required was about 7 people (Korte & Milgram, 1970; Milgram, 1967)!

Question: How is that possible?

Actually, the 7-link average is not as astounding as it might seem. Each of us is enmeshed in a complex network of social relationships, and each person's network overlaps with many others. If you know hundreds of people, and each of them knows hundreds more, a chain of 7 people can create millions of possible interconnections. Undeniably, humans are social animals.

Social psychology *is the study of how people behave in the presence (actual or implied) of others. Some groups are formal and organized. Others are unorganized. All influence the behavior of their members. The fascinating interplay of individual and group behavior has been the target of an immense amount of psychological study—too much, in fact, for us to cover in detail. Therefore, this chapter and the next are social psychology "samplers." It is hoped that you will find the topics interesting and thought provoking.*

Survey Questions

- How does group membership affect individual behavior?
- What unspoken rules govern the use of personal space?
- How do we perceive the motives of others and the causes of our own behavior?
- Why do people affiliate?
- What factors influence interpersonal attraction?
- What have social psychologists learned about conformity, social power, obedience, and compliance?
- How does self-assertion differ from aggression?
- What is a social trap?

Humans in a Social Context—People, People, Everywhere

We are born into an organized society. Established values, expectations, and behavior patterns are present when we arrive. So too is **culture,** an ongoing pattern of life that is passed from one generation to the next. Some readily visible aspects of culture are language, marriage customs, concepts of ownership, and sex roles.

Groups The groups to which you belong form your most immediate day-to-day social environment. Each person is a member of many groups: the family, teams, church groups, work groups, and so on. In each group we occupy a *position* in the *structure* of the group. **Roles** are expected behavior patterns linked with various social positions. There are expectations associated with playing each of the following roles: mother, teacher, employer, student. Some roles are **ascribed,** meaning they are not under the individual's control: male or female, adolescent, inmate. **Achieved** roles are those attained voluntarily or by special effort: wife, teacher, scientist, band leader (Fig. 23–1).

Question: What effect does role playing have on behavior?

Roles allow us to anticipate the behavior of others. When a person is acting as a physician, mother, clerk, or police officer, we expect certain behaviors. In general, roles are quite useful because they streamline many of our daily interactions with others. However, roles have a negative side, too. It is not unusual for a person to occupy two or more conflicting roles. Getting caught in a **role conflict** can be quite uncomfortable or frustrating. Consider, for example, the traffic court judge whose son is brought before her with a violation, or the teacher who must flunk a close friend's daughter.

The impact of roles is dramatically illustrated by an experiment conducted by psychologist Philip Zimbardo and his students at Stanford University. In this experiment, normal, healthy, male college students were paid $15 a day to serve as "inmates" and "guards" in a simulated prison (Zimbardo et al., 1973).

On the second day of their "imprisonment," the prisoners staged a number of disturbances, but their rebellion was quickly suppressed by the guards. Over the next few days, the guards behaved with increasing brutality and the prisoners became more traumatized, passive, and dehumanized. Four prisoners had to be released in the first 4 days because of reactions such as hysterical crying, confusion, and severe depression. Each day the guards tormented the prisoners with more frequent commands, insults, and demeaning tasks. After 6 days the experiment was halted.

What had happened? Zimbardo's interpretation is that the roles—prisoner and guard—assigned to participants were so powerful that in just a matter of days the experiment had become "reality" for those involved. After-

Fig. 23–1 *Roles have a powerful impact on social behavior. What kinds of behavior do you expect from your teachers? What behaviors do they expect from you? What happens if either of you fails to match the other's expectations?*

ward, many of the guards found it hard to believe their own behavior. As one recalls, "I was surprised at myself. I made them call each other names and clean toilets out with their bare hands. I practically considered the prisoners cattle" (Zimbardo, 1973). It would seem that the source of many destructive human relationships can be found in destructive roles.

Position in a group also determines one's **status.** In most groups, higher status is associated with special privileges and respect. Status can operate very subtly to influence behavior in many situations. For example, in one interesting experiment, researchers left dimes in phone booths. When subjects entered the booths, they were approached by a researcher who said, "Excuse me, I think I left a dime in this phone booth a few minutes ago. Did you find it?" Seventy-seven percent of the people returned the dime when the researcher was well dressed, but only 38 percent returned it to poorly dressed researchers (Bickman, 1974). Perhaps the better treatment given "higher-status" individuals in this example explains some of the modern preoccupation with status symbols.

Question: Are there other dimensions of group membership?

Groups are made up of people who are in some way interrelated. Two very important dimensions of any group are its *structure* and *cohesiveness*. **Group structure** is the organization of roles, communication pathways, and power in the group. Organized groups such as an army or an athletic team have a high degree of structure. Informal friendship groups may or may not be highly structured. **Group cohesiveness** is basically an indication of the degree of attraction among group members. Cohesiveness is the basis for much of the power that groups exert over their members.

A very important aspect of the functioning of any group is its norms. **Norms** are standards of conduct that prescribe appropriate behavior in various situations. If you have the slightest doubt about the existence of powerful group norms, Stanley Milgram suggests this test: Board a crowded bus, find a seat, and begin singing loudly in your fullest voice. Milgram's guess is that not more than 1 person in 100 could actually carry out these instructions.

Question: How are norms formed?

One early study of how group norms are formed made use of a striking illusion called the **autokinetic effect.** In a completely darkened room, a stationary pinpoint of light will appear to drift or move about (it is therefore "autokinetic," or "self-moving"). Muzafer Sherif (1935) found that estimates of how far the light moves vary widely from person to person. However, when two or more people give estimates at the same time, their judgments rapidly converge. A similar convergence of attitudes, beliefs, and behavior takes place among members of most groups. A good example of such convergence can be found in norms governing the use of *personal space*. Since personal space is an intriguing topic in its own right, let's take a moment to examine it.

● Personal Space—Invisible Boundaries

An interesting aspect of social behavior is the effort people expend to regulate the space around their bodies. Each person has an invisible "spatial envelope" that defines his or her **personal space** and extends "I" or "me" boundaries past the skin.

Question: What effect does personal space have on behavior?

Maintaining and regulating personal space directly affects many social interactions. There are unspoken rules covering the interpersonal distance considered appropriate for formal business, casual conversation, waiting in line with strangers, and other situations. The study of rules for the personal use of space is called **proxemics** (Hall, 1974) (Fig. 23–2).

The existence of personal space and the nature of proxemics can be demonstrated by "invading" the space of another person. The next time you are talking with an acquaintance, move closer and watch the reaction. Most people show immediate signs of discomfort and step back to reestablish their original distance. Those who hold their ground will turn to the side, look away, or position an arm in front of themselves as a kind of barrier to intrusion. If you persistently edge toward your subjects, you should find it easy to move them several feet from their original positions.

Question: Would this technique work with a good friend?

Possibly not. Conventions governing comfortable or acceptable distances vary according to relationships as well as activities. Hall (1966) identified four basic zones. (Listed distances apply to face-to-face interactions in North American culture.)

1. Intimate distance. For the majority of American adults, the most private personal space extends about 18 inches out from the skin. Entry within this space (face to face) is reserved for special people or special circumstances. Lovemaking, comforting others, cuddling children, and massage all take place within this space. So does wrestling!

2. Personal distance. This is the distance maintained in comfortable interaction with friends. It extends from about 1½ to 4 feet from the body. Personal distance basically keeps people within "arm's reach" of each other.

3. Social distance. Impersonal business and casual social gatherings take place in a range of about 4 to 12 feet. This distance eliminates most touching, and it formalizes conversation by requiring greater voice projection. "Important people" in many business offices use the imposing width of their desks to maintain social distance.

4. Public distance. When people are separated by more than 12 feet, interactions take on a decidedly formal quality. At this distance people look "flat" and the voice must be raised. Formal speeches, lectures, business meetings, and the like, are conducted at public distance.

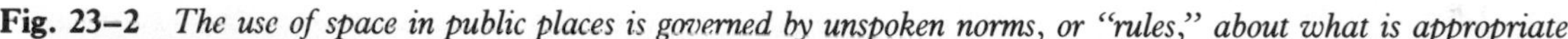

Fig. 23–2 *The use of space in public places is governed by unspoken norms, or "rules," about what is appropriate.*

Because spatial behavior is very consistent, you can learn much about your relationship to others by observing the distance you comfortably hold between yourselves. Watch for this dimension in your daily social activities.

We have now explored some basic facts of social life and a striking example of group norms. In the next section we will consider a kind of impromptu detective work that we engage in as we try to guess the motives of others and the causes of their actions. Let's see how this is done.

● Social Perception—Behind the Mask

As much as we might like to think otherwise, it is probably impossible to completely know another person. In fact, in many instances we must form impressions of people from only the smallest shreds of evidence. How do we form such impressions? How do they affect our behavior? Many of the answers lie in **attribution,** the process of making inferences about behavior. (Attribution was also discussed briefly in Chapter 12.) To learn how we fill in the "person behind the mask," let's further explore the making of attributions.

Attribution Theory

Two people enter a restaurant and order different meals. One person tastes her food, then salts it. The second salts his food before tasting it. How would you explain their behavior? In the first instance, you might assume that the *food* needed salt. If so, you have attributed the woman's actions to an **external** cause. In the second case, you might be more inclined to conclude that the man must really *like* salt. If so, you would be saying that the cause of his behavior is **internal** (McGee & Snyder, 1975).

Question: What effects do such interpretations have?

It is difficult to fully understand social behavior without considering internal and external attributions. For instance, let's say that Jim, who is in one of your classes, seems to avoid you. You see Jim at a market. Do you say hello to him? It could depend on how you have explained Jim's actions to yourself (Wegner & Vallacher, 1977). Have you assumed his avoidance is caused by shyness? Coincidence? Dislike?

Question: How do people make such judgments?

Making Attributions Two factors that greatly influence attribution are the **consistency** and **distinctiveness** of a person's behavior (Kelly, 1967). If Jim has consistently avoided you, it is clear that he was not just in a bad mood on each occasion, so coincidence is ruled out. Still, Jim's avoidance could mean he is shy, not that he dislikes you. This is why distinctiveness is also important. If Jim seems to avoid others, too, you may conclude that he is shy. If his avoidance is consistently and distinctively linked with you, you will probably assume that he dislikes you. You could be wrong, of course, but your behavior toward Jim will change just the same.

To infer causes, we typically take into account the behavior of the **actor,** the **object** of the action, and the **setting** in which the action occurs (Kelly, 1967). Imagine, for example, that someone compliments your taste in clothes. If you are at a picnic, you may attribute this compliment to what you are wearing (the "object"), unless, of course, you're wearing your worst "grubbies." If you are, you may simply assume that the person (or "actor") is friendly, or tactful. However, if you are at a clothing store and a salesperson compliments you, you will probably attribute it to the setting—not to what you are wearing or to the salesperson's true feelings. In making attributions, we are very sensitive to **situational demands.** When a person is quiet and polite in church or at a funeral, it tells us little about the individual's motives. The situation demands such behavior.

When situational demands are quite strong, we tend to **discount** claims that a person's actions are internally caused (also see Highlight 23–1). For example, you have probably discounted the sincerity of professional athletes who endorse shaving creams, hair tonics, deodorants, and the like. Obviously, the athletes' endorsements are well explained by the large sums of money they receive. It's not necessary to assume they actually *like* the potions they sell.

Consensus (or agreement) is another factor affecting attribution. A consensus in the behavior of a number of people implies that the behavior has an external cause. If millions of people go to see a particular movie, we tend to say *the movie* is good. If someone you know goes to see a movie 6 times, when others are staying away in droves, the tendency is to assume that *the person* likes "that type of movie."

Actor and Observer Let's say that at the last 5 parties you have attended, you've seen a woman named Pam. Based on this, you assume that Pam is very outgoing and likes to socialize. You see Pam at yet another gathering and mention that she seems to like parties. She says, "Actually, I hate these parties, but I get invited to play my tuba at them. My music teacher says I need to practice in front of an audience, so I keep attending these dumb events. Want to hear a Sousa march?"

● HIGHLIGHT 23–1
Self-Handicapping—Smoke Screen for Failure

Have you ever known someone who got drunk before taking an exam? Why would a person risk failure in this way? Often, the reason lies in an interesting effect called **self-handicapping.**

Steven Berglas (1986) has done studies showing that self-handicapping occurs when a person does not feel very confident about succeeding. To protect a fragile self-image, people sometimes arrange to be evaluated while "handicapped." That way, they can attribute failure to the handicap. And what if they succeed? Well, so much the better. Their self-image then gets a boost because they succeeded under conditions that everyone knows hinder performance. In other words, self-handicappers try to arrange a no-lose situation in which their positive image of themselves is protected no matter what the outcome.

There are many ways to arrange self-handicapping. In Chapter 1, for example, we discussed how procrastination on school assignments may actually be an attempt to protect one's self-image. Of the many ways to self-handicap, however, drinking alcohol is among the most popular—and dangerous. In the eyes of many, alcohol reduces personal responsibility for performance. Therefore, a person who is drunk can attribute failure to being "loaded," while accepting success if it occurs.

A person who gets drunk at times when he or she will be evaluated should be aware that this represents self-handicapping. Examples include being drunk for school exams, job interviews, and an important first date. Those who cope with anxiety in this way run a high risk of developing a pattern of alcohol abuse.

Any time you set up reasonable excuses for a poor performance, you are self-handicapping. Most of us have used self-handicapping at times when we faced a difficult challenge and were doubtful about success. Indeed, life would be harsh if we didn't sometimes give ourselves a break from accepting total responsibility for success or failure. Self-handicapping, therefore, becomes a problem when it turns into a habit, rather than a way of coping with life's harshest demands (Kleinke, 1986). So, watch out for self-handicapping, but don't be too hard on yourself.

We seldom know the real reasons for others' actions. This is why we tend to infer causes from *circumstances*. However, in doing so, we often make mistakes of the type just described. The most common error is to attribute the actions of *others* to *internal causes*, while attributing our *own* behavior to situations (*external causes*) (Jones & Nisbett, 1971; Kelly, 1971). This mistake is made so often that it is called the **fundamental attributional error** (Ross, 1977).

Psychologists have found that we consistently attribute the behavior of others to their wants, motives, and personality traits. In contrast, we tend to find external explanations for our own behavior. No doubt you chose *your* major in school because of what it has to offer. Other students choose *their* majors because of the kind of people they are (Wegner & Vallacher, 1977). And, of course, other people who don't leave tips in restaurants are cheapskates. If you don't leave a tip, it's because the service was bad.

Compare: Some Core Concepts of Attribution Theory

Attribution The process of mentally ascribing one's own behavior, and that of others, to various causes.

External cause A cause of behavior that is assumed to lie outside a person.

Internal cause A cause of behavior that is assumed to lie within a person; for instance, a need, preference, or personality trait.

Consistency As a basis for making causal attributions, noticing that a behavior changes very little in similar situations on different occasions.

Distinctiveness As a basis for making causal attributions, noticing that a behavior occurs only under a specific (distinct) set of circumstances.

Situational demands Unstated expectations that define desirable or appropriate behavior in various settings and social situations.

Discounting When making attributions, the tendency to downgrade internal explanations of behaviors that appear to have strong external causes.

Fundamental attributional error The tendency to attribute the behavior of others to internal causes (personality, likes, emotions, and so forth) while attributing one's own behavior to external causes (situations and circumstances).

Implications As you can see, attribution theory attempts to summarize how we think about ourselves and others. It also tries to identify some of the consistent errors or biases in our interpretations. In addition to providing a better understanding of behavior, attribution theory has helped identify some practical problems. Let's conclude with a brief example.

Ye Old Double Standard Attribution research has uncovered an interesting double standard for men and women. In a study by Deaux and Emswiller (1974), men and women overheard a male or female perform extremely well on a perception task. Subjects were then asked to rate whether the test taker's success was due to his or her ability, to luck, or to some combination of the two. Both men and women attributed male success mainly to skill and women's performances mainly to luck! This was true even though male and female performances were identical. Such attributions no doubt dog the heels of many talented and successful women.

Learning Check

1. *Male, female,* and *adolescent* are examples of ______________________ roles.
2. Status refers to a set of expected behaviors associated with a social position. T or F?
3. Research has shown that the number of first-name acquaintances needed to interconnect two widely separated strangers averages about 7 people. T or F?
4. The Stanford prison experiment demonstrated the powerful influence of the autokinetic effect on behavior. T or F?
5. Social psychology is the study of how people behave ______________________________________.
6. If two people position themselves 5 feet apart while conversing, they are separated by a gap referred to as ____________ distance.
7. When situational demands are strong, we tend to attribute a person's actions to internal causes. T or F?
8. The fundamental attributional error is to attribute the actions of others to internal causes, while attributing our own behavior to external causes. T or F?

Answers:
1. ascribed 2. F 3. T 4. F 5. in the presence of others 6. social 7. F 8. T

The Need for Affiliation—Come Together

Question: Why do people choose to associate with others?

We have already observed that the **need to affiliate** appears to be a basic human characteristic. But why? Probably because affiliation helps meet needs for approval, support, friendship, and information. We also seek company to alleviate fear or anxiety. An experiment in which college women were threatened with painful electric shock serves as an illustration.

Zilstein's Shock Shop

A man introduced as Dr. Gregor Zilstein ominously explained to arriving subjects, "We would like to give each of you a series of electric shocks . . . these shocks will hurt, they will be painful." In the room was a frightening electrical device that seemed to verify Zilstein's plans. While waiting to be shocked, each subject was given a choice of waiting alone or with other subjects. Women frightened in this way more often chose to wait with others than did subjects told that the shock would be a mild tickle or tingle (Schachter, 1959).

Apparently, the frightened women found it comforting or reassuring to be with others. The tempting conclusion is that "misery loves company." But this is not completely accurate.

In a later experiment, women expecting to be shocked were given the option of waiting with other shock subjects, with women waiting to see their advisors, or alone. Most subjects chose to wait with other future "victims." In short, misery seems to love miserable company! In general, we tend to seek the company of people in circumstances similar to our own.

Question: Is there a reason for this?

Yes. Other people provide information for evaluating one's own reactions. When a situation is threatening or unfamiliar, or when a person is in doubt, *social comparisons* serve as a guide for behavior.

Social Comparison Theory In some cases objective standards for self-evaluation exist. If I want to know how tall I am, I simply get out a yardstick. But how do I know if I am a good athlete, guitarist, worker, parent, or friend? How do I know if my views on politics, religion, or the latest rock album are correct? The only yardstick available for such evaluations is provided by comparing myself to others.

Eminent social psychologist Leon Festinger (1954) was among the first to point out that group membership fills needs for **social comparison.** When there are no objective standards, we must turn to others to evaluate our actions, feelings, opinions, or abilities. When students gather to compare notes after a classroom exam, they satisfy needs for social comparison.

Festinger emphasizes that social comparisons are not made randomly or on some ultimate scale. To illustrate, let's say we ask a student if she is a good tennis player. If she were to compare herself to a professional, the answer would be no. But this tells little about her relative ability. In her group of tennis partners, she might be considered an excellent player. Useful personal evaluation requires comparison with people of similar backgrounds, abilities, and circumstances. On a fair scale of comparison, our tennis player knows she is good and takes pride in her skills.

In the same way, thinking of yourself as successful, talented, responsible, or fairly paid depends entirely on whom you compare yourself with. Social comparison theory holds that a desire for self-evaluation provides a general motive for associating with others and determines which groups we join.

Question: Don't people also affiliate out of attraction for one another?

They do, of course. The next section tells why.

Interpersonal Attraction—Social Magnetism?

"Birds of a feather flock together." "Familiarity breeds contempt." "Opposites attract." "Absence makes the heart grow fonder." Interest in what attracts people to one another has spawned an extensive folklore about what factors are important. This is understandable, since **interpersonal attraction** is the basis for most voluntary social relationships.

Question: What attracts people to each other?

Social psychologist Elliot Aronson (1969) lists several factors that determine with whom you are likely to become friends.

1. Physical proximity. It may be difficult to admit, but our friends (and even lovers) are selected more on the basis of opportunity than we might like to believe. Nearness plays a powerful role in determining friendships. In a study of friendship patterns in a campus married-student housing complex, it was found that the closer people lived to each other, the more likely they were to be friends (Festinger et al., 1950). People in love like to think they have found the "one and only" person in the universe for them. In reality, they have probably found the one and only person in a 5-mile radius—or at least within driving distance (Buss, 1985)!

A main reason for proximity's effect is that it increases the *frequency of contact* between people. A variety of experiments show that we are generally attracted to people with whom we have had frequent contact (Saegert et al., 1973). In other words, there does seem to be a "boy-next-door" or "girl-next-door" effect in friendship (Fig. 23–3).

2. Physical attractiveness. As might be expected, beautiful people are consistently rated more attractive than those of average appearance. This is another example of the *halo effect* (see Chapter 16), in which it is assumed that attractive people are also intelligent, witty, honest, and so on.

Being physically attractive seems to be an advantage for both males and females, but in our culture beauty has more influence on a woman's fate than on a man's. For instance, a study of dating patterns of college dormitory residents found a strong relationship between

Fig. 23–3 *What attracts people to each other? Proximity and frequency of contact have a surprisingly large impact.*

physical beauty in women and their frequency of dating. For men, looks were unrelated to dating frequency (Krebs & Adinolfi, 1975). After marriage there is a tendency for attractive women to be paired with highly educated men with high incomes. For men, however, there is little relationship between attractiveness and the achievement of status (Udry & Eckland, 1984).

If you view this state of affairs as rather shallow and sexist, it may be reassuring to know that beauty is a factor mainly in initial acquaintance. Later, more substantial personal qualities become important (Berscheid & Walster, 1974). It takes more than appearance to make a lasting relationship.

3. Competence. We are also attracted to those who are talented or competent, but there is an interesting twist to this.

Clever but Clumsy

In an experiment on attraction, college students listened to one of four tapes of a supposed candidate for the "College Quiz Bowl." On two of the tapes the person was represented as highly intelligent; on the other two he was depicted as average in ability. One of the "intelligent" and one of the "average" tapes include an incident in which the candidate clumsily spilled coffee on himself. Those listening to the tapes rated as *most* attractive the superior candidate who blundered, and as *least* attractive the student who was average and clumsy. The superior but clumsy student was more attractive than the student who was only superior. (Aronson, 1969)

The upshot of this experiment seems to be that we like people who are competent but human.

4. Similarity. Take a moment to mentally list as many of your friends as you can. What do they have in common (other than the joy of knowing you)? It is highly likely that most are close to you in age and of the same sex and race as you. There will be exceptions, of course. However, similarity on these three dimensions is the general rule for friendships (Huston & Levinger, 1978).

One of the most consistent findings about interpersonal attraction is that people with similar backgrounds, interests, attitudes, or beliefs are attracted to each other (Byrne, 1971). This is probably at least partially due to the reinforcing value of seeing our beliefs and attitudes affirmed by others. It shows we are "right" and reveals that they are clever people as well! Similarity also affects mate selection (see Highlight 23–2).

Question: How do people who are not yet friends learn if they are similar?

Self-Disclosure Getting to know others requires a willingness to talk about more than just the weather, sports, or nuclear physics. At some point you must begin to share private thoughts and feelings and reveal more of your true self. Engaging in such **self-disclosure** is a major step toward friendship. Experimental work confirms that we more often reveal ourselves to persons we like than to those we find less attractive (Chaiken & Derlega, 1974).

Disclosing oneself to others requires a degree of trust. Many people play it safe, or "close to the vest," with people they do not know well. Indeed, there are definite norms about when self-disclosure is acceptable and when it is not. Moderate self-disclosure leads to **reciprocity** (a return in kind) (Huston & Levinger, 1978). **Overdisclosure,** however, gives rise to suspicion and reduced attraction (Rubin, 1975). (Imagine standing in line at a market and having the person in front of you say, "Lately I've been thinking about how I really feel about myself. I think that I'm pretty well adjusted, but I occasionally

● HIGHLIGHT 23–2
Selecting a Mate—Reflections in a Social Mirror

Ninety percent of all people in Western societies marry at some point. What, beyond attraction, determines how people pair up? The answer is that we tend to marry someone who is like us in almost every way.

A variety of studies show that people who marry are highly similar in age, education, race, religion, and ethnic background. In addition, the correlation of attitudes and opinions for married couples is .5. For mental abilities it is .4, and for socioeconomic status, height, weight, and eye color it is .3. In general, you are far more likely to choose someone similar to yourself as a mate than someone very different.

A second question of interest concerns what traits people look for in a mate. In the United States, both men and women agree that the following are the first 6 most important qualities: kindness and understanding, intelligence, exciting personality, good health, adaptability, and physical attractiveness.

Despite such agreement, men and women do differ on some rankings. Men, for instance, rank physical attractiveness as the third most important feature, whereas women rank it sixth. A second major difference concerns good earning capacity: Men rank it eleventh; women rank it eighth. Apparently, for most people, romance is leavened with a dash of practicality. Even so, kindness and understanding are ranked first by almost everyone. (Source: Buss, 1985) have some questions about my sexual adequacy.") When self-disclosure proceeds at a moderate pace, it is accompanied by growing trust and intimacy. When it is too rapid or inappropriate, we are likely to "back off" and wonder about the person's motives.

Social Exchange Theory As relationships progress, quite often they can be understood in terms of maximizing rewards while minimizing "costs" in any **social exchange.** When a relationship ceases to be attractive, people often say, "I'm not getting anything out of it any more." Actually, they probably are, but their costs—in terms of effort, irritation, or lowered self-esteem—have exceeded their rewards. According to social exchange theory, we unconsciously weigh such rewards and costs. For a relationship to last, it must be *profitable* (its rewards must exceed its costs) for both parties.

Question: Does romantic attraction differ from interpersonal attraction?

In an earlier discussion, we treated love as an emotion (see Chapter 12) and pointed out that passionate or romantic love is marked by heightened arousal. To get another angle on love, psychologist Zick Rubin (1973) chose to think of it as an attitude held by one person toward another. This allowed him to develop "liking" and "love" scales to measure each "attitude" (see Box 23–1). Next, he asked dating couples to complete each scale twice, once with their date in mind and once for a close friend of the same sex.

Question: What were the results?

Scores for love of partner and love of friend differed more than those for liking (Table 23–1). In other words, dating couples liked *and* loved their partners, but mostly liked their friends. Women, however, were a little more "loving" of their friends than were men. Does this reflect real differences in the strength of male friendships and female friendships? Probably not, since it is more acceptable in our culture for women to express love for one another than it is for men.

Another way in which love and friendship differ is mutual absorption. Romantic love, in contrast to simple liking, usually involves deep **mutual absorption** of the lovers. In other words, lovers (unlike friends) attend almost exclusively to one another. It's not surprising, then, that couples scoring high on Rubin's love scale spend more time gazing into each other's eyes than do couples who score low on the scale. As the song says, "Millions of people go by, but they all disappear from view—'cause I only have eyes for you" (Rubin, 1970).

Love Scale

1. If ____________ were feeling bad, my first duty would be to cheer him (her) up.
2. I feel that I can confide in ____________ about virtually everything.
3. I find it easy to ignore ____________'s faults.

Liking Scale

1. When I am with ____________, we are almost always in the same mood.
2. I think that ____________ is unusually well adjusted.
3. I would highly recommend ____________ for a responsible job.

Box 23–1 *Sample love-scale and liking-scale items. Each scale consists of 13 items similar to those shown. Scores on these scales correspond to other indications of love and liking. (Reprinted by permission of Zick Rubin.)*

Table 23–1 Love and Liking for Date and Same-Sex Close Friend

	MEAN SCORES	
CONDITION	**WOMEN**	**MEN**
Love for partner	89.46	89.37
Liking for partner	88.48	84.65
Love for friend	65.27	55.07
Liking for friend	80.47	79.10

Source: Rubin, 1970.

Learning Check

Before reading more, check your comprehension with the following questions.

1. Women threatened with electric shock in an experiment generally chose to wait alone or with other women not taking part in the experiment. T or F?

2. The need to affiliate is related to interest in social comparison. T or F?

3. Social comparisons are made pretty much at random. T or F?
4. Interpersonal attraction is increased by all but one of the following. (Which does not fit?)
   a. physical proximity *b.* competence *c.* similarity *d.* social costs
5. High levels of self-disclosure are reciprocated in most social encounters. T or F?
6. Women rate their friends higher on the love scale than do men. T or F?
7. The most striking finding about marriage patterns in the United States is that most people choose mates whose personalities are quite unlike their own. T or F?

Answers:
1. F 2. T 3. F 4. *d* 5. F 6. T 7. F

Social Influence—Follow the Leader

Question: What is social influence?

Imagine a traffic signal brightly flashing the word WAIT. As you and a number of other pedestrians wait for it to change, a well-dressed man in a suit crosses against the light. How many people follow him? Do you think the answer would be different if the man were dressed in a denim shirt, patched pants, and scuffed shoes?

One of the most heavily researched topics in social psychology concerns the effects of **social influence.** When people interact, they almost always affect one another's behavior. The street-corner setting was used in an early experiment on social influence. As you might have guessed, more people followed the well-dressed man than the one dressed in shabby clothes (Lefkowitz et al., 1955).

In another sidewalk experiment, various numbers of people were assembled on a busy New York City street. On cue they all looked at a sixth-floor window across the street. A camera recorded the number of passersby who also stopped to stare. The larger the influencing group, the more people were swayed to join in staring at the window (Milgram et al., 1969).

Question: Are there different kinds of social influence?

Social influence ranges from simple suggestion to intensive indoctrination (brainwashing). Everyday behavior is probably most influenced by group pressures for conformity. Conformity situations develop when individuals become aware of differences between themselves and group actions, norms, or values (McGuire, 1969). Let us consider this important dimension of social life in more detail.

Conformity

When John first started working at the Fleegle Flange Factory, he found it easy to process 300 flanges an hour, while those around him averaged only 200. Other workers told him to slow down and take it easy. "I get bored," he said and continued to do 300 flanges an hour. At first John had been welcomed, but now conversations broke up when he approached, and other workers laughed at him or ignored him when he spoke. Although he never made a conscious decision to conform, in another week John's output had slowed to 200 flanges an hour.

As mentioned earlier, all groups have unspoken shared rules of conduct called *norms*. The broadest norms, defined by society as a whole, establish "normal" or acceptable behavior in most situations. Comparing hair styles, habits of speech, dress, eating habits, and social customs in two or more cultures makes it clear that we all conform to social norms. In fact, a degree of uniformity is necessary if we are to interact comfortably. Imagine being totally unable to anticipate the actions of others. In stores, schools, and homes this would be frustrating and disturbing. On the highways it would be lethal.

Perhaps the most basic of all group norms is, as John discovered, "Thou shalt conform!" (Suedfeld, 1966). This is equally true for the Hell's Angels, and Daughters of the American Revolution, a street-corner gang, or the board of directors of a large corporation. Groups of all kinds exert considerable pressures toward uniformity on their members. Like it or not, everyday life is filled with instances of conformity (Fig. 23–4).

Question: How strong are group pressures for conformity?

The Asch Experiment One of the better-known experiments on conformity was staged by Solomon Asch in the early 1950s. Asch's experiment is best appreciated by placing yourself in the position of a subject. Assume that you are seated at a table with 6 other students. Your task is actually quite simple. On each trial, you are asked to select from among 3 lines the one that matches a standard line (Fig. 23–5).

Fig. 23–4 *Conformity is a subtle dimension of daily life. Notice the similarities in clothing and hair styles among these couples.*

As the testing begins, each subject announces an answer for the first card. When your turn comes, you find yourself in complete agreement with the others. "This isn't hard at all," you say to yourself. For several more trials your answers correspond to those of the group. Then comes a shock. All 6 people announce that line 1 matches the standard, and you were about to say line 3 matches. Suddenly you feel alone and upset. You nervously look at the lines again as the room falls silent. Everyone seems to be staring at you as the experimenter awaits your answer. Do you yield to the group?

Fig. 23–5 *Stimuli used in Solomon Asch's conformity experiments.*

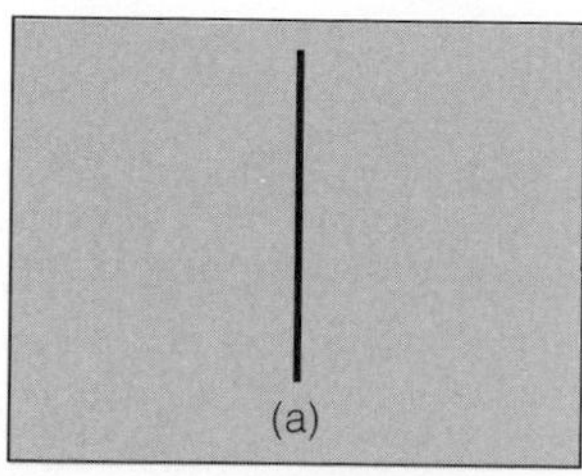

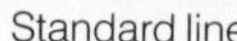

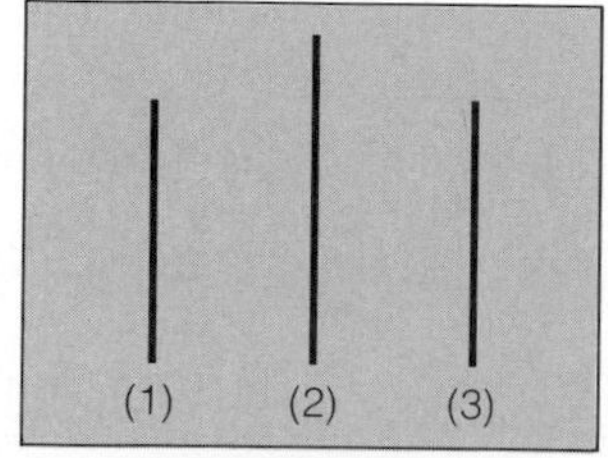

In this experiment the other "students" were all accomplices coached to give the wrong answer on about a third of the trials. Few real subjects suspected trickery; hence, the group pressure created was very realistic (Asch, 1956).

Question: How many people yielded to group pressure?

Subjects conformed to the group on about one-third of the critical trials. Of those tested, 75 percent yielded at least once. The significance of these results is underscored by the fact that the other subjects tested alone erred in less than 1 percent of their judgments. Those who yielded to group pressures were clearly denying what their eyes told them.

Question: Are some people more susceptible to group pressures than others?

A variety of experiments have shown that people with high needs for structure or certainty are more likely to be influenced. People who are anxious, low in self-confidence, or concerned with the opinions or approval of others are also more susceptible. Certain situations also encourage conformity, sometimes with disastrous results (see Highlight 23–3).

Group Factors in Conformity In most of our experiences with groups, we have been rewarded with acceptance and approval for conformity and threatened with rejection or ridicule for nonconformity. These reactions are called **group sanctions.** Negative sanctions (or punishments) for nonconformity range from laughter, staring, or social disapproval to complete rejection or formal ostracism. This is illustrated by later experiments in which Asch made up groups of 6 real subjects and 1 trained dissenter. When "Mr. Odd" announced his wrong answers, he was greeted with derisive laughter and sidelong glances.

Question: Wouldn't the effectiveness of group sanctions depend on the importance of the group?

Yes. And this is why the Asch experiments are impressive. Since these were only temporary groups, sanctions were informal and rejection had no lasting importance, and yet the power of the group was evident.

Question: What factors, besides importance of the group, affect the degree of conformity?

Earlier we described an experiment in which passersby were influenced by a group of people staring at a building.

HIGHLIGHT 23–3
Groupthink—Agreement at Any Cost

What happens when people in positions of power fall prey to pressures for conformity? To find out, Yale psychologist Irving Janis analyzed a collection of disastrous decisions made by government officials. His conclusion? Many such fiascoes are the result of **groupthink**—a compulsion by decision-makers to maintain each other's approval, even at the cost of critical thinking. Groupthink has been blamed for many embarrassments, such as the Susan B. Anthony dollar and John F. Kennedy's backing of the Bay of Pigs invasion in Cuba. It also seems to have contributed to the *Challenger* space shuttle disaster.

The core of groupthink is misguided group loyalty that prevents members from "rocking the boat" or questioning weak arguments and sloppy thinking. The resulting conformity pressures and self-censorship cause members to believe that greater agreement and unanimity exists than actually does (Janis & Mann, 1977).

To prevent groupthink, Janis suggests that group leaders should (1) define each group member's role as that of critical evaluator; (2) avoid stating any personal preferences in the beginning; (3) state the problem factually, without bias; (4) invite a group member or outside person to play devil's advocate. In addition, Janis suggests that there should be a "second-chance" meeting to reevaluate important decisions. That is, each decision should be reached twice. In an age clouded by the threat of nuclear war and similar disasters, even stronger solutions to the problem of groupthink would be welcome. Perhaps we should form a group to think about it?!

We noted that the larger the group, the greater the number of people influenced. In Asch's face-to-face groups the size of the majority also made a difference, but a surprisingly small one. In other experiments, the number of conforming subjects increased dramatically as the majority was increased from 2 to 3 people. However, a majority of 3 produced about as much yielding as a majority of 8. Next time you want to talk someone into (or out of) something, take two friends along and see what a difference it makes! (Sometimes it helps if the two are large and mean looking.)

Even more important than the size of the majority is its **unanimity.** Having at least one person in your corner can greatly reduce pressures to conform. When Asch provided subjects with an ally (who also opposed the majority by giving the correct answer), conformity was lessened. In terms of numbers, a unanimous majority of 3 is more powerful than a majority of 8 with 1 dissenting. Perhaps this accounts for the rich diversity of human attitudes, beliefs, opinions, and lifestyles. If you can find at least one other person who sees things as you do (no matter how weird), you can be relatively secure in your opposition to other viewpoints.

Learning Check

1. The effect one person's behavior has on another is called ______________.
2. Conformity is a normal aspect of social life. T or F?
3. Subjects in Solomon Asch's conformity study yielded on about 75 percent of the critical trials. T or F?
4. Nonconformity is punished by negative group ______________.
5. Janis uses the term ______________ to describe a compulsion among decision-making groups to maintain an illusion of unanimity.

Answers:

1. social influence 2. T 3. F 4. sanctions 5. groupthink

Social Power—Who Can Do What to Whom?

Here's something to think about: Whereas *strength* is a quality possessed by individuals, *power* is always social—it arises when people come together and disappears when they disperse. In trying to understand the ways in which people are able to influence each other, it is helpful to distinguish among five types of **social power** (Raven, 1974).

Reward power lies in the ability to reward a person for complying with desired behavior. Teachers try to exert reward power over their students through the use of grades. Employers command reward power by their control of wages and bonuses.

Coercive power is based on the ability to punish a person for failure to comply. Coercive power is the basis for most statute law, in that fines or imprisonment are used to control behavior.

Legitimate power comes from acceptance of a person as an agent of an established social order. For example, elected leaders and supervisors have legitimate power. So does a teacher in the classroom, but outside the classroom that power would have to come from another source.

Referent power is based on respect for or identification with a person or a group. The person "refers to" the source of referent power for direction. Referent power is responsible for much of the conformity observed in groups.

Expert power is based on recognition that another person has knowledge or expertise necessary for achieving a goal. Allowing teachers or experts to guide behavior because you believe in their ability to produce desirable results is an example. Physicians, lawyers, psychologists, and plumbers have expert power.

A person who has power in one situation may have very little in another. In those situations where a person has power, he or she is described as an *authority*. In the next section we will investigate *obedience*. Obedience is a special type of conformity to the demands of an authority.

Obedience—Would You Electrocute a Stranger?

The question is this: If ordered to do so, would you shock a man with a known heart condition who is screaming and asking to be released? Certainly we can assume that few people would do so. Or can we? In Nazi Germany, obedient soldiers (once average citizens) helped slaughter over 9 million people in concentration camps. Another example of the same phenomenon was an infamous incident during the Vietnam War when Lt. William Calley led a bloody massacre of helpless civilians at My Lai. Do such inhumane acts reflect deep character flaws? Are they the acts of heartless psychopaths or crazed killers? Or are they simply the result of obedience to authority? What are the limits of such obedience? These are questions that puzzled social psychologist Stanley Milgram (1965) when he began a provocative series of studies on obedience.

Question: How did Milgram study obedience?

As was true of the Asch experiments, Milgram's research is best appreciated by imagining yourself as a subject. Place yourself in this situation.

Milgram's Study Imagine answering a newspaper ad to take part in a "learning" experiment at Yale University. When you arrive, a coin is flipped and a second subject, a pleasant-looking man in his 50s, is designated the "learner." By chance you have become the "teacher."

Your task is to read a list of word pairs to be memorized by the learner. You are to punish him with an electric shock each time he makes a mistake. The learner is taken to an adjacent room and you watch as he is seated in an "electric chair" apparatus, and electrodes are attached to his wrists. You are then escorted to your position in front of a "shock generator." On this device is a row of 30 switches labeled from 15 to 450 volts and accompanied by descriptions ranging from "Slight Shock" to "Extreme Intensity Shock" and finally "Danger Severe Shock." Your instructions are to administer a shock each time the learner makes a mistake. You are to begin with 15 volts and then move one switch (15 volts) higher for each additional mistake.

The experiment begins, and the learner soon makes his first error. You flip a switch. More mistakes. Rapidly you reach the 75-volt level. The learner moans after each shock. At 100 volts he complains he has a heart condition. At 150 volts he says he no longer wants to continue and demands release. At 300 volts he screams and says he can no longer give answers.

At some point during the experiment, you begin to protest to the experimenter. "That man has a heart condition," you say; "I'm not going to kill that man." The experimenter says, "Please continue." Another shock and another scream from the learner and you say, "You mean I've got to keep going up the scale? No, sir. I'm not going to give him 450 volts!" The experimenter says, "The experiment requires that you continue." For a time the learner refuses to answer any more questions and screams with each shock (Milgram, 1965). Then he falls chillingly silent for the remainder of the experiment.

Question: I can't believe many people would do this. What happened?

Milgram also doubted that many people would obey his orders, and when he polled a group of psychiatrists before the experiment, they predicted that less than 1 percent of those tested would obey. The astounding fact is that 65 percent of those tested obeyed completely by going all the way to the 450-volt level. Virtually no one stopped short of 300 volts ("Severe Shock") (Fig. 23–6).

Question: Was the learner injured?

The time has come to reveal that the "learner" was actually an actor who turned a tape recorder on and off in the shock room. No shocks were ever administered, but the dilemma for the "teacher" was quite real. Subjects protested, sweated, trembled, stuttered, bit their lips, and laughed nervously. Clearly, they were disturbed by what they were doing, but most obeyed the experimenter's orders.

Question: Why did so many people obey?

Milgram's Follow-Up Some have suggested that the prestige of Yale University contributed to subjects' willingness to obey. Could subjects have assumed that the professor running the experiment would not really allow anyone to be hurt? To investigate this possibility, the experiment was rerun in a shabby office building in nearby Bridgeport, Connecticut. There was nothing in either the location or the experimenter's appearance to inspire confidence. Under these conditions fewer people obeyed (48 percent), but the reduction was minor.

Milgram was quite disturbed by the willingness of people to knuckle under to authority and to senselessly shock someone. In later experiments, he tried in various ways to reduce obedience. He found that distance between the teacher and the learner was of importance. When subjects were in the *same room* as the learner, only 40 percent were fully obedient. When they were *face to face* with the learner and required to force his hand down on a simulated "shock plate," only 30 percent obeyed (Fig. 23–7). *Distance* from the authority also had an effect. When the experimenter delivered his orders over the phone, only 22 percent obeyed. You may doubt that Milgram's study of obedience applies to you. If so, take a moment to read Highlight 23–4.

Milgram's research raises nagging questions about our willingness to commit antisocial or inhumane acts commanded by a "legitimate authority." The excuse so often given by war criminals—"I was only following orders"—takes on new meaning in this light. Milgram suggested that when directions come from an authority, people rationalize that they are not personally responsible for their actions (Fig. 23–8).

Question: Aren't you taking an overly dim view of obedience?

Fig. 23–6 *Results of Milgram's obedience experiment. Only a minority of subjects refused to provide shocks, even at the most extreme intensities. The first substantial drop in obedience occurred at the 300-volt level (Milgram, 1963).*

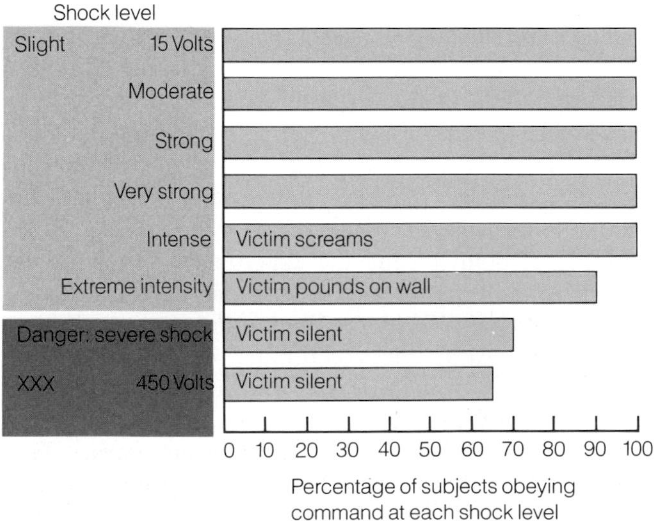

Fig. 23–7 *Physical distance from the "learner" had a significant effect on the percentage of subjects obeying orders.*

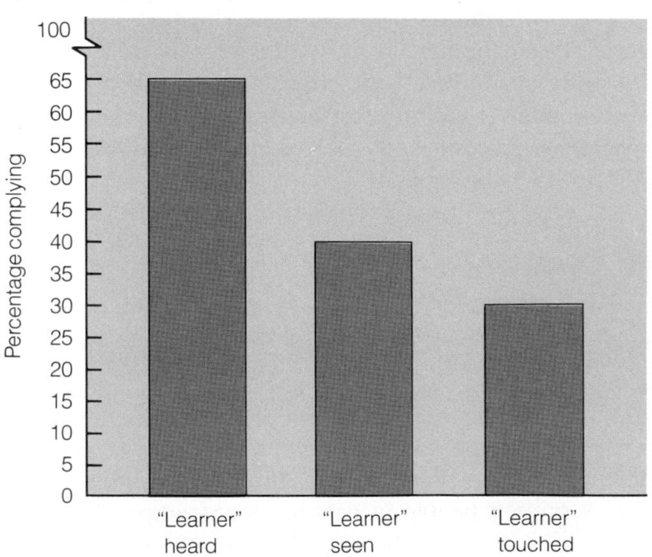

HIGHLIGHT 23–4
Quack Like a Duck

The demonstration described here has become a favorite of many psychology teachers (Halonen, 1986). Imagine your response to the following events. On the first day of class, your professor begins to establish the basic rules of behavior for the course. Seats are assigned, and you must move to a new location. You are told not to talk during class. Your professor tells you that you must have permission to leave early. You are told to bring your textbook to class at all times.

Up to this point, you might have no problem with your professor's orders. Then the demands become less reasonable. The professor says, "Use only a pencil for taking notes. Borrow one if you must." "Take off your watch." "Keep both hands on your desk top at all times." "All students who are freshmen stand at the back of the class." The demonstration is capped by orders that you cannot follow without looking silly: "Stick two fingers up your nose and quack like a duck."

Where do you think you would draw the line in obeying such orders? In reality, you might find yourself obeying a legitimate authority long after that person's demands had become unreasonable. What would happen, though, if a few students resisted orders given early in the sequence? Would that help free others to disobey? For an answer, return to the concluding remarks on Milgram's experiment.

Fig. 23–8 *Obedience to authority is often necessary and reasonable; however, it can also be destructive.*

Obedience to authority is obviously necessary and desirable in many circumstances. Just the same, it is probably true, as C. P. Snow (1961) has observed, "When you think of the long and gloomy history of man, you will find more hideous crimes have been committed in the name of obedience than in the name of rebellion." With this in mind, let us end this discussion on a more positive note. In one of his experiments, Milgram found that group support can greatly reduce destructive obedience. When real subjects saw two other "teachers" (both actors) resist orders and walk out of the experiment, only 10 percent continued to obey. Thus, a personal act of courage or moral fortitude by one or two members of a group may free others to disobey misguided or unjust authority.

Compliance—A Foot in the Door

In *conformity* situations the pressure to "get in line" is usually indirect. When an authority commands *obedience* the pressure is direct and difficult to resist. There is a third interesting possibility. The term **compliance** has been used to describe situations in which a person with little or no authority makes a direct request to another person (Wrightsman & Deaux, 1981).

Pressures to comply are quite common. For example, a stranger might ask you to yield a phone booth so he can make a call, a saleswoman might suggest that you buy a more expensive watch than you had planned on, or a co-worker might ask you for a quarter to buy a cup of coffee.

Question: What determines whether a person will comply with a request?

Many factors could be listed but three stand out as especially interesting. Let's briefly consider each.

The Foot-in-the-Door Effect People who sell door-to-door have long recognized that once they get a foot in the door, a sale is almost a sure thing. To state the **foot-in-the-door principle** more formally, a person who agrees to a small request is later more likely to comply with a larger demand. Evidence suggests, for instance, that if someone asked you to put a large, ugly sign in your front yard to promote safe driving, you would refuse. If, however, you had first agreed to put a small sign in your window, you would later be much more likely to allow the big sign to be placed in your yard (Freedman & Fraser, 1966).

The Door-in-the-Face Effect Let's say that a neighbor comes to your door and asks you to feed his dogs, water his plants, and mow his yard while he is out of town for a month. This is quite a major request—one that most people would probably turn down. Feeling only slightly guilty, you tell your neighbor that you're sorry but you can't help him out. Now, what if the same neighbor returned the next day and asked you if you would at least pick up his mail while he was gone. Chances are very good that you would honor this request, even if you might have resisted it otherwise.

Psychologist Robert Cialdini and his associates coined the term **door-in-the-face effect** to describe the reverse of the foot-in-the-door effect (Cialdini et al., 1975). On some occasions, the best way to get a person to agree to a small request is to first make a major request. After the person has turned down the major request ("slammed the door in your face"), he or she may be more willing to agree to a lesser demand.

The Low-Ball Technique Anyone who has purchased an automobile will recognize a third way of inducing compliance. Automobile dealers are notorious for convincing customers to buy a car by offering "low-ball" prices that undercut the competition. The dealer first gets the customer to agree to buy at an attractively low price. Then, once the customer is committed, various techniques are used to bump the price up before the sale is concluded (see Highlight 23–5). The **low-ball technique,** then, consists of getting a person committed to act and then making the terms of acting less desirable. Another example would be asking someone to lend you $5 and then upping it to $15. Or you might ask someone to give you a ride to school in the morning. Only after the person has agreed would you tell her or him that you had to be there at 6 A.M.

Passive Compliance Complying with requests is a normal part of daily social life. At times, however, a willingness to comply can exceed what is reasonable. Researcher Thomas Moriarty (1975) has demonstrated excessive, passive compliance under realistic conditions. Moriarty became interested in the "little murders" of daily life—the personal insults, rebuffs, and sacrifices of dignity that have become so common. Moriarty observed that many people will put up with almost anything to avoid a confrontation. He decided to put this passive, "no-hassle" attitude to experimental test.

HIGHLIGHT 23–5
How To Drive a Hard Bargain

Your local car lot is a good place to see compliance take place. Automobile salespersons play the compliance game daily and get very good at it. If you understand what they are up to, you will have a far better chance of resisting their tactics.

A Foot in the Door The salesperson offers you a test drive. If you accept, you will have made a small commitment of time to a particular car and to the salesperson. The salesperson will then ask you to go to an office and fill out some papers, "just to see what kind of a price" he or she can offer. If you go along, you will be further committed.

The Low-Ball Technique To get things under way, the salesperson will offer you a very good price for your trade-in or will ask you to make an offer on the new car, "any offer, no matter how low." The salesperson will then ask if you will buy the car if she or he can sell it for the price you state. If you say yes, you have virtually bought the car. Most people find it very difficult to walk away once bargaining has reached this stage.

The Hook Is Set Once buyers are "hooked" by a low-ball offer, the salesperson goes to the manager to have the sale "approved." On returning, the salesperson will tell you with great disappointment that the dealership would lose money on the deal. "Couldn't you just take a little less for the trade-in or pay a little more for the car?" the salesperson will ask. At this point, many people hesitate and grumble, but most give in and accept some "compromise" price or trade-in amount.

Milking the Sale By the time you strike a deal, you can be sure that the price you accept will give the dealership the minimum profit it requires on all sales—and probably much more. To add insult to injury, the salesperson will then try to increase the profit by convincing you to add various options to your car—extra mirrors, a stereo system, cruise control, and so forth. All of these items cost less from independent suppliers, so many people pay hundreds of dollars too much for them alone.

Evening the Odds To combat all of the preceding, get a final "best offer" in writing. Then walk out. Go to another dealer and see if the salesperson will better the price, in writing. When he or she does, return to the first dealership and negotiate for an even better price. Then decide where to buy.

In one experiment, two subjects (one actually an accomplice) were given a difficult test in a very small room. The subjects were seated back to back and left alone to work. As soon as the experimenter left, the phony subject turned on a portable cassette player at full volume. Real subjects who failed to complain were treated to a 17-minute blast of nerve-wracking rock music. The accomplice was instructed to turn the music off only after a third request. In this particular experiment, 80 percent of the subjects said nothing, although they glared, covered their ears, stopped work, and so forth. An interview later showed that most were angry or annoyed, but were afraid to tell the other "subject" to be quiet.

Question: Could it be that people failed to complain because they didn't want to disrupt the testing?

Yes, it is possible that the passivity observed in this study is unique to the experimental setting. However, when Moriarty and his students staged loud conversations behind theater patrons or people studying in a library, very few protested. In other naturalistic experiments, people were accosted in phone booths. The experimenter explained that he had left a ring in the booth and asked if the subject had found it. When the subject said no, the experimenter demanded that the subject empty his pockets. Most did.

In these and similar situations, people passively accepted having their personal rights trampled, even when objecting presented no threat to their safety. Have we become, as Moriarty puts it, "a nation of willing victims?" Certainly, we hope not. Nevertheless, researchers such as Milgram and Moriarty have identified a significant social problem. We will address this problem again in the Applications section that follows.

Learning Check

1. An ability to punish others for failure to obey is the basis for
a. referent power *b.* legitimate power *c.* expert power *d.* coercive power

2. The term *compliance* refers to situations in which a person complies with commands made by a person who has authority. T or F?

3. Obedience in Milgram's experiments was related to
a. distance between learner and teacher
b. distance between experimenter and teacher
c. obedience of others teachers
d. all of these

4. Obedience is conformity to the commands of an ______________.

5. By repeating his obedience experiment in a downtown office building, Milgram demonstrated that the prestige of Yale University was the main reason for subjects' willingness to obey in the original experiment. T or F?

6. The research of Thomas Moriarty and others has recently shifted to an interest in ______________ rather than obedience to authority.

Answers:
1. *d* 2. F 3. *d* 4. authority 5. F 6. passive compliance

Applications: Assertiveness Training—Standing Up for Your Rights

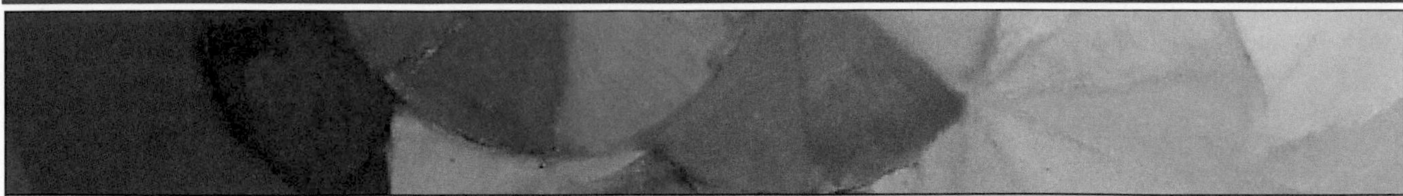

Have you ever:

- Hesitated to question an error on a restaurant bill because you were afraid of making a scene?
- Backed out of asking for a raise or a change in working conditions?
- Said yes when you wanted to say no?
- Been afraid to question a grade that seemed unfair?

Most of us have been rewarded, first as children and later as adults, for compliant, obedient, or "good" behavior. Perhaps this is why so many people find it difficult to assert themselves. Or perhaps non-assertion is related to anxiety about "making a scene" or feeling disliked by others. Whatever the causes, some people suffer tremendous anguish in any situation requiring poise, self-confidence, or self-assertion. Fortunately for these people, behavior therapist Joseph Wolpe (and others) pioneered a therapeutic technique called assertiveness training.

Question: What is done in assertiveness training?

Assertiveness training is a very direct procedure. By using group exercises, videotapes, mirrors, and staged conflicts, the behavior therapist teaches assertive behavior. People learn to practice honesty, disagreeing, questioning authority, and assertive postures and gestures. As their self-confidence improves, non-assertive clients are taken on "field trips" to shops and restaurants where they practice what they have learned.

Non-assertion requiring therapy is unusual. Nevertheless, many people become tense or upset in at least some situations in which they must stand up for their rights. For this reason, many people have found the techniques and exercises of assertiveness training helpful. If you have ever eaten a carbonized steak when you ordered it rare, or stood in silent rage as a clerk ignored you, the following discussion will be of interest.

Self-Assertion The first step in assertiveness training is to convince yourself of three basic rights: You have the right to refuse, to request, and to right a wrong. Self-assertion involves standing up for these rights by speaking out in your own behalf.

Question: Is self-assertion just getting things your own way?

Not at all. A basic distinction can be made between *self-assertion* and *aggressive* behavior. Assertion is a direct, honest expression of feelings and desires. It is not exclusively self-serving, since pent up anger can be very destructive to relationships. People who are non-assertive are usually patient to a fault. In contrast, aggression does not take into account the feelings or rights of others. Aggression is an attempt to get one's own way no matter what. Assertion techniques emphasize firmness, not attack (Table 23–2).

The basic idea in assertiveness training is that each assertive action is practiced until it can be repeated even under stress. For example, let's say it really angers you when a store clerk waits on several people who arrived after you did. To improve

Table 23–2 Comparison of Assertive, Aggressive, and Non-assertive Behavior

	ACTOR	RECEIVER OF BEHAVIOR
Non-assertive behavior	Self-denying, inhibited, hurt, and anxious; lets others make choices; goals not achieved	Feels sympathy, guilt, or contempt for actor; achieves goals at actor's expense
Aggressive behavior	Achieves goals at others' expense; expresses feelings, but hurts others; chooses for others or puts them down	Feels hurt, defensive, humiliated, or taken advantage of; does not meet own needs
Assertive behavior	Self-enhancing; acts in own best interests; expresses feelings; respects rights of others; goals usually achieved, self-respect maintained	Needs respected and feelings expressed; may achieve goal; self-worth maintained

After Alberti & Emmons, 1978.

Applications

your assertiveness in this situation, you would begin by *rehearsing* the dialogue, posture, and gestures you would use to confront the clerk or the other customer. Working in front of a mirror can be very helpful. If possible, you should *role play* the scene with a friend. Be sure to have your friend take the part of a really aggressive or irresponsible clerk, as well as a cooperative one. Rehearsal and role playing should also be used when you expect a possible confrontation with someone—for example, if you are going to ask for a raise, challenge a grade, or confront a landlord.

Question: Is that all there is to it?

No. Another important principle is *overlearning*. When you rehearse or role play assertive behavior, it is essential to continue practice until your responses become almost automatic. This helps prevent you from getting flustered in the actual situation.

One more technique you may find useful is the *broken record*. A good way to prevent assertion from becoming aggression is to simply restate your request as many times and in as many ways as necessary. As an illustration, let's say you are returning a pair of shoes to a store. After two wearings, the shoes fell apart, but you bought them 2 months ago and no longer have a receipt. The broken record could sound something like this:

Customer: I would like to have these shoes replaced.
Clerk: Do you have a receipt?
Customer: No, but I bought them here, and since they are defective, I would like to have you replace them.
Clerk: I can't do that without a receipt.
Customer: I understand that, but I want them replaced.
Clerk: Well, if you'll come back this afternoon and talk to the manager.
Customer: I've brought these shoes in because they are defective.
Clerk: Well, I'm not authorized to replace them.
Customer: Yes, well, if you'll replace these, I'll be on my way.

Notice that the customer did not attack the clerk or create an angry confrontation. Simple persistence is often all that is necessary for successful self-assertion.

Question: How would I respond assertively to a put-down?

Responding assertively to verbal aggression (a "put-down") is a real challenge. The tendency is to respond aggressively, which usually makes things worse. A good way to respond to a put-down uses the following steps. (1) If you are wrong, admit it; (2) acknowledge the person's feelings; (3) assert yourself about the other person's aggression; (4) briskly end the interchange.

Psychologists Robert Alberti and Michael Emmons (1978) offer an example of how to use the four steps. Let's say you accidentally bump into someone. The person responds angrily, "Damn it! Why don't you watch where you're going! You fool, you could have hurt me!" A good response would be to say, "I'm sorry I bumped you. I didn't do it intentionally. It's obvious you're upset, but I don't like your calling me names, or yelling. I can get your point without that."

Now, what if someone insults you indirectly ("I love your taste in clothes, it's so 'folksy' ")? Alberti and Emmons suggest you ask for a clarification ("What are you trying to say?"). This will force the person to take responsibility for the aggression. It can also provide an opportunity to change the way the person interacts with you: "If you really don't like what I'm wearing, I'd like to know it. I'm not always sure I like the things I buy, and I value your opinion."

To summarize, self-assertion does not supply instant poise, confidence, or self-assurance. However, it is a way of combating anxieties associated with life in an impersonal and sometimes intimidating society. If you are interested in more information, you can consult a book entitled *Your Perfect Right* by Alberti and Emmons (1978).

Learning Check

1. In assertiveness training, people learn techniques for getting their way in social situations and angry interchanges. T or F?

2. Non-assertive behavior causes hurt, anxiety, and self-denial in the actor and sympathy, guilt, or contempt in the receiver. T or F?

3. Overlearning should be avoided when rehearsing assertive behaviors. T or F?

4. The "broken record" must be avoided, because it is a basic non-assertive behavior. T or F?

Answers:
1. F 2. T 3. F 4. F

Exploration: Social Traps—The Tragedy of the Commons

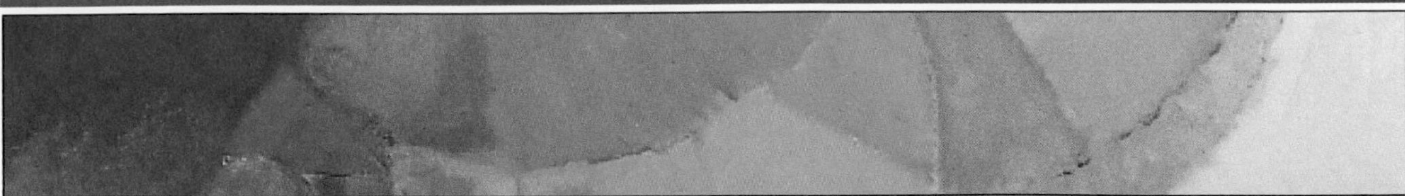

You are in a packed theater in an older building. Halfway through the feature movie *(Bambi Meets Godzilla)* you begin to smell smoke. The screen goes dark. You try to stay calm as you shuffle toward a distant exit sign. Suddenly someone screams. You lunge for the door. Instantly, you are caught in a crush of people. The crowd jams together so tightly that only a few people can squeeze through the door. If the fire moves swiftly, many lives will be lost.

This situation—panic during a fire—is a classic example of a *social trap*. Each person in a theater who runs toward the exits has acted in his or her immediate self-interest. Yet if *everyone* bolts at once the chances that anyone will survive may be very low.

Social Traps

Question: What exactly is a social trap?

A **social trap** is any social situation that rewards actions that have undesired effects in the long run (Cross & Guyer, 1980). Personal examples of social traps are quite common. For instance, many people are enticed into drinking too much at parties because their pleasure is immediate and their discomfort (a hangover) comes later. Many people go into debt because they get the immediate reward of owning desirable goods; only later do they suffer when a staggering credit card bill arrives. For the immediate pleasure of intimacy, many teenagers later pay the price of pregnancy, forced marriage, early divorce, curtailed education, and so on.

Psychologists have been especially interested in *collective* social traps. In such traps, no one individual acts against the group interest, but if many people act alike, collective harm is done. For example, each person who leaves work at 5 P.M. in a congested city expects to gain by getting home earlier. Yet if everyone leaves at 5:00, the resulting traffic jam ensures that everyone will, in fact, arrive home late and emotionally frazzled. The problem could be solved if some people would wait a half hour or more before leaving. However, no one does this because immediate self-interest encourages a "fast getaway."

A related example is the fact that many large cities now have rapid transit systems that are underused by its citizens. Each person decides that it is more convenient to own and drive a separate car (in order to run errands and so on). However, we see again that individual behavior affects the welfare of others. Because everyone wants to drive for "convenience," driving becomes inconvenient: The mass of cars in most cities causes irritating traffic snarls and a lack of parking spaces. Each car owner has been drawn into a trap.

The Tragedy of the Commons

Social traps are especially damaging when we are enticed into overuse of scarce resources. This is exactly what happened a few years ago to crab fishermen in Alaska.

Initially, crabs were plentiful and fishermen were few. Each fisherman was therefore able to make large, lucrative catches. To raise their profits, fishermen began to add second, third, and fourth boats to their operations. For a while this did, in fact, increase individual profits. But as the size of the fishing fleet continued to grow, the number of crabs available to be caught by any boat decreased.

Eventually, so many crabs were caught that their rate of reproduction slowed. As a result, crab fishermen began to go bankrupt in large numbers. Individually their actions made sense. But collectively the group suffered greatly.

Ecologist Garrett Hardin (1968; 1985) calls situations like the one just described the **tragedy of the commons.** Tragedies of this sort often occur when people share a scarce resource. Each person acts in his or her self-interest, which causes the resource to be used up so that everyone suffers. More familiar examples of this dilemma are the lack of individual incentives to conserve gasoline, water, or electricity. Whenever one's personal comfort or convenience is involved, it is highly tempting to "let others worry about it." Yet in the long run everyone stands to lose.

Social Problems Many major social problems can be thought of as social traps. In most cases of environmental pollution, for instance, there are immediate benefits for polluting and major long-term costs. If

Exploration

one person pollutes a river or trashes the roadside, it has little noticeable effect. But as many people do the same, problems that affect everyone quickly mount. As another example, consider the farmer who applies DDT to a crop to save it from insect damage. The farmer benefits immediately. However, if other farmers follow suit, the local water system may be permanently damaged.

Traps also exist at the international level. Countries continue to add to their nuclear stockpiles in order to be more "secure." Yet, doing so may eventually increase the chances of a final nuclear holocaust. It's no wonder that people who study international conflicts often come away shaking their heads and wondering, "How did we get into this mess?"

Question: What can be done to avoid social traps?

Escaping Traps In some situations it might be possible to dismantle social traps by rearranging rewards and costs. For example, many companies are tempted to pollute because it saves them money and increases profits. To reverse the situation, a pollution tax could be levied so that it would cost more, not less, for a business to pollute. As another example, we could reward lower individual consumption of resources. Some power companies have already experimented with a meter that charges lower rates for using power at "off-peak" periods (also see Chapter 26).

There is evidence that in real social traps, people are more likely to restrain themselves when they believe others will, too (Messick et al., 1983). Otherwise they are likely to think, "Why should I be a sucker? I don't think anyone else is going to conserve" (fuel, electricity, water, crabs, or whatever).

Other problems may be harder to solve. What, for instance, can be done about truck drivers who cause dangerous traffic jams because they will not pull over on narrow roads? How can littering be discouraged or prevented? How would you make carpooling or using public transportation the first choice for most people? Or how could people simply be encouraged to stagger their departure times to and from work? All of these and more are social traps that need springing. It is important that we not fall into the trap of ignoring them.

Learning Check

1. A social trap is any situation in which undesired actions are rewarded in the long run. T or F?
2. Individuals in a collective social trap act in ways that appear to be rational, but that create problems for the group as a whole. T or F?
3. The tragedy of the commons occurs when individuals use a shared resource too quickly because they get immediate rewards for doing so. T or F?
4. Rearranging individual rewards and costs is one way to dismantle social traps. T or F?

Answers:

1. F 2. T 3. T 4. T

Chapter Summary

- Humans are social animals enmeshed in a complex network of social relationships. **Social psychology** studies humans as members of groups. Its focus is on how people behave in the presence (actual or implied) of others.
- **Culture** provides a broad social context for our behavior. One's *position* in groups defines a variety of **roles** to be played. Roles, which may be *achieved* or *ascribed,* are particular behavior patterns associated with social positions. When two or more contradictory roles are held, **role conflict** may occur. The Stanford prison experiment showed that destructive roles may override individual motives for behavior.
- Positions within groups typically carry higher or lower levels of **status.** High status is associated with special privileges and respect.
- **Group structure** refers to the organization of roles, communication pathways, and power within a group. **Group cohesiveness** is basically the degree of attraction among group members. **Norms** are standards of conduct enforced (formally or informally) by groups. The **autokinetic effect** has been used to demonstrate that norms rapidly form even in temporary groups.
- The study of personal space is called **proxemics.** Four basic spatial zones around each person's body are **intimate distance** (0–18 inches), **personal distance** (1½–4 feet), **social distance** (4–12 feet), and **public distance** (12 feet or more).
- **Attribution theory** is concerned with how we make inferences about behavior. A variety of factors affect attribution, including **consistency, distinctiveness, situational demands,** and **consensus.** The **fundamental attributional error** is to ascribe the actions of others to internal causes, while attributing one's own behavior to external causes. **Self-handicapping** involves arranging excuses for poor performance as a way to protect one's self-image or self-esteem.
- The **need to affiliate** is tied to additional needs for approval, support, friendship, and information. Additionally, research indicates that affiliation is related to reducing anxiety and uncertainty. **Social comparison theory** holds that we also affiliate to evaluate our actions, feelings, and abilities.
- **Interpersonal attraction** is increased by **physical proximity** (nearness), **frequent contact, physical attractiveness, competence,** and **similarity.** A large degree of similarity on many dimensions is characteristic of mate selection in most marriages.
- **Self-disclosure** occurs more when two people like one another. A **reciprocity norm** exists for self-disclosure: Low levels of self-disclosure are met with low levels in return, whereas moderate self-disclosure elicits more personal replies. However, **overdisclosure** tends to inhibit self-disclosure by others.
- According to **social exchange theory,** we tend to maintain relationships that are *profitable,* that is, those for which perceived rewards exceed perceived costs.
- **Romantic love** has been studied as a special kind of attitude. Love can be distinguished from liking by the use of attitude scales. Dating couples like *and* love their partners but only like their friends. Love is also associated with greater *mutual absorption* between people.
- In general, **social influence** refers to alterations in behavior brought about by the behavior of others. **Conformity** to group pressure is a familiar example of social influence.
- Virtually everyone conforms to a variety of broad social and cultural norms. **Conformity pressures** also exist within smaller groups. The famous Asch experiments demonstrated that various **group sanctions** encourage conformity.
- **Groupthink** refers to compulsive conformity in group decision making. Victims of groupthink seek to maintain each other's approval, even at the cost of critical thinking.
- Social influence is also related to five types of **social power: reward power, coercive power, legitimate power, referent power,** and **expert power.**
- **Obedience** to authority has been investigated in a variety of experiments, particularly those by Milgram. Obedience in Milgram's studies decreased when the victim was in the same room, when the victim and subject were face to face, when the authority figure was absent, and when others refused to obey.
- **Compliance** with direct requests is another means by which behavior is influenced. Three strategies for inducing compliance are the **foot-in-the-door technique,** the **door-in-the-face approach,** and the **low-ball technique.**
- Recent research suggests that in addition to excessive obedience to authority, many people show a surprising **passive compliance** to unreasonable requests.
- **Self-assertion,** as opposed to **aggression,** involves clearly stating one's wants and needs to others. Learning to be assertive is accomplished by *role playing, rehearsing* assertive actions, *overlearning,* and use of specific techniques, such as the *"broken record."*
- A **social trap** is a social situation in which immediately rewarded actions have undesired effects in the long run. One prominent social trap occurs when limited public resources are overused, a problem called the **tragedy of the commons.**

Questions For Discussion

1. Reread the experiments performed on passive compliance. What would have been an assertive response to the situations described? An aggressive response?

2. Would it be possible to be completely nonconforming (that is, to not conform to *some* group norm)?

3. How serious, in your estimation, are problems of conformity, obedience, and passive compliance?

4. How has physical proximity influenced your choice of friends?

5. Modern warfare allows killing to take place impersonally and at a distance. How does this relate to Milgram's experiments?

6. People of different nationalites often have different norms for personal space. What would you expect to happen in a conversation between two people with very different proxemic habits?

7. Can you think of a personal experience in which you were subjected to group pressures similar to those in the Asch experiment? How did you feel? Did you yield?

8. In view of the Milgram obedience experiment, do you think the civil disobedience of the civil rights and antiwar movements was justified? Why or why not?

9. If you were placed in charge of an important decision-making group, what would you do to minimize groupthink? Do you think that some types of committees or groups are especially prone to groupthink? How serious a problem do you think groupthink is in the government? In the military? In business? In schools? In community groups?

10. What social traps can you identify in day-to-day experience? What could be done to change them?

11. Garrett Hardin believed that it is a mistake to send food to countries wracked by famine. According to Hardin, this only allows the population of such countries to expand so that a later, larger disaster becomes inevitable. In your opinion, is it more or less humane to supply food under such circumstances?

Chapter 24

Social Psychology II

In This Chapter

Attitudes
Persuasion
Cognitive dissonance
Brainwashing and cults
Prejudice
Group conflict
Aggression

Applications

Helping others

Exploration

Sociobiology

Chapter Preview

Doomsday for the Seekers

Hardly a year passes, it seems, without a doomsday group of one kind or another making the news. In one classic example of such groups, a woman named Mrs. Keech claimed she was receiving messages from beings on a planet called Clarion. The beings told Mrs. Keech that they had detected a fault in the earth's crust that would submerge North America, causing an unimaginable natural disaster. The date of this event would be December 21. However, Mrs. Keech and her band of followers, who called themselves the Seekers, had no fear: On December 20 they expected to be met at midnight by a flying saucer and taken to safety in outer space.

The night of December 20 arrived, and the Seekers gathered at Mrs. Keech's house. Many had given up jobs and possessions to prepare for departure. Expectations were high and commitment was total. But as the night wore on, midnight passed and the world continued to exist. It was a bitter and embarrassing disappointment for the Seekers.

Question: Did the group break up then?

The story now takes an amazing twist—one that intrigued social psychologists. Instead of breaking up, the Seekers became more *convinced than even before that they had been right. At about 5* A.M. *Mrs. Keech announced that she had received a message explaining that the Seekers had saved the world.*

Before the night of December 20, the Seekers had been uninterested in convincing other people that the world was coming to an end. Now they called newspapers, magazines, and radio stations to explain what had happened and to convince others of their accomplishment.

How do we explain this strange turn in the behavior of Mrs. Keech's doomsday group? An answer may lie in the concept of cognitive dissonance. *Cognitive dissonance also helps to explain many aspects of attitude change. Watch for a discussion of cognitive dissonance later in this chapter.*

Survey Questions

- What are attitudes? How are they acquired, measured, and changed?
- Under what conditions is persuasion most effective?
- What is cognitive dissonance? What does it have to do with attitudes and behavior?
- Is brainwashing actually possible? How are people converted to cult membership?
- What causes prejudice and intergroup conflict? What can be done about these problems?
- How do psychologists explain human aggression?
- Why are bystanders so often unwilling to help in an emergency?
- How does the theory of sociobiology try to explain social behavior?

Attitudes—Belief + Emotion + Action

What is your attitude toward birth control, marijuana, Republicans, higher education, Chevrolets, psychology? The answers have far-reaching effects on your behavior. The effects of attitudes are intimately woven into our actions and views of the world. Our tastes, friendships, votes, preferences, and goals are all touched by attitudes.

Question: What specifically is an attitude?

An **attitude** is a mixture of belief and emotion that predisposes a person to respond to other people, objects, or institutions in a positive or negative way. Attitudes summarize past experience and *predict* or direct future actions. For example, an approach known as the **misdirected letter technique** demonstrates that actions are closely connected to attitudes.

The Luck of the Irish

During a period of civil violence in Ireland, attitudes held toward the Irish were measured in a sample of English households. Later, wrongly addressed letters were sent to the same households. Each letter had either an English name or an Irish name on it. The question was: Would the "Irish" letters be returned to the Post Office or thrown away? As predicted, the number of "Irish" letters returned corresponded directly to pro-Irish or anti-Irish attitudes measured earlier (Howitt et al., 1977).

"Your attitude is showing," is sometimes said. This statement seems simple, but actually there are three ways in which attitudes are expressed. Most attitudes have a **belief component,** an **emotional component,** and an **action component.** Consider, for example, your attitude toward gun control. You will have beliefs about whether or not gun control would affect rates of crime or violence. You will have emotional responses to guns, finding them either attractive and desirable or threatening and destructive. And you will have a tendency to seek out or to avoid gun ownership. The action component of your attitude will probably also include support of organizations that urge or oppose gun control.

Question: How do people acquire attitudes?

Attitude Formation Attitudes are acquired in several basic ways. Sometimes, attitudes come from **direct contact** with the object of the attitude—such as opposing pollution when a nearby factory ruins your favorite river. Attitudes are also learned through **interaction with others** holding the same attitude: If you live in a vegetarian household, chances are good that you will become a vegetarian. Attitudes are also acquired through the effects of **child rearing.** For example, if both parents belong to the same political party, chances are 2 out of 3 that the child will belong to the same party as an adult (Campbell et al., 1954).

In the previous chapter, we discussed group forces that operate to bring about conformity. There is little doubt that many of the attitudes we hold are influenced by **group membership** (Fig. 24–1). In one classic study, for example, groups were formed to discuss the case of a juvenile delinquent. Most participants believed that what the boy needed was love, kindness, and friendship. To test group pressures on attitudes, a person who advocated severe punishment was added to each group.

Question: How did group members react to the "deviate"?

At first they directed almost all of their comments to him. But when the deviate stuck to his position, an interesting thing happened. Soon, he was almost completely ex-

Fig. 24–1 *Attitudes are an important dimension of social behavior. They are often rooted in reference groups.*

cluded from conversation. And later, the deviate was strongly rejected in ratings made by other group members (Schachter, 1951). Group pressures for conformity and the difficulty of holding deviant attitudes can be clearly seen in this outcome.

Attitudes are also influenced by the **mass media.** As Marshall McLuhan put it, we are "massaged" by the media, meaning we are threatened, urged, cajoled, persuaded, and otherwise influenced. Ninety-eight percent of American homes have a television set, which is on an average of over 7 hours a day (Oskamp, 1984). As we noted in Chapter 8, the values and information thus channeled into homes exert a powerful influence on how people perceive, think about, and react to their world. For instance, the heavy dose of violence on television may lead viewers to develop a **"mean" world view** (Heath & Petraitis, 1987). That is, frequent viewers overestimate their chances of being involved in a violent incident (Roberts & Bachen, 1981). Heavy viewers are also less likely to feel that most people can be trusted (Gerbner & Gross, 1976).

Some attitudes are inadvertently formed by **chance conditioning.** Let's say, for instance, that you have had three encounters in your lifetime with psychologists. If by chance all three were negative, you might take an unduly dim view of psychology and psychologists. In the same way, people often develop strong attitudes toward cities, restaurants, or parts of the country on the basis of one or two unusually good or bad experiences with each.

Question: Why are some attitudes acted on, while others are not?

To answer this question, let's consider an example. Assume that a person agrees that automobiles add to pollution, and strongly objects to smog. Why would the person continue to drive to work every day? Probably it is because the *immediate consequences* of our actions weigh heavily on the choices we make. No matter what the person's attitude, it is difficult to resist the immediate convenience of driving. Also important is our expectation of how *others will evaluate* our actions (Fishbein & Ajzen, 1975). By taking this factor into account, researchers have been able to predict family planning choices, alcohol use by adolescents, re-enlistment in the National Guard, voting on a nuclear power plant initiative, and so forth (Cialdini et al., 1981). Finally, we must not overlook the effect that long-standing *habits* have on action (Triandis, 1977). Say a "male chauvinist" boss vows to change his sexist attitudes toward female employees. Two months later, it would not be unusual for his behavior to show the effects of habit rather than his intention to change.

In short, there are often large differences between attitudes and behavior—particularly between privately held attitudes and public behavior. However, barriers to action typically fall when a person holds an attitude with conviction. To have *conviction* means that an attitude is of central importance to a person. The issues about which you have conviction are those that you feel strongly about (emotionally), that you believe are important, that you frequently think about and discuss, and that you feel knowledgeable about (Ableson, 1988). Attitudes that are held with passionate conviction often lead to major changes in personal behavior.

Question: Can attitudes be measured?

Attitude Measurement There are a number of approaches to the measurement of attitudes. In some cases, individuals are simply asked in a straightforward way to express attitudes toward a particular issue. For example, a person might be asked in an **open-ended interview,** "What are your thoughts about the 'Star Wars' missile defense?" The second approach, which has been very useful as a measure of attitudes toward groups, uses a **social distance scale.** Social distance indicates the degree to which one person would be willing to have contact with another person. That is, the individual is asked to state his or her willingness to admit members of a particular group to various levels of social closeness. These levels range from "would exclude from my country" to "would admit to marriage in my family."

The use of **attitude scales** is one of the most common methods of measurement. Attitude scales consist of statements expressing various possible views on an issue. For example: "Socialized medicine would destroy the quality of health care in this country" or "This country needs a national health care program." People are asked to agree or disagree with each item on a 5-point scale by ranking it from "strongly agree" to "strongly disagree." By computing scores on all items, a person can be rated for overall acceptance or rejection of a particular issue. When used in public polls, attitude scales have provided much useful information about the feelings of large segments of the population.

Attitude Change—Why the "Seekers" Went Public

Although attitudes are relatively stable, they are subject to change. Some attitude change can be understood in terms of the concept of **reference groups.** A reference group is a group whose values and attitudes a person regards as relevant to his or her own. It is not necessary to be in face-to-face contact with others for them to serve as a reference group. It depends instead on whom you identify with or care about.

In the 1930s, Theodore Newcomb studied real-life attitude change among students at Bennington College. Most students came from conservative homes, but Bennington was a very liberal school. Newcomb found that most students shifted significantly toward more liberal attitudes during their 4 years at Bennington. Those who did not change kept parents and hometown friends as their primary reference group. This is typified by one student's statement, "I decided I'd rather stick to my father's ideas." Those who did change primarily identified with the campus community. Notice that all students could count the college and their families as *membership* groups. However, one group or the other tended to become their point of reference.

Question: What about advertising and other direct attempts to change attitudes? Are they effective?

Businesses, politicians, and others who seek to persuade us obviously believe that attitude change can be induced. Over $5 billion is spent yearly on television advertising in the United States alone. **Persuasion** refers to any deliberate attempt to change attitudes by imparting information. Persuasion can range from the daily blitz of media commercials to personal discussion among friends. In most cases, the success or failure of attempted persuasion can be understood if we consider characteristics of the **communicator,** the **message,** and the **audience** (Fig. 24–2).

Let's say you have a chance to promote an issue important to you (for or against nuclear power, for instance) at a community gathering. Whom should you choose to make the presentation, and how should that person present it?

Research on persuasion suggests that attitude change is encouraged when (1) the communicator is likable, trustworthy, an expert on the topic, and similar to the audience in some respect; (2) the message appeals to emotions, particularly to fear or anxiety; (3) the message also provides a clear course of action that will, if followed, reduce fear or anxiety; (4) the message states clear-cut conclusions; (5) both sides of the argument are presented in the case of a well-informed audience; (6) only one side of the argument is presented in the case of a poorly informed audience; (7) the persuader appears to have nothing to gain if the audience accepts the message; and (8) the message is repeated as frequently as possible (Aronson, 1972; McGuire, 1969). You should have little difficulty

Fig. 24–2 *Persuasion. Would you be likely to be swayed by this person's message? Successful persuasion is related to characteristics of the communicator, the message, and the audience.*

seeing how these principles are applied in the selling of everything from underarm deodorants to presidents.

We all know from personal observation that emotional experiences can dramatically alter attitudes. A person who gives up drinking after nearly dying in an automobile accident caused by drunkenness serves as an example. To actively bring about such attitude change, psychologists have experimented with creating similar experiences through role playing.

Janis and Mann (1965) asked women who were known smokers to play the role of cancer patients. A doctor told each of the women that he had some bad news: She had lung cancer and would have to undergo immediate surgery. The women played out the part by asking questions about the surgery, if it might fail, and so on. Women in the role-playing group drastically reduced their smoking. Those who listened to a tape recording of similar information showed little change.

Question: Why should role playing have more effect than hearing the same information?

Cognitive Dissonance Theory Certainly emotional impact and realism have some effect, but part of the explanation also lies in the concept of **cognitive dissonance.**

Cognitions are thoughts. Dissonance means clashing. The influential theory of cognitive dissonance (Festinger, 1957) states that contradicting or clashing thoughts cause discomfort. We have a need for *consistency* in our thoughts and our perceptions.

If individuals can be made to act in ways that are inconsistent with their attitudes, they may change their thoughts to bring them into agreement with their actions. For example, smokers are told on every pack that cigarettes endanger their lives. They light up and smoke. How do they resolve the tension between this information and their actions? They could quit smoking, but it may be easier to convince themselves that smoking is not really so dangerous. To do this, many smokers seek examples of people who have lived long lives as heavy smokers, and they associate with other smokers who support their choice. Many smokers also avoid information concerning the link between smoking and cancer. Cognitive dissonance theory also suggests that people tend to reject new information that contradicts ideas they already hold, in a sort of "don't bother me with the facts, my mind is made up" strategy.

Now recall Mrs. Keech and her doomsday group. Why did their belief in Mrs. Keech's messages *increase* after the world failed to end? Why did they suddenly become interested in convincing others that their beliefs were correct? Cognitive dissonance theory explains that after publicly committing themselves to their beliefs, they had a strong need to maintain their stand. In effect, convincing others served as a way of adding proof that they were right.

Question: Acting contrary to one's attitudes does not always bring about change. How does cognitive dissonance account for this?

The amount of **reward,** or **justification,** for acting contrary to one's attitudes and beliefs can influence the amount of dissonance created. In a now classic study, college students performed an extremely boring task that consisted of turning wooden pegs on a board for an extended time. Afterward, they were asked to help lure others into the experiment by pretending it was interesting and en-

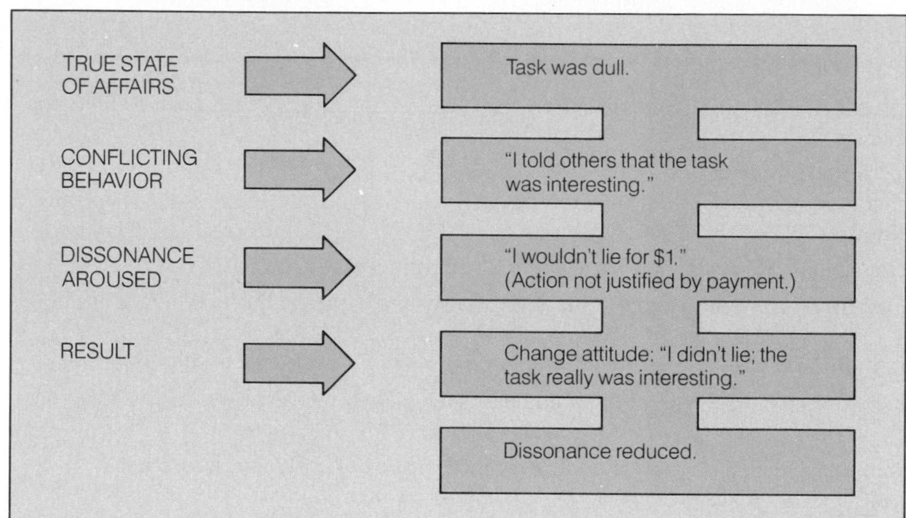

Fig. 24–3 *Summary of the Festinger and Carlsmith (1959) study from the viewpoint of a person experiencing cognitive dissonance.*

joyable. Students paid $20 for lying to others did not change their own negative opinion of the task. Those who were paid only $1 later rated the experience as actually being pleasant and interesting. In other words, those paid $20 experienced no dissonance. These students could reassure themselves that anybody would tell a little white lie for $20. Those paid $1 were faced with the conflicting thought, "I lied, but I had no good reason to do it." Rather than admit to themselves that they had lied, these students changed their attitude toward what they had done (Festinger & Carlsmith, 1959) (Fig. 24–3).

More recent studies indicate that we are especially likely to experience dissonance when we cause an event to occur that we would rather hadn't occurred (Cooper & Fazio, 1984). Let's say, for example, that you agree to help a friend move to a new apartment. The big day arrives and you feel like staying in bed. Actually, you wish you hadn't promised to help. To reduce dissonance, you may convince yourself that the work will actually be "sort of fun" or that your friend really deserves the help. We often make such adjustments in attitudes to minimize cognitive dissonance (Fig. 24–4).

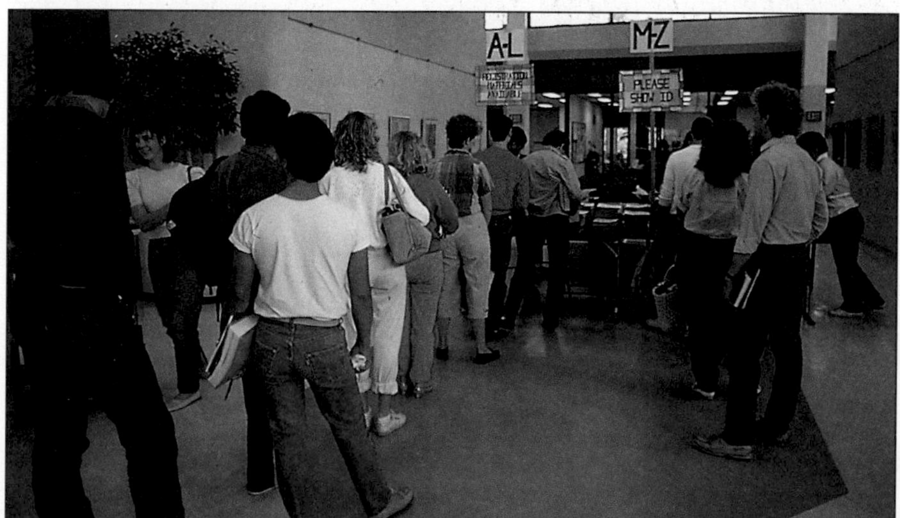

Fig. 24–4 *Making choices often causes dissonance. This is especially true if the rejected alternative is perceived as better than the one selected. To minimize such dissonance, we tend to emphasize positive aspects of what we choose, while downgrading other alternatives. Thus, college students are more likely to think their courses will be good after they have registered than they did before making a commitment (Rosenfeld et al., 1983).*

Learning Check

1. Attitudes have three parts: a ____________ component, an ____________ component, and an ____________ component.
2. Which of the following is associated with attitude formation?
   a. group membership *c.* chance conditioning *e.* all of the preceding
   b. mass media *d.* child rearing *f.* *a* and *d* only
3. Because of the immediate consequences of actions, behavior contrary to one's stated attitudes is often enacted. T or F?
4. Items such as "would exclude from my country" or "would admit to marriage in my family" are found in which attitude measure?
   a. a reference group scale *b.* a social distance scale *c.* an attitude scale *d.* an open-ended interview
5. In presenting a persuasive message, it is best to give both sides of the argument if the audience is already well informed on the topic. T or F?
6. Much attitude change is related to a desire to avoid clashing, or contradictory, thoughts, an idea summarized by ____________ theory.

Answers:
1. belief, emotional, action **2.** *e* **3.** T **4.** *b* **5.** T **6.** cognitive dissonance

Forced Attitude Change—Brainwashing and Cults

Many people associate *brainwashing* with techniques used by the Chinese on American prisoners during the Korean War. Through various types of "thought reform," the Chinese were able to coerce approximately 16 percent of these prisoners to sign false confessions (Schein et al., 1957). More recently, the mass murder/suicide at Jonestown rekindled public interest in the subject of forced changes in attitudes, beliefs, and personal loyalties.

Question: What is brainwashing? How does it differ from other persuasive techniques?

As we have noted, advertisers, politicians, educators, religious organizations, and others actively seek to alter attitudes and opinions. To an extent, their persuasive efforts resemble brainwashing, but there is an important difference: **Brainwashing** requires a *captive* audience. If you are offended by a television commercial, you can tune it out. Prisoners in the POW camps in Korea (and later in Vietnam) were completely at the mercy of their captors. James McConnell has noted that complete control over the environment allows a degree of psychological manipulation that would be impossible in a normal setting.

Question: How does captivity facilitate persuasion?

Brainwashing McConnell identifies three techniques used in brainwashing: (1) The target person is isolated from other people who would support his or her original attitudes; (2) the target is made completely dependent on his or her captors for satisfaction of needs; and (3) the indoctrinating agent is in a position to reward the target for changes in attitude or behavior.

Brainwashing typically begins with an attempt to make the target person feel completely helpless. Physical and psychological abuse, lack of sleep, humiliation, and isolation serve to **unfreeze** former values and beliefs. **Change** comes about when exhaustion, pressure, and fear become unbearable. At this point, prisoners reach the breaking point and sign a false confession or cooperate to gain relief. When they do, they are suddenly rewarded with praise, privileges, food, or rest. Continued coupling of hope and fear with additional pressures to conform then serve to **refreeze** new attitudes (Schein et al., 1961).

Question: How permanent are changes caused by brainwashing?

In most cases, the dramatic shift in attitudes brought about by brainwashing is temporary. Most "converted" prisoners who returned to the United States after the Korean War eventually reverted to their original beliefs and repudiated their indoctrinators.

Cults Exhorted by their leader, some 900 members of the Reverend Jim Jones' People's Temple picked up paper cups and drank purple Kool-Aid laced with the deadly poison cyanide. Psychologically, the mass suicide at Jonestown in 1978 is not so incredible as it might seem.

The inhabitants of Jonestown were isolated in the jungles of Guyana, intimidated by guards and lulled with sedatives. They were also cut off from friends and relatives and totally accustomed to obeying rigid rules of conduct, which primed them for Jones' final "loyalty test." Of greater psychological interest is the question of how people reach such a state of commitment and dependency.

Question: Why do people join groups such as the People's Temple?

Psychologist Margaret Singer (1979) has studied and aided hundreds of former cult members. Her interviews reveal that in recruiting new members, cults make use of a powerful blend of guilt, manipulation, isolation, deception, fear, and escalating commitment. In this respect, cults employ high-pressure indoctrination techniques not unlike those used in brainwashing.

Some of those interviewed by Singer were suffering from marked psychological distress when they joined a cult. Most, however, were simply undergoing a period of mild depression, indecision, or alienation from family and friends. Cult members try to catch potential converts at a time of need—especially when a sense of belonging will be attractive to the convert. For instance, many converts were approached just after a romance had broken up, or when they were struggling with exams or choice of a major, or were simply at loose ends and "on the street."

Question: How is conversion achieved?

Often it begins with intense displays of affection and understanding ("Love bombing"). Next comes isolation from non–cult members and drills, discipline, and rituals (all-night meditation or continuous chanting, for instance) to wear down physical and emotional resistance, as well as to generate commitment.

At first, recruits make small commitments (to stay after a meeting, for example). Then, large commitments are encouraged (to stay an extra day, to call in sick at work, and so forth). Making a major commitment is usually the final step. The new devotee signs over a bank account or property to the group, takes up residence with the group, and so forth. Such major public commitments create a powerful cognitive dissonance effect in which it becomes virtually impossible for converts to admit that they have made a mistake.

Once in the group, members are cut off from family and friends (former reference groups), and the cult can control the flow and interpretation of information to them. Members are isolated physically (by continuous activity) and psychologically from their former value systems and social structure.

Question: Why do people stay in cults?

Most former members mention guilt and fear as the main reasons for not leaving when they wished they could. Most had been reduced to childlike dependency on the group for meeting all their daily needs (Singer, 1979). Behind the "throne" from which Jim Jones ruled Jonestown was a sign bearing these words: "Those who do not remember the past are condemned to repeat it" (Fig. 24–5). If we are to take the Reverend Jones at his word, then we should remember that cults are but one example of the danger of trading independence for security. Cults are merely the most visible sign of how we all can be influenced by sophisticated psychological coercion and by our need for approval from others.

Fig. 24–5 *Aftermath of the mass suicide at Jonestown. How do cultlike groups recruit new devotees? (See text.)*

Prejudice—Attitudes That Injure

Prejudice is a negative attitude or prejudgment tinged with unreasonable suspicion, fear, or hatred. Often, prejudice is institutionalized and backed by social power structures. In such cases it is referred to as **racism, sexism,** or **ageism,** depending on the group affected. Since sexism and ageism were discussed in earlier chapters, let's focus on racial prejudice and racism. Both racial prejudice and institutionalized racism may lead to *discrimination.* **Discrimination** refers to behavior that prevents individuals from doing things they might reasonably expect to be able to do, such as buying a house, riding a bus, or attending a high-quality school. Discrimination is often deeply woven into society. One remarkable study, for instance, involved 15 college students who had received no traffic citations in the previous year. Each student attached a bumper sticker for a well-known, militant black organization to his or her car (Heussenstamm, 1971). During the next 17 days the group received a total of 33 traffic citations! The power relationship between the white establishment and black militants (at least as interpreted by individual police officers) is clear.

Question: How do prejudices develop?

Becoming Prejudiced One theory suggests that prejudice is a form of **scapegoating.** Scapegoating, you may recall, is a type of displaced aggression in which hostilities generated by frustration are redirected to other targets. One interesting test of this hypothesis was conducted at a summer camp for young men. Subjects were given a difficult test they were sure to fail. Additionally, completing the test caused them to miss a trip to the theater (normally the high point of their weekly entertainment). Attitudes toward Mexicans and Japanese were measured before the test and after the men had failed the test and missed the entertainment. Subjects in this study consistently rated members of these two groups lower after being frustrated (Miller & Bugelski, 1970).

At times, the development of prejudice (like other attitudes) can be traced to direct experiences with members of the rejected group. A child who is repeatedly bullied by members of a particular racial or ethnic group may develop resentment that forms the core of a lifelong dislike for all members of the group. The tragedy in such cases is that once dislike is established, it prevents accepting additional, more positive experiences that could reverse the damage. Gordon Allport (1958) concluded that there are two important sources of prejudice. **Personal prejudice** occurs when members of another racial or ethnic group represent a threat to the individual's security or comfort. For example, members of another group may be viewed as competitors for jobs. **Group prejudice** occurs simply through a person's adherence to *group norms.* In other words, you may have no personal reason for disliking out-group members, but your friends, acquaintances, or co-workers expect it of you.

The Prejudiced Personality Other research suggests that prejudice at times is a general personality characteristic.

Question: Do you mean some people are more prone to prejudice than others?

Apparently, some are. Theodore Adorno and his associates (1950) carefully probed what they called the **authoritarian personality.** These researchers started out by studying anti-Semitism as a means of understanding the social climate that existed in Germany during World War II. In the process, they found that people who are prejudiced against one group tend to be prejudiced against *all* out-groups.

Question: What are the characteristics of the prejudice-prone personality?

The authoritarian personality has a collection of personal attitudes and values marked by rigidity, inhibition, and over-simplification. Authoritarians tend to be very **ethnocentric.** That is, they use their own national, ethnic, or religious group as a basis for judging all other groups, and they consider their own group superior to others. In addition to rejecting out-groups, authoritarians are overwhelmingly concerned with power, authority, and obedience. To measure these qualities, the *F scale* was created (the *F* stands for "fascism"). This attitude scale is made up of statements such as the ones that follow—to which the authoritarian readily agrees (Adorno et al., 1950).

Authoritarian Beliefs

Obedience and respect for authority are the most important virtues children should learn.

People can be divided into two distinct classes: the weak and the strong.

If people would talk less and work more, everybody would be better off.

What this country needs most, more than laws and political programs, is a few courageous, tireless, devoted leaders, in whom the people can put their faith.

Nobody ever learns anything really important except through suffering.

Every person should have complete faith in some supernatural power whose decisions are obeyed without question.

Certain religious sects that refuse to salute the flag should be forced to conform to such patriotic action or else be abolished.

As children, authoritarians were usually severely punished. Most learned to fear authority (and to covet it) at an early age. Authoritarians are not happy people.

It should be readily apparent from the list of authoritarian beliefs that the F scale is slanted toward politically conservative authoritarians. To be fair, psychologist Milton Rokeach (1960) noted that rigid and authoritarian personalities can be found at both ends of the political spectrum. Rokeach, therefore, prefers to describe rigid and intolerant thinking as **dogmatism.** (Dogmatism is an unwarranted positiveness or certainty in matters of belief or opinion.)

Even if we discount the obvious bigotry of the dogmatic or authoritarian personality, racial prejudice runs deep in many nations. To illustrate, one experiment showed that liberal, white, male college students were more willing to give shocks (under laboratory conditions) to a black victim than to a white victim (Shulman, 1974). We will probe deeper into the roots of such prejudiced behavior in an upcoming discussion, but first let's stop for a Learning Check.

Learning Check

1. Brainwashing differs from other persuasive attempts in that brainwashing requires a ____________________.

2. Which statement about brainwashing is *false*?
a. The target person is isolated from others.
b. Attitude changes brought about by brainwashing are usually permanent.
c. The first step is unfreezing former values and beliefs.
d. Cooperation with the indoctrinating agent is rewarded.

3. Margaret Singer found that most former cult members had experienced a major psychological disturbance just prior to joining the cult. T or F?

4. Which of the following is *not* a technique typically used by cults to recruit new members?
a. "love bombing" and isolation
b. drills and rituals to wear down resistance
c. physical intimidation and veiled threats
d. a succession of smaller to larger commitments

5. The authoritarian personality tends to be prejudiced against all out-groups, a quality referred to as ____________________.

Answers:
1. captive audience **2.** *b.* **3.** F **4.** *c* **5.** ethnocentrism

Intergroup Conflict—The Roots of Prejudice

An unfortunate by-product of group membership is that it often limits contact with people in other groups. Additionally, groups themselves may come into conflict. Both events tend to foster unpleasant feelings and prejudices toward the out-group. The bloody clash of opposing forces in Ireland, South Africa, and hometown U.S.A. are reminders that intergroup conflict is a widespread problem of modern life. Daily we read of jarring clashes between nations, communities, races, and political, religious, or ethnic groups. In many cases, intergroup conflict is accompanied by *stereotyped* images of out-group members and by bitter prejudice.

Question: What exactly do you mean by a stereotype?

Social stereotypes are oversimplified images of people who fall into a particular category. As psychologist Gordon Allport (1958) put it: "Given a thimbleful of facts . . . [we] rush to make generalizations as large as a tub." Stereotypes tend to simplify people into "us" and "them" categories. Actually, aside from the fact that they always oversimplify, stereotypes may be either *positive* or *negative*. Table 24–1 shows stereotyped images of various national and ethnic groups and their changes over a 34-year period (Fig. 24–6). Notice that many of the qualities listed are desirable. Note too, that while the overall trend was a decrease in negative stereotypes, belief in the existence of some negative traits increased.

Table 24–1 University Students' Characterization of Ethnic Groups, 1933 and 1967

TRAIT	PERCENT CHECKING TRAIT 1933	1967	TRAIT	PERCENT CHECKING TRAIT 1933	1967	TRAIT	PERCENT CHECKING TRAIT 1933	1967
Americans			**Italians**			**Jews**		
Industrious	48	23	Artistic	53	30	Shrewd	79	30
Intelligent	47	20	Impulsive	44	28	Mercenary	49	15
Materialistic	33	67	Musical	32	9	Grasping	34	17
Progressive	27	17	Imaginative	30	7	Intelligent	29	37
			Revengeful	17	0			
Germans			**Irish**			**Blacks**		
Scientific	78	47	Pugnacious	45	13	Superstitious	84	13
Stolid	44	9	Witty	38	7	Lazy	75	26
Methodical	31	21	Honest	32	17	Ignorant	38	11
Efficient	16	46	Nationalistic	21	41	Religious	24	8

Source: M. Karlins, T. L. Coffman, and G. Walters, "On the fading of social stereotypes: Studies in three generations of college students." *Journal of Personality and Social Psychology* 13 (1969): 1–16.

In the years since 1967, there have been further declines in negative stereotypes, but also some recent reversals. Some observers believe that racial and ethnic prejudice is on the upswing in the United States. But often, today's racism takes the form of **symbolic prejudice** (also sometimes called "modern prejudice") (Brewer & Kramer, 1985). That is, many people realize that crude and obvious racism is socially unacceptable. However, this may not stop them from expressing prejudice in disguised forms when they give their opinions on issues such as affirmative action programs, busing, "law and order" issues, and so on.

Fig. 24–6 *Racial and ethnic pride are gradually replacing stereotypes and discrimination, but the problem of prejudice is far from solved.*

Stereotypes held by the prejudiced tend to be unusually irrational. When given a list of negative statements about other groups, prejudiced individuals agree with most of them. Particularly revealing is the fact that they often agree with conflicting statements. Thus, a prejudiced person may say that Jews are both "pushy" and "standoffish" or that blacks are both "ignorant" and "sly." In one study, prejudiced subjects even expressed negative attitudes toward two nonexistent groups, the "Piraneans" and the "Danirians." Note, too, that when a prejudiced person meets a pleasant or likable member of a rejected group, the out-group member tends to be perceived as "an exception to the rule," not as evidence against the stereotype. Even when such "exceptional" experiences begin to accumulate, a prejudiced person may not change his or her stereotyped belief.

Question: How do stereotypes and intergroup tensions develop?

Two experiments, both in unlikely settings and both using children as subjects, offer some insight into these problems.

An Experiment in Prejudice What is it like to be discriminated against? Those who have never experienced discrimination probably can't imagine it. In a unique experiment, elementary school teacher Jane Elliot sought to give her pupils direct experience with prejudice.

On the first day of the experiment, Elliot announced that brown-eyed children were to sit in the back of the room and that they could not use the drinking fountain. Blue-eyed children were given extra recess time and got to leave first for lunch. At lunch, brown-eyed children were prevented from taking second helpings because they would "just waste it." Brown-eyed and blue-eyed children were kept from mingling, and the blue-eyed children were told they were "cleaner" and "smarter" (Peters, 1971).

At first, Elliot had to maintain these imposed conditions of prejudice. She also made an effort to constantly criticize and belittle the brown-eyed children. To her surprise, the blue-eyed children rapidly joined in and were soon outdoing her in the viciousness of their attacks. The blue-eyed children began to feel superior, and the brown-eyed children felt just plain awful. Fights broke out. Test scores of the brown-eyed children fell.

Question: How lasting were the effects of this experiment?

The effects were short-lived, because 2 days later the roles of the children were reversed. Before long, the same destructive effects occurred again, but this time in reverse. The implications of this experiment are unmistakable. In less than 1 day, it was possible to get children to hate each other because of **status inequalities** and eye color. (Status inequalities are differences in the power, prestige, or privileges of two or more persons or groups.) Certainly the effects of a lifetime of real racial or ethnic prejudice are infinitely more powerful and destructive.

Question: What can be done to combat prejudice?

Equal-Status Contact Progress has been made through attempts to educate the general public about the lack of justification for prejudicial attitudes. Changing the belief component of an attitude has long been known to be one of the most direct means of changing the entire attitude. Thus, when people are made aware that minority group members share the same goals, ambitions, feelings, and frustrations as they do, intergroup relations may be improved.

However, this is not the whole answer. As we noted earlier, there is often a wide difference between attitudes and actual behavior. Until non-prejudiced behavior is engineered, changes can be quite superficial. Several lines of thought (including cognitive dissonance theory) suggest that more frequent **equal-status contact** between groups in conflict should reduce prejudice and stereotypes.

Question: But does it?

Much evidence suggests that it does. For example, in one early study white women who lived in integrated and segregated housing projects were compared for changes in attitude toward their black neighbors. Women in the integrated project showed a favorable shift in attitudes toward members of the other racial group. Those in the segregated project showed no change or actually became more prejudiced than before (Deutsch & Collins, 1951). In other studies, mixed-race groups have been formed at work, in the laboratory, and at schools. The conclusion from such research is that personal contact with a disliked group will induce friendly interracial behavior, respect, and liking. However, these benefits occur only when personal contact is on an equal footing (Cook, 1985).

To test the importance of equal-status contact directly, Gerald Clore and his associates set up a unique summer camp for children. The camp was directed by 1 white male, 1 white female, 1 black male, and 1 black female. Each campsite had 3 black and 3 white campers and 1 black and 1 white counselor. Thus, blacks and whites were equally divided in number, power, privileges, and duties. Did the experience make a difference? Apparently it did: Testing showed that the children had significantly more positive attitudes toward opposite-race children after the camp than they did before (Clore, 1976).

Superordinate Goals Let us now consider a revealing study of intergroup conflict and its reduction. Muzafer Sherif and his associates did an ingenious experiment, also at a summer camp, with 11-year-old boys. When the boys arrived at camp, they were split into two groups and housed in separate cabins. At first the groups were kept apart to build up in-group friendships. During this time, cooperative games and activities were used to develop group pride and identification. Soon each group had a flag and a name (the "Rattlers" and the "Eagles") and had staked out its own territory. At this point the two groups were placed in competition with each other. After a number of clashes, disliking between the two groups bordered on hatred. Outright hostility erupted as the boys baited each other, started fights, and raided each other's cabins (Sherif et al., 1961).

Question: Where they allowed to go home hating each other?

As an experiment in reducing intergroup conflict, and to prevent the boys from remaining enemies, various strategies were tried to reduce tensions. Holding meetings between leaders from each group did nothing. Just getting the groups together also did little. When the groups were invited to eat together, the event became a free-for-all.

Finally, emergencies that required cooperation among members of both groups were staged at the camp. For example, the water supply was damaged in a way so that all the boys had to work together to repair it. Creation of this and other **superordinate goals** helped restore peace between the two groups. As members were forced to cooperate, hostilities subsided (see Highlight 24–1).

"Jigsaw" Classrooms Contrary to the hopes of many, integrating public schools often has little positive effect on racial prejudice. In fact, prejudice may be made worse, and the self-esteem of minority students frequently decreases (Aronson, 1980).

Question: If integrated schools provide equal-status contact, shouldn't prejudice be reduced?

Theoretically, yes. But in practice, minority group children often enter newly integrated schools unprepared to compete on an equal footing. Elliot Aronson and his colleagues (1978) argue that the competitive nature of schools almost guarantees that children will *not* learn to like and understand each other. In the typical classroom, children compete fiercely for the approval of the teacher. Successful students learn to feel superior and often hold unsuccessful students in contempt. This is a high-stakes game in which only a few can win. It is clearly not a good way to reduce prejudice.

With the preceding in mind, Aronson has pioneered a way to apply the concept of superordinate goals to ordinary classrooms. According to Aronson, such goals are effective because they make people **mutually interdependent.** Each person's needs are linked to those of others in the group, and cooperation is encouraged.

Question: How has this idea been applied?

Aronson has successfully created **"jigsaw" classrooms** that emphasize cooperation rather than competition. The term *jigsaw* refers to the pieces of a jigsaw puzzle. In Aronson's method, each child is given a "piece" of the information needed to prepare for a test (Fig. 24–7).

In a typical session, children are divided into groups of 5 or 6 and given a topic to study for a later exam. Each child is given his or her "piece" of information and asked to learn it. For example, one child might have information on Thomas Edison's invention of the light bulb; another, facts about his invention of the long-playing phonograph record; and a third, information on Edison's childhood. After the children have learned their individual parts, they teach them to others in the group. Even the most competitive children quickly realize that they cannot do well without the aid of everyone in the group. Each child

HIGHLIGHT 24–1
Finding Common Ground

A superordinate goal exceeds or overrides all others. Can such goals exist on a global scale? One example might be a desire to avoid nuclear holocaust. Politically, this goal may be far from universal. But its superordinate quality is increasingly evident. Scientists now project that if *any* country suffers a nuclear attack, all other countries would suffer a terrifying "nuclear winter." In effect, almost everyone, friend and foe alike, would share the same fate.

Nuclear winter refers to a devastating drop in global temperature that would follow the fire storms, dust, and smoke of a nuclear strike. The probable result would be global crop failure, famine, and death on a large scale. Even if there were no counter-attack, a hostile country could pay dearly for its aggression (Turco et al., 1983).

It is probably fair to say that nations need to find more commonalities and shared goals. In view of predictions of a nuclear winter, perhaps finding a way to reduce the threat of nuclear warfare will prove to be one such superordinate goal.

Fig. 24–7 *In a "jigsaw" classroom, children help each other prepare for tests. As they teach each other what they know, the children learn to cooperate and to respect the unique strengths of each individual.*

makes a unique and essential contribution, so the children learn to listen to, and respect, each other.

Does the jigsaw method work? Compared to children in traditional classrooms, children in jigsaw groups were less prejudiced, they liked their classmates more, they had more positive attitudes toward school, their grades improved, and their self-esteem increased (Aronson et al., 1979). Incidentally, the work of brighter students is not sacrificed by this method. High achievers working in cooperative groups do at least as well as when learning alone, and often they do better (Johnson & Johnson, 1987). Such results are quite encouraging. As Kenneth Clark (1965) has said, "Racial prejudice . . . debases all human beings—those who are its victims, those who victimize, and in quite subtle ways, those who are merely accessories."

● Aggression—The World's Most Dangerous Animal

For a time, the City Zoo of Los Angeles, California, had on display two examples of the world's most dangerous animal—the only animal capable of destroying the earth and all other animal species. Perhaps you have already guessed which animal it was. In the cage were two college students, representing the species *Homo sapiens!*

The human capacity for aggression seems staggering. It has been estimated that during the 125-year period ending with World War II, 58 million humans were killed by other humans (an average of nearly 1 person per minute). Murder now ranks as a major cause of death in the United States. One American kills another every 23 minutes—making the United States one of the world's most violent nations (Meredith, 1984). It is estimated that more than 1.7 million American children are subjected to physical abuse by parents each year. War, homicide, riots, family violence, assassination, rape, assault, forcible robbery, and other violent acts offer further testimony to the realities of human aggression (Fig. 24–8).

Question: What causes aggression?

The complexity of aggression has given rise to a number of potential explanations for its occurrence. Brief descriptions of some of the major possibilities follow.

Instincts Some theorists argue that as humans, we are naturally aggressive, having inherited a "killer instinct" from our animal ancestors. Ethologists such as Konrad Lorenz (1966, 1974) believe that aggression is a biologically rooted behavior observed in all animals, including humans. Lorenz also believes that humans lack certain

Fig. 24–8 *Ritualized human aggression. Violent and aggressive behavior is so commonplace it may be viewed as entertainment. How "natural" is aggressive behavior?*

innate patterns that inhibit aggression in other animal species. For example, in a dispute over territory or dominance, two wolves may growl, lunge, bare their teeth, and fiercely threaten each other. In most instances, though, neither is killed or even wounded. One wolf, recognizing the dominance of the other, will typically bare its throat in a gesture of submission. The dominant wolf could kill in an instant, but it is inhibited by the submissive gesture. In contrast, human confrontations of equal intensity almost always end in injury or homicide.

The idea that humans are "naturally" aggressive has an intuitive appeal, but many psychologists question it. Many of Lorenz's "explanations" of aggression are little more than loose comparisons between human and animal behavior. Just labeling a behavior as "instinctive" does little to explain it. More important, we are left with the question of why some individuals or human groups (the Arapesh, the Senoi, and Navajo, the Eskimo, and others) show little hostility or aggression. And, thankfully, the vast majority of humans *do not* kill or harm others.

Biology Despite problems with the instinctive view, there is evidence that a biological basis for aggression may exist. Physiological studies have shown that there are brain areas capable of triggering or ending aggressive behavior (see Chapter 3). Also, researchers have found a relationship between aggression and such physical factors as hypoglycemia (low blood sugar), allergy, and specific brain injuries and disorders (Bandura, 1973; Bolton, 1976;

Mark & Ervin, 1970). None of these conditions, however, can be considered a direct *cause* of aggression. Instead, they probably lower the threshold for aggression, making hostile behavior more likely to occur.

The effects of alcohol and other drugs provide another indication of the role of the brain and biology in violence and aggression. A variety of studies show that alcohol is involved in large percentages of murders and violent crimes (Collins, 1981; Lagerspetz, 1981). Intoxicating drugs lower inhibitions to act aggressively—too often with tragic results.

To summarize, the fact that we are biologically *capable* of aggression does not mean that aggression is inevitable or "part of human nature." In 1986, a group of 20 eminent scientists gathered to examine the evidence and hammer out a statement on this issue. They concluded that, "Biology does not condemn humanity to war. . . . Violence is neither in our evolutionary legacy nor in our genes. The same species that invented war is capable of inventing peace" (Kohn, 1988).

Frustration Step on a dog's tail and you may get nipped. Frustrate a human and you may get insulted. The **frustration-aggression hypothesis** states that frustration is closely associated with aggression (Dollard et al., 1939). At several points in earlier chapters, we have considered examples of the link between frustration and aggression.

Question: Does frustration always produce aggression?

Although the connection is strong, a moment's thought will show that frustration does not *always* lead to aggression. Frustration, for instance, may lead to stereotyped responding or perhaps to a state of "learned helplessness" (see Chapters 12 and 13). Also, aggression can occur in the absence of frustration. This possibility is illustrated by sports spectators who start fights, throw bottles, tear down goal posts, and so forth, after their team has *won*.

Frustration probably encourages aggression because it is aversive (uncomfortable). Many experiments have shown that unpleasant stimuli, such as pain, insults, sweltering rooms, and disgusting scenes or odors, tend to increase aggression. Such stimuli probably raise overall arousal levels so that we become more sensitive to **aggression cues** (Berkowitz, 1976, 1982).

Question: What do you mean by "aggression cues"?

Some cues, or signals, for aggression are internal (angry thoughts, for instance). Many are external: Certain words, actions, and gestures of others are strongly associated with aggressive response. A raised middle finger, for instance, is an almost universal invitation to aggression in North America.

Even inanimate objects may serve as cues for aggression. In one classic experiment, subjects gave shocks to another person in a laboratory. Before doing so, they were ridiculed and shocked by the other person. Just before subjects got a chance to "return the favor," they saw either a couple of badminton rackets or a shotgun and a revolver on a table in the testing room. In either case, the experimenter explained that someone had left the objects there, and he casually moved them aside. Subjects who glimpsed the guns gave stronger shocks to the person who had angered them than did subjects who saw the sports equipment (Berkowitz, 1968). The implication of this **weapons effect** seems to be that the symbols and trappings of aggression encourage aggression (Fig. 25–9).

Social Learning One of the most widely accepted explanations of aggression is also the simplest. **Social learning theory** holds that we learn to be aggressive by observing aggression in others (Bandura, 1973). According to this view, there is no instinctive human programming for fistfighting, pipe-bombing, knife wielding, gun loading, or other elements of violent or aggressive behavior. Hence, aggression must be learned.

Social learning theorists predict that individuals growing up in non-aggressive cultures will themselves be non-aggressive. Those raised in a culture with aggressive models and heroes will learn aggressive responses.

Considered in such terms, it is no wonder that America has become one of the most violent of all countries. It is estimated that a violent crime occurs every 54 seconds in the United States. Approximately 40 percent of the pop-

Fig. 24–9 *Freeway shootings are a disturbing affliction of modern life. Some shootings may be a reaction to the frustration of traffic congestion. The fact that automobiles provide an anonymity may also encourage aggressive actions.*

ulation owns firearms. Nationally, 70 percent agree that "When a boy is growing up, it is very important for him to have a few fistfights." Eighteen percent of the population admit to having slapped or kicked another person (Stark & McEvoy, 1970). Children and adults are treated to an almost nonstop parade of aggressive models (in the media as well as in actual behavior—see Highlight 24–2). We are, without a doubt, an aggressive culture.

Question: What can be done about aggression?

Social learning theory implies that "aggression begets aggression." In other words, watching a prize fight, sporting event, or violent television program may increase aggression, rather than drain off aggressive urges. A case in point is provided by psychologist Leonard Eron, who spent 22 years following over 600 children into adulthood. Eron (1987) observes, "Among the most influential models for children were those observed on television. One of the best predictors of how aggressive a young man would be at age 19 was the violence of the television programs he preferred when he was 8 years old" (Fig. 24–10). According to Eron, children learn aggressive strategies and actions from TV violence (also see Chapter 8). Because of this, they are more prone to aggression when they face frustrating situations or cues. Thus, the spiral of aggression might be broken if we did not so often portray it, reward it, and glorify it.

Fig. 24–10 *Although TV violence does not cause aggression, it can encourage it. The likelihood of committing criminal acts by age 30 is related to the amount of TV watching a person did when he or she was a child (Eron, 1987). (Graph copyright 1987 by the American Psychological Association, Inc. Reprinted by permission of the author.)*

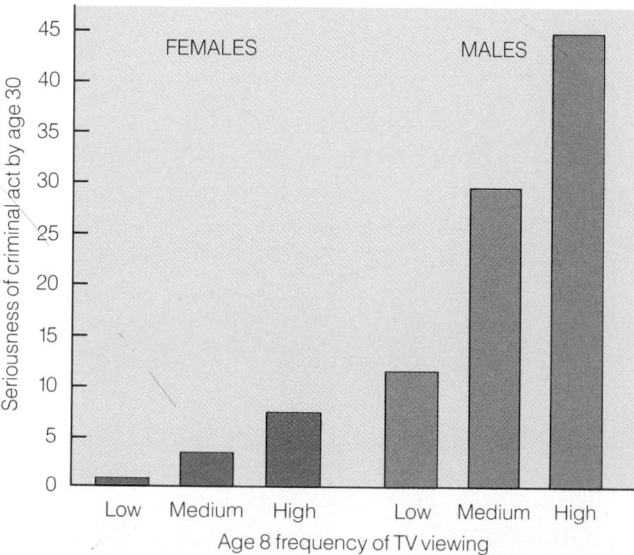

● HIGHLIGHT 24–2
Aggression and Pornography—Is there a Link?

The debate on the effects of pornography is heating up again. Until recently, most evidence suggested that viewing pornography has no major adverse effects. This conclusion appears to remain valid for stimuli that can be described as merely erotic or sexual in content. However, in the last 10 years, there has been a dramatic increase in the number of aggressive-pornographic stimuli appearing in the mass media. **Aggressive pornography** refers to depictions in which violence, threats, or obvious power differences are used to force someone (usually a woman) to engage in sex.

The principal finding of studies on aggressive-pornographic stimuli is that they do increase aggression by males against females. In a summary of various experiments, researchers Neil Malamuth and Ed Donnerstein (1982) concluded that "exposure to mass media stimuli that have violent and sexual content increases the audience's aggressive-sexual fantasies, beliefs in rape myths, and aggressive behavior." Donnerstein and Daniel Linz (1986) further conclude that it is media *violence* that is most damaging. As they put it, "Violent images, rather than sexual ones, are most responsible for people's attitudes about women and rape." The problem, then, extends far beyond X-rated films and books. Mainstream movies, magazines, videos, and television programs are equally to blame for reinforcing the myth that women find force or aggression pleasurable.

Anger Control On a personal level, some psychologists have succeeded in teaching people to control their anger and aggressive impulses. The key to **anger control** is the fact that people who respond calmly to upsetting situations tend to see them as *problems to be solved*. Therefore, to limit anger, people are taught to:

1. Define the problem as precisely as possible.
2. Make a list of possible solutions.
3. Rank the likely success of each solution.
4. Choose a solution and try it.
5. Assess how successful the solution was, and make adjustments if necessary.

Taking these steps has helped many people to lessen tendencies toward child abuse, family violence, and other destructive outbursts (Meichenbaum et al., 1982).

Beyond this, the question remains, How shall we tame the world's most dangerous animal? There is no easy answer. Only a challenge of pressing importance. The solution will undoubtedly involve the best efforts of thinkers and researchers from many disciplines.

For the more immediate future, it is clear that we need more people who are willing to engage in helpful, altruistic, *prosocial* behavior. In the following Applications section we will examine some of the forces that operate to prevent people from helping others. Also discussed are a few glimmerings about how to encourage prosocial behavior.

Learning Check

1. Social stereotypes may be both positive and negative. T or F?

2. The stereotypes underlying racial and ethnic prejudice tend to evolve from the superordinate goals that often separate groups. T or F?

3. The term *symbolic prejudice* refers to racism or prejudice that is expressed in disguised or hidden form. T or F?

4. Jane Elliot's classroom experiment in prejudice showed that children could be made to dislike one another
a. by setting up group competition
b. by imposing status inequalities
c. by role playing
d. by frustrating all the students

5. Research suggests that prejudice and intergroup conflict may be reduced by ____________ interaction and ____________ goals.

6. Social learning theorists view aggression as related to biological instincts for aggression. T or F?

7. Frustration is more likely to produce aggression when cues for aggressive behavior are present. T or F?

8. Social learning theory holds that exposure to aggressive models helps drain off aggressive energies. T or F?

Answers:
1. T **2.** F **3.** T **4.** *b* **5.** equal-status, superordinate **6.** F **7.** T **8.** F

Applications: Helping—Promoting Prosocial Behavior

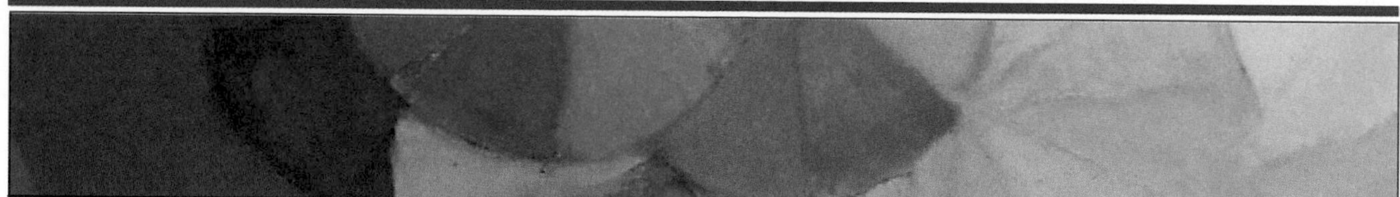

Late one night in March, 1964, tenants of a Queens, New York, apartment building watched and listened in horror as a young woman named Kitty Genovese was murdered on the sidewalk outside. From the safety of their rooms, no fewer than 38 people heard the agonized screams as her assailant stabbed her, was frightened off, and returned to stab her again.

Kitty Genovese's murder took over 30 minutes, but none of her neighbors tried to help. None even called the police. Perhaps it is understandable that no one wanted to get involved. After all, it could have been a violent lovers' quarrel, or helping might have meant risking personal injury. But what prevented these people from at least calling the police?

Question: Isn't this an example of the alienation of city life?

News reports treated this incident as evidence of a breakdown in social ties caused by the impersonality of the city. While it is true that urban living can be dehumanizing, this does not fully explain such **bystander apathy.** According to psychologists Bibb Latané and John Darley (1968), failure to help is related to the number of people present. Over the years many studies have shown that the *more* potential helpers present, the *lower* the chances that help will be given (Latané et al., 1981).

Question: Why would people be less willing to help when others are present?

In Kitty Genovese's case, the answer is that everyone thought *someone else* would help. The dynamics of this effect can be illustrated in this way: Suppose that two motorists have stalled at roadside, one on a sparsely traveled country road and the other on a busy freeway. Who gets help first? On the freeway, where hundreds of cars pass every minute, each driver can assume that someone else will help. Personal responsibility for helping is spread so thin that no one takes action. On the country road, one of the first few people to arrive will probably stop, since the responsibility is clearly theirs. In general, Latané and Darley assume that bystanders are not apathetic or uncaring; they are inhibited by the presence of others.

Bystander Intervention There are four decision points individuals must pass through before giving help. First they must notice that something is happening. Next they must define the event as an emergency. Then they must take responsibility. Finally, they must select a course of action (Fig. 24–11). Laboratory experiments have shown that each step can be influenced by the presence of other people.

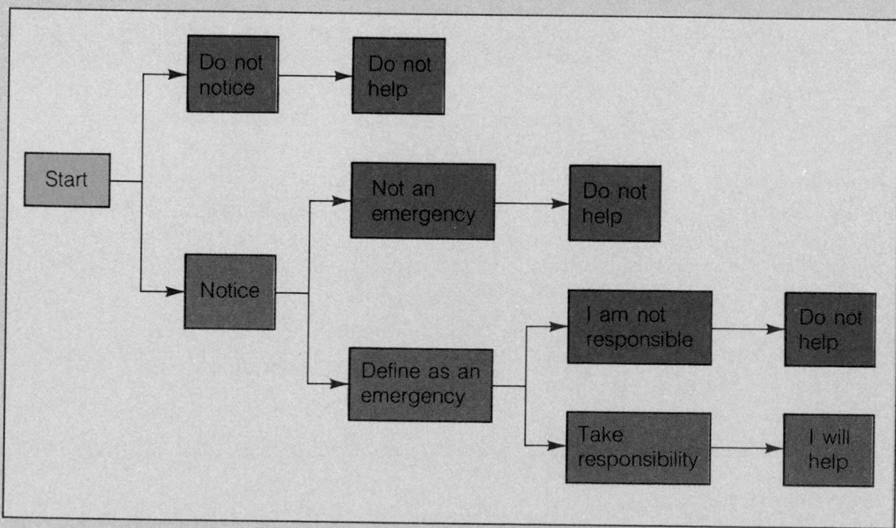

Fig. 24–11 *This decision tree summarizes the steps a person must take before making a commitment to offer help, according to Latané and Darley's model.*

Applications

Noticing What would happen if you fainted and collapsed on the sidewalk? Would someone stop to help? Would people think you were drunk? Would they even notice you? Latané and Darley suggest that if the sidewalk is crowded, few people will even see you. This has nothing to do with people blocking each other's vision. Instead, it is related to widely accepted norms against staring at others in public. People in crowds typically "keep their eyes to themselves."

Question: Is there any way to show that this is a factor in bystander apathy?

To test this idea, students were asked to fill out a questionnaire either alone or in a room full of people. While the students worked, a thick cloud of smoke was blown into the room through a vent.

Most students alone in the room noticed the smoke immediately. Few of the people in groups noticed the smoke until it actually became difficult to see through it. Subjects working in groups politely kept their eyes on their papers and avoided looking at others (or the smoke). In contrast, those who were alone scanned the room from time to time.

Defining an Emergency The smoke-filled room also shows the influence others have on defining a situation as an emergency. When subjects in groups finally noticed the smoke, they cast sidelong glances at others in the room. Apparently, they were searching for clues to help interpret what was happening. No one wanted to overreact or act like a fool if there was no emergency. However, as subjects coolly surveyed the reactions of others, they were themselves being watched. In real emergencies, people sometimes underestimate the need for action because each person attempts to appear calm. In short, until someone acts, no one acts.

Taking Responsibility Perhaps the most crucial step in the helping sequence is assuming responsibility. In this case, groups limit helping by causing a **diffusion of responsibility.**

Question: Is that like the unwillingness of drivers to offer help on a crowded freeway?

Exactly. It is the feeling that no one is personally responsible for helping. This problem was demonstrated in an experiment in which students took part in a group discussion over an intercom system. Actually, there was only one real subject in each group; the others were tape-recorded confederates of the experimenter. Each subject was placed in a separate room (supposedly to maintain confidentiality), and discussions of college life were begun. During the discussion, one of the "students" simulated an epileptic-like seizure and called out for help. In some cases, subjects thought they were alone with the seizure victim. Others believed they were members of 3- or 6-person groups.

Subjects who thought they were alone with the "victim" of this staged emergency reported it immediately or tried to help. Some subjects in the 3-person groups failed to respond, and those who did were slower. In the 6-person groups, over a third of the subjects took no action at all. People in this experiment were obviously faced with a conflict like that in many real emergencies: Should they be helpful and responsible, or should they mind their own business? Many were influenced toward inaction by the presence of others.

Question: People do help in some emergencies. How are these situations different?

It is not always clear what makes the difference. Helping behavior is a complex event, influenced by many variables. One naturalistic experiment staged in a New York City subway gives a hint of the kinds of things that may be important. When a "victim" (actor) "passed out" in a subway car, he received more help when carrying a cane than when carrying a liquor bottle. More important, however, was the fact that most people were willing to help in either case (Piliavin et al., 1969).

To better answer the question, we need to consider some factors not included in Latané and Darley's account of helping.

Who Will Help Whom? Psychologist John Dovido (1984) has nicely summarized some of the major factors that affect helping behavior. Many studies suggest that when we see a person in trouble, it tends to cause *heightened arousal.* This aroused, keyed-up feeling can motivate us to give aid, but only if the rewards of helping outweigh the costs. Higher costs (such as great effort, personal risk, or possible embarrassment) almost always decrease helping (Foss, 1986). In addition to general arousal, potential helpers may feel **empathic arousal.** This means that they empathize with the person in need or feel some of the person's pain, fear, or anguish.

Empathic arousal also motivates helping—especially when the person in need seems to be similar to ourselves (Eisenberg & Miller, 1987). In fact, feeling a connection to the victim may be one of the most important factors in helping. This, perhaps, is why being in a good mood also increases helping. When we are feeling successful, happy, or fortunate, we may also feel more connected to others (Dovido, 1984).

Question: Is there anything that can be done to encourage prosocial behavior?

There is evidence that people who see others helping are more likely to offer help themselves. As you may recall from Chapter

Applications

2, for example, motorists were much more likely to stop to help a woman fix a tire when they had just passed another woman being helped by someone (Bryan & Test, 1967). Also, persons who give help in one situation tend to perceive themselves as helpful people. This change in self-image encourages them to help in other situations. One more point is that norms of fairness encourage us to help others who have helped us (Dovido, 1984). For all these reasons, helping others not only assists them directly; it encourages others to help, too.

Learning Check

1. Psychologists have shown that the dehumanizing qualities of urban living explain most instances of bystander apathy. T or F?

2. Defining an event as an emergency is the first step toward bystander intervention. T or F?

3. People sometimes fail to define an event as an emergency because they are misled by a seeming lack of concern displayed by others. T or F?

4. In laboratory experiments, a large number of potential helpers tends to reduce the likelihood that help will be given. T or F?

Answers:
1. F 2. F 3. T 4. T

Exploration: Sociobiology—Do Genes Guide Social Behavior?

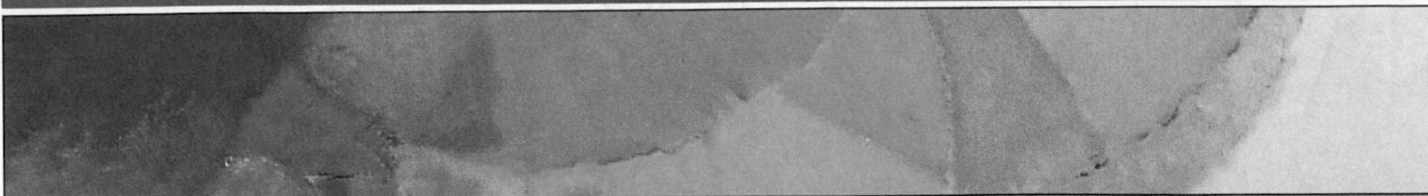

A small band of men moves cautiously through a rubble-strewn battlefield. Without warning, a grenade sails overhead and lands at their feet. There is no time for escape. Instinctively, one of the men dives at the grenade, covers it with his own body, and shields his comrades from certain death. Scenes such as this have occurred in almost every modern war. How are such altruistic actions explained?

Sociobiology According to a viewpoint called **sociobiology,** many human social behaviors have roots in heredity. Sociobiologists, such as Harvard zoologist Edward Wilson, believe that competition, war, territoriality, aggression, sibling rivalry, conformity, male-female differences, fear of strangers, altruism, and many other behaviors are "in our genes."

The core idea in sociobiology is that social behavior evolves in ways that maximize fitness for survival. For instance, animals who compete successfully for food, territory, mates, and so forth, are more likely to survive and reproduce. Thus, competitiveness gradually becomes a trait of following generations. Sociobiologists believe that many human traits evolved through similar patterns of natural selection.

Applying the concept of natural selection to explain human nature may make sense for some behaviors. But how do sociobiologists explain altruistic actions like the selfless heroism of the soldier described earlier? The answer is intriguing. Sociobiologists point out that altruistic suicides can be observed in many animal species. For example, if a honeybee stings an intruder to protect its hive, the bee will die. How could such behavior evolve if altruistic bees never get a chance to reproduce and pass on their genes? Sociobiologists reply that altruistic actions help improve chances that an animal's *kin* will survive.

Each individual shares some genes in common with close family members. So, while the altruistic individual's genes may not be passed on directly, they are perpetuated by close kin. In human terms, sociobiologists argue that a person might sacrifice his or her own chance of survival to ensure the survival of a number of close relatives. Of course, heroic soldiers are typically unrelated to their comrades. Nevertheless, a soldier may act for the good of the group because altruism has been "bred into" humans during eons of evolution.

Biological Determinism Sociobiology deserves credit for offering a fresh perspective on human behavior. In fact, sociobiology produces some fascinating images when it is taken to its logical extremes: It is almost as if genes are at the helms of great hulking machines (our bodies) that they use for protection and self-preservation. Sociobiology seems to say that genes manipulate our behavior to ensure *their* survival (or at least the survival of duplicate genes in the bodies of our relatives).

Sociobiology's major strength is that it helps relate human behavior to biology. Its major weakness is that it probably overstates its case. The degree of biological determinism assumed by sociobiologists is so extreme that even most biologists question it.

Critique Thinking about the biological foundations of human behavior is always interesting. However, the conclusions drawn by sociobiologists are highly questionable. Evolution and natural selection, for instance, may have favored development of the human brain, rather than of specific behavioral traits. Humans equipped with large brains are resourceful, adaptable, and flexible. Our intelligence, in fact, would seem to have much more to do with our survival as individuals and as a group than could be provided by strict genetic programming.

Along the same line, many critics of sociobiology point out that evolution progresses too slowly to account for many behavioral adaptations. The spread of ideas, traditions, and cultural patterns is much more rapid. To return to our earlier example, altruism may indeed be a necessity for a society to endure. However, selfless acts need not be coded into our nature by genes; they may be explained equally well by learning.

The danger inherent in sociobiology is that it can be used to support

Exploration

the social status quo. By defining human nature as relatively fixed and (in the short run) unchanging, sociobiology discourages attempts to change current cultural practices. Edward Wilson has said, for instance, that since males are typically more aggressive than females, "Even with identical education and equal access to all professions, men are more likely to continue to play a disproportionate role in political life, business, and science." If you are female, that should make you angry. If you are a male, it should make you angry on behalf of your mother, sisters, daughters, wife, lover, or female friends.

Conclusion In the realm of ideas, it's also a matter of survival of the fittest. To many observers it appears that sociobiology will have to evolve greatly if it is going to survive. In the meantime, the sociobiology debate should prove interesting. (Sources: Blaustein, 1983; Gould, 1976; Kamin, 1985; Kitchner, 1985; Lumsden & Wilson, 1983; Snowdon, 1983; Wilson, 1975)

Learning Check

1. The core idea of sociobiology is that social behavior evolved in ways that maximize individual fitness for survival. T or F?
2. Sociobiologists believe that altruistic behavior evolved because individual sacrifice improved chances that immediate family members and close kin would survive. T or F?
3. The majority of biologists endorse sociobiological explanations of behavior. T or F?
4. Critics of sociobiology point out that natural selection among humans might have favored enlargement of the brain and behavioral flexibility—not selection of specific behavioral traits. T or F?

Answers:

1. F 2. T 3. F 4. T

Chapter Summary

- **Attitudes** are learned dispositions made up of a **belief component,** an **emotional component,** and an **action component.**
- Attitudes may be formed by *direct contact, interaction* with others, and *child-rearing practices*. Groups also exert pressures on attitudes held by their members. *Peer group influences*, the *mass media*, and *chance conditioning* also appear to be important in attitude formation.
- Attitudes are typically measured by use of techniques such as **open-ended interviews, social distance scales,** and **attitude scales.** Attitudes expressed in these ways do not always correspond to actual behavior.
- Attitude change is related to **reference group** membership, to deliberate **persuasion,** and to significant personal experiences (which may be engineered through *role playing*).
- The maintenance and change of attitudes is closely related to needs for consistency in thoughts and actions. **Cognitive dissonance theory** explains the dynamics of such needs.
- **Brainwashing** is a form of forced attitude change. It depends on control of the target person's total environment. Three steps in brainwashing are **unfreezing, changing,** and **refreezing** attitudes and beliefs.
- Many religious and quasi-religious cults recruit new members with high-pressure indoctrination techniques resembling brainwashing. Such groups attempt to catch people when they are vulnerable. Then they combine

isolation, displays of *affection, discipline and rituals, intimidation,* and *escalating commitment* to bring about conversion.

• **Prejudice** is a negative attitude held toward members of various out-groups. One theory attributes prejudice to **scapegoating.** A second account says that prejudices may be held for personal reasons **(personal prejudice)** or simply through adherence to group norms **(group prejudice).**

• Prejudiced individuals tend to have an **authoritarian** or **dogmatic personality,** characterized by rigidity, inhibition, intolerance, over-simplification, and **ethnocentrism.**

• Intergroup conflict gives rise to hostility and the formation of **social stereotypes. Status inequalities** tend to build prejudices. **Equal-status contact** tends to reduce it. Muzafer Sherif and others have emphasized the concept of **superordinate goals** as a key to reducing intergroup conflict, be it racial, religious, ethnic, or national. On a smaller scale, **jigsaw classrooms** (which encourage cooperation through **mutual interdependence**) have been shown to be an effective way of combating prejudice.

• **Aggression** and violence are serious social problems and the subject of much current research. **Ethological explanations** of aggression attribute it to inherited instincts. **Biological explanations** emphasize brain mechanisms and physical factors related to thresholds for aggression. According to the **frustration-aggression hypothesis,** frustration and aggression are closely linked, especially when **aggression cues** are present. **Social learning theory** has focused attention on the role of **aggressive models** in the development of aggressive behavior.

• Four decision points that must be passed before a person gives help are: **noticing, defining an emergency, taking responsibility,** and **selecting a course of action.** Helping is less likely at each point when other potential helpers are present. Helping is encouraged by general arousal, **empathic arousal,** being in a good mood, low effort or risk, and similarity between the victim and the helper. For several reasons, giving help tends to encourage others to help too.

• **Sociobiology** attempts to explain human social behavior by relating it to natural selection and human evolution. Although some elements of the theory are difficult to defend, sociobiology has prompted a healthy debate about the biological origins of human behavior.

Questions For Discussion

1. Choose an issue you feel strongly about. State your attitudes concerning the issue. How did you come to hold your present attitudes? What types of experiences or variables influenced you?

2. If you were asked to establish a program to end conflict between students attending two rival high schools, what steps would you take?

3. What do you think are the superordinate goals facing the nation and the world? (To be truly superordinate, a goal would have to be seen as valid by nearly everyone.) Do such goals exist? How could such a goal be converted into greater intergroup cooperation?

4. Describe a situation in which you did or did not offer help to someone who was, or might have been, in need. What influenced your decision? In view of what you know about helping behavior, can you explain why rape or assault victims are advised to shout "Fire!"?

5. Kenneth Clark has said, "Prejudice is a way that human beings have of betraying the fragility of their egos." What do you think Clark meant? Do you agree?

6. How has the anti-smoking campaign of the American Cancer Society made use of cognitive dissonance to discourage smoking?

7. In what ways do magazine and television advertisements apply the principles of persuasion? (Consider the communicator, the message, and the audience.)

8. The view that humans are instinctively aggressive "naked apes" has been quite popular. To what do you attribute this popularity? Do you consider humans naturally aggressive? What evidence can you give for or against this view?

9. Studies of capital punishment show that it has either no effect on deterring homicides, or that there is a slight *decline* after it is abolished. How would a social learning theorist explain this decline? If capital punishment does not deter homicides, do you think it can be justified for other reasons? If so, what, in your opinion, are they?

10. Sociobiologists have been accused of making a basic error by assuming that human nature is revealed by the behavior of citizens in modern societies. What do you think are the basic, universal characteristics of human nature?

Chapter 25

Sexuality and Gender

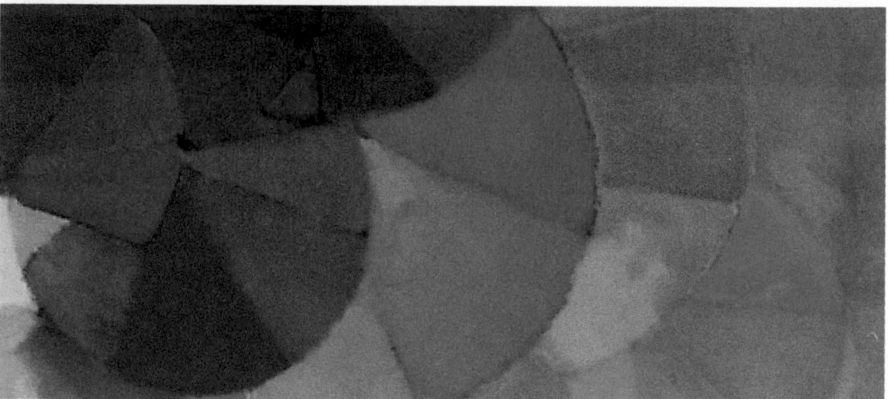

In This Chapter
Dimensions of gender
Sexual behavior
Human sexual response
Attitudes and sexual behavior
AIDS and STDs
Applications
Sexual problems
Sexual adjustment
Exploration
Patterns of touching

Chapter Preview

That Magic Word

Sex\seks n 1. One of the two divisions of organisms formed on the distinction of male and female.

"Sex" has many meanings: reproduction, gender, sexual identity, intimacy, and much more. Of the various meanings, the simplest would seem to be the reference to gender. What, really, could be simpler? Males are males and females are females, right? Wrong. Even something as basic as gender is complicated and many-sided.

Gender *The complexity of gender is illustrated by the attempt (1976) of Dr. Renée Richards to enter a women's tennis tournament. You may recall from news stories that Dr. Richards is a transsexual. Formerly she was Dr. Richard Raskin, an opthalmologist. As a man, Richard Raskin was a modestly successful tennis player. After a sex change operation, Dr. Richards tried to launch a new tennis career as a woman. Understandably, other women players protested. Officials finally decided to use a genetic sex test to determine if Dr. Richards could compete. She, in turn, protested this test. Genetically she would still be considered male, but psychologically she is female—she has female genitals, and she functions socially as a female (Hyde, 1984). Is Dr. Richards, then, male or female?*

You might view the case of Renée Richards as an unfair example because transsexuals seek to alter natural gender. For most people, the various indicators of gender are in agreement. Nevertheless, it is not unusual to find occasional ambiguities among the dimensions of a person's "sex." Contrary to common belief, gender is not a simple either-or classification. In the first part of this chapter, we will consider some basic dimensions of "maleness" and "femaleness." An essential question we will address is, How does one become male or female?

Sexual Behavior *Each of us is by nature a sexual creature. This inescapable reality springs from the basic biology of reproduction. With this reality in mind, later sections of this chapter discuss sexual behavior, sexual arousal and response, sexual problems, and attitudes toward sexuality. These are topics you may feel you already know a lot about. Therefore, before reading further, you may find it interesting to see if you can correctly answer the* Human Sexuality Quiz. *Answers follow the quiz. The reasons for the answers can be found in this chapter.*

Human Sexuality Quiz *Indicate which of the statements are true and which are false.*

1. *Women are generally incapable of multiple orgasm.*
2. *More than half of all cases of impotence in males are psychologically caused.*
3. *Frequent nocturnal emissions ("wet dreams") in males indicate the existence of a sexual disorder.*
4. *Male sexual potency and female pleasure in intercourse are closely related to penis size.*
5. *Of the various sexual dysfunctions, premature ejaculation is one of the easiest to treat.*
6. *In recent years, medical advances have brought about a decline in the overall occurrence of sexually transmitted diseases.*
7. *For women, masturbation typically involves stimulation of the clitoris.*
8. *Sterilization in both men and women usually abolishes the sex drive.*
9. *Women have two kinds of orgasm, vaginal and clitoral.*
10. *The "sexual revolution" has brought about greater changes in women's sexual behavior than men's.*
11. *Men are more physically aroused by explicit erotic stimuli (such as pornographic films) than are women.*
12. *Maximum sexual responsiveness generally occurs at a later age for women than it does for men.*

Answers:

1. F **2.** T **3.** F **4.** F **5.** T **6.** F **7.** T **8.** F **9.** F **10.** T **11.** F **12.** T

Survey Questions

- What are the basic dimensions of gender?
- How does one's sense of maleness or femaleness develop?
- How are sex roles acquired?
- What are the most typical patterns of human sexual behavior?
- To what extent do males and females differ in sexual response?
- Have recent changes in attitudes affected sexual behavior?
- What impact have sexually transmitted diseases had on sexual behavior?
- What are the most common sexual adjustment problems? How are they treated?
- What is the role of touching in personal relationships?

The Development of Sex Differences

It has been said that the one thing you will never forget about a person is that person's sex. Considering the number of activities, relationships, conflicts, and choices influenced by gender, it is no wonder that we pay close attention to it. Let's begin with a few basic questions: What does it mean to be male or female? What are the dimensions of gender? How do gender and sex role differences develop?

Male or Female?

Traditionally, the basic physical differences between males and females have been divided into *primary* and *secondary* sexual characteristics. **Primary sexual characteristics** refer to the sexual and reproductive organs themselves: the penis, testes, and scrotum in males and the vagina, ovaries, and uterus in females (Figs. 25–1 and 25–2). As described in Chapter 15, **secondary sexual characteristics** appear at puberty in response to hormonal signals from the pituitary gland. In females, secondary sexual characteristics involve development of the breasts, broadening of the hips, and other changes in body shape. Males develop facial and body hair, and the voice deepens. These changes signal readiness for reproduction. Reproductive maturity is especially evident in the female **menarche** (MEN-ar-kee: the onset of menstruation). Soon after menarche, monthly **ovulation** begins. Ovulation refers to the release of ova (eggs) from the ovaries. From the first ovulation until **menopause** (the end of regular monthly fertility cycles), women can bear children.

Question: What causes the development of sex differences?

In general terms, both primary and secondary sexual characteristics are related to the action of sex hormones in the body. (*Hormones* are chemical substances secreted by glands of the endocrine system.) The **gonads** (or sex glands) affect sexual development and behavior by secreting **estrogens** (female hormones) and **androgens** (male hormones). The gonads in the male are the testes; the female gonads are the ovaries. The adrenal glands (located above the kidneys) also supply sex hormones in both males and females. At puberty, adrenal secretions add to the development of secondary sexual characteristics.

Interestingly, all individuals normally produce both estrogens and androgens. It is the proportion of these hormones that influences sex differences. In fact, the development of male or female anatomy is largely due to the presence or absence—before birth—of **testosterone** (one of the androgens).

Question: Then is biological sex determined by the sex hormones?

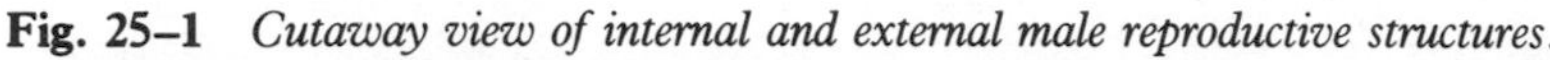

Fig. 25–1 *Cutaway view of internal and external male reproductive structures.*

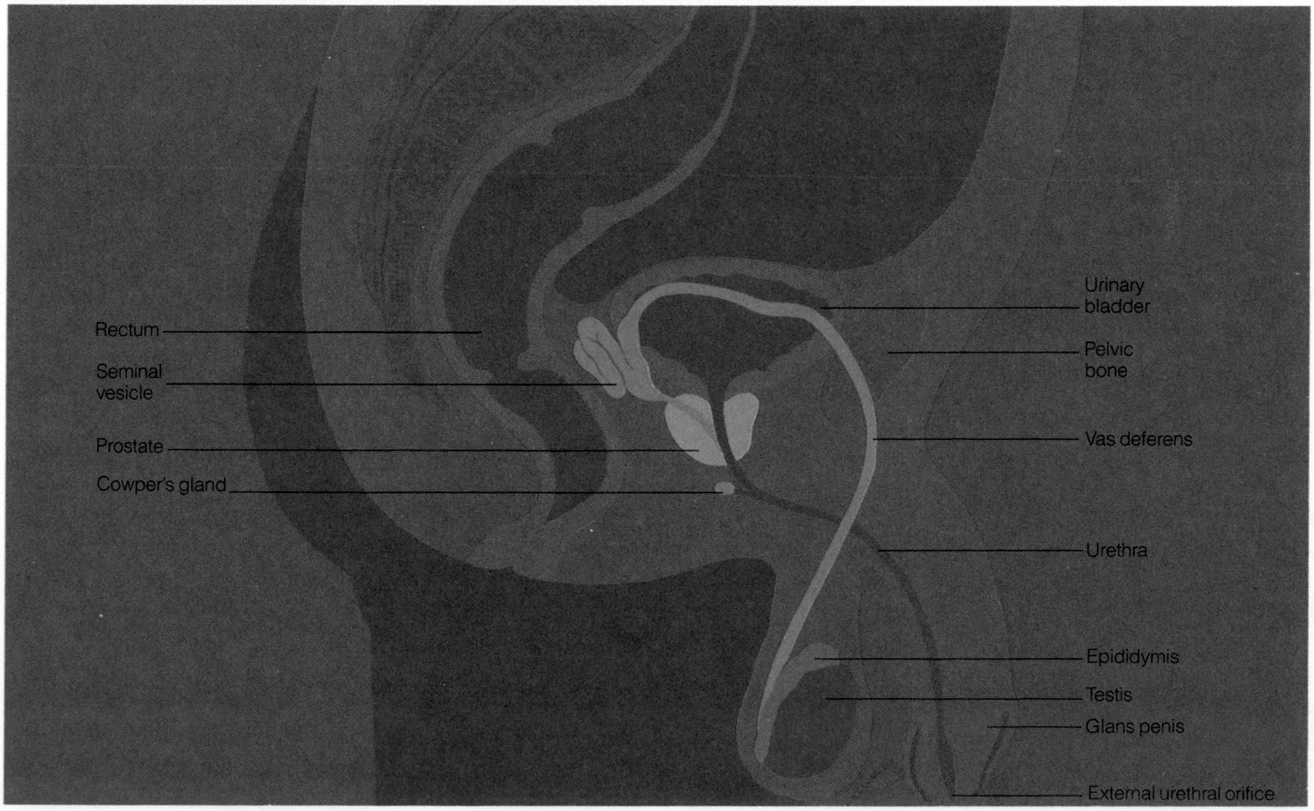

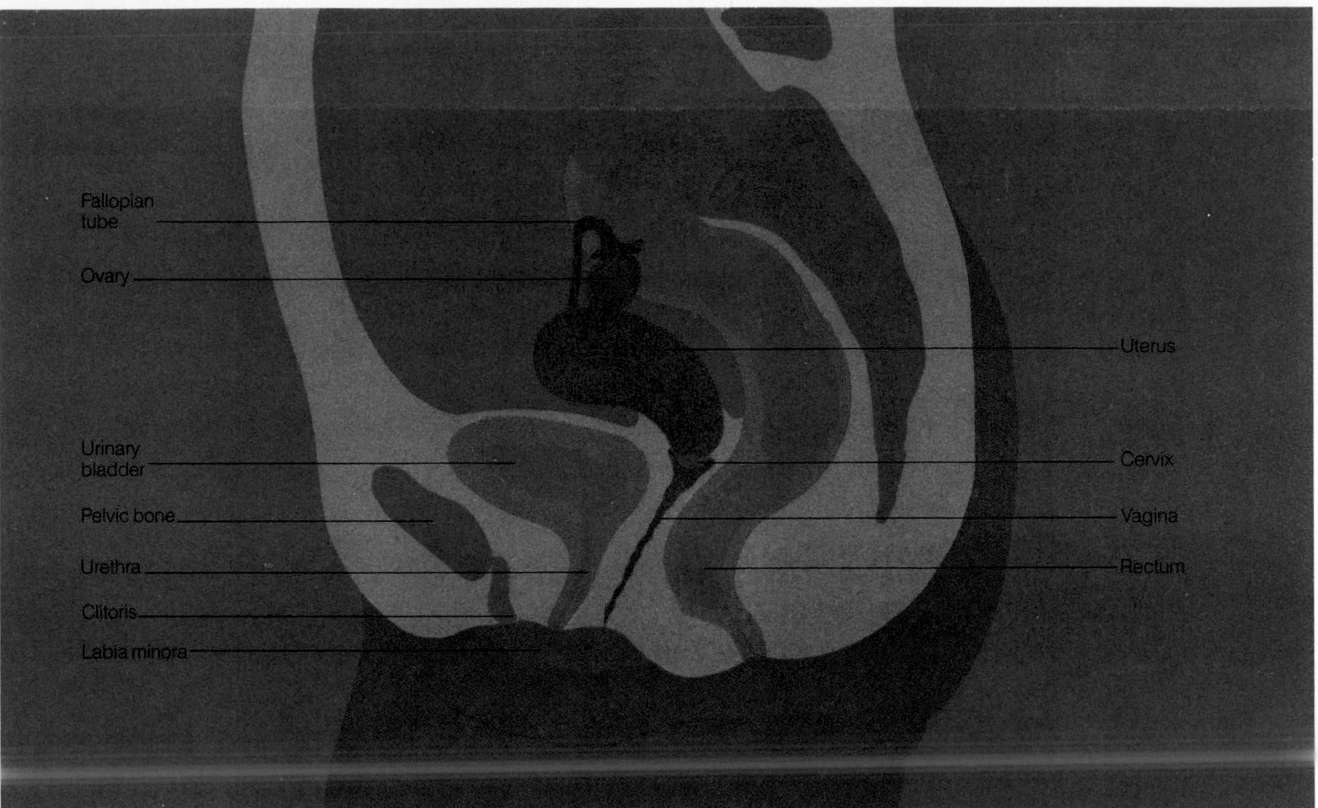

Fig. 25–2 *Cutaway view of internal and external female reproductive structures.*

Not entirely. As suggested by our discussion in the Chapter Preview, gender cannot be reduced to a single dimension.

Dimensions of Gender At the very least, any evaluation of gender must include (1) **genetic sex** (*XX* or *XY* chromosomes), (2) **gonadal sex** (ovaries or testes), (3) **hormonal sex** (predominance of androgens or estrogens), (4) **genital sex** (clitoris and vagina in females, penis and scrotum in males), and (5) **gender identity** (one's personal sense of maleness or femaleness) (Money & Ehrhardt, 1972). To see why gender must be defined along several dimensions, let's follow the sequence of events involved in becoming male or female.

Gender Development

Becoming male or female starts simply enough. Genetic sex is determined at the instant of conception: Two *X* chromosomes initiate development of a female; an *X* chromosome plus a *Y* chromosome produces a male. Genetic sex remains the same throughout life. But it alone does not determine gender. We must also consider hormonal effects before birth.

For the first 6 weeks of prenatal growth, there is no difference between a genetically male and a genetically female embryo. However, if a *Y* chromosome is present, testes develop in the embryo and supply testosterone. This stimulates growth of the penis and other male structures (Fig. 25–3). In the absence of testosterone, the embryo will develop female reproductive organs and genitals, regardless of genetic sex. It might be said, then, that nature's primary impulse is to make a female (Money, 1965).

Development of the embryo usually matches genetic sex, but not always. A genetic male will fail to develop male genitals if too little testosterone is formed during prenatal growth. Even if testosterone is present, an inherited *androgen insensitivity* may exist, again resulting in female development.

Similarly, androgens must be either at low levels or absent for an *XX* embryo to develop as a female. Thus, for both genetic males and females, hormonal problems before birth may result in **hermaphroditism** (her-MAF-

havior because it is "expected." However, pressures such as these probably come as much from the individual as from others. If a greater acceptance of human sexuality is to be constructive, it must be perceived as a general increase in personal freedom—as the right to say no, as well as the right to choose when, where, how, and with whom one's sexuality will be expressed.

The importance of respecting the right to say no is underscored by the recent dramatic increase in cases of **acquaintance** (or **date**) **rape.** One recent study found that 15 percent of all female college students had been raped. Roughly one-half of these rapes were by first dates, casual dates, or romantic acquaintances (Koss et al., 1987). Men who commit date rape often believe they have done nothing wrong. A typical explanation is, "Her words were saying no, but her body was saying yes." But forced sex is rape, even if the rapist doesn't use a knife or become violent. The effects of acquaintance rape are no less devastating than rape committed by a stranger.

In general, most adults favor greater freedom of choice for themselves, including choice about sexual behavior (Sadock, 1987). Yet, as noted, there is some ambivalence toward greater sexual freedom. As the upcoming discussion of AIDS suggests, there are new and compelling reasons for caution in sexual behavior. As is true elsewhere, freedom must be combined with responsibility, commitment, and caring if it is to have meaning.

AIDS, STD, and Sexual Responsibility The incidence of **sexually transmitted disease (STD)** has been rising in the United States for the last 20 years. Today, sexually active individuals run an elevated risk of getting chlamydia, gonorrhea, hepatitis B, herpes, syphilis, and other STDs. For many people, **acquired immune deficiency syndrome (AIDS)** has added a new fear. Whereas most other STDs are treatable, AIDS is almost always fatal once symptoms appear. You probably already know about AIDS. Even so, it might be a good idea to check your knowledge against the following summary.

AIDS is caused by a virus. In time, the disease disables the immune system. This allows various other "opportunistic" diseases to invade the body without resistance. Most AIDS victims eventually die of multiple infections. The first symptoms of AIDS may show up as little as 2 months after infection, or they may not appear for up to 7 years. Because of this long incubation period, infected persons often pass AIDS on to others without knowing it.

AIDS is spread by direct contact with body fluids—especially blood, semen, and vaginal secretions. The AIDS virus cannot be transmitted by casual contact. People do not get AIDS from shaking hands, touching or using objects used by an AIDS patient, social kissing, sharing drinking glasses, sharing towels, and so forth.

AIDS has been called the gay plague because male homosexuals were its first highly visible victims. However, this label is in error. AIDS can be spread by all forms of sexual intercourse, and it has affected persons of all sexual orientations (Denning, 1987; Koop, 1988b). Those who are at greatest risk include men who have had sex with other men (homosexual and bisexual men), people who have shared needles (for tattoos or for intravenous drug use), blood transfusion recipients (between 1977 and spring 1985), hemophiliacs (who require frequent blood transfusions), sexual partners of people in the preceding groups, and heterosexuals with a history of multiple partners.

The U.S. Public Health Service notes that the behaviors listed here are risky when performed with an infected person (Koop, 1988b).

Risky Behaviors

- Sharing drug needles and syringes
- Anal sex, with or without a condom
- Vaginal or oral sex with someone who injects drugs or engages in anal sex
- Sex with someone you don't know well or with someone you know has several partners
- Unprotected sex (without a condom) with an infected partner

With respect to the preceding, it's important to remember that you can't tell from appearance if a person is infected.

The preceding high-risk behaviors can be contrasted with the following list of safe sexual practices.

Safe Behaviors

- Not having sex
- Sex with one mutually faithful, uninfected partner
- Not injecting drugs

Perhaps because it is fatal, AIDS is having a strong impact on sexual behavior in some groups. Among gay men there has been a sharp increase in monogamous relationships and in abstention from sex. Gay men have also significantly reduced their participation in high-risk sexual behaviors ("High risk," 1987). Evidence is growing that the risk of AIDS infection is lower for heterosexuals than once predicted (Scheer, 1987). Nevertheless, all sexually active persons are at risk, and the total number of heterosexual cases *is* growing (Koop, 1988b). This has forced many people to face new issues of risk and responsibility.

The sexual revolution was fueled, in part, by the "pill" and other birth control methods. Will the threat of AIDS reverse the tide of changes that occurred in previous decades? Will STD come to mean Sudden Total Disinterest in sex? Will the "germs of endearment" change the terms of endearment? The answers may depend on how quickly AIDS spreads into the general population and how soon its prevention or cure can be achieved.

Learning Check

1. List the four phases of sexual response identified by Masters and Johnson: ______________________________

____

2. Males typically experience ______________________ after ejaculation.
a. an increased potential for orgasm *c.* the excitement phase
b. a short refractory period *d.* muscular contractions of the uterus

3. The research of Masters and Johnson suggests that the similarities between male and female sexual responses outweigh the differences. T or F?

4. During lovemaking, from 10 to 20 minutes is often required for a woman to go from excitement to orgasm, while the male may experience all four stages of sexual response in as little as 4 minutes. T or F?

5. Stimultaneous orgasm of the male and female should be the ultimate goal in lovemaking. T or F?

6. Recent research shows that more liberal views regarding sexual behavior have erased the traditional values that link sexual involvement with committed relationships. T or F?

7. Contrary to long-standing belief, it now appears that much female sexual pleasure is focused on
a. the uterus *b.* the clitoris *c.* the urethra *d.* the cervix

8. The term ______________ ______________ describes the long-standing tendency for the sexual behavior of men and women to be judged differently.

9. Because AIDS is spread by direct contact with body fluids, it can be transmitted by social kissing or contact with food or dishes handled by an AIDS patient. T or F?

Answers:

1. excitement, plateau, orgasm, resolution **2.** *b* **3.** T **4.** T **5.** F **6.** F **7.** *b* **8.** double standard **9.** F

Applications: Sexual Problems

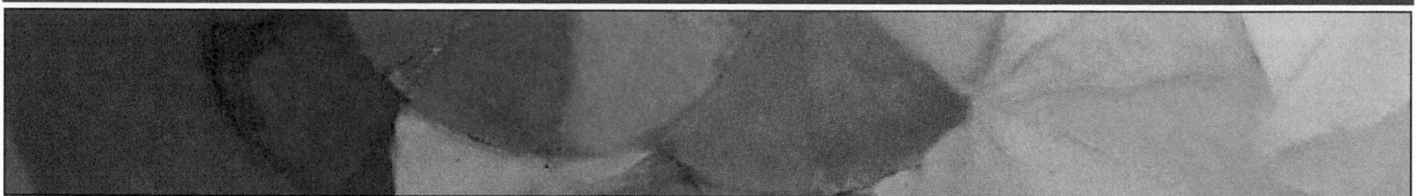

Question: What are the most common sexual problems? How are they treated?

Most people who seek sexual counseling have one or more of the following six problems (Kaplan, 1974):

A. For the male:

1. **Impotence:** an inability to produce or maintain an erection
2. **Premature ejaculation:** an inability to delay or control orgasm
3. **Retarded ejaculation:** an inability to reach orgasm

B. For the female:

1. **General sexual dysfunction:** a lack of erotic response to sexual stimulation (frigidity)
2. **Orgasmic dysfunction:** an inability to reach orgasm
3. **Vaginismus:** a spasm of muscles at the entrance of the vagina that prevents intercourse

There was a time when people endured such dysfunctions in silence. However, in recent years effective treatments have been found for each major problem. Let's briefly investigate the causes and treatments of the six barriers to sexual adjustment and fulfillment.

Male Impotence Impotence (also known as erectile dysfunction) is the inability to maintain an erection for sexual intercourse. Males suffering from primary impotence have never had an erection. Those who have previously performed successfully, but then have become impotent, are said to suffer from secondary impotence. In either case, when impotence becomes a repeated problem, it is usually very disturbing to the man and his sexual partner.

Question: How often must a man experience failure to be considered impotent?

Sex therapists Masters and Johnson (1970) believe that a problem exists when failure occurs on 25 percent or more of a man's lovemaking attempts. Repeated impotence should therefore be distinguished from *occasional* erectile problems. Fatigue, anger, anxiety, and excessive consumption of alcohol can cause temporary impotence in healthy males. True impotence typically persists for months or years.

It is important to recognize that occasional impotence is normal. In fact, overreaction to it may generate fears and doubts that can contribute to further impotence. At such times, it is particularly important for the man's partner to avoid expressing anger, disappointment, or embarrassment. Patient reassurance helps prevent the establishment of a vicious cycle.

Question: What causes impotence?

For years, experts held that impotence rarely was caused by physical illness, disease, or damage. Now it is recognized that roughly 40 percent of cases are organic, or physically caused. The origin of the remaining cases is psychogenic (a result of emotional factors). Even when impotence is organic, however, it is almost always made worse by anxiety and other emotional reactions. If a man can have an erection at times other than lovemaking (during sleep, for instance) the problem probably is not physical (Knox, 1984).

Organic impotence has many causes. Typical problems include alcohol or drug abuse, diabetes, vascular disease, prostate and urological disorders, neurological problems, and reactions to medication for high blood pressure, heart disease, or stomach ulcers.

According to Masters and Johnson (1970), primary psychogenic impotence is often related to harsh religious training, early sexual experience with a seductive mother, or other experiences leading to guilt, fear, and sexual inhibition. In a few instances, unrecognized homosexual feelings may also be a source of conflicts.

Secondary psychogenic impotence may be related to anxiety about sex in general, guilt because of an extramarital affair, resentment or hostility toward a sexual partner, fear of inability to perform, and similar emotions and conflicts. Often the problem starts with repeated sexual failures caused by drinking too much alcohol or by the presence of premature ejaculation. In either case, initial doubts soon become severe fears of failure—which further inhibit sexual response.

Medical treatment for organic impotence may employ drugs or surgery. Treatment for both organic and psychogenic impotence also usually includes counseling to remove fears and psychological blocks. The man learns that he cannot consciously will an erection and that his disability is not a reflection on his manhood. To further free him of his fears (particularly fear of failure), the man and his partner are usually assigned a series of exercises to perform. This technique, called sensate focus, directs attention to natural sensations of pleasure and builds communication skills.

Applications

In sensate focus, the couple is initially told to take turns stroking various parts of each other's bodies. They are instructed to carefully avoid any genital contact at first. Instead, they are to concentrate on giving pleasure and on signaling what is most gratifying to them. This takes the pressure to perform off the male and allows him to learn to give pleasure as a means of receiving it.

Over a period of days or weeks, the couple proceeds to more intense physical contact involving the breasts and genitals. As inhibitions are reduced and natural arousal begins to replace fear, the successful couple moves on to intercourse.

Premature Ejaculation Masters and Johnson (1970) consider ejaculation to be premature if a man cannot delay sexual climax long enough to satisfy his partner in at least one-half of their lovemaking attempts. However, Helen Kaplan, of Cornell University Medical School, finds this definition unsatisfactory because of large variations in the time different women take to reach orgasm. Kaplan (1974) says that prematurity exists when ejaculation occurs reflexively or when there is an inability to tolerate high levels of excitement at the plateau stage of arousal.

Question: Do many men have difficulties with premature ejaculation?

Premature ejaculation is a common problem in male sexual adjustment. Theories advanced to explain it have ranged from the idea that it may represent hostility toward the man's sexual partner (since it deprives the partner of satisfaction) to the suggestion that most early male sexual experiences tend to encourage rapid climax (such as those taking place in the back seat of a car and masturbation). Kaplan (1974) adds that excessive arousal and anxiety over performance are usually present, and that some men simply engage in techniques that maximize sensation and make rapid orgasm inevitable. Whatever the causes, premature ejaculation can be a serious difficulty, especially in the context of long-term relationships.

Treatment for premature ejaculation is highly successful and relatively simple. The most common treatment procedure is the *squeeze technique* used by Masters and Johnson. The man's sexual partner stimulates him manually until he signals that ejaculation is about to occur. The man's partner then firmly squeezes the tip of his penis to inhibit orgasm. When the man feels he has control, stimulation is repeated. Gradually, the man acquires the ability to delay orgasm sufficiently for satisfactory intercourse. During treatment, skills that improve communication between partners are developed, along with a better understanding of the male's sexual response cues.

Retarded Ejaculation Among males, an inability to reach orgasm was once considered a rare problem. But milder forms of this dysfunction have recently accounted for increasing numbers of clients seeking therapy (Kaplan, 1974). Typical background factors are strict religious training, fear of impregnating, lack of interest in the sexual partner, symbolic inability to give of oneself, unacknowledged homosexuality, or the recent occurrence of traumatic life events. Power and commitment struggles within relationships may be important added factors.

Treatment for retarded ejaculation consists of sensate focus, manual stimulation by the man's partner (which is designed to orient the male to his partner as a source of pleasure), and stimulation to the point of orgasm followed by immediate intercourse and ejaculation. Work also focuses on resolving personal conflicts and marital difficulties underlying the problem.

Female General Sexual Dysfunction This difficulty, commonly referred to as frigidity, is usually defined as a persistent inability to derive pleasure from sexual stimulation. Women who show general sexual dysfunction respond with little or no physical arousal to sexual stimulation. The problem thus appears to correspond directly to male impotence (Kaplan, 1974). As in male impotence, general female sexual dysfunction may be primary or secondary.

The causes of female general sexual dysfunction bear some similarity to those seen in psychogenic impotence. Frigidity can often be traced to frightening childhood experiences, such as molestations (often by older relatives), incestuous relations that produced lasting guilt, a harshly religious background in which sex was considered evil, or cold, unloving childhood relationships. Also common is the need to maintain control over emotions, deep-seated conflicts over being female, and extreme distrust of others, especially males (Masters & Johnson, 1970).

Question: How does treatment proceed?

Treatment at the Cornell clinic includes sensate focus, genital stimulation by the woman's partner, and "non-demanding" intercourse controlled by the woman. With success in these initial stages, full intercourse is gradually instituted. As sexual training proceeds, psychological conflicts and dynamics typically appear, and as they do, they are treated in separate counseling sessions (Kaplan, 1974).

Female Orgasmic Dysfunction The most prevalent sexual complaint among women is orgasmic dysfunction, an in-

Applications

ability to reach orgasm during intercourse. It is often clear in such cases that the woman is not completely unresponsive; rather, she is unresponsive in the context of a relationship—she may easily reach orgasm by masturbation, but not in sexual intercourse.

Question: Then couldn't the woman's partner be at fault?

Sex therapists try to avoid finding fault or placing blame. However, it is true that the male partner must be sexually adequate in terms of freedom from premature ejaculation, and he must have a commitment to ensuring gratification of the woman. Some apparent instances of orgasmic dysfunction can be traced to inadequate stimulation or faulty technique on the part of the woman's partner. Even when this is the case, sexual adjustment difficulties are best viewed as a problem the couple shares, not just as the "woman's problem" or the "man's problem."

If we focus only on the woman, the most common source of orgasmic difficulties is overcontrol of sexual response. Female orgasm requires a degree of abandonment to erotic feelings. It is therefore inhibited by ambivalence or hostility toward the relationship, by guilt, by fears of expressing sexual needs, and by tendencies to control and intellectualize erotic feelings. The woman is unable to let go and enjoy the flow of pleasurable sensations.

In Helen Kaplan's treatment program, anorgasmic women are first trained to focus on their sexual responsiveness through masturbation or vigorous stimulation by a partner. As the woman becomes consistently orgasmic in these circumstances, her responsiveness is gradually transferred to intercourse. Couples also typically learn alternative positions and techniques of lovemaking designed to increase clitoral stimulation. At the same time, communication between partners is stressed, especially with reference to the woman's sexual value system (expectations, motivations, and preferences).

Vaginismus In the condition known as vaginismus, muscle spasms make intercourse impossible. Vaginismus is often accompanied by obvious fears of intercourse, and where fear is absent, high levels of anxiety are present. Vaginismus therefore appears to be a phobic response to intercourse. Predictably, causative factors include experiences of painful intercourse, rape and/or brutal and frightening sexual encounters, fear of men, misinformation about sex (belief that it is injurious), fear of pregnancy, and fear of the specific male partner (Kaplan, 1974).

Treatment of vaginismus is similar to what might be done for a nonsexual phobia. It includes extinction of conditioned muscle spasms by progressive relaxation of the vagina, desensitization of fears of intercourse, and masturbation or manual stimulation to associate pleasure with sexual approach by the male partner. Hypnosis has also been used successfully in some cases (Kaplan, 1974).

Summary Solving sexual problems can be difficult. The problems described here are rarely solved without professional help (a possible exception is premature ejaculation). If a serious sexual difficulty is not resolved in a reasonable amount of time, the aid of an appropriately trained psychologist, physician, or counselor should be sought. The longer the problem is ignored, the more difficult it is to solve. But professional help is available.

Sexual Adjustment

Question: What can be done to improve sexual adjustment?

Often, it is best to view sexual adjustment within the broader context of a relationship. Conflict and unresolved anger in other areas frequently take their toll in sexual adjustment, and mutually satisfying relationships tend to carry over into sexual relations. Sex is not a performance or a skill to be mastered like playing tennis. It is a form of communication within a relationship. Couples with strong and caring relationships can probably survive most sexual problems. A couple with a satisfactory sex life but a poor relationship rarely lasts.

Sex researchers and therapists Masters and Johnson (1970) have discussed how sexual partners can best approach disagreements about each other's sexual needs and wishes. When disagreements arise over issues such as frequency of intercourse, who initiates lovemaking, or what behavior is appropriate, Masters and Johnson believe that the rule should be, "Each partner must accept the other as the final authority on his or her own feelings."

Partners are urged to give feedback about their feelings by following what therapists call the "touch and ask" rule: Touching and caressing should often be followed by questions such as, "Does that feel good?" "Do you like that?" and so forth (Knox, 1984). When problems do arise, partners are urged to be *responsive* to each other's needs at an *emotional* level and to recognize that all sexual problems are *mutual.* "Failures" should always be shared without placing blame. Masters and Johnson believe that it is particularly important to avoid the "numbers game." That is, couples should avoid being influenced by statistics on the average frequency of intercourse, by stereotypes about sexual potency, and by the

Applications

superhuman sexual exploits portrayed in movies and magazines.

Question: Are there any other guidelines for maintaining a healthy emotional relationship?

Intimacy and Communication In a study that compared happily married couples with unhappily married couples, Navran (1967) found that in almost every regard, the happily married couples showed superior *communication* skills. Many couples find that communication is facilitated by observing the following guidelines (after Bach & Wyden, 1969).

Avoid "Gunnysacking" Persistent feelings, whether positive or negative, need to be expressed. Gunnysacking refers to saving up feelings and complaints. These are then "dumped" during an argument or are used as ammunition in a fight. Gunnysacking is very destructive to a relationship.

Be Open About Feelings Happy couples not only talk more, they convey more personal feelings and show greater sensitivity to their partners' feelings. As one expert put it, "In a healthy relationship, each partner feels free to express his likes, dislikes, wants, wishes, feelings, impulses, and the other person feels free to react with like honesty to these. In such a relationship, there will be tears, laughter, sensuality, irritation, anger, fear, babylike behavior, and so on" (Jourard, 1963).

Don't Attack the Other Person's Character Whenever possible, expressions of negative feelings should be given as statements of one's own feelings, not as statements of blame. It is far more constructive to say, "It makes me angry when you leave things around the house" than it is to say, "You're a slob!"

Don't Try to "Win" a Fight Constructive fights are aimed at resolving shared differences, not at establishing who is right or wrong, superior or inferior.

Recognize That Anger Is Appropriate Constructive and destructive fights are not distinguished by whether or not anger is expressed. A fight is a fight, and anger is appropriate. As is the case with any other emotion in a relationship, anger should be expressed. However, constructive expression of anger requires that couples fight fair by sticking to the real issues and not "hitting below the belt."

To add to these guidelines, Bryan Strong and Christine DeVault (1988) suggest that if you really want to mess up a relationship, you can almost totally avoid intimacy and communication by doing the following.

Ten Ways to Avoid Intimacy

1. Don't talk about anything meaningful, especially about feelings.
2. Never show your feelings; remain as expressionless as possible.
3. Always be pleasant and pretend everything is okay even when you are upset or dissatisfied.
4. Always win, never compromise.
5. Always keep busy; that way you can avoid intimacy and make your partner feel unimportant in your life.
6. Always be right; don't let on that you are human.
7. Never argue or you may have to reveal differences and make changes.
8. Make your partner guess what you want. That way, you can tell your partner that he or she doesn't really understand or love you.
9. Always take care of your own needs first.
10. Keep the television set on. Wouldn't you rather be watching TV than talking with your partner?

Remember, to encourage intimacy, wise couples *avoid* the practices in the preceding list.

As a last point, it is worth restating that sexual adjustment and loving relationships are interdependent. As one observer put it, when sex goes well, it's 15 percent of a relationship, and when it goes badly, it's 85 percent (Knox, 1984). As a shared pleasure, a form of intimacy, a means of communication, and a haven from everyday tensions, a positive sexual relationship can do much to enhance a couple's mutual understanding and caring. Likewise, an honest, equitable, and affectionate out-of-bed relationship contributes greatly to sexual satisfaction (Hatfield et al., 1982).

Applications

Learning Check

1. Males suffering from primary impotence have never been able to have or maintain an erection. T or F?
2. According to the latest figures, most cases of impotence are caused by physical problems. T or F?
3. Sensate focus is the most common treatment for premature ejaculation. T or F?
4. Premature ejaculation is considered the rarest of the male sexual adjustment problems. T or F?
5. As it is for psychogenic impotence, the sensate focus technique is a primary treatment mode for female general sexual dysfunction. T for F?
6. Vaginismus appears to be a phobic response to sexual intercourse. T or F?
7. Masters and Johnson urge sexual partners to recognize that all sexual problems are mutual and not just one partner's problem. T or F?
8. The term *gunnysacking* refers to the constructive practice of hiding anger until it is appropriate to express it. T or F?

Answers:
1. T 2. F 3. F 4. F 5. T 6. T 7. T 8. F

Exploration: Touching—Does It Always Have Sexual Implications?

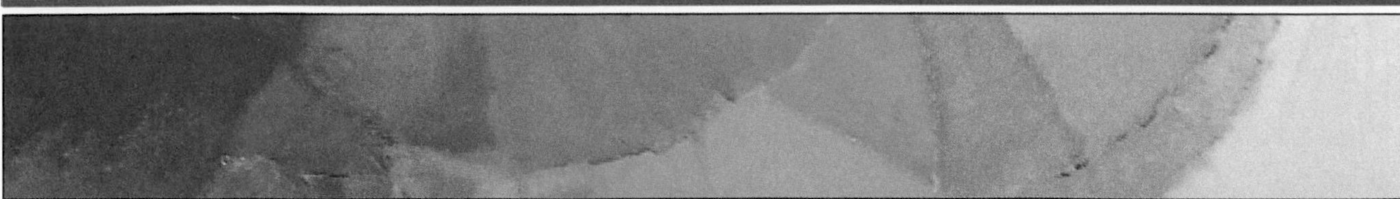

The whole thing began because Sidney Jourard is a people watcher. One day, sitting in a coffeehouse in San Juan, Puerto Rico, where he was a Peace Corps consultant, he wondered how many times the couple at the next table would touch each other in 1 hour. During the next 2 years, he did the same thing in London and Paris while studying at London's Tavistock Clinic. When he went to Gainesville, Florida, to teach psychology at the University of Florida, he checked out an American couple for the 1 hour. The two people at the Gainesville table touched each other 2 times in 1 hour. In Paris the touch total for 1 hour was 110. In San Juan, 180. And in London? In London, the two people touched each other not at all.

From this information you must draw your own conclusions. Jourard—back at Gainesville, Florida, teaching, being a therapist, and practicing hatha-yoga—refused to. But his interest led him to make further surveys.

He gave booklets to his Gainesville students, 54 males and 84 females. Each booklet contained four diagrams of the body divided into 24 zones, the idea lifted (he says with a straight face) from a butcher's meat chart. He then asked his students to report, anonymously of course, which area of their bodies had been touched by mother, father, best-friend-same-sex, and best-friend-opposite-sex. Furthermore, each student was asked to show which zones he or she had touched on these four persons. Time range: within the last year. The charts in Figure 25–6 show the result.

Here Jourard *will* draw conclusions about "body accessibility."

"If you're out of love," says the professor, "you're out of touch."

"There isn't a great deal of body contact going on outside the strictly sexual context. It's almost as if all possible meanings of a touch are eliminated except the caress with the sexually arousing intent. . . . Most regions of a young adult's body remain untouched unless one has a close friend of the opposite sex, and that depends on the relationship going on between them."

One of our touch taboos, then, is that we equate touch with sexuality. Therefore, unless the relationship is sexual, *mustn't touch*.

Jourard goes on to say that in family physical contact, the daughters are "the favored ones." A girl's parents touch her more than they would if she were a boy. Right up into her 20s. Parents stop touching boys about the time they reach what used to be called the Age of Reason—when one can commit sin. Furthermore, a girl's mother is allowed, or allows herself (having herself once been a favored one), to give frequent touches to a girl's hair. One-half of the parents get to touch her on the lips, and half manage a literal pat on the back. But—taboo, taboo—only 13 percent of the girls received a paternal pat on the bottom, and none of the girls touched or were touched by their fathers in the genital area. (Not quite the case with regard to male students and Mamma.)

Outside the best-friend-opposite-sex category, very little touching goes on, but when it does happen between lovers, the professor says, "There is a virtual deluge of physical contact all over the body. . . . I suspect that the transformation from virginity or even preorgasmic existence to the experience of having a sexual climax is so radical as to be equivalent to a kind of rebirth."

For Jourard, in our maddeningly crowded world, touch may be our salvation. "I think that body contact has the function of confirming one's bodily being," he says. Yet, how can one learn to touch lovingly if one is not permitted to touch and be touched when young? To touch and be touched at times other than when making love?

"It's a blunted way of life," Jourard says. "People need physical contact to increase awareness and sensitivity to the body. But, instead, we use our relationship with others as a means to increase our status and social position. We are afraid to let others get close because then we are trapped. . . . The price we pay for this estrangement is loneliness." (The preceding article was written by H.E.F. Donohue, 1968.)

Exploration

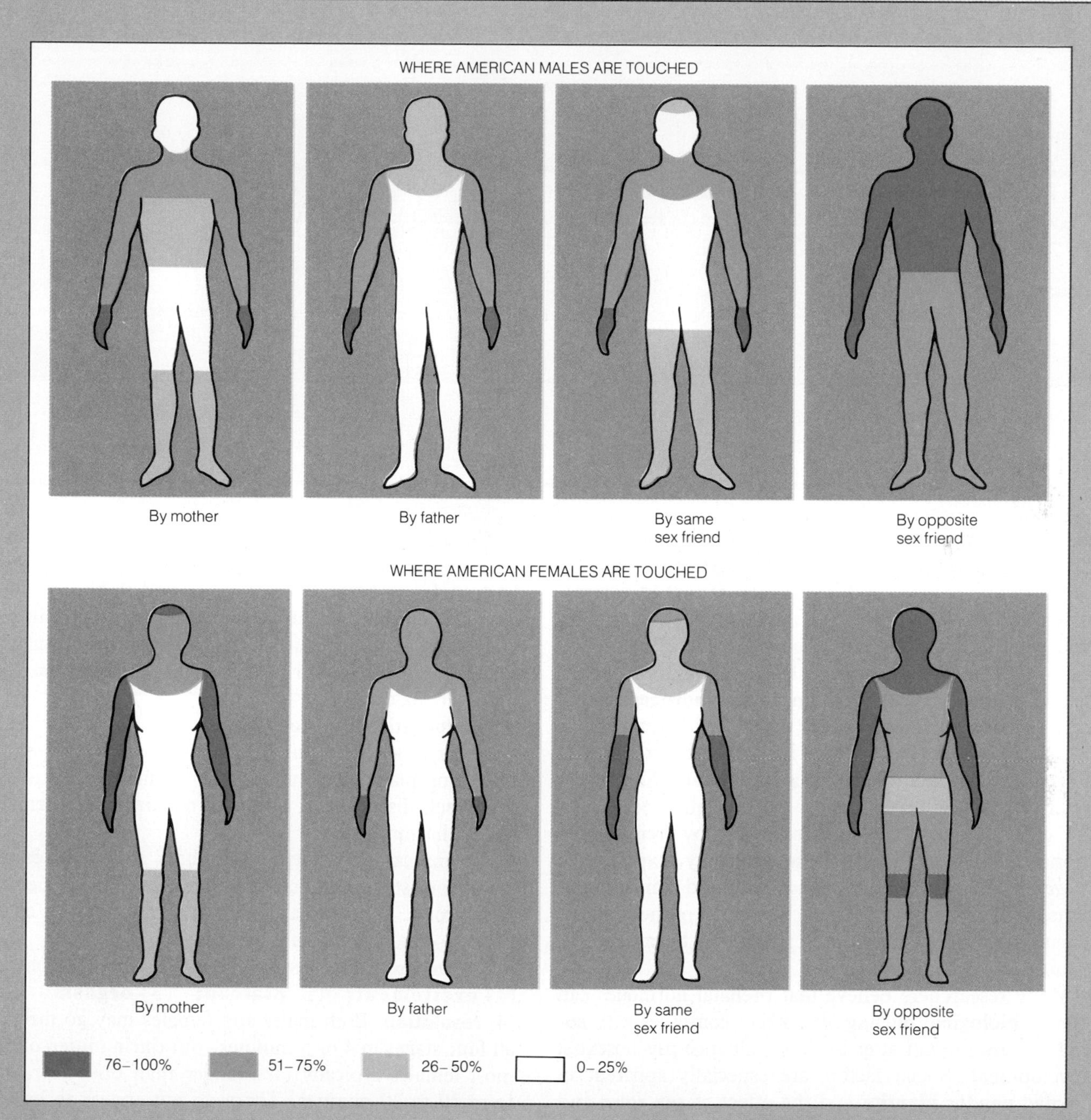

Fig. 25–6 *Results of Jourard's study of body accessibility. Figures shown are the percentages of young adults touched in each body area, during a 1-year period, by the persons listed. Touching patterns are highly influenced by culture. People in other countries touch much more, or less, than is customary in the United States. (After Jourard, 1966.)*

Exploration

Learning Check

1. In his first casual observations, Jourard noted the highest rates of touching in
a. Florida *b.* France *c.* Puerto Rico *d.* England

2. Within the family, boys are typically touched more by parents than girls are. T or F?

3. Jourard recorded the highest rates of touching by
a. mothers *b.* fathers *c.* same-sex friends *d.* opposite-sex friends

4. In American culture, the hands are the most accepted areas of the body for touching by others. T or F?

Answers:
1. *c* 2. F 3. *d* 4. T

Chapter Summary

• Physical differences between males and females can be divided into **primary sexual characteristics** (genital and reproductive organs) and **secondary sexual characteristics** (other bodily features). Reproductive maturity in females is signaled by **menarche** (the onset of menstruation). The development of both primary and secondary sexual characteristics is influenced by **androgens** (male sex hormones) and **estrogens** (female sex hormones).

• Gender can be broken down into **genetic sex, gonadal sex, hormonal sex, genital sex,** and **gender identity.**

• Gender development begins with genetic sex (*XX* or *XY* chromosomes). It is then influenced by prenatal hormonal influences. **Androgen insensitivity,** exposure to *progestin,* the **androgenital syndrome,** and similar problems can cause problems in the formation of the genitals. Resulting gender ambiguities are called **hermaphroditism.**

• Many researchers believe that prenatal hormones can exert a **biological biasing effect** that combines with **social factors** present after birth to influence psychosexual development. Social factors are especially apparent in learned **gender identity** and the effect of **sex roles** and **sex role socialization** on behavior. Sex role socialization, in particular, seems to account for most observed male/female differences.

• Sexual behavior is quite "natural," being apparent soon after birth and expressed in various ways throughout life. There appears to be little difference in sexual responsiveness between males and females.

• There is some evidence that the sex drive peaks at a later age for females than it does for males. Sex drive in both males and females may be related to bodily levels of androgen. **Nocturnal orgasms** are a normal, but relatively minor, form of sexual release. **Castration** may or may not influence sex drive in humans. **Sterilization** does not alter sex drive.

• **Masturbation** is a normal and completely acceptable behavior practiced by a large percentage of the population. For many, masturbation is an important part of sexual self-discovery. It is valid in marriage and normally has no harmful effects.

• A significant minority of all adults are **homosexual,** being consistently attracted to members of the same sex. As a group, homosexual men and women do not differ psychologically from heterosexuals.

• Human sexual response can be divided into four phases: (1) **excitement;** (2) **plateau;** (3) **orgasm;** and (4) **resolution.** Both males and females may go through all four stages in 4 or 5 minutes. But during intercourse, most females typically take longer than this, averaging from 10 to 20 minutes. There do not appear to be any differences between "vaginal orgasms" and "clitoral orgasms" in the female. Mutual orgasm has been abandoned by most sex counselors as the ideal in lovemaking.

• Attitudes toward sex have been significantly liberalized, but actual changes in sexual behavior have been more gradual. The next greatest change has been earlier and more frequent sexual activity among adolescents and young adults. Also evident are a greater acceptance of female sexuality and a narrowing of differences in male and female patterns of sexual behavior.

• During the last 20 years, there has been a steady increase in the incidence of **sexually transmitted diseases.** This increase, coupled with the emergence of **acquired immune deficiency syndrome,** has had a sizable impact on patterns of sexual behavior.

• The principal male problems in sexual adjustment are **impotence, premature ejaculation,** and **retarded ejaculation.** For women they are **general sexual dysfunction, orgasmic dysfunction,** and **vaginismus.** Behavioral methods and counseling techniques have been developed to alleviate each problem. However, most sexual adjustment problems are closely linked to the general health of a couple's relationship. For this reason, communication skills that foster and maintain intimacy are the key to successful relationships.

• Patterns of touching vary from culture to culture, and they depend on the nature of the relationship between two people. Touch can therefore have a variety of meanings, most of which are nonsexual.

Questions for Discussion

1. Do your patterns of touching and being touched correspond to those found by Jourard?

2. In what ways does sexual contact differ from nonsexual touching? Do you feel, as Jourard does, that people should touch more? Why or why not?

3. Would you be jealous if your spouse or lover were touched (in a nonsexual way) by a person of the same sex? Opposite sex?

4. Do you think the sexual revolution has increased touching by encouraging openness or decreased it by defining more casual touching as potentially sexual?

5. In recent years, there has been a dramatic increase in child molestation trials involving day-care workers. Some teachers and child-care workers complain that they are now afraid to touch or hug children. Is this new reticence to touch an overdue correction or a saddening loss?

6. Imagine that you were born as a member of the opposite sex. In what ways would your life so far have been different? (Consider relationships, self-image, clothing, recreation, interests, career plans, and so forth.)

7. In your opinion, what are the advantages and disadvantages of distinctly different male/female sex roles?

8. Mentally change your male friends to females and your female friends to males. Can you separate the "human being" or "core person" from your friends' normal gender identities and sex roles? What effect does this have on your perception of others?

9. Female sexual behavior appears to be changing more rapidly than male behavior. To what do you attribute the different rate of change?

10. Recall your own education about sexuality. In what ways and at what age would your recommend that children learn about sex?

Chapter 26

Applied Psychology

In This Chapter

Industrial psychology
Engineering psychology
Organizational psychology
Environmental psychology
Educational psychology
Consumer psychology
Law and psychology
Sports psychology
Applications: Career choice and occupational survival
Exploration: Space psychology

Chapter Preview

Bird Brains

Imagine yourself lost at sea in a tiny rubber raft, the victim of a boating accident. After 10 hours adrift, you begin to lose all hope of being found. Then, seemingly out of nowhere, a Coast Guard helicopter swoops in and lifts you from the waves. Gratefully, you thank your rescuers. But with a laugh, they insist the real credit belongs to three "bird brains."

Sound far-fetched? In recent tests, pigeons—who are sharp-eyed and nearly immune to boredom—have been taught to aid search-and-rescue crews. The pigeons are first conditioned in Skinner boxes to peck images of red or yellow rafts, life vests, and life preservers. During rescues, they ride in a chamber under a helicopter, where their pecking is monitored electronically. A buzzer in the cockpit, activated by the pecking, guides pilots to the target (Japenga, 1982; Stark, 1981).

Applied psychology *refers to the use of psychological principles and research methods to solve practical problems, such as finding victims lost at sea. Increasingly, psychology is being used to enhance the quality of life and improve human performance. And, as we will soon see, the ocean is not the only place where applied psychology can make a life-or-death difference.*

The Towering Inferno *All too often, fires in high-rise buildings lead to needless deaths. Using the elevators, for instance, can be fatal because they act as chimneys for smoke and poisonous fumes (Keating & Loftus, 1981).*

Question: How can psychology improve the odds for survival?

In the confusion following a fire alarm, many people ignore posted instructions for safe escape. To remedy the situation, psychologists Jack Keating and Elizabeth Loftus created an unusual, life-saving "fire alarm." The best alarm, they found, is a voice *that tells people exactly what to do. After much research, they designed the following message to be broadcast during fires.*

> *Female voice:* "May I have your attention, please. May I have your attention, please."
> *Male voice:* "There has been a fire reported on the 20th floor. While this report is being verified, the building manager would like you to proceed to the stairways and walk down to the 18th floor. Please do not use the elevators, as they may be needed. Please do not use the elevators, but proceed to the stairways." (Loftus, 1979)

As simple as this message seems, it contains certain key elements: (1) Research has shown that switching from a female to a male voice (or the reverse) is very attention-getting; *(2) during emergencies, people like to feel that some* authority *is in control (the "building manager," in this case); (3) the crucial reminder to avoid the elevators is* repeated, *so it will be remembered.*

Sea rescues and escaping fires may be dramatic examples of applying psychology, but they are far from unusual. In fields as diverse as industry, sports, law, and medicine, psychology is being applied to our lives. Let's see how.

Survey Questions

- What are the major areas of applied psychology?
- How is psychology applied in business, engineering, and industry?
- What have psychologists learned about the effects of our physical and social environments?
- How does psychology apply to education, consumer behavior, law, and sports?
- What are the typical stages in choosing a career? How can career choices be improved?
- How is psychology being applied in space missions?

Introduction to Applied Psychology

Question: What are the major areas of applied psychology?

The largest areas are clinical and counseling psychology (see Chapter 1). A closely related specialty is **community psychology.** Instead of focusing on individuals (as clinical and counseling psychologists do), community psychologists treat whole neighborhoods or communities as their "clients" (Conyne & Clack, 1981). (Community psychologists have BIG offices!) Typically, community psychologists emphasize prevention, education, and consultation to promote community mental health. Often, they target drug abuse, child neglect, unemployment, prejudice, and similar problems for solution. Such efforts, they believe, help prevent mental health problems before they begin.

Beyond the clinical areas of psychology, the list of applications grows large. In this chapter we will cover the psychology of work, environmental behavior, education, consumer behavior, law, and sports. To begin, let's see how psychology is applied in business and industry.

Industrial/Organizational Psychology—Psychology at Work

Do you consider work a blessing? Or a curse? Or do you simply agree that it is "better to wear out than to rust out"? Whatever your attitude, the simple fact is that most adults work for a living. From the 1920s until the present, **industrial/organizational psychologists** have studied the problems people face at work. Very likely, their efforts will affect how you are selected for a job and how you are tested, trained, and evaluated for promotions. A psychologist may even help design the machines you use at work, or the work environment itself.

Industrial/organizational psychologists are employed mostly by government, industry, and businesses. Typically, they work in three major areas. These are (1) testing and placement (personnel psychology), (2) human relations at work, and (3) industrial engineering (the design of machines and work environments) (Landy & Trumbo, 1980). To get a fuller flavor of what I-O psychologists do, look at Table 26–1. As you can see, their interests are quite varied. As a further illustration, see Box 26–1 for an interesting sample of I-O research.

Question: You mentioned that industrial psychologists sometimes help design machines. What does a "shrink for machines" do?!

Engineering Psychology

However helpful a machine may be in theory, it is of little value until it can be operated by humans. A pocket calculator that is difficult to handle might just as well be a paperweight. An automobile design that blocks large areas of the driver's vision could be deadly. To adapt machines for human use, the **engineering psychologist** (or **human factors engineer**) must make them *compatible* with our sensory and motor capacities (Neff, 1977; Wickens & Kramer, 1985). For example, *displays* must be easy to perceive, *controls* must be easy to use, and the tendency to make errors must be minimized (Figure 26–1). Many of the machines we rely on each day were designed, in part, by human factors engineers. Some familiar examples include push-button telephones, "user-friendly" computers, home appliances, cameras, airplane controls, and traffic signals. More elaborate machines, such as the United States space shuttle, stretch human capacities to their limits—and require *extensive* human factors engineering.

Donald Norman (1988) refers to effective human factors engineering as **natural design.** Effective design makes use of signals that are naturally understood by people without any need to learn them. An example of natural design is the row of vertical buttons in elevators. The pattern of the buttons mimics the layout of the floors. This is simple, natural, and clear. In contrast, Norman tells about a friend who became trapped for a few moments by a double set of glass doors at the front of a public building. None of the doors had visible handles or hinges, and the poor man tried repeatedly to push on the wrong (hinged) side of the doors. An effective natural design would have included a visible plate, handle, or hinge to signal where to push.

Another major point that Norman emphasizes will be familiar to you from Chapter 8. Effective design provides clear **feedback.** That is, in good design each control produces an immediate and obvious effect. The audible click designed into many computer keyboards is a good example. As Norman points out, the "human error" cited as the cause of many accidents and disasters often misses the real culprit: poor design.

Table 26–1 Topics of Special Interest to Industrial/Organizational Psychologists

Absenteeism	Pay schedules
Decision making	Personnel selection
Designs of organizations	Personnel training
Employee stress	Productivity
Employee turnover	Promotion
Interviewing	Task analysis
Job enrichment	Task design
Job satisfaction	Work behavior
Labor relations	Work environment
Machine design	Worker evaluations
Management styles	Work motivation
Minority workers	

BOX 26–1 Flexitime

If you've ever worked "9 to 5," you know that traditional time schedules can be confining. They also doom many workers to a daily battle with rush-hour traffic. To improve worker morale, industrial psychologists have proposed the use of flexible working hours, or **flexitime.** The basic idea of flexitime is that starting and quitting times are flexible, as long as employees are present during a core work period (Owen 1976). For example, employees might be allowed to arrive between 7:30 A.M. and 10:30 A.M. and to depart between 3:30 P.M. and 6:30 P.M.

Is flexitime really an improvement? Recent studies of two groups of clerical workers suggest that in many cases it is. After a switch to flexitime, a number of benefits were observed, including more job satisfaction, better work-group relations, better relations with supervisors, and less absenteeism (Narayan & Nath, 1982; Orpen, 1981). Although more research is needed, perhaps we can say that it is better, when possible, to bend hours instead of people.

Personnel Psychology

The mark of maturity, Sigmund Freud said, is a capacity for love and work. While most people gladly embrace love, many would just as soon forget work. Yet the fact is, employed adults spend an average of over 2000 hours a year at their jobs. With so much time at stake, understanding the world of work is clearly a "survival skill."

At present, the odds are 9 out of 10 that you are, or will be, employed in business or industry. Thus, nearly everyone who holds a job is sooner or later placed under the "psychological microscope" of personnel selection. Clearly, there is value in knowing how selection for hiring and promotion is done.

Question: How do personnel psychologists make employee selections?

Personnel selection begins with a **job analysis** to find out exactly what workers do and what skills or knowledge they need to succeed in a job (Tenopyr & Oeltjen, 1982). A job analysis may be done by interviewing workers or supervisors, by giving them questionnaires, by directly observing work, or by identifying **critical incidents.** Critical incidents are situations that an employee *must* be able to cope with if he or she is going to succeed in a particular job. The ability to deal calmly with a mechanical emergency, for example, is a critical incident for an airline pilot. Once job requirements are known, psychologists can state what skills, aptitudes, and interests are needed (Fig. 26–2).

Selection Procedures After desirable skills and traits are identified, the next step is to learn which job applicants have them. Today, the methods most often used for evaluating job candidates include the collection of *biodata, interviews, standarized psychological tests,* and the *assessment center* approach. Let's see what each entails.

As simple as it may seem, one good way to predict job success is to collect **biodata** (detailed biographical information) from applicants. The idea behind biodata is that past behavior is a good predictor of future behavior. Thus, by learning in detail about a person's life, it is often possible to say whether the person is suited for a particular type of work (Owens & Shoenfeldt, 1979). Some of the most useful items of biodata include past athletic interest, academic achievement, scientific interest, extracurricular activities, religious activities, social popularity, friction with brothers and sisters, attitude toward school, and parents' socioeconomic status (Eberhardt & Muchinsky, 1982). Such facts tell quite a lot about personality, interests, and abilities.

The traditional **personal interview** is still one of the most popular ways to select people for jobs or promotions. However, as we discussed in Chapter 16, interviews are subject to the *halo effect* and similar problems. For this reason, psychologists continue to study factors

Fig. 26–1 *Human Factors Engineering.* (a) *Early roll indicators in airplanes were perceptually confusing and difficult to read* (top). *Improved displays are clear even to nonpilots. Which would you prefer if you were flying an airplane in heavy fog?* (b) *Even on a stove, the placement of controls is important. During simulated emergencies, subjects made no errors in reaching for the controls on the top stove. In contrast, they erred 38 percent of the time with the bottom arrangement (Chapanis & Lindenbaum, 1959).* (c) *Sometimes, the shape of a control is used to indicate its function, so as to discourage errors. For example, the left control might be used to engage and disengage the gears of an industrial machine, whereas the right control might operate the landing flaps on an airplane.*

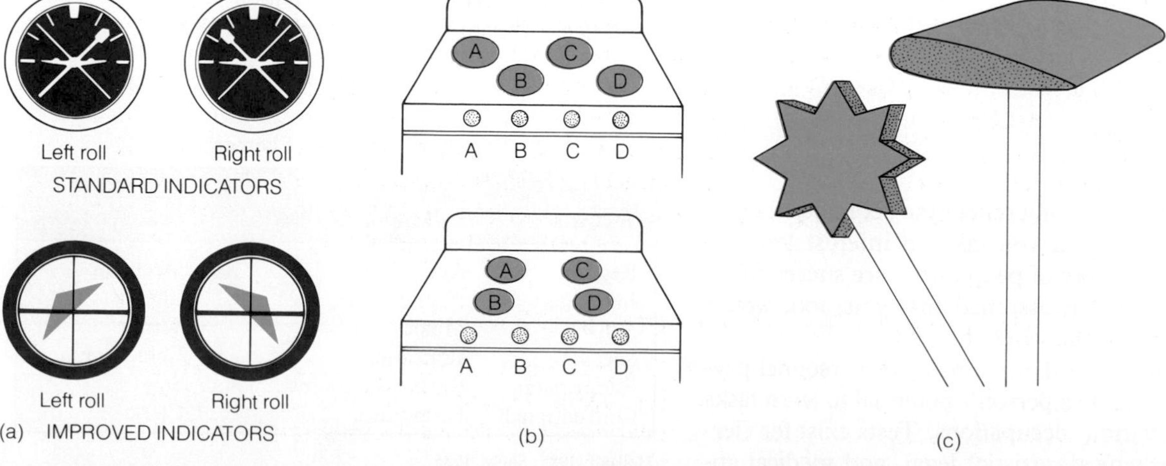

Fig. 26–2 *Analyzing complex skills has also been valuable to the U.S. Air Force. When million-dollar aircraft and the lives of pilots are at stake, it makes good sense to do as much training and research as possible on the ground. Air force psychologists use flight simulators like the one pictured here to analyze the complex skills needed to fly jet fighters. Skills can then be taught without risk on the ground. The General Electric simulator shown here uses a computer to generate full-color images that respond realistically to a pilot's use of the controls. (Photograph supplied courtesy of General Electric Company.)*

that affect interviews, with an eye on improving their value (see Box 26–2).

Question: What kinds of tests do personnel psychologists use?

In addition to general intelligence and personality tests (described in earlier chapters), personnel psychologists often use **vocational interest tests.** Tests such as the *Kuder Occupational Interest Survey* and the *Strong-Campbell Interest Inventory* probe interests with items like the following:

I would prefer to
a. visit a museum
b. read a good book
c. take a walk outdoors

Interest inventories typically reflect the six major themes shown in Table 26–2. If you take an interest test and your choices match those of people who are successful in a given occupation, it is assumed that you, too, would be comfortable doing the work they do.

Aptitude tests are another mainstay of personnel psychology. Such tests rate a person's potential to learn tasks or skills used in various occupations. Tests exist for clerical, verbal, mechanical, artistic, legal, and medical aptitudes, plus many others. For example, tests of clerical aptitude emphasize the capacity to do rapid, precise, and accurate office work. One section of a clerical aptitude test might therefore ask a person to mark all identical numbers and names in a long list of pairs like those shown here (Schultz, 1979). (Also see Fig. 26–3.)

49837266	49832766
Global Widgets, Inc.	Global Wigets, Inc.
874583725	874583725
Sevanden Corp.	Sevanden Corp.
Perlee Publishing	Perlee Puhlishing

Table 26–2 Vocational Interest Themes

THEME	SAMPLE COLLEGE MAJOR	SAMPLE OCCUPATION
Realistic	Agriculture	Mechanic
Investigative	Physics	Chemist
Artistic	Music	Writer
Social	Education	Counselor
Enterprising	Business administration	Sales
Conventional	Economics	Clerk

Holland, 1985; Snow, 1986.

● BOX 26–2
The Sweet Smell of Success? Not Always

Each year, clothing and cosmetics manufacturers spend huge sums to convince us that their products make us more attractive. Actually, such claims are somewhat justified. You might recall from Chapter 16, for instance, that physically attractive people are often given more positive evaluations in interviews—even on traits that have no connection with appearance. Presumably, this might even apply to the effects of wearing a pleasant perfume or cologne. But does it? In an interesting study, *female* interviewers did, in fact, give higher ratings to job applicants who wore pleasant scents. But *males,* in contrast, gave *lower* ratings to persons who wore perfume or cologne (Baron, 1983).

Psychologist Robert Baron, who did this experiment, speculates that the male interviewers were more aware of the scents and resented the implied attempt to influence their ratings. Whatever the case, one thing is clear: If possible, you should learn an interviewer's sex beforehand—if you want to avoid making a flagrant, fragrant error, that is.

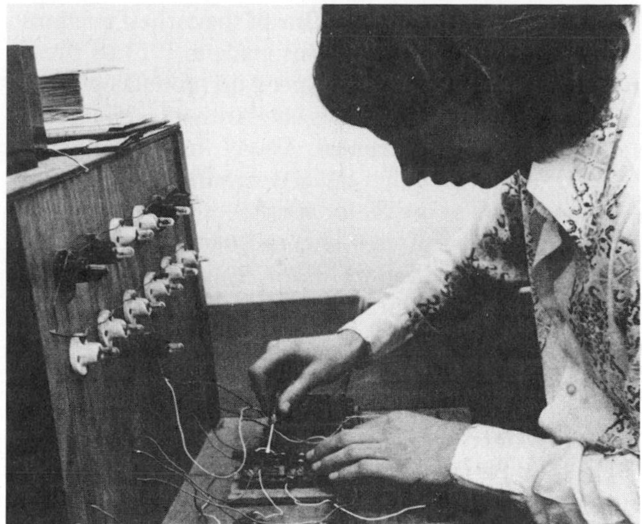

Fig. 26–3 *Not all aptitude tests are of the paper-and-pencil variety. Here, a job applicant takes a mechanical aptitude test.*

As a college graduate, you will quite likely encounter the **assessment center** approach to personnel selection. Assessment centers are set up by many large organizations to do in-depth evaluations of job candidates. This approach has become so popular that the list of businesses using it—Ford, IBM, Kodak, Exxon, Sears, Bell Telephone, and over 1000 others—reads like a corporate *Who's Who.*

Question: How do assessment centers differ from the selection methods already described?

Assessment centers are primarily used to fill management and executive positions. Applicants are first tested and interviewed at an assessment center. Then they are observed and evaluated in simulated work situations. For example, in one exercise, applicants are given an **in-basket test.** This test consists of a basket full of memos, requests, and problems typical of those faced by executives. Each applicant is asked to quickly read all of the materials and to take appropriate action. In another, more stressful test, applicants take part in a **leaderless group discussion** in which they try to solve a realistic business problem (Schultz, 1979). While the group grapples with the problem, "clerks" bring in price changes, notices about delayed supplies, and so forth. By observing applicants, it is possible to evaluate leadership skills and to see how job candidates cope with stress.

Question: How well does this approach work?

Assessment centers have had considerable success in predicting performance in a variety of jobs, careers, and advanced positions (Borman et al., 1983). One study of women, for instance, found that assessment center predictions of management potential were closely related to career progress 7 years later (Ritchie & Moses, 1983). On the basis of long-range studies, it appears that future success is most clearly predicted by oral communication skills, leadership, energy, resistance to stress, tolerance for uncertainty, need for advancement, and planning skills (Bray et al., 1974; Ritchie & Moses, 1983).

As you will soon learn, psychologists working in business do far more than match people with jobs. Let's see how they contribute to management and the quality of work.

Theories of Management and Job Satisfaction

At 7 A.M. each morning at a major manufacturing plant, more than 400 assembly line workers, supervisors, and top executives begin their work day talking, joking, and exercising together, all to the beat of amplified music. To say the least, these are unusual working conditions. To understand the rationale behind them, let's consider 2 basic theories of employee management.

Theory X and Theory Y One of the earliest attempts to improve worker efficiency was made in 1923 by Frederick Taylor, an engineer. To speed up production, Taylor standardized work routines and stressed careful planning, control, and orderliness. Today, modern versions of Taylor's approach are called **scientific management** (also known as **Theory X,** for reasons explained shortly). Scientific management uses time-and-motion studies, task analysis, job specialization, assembly lines, pay schedules, and the like, to increase productivity.

Question: It sounds like scientific management treats people as if they were machines. Is that true?

To some extent it is. Managers who follow Theory X tend to assume that workers must be goaded or guided into being productive. Many psychologists working in business, of course, are concerned with improving **work efficiency** (defined as maximum output at lowest cost). As a result, they alter conditions they believe will affect workers (such as time schedules, work quotas, bonuses, and so on). Some might even occasionally wish that people would act like well-oiled machines. However, most recognize that **psychological efficiency** is just as important as work efficiency. In addition to achieving high productivity, businesses that prosper must be able to retain workers, minimize absenteeism, sustain good morale and labor relations, and so forth. Management that ignores or mishandles the human element can be devastatingly costly.

The term *Theory X* was coined by psychologist Douglas McGregor (1960) as a way to distinguish scientific management from a newer management style. McGregor dubbed this newer approach, which emphasizes human relations at work, **Theory Y.**

Question: How is this approach different?

Theory Y managers assume that workers enjoy autonomy and are willing to accept responsibility. They also assume that worker needs and goals can be meshed with the company's goals, and that people are not naturally passive or lazy. In short, Theory Y assumes that people are industrious, creative, and rewarded by challenging work. It appears that given the proper conditions of freedom and responsibility, many people *will* work hard to gain competence and use their talents fully.

Many features of Theory Y are illustrated by the Honda plant at Marysville, Ohio. As you may already know, the automobile industry has a long history of labor-management clashes and worker discontent. In fact, outright sabotage by assembly line workers is not uncommon. To avoid such problems, Honda initiated a series of simple, seemingly successful measures. They include the following practices:

- Regardless of their position, all employees wear identical white uniforms. This allows workers and supervisors to interact on a more equal footing and builds feelings of teamwork.
- To further minimize status differences, all employees hold the title *associate*.
- Private offices, separate dining halls, and reserved parking spaces for executives were abolished.
- Employees work alongside company executives, to whom they have easy access.
- Every employee has a say in, and responsibility for, quality control and safety.
- Departmental meetings are held daily. At this time, announcements are discussed, decisions are made, and thoughts are freely shared (Abrams, 1983).

Two elements that make Theory Y methods effective are *participative management* and *management by objectives*. In **participative management,** employees at all levels are directly involved in decision making (Fig. 26–4). By taking part in decisions that affect them, employees like those at the Honda factory come to see work as a cooperative effort—not as something imposed on them by an egotistical boss. The benefits include greater productivity, greater job satisfaction, and less job-related stress (Jackson, 1983).

Question: What does "management by objectives" refer to?

In **management by objectives,** workers are given specific goals to meet, so they can tell if they are doing a good job. Typical objectives include reaching a certain sales total, making a certain number of items, or reducing waste by a specific percentage. In any case, workers are free to choose (within limits) how they will achieve their goals. As a result, they feel a greater sense of independence and personal responsibility for their work.

How can workers below the management level be involved more in their work? One popular answer is by the creation of **quality circles.** These are voluntary discussion groups that meet regularly, with or without supervision. Members of quality circles try to find ways to solve business problems or to improve efficiency (Jewell, 1985). Usually such groups do not have the power to put their suggestions into practice directly. But good ideas speak for themselves, and many are adopted by management. Quality circles and similar worker involvement programs have many limitations. Nevertheless, studies verify that greater involvement can have a positive impact on organizations and employees (Marks, 1986).

Fig. 26–4 *Participative management techniques encourage employees at all levels to become involved in decision making. Quite often, this arrangement leads to greater job satisfaction.*

Job Satisfaction

It often makes perfect sense to apply Theory X methods to work. However, doing so without taking worker needs into account can be a case of winning the battle while losing the war. That is, immediate productivity may be enhanced while job satisfaction is lowered. And when job satisfaction is low, absenteeism skyrockets, morale falls, and there is a high rate of employee turnover (leading to higher training costs and inefficiency). Understandably, many of the methods used by enlightened Theory Y managers ultimately improve **job satisfaction.**

Question: Under what conditions is job satisfaction highest?

Basically, job satisfaction comes from a good fit between work and a person's interests, abilities, needs, and expectations. What, then, do workers consider important? In the early 1970s, when American workers were asked to rate the importance of 25 aspects of work, their first 8 choices were as follows:

1. Interesting work
2. Enough help and equipment to get the job done
3. Enough information to get the job done
4. Enough authority to get the job done
5. Good pay
6. Opportunity to develop special abilities
7. Job security
8. Seeing the results of one's work

(*Work in America*, 1973).

A second survey in the early 1980s again found that satisfying, rewarding work ranked first in worker preference. However, high income rose to second place (Weaver & Mathews, 1985). Some observers worry that a swing toward greater materialism has occurred in the last 10 to 15 years. Even if this is true, intrinsically interesting work still tops the list. To summarize much research, we can say that job satisfaction is highest when workers are (1) allowed ordinary social contacts with others; (2) given opportunities to use their own judgment and intelligence; (3) recognized for doing well; (4) given a chance to apply their skills; (5) given relative freedom from close supervision; and (6) given opportunities for promotion and advancement.

Job Enrichment For years, the trend in business and industry was to make work more streamlined and efficient and to tie better pay to better work. There is now ample evidence that incentives such as bonuses, earned time off, and profit sharing can increase productivity (Horn, 1987). However, in recent years far too many jobs have become routine, repetitive, boring, and unfulfilling. To combat the discontent this can breed, many psychologists recommend a strategy called **job enrichment.**

Question: How is job enrichment done?

Job enrichment applies many of the principles we have discussed. Usually it involves removing some of the controls and restrictions on employees, giving them greater responsibility, freedom, choice, and authority. Employees also switch to doing a complete cycle of work. That is, they complete an entire item or project, instead of doing an isolated part of a larger process. Whenever possible, workers are given feedback about their work or progress. This feedback comes to them directly, instead of to a supervisor. Workers are encouraged to learn new and more difficult tasks and to learn a broad range of skills.

Job enrichment has been used with great success by large corporations such as IBM, Maytag, Western Electric, Chrysler, and Polaroid. It usually leads to lower production costs, increased job satisfaction, reduced boredom, and less absenteeism (Schultz, 1979).

Although we have only scratched the surface of industrial/organizational psychology, it is time to move on for a look at another applied area of great personal relevance. Before we begin, here's a Learning Check on the preceding discussion.

Learning Check

1. To gain attention for an emergency announcement, it is better to switch from a male voice to a female voice than it is to do the reverse. T or F?
2. An important element of engineering psychology is making __________ and __________ compatible with human use. This is often best accomplished through __________ design.
3. Identifying critical work incidents is sometimes included in a thorough __________ __________.
4. Detailed biographical information about a job applicant is referred to as __________.
5. The Strong-Campbell Inventory is a typical aptitude test. T or F?
6. A leaderless group discussion is most closely associated with which approach to employee selection?
   a. aptitude testing *b.* personal interviews *c.* job analysis *d.* assessment center
7. Theory X, or scientific management, is concerned primarily with improving __________.
8. Participative management is often a feature of businesses that adhere to Theory Y. T or F?
9. For the majority of workers, job satisfaction is almost exclusively related to the amount of pay received. T or F?
10. Job enrichment is a direct expression of scientific management principles. T or F?

Answers:

1. F **2.** displays, controls, natural **3.** job analysis **4.** biodata **5.** F **6.** *d* **7.** work efficiency **8.** T **9.** F **10.** F

Environmental Psychology—Life in the Big City

For the last decade, psychologist Terry Daniel has pursued an unusual and very interesting line of research. Using a variety of special techniques, Daniel and his colleagues have helped the U.S. Forest Service analyze the psychological effects of harvesting timber from forest lands (Daniel & Boster, 1976). The Forest Service was interested in how to harvest timber (especially dead trees) from forests without damaging their appeal. By doing a psychological analysis of scenic beauty, Daniel and his colleagues helped guide harvesting plans. Loosely speaking, what they found is that in the public eye, the ideal forest scene consists of a green meadow, a few young, healthy pine trees, and one or two picturesque fallen logs. This description, obviously, suggests that considerable thinning of natural forestation can be done without hurting forest aesthetics—at least as far as the general public is concerned.

The work of Terry Daniel, and psychologists like him, falls into an area known as **environmental psychology,** a specialty concerned with how environments influence our behavior. Environmental psychologists are interested in both **physical environments** (natural or constructed) and **social environments** (such as a dance, business meeting, or party) (Conyne & Clack, 1981). They also give special attention to **behavioral settings** (for example, an office, locker room, church, casino, or classroom). As you have no doubt noticed, various environments and behavioral settings tend to "demand" certain actions (Fig. 26–5). Consider for example, the difference between a library and a campus center lounge. In which would a conversation be more likely to occur?

Fig. 26–5 *Various behavioral settings place strong demands on people to act in expected ways.*

Other major interests of environmental psychologists are personal space, territorial behavior (see Box 26–3), stressful environments, architectural design, environmental protection, and many related topics (Table 26–3).

Environmental Influences A major finding of environmental research is that much of our behavior is controlled, in part, by the environment (Conyne & Clack, 1981). A case in point is the seismograph (earthquake detector) housed at a museum in the author's home town. Even though this instrument is encased in solid concrete, its lure is apparently irresistible. Below it are countless

Table 26–3 Topics of Special Interest to Environmental Psychologists

Architectural design	Noise
Behavioral settings	Personal space
Cognitive maps	Personality and environment
Constructed environments	Pollution
Crowding	Privacy
Energy conservation	Proxemics
Environmental stressors	Resource management
Heat	Territoriality
Human ecology	Urban planning
Littering	Vandalism
Natural environment	

● BOX 26–3 Territoriality

In Chapter 23 we noted that powerful norms govern the use of the space immediately surrounding each person's body. As we move farther from the body, it becomes apparent that personal space also extends to adjacent areas that we claim as our "territory." For example, in the library, **territorial behavior** might include protecting your space with a coat, handbag, book, or other personal belonging (Sommer, 1969). "Saving a place" at a theater or a beach also demonstrates the tendency to identify a space as "ours."

Respect for the temporary ownership of space is widespread. It is not unusual for a person to "take over" an entire table or study room by looking annoyed when others intrude. Your own personal territory may include your room, specific seats in many of your classes, or a particular table in the cafeteria or library that "belongs" to you and your friends.

Researchers have found that the more attached you are to an area, the more likely you are to signal your "ownership" with obvious **territorial markers,** such as decorations, plants, photographs, posters, or even graffiti (Hansen & Altman, 1976). College dorms and business offices are prime places to observe this type of territorial marking.

shoe marks made by visitors who kicked the wall to see if the needle would move! (It doesn't.) Similarly, psychologists have found that a variety of factors influence the amount of vandalism that occurs in public places.

On the basis of psychological research, many architects now "harden" and "de-opportunize" public settings to discourage vandalism and graffiti (Wise, 1982). Some such efforts limit opportunities for vandalism (doorless toilet stalls, tiled walls). Others weaken the lure of likely targets. (Strangely enough, a raised flower bed around signs helps protect them because people resist trampling the flowers to get to the sign.)

Given the personal impact that environments have, it is important to know how we are affected by stressful or unhealthy environments—a topic we will consider next.

Stressful Environments

Everyone has his or her own list of complaints about large cities. Traffic congestion, pollution, crime, and impersonality are urban problems that immediately come to mind. To this list psychologists have added crowding, noise, and over-stimulation as major sources of urban stress. Recent psychological research has begun to clarify the impact of each of these conditions on human functioning.

Crowding Over-population ranks as one of the most serious problems facing the world today. The world's population is now well over 5 billion, and it will more than double in the next 40 years. Nowhere are the effects of over-population more evident than in the teeming cities of many under-developed nations. Closer to home, the jammed buses, subways, and living quarters of our own large cities are ample testimony to the stresses of crowding.

Question: Is there any way to assess the effect crowding has on people?

One approach is to study the effects of overcrowding among animals. Although the results of animal experiments cannot be considered conclusive for humans, they point to some disturbing effects.

Question: For example?

In an interesting experiment, John Calhoun (1962) let a group of laboratory rats breed without limit in a confined space. Calhoun provided plenty of food, water, and nesting material for the rats. All that the rats lacked was space. At its peak, the colony numbered 80 rats. Yet, it was housed in a cage designed to comfortably hold about 50. Overcrowding in the cage was heightened by the actions of the 2 most dominant males. These rascals staked out private territory at opposite ends of the cage, gathered harems of 8 to 10 females, and prospered. Their actions forced the remaining rats into a small, severely crowded middle area.

Question: What effect did crowding have on the animals?

A high rate of pathological behavior developed in both males and females. Females gave up nest building and caring for their young. Pregnancies decreased, and infant mortality ran extremely high. Many of the animals became indiscriminately aggressive and went on rampaging attacks against others. Abnormal sexual behavior was rampant, with some animals displaying hypersexuality, bisexuality, homosexuality, or total sexual passivity. Many of the animals died, apparently from stress-caused diseases. The link between these problems and overcrowding is unmistakable.

Question: But does this apply to humans?

Many of the same pathological behaviors can be observed in crowded inner-city ghettos. It is therefore tempting to assume that violence, social disorganization, and declining birthrates as seen in these areas are directly related to crowding. However, the connection has not yet been demonstrated with humans. People living in the inner city suffer disadvantages in nutrition, education, income, and health care. These, more than crowding, may deserve the blame (Freedman, 1975). In fact, most laboratory studies using human subjects have failed to produce any serious ill effects by crowding people into small places. Most likely, this is because *crowding* is a psychological condition that is separate from **density** (the number of people in a given space).

Question: How does crowding differ from density?

Crowding refers to *subjective* feelings of being over-stimulated by social inputs or by a loss of privacy. Whether high density is experienced as crowding may depend on relationships among those involved (Fig. 26–6). In an elevator, subway, or prison, high densities may be uncomfortable. In contrast, a musical concert, party, or reunion may be most pleasant at high density levels (Freedman, 1975). Thus, physical crowding may interact with situations to intensify existing stresses or pleasures. Along this line, researcher Garvin McCain and his colleagues recently reported that death rates increase among prison inmates and mental hospital patients who live in crowded conditions.

Fig. 26–6 *High densities do not automatically produce feelings of crowding. The nature of the situation and the relationship between crowd members are also important.*

BOX 26–4
The High Cost of Noise

How serious are the effects of daily exposure to noise? A study of children attending schools near Los Angeles International Airport suggests that constant noise can be quite damaging. Children from the noisy schools were compared with similar students attending schools farther from the airport (Cohen et al., 1980). These comparison students were from families of comparable social and economic makeup. Testing showed that children attending the noisy schools had higher blood pressure than those from the quieter schools. They were more likely to give up attempts to solve a difficult puzzle. And they were poorer at proofreading a printed paragraph—a task that requires close attention and concentration.

The greater tendency of the noisy-school children to give up or become distracted is a serious handicap. It may even reveal a state of "learned helplessness" (described in Chapter 12) caused by daily, uncontrollable blasts of sound. Even if such damage proves to be temporary, it is clear that *noise pollution* is a major source of environmental stress.

Overload One unmistakable result of high densities and crowding is a condition that psychologist Stanley Milgram called **attentional overload.** Large cities tend to bombard residents with continuous sensory stimulation, information, and contact with others. The resulting sensory and cognitive overload can be quite stressful (see Box 26–4). Milgram (1970) believed that city dwellers learn to prevent overload by engaging in only brief, superficial social contacts, by ignoring nonessential events, and by fending off others with cold and unfriendly expressions. In short, many city dwellers find that a degree of callousness is essential for survival.

Question: Is there any evidence that such strategies are actually adopted?

A fascinating study suggests that they are. In several large American cities and smaller nearby towns, a young child stood on a busy street corner and asked passing strangers for help, saying, "I'm lost. Can you call my house?" About 72 percent of those approached in small towns offered to help. Only about 46 percent of those who were asked for help in the cities gave aid. In some cities (Boston and Philadelphia) only about one-third were willing to help (Takooshian et al., 1977). A more recent analysis of 65 studies confirmed that "country people are more likely to help than city people" (Steblay, 1987). Thus, a blunting of sensitivity to the needs of others may be one of the more serious costs of urban stresses and crowding.

Environmental Problem Solving

While overcrowding ranks high on the list of environmental stresses, it is only one of the many problems that press for attention. Other major difficulties center on pollution, the effects of noise, energy usage, poor architectural design, and related problems. Although the challenge is sizable, environmental psychology has begun to provide many solutions. To conclude, let's examine some sample problems and their possible solutions.

Problem The way people think about the environment greatly affects their behavior. Mental "maps" of various areas, for instance, often guide actions and alter decisions. A case in point is a study done in Philadelphia. There, researchers found that an existing school bus route contributed to truancy. The problem was that many of its stops were at corners where children were afraid of being attacked and beaten (Conyne & Clack, 1981).

Solution By doing an **environmental assessment,** psychologists develop a picture of environments as they are perceived by the people using them. An assessment often includes such things as charting areas of highest use in buildings, using attitude scales to measure reactions to various settings (such as schools, businesses, and parks), and even having people draw a version of their cognitive map of a building, campus, or city (Stokols, 1978).

In the case of the school children, residents of the neighborhood were asked to rate how much stress they felt when walking in various areas. The result was a contour map (somewhat like a high- and low-pressure weather map) that showed the areas of highest perceived stress. This "stress map" was then used to reroute school buses to "low-pressure" areas.

Problem Anyone who has ever lived in a college dorm knows that at times a dorm hall can be quite a "zoo." Most architects aim to create buildings in which people will be comfortable, happy, and healthy. But sometimes they miss the mark with human behavior. In one well-known experiment, Baum and Valins (1977) found that students housed in long, narrow, corridor-design dormitories often feel crowded and stressed. The crowded students tended to withdraw from others and even made more trips to the campus health center than students living in less crowded buildings.

Solution **Architectural psychology** is a specialty of growing importance for designing buildings. By studying the effects of existing buildings, psychologists are often able to suggest design changes that solve or avoid problems. For example, Baum and Valins (1979) studied 2 basic dorm arrangements. One dorm had a long corridor with one central bathroom. As a result, residents were constantly forced into contact with one another. The other dorm had rooms clustered in threes. Each of these suites shared a small bathroom. Even though the amount of space available to each student was the same in both dorms, students in the long-corridor dorm reported feeling more crowded. They also made fewer friends in their dorm and showed greater signs of withdrawing from social contact.

Question: What sort of solution does this suggest?

A later study showed that small architectural changes can greatly reduce stress in high-density living conditions. Baum and Davis (1980) compared students living in a long-corridor dorm housing 40 students to those living in an altered long-corridor dorm. In the altered dorm, Baum and Davis divided the hallway in half with unlocked doors and made 3 center bedrooms into a lounge area (Fig. 26–7). At the end of the term, students living in the divided dorm reported less stress from crowding. They also formed more friendships and were more open to social contacts. In comparison, students in the long-corridor dorm felt more crowded, stressed, and unfriendly, and they kept their doors shut much more frequently—presumably because they "vahnted to be alone." Similar improvements have been made by altering the interior design of businesses, schools, apartment buildings, mental hospitals, and prisons.

Problem The rapid worldwide consumption of natural resources is one of the most devastating of all social problems. The energy crisis of the early 1980s may have been a small taste of what lies ahead. In the face of projected shortages and squandered resources, what can be done to encourage conservation on a personal level?

Solution Try as you might to reduce your use of energy (electricity, for instance), you would probably find it difficult to do. A major problem is that *feedback* about

Fig. 26–7 *An architectural solution for crowding. Psychologists divided a dorm hall like that shown in the left diagram* (a) *into two shorter halls separated by unlocked doors and a lounge area* (b). *This simple change minimized unwanted social contacts and greatly reduced feelings of crowding among dorm residents. (Adapted from Baum & Davis, 1980.)*

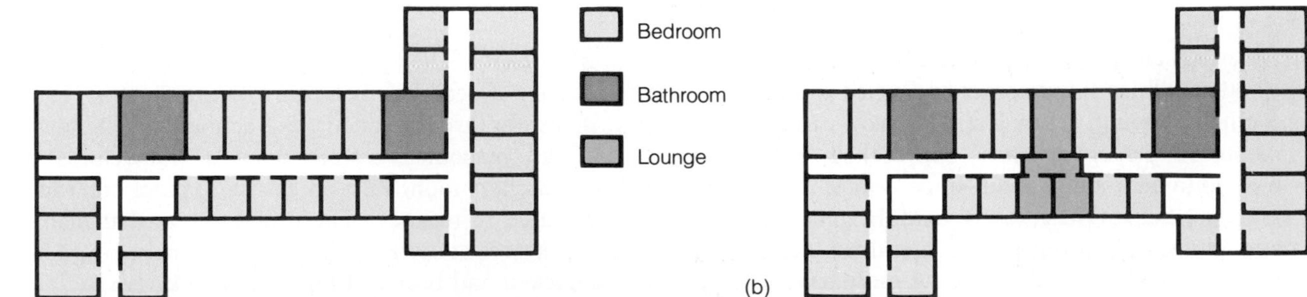

energy use (the monthly bill) arrives long after the temptation to turn up the heat or to leave lights on (see Chapter 8). Psychologists aware of this problem have shown that moderately lower energy bills result from simply giving families daily feedback about their use of gas or electricity (Seligman & Darley, 1978).

Programs that give monetary rewards for energy conservation are even more effective (Cone & Hayes, 1980). This is especially true for "master-metered" apartment complexes. In such apartments, families do not receive individual bills for their utilities. Consequently, they have no reason to save gas and electricity. Often, they consume about 25 percent more energy than they would in an individually metered apartment (McClelland & Cook, 1980). At this rate of waste, apartment owners can split any savings (from reduced consumption) with their tenants—and still be ahead.

Conclusion We have had room here only to hint at the creative and highly useful work being done in environmental psychology. While many environmental problems remain, it is encouraging to see that behavioral solutions exist for at least some of them. Surely, creating and maintaining healthy environments is one of the major challenges facing coming generations.

Learning Check

1. Although male rats in Calhoun's crowded animal colony became quite pathological, female rats continued to behave in a relatively normal fashion. T or F?
2. To clearly understand behavior, it is necessary to make a distinction between crowding and ________________ (the number of people in a given space).
3. Milgram believed that many city dwellers prevent attentional overload by limiting themselves to superficial social contacts. T or F?
4. Performing an environmental ________________ might be a good prelude to redesigning college classrooms to make them more comfortable and conducive to learning.
5. So far, the most successful approach for bringing about energy conservation is to add monetary penalties to monthly bills for excessive consumption. T or F?

Answers:

1. F 2. density 3. T 4. assessment 5. F

A Panorama of Applied Psychology

We have discussed work and the environment at some length because both have major effects on our lives. To provide a fuller account of the diversity of applied psychology, let's conclude by briefly sampling some additional topics of interest.

Educational Psychology

You have just been asked to teach a class of fourth-graders for a day. What will you do? (Assume that bribery, showing them films, and a field trip to a video arcade are out.) If you ever do try teaching, you might be surprised at how challenging it can be. Effective teachers must understand processes involved in learning, instruction, classroom dynamics, and testing. Fortunately, teachers (and their students) have benefited greatly from the work of educational psychologists (see Box 26–5). Specifically, **educational psychology** seeks to understand how people learn and how teachers instruct (Thornburg, 1984) (Fig. 26–8).

What are the best ways to teach? Is there an optimal teaching style for different age groups, topics, or individuals? These and many related questions lie at the heart of educational psychology (Table 26–4). In addition to studying such questions, educational psychologists design aptitude and achievement tests, evaluate educational programs, and participate in teacher training at colleges and universities.

Question: As a student, I've encountered many different teaching styles. Do different styles affect classroom learning?

There is little doubt that teachers can greatly affect student interest, motivation, and creativity. But what styles

BOX 26–5 Elements of a Teaching Strategy

Whether it's "breaking in" a new co-worker, instructing a friend in a hobby, or helping a child learn to read, the fact is, we all teach at times. The next time you are asked to share your knowledge, how will you do it? One good way to become more effective is to use a specific **teaching strategy.** The example that follows was designed for classroom use, but it applies to many other situations as well (adapted from Thornburg, 1984).

Step 1: Learner preparation Begin by gaining the learner's attention, and focus interest on the topic at hand.

Step 2: Stimulus presentation Present instructional stimuli (information, examples, and illustrations) deliberately and clearly.

Step 3: Learner response Allow time for the learner to respond to the information presented (by repeating correct responses or asking questions, for example).

Step 4: Reinforcement Give positive reinforcement (praise, encouragement) and feedback ("Yes, that's right," "No, this way," and so on) to strengthen correct responses.

Step 5: Evaluation Test or assess the learner's progress so that both you and the learner can make adjustments when needed.

Step 6: Spaced review Periodic review is an important step in teaching because it helps strengthen responses to key stimuli.

have what effects? To answer this question, psychologists have compared a number of teaching styles. Two of the most basic are direct instruction and open teaching.

In **direct instruction,** factual information is presented by lecture, demonstration, and rote practice. In **open teaching,** active teacher-student discussion is emphasized (Peterson, 1979). And now, the winner: As it turns out, both approaches have certain advantages. Students of direct instruction do slightly better on achievement tests than students in open classrooms (Thornburg, 1984). However, students of open teaching do somewhat better on tests of abstract thinking, creativity, and problem solving. They also tend to be more independent, curious, and positive in their attitudes toward school (Peterson, 1979). At present, it looks as if a balance of teaching styles goes hand in hand with a balanced education.

Fig. 26–8 *Educational psychologists are interested in enhancing learning and improving teaching.*

Although we have viewed only a small sample of educational research, its value for improving teaching and learning should be apparent. In the next section, we will consider how psychology is applied in a very different context—the highly competitive world of consumer affairs.

Consumer Psychology

Whether it's buying a car, toothpaste, a record, or lunch, we are all consumers. **Consumer psychology** is an applied field that focuses on why consumers act as they do (Robertson et al., 1984) (Table 26–5). Consumer psy-

Table 26–4 Topics of Special Interest to Educational Psychologists

Aptitude testing	Language learning
Classroom management	Learning theory
Classroom motivation	Moral development
Classroom organization	Student adjustment
Concept learning	Student attitudes
Curriculum development	Student needs
Disabled students	Teacher attitudes
Exceptional students	Teaching strategies
Gifted students	Teaching styles
Individualized instruction	Test writing
Intellectual development	Transfer of learning
Intelligence testing	

Table 26–5 Topics of Special Interest to Consumer Psychologists

Attitude change	Marketing research
Brand loyalty	Marketing strategies
Brand recognition	Mass media effects
Buying habits	Opinion leaders
Consumer attitudes	Opinion polling
Consumer complaints	Package design
Consumer needs	Product image
Consumer protection	Promotional schemes
Consumer values	Shopping behavior
Effects of advertising	Subcultural markets
Family decision making	

chology is a rapidly growing specialty, especially as it is applied to business and advertising (Kassarjian, 1982).

Many people give little thought to why they buy what they do. But in fact, **consumer behavior** can be separated into several steps. These include deciding to spend, selecting a brand, shopping, making the purchase, and evaluating the product in use (Robertson, et al., 1984). At each step, advertising, packaging, and a host of other factors affect our behavior. To pinpoint such factors, a type of public opinion polling called **marketing research** is often done.

In marketing research, people in a representative sample are asked to give their personal impressions of products, services, and advertising. In this way, researchers have learned, among other things, that powerful, widely held **brand images** often develop. A case in point is the images many people have of automobiles, such as: Mercedes-Benz (high status), Corvette (power and sportiness), Buick (conservatism), and so forth (Robertson et al., 1984). Brand images often direct buying behavior and help explain why many people purchase products for their labels as much as for their performance.

In addition to marketing research, consumer psychologists do laboratory testing of products (see Box 26–6). They also try to match products to consumer needs. They test public acceptance of new products, brand names,* and packaging. And they design various strategies to change buying habits (through the use of TV commercials, printed advertisements, premiums, contests, promotional schemes and the like).

*The importance of product names is illustrated by the difficulty Chevrolet had in initial attempts to market its *Nova* model in South America. Until the name was changed, consumers shunned the car. The problem? In Spanish, *no va* means "doesn't go"!

● BOX 26–6 Name That Beer

It is quite common for products to be promoted as "superior," "the best," "unmistakably different," and the like. How well do such claims hold up? In one recent test, 3 nationally advertised brands of beer were compared. The results are typical of many similar tests: When consumers sampled beer under controlled conditions—where taste was the only cue available—there was no evidence of any noticeable difference in brands (Fowler, 1982).

Although beer lovers would probably disagree, it appears that the labels could be interchanged on many major brands and no one would notice the difference. It is minimal differences of this sort that spur massive, image-conscious advertising campaigns.

Question: It sounds like consumer psychology is concerned with getting people to buy things they don't need. Is that the case?

It is true that many consumer psychologists use their knowledge to increase sales. However, not all consumer psychology is profit-oriented. For instance, principles of consumer behavior may be used to encourage the conservation of gasoline, water, or electricity. Also, many consumer psychologists are interested in protecting and enhancing consumer welfare by persuading people to act in their own best interest. Advertising campaigns concerning auto seat belt use, highway safety, drug abuse prevention, and the like, all draw on an understanding of consumer behavior.

As a final example, it was consumer psychologists who documented the large number of commercials on "kid vid" (children's television programs). Each year, the average child sees over 20,000 commercials—most of which are for highly sugared cereals and overpriced toys. Related research showed that children under age 6 are easily victimized because they often cannot distinguish commercials from the program itself (Oskamp, 1984). Such findings have helped advance the cause of **consumerism** (attempts to enhance consumer knowledge, rights, and welfare) for both children and adults.

Psychology and Law

One of the best places to see psychology in action is the local courthouse. Jury trials are often fascinating studies in human behavior. Does the defendant's appearance affect the jury's decision? Do the personality characteristics or attitudes of jurors influence how they vote? These and many more questions have been investigated in recent years by psychologists interested in law (Oskamp, 1984) (Table 26–6).

Jury Behavior When a case goes to trial, jurors must listen to days or weeks of testimony and then decide guilt or innocence. How do they reach their decision? Psychologists use **mock juries** made up of volunteers to probe such behavior. Some mock juries are simply given written evidence and arguments to read before making a decision. Others are shown videotaped trials staged by actors. Either way, studying the behavior of mock juries helps us understand what determines how real jurors vote.

Some of the findings of jury research are unsettling. Studies show that jurors are rarely able to put aside their biases, attitudes, and values while making a decision (Watson et al., 1984). For example, jurors are less likely to find attractive defendants guilty (on the basis of the same evidence) than unattractive defendants (Perlman & Cozby, 1983). There is an interesting twist, however. If it appears that being attractive helped a person commit a crime, it can work against her or him in court (Tedeschi et al., 1985). An example would be a handsome man on trial for swindling money from an unmarried middle-aged woman.

A second major problem is that jurors are not very good at separating evidence from other information, such as their perceptions of the defendant, attorneys, witnesses, and what they think the judge wants. When jurors are told to ignore information that slips out in court, they find it hard to do so. Often, their final verdict is influenced by inadmissible evidence, such as mention of a defendant's prior conviction (Watson et al., 1984). A related problem occurs when jurors take into account the severity of the punishment a defendant faces (Sales & Hafemeister, 1985). Jurors are not supposed to let this affect their verdict, but many do.

A third area of difficulty arises because jurors usually cannot suspend judgment until all the evidence is in. Typically, jurors form an opinion early in the trial. It then becomes hard for them to fairly judge evidence that contradicts their opinion.

Problems like these are troubling in a legal system that prides itself on fairness. However, all is not lost. Each of the factors discussed has much less effect as a crime becomes more severe or the evidence becomes more clear-cut (Tedeschi et al., 1985). Although it is far from perfect, the jury system works reasonably well in most cases.

Jury Selection Before a trial begins, opposing attorneys are allowed to disqualify potential jurors who may be biased (Fig. 26–9). For example, a person who knows anyone connected with the trial can be excluded. Beyond this, however, attorneys try to use jury selection to re-

Table 26–6 Topics of Special Interest in the Psychology of Law

Arbitration	Juror attitudes
Attitudes toward law	Jury decisions
Bail setting	Jury selection
Capital punishment	Mediation
Conflict resolution	Memory
Criminal personality	Parole board decisions
Diversion programs	Police selection
Effects of parole	Police stress
Expert testimony	Police training
Eyewitness testimony	Polygraph accuracy
Forensic hypnosis	Sentencing decisions
Insanity plea	White-collar crime

Fig. 26–9 *The behavior of juries and jurors has been extensively studied. The findings of such studies are applied by psychologists who act as advisors to attorneys during the jury selection process.*

move people who may cause trouble for them. For instance, jurors who believe in rape myths (that a woman may "ask for it" by her actions or style of dress, for example) are less likely to convict an accused rapist (Watson et al., 1984).

Only a limited number of potential jurors can be excused. As a result, many attorneys are now asking psychologists for help in identifying people who will favor or harm their efforts. Several techniques are typically used. As a first step, *demographic information* is frequently collected for each juror. Much can be guessed by knowing a juror's age, sex, race, occupation, education, political affiliation, religion, and socioeconomic status. Most of this information is available from public records.

To supplement demographic information, a *community survey* may be done to find out how local citizens feel about the case. The assumption is that jurors probably have attitudes similar to people with backgrounds like their own. Although talking with potential jurors outside the courtroom is not permitted, other information networks are available. If possible, a psychologist may interview relatives, acquaintances, neighbors, and co-workers of potential jurors.

Back in court, psychologists also often watch for *authoritarian personality* traits in potential jurors (see Chapter 24). (Authoritarians tend to believe that punishment is effective, and they are more likely to vote for conviction.) At the same time, the psychologist typically observes potential jurors' *nonverbal behavior*. The idea is to try to learn from body language which side the person favors (Sales & Hafemeister, 1985).

Some of these techniques were used a few years ago in the defense of automaker John DeLorean. As you may recall, DeLorean was charged with setting up a $25 million cocaine deal. Before the trial, DeLorean's attorneys had a national survey done to see if he would have a better chance if the trial were held away from Los Angeles. As it turned out, the public attitude was the same all over the country. Everyone thought DeLorean was guilty. (He was eventually acquitted.)

Cases like DeLorean's, in which wealthy clients have the advantage of psychological jury selection, raise ethical questions about the practice. Attorneys, of course, can't be blamed for trying to improve their odds of winning a case. And since both sides help select jurors, the net effect in most instances is a more balanced jury (Sales & Hafemeister, 1985). Rather than trying to tip the scales of justice, psychologists who analyze juries believe that they are helping to identify and remove only people who would be highly biased.

Jury research is perhaps the most direct link between psychology and law, but there are others. Psychologists evaluate people for sanity hearings, do counseling in prisons, advise lawmakers on public policy, help train police cadets, and more. In the future, it is quite likely that psychology will have a growing impact on law and the courts.

Sports Psychology

Question: What does psychology have to do with sports?

As almost all serious athletes soon learn, peak performance requires more than physical training. Mental and emotional "conditioning" are also important. Recognizing this fact, many teams, both professional and amateur, now include psychologists on their staffs (Greenspan, 1983). On any given day, a sports psychologist might teach an athlete how to relax, how to ignore distractions, or how to cope with emotions. The sports psychologist might also provide personal counseling for performance-lowering stresses and conflicts (Rushall, 1975). Other psychologists are interested in studying factors that affect athletic achievement, such as skill learning, the personality profiles of champion athletes, the effects of spectators, and related topics (Table 26–7). In short, **sports psychologists** seek to understand and improve sports performance and to enhance the benefits of participating in sports.

Before the advent of sports psychology, it was debatable whether athletes improved because of "homespun" coaching methods, or in spite of them. For example, in early studies of volleyball and gymnastics, it became clear that people teaching these sports had very little knowledge of crucial, underlying skills (Salmela, 1974, 1975).

Question: How has psychology helped?

An ability to do detailed studies of complex skills has been one of the major contributions (Desharhais, 1975).

Table 26–7 Topics of Special Interest to Sports Psychologists

Achievement motivation	Hypnosis
Athletic personality	Mental practice
Athletic task analysis	Motor learning
Coaching styles	Peak performance
Competition	Positive visualization
Control of attention	Self-regulation
Coping strategies	Skill acquisition
Emotions and performance	Social facilitation
Exercise and mental health	Stress reduction
Goal setting	Team cooperation
Group (team) dynamics	Training procedures

In a psychological **task analysis,** sports skills are broken into subparts, so that key elements can be identified and taught (see Box 26–7). Such methods are an extension of techniques first used for job analyses, as described earlier.

Because sports have strong positive or negative effects on participants, they often provide valuable information on human behavior in general. For example, a study of Little League baseball found that children's self-esteem improved significantly after a season of play (Hawkins & Gruber, 1982). In other work, psychologists have learned that such benefits are most likely to occur when competition, rejection, criticism, and the "one-winner mentality" are minimized. When working with children in sports, it is also important to emphasize fair play, intrinsic rewards, self-control of emotions, independence, and self-reliance (Orlick, 1975).

Adults, of course, may also benefit from sports. For many, the payoffs are stress reduction, a better self-image, and improved general health. Researchers have reported, for instance, that distance running is associated with lower levels of tension, anxiety, fatigue, and depression than is found in the nonrunning population (Gondola & Tuckman, 1982; Morgan, 1978).

One of the most interesting topics in sports psychology is the phenomenon of **peak performance.** Many athletes report episodes during which they felt almost as if they were in a trance. The experience has also been called "flow" because the athlete becomes one with his or her performance and flows with it. At such times, athletes

BOX 26–7
Taking the Pulse of a Bull's-Eye

It doesn't take much to be off target in the Olympic sport of marksmanship. The object is to hit a bull's-eye the size of a dime at the end of a 165-foot-long shooting range. Nevertheless, an average of 50 bulls'-eyes out of 60 shots is not unusual in international competition (prone position).

What does it take—beyond keen eyes and steady hands—to achieve such accuracy? The answer is surprising. Sports psychologists have found that top marksmen consistently squeeze the trigger *between* heartbeats (Fig. 26–10). Apparently the tiny tremor induced by a heartbeat is enough to send the shot astray (Pelton, 1983). Without careful psychological study, it is doubtful that this element of marksmanship would have been identified. Now that its importance is known, competitors have begun to use various techniques—from relaxation training to biofeedback—to steady and control their heartbeat. In the future, the best marksmen may be those who set their sights on mastering their hearts.

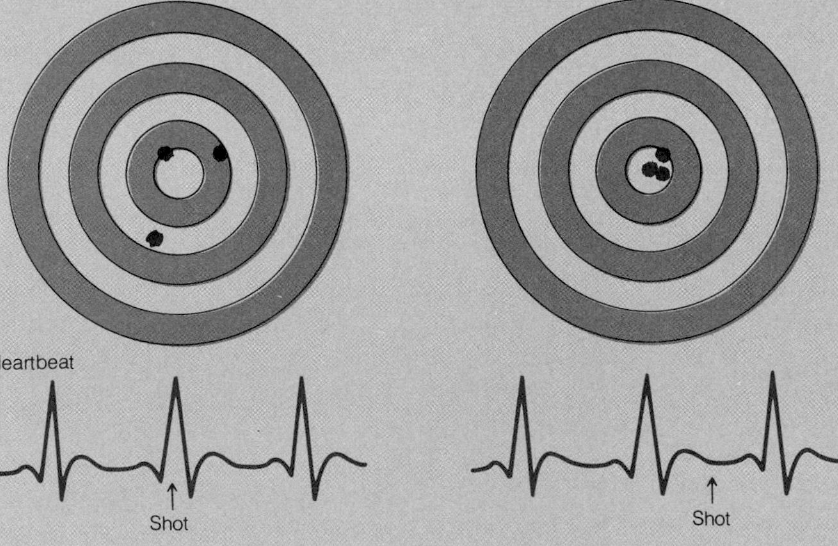

Fig. 26–10 *The target on the left shows what happens when a marksman fires during the heart's contraction. Higher scores, as shown by the 3 shots on the right, are more likely when shots are made between heartbeats. (Adapted from Pelton, 1983.)*

experience intense concentration, detachment from surroundings, a lack of fatigue and pain, a subjective slowing of time, and feelings of unusual power and control (Browne & Mahoney, 1984). It is at just such times that "personal bests" tend to occur.

A curious aspect of flow is that it cannot be forced to happen. In fact, if a person stops to think about it, the flow state goes away. Psychologists are now seeking to identify conditions that facilitate peak performance and the unusual mental state that usually accompanies it. Promising work is being done to train athletes to use physical relaxation, guided imagery, mental rehearsal, self-hypnosis, and the like, to attain peak performance.

At present, sports psychology is a very young field and still much more an art than a science (Greenspan, 1983). Nevertheless, interest in the field is rapidly expanding.

Summary Although we have sampled several major areas of applied psychology, they are by no means the only applied specialities. Others that immediately come to mind are school psychology, military psychology, health psychology (discussed in Chapter 13), and space psychology (a skyrocketing field that is really looking up—see this chapter's Exploration).

In the Applications section that follows, we will discuss the psychology of making vocational choices—a topic that has a great deal of personal impact. But first, a word from your conscience: It's time for a Learning Check.

Learning Check

Match the term on the left with one or more related topics or concepts from the list on the right.

____ **1.** Educational psychology
____ **2.** Consumer psychology
____ **3.** Psychology of law
____ **4.** Sports psychology

A. nonverbal ratings
B. teaching strategies
C. peak performance
D. marketing research
E. eyewitnesses
F. brand image
G. styles of instruction
H. community campaigns
I. task analysis

5. Compared to direct instruction, open teaching produces better scores on achievement tests. T or F?

6. Which of the following is *not* commonly used by psychologists to aid jury selection?
a. mock testimony *b.* information networks *c.* community surveys *d.* demographic data

Answers:
1. B, G 2. D, F 3. A, E 4. C, I 5. F 6. *a*

Applications: Vocational Choice and Occupational Survival—Charting Your Course in the World of Work

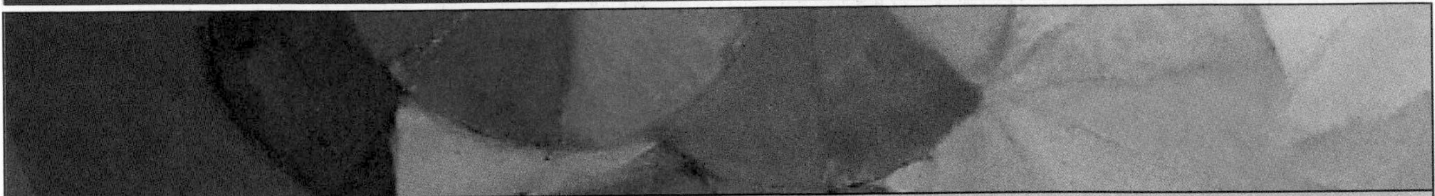

Within 5 years after starting work, more than half of all college graduates change jobs. Why? Contrary to what might be expected, higher pay is not the prime reason. Needs for recognition and challenge, the desire to do something worthwhile, opportunities to learn, and needs to use skills and abilities are all ranked higher than money by workers (Renwick & Lawler, 1978).

The message in these findings seems to be that work needs to be satisfying on a day-to-day basis. When it's not, many people quickly tire of trading their time and energy for money. Professionals, in particular—such as accountants, nurses, engineers, architects, biologists, and teachers—rate the nature of their work as the greatest source of their job satisfaction (Bird, 1975).

In recognition of the likely importance of work in your life, this final Applications provides a look at how vocational choices are made and how they can be improved. Let's begin with a short case history.

John's Story John was always an excellent student, but his real love was sports. Being on the track team was, in fact, the high point of his college career. (About 7 feet high, to be exact. John was a high jumper.) After he graduated, John was hired by a large accounting firm at an enviable starting salary. Yet within 2 years, John knew he had made a mistake. Accounting left him dissatisfied, restless, and often bored.

In college, John's career choice had seemed highly practical. Now he was miserable. What could he do about it? John decided to take a chance. He quit his job, and after several years of additional education, financial hardship, and personal sacrifice, he accepted his first college coaching position.

Vocational Choice

As John's story illustrates, vocational decisions are neither permanent nor easily undone. Usually, by the time a person has selected a career path, it takes a big effort to change course. Moreover, changing careers can be a major risk. (What if John had discovered that he also disliked coaching?) The reality that John faced is illustrated by a survey in which 44 percent of those polled said that for better or worse, they felt "locked into" their current jobs (Renwick & Lawler, 1978). Clearly, there is value in making good vocational choices, and in making them early, if possible.

Career Development John's abrupt change is somewhat unusual. For most people who enter professions, career development tends to flow through four broad phases. These are: (1) the **exploration phase,** during which an initial search for career possibilities is made; (2) the **establishment phase,** during which the person finds a job, enters a career, develops competence, and gains status; (3) the **midcareer phase,** which is a time of high productivity and acceptance by co-workers; and (4) the **later career phase,** when the individual serves as a respected expert and often as a mentor (role model and guide) for younger workers (Van Maanen & Schein, 1977).

Of the four phases, the two most likely to be of immediate relevance to you are exploration and establishment. Let's probe them in greater depth.

Question: How do most people choose their vocations?

During the exploration phase, most people go through a recognizable series of stages as they choose a vocation (Weiten, 1983).

In the **fantasy stage,** children under age 10 simply *imagine* what they want to be when they grow up. The roles they fantasize—such as president, pilot, rock star, rodeo rider, or TV announcer—may be unrealistic, but they do show that children realize that they will need to work someday.

During the **tentative stage** (roughly, ages 10 to 18), adolescents begin to form more realistic, if somewhat general, ideas about what they want to do. However, their plans may shift several times during this period, and they typically remain tentative. Toward the end of high school, many students begin to more fully appreciate the importance of choosing a vocation. They also become aware that there are limits to their options and barriers to certain careers.

After high school, various social and practical pressures lead most people to narrow their range of vocational options. During this **realistic stage,** the first steps are taken to find out what specific jobs are like and to prepare for them. At this time, many college students use course work as a way to discover what they are good at and what holds their interest.

By the early 20s, most people begin to carry out their vocational plans. This involves completing necessary training and landing that important first job.

The preceding description implies that most people carefully choose a vocation or career. Actually, there is evidence

Applications

that vocational choice is often rather haphazard (Janis & Wheeler, 1978). For example, it is not unusual for students to allow a tentative choice of a major to determine school course work. Soon, they find themselves channeled into a career path—without really having made a clear decision.

Question: How would a person go about improving the quality of his or her vocational choice?

To begin with, it helps to recognize that our attraction to certain jobs or careers is influenced by many factors. Some of the more important influences are socioeconomic status, intelligence, school achievement, family background, gender, and personal interests (Kaplan & Stein, 1984). As much as these factors may influence your own choice, it is also important to realize that you have the potential to succeed in a variety of occupations. This is reflected by the fact that the best single predictor of what job category you will enter is your **vocational aspiration,** which is simply what you tell yourself you would like to do.

The world of work is complex and rapidly changing. In the face of such changes, it is becoming more important to make careful, informed decisions about what kind of work you would like to do. To make sure your vocational choice will be realistic and personally rewarding, you must (1) gain an accurate understanding of various occupations and (2) get a clear picture of your own interests, needs, and goals.

Question: That seems obvious. But how?

Vocational Counseling The easiest way to improve occupational choice is to consult a **vocational counselor.**

Vocational counselors are counseling psychologists who have the specialized skills and knowledge needed to match people with jobs. A vocational counselor can help you clarify your career goals, and he or she can administer interest and aptitude tests to guide your choice. Many colleges now offer vocational counseling at campus **career centers.** These centers also typically hold a wealth of information about various jobs and careers. (An introductory discussion of careers in psychology follows this chapter in Appendix A.)

If formal guidance is unavailable, you will have to serve as your own "vocational counselor." A good way to start is to consult the *Occupational Outlook Handbook,* available in most libraries. This book, published yearly by the U.S. Department of Labor, provides objective information about the outlook for various occupations. The *Handbook* includes job descriptions, information on training requirements, average earnings, and the number of jobs likely to be available in coming years. A simple look at such facts could prevent many students from pursuing over-populated careers (law, for instance).

To find out what a particular job is really like may require more initiative. In many occupations the nature of the work is not what it seems from the outside. For instance, medical students are often dismayed when they first begin to realize that disease is ugly and that many medical procedures are distasteful. To find out beforehand what an occupation is like, it is advisable to talk to several people in that line of work. Be sure to ask your informants what they dislike about their jobs, as well as what they like. If possible, you might even spend a day observing people in an occupation that interests you.

After you have selected, prepared for, and begun a career, many challenges remain—far too many, in fact, to discuss here. To conclude, let us briefly consider the challenge of maintaining a healthy attitude at work.

Occupational Survival

Many businesses are now trying to reduce stresses at work by altering management practices and redefining roles. Some also hire psychologists to teach employees to cope better with stress—an approach that seems to have merit. For instance, one study found that teaching employees stress inoculation techniques (see Chapter 13) and progressive relaxation (see Chapter 22) lowered adrenaline levels and depression ratings at work (Ganster et al., 1982).

If an employer does not provide for occupational stress reduction, it may be up to you to ensure your own health by practicing stress-coping strategies. Sometimes, it is also possible to carry out a personal program of job enrichment to make work more rewarding. If such strategies fail to keep job satisfaction high and work stresses within bounds, it may be time to consider a change in jobs or even careers.

Making Career Decisions

Another way of improving work adjustment is to examine your approach to making career decisions. Psychologist Irving Janis and Dan Wheeler (1978) have described the ways in which people typically deal with work dilemmas, especially those that lead to a change in careers. Their analysis suggests that there are four basic coping styles. See if you recognize yourself in any of the following descriptions.

The Vigilant Style This style is the most effective of the four. It describes individuals who evaluate information objectively and make decisions with a clear understanding of the alternatives. Persons using this style make mental "balance sheets" to weigh possible gains and losses before taking action.

The Complacent Style Persons of this type drift along with a nonchalant attitude toward job decisions. They tend

Applications

to let chance direct their careers and to take whatever comes along without really making plans.

The Defensive-Avoidant Style These people are fully aware of the risks and opportunities presented by career choices and dilemmas. However, they are uncomfortable making decisions. This leads them to procrastinate, rationalize, and make excuses for their inaction and indecision.

The Hypervigilant Style People with this style more or less panic when forced to make career decisions. They may collect hundreds of job announcements and brochures, but they become so frantic that making logical decisions is nearly impossible.

These coping styles may seem exaggerated, but they are easy to observe when people are forced to change jobs or make major alterations in career plans. To relate them to yourself, think about how you have handled vocational decisions to date, or decisions about your college career. Of the four, Janis and Wheeler consider only the vigilant style to be constructive. With this insight, you may be able to greatly improve the quality of your career choices.

Conclusion Work, leisure, family, community, and environment all contribute to the quality of our lives. And as we have seen throughout this text, psychology has much to offer in each of these areas. It is my sincere hope that you have found enough relevance and value in this book to kindle a lifelong interest in psychology. Psychology's future looks exciting. What role will it play in your life?

Learning Check

1. Those working in professions generally place greater emphasis on the nature of their work than on money as the source of job satisfaction. T or F?
2. The establishment phase of career development is a time during which an initial search for career possibilities is made. T or F?
3. Many people go through a fantasy stage and a tentative stage before they become more realistic about choosing a career. T or F?
4. The best single predictor of what occupations college students will enter is their IQ scores. T or F?
5. Stress inoculation techniques have proved capable of lowering stress levels at work. T or F?
6. The vigilant style of making career choices is characterized by panic and illogical decisions. T or F?

Answers:
1. T 2. F 3. T 4. F 5. T 6. F

Exploration: Space Psychology—Life on the High Frontier

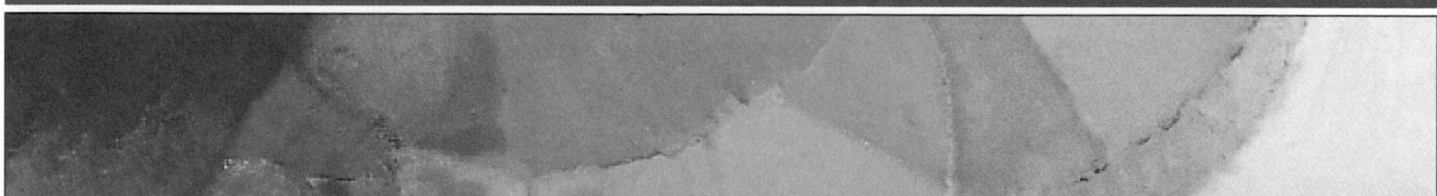

The first human outpost in space is drawing nearer. By the late 1990s the United States plans to orbit a continuously inhabited space station. Many engineering problems must be solved before a permanent space habitat becomes a reality. Yet, the real challenge may lie in the psychological adjustments needed for men and women to live in space.

The Challenge of Living Aloft

Life in the "mini-world" of a space station won't be easy, physically or mentally. For months at a time, space station residents will be restricted to tiny living quarters with little privacy. During an interplanetary trip, explorers would be confined for nearly 2 years.

No doubt the first long-term space residents will find life in orbit stressful. Even small disagreements can lead to tense clashes when people must live in cramped quarters. Living aloft would be similar to spending several months among a group of strangers in a small room from which you cannot escape.

In addition to confinement, long-term space inhabitants will face other trying conditions. These include restricted movement, separation from loved ones, isolation from recreation and hobbies, sensory monotony, noise, and many other stresses. It's no wonder that some astronauts reported restlessness, depression, and boredom after spending months aboard Skylab, a small space station orbited in the early 1970s.

Space Strike America's third Skylab crew spent a highly productive 3½ months in space. The crew—Edward Gibson, Gerald Carr, and William Pogue—also staged the world's first "space strike." Along with the pesky irritations of confined living, the crew felt pressured by an 18-hour-per-day work schedule. After 6 weeks the crew had fallen far behind in chores and experiments. The first signs of trouble surfaced at that time: Carr told Mission Control, "There's nothing worse than having to gobble your meal in order to get some task done that really should have been scheduled some other time, so please loosen up!" In a sudden burst of defiance, the astronauts went on strike and did exactly as they pleased. Gibson went to the solar console. Carr and Pogue sat in the wardroom, looked out the window, and took photographs.

Obviously, no one on earth was going to fly up and punish the astronauts for skipping their chores. The crisis was finally resolved when the crew was given more time to do experiments and fewer tasks to complete. Although the Skylab-3 strike was brief, it shows how important the human element will be in space.

Space Habitats

Clearly, space habitats must be designed with human behavior in mind. What will it take to make a congenial space station—one capable of sustaining emotional well-being and efficient performance? To begin, the *social* environment or "micro-society" in a space station will need to operate as smoothly as possible. For this reason, many problems may be avoided by carefully selecting and training future space residents *before* they go aloft.

It also would be wise to identify—and ease—stressors in space living quarters. To this end, psychologists have pinpointed several key areas of concern. Much has been learned by studying people confined to submarines, missile silos, Antarctic stations, simulated space stations on earth, and the like. Let's sample some expected problems and possible solutions.

General Environment Design of a space station as a living environment must take many human factors into account. For instance, researchers have learned that astronauts prefer rooms with clearly defined "up" and "down"—even in the weightlessness of space. Provisions must be made for regular exercise and full-body showers. As trivial as it might seem, a lack of showers was a major complaint among subjects in earlier confinement experiments.

Inside a space station there should be some flexibility in the use of living and work areas. Behavior patterns change over time, and control of one's environment helps lower stress. At the same time, people need stability. Psychologists have found, for instance, that eating becomes an important high point in monotonous environments. Eating at least one meal

Exploration

together each day can help keep a crew working as a social unit.

Sleep cycles will need to be carefully controlled in space to avoid disrupting bodily rhythms. In earlier space missions, astronauts had difficulty sleeping while the remainder of the crew continued to work and talk. Problems with sleep will be worsened by the constant noise on a space station. Fans, pumps, switches, lights, and the like, constantly click, hum, or throb on a spacecraft. At best, a space station will be at least as noisy as the typical office. At first, such noise is annoying. After weeks or months, it can become a serious stressor. Researchers are experimenting with various earmuffs, eyeshades, and sleeping arrangements to alleviate such difficulties.

Privacy Psychologists are helping engineers design space habitats that meet human needs for privacy. However, privacy will have to be based mainly on temporarily blocking out visual and auditory contact with others. In the first permanent space stations, there will be too little room for separate quarters.

Forced togetherness is stressful mainly because temporary retreat from contact with the group is difficult or impossible. Thus, control over the amount of contact one has with others is more important than having a private room. Designers do recognize, however, the need to define private territories. It will be important to identify small areas that can be personalized and "owned" by each individual. Desks, lockers, sleep stations, and the like, could fill this need if they are not shared with others.

Sensory Restriction Sensory monotony will be a problem in space, even with the magnificent vistas of earth below. (How many times would you have to see the North American continent before you lost interest?)

Researchers are developing stimulus environments that will use music, videotapes, and other diversions to combat monotony and boredom. Again, they are trying to provide choice and control for workers. Studies of confined living make it clear that one person's symphony is another's grating noise. Where music is concerned, individual earphones may be all that is required.

Most people in restricted environments find that they prefer non-interactive pastimes such as reading, listening to music, looking out windows, writing, and watching films or television. As much as anything, this preference may show again the need for privacy. A person can psychologically withdraw from the group by reading or listening to music. A good selection of passive entertainments looks like a must for any space station. Interestingly, Soviet astronauts, who make much use of music, have also reacted with delight to grab bags containing unexpected toys or novelties.

Social Isolation Separation from family, friends, and one's home community is a major stressor. However, the ability to talk regularly with family via two-way televised meetings should help ease feelings of social isolation. Some psychologists also believe that there should be a psychological support group on earth with whom a space station crew would talk to prevent emotional problems. In short, the best antidote for social isolation will probably be abundant opportunities to communicate with associates and loved ones on earth.

Conflict Resolution and Mental Health Many studies of long-term isolation show steady declines in motivation. Most inhabitants intend to use their free time for creative pursuits. But in reality they end up marking time and many become apathetic. Judging from submarine missions and Antarctic bases, as many as 5 percent of space inhabitants may experience some psychological disturbance. Most often, the problem will be depression. However, in rare instances people have become paranoid, psychotic, suicidal, or uncontrollably aggressive. As stated earlier, the risk of such problems may be minimized by carefully selecting personnel. Even so, it will be important to teach crew members basic counseling skills for solving conflicts.

Life on Spaceship Earth

Why is the idea of living in space so fascinating? Perhaps it is because human strengths and weaknesses will be magnified in the miniature world of a space station. As psychologist Yvonne Clearwater (1985) says:

> The space station represents the first glimmerings of recognition that some of the toughest challenges in space—as on earth—concern human behavior, not technology. . . . Ironically, the farther we go from earth and the longer we stay away, the more we will need to know about ourselves. Scientists working on the space effort believe that psycholog-

Exploration

ical factors will become increasingly important for the success or failure of future space missions.

It is curiously fitting that the dazzling technology of space travel has highlighted the inevitable importance of human behavior. Here on earth, as in space, we cannot count on technology alone to solve problems. The threat of nuclear war, social conflict, crime, prejudice, over-population, environmental damage, famine, homicide, economic disaster—these and most other major problems facing us are behavioral. Will spaceship earth endure? It's a psychological question. (Sources: Chaikin, 1985; Clearwater, 1985; Connors, Harrison, & Akins, 1985; Engle & Lott, 1980; Joyce, 1984.)

Learning Check

1. The Skylab-3 space strike was caused mainly by dissatisfaction with the poor quality of meals in space. T or F?
2. Researchers have learned that astronauts have no preference for living quarters with clearly defined "up" and "down" orientations. T or F?
3. Research shows that needs for privacy can be met by providing ways to temporarily withdraw from social contact with a group, even when physical withdrawal is impossible. T or F?
4. Most people in restricted environments prefer group pastimes, such as playing card games, skits, or group singing. T or F?

Answers:
1. F 2. F 3. T 4. F

Chapter Summary

• **Applied psychology** refers to the use of psychological principles and research methods to solve practical problems.

• **Community psychologists** treat entire communities as their "clients" and engage in activities that help promote community-wide mental health.

• **Industrial/organizational psychologists** are interested in the problems people face at work. Typically they specialize in **personnel psychology, human relations** at work, and/or **engineering psychology** (the design of machines and work environments for human use).

• Personnel psychologists try to match people with jobs by combining **job analysis** with a variety of selection procedures, including gathering **biodata, interviewing,** giving **standardized psychological tests** (especially **interest inventories** and **aptitude tests),** and using the **assessment center** approach.

• Two basic approaches to business and industrial management are **scientific management (Theory X)** and **human relations** approaches **(Theory Y).** Theory X is most concerned with *work efficiency,* whereas, Theory Y emphasizes *psychological efficiency*.

• **Job satisfaction** is not directly related to productivity, but it is linked to absenteeism, morale, employee turnover, and other factors that affect overall business efficiency. Job satisfaction is usually enhanced by Theory Y–oriented **job enrichment.**

• **Environmental psychologists** are interested in the effects of **behavioral settings, physical** or **social environments,** and human **territoriality,** among many other major topics.

• Over-population is a major world problem, often reflected at an individual level in crowding. Animal experiments indicate that excessive crowding can be unhealthy. However, human research shows that psychological feelings of **crowding** do not always correspond to **density** (the number of people in a given space). One major consequence of crowding is **attentional overload.**

• A large number of practical problems—from *noise pollution* to architectural design—have come under the scrutiny of environmental psychologists. In many cases, effective behavioral solutions to such problems have been found, often as a result of first doing a careful **environmental assessment.**

• **Educational psychologists** seek to understand how people learn and teachers instruct. They are particularly interested in **teaching styles,** such as *direct instruction* and *open teaching,* and **teaching strategies.**

• **Consumer psychologists** study *consumer behavior* and serve as consultants to businesses and advertising agencies. Consumer psychologists often do **marketing research** to aid the promotion of various products. Some also do research that helps advance the cause of **consumerism** and consumer welfare.

• The **psychology of law** includes studies of courtroom behavior and other topics that pertain to the legal system. Psychologists also serve various consulting and counseling roles in legal, law enforcement, and criminal justice settings. Studies of **jury behavior** show that jury decisions are often far from objective.

• **Sports psychologists** seek to enhance sports performance and the benefits of sports participation. A careful **task analysis** of sports skills is one of the major tools for improving coaching and performance.

• Four broad periods in **career development** are the **exploration phase,** the **establishment phase,** the **mid-career phase,** and the **later career phase.** The exploration phase can be further divided into a **fantasy stage,** a **tentative stage,** and a **realistic stage. Vocational counseling** can greatly aid career decision making.

• Styles of making career decisions have been classified as **vigilant, complacent, defensive-avoidant,** and **hypervigilant.** Of these four, only the vigilant style is consistently constructive.

• **Space psychologists** study the many behavioral challenges that accompany space flight and life in restricted environments. Space habitats must be designed with special attention to environmental stressors, privacy, social isolation, conflict resolution, and the maintenance of mental health.

Appendix A

Careers in Psychology

Let's say that you have taken the first step toward a career in psychology: Your introductory course has convinced you that you want to learn more about human behavior. The next step is to learn more about careers in psychology—something you can begin doing right here.

First Questions Are you suited to a career in psychology? What kinds of jobs are available to persons with associate, bachelor's, master's, or doctoral degrees in psychology? What is the employment outlook for psychology and related fields? These are questions to ask if you are thinking about majoring in psychology. Although this appendix can only provide preliminary answers, it should help you get started. First, let's see if you are on the right track at all:

- Do you have a strong interest in human behavior?
- Are you emotionally stable?
- Do you have good communication skills?
- Do you find theories and ideas challenging and stimulating?
- Do your friends regard you as especially sensitive to the feelings of others?
- Have you read popular books on psychology and found them interesting?
- Have discussions in this text matched some of your own insights about human behavior?
- Do you enjoy working with other people?

If you answered yes to most of these questions, a career in psychology or a related field may be a good choice for you.

Majoring in Psychology

As a quick survey of your classmates might show, the majority of students studying introductory psychology are not psychology majors. More surprising is the fact that about half of all undergraduate psychology majors do not plan to work as psychologists: Nearly 50 percent of all psychology majors seek full-time jobs immediately after they graduate (Woods & Wilkinson, 1987). Many of today's psychology majors recognize that a psychology degree does not limit them to a career in psychology. Learning psychology can provide a general knowledge of behavior that aids success in various occupations.

If you think you would like to major in psychology, but are not interested in graduate training, here are some points to consider:

- Few workers hold one job forever, or even remain in a single line of work for life.
- The nature of work is likely to change greatly in your lifetime, and adaptability will be important.
- A broad education that develops many skills makes a person more vocationally adaptable.
- It is a major myth that every job requires a precise set of skills. Apart from highly technical or specialized jobs, many positions can be filled by persons with differing combinations of skills.
- Specific undergraduate programs do not exist for many mental health professions, making psychology a good undergraduate major leading to later specialized training.
- Job recruiters look primarily for general competence in verbal and written communication, plus social skills and facility in meeting the public.

General Skills For reasons like those listed here, a general education in psychology can lead to a variety of interesting jobs and professions. Even a brief list of "marketable" abilities provided by a psychology degree would include the following: clear, analytic thinking; objectivity and keen observation; an ability to handle data, recognize patterns, and draw conclusions; ability to plan and organize complex activities; ability to communicate clearly, both verbally and in writing; the capacity to comprehend abstract principles and the subtleties of human behavior; ability to critically evaluate evidence; interpersonal skills; and general knowledge relevant to success in many settings.

Again, the point is that even if you do not plan to work as a psychologist, psychology can be a practical undergraduate major.

Education and Options

If you do decide to major in psychology, it is important to be aware of the level of training required for various jobs. While opportunities exist for those with an A.A. or B.A. degree in psychology, many of the most rewarding positions require further education. The discussion that follows should give you some idea of the options at each level.

Associate Degree Level Training in psychology at the associate degree level tends to yield fewer choices than those available to graduates with bachelor's degrees or more advanced training. Even so, all of the jobs listed here are open to persons with a 2-year, A.A. degree.

child care worker
human services worker
mental health assistant
nursing home attendant
playground supervisor
preschool aide
psychiatric technician
public survey worker
recreation aide
rehabilitation aide
senior citizen aide
teacher's aide
ward attendant
youth supervisor

The jobs listed here are only a sample of what is available. People with associate degrees in psychology are qualified to do interviewing, to give and score specific psychological tests, and to communicate the needs of clients to psychologists and other professionals. In general, a person with an associate degree can expect to work directly with clients, but under the supervision of more highly trained professionals.

In some communities, there are specific training programs for students interested in working as psychiatric (or psychological) technicians at hospitals or clinics. Often, a year or two of training can lead directly to a job in a local mental health facility. In some cases, provisions have been made for "psych-tech" trainees to combine classroom study with on-the-job training.

Bachelor's Degree As already mentioned, a bachelor's degree in psychology can be considered preparation for a variety of jobs or occupations. An undergraduate psychology major is also a good prelude to advanced training in several related professions. And, of course, a bachelor's degree is the first step toward a master's or doctoral degree in psychology.

Most of the jobs listed here are available to persons with bachelor's degrees in psychology. Some, however, require additional training (becoming a high school teacher, for example). Also, you would be most competitive for many of these jobs if you were to combine a psychology major with a minor in another area, such as business (Carducci et al., 1987). In other cases, it would be better to make psychology your minor, in combination with a major in a related area (law enforcement and nursing are examples).

advertising agent
art therapist
assistant youth coordinator
biofeedback technician
business management trainee
case worker
child development specialist
child welfare agent
college admissions representative
counselor aide
crisis intervention team member
customer relations specialist
director of daycare center
drug counselor
educational salesperson
employment counselor
employment interviewer
family services worker
geriatric technician
group home coordinator
high school psychology teacher
human relations director
job analyst
labor relations specialist
management consultant
marketing researcher
music therapist
occupational therapist
patient service representative
personnel worker
probation/parole officer
psychiatric nurse
public health assistant
public relations specialist
recreational therapist
research assistant
sales representative
social worker
special education teacher
statistical assistant
veterans' advisor

Again, these are only some of the possibilities. As the diversity of the list suggests, it is important to remain flexible when pursuing a psychology major. Plan your education so that you are exposed to psychology's many areas of knowledge, and avoid specializing too soon. To further broaden your employment options, consider taking classes in computer programming, mathematics, statistics, accounting, finance, business, marketing, advertising, education, technical writing, or law enforcement.

Master's Level A master's degree in psychology usually requires from 1 to 2 years of graduate-level training beyond the bachelor's degree. The master's degree usually requires completion of a research thesis and/or a certain number of hours of supervised practical experience in an applied setting.

At present, the most popular master's-level specialty is counseling psychology. Undoubtedly, this is because a master's degree in counseling is one of the most direct routes to a career as a mental health professional. Those with a master's degree in counseling psychology may further specialize in marriage and family counseling, vocational or educational counseling, child counseling, or rehabilitation counseling—to name only major possibilities.

Many counselors are self-employed, but some work for human service agencies, at mental health clinics, and occasionally for the military or large businesses. Recently, counselors have begun to move into new areas, such as hospices, child abuse clinics, rape counseling centers, and stress clinics.

Other master's-level specialties, such as human factors engineering, school psychology, psychometrics, clinical psychology, industrial psychology, and general psychology, are also offered. But recently, employment opportunities have become more limited for new master's-level psychologists. When positions open in such areas, they are most often filled by doctoral-level psychologists. (However, master's-level psychologists with prior work experience often are competitive for such positions.) On the other hand, a master's degree could make you more competitive for all of the bachelor's-level jobs listed earlier. It might also help you qualify for higher pay. If you are interested in teaching, a master's degree would qualify you to teach at a community college. For such reasons, a master's degree in psychology remains valuable, even in areas other than counseling.

Doctoral Level Earning a doctorate in psychology requires commitment. (That's personal commitment, not commitment to a mental hospital—although some doctoral candidates might disagree!) It usually takes at least 3 years of education beyond a bachelor's degree to attain a doctorate (Ph.D., Psy.D., or Ed.D.). More often, a doctorate takes 4 or more years to complete, and some specialties, such as clinical and counseling psychology, require at least 1 more year of internship. (An internship is a closely supervised, on-the-job training experience for professionals entering the field.)

How do the three doctoral degrees differ? The answer may help you decide which would be most appropriate for you if you want to become a psychologist. A Ph.D. is a research degree. As such, it requires completion of a dissertation (an original research contribution to the field).

Psychologists holding Ph.D. degrees are active in all areas of psychology, including clinical psychology. However, some psychologists who primarily want to work as therapists now earn a Psy.D. degree (Doctor of Psychology) instead of a Ph.D. This newly created degree allows students in clinical psychology to gain practical experience as a psychotherapist rather than doing a dissertation. The Ed.D. (Doctor of Education) is also typically more applied in orientation than the Ph.D. The Ed.D. is usually awarded after completion of an advanced series of courses focused on the psychology of learning and education.

It is also worth mentioning that in most states a doctoral degree alone does not automatically allow a person to practice psychology. Usually, to be legally licensed or certified as a psychologist, a person must have a doctorate in psychology, plus at least 1 year of internship, and he or she must pass written and oral state licensing exams. As you can see, becoming a psychologist is a major achievement, reflecting the attainment of a high level of knowledge.

Understandably, doctoral-level psychologists have the widest range of work choices. These include settings such as colleges and universities, clinics, rehabilitation centers, government agencies, businesses, industry, the military, and private practice. Also, as you can see in Table A–1, psychologists holding doctoral degrees average several thousand dollars per year greater income in most professional positions.

If you wish to pursue a doctorate in psychology, it is not absolutely necessary to make plans now for attending

Table A–1 Average Income for American Psychologists

AREA	MASTER'S	DOCTORATE
College faculty		
Assistant professor	24,000*	25,000*
Associate professor	29,000*	31,000*
Full professor	35,000*	43,000*
Educational administration	42,000	42,000
Clinical psychology	28,000	40,000
Counseling psychology	26,000	34,000
Research	34,000	38,000
School psychology	28,000*	29,000*
Applied (I-O) psychology	38,000	48,000

*For 9- to 10-month academic year.

Faculty data from Goodstein, 1986; remaining data from Stapp & Fulcher, 1983, are projections based on a 6 percent average increase since last assessment. All figures are rounded to nearest thousand dollars.

graduate school—but it helps! Getting admitted to a doctoral program in psychology is as difficult as getting into medical school. The sooner you know what kind of program you would like to enter, the better your chances will be of meeting all of its requirements. To learn more, consult the book *Graduate Study in Psychology*, published by the American Psychological Association. This book is loaded with information to help you plan your graduate education. Be sure to read that book's Appendix D, which gives practical, step-by-step information on how to get accepted to graduate school. (An address for APA publications is given at the end of this appendix.)

Table A–2 shows why there is value in deciding early if you intend to seek employment or if you plan to enter graduate school (Milton et al., 1986). The table gives the results of a national survey of college faculty members and people in business involved in hiring college graduates. As you can see, businesspeople and faculty members differ greatly in what they believe is most important when considering students for employment or admission. Personality and an ability to present oneself effectively are highly valued in the business world. Public speaking ability, interviewing skills, writing skills, and job experience—all these should be high on your list of priorities if you plan to seek immediate employment when you graduate. Notice too, that grades do count. The list for graduate school admission in Table A–2 speaks for itself.

Employment Outlook

The good news is that overall, jobs for people with psychology degrees are expected to increase faster than average in coming years. However, professional-level jobs (master's and doctorate) will account for a relatively small percentage of total new positions. With projections for a decline in college enrollments, academic positions will be in especially short supply. Even in industrial, clinical, and other applied areas, there will be much competition for positions. However, this should not deter a person who is strongly interested in psychology from pursuing a doctoral-level career. It simply means that it is wise to take steps to make yourself highly employable. These include (1) attending an APA accredited graduate school; (2) gaining work experience while in school (by working as a research assistant, teaching assistant, or even as a volunteer, if necessary); and (3) specializing in additional skills that are in demand, such as computer programming, therapy for special populations (such as the mentally retarded), and research in heavily funded areas (such as drug abuse research).

Table A–2 Important Factors Influencing Employment and Admission to Graduate School

Business Employment
1. Personality/self-presentation
2. Grades in major subject
3. Non-college jobs held
Graduate School
1. Number of difficult courses taken
2. Breadth of courses taken
3. Samples of writing ability
4. Overall grade point average
5. Letters of recommendation
6. Publications, honors, awards

Source: Milton et al., 1986.

Best Bets At all degree levels, applied areas are probably the best bet for employment in the near future. The prospects remain reasonably good for clinical and counseling psychologists, industrial/organizational psychologists, and clinical or psychiatric social workers. Health psychology and health-related jobs also look good, especially anything associated with senior citizens, as the "graying of America" continues. Two of the fastest growing jobs for the next decade are projected to be employment interviewers and occupational therapists. Both positions are open to holders of bachelor's and master's degrees.

For further information on careers in psychology, talk with your psychology teacher or visit the campus career center if your school has one. Additional sources of information follow shortly.

The Future In addition to the jobs discussed here, there are a number of emerging specialties that are likely to grow rapidly. It shouldn't be long before job titles such as the following become more common: shyness counselor, thanatologist, retirement counselor, jury selection specialist, weight control counselor, stress reduction counselor, executive recruiter, and sleep disorders therapist. In short, psychology should remain a stimulating and innovative field as the demand for psychological skills and services continues to grow. Perhaps psychology holds a future for you.

Additional Sources of Information

American Psychological Association. *Careers in psychology*. Washington, DC: Author, 1980. (Address: 1200 Seventeenth St. N.W., Washington, DC 20036. One copy of this pamphlet will be sent free, upon request.)

American Psychological Association. *Graduate study in psychology* (revised annually). Washington, DC: Author, 1989. (Address given above.)

Fretz, B. R., and D. J. Stang. *Preparing for graduate study in psychology: Not for seniors only!* Washington, DC: American Psychological Association, 1980.

Woods, P. J. (Ed.) *The psychology major: Training and employment strategies*. Washington, D.C.: American Psychological Association, 1979.

Woods, P. J. (Ed.), with C. S. Wilkinson. *Is psychology the major for you? Planning for your undergraduate years*. Washington, DC: American Psychological Association, 1987.

Appendix B

Statistics*

Statistics from "Heads" to "Tails"

Let's say a friend of yours invites you to try your hand at a "game of chance." He offers to flip a coin and pay you a dollar if the coin comes up heads. If the coin shows tails, you must pay him a dollar. He flips the coin: tails—you pay him a dollar. He flips it again: tails. Again: tails. And again: tails. And again: tails.

At this point you are faced with a choice. Should you continue the game in an attempt to recoup your losses? Or should you assume that the coin is biased and quit before you really get "skinned"? Taking out a pocket calculator (and the statistics book you carry with you at all times), you compute the odds of obtaining 5 tails in a row from an unbiased coin. The probability is 0.031 (roughly 3 times out of 100).

If the coin really is honest, 5 consecutive tails is a rare event. Wisely, you decide that the coin is probably biased and refuse to play again. (Unless, of course, your "friend" is willing to take "tails" for the next 5 tosses!)

Perhaps a decision could have been made in this hypothetical example without using statistics. But notice how much clearer the situation becomes when it is expressed statistically.

Statistics in Psychology Psychologists try to extract and summarize useful information from the observations they make. To do so, they use two major types of statistics. The first type, called **descriptive statistics,** summarizes or "boils down" numbers so they become more meaningful and easier to communicate to others. The second type, known as **inferential statistics,** is used for decision making, for generalizing from small samples, and for drawing conclusions. As was the case in the coin-flipping example, psychologists must often base decisions on limited data. Such decisions are much easier to make with the help of inferential statistics.

*Portions of this appendix were contributed by Danniel Downey, Ph.D.

Descriptive Statistics

Statistics bring greater clarity and precision to psychological thought and research. To see how, let's begin by considering three basic types of descriptive statistics: **graphical statistics,** measures of **central tendency,** and measures of **variability.**

Graphical Statistics Table B–1 shows simulated scores on a test of hypnotic susceptibility given to 100 college students.

With such disorganized data, it is hard to form an overall "picture" of the differences in hypnotic susceptibility. But by using a **frequency distribution,** large amounts of information can be neatly organized and summarized. A frequency distribution is made by breaking down the entire range of possible scores into *classes* of equal size. Next, the number of scores falling into each class is recorded. In Table B–2, the raw data from Table B–1 have been condensed into a frequency distribution. Notice how much clearer the pattern of scores for the entire group becomes.

Frequency distributions are often shown *graphically* to make them more "visual." **Histograms,** as these graphs are called, are made by labeling class intervals on the *abscissa* (horizontal line) and frequencies (the number of scores in each class) on the *ordinate* (vertical line). Next, bars are drawn for each class interval; the height of each bar is determined by the number of scores in each class (Fig. B–1). An alternate way of graphing scores is the more familiar **frequency polygon** (Fig. B–2). Here, points

Table B–1 Raw Scores of Hypnotic Susceptibility

55	86	52	17	61	57	84	51	16	64
22	56	25	38	35	24	54	26	37	38
52	42	59	26	21	55	40	59	25	57
91	27	38	53	19	93	25	39	52	56
66	14	18	63	59	68	12	19	62	45
47	98	88	72	50	49	96	89	71	66
50	44	71	57	90	53	41	72	56	93
57	38	55	49	87	59	36	56	48	70
33	69	50	50	60	35	67	51	50	52
11	73	46	16	67	13	71	47	25	77

are placed at the center of each class interval to indicate the number of classes. Then the dots are connected by straight lines.

Measures of Central Tendency Notice in Table B–2 that more scores fall in the range 40–59 than elsewhere. How can we show this fact? A measure of **central tendency** is simply a number describing a "middle score" around which other scores fall. A familiar measure of central tendency is the mean, or "average." But as we shall see in a moment, there are other types of "averages" that can be used. To illustrate each we need an example: Table B–3 shows the raw data for an imaginary experiment in which 2 groups of subjects were given a test of memory. Assume that one group was given a drug that might improve memory (let's call the drug Rememberine). The second group received a placebo. Is there a difference in memory scores between the two groups? It's difficult to tell without computing an average.

As one type of "average," the **mean** is calculated by adding all the scores for each group and then dividing by the total number of scores. Notice in Table B–3 that the means reveal a difference between the two groups.

The mean is sensitive to extremely high or low scores in a distribution. For this reason it is not always the best measure of central tendency. (Imagine how distorted it would be to calculate average yearly income from a small sample of people that happened to include a multimillionaire.) In such cases, the *middle score* in a group of scores—called the **median**—is used instead.

The median is found by arranging scores from the highest to the lowest and selecting the score that falls in the middle. Consider for example, the following weights obtained from a small class of college students: 105, 111,

Table B–2 Frequency Distribution of Hypnotic Susceptibility Scores

CLASS INTERVAL	NUMBER OF PERSONS IN CLASS
0–19	10
20–39	20
40–59	40
60–79	20
80–99	10

Fig. B–1 *Frequency histogram of hypnotic susceptibility scores contained in Table B–2.*

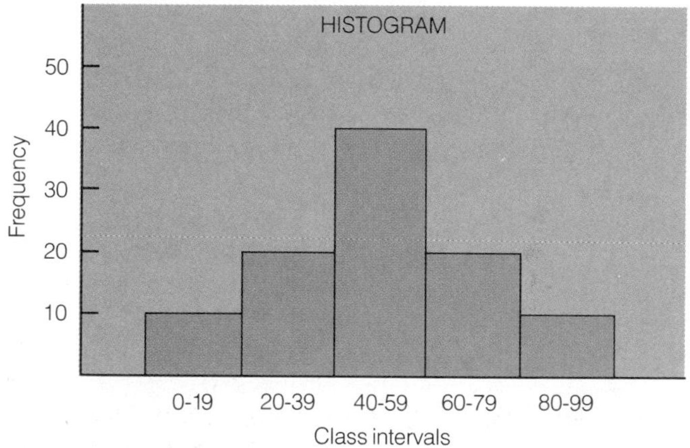

Fig. B–2 *Frequency polygon of hypnotic susceptibility scores contained in Table B–2.*

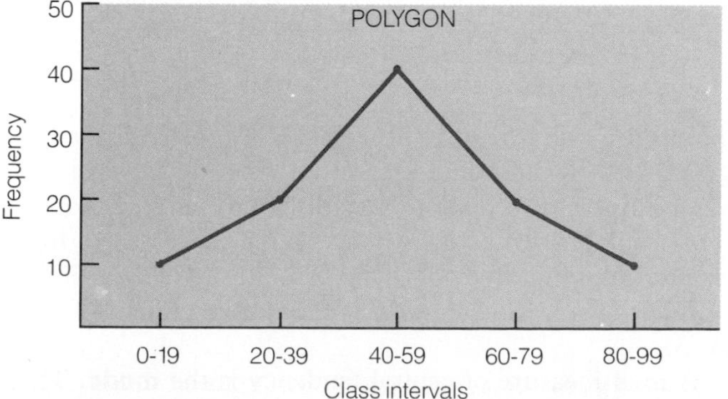

Table B–3 Raw Scores on a Memory Test for Subjects Taking Rememberine or a Placebo

SUBJECT	GROUP 1 REMEMBERINE	GROUP 2 PLACEBO
1	65	54
2	67	60
3	73	63
4	65	33
5	58	56
6	55	60
7	70	60
8	69	31
9	60	62
10	68	61
Sum	650	540
Mean	65	54
Median	66	60

$$\text{Mean} = \frac{\Sigma X}{N} \text{ or } \frac{\text{sum of all scores, X}}{\text{number of scores}}$$

$$\begin{array}{l}\text{Mean}\\ \text{Group 1}\end{array} = \frac{65 = 67 + 73 + 65 + 58 + 55 + 70 + 69 + 60 + 68}{10}$$

$$= \frac{650}{10} = 65$$

$$\begin{array}{l}\text{Mean}\\ \text{Group 2}\end{array} = \frac{54 + 60 + 63 + 33 + 56 + 60 + 60 + 31 + 62 + 61}{10}$$

$$= \frac{540}{10} = 54$$

Median = the middle score or the mean of the 2 middle scores*

$$\begin{array}{l}\text{Median}\\ \text{Group 1}\end{array} = 55 \quad 58 \quad 60 \quad 65 \quad \boxed{65 \quad 67} \quad 68 \quad 69 \quad 70 \quad 73$$

$$= \frac{65 + 67}{2} = 66$$

$$\begin{array}{l}\text{Median}\\ \text{Group 2}\end{array} = 31 \quad 33 \quad 54 \quad 56 \quad \boxed{60 \quad 60} \quad 60 \quad 61 \quad 62 \quad 63$$

$$= \frac{60 + 60}{2} = 60$$

*☐ indicates middle score(s).

123, 126, 148, 151, 154, 162, 182. The median for the group is 148, the middle score. Of course, if there is an even number of scores, there will be no "middle score." This problem is handled by averaging the 2 scores that "share" the middle spot. This procedure yields a single number to serve as the median (see bottom panel of Table B–3).

A final measure of central tendency is the **mode.** The mode is simply the most frequently occurring score in a group of scores. If you were to take the time to count the scores in Table B–3, you would find that the mode of Group 1 is 65, and the mode of Group 2 is 60. The mode is usually easy to obtain. However, the mode can be an unreliable measure, especially in a small group of scores. The mode's advantage is that it gives the score actually obtained by the greatest number of people.

Measures of Variability Let's say a researcher discovers two drugs that lower anxiety in agitated patients. However, let's also assume that one drug consistently lowers anxiety by moderate amounts, whereas the second sometimes lowers it by large amounts, sometimes has no effect, or may even increase anxiety in some patients. Overall, there is no difference in the *average* (mean) amount of anxiety reduction. Even so, an important difference exists between the two drugs. As this example shows, it is not enough to simply know the average score in a distribution. Usually, we would also like to know if scores are grouped closely together or scattered widely.

Measures of **variability** provide a single number that tells how "spread out" scores are. When the scores are widely spread, this number gets larger. When they are close together, it gets smaller. If you look again at the example in Table B–3, you will notice that the scores within each group vary widely. How can we show this fact?

The simplest way would be to use the **range,** which is the difference between the highest and lowest scores. In Group 1 of our experiment, the highest score is 73, and the lowest is 55; thus, the range is 18 (73 − 55 = 18). In Group 2, the highest score is 63, and the lowest is 31; this makes the range 32. Scores in Group 2 are more spread out than those in Group 1.

A better measure of variability is the **standard deviation.** To obtain the standard deviation, we find the deviation (or difference) of each score from the mean and then square it (multiply it by itself). These squared deviations are then added and averaged (the total is divided by the number of deviations). Taking the square root of this average yields the standard deviation (Table B–4). Notice again that the variability for Group 1 (5.4) is smaller than that for Group 2 (where the standard deviation is 11.3).

Table B–4 Computation of the Standard Deviation (for Table B–3 Data)

GROUP 1 MEAN = 65

SCORE	MEAN	DEVIATION (d)	DEVIATION SQUARED (d^2)
65 −	65 =	0	0
67 −	65 =	2	4
73 −	65 =	8	64
65 −	65 =	0	0
58 −	65 =	−7	49
55 −	65 =	−10	100
70 −	65 =	5	25
69 −	65 =	4	16
60 −	65 =	−5	25
68 −	65 =	3	9
			291

$$SD = \sqrt{\frac{\text{sum of } d^2}{n}} = \sqrt{\frac{291}{10}} = \sqrt{29.1} = 5.4$$

GROUP 2 MEAN = 54

SCORE	MEAN	DEVIATION (d)	DEVIATION SQUARED (d^2)
54 −	54 =	0	0
60 −	54 =	6	36
63 −	54 =	9	81
33 −	54 =	−21	441
56 −	54 =	2	4
60 −	54 =	6	36
60 −	54 =	6	36
31 −	54 =	−23	529
62 −	54 =	8	64
61 −	54 =	7	49
			1276

$$SD = \sqrt{\frac{\text{sum of } d^2}{n}} = \sqrt{\frac{1276}{10}} = \sqrt{127.6} = 11.3$$

Standard Scores A particular advantage of the standard deviation is that it can be used to "standardize" scores in a way that gives them greater meaning. For example, John and Susan both took psychology midterms, but in different classes. John earned a score of 118, and Susan scored 110. Who did better? It is impossible to tell without knowing what the average score was on each test, and whether John and Susan scored at the top, middle, or bottom of their classes. We would like to have one number that gives all this information. A number that does this is the **z-score.**

To convert original scores to z-scores, we subtract the mean from the score. The resulting number is then divided by the standard deviation for that group of scores. To illustrate, Susan had a score of 110 in a class with a mean of 100 and a standard deviation of 10. Therefore, her z-score is +1.0 (Table B–5). John's score of 118 came from a class having a mean of 100 and a standard deviation of 18; thus, his z-score is also +1.0 (see Table B–5).

Originally it looked as if John did better on his midterm than Susan did. But we now see that relatively speaking, their scores were equivalent. Compared to other students, each was an equal distance above average.

Table B–5 Computation of a z-Score

$$z = \frac{X - \bar{X}}{SD} \text{ or } \frac{\text{score} - \text{mean}}{\text{standard deviation}}$$

$$\text{Susan: } z = \frac{110 - 100}{10} = \frac{+10}{10} = +1.0$$

$$\text{John: } z = \frac{118 - 100}{18} = \frac{+18}{18} = +1.0$$

The Normal Curve

When chance events are recorded, we find that some outcomes have a high probability and occur very often; others have a low probability and occur infrequently; still others have little probability and occur rarely. As a result, the distribution (or tally) of chance events typically resembles a **normal curve** (Fig. B–3). Most psychological traits or events are determined by the action of a large number of factors. Therefore, like chance events, measures of psychological variables tend to roughly match a normal curve. For example, direct measurement has shown such characteristics as height, memory span, and intelligence to be distributed approximately along a normal curve. In other words, many people have average height, memory ability, and intelligence. However, as we move above or below average, fewer and fewer people are found.

It is very fortunate that so many psychological variables tend to form a normal curve, because much is known about the curve. One valuable property concerns the relationship between the standard deviation and the normal curve. Specifically, the standard deviation measures off set proportions of the curve above and below the mean. For example, in Figure B–4, notice that roughly 68 percent of all cases (IQ scores, memory scores, heights, or whatever) fall between one standard deviation above and below the mean (± 1 SD); 95 percent of all cases fall between ± 2 SD; and 99 percent of the cases can be found between ± 3 SD from the mean.

Table B–6 gives a more complete account of the relationship between z-scores and the percentage of cases found in a particular area of the normal curve. Notice for example, that 93.3 percent of all cases fall below a z-score of +1.5. A z-score of 1.5 on a test (no matter what the original, or "raw," score was) would be a good performance, since roughly 93 percent of all scores fall below this mark. Relationships between the standard deviation (or z-scores) and the normal curve do not change. This makes it possible to compare various tests or groups of scores if they come from distributions that are approximately normal.

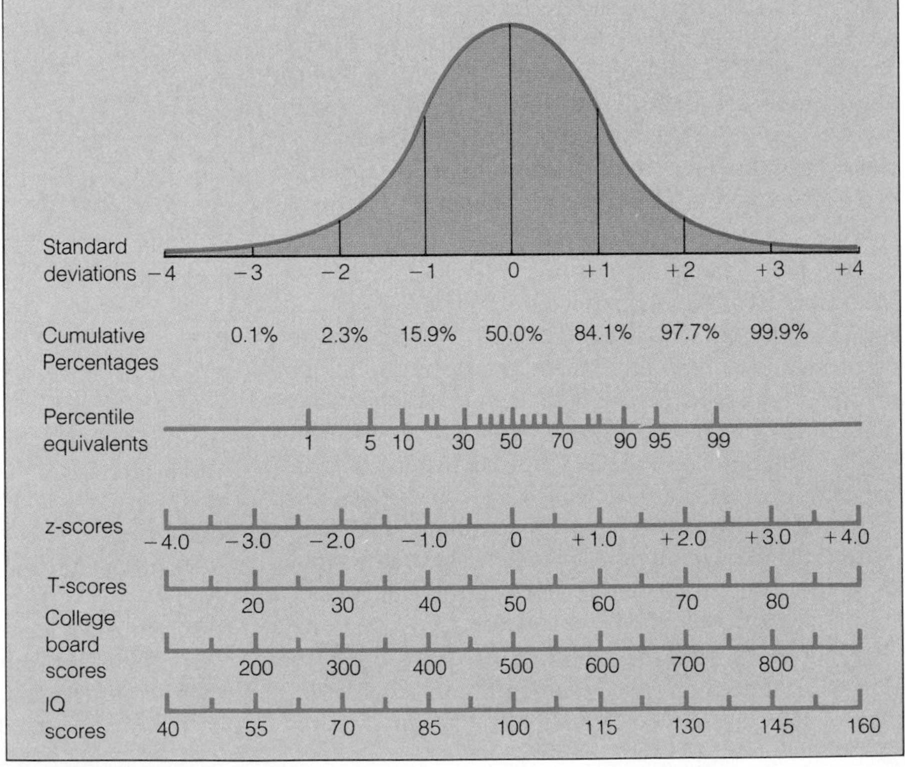

Fig. B–3 *The normal curve. The normal curve is an idealized mathematical model. However, many measurements in psychology closely approximate a normal curve. The scales you see here show the relationship of standard deviations, z-scores, and other measures to the curve.*

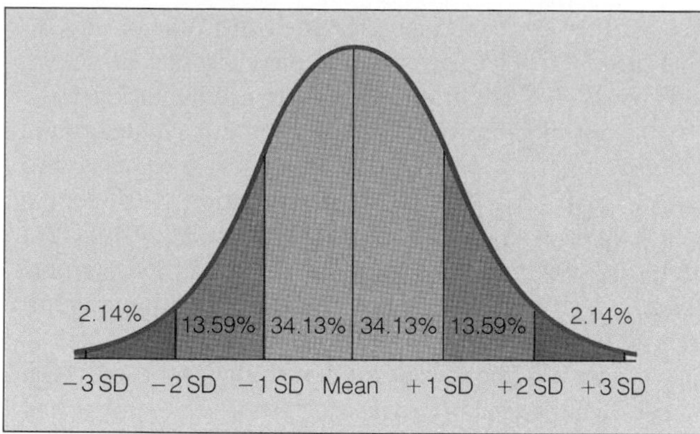

Fig. B–4 *Relationship between the standard deviation and the normal curve.*

Inferential Statistics

Let's say that a researcher studies the effects of a new therapy on a small group of depressed individuals. Is he or she interested only in these particular individuals? Usually not, since except in rare instances, psychologists seek to discover general laws of behavior that apply widely to humans and animals. Undoubtedly, the researcher would like to know if the therapy holds any promise for all depressed people. As stated earlier, **inferential statistics** are techniques that allow us to make inferences. That is, they allow us to generalize from the behavior of small groups of subjects to that of the larger groups they represent.

Table B–6 Area Under the Normal Curve as a Percentage of Total Area for a Variety of z-Scores

Z-SCORE	PERCENTAGE OF AREA TO THE LEFT OF THIS VALUE	PERCENTAGE OF AREA TO THE RIGHT OF THIS VALUE
−3.0 SD	00.1	99.9
−2.5 SD	00.6	99.4
−2.0 SD	02.3	97.7
−1.5 SD	06.7	93.3
−1.0 SD	15.9	84.1
−0.5 SD	30.9	69.1
0.0 SD	50.0	50.0
+0.5 SD	69.1	30.9
+1.0 SD	84.1	15.9
+1.5 SD	93.3	06.7
+2.0 SD	97.7	02.3
+2.5 SD	99.4	00.6
+3.0 SD	99.9	00.1

Samples and Populations In any scientific study, we would like to observe the entire set, or **population,** of subjects, objects, or events of interest. However, this is usually impossible or impractical. Observing all Catholics, all cancer patients, or all mothers-in-law could be both impractical (since all are large populations) and impossible (since people change denominations, may be unaware of having cancer, and change their status as relatives). In such cases, **samples,** or smaller cross sections of a population, are selected, and observations of the sample are used to draw conclusions about the entire population.

For any sample to be meaningful, it must be **representative.** That is, the sample group must truly reflect the membership and characteristics of the larger population. In our earlier hypothetical study of a memory drug, it would be essential for the sample of 20 people to be representative of the general population. A very important aspect of representative samples is that their members are chosen at **random.** In other words, each member of the population must have an equal chance of being included in the sample.

Significant Differences In our imaginary drug experiment, we found that the average memory score was higher for the group given the drug than it was for persons who didn't take the drug (the placebo group). Certainly this result is interesting, but could it have occurred by chance? If two groups were repeatedly tested (with neither receiving any drug), their average memory scores would sometimes differ. How much must two means differ before we can consider the difference "real" (not due to chance)?

Notice that the question is similar to one discussed earlier: How many tails in a row must we obtain when flipping a coin before we can conclude that the coin is biased? In the case of the coin, we noted that obtaining 5 tails in a row is a rare event. Thus, it became reasonable to assume that the coin was biased. Of course, it is possible to get 5 tails in a row when flipping an honest coin. But since this outcome is unlikely, we have good reason to suspect that something other than chance (a loaded coin, for instance) caused the results. Similar reasoning is used in tests of statistical significance.

Tests of **statistical significance** provide an estimate of how often experimental results could have occurred by chance alone. The results of a significance test are stated as a probability. This probability gives the odds that the observed difference was due to chance. In psychology, any experimental result that could have occurred by chance 5 times (or less) out of 100 (in other words, a probability of .05 or less) is considered *significant*. In our memory experiment, the probability is .025 ($p = .025$) that the group means would differ as they do by chance alone. This allows us to conclude with reasonable certainty that the drug actually did improve memory scores.

Correlation

Many of the statements that psychologists make about behavior do not result from the use of experimental methods. Rather, they come from keen observations and measures of existing phenomena. A psychologist might note, for example, that the higher a couple's socioeconomic and educational status, the smaller the number of children they are likely to have. Or that grades in high school are related to how well a person is likely to do in college. Or even that as rainfall levels increase within a given metropolitan area, crime rates decline. In these instances, we are dealing with the fact that two variables are **correlating** (varying together in some orderly fashion).

As discussed in Chapter 2, the simplest way of visualizing a correlation is to construct a **scatter diagram.** In a scatter diagram, two measures (grades in high school and grades in college, for instance) are obtained. One measure is indicated by the X axis and the second by the Y axis. The scatter diagram plots the intersection (crossing) of each pair of measurements as a single point. Many such measurement pairs give pictures like those shown in Figure B–5.

Figure B–5 also shows scatter diagrams of three basic kinds of relationships between variables (or measures). Graphs A, B, and C show **positive relationships** of varying strength. As you can see, in a positive relationship, increases in the X measure (or score) are matched by increases on the Y measure (or score). An example would be finding that higher IQ scores (X) are associated with higher college grades (Y). A **zero correlation** (or relationship) is pictured in graph D. This might be the result of comparing subjects' hat sizes (X) to their college grades (Y). Graphs E and F both show a **negative relationship** (or correlation). Notice that as values of one measure increase, those of the second become smaller. An example might be the relationship between amount of alcohol consumed and scores on a test of coordination: Higher alcohol levels are correlated with lower coordination scores.

Correlations can also be expressed as a **coefficient of correlation.** This coefficient is simply a number falling somewhere between +1.00 and −1.00. If the number is zero or close to zero, it indicates a weak or nonexistent relationship. If the correlation is +1.00, a **perfect positive relationship** exists; if it is −1.00, a **perfect negative relationship** has been discovered. The most commonly used correlation coefficient is called the Pearson *r*. Calculation of the Pearson *r* is relatively simple, as shown in Table B–7. (The numbers shown are hypothetical.)

As stated in Chapter 2, correlations in psychology are rarely perfect. Most fall somewhere between zero and plus or minus 1. The closer the correlation coefficient is to +1.00 or −1.00, the stronger the relationship. An interesting example of some typical correlations is provided by a study that compared the IQs of adopted children with the IQs of their biological mothers. At age 4, the children's IQs correlated .28 with their mothers' IQs. By age 7, the correlation was .35. And by age 13, it had grown to .38.

Correlations often provide highly useful information. For instance, it is valuable to know that there is a cor-

Table B–7 IQ and Grade Point Average for Computing Pearson *r*

Student No.	IQ X	Grade Point Average Y	X Score Squared X^2	Y Score Squared Y^2	X Times Y XY
1	110	1.0	12,100	1.00	110.0
2	112	1.6	12,544	2.56	179.2
3	118	1.2	13,924	1.44	141.6
4	119	2.1	14,161	4.41	249.9
5	122	2.6	14,884	6.76	317.2
6	125	1.8	15,625	3.24	225.0
7	127	2.6	16,124	6.76	330.2
8	130	2.0	16,900	4.00	260.0
9	132	3.2	17,424	10.24	422.4
10	134	2.6	17,956	6.76	348.4
11	136	3.0	18,496	9.00	408.0
12	138	3.6	19,044	12.96	496.8
Total	1503	27.3	189,187	69.13	3488.7

$$r = \frac{\Sigma XY - \frac{(\Sigma X)(\Sigma Y)}{N}}{\sqrt{\left[\Sigma X^2 - \frac{(\Sigma X)^2}{N}\right]\left[\Sigma Y^2 - \frac{(\Sigma Y)^2}{N}\right]}}$$

$$= \frac{3488.7 - \frac{1503(27.3)}{12}}{\sqrt{\left[189{,}187 - \frac{(1503)^2}{12}\right]\left[69.13 - \frac{(27.3)^2}{12}\right]}}$$

$$= \frac{69.375}{81.088} = 0.856 = 0.86$$

Adapted from Pagano, 1981.

relation between cigarette smoking and lung cancer rates. Another example is the fact that higher consumption of alcohol during pregnancy is correlated with lower birth weight and a higher rate of birth defects. There is a correlation between the number of recent life stresses experienced and the likelihood of emotional disturbance. Many more examples could be cited, but the point is, correlations help us to identify relationships that are worth knowing.

Correlations are particularly valuable for making **predictions.** If we know that two measures are correlated, and we know a person's score on one measure, we can predict his or her score on the other. For example, most colleges have formulas that use multiple correlations to decide which applicants have the best chances for success. Usually the formula includes such predictors as high school GPA, teacher ratings, extracurricular activities, and scores on the *Scholastic Aptitude Test* (SAT) or some similar test. Although no single predictor is perfectly correlated with success in college, together the various predictors correlate highly and provide a useful technique for screening applicants.

There is an interesting "trick" you can do with correlations that you may find useful. It works like this: If

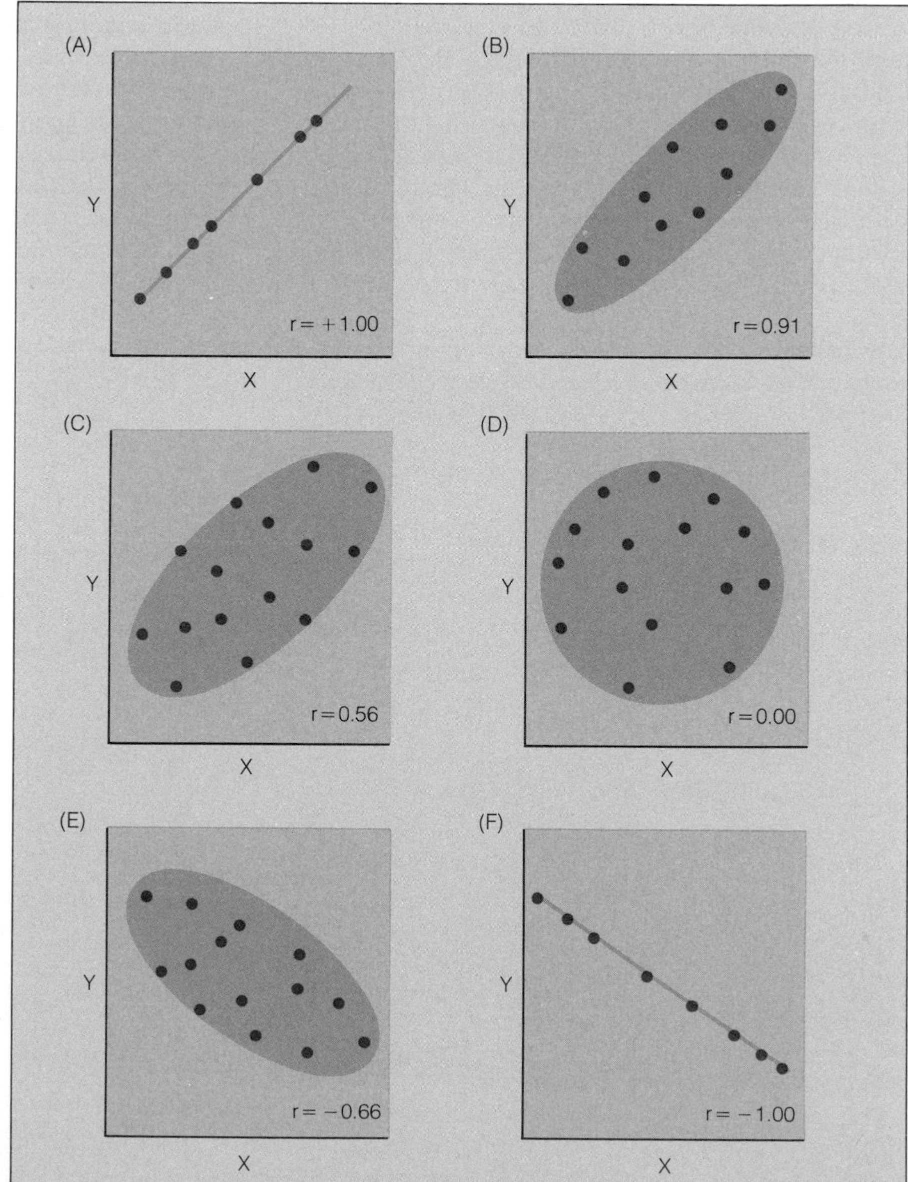

Fig. B–5 *Scatter diagrams showing various degrees of relationship for a positive, zero, and negative correlation. (Adapted from Pagano, 1981.)*

you *square* the correlation coefficient (multiply *r* by itself), you will get a number telling the **percent of variance** accounted for by the correlation. For example, the correlation between IQ scores and college grade point average is .5. Multiplying .5 times .5 gives .25, or 25 percent. This means that 25 percent of the variation in college grades is accounted for by knowing IQ scores. In other words, with a correlation of .5, college grades are "squeezed" into an oval like the one shown in graph C, Figure B–5. IQ scores take away some of the possible variation in corresponding grade point averages. If there were no correlation between IQ and grades, grades would be completely free to vary, as shown in Figure B–5, graph D.

Along the same line, a correlation of +1.00 or −1.00 means that 100 percent of the variation in the Y measure is accounted for by knowing the X measure: If you know a person's X score, you can tell exactly what the Y score is. An example that comes close to this state of affairs is the high correlation (.86) between the IQs of identical twins. In any group of identical twins, 74 percent of the variation in the "Y" twins' IQs is accounted for by knowing the IQs of their siblings (the "X's").

Correlation and Causation It is very important to recognize that finding a correlation between two measures does not automatically mean that one causes the other: *Correlation does not demonstrate causation.* When a correlation exists, the best we can say is that two variables are related. Of course, this does not mean that it is impossible for two correlated variables to have a cause-and-effect relationship. Rather, it means that we cannot *conclude,* solely on the basis of correlation, that a causal link exists. To gain greater confidence that a cause-and-effect relationship exists, an experiment must be performed (see Chapter 2).

Often, two correlated measures are related due to the influence of a third variable. For example, we might observe that the more hours students devote to studying, the better their grades. Although it is tempting to conclude that more studying produces (causes) better grades, it is possible (indeed, it is probable) that grades and the amount of study time are both related to the amount of motivation or interest a student has.

The difference between cause-and-effect data and data that reveal a relationship of unknown origin is one that should not be forgotten. Since we rarely run experiments in daily life, the information on which we act is largely correlational. This should make us more humble and more tentative in the confidence with which we make pronouncements about human behavior.

Glossary

Absolute threshold A point indicating the minimum amount of physical energy necessary to produce a sensation.

Accommodation Changes in the shape of the lens of the eye that serve to focus objects at varying distances. Also, modifying old concepts and thinking habits to fit new information or demands (Piaget).

Acetylcholine (uh-SEET-ul-COH-leen) A neurotransmitter substance that is released at synapses and at the neuromuscular junction (point of contact between a neuron and a muscle fiber). Acetylcholine can initiate a nerve impulse or a muscle contraction, depending on its point of release.

Achievement motivation A need for success or the attainment of excellence.

Acromegaly (ak-row-MEG-uh-lee) A condition involving progressive enlargement of the hands, face, and feet due to excessive secretion of growth hormones by the pituitary.

Acuity (ah-CUE-ih-tee) That aspect of visual perception having to do with the sharpness or resolution of images.

Acupuncture (AK-you-punk-chur) The Chinese medical art of relieving pain and treating illness by inserting thin hairlike needles at various points on the body.

Adaptation In general, adjustment to environmental demands. In connection with the senses, a gradual decline in response to a constant stimulus.

Adaptation level An internal or mental medium point that we use to judge amounts.

Addiction Development of physical dependence on a drug such that craving and physical discomfort (withdrawal symptoms) occur in its absence.

Adjustment disorder A combination of emotional, psychological, and physical disturbances caused by identifiable life stresses.

Adrenal glands (ah-DREE-nal) Source of adrenaline, a hormone secreted during emotional arousal. Also, a source of other important hormones.

Adrenaline (ah-DREN-ul-in) A hormone produced by the adrenal glands similar in its effect to sympathetic nervous system activation; produces diffuse activation throughout the body.

Affect Pertaining to emotion or feelings.

Affective disorders A form of psychopathology characterized by mania or severe depression; disorders involving extremes of emotion.

Affective psychosis A loss of contact with reality involving extremes of emotional response, such as mania, depression, or manic-depressive mood swings.

Afferent (AF-er-ent) Carrying or conducting inward, as in nerves or neurons conveying impulses toward the brain or central nervous system; opposite of *efferent.*

Afferent or sensory nerves Incoming sensory fibers.

Affiliation motive The desire to associate with other people.

Ageism A prejudice held on the basis of age; hence, any tendency to discriminate on the basis of age.

Age regression Return of a hypnotized subject to a younger age.

Aggression Any response made with the intention of bringing harm to another person.

Agnosias (ag-NO-zyahs) In perception, disturbances of the meaning of sensory stimuli; hence, an inability to know; for example, an inability to recognize objects or pictures.

Alpha wave A relatively large, slow brain wave pattern indicating a passive state of relaxed awareness.

Altered state of consciousness Any nonordinary mental state, including meditation, hypnosis, and drug-induced states.

Ambivalence (am-BIV-ah-lence) Holding opposite emotions such as love and hate toward some person or object.

Amnesia Loss of memory (partial or complete) for past events.

Amniocentesis (AM-nee-oh-sen-TEE-sus) The extraction and analysis of amniotic fluid from the womb in the early stages of pregnancy; used for the detection of genetic anomalies in the fetus.

Amphetamines Class of drugs acting as central nervous system stimulants. May be physically addictive and can definitely cause strong psychological dependency.

Anal stage In Freud's theory, the second stage of psychosexual development corresponding roughly to the period of toilet training between the second and third year. (See also *genital stage; oral stage; phallic stage.*)

Androgen (AN-dro-jen) Any of a number of male sex hormones.

Androgyny (an-DROJ-ih-nee) The condition of having both

male and female behavioral traits or a balance between "masculinity" and "femininity" as they are defined by one's culture.

Anesthesia (an-es-THEE-zyah) Loss of bodily sensations.

Anima (AN-ih-muh) In Jung's theory, an archetype representing femaleness or the female principle within the psyche. (See *archetype*.)

Animus (AN-ih-mus) In Jung's theory, an archetype representing maleness or the male principle within the psyche. (See *archetype*.)

Anorexia nervosa (AN-uh-REX-see-ah ner-VOH-sah) A condition in which a person will eat, but with great reluctance, and typically not enough to sustain normal weight. A serious loss of appetite apparently of psychological origin.

Anosmia (a-NAHZ-me-ah) Loss of the sense of smell, particularly for a specific type of odor.

Anthropomorphic fallacy (AN-thro-po-MORE-fik) The error of attributing human thoughts, feelings, and motives to animals.

Antidepressants Drugs that counteract depression or despondency by elevating the individual's mood.

Antipsychotics (An-tie-sie-KOT-iks) Drugs that alleviate psychotic symptoms, making it easier to treat psychiatric problems.

Anxiety A feeling of painful or apprehensive uneasiness closely related to fear; especially, that characterized by dread or anticipation of some unclear threat.

Anxiety disorders A class of personal disturbances characterized by excessive and chronic anxiety states. Formerly referred to as neurosis.

Aphasias (ah-FAZE-yahs) Speech disturbances resulting from damage to certain areas in the temporal lobe of the brain.

Apnea (ap-NEE-uh) To be without breath; an interruption in breathing.

Approach-avoidance conflict Unpleasant situation in which a person is simultaneously attracted to and repelled by the same goal. (See *conflict*.)

Aptitude test A test that rates a person's potential for learning skills required by various occupations.

Architectural psychology Study of the effects buildings have on behavior; the design of buildings using behavioral principles.

Archetype (AR-keh-type) An original pattern, prototype, or idea on which others are modeled. In Jung's theory, universal primordial images found in the collective unconscious.

Arousal The overall level of excitation or activation present at any given time for a person or animal.

Assessment Evaluation or measurement.

Assimilation In Piaget's theory, the application of existing mental patterns to new situations. (Compare *accommodation*.)

Astigmatism (ah-STIG-mah-tiz-im) A defect in the shape of the cornea, the lens, or the eye as a whole that causes some parts of vision to be out of focus.

Attention Orienting toward or focusing on some stimulus.

Attitude A predisposition having emotional, belief, and behavioral components that determines a person's reaction toward a particular social stimulus.

Attribution The process of mentally ascribing one's own behavior, and that of others, to various causes.

Autism (OT-is-im) A severe disorder of childhood involving mutism, sensory spinouts, sensory blocking, tantrums, lack of awareness of others, echolalia, and other difficulties.

Autokinetic effect (OT-oh-kih-NET-ik) The apparent movement of a stationary pinpoint of light displayed in a dark room; often occurs as a result of suggestion.

Autonomic nervous system (ANS) Division of the peripheral nervous system concerned with involuntary functions of the body.

Aversive conditioning (ah-VER-siv) Use of an unpleasant or painful stimulus to reinforce learning.

Avoidance learning Learning procedure in which the occurrence of a particular response results in postponement or prevention of an unpleasant stimulus.

Axon (AK-sahn) A thin fiber process extending from the cell body of a neuron (nerve cell); normally conducts information away from the cell body.

Babinski reflex Curling and spreading of the toes that occurs when the sole of an infant's foot is stroked.

Bait shyness An unwillingness or hesitation on the part of animals to accept a particular food. Often caused by the presence of a taste aversion. (See *taste aversion*.)

Barbiturates Addictive drugs that depress activity of the central nervous system. Barbiturate intoxication resembles intoxication caused by alcohol.

Behavioral medicine The study of behavioral factors in physical illness and the use of behavioral methods to preserve health and treat disease.

Behaviorism The school of psychology that emphasizes the study of overt, observable behavior.

Behavior modification Application of principles of learning to change or eliminate maladaptive or abnormal behavior.

Beta waves (BAY-tah) Fast, low-voltage activity of a more or less random character recorded on the EEG when an organism is alert and attending to stimuli. (See *EEG*.)

Biased sampling Selection of subjects for an experiment or public opinion poll that gives some subjects a greater chance of being included than others. (See also *randomization*.)

Binocular cues Any cue for depth perception that requires two eyes.

Biodata Detailed biographical information about a job applicant used to predict suitability for various occupations.

Biofeedback A technique allowing a subject to monitor and control his or her own internal bodily functions.

Bipolar disorders Emotional disorders in which a person is manic (excited) or depressed, or swings between mania and depression.

Blind spot A portion of the retina where the optic nerve leaves the eye and therefore there are no visual receptors.

Brain lesion (LEE-zhun) Destruction of brain tissue experimentally, accidentally, or through disease.

Brainstorming A group problem-solving technique in which ideas are offered freely, imaginatively, and without evaluation as to their practicality.

Brainwashing Engineered or forced change in attitudes and beliefs.

Brightness In perception, the relative amount of light reflected from or emanating from the surface of a stimulus or objects.

Caffeine A natural drug with stimulant properties that is found in coffee, tea, and synthetic beverages and medicines.

Carcinogen (Kar-SIN-oh-jen) Any cancer-producing substance.

Case study An intensive investigation of the behavior of a single person.

Cataplexy (CAT-ah-plek-see) A sudden loss of all muscle tone and voluntary movement in the body causing complete collapse.

Catatonic (CAT-ih-TAWN-ik) A schizophrenic state marked by alternate periods of stupor and activity, also by mutism and waxy flexibility of the body.

Central nervous system (CNS) The brain and spinal cord.

Character A subjective evaluation of an individual's personality, often as to its desirable and undesirable attributes.

Chemotherapy (KEE-mo-therapy or CHEM-oh-therapy) Use of psychoactive drugs for the treatment of mental disturbances.

Chromosomes (KRO-muh-somz) Threadlike structures ("colored bodies") within the nucleus of each cell that carry the genes. Normal human cells each have 23 pairs of chromosomes.

Circadian rhythms (SUR-kay-dee-an) Cyclical changes in bodily function that vary on a schedule approximating one 24-hour day.

Clairvoyance (klare-VOY-ans) Purported form of extrasensory perception (ESP) in which objects or events are perceived without the aid of normal sensory systems.

Classical conditioning A basic form of learning discovered by Pavlov in which existing (reflex) responses are attached to new stimuli by pairing the new stimuli with stimuli that naturally elicit the response.

Client-centered therapy A form of therapy designed by Rogers in which the client assumes responsibility for solving his or her own problems. The therapist's role is to clarify and assist, not to give advice.

Climacteric (kly-MAK-ter-ik) A period or point during late middle age in males in which a significant change in health, vigor, appearance, or potency takes place. Roughly analogous to *menopause* in women.

Clinical psychologist A psychologist who specializes in treating psychological and behavioral disturbances or who does research on such disturbances.

Cloning (KLO-ning) The reproduction of an entire plant or organism from a single cell of the original plant or organism.

Closure Gestalt term for the perceptual tendency to complete figures by "closing," or ignoring, small gaps.

Cocaine A crystalline drug derived from coca leaves; used as a central nervous system stimulant and local anesthetic.

Cochlea (KOCK-lee-ah) The snail-shaped organ of hearing in the inner ear containing the ultimate sensory receptors for hearing.

Coding Organizing information for efficient memory storage and retrieval.

Coefficient of correlation (KOE-eh-FISH-ent of KORE-eh-LAY-shun) An index of the degree of relationship between two sets of measures or two variables. Coefficients are expressed as a number ranging from −1.00 to +1.00.

Cognition (Cog-NISH-un) The process of thinking, knowing, or processing information.

Cognitive (COG-nuh-tiv) Of or pertaining to thinking, knowing, understanding, or the internal processing of information.

Cognitive dissonance (COG-nuh-tiv DIS-uh-nuns) An imbalance between one's thoughts, beliefs, attitudes, or behavior; a tension state that people are motivated to reduce.

Cognitive map Internal images of an area (maze, city, campus, and so forth) that presumably underlie an ability to choose alternate paths to the same goal.

Collective unconscious According to Jung's theory, a portion of the psyche that is common to all people and that contains archetypal images. (See *archetype*.)

Colostrum (kuh-LOSS-trum) The milklike substance secreted by women during the first few days after childbirth. Colostrum is rich in antibodies to disease.

Community psychology A specialty that seeks to improve community-wide mental health through direct services, prevention, education, and consultation.

Comparative psychology The study and comparison of the behavior of different species, especially animals.

Compensation Counteracting a real or imagined weakness by emphasizing desirable traits or seeking to excel in other areas.

Compression In hearing, the squeezing together of air molecules at the front of a sound wave. Collision of the compressed wave front with the auditory apparatus then sets the auditory apparatus in motion.

Compulsion An act the individual feels driven to repeat, often against his or her will.

Concept A generalized idea representing a class of objects or events that are grouped together on the basis of some common feature or property characteristic of each.

Condensation In the Freudian theory of dream interpretation, a tendency to combine images from several sources into a single complex image.

Conditioned emotional response The conditioning of autonomic nervous system response and/or visceral response to a previously non-emotional stimulus.

Conditioned response In classical conditioning, a learned response that becomes attached to the conditioned stimulus.

Conditioned stimulus In classical conditioning, a previously neural stimulus that acquires the capacity to evoke a response as the result of association with an unconditioned stimulus.

Conditioning The process of learning by association discovered by Pavlov. Also sometimes used to refer to operant learning. (See *classical conditioning* and *operant conditioning*.)

Cones Visual receptors in the eye responsible for color vision and daylight visual acuity. (See *rods*.)

Conflict A mental or behavioral state characterized by clashing or incompatible motives, desires, goals, and so forth. The four most basic conflicts are: approach conflicts, avoidance conflicts, approach-avoidance conflicts, and double approach-avoidance conflicts.

Congenital problems (kon-JEN-ih-tal) A defect acquired

during development in the uterus; hence, a problem existing at birth (a "birth defect"). Distinct from a *hereditary* problem (that is, one transmitted by genes).
Conjunctive concept (kon-JUNK-tiv) A concept defined as having one value on one dimension *and* a second value on another dimension (for example, red triangles). (Compare with *disjunctive* and *relational* concepts.)
Connotative meaning (KON-oh-TAY-tiv) The subjective personal or emotional significance of a word or concept apart from its explicit and recognized meaning.
Conscience (KON-chuns) Internalized sense of right and wrong; in Freudian theory, the superego.
Consolidation (kon-sol-ih-DAY-shun) Theoretical process by which material is solidified as a permanent memory in the brain after being learned.
Constructs Explanatory concepts inferred from observable events but not directly observable themselves.
Consumer psychology Specialty area that focuses on understanding consumer behavior; often applied to advertising, marketing, product testing, and the like.
Contact comfort A pleasant and reassuring feeling human and animal infants derive from touching or clinging to something soft and warm, usually the mother.
Contiguity (kon-tih-GEW-ih-tee) In close proximity or contact; very near in time or space.
Continuous reinforcement A schedule of reinforcement in which every response is reinforced.
Control Eliminating, identifying, or equalizing all factors in an experiment that could affect its outcome.
Control group A group in a psychological experiment that is exposed to all experimental conditions except the independent variable. (See *experimental group*.)
Convergence The simultaneous turning inward of the two eyes as they focus on nearby objects.
Convergent thought Thinking directed toward discovery of a single established correct answer; conventional thinking.
Conversion reaction A symptom or disability that appears to be physical but that actually results from anxiety, stress, or emotional conflict.
Cornea (KOR-nee-ah) The clear outer membrane covering the eyeball.
Corpus callosum (KOR-pus cah-LO-sum) A large nerve unit in the middle of the brain connecting the two hemispheres; serves to transfer information from one hemisphere to the other.
Correlation (KOR-eh-LAY-shun) The existence of a consistent (non-random) relation between two variables or measure.
Correlational study A nonexperimental study designed to assess the degree of relationship between two or more variables.
Corticalization (KOR-tih-kal-ih-ZAY-shun) The increase in the relative size and importance of the cerebral cortex observed as one ascends the biological scale from lower animals to humans.
Counseling psychologist A psychologist who specializes in the treatment of milder emotional and behavioral disturbances.
Counselor A mental health professional who specializes in adjustment problems not involving serious mental disorder; for example, marriage counselors, occupational counselors, or school counselors.
Cretinism (KREET-un-ism) A form of mental retardation resulting from a malfunction of the thyroid gland.
Critical period A time during which a certain event must occur in an organism's life if development is to occur normally.
CT scan Computed tomography scan; a computer-enhanced X-ray image of the brain.
Culture An ongoing pattern of life characterizing a society at a particular historical period or stage in its development.

Dark adaptation The process by which the eye adapts to conditions of low illumination, principally, by a shift to rod vision. (See *rods*.)
Decibel (DES-ih-bel) A unit used to measure the loudness of sounds; ordinary speech registers around 60 decibels.
Deductive thought A pattern of thought in which the thinker must use a general set of rules to draw a logical conclusion. (Compare with *inductive thought*.)
Defense mechanisms Habitual and unconscious psychological devices used to reduce or avoid anxiety.
Delayed speech A significant delay in the development of speech capacity in early childhood.
Delta waves Large, slow, regular waves of brain activity recorded on the EEG during the deeper stages of sleep.
Delusions False beliefs held against all evidence to the contrary; symptomatic of some psychotic disorders.
Demonology (DEE-mon-OL-oh-gee) In Medieval Europe, that branch of knowledge dealing with the study of demons and the treatment of those "possessed" by demons.
Dendrites (DEN-drites) Branching projections of nerve cell bodies (neurons) that form synapses with other neurons and conduct information toward the cell body. (See *neurons*.)
Denial A defense mechanism used to deny the existence of a problem or an unpleasant reality.
Denotative (DEE-no-TATE-iv) The objective dictionary meaning of a word or concept.
Dependent variable The variable (usually a behavior) that reflects changes in the independent variable. (See *independent variable*.)
Depressant A drug or chemical agent that lowers bodily or nervous system function.
Depressive neurosis (new-ROW-sis) Prolonged and severe depression triggered by a stressful event but representing an overreaction to it.
Depressive psychosis (sie-KOH-sis) A form of psychosis characterized by the deepest possible despondency.
Deprivation In development, the loss or withholding of normal stimulation, nutrition, comfort, love, and so forth. A condition of lacking.
Depth perception The ability to see three-dimensional space and to accurately estimate distances.
Detoxification (de-TOKS-ih-fih-KAY-shun) To remove poison or the effects of poison. In the treatment of alcoholism, the physical withdrawal of the patient from alcohol.

Developmental tasks Any of the countless personal changes that must be made throughout life for optimal development.
Developmental psychologist A psychologist interested in the course of human growth and development, from before birth until death.
Difference threshold The smallest change in a physical stimulus that can be detected by an observer.
Digit span test A test of attention and short-term memory. Subjects are asked to recall a series of random digits of varying lengths that has just been read to them.
Discrimination (learning) The ability to detect differences between two or more objects or events; often brought about by reinforcement of responses to one stimulus but not the other.
Dishabituation (DIS-ha-bit-you-AY-shun) A reinstatement of sensory response lost or reduced by the occurrence of habituation. (See *habituation*.)
Disjunctive concept A concept defined by the presence of at least one of a number of features, or a concept defined as having one value on one dimension *or* a different value on another dimension (for example, blue *or* triangular). (Compare with *conjunctive* and *relational* concepts).
Disorganized schizophrenia (SKIT-suh-FREE-nee-ah) A form of psychosis characterized by giddy, obscene, or silly behavior and including a severe disintegration of personality.
Displacement In Freudian theory, the rechanneling of energy from one target or activity to another. Often used as a defense mechanism, as when aggression is displaced on someone or something other than the actual source of frustration.
Dissociative reaction (dih-SOSH-ih-tiv) Unusual disorders including amnesia, fugue, and multiple personality that allow individuals to separate themselves from upsetting thoughts and actions.
Divergent thinking Thinking that produces many ideas or alternatives; creative or unconventional thinking.
DNA (deoxyribonucleic acid) Large and complex chemical molecules found in chromosomes and believed to be the substance of which genes are composed.
Dogmatism (DOG-mah-tizm) An unwarranted positiveness or certainty in matters of opinion.
Dominant gene A gene whose influence will be expressed on every occasion in which it is present. (Compare *recessive gene*.)
Dopamine (DOPE-ah-meen) An important neurotransmitter found in the brain, particularly at sites within the limbic system.
Double-bind communication A message that contradicts itself and places the person who receives it in an unsolvable conflict.
Down syndrome A hereditary abnormality associated with the presence of 47 chromosomes rather than the usual 46 and characterized by a shortened life expectancy, mental retardation, and unusual physical features.
Drive The psychological representation of internal need states; for example, hunger, thirst, and so forth.
Drug interaction The outcome of combining two or more drugs within the body producing effects above and beyond what would be expected from the mere addition of the effects of one to the effects of the other.
Dual personality A form of dissociative disorder in which the person maintains two separate personalities, one of which typically is unaware of the existence of the other.
Dyslexia (dis-LEK-see-ah) An inability to read with understanding, often caused by a tendency to misread letters (by seeing their mirror images, for instance).

Echolalia (ek-oh-LAY-lee-ah) A tendency, sometimes observed in autistic children, to repeat, or echo back, whatever is said to them.
Eclectic Selected or chosen from many sources.
Educational psychology The psychological study of learning, teaching, and related topics.
EEG (electroencephalogram) Record of the electrical activity of the brain; made by attaching electrodes to the scalp.
Efferent (EF-er-ent) Carrying or conducting outward, as in nerves or neurons conveying impulses away from the brain or central nervous system: opposite of *afferent*.
Ego (EE-go) In Freudian terminology, the portion of personality that is in conscious control of behavior and that reconciles the demands of the id, superego, and external reality.
Egocentric (EE-go-SEN-trik) Unable to take a viewpoint other than one's own.
Eidetic imagery (eye-DET-ik IM-ij-ree) The ability to retain an image long enough to use it as a source of information; basically, a photographic memory.
Ejaculation (EE-jac-you-LAY-shun) The release of sperm and seminal fluid by the male at the time of orgasm.
Electra conflict (ih-LEK-trah) In Freudian theory, a conflict experienced by female children when they become attracted to their fathers and feel themselves to be in competition with their mothers. (See *Oedipus conflict*.)
Electroconvulsive shock (ECS) (ih-LEK-tro-cun-VUL-siv) An electric shock passed directly through the brain, producing a convulsion. ECS can impair memory and produce amnesia in experimental animals. Clinically, it is used in the treatment of severe depression.
Electrode Any needle, wire, metal plate, or saltwater-filled glass tube used to apply electrical current to the body, especially to neural tissue.
Electromagnetic radiation (ih-LEK-tro-mag-NET-ik) Waves of energy produced by electric and magnetic oscillations. Radio waves, light waves, X rays, and gamma rays are all electromagnetic waves differing only in their wavelength.
Empathy (EM-puh-thee) A capacity for taking another's point of view or sharing another's state of consciousness; to feel what another is feeling.
Empirical (im-PIR-ih-cul) Founded on experiment or experience; based on direct observation.
Encoding Changing information into a form that allows it to be stored in memory and manipulated in thought.
Encopresis (en-coh-PREE-sis) An inability to control defecation (elimination of solid wastes); hence, "soiling."
Encounter group A group experience that emphasizes intensely honest interchanges among participants regarding feelings and reactions to one another.

Endorcrine system (EN-duh-krin) Bodily system made up of those glands whose secretions pass directly into the bloodstream or lymph system.
Endogenous depression (en-DAHJ-eh-nus) Depression that appears to be produced from within, rather than as a reaction to life events.
Endorphins (en-DOR-funz) A class of brain peptides (proteins) having an apparent link to the control of pain and possibly to psychiatric disturbances.
Engineering psychology A specialty concerned with the design of machines and work environments so that they are compatible with human sensory and motor capabilities.
Engrams (EN-gramz) "Memory traces" or physical changes taking place in the brain; a general term referring to the theoretical basis for learning and memory.
Enkephalins (en-KEF-ah-lins) Recently discovered brain peptides (proteins) having an apparent link to emotional functioning.
Enuresis (EN-you-REE-sis) An inability to control urnination, particularly with reference to bed-wetting.
Environmental psychology The formal study of how environments affect behavior.
Episodic drive (ep-ih-SOD-ik) A noncyclical drive state occurring in distinctly separate episodes associated with particular conditions (for example, pain avoidance, specific hungers, sexual motivation).
Episodic memory (ep-ih-SOD-ik) A hypothesized "autobiographical" subpart of memory that records life events or "episodes."
Erogenous zone (eh-ROJ-ih-nus) Any bodily area productive of pleasurable sensations and particularly those areas producing erotic desire when stimulated.
Escape learning Learning to make a response to escape or to terminate an aversive (painful) stimulus. Escape learning is negatively reinforced by termination of the aversive stimulus.
Escapism Reducing discomfort by leaving frustrating situations or by psychologically withdrawing from them.
Estrogen (Es-truh-jen) Any of a number of female sex hormones.
Estrus (ES-trus) Changes in the reproductive organs and sexual drives of animals associated with a desire for mating, particularly used to refer to female animals "in heat."
Ethnocentric (ETH-no-CEN-trik) Placing one's own group or race at the center; that is, tending to reject all other groups but one's own.
Ethologist (ETH-all-oh-jist) A person who studies the natural behavior patterns of animals.
Eugenics (you-GEN-iks) The science that deals with the improvement of an animal species or race.
Exorcism In Medieval Europe, the practice of expelling or driving off an "evil spirit," particularly one residing in the body of an individual who is "possessed."
Experiment A scientific technique whereby all relevant variables are manipulated, measured, or controlled so that cause-effect relationships may be observed. Simple experiments typically involve both an *experimental group* and a *control group*.
Experimental group In a controlled experiment, the group of subjects exposed to the independent variable or experimental manipulation (See control group.)
Experimental psychologist A psychologist primarily interested in the scientific study of human and animal behavior.
Experimenter effect Changes in subjects' behavior caused by the unintended influence of an experimenter's presence and actions.
Extinction The process of consistently not reinforcing a learned response, leading to a gradual decrease in the frequency with which the response occurs.
Extraneous variables (ex-TRAY-nee-us) Those conditions or factors to be excluded from possible influence on the outcome of a controlled experiment (that is, variables the experimenter is not interested in).
Extrasensory perception The purported ability to perceive events in ways that cannot be explained by known capacities of the sensory organs.
Extrinsic motivation Motivation based on obvious external rewards, obligations, or similar factors, not on the inherent satisfactions of the task or activity.
Extrovert (EK-struh-vert) An individual whose energies and interests are directed outward; a person who seeks social contact or is outgoing. (Compare introvert.)

Factor analysis A statistical technique whereby multiple measures are intercorrelated. Measures that form "clusters" of correlations are assumed to represent some more general underlying factor.
Family therapy Therapeutic technique in which all family members participate, both individually and as a group, to change destructive relationships.
Fantasy A product of the imagination determined mainly by one's motives or feelings. Fantasy may be used as an escape mechanism.
Feedback Knowledge of results or relaying the effect of some action to the person controlling it.
Figure-ground Gestaltist's observation that some aspects of a stimulus pattern appear to stand out as an object (figure) while others appear to stand in the background (ground).
Fixation The tendency to repeat wrong solutions or faulty responses as a consequence of frustration. In Freudian theory, lasting conflicts developed during a particular stage of development as a result of frustration or overindulgence during that stage.
Fixed-action pattern A genetically programmed sequence of movements occurring mechanically and virtually universally in members of a particular species.
Fixed-interval schedule A schedule of reinforcement in which reinforcement is administered following a fixed period of time after the previous reinforcement; for example, every 3 minutes.
Fixed-ratio schedule A schedule of reinforcement in which a predetermined number of responses must be made before reinforcement is delivered; for example, one reinforcement for every five responses.

Flat affect A seemingly total lack of emotional responsiveness.
Fovea (FOE-vee-ah) A small depression in the center of the retina containing the greatest concentration of *cones* and providing the sharpest vision.
Frame of reference A mental and emotional perspective, relative to which events are preceived and evaluated.
Fraternal twins Twins conceived from two separate eggs. Fraternal twins are no more alike genetically than other siblings. (See *identical twins.*)
Free association A technique of *psychoanalysis* in which persons say anything that comes into their minds regardless of how embarrassing or unimportant it may seem.
Free-floating anxiety Feelings of dread or apprehension that cannot be traced to any particular source.
Free will The doctrine that humans are capable of freely making choices or decisions.
Frigidity An abnormal lack of sexual desire.
Frontal lobotomy Surgical destruction of the frontal lobes of the brain, or separation of the frontal lobes from the remainder of the brain.
Frustration An internal emotional state resulting from interference with satisfaction of a motive or blocking of goal-directed behavior.
Fugue (FEWG) A dissociative reaction characterized by taking flight and by a loss of memory for events before or during the act of fleeing.
Functional fixedness Rigidity in problem solving caused by an inability to see novel uses for familiar objects.
Functionalism (FUNK-shun-ul-ism) School of psychology concerned with how behavior and mental abilities help people adapt to their environments.
Functional psychosis A psychosis with no apparent biological basis.

Galvanic skin response (GSR) (gal-VAN-ik) A change in the electrical resistance of the skin associated with arousal or anxiety.
General adaptation syndrome (GAS) Selye's description of a consistent pattern of reactions to prolonged stress occurring in three stages: alarm, resistance, and finally, exhaustion.
General paresis (pah-REE-sis) An organic psychosis that results when syphilis attacks the brain.
Generalization The transfer of a learned response from one stimulus or set of circumstances to others that are in some way like the original stimulus.
Generalized anxiety disorder Defined as at least 6 months of persistent anxiety.
Genes Areas on the chromosomes that carry hereditary instructions affecting various personal characteristics.
Genital stage The final stage in psychosexual development (according to Freud); typically attained in late adolescence and representing full psychosexual maturity. (See also *anal stage; oral stage; phallic stage.*)
Gerontologist (JER-un-TOL-uh-jist) One who studies the effects of aging.
Gestalt (guh-SHTALT) A German word meaning form or pattern. The school of psychology emphasizing the study of perception, learning, and thinking in whole units, not by analysis into parts.
Gestalt therapy A psychotherapy developed by Perls and others that emphasizes immediate experience and participation of the whole person in any activity.
Goal The object of a motivated and directed sequence of behavior.
Gonads The sex glands—testes in males and ovaries in females.
Grammar The study of classes of words and their functions and relations within sentences.
Graphology (gra-FALL-uh-jee) The legitimate study of handwriting to detect forgeries; also, the discredited notion that personality characteristics are revealed by handwriting.
Group sanctions Any rewards or punishments (real or symbolic) applied to members of a group for adherence to, or deviation from, group norms for acceptable conduct.
Group therapy Any form of psychotherapy taking advantage of the special characteristics of group interaction. Individuals work out personal problems with the guidance of a trained therapist and the help of other group members.
Gustation (gus-TAY-shun) The sense of taste or the act of tasting.

Habituation (ha-bich-oo-WAY-shun) A decrease in the strength of a reflex caused by its repeated elicitation. Also, a decrease in sensory response to repeated presentation of a stimulus.
Hallucinations (ha-loos-un-AY-shuns) Imaginary sensations such as seeing, hearing, or smelling things that don't exist in the real world.
Hallucinogen (ha-lu-SIN-oh-jen) Any substance or drug that causes hallucinations.
Halo effect The tendency to generalize a favorable or unfavorable impression to unrelated details of personality.
Heredity A transmission of physical and psychological characteristics from parents to offspring through genes.
Hermaphroditism (hur-MAF-roh-dite-ism) The condition of having genitals suggestive of both sexes; ambiguous genital sexuality.
Hippocampus A structure in the brain associated with the regulation of emotion and the transfer of information from short-term memory to long-term memory.
Homeostasis (HOE-me-oh-STAY-sis) Steady state of physiological equilibrium maintained by various bodily mechanisms.
Hormone A bodily chemical transported by body fluids that has an effect on physiological functioning or psychological behavior.
Hospitalism A pattern of deep depression observed in institutionalized infants; marked by weeping and sadness and a lack of normal response to other humans.
Hue That property of color represented by its classification into basic categories of red, orange, yellow, green, blue, indigo, and violet or intermediaries of these.

Humanism An approach to psychology that focuses on human experience, problems, potentials, or ideals.
Hydrocephaly (HI-dro-SEF-ah-lee) A type of mental retardation caused by accumulation of cerebrospinal fluid within the brain.
Hyperactivity A behavioral state characterized by short attention span, restless movement, and impaired learning capacity. Sometimes referred to as minimal brain dysfunction (MBD).
Hyperopia (HI-per-OH-pea-ah) A visual defect causing farsightedness.
Hypnogogic images (hip-no-GAH-jik) Unusually vivid mental imagery associated with hypnosis, the period immediately preceding sleep, and other unusual states of consciousness.
Hypnosis An altered state of consciousness characterized by relaxation, focused attention, and increased susceptibility to suggestion.
Hypochondria (HI-po-KON-dree-ah) An excessive preoccupation with minor bodily problems or complaints about illnesses that seem to be imaginary.
Hypoglycemia (HI-po-gly-SEE-me-ah) Below-normal blood sugar level.
Hypothalamus (HI-po-THAL-ah-mus) A small area at the base of the brain that regulates many aspects of motivation and emotion, particularly hunger, thirst, and sexual behavior.
Hypothesis (hi-POTH-eh-sis) The predicted outcome of an experiment or an educated guess about the relationship between variables.
Hysteria (his-TAIR-ee-ah) Wild emotional excitability sometimes associated with the development of apparent physical disabilities (numbness, blindness, and so forth) without known physical cause.

Icon (EYE-con) A mental image or representation.
Id According to Freud, the most primitive part of the personality, which supplies energy and which demands immediate gratification of needs, drives, and desires.
Identical twins Twins who develop from the same egg and who, therefore, have an identical hereditary makeup. (See *fraternal twins*.)
Identification A process in personality development in which a person becomes like an admired adult by incorporating the adult's goals and values into his or her own behavior. Also used as a defense mechanism in adulthood.
Illusion In perception, an unreal or misleading impression presented to vision or other senses; thus, a perception that fails to give a true representation of the stimulus. (Compare with *hallucination*.)
Implicit trial and error In problem solving, the internal elimination (by covert trial and error) of wrong solutions.
Imprinting A rapid and relatively permanent type of learning that occurs within a limited period of time early in life.
Incentive A goal object valued by an individual that can be employed to motivate behavior.
Incentive value The value a goal holds for a person or animal above and beyond its ability to fill a need.
Independent variable In a controlled experiment, the condition under investigation as a potential cause of some change in behavior; the variable manipulated (changed) by the experimenter. (See *dependent variable*.)
Inductive thought A type of thinking in which one is given a series of specific examples and must infer from them a general rule. (Compare with *deductive thought*.)
Industrial psychology The application of psychology to work, especially to personnel selection, human relations, and machine design.
Innate Inborn or hereditary traits.
Insanity Mental disability resulting in an inability to manage one's affairs or to be aware of the consequences of one's actions. Legally, persons declared insane may not be held fully responsible for their actions.
Insight A sudden reorganization of the elements of a problem causing the solution to become self-evident. Also, one's understanding of one's own behavior or motives.
Insomnia A consistent or prolonged inability to sleep; insufficient sleep or poor quality sleep.
Instinct Complex unlearned behaviors that are species-specific and relatively uniform.
Instrumental conditioning Learning brought about when voluntary responses are affected by their consequences, as when an animal learns its way through a maze to get food; specifically, the effects of positive and negative reinforcement, nonreinforcement, and punishment.
Intellectualization A psychological defense mechanism in which anxiety or emotion is removed from a situation by thinking or speaking of the situation in very formal or abstract terms.
Intelligence quotient (IQ) An index of intelligence defined as a person's mental age divided by his or her chronological age and multiplied by 100.
Interference theory The theory of forgetting that holds that previously learned materials interfere with the storage of new material or that the recall of previous learning is prevented by recent learning.
Intermittent reinforcement Reinforcement occurring irregularly or unexpectedly (partial reinforcement).
Intrauterine environment (IN-tra-YOOT-uh-run) The chemical and physical environment existing in the womb before birth.
Intrinsic motivation Motivation that comes from within, rather than from the presence of external rewards; the motivation that derives from enjoyment of a task or activity.
Introspection (IN-tro-SPEK-shun) A psychological technique used to examine one's own conscious experience; self-observation of one's thoughts, feelings, and sensations.
Introvert (IN-truh-vert) An individual who prefers being alone, who withdraws from social contact, or who is self-centered. (Compare *extrovert*.)
Iris Colored circular muscle of the eye that opens and closes to admit more or less light into the eye.
Isolation A psychological defense involving the separation of contratory feelings or ideas in "logic-tight" compartments.

Just noticeable difference The amount of increase or decrease in a stimulus that can be reliably detected as a change in amount, value, or intensity.

Kinesics (kih-NEE-siks) The study of the meaning of body movements, posture, hand gestures, and facial expressions.
Kinesthesis (KIN-es-THEE-sus) The sense of one's own bodily position, muscle movement, or equilibrium.

Latency (LATE-un-see) In Freudian theory, the period from age 6 until puberty characterized as a quiet interruption of psychosexual development.
Latent learning Learning that occurs without obvious reinforcement and that is not apparent until reinforcement is provided.
Lateralization Refers to the concentration of specific mental functions or abilities on one side of the brain or the other.
Learned helplessness A learned inability to overcome environmental obstacles or to avoid punishment.
Learning In general, any relatively permanent change in behavior that can be attributed to experience but not to such factors as fatigue, maturation, injury, and so forth.
Learning set A readiness for learning a task or mastering a problem established by prior learning of similar tasks or solution of similar problems.
Lens A transparent structure at the front of the eye that focuses images on the retina.
Libido (lih-BEE-doe) In Freudian terminology, the sexual energy involved in the functioning of personality; primarily sexual in nature.
Limbic system A collection of interconnected brain structures whose functions include smell and emotional reactions.
Linguistic determinism Hypothesis proposed by Whorf that the language one speaks shapes one's perception of reality and influences one's thought.
Localization of function The theory that particular psychological functions are represented by particular parts of the brain.
Logotherapy (LO-go-therapy) Therapy that emphasizes the need to find meaning in life.
Long-term memory Memory of events for relatively long periods, usually presumed to be based on permanent storage of information transferred from short-term memory. (See also *short-term memory*.)

Major affective disorders Psychotic disorders marked by lasting extremes of mood or emotion.
Major depression A severe and lasting depression accompanied by the symptoms of psychosis.
Major tranquilizers Drugs that in addition to having tranquilizing properties also serve as antipsychotics by reducing hallucinations, sensory distortions, and delusional thinking. (Compare with *minor tranquilizers*.)
Manic Extremely excited, hyperactive, or irritable.
Manic-depressive psychosis A psychosis in which a person's moods swing from elation or excitement to deep depression. (See *psychosis*.)
Mantra A flowing word or sound repeated silently to oneself as the focus of attention in mediation.
Masochism (MAS-oh-kizm) Deriving sexual gratification from pain inflicted on oneself by others.
Massed practice Continuous practice without rest periods or interruption, as distinct from distributed practice.
Mass media Major channels of public communication and information flow, such as radio, television, newspapers, magazines.
Masturbation Erotic stimulation of the genitals other than by intercourse, usually resulting in orgasm.
Maternal influences The aggregate of all psychological effects mothers have on their children. (See *paternal influences*.)
Maturation The emergence and development of personal characteristics in an orderly sequence as a result of underlying physical growth.
Meditation A contemplative exercise for the production of relaxation, heightened awareness, or spiritual revelation.
Memory The mental capacity for storing, organizing, and recovering information.
Menarche (MEN-ar-kee) The onset of menstruation; a woman's first period.
Menopause (MEN-oh-paws) In females, the time during middle age when regular monthly menstrual periods end. (See also *climacteric*.)
Mental age An indication of mental ability defined in terms of the average capabilities of individuals at each age; that is, mental ability apart from actual age in years.
Mental retardation The presence of a developmental disability; a formal IQ score below 70; or a significant impairment of adaptive behavior.
Mescaline (MES-kuh-lin) A psychoactive drug derived from the peyote cactus that has properties similar to LSD.
Mesmerize An archaic term for hypnotize.
Metabolism (meh-TAB-oh-lizm) The rate of energy production and expenditure in the body.
Microcephaly (MY-kro-CEF-ah-lee) A type of mental retardation characterized by a very small skull that prevents normal brain development.
Microsleep A momentary shift in brain wave patterns to those of sleep.
Minimal brain dysfunction A condition of brain immaturity believed by some to underlie hyperactivity in children. (See *hyperactivity*.)
Minor tranquilizers Drugs capable of producing relaxation or a reduction of general tension or activation, and those that have an antianxiety property such as Valium. (Compare with *major tranquilizers*.)
MMPI (Minnesota Multiphasic Personality Inventory) The most widely used self-rating personality test.
Mnemonic device (nee-MON-ik or ni-MON-ik) Any technique or strategy to assist remembering.
Model A system of ideas and concepts designed to interrelate known facts and to provide an explanatory system.
Modeling A type of imitation in which an individual mimics behavior performed by another person (the model).
Monocular (mah-NOCK-you-ler) Pertaining to the function of one eye. For example, monocular cues for depth perception are those involving the use of only one eye.
Morphemes (MORE-feems) The smallest meaningful units in a language.

Motive A drive or force within the organism that activates behavior or directs it toward a goal.
Motor neuron An efferent neuron that carries motor commands from the central nervous system to muscles and glands. (See *efferent; neurons.*)
Motor program A mental representation or model of a skilled movement; similar in some ways to a computer program.
Motor skills Learned skills having an element of physical dexterity or requiring the coordination of muscular movements.
Multiple personality A rare form of emotional disturbance in which an individual maintains two or more distinct personalities; formally classified as a dissociative reaction.
Myoclonus (MY-ahk-luh-nus) Reflex contractions of muscles, causing a jerking motion.
Myopia (my-OH-pea-ah) A visual defect making it difficult to focus distant objects (nearsightedness).

Narcolepsy (NAR-co-lep-see) A serious sleep disturbance in which the individual suffers uncontrollable sleep attacks, which can occur even when the person is standing or driving.
Natural selection Charles Darwin's theory that evolution favors the survival of those plants and animals best adjusted to the conditions under which they live (survival of the fittest).
Naturalistic observation Observation and recording of naturally occurring behavior that is not manipulated experimentally.
Need In motivational theory, a specific state within the organism that may elicit behavior appropriate to the need (often related to the depletion of essential bodily substances or the disruption of homeostasis).
Negative practice The deliberate repetition of an unwanted response until it becomes aversive or painful.
Negative reinforcement Increasing the probability of a response by terminating or withdrawing an unpleasant stimulus on completion of the response.
Negative transfer A carryover of skills or responses from one task to another when such carryover impairs performance on the second task. (Compare *positive transfer*.)
Neo-Freudians (NEE-oh-Freudians) Personality theorists who accept the broad features of Freud's psychodynamic approach but who have revised his theory to fit their own concepts.
Neonate (NEE-oh-nate) The human newborn.
Nervous system A network of neurons that interconnects sensory receptors and effector organs to produce behavior and conscious experience.
Neurilemma (NEW-rih-LEM-ah) A thin layer of cells wrapped around the axons of some neurons.
Neurons Individual nerve cells that form the basic structure of the nervous system.
Neurosis (new-ROW-sis) A behavior disturbance primarily characterized by excessive anxiety, minor distortions of reality, and subjective discomfort. The term is now considered outdated.
Neuropeptides (NEW-roh-PEP-tides) A newly discovered class of brain chemicals consisting of simple proteins capable of a wide range of effects on moods and behavior.
Neurotransmitter (NEW-roh-transmitter) Any one of a number of chemical substances secreted by neurons, which cross the synapse and alter activity in the receiving neuron.
Night blindness A condition in which vision becomes impaired in low levels of illumination.
Nondirective therapy (See *client-centered therapy.*)
Nonhomeostatic Not subject to the maintenance of homeostatic balance. (See *homeostasis.*)
Nonsense syllable A meaningless syllable usually consisting of a consonant, a vowel, and a consonant; used in experiments on retention and memory.
Noradrenaline (NOR-ah-DREN-ah-lin) A neurotransmitter secreted by neurons of the sympathetic nervous system; also produced at various locations within the brain. Increased noradrenaline output is associated with anger.
Normal curve A bell-shaped curve having known mathematical properties and characterized by a large number of scores in the middle, tapering toward very few extremely high and low scores at either end.
Norms Accepted social rules for behavior to which the individual members of a group tend to conform.
NREM sleep Sleep periods during which there is a minimum of eye movement and little or no dreaming.
Nystagmus (nis-TAG-mus) Involuntary vibration or movement of the eyeball, including tiny oscillations (physiological nystagmus) and larger reflex movements seen in the blind.

Object constancy Tendency to perceive objects in the same way even when one's view of them changes.
Object permanence Recognition that objects continue to exist when they cannot be seen. Very young children appear to believe that objects cease to exist when the objects are out of sight.
Obsessions Recurring irrational or disturbing thoughts a person cannot prevent.
Obsessive-compulsive disorder Extreme preoccupation with certain thoughts and compulsive performance of certain behaviors, both of which occur in ritualistic or unavoidable fashion.
Oedipus conflict (ED-ih-pus) A Freudian concept referring to a boy's sexual attachment to his mother. (See *Electra conflict.*)
Olfaction (ol-FAK-shun) The sense of smell.
Operant conditioning (OP-er-unt) Type of learning that occurs when an organism "operates" on the environment. The consequences of a response affect its probability of recurrence.
Operational definition Definition of a concept or variable that specifies the operations (actions or procedures) used to measure the concept or manipulate the variable.
Optic nerve The large nerve carrying visual impulses from each eye to the brain.
Oral stage The Freudian stage of psychosexual development in which the individual is preoccupied with his or her mouth. (See also *anal stage; genital stage; phallic stage.*)
Organic mental disorder A mental or emotional problem caused by clearly identifiable physiological or genetic factors.
Organismic valuing (or-gan-IS-mik) The process of evaluating events on the basis of spontaneous personal reaction rather than by reference to learned systems of values.

Orgasm A climax and release of sexual excitement.
Orientation response The pattern of changes occurring throughout the body that prepares an organism to receive information from a particular stimulus.
Ovaries Female sex organs that produce hormones and ova (eggs).
Overlearning Practice that is continued beyond the point of mere mastery of memorized material or of a skill.

Palmistry (PALM-is-tree) A false system that claims to be able to identify personality traits or to predict the future by analyzing the lines on the palms of the hand.
Panic disorder Persistently high levels of anxiety coupled with sudden episodes of intense, but unfocused, panic.
Paradoxical sleep A sleep pattern in which the individual produces an EEG record similar to Stage 1 sleep, or even to waking, yet remains behaviorally asleep (and typically dreaming).
Paranoia (pair-ih-NOY-yah) A psychotic state characterized by delusions of persecution or grandeur.
Paranoid schizophrenia (PAIR-ih-noid SKIT-suh-FREE-nee-ah) A psychosis characterized by delusions of persecution or grandeur and accompanied by severe disturbances of thought and emotion. (See *psychosis*.)
Paraprofessional An individual who works in a near-professional capacity under the supervision of a more highly trained person.
Parapsychology (PAIR-ah-sie-COLL-uh-jee) The scientific study of extranormal psychological events; for example, extrasensory perception.
Parasympathetic nervous system (PAIR-ah-sim-pah-THET-ik) The division of the autonomic nervous system associated with production of relaxation, bodily deactivation, and conservation of energy.
Partial reinforcement Reinforcement administered only after a portion of the total responses in a particular situation (also called intermittent reinforcement).
Partial reinforcement effect A greater resistance to extinction observed in responses acquired on a schedule of partial reinforcement (responses rewarded on only a portion of their occurrences).
Paternal influences The aggregate of all psychological effects fathers have on their children. (See *maternal influences*.)
Pedophilia Sex with children; child molesting.
Peer group A group of people of one's own age and of equal or similar background.
Perception The process of meaningfully organizing sensation.
Peripheral nervous system (peh-RIF-er-al) All portions of the nervous system lying outside the brain and spinal cord, including sensory neurons, motor neurons, the spinal nerves, cranial nerves, skeletal nervous system, and autonomic nervous system.
Peripheral vision Vision at the periphery (edges) of the visual field.
Persona (per-SO-nah) In Jung's system, an archetype representing the "mask" or public self presented to others.
Personality An individual's unique and enduring traits and psychological characteristics and the dynamic relationship among them. (See *traits*.)
Personality disorder Disturbances involving maladaptive and long-standing distortions of personality characteristics.
Personality types Systems of personality description employing only a few categories, with each category representing a collection of related traits. (See *traits*.)
Personnel psychology Branch of industrial/organizational psychology concerned with testing, selection, placement, and promotion of employees.
PET scan Positron emission tomography; the colored image of brain areas and their activity produced by the scanning process.
Phallic stage (FAL-ik) The Freudian developmental stage in which the individual is preoccupied with pleasure derived from the genital organs. (See also *anal stage; genital stage; oral stage*.)
Phenomenal field (fi-NOM-un-ul) One's complete field of subjective awareness.
Phenylketonuria (PKU) (FEN-ul-KEET-un-YURE-ee-ah or FEEN-ul-KEET-un-YURE-ee-ah) A metabolic disorder causing the accumulation of phenylalanine in the body and leading to mental retardation.
Phi phenomenon (FIE fie-NOM-uh-non) The apparent movement of two stationary lights caused when they are lighted in quick succession.
Phobia (FOE-bee-ah) An intense and unrealistic fear of some specific object or situation.
Phobic disorder (FOE-bik) A type of anxiety disorder in which irrational fears predominate.
Phonemes (FOE-neems) The basic sounds of a language that can be distinguished from one another.
Phosphene (FOSS-feen) A luminous visual impression caused by activation of the retina by any means, including pressure and electrical stimulation.
Photoreceptors Sensory receptors sensitive to light and specialized for transforming light waves into neural impulses.
Phrenology (freh-NOL-oh-jee) A false system that holds that the shape of the skull indicates mental faculties or personal characteristics.
Physiological psychologist A psychologist who studies the relationship between the nervous system and behavior.
Pica (PIE-kah) A craving for unnatural foods or substances such as chalk, ashes, and so forth.
Pitch Psychological experience of high or low tones corresponding to the physical dimension of frequency.
Placebo (pla-SEE-bo) An inactive substance given in the place of a drug in psychological research or by physicians who wish to treat chronic aches and pains by suggestion.
Placebo effect Changes in behavior due to one's expectations that a drug (or other treatment) will have some effect.
Polygenetic Any physical or behavioral trait influenced by three or more (often many) genes.
Polygraph An instrument for recording several measures of bodily activity simultaneously; commonly used to refer to the records of emotional response made by a "lie detector."

Population An entire defined group, all members of a class or set from which a smaller sample may be drawn. (See *sample*.)
Positive reinforcement Rewards or stimuli that increase the probability of a response they have followed.
Positive transfer The carryover of skills or responses from one task to another when such carryover improves performance on the second task. (Compare *negative transfer*.)
Post-traumatic stress disorder Psychological and emotional disturbance following exposure to stresses outside the range of normal human experience, such as natural disasters and military combat.
Precognition (PREE-kog-nish-un) Literally, knowing beforehand; hence, any foretelling of the future or any prior knowledge of events unknowable by normal means.
Prejudice A negative attitude or prejudgment held against members of a particular group of people. Most often, attitudes held about racial or ethnic groups, but also frequently applied to other groups as well.
Prenatal Events occurring before the birth of a child.
Presbyopia (prez-by-OH-pea-ah) Farsightedness caused by aging.
Pressure In psychological terms, pressure is said to exist when extended vigilance must be maintained, when events must be speeded up, or when a person must work at or near maximum capacity for an extended period.
Primary impotence (IM-puh-tens) In the male, total inability to perform sexually. (See also *secondary impotence*.)
Primary motives Innate motives based on biological needs.
Primary reinforcers Unlearned reinforcers; usually those that satisfy physiological needs.
Primate A member of the family of mammals, including humans, apes, and monkeys.
Proactive inhibition (pro-AK-tiv) Forgetting that occurs when previous learning interferes with more recent learning.
Projection Attributing one's own feelings, shortcomings, or unacceptable impulses to others as a means of defending against anxiety.
Projective tests Psychological tests making use of unstructured stimuli, wherein the subject is presumed to project his or her own thoughts and impulses onto the stimulus.
Proxemics (prox-EM-iks) Systematic study of the human use of space; particularly, interpersonal space in various social settings.
Pseudo-memories (SUE-doe) False memories that a person believes to be true or accurate.
Pseudo-psychologies (SUE-doe) False or dubious systems that purport to explain behavior.
Psi events (SEYE events) Paranormal events falling outside the traditional bounds of psychology and science. Includes clairvoyance, telepathy, precognition, psychokinesis, astral projection, out-of-body experiences, and the like.
Psyche (SIE-kee) The mind, mental life, and personality as a whole.
Psychiatrist A medical doctor who has additional training in the diagnosis and treatment of mental illness.
Psychoactive drugs (SIE-co-AK-tiv) Any of a large number of substances (often quite potent) capable of altering sensation, perception, cognition, memory, or other psychological events.
Psychoanalysis (SIE-co-ah-NAL-ih-sis) A Freudian approach to therapy emphasizing free association, dream interpretation, and transference.
Psychoanalyst (SIE-co-AN-ah-list) A mental health professional (usually a medical doctor) trained to practice psychoanalysis.
Psychodrama (SIE-co-DRAH-ma) A technique of psychotherapy in which people act out personal conflicts in the presence of other people who play supporting parts.
Psychodynamic (SIE-co-die-NAM-ik) Pertaining to internal motives, unconscious forces, and other aspects of mental functioning.
Psychokinesis (SIE-co-kih-NEE-sis) The ability to influence physical events by mental activity or the act of exerting mental control over inanimate objects.
Psycholinguist (SIE-co-LING-wist) A psychologist who specializes in the study of language.
Psychologist An individual highly trained in the philosophy, methods, factual knowledge, and theories of psychology; usually has at least a master's degree and frequently a doctorate.
Psychology The scientific study of behavior and conscious experience.
Psychometrics (SIE-co-MET-riks) Specialty that focuses on mental measurement or psychological testing, such as personality and intelligence testing.
Psychopath (SIE-co-path) An individual who appears to make no distinctions between right and wrong and to feel no guilt about destructive or antisocial behavior.
Psychopathology (SIE-co-pah-THOL-ih-jee) Abnormal or maladaptive behavior; literally, mental sickness.
Psychophysics (SIE-co-fiz-iks) The study of the relationship between physical stimuli and the sensations evoked by them in a human observer.
Psychosexual stages (SIE-co-sexual) In Freudian theory, development of the personality according to the following stages: *oral stage, anal stage, phallic stage, and genital stage.*
Psychosis (sie-CO-sis) A severe psychological disturbance characterized by withdrawal from reality, by hallucinations and delusions, by disturbed emotions, and often by personality disorganization.
Psychosomatic illnesses (SIE-co-so-MAT-ik) Disorders in which actual physical damage results from psychological stress.
Psychosurgery (SIE-co-surgery) Surgical alterations of the brain designed to bring about certain behavioral or emotional changes; may be performed with traditional surgical instruments or by the removal of brain tissue through use of electrical currents and electrodes.
Psychotherapy (SIE-co-therapy) General term referring to any form of psychological treatment for behavioral disorders; most often used to refer to verbal interaction between the client and a trained mental health professional.
Punishment After a response, the delivery of an event or stim-

ulus that tends to reduce the future probability of that response.
Pupil The dark spot at the front of the eye through which light moves in to reach the retina.

Racism Racial prejudice that has become institutional (that is, reflected in government policy, schools, and so forth) and that is enforced by the existing social power structure.
Random Haphazard and without definite pattern. Random numbers represent a series in which each digit from 0 to 9 has an equal probability of appearing in any particular position.
Randomization The use of random numbers or a random procedure (for example, flipping a coin) to assign subjects to the experimental and control groups in an experiment or a similar situation.
Rarefaction (rare-eh-FAK-shun) In hearing, the spreading or thinning of air molecules between the crests of successive sound waves.
Rational emotive therapy A direct and forceful therapy in which clients learn to abandon irrational an self-defeating behavior and beliefs.
Rationalization Explaining away one's shortcomings in such a way as to avoid responsibility.
Reaction formation A psychological defense mechanism in which an individual controls unconscious anxiety-producing impulses by behaving in exactly the opposite way.
Recall Detailed remembering with a minimum of memory cues.
Recessive gene A gene whose influence will only be expressed when it is paired with a second recessive gene (that is, it cannot be expressed in the presence of a dominant gene). (See *dominant gene*.)
Recitation (RES-ih-TAY-shun) Repeating aloud material that is to be learned as a means for improving memory of the material.
Recognition Memory in which previously learned material is correctly identified as that which has been seen before.
Redintegration (ruh-DIN-tuh-GRAY-shun) The process of inferring or reconstructing an entire complex memory after first observing or remembering only a part of it.
Reference group Any group with which the individual identifies psychologically and uses as a standard for social comparison.
Reflex An automatic response to a stimulus; for example, an eye blink, knee jerk, or dilation of the pupil.
Regression Return to earlier behavior patterns appropriate to a child or younger person, particularly as a response to stress.
Reinforcement Any stimulus that brings about learning or increases the frequency of the response. Often simply a reward.
Reinforcer Any stimulus that reliably increases the frequency or probability of responses it follows.
Relational concept A concept defined by the relationship of one or more dimensions to a second (or other) dimension (for example, "greater than," "above," "equal to"). (Compare with *conjunctive* and *disjunctive* concepts.)
Relearning Learning again something previously learned; used as a measure of memory for prior learning.
Reliability An important characteristic of any test. A test that is reliable gives the same score each time it is administered.
Remission (reh-MISH-un) Disappearance of symptoms of a psychological disorder.
REMs An abbreviation for rapid eye movements characteristics of Stage 1 dream sleep.
REM sleep Rapid-eye-movement sleep corresponding to periods of dreaming.
Replicate To reproduce or repeat, as in duplicating the results of an experiment.
Representative sample A sample of a larger population of subjects or observations that accurately reflects the characteristics of the larger population. Representative samples are frequently achieved by random selection of subjects or observations. (See *randomization* and *sample*.)
Repression Pushing out or barring from consciousness unwanted memories, impulses, or feelings.
Resistance Blocks that occur in psychoanalysis during free association.
Respondent conditioning Another term for classical conditioning. (See *classical conditioning*.)
Response Any muscular action, glandular activity, or other objectively identifiable aspect of behavior.
Retardation Mental capacity significantly below average; traditionally defined as an IQ score below 70.
Retention Storage or memorization of information.
Retina The photosensitive lining at the back of the eye containing rods and cones.
Retrieval Extracting stored information from memory.
Retroactive inhibition (RET-ro-AK-tiv) The interference of new learning with the memory of previously learned material.
Retrograde amnesia (RET-ro-grade) Loss of memory for events that happened before a head injury or other amnesia-producing events.
Rhodopsin (row-DOP-sin) The photosensitive pigment in the rods of the retina. A chemical composed of retinene and opsin that breaks down into retinene and opsin when struck by light.
RNA (ribonucleic acid) A chemical substance similar to DNA and believed to be involved in learning and memory.
Rods Visual receptors in the retina that are responsive to low levels of illumination but that produce only black-white vision. (See *cones*.)
Role Pattern of behavior one is expected to exhibit when occupying a particular position within a group.
Role reversal Taking the role of another person to learn how one's own behavior appears from the other person's perspective.

Sadism (SADE-izm) Deriving erotic satisfaction by the infliction of pain on another; more broadly, love of cruelty.
Sample A subset or portion of a population.
Saturation As applied to colors, saturation refers to colors that are free from the mixture of white, that are very pure, and that represent a concentrated area of the spectrum.

Savings score In testing memory by relearning, the score that is obtained by subtracting the amount of time necessary to remaster material from the amount of time necessary to master it originally.
Scapegoating The act of causing a person or group of people to bear the blame for others or for conditions not of their making; habitual redirection of aggression toward some person or group.
Schedule of reinforcement A rule for determining which response will be reinforced.
Schizophrenia (SKIT-suh-FREE-nee-uh) A form of psychosis characterized by withdrawal from reality, apathy or inappropriate emotion, and, in many cases, delusions and hallucinations.
Schizotypal personality (SKIT-suh-TYPE-al) A serious personality disorder involving withdrawal, odd behavior, and eccentric thought but lacking the hallucinations and delusions of true schizophrenia.
Scientific method A technique for testing the truth of a proposition through careful measurement and controlled observation.
Secondary elaboration In Freudian dream theory, a tendency to fill in gaps and missing details in the recall or retelling of dreams, thus making dream accounts more logical and organized.
Secondary impotence (IM-puh-tens) In the male, unsatisfactory sexual performance caused by premature ejaculation. (See also *primary impotence.*)
Secondary motives Motives based on learned psychological needs.
Secondary reinforcement A previously neutral stimulus that acquires reinforcement value through association with primary reinforcers. (See also *primary reinforcers.*)
Sedative A drug that tends to calm, tranquilize, or to encourage sleep.
Self-actualization The full development of personal potential, especially emotional potential.
Self-disclosure The process of revealing private thoughts, feelings, and personal history to others.
Self-image Total subjective perception of oneself, including an image of one's body and perceptions of one's personality, capabilities, and so forth.
Semantics The study of meanings in language.
Semantic memory A hypothetical "mental dictionary" of basic facts and knowledge said to be a subpart of long-term memory.
Senile dementia Serious mental impairment in old age caused by physical deterioration of the brain.
Sensation The immediate response to stimulation of the sensory receptors and the transduction of environmental or internal events into neural response.
Sensitivity group A group experience consisting of exercises designed to increase self-awareness and sensitivity to others.
Sensory adaptation A reduction in sensory responses to any unchanging form of stimulation.
Sensory memory The first stage in memory storage that holds detailed and literal images of incoming information for a half-second or less.
Sensory neuron An afferent neuron that carries sensory information toward the brain or central nervous system.
Separation anxiety Distress displayed by infants when they are separated from their parents or principal caregivers.
Serial position effect The tendency for the greatest number of memory errors to occur for the middle portions of an ordered list.
Set A predisposition to respond in a certain way.
Set point A theoretical proportion of body fat that tends to be maintained by alterations in hunger and eating.
Sexism Prejudice and discrimination based on gender, particularly that which is reflected in existing social power structures, but also in more subtle attitudes and actions.
Sex roles Learned behavior that fits societal expectations of proper behavior for males and females.
Shaping Gradual molding of responses to a final desired behavior by reinforcing successive approximations of the behavior.
Short-term memory (STM) The retention of information for brief periods without rehearsal, the first step in the creation of permanent memories. (See also *long-term memory.*)
Skin senses The senses of touch, pressure, pain, heat, and cold.
Social comparison Making judgments about ourselves through comparison with others.
Social learning theory An approach that combines learning principles with cognitive processes (perception, thinking, anticipation), plus the effects of observational learning, to explain behavior.
Social influence Changes in a person's behavior induced by the presence or actions of others.
Social motives Learned motives that are acquired as part of growing up in a particular society or culture.
Socialization The process of learning to live in a particular culture by adopting socially acceptable behavior.
Social psychologist A psychologist particularly interested in the effects of other people on individual behavior.
Sociopath Another name for the psychopath or antisocial personality. (See *psychopath.*)
Soma (SO-ma) The body of any living cell, particularly the body of a nerve cell (neuron).
Somatic therapy (so-MAT-ik) Any therapy directly involving bodily processes; for example, drug therapy, electroconvulsive therapy, psychosurgery, and so forth.
Somatoform disorders (so-MAT-oh-form) A class of disturbances characterized by exaggerated bodily complaints (hypochondria) or by the presence of physical disability without apparent cause.
Somesthetic (som-es-THET-ik) Pertaining to sensations produced in the skin, muscles, joints, and viscera.
Somnambulism (som-NAM-bue-lizm) The formal term for sleepwalking.
Spaced practice Learning trials or practice sessions spread

over an extended period of time and including a number of rest periods.

Species A classification comprising closely related plants or animals potentially able to breed with one another.

Species-specific behavior Patterned behavior that is exhibited by all normal members of a particular species. (See also *species.*)

Specific hunger A heightened desire for, or consumption of, a particular food item, especially one that remedies a nutritional deficiency.

Spontaneous recovery The sudden reappearance of a learned response after apparent extinction.

Spontaneous remission In psychiatry or clinical psychology, the spontaneous disappearance of psychological symptoms or behavioral disturbances (for example, clients placed on waiting lists sometimes improve at the same rate as those accepted into therapy).

Sports psychology A specialty that combines study of sports skills with clinical techniques to enhance sports performance and the benefits of sports participation.

Status An individual's position in a group or social system.

Stereoscopic vision The seeing of objects as three-dimensional and the perception of space made possible chiefly by the separation of the eyes.

Stereotype An inaccurate or oversimplified image of the traits of individuals who belong to a particular social group.

Stereotyped response A rigid, repetitive, and nonproductive response made mechanically and without regard for its appropriateness.

Stimulant A substance that produces temporary excitation of the body and/or nervous system.

Stimulus Any physical energy that has some effect on an organism and that evokes a response.

Stimulus generalization The tendency to make a learned response to stimuli similar to the stimulus an organism was originally conditioned to respond to.

Stimulus motives Innate need for stimulation and information.

Stress A condition in which an organism is subjected to external conditions to which it must adjust or adapt.

Stroboscopic movement (strobe-oh-SKOP-ik) An illusion of movement caused by the rapid presentation of a series of photographs or other representations of phases of a continuous movement. More commonly, the illusion of movement created by cartoon animation and by movie films.

Structuralism (STRUK-chur-al-izm) An early school of thought in psychology that tried to analyze sensations and to break down subjective experience into its basic building blocks.

Sublimation (SUB-lih-may-shun) A psychological defense mechanism involving the expression of socially unacceptable impulses in a socially acceptable way; for example, converting greed into a successful business career.

Subliminal (sub-LIM-ih-nal) Perception of a stimulus that is presented below the threshold for conscious recognition.

Superego (super-EE-go) In Freud's theory of personality, the representation of parental values and the rules of society; basically, the unit that acts as the conscience.

Superordinate goals (super-ORD-ih-nate) Goals that exceed or override all others; goals that render other goals relatively less important.

Survey method The use of public polling techniques to answer psychological questions.

Syllogism (SIL-oh-jizm) A logical format for reasoning consisting of a major premise, a minor premise, and a conclusion.

Symbolization In dream imagery, the tendency for images to stand for or suggest something else by reason of similarity, relationship, appearance, or unconscious association.

Sympathetic nervous system A division of the autonomic nervous system responsible for activating the body at times of emotion or stress by speeding up energy consumption and preparing the body for action.

Synapse (SIN-aps) The microscopic space over which nerve impulses travel in the junction of two neurons.

Synesthesia (sin-es-THEE-zyah) Experiencing one sensory modality in terms of another, for example, "seeing" sounds as colors.

Synesthete (sin-es-THEET) A person who regularly experiences synesthesia. (See *synesthesia.*)

Syntax The study of the word order used in the formation of phrases, clauses, and sentences.

Tachistoscope (tuh-KIS-toh-scope) A mechanical device capable of flashing words or pictures on a screen for very short periods of time; used in perceptual testing, especially in studies of subliminal perception.

Taste aversion An active dislike for a particular food frequently when the food is associated with sickness or discomfort. (See *bait shyness.*)

Telepathy (teh-LEP-ah-thee) A purported form of extrasensory perception in which thoughts are transferred from a sender to a receiver without direct contact. (See *extrasensory perception.*)

Telodendria (tel-oh-DEN-dree-ah) A branching network of fibers at the end of the axon in nerve cells that forms multiple synapses with other neurons.

Temperament The physical foundation of personality including such things as prevailing mood, sensitivity, energy levels, and so forth.

Terminal decline A significant decline in mental capacity observed before death and in some cases anticipating the occurrence of death.

Testes The male sex organs, located in the scrotum; the source of sperm and male sex hormones.

Testosterone (tes-TOS-ter-own) Male sex hormone responsible for the development of secondary sexual characteristics.

Thanatologist (THAN-ah-TOL-oh-jist) One who studies death and the process of dying.

Theory A system of ideas and concepts designed to set forth and interrelate concepts and facts in a way that summarizes existing data and predicts future observations.

Timbre (TIM-ber) The psychological aspect of sound that corresponds to the complexity of a tone.
Tinnitus (tin-NYE-tus) A ringing or whistling sensation in the ears due to disease, injury, drugs or unknown causes.
Tip-of-the-tongue phenomenon The experience of feeling that a memory is available but being unable to retrieve it.
Tolerance A condition in drug addiction brought about by the body's ability to withstand increased amounts of the drug. As tolerance develops, the dosage must be increased to produce the same reaction a smaller dosage once produced.
Traits (personality) Enduring attitudes and personal qualities that an individual tends to display in most life situations.
Transactional analysis (TA) A therapeutic technique designed to improve awareness of one's transactions (interchanges) with others.
Transduction Changing one form of energy into another.
Transference Refers to the tendency of a patient to transfer feelings to the therapist that correspond to feelings held toward important figures in the patient's past.
Trepanning (treh-PAN-ing) In modern usage, any surgical procedure in which a hole is bored into the skull. Historically, the chipping or boring of holes in the skull by primitive people as a means of treating mental disturbances.
Trichromatic color theory (TRY-kroe-MAT-ik) Theory of color vision that states that there are three types of cones, each type maximally sensitive to either red, green, or blue.

Unconditioned response In classical conditioning, the unlearned response that is innately elicited by the unconditioned stimulus; usually a reflex response.
Unconditioned stimulus A stimulus innately capable of eliciting a response.
Unconscious (un-KON-shus) That part of a person's mind or personality that contains impulses and desires not directly known to the person.
Unipolar disorder An emotional disorder in which a person experiences extended periods of deep depression but has no history of ever having been manic.

Vacillation (VAS-ih-LAY-shun) Wavering in aim or action, especially in conflict situations.
Validity The ability of a test to measure what it purports to measure.
Variable interval schedule A schedule of reinforcement that varies the time period between reinforcements.
Variable ratio schedule A schedule in which the number of responses required to produce reinforcement varies.
Vestibular senses (ves-TIB-you-ler) Concerned with balance or equilibrium; senses that are produced by the semicircular canals located close to the inner ear.
Vicarious conditioning (vic-CARE-ee-us) The establishment of a conditioned response (often an emotional response) by observing the reactions of another person to a particular stimulus.
Visual acuity The clarity of visual perception.
Vocational interest test A paper-and-pencil test that assesses a person's interests and matches them to interests found among successful workers in various occupations.

White noise An auditory stimulus that is made up of all audible frequencies of sound and that sounds like a hiss or a waterfall.

References

Aarons, L. (1976). Sleep-assisted instruction. *Psychological Bulletin, 83,* 1–40.

Abe, K., Amatomi, M., & Oda, N. (1984). Sleepwalking and recurrent sleeptalking in children of childhood sleepwalkers. *American Journal of Psychiatry, 141,* 800–801.

Ableson, R. P. (1988). Conviction. *American Psychologist. 43*(4), 267–275.

Abrams, A. (1983, January 7). Honda Ohio plant transplants Japan methods, harmony. *Los Angeles Times,* Part IV, pp. 1–2.

Abramson, L. Y., Seligman, M. E. P., & Teasdale, J. D. (1985) Learned helplessness in humans: Critique and reformulation. In J. C. Coyne (Ed.) *Essential papers on depression.* New York: New York University Press, 259–301.

Adams, J. (1980). *Conceptual blockbusting* (2nd ed). New York: Norton.

Adams, J. A. (1967). *Human memory.* New York: McGraw-Hill.

Adams, J. A. (1980). *Learning and memory.* Homewood, Illinois: Dorsey Press.

Ader, R. (1981). *Psychoneuroimmunology.* New York: Academic Press.

Adler, C. S., & Adler, S. M. (1976). Biofeedback—psychotherapy for the treatment of headaches: A 5-year follow-up. *Headache, 16,* 189–191.

Adorno, T. W., Frenkel-Brunswik, E., Levinson, D. J., & Sanford, R. N. (1950). *The authoritarian personality.* New York: Harper.

Ahles, T. A., Blanchard, E. B., & Leventhal, H. (1983). Cognitive control of pain: Attention to the sensory aspects of the cold pressor stimulus. *Cognitive Therapy and Research, 7,* 159–178.

Ainsworth, M. D. S. (1979). Infant-mother attachment. *American Psychologist, 34,* 932–937.

Akerstedt, T., Torsvall, L., & Gillberg, M. (1982). Sleepiness and shift work: Field studies. *Sleep, 5,* S95-S106.

Albert, E. M. (1963). The roles of women: Question of values. In Farber & Wilson (Eds.), *The potential of women.* New York: McGraw-Hill.

Alberti, R., & Emmons, M. (1978). *Your perfect right.* San Luis Obispo, CA: Impact.

Alcock, J. E. (1981). *Parapsychology, science or magic?* New York: Pergamon.

Alessi, S. M. & Trollip, S. R. (1985). *Computer-based instruction.* New York: Prentice-Hall.

Alevizos, P. N., & Callahan, E. J. (1977). Assessment of psychotic behavior. In A. R. Ciminero, K. S. Callhoun, & H. E. Adams (Eds.), *Handbook of behavioral assessment,* New York: Wiley.

Alexander, G. (1978, Sept.). Terminal therapy. *Psychology Today,* pp. 50–60.

Allen, B. (1979). Winged victory of 'Gossamer Albatross.' *National Geographic, 156,* pp. 652–651.

Allison, T., & Van Twyver, H. (1970, Feb.). The evolution of sleep. *Natural History,* The American Museum of Natural History.

Alloy, L. B., Peterson, C., Abramson, L. Y., & Seligman, M. E. (1984). Attributional style and the generality of learned helplessness. *Journal of Personality and Social Psychology, 46,* 681–687.

Allport, G. W. (1958). *The nature of prejudice.* Garden City, N.Y.: Anchor Books, Doubleday.

Allport, G. W. (1961). *Pattern and growth in personality.* New York: Holt, Rinehart, and Winston.

Allport, G. W., & Odbert, H. S. (1936). Trait-names: A psycholexical study. *Psychological Monographs,* (221).

Alvino, J., and the Editors of Gifted Children Monthly. (1985). *Parents' Guide to Raising a Gifted Child.* Boston, Little, Brown and Co.

Amabile, T. M. (1983). *The social psychology of creativity.* New York: Springer-Verlag.

Amabile, T. M. (1985). Motivation and creativity: Effects of motivational orientation on creative writers. *Journal of Personality and Social Psychology, 48,* 393–397.

Americans liberal about sex—survey (1985, April 25). *Santa Barbara News-Press,* B–3.

Anand, B. K., & Brobeck, J. R. (1951). Hypothalamic control of food intake in rats and cats. *Yale Journal of Biological Medicine,* 123–140.

Anastasi, A., & Foley, J. P., Jr. (1958). *Differential psychology* (3rd ed.). New York: Macmillan.

Anderson, R. H., Anderson, K., Fleming, D. E., & Kinghorn, E. (1984). A multidimensional test of the attributional reformulation of learned helplessness. *Bulletin of the Psychonomic Society, 22,* 221–213.

Annett, J. (1979). Memory for skill. In M. M. Gruneberg, & P. E. Morris (Eds.) *Applied problems in memory,* London: Academic Press.

Apfel, R. E. (1977, Nov.). Resounding facts on hearing loss. *The Science Teacher, 44*(8), 31–34.

Arndt, S. & Berger, D. E. (1978). Cognitive mode and asymmetry in cerebral functioning. *Cortex, 14,* 78–86.

Aronson, E. (1969). Some antecedents of interpersonal attraction. In W. J. Arnold & D. Levine (Eds.). *Nebraska Symposium on Motivation,* Lincoln: University of Nebraska Press.

Aronson, E. (1972). *The social animal.* San Francisco: W. H. Freeman.

Aronson, E. (1980). *The social animal.* San Francisco: W. H. Freeman.

Aronson, E., Stephan, C., Sikes, J., Blaney, N., & Snapp, M. (1978). *The jigsaw classroom.* Beverly Hills, CA: Sage Publications.

Aronson, E. with Blaney, N., Sikes, J., Stephan, C., & Snapp, M. (1979). Busing and racial tension: The jigsaw route to learning and liking. In V. J. Derlega & L. H. Janda (Eds.). *Personal adjustment, selected readings,* Glenview, Ill.: Scott, Foresman.

Asch, S. E. (1956). Studies of independence and conformity: A minority of one against a unanimous majority. *Psychological Monographs, 70*(416).

Asimov, I. (1967). *Is anyone there?* Garden City, N.Y.: Doubleday.

Aslin, R. N. & Smith, L. B. (1988). Perceptual development. *Annual Review of Psychology, 39,* 435–473.

Astronomical Society of the Pacific. (1983). *Astrology and astronomy,* San Francisco, 1983.

Athenasiou, R., Shaver, P., & Tavris, C. (1970). Sex. *Psychology Today, 4*(2), pp. 37–52.

Atkinson, R. C., & Shiffrin, R. M. (1971, Aug.) The control of short-term memory. *Scientific American*, pp. 89–90.

Ayllon, T. (1963). Intensive treatment of psychotic behavior by stimulus satiation and food reinforcement. *Behavior Research and Therapy, 1,* 53–61.

Ayllon, T., & Azrin, N. H. (1965). The measurement and reinforcement of behavior of psychotics. *Journal of the Experimental Analysis of Behavior, 8,* 357–383.

Ayllon, T., Haughton, E., & Hughes, H. B. (1965). Interpretation of symptoms: Fact or fiction? *Behavior and Therapy, 3,* 1–7.

Azrin, N. H., Hutchinson, R. R., & McLaughlin, R. (1965). The opportunity for aggression as an operant reinforcer during aversive stimulation. *Journal of Experimental Analysis of Behavior, 8,* 171–180.

Bach, G., & Wyden, P. (1969). *The intimate enemy*. New York: Morrow.

Bachman, J. G., & Johnson, L. D. (1979). The freshmen. *Psychology Today, 13,* pp. 78–87.

Bachrach, L. L. (1984). Asylum and chronically ill psychiatric patients. *American Journal of Psychiatry, 141,* 975–978.

Back, K. W. (1972). The group can comfort but it can't cure. *Psychology Today, 6*(7), pp. 28–35.

Baddeley, A. D. (1976). *The psychology of memory*. New York: Basic Books.

Baer, D. M. (1971, Oct.). Let's take another look at punishment. *Psychology Today*.

Bahrick, H. P. (1984). Semantic memory content in permastore: Fifty years of memory for Spanish learned in school. *Journal of Experimental Psychology: General, 113*(1), 1–37.

Baillargeon, R. (1987). Object permanence in 3½- and 4½-month old infants. *Developmental Psychology, 23*(5).

Baillargeon, R., Spelke, E. S., & Wasserman, S. (1985). Object permanence in five-month-old infants. *Cognition, 20,* 191–208.

Baker, B. (1988, March 14) "Electronic inner ear" gives shower of noise. *Los Angeles Times*, Part II, pp. 4.

Ball, G. G., & Grinker, J. A. (1981). Overeating and obesity. In S. J. Mule (Ed.), *Behavior in Excess* (pp. 194–220). New York: The Free Press.

Baltes, P. B. (1987). Theoretical propositions of life-span developmental psychology: On the dynamics between growth and decline. *Developmental Psychology, 23*(5), 611–626.

Baltes, P. B., & Schaie, K. W. (1974). Aging and I.Q.: The myth of the twilight years. *Psychology Today, 7*(10), pp. 35–40.

Bandura, A. (1965). Vicarious processes: A case of no-trial learning. In L. Berkowitz (Ed.), *Advances in experimental social psychology, Vol. 2,* (pp. 1–55). New York: Academic Press.

Bandura, A. (1971). *Social learning theory*. New York: General Learning Press.

Bandura, A. (1973). *Aggression: A social learning analysis*. Englewood Cliffs, N.J.: Prentice-Hall.

Bandura, A. (1977). Self-efficacy: Toward a unifying theory of behavioral change. *Psychological Review, 84,* 191–215.

Bandura, A. (1982). Self-efficacy mechanism in human agency. *American Psychologist*, 37, 122–147.

Bandura, A. (1986). *Social foundations of thought and action: A social cognitive theory*. Englewood Cliffs, NJ: Prentice-Hall.

Bandura, A., & Rosenthal, T. L. (1966). Vicarious classical conditioning as a function of arousal level. *Journal of Personality and Social Psychology, 3,* 54–62.

Bandura, A., Ross, D., & Ross, S. A. (1963). Vicarious reinforcement and imitative learning. *Journal of Abnormal and Social Psychology, 67,* 601–607.

Bandura, A., & Walters, R. (1959). *Adolescent aggression*. New York: Ronald.

Bandura, A., & Walters, R. (1963). Aggression. In H. W. Stevenson (Ed.), *Child psychology*. Chicago: University of Chicago Press.

Bandura, A., & Walters, R. (1963). *Social learning and personality development*. New York: Holt.

Bank, S. P., & Kahn, M. D. (1982). *The sibling bond*. New York: Basic Books.

Barahal, H. S. (1958). 1000 prefrontal lobotomies: Five to ten year follow-up study. *Psychiatric Quarterly, 32,* 653–678.

Barber, T. X. (1959). Toward a theory of pain: Relief of chronic pain by prefrontal leucotomy, opiates, placebos, and hypnosis. *Psychological Bulletin, 56,* 430–460.

Barber, T. X. (1970). Suggested ('hypnotic') behavior: The trance paradigm versus an alternative paradigm. Harding, Mass. Medfield Foundation, Report No. 103.

Barchas, J. D., Elliot, G. R., & Berger, P. A. (1978). Biogenic amine hypothesis of schizophrenia. In L. C. Wynne, R. L. Cromwell, and S. Matthysse (Eds.), *The nature of schizophrenia: New approaches to research and treatment*. New York: John Wiley and Sons.

Barglow, P. Vaughn, B. E., & Monitor, N. (1987). *Child Development, 58*(4), 945–954.

Baron, R. A. (1983). "Sweet smell of success"? The impact of pleasant artificial scents on evaluations of job applicants. *Journal of Applied Psychology, 68,* 709–713.

Barrett, R. J. (1985). Behavioral approaches to individual differences in substance abuse. In Galizio, M. & Maisto, S. A. (Eds.), *Determinants of substance abuse treatment: Biological, psychological, and environmental factors*. New York: Plenum.

Barron, F. (1958). The psychology of imagination. *Scientific American, 199*(3), pp. 150–170.

Barrow, G. M., & Smith, P. A. (1979). *Aging, ageism, and society*. St. Paul: West.

Bart, P. B., & O'Brien, P. H. (1985). *Stopping rape: Successful survival strategies*. New York: Pergamon Press.

Basedow, R. A. (1925). *The australian aborigine*. Adelaide, Australia: F. W. Peerce and Sons.

Bassuk, E. L., & Gerson, S. (1978) Deinstitutionalization and mental health services. *Scientific American, 238*(2), pp. 46–53.

Bassuk, E. L., Rubin, L., & Lauriat, A. (1984). Is homelessness a mental health problem? *American Journal of Psychiatry, 141,* 1546–1550.

Bateson. G., Jackson, D. D., Haley, J. & Weakland, J. (1956). Toward a theory of schizophrenia. *Behavioral Science, 1,* 251–264.

Bauer, W. D., & Twentyman, C. T. (1985). Abusing, neglectful, and comparison mothers' response to child-related and non-child-related stressors. *Journal of Consulting and Clinical Psychology, 53,* 335–343.

Baum, A., & Davis, G. E. (1980). Reducing the stress of high-density living: An architectural intervention. *Journal of Personality and Social Psychology, 38,* 471–481.

Baum, A., & Valins, S. (Eds.). (1977). *Human response to crowding: Studies of the effects of residential group size*. Hillsdale, N.J.: Lawrence Erlbaum Associates.

Baum, A., & Valins, S. (1979). Architectural mediation of residential density and control: Crowding and the regulation of social contact. *Advances in Experimental and Social Psychology, 12,* 131–175.

Baumeister, A. A. (1987). Mental retardation: Some conceptions and dilemmas. *American Psychologist, 42*(2), 796–800.

Baumrind, D. (1980, July). New directions in socialization research. *American Psychologist, 35,* 639–652.

Beach, F. A. (1975). Behavioral endocrinology: An emerging discipline. *American Scientist, 63,* pp. 178–187.

Beck, A. T. (1985). Cognitive therapy of depression: New perspectives. In P. Clayton (Ed.), *Depression*. New York: Raven.

Beck, A. T., & Greenberg, R. L. (1974). *Coping with depression*. Institute For Rational Living, Inc.

Beck, A. T., Rush, A. J., Shaw, B., & Emery, G. (1979). *Cognitive therapy of depression: A treatment manual*. New York: Gilford Press.

Beck, A. T., & Young, J. E. (1978, Sept.). College blues. *Psychology Today*, pp. 80–92.

Becker, P. (1982). Fear reactions and achievement behavior of students approaching an examination. In H. W. Krohne, & L. Laux (Eds.), *Achievement, stress, and anxiety* (pp. 275–290). Washington: Hemisphere.

Beebe, B., Gerstman, L., Carson, B., Dolins, M., Zigman, A., Rosensweig, H., Faughey K., & Korman, M. (1982). Rhythmic communication in the mother-infant dyad. In M. Davis (Ed.), *Interaction rhythms, periodicity in communicative behavior*. New York: Human Sciences Press.

Beecher, H. K. (1959). *Measurement of subjective responses: Quantitative effects of drugs*. New York: Oxford University Press.

Been, H., & Sklar, I. (1985). Transference in short-term dynamic psychotherapy. In A. Winston (Ed.), *Short-term dynamic psychotherapy* (pp. 2–18). Washington, DC: American Psychiatric Press, Inc.

Beidler, L. M. (1963). Dyanmics of taste cells. In Y. Zotterman (Ed.), *Olfaction and taste. Vol. 1*. New York: Macmillan.

Beljan, J. R., Rosenblatt, L. S., Hetherington, N. W., Layman, J., Flaim, S. E. T., Dale, G. T., & Holley, D. C. (1972). *Human performance in the aviation environment*. NASA Contract no. 2-6657, Pt. Ia, 253–259.

Bell, A. P., Weinberg, M. S., & Hammersmith, S. K. (1981). *Sexual preference*. Indiana University Press.

Belloc, N. B. (1973). Relationship of physical health practices and mortality. *Preventive Medicine,* 2, 67–81.

Belloc, N. B. & Breslow, L. (1972). Relationship of physical health status and healthy practices. *Preventive Medicine,* 1, 409–421.

Belmont, L., & Marolla, F. A. (1973). Birth order, family size, and intelligence. *Science, 182,* 1096–1101.

Belsky, J., Gilstrap, B., & Rovine, M. (1984). The Pennsylvania infant and family development project, I: Stability and change in mother-infant and father-infant interactions in a family setting at one, three, and nine months. *Child Development, 55,* 692–705.

Belsky, J. & Rovine, M. J. (1988). Nonmaternal care in the first year of life and the security of infant-parent attachment. *Child Development, 59*(1), 157–167.

Belsky, J., Rovine, M., & Taylor, D. G. (1984). The Pennsylvania infant and family development project, III: The origins of individual differences in infant-mother attachment: Maternal and infant contributions. *Child Development, 55,* 718–728.

Bem, S. L. (1974). The measurement of psychological androgyny. *Journal of consulting and clinical psychology, 42,* 155–162.

Bem, S. L. (1975a). Sex-role adaptability: One consequence of psychological androgyny. *Journal of Personality and Social Psychology, 31,* 634–643.

Bem, S. L. (1977). Psychological androgyny. In A. G. Sargent (Ed.), *Beyond Sex Roles*. St. Paul: West.

Bem, S. L. (1981). Gender schema theory. A cognitive account of sex typing. *Psychological Review, 88,* 354–364.

Bem, S. L. (1975b, Sept.). Androgyny vs. the tight little lives of fluffy women and chesty men. *Psychology Today,* pp. 58–62.

Benbow, C. P. (1986). Physiological correlates of extreme intellectual precocity. *Neuropsychologia, 24*(5), 719–725.

Beneke, W. M., & Harris, M. B. (1972). Teaching self-control of study behavior. *Behavior Research and Therapy, 10,* 35–41.

Benjamin, L. T., Cavell, T. A., & Shallenberger, W. R., III. (1984). Staying with initial answers on objective tests: Is it a myth? *Teaching of Psychology, 11,* 133–141.

Bennett, W., & Gurin, J. (1982). *The dieter's dilemma*. New York: Basic Books.

Ben-Shakhar, G., Bar-Hillel, M., Bilu, Y., Ben-Abba, E., & Flug, A. (1986). Can graphology predict occupational success? Two empirical studies and some methodological ruminations. *Journal of Applied Psychology, 71, 4,* 645–653.

Benson, H. (1977). Systematic hypertension and the relaxation response. *The New England Journal of Medicine, 296,* 1152–1156.

Benson, H. (1975). *The relaxation response*. New York: William Morrow.

Benton, A. L. (1980, Feb.). The neuropsychology of facial recognition. *American Psychologist, 35,* 176–186.

Bergin, A., & Suinn, R. M. (1975). Individual psychotherapy and behavior therapy. *Annual Review of Psychology, 26,* 509–556.

Berglas, S. (1986). "A typology of self-handicapping alcohol abusers." In Saks, M. J. & Saxe, L. (Eds.), *Advances in applied social psychology, Vol. 3*. Hillsdale, N.J.: Lawrence Erlbaum, 29–56.

Berkowitz, L. (1984). Some effects of thoughts on anti- and prosocial influences of media events: A cognitive-neoassociation analysis. *Psychological Bulletin, 95,* 410–427.

Berkowitz, L. (1982). Aversive conditions as stimuli to aggression. In L. Berkowitz (Ed.), *Advances in experimental social psychology, vol 15*. New York: Academic Press.

Berkowitz, L. (1968). The frustration-aggression hypothesis revisited. In L. Berkowitz (Ed.), *Roots of aggression: A re-examination of the frustration-aggression hypothesis*. New York: Atherton Press.

Berlyne, D. (1966). Curiosity and exploration. *Science, 153* 25–33.

Berman, L. H. (1982). Family therapy. In L. E. Abt, & I. R. Stuart (Eds), *The newer therapies: A sourcebook*. New York: Van Nostrand, Reinhold.

Berne, E. (1961). *Transactional analysis in psychotherapy*. New York: Grove Press.

Berne, E. (1964). *Games people play*. New York: Grove Press.

Bernstein, I. L. (1978). Learned taste aversions in children receiving chemotherapy. *Science, 200,* 1302–1303.

Berry, P., Groeneweg, G., Gibson, D., & Brown, R. I. (1984). Mental development of adults with Down syndrome. *American Journal of Mental Deficiency, 89,* 252–256.

Bersheid, E., & Walster, E. (1974a). Physical attractiveness. In L. Berkowitz (Ed.), *Advances in experimental social psychology, Vol. 7*. New York: Academic Press.

Bersheid, E., & Walster, E. (1974b). A little bit about love. In T. L. Huston (Ed.), *Foundations of interpersonal attraction*. New York: Academic Press.

Bertsch, G. J. (1976). Punishment of consummatory and instrumental behavior: A review. *Psychological Record, 26,* 13–31.

Best, J. B. (1986). *Cognitive psychology*. St. Paul, MN: West Publishing Company.

Bettelheim, B. (1960). *The informed heart*. New York: Free Press.

Beyerstein, B. (1985, Fall). The myth of alpha consciousness. *The Skeptical Inquirer, 10,* 42–59.

Biblow, E. (1973). Imaginative play and the control of aggressive behavior. In J. L. Singer (ed.), *The child's world of make-believe: Experimental studies of imaginative play*. New York: Academic Press.

Bickman, L. (1974, April). Clothes make the person. *Psychology Today*.

Bierley, C., McSweeney, F. K., & Vannieuwerk, R. (1985). Classical conditioning of preferences for stimuli. *Journal of Consumer Research, 12,* 316–323.

Biller, H. B. (1982). Fatherhood: Implications for child and adult development. In B. B. Wolman (Ed.), *Handbook of developmental psychology*. Englewood Cliffs, N.J.: Prentice-Hall.

Binder, V. (1976). Behavior modification: Operant approaches to therapy. In V. Binder, A. Binder, & B. Rimland (Eds.), *Modern therapies* (pp. 150–165). Englewood Cliffs, N.J.: Prentice-Hall.

Bird, D. (1975). *The case against college*. New York: David McKay Co.

Birnbaum, I. M., Parker, E. S., Hartley J. T., & Nobel, E. P. (1978). Alcohol and memory: Retrieval processes. *Journal of Verbal Learning and Verbal Behavior, 17,* 325–335.

Blackwell, R. T. Galassi, J. P., Galassi, M. D., & Watson, T. E. (1985). Are cognitive assessments equal? A comparison of think aloud and thought listing. *Cognitive Therapy and Research, 9,* 399–413.

Blanchard, E., Andrasik, F., Neff, D., Arena, J., Ahles, T., Jurish, S., Pallmayer, T., Saunders, N., Teders, S., Barron, K., & Rodichock, L. (1982). Biofeedback and relaxation training with three kinds of headache: Treatment effects and their prediction. *Journal of Consulting and Clinical Psychology, 50,* 562–576.

Blanchard, E., McCoy, G., Andrasik, F., Acerra, M., Pallmeyer, T., Gerardi, R., Halpern, M., & Musso, A. (1984). Preliminary results from a controlled evaluation of thermal biofeedback as a treatment for essential hypertension. *Biofeedback & Self-Regulation, 9,* 471–495.

Blanchard, E. B., & Epstein, L. H. (1978). *A biofeedback primer*. Reading, Mass: Addison-Wesley. B K

Blaske, D. M. (1984). Occupational sex-typing by kindergarten and fourth-grade children. *Psychological Reports, 54,* 795–801.

Blaustein, A. R. (1983). The situation of sociobiology. *Science, 220,* 188–189.

Block, J. (1979, Sept.). Socialization influence of personality development in males and females. American Psychological Association Master Lecture, Convention of the American Psychological Association, New York City.

Bloom, B. (1985). *Developing talent in young people*. New York: Ballantine.

Bloom, B. L., & Parad, H. J. (1977). Professional activity patterns in community mental health centers. In I. Iscoe, B. L. Bloom and C. D. Spielberger (Eds.), *Community psychology in transition*. Washington, D.C.: Hemisphere.

Bloom, K., Russell, A., & Wassenberg, K. (1987). Turn taking affects the quality of infant vocalizations. *Journal of Child Language, 14*(2), 211–227.

Bloom, L., & Lahey, M. (1978). *Language development and language disorders*. New York: Wiley.

Blumenthal, A. L. (1979). The founding father we never knew. *Contemporary Psychology, 24*, 547–550.

Blumenthal, A. L. (1976). *The process of cognition*. Englewood Cliffs, NJ: Prentice-Hall.

Bocher, J., & Carlson, G. (1980). Recognition of facial expression in three cultures. *Journal of cross-cultural psychology, 11*, 263–280.

Bock, F. G. (1980). Cocarcinogenic properties of nicotine. In G. B. Gori & F. G. Bock (Eds.), *Banbury report*. Cold Spring Harbor Laboratory.

Boker, J. R. (1974). Immediate and delayed retention effects of interspersing questions in written instructional passages. *Journal of Educational Psychology, 66*, 96–98.

Bolles, R. C. (1979). *Learning theory* (2nd ed.). New York: Holt, Rinehart & Winston.

Bolton, R. (1976). Hostility in fantasy: A further test of the hypoglycemia-aggression hypothesis. *Aggressive Behavior, 2*, 257–274.

Bonnet, M. H., & Moore, S. E. (1982). The threshold of sleep: Perception of sleep as a function of time asleep and auditory threshold. *Sleep, 5*(3), 267–276.

Bootzin, R. (1973, Aug.). *Stimulus control of insomnia*. Paper presented at the meeting of the American Psychological Association, Montreal.

Borkovec, T. D. (1982). Insomnia. *Journal of Consulting and Clinical Psychology, 50*, 880–895.

Borman, W. C., Eaton, N. K., Bryan, J. D., & Rosse, R. S. (1983). Validity of army recruiter behavioral assessment. Does the assessor make a difference? *Journal of Applied Psychology, 68*, 415–419.

Bornstein, M. H. (1975). Qualities of color vision in infancy. *Journal of Experimental Child Psychology, 19*, 401–419.

Borrie, R. A., & Suedfeld, P. (1980). Restricted environmental stimulation therapy in a weight reduction program. *Journal of Behavioral Medicine, 3*, 147–161.

Botwinick, J. (1984). *Aging and behavior*. New York: Springer.

Bouchard, T. J., Jr. (1983). Twins-Nature's twice-told tale. *Yearbook of science and the future* (pp. 66–81). Chicago: Encyclopedia Britannica.

Bouchard, T. J. Jr., Heston L., Eckert, E., Keyes, M., & Resnick, S. (1981). The Minnesota study of twins reared apart: Project description and sample results in the developmental domain. In L. Gedda, P. Parisi, & W. E. Nance (Eds.), *Twin research 3: Part B. Intelligence, personality, and development* (pp. 227–233). New York: Alan R. Liss.

Bouzid, N. & Crawshaw, C. M. (1987). Massed versus distributed word-processor training. *Applied Ergonomics, 18*(3), 220–222.

Bower, B. (1984, Oct. 6). Not popular by reason of insanity. *Science News, 126*(14), pp. 218–219.

Bower, G. H. (1981). Mood and memory. *American Psychologist, 36*, 129–148.

Bower, G. H. (1973, Oct.). How to . . . uh . . . remember. *Psychology Today*, pp. 63–70.

Bower, G. H., & Clark, M. C. (1969). Narrative stories as mediators for serial learning. *Psychonomic Science, 14*, 181–182.

Bower, G. H., & Springston, F. (1970). Pauses as recoding points in letter series. *Journal of Experimental Psychology, 83* 421–430.

Bowerman, M. (1977). The acquistion of word meaning: An investigation of some current concepts. *Thinking*.

Bowlby, J. (1969). *Attachment and loss, Volume I: Attachment*. New York: Basic Books.

Bowlby, J. (1973). *Attachment and loss, Volume II: Separation and anxiety*. New York: Basic Books.

Boyd, J. H. & M. M. Weissman (1982). Epidemiology. In E. S. Paykel (Ed.) *Handbook of affective disorders*. New York: Guilford Press, pp. 109–125.

Brackbill, Y. (1979). Obstetrical medication and infant behavior. In J. D. Osofsky (Ed.) *Handbook of infant development*. New York: Wiley.

Braginsky, B. M., & Braginsky, D. D. (1967). Schizophrenic patients in the psychiatric interview: An experimental study of their effectiveness at manipulation. *Journal of Consulting Psychology, 31*, 543–547.B K

Bransford, J. & Stein, B. S. (1984). *The IDEAL problem solver*. New York: W. H. Freeman.

Bransford, J., Sherwood, R., Vye, N., & Rieser, J. (1986). Teaching thinking and problem solving. *American Psychologist, 41*(10), 1078–1089.

Bransford, J. D., & McCarrell, N. S. (1977). A sketch of cognitive approach to comprehension: Some thoughts about understanding what it means to comprehend. In P. N. Johnson-Laird & P. C. Wason (Eds.), *Thinking: Readings in cognitive science*. Cambridge: Cambridge University Press.

Braun, B. G. (1986). Issues in the psychotherapy of multiple personality disorder. In B. G. Braun (Ed.) *Treatment of multiple personality disorder*. Washington, D.C.: American Psychiatric Press.

Bray, D. W., Campbell, R. J., & Grant, D. (1974). *Formative years in business: A long term study of managerial lives*. New York: Wiley.

Brazelton, T. B., Koslowski, B., & Main, M. (1974). The origins of reciprocity: The early mother-infant interaction. In M. Lewis, & L. A. Rosenblum, (Eds.), *The effect of the infant on its caregiver*. New York: Wiley-Interscience.

Brazelton, T. B., et al., (1975). Early mother-infant reciprocity. In *Parent-infant interaction*, Ciba Foundation Symposium 33. Amsterdam: Associated Scientific Publishers.

Brecher, E. M., & the Editors of *Consumer Reports*. (1972). *Licit and illicit drugs*. Boston: Little, Brown.

Brecher, E. M. (1975a, March). Marijuana: The health questions. *Consumer Reports, 40*, pp. 143–149.B K

Breier, A., & Strauss, J. S. (1983, October). Self control in psychotic disorders. *Archives of General Psychiatry, 40*, 1141.

Breland, K., & Breland, M. (1961). The misbehavior of organisms. *American Psychologist, 16*, 681–684.

Bresler, D. E., & Trubo, R. (1979). *Free yourself from pain*. New York: Simon & Schuster.

Breslow, L. & Enstrom, J. E. (1980). Persistence of health habits and their relationship to mortality. *Preventive Medicine, 9*, 469–483.

Brewer, M. B. & Kramer, R. K. (1985). The psychology of intergroup attitudes and behavior. *Annual Review of Psychology, 36*, 219–243.

Brewer, J. S. (1981). Duration of intromission and female orgasm rates. *Medical Aspects of Human Sexuality, 15*(4), 70–71.

Bridges, K. M. B. (1932). Emotional development in early infancy. *Child Development, 3*, 324–334.

Brookfield, S. D. (1987). *Developing critical thinkers*. San Francisco: Jossey-Bass.

Brown, A. S. (1974). Satisfying relationships for elderly and their patterns of disengagement. *Gerontologist, 14*, 258–262.

Brown, B. (1980). Perspectives on social stress. In H. Selye (Ed.), *Selye's guide to stress research, vol. 1*. New York: Van Nostrand Reinhold.

Brown, G. W. (1985) A three-factor causal model of depression. In J. C. Coyne (Ed.) *Essential papers on depression*. New York: New York University Press, pp. 390–420.

Brown, J. D. (1986, Winter). Sex in the media. *Planned Parenthood Review*, pp. 4–7.

Brown, R., & Kulik, J. (1977). Flashbulb memories. *Cognition, 5*, 73–99.B K

Brown, R., & McNeill, D. (1966). The "tip of the tongue" phenomenon. *Journal of Verbal Learning and Verbal Behavior, 5*, 325–337.

Brown, S. A., Goldman, M. S., & Christiansen, B. A. (1985). Do alcohol expectancies mediate drinking patterns of adults? *Journal of Consulting and Clinical Psychology, 53*(4), 512–519.

Browne, A. (1986). "Assault and homicide at home: When battered women kill." In Saks, M. J. & Saxe, L. (Eds.), *Advances in applied social psychology, Vol. 3*. Hillsdale, N.J.: Lawrence Erlbaum, 57–79.

Browne, M. A., & Mahoney, M. J. (1984). Sport psychology. *Annual Review of Psychology, 35*, 605–625.

Brownell, K. (1988, January). Yo-yo dieting. *Psychology Today*, pp. 20–23.

Brownell, K. D. (1982). Obesity: Understanding and treating a serious, prevalent, and refractory disorder. *Journal of Consulting and Clinical Psychology, 50*, 820–840.

Brownell, K. D., Greenwood, M. R. C., Stellar, E. & Shrager, E. E. (1986). The effects of repeated cycles of weight loss and regain in rats. *Physiology and Behavior, 38*, 459–464.

Brownell, K. D., Marlatt, G. A., Lichtenstein, E., & Wilson, G. T. (1986). Understanding and preventing relapse. *American Psychologist, 41*, 765–782.

Bruch, H. (1973). *Eating disorders*. New York: Basic Books.

Bruner, J. (1983). *Child's Talk*. New York: W. W. Norton.

Bruner, J. S. (1968). *Toward a theory of instruction*. New York: Norton.

Bruner, J. S., et al. (1966). *Studies in cognitive growth*. New York: Wiley.

Bruner, J. S., & Postman, L. (1949). On the perception of incongruity: A paradigm. *Journal of Personality, 18*, 206–223

Bryan, J. H., & Test, M. A. (1967). Models and helping. Naturalistic studies in aiding behavior. *Journal of Personality and Social Psychology, 6*, 400–407.

Bryan, J. H., & Walbek, N. H. (1970). Preaching and practicing generosity: Children's actions and reactions. *Child Development, 41*, 329–353.

Buchwald, A. (1965, June 20). Psyching out. *The Washington Post*.

Buckalew, L. W., & Buckalew, P. B. (1983). Behavioral management of exceptional children using video games as reward. *Perceptual Motor Skills, 56*, 580.

Buckhout, R. (1974, Dec.). Eyewitness testimony. *Scientific American, 231*, pp. 23–31.

Budzynski, T. H. (1977). Biofeedback strategies in headache treatment. In J. V. Basmajian (Ed.), *Biofeedback: A handbook for clinicians*. Baltimore; Williams and Wilkins.

Burka, J. B., & Yuen, L. M. (1983). *Procrastination*. Menlo Park, CA: Addison-Wesley.

Burns, D. D., & Persons, J. (1982). Hope and hopelessness: A cognitive approach. In L. E. Abt, & I. R. Stuart (Eds.), *The newer therapies: A sourcebook*, pp. 33–57. New York: Van Nostrand Reinhold.

Burt, M. R. (1980). Cultural myths and supports for rape. *Journal of Personality and Social Psychology, 38*, 217–230.

Burtt, H. E. (1941). An experimental study of early childhood memory: Final report. *Journal of General Psychology, 58*, 435–439.

Bushsbaum, M. S., & Haier, R. J. (1983). Psychopathology: Biological approaches. *Annual Review of Psychology, 34*, 401–430.

Buss, A. H. (1980). *Self-consciousness and social anxiety*. San Francisco: W. H. Freeman.

Buss, A. H. (1986). A theory of shyness. In Jones, W. H., Cheek, J. M., & Briggs, S. R., *Shyness: Perspectives on research and treatment*. New York: Plenum.

Buss, D. M. (1985). Human mate selection. *American Scientist, 73*, 47–51.

Butler, R. (1954). Curiosity in monkeys. *Scientific American, 190*(18), pp. 70–75.

Butler, R., & Harlow, H. F. (1954). Persistence of visual exploration in monkeys. *Journal of Comparative Physiological Psychology, 47*, 258–263.

Byck, R. (1987). Cocaine use and research: Three histories. In Fisher, S., Raskin, A. & Uhlenhuth, E. H. (Eds.), *Cocaine: Clinical and behavioral aspects*. N.Y.: Oxford University Press, 1–20.

Byrne, D. (1971). *The attraction paradigm*. New York: Academic Press.

Cabanac, M., & Duclaux, P. (1970). Obesity: Absence of satiety aversion to sucrose. *Science, 168*, 496–497.

Calhoun, J. B. (1962). A "behavioral sink." In E. L. Bliss (Ed.), *Roots of behavior*. New York: Harper & Row.

Campbell, A., Gurin, G. & Miller, W. E. (1954). *The voter decides*. New York: Harper & Row.

Campbell, J. B., & Hawley, C. W. (1982). Study habits and Eysenck's theory of extraversion—introversion. *Journal of Research in Personality, 16*, 139–146.

Campos, J. J., Hiatt, S., Ramsay, D., Henderson, C., & Svejda, M. (1978). The emergence of fear on the visual cliff. In M. Lewis, & L. A. Rosenblum (Eds.), *The development of affect* (pp. 149–182). New York: Plenum Press.

Canadian Government's Commission of Inquiry. (1971). *The non-medical use of drugs*. Baltimore: Penguin.

Canavan, A. G., Dunn, G., & McMillan, T. M. (1986). Principal components of the WAIS-R. *British Journal of Clinical Psychology, 25*(2), 81–85.

Cannon, J. T., Liebeskind, J. C., & Frenk, H. Neural and neurochemical mechanisms of pain inhibition. In R. A. Sternbach (Ed.), *The psychology of pain*. New York: Raven Press.

Cannon, W. B. (1932). *The wisdom of the body*. New York: Norton.

Cannon, W. B. (1942). "Voodoo" death. *American Anthropologist, 44*, 169–181.

Cannon, W. B., & Washburn, A. L. (1912). An exploration of hunger. *American Journal of Physiology, 29*, 441–454.

Cannon, W. B. (1934). Hunger and thirst. In C. Murchinson (Ed.), *Handbook of general experimental psychology*, Worcester, Mass: Clark University Press.

Caplan, P. J., MacPherson, G. M., & Tobin, P. (1985). Do sex-related differences in spatial abilities exist? A multilever critique with new data. *American Psychologist, 40*, 786–799.

Caplan, P. J., MacPherson, G. M., & Tobin, P. (1986). The magnified molehill and the misplaced focus: Sex-related differences in spatial ability revisited. *American Psychologist, 41*, 1016–1018.

Carducci, B. J., Deeds, W. C., Jones, J. W., Moretti, D. M., Reed, J. G., Saal, F. E., & Wheat, J. E. (1987). Preparing undergraduate psychology students for careers in business. *Teaching of Psychology, 14*, 16–20.

Carelli, R. (1982, May 31). Insanity: A legal lever that tips justice scales. Associated Press news article, Santa Barbara News Press.

Carew, J. V., Chan, I., & Halfor, C. (1976). *Observing intelligence in young children: Eight case studies*. Englewood Cliffs, N.J.: Prentice-Hall.

Carey, S. (1986). Cognitive science and science education. *American Psychologist, 41*(10), 1123–1130.

Carlson, J. M. (1986). *Prime time law enforcement*. New York: Praeger.

Carlson, N. R. (1981). *Physiology of behavior (2nd Ed.)*. Boston: Allyn and Bacon.

Carmen, R., & Adams, W. R. (1985). *Study skills: A student's guide for survival*. New York: Wiley.

Carr, R. R., & Meyers, E. J. (1980). Marijuana and cocaine: The process of change in drug policy. In *The facts about "drug abuse."* The Drug Abuse Council. New York: The Free Press.

Carroll, J. B. (1985). Second language abilities. In Sternberg, R. J. (Ed.), *Human abilities*. New York: W. H. Freeman.

Carson, R. C., Butchers, J. N., & Coleman, J. C. (1988) *Abnormal psychology and modern life*. Glenview, IL: Scott Foresman.

Carter, W. E. (Ed.) (1980). *Cannabis in Costa Rica: A study of chronic marihuana use*. Philadelphia: Institute for the Study of Human Issues.

Cartwright, R. (1969). In M. Kramer (Ed.), *Dream psychology and the new biology of dreaming*. Springfield, Ill.: Charles C. Thomas.

Cartwright, R. D. (1978). Sleep and dreams, Part II. *Annual Review of Psychology, 29*, 223–252.

Cartwright, R. D. (1978, Dec.). Happy endings for our dreams. *Psychology Today*, pp. 66–77.

Case, R. B., S. S. Heller, Case, N. B., Moss, A. J., & The Multicenter Post-Infarction Research Group. (1985). Type A behavior and survival after acute myocardial infarction. *New England Journal of Medicine, 312*(12).

Casler, L. (1965). The effects of extra tactile stimulation on a group of institutionalized infants. *Genetic Psychology Monographs 71*, 137–175.

Cattell, R. B. (1965). *The scientific analysis of personality*. Baltimore: Penguin.

Cattell, R. B. (1973, July). Personality pinned down. *Psychology Today*, pp. 40–46.

Cautela, J. R. & Kearney, A. J. (1986). *The covert conditioning handbook*. New York: Springer.

Cautela, J. R., & Bennett, A. K. (1981). Covert conditioning. In R. J. Corsini (Ed.), *Handbook of innovative psychotherapies*, pp. 189–204. New York: Wiley.

Chaikin, A. (1985, Feb.). The loneliness of the long-distance astronaut. *Discover*, pp. 20–31.

Chaikin, A. L., & Derlega, V. J. (1974). *Self-disclosure*. Morristown, N. J.: General Learning Press.

Challinor, M. E. (1980, Dec.). *Science 80,* p. 27.

Chance, P. (1982, Jan.). Your child's self-esteem. *Parents.*

Chapanis, A., & Lindenbaum, L. E. "A reaction time study of four control-display linkages. *Human Factors, 1,* 1–7.

Charren, P. & Sandler, M. W. (1983). *Changing channels.* Reading, Mass.: Addison-Wesley.

Check, J. V. P., & Malamuth, N. M. (1983). Sex role stereotyping and reactions to depictions of stranger versus acquaintance rape. *Journal of Personality and Social Psychology, 45,* 344–356.

Cheek, J. & Buss, A. H. (1979). Scales of shyness, sociability and self-esteem and correlations among them. Unpublished research, University of Texas. (Cited by Buss, 1980).

Chesney, M. A., & Rosenman, R. H. (Eds.). (1985). *Anger and hostility in cardiovascular and behavioral disorders.* Washington, D.C.: Hemisphere.

Chess, S. & Thomas, A. (1986). *Know your child.* New York: Basic Books.

Chess, S., Thomas, A. & Birch, H. G. (1965). *Your child is a person: A psychological approach to parenthood without guilt.* New York: Viking.

Chomsky, N. (1968). *Language and mind.* New York: Harcourt Brace Jovanovich.

Chomsky, N. (1975). *Reflections on language.* New York: Pantheon Books.

Christian, A. G. & McDonald, J. L. (1987). Smokeless tobacco country: From nicotine dependency to oral problems and cancer. *Aviation, Space, & Environmental Medicine, 58*(2), 97–104.

Cialdini, R. B., Petty, R. E., & Cacippo. T. J. (1981). Attitude and attitude change. *Annual Review of Psychology, 32,* 357–404.

Cialdini, R. B., Vincent, J. E., Lewis, S. K., Catalan, J., Wheeler, D., & Darby, B. L. (1975). A reciprocal concessions procedure for inducing compliance. The door-in-the-face technique. *Journal of Personality and Social Psychology, 21,* 206–215.

Clark, K. B. (1965). *Dark ghetto.* New York: Harper & Row.

Clark, M. S. & Reis, H. T. (1988). Interpersonal processes in close relationships. *Annual Review of Psychology, 39,* 609–672.

Clarke-Steward, A., & Koch, J. B. (1983). *Children, development through adolescence.* New York: John Wiley & Sons.

Clearwater, Y. (1985, July). A human place in outer space. *Psychology Today,* pp. 34–43.

Cline, V. B., Croft, R. G., & Courrier, S. (1972). Desensitization of children to television violence. *Journal of Personality and Social Psychology, 27,* 360–365.

Clore, G. L. (1976). Interpersonal attraction: An overview. In *Contemporary topics in social psychology.* Morristown, N.J. General Learning Press.

Coates, D. L., & Lewis, M. (1984). Early mother-infant interaction and infant cognitive status as predictors of school performance and cognitive behavior in six-year-olds. *Child Development, 55,* 1219–1230.

Cobb, S. (1976). Social support as a moderator of life stresses. *Psychosomatic Medicine, 38,* 300–314.

Cocaine use by students declines. (1988). *Santa Barbara News-Press,* Jan. 14, A–1.

Cofer, C. N. (Ed.). (1975). *The structure of human memory.* San Francisco: W. H. Freeman.

Cohen, D. (1974). *Intelligence.* New York: M. Evans.

Cohen, J. (1970). *Secondary motivation.* Chicago: Rand McNally.

Cohen, S. (1977, Sept.). Internal opioid-like compounds. *Drug Abuse and Alcoholism Newsletter, 6*(7).

Cohen, S., Evans, G. W., Krantz, D. S., & Stokols, D. (1981). Cardiovascular and behavioral effects of community noise. *American Scientist, 69,* pp. 528–535.

Cohen, S. (1969). *The drug dilemma.* New York: McGraw-Hill.

Coleman, J. S., Hersberg, J., & Morris, M. (1977). Identity in adolescence: Present and future self-concepts. *Journal of Youth and Adolescence, 6*(1), 63–75.

Coleman, J., Butcher, J. N., & Carson, R. C. (1984). *Abnormal psychology and modern life (7th ed.).* Glenview, Ill.: Scott Foresman.

Collins, A. M., & Quillian, M. R. (1969). Retrieval time from semantic memory. *Journal of Verbal Learning and Verbal Behavior, 8,* 240–247.

Collins, J. J. (1981). Alcohol use and criminal behavior: An empirical, theoretical, and methodological overview. In J. J. Collins (Ed.), *Drinking and crime: Perspectives on the relationship between alcohol consumption and criminal behavior.* New York: Guilford.

Comfort, A. (1976). *A good age.* New York: Crown.

Comstock, G., Chaffee, S., Katzman, N., McCombs, M., & Roberts, D. (1978). *Television and human behavior.* New York: Columbia University Press.

Condon, W. S., & Sander, L. W. (1974). Neonate movement is synchronized with adult speech: Interactional participation and language acquisition. *Science, 183,* 99–101.

Cone, J. D., & Hayes, S. C. (1980). *Environmental problems/behavioral solutions.* Monterey, CA.: Brooks/Cole.

Coni, N., Davison, W., & Webster, S. (1984). *Ageing.* Oxford: Oxford University Press.

Conley, J. J. (1984). Longitudinal consistency of adult personality: Self-reported psychological characteristics across 45 years. *Journal of Personality and Social Psychology, 47,* 1325–1333.

Connors, M. M., Harrison, A. A., & Akins, F. R. (1985). *Living Aloft.* Washington, D.C.: National Aeronautics and Space Administration.

Conte, H. R., Weiner, M. B., & Plutchik, R. (1982). Measuring death anxiety: Conceptual, psychometric, and factor-analytic aspects. *Journal of Personality and Social Psychology, 43,* 775–785.

Conyne, R. K., & Clack, R. J. (1981). *Environmental assessment and design.* New York: Praeger.

Cook, S. W. (1985). Experimenting on social issues. *American Psychologist, 40,* 452–460.

Cooper, J., & Fazio, R. H. (1984). A new look at dissonance theory. *Advances in Experimental Social Psychology, 17,* 229–226.

Coopersmith, S. (1968). Studies in self-esteem. *Scientific American, 218,* pp. 96–106.

Corballis, M. C. (1980, March). Laterality and myth. *American Psychologist, 35,* 284–295.

Coren, S., & Porac, C. (1977, Nov.). Fifty centuries of right-handedness: The historical record. *Science, 198,* 631–632.

Cornsweet, T. N. (1970). *Visual perception.* New York: Academic Press.

Corteen, R. S. & Williams, T. M. (1986). Television and reading skills. In T. M. Williams (Ed.), *The impact of television: A natural experiment in three communities.* Orlando, Florida: Academic Press, 39–86.

Cowles, J. T. (1937). Food tokens as incentives for learning by chimpanzees. *Comparative Psychology, Monograph, 14*(5, Whole No. 71).

Cox, F. D. (1984). *Human intimacy.* St. Paul, Minn.: West Publishing.

Cox, T. (1979). *Stress.* Baltimore: University Park Press.

Coyle, J. T., Price, D. L., & DeLong, M. R. (1983). Alzheimer's disease: A disorder of cortical cholinergic innervation. *Science, 219,* 1184–1190.

Craig, K. (1978). Social modeling influences on pain. In R. A. Sternbach (Ed.), *The psychology of pain.* New York: Raven Press.

Craik, F. I. M. (1970). The fate of primary items in free recall. *Journal of Verbal Learning and Verbal Behavior, 9,* 143–148.

Crawley, S. B., & Sherrod, K. B. (1984). Parent-infant play during the first year of life. *Infant Behavior & Development, 7,* 65–75.

Cregler, L. L., & Mark, H. (1985). Medical Complications of Cocaine Abuse. *New England Journal of Medicine, 315*(23), 1495–1500.

Crits-Christoph, P., & Singer, J. L. (1984). An experimental investigation of the use of positive imagery in the treatment of phobias. *Imagination, Cognition and Personality, 3,* 305.

Croll, C. (1986). Personal communication.

Cronbach, L. (1970). *Essentials of Psychological testing (3rd ed.).* New York: Harper & Row.

Cross, J. G. & Guyer, M. J. (1980). *Social traps.* Ann Arbor: The University of Michigan Press.

Crowley, T. J. (1987). Clinical issues in cocaine abuse. In Fisher, S., Raskin, A. & Uhlenhuth, E. H. (Eds.), *Cocaine: Clinical and behavioral aspects.* N.Y.: Oxford University Press, 193–211.

Culver, B., & Ianna, P. (1979). *The gemini syndrome.* Tucson, AZ: Pachart Publishing.

Cumming, E., & Henry, W. E. (1961). *Growing old: The process of disengagement.* New York: Basic Books.

Cutrona, C. E., & Troutman, B. R. (1986). Social support, infant temperament and parenting self-efficacy: A mediational model of postpartum depression. *Child Development, 57,* 1507–1518.

Czeisler, C. A., Richardson, G. S., Zimmerman, J. C., Moore-Ede, M. C., & Weitzman, E. D. (1981). Entrainment of human circadian rhythms by light-dark cycles: A reassessment. *Photochemistry, Photobiology, 34,* 239–247.

Daniel, T. C., & Boster, R. S. (1978). Measuring landscape esthetics: The scenic beauty estimation method. *USDA Forestry Service Research Paper, RM-167.* Rocky Mt. Forest Range Station, Ft. Collins, Colorado, 66.

Daniel, T. L., & Esser, J. K. (1980). Intrinsic motivation as influenced by rewards, task interest, and task structure. *Journal of Applied Psychology, 65,* 566–573.

Darley, J. M., & Latane, B. (1968). Bystander intervention in emergencies: Diffusion of responsibility. *Journal of Personality and Social Psychology, 8,* 377–383.

Darwin, C. (1872). The *expression of emotion in man and animals.* Chicago: The University of Chicago Press.

Davanloo, H. (1980). *Short-term dynamic psychotherapy.* New York: Jason Aronson.

Davies, P. (1988). Alzheimer's Disease and related disorders: An overview. In M. K. Aronson (Ed.), *Understanding Alzheimer's Disease.* New York: Charles Scribner's Sons, 3–14.

Davis, D. M. (1928). Self-selection of diet by newly weaned infants. *American Journal of diseases of Children, 36,* 651–679.

Davis, J. M. (1978). Dopamine theory of schizophrenia: A two-factor theory. In L. C. Wynne, R. L. Cromwell, & S. Matthysse (Eds.), *The nature of schizophrenia: New approaches to research and treatment.*

Davis, M., McKay, M. & Eshelman, E. R. (1980). *The relaxation and stress reduction workbook.* Richmond, CA.: New Harbinger.

Deaux, K. (1985). Sex and gender. *Annual Review of Psychology, 36,* 49–81.

Deaux, K., & Emswiller, T. (1974). Explanation of successful performance on sex-linked tasks: What is skill for the male is luck for the female. *Journal of Personality and Social Psychology, 29,* 80–85.

de Bono, E. (1970). *Lateral Thinking: Creativity step by step.* New York: Harper & Row.

DeCharms, R., & Muir, M. S. (1978). Motivation: Social Approaches. *Annual Review of Psychology, 29,* 91–113.

Deese, J., & Hulse, S. J. (1967). *The psychology of learning (3rd. Ed.).* New York: McGraw-Hill.

DeFries, J. C., Plomin, R., & LaBuda, M. C. (1987). Genetic stability of cognitive development from childhood to adulthood. *Developmental Psychology, 23,* 4–12.

DeGood, D. E. (1975). Cognitive factors in vascular stress responses. *Psychophysiology, 12,* 399–401.

De Koninck, J., Gagnon, P., & Lallier, S. (1983). Sleep positions in the young adult and their relationship with the subjective quality of sleep. *Sleep, 6*(1), 52–59.

De La Cruz, F. F., & Muller, J. Z. (1983, Nov.–Dec.). Facts about Down syndrome. *Children Today, 12*(6), pp. 2–7.

Delgado, J. (1969). *Physical control of the mind.* New York: Harper & Row.

Delgado, J. (1970, May). ESB. *Psychology Today.*

Dember, W. N., & Warm, J. S. (1979). *Psychology of perception, 2nd ed.* New York: Holt.

Dement, W. (1960). The effect of dream deprivation. *Science, 131,* 1705–1707.

Dement, W. (1972). *Some must watch while some must sleep.* Stanford, CA: Stanford Alumni Association.

Denning, P. J. (1988). Blindness in designing intelligent systems. *American Scientist, 76,* 118–120.

Denning, P. J. (1987). Computer models of aids epidemiology. *American Scientist, 75,* 347–352.

Deregowski, J. B. (1972, Nov.). Pictorial perception and culture. *Scientific American,* pp. 82–88.

Desharnais, R. (1975). Sport psychology in athletic training: Programs for maximum performance. In B. S. Rushall (Ed.), *The status of psychomotor learning and sport psychology research.* Dartmouth, Nova Scotia: Sport Science Associates.

DeSpelder, L. A., & Strikland, A. L. (1983). *The last dance.* Palo Alto, CA: Mayfield Publishing Co.

Deutsch, D. (1978). Pitch memory: An advantage for the left-handed. *Science, 199,* 559–560.

Deutsch, M., & Collins, M. E. (1951). *Interracial housing;* Minneapolis: University of Minnesota Press.

Diamond, M. (1977). Human sexual development: Biological foundations for social development. In F. A. Beach (Ed.), *Human sexuality in four perspectives* (pp. 22–61). Baltimore: Johns Hopkins University Press.

Dixon, J. (1975, Sept. 30). Jeanne Dixon strikes back at scientists who knock astrology. National Star, p. 5.

Dobelle, W. H. (1977). Current status of research on providing sight to the blind by electrical stimulation of the brain. *Journal of Visual Impairment and Blindness, 71,* 290–297.

Dobelle, W. H., Mladejovsky, M. G., & Girvin, J. P. (1974). Artificial vision for the blind: electrical stimulation of visual cortex offers a hope for a functional prosthesis. *Science, 183,* 440–444.

Dollard, J., et al. (1939). *Frustration and aggression.* New Haven: Yale University Press.

Dollard, J., & Miller, N. E. (1950). *Personality and psychotherapy: An analysis in terms of learning, thinking and culture.* New York: McGraw-Hill.

Donnerstein, E. I., & Linz, D. G. (1986, Dec.). The question of pornography. *Psychology Today,* pp. 56–59.

Donohue, H. E. F. (1968). *Where should you touch?* New York: The Hearst Corporation.

Dooling, D. J., & Lachman, R. (1971). Effects of comprehension on retention of prose. *Journal of Experimental Psychology, 88,* 216–222.

Dornbush, S. M., Ritter, P. L., Leiderman, P. H., & Roberts, D. F. (1987). The relation of parenting style to adolescent school performance. *Child Development, 58*(5), 1244–1257.

Dossett, D. L., & Hulvershorn, P. (1983). Increasing technical training efficiency: Peer training via computer-assisted instruction. *Journal of Applied Psychology, 68,* 552–558.

Dovidio, J. F. (1984). Helping behavior and altruism: An empirical and conceptual overview. In L. Berkowitz (Ed.), *Advances in experimental social psychology, vol. 17.* New York: Academic Press.

Dreyfus, H. L. & Dreyfus, S. E. (1986). Mind over machine: The power of human intuition and expertise in the era of the computer. City: Macmillian/The Free Press.

Dreyfuss, J. (1985, Jan. 29). Implant liberates the deaf from silence. *Los Angeles Times,* Part V, page 1.

Driskell, J. L., & Kelly, E. L. A. (1980). A guided notetaking and study skills system for use with university freshmen predicted to fail. *Journal of Reading, 1,* 4–5.

Drowatzky, J. N. (1975). *Motor learning: Principles and practices.* Minneapolis, Minn.: Burgess.

Drug Abuse Council. (1980) *The facts about "drug abuse".* New York: The Free Press.

DSM-III-R: Diagnostic and Statistical Manual of Mental Disorders (3rd ed.). American Psychiatric Association. Washington, D. C., 1987.

Duncker, K. (1945). On problem solving. *Psychological Monographs, 58*(270).

Dunkle, T. (1982). The sound of silence. *Science 82,* pp. 30–33.

Dunner, D. L. (1985). Recent genetic studies of bipolar and unipolar depression. In J. C. Coyne (Ed.) *Essential papers on depression.* N.Y.: New York University Press, 140–149.

Durden-Smith, J., & DeSimone, D. (1984, Jan.). Hidden threads of illness. *Science Digest,* pp. 51–53.

Dutton, D. G., & Aron, A. P. (1974). Some evidence for heightened sexual attraction under conditions of high anxiety. *Journal of Personality and Social Psychology, 30,* 510–517.

Dyck, M. J. (1987). Assessing logotherapeutic constructs: Conceptual and psychometric status of Purpose in Life and Seeking of Noetic Goals tests. *Clinical Psychology, 7*(4), 439–447.

Dywan, J., & Bowers, K. S. (1983). The use of hypnosis to enhance recall. *Science, 222,* 184–185. K

Ebbinghaus, H. (1885). *Memory: A contribution to experimental psychology.* Translated by H. A. Ruger, & C. E. Bussenius, 1913. New York: New York Teacher's College, Columbia University.

Eberhardt, B. J., & Muchinsky, P. M. (1982). An empirical investigation of the factor stability of owens' biographical questionnaire. *Journal of Applied Psychology, 67,* 138–145.

Edelson, S. M. (1984). Implications of sensory stimulation in self-destructive behavior. *American Journal of Mental Deficiency, 89,* 140–145.

Egar, G. (1984). Skilled helping: A problem-management framework for helper training. In D. Larson (Ed), *Teaching Psychological Skills* (pp. 133–150). Monterey: Brooks/Cole.

Ehara, T. H. (1980, Dec.). On the electronic chess circuit., *Science 80,* pp. 78–79.

Eichorn, D. H., Hunt, J. V., & Honzik, M. P. (1981). Experience, personality and IQ: Adolescence to middle age. In D. H. Eichorn, J. A. Clausen, N. Haan, M. P. Honzik, & P. H. Mussen (Eds.), *Present and past in middle life* (pp. 89–116). New York: Academic.

Einstein, D. (1981, Feb. 26). Results of sanity trials show weakness in system. Associated Press news article, Santa Barbara News Press.

Eisenberg, N. & Miller, P. A. (1987). The relation of empathy to prosocial and related behaviors. *Psychological Bulletin, 101*(1), 91–119.

Eiser, J. R. (1980). *Cognitive social psychology.* Maidenhead, Berkshire England: McGraw-Hill (UK).

Ekman, P. (1986). *Telling Lies.* New York: Berkley Publishing Company.

Ekman, P. (1980). *The face of man: Expressions of universal emotions in a New Guinea village.* New York: Garland STPM Press.

Ekman, P., & Friesen, W. V. (1975). *Unmasking the face.* Englewood Cliffs, N.J.: Prentice-Hall.

Ekman, P., Friesen, W. V., & Bear, J. (1984). The international language of gestures. *Psychology Today,* May, 64–69.

Ekman, P., Levenson, R. W., & Friesen, W. V. (1983). Autonomic nervous system activity distinguishes among emotions. *Science, 221,* 1208–1210.

Elkind, D. (1984). *All grown up & no place to go.* Reading, Mass: Addison-Wesley.

Elkind, D. (1981). *The hurried child.* Reading Mass: Addison-Wesley.

Elkind, D. (1968, May 26). Giant in the nursery—Jean Piaget. *The New York Times Magazine.*

Ellis, A. (1987). A sadly neglected cognitive component in depression. *Cognitive Therapy & Research, 11*(1), 121–145.

Ellis, A. (1979). The practice of rational-emotive therapy in A. Ellis, & J. Whiteley (Eds.) *Theoretical and empirical foundations of rational-emotive therapy.* Monterey, CA: Brooks/Cole.

Ellis, A. (1962). *Reason and emotion in psychotherapy.* New York: Lyle Stuart.

Ellis, A. (1973, Feb.). The no cop-out therapy. *Psychology Today, 7,* pp. 56–60, 62.

Ellis, A. (1976). Rational-emotive therapy. In V. Binder, A. Binder, & B. Rimland (Eds.), Modern Therapies (pp. 21–34). Englewood Cliffs, N. J.: Prentice-Hall.

Ellis, H. C. & Hunt, R. R. (1983). *Fundamentals of human memory and cognition.* Dubuque, Iowa: Wm. C. Brown.

Engel, G. (1977, Nov.). Emotional stress and sudden death. *Psychology Today,* p. 144.

Engen, T. (1987). Remembering odors and their names. *American Scientist, 75,* 497–503.

Engle, E., & Lott, A. S. (1980). *Man in flight.* Annapolis, Maryland: Leeward Publications.

Epstein, R., Langa, R. P., & Skinner, B. F. (1981). "Self-awareness" in the pigeon. *Science, 212,* 695–696.

Erdelyi, M. H. (1974). A new look at the new look: Perceptual defense and vigilance. *Psychological Review, 81,* 1–25.

Erdelyi, M. H., & Appelbaum, A. G., (1973). Cognitive masking: The disruptive effect of an emotional stimulus upon the perception of contiguous neutral items. *Bulletin of the Psychonomic Society, 1,* 59–61.

Ericsson, K. A., & Chase, W. G. (1982). Exceptional memory. *American Scientist, 70,* 607–615.

Erikson, E. H. (1963). *Childhood and society* (2nd ed.). New York: Norton.

Ernst, C., & Angst, J. (1983). *Birth order.* New York: Springer-Verlag.

Eron, L. D. (1987). The development of aggressive behavior from the perspective of a developing behaviorism. *American Psychologist, 42,* 435–442.

Eron, L. D. (1986). Interventions to mitigate the psychological effects of media violence on aggressive behavior. *Journal of Social Issues, 42*(3), 155–169.

Etaugh, C. (1980, April). Effects of nonmaternal care on children. *American Psychologist, 35,* 309–319.

Evans, L. (1984). *Landscapes of the night.* P. Evans (Ed.), New York: Viking Press.

Evarts, E. V. (1979). Brain mechanisms of movement. *Scientific American, 241*(3), pp. 164–179.

Eysenck, H. J. (1967, June). New ways in psychotherapy. *Psychology Today,* p. 40.

Eysenck, M. W. (1984). *Attention and arousal.* New York: Academic Press.

Fantz, R. L. (1963). Pattern vision in newborn infants. *Science, 140,* 296–297.

Fantz, R. L. (1961, May). The origin of form perception. *Scientific American,* p. 71.

Faraday, A. (1972). *Dream power.* New York: Coward.

Farber, B. A. (1983). Introduction: A critical perspective on burnout. In B. A. Farber (Ed.), *Stress and burnout in the human service professions* (pp. 1–22). New York: Pergamon.

Farber, L. H. (1966, Dec. 11). Ours is the addicted society. *The New York Times Magazine.*

Farber, S. L. (1981). *Identical twins reared apart.* New York: Basic Books.

Farquhar, J. W., Fortmann, S. P., Maccoby, N., Wood, P. D., Haskell, W. L., Taylor, C. B., Flora, J. A., Solomon, D. S., Rogers, T., Adler, E., Breitrose, P., & Weiner, L. (1984). The Stanford Five City Project: An overview. In J. D. Matarazzo, S. M. Weiss, J. A. Herd, N. E. Miller, & S. M. Weiss (Eds.). *Behavioral health: A handbook of health enhancement and disease prevention.* New York: Wiley, 1154–1165.

Fast, J. (1970). *Body language.* New York: M. Evans.

Fate, IRS, link 2 women. (1983, May, 2). *Santa Barbara News-Press,* B–7.

Fehr, L. (1976). J. Piaget and S. Claus: Psychology makes strange bedfellows. *Psychological Reports, 39,* 740–742.

Feinberg, I., & Carlson, V. R. (1967). Sleep variables as a function of normal and pathological aging in man. *Journal of Psychiatric Research, 5,* 107–144.

Feingold, A. (1988). Cognitive gender differences are disappearing. *American Psychologist, 43*(2), 95–103.

Feldman, D. H., & Bratton, J. S. (1972). Relativity and giftedness: Implications for equality of educational opportunity. *Exceptional Children, 38,* 491–492.

Feldman, P. (1984). The homosexual preference. In K. Howells (Ed.) *The psychology of sexual diversity.* Oxford, U.K.: Basil Blackwell. pp. 5–41.

Feldman, R. D. (1982). *Whatever happened to the quiz kids: Perils and profits of growing up gifted.* Chicago: Chicago Review Press.

Feldman, R. S. & Quenzer, L. F. (1984). *Fundamentals of neuropsychopharmacology.* Sunderland, Mass.: Sinauer Associates.

Ferster, C. B. (1968, Feb.). The autistic child. *Psychology Today,* pp. 35–37, 61.

Ferster, C. B., Nurnberger, J. I., & Levitt, E. B. (1962). The control of eating. *Journal of Mathematics, 1,* 87–109.

Festinger, L. (1954). A theory of social comparison processes. *Human Relations, 7,* 117–140.

Festinger, L. (1957). *A theory of cognitive dissonance.* Stanford, CA: Stanford University Press.

Festinger, L., & Carlsmith, J. M. (1959). Cognitive consequences of forced compliance. *Journal of Abnormal and Social Psychology, 58,* 203–210.

Festinger, L., Schachter, S., & Back, K. (1950). *Social pressures in informal groups: A study of a housing project.* New York: Harper.

Feuerstein, M., Labbé, E. E., & Kuczmierczyk, A. R. (1986). *Health psychology: A psychobiological perspective.* New York: Plenum Press.

Feuerstein, R., Rand, Y., & Hoffman, M. B. (1980). *Instrumental enrich-*

ment: An intervention program for cognitive modifiability. Baltimore: University Park.

Fink, M. (1977). Myths of shock therapy. *American Journal of Psychiatry, 134,* 991–996.

Finkelstein, P., Wenegrat, B., & Yalom, I. (1982). Large group awareness training. *Annual Review of Psychology, 33,* 515–539.

Fischer, K. W. & Pipp, S. L. (1984). Process of cognitive development: Optimal level and skill acquisition. In R. J. Sternberg (Ed.) *Mechanisms of cognitive development.* New York: W. H. Freeman, 45–80.

Fishbein, M., & Ajzen, I. (1975). *Belief, attitude, intention, and behavior: An introduction to theory and research.* Reading, Mass.: Addison-Wesley.

Fisher, K. (1984, Dec.). Berkeley study finds stress is value-laden. *APA Monitor,* pp. 26 & 30.

Fisher, K. (1986, March). Animal research: Few alternatives seen for behavioral studies. *APA Monitor,* pp. 16–17.

Fisher, R. P. & Geiselman, R. E. (1987). Enhancing eyewitness memory with the cognitive interview. In M. M. Grunegerg, P. E. Morris, & R. N. Sykes (Eds.), *Practical aspects of memory: Current research and issues.* Chinchester, England: John Wiley & Sons, 34–39.

Fisher, S. (1973). *The female orgasm.* New York: Basic Books.

Fitzgerald, L. F., & Osipow, S. H. (1986). An occupational analysis of counseling psychology. *American Psychologist, 41,* 535–544.

Fleming, J. (1974, Jan.). Field report: The state of the apes. *Psychology Today,* p. 46.

Flint, B. M. (1978). *New hope for deprived children.* Toronto: University of Toronto Press.

Flynn, J. R. (1987). Massive IQ gains in 14 nations: What IQ tests really measure. *Psychological Bulletin, 101*(2), 171–191.

Foos, P., & Clark, M. C. (1984). *Human Learning, 2*(3).

Foreyt, J. P. (1987b). The addictive disorders. In Wilson, G. T., Franks, C. M., Kendall, P. C. & Foreyt, J. P. *Review of behavior therapy: Theory and practice, Vol. II.* New York: Guilford Press, 187–233.

Foreyt, J. P. (1987). Behavioral medicine. In Wilson, G. T., Franks, C. M., Kendall, P. C. & Foreyt, J. P. *Review of behavior therapy: Theory and practice, Vol. II.* New York: Guilford Press, 154–186.

Forgays, D. G. & Belinson, M. J. (1986). Is flotation isolation a relaxing environment? *Journal of Environmental Psychology, 6*(1), 19–34.

Foss, R. D. (1986). Using social psychology to increase altruistic behavior: Will it help?. In Saks, M. J. & Saxe, L. (Eds.), *Advances in applied social psychology, Vol. 3.* Hillsdale, N.J.: Lawrence Erlbaum, 127–151.

Foster, G., & Ysseldyke, J. (1976). Expectancy and halo effects as a result of artificially induced teacher bias. *Contemporary Educational Psychology, 1,* 37–45.

Foulkes, D. (1985). *Dreaming: A cognitive-psychological analysis.* Hillsdale, N.J.: Lawrence Erlbaum Associates.

Foulkes, D., & Schmidt, M. (1983). Temporal sequence and unit composition in dream reports from different stages of sleep. *Sleep, 6*(3), 265–280.

Fouts, R., Fouts, D., & Schoenfield, D. (1984). Sign language conversational interaction between chimpanzees. *Sign Language Studies, 42,* 1–12.

Fowler, R. L. (1982). Detection of differences in beer composition by brand and level of calorie content. *Perceptual and Motor Skills, 55,* 967–970.

Fox, P., & Oakes, W. (1984). Learned helplessness: Non contingent reinforcement in video game performance produces a decrement in performance on a lexical decision task. *Bulletin of the Psychonomic Society, 22,* 113–166.

Frank, J. D. (1973). The demoralized mind. *Psychology Today, 6*(11), pp. 22–31, 100–101.

Frankenburg, W. K., & Dodds, J. B. (1967). The Denver Developmental Screening Test." *The Journal of Pediatrics, 1,* 181–191.

Frankl, F. H. (1977). Current perspectives on ECT: A discussion. *American Journal of Psychiatry, 134,* 1014–1019.

Frankl, V. (1955). *The doctor and the soul.* New York: Knopf.

Franklin, D. (1984). Growing up short. *Science News, 125*(6), pp. 92–94.

Franklin, D. (1984, Oct. 20). Crafting sound from silence. *Science News, 126,* pp. 252–254.

Franks, C. M. (1987). Behavior therapy with children and adolescents. In Wilson, G. T., Franks, C. M., Kendall, P. C. & Foreyt, J. P. *Review of behavior therapy: Theory and practice, Vol. II.* New York: Guilford Press, 234–287.

Frederick, C. J. (1987) Psychic trauma in victims of crime and terrorism. In VandenBos, G. R. & Bryant, B. K. (Eds.) *Cataclysms, crises, and catastrophes: Psychology in action.* Washington, DC: American Psychological Association. pp. 59–108.

Freedman, J. L. (1984). Effect of television violence on aggressiveness. *Psychological Bulletin, 96,* 227–246.

Freedman, J. L. (1975). *Crowding and behavior.* San Francisco: W. H. Freeman.

Freedman, J. L., & Fraser, S. C. (1966). Compliance without pressure: The foot-in-the-door technique. *Journal of Personality and Social Psychology, 4,* 195–202.

Freize, I. H. (1987). The female victim. In VandenBos, G. R. & Bryant, B. K. (Eds.) *Cataclysms, crises, and catastrophes: Psychology in action.* Washington, DC: American Psychological Association, pp. 113–145.

Freud, S. (1900). *The interpretation of dreams.* London: Hogarth.

Freud, S. (1949). *An outline of psychoanalysis.* New York: Norton.

Friedberg, J. (1977). Shock treatment, brain damage, and memory loss: A neurological perspective. *American Journal of Psychiatry, 134,* 1010–1014.

Friedman, H. S. & Booth-Kewley, S. (1987). The "disease-prone personality." *American Psychologist, 42*(6), 539–555.

Friedman, M., & Rosenman, R. (1974). *Type A behavior and your heart.* New York: Knopf.

Friedman, M., & Stricker, E. M. (1976). The physiological psychology of hunger: A physiological perspective. *Psychological Review, 83,* 409–431.

Friedman, M., Thoresen, C. E., Gill, J. J., Powell, L. H., Ulmer, D., Thompson, L., Price, V. A., Rabin, D. D., Breall, W. S., Dixon, T., Levy, R., & Bourg, E. (1984). Alteration of Type A behavior and reduction in cardiac recurrences in postmyocardial infarction patients. *American Heart Journal, 108*(2), 237–248.

Frodi, A. N., Lamb, M. E., Leavitt, L. A., Donovan, W. L., Neff, C. & Sherry, D. (1978). Fathers' and mothers' responses to the faces and cries of normal and premature infants. *Developmental Psychology, 14,* 190–198.

Fuastman, W. O. (1976, Nov.). Aversive control of maladaptive sexual behavior: Past developments and future trends. *Psychology, 13*(4), 53–60.

Fuchs, C., & Rehm, L. (1977). A self-control behavior therapy program for depression. *Journal of Consulting and Clinical Psychology, 45,* 206–215.

Fulgosi, A., & Guilford, J. P. (1968). Short-term incubation in divergent production. *American Journal of Psychology, 7,* 1016–1023.

Fuller, B. (1969). *Utopia or oblivion: The prospects for humanity.* New York: Bantam Matrix.

Fulton, R. (1979, Jan. 21). Death and dying in a changing world. *Santa Barbara News Press.*

Furey, E. M. (1982). The effects of alcohol on the fetus. *Exceptional Children, 49,* 30–34.

Furumoto, L., & Scarborough, E. (1986). Placing women in the history of psychology. *American Psychologist, 41,* 35–42.

Gadow, K. D. (1985). Relative efficacy of pharamacological, behavioral, and combination treatments for enhancing academic performance. *Clinical Psychology Review, 5,* 513–533.

Gagne, R. M., & Fleishman, E. A. (1959). *Psychology and human performance.* New York: Holt, Rinehart & Winston.

Gagnon, J. H. (1977). *Human sexualities.* Glenview, Ill.: Scott, Foresman.

Galanter, E. (1962). Contemporary psychophysics. In *New directions in psychology,* Vol. 1 (pp. 87–156). New York: Holt, Rinehart & Winston.

Galston, A. W., & Slayman, C. L. (1983). Plant sensitivity and sensation. In G. O Abell & B. Singer (Eds.), *Science and the paranormal* (40–55). New York: Charles Scribner's Sons.

Ganster, D. C., Mayes, B. T., Sime, W. E., & Tharp, G. D. (1982). Managing organizational stress: A field experiment. *Journal of Applied Psychology, 67,* 533–542.

Garcia, J. (1977). Intelligence testing: Quotients, quotas and quackery. In J. L. Martinez (Ed.), *Chicano psychology.* New York: Academic Press.

Garcia, J., Hankins, W. G., & Rusiniak, K. W. (1974). Behavioral regulation of the milieu interne in man and rat. *Science, 185,* 824–831.

Gardner, H. (1985). *Frames of mind.* New York: Basic Books.

Gardner, H. (1975). *The shattered mind: The person after brain damage.* New York: Knopf.

Gardner, M. (1966). Dermo-optical perception: A peek down the nose. *Science, 151,* 654–657.

Gardener, M. (1977, Nov./Dec.). A skeptic's view of parapsychology. *The Humanist.*

Gardener, R. A., & Gardner, B. T. (1969). Teaching sign language to a chimpanzee. *Science, 165,* 664–672.

Gates, A. I. (1958). Recitation as a factor in memorizing. In J. Deese (Ed.), *The psychology of learning* (2nd ed.). New York: McGraw-Hill.

Gatz, M. & Pearson, C. G. (1988). Agesim revised and the provision of psychological services. *American Psychologist.* 43:3, 184–188.

Gazzaniga, M. S. (1988). *Mind matters.* Boston: Houghton Mifflin.

Gazzaniga, M. S. (1970). *The bisected brain.* New York: Plenum.

Gazzaniga, M. S., & LeDoux, J. E. (1978). *The integrated mind.* New York: Plenum.

Geiselman, R. E., Fisher, R. P., MacKinnon, D. P., & Holland, H. L. (1986). Eyewitness memory enhancement with the cognitive interview. *American Journal of Psychology, 99,* 385–401.

Geldard, F. A. (1972). *The human senses* (2nd ed.). New York: John Wiley.

Gerbner, G., & Gross, L. (1976). Living with television: The violen profile. *Journal of Communication, 26,* 173–199.

Gersh, R. D. (1982, June 20). Learning when not to shoot. *Santa Barbara News Press.*

Geschwind, N. (1975). The apraxias: neural mechanisms of disorders of learned movement. *American Scientist, 63,* 188–195.

Geschwind, N. (1979, Sept.). Specializations of the human brain. *Scientific American, 241,* pp. 180–199.

Gesell, A., et al. (1940). *The first five years of life.* New York: Harper Bros.

Gesteland, R. C. (1986). Speculations on receptor cells as analyzers and filters. *Experientia, 42,* 287–291.

Gibson, E. J., & Walk, R. D. (1960). The "Visual Cliff." *Scientific American, 202*(4), pp. 67–71.

Gilbert, A. N. & Wysocki, C. J. (1987). The smell survey results. *National Geographic,* Oct., 514–524.

Gillam, B. (1980). Geometrical illusions. *American Psychologist, 242,* 102–111.

Gilligan, C. (1982). *In a different voice.* Cambridge, Mass: Harvard University Press.

Giniger, S., Dispenzieri, A., & Eisenberg, J. (1983). Age experience, and performance on speed and skill jobs in an applied setting. *Journal of Applied Psychology, 68,* 469–475.

Ginott, H. G. (1965). *Between parent and child: New solutions to old problems.* New York: Macmillan.

Giovannoni, J. M., & Becerra, R. M. (1979). *Defining child abuse.* New York: The Free Press.

Girodo, M. (1978). *Shy? (You don't have to be!).* New York: Pocket Books.

Gladue, B. A. (1987) Psychobiological contributions. In L. Diamant (Ed.) *Male and female homosexuality: Psychological approaches.* Washington: Hemisphere Publishing.

Glaser, R. (1977, Sept./Oct.). Adapting to individual differences. *Social Policy,* pp. 27–33.

Glass, A. L., Holyoak, K. J., & Santa, J. L. (1979). *Cognition.* Reading Mass.: Addison-Wesley.

Glass, D. C. (1977). Stress, behavior patterns, and coronary disease. *American Scientist, 65,* 177–187.

Glick, D., & Hargreaves, W. A., with Drues, J., & Showstack, J. (1979). *Psychiatric hospital treatment for the 1980s: A controlled study of short versus long hospitalization.* Lexington, Mass.: Lexington Books.

Globus, G. (1987). *Dream life, wake life: The human condition through dreams.* Albany, N.Y.: State University of New York Press.

Goering, P., Wasylenki, D., Lancee, W., & Freeman, S. J. (1984). From hospital to community: Six-month and two-year outcomes for 505 patients. *Journal of Nervous & Mental Disease, 172,* 667–673.

Gold, P. E. (1987). Sweet Memories. *American Scientist, 75,* March-April, 151–155.

Goldenson, R. M. (1970b). *The encyclopedia of human behavior,* Vol. 2. Garden City, N.Y.: Doubleday. K

Goldiamond, I. (1965). Fluent and non-fluent speech (stuttering): Analysis and operant techniques for control. In L. Krasner, & L. P. Ullman (Eds.), *Research in behavior modification.* New York: Holt, Rinehart & Winston.

Goldiamond, I. (1971). Self-control procedures in personal behavior problems. In M. S. Gazzaniga, & E. P. Lovejoy (Eds.), *Good reading in psychology.* Englewood Cliffs, N.J.: Prentice-Hall.

Goldstein, E. B. (1984). *Sensation and perception.* Belmont, CA: Wadsworth.

Goldstein, M. J. (1985). *The UCLA family project.* Presented at NIMH High-Risk Consortium, San Francisco. Cited by Mirsky & Duncan, 1986.

Goleman, D. (1982, March). Staying up: The rebellion against sleep's gentle tyranny. *Psychology Today,* pp. 24–35.

Gomes-Schwartz, B., Hadley, S. W., & Strupp, H. H. (1978). Individual psychotherapy and behavior therapy. *Annual Review of Psychology, 29,* 435–471.

Gondola, J. C., & Tuckman, B. W. (1982). Psychological mood state in "average" marathon runners. *Perceptual and Motor Skills, 55,* 1295–1300.

Goodglass, H. (1980). Disorders of naming following brain injury. *American Scientist, 68,* 647–655.

Goodman, G. (1984). SASHAtapes: Expanding options for help-intended communication. In D. Larson (Ed.), *Teaching psychological skills* (pp. 271–286). Monterey: Brooks/Cole.

Goodstein, L. D. (1986). 1985–86 faculty salary survey. *APA Monitor,* March, 37.

Gordon, T. (1970). *P.E.T. parent effectiveness training: A tested new way to raise children.* New York: Peter H. Wyden.

Gorman, J. (1985, Feb.). My fair software. *Discover,* pp. 64–65.

Gottesman, I. I. (1978). Schizophrenia and genetics: Where are we? Are you sure? In L. C. Wynne, R. L. Cromwell, & S. Matthysse (Eds.), *The nature of schizophrenia: New approaches to research and treatment.* New York: Wiley.

Gottesman, I. I., & Shields, J. (1982). *The schizophrenic puzzle.* New York: Cambridge University Press.

Gottfried, A. W., & Bathurst, K. (1983). Hand preference across time is related to intelligence in young girls, not boys. *Science, 221,* 1074–1075.

Gough, H. G., Fioravanti, M., & Lazzari, R. (1983). Some implications of self versus ideal-self congruence on the revised adjective check list. *Journal of Personality and Social Psychology, 44,* 1214–1220.

Gould, R. (1975, Feb.). Growth toward self-tolerance. *Psychology Today.*

Gould, S. J. (1976). Biological potential vs. biological determinism. *Natural History, 85*(5).

Grady, D. (1986, July). Don't get jittery over caffeine. *Discover,* pp. 73–79.

Graubard, P. S., & Rosenberg, H. (1974, March). Little brother is changing you. *Psychology Today.*

Green, J. A., & Shellenberger, R. D. (1986, Sept.). Biofeedback research and the ghost in the box: A reply to Roberts. *American Psychologist,* 1003–1005.

Greenberg, J. (1977, July, 30) The brain and emotions: Crossing a new frontier. *Science News, 112*(5), pp. 74–75.

Greene, D., & Lepper, M. R. (1974, Sept.). How to turn play into work. *Psychology Today,* p. 49.

Greeno, C. G. & Maccoby, E. E. (1986). How different is the "different voice"? *Signs: Journal of Women, Culture, and Society, 11*(2), 310–316.

Greenspan, E. (1983, Aug. 28). Conditioning athlete's minds. *New York Times Magazine,* pp. 32–34.

Gregory, R. L. (1970). *The intelligent eye.* New York: McGraw-Hill.

Griffin, D. R. (1984). Animal Thinking. *American Scientist, 72,* 456–463.

Grings, W. W., & Lockhart, R. A. Effects of anxiety-lessening instructions and differential set development on the extinction of GSR. *Journal of Experimental Psychology,* 66, 292–299.

Grinspoon, L. & Bakalar, J. B. (1985). *Cocaine: A drug and its social evolution.* New York: Basic Books.

Grinspoon, L., & Bakalar, J. B. (1977). *Cocaine, a drug and its social evolution.* New York: Basic Books.

Grobstein, P., & Chow, K. L. (1975). Perceptive field development and individual experience. *Science, 190,* 352–358.

Grossman, F. K., Eichler, L. S., & Winicoff, S. A. (1980). *Pregnancy, Birth and Parenthood*. San Francisco,: Jossey-Bass.

Grossmann, K. E., & Volkmer, H. (1984). Fathers' presence during birth of their infants and paternal involvement. *International Journal of Behavioral Development*, *7*, 157–165.

Grover, S. C. (1983). *The cognitive basis of the intellect: A response to Jensen's "Bias in mental testing."* Calgary, Alberta: University of Calgary.

Guilford, J. P. (1950). Creativity. *American Psychologist*, *5*, 444–454.B K

Guilford, J. P. (1959). *Personality*. New York: McGraw-Hill.

Guilleminault, C. (1979, June). The sleep apnea syndrome. *Medical Times*, pp. 59–67.

Guilleminault, C., Passouant, P., & Dement, W. C. (1976). *Narcolepsy*. New York: Spectrum.

Gustavson, C. R., & Garcia, J. (1974, May). Pulling a gag on the wily coyote. *Psychology Today*, pp. 68–72.

Gutek, B. A. (1981, Aug.). Experiences of sexual harassment: Results from a representative survey. Paper presented at symposium of the annual convention, American Psychological Association, Los Angeles, California.

Haber, R. N. (1969). Eidetic images; with biographical sketches. *Scientific American*, *220*(12), pp. 36–44.

Haber, R. N. (1970, May). How we remember what we see. *Scientific American*, pp. 104–112.

Haber, R. N. (1974). Eidetic images. In *Image object and illusion*. San Francisco: W. H. Freeman.

Haber, R. N. (1980). How we perceive depth from flat pictures. *American Scientist*, *68*, 370–380.

Haefele, J. W. (1962). *Creativity and innovation*. New York: Reinhold.

Haier, R. J., Siegel, B. V., Nuechterlein, K. H., Hazlett, E., Wu, J. C., Paek, J. Browning, H. L., & Buchsbaum, M. S. (1988). Cortical glucose metabolic rate correlates of abstract reasoning and attention studied with positron emission tomography. *Intelligence*, *12*, 199–217.

Hales, D. (1980). *The complete book of sleep*. Reading, Mass.: Addison-Wesley.

Hall, C. (1966). *The meaning of dreams*. New York: McGraw-Hill.

Hall, C. (1974). What people dream about. In R. L. Woods, & H. B. Greenhouse (Eds.), *The new world of dreams: An anthology*. New York: Macmillan.

Hall, C., Domhoff, G. W., Blick, K. A., & Weesner, K. E. (1982). The dreams of college men and women in 1950 and 1980: A comparison of dream contents and sex differences. *Sleep*, *5*(2), 188–194.

Hall, E. T. (1966). *The hidden dimension*. Garden City, N.Y.: Doubleday.

Hall, E. T. (1974). *Handbook for proxemic research*. Washington, D.C.: Social Anthropology and Visual Communication.

Hall, G. S. (1922). *Senescence, the last half of life*. New York: Appleton-Century-Crofts.

Hall, R. G., Sachs, D. P., Hall, S. M., & Benowitz, N. L. (1984). Two-year efficacy and safety of rapid smoking therapy in patients with cardiac and pulmonary disease. *Journal of Consulting and Clinical Psychology*, *52*, 574–581.

Halonen, J. S. (1986). *Teaching critical thinking in psychology*. Milwaukee, Wis.: Alverno Productions.

Hamilton, S. B., & Waldman, D. A. (1983). Self-modification of depression via cognitive-behavioral intervention strategies: A time series analysis. *Cognitive Therapy and Research*, *7*, 99–106.

Hammer, S., & Hazelton, L. (1984, Oct.). Cocaine and the chemical brain. *Science Digest*, *92*, pp. 58–61, 100–103.

Hansel, C. E. M. (1980). *ESP and parapsychology: A critical reevaluation*. Buffalo, N.Y.: Prometheus.

Hansen, W. B., & Altman, I. (1976). Decorating personal places: A descriptive analysis. *Environmental Behavior*, *8*, pp. 491–505.

Hardin, G. (1985) *Filters against folly*. New York: Viking.

Hardin, G. (1968). The tragedy of the commons. *Science*, *162*, 1243–1248.

Hardy, A. B. (1976). *Agoraphobia: Symptoms, causes, treatment*. Menlo Park, Ca.: Terrap, Inc.

Hardyck, C., Petrinovich, L. F., & Goldman, R. (1976). Left handedness and cognitive deficit. *Cortex*, *12*, 266–278.

Hare, R. D., & Cox, D. N. (1978). Psychophysiological research on psychopathy. In W. H. Reid (Ed.), *The psychopath: A comprehensive study of anti-social disorders and behaviors*. New York: Brunner-Mazel.

Hare-Mustin, R. T. & Marecek, J. (1988). The meaning of difference. *American Psychologist*, *43*(6), 455–464.

Harlow, H. F. (1966). Learning to love. *American Scientist*, *54*, pp. 244–272.

Harlow, H. F. (1967). The young monkeys. *Psychology Today*, *1*(5), pp. 40–47.

Harlow, H. F., & Harlow, M. K. (1962). Social deprivation in monkeys. *Scientific American*, *207*, pp. 136–146.

Harlow, H. F., & Zimmerman, R. R. (1958). The development of affectional responses in infant monkeys. *Proceedings of the American Philosophical Society*, *102*, 501–509.

Harlow, J. M. (1868). Recovery from the passage of an iron bar through the head. *Massachusetts Medical Society*, *2*, 327.

Harper, (1959). *Psychoanalysis and psychotherapy*. Englewood Cliffs, N.J.: Prentice-Hall.

Harris, A. C. (1986). *Child development*. St. Paul, MN: West Publishing.

Harris, I. D. (1964). *The promised seed: A complete study of eminent first and later sons*. New York: Free Press.

Harrison, G. P. & Katz, D. L. (1987) Letter. *The Lancet*, *1*, 863.

Harrison, L. F. & Williams, T. M. (1986). Television and cognitive development. In T. M. Williams (Ed.), *The impact of television: A natural experiment in three communities*. Orlando, Florida: Academic Press, 87–142.

Hart, K. J., & Ollendick, T. H. (1985). Prevalence of bulemia in working and university women. *American Journal of Psychiatry*, *142*, 851–854.

Hartmann, E. L. (1973). *The functions of sleep*. New Haven: Yale University Press.

Hartmann, E. L. (1978). *The sleeping pill*. New Haven: Yale University Press.

Hartmann, E. L. (1981). The functions of sleep and memory processing. In W. Fishbein (Ed.) *Sleep, dreams and memory* (pp. 111–124). New York: Sp Medical & Scientific Books.

Hatch, J. A. (1987). Peer interaction and the development of social competence. *Child Study Journal*, *17*(3), 169–183.

Hatfield, E., Greenberger, D., Traupmann, J., & Lambert, P. (1982). Equity and sexual satisfaction in recently married couples. *Journal of Sex Research*, *18*, 18–32.

Hattie, J. A., Sharpley, C. F., & Rogers, H. J. (1984). Comparative effectiveness of professional and paraprofessional helpers. *Psychological Bulletin*, *95*, 534–541.

Havighurst, R. J. (1979). *Developmental tasks and education*, 4th ed. New York: David McKay Co.

Havighurst, R. J. (1961). Successful aging. *Gerontologist*, *1*, 8–13.

Havighurst, R. J. (1976). Choosing a middle path for the use of drugs with hyperactive children. *School Review*, *85*(1), pp. 60–77.

Hawkins, D. B., & Gruber, J. J. (1982). Little league baseball and players' self-esteem. *Perceptual and Motor Skills*, *55*, 1335–1340.

Hayakawa, S. I. (1965). The use and misuse of language. In R. E. Farson (Ed.), *Science and human affairs* (pp. 95–113). Palo Alto, Calif: Science and Behavior Books.

Hayes, C. (1951). *The ape in our house*. New York: Harper & Row.

Hayes, J. R. (1978). *Cognitive psychology: Thinking and creating*. Homewood, Ill.: Dorsey.

Haywood, H. C., Meyers, C. E., & Switzby, H. N. (1982). Mental retardation. *Annual Review of Psychology*, *33*, 309–342.

Hearold, S. L. (1987). Meta-analysis of the effects of television on social behavior. In G. Comstock (Ed.), *Public communication and behavior: Volume 1*. N.Y.: Academic Press.

Hearst, E. (1969). Psychology across the chess board. In *Readings in Psychology Today* (pp. 16–23). Del Mar, Calif.: CRM.

Heath, L. & Petraitis, J. (1987). Television viewing and fear of crime: Where is the mean world? *Basic & Applied Social Psychology*, *8*(1–2), 97–123.

Hebb, D. O. (1949). *Organization of behavior*. New York: Wiley.

Hebb, D. O. (1966). *A textbook of psychology* (2nd ed.). Philadelphia: Saunders.

Hebb, D. O. (1974). What psychology is about. *American Psychologist*, *29*, 71–79.

Heckhausen, J. (1987). Balancing for weaknesses and challenging developmental potential. *Developmental Psychology*, *23*(6), 762–770.

Heiby, E. M. (1983). Assessment of frequency of self-reinforcement. *Journal of Personality and Social Psychology, 44,* 1304–1307.

Heiman, J. R. (1977). A pscyhophysiological exploration of sexual arousal patterns in females and males. *Psychophysiology, 14*(3), 266–274.

Heinstein, M. I. (1963). Behavioral correlates to breast-bottle regimes under varying parent-infant relationships. *Monographs of the Society for Research in Child Development, 28*(4), 1–61.

Held, R. (1971). Plasticity in sensory-motor systems. In *Contemporary psychology*. San Francisco: W. H. Freeman.

Helfrich, A. A., Crowley, T. J., Atkinson, C. A., & Post, R. D. (1983). A clinical profile of 136 cocaine abusers. In *Problems of drug dependency, 1983*. NIDA Research Monograph Series, No. 43. Washington, D.C., United States Government Printing Office, 343–350.

Hellekson, C. & Rosenthal, N. (1987). New light on seasonal mood changes. *The Harvard Medical School Mental Health Letter, 3*(10), 4–6.

Heller, J. (1961). *Catch 22*. New York: Simon & Schuster.

Helson, H. (1964). *Adaptation-level theory*. New York: Harper & Row.

Henderson, N. D. (1982). Human behavior genetics. *Annual Review of Psychology, 33,* 403–440.

Herbert, W., & Greenberg, J. (1983, Sept. 10). Behavior: Sex roles remain. *Science News, 124,* p. 172.

Heron, W. (1957). The pathology of boredom. *Scientific American, 196,* pp. 52–56.

Herrnstein, R. J. (1979). Acquisition, generalization, and discrimination reversal of a natural concept. *Journal of Experimental Psychology: Animal Behavior Processes, 5,* 116–129.

Herrnstein, R. J., Nickerson, R. S., de Sanchez, M., & Swets, J. (1986). Teaching thinking skills. *American Psychologist, 41*(11), 1279–1289.

Herron, J. (1980). *Neuropsychology of left-handedness*. New York: Academic Press.

Hertel, P. T. (1987). Monitoring external memory. In M. M. Grunegerg, P. E. Morris, & R. N. Sykes (Eds.), *Practical aspects of memory: Current research and issues*. Chinchester, England: John Wiley & Sons, 221–226.

Hess, E. H. (1959). Imprinting. *Science, 130,* 133–141.

Hess, E. H. (1975a). *The tell-tale eye: How your eyes reveal hidden thoughts and emotions*. New York: Van Nostrand Reinhold.

Hess, E. H. (1975b, Nov.). The role of pupil size in communication. *Scientific American,* pp. 110–119.

Heussenstamm, F. K. (1971). Bumper stickers and the cops. *Transaction, 8,* pp. 32–33.

High-risk sex less common. (1987, Aug.). *APA Monitor,* p. 16.

Hilgard, E. R. (1968). *The experience of hypnosis*. New York: Harcourt Brace Jovanovich.

Hilgard, E. R. (1974, Nov.). Weapon against pain—Hypnosis is no mirage. *Psychology Today*.

Hilgard, E. R. (1977). *Divided consciousness*. New York: Wiley.

Hilgard, E. R. (1978). Hypnosis and Pain. In R. A. Sternbach (Ed.), *The psychology of pain*. New York: Raven Press.

Hilgard, E. R., & Hilgard J. R. (1983). *Hypnosis in the Relief of Pain*. Los Altos, CA: Kaufmann.

Hilton, I. (1967). Differences in the behavior of mothers toward first and later born children. *Journal of Personality and Social Psychology, 7,* 282–290.

Hite, S. (1976). *The Hite report*. New York: Macmillan.

Hobson, J. A. (1988). *The dreaming brain*. New York: Basic Books.

Hobson, J. A., & McCarley, R. W. (1977). The brain as a dream state generator: An activation-synthesis hypothesis of the dream process. *American Journal of Psychiatry, 134,* 1335–1348.

Hodgson, R., & Miller, P. (1982). *Selfwatching*. New York: Facts on File, Inc.

Hoffman, L. W. (1977). Changes in family roles, socialization, and sex differencies. *American Psychologist, 32,* 644–657.

Hoffman, M. L. (1975). Altruistic behavior and the parent-child relationship. *Journal of Personality and Social Psychology, 31,* 937–943.

Hoffman, M. L. (1977). Moral internalization: Current theory and research. In L. Berkowitz (Ed.), *Advances in experimental and social psychology* Vol. 10. New York: Academic Press.

Holden, C. (1980, Nov.). Twins reunited. *Science 80,* pp. 55–59.

Holland, J. (1985). *Making vocational choices: A theory of careers*. Englewood Cliffs, NJ: Prentice-Hall.

Holland, M. K. (1975). *Using psychology: Principles of behavior and your life*. Boston: Little, Brown.

Holmes, D. S. (1984). Meditation and somatic arousal reduction: A review of the experimental evidence. *American Psychologist, 39*(1), 1–10.

Holmes, D. S., Curtright, C. A., McCaul, K. D., & Thissen, D. (1980). Biorhythms: Their utility for predicting postoperative recuperative time, death, and athletic performance. *Journal of Applied Psychology, 65,* 233–236.

Holmes, D. S., Solomon, S., Cappo, B. M., & Greenberg, J. L. (1983). Effects of transcendental meditation versus resting on physiological and subjective arousal. *Journal of Personality and Social Psychology, 44,* 1245–1252.

Holmes, T., & Masuda, M. (1972, April). Psychosomatic syndrome. *Psychology Today,* p. 71.

Holmes, T. H., & Rahe, R. H. (1957). Social readjustment rating scale. *Journal of Psychosomatic Research*.

Honzik, M. P. (1984). Life-span development. *Annual Review of Psychology, 35,* 309–331.

Honzik, M. P. (1983). Measuring abilities in infancy: Value and limitations. In M. Lewis (Ed.), *Origins of intelligence*. New York: Plenum.

Hopkins, J., Marcus, M., & Campbell, S. B. (1984). Postpartum depression: A critical review. *Psychological Bulletin, 95,* 498–515.

Hopson, J. L. (1986, June). The unraveling of insomnia. *Psychology Today,* pp. 43–49.

Horn, J. C. (1987). Bigger pay for better work. *Psychology Today,* July, 54–57.

Horn, J. C. & Meer, J. (1987, May). The vintage years. *Psychology Today,* 76–93*ff*.

Horn, J. M., Loehlin, J. C., & Willerman, L. (1979). Intellectual resemblance among adoptive and biological relatives: The Texas adoption project. *Behavior Genetics, 9,* 177–207.

Horn, J. M., Plomine, R., & Rosenman, R. (1976). Heritability of personality traits in adult male twins. *Behavior Genetics, 6,* 17–30.

Horne, J. A., Brass, C. G., Pettitt, A. N. (1980). Circadian performance differences between morning and evening "types." *Ergonomics, 23,* 29–36.

Horne, J. A., & Staff, L. H. E. (1983). Exercise and sleep: Body-heating effects. *Sleep, 6,* 36–46.

Horowitz, F. D. & O'Brien, M. (1986). Gifted and talented children. *American Psychologist, 41*(10), 1147–1152.

Horowitz, M. J. (1970). *Image formation and cognition*. New York: Appleton-Century-Crofts.

Horwitz, W. A., Kestenbaum, C., Person, E., & Jarvik, L. (1965). Identical twin—"Idiot savants" calendar calculators. *The American Journal of Psychiatry, 121,* 1075–1079.

Hosch, H. M., & Cooper, D. S. (1982). Victimization as a determinant of eyewitness accuracy. *Journal of Applied Psychology, 67,* 649–652.

Houston, J. P. (1985). *Motivation*. New York: Macmillan.

Howard, A., Pion, G. M., Gottfredson, G. D., Flattau, P. E., Oskamp, S., Pfafflin, S. M., Bray, D. W., Y Burstein, A. G. (1986) The changing face of American psychology. *American Psychologist, 41,* 1311–1327).

Howard, K. I., Kopta, S. M., Krause, M. S., & Orlinsky, D. E. (1986). The dose-effect relationship in psychotherapy. *American Psychologist, 41,* 159–164.

Howarth, E. (1980). Birth order, family structure and personality variables. *Journal of Personality Assessment, 44,* 299–301.

Howitt, D., Craven, G., Iveson, C., Kremer, J., McCabe, J., & Rolph, T. (1977). The misdirected letter. *British Journal of Social and Clinical Psychology, 16,* 285–286.

Hoyenga, K. B., & Hoyenga, K. T. (1984). *Motivational explanations of behavior*. Monterey CA.: Brooks Cole.

Hsia, Y., & Graham, C. H. (1965). Color blindness. In C. H. Graham (Ed.), *Vision and visual perception* (pp. 395–413). New York: Wiley.

Hubel, D. H. (1979, Sept.). The brain. *Scientific American, 241,* pp. 45–53.

Hubel, D. H. (1979 b). The visual cortex of normal and deprived monkeys.

American Scientist, 67, 532–543.

Hubel, D. H., & Wiesel, T. N. (1979). Brain mechanisms of vision. *Scientific American, 241,* pp. 150–162.

Huesmann, L. R. & Eron, L. D. (1986). The development of aggression in American children as a consequence of television violence viewing. In L. R. Huesmann & L. D. Eron (Eds.), *Television and the aggressive child: A cross-national comparison.* Hillsdale, New Jersey: Lawrence Erlbaum.

Huesmann, L. R., Eron, L., Klein, L., Brice, P., & Fischer, P. (1983). Mitigating the imitation of aggressive behaviors by changing children's attitudes about media violence. *Journal of Personality and Social Psychology, 44,* 899–910.

Huesmann, L. R. & Malamuth, N. M. (1986). Media violence and antisocial behavior: An overview. *Journal of Social Issues, 42*(3) 1–6.

Hugdahl, K., & Karker, A. C. (1981). Biological vs. experimental factors in phobic conditioning. *Behavior Research and Therapy,* 19, 109–115.

Huges, J. (1974). Acquisition of a non-vocal "language" by aphasic children. *Cognition 3,* 41–55.

Hull, J. G., VanTreuren, R. R., & Virnelli, S. (1987). Hardiness and health: A critique and alternative approach. *Journal of Personality and Social Psychology, 53,* 518–530..

Humphrey, J. A., Puccio, D., Niswander, G. D., & Casey, T. M. (1972). An analysis of the sequence of selected events in the lives of a suicidal population: A preliminary report. *Journal of Nervous Mental Disorders, 154,* 137–140.

Hunt, M. (1982). *The universe within.* New York: Simon and Schuster.

Hunt, M. (1974). *Sexual behavior in the 1970s.* Chicago: Playboy Press.

Hurd, P., Johnson, C. A., Pechacek, T., Bast, L. P., Jacobs, D. R., & Luepker, R. V. (1980). Prevention of smoking in seventh grade students. *Journal of Behavioral Medicine, 3,* 15–28.

Hurst, M. W., Jenkins, C. D., & Rose, R. M. (1979). The relation of psychological stress to onset of medical illness. In C. A. Garfield (Ed.), *Stress and survival: The emotional realities of life-threatening illness.* St. Louis: C. V. Mosby.

Huston, T. L., & Levinger, G. (1978). Interpersonal attraction and relationships. *Annual Review of Psychology, 29,* 115–156.

Hutchison, M. (1984). *The book of floating.* New York: Quill.

Huxley, A. (1965). Human potentialities. In R. E. Farson (Ed.), *Science and human affairs.* Palo Alto, CA: Science and Behavior Books.

Hyde, J. S. (1984). *Understanding human sexuality.* New York: McGraw-Hill.

Hyman, R. (1977). The case against parapsychology. *The Humanist, 37,* pp. 47–49.

Iavecchia, J. H., Iavecchia, H. P. & Roscoe, S. N. (1983). The moon illusion revisited. *Aviation, Space, and Environmental Medicine, 54,* 39–46.

Ickes, W., & Turner, M. (1983). On the social advantages of having and older, opposite-sex sibling: Birth order influences in mixed-sex dyads. *Journal of Personality and Social Psychology, 45,* 210–222.

Isen, A. M., & Means, B. (1983). The influence of positive affect on decision-making strategy. *Social Cognition, 2,* 18–31.

Isenberg, P. L., & Schatzberg, A. F. (1976). Psychoanalytic contribution to a theory of depression. In J. O. Cole, A. F. Schatzberg, & S. H. Frazier (Eds.), *Depression: Biology, psychodynamics, and treatment.* New York: Plenum Press.

Isner, J. M., Estes, N. A. M, Thompson, P. D., Costanzo-Nordin, M. R., Subramanian, R., Miller, G., Katsas, G., Sweeney, K., & Sturner, W. Q. (1986). Acute cardiac events temporally related to cocaine abuse. *New England Journal of Medicine, 315*(23), 1438–1443.

Iversen, L. L. (1979, Sept.). The chemistry of the brain. *Scientific American, 241*(3), pp. 134–147.

Ivey, A. E., & Galvin, M. (1984). Microcounseling: A metamodel for counseling, theapy, business, and medical interviews. In D. Larson (Ed.), *Teaching Psychological Skills* (pp., 207–225). Monterey: Brooks/Cole.

Izard, C. E. (1977). *Human emotions.* New York: Plenum.

Jackson, B. (1973, Sept. 22). Our prisons are criminal. *New York Times Magazine,* pp. 54, 57.

Jackson, S. E. (1983). Participation in decision making as a strategy for reducing job-related strain. *Journal of Applied Psychology, 68,* 3–19.

Jacobs, B. L. (1987). How hallucinogenic drugs work. *American Scientist, 75,* 386–391.

Jacobson, L. E. (1932). The electrophysiology of mental activities. *American Journal of Psychology, 44,* 677–694.

Jacobson, S. W., et al. (1984). Neonatal correlates of prenatal exposure to smoking, caffeine, and alcohol. *Infant Behavior & Development,* 7, 253–265.

Jahn, R. G. (1982). The persistent paradox of psychic phenomena. *Proceedings of the IEEE, 70*(2), 136–166.

Janis, I. L., & Mann, L. (1965). Effectiveness of emotional role-playing in modifying smoking habits and attitudes. *Journal of Experimental Research in Personality, 1,* 84–90.

Janis, I. L., & Mann, L. (1977). *Decision making.* New York: The Free Press.

Janis, I. L., & Wheeler, D. (1978, May). Thinking clearly about career choices. *Psychology Today, 11,* pp. 66–78.

Janos, P. M. & Robinson, N. M. (1985). Psychosocial development in intellectually gifted children. In F. D. Horowitz & M. O'Brien (Eds.), *The gifted and talented: Developmental perspectives,* 149–195, Washington, DC: American Psychological Association.

Japenga, A. (1982, May 19). The birds that hunt people. *Los Angeles Times,* Part V, pp. 1,2.

Jarvik, L. F., Eisdorfer, C., & Blum, J. E. (Eds.). (1973). *Intellectual functioning in adults.* New York: Springer.

Jarvik, E. M. (1964). Ciba found. In H. Steinberg et at., *Symposium of Animal Pharmacology Drug Action.*

Jehu, D. (1984) Sexual inadequacy. In K. Howells (Ed.) *The psychology of sexual diversity.* Oxford, U.K.: Basil Blackwell. pp. 135–160.

Jellinik, E. M. (1960). *The disease concept of alcoholism.* New Haven: Hill House Press.

Jemmott, J. B., III, Borysenkco, J. Z., Borysenko, M., McDlelland, D. C., Chapman, R., Meyer, D., & Bensen, H. (1983, June 25). Academic stress, power motivation, and decrease in secretion rate of salivary secretory immunoglobulin A. *The Lancet, 1:* 839, 1400–1402.

Jemmott, J. B. III, & Locke, S. E. (1984). Psychological factors, immunologic mediation, and human susceptibility to infectious disease: How much do we know? *Psychological Bulletin, 95,* 78–108.

Jenkins, J. G., & Dallenbach, K. M. (1924). Oblivescence during sleep and waking. *American Journal of Psychology, 35,* 605–612.

Jensen, M. D., Benson, R. C., & Bobak, I. M. (1981). *Maternity care. The nurse and the family* (2nd ed.). St. Louis: Mosby.

Jerome, L. E. (1975). Astrology: Magic or science? In *Objections to astrology,* Prometheus Books.

Jewell, L. N. (1985). *Contemporary industrial/organizational psychology.* St. Paul: West.

John, E. R. (1967). *Mechanisms of memory.* New York: Academic Press.

Johnson, D. W. & Johnson, R. T. (1987). *Learning together and alone: Cooperive, competitive, and individualistic learning.* Englewood Cliffs, NJ: Prentice-Hall.

Johnson, J. J. (1975). Sticking with first responses on multiple-choice exams: For better or for worse? *Teaching of Psychology,* 2(4).

Johnson, L., Naitoh, P., Lubin, A., & Moses, J. Sleep stages and performance. In W. P. Colquhoun (Ed.). *Aspects of human efficiency* (pp. 81–100). London: English University Press.

Johnson, M. K. & Hasher, L. (1987). Human learning and memory. *Annual Review of Psychology, 38,* 631–668.

Johnson, P. C., Jr. (1984). Space medicine. *American Scientist, 72,* 495–498.

Johnson, S. M., & White, G. (1971). Self-observation as an agent of behavioral change. *Behavior Therapy, 2,* 488–497.

Johnston, W. A. & Dark, V. J. (1986). Selective attention. *Annual Review of Psychology, 37,* 43–75.

Jones, E. (1953). *The life and work of Sigmund Freud.* New York: Basic Books.

Jones, E. E., & Nisbett, R. E. (1971). The actor and observer: Divergent perceptions of the causes of behavior. In E. E. Jones, D. E. Kanouse,

H. H. Kelley, R. E. Nisbett, S. Valins, & B. Weiner (Eds.). *Attribution: Perceiving the causes of behavior*. Morristown, N.J.: General Learning Press.

Jones, W. R., & Ellis, N. R. (1962). Inhibitory potential in rotary pursuit acquisition. *Journal of Experimental Psychology, 63*, 534–537.

Jospe, M. (1978). *The placebo effect in healing*. Lexington, Mass.: Lexington Books.

Jourard, S. M. (1963). *Personal adjustment* (2nd ed.). New York: Macmillan.

Jourard, S. M. (1966). An exploratory study of body-accessibility. *British Journal of Social and Clinical Psychology, 5*, 221–231.

Jourard, S. M. (1974). *Healthy personality*. New York: Macmillan.

Joy, L. A., Kimball, M. M., & Zabrack, M. L. (1986). Television and aggressive behavior. In T. M. Williams (Ed.), *The impact of television: A natural experiment involving three towns*. N.Y.: Academic Press, 303–360.

Joyce, C. (1988, Feb.). This machine wants to help you. *Psychology Today*, 44–50.

Joyce, C. (1984, May). Space travel is no joyride. *Psychology Today*, pp. 30–37.

Judson, A. I., & Cofer, C. N. (1956). Reasoning as an associative process: I. "direction" in a simple verbal problem. *Psychological Reports, 2*, 469–476.

Julesz, B. (1971). *Foundations of cyclopean perception*. Chicago: University of Chicago Press.

Julesz, B. (1975, April). Experiments in the visual perception of texture. *Scientific American, 232*, pp. 34–43.

Julien, R. M. (1985). *A primer of drug action* (4th ed.). San Francisco: Freeman.

Kagan, J. (1969). *Personality development*. New York: Harcourt, Brace, Jovanovich.

Kagan, J. (1971). *Change and continuity in infancy*. New York: Wiley.

Kagan, J. (1976). Emergent themes in human development. *American Scientist, 64*, 186–196.

Kagan, J., & Klein, R. E. (1973). Cross-cultural perspectives on early development. *American Psychologist, 28*, 947–961.

Kahneman, D., Slovic, P., & Tversky, A. (1982). *Judgment under uncertainty: Heuristics and Biases*. Cambridge: Cambridge University Press.

Kahneman, D., & Tversky, A. (1973). On the psychology of prediction. *Psychological Review, 80*, 237–251.

Kahneman, D., & Tversky, A. (1972). Subjective probability: A judgment of representativeness. *Cognitive Psychology, 3*, 430–454.

Kales, A., & Kales, J. (1973). Recent advances in the diagnosis and treatment of sleep disorders. In G. Usdin (Ed.). *Sleep research and clinical practice*. New York: Brunner/Mazel.

Kaluger, G., & Kaluger, M. F. (1984). *Human Development*. St. Louis: Times Mirror/Mosby.

Kamin, L. J. (1981). *The intelligence controversy*. New York: Wiley.

Kamin, L. J. (1985, Oct.). Genes and behavior: The missing link. *Psychology Today*, pp. 76–78.

Kamiya, J. (1968). Conscious control of brain waves. *Psychology Today 1*, pp. 57–66.

Kandel, E. R. (1976). *Cellular basis of behavior: An introduction to behavioral neurobiology*. San Francisco: Freeman.

Kanfer, F. H., & Goldfoot, D. A. (1966). Self-control and tolerance of noxious stimulation. *Psychological Reports, 18*, 79–85.

Kaplan, H. S. (1974). *The new sex therapy*. New York: Brunner/Mazel.

Kaplan, M. (1983). The issue of sex bias in DSM-III: Comments on the articles by Spitzer, Williams, and Kass. *American Psychologist, 38*, 802–803.

Kaplan, P. S., & Stein, J. (1984). *Psychology of adjustment*. Belmont, CA.: Wadsworth.

Kapleau, P. (1966). *The three pillars of Zen*. New York: Harper & Row.

Karlins, M., Coffman, T. L., & Walters, G. (1969). On the fading of social stereotypes: Studies in three generations of college students. *Journal of Personality and Social Psychology, 13*, 1–16.

Kasamatsu, A., & Hirai, T. (1966). An electroencephalographic study of Zen meditation (Zazen)." *Folia Psychiatria et Neurologia Japonica, 20*, 315–336. Reprinted in Tart, *Altered states of consciousness*.

Kastenbaum, R., & Aisenberg R. (1972). *The psychology of death*. New York: Springer.

Kassarjian, H. H. (1982). Consumer psychology. *Annual Review of Psychology, 33*, 619–649.

Katahn, M. (1984). *Beyond diet*. New York: W. W. Norton.

Katz, B. J. (1972). Finding psychiatric help can be traumatic itself. *The National Observer*.

Katzmann, R. (1988). Research directions in Alzheimer's Disease: Advances and opportunities. In M. K. Aronson (Ed.), *Understanding Alzheimer's Disease*. New York: Charles Scribner's Sons, 345–357.

Kaufman, J. & Zigler, E. (1987). *American Journal of Orthopsychiatry, 57*(2), 186–192.

Kazdin, A. E. (1975). *Behavior modification in applied settings*. Homewood, Ill.: Dorsey Press.

Kearney, M. (1984). A comparison of motivation to avoid success in males and females. *Journal of Clinical Psychology, 40*, 1005–1007.

Keating, J. P., & Loftus, E. F. (1981, June). The logic of fire escape. *Psychology Today*, pp. 14–19.

Keefe, F. J. (1982). Behavioral assessment and treatment of chronic pain: Current status and future directions. *Journal of Consulting and Clinical Psychology, 50*, 896–911.

Keeffe, P. (1977, Sept.). Ice after death. *Novus*, pp. 29–33.

Kelley, H. H. (1950). The warm-cold variable in first impressions of persons. *Journal of Personality, 18*, 431–439.

Kelley, H. H. (1967). Attribution in social psychology. *Nebraska Symposium on Motivation, 15*, 192–238.

Kelley, H. H. (1971). *Attribution in social interaction*. Morristown, N.J.: General Learning Press.

Kemeny, A., & Maltzman, I. (1987). *The role of individual differences in mental practice*. Paper presented at the Western Psychological Association Convention, Long Beach, CA, 1987.

Kemp, M. (1988). Fountains of lead. *Discover*, May, 20.

Kendall, P. C. (1987). Cognitive processes and procedures in behavior therapy. In, Wilson, G. T., Franks, C. M., Kendall, P. C. & Foreyt, J. P. *Review of behavior therapy: Theory and practice, Vol. II*. New York: Guilford Press, 114–153.

Kendrick, D. T. & MacFarlane, S. W. (1986). Ambient temperature and horn honking: A field study of the heat/aggression relationship. *Environment and Behavior, 18*(2), 1986, 179–191.

Kennedy, J. M. (1983). What can we learn about pictures from the blind? *American Scientist, 71*, 19–26.

Kennell, J. H., & Klaus, M. H. (1984). Mother-infant bonding: Weighing the evidence. *Developmental Review, 4*, 275–282.

Kessen, W. & Cahan, E. D. (1986). A century of psychology: From subject to object to agent. *American Scientist, 74*, 640–649.

Kety, S. S. (1979, Sept.). Disorders of the human brain. *Scientific American, 241*, pp. 202–214.

Key, B. W. (1980). *The clam-plate orgy and other subliminal techniques for manipulating your behavior*. Englewood Cliffs, NJ: Prentice-Hall.

Keys, A., Brozek, J., Henschel, A., Mickelson, O., & Taylor, H. L. (1950). *The biology of human starvation*. Minneapolis: University of Minnesota Press.

Kiell, N. (Ed.). (1973). *The psychology of obesity: Dynamics and treatment*. Springfield, Ill.: Charles C Thomas.

Kihlstrom, J. F. (1985). Hypnosis. *Annual Review of Psychology 36*, (385–418).

Kimball, M. M. (1986). Television and sex-role attitudes. In T. M. Williams (Ed.), *The impact of television: A natural experiment in three communities*. Orlando, Florida: Academic Press, 265–301.

Kimble, G. A. (1961). *Hilgard and Marquis' conditioning and learning* (2nd ed.). New York: Appleton-Century-Crofts.

Kimmel, D. C. (1988). Ageism, psychology, and public policy. *American Psychologist, 43:3*, 175–178.

Kimura, D. (1985, Nov.). Male brain, female brain: The hidden difference. *Psychology Today*, pp. 50–58.

King, H. E. (1961). Psychological effects of excitation in the limbic system. In D. E. Sheer (Ed.). *Electrical stimulation of the brain*. Austin: University of Texas Press.

Kinsey, A., Pomeroy, W., & Martin, C. (1948). *Sexual behavior in the human male*. Philadelphia: Saunders.

Kinsey, A., Pomeroy, W., & Martin, C. (1953). *Sexual behavior in the human female*. Philadelphia: Saunders.

Kipnis, D. (1987). Psychology and behavioral technology. *American Psychologist, 42,* 30–36.

Kitcher, P. (1985). *Vaulting ambition: Sociolobiology and the quest for human nature*. Cambridge, Mass: MIT Press.

Klatzky, R. L. (1980). *Human memory structures and processes,* (2nd ed.). San Francisco: W. H. Freeman.

Klaus, M. H., & Kennell, J. H. (1982). *Parent-infant bonding*. St. Louis: Mosby.

Klausmeir, H. J., & Goodwin, W. (1975). *Learning and human abilities* (4th ed.). New York: Harper & Row.

Kleinke, C. L. (1986). *Meeting and understanding people*. New York: W. H. Freeman and Company.

Kleinke, C. L. (1978). *Self-perception: The psychology of personal awareness*. San Francisco: W. H. Freeman.

Kleinknecht, R. A. (1986) *The anxious self: Diagnosis and treatment of fears and phobias*. New York: Humans Sciences Press.

Kleitman, N. (1982). Basic rest-activity cycle—22 years later. *Sleep, 5,* 311–317.

Kleitman, N. (1963). *Sleep and wakefulness* (2nd ed.). Chicago: University of Chicago Press.

Kleitman, N., & Kleitman, E. (1953). Effect of non-24-hour routines of living on oral temperature and heart rate. *Journal of Applied Physiology, 6,* 283–291.

Klinnert, M. D. (1984). The regulation of infant behavior by maternal facial expression. *Infant Behavior & Development, 77,* 447–465.

Knapp, M. L. (1978). *Nonverbal communication in human interaction* (2nd ed.) New York: Holt, Rinehart and Winston.

Knight, R. P. (1949). A critique of the present status of the psychotherapies. *Bulletin of the New York Academy of Medicine, 25,* 100–114.

Knox, D. (1984). *Human sexuality*. St. Paul: West.

Kohlberg, L. (1981a). *Essays on moral development. Vol. 1. The philosophy of moral development*. San Francisco: Harper.

Kohlberg, L. (1981b). *The meaning and measurement of moral development*. Worcester, Mass: Clark University Press.

Kohlberg, L. (1976). Moral stages and moralization: The cognitive-developmental approach. In T. Lickona (Ed.), *Moral development and behavior*. New York: Holt, Rinehart & Winston.

Kohlberg, L. (1969). The cognitive-developmental approach to socialization. In A. Goslin (Ed.). *Handbook of socialization theory and research*. Chicago: Rand McNally.

Kohler, I. (1962). Experiments with goggles. *Scientific American,* Offprint No. 465, pp. 62–72. K

Kohler, W. (1925). *The mentality of apes*. New York: Harcourt Brace Jovanovich.

Kohn, A. (1988). Schock therapy makes a comeback. *Los Angeles Times,* March 21, 1988, Part II, 5.

Kohn, A. (1988). Make love not war. *Psychology Today,* June, 35–38.

Kohn, A. (1987). Art for art's sake. *Psychology Today,* September, 52–57.

Kolata, G. (1983). Braingrafting work shows promise. *Science, 221,* 1277.

Koocher, G. P. (1977). Bathroom behavior and human dignity. *Journal of Personality and Social Psychology, 35,* 120–121.

Koop, C. E. (1988a). *The health consequences of smoking: Addiction*. United States Surgeon General's Report Washington D.C.: United States Government Printing Office.

Koop, C. E. (1988b). *Understanding AIDS*. HHS Publication No. (CDC) HHS-88-8404. U.S. Department of Health and Human Services, Rockville, MD.

Kopp, C. B., & Parmelee, A. H. (1979). Prenatal and perinatal influences on infant behavior. In J. D. Ofsky (Ed.). *Handbook of infant development*. New York: John Wiley.

Korte, C., & Milgram, S. (1970). Acquaintance networks between racial groups. *Journal of Personality and Social Psychology, 15,* 101–108.

Koss, M., Gidycz, C. A., & Wisniewski, N. (1987). The scope of rape: Incidence and prevalence of sexual aggression and victimization in a national sample of higher education students. *Journal of Consulting and Clinical Psychology, 55*(2), 162–170.

Kosslyn, S. M. (1983). *Ghosts in the mind's machine*. New York: W. W. Norton.

Kosslyn, S. M. (1975). Information representation in visual images. *Cognitive Psychology, 7,* 341–370.

Kosslyn, S. M. (1985). Stalking the mental image. *Psychology Today,* May, 23–28.

Kosslyn, S. M., Ball, T. M., & Reiser, B. J. (1978). Visual images preserve metric spatial information: Evidence from studies of image scanning. *Journal of Experimental Psychology: Human Perception and Performance, 4,* 47–60.

Kottler, J. A., & Brown, R. W. (1985). *Introduction to therapeutic counseling*. Monterey: Brooks/Cole.

Koukkou, M., & Lehmann, D. (1968). EEG and memory storage in sleep experiments with humans. *Electroencephalography and Clinical Neurophysiology, 25,* 455–462.

Krebs, D., & Adinolfi, A. A. (1975). Physical attractiveness, social relations, and personality style. *Journal of Personality and Social Psychology, 31,* 245–253.

Krech, D., Rosenzweig, M. R., & Bennett, E. L. (1962). Relations between brain chemistry and problem solving among rats raised in enriched and impoverished environments. *Journal of Comparative and Physiological Psychology, 55,* 801–807.

Krieger, D. T. (1983). Brain peptides: What, where, and why? *Science, 222,* 975–985.

Kristt, D. A., & Engel, B. T. (1975). Learned control of blood pressure in patients with high blood pressure. *Circulation, 51,* 370–378.

Kroll, N. E. A., Schepeler, E. M. & Angin, K. T. (1986). Bizarre imagery: The misremembered mnemonic. *Journal of Experimental Psychology: Learning, Memory, and Cognition. 12,* 42–53.

Kruger, L., & Liebeskind, J. C. (eds.). (1984). *Advances in pain research and therapy*. New York: Raven Press.

Kubler-Ross, E. (1975). *Death: The final stage of growth*. Englewood Cliffs, N. J.: Prentice-Hall.

Kulik, J. A., Bangert-Drowns, R. L., & Kulik, C. C. (1984). Effectiveness of coaching for aptitude tests. *Psychological Bulletin, 95,* 179–188.

Kulik, J. A., Kulik, C. C., & Cohen, P. A. (1980). Effectiveness of computer-based college teaching: A meta-analysis of findings. *Review of Educational Research, 50,* 525–544.

Kunst-Wilson, W., & R. Zajonc. (1980). Affective discrimination of stimuli that cannot be recognized. *Science, 207,* 557–558.

Kushe, L. (1975). *The Bermuda Triangle mystery—Solved*. New York: Warner Books.

Labbe, R., Firl, A., Jr., Mufson, E. J., & Stein, D. G. (1983). Fetal brain transplants: Reduction of cognitive deficits in rats with frontal cortex lesions. *Science, 221,* 470–472.

La Berge, S. P. (1980) Lucid dreaming as a learnable skill: A case study. *Perceptual and Motor Skills, 51,* 1039–1042.

La Berge, S. P. (1981b, January). Lucid dreaming: Directing the action as it happens. *Psychology Today,* 48–57.

La Berge, S. P. (1985). *Lucid dreaming*. Los Angeles: J. P. Tarcher.

La Berge, S. P., Nagel, L. E., Dement, W. C., & Zarcone, V. (1981a). Lucid dreaming verified by voluntional communication during REM sleep. *Perceptual and Motor Skills, 52,* 727–732.

Labov, W. (1973). The boundaries of words and their meanings. In C. J. N. Bailey & R. W. Shuy (Eds.) *New Ways of analyzing variation in English*. Washington, D.C.: Georgetown University Press.

Labovitz, S., & Hagedorn, R. (1971). An analysis of suicide rates among occupational categories. *Social Inquiry, 41,* 67–72.

Lagerspetz, K. (1981). Coming aggressions studies in infra-humans and man. In P. F. Brain & D. Benton (Eds.), *Multidicidiplinary approaches to aggression research*, pp. 389–400. New York: Elsevier/North-Holland.

Laing, R. D. (1970). *The divided self*. New York: Pantheon.

Laing, R. D. (1967). *The politics of experience*. New York: Pantheon.

Laird, J. D. (1984). The real role of facial response in the experience of emotion. *Journal of Personality and Social Psychology, 47*, 909–917.

Laird, J. D. (1974). Self-attribution of emotion: the effects of expressive behavior on the quality of emotional experience. *Journal of Personality and Social Psychology, 29*, 475–486.

Lake, A. (1973). Get thin, stay thin. *McCalls, 100*(4).

Landers, S. (1986). Judge reiterates I.Q. test ban. *APA Monitor*, December, 18.

Landis, D. (1980, Dec.). A scan for mental illness. *Discover*, pp. 26–27.

Landy, F. J., & Trumbo, D. A. (1980). Psychology of work behavior. Homewood, Ill.: Dorsey.

Lang, P. J., & Melamed, B. G. (1969). Avoidance conditioning therapy of an infant with chronic ruminative vomiting. *Journal of Abnormal Psychology, 74*, 1–8.

Langer, E. J., & Piper, A. I. (1987). Prevention of mindblindness. *Journal of Personality and Social Psychology, 53*, 280–287.

Last, C. G., Barlow, D. H., & O'Brian, G. T. (1984). Precipitants of agoraphobia: Role of stressful life events. *Psychological Reports, 54*, 567–570.

Latane, L., Nida, S. A., & Wilson, D. W. (1981). The effects of group size on helping behavior. In J. P. Rushton & R. M. Sorrentino (Eds.), *Altruism and helping behavior: Social, personality and developmental perspectives*. Hillsdale, NJ: Erlbaum.

Laudenslager, M. L., Ryan, S. M., Drugan, R. C., Hyson, R. L., & Maier, S. F. (1983). Coping and immunosuppression: Inescapable but not escapable shock suppresses lymphocyte proliferation. *Science, 221*, 568–570.

Laurence, J., & Perry, C. (1983). Hypnotically created memory among highly hypnotizable subjects. *Science, 222*, 523–524.

Lazarus, A. H. (1964). The treatment of chronic frigidity by systematic desensitization. In H. J. Eysenck (Ed.). *Experiments in behavior therapy*. New York: Pergamon.

Lazarus, R. S. (1975). A cognitively oriented psychologist looks at feedback. *American Psychologist, 30*, 553–561.

Lazarus, R. S. (1981, July). Little hassles can be hazardous to health. *Psychology Today*, pp. 58–62.

Lazarus, R. S. (1981). The stress and coping paradigm. In C. Eisdorfer, D. Cohen, A. Kleinman, & P. Maxim (Eds.). *Models for clinical psychopathology*. New York: Spectrum.

Lazarus, R. S. (1984). The trivialization of distress. In B. L. Hammonds & C. J. Scheirer (Eds.), *Psychology and Health*. Washington, D. C.: American Psychological Association. pp. 12 5–14.

Lazarus, R. S., DeLongis, A., Folkman, S., & Gruen, R. (1985). Stress and adaptational outcomes. *American Psychologist, 40*, 770–779.

Lazarus, R. S., & Folkman, S. (1984). *Stress, appraisal, and coping*. New York: Springer.

Leboyer, F. (1975). *Birth without violence*. New York: Knopf.

Lee, M., Zimbardo, P. G., & Bertholf, M. (1977, Nov.). Shy murderers. *Psychology Today*.

Lee, T., & Seeman, P. (1980). Elevation of brain neuroleptic/dopamine receptors in schizophrenia. *American Journal of Psychiatry, 137*, 191–197.

Leeper, R. W. (1935). A study of a neglected portion of the field of learning: The development of sensory organization. *Pedagogical Seminary and Journal of Genetic Psychology, 46*, 41–75.

Lefkowitz, M., Blake, R. R., & Mouton, J. S. (1955). Status factors in pedestrian violation of traffic signals. *Journal of Abnormal and Social Psychology, 51*, 704–706.

Le Magnen, J. (1980). The body energy regulation: The role of three brain responses to glucopenia. *Neuroscience and Biobehavioral Reviews, 4*, 65–72.

Lemley, B. (1986). I'm not a nerd. *Parade Magazine*, June, 22, 8–9.

Lenfant, C., & Schweizer, M. (1985). Contributions of health-related biobehavioral research to the prevention of cardiovascular diseases. *American Psychologist, 40*, 217–220.

Lepper, M. R. (1985). Microcomputers in Education. American Psychologist, 40, 1–18.

Lerner, R. M., & Shea, J. A. (1982). Social behavior in adolescence. In B. B. Wolman, G. Stricker, S. J. Ellman, P. Keith-Spiegel, & D. S. Palermo (Eds.), *Handbook of developmental psychology*, pp. 503–525. Englewood Cliffs, NJ: Prentice-Hall.

Lester, D. (1971b). Relationship of mental disorder to suicidal behavior. *New York State Journal of Medicine, 71*, 1503–1505.

Lester, D. (1972). *Why people kill themselves: A summary of research on suicidal behavior*. Springfield, Ill.: Charles C. Thomas.

Lester, G., & Lester, D. (1971). *Suicide: The gamble with death*. Englewood Cliffs, N.J.: Prentice-Hall.

Lettvin, J. Y. (1961). Two remarks on the visual system of the frog. In W. Rosenblith (Ed.). *Sensory communication*. Cambridge, Mass: MIT Press.

Levanthal, H. & Tomarken, A. J. (1986). "Emotion: Today's problems." *Annual Review of Psychology, 37*, 565–610.

Leveton, E. (1977). *Psychodrama for the timid clinician*. New York: Springer.

Levin, R. J., & Levin, A. (1975, Oct.). The redbook report on premarital and extramarital sex. *Redbook*, p. 38.

Levin, R. J., & Levin, A. (1975, September). Sexual pleasure: The preference of 100,000 women. *Redbook*, 51.

Levine, J. D., Gordon, N. C., & Fields, H. L. (1979). The role of endorphins in placebo analgesia. In J. J. Bonica, J. C. Liseskind, & D. Albe-Fessard (Eds.). *Advances in pain research and therapy* (Vol. 3). New York: Raven Press.

Levinger, G. (1986). Editor's Page. *Journal of Social Issues, 42*(3).

Levinson, D. J. (1986). A conception of adult development. *American Psychologist, 41*(1), 3–13.

Levinson, D. J. with Darrow, C. N., Klein, E. B., Levinson, M. H., & McKee, B. (1979). *The seasons of a man's life*. New York: Alfred A. Knopf.

Levitt, R. A. (1977). Recreational drug use and abuse. In D. C. Rimm, & J. W. Somervill (Eds.). *Abnormal psychology*. New York: Academic Press.

Levy, J., & Redd, M. (1976). Cerebral organization. *Science*, 337–339.

Lewin, K. (1935). *A dynamic theory of personality*. New York: McGraw-Hill.

Lewin, R. (1974, Oct. 5). The brain through a cat's eyes. *Saturday Review/World*.

Lewinsohn, P. M. (1985). A behavioral approach to depression. In J. C. Coyne (Ed.) *Essential papers on depression*. New York: New York University Press, 150–172.

Lewinsohn, P. M., & Hoverman, H. M. (1982). Depression. In A. S. Bellack, M. Hersen, & A. E. Kazdin (Eds.) *International handbook of behavior modification and therapy*. New York: Plenum Press.

Lewis, M., & Brooks-Gunn, J. (1979). *Social cognition and the acquisition of self*. New York: Plenum Press.

Lichtenstein, E. (1982). The smoking problem: A behavioral perspective. *Journal of Consulting and Clinical Psychology, 50*, 804–819.

Lichtenstein, E., & Brown, R. A. (1982). Current trends in the modification of cigarette dependence. In A. S. Bellack, M. Hersen, & A. E. Kazdin (Eds.), *International handbook of behavior modification and therapy*. New York: Plenum.

Lieberman, D. A. (1979). Behaviorism and the mind: A (limited) call for a return to introspection. *American Psychologist, 34*, 319–333.

Lieberman, R. P., Fearn, C. H., Derisi, W., Roberts, J., & Carmona, M. (1976). The credit-incentive system: Motivating the participation of patients in a day hospital. *British Journal of Clinical Psychology, 15*.

Liebert, R. M., Neale, J. M., & Davidson, E. S. (1973). *The early window: Effects of television on children and youth*. Elmsford, N.Y.: Pergamon Press.

Lilly, J. C. (1972). *The center of the cyclone*. New York: Julian Press.

Lindsley, D. B., Bowden, J., & Magoun, H. W. (1949). Effect upon the EEG of acute injury to the brain stem activating system. *EEG and Clinical Neurophysiology, 1*, 475–486.

Lindsley, J. G., Hartmann, E. L., & Mitchell, W. (1983). Selectivity in response to L-tryptophan among insomniac subjects: A preliminary report. *Sleep, 6*(3), 247–256.

Linton, M. (1979, July). I remember it well. *Psychology Today*, pp. 81–86.

Lintz, D., Donnerstein, E., & Penrod, S. (1984). The effects of multiple exposures to filmed violence against women. *Journal of Communication, 34,* 130–147.

Lipinski, E., & Lipinski, B. G. (1970). Motivational factors in psychedelic drug use by male college students. In R. E. Hormon, & A. M. Fox (Eds.). *Drug awareness.* New York: Discuss Books, Avon.

Lipscomb, D. M. (1974). *Noise: The unwanted sounds.* Chicago: Nelson-Hall.

Loehlin, J. C., Willerman, L., & Horn, J. M. (1988). Human behavior genetics. *Annual Review of Psychology, 39,* 101–133.

Loevinger, J., & Knoll, E. (1983). Personality: Stages, traits, and the self. *Annual Review of Psychology, 34,* 195–222.

Loftus, E. F. (1979, Nov.). Words that could save your life. *Psychology Today,* pp. 102, 105–6.

Loftus, E. (1977). Shifting human color memory. *Memory & Cognition, 5,* 696–699.

Loftus, E. (1979). *Eyewitness testimony.* Cambridge, Mass.: Harvard University Press.

Loftus, E. (1980). *Memory.* Reading, Mass.: Addison-Wesley.

Loftus, E., & Loftus, G. (1980). On the permanence of stored information in the human brain. *American Psychologist, 35,* 409–420.

Loftus, E., & Monahan, J. (1980). Trial by data: Psychological research as legal evidence. *American Psychologist, 35,* 270–283.

Loftus, E., & Palmer, J. C. (1974). Reconstruction of automobile destruction: An example of interaction between language and memory. *Journal of Verbal Learning and Verbal Behavior, 13,* 585–589.

Loftus, G. R. & Mackworth, N. H. (1978). Cognitive determinants of fixation location during picture viewing. *Journal of Experimental Psychology: Human Perception and Performance, 4,* 565–572.

Lord, L. (1985). Morality. *U. S. News & World Report,* December 9, 52–59.

Lorenz, K. (1937). Imprinting. *The Auk, 54,* pp. 245–273.

Lorenz, K. (1962). *King Solomon's ring.* New York: Time.

Lorenz, K. (1966). *On aggression.* Translated by M. Kerr-Wilson. New York: Harcourt Brace Jovanovich.

Lorenz, K. (1974). *The eight deadly sins of civilized man.* Translated by M. Kerr-Wilson. New York: Harcourt Brace Jovanovich.

Los Angeles Times. (1981, Sept. 24). Man tells how rod ran through head, p. 3.

Louis, A. M. (1978, April). Should you buy biorhythms? *Psychology Today,* pp. 93–96.

Lovaas, O., & Simmons, J. (1969). Manipulation of self-destruction in three retarded children. *Journal of Applied Behavior Analysis, 2,* 143–157.

Luborsky, L., Crits-Christoph, P., McLellan, A. T., Woody, G. et al., (1986). Do therapists vary much in their success? *American Journal of Orthopsychiatry,* 56(4), 501–512.

Luce, G. G. (1965). Current research on sleep and dreams. *Heath Service Publication* No. 1389, U.S. Department of Health, Education and Welfare.

Luce, G. G. (1974). Sleepwalking not related to dreams. In R. L. Woods, & H. B. Greenhouse (Eds.). *The new world of dreams.* New York: Macmillan.

Luce, G. G., & Peper, E. (1971, Sept. 12). Mind over body, mind over mind. *The New York Times Magazine.*

Ludwig, A. M. (1966). Altered states of consciousness. *Archives of General Psychiatry, 15,* 225–233.

Lueptow, L. B. (1980). Social change and sex-role changes in adolescent orientations toward life, work, and achievement: 1964–1975. *Social Psychology Quarterly, 43,* 48–59.

Lumsden, C., & Wilson, E. O. (1983). *Promethean fire.* Cambridge, MA: Harvard University Press.

Luria, A. R. (1968). *The mind of a mnemonist.* New York: Basic Books.

Luthans, F., Paul, R., & Baker, D. (1981). An experimental analysis of the impact of contingent reinforcement on salespersons' performance behavior. *Journal of Applied Psychology, 66,* 314–323.

Lykken, D. T. (1987). Genes and the mind. *The Harvard Medical School Mental Health Letter,* 4(2), 4–6.

Lykken, D. T. (1974). Psychology and the lie detector industry. *American Psychologist, 29,* 725–739.

Lykken, D. T. (1981). *A tremor in the blood, uses and abuses of the lie detector.* New York: McGraw-Hill.

Lynch, G., & Baudry, M. (1984). The biochemistry of memory: A new and specific hypothesis. *Science, 224,* 1057–1163.

Lynn, S. J. & Rhue, J. W. (1988). Fantasy proneness. *American Psychologist,* 43(1), 35–44.

Maccoby, E. E., & Jacklin, C. N. (1974). *The psychology of sex differences.* Stanford, CA.: Stanford University Press.

Mack, J. E. (1986). Adolescent suicide: An architectural model. In G. L. Klerman (Ed.), *Suicide and depression among adolescents and young adults.* Washington, D. C.: American Psychiatric Press.

MacKinnon, D. W. (1962). The nature and nurture of creative talent. *American Psychologist, 1,* 484–495.

MacKinnon, D. W. (1968). Selecting students with creative potential. In P. Heist (Ed.). *The creative college student: An unmet challenge.* San Francisco: Jossey-Bass.

Maddi, S. R. & Kobasa, S. C. (1984). *The hardy executive: Health under stress.* Homewood, Il: The Dorsey Press.

Madsen, C. H., Jr., Becher, W. C., Thomas, D. R., Koser, L., & Plager, E. (1968). An analysis of the reinforcing function of "sit down" commands. In R. K. Parker (Ed.). *Readings in educational psychology.* Boston: Allyn & Bacon.

Magid, K. (1988). *High risk: Children without a conscience.* New York: Bantam.

Maier, N. R. F. (1949). *Frustration.* New York: McGraw-Hill.

Main, M., & George, C. (1985). Responses of abused and disadvantaged toddlers to distress and agemates: A study in day care. *Developmental Psychology, 21,* 407–412.

Malamuth, N. M., & Donnerstein, E. (1982). The effects of aggressive-pornographic mass media stimuli. In L. Berkowitz (Ed.), *Advances in Experimental Social Psychology, 15,* 103–136. New York: Academic Press.

Malatesta, C. Z. (1982). "The expression and regulation of emotion: A lifespan perspective." In T. Field & A. Fogel (Eds.), *Emotion and early interation.* Hillsdale, N.J.: Lawrence Erlbaum.

Malatesta, V. J., Pollack, R. H., Wilbanks, W. A., & Adams, H. E. (1979). *Journal of Sex Research, 15,* 101.

Malmo, R. B. (1975). *On emotions, needs, and our archaic brain.* New York: Holt, Rinehart & Winston.

Mandell, A. J., Segal, D. S., Kuczenski, R. T., & Knapp, S. (1972, Oct.). The search for the schizococcus. *Psychology Today,* pp. 68–72.

Mandler, G. (1968). Association and organization: Fact, fancies, and theories. In T. R. Dixon, & D. L. Horton (Eds.) *Verbal behavior and general behavior theory* (pp. 109–119). Englewood Cliffs, N.J.: Prentice-Hall.

Mandler, G. (1984). *Mind and body: Psychology of emotion and stress.* New York: W. W. Norton.

Mannuzza, S. Klein, R. G. Bonagura, N., & Konig, P. H. (1988). Hyperactive boys almost grown up: II. Status of subjects without a mental disorder. *Archives of General Psychiatry,* 45(1), 13–18.

Mantyla, T. (1986). Optimizing cue effectiveness: Recall of 600 incidentally learned words. *Journal of Experimental Psychology: Learning, Memory, and Cognition,* 12(1), 66–71.

Mark, V. H., & Ervin, F. R. (1970). *Violence and the brain.* New York: Harper & Row.

Markman, E. M., Seibert, J. (1976). Classes and collections: Internal organization and resulting holistic properties. *Cognitive Psychology,* 8, 561–577.

Marks, D., & Kammann, R. (1979). *The psychology of the psychic.* Buffalo, N.Y.: Prometheus Books.

Marks, L. (1978). *The unity of the senses: Interrelations among the modalities.* New York: Academic Press.

Marks, M. T. (1986). The question of quality circles. *Psychology Today,* March, 36–46*ff.*

Markus, H. (1981, June). Sibling personalities: The luck of the draw. *Psychology Today,* pp. 35–37.

Markus, H., & Nurius, P. (1986). Possible selves. *American Psychologist, 41,* 954–969.

Marlatt, G. A., Baer, J. S., Dononovan, D. M., & Kivlahan, D. R. (1988). Addictive behaviors: Etiology and treatment. *Annual Review of Psychology, 39,* 223–252.

Marlatt, G. A., & Gordon, J. R. (Eds.) (1985). *Relapse prevention: Maintenance strategies in the treatment of addictive behaviors.* New York: Guilford Press.

Marmon, J. (1975). Psychiatrists and their patients, a national study of private office practice. Joint Information Service of the American Psychiatric Association and the National Association for Mental Health. Washington, D.C.

Marmor, J. (ed.) (1980). *Homosexual behavior: A modern reappraisal.* New York: Basic Books.

Marmor, J. (1985). Homosexuality: Nature vs. nurture. *The Harvard Medical School Mental Health Letter, 2*(4), 5–6.

Marques, P., Bradley, J., Shappee, J., & Marques, C. (1982). *Bienestar: Health, well-being and lifestyle choices for Pinal County.* Project West Pinal, University of Arizona Health Sciences Center.

Marsh, C. (1977). A framework for describing subjective states of consciousness. In N. E. Zinberg (Ed.). *Altered states of consciousness* (pp. 121–144). New York: Free Press.

Martin, B. M., Garrity, T. F., & Bowers, F. R. (1975). The influence of recent life experience on the health of college freshman. *Journal of Psychosomatic Research, 19,* 87–98.

Martin, J. A., King, D. R., Maccoby, E. E., & Jacklin, C. N. (1984). Secular trends and individual differences in toilet-training progress. *Journal of Pediatric Psychology, 9,* 457–467.

Marx, J. L. (1983). The two sides of the brain. *Science, 220,* 488–490.

Maslach, C. (1982). *Burnout: The cost of caring.* Englewood Cliffs, N. J.: Prentice-Hall.

Maslow, A. H. (1954). *Motivation and personality.* New York: Harper.

Maslow, A. H. (1967). Self-actualization and beyond. In J. F. T. Bugental (Ed.). *Challenges of humanistic psychology.* New York: McGraw-Hill.

Maslow, A. H. (1968). *Toward a psychology of being* (2nd ed.). New York: Van Nostrand.

Maslow, A. H. (1969). *The psychology of science.* Chicago: Henry Regnery.

Maslow, A. H. (1970). *Motivation and personality* (2nd ed.). New York: Harper & Row.

Maslow, A. H. (1971). *The farther reaches of human nature.* New York: Viking.

Masters, W. H., & Johnson, V. E. (1966). *Human sexual response.* Boston: Little, Brown.

Masters, W. H., & Johnson, V. E. (1970). *The pleasure bond: A new look at sexuality and commitment.* Boston: Little, Brown.

Masur, E. F. (1987). Imitative interchanges in a social context: Mother-infant matching behavior at the beginning of the second year. *Merrill-Plamer Quarterly, 33*(4), 453–472.

Matarazzo, J. D. (1984). Behavioral immunogens and pathogens in health and illness. In B. L. Hammonds & C. J. Scheirer (Eds.), *Psychology and Health.* Washington, D. C.: American Psychological Association. pp. 5–43.

Matheny, A. P., Jr., Wilson, R. S., & Nuss, S. M. (1984). Toddler Temperament: Stability across settings and over ages. *Child Development, 55,* 1200–1211.

Matossian, M. K. (1982). Ergot and the Salem witchcraft affair. *American Scientist, 70,* 355–357.

Matthews, L. H., & Knight, M. (1963). *The senses of animals.* London: Museum Press.

Maugh, T. H. (1988). Researcher uses bit, bytes and Bach for program of note. *Los Angeles Times,* August 20, Part I, 30.

Maupin, E. W. (1965). Individual differences in response to a Zen meditation exercise. *Journal of Consulting Psychology, 29,* 139–145.

Mayer, J. (1968). *Overweight: Causes, cost, and control.* Englewood Cliffs, N.J.: Prentice-Hall.

McAlister, A. L., (1983). Social psychological approaches. In T. Glynn, C. Leukefeld, & J. Lundford (Eds.), *Preventing adolescent drug abuse: Intervention strategies.* (NIDA) Research Monograph No. 47, D.H.H.S. Publication No. ADM 83-1280). Washington, DC: U. S. Government Printing Office.

McBurney, D. H. & Collings, V. B. (1984). *Introduction to sensation/perception,* 2nd ed. Englewood Cliffs, NJ: Prentice-Hall.

McCabe, P., & Schneiderman, N. (1984). Psychophysiologic reactions to stress. In N. S. Schneiderman & J. J. Tapp (Eds.), *Behavioral medicine: The biopsychosocial approach.* Hillsdale, N.J.: Lawrence Erlbaum.

McCabe, M. S. (1976). Reactive psychoses and schizophrenia with good prognosis. *Archives of General Psychiatry, 33*(5), 571–576.

McCain, G., & Segal, E. M. (1969). *The game of science.* Belmont, Ca.: Brooks Cole.

McCall, R. B. (1984). Developmental changes in mental performance: The effect of the birth of a sibling. *Child Development, 55,* 1317–1321.

McCardel, J., & Murray, E. J. (1974). Nonspecific factors in weekend encounter groups. *Journal of Consulting Psychology, 42,* 337–345.

McCaul, K. D. & Malott, J. M. (1984). Distraction and coping with pain. *Psychological Bulletin, 95,* 516–533.

McCauley, E., & Ehrhardt, A. A. (1976). Female sexual response: Hormonal and behavioral interactions. *Primary Care, 3,* 455.

McClelland, D. C. (1958). Risk taking in children with high and low need for achievement. In J. W. Atkinson (Ed.). *Motives in fantasy action and society.* New York: Van Nostrand.

McClelland, D. C. (1961). *The achieving society.* New York: Van Nostrand.

McClelland, D. C. (1965). Achievement and entrepreneurship. *Journal of Personality and Social Psychology, 1,* 389–393.

McClelland, D. C. (1973). Testing for competence rather than "intelligence." *American Psychologist, 28,* 1–14.

McClelland, D. C. (1975). *Power the inner experience.* New York: Irvington.

McClelland, D. C. & Pilon, D. A. (1983). Sources of adult motives in patterns of parent behavior in early childhood. *Journal of Personality and Social Psychology, 44,* 564–574.

McClelland, L., & Cook, S. W. (1980). Promoting energy conservation in master-metered apartments through group financial incentives. *Journal of Applied and Social Psychology, 10,* 20–31.

McFadden, D., & Wightman, F. L. (1983). Audition. *Annual Review of Psychology, 34,* 95–128.

McGaugh, J. L. (1983). Hormonal influences on memory. *Annual Review of Psychology, 34,* 297–323.

McGaugh, J. L. (1970) Time-dependent processes in memory storage. In J. L. McGaugh & M. J. Herz (Eds.), *Controversial issues in consolidation of the memory trace.* New York: Atherton.

McGee, M. G., & Snyder, M. (1975). Attribution and behavior: Two field studies. *Journal of Personality and Social Psychology, 32,* 185–190.

McGinnies, E. (1949). Emotionality and perceptual defense. *Psychological Review, 56,* 244–251.

McGregor, D. (1960). *The human side of enterprise.* New York: McGraw-Hill.

McGuire, W. J. (1969). The nature of attitudes and attitude change. In G. Lindzey, & E. Aronson (Eds.). *The handbook of social psychology* Vol. 3. Reading, Mass.: Addison-Wesley.

McKean, K. (1985, April). Of two minds: Selling the right brain. *Discover,* pp. 30–40.

McKean, K. (1982, Dec.). Anatomy of an air crash. *Discover,* pp. 19–21.

McKean, K. (1982, Aug.). A picture of Hinckley's brain. *Discover, 3,* pp. 78–80.

McKean, K. (1984, May). The fine art of reading voters' minds. *Discover,* pp. 66–69.

McKean, K. (1983, November). Memory. *Discover,* pp. 19–27.

McKellar, P. (1965). The investigation of mental images. In S. A. Barnett, & A. McLaren (Eds.). *Penguin science journal.* Harmondsworth: Penguin.

McMullan, W. E., & Stocking, J. R. (1978). Conceptualizing creativity in three dimensions. *The Journal of Creative Behavior, 12,* 161–167.

McNett, I. (1982, Jan.). Psy.D. fills demand for practitioners. *APA Psychology Monitor, 13,* pp. 10–11.

Mead, M. (1935). *Sex and temperament in three primitive societies.* New York: Morrow.

Meeker, M. (1978). Measuring creativity from the child's point of view. *The Journal of Creative Behavior, 12,* 52–62.

Mehrabian, A. (1969). Significance of posture and position in the communication of attitude and status relationships. *Psychological Bulletin, 71,* 359–372.

Meichenbaum, D. (1977). *Cognitive behavior modification: An integrative approach.* New York: Plenum Press.

Meichenbaum, D., Henshaw, D., & Himel, N. (1982). Coping with stress as a problem-solving process. In H. W. Krohne & L. Laux (Eds.), *Achievement, stress, and anxiety.* New York: Hemisphere.

Melton, R. F., (1978). Resolution of conflicting claims concerning the effect of behavioral objectives on student learning. *Review of Educational Research, 48,* 291–302.

Meltzoff, A. N. (1988). Infant imitation and memory: Nine-month-olds in immediate and deferred tests. *Child Development, 59*(1), 217–225.

Meltzoff, A., & Moore, M. K. (1977, Oct.). Imitation of facial and manual gestures by human neonates. *Science,* 75–78,.

Meltzoff, A. N. & Moore, M. K. (1983). Newborn infants imitate adult facial gestures. *Child Development, 54,* 702–709.

Melzack, R. (1974). Shutting the gate on pain. *Science Year: The World Book Science Annual.* Palo Alto, Ca.: Field.

Melzack, R. (1984). The myth of painless childbirth. *Pain, 19,* 321–337.

Melzack, R., & Dennis, S. G. (1978). Neurophysical foundations of pain. In edited by R. A. Sternbach (Ed.). *The psychology of pain.* New York: Raven Press.

Melzack, R., & Scott, T. H. (1957). The effects of early experience on the response to pain. *Journal of Comparative and Physiological Psychology, 50,* 155–161.

Melzack, R. & Wall, P. D. (1983). *The challenge of pain.* New York: Basic Books.

Menninger, K. (1964, April 25). Psychiatrists use dangerous words. *Saturday Evening Post.*

Menzel, E. W. (1978). Cognitive mapping in chimpanzees. In S. H. Hulse, H. Fowler, & W. K. Honig (Eds.). *Cognitive processes in animal behavior.* Hillsdale: Erlbaum.

Mercer, J. R. (1977). Identifying the gifted Chicano child. In J. L. Martinez (Ed.), *Chicano psychology.* New York: Academic Press.

Meredith, N. (1984, Dec.). The murder epidemic. *Science 84,* pp. 43–48.

Mermelstein, R. (1986). Social support and smoking cessation and maintenance. *Journal of Consulting & Clinical Psychology, 54*(4), 447–453.

Messerer, J., Hunt, E., Meyers, G., & Lerner, J. (1984) Feuerstein's instrumental enrichment: A new approach for activating intellectual potential in learning disabled youth. *Journal of Learning Disabilities, 17,* 322–325.

Messick, D. M., Wilke, H., Brewer, M., Kramer, R. M., Zemke, P. E., & Lui, L. (1983). Individual adaptations and structural change as solutions to social dilemmas. *Journal of Personality and Social Psychology, 44,* 294–309.

Metcalfe, J. (1986). Premonitions of insight predict impending error. *Journal of Experimental Psychology: Learning, Memory, and Cognition, 12,* 623–634.

Meyer, A. J., Nash, J. D., McAlister, A. L., Maccoby, N., & Farquhar, J. W. (1980). Skills training in a cardiovascular health education campaign. *Journal of Consulting and Clinical Psychology, 48,* 129–142.

Michotte, A. (1963). *The perception of causality.* New York: Methuen & Co., Ltd. Basic Books.

Middlemist, R. D., Knowles, E. S., & Matter, C. F. (1976). Personal space invasions in the lavatory: Suggestive evidence for arousal. *Journal of Personality and Social Psychology, 33,* 541–546.

Milgram, S. (1963). Behavioral study of obedience. *Journal of Abnormal and Social Psychology, 67,* 371–378.

Milgram, S. (1965). Some conditions of obedience and disobedience to authority. *Human Relations, 18,* 57–76.

Milgram, S. (1967, May). The small-world problem. *Psychology Today,* pp. 61–67.

Milgram, S. (1970). The experience of living in the cities: A psychological analysis. *Science, 167,* 1461–1468.

Milgram, S. (1974). *Obedience to authority: An experimental view.* New York: Harper & Row.

Milgram, S., Bickman, L., & Berkowitz, L. (1969). Note on the drawing power of crowds of different size. *Journal of Personality and Social Psychology, 13,* 79–82.

Miller, G. (1956). The magical number seven, plus or minus two: Some limits on our capacity for processing information. *Psychological Review, 63,* 81–87.

Miller, G. (1964). Language and psychology. In E. H. Lennenberg (Ed.). *New directions in the study of language* (pp. 89–107). Cambridge, Mass.: MIT Press.

Miller, G. (1969). On turning psychology over to the unwashed. American Psychological Association paper.

Miller, G. (1977). *Spontaneous apprentices: children and language.* The Seabury Press.

Miller, G. (1980, Jan.). Giving away psychology in the 80's. *Psychology Today,* p. 38.

Miller, L. K. (1976). The design of better communities through the application of behavioral principles. In W. E. Craighead, A. E. Kazdin, & M. J. Mahone (Eds.). *Behavior modification: Principles, issues, and applications.* Boston: Houghton Mifflin.

Miller, N. E. (1941). The frustration-aggression hypothesis. *Psychological Review, 48,* 337–342.

Miller, N. E. (1944). Experimental studies of conflict. In J. McV. Hunt (Ed.). *Personality and the behavior disorders,* Vol. I (pp. 431–465). New York: Ronald Press.

Miller, N. E. (1969). Learning of visceral and glandular responses. *Science, 163,* 434–445.

Miller, N. E. (1983). Behavioral medicine: Symbiosis between laboratory and clinic. *Annual Review of Psychology, 34,* 1–31.

Miller, N. E. (1985). The value of behavioral research on animals. *American Psychologist, 40,* 423–440.

Miller, N. E. (1985). Rx: Biofeedback. Psychology Today, 19, (Feb.), 54–59.

Miller, N. E., & Bugelski. R. (1970). The influence of frustration imposed by the in-group on attitudes expressed toward out-groups. In R. I. Evans, & R. M. Rozelle (Eds.). *Social psychology in life.* Boston: Allyn & Bacon.

Miller, W. R., Rosellini, R. A., & Seligman, M. E. P. (1977). In J. D. Maser, & M. E. P. Seligman (Eds.). *Psychopathology: Experimental models* (pp. 104–120). San Francisco: W. H. Freeman.

Millon, T., (1981) *Disorders of personality: DSM-III: Axis II.* New York: Wiley.

Milner, B. (1965). Memory disturbance after bilateral hippocampal lesions. In P. Milner, & S. Glickman (Eds.). *Cognitive processes and the brain* (pp. 97–111). Princeton, N.J.: Van Nostrand.

Milton, O., Pollio, H., & Eison, J. (1986). *Making sense of college grades: Why the grading system does not work and what can be done about it.* San Francisco, CA: Josey-Bass.

Milunsky, A. (1977). *Know your genes.* Boston: Houghton Mifflin.

Mirsky, A. F. & Duncan, C. C. (1986). Etiology and expression of schizophrenia. *Annual Review of Psychology, 37,* 291–319.

Mischel, W. (1968). *Personality and assessment.* New York: Wiley.

Mischel, W. (1973). Toward a cognitive social learning reconceptualization of personality. *Psychological Review, 80,* 252–283.

Mitchell, D. (1987). Firewalking cults: Nothing but hot air. *Laser* (Journal of the Southern California Skeptics), Feb. 1987, 7–8.

Mithcell-Heggs, N., Kelly, D., & Richardson, A. (1976). Stereotactic limbic leucotomy—A follow up at 16 months. *British Journal of Psychiatry, 128,* 226–240.

Money, J. (1965). Psychosexual differentiation. In J. Money (Ed.). *Sex research: New developments* (pp. 3–23). New York: Holt, Rinehart & Winston.

Money, J. (1977). Human hermaphroditism. In F. A. Beach (Ed.). *Human sexuality in four perspectives.* Baltimore: Johns Hopkins University Press.

Money, J. (1987). Sin, sickness, or status? *American Psychologist, 42*(4), 384–399.

Money, J., & Ehrhardt, A. (1972). *Man and woman, boy and girl.* Baltimore: Johns Hopkins Press.

Money, J., & Mathews, D. (1982). Prenatal exposure to virilizing progestins: An adult follow-up study of twelve women. *Archives of Sexual Behavior, 11,* 73–83.

Monmaney, T. (1987). Are we led by the nose? *Discover,* Sept., 48–56.

Moore, D. C. (1981). Anorexia nervosa. In S. J. Mule (Ed.), *Behavior in excess.* New York: The Free Press.

Moore-Ede, M. C., Sulzman, F. M., & Fuller, C. A. (1982). *The clocks that time us.* Cambridge, Mass: Harvard University Press.

Morain, D. (1988). In figuring, she plays it by the numbers. *Los Angeles Times,* March 1, Part I, 3.

Moreno, J. L. (1953). *Who shall survive?* New York: Beacon.

Morgan, W. P. (1978). The mind of the marathoner. *Psychology Today,* pp. 43–50.

Moriarty, T. (1975, April). A nation of willing victims. *Psychology Today,* pp. 43–50.

Moritz, A. P., & Zamchech, N. (1946). Sudden and unexpected deaths of young soldiers. *American Medical Association Archives of Pathology, 42,* 459–494.

Morse, S. J. (1986). We can't win a drug war. *Los Angeles Times,* Aug. 14, Part II, 7.

Moruzzi, G., & Magoun, H. W. (1949). Brain stem reticular formation and activation of the EEG. *EEG and Clinical Neurophysiology, 1,* 455–473.

Moser, D. (1965, May 7). The nightmare of life with Billy. *Life.*

Moss, H. A., & Susman, E. J. (1980). Longitudinal study of personality development. In O. G. Brim, Jr., & J. Kagan (Eds.), *Constancy and change in human development,* pp. 530–595. Cambridge, Mass: Harvard University Press.

Moss, S., & D. C. Butler. (1978). The scientific credibility of ESP. *Perceptual and Motor Skills, 46.*

Moyer, R. S., & Bayer, R. H. (1976). Mental comparison and the symbolic distance effect. *Cognitive Psychology, 8,* 228–246.

Mueller, J. H., & Thompson, W. B. (1984). Test anxiety and distinctiveness of personal information. In H. M. Van Der Ploeg, R. Schwarzer, & C. D. Spielberger (Eds.), *Advances in test anxiety research,* vol. 3 (pp. 21–37). Hillsdale, NJ: Erlbaum.

Munn, N. L., Fernald, L. D., Jr., & Fernald, P. S. (1969). *Introduction to psychology* (2nd ed.). Boston: Houghton Mifflin.

Murphy, K. R. (1987). Detecting infrequent deception. *Journal of Applied Psychology, 72*(4), 611–614.

Murphy, L. B., & Moriarty, A. E. (1976). *Vulnerability, coping and growth.* New Haven: Yale University Press.

Murray, F. S. (1980). Estimation of performance levels by students in introductory psychology. *Teaching of Psychology, 7,* 61–62.

Mussen, P. H., Conger, J. J., & Kagan, J. (1969). *Child development and personality* (3rd ed.). New York: Harper & Row.

Mussen, P. H., Conger, J. J., Kagan, J., & Geiwitz, J. (1979). *Psychological development: A life span approach.* New York: Harper & Row.

Myers, A. (1980) *Psychology.* New York: Van Nostrand.

Myers, B. J., Jarvis, P. A., & Creasey, G. L. (1987). Infants' behavior with their mothers and grandmothers. *Infant Behavior & Development, 10*(3), 245–259.

Nachman, M. (1970). Learned taste and temperature aversions due to lithium chloride sickness after temporal delays. *Journal of Comparative and Physiological Psychology, 73,* 22–30.

Naeye, R L. (1980). Sudden infant death. *Scientific American, 4*(242), pp. 56–62.

Nahas, G. G. (1979b). *Keep off the grass.* Elmsford, N.Y.: Pergamon Press.

Nahas, G. G., & Paton, W. D. M. (1979a). *Marihuana, biological effects.* Elmsford, N. Y.: Pergamon Press.

Naranjo, C. (1970). Present-centeredness: Technique, prescription, and ideal. In J. Fagan, & I. L. Shepherd (Eds). *What is Gestalt therapy?* (pp. 63–97). New York: Harper & Row.

Narayanan, V. K., & Nath, R. (1982). A field test of some attitudinal and behavioral consequences of flexitime. *Journal of Applied Psychology, 67,* 214–218.

Nathans, J., Thomas, P. Piantandia, R. L., Eddy, T. B., Shows, D. S. & Hogness, D. S. (1986). Molecular genetics of inherited variations in human color vision. *Science, 232,* 203–210.

National Commission on Marihuana and Drug Abuse, R. P. Shafer, Chairman. (1973). *Drug use in America: The problem in perspective.* Washington, D.C.: U.S. Government Printing Office.

National Institute on Drug Abuse (NIDA) (1976). *Marihuana and health.* Princeton, N. J.: Response Analysis Corporation.

National Institute of Mental Health. (1982). Television and behavior: Ten years of scientific progress and implications for the eighties. Washington, D.C.: U.S. Government Printing Office.

Nauta, W. J. H., & Feirtag, M. (1979). The organization of the brain. *Scientific American,* pp. 88–111.

Navran, L. (1967). Communication and adjustment in marriage. *Family Process, 6,* 173–184.

Neff, W. S. (1977). *Work and human behavior* (2nd ed.). Chicago: Aldine.

Nelson, E. (1976, May). New facts on biorhythms. *Science Digent,* pp. 71–75.

Nelson, H. (1982, April 16). Twins: Studies of striking similarities. *Los Angeles Times,* p. 24.

Nelson, N., Enkin, M., Saigal, S., Bennett, K., Milner, R., & Sackett, D. (1980). A randomized clinical trial of the Leboyer approach to childbirth. *New England Journal of Medicine, 302,* 655–660.

Nelson, R., & Crutchfield, R. S. (1970). Mathematicians: The creative researcher and the average Ph.D. *Journal of Consulting and Clinical Psychology, 34,* 250–257.

Nelson, T. O. (1987). Predictive accuracy of the feeling of knowing across different tasks and across different subject populations and individuals. In M. M. Grunegerg, P. E. Morris, & R. N. Sykes (Eds.), *Practical aspects of memory: Current research and issues.* Chinchester, England: John Wiley & Sons, 190–196.

Neufeld, R. W. (1970). The effect of experimentally altered cognitive appraisal on pain tolerance. *Psychonomic Science, 20*(2), 106–107.

Neugarten, B. (1971, Dec.). Grow old along with me! The best is yet to be. *Psychology Today,* p. 45.

Neuringer, A. J. (1970). Superstitious key pecking after three peck-produced reinforcements. *Journal of the Experimental Analysis of Behavior, 13,* 127–134.

Newman, B. M. & Newman, P. R. (1987). The impact of high school on social development. *Adolescence, 22*(87), 525–534.

Newman, P. R. (1982). The peer group. In B. B. Wolman, G. Stricker, S. J. Ellman, P. Keith-Spiegel, & D. S. Palermo, (Eds.), *Handbook of developmental psychology.* Englewood Cliffs, NJ: Prentice-Hall.

Nickerson, R. S., & Adams, M. J. (1979). Long-term memory for a common object. *Cognitive Psychology, 11,* 287–307.

Nicogossian, A. E., & Parker, J. F. (1982). *Space physiology and medicine.* NASA.

Nicol, S. E., & Gottesman, I. I. (1983). Clues to the genetics and neurobiology of schizophrenia. *American Scientist, 71,* 398–404.

Noel, J. G., Forsyth, D. R., & Kelley, K. N. (1987). Improving the performance of failing students by overcoming their self-serving attributional biases. *Basic and Applied Social Psychology, 8*(1–2), 151–162.

Nomellini, S., & Katz, R. C. (1983). Effects of anger control training on abusive parents. *Cognitive Therapy and Research, 7,* 57–68.

Norman, D. A. (1988) *The psychology of everyday things.* New York: Basic Books.

Norris, P. A. (1986, Sept.) On the status of biofeedback and clinical practice. *American Psychologist,* 1009–1010.

Nurnberger, J. I. & Gershon, E. S. (1982). Genetics. In E. S. Paykel (Ed.) *Handbook of affective disorders.* New York: Guilford Press, pp. 126–145.

Nurnberger, J. I., & Zimmerman, J. (1970). Applied analysis of human behaviors: An alternative to conventional motivational inferences and unconscious determination in therapeutic programming. *Behavior Therapy, 1,* 59–69.

O'Brien, R. M., Figlerski, R. W., Howard, S. R., & Caggiano, J. (1981. Aug.). The effects of multi-year, guaranteed contracts on the performance of pitchers in major league baseball. Paper presented at the annual meeting of the American Psychological Association, Los Angeles.

O'Connell, K. A. & Martin, E. J. (1987). Highly tempting situations associated with abstinence, temporary relapse, and relapse among participants in smoking cessation programs. *Journal of Consulting & Clinical Psychology, 55*(3), 367–371.

Olds, J. (1977). *Drives and reinforcements: Behavioral studies of hypothalamic functions.* New York: Raven Press.

Olds, J., & Milner, P. (1954). Positive reinforcement produced by electrical stimulation of septal area and other regions of rat brain. *Journal of Comparative and Physiological Psychology, 47,* 419–427.

Olds, M. E., & Fobes, J. L. (1981). The central basis of motivation: Intracranial self-stimulation studies. *Annual Review of Psychology, 32,* 523–574.

O'Leary, K. D., & Becker, W. C. (1967). Behavior modification of an adjustment class: A token reinforcement program. *Exceptional Children, 33,* 637–642.

Oliver, C. M., & Oliver, G. M. (1978). Gentle Birth: Its safety and its effect on neonatal behavior. *Journal of Obstetrical, Gynecological and Neonatal Nursing.*

Olmstead, B. (1983, Feb. 17). More heaving drinking in colleges. *Los Angeles Times.*

Olson, R. L. & Roberts, N. W. (1987). Alternative treatments for sibling aggression. *Behavior Therapy, 18*(3), 243–250.

O'Malley, M. N., & Andrews, L. (1983). The effect of mood and incentives on helping: Are there some things money can't buy? *Motivation and Emotion, 7,* 179.

Orlick, T. D. (1975). The sports environment: A capacity to enhance- a capacity to destroy. In B. S. Rushall (Ed.). *The status of psychomotor learning and sport psychology research.* Dartmouth, Nova Scotia: Sport Science Associates.

Orne, M. T. (1982). Perspectives in biofeedback: Ten years ago, today, and . . . In L. White & B. Tursky (Eds.), *Clinical biofeedback: Efficacy and mechanisms* (pp. 422–437). New York: Guilford.

Orne, M. T., & Wilson, S. K. (1978). On the nature of alpha feedback training. In G. E. Schwartz & D. Shapiro (Eds.) *Consciousness and self-regulation* (pp. 359–400.). New York: Plenum.

Ornstein, R. E. (1972). *The psychology of consciousness.* San Francisco: Freeman.

Ornstein, R. E., & Galin, D. (1976). Physiological studies of consciousness. In P. Lec, R. E. Ornstein, D. Galin, A. Deichman, & C. Tart (Eds.). *Symposium on consciousness.* New York: Viking Press.

Orpen, C. (1981). Effect of flexible working hours on employee satisfaction and performance: A field experiment. *Journal of Applied Psychology, 66,* 113–115.

Orvaschel. H., Weissman, M. M. & Kidd, K. K. (1980) Children and depression: The children of depressed parents; the childhood of depressed patients; depression in children. *Journal of Affective Disorders,* 2, 1–16.

Osgood, C. E. (1952). The nature and measurement of meaning. *Psychological Bulletin, 49,* 197–237.

Osgood, C. E. (1962). Studies on the generality of affective meaning systems. *American Psychologist, 17,* 10–28.

Oskamp, S. (1984). *Applied social psychology.* Englewood Cliffs, N.J.: Prentice-Hall.

Oster, G. (1984). Muscle sounds. *Scientific American,* 250(3), pp. 108–114.

Overmier, J. B., & Seligman, M. E. P. (1967). Effects of inescapable shock upon subsequent escape and avoidance learning. *Journal of Comparative and Physiological Psychology, 63,* 23–33.

Overton, D. A. (1985). Contextual stimulus effects of drugs and internal states. In P. D. Balsam, & A. Tomie (Eds.), *Context and learning* (pp. 357–384). Hillsdale, N.J.: Lawrence Erlbaum.

Owen, J. D. (1976). Flextime: Some problems and solutions. *Industrial and Labor Relations Review, 29,* 152–160.

Owens, W. A., & Schoenfeldt, L. F. (1979). Toward a classification of persons. *Journal of Applied Psychology Monograph, 64,* 569–607.

Pagano, R. R. (1981). *Understanding statistics.* St. Paul: West Publishing Co.

Pagano, R. R., & Warrenburg, S. (1983) Meditation. In R. J. Davidson, G. E. Schwartz, & D. Shapiro (Eds.), *Consciousness and self-regulation* (153–210). New York: Plenum.

Page, J. D. (1971). *Psychopathology.* Chicago: Aldine.

Paivio, A. (1969). Mental imagery in associative learning and memory. *Psychological Review, 76,* 241–263.

Palazolli, M. (1978). *Self starvation,* Jason Aronson.

Palkovitz, R. J., & Lore, R. K. (1980). Note taking and note review: Why students fail questions based on lecture material. *Teaching of Psychology,* 7, 159–160.

Palmer, E. L. (1987). *Children in the cradle of television.* Lexington, Mass.: Lexington Books.

Palmer, M. H., Lloyd, M. E., & Lloyd, K. E. (1977). An experimental analysis of electricity conservation procedures. *Journal of Applied Behavior Analysis, 10,* 665–671.

Pappenheimer, J. R. (1976, Aug.). The sleep factor. *Scientific American.*

Parachini, A. (1986). '84 youth suicides a blip in 7-year drop, report says. *Los Angeles Times,* Nov. 19, V, 1,6.

Pardine, P., Napoli, A., Goodman, M., & Schure, M. (1981, Aug.). Physiological correlates of recent life stress experience. Paper presented at the annual convention of the American Psychological Association, Los Angeles, CA.

Parke, R. D., & Asher, S. R. (1983). Social and personality development. *Annual Review of Psychology, 34,* 465–509.

Parke, R. D., & Sawin, D. B. (1977, Nov.). Fathering: It's a major role. *Psychology Today.*

Parkes, C. M. (1979). Grief: The painful reaction to the loss of a loved one. Monograph, University of California, San Diego.

Parks, T. E. (1984). Illusory figures: A (mostly) theoretical review. *Psychological Bulletin, 95,* 282–300.

Parlee, M. B., & the Editors of *Psychology Today* Magazine. (1979, Oct.). The friendship bond. *Psychology Today.*

Parlee, M. B. (1979). Psychology and women. *Journal of Women in Culture and Society, 5,* 121–133.

Parnes, S. J. (1967). *Creative behavior workbook.* New York: Scribners.

Pasachoff, J. (1981). *Contemporary Astronomy,* 2nd ed. New York: Holt, Rinehart and Winston.

Passman, R. H. (1987). Attachments to inanimate objects: Are children who have security blankets insecure? *Journal of Consulting and Clinical Psychology, 55*(6), 825–830.

Patterson, G. R. (1982). *Coercive family process.* Eugene: Castilia Press.

Patterson, F. (1978). Conversations with a gorilla. *National Geographic, 154*(4), pp. 438–465.

Patterson, F. G., Patterson, C. H., & Brentari, D. K. (1987). Language in child, chimp, and gorilla. *American Psychologist,* March, 270–272.

Patton, R. W., Corry, J. M., Gettman, L. R., & Graf, J. S. (1986). *Implementing health/fitness programs.* Champaign, Ill.: Human Kinetics Publishers.

Pavlov, I. P. (1927). *Conditioned reflexes.* Translated by G. V. Anrep. New York: Dover.

Paykel, E. S. (1982) Life events and early environment. In E. S. Paykel (Ed.) *Handbook of affective disorders.* New York: Guilford Press, pp. 146–161.

Pelham, W. E. (1977). Withdrawal of a stimulant drug and concurrent behavioral intervention in the treatment of a hyperactive child. *Behavior Therapy, 8,* 473–479.

Pellegrino, J. W. (1985, Oct.). Anatomy of analogy. *Psychology Today,* pp. 49–54.

Pelton, T. (1983, May). The shootists. *Science 83, 4*(4), pp. 84–86.

Penfield, W. (1957, April 27). Brain's record of past a continuous movie film. *Science News Letter,* p. 265.

Penfield, W. (1958). *The excitable cortex in conscious man.* Springfield, Ill.: Charles C Thomas.

Penfield, W. (1975). *The mystery of the mind: A critical study of consciousness and the human brain.* Princeton, N.J.: Princeton University Press.

Penfield, W., & Roberts, L. (1959). *Speech and brain mechanisms.* Princeton, N.J.: Princeton University Press.

Perfetto, G. A., Bransford, J., & Franks, J. J. (1983). Constraints on access in a problem solving context. *Memory and Cognition, 11,* 24–31.

Perin, C. T. (1943). A quantitative investigation of the delay of reinforcement gradient. *Journal of Experimental Psychology, 32,* 37–51.

Perkins, D. G., & Perkins, F. M. (1976). *Nailbiting and cuticlebiting: Kicking the habit*. Richardson, TX: Self Control Press.

Perkoff, G. T. (1980). The meaning of "experimental." In E. S. Valenstein (Ed.), *The psychosurgery debate*. San Francisco: W. H. Freeman.

Perlman, D. & Coxby, P. C. (1983). *Social psychology*. NY: Holt, Rinehart & Winston.wc

Perls, F. (1969). *Gestalt therapy verbatim*. Lafayette, Ca.: Real People Press.

Persky, H., Lief, H. I., Straus, D., Miller, W. R., & O'Brien, C. P. (1978). Plasma testosterone level and sexual behavior of couples. *Archives of Sexual Behavior, 7*, 157–173.

Peters, W. A. (1971). *A class divided*. Garden City, N.Y.: Doubleday.

Petersen, A. C. (1987, Sept.). Those gangly years. *Psychology Today*, 28–34.

Peterson, L. R., & Peterson, M. J. (1959). Short-term retention of individual verbal items. *Journal of Experimental Psychology, 58*, 193–198.

Peterson, P. L. (1979). Direct instruction: Effective for what and for whom? *Educational Leadership, 37*, 46–48.

Phillips, D. (1982). The impact of fictional television stories on U.S. adult fatalities: New evidence on the effect of mass media on violence. *American Journal of Sociology, 87*, 1340–1359.

Phillips, D. P. & Wills, J. S. (1987). A drop in suicides around major national holidays. *Suicide and Life-Threatening Behavior, 17*, 1–12.

Phillips, J. L. (1969). *Origins of intellect: Piaget's theory*. San Francisco: Freeman.

Piaget, J. (1951, original French, 1945). *The psychology of intelligence*. New York: Norton.

Piaget, J. (1952). *The origins of intelligence in children*. New York: International University Press.

Pierrel, R., & Sherman, J. G. (1963, Feb.). Train your pet the Barnabus way. *Brown Alumni Monthly*.

Piliavin, I. M., Rodin, J., & Piliavin, J. A. (1969). Good samaritanism: An underground phenomenon? *Journal of Personality and Social Psychology, 13*, 289–299.

Pilkonis, P. A. (1977). The behavioral consequences of shyness. *Journal of Personality, 45*, 596–611.

Pines, M. (1969, July 6). Why some three-year-olds get A's and some get C's. *The New York Times Magazine*, pp. 4–5, 10–17.

Pines, M. (1980, Dec.). The sinister hand. *Science 80*, pp. 26–27.

Pintrich, P. R. & McKeachie, W. J. (1987). Teaching a course in learning to learn. *Teaching of Psychology, 14*(2), 81–85.

Pion, G. (1986, Jan.). Job focus shifts to service, policy. *APA Monitor*, p. 25.

Pittman, T. & Heller, J. F. (1987). Social motivation. *Annual Review of Psychology, 38*, 461–489.

Playboy, (1969). *16*(2), p. 46.

Plutchik, R. (1980). *Emotion*. New York: Harper & Row.

Polivy, J., & Herman, C. P. (1985). Dieting and Binging. *American Psychologist, 40*, 193–201.

Potkay, C. R., & Allen, B. P. (1986). *Personality: Theory, research, and applications*. Monterey: Brooks Cole.

Premack, A. J., & Premack, D. (1972, Oct.). Teaching language to an ape. *Scientific American*, pp. 92–99.

Premack, D. (1965). Reinforcement theory. In D. Levine (Ed.). *Nebraska symposium on motivation*. Lincoln: University of Nebraska Press.

Premack, D. (1970, Sept.). The education of S*A*R*A*H. *Psychology Today*, pp. 54–58.

Premack, D. (1983). Animal cognition. *Annual Review of Psychology, 34*, 351–362.

Premack, D., & Premack, A. J. (1983). *The mind of an ape*. New York: W. Norton.

Pressley, M., Levine, J. R., Nakamura, G. V., Hope, D. J., Bispo, J. G., & Toye, A. R. (1980). The keyword method of foreign vocabulary learning: An investigation of its generalizability. *Journal of Applied Psychology, 65*, 635–642.

Pritchard, R. M. (1961). A collimator stabilizing system. *Quarterly Journal of Experimental Psychology, 13*, 181–183.

Pueschel, S. M., Canning, C. D., Murphy, A., & Zausmer, E. (1978). *Down syndrome: Growing and learning*. Kansas City, Mo.: Sheed Andrews & McMeel.

Pursch, J. A. (1983, June 12). Cocaine can give you the business. *Los Angeles Times*, Part VII, p. 12.

Rader, P. E., & Hicks, R. A. (1987). Jet lag desynchronization and self assessment of business related performance. Paper presented at the Western Psychological Association meeting in Long Beach, CA, April 1987.

Radloff, L. S. (1985). Risk factors for depression: What do we learn from them? In J. C. Coyne (Ed.) *Essential papers on depression*. New York: New York University Press, 140–149.

Rafaeli, A., & Klimoski, R. J. (1983). Predicting sales success through handwriting analysis: An evaluation of the effects of training and handwriting sample content. *Journal of Applied Psychology, 68*, 212–217.

Rahe, R. H. (1972). Subjects' recent life changes and their near-future illness reports. *Annals of Clinical Research, 4*, 250–265.

Ramsey, P. H., Ramsey, P. P., & Barnes, M. J. (1987). Effects of student confidence and item difficulty on test score gains due to answer changing. *Teaching of Psychology, 14*(4), 206–209.

Randi, J. (1980). *Film-flam!* New York: Lippincott & Crowell.

Randi, J. (1983). Science and the chimera. In G. O. Abell & B. Singer (Eds.), *Science and the paranormal*. New York: Scribner's Sons.

Raven, B. H. (1974). The analysis of power and power preference. In J. T. Tebeschi (Ed.) *Prospectus on social power*. Chicago: Aldine.

Rea, C P. & Modigliani, V. (1987). Educational implications of the spacing effect. In M. M. Grunegerg, P. E. Morris, & R. N. Sykes (Eds.), *Practical aspects of memory: Current research and issues*. Chinchester, England: John Wiley & Sons, 402–406.

Read, J. D. & Bruce, D. (1982). Longitudinal tracking of difficult memory retrievals. *Cognitive Psychology*, 14, 280–300.

Rechtschaffen, A., Gilliland, M. A., Bergmann, B. M., & Winter, J. B. (1983). Physiological correlates of prolonged sleep deprivation in rats. *Science, 221*, 182–184.

Reed, S. K. (1988). *Cognition: theory and applications (2ed)*. Pacific Grove, Calif.: Brooks/Cole.

Reif A. E. (1981). The causes of cancer. *American Scientist, 69*, 437–447.

Reiser, M. (1985). *Mind, brain, body: Toward a convergence of psychoanalysis*. New York: Basic.

Reiss, D. (1974, Spring). Competing hypothesis and waring factions: Applying knowledge of schizophrenia. *Schizophrenia Bulletin* (8).

Renwick, P. A., & Lawler, E. E. (1979). What you really want from your job. *Psychology Today, 11*(12), pp. 53–65.

Rescorla, R. A. (1988). Pavlovian conditioning: It's not what you think it is. *American Psychologist, 43*:3, 151–160.

Rescorla, R. A. (1987). A Pavlovian analysis of goal-directed behavior. *American Psychologist, 42*, 119–126.

Rescorla, R. (1980). *Pavlovian second-order conditioning: Studies in associative learning*. MacEachren Lectures, Halsted Press.

Resnick, R. B., Kestenbaum, R. S., & Schwartz, K. L. (1977). Acute systemic effects of cocaine in man: A controlled study in intranasal and intravenous routes. *Science, 195*, 696–698.

Reybowski, J. (1982). Social motivation. *Annual Review of Psychology, 33*, 123–154.

Rhine, J. B. (1953). *New world of the mind*. New York: Sloane.

Rhine, J. B. (1974). Security versus deception in parapsychology. *Journal of Parapsychology, 38*, 99–121.

Rhine, J. B. (1977). History of experimental studies. In B. B. Wolman (Ed.). *Handbook of parapsychology*. Van Nostrand Reinhold.

Ricketts, M. S., & Galloway, R. E. (1984). Effects of three different one-hour single-session treatments for test anxiety. *Psychological Reports, 54*, 113–119.

Rieger, M. G. (1976, Oct. 30). Pain control through hypnosis. *Science News*.

Rimland, B. (1978). Inside the mind of the autistic savant. *Psychology Today, 12*, pp. 68–80.

Ristow, W. (1978, Nov.). Larry P. versus IQ tests. *The Progressive, 42*, pp. 48–50.

Ritchie, R. J., & Moses, J. L. (1983). Assessment center correlates of women's advancement into middle management: A 7-year longitudinal analysis. *Journal of Applied Psychology, 68*, 227–231.

Roach, M. (1985, Aug.). Reflection in a fatal mirror. *Discover,* pp. 76–85.
Roberts, D. F., & Bachen, C. M. (1981). Mass communication effects. *Annual Review of Psychology, 32,* 307–356.
Robertson, T. S., Zielinski, J., & Ward, S. (1984). *Consumer behavior.* Glenview, Ill: Scott, Foresman.
Robinson, F. P. (1941). *Effective behavior.* New York: Harper & Row.
Robinson, H. B., & Robinson, N. M. (1976). Mental retardation. In P. H. Mussen (Ed.). *Carmichael's manual of child psychology* Vol. 2 (3rd ed.), New York: Wiley.
Robson, P. (1984). Prewalking locomotor movements and their use in predicting standing and walking. *Child Care, Health & Development, 10,* 317–330.
Rock, I., & Kaufman, L. (1962). The moon illusion II. *Science, 136,* 1023–1031.
Rodgers, J. L. (1988). Birth order, SAT, and confluence: Spurious correlations and no causality. *American Psychologist,* June, 476–477.
Rodin, J. (1981). Current status of the internal-external hypothesis for obesity: What went wrong? *American Psychologist, 36,* 361–372.
Rodin, J. (1978). Stimulus-bound behavior and biological self-regulation: Feeding, obesity, and external control. In G. E. Schwartz, & D. Shapiro (Eds.), *Consciousness and self-regulation* (pp. 215–239). New York: Plenum.
Rogers, C. R. (1957). The necessary and sufficient conditions of therapeutic personality change. *Journal of Consulting Psychology, 21,* 95–103.
Rogers, C. R. (1959). A theory of therapy, personality and interpersonal relationships, as developed in the client-centered framework. In S. Koch (Ed.). *Psychology: A study of a science* Vol. 3. New York: McGraw-Hill.
Rogers, C. R. (1961). *On becoming a person: A therapist's view of psychotherapy.* Boston: Houghton Mifflin.
Rogers, C. R. (1962, Jan. 28). Learning to be free. A paper given at a session on "Conformity and Diversity" in the conference on "Man and Civilization," sponsored by the University of California School of Medicine, San Francisco, Ca.
Rogers, C. R. (1980). *A way of being.* Boston: Houghton Mifflin.
Rogers, J. M. (1971, Sept.). Drug abuse—Just what the doctor ordered. *Psychology Today,* pp. 16–24.
Roggman, L. A., Langlois, J. H., & Hubbs-Tait, L. (1987). Mothers, infants, and toys: Social play correlates of attachment. *Infant Behavior & Development, 10*(2), 233–237.
Rohsenow, D. J., & Smith R. E. (1982). Irrational beliefs as predictors of negative affective states. *Motivation and Emotion, 6,* 299–301.
Rokeach, M. (1960). *The open and closed mind.* New York: Basic Books.
Rorer, L. G., & Widiger, T. A. (1983). Personality structure and assessment. *Annual Review of Psychology, 34,* 431–463.
Rosch, E. (1977). Classification of real-world objects: Origins and representations in cognition. In P. N. Johnson-Laird, & P. C. Wason (Eds.). *Thinking: Reading in cognitive science.* Cambridge: Cambridge University Press.
Roscoe, S. N. (1985). Bigness is in the eye of the beholder. *Human Factors, 27*(6), 615–636.
Rose, K. J. (1984, Feb.). How animals think. *Science Digest, 89,* pp. 59–61.
Rosen, J. C., & Leitenberg, H. (1982). Bulimia nervosa: Treatment with exposure and response prevention. *Behavior Therapy, 13,* 117–124.
Rosenbaum, M. B. (1979). The changing body image of the adolescent girl. In M. Sugar (Ed.), *Female adolescent development.* New York: Brunner/Mazel.
Rosenberg, J., & Pettinati, H. M. (1984). Differential memory complaints after bilateral and unilateral ECT. *American Journal of Psychiatry, 14,* 1071–1074.
Rosenfeld, P., Giacalone, R. A., & Tedeschi, J. T. (1983). Cognitive dissonance vs. impression management. *Journal of Social Psychology, 120,* 203–211.
Rosenhan, D. L. (1973). On being sane in insane places. *Science, 179,* 250–258.
Rosenman, R. H., Brand, R. J., Jenkins, C. D., Friedman, M., Straus, R., & Wurm, M. (1975). Coronary heart disease in the Western Collaborative Group Study: Final follow-up experience of 8½ years. *Journal of the American Medical Association, 233,* 872–877.
Rosenthal, D. (1963). *The Genain quadruplets.* New York: Basic Books.
Rosenthal, D., & Quinn, O. W. (1977). Quadruplet hallucinations: Phenotypic variations of a schizophrenic genotype. *Archives of General Psychiatry, 34*(7), 817–827.
Rosenthal, N. E., Sack, D. A., Gillin, J. C., Levy, A. J., et al., (1984). Seasonal affective disorder. *Archives of General Psychiatry, 41*(72), 72–80.
Rosenthal, R. (1965). *Clever Hans: A case study of scientific method. Introduction to Clever Hans: (The horse of Mr. Von Osten),* O. Pfungst. New York: Holt, Rinehart & Winston.
Rosenthal, R. (1976). *Experimenter effects in behavioral research.* New York: Appleton-Century-Crofts.
Rosenthal, R. (1973, Sept.). The Pygmalion effect lives. *Psychology Today,* pp. 56–63.
Rosenthal, T. L., Linehan, K. S., Kelley, J. E. Rosenthal, R. H., Theobald, D. E., & Davis, A. F. (1978). Group aversion by imaginal, vicarious and shared recipient-observer schocks. *Behavior Research and Therapy, 16,* 421–427.
Rosenthal, T. L., & Rosenthal, R. (1980). The vicious cycle of stress reaction. Copyright, Renate and Ted Rosenthal, Stress Management Clinic, Department of Psychiatry, University of Tennessee College of Medicine, Memphis, Tennessee.
Rosenthal, T. L., & Zimmerman, B. J. (1978). *Social learning and cognition.* New York: Academic Press.
Ross, J. (1976, March). The resources of binocular perception. *Scientific American,* pp. 80–86.
Ross, L. (1977). The intuitive psychologist and his shortcomings: Distortions in the attribution process. In L. Berkowitz (Ed.). *Advances in experimental social psychology.* New York: Academic Press.
Ross, M., Karniol, R., & Rothstein, M. (1976). Reward contingency and intrinsic motivation in children. *Journal of Personality and Social Psychology, 33,* 442–447.
Rotter, J. B., & Hochreich, D. J. (1975). *Personality.* Glenview, Ill.: Scott, Foresman.
Rotton, J. & Kelly, I. W. (1985). Much ado about the full moon: A meta-analysis of lunar-lunacy research. *Psychological Bulletin, 97,* 286–306.
Rowe, D. C. (1987). Resolving the person-situation debate. *American Psychologist, 42,* 218–227.
Rowley, P. T. (1984). Genetic screening: Marvel or menace? *Science, 225,* 138–144.
Rubenstein, C. (1983, July). The modern art of courtly love. *Psychology Today.*
Rubenstein, C. & Tavris, C. (1987). Special survey results: 2600 women reveal the secrets of intimacy. *Redbook, 159,* 147–149*ff.*
Rubin, D. C. (1985). The subtle deceiver: Recalling our past. *Psychology Today,* September, 38–46.
Rubin, V., & Comitas, L. (Eds.). (1975). *Ganja in Jamaica.* The Hague: Mouton.
Rubin, Z. (1970, Dec.). Jokers wild in the lab. *Psychology Today.*
Rubin, Z. (1970). Measurement of romantic love. *Journal of Personality and Social Psychology, 16,* 265–273.
Rubin, Z. (1973). *Liking and loving: An invitation to social psychology.* New York: Holt.
Rubin, Z. (1975). Disclosing oneself to a stranger: Reciprocity and its limits. *Journal of Experimental and Social Psychology, 11,* 233–260.
Rubinstein, E. A. (1978). Television and the young viewer. *American Scientist, 66,* 685–693.
Rubinstein, E. A., Liebert, R. M., Neale, J. M., & Poulos, R. W. (1974). *Assessing television's influence on children's prosocial behavior.* New York: Brookdale International Institute.
Ruch, F. L., Zimbardo, P. G. (1971). *Psychology and life* (8th ed.). Glenview, Ill.: Scott, Foresman.
Rudestam, K. E. (1971). Stockholm and Los Angeles: A cross-cultural study of the communication of suicidal intent. *Journal of Consulting and Clinical Psychology, 36,* 82–90.
Ruff, H. A., & Birch, H. G. (1974). Infant visual fixation: The effect of concentricity, curvilinearity, and number of directions. *Journal of Experimental Child Psychology, 17,* 460–473.
Rushall, B. S. (1975). Applied psychology in sports. In B. S. Rushall (Ed.). *The status of psychomotor learning and sport psychology research.* Dartmouth, Nova Scotia: Sports Science Associates.

Rushton, N. A. H. (1975, March). Visual pigments and color blindness. *Scientific American*, pp. 64–74.

Russell, G. & Russell, A. (1987). Mother-child and father-child relationships in middle childhood. *Child Development, 58*(6), 1573–1585.

Saarni, C. (1982). Social and affective functions of nonverbal behavior: Developmental concerns. In R. S. Feldman (Ed.), *Development of nonverbal behavior in children* (pp. 123–148). New York: Springer-Verlag.

Sackheim, H. A., Decina, P., Kanzler, M., & Kerr, B. (1987). Effects of electrode placement on the efficacy of titrated, low-dose ECT. *American Journal of Psychiatry, 144*(11), 1449–1455.

Saegert, S., Swap, W., & Zajonc, R. B. (1973). Exposure, context, and interpersonal attraction. *Journal of Personality and Social Psychology, 25*, 234–242.

Sadock, V. A. (1987). Adolescent sexuality. *The Harvard Medical School Mental Health Letter, 3*(9), 6.

Salame, R. F. (1984). Test anxiety: Its determinants, manifestations and consequences. In H. M. Van Der Ploeg, R. Schwarzer, & C. D. Spielberger (Eds.), *Advances in test anxiety research*, vol. 3 (pp. 83–119). Hillsdale, NJ: Erlbaum.

Sales, B. D. & Hafemeister, T. L. (1985). Law and psychology. In Altmeir, E. M. & Meyer, M. E. (Eds.), *Applied specialties in psychology*, NY: Random House.

Salmela, J. H. (1974). An information processing approach to volleyball. *C.V.A. Technical Journal, 1*, 49–62.

Salmela, J. H. (1975). Psycho-motor task demands of artistic gymnastics. In J. H. Salmela (Ed.). *The advanced study of gymnastics: A textbook*. Sundby Publications.

Salmoni, A. W., Schmidt, R. A., & Walter, C. B. (1984). Knowledge of results and motor learning: A review and critical reappraisal. *Psychological Bulletin, 95*, 355–386.

Salthouse, T. A. (1987). Age, experience, and compensation. In C. Schooler & K. W. Schaie (Eds.), *Cognitive functioning and social structure over the life course* (pp. 142–150). New York: Ablex.

Sanders, G. S., & Simmons, W. L. (1983). Use of hypnosis to enhance eyewitness accuracy: Does it work? *Journal of Applied Psychology, 68*, 70–77.

Santrock, J. W. (1984). *Adolescence*. Dubuque, Iowa: Wm. C. Brown.

Sapolsky, R. M. (1987). The case of the falling nightwatchmen. *Discover*, July, 42–45.

Sarason, I. G. (1981). Test anxiety, stress, and social support. *Journal of Personality, 49*, 101–114.

Sarason, I. G. (1975). Test anxiety, attention, and the general problem of anxiety. In C. D. Spielberger, & I. G. Sarason (Eds.). *Stress and anxiety* Vol. 1. Washington, D.C.: Hemisphere.

Savage-Rumbaugh, E. S., Rumbaugh, D. M., & Boysen, S. (1980). Do apes use language? *American Scientist, 68*, 49–61.

Saxe, L., Dougherty, D., & Cross, T. (1985). The validity of polygraph testing. *American Psychologist, 40*, 355–366.

Scarr, S., Webber, P. L., Weinberg, R. A., & Wittig, M. A. (1981). Personality resemblance among adolescents and their parents in biologically related and adoptive families. *Journal of Personality and Social Psychology, 40*, 885–898.

Scarr, S. & Weinberg, R. A. (1986). The early childhood enterprise: Care and education of the young. *American Psychologist, 41*(10), 1140–1146.

Scarr, S., & Weinberg, R. A. (1983). The Minnesota adoption studies: genetic differences and malleability. *Child Development, 54*, 260–267.

Scarr, S., & Weinberg, R. A. (1977). Intellectual similarities within families of both adopted and biological children. *Intelligence, 1*, 170–191.

Scarr-Salapatek, S. (1971). Race, social class, and I.Q. *Science, 174*, 1223–1228.

Scarr-Salapatek, S., & Weinberg, R. A. (1975, Dec.). When black children grow up in white homes . . . *Psychology Today*.

Schachter, S. (1959). *Psychology of affiliation*. Stanford, Ca.: Stanford University Press.

Schachter, S. (1971). *Emotion, obesity and crime*. New York: Academic Press.

Schachter, S. (1978). Pharmacological and psychological determinants of smoking. In R. E. Thornton (Ed.). *Smoking behavior*. Edinburgh: Churchill Livingston.

Schachter, S., & Grose, L. P. (1968). Manipulated time and eating behavior. *Journal of Personality and Social Psychology, 10*, 98–106.

Schachter, S., & Rodin, J. (1974). *Obese humans and rats*. Potomac, Md.: Lawrence Earlbaum.

Schachter, S., & Wheeler, L. (1962). Epinephine, chlorpromazine and amusement. *Journal of Abnormal and Social Psychology, 65*, 121–128.

Schaie, K. W. (1980). Age changes in intelligence. In R. L. Sprott (Ed.). *Age, learning ability, and intelligence*. New York: Von Nostrand Reinhold.

Schaie, K. W. (1988). Ageism in psychological research. *American Psychologist*. 43:3, 179–183.

Schally, A. V., Kastin, A. J., & Arimura, A. (1977). Hypothalamic hormones: The link between brain and body. *American Scientist, 65*, 712–719.

Scheer, R. (1987, August 14). AIDS threat to all—How Serious? *Los Angeles Times*, p. 1.

Schein, E. H., Hill, W. F., Lubin, A., & Williams, H. L. (1957). Distinguishing characteristics of collaborators and resistors among American prisoners of war. *Journal of Abnormal and Social Psychology, 55*, 197–201.

Schein, E. H., Schneier, I., & Barker, C. H. (1961). *Coercive persuasion*. New York: Norton.

Schlesier-Stropp, B. (1984). Bulimia: A review of the literature. *Psychological Bulletin, 38*, 247–257.

Schless, A. P. (1977). Life events and illness: A three year prospective study. *British Journal of Psychiatry, 131*, 26–34.

Schlosberg, H. (1954). Three dimensions of emotion. *Psychological Review, 61*, 81–88.

Schmeidler, G. R. (1977). Methods for controlled research on ESP and PK. In B. B. Wolman (Ed.). *Handbook of parapsychology*. New York: Van Nostrand Reinhold.

Schmid, R. E. (1988). Number of unmarried couples tops 2.3 million. *Santa Barbara News-Press*, May 14, A-9.

Schmidt, J. A. (1976). *Help yourself: A guide to self-change*. Champaign, Ill.: Research Press.

Schneider, A. M., & Tarshis, B. (1975). *Physiological psychology*. New York: Random House.

Schneider, C. (1987). *Children's television: The art, the business, and how it works*. Chicago: NTC Business Books.

Schommer, N. (1984, Oct.). Shrinks on the air. *Discover*, pp. 68–70.

Schopler, E. (1978). Changing parental involvement in behavioral treatment. In M. Rutter, & E. Schopler (Eds). *Autism: A reappraisal of concepts and treatment*. New York: Plenum.

Schreiber, F. R. (1973). *Sybil*. Chicago: Regency.

Schuele, J. G., & Wiesenfeld, A. R. (1983). Autonomic response to self-critical thought. *Cognitive Therapy and Research, 7*, 189–194.

Schultz, D. P. (1979). *Psychology in use, an introduction to applied psychology*. New York: Macmillan.

Schutz, W. (1986). Encounter groups. In Kutash, I. L. & Wolf, A. (Eds.), *Psychotherapist's casebook*, 364–377, San Francisco: Jossey-Bass.

Schulz, R. (1978). *The psychology of death, dying and bereavement*. Reading, Mass.: Addison-Wesley.

Schwartz, B. (1984). *Psychology of learning & behavior*, 2nd. ed. New York: Norton.

Schwartz, G. E. (1984). Psychobiology of health: A new synthesis. In B. L. Hammonds & C. J. Scheirer (Eds.), *Psychology and Health*. Washington, D. C.: American Psychological Association. pp. 5–43.

Sclafani, A., & Springer, D. (1976). Dietary obesity in adult rats: Similarities to hypothalamic and human obesity syndromes. *Physiology and Behavior, 17*, 461–471.

Scrima, L., Broudy, M., Nay, K. N., & Cohn, M. A. (1982). Increased severity of obstructive sleep apnea after bedtime alcohol ingestion: Diagnostic potential and proposed mechanism of action. *Sleep, 5*, 318–328.

Sears, R. R., Maccoby, E. E., & Levin, H. (1957). *Patterns of child rearing*. Evanston, Ill.: Row, Peterson.

Seidel, W. F., Roth, T., Roehrs, T., Zorick, F., & Dement, W. C. (1984). Treatment of a 12-hour shift of sleep schedule with benzodiazepines. *Science, 224*, 1262–1264.

Seiden, R. H. (1966). Campus tragedy: A study of student suicide. *Journal of Abnormal Psychology, 1,* 389–399.

Seidenberg, M. S., & Petitto, L. A. (1979). Signing behavior in apes: A critical review. *Cognition, 7,* 177–215.

Seligman, C., & Darley, J. M. (1977). Feedback as a means of decreasing residential energy consumption. *Journal of Applied Psychology, 62,* 363–368.

Seligman, M. E. P. (1972) Phobias and preparedness. In M. E. P. Seligman & J. L. Hager (Eds). *Biological boundaries of learning.* New York: Appleton-Century-Crofts, pp. 451–462.

Seligman, M. E. P. (1972). For helplessness: Can we immunize the weak? In *Readings in psychology today* (2nd ed.). Del Mar, CA.: CRM.

Seligman, M. E. P. (1974). Submissive death: Giving up on life. *Psychology Today, 7,* pp. 80–85. K

Seligman, M. E. P., Maier, S. F., & Solomon, R. L. (1971). Unpredictable and uncontrollable aversive events. In F. R. Brush (Ed.). *Aversive conditioning and learning.* New York: Academic Press.

Selye, H. (1956, 1976). *The stress of life.* New York: Knopf.

Selye, H. (1976). *Stress in health and disease.* Boston: Butterworth.

Senden, M. V. (1960). *Space and sight.* Translated by P. Heath. Glencoe, Ill.: Free Press.

Serban, G. (1982). *The tyranny of magical thinking.* New York: Dutton.

Serbin, L. A., & O'Leary, K. D. (1975, Dec.). How nursery schools teach girls to shut up. *Psychology Today,* pp. 57–58, 102–103.

Sexual Medicine Today (1980, April) p. 17.

Shaffer, L. F. (1947). Fear and courage in aeriel combat. *Journal of Consulting Psychology, 11,* 137–143.

Shapiro, D. A., & Shapiro, D. (1982). Meta-analysis of comparative therapy outcome studies: A replication and refinement. *Psychological Bulletin, 92,* 581–604.

Shapiro, D. H. (1984). Overview: Clinical and physiological comparison of meditation with other self-control strategies. In Shapiro, D. H. & Walsh, R. N. (Eds.), *Meditation: Classic and contemporary perspectives.* New York: Aldine.

Shatz, M. (1985). Students' guessing strategies: Do they work? *Psychological Reports, 57*(3), 1167–1168.

Shaw, G. A., & Belmore, S. M. (1983). The relationship between imagery and creativity. *Imagination, Cognition and Personality, 2,* 115–123.

Sheehan, J. G., & Costley, M. S. (1977). A reexamination of the role of heredity in stuttering. *Journal of Speech and Hearing Disorders, 42,* 47–59.

Sheehan, P. W., Grigg, L., & McCann, T. (1984). Memory distortion following exposure to false information in hypnosis. *Journal of Abnormal Psychology, 93,* 259–265.

Sheehy, G. (1976). *Passages: Predictable crises from adult life.* New York: Dutton.

Sheils, M., & Monroe, S. (1976, March 22). A ban on I.Q. tests? *Newsweek,* p. 49.

Shepard, R. N. (1975). Form, formation, and transformation of internal representations. In R. L. Solso (Ed.). *Information processing and cognition: The Loyola Symposium.* Hillsdale, NJ: Erlbaum.

Sherif, M. (1935). A study of some social factors in perception. *Archives of Psychology, 27*(187).

Sherif, M., Harvey, O. J., White, B. J., Hood, W. R., & Sherif, C. W. (1961). *Intergroup conflict and cooperation: The Robbers Cave experiment.* Institute of Group Relations, University of Oklahoma.

Shiffman, S. M. (1980). Diminished smoking, withdrawal symptoms, and cessation: A cautionary note. In G. B. Gori, & F. G. Bock (Eds.). *Banbury report.* Cold Spring Harbor Laboratory.

Shiffrin, R. M. (1970). Forgetting: Trace erosion or retrieval failure? *Science, 168,* 1601–1603.

Shiffrin, R. M., & Cook, J. R. (1978). Short-term forgetting of item and order information. *Journal of Verbal Learning and Verbal Behavior, 17,* 189–218.

Shneidman, E. (1987, March). At the point of no return. *Psychology Today,* pp. 54–58.

Schneidman, E. (1980). *Voices of death.* New York: Harper & Row.

Shneidman, E. S. (1971). You and death. *Psychology Today,* 5(1), pp. 43–45, 74–80.

Shneidman, E. S., Farherow, N. L., & Cabista, L. (1965). *Some facts about suicide causes and prevention.* Washington, D.C.: U.S. Government Printing Office.

Shneidman, E. S. (1987). Psychological approaches to suicide. In VandenBos, G. R. & Bryant, B. K. (Eds.) *Cataclysms, crises, and catastrophes: Psychology in action.* Washington, DC: American Psychological Association, 151–183.

Shodell, M. (1984). The clouded mind. *Science 84.*

Short, A. B. (1984). Short-term treatment outcome using parents as cotherapists for their own autistic children. *Journal of Child Psychology & Psychiatry, 25,* 443–458.

Shulman, G. I. (1974). Race, sex and violence: A laboratory test of the sexual threat of the black male hypothesis. *American Journal of Sociology, 79,* 1260–1277.

Siegal, M. (1987). Are sons and daughters treated more differently by fathers than by mothers? *Developmental Review,* 7(3), 183–209.

Siegel, S., Hearst, E., George, N., & O'Neal, E. (1968). Generalization gradients obtained from individual subjects following classical conditioning. *Journal of Experimental Psychology, 78,* 171 171.

Siegel, O. (1982). Personality development in adolescence. In B. B. Wolman, G. Stricker, S. J. Ellman, P. Keith-Spiegel, & D. S. Palermo (Eds), *Handbook of developmental psychology,* pp. 537–548. Englewood Cliffs, NJ: Prentice Hall.

Siegelman, M. (1987). Kinsey and others: Empirical input. In L. Diamant (Ed.) *Male and female homosexuality: Psychological approaches.* Washington: Hemisphere Publishing.

Singer, J. L. (1974). Daydreaming and the stream of thought. *American Scientist, 62,* 417–425.

Singer, M. T. (1979, Jan.). Coming out of the cults. *Psychology Today,* pp. 72–82.

Singer, R. N. (1978). Motor skills and learning strategies. In H. F. O'Neil, Jr. (Ed.). *Learning strategies.* New York: Academic Press.

Skeels, H. M. (1966). Adult status of children with contrasting early life experiences. *Monograph of the Society for Research in Child Development, 31*(3).

Skinner, B. F. (1938). *The behavior of organisms.* Englewood Cliffs, N.J.: Prentice-Hall.

Skinner, B. F. (1971). *Beyond freedom and dignity.* New York: Bantam.

Smith, A., & Sugar, O. (1975). Development of above normal language and intelligence 21 years after left hemispherectomy. *Neurology, 25,* 813–818.

Smith, B. M. (1971). *The polygraph in contemporary psychology.* San Francisco: Freeman.

Smith, C., Carey, S., & Wiser, M. (1985). On differentiation: A case study of the development of the concepts of size, weight, and density. *Cognition, 21*(3), 177–237.

Smith, J. C. (1986). Meditation, biofeedback, and the relaxation controversy: A cognitive-behavioral perspective. *American Psychologist,* Sept., 1007–1009.

Smith, M. L., & Glass, G. V. (1977). Meta-analysis of psychotherapy outcome studies. *American Psychologist, 32,* 752–760.

Smith, S. M. (1985). Background music and context-dependent memory. *American Journal of Psychology, 98,* 591–603.

Smith, V. L. & Ellsworth, P. C. (1987). The social psychology of eyewitness accuracy: Misleading questions and communicator expertise. *Journal of Applied Social Psychology,* 72(2), 294–300.

Snider, J. G., Davis, M. H., & Brown, R. (1984). Effects of self-tape recording on self-awareness in a context of self-counseling. *Psychological Reports, 54,* 311–315.

Snow, C. E. (1977). The development of conversation between mothers and babies. *Journal of Child Language, 4,* 1–22.

Snow, C. P. (1961, Feb.). Either-or. *Progressive,* p. 24.

Snow, R. E. (1986). Individual differences and the design of educational programs. *American Psychologist, 41,* 1029–1039.

Snowdon, C. T. (1983). Ethology, comparative psychology, and animal behavior. *Annual Review of Psychology, 34,* 63–94.

Snyder, C. R., & Shenkel, R. J. (1975, March). P. T. Barnum effect. *Psychology Today, 8,* pp. 52–54.

Snyder, M. (1987). *Public appearances and private realities*. New York: W. F. Freeman.

Snyder, M. & Harkness, A. R. (1984). *E = f(p): The impact of personality on choice of situation*. Paper presented at the annual meeting of the Midwestern Psychological Association, Chicago.

Snyder, M. & Smith, D. (1984). *Self-monitoring and depression: Precipitating events and copying strategies*. Paper presented at the annual meeting of the Midwestern Psychological Association, Chicago.

Snyder, S. H. (1972, Jan.). The true speed trip: schizophrenia. *Psychology Today*.

Snyder, S. H., & Childers, S. R. (1979). Opiate receptors and opioid peptides. *Annual Review of Neuroscience, 2*, 35–64.

Snyderman, M. & Rothman, S. (1987). Survey of expert opinion on intelligence and aptitude testing. *American Psychologist, 42*(2), 137–144.

Solanto, M. V. (1984). Neuropharmacological basis of stimulant drug action in attention deficit disorder with hyperactivity: A review and synthesis. *Psychological Bulletin, 95*, 387–409.

Solomon, R. C., & Wynne, L. C. (1953). Traumatic avoidance learning: Acquisition in normal dogs. *Psychological Monographs, 67*(4, Whole No. 354).

Solomon, R. L. (1980, Aug.). The opponent-process theory of acquired motivation. *American Psychologist*, 691–721.

Sommer, R. (1969). *Personal space: The behavioral basis of design*. Englewood Cliffs, N.J.: Prentice-Hall.

Sommer, R. (1977, Jan.). Toward a psychology of natural behavior. *APA Monitor*.

Sorce, J. F., Emde, R. N., Campos, J. J., & Klinnert, M. D. (1985). Maternal emotional signaling: Its effect on the visual cliff behavior of 1-year-olds. *Developmental Psychology, 21*, 195–200.

Spence, J. T. (1984). Masculinity, femininity, and gender-related traits: A conceptual analysis and critique of current research. In B. A. Maker, & W. B. Maker (Eds.). *Progress in experimental personality research: Normal personality processes* (Vol. 13). New York: Academic Press.

Sperry, R. W. (1956). The eye and the brain. *Scientific American*, Offprint No. 465, pp. 48–52.

Sperry, R. W. (1968). Hemisphere deconnection and unity in conscious awareness. *American Psychologist, 23*, 723–733.

Sperry, R. W. (1974). Lateral specialization in the surgically separated hemispheres. In F. S. Schmitt, & F. G. Worden (Eds.). *The neurosciences*. Cambridge, Mass.: MIT Press.

Spiegel, D. (1986). Dissociation, double binds, and posttraumatic stress in multiple personality disorder. In B. G. Braun (Ed.) *Treatment of multiple personality disorder*. Washington, D.C.: American Psychiatric Press.

Spielberger, C. D., Anton, W. D., & Bedell, J. (1976). The nature and treatment of test anxiety. In M. Zuckerman, & C. D. Spielberger (Eds.). *Emotions and anxiety: New concepts, methods, and applications* (pp. 317–345). Hillsdale, NJ: Lawrence Erlbaum.

Spielberger, C. C. & Stenmark, D. E. (1985). Community psychology. In Altmaier, E. M. & Meyer, M. E. (Eds.), *Applied specialties in psychology*. New York: Random House.

Spiesman, J. C., Lazarus, R. S., Mordkoff, A. M., & Davidson, L. A. (1964). The experimental reduction of stress based on ego-defense theory. *Journal of Abnormal and Social Psychology, 68*, 367–380.

Spitz, R. A. (1945). Hospitalism: An inquiry into the genesis of psychiatric conditions in early childhood. In *The psychoanalytic study of the child* (Vol. I), pp. 53–74. New York: International University Press.

Spotts, J. V., & Shontz, F. C. (1980). *Cocaine users*. New York: The Free Press. K

Springer, S. P. & Deutsch, G. (1985). *Left brain, right brain*. New York: W. H. Freeman.

Sprott, R. L., & Staats, J. (1975). Behavioral studies using genetically-defined mice—A bibliography. *Behavior Genetics, 5*, 27–82.

Stanovich, K. E. (1986). *How to think straight about psychology*. Glenview, Ill.: Scott, Foresman.

Staples, F. R., Sloane, B., Whipple, K., Cristol, A. H., & Yorkston, N. J. (1975). Differences between behavior therapists and psychotherapists. *Archives of General Psychiatry, 32*, 1515–1522.

Stapp, J., & Fulcher, R. (1983). *Salaries in psychology*. Washington, D.C.: American Psychological Association.

Stark, E. (1981, Sept.). Pigeon patrol. *Science 81*, pp. 85–86.

Stark, R., & McEvoy, J. (1970, Nov.). Middle-class violence. *Psychology Today*.

Steblay, N. M. (1987). Helping behavior in rural and urban environments: A meta-analysis. *Psychological Bulletin, 102*(3), 346–356.

Stefanis, C., Dornbush, R. L., & Fink, M. (1977). *Hashish: A study of long-term use*. New York: Raven Press.

Stein, M. I. (1974). *Stimulating creativity* (Vol. 1). New York: Academic Press.

Steinberg, L. D., Catalano, R., & Dooley, P. (1981). Economic antecedents of child abuse and neglect. *Child Development, 52*, 975–985.

Sterman, M. B. (1977). Effects of sensorimotor EEG feedback training on sleep and clinical manifestations of epilepsy. In J. Beatty, & H. Legewie (Eds.). *Biofeedback and behavior*. New York: Plenum.

Stern, C. (1956). Hereditary factors affecting adoption: A study of adoption practices. *Child Welfare League of America, 2*, p. 53.

Stern, D. (1982). Some interactive functions of rhythm changes between mother and infant. In M. Davis (Ed.). *Interaction rhythms, periodicity in communicative behavior*. New York: Human Sciences Press.

Stern, D., Jaffe, J., Beebe, B., & Bennett, S. (1975). Vocalizing in unison and in alternation: Two modes of communication within the mother-infant dyad. In D. Aronson, & R. Rieber (Eds.). *Developmental psycholinguistics and communication disorders* (pp. 89–100). Annals of the New York Academy of Sciences.

Stern, W. C. (1981). REM sleep and behavioral plasticity: Evidence for involvement of brain catecholamines. In W. Fishbein (Ed.). *Sleep, dreams and memory* (99–109). New York: SP Medical and Scientific Books.

Sternberg, R. J. (1986). A triangular theory of love. *Psychological Review, 93*, 119–135.

Sternberg, R. J. (1985a). *Beyond IQ*. Cambridge University Press.

Sternberg, R. J. (1987). Liking versus loving: A comparative evaluation of theories. *Psychological Bulletin, 102*(3), 331–345.

Sternberg, R. J. & Barnes, M. (1986). Real and ideal others in romantic relationships: Is four a crowd? *Journal of Personality and Social Psychology, 49*, 1586–1608.

Sternberg, R. J. & Davidson, J. D. (1985). Cognitive development in the gifted and talented. In F. D. Horowitz & M. O'Brien (Eds.) *The gifted and talented: Developmental perspectives*, Washington, DC: American Psychological Association, 37–74.

Sternberg, R. J. & Davidson, J. D. (1983). Insight in the gifted. *Educational Psychologist, 18*, 51–57.

Sternberg, R. J., & Davidson, J. D. (1982, June). The mind of the puzzler. *Psychology Today*.

Sternberg, R. J., & Grajek, S. (1984). The nature of love. *Journal of Personality and Social Psychology, 47*, 312–329.

Steuer, J. La Rue, A., Blum, J. & Jarvik, L. F. "Critical loss" in the eight and ninth decades. *Journal of Gerontology, 36*(2), 1981, 211–213.

Stevens, C. F. (1979). The neuron. *Scientific American, 241*(3), pp. 54–65.

Stevens, J. O. (1971). *Awareness: Exploring, experimenting, experiencing*. Lafayette, CA: Real People Press.

Stiles, W. B., Shapiro, D. A., & Elliott, R. (1986). Are all psychotherapies equivalent? *American Psychologist, 41*, 165–180.

Stokols, D. (1978). Environmental psychology. *Annual Review of Psychology, 29*, 253–295.

Stoller, F. H. (1967). The long weekend. *Psychology Today, 1*(7), pp. 28–33.

Stoller, F. H. (1972). Marathon groups: Toward a conceptual model. In L. N. Solomon, & B. Berzon (Eds.). *New Perspectives on Encounter Groups* (pp. 171–194). San Francisco: Jossey-Bass.

Story, M. & Brown, J. E. (1987). Do young children instinctively know what to eat? *The New England Journal of Medicine, 316*, 103–106.

Strange, J. R. (1965). *Abnormal psychology*. New York: McGraw-Hill.

Streissguth, A. P., et al. (1984). Intrauterine alcohol and nicotine exposure: Attention and reaction time in 4-year-old children. *Developmental Psychology, 20*, 533–541.

Strickler, E. M. & Verbalis, J. G. (1988). Hormones and behavior: The biology of thirst and sodium appetite. *American Scientist*, May–June, 261–267.

Strong, B. & DeVault, C. (1988). *Understanding our sexuality*. St. Paul, MN: West Publishing Company.

Strongman, K. T. (1987). *The psychology of emotion*. New York: John Wiley & Sons.

Stunkard, A. (1980). *Obesity*. Philadelphia: Saunders.

Stunkard, A. J., Sorenson, T. I. A., Hanis, C., Teasdale, T. W., Chakraborty, R., Schull, W. J. & Schulsinger, F. (1986). An adoption study of human obesity. *New England Journal of Medicine, 314,* 193–198.

Sue, D., Sue, D. W., & Sue, S. (1981). *Understanding abnormal behavior*. Boston: Houghton Mifflin.

Suedfeld, P. (1966). *Social processes*. Dubuque, Iowa: Brown.

Suedfeld, P. (1975, Jan.–Feb.). The benefits of boredom: Sensory deprivation reconsidered. *American Scientist, 63*.

Suedfeld, P. (1980). *Restricted environmental stimulation: Research and clinical applications*. New York: Wiley-Interscience.

Suedfeld, P., & Piedrahita, L. E. (1984). Intimations of mortality: Integrative simplification as a precursor of death. *Journal of Personality and Social Psychology, 47,* 848–852.

Suinn, R. M. (1982). Intervention with Type A behaviors. *Journal of Consulting and Clinical Psychology, 50,* 933–949.

Suinn, R. M. (1970). *Fundamentals of behavior pathology*. New York: Wiley.

Suinn, R. M. (1975). *Fundamentals of behavior pathology* (2nd ed.). New York: Wiley.

Sully, R. (1983). The work-setting support group: A means of preventing burnout. In B. A. Farber (Ed.), *Stress and burnout in the human service professions* (pp. 188–197). New York: Pergamon.

Sulzman, F. M. (1983). Primate circadian rhythms. *BioScience, 33*(7), 445–450.

Sutton-Smith, B. (1982). Birth order and sibling status effects. In M. E. Lanb, & B. Sutton-Smith (Eds.), *Sibling relationships: Their nature and significance across the life-span*. Hillsdale, NJ: Erlbaum.

Swan, G. E. & Denk, C. E. (1987). Dynamic models for the maintenance of smoking cessation: Event history analysis of late relapse. *Journal of Behavioral Medicine, 10*(6), 527–554.

Swensen, C. H. (1973). *Introduction to interpersonal relations*. Glenview, Ill., Scott, Foresman.

Swets, J., Bjork, R. A., Cook, T. D., Davison, G. C., Humphreys, L. G., Hayman, R., Landers, D., Mobley, S. A., Porter, L. W., Posner, M., Schneider, W., Singer, J. E., Springer, S. P., and Thompson, R. F. (1988). *Enhancing human performance: Issues, theories, and techniques*. Washington, DC: National Academy Press of the United States National Research Council.

Szasz, T. S. (1966, June 12). Mental illness is a myth. *The New York Times Magazine*.

Szasz, T. S. (1969). The crime of commitment. *Psychology Today, 2*(10), pp. 55–57.

Szasz, T. S. (1972, April). The ethics of addiction. *Harpers*.

Szasz, T. S. (1987). *Insanity: The idea and its consequences*. New York: Wiley.

Szasz, T. S. (1983). *Thomas Szasz: Primary values and major contentions*. Buffalo, NY: Prometheus Books.

Takooshian, H., Haber, S., & Lucido, D. J. (1977, Feb.). Who wouldn't help a lost child? You, maybe. *Psychology Today*, p. 67.

Tanner, J. M. (1973, Sept.). Growing up. *Scientific American*, pp. 34–43.

Tanzer, D., & Block, J. L. (1976). *Why natural childbirth?* New York: Schocken.

Tarpy, R. M., & Mayer, R. E. (1978). *Foundations of learning and memory*. Glenview, Ill.: Scott, Foresman.

Tart, C. T. (1975). *States of consciousness*. New York: Dutton.

Taylor, C. W. (1978). How many types of giftedness can your program tolerate? *The Journal of Creative Behavior, 12,* 39–51.

Taylor, T. E. (1983, March 17). Learning studies of higher cognitive levels in short-term sensory isolation environment. Paper delivered at First International Conference on REST and Self-regulation, Denver, Colorado.

Tedeschi, J. T., Lindskold, S., & Rosenfeld, P. (1985). *Introduction to social psychology*. St. Paul: West Publishing.

Tenopyr, M. L., & Oeltjen, P. D. (1982). Personnel selection and classification. *Annual Review of Psychology, 33,* 581–618.

Tephly, J. B., & Elardo, R. (1984). Mothers and day-care teachers: Young children's perceptions. *British Journal of Developmental Psychology, 2,* 251–256.

Terman, L. M., & Oden, M. (1959). *The gifted group in mid-life. Vol. 5, Genetic studies of genius*. Stanford: Stanford University Press.

Terman, L. M., & Merrill, M. A. (1937, revised ed., 1960). *Stanford-Binet Intelligence Scale*. Boston: Houghton Mifflin.

Terrace, H. S. (1985). In the beginning was the "name." *American Psychologist, 40,* 1011–1028.

Thatcher, R. W., Walker, R. A., & Giudice, S. (1987). Human cerebral hemispheres develop at different rates and ages. *Science, 236,* 1110–1113.

Thielens, W., Jr. (1987, April). *The disciplines and undergraduate lecturing*. Paper presented at the meeting of the American Educational Research Association, Washington, D.C.

Thigpen, C. H., & Cleckley, H. M. (1957). *The three faces of Eve*. New York: McGraw-Hill.

Thomas, A., & Chess, S. (1977). *Temperament and development*. New York: Brunner/Mazel.

Thomas, A., Chess, S., & Birch, H. G. (1968). *Temperament and behavior disorders in children*. New York: New York University Press.

Thompson, R. F. (1985). *The brain*. New York: W. H. Freeman.

Thornburg, H. D. (1984). *Introduction to educational psychology*. St. Paul: West.

Tierney, J. (1982, June). Doctor is this man dangerous? *Science 82*, pp. 28–31.

Tiffany, S. T., Martin, E. M., & Baker, T. B. (1986). Treatments for cigarette smoking: An evaluation of the contributions of aversion and counseling procedures. *Behaviour Research & Therapy, 24*(4), 437–452.

Time, (1973, Jan. 8).

Tolman, E. C., & Honzik, C. H. (1930). Introduction and removal of reward and maze performance in rats. *University of California Publications in Psychology, 4,* 257–275.

Tolman, E. C., Ritchie, B. F., & Kalish, D. (1946). Studies in spatial learning: II. Place learning versus response learning. *Journal of Experimental Psychology, 36,* 221–229.

Torrey, E. F. (1988). *Surviving schizophrenia: A family manual*. New York: Harper & Row.

Tresemer, D. W. (1977). *Fear of success: An intriguing set of questions*. New York: Plenum.

Triandis, H. C. (1977). *Interpersonal behavior*. Monterey: Brooks/Cole.

Trotter, R. J. (1986). The three faces of love. *Psychology Today*, Sept. 44–54.

Trotter, R. J. (1974, Aug. 3). *Obesity and behavior*. Science News.

Truax, S. R. (1983). Active search, mediation, and the manipulation of cue dimensions: Emotion attribution in the false feedback paradigm. *Motivation and Emotion, 7,* 41–60.

Trujillo, M. (1986). Short-term dynamic psychotherapy. In Kutash, I. L. & Wolf, A. (Eds.), *Psychotherapist's casebook*, 78–98, San Francisco, Jossey-Bass.

Tryon, R. C. (1929). The genetics of learning ability in rats. *University of California Publications in Psychology, 4,* pp. 71–89.

Tulving, E. (1986). What kind of a hypothesis is the distinction between episodic and semantic memory? *Journal of Experimental Psychology: Learning, Memory, and Cognition, 12*(2), 307–311.

Tulving, E. (1985). How many memory systems are there? *American Psychologist, 40,* 385–398.

Turco, R. P., Toon, O. B., Ackerman, T. P., Pollack, J. B., & Sagan, C. (1983). Nuclear winter: Global consequences of multiple nuclear explosions. *Science, 222,* 1, 283–292.

Turkington, C. (1986). Pot and the immune system. *APA Monitor*, Aug., 22.

Turnbull, C. M. (1961). Some observations regarding the experiences and behavior of the Bambuti Pygmies. *American Journal of Psychology, 74,* 304–308.

Tversky, A., & Kahneman, D. (1982). Judgments of and by representativeness. In D. Kahneman, P. Slovic, & A. Tversky, *Judgment under uncertainty: Heuristics and biases* (84–98). Cambridge: Cambridge University Press.

Tversky, A., & Kahneman, D. (1981). The framing of decisions and the psychology of choice. *Science, 211,* 453–458.

Udry, J. R., & Eckland, B. K. (1984). Benefits of being attractive: Differential payoffs for men and women. *Psychological Reports, 54,* 47–56.

Udry, J. R., & Morris, N. M. (1977). Human sexual behavior at different stages of the menstrual cycle. *Journal of Reproduction and Fertility, 51,* 419.

Uhlenhuth, D. H., Balter, M. B., Mellinger, G. D., Cisin, I. H., & Clinthorne, J. (1983). Symptom checklist syndromes in the general population: Correlations with psychotherapeutic drug use. *Archives of General Psychiatry,* 40 1167–1173.

Ulrich, R. E., Stachnik, T. J., & Stainton, N. R. (1963). Student acceptance of generalized personality interpretations. *Psychological Reports, 131,* 831–834.

Underwood, B. J. (1957). Interference and forgetting. *Psychological Review, 64,* 49–60.

Unger, R. K. (1979). Toward a redefinition of sex and gender. *American Psychologist, 34,* 1085–1094.

U.S. Commission on Civil Rights. (1977). *Window dressing on the set: Women and minorities in television.* Washington, D.C.: Government Printing Office.

Valenstein, E. S. (1980). Extent of psychosurgery worldwide. In E. S. Valenstein (Ed.), *The psychosurgery debate.* San Francisco: W. H. Freeman.

Valins, S. (1966). Cognitive effects of false heart-rate feedback. *Journal of Personality and Social Psychology, 4,* 400–408.

Valins, S. (1967). Emotionality and information concerning internal reactions. *Journal of Personality and Social Psychology, 6,* 458–463.

VandenBos, G. R. & Bryant, B. K. (1987). Preface. In VandenBos, G. R. & Bryant, B. K. (Eds.) *Cataclysms, crises, and catastrophes: Psychology in action.* Washington, DC: American Psychological Association.

van Lawick-Goodall, J. (1971). *In the shadow of man.* New York: Houghton Mifflin.

Van Maanen, J., & Schein, E. H. (1977). Career development. In J. R. Hackman, & J. L. Suttle (Eds.). *Improving life at work.* Santa Monica, CA.: Goodyear Publishing Co.

Van Riper, C. & Emerick, L. (1984). *Speech correction: An introduction to speech pathology and audiology.* Englewood Cliffs, N.J.: Prentice-Hall.

Varley, C. K. (1984). Attention deficit disorder (the hyperactivity syndrome): A review of selected issues. *Journal of Developmental & Behavioral Pediatrics, 5,* 254–258.

Vera, J. M. (1988). Supplying the 40 million who won't say no. *World Press Review,* May, 26–28.

Verhave, T. (1966). The pigeon as a quality control inspector. *American Psychologist, 21,* 109–115.

Vils, U. (1976, Feb. 26). Alcoholism: Tempest in a shot glass. *Los Angeles Times.*

Voeller, K. K. S. (1986). Right-hemisphere deficit syndrome in children. *American Journal of Psychiatry, 143,* 1004–1009.

Vogel, S. (1988, Feb.). Cold storage. *Discover,* 52–54.

Vogler, R. E., & Bartz, W. R. (1982). *The better way to drink.* New York: Simon and Schuster.

Vogler, R. E., Weissbach, T. A., Comptom, J. V., & Martin, G. T. (1977). Integrated behavior change techniques for problem drinkers in the community. *Journal of Consulting and Clinical Psychology, 45,* 267–279.

Vokey, J. R. & Read, J. D. (1985). Subliminal messages: Between the Devil and the media. *American Psychologist, 40*(11), 1231–1239.

Volpicelli, J. R., Ulm, R. R., Altenor, A., & Seligman, M. E. P. (1983). Learned mastery in the rat. *Learning and Motivation, 14,* 204–222.

von Baumgarten, R., Benson, A., Berthoz, A., Brandt, T., Brand, U., Bruzek, W., Dichgans, J., Kass, J., Probst, T., Scherer, H., Vieville, T., Vogel, H., & Wetzig, J. (1984). Spatial orientation in weightlessness and readaptation to earth's gravity. *Science, 225,* 205–225.

Waid, W. M., & Orne, M. T. (1982, July/Aug.). The physiological detection of deception. *American Scientist, 70,* 402–409.

Wallach, M. A. (1985). Creativity testing and giftedness. In F. D. Horowitz & M. O'Brien (Eds.) *The gifted and talented: Developmental perspectives,* Washington, DC: American Psychological Association, 99–123.

Wallach, M. A., & Kogan, N. (1965). *Modes of thinking in young children.* New York: Holt.

Walsh, R. (1984). An evolutionary model of meditation research. In Shapiro, D. H. & Walsh, R. N. (Eds.), *Meditation: Classic and contemporary perspectives.* New York: Aldine.

Walster, E. (1971). Passionate Love. In B. I. Murstein (Ed.). *Theories of attraction and love.* New York: Springer.

Walster, E., & Walster, G. W. (1978). *A new look at love.* Reading, Mass.: Addison-Wesley.

Warrenburg, S., & R. Pagano. (1983). Meditation and hemispheric specialization: Absorbed attention in long-term adherence. *Imagination, Cognition and Personality, 2,* 211–229.

Washton, A. M. & Gold, M. S. (1984). Chronic cocaine abuse: Evidence for adverse effects on health and functioning. *Psychiatric Annals,* 14: 733–743.

Watkins, C. E., Jr., Lopez, F. G., Campbell, V. L., & Himmell, C. D. (1986. May). Counseling psychology and clinical psychology: Some preliminary comparative data. *American Psychologist,* 581–582.

Watson, D. L., deBortali-Tregerthan, G., & Frank, J. (1984). *Social Psychology: Science and application.* Glenview, IL: Scott, Foresman.

Watson, D. L., & Tharp, R. G. (1981). *Self-directed behavior: Self-modification for personal adjustment, 3rd ed.* Monterey, CA: Brooks/Cole.

Watson, J. B. (1913). Psychology as the behaviorist views it. *Psychological Review, 20,* 158–177.

Watts, B. (1982). Individual differences in circadian activity rhythms and their effects on roommate relationships. *Journal of Personality, 50,* 374–384.

Weaver, C. N. and Matthews, M. D. (1987). What white males want from their jobs: Ten years later. *Personnel, 4*(9), 62–65.

Webb, W. (1975). *Sleep the gentle tyrant.* Englewood Cliffs, N.J.: Prentice-Hall.

Webb, W. (1978). Sleep and dreams, Part I. *Annual Review of Psychology, 29,* 223–252.

Wechsler, D. (1958). *The measurement and appraisal of adult intelligence (4th ed.).* Baltimore: Williams & Wilkins.

Wegner, D. M., & Vallacher, R. R. (1977). *Implicit psychology.* New York: Oxford University Press.

Weinberg, M. S., & Williams, C. J. (1974). *Male homosexuals.* New York: Oxford University Press.

Weinberger, M., Hiner, S. L., & Tierney, W. M. (1987). In support of hassles as a measure of stress in predicting health outcomes. *Journal of Behavioral Medicine, 10*(1), 19–31.

Weiner, R. D. (1984). Convulsive therapy: 50 years later. *American Journal of Psychiatry, 14,* 1078–1079.

Weintraub, M. I. (1983). *Hysterical conversion reactions.* New York: SP Medical & Scientific Books.

Weisfeld, G. E., & Beresford, J. M. (1982). Erectness of posture as an indicator of dominance or success in humans. *Motivation and Emotion, 6,* 113–131.

Weiss, J. M. (1972). Psychological factors in stress and disease. *Scientific American, 26,* pp. 104–113.

Weiten, W. (1983). *Psychology applied to modern life: Adjustment in the 80's.* Monterey, CA.: Brooks/Cole.

Weitzenhoffer, A. M., & Hilgard, E. R. (1959). *Stanford Hypnotic susceptibility Scales Forms A and B.* Palo Alto, CA: Consulting Psychologists Press.

Weizenbaum, J. (1966, Jan.). ELIZA—A computer program for the study of natural language communication between man and machine. *Communications of The Association For Computing Machinery, 9,* 36–43.

Wells, G. L. & Loftus, E. F. (1984). *Eyewitness testimony: Psychological perspectives*. Cambridge University Press.

Wells, G. L., & Murray, D. M. (1983). What can psychology say about Neil v. Biggers criteria for judging eyewitness accuracy? *Journal of Applied Psychology*, 68, 347–362.

Wertheimer, M. (1959). *Productive thinking*. New York: Harper & Row.

Wexley, K. N. (1984). Personnel training. *Annual Review of Psychology, 35,* 519–551.

Whimbey, A., with Whimbey, L. S. (1980). *Intelligence can be taught*. New York: Dutton.

White, B. L., & Held, R. (1966). Plasticity of sensorimotor development in the human infant. In J. F. Rosenblith, & W. Allinsmith (Eds.). *The causes of behavior Vol. I (2nd ed.)*. Boston: Allyn & Bacon.

White, B. L., & Watts, J. C. (1973). *Experience and environment Vol. I*. Englewood Cliffs, NJ: Prentice-Hall.

White, T. (1981, Sept.). What is a decibel? *Journal of Guitar Acoustics, 4,* 31–35.

Wickens, C. D., & Kramer, A. (1985). Engineering psychology. *Annual Review of Psychology, 36,* 307–348.

Wicken, D. D., Allen, C. K., & Hill, F. A. (1963). Effects of instruction and UCS strength on extinction of the conditioned GSR. *Journal of Experimental Psychology, 66,* 235–240.

Wickes, I. G. (1958). Treatment of persistent enuresis with the electric buzzer. *Archives of Diseases in Childhood, 33,* 160–164.

Wilber, R. (1986, March). A drug to fight cocaine. *Science 86,* pp. 42–46.

Wilhelm, J. L. (1976). *The search for superman*. New York: Simon & Schuster.

Williams, B. A. (1984, Nov. 30). U.S. approves implants to aid the totally deaf. *Santa Barbara News Press,* part C, p. 6.

Williams, B. M. (1974, Nov.). Promise and caution—"Hypnosis is like a scalpel. You wouldn't want it wielded by your janitor." *Psychology Today*.

Williams, R. L. (1975). The Bitch-100: A culture-specific test. *Journal of Afro-American Issues, 3,* 103–116.

Williams, R. L., et al. (1964). Sleep patterns in young adults: An EEG study. *Electroencephalography and Clinical Neurophysiology,* 376–381.

Williams, R. L., & Long, J. D. (1979). *Toward a self-managed life style*. Boston: Houghton Mifflin.

Williams, S. (1984, April). Disk therapy. *Science 84,* 81, 94.

Williams, T. M. & Handford, A. G. (1986). Television and other leisure activities. In T. M. Williams (Ed.), *The impact of television: A natural experiment in three communities*. Orlando, Florida: Academic Press, 143–213.

Williamson, A. M. & Sanderson, J. W. (1986). Changing the speed of shift rotations: A field study. *Ergonomics, 29*(9), 1085–1095.

Wilson, E. O. (1975, Oct. 12). Human decency is animal. *New York Times Magazine*.

Wilson, R. R. (1986). *Don't panic: Taking control of anxiety attacks*. New York: Harper & Row.

Wilson, R. R. (1968). Perceptual distinction of height as a function of ascribed academic status. *Journal of Social Psychology, 74,* 97–102.

Wilson, S., Strong, B., Clarke, L. M., & Thomas, J. (1984). *Human sexuality*. St. Paul: West Publishing Co.

Winget, C., & Kramer, M. (1979). *Dimensions of dreams*. Gainesville: University Presses of Florida.

Winson, J. (1985). *Brain and psyche: The biology of the unconscious*. Garden City, NY: Doubleday.

Wise, E. H., & Haynes, S. N. (1983). Cognitive treatment of test anxiety: Rational restructuring versus attentional training. *Cognitive Therapy and Research,* 7, 69–78.

Wise, J. (1982, Sept.). A gentle deterrent to vandalism. *Psychology Today,* pp. 31–38.

Wolcott, J. H., McNeekin, R. R., Burgin, R. E., & Yanowitch, R. E. (1977). Correlation of general aviation accidents with the biorhythm theory. *Human factors, 19,* 283–293.

Wolfe, J. B. (1936). Effectiveness of token rewards for chimpanzees. *Comparative Psychology Monographs, 12*(5), Whole No. 60.

Wolpe, J. (1974). *The practice of behavior therapy (2nd ed.)*. New York: Pergamon.

Wood, M. M., & Greenfield, S. T. (1976). Women managers and fear of success: A study in the field. *Sex Roles, 2,* 375–387.

Woodmansee, J. J. (1970). The pupil response as a measure of social attitudes. In G. F. Summers (Ed.). *Attitude measurement*. Chicago: Rand McNally.

Woods, J. H., Winger, G. D., & France, C. P. (1987). Reinforcing and discriminative stimuli effects of cocaine: Analysis of pharmacological mechanisms. In Fisher, S., Raskin, A. & Uhlenhuth, E. H. (Eds.), *Cocaine: Clinical and behavioral aspects*. N.Y.: Oxford University Press. 21–65.

Woods, P. J. (Ed.) with C. S. Wilkinson (1987). *Is psychology the major for you? Planning for your undergraduate years*. Washington, D.C.: American Psychological Association.

Woolfolk, R., & Richardson, F. (1978). *Stress, sanity and survival*. New York: Signet.

Work In America. (1973). Special Task Force, Department of Health, Education and Welfare. Cambridge, Mass.: MIT Press.

Wortman, C. B. & Silver, R. C. (1987). Coping with irrevocable loss. In VandenBos, G. R. & Bryant, B. K. (Eds.) *Cataclysms, crises, and catastrophes: Psychology in action*. Washington, DC: American Psychological Association, 185–235.

Wright, L. (1988). The Type A behavior pattern and coronary artery disease: Quest for the active ingredients and the elusive mechanism. *American Psychologist, 43*(1), 2–14.

Wrightsman, L. S., & Deaux, K. (1981). *Social psychology in the 80s*. Monterey, CA: Brooks/Cole.

Wu, T. C., Tashkin, D., Djahed, B., & Ross, J. E. (1988). The pulmonary hazards of smoking marijuana as compared with tobacco. *The New England Journal of Medicine, 318*(6), 347–351.

Wursig, B. (1979, March). Dolphins. *Scientific American, 240*(3), pp. 136–148.

Wyatt, J. W., Posey, A., Welker, W., & Seamonds, C. (1984). Natural levels of similarities between identical twins and between unrelated people. *The Skeptical Inquirer, 9,* 62–66.

Yalom, I. D. (1980). *Existential psychotherapy*. New York: Basic Books.

Yule, W., Urbanowicz, M., Lansdown, R., & Millar, I. B. (1984). Teachers' ratings of children's behavior in relation to blood lead levels. *British Journal of Developmental Psychology, 2,* 295–305.

Zajonc, R. B. (1986). The decline and rise of Scholastic Aptitude Scores. *American Psychologist, 41*(8), 862–867.

Zajonc, R. B. (1975, Jan.). Dumber by the dozen. *Psychology Today,* pp. 37–43.

Zajonc, R. B., & Markus, G. B. (1975). Birth order and intellectual development. *Psychological Review, 82,* 74–88.

Zaludek, G. M. (1976, Feb.). How to cope with male menopause. *Science Digest,* pp. 74–79.

Zane, M. D., & Milt, H. (1984). *Your phobia*. Washington, D.C.: American Psychiatric Press.

Zilbergeld, B. (1983). *The shrinking of America: Myths of psychological change*. Boston: Little Brown.

Zimbardo, P. G. (1975). *Psychology and life* (9th ed.). Glenview, Ill.: Scott, Foresman.

Zimbardo, P. G., Haney, C., & Banks, W. C. (1973, April 8). A pirandellian prison. *The New York Times Magazine*.

Zimbardo, P. G., Pilkonis, P. A., & Norwood, R. M. (1978). The social disease called shyness. In *Annual editions, personality and adjustment 78/79*. Guilford CT: Dushkin.

Zinberg, N. E. (1976, Dec.). The war over marijuana. *Psychology Today,* pp. 92–98.

Zubek, J. (1969b). Sensory and perceptual-motor processes. In J. Zubek (Ed.). *Sensory deprivation: Fifteen years of research* (pp. 207–253). New York: Appleton-Century-Crofts.

Zuckerman, M. (1972, April). *Manual and research report for the Sensation Seeking Scale (SSS)*. Mimeograph, University of Delaware, Newark, Del.

Zuckerman, M., & Allison, S. (1976). An objective measure of fear of success: Construction and validation. *Journal of Personality, 40*, 422–430.

Zuckerman, M., Eysenck, S., & Eysenck, H. J. (1978). Sensation seeking in England and America: Cross-cultural, age, and sex comparisons. *Journal of Consulting and Clinical Psychology, 46*, 139–149.

Zung, W. W. K., & Green, R. H., Jr. (1974). Seasonal variation of suicide and depression. *Archives of General Psychiatry, 30*, 89–91.

Index

Acknowledgments, continued

Table 6–3 Facts About Drugs from *The Resource Book for Drug Abuse Education*. National Education Association, 1969.
Fig. 6–11 Spectrum and Continuum of Drugs, Dr. Robert W. Earle, University of California, Irvine.
Fig. 6–12 D. Coon.
P. 161 Gary Larson's cartoon is reproduced by permission of Chronical Features, San Francisco.
Fig. 6–13 Blood Alcohol Content Chart, courtesy of Jozef Cohen.
Fig. 6–14 "Beware Marijuana" poster courtesy of Dr. Lester Grinspoon, Harvard Medical School.
Fig. 7–4 © Dan Francis, Mardan Photography.
Fig. 7–6 *(left)* J. Albertson, Stock, Boston; *(right)* D. Coon.
Fig. 7–9 Ira Kirschenbaum, Stock Boston.
Fig. 7–10 Yale Joel, LIFE Magazine, © Time Inc.
Fig. 7–12 Chimp-O-Mat. Yerkes Regional, Primate Research Center, Emory University.
Fig. 7–15 Dan Francis, Mardan Photography.
Fig. 7–16 Loomis Dean, LIFE Magazine, © Time Inc.
Fig. 7–18 Photos by Barbara Martin, courtesy of the *Los Angeles Times*, © 1984.
Fig. 7–19 Alain Dejean, Sygma.
Fig. 8–5 "Effects of Punishment on Extinction." Chart from B. F. Skinner, *The Behavior of Organism*, 1938. Permission from Prentice Hall, Inc.
Fig. 8–6 © Ellis Herwig, The Picture Cube.
P. 212 Cartoon courtesy of Ed Arno and *Science 80*.
Fig. 8–9 Nursery School Children, Dr. Albert Bandura, Stanford University.
Fig. 8–10 © Rick Smolan, Stock Boston.
Fig. 8–12 Owen Franken, Stock Boston.
Fig. 8–13 Steven Stone, The Picture Cube.
Fig. 9–1 Courtesy of IBM.
Fig. 9–3 Penfield, W. *The Excitable Cortex in Conscious Man*, 1958. Courtesy of Charles C Thomas Publisher, Springfield, Illinois.
Fig. 9–6 © Larry Day.
Fig. 9–11 © Dan Francis, Mardan Photography.
Fig. 9–16 © Animals, Animals.
Fig. 10–2 © Ralph Reinhold, Animals, Animals.
Fig. 10–6 Osgood, C. E. "The Nature and Measurement of Meaning." *Psychological Bulletin*, 49, Copyright, 1952 by The American Psychological Association. Reprinted by permission.
Fig. 10–15 U.S. Patent No. 556,248. From *Absolutely Mad Inventions* by A. E. Brown and H. A. Jeffcott, Jr. Dover, 1970.
Fig. 11–1 © David Lausten, Woodfin Camp.
Fig. 11–4 Hyperphagic Rat photograph courtesy of Dr. Neal E. Miller, Rockefeller University.
Fig. 11–5 UPI/Bettmann Newsphotos.
Fig. 11–6 © Peter Menzel, Stock Boston.
Fig. 11–7 "Monkeys and Locks." Harry F. Harlow, University of Wisconsin Primate Laboratory.
Fig. 11–8 Berlyne, D. E. "Curiosity and Exploration." *Science*, Vol. 153, pp. 25–33, Figure 4, 1 July, 1966, Copyright 1966 by the American Association for the Advancement of Science.
P. 293 Zuckerman, M. *Manual and Research Report for the Sensation-Seeking Scale (SSS)*. Mimeograph, University of Delaware, Newark, Delaware, April 1972. Reproduced by permission.
Fig. 11–9 © David F. Hughes, The Picture Cube.
Fig. 11–12 © Ellis Herwig, The Picture Cube.
Fig. 11–13 © duomo, David Madison, 1988.
Fig. 11–15 © Marty Heitner, Taurus.
Fig. 12–1, 12–7 Courtesy of The Record, Hackensack, New Jersey.
Fig. 12–4 Photo courtesy of the Stoelting Company, Chicago, Illinois.
Fig. 12–5 Bridges, K. M. B. "Emotional Development in Early Infancy." *Child Development*, 3, 324–341. Figure 1, p. 340. Copyright 1932.
Fig. 12–6 Zoological Society of San Diego.
Fig. 12–8 © Laimute Druskis, Taurus.
Fig. 12–10 Michael Grecco, Stock Boston.
Fig. 12–11 © Dan Francis, Mardan Photography.
P. 323 The Far Side © 1985 Universal Press Syndicate. Reprinted with permission. All rights reserved.
Fig. 12–13 © David Woo, Stock Boston.
PP. 329–30 The Danger Signals of Depression, National Association of Mental Health.
Fig. 13–1 © Liane Enkilis, Stock Boston.
Table 13–1 Reprinted with permission from the *Journal of Psychosomatic Research,* Vol. 11. T. H. Holmes and R. H. Rahe. "Social Readjustment Rating Scale, " 1957, Pergamon Press, Ltd.
Fig. 13–5 © Cary Wolinsky, Stock Boston.
Table 13–2 Friedman, M. and R. Roseman. *Type A Behavior and Your Heart*, Alfred A. Knopf, Inc. 1974. Reprinted by permission.
Fig. 13–6 The General Adaptation Syndrome graph from *The Stress of Life* by Hans Selye. Copyright © 1956, 1976 by Hans Selye. Used by permission of McGraw-Hill Book Company.
Fig. 13–7 *(top)* Dennis Brack, Black Star; *(bottom)* Sandy Herring, The Picture Cube.
Fig. 13–8 Reproduced courtesy of Paul Marques. Bienestar Health, Well-Being and Life Style Choices for Pinal County. Project West Pinal, University of Arizona Health Services Center, 1982.
P. 356 H. Benson. "Systematic hypertension and the relaxation response." Reprinted by permission from *The New England Journal of Medicine*, 296, pp. 1152–1156, 1977.
Fig. 14–1 "Imitation of Facial and Manual Gestures by Human Neonates." by A. M. Meltzoff and M. K. Moore. *Science* Vol 198, pp. 75–78, Fig. 1, October 7, 1977. Copyright 1977 by The American Association for the Advancement of Science.
Fig. 14–2 From "The Origin of Form Perception," by Rob-

ert L. Fantz. Copyright © 1961 by Scientific American, Inc. All rights reserved. Photograph of Fantz's Looking Chamber by David Linton.
Fig. 14–5 © Michael Grecco, Stock Boston.
Fig. 14–5 © Petit Format/Nestle, Science Source, Photo Researchers.
Fig. 14–7 © A. Glauberman, Photo Researchers.
Fig. 14–8 © Frank Siteman, Taurus.
Fig. 14–10 Nina Leen © 1964 Time inc.
Fig. 14–12 Jerome Bruner, Child's Talk, Learning to Use Language, W. W. Norton & Co., 1981. Reprinted by permission.
Fig. 14–13 © Mimi Forsyth, Monkmeyer.
Fig. 14–14 © Yves Debraine, Black Star.
P. 385 Associated Press news article courtesy of the Associated Press.
Fig. 14–15 Photograph courtesy of H. Harlow, University of Wisconsin Primate Laboratory.
Fig. 15–1 © Gabor Demjen., Stock Boston.
Fig. 15–3 © Lenore Wever, Taurus.
Fig. 15–4 © Bohdan Hrynewych, Stock Boston.
Fig. 15–5 © Mark M. Walker, The Picture Cube.
Fig. 15–7 © Rhoda Sidney, Monkmeyer.
Fig. 15–8 © 1987 Lynn Johnson, Black Star.
Fig. 15–9 © A. Tannenbaum, Sygma.
P. 413 Ginott, H. *Between Parent and Child,* 1965. Reprinted by permission of Dr. Alice Ginott.
Fig. 16–1 © Arthur Grace, Sygma.
Fig. 16–2 Cattell, R. B. "Personality Pinned Down." 1973. Reprinted by permission of Dr. R. B. Cattell.
Fig. 16–3 © Dan Francis, Mardan Photograhy.
Fig. 16–4 Daemmrich, Stock Boston.
Table 16–2 Reproduced by permission. Copyright 1943, renewed 1970 by the University of Minnesota. Published by the Psychological Corporation, New York, New York. All rights reserved.
Fig. 16–5 Woodfin Camp.
P. 432 Art Buchwald quotation courtesy of Art Buchwald, Los Angeles Times.
Fig. 16–9 © Alvis Upitis, Black Star.
Fig. 17–1 "All Is Vanity." Courtesy of Illusions, Park Ridge, Illinois.
Fig. 17–3 UPI/Bettmann News Photo.
Fig. 17–5 © Dan Francis, Mardan Photography.
Fig. 17–6 © 1987 Jeffrey D. Hetler, Stock Boston.
Fig. 17–7 © Frank Siteman, Stock Boston.
Fig. 17–8 © Charles E. Schmidt, Taurus.
Fig. 18–1 © Mimi Forsyth, Monkmeyer.
Table 18–2 Terman, L. & M. Merrill, *Stanford–Binet Intelligence Scale.* 1937 (Revised ed. 1960b). Houghton Mifflin Co.
Fig. 18–2 © 1986 Devin Horan, Picture Group.
Table 18–3 Wechsler Scale, The Psychological Corporation 1958.
Fig. 18–4 Wide World Photos.
Fig. 18–5 *(left)* © Karen R. Preuss, Taurus; *(middle)* © Dan Francis, Mardan Photography; *(right)* © David M. Campione, Taurus.
Fig. 18–6 Special Olympics Photograph courtesy of Priscilla Copass & Steve Neighbors.
Fig. 18–9 Culture Fair Test Sample Items from R. B. Cattell, "Are I.Q. Tests Intelligent?" Reprinted by permission of Dr. R. B. Cattell.
PP. 494–95 *Catch 22* Copyright © 1955, 1961 by Joseph Heller. Reprinted by permission of Simon and Schuster, Inc.
Fig. 19–1 Photographs courtesy of Ulrike Kanton Gallery.
Fig. 19–3 © Laimute Druskis, Taurus.
P. 504 Suinn, Richard M. *Fundamentals of Behavior Pathology,* 2nd ed. Copyright © 1975 by Richard Suinn. Reprinted by permission of John Wiley & Sons, Inc.
Fig. 19–4 © Cary Wolinsky, Stock Boston.
Fig. 19–5 *(left)* UPI/Bettmann News Photos; *(right)* D. Coon.
Fig. 19–6 © Charles Gupton, Stock Boston.
Fig. 20–1 Zalesky/Clemmer, Black Star.
Fig. 20–2 The Bettmann Archive.
Fig. 20–3 D. Coon.
Fig. 20–4 Benyas, Black Star.
P. 528 Suinn, Richard M. *Fundamentals of Behavior Pathology,* 1st ed. Copyright © 1970 by Richard Suinn. Reprinted by permission of John Wiley & Sons, Inc.
Fig. 20–5 Grunnitus, Monkmeyer.'
Fig. 20–7 Derik Bayes/Courtesy Guttmann-Maclay Life Picture Service.
Fig. 20–8 *(left)* Dennis Brack, Black Star; *(right)* Duke University Hospital.
Fig. 20–9 The Brookhaven Institute.
Fig. 20–10 © Will McIntyre, Photo Researchers.
Fig. 20–11 © Peter Southwick, Stock Boston.
PP. 541–542 Jackson, B. "Our Prisons Are Criminal," September 22, 1968. © 1960 by the New York Times Company. Reprinted by permission.
Fig. 21–1 *(a)* University Museum of the University of Pennsylvania; *(b)* courtesy of the New York Public Library; *(c)* The Bettman Archive.
Fig. 21–3 Historical Pictures Service, Chicago.
Fig. 21–4 Michael Routgier, Life Magazine © Time, Inc.
Fig. 21–5 © Stacy Pick, Stock Boston.
P. 559 Stevens, J. O. *Awareness: Exploring, Experimenting, Experiencing.* Real People Press, 1971.
PP. 562–63 Weizenbaum, J. "ELIZA—A computer program for the study of natural language communication between man and machine." *Communications of the Association for Computing Machinery,* January, 1966, Volume 9, No. 1, pp. 36–43. Copyright 1966, Association for Computing Machinery, Inc. Reprinted by permission.
Fig. 22–1 Curt Gunther, Camera 5.
Fig. 22–2 © Peter Menzel, Stock Boston.
Fig. 22–3 Photograph courtesy of Albert Bandura and the American Psychological Association. Copyright 1969 by the American Psychological Association. Reprinted by permission. From the *Journal of Personality and Social Psychology,* 1969, 13, pp. 173–199.

P. 570 Lazarus, Arnold. "The Treatment of Chronic Frigidity by Systematic Desensitization." In *Experiments in Behavior Therapy,* H. J. Eysenck, (ed). Reprinted by permission of the author. Copyright © 1964 Pergamon Press, Ltd.
P. 572 Lovaas, O. I. and Simmons, J. Q. "Manipulation of Self–destruction in Three Retarded Children." *Journal of Applied Behavior Analysis,* 1969, 2, pp. 143–157. Reprinted by permission.
P. 573 Token Economy photograph courtesy of Robert Liberman, M.D.
Fig. 23–1 © Charles Gupton, Stock Boston.
Fig. 23–2 © Gregg Mancusco, Stock Boston.
Fig. 23–3 © Stacy Pick, Stock Boston.
Box 23–1 From Zick Rubin, *Liking and Loving: An Invitation to Social Psychology,* 1973, Holt Rinehart and Winston.
Table 23–1 From Zick Rubin. "Measurement of Romantic Love." *Journal of Personality and Social Psychology.* Copyright 1970 by the American Psychological Association. Reprinted by permission.
Fig. 23–4 © Janeart 1983, The Image Bank.
Fig. 23–8 © Robert Y. Eckert, Stock Boston.
Fig. 24–1 © C. Kuhn, The Image Bank West.
Fig. 24–2 © Mark Mittelman, Taurus.
Fig. 24–4 Ellis Herwig, Taurus.
Fig. 24–5 Wide World Photos.
PP. 616–17 Adorno, Theodore, E. Frenkel–Brunswik, D. J. Levinson and R. N. Stanford. *The Authoritarian Personality.* Copyright 1950. Harper & Row.
Table 24–1 M. Karlins, T. L. Coffman and G. Walters. "On the Fading of Social Stereotypes: Studies in Three Generations of College Students." *Journal of Personality and Social Psychology.* Copyright 1969 by the American Psychological Association. Reprinted by permission.
Fig. 24–6 © Bill Gallery, Stock Boston.
Fig. 24–7 © Charles Gupton, Stock Boston.
Fig. 24–8 © Dennis Brack, Black Star.
Fig. 24–9 © Chris Gulker, Picture Group.
Fig. 24–10 Eron, L. D. 'The Development of Aggressive Behavior from the Perspective of a Developing Behaviorism, American Psychologist, May 1987, *42,* 435–442. Copyright 1987 by the American Psychological Association. Reprinted by permission.
Figs. 25–4 and 25–5 Beach, Frank A., ed. *Sex and Behavior,* New York, John Wiley & Sons, Inc., 1965.
Fig. 25–6 From "Where Should You Touch?" by H. E. F. Donohue. Copyright © 1965 Hearst Corporation. Reprinted by permission.
Fig. 26–2 Photograph reproduced courtesy of General Electric.
Fig. 26–3 © David Strickler, Monkmeyer.
Fig. 26–4 © Charles Feil, Stock Boston.
Fig. 26–5 © Steve Hanson, Stock Boston.
Fig. 26–6 © 1986 James Kamp, Black Star.
Fig. 26–8 © Charles Gupton, Stock Boston.
Fig. 26–9 © Jim Pickerell, Black Star.
P. 680 © Taurus.